Contemporary Mathematics
for Business and Consumers

Contemporary Mathematics
for Business and Consumers

Robert A. Brechner
Miami-Dade Community College

THE DRYDEN PRESS

HARCOURT BRACE COLLEGE PUBLISHERS

Fort Worth   Philadelphia   San Diego   New York   Orlando   Austin   San Antonio
Toronto   Montreal   London   Sydney   Tokyo

Acquisitions Editor: Lyn Maize
Developmental Editor: Traci Keller
Project Editor: Cheryl Hauser
Designer: Linda Wooton
Production Managers: Erin Gregg and Eddie Dawson
Product Manager: Nick Agnew
Picture & Literary Rights Editor: Adele Krause

Copy Editor: Colleen Cranney
Proofreaders: D. Teddy Diggs, Judi McClellan
Math Checkers: Nancy Weaver, Rick Roehrich
Indexer: Leslie Leland Frank
Compositor: TSI Graphics
Text Type: 10/12 Times Roman

Address for orders:
The Dryden Press
6277 Sea Harbor Drive
Orlando, FL 32887-6777
1-800-782-4479 or 1-800-433-0001 (in Florida)

Address for editorial correspondence:
The Dryden Press
301 Commerce Street, Suite 3700
Fort Worth, TX 76102

ISBN: 0-03-017247-0 (main)
ISBN: 0-03-097876-9 (AIE)

Library of Congress Catalog Card Number: 96-85464

Printed in the United States of America

6 7 8 9 0 1 2 3 4 5   048   9 8 7 6 5 4 3 2 1

The Dryden Press
Harcourt Brace College Publishers

DEDICATION

This book is dedicated to my beloved wife Shari Joy for her unending support over the past five years in making this dream become a reality. You have played every role from coach to cheerleader. I couldn't have done it without you.

THE DRYDEN PRESS SERIES IN MANAGEMENT

Contemporary Mathematics for Business and Consumers is a 21-chapter adventure into today's business world and its associated mathematical procedures. This book was written for an extensive post-secondary market, including community colleges, vocational and technical schools, business schools, entry-level courses at four-year colleges and universities, corporate employee training courses, and continuing education classes. Written in an interesting and easy to comprehend style, the book is designed to provide solid preparation and foundation for students going on to courses and careers in accounting, marketing, retailing, banking, office administration, finance, insurance, real estate, business, and for use in small businesses or for personal consumer needs.

The book begins with a business-oriented review of the basic operations, including whole numbers, fractions, and decimals. Once students have mastered these operations, they are introduced to the concept of basic equations and how equations are used to solve business problems. From that point, each chapter presents a business math topic that utilizes the student's knowledge of the basic operations and equations.

In keeping with the philosophy of "practice makes perfect," the book contains over 2,000 realistic business math exercises—many with multiple steps and answers—designed to prepare students to use math to make business decisions and develop critical-thinking and problem-solving skills. Many of the exercises in each chapter are written in a "you are the manager of" format, to enhance student involvement. The exercises cover a full range of difficulty levels, from those designed for beginners to those requiring moderate to challenge-level skills. The exercises also reflect today's changing American workplace, from heavy industry to the increasingly important service sector.

Text Organization

Sections and Performance Objectives

Each chapter is divided into *sections,* with each section broken into *performance objectives* that are easy to learn and evaluate. This modular approach allows instructors to choose the material and order of coverage, providing the flexibility to customize the course to the requirements of their school and the learning needs of their students.

Each section and performance objective includes an in-depth description of the topic, a step-by-step explanation of the math calculations required, a worked-out sample exercise and solution, an exercise for students to try, and a full complement of review exercises.

Each chapter ends with a summary of the relevant formulas and a recap of the topics discussed by section. Solutions to all of the Try-It Exercises follow the summary charts. The final element of each chapter is the Assessment Test, which provides students with extensive and varied exercises to practice the math skills covered in the chapter.

In addition to all of these excellent features, many real-company and real-people names in the problem material are used in order to make the problems realistic. However, to make the problems workable for students, some of the quantitative information used in problems, exercises, and examples was invented rather than taken from real companies, organizations, or people.

Text Explanations and Marginal Glossary

Each section and performance objective begins with a description of the business aspect of each topic. These synopses provide an in-depth look at how each topic relates to today's business world. Extensive research has been done to make these explanations as realistic and current as possible.

Important terminology is highlighted in boldface type, with a corresponding marginal glossary for each term for easy reference and review. In addition, each section contains pertinent charts, graphs, tables, photographs, and illustrations, to further enhance student comprehension and retention.

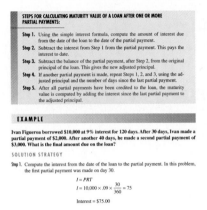

STEPS FOR CALCULATING MATURITY VALUE OF A LOAN AFTER ONE OR MORE PARTIAL PAYMENTS:

Step 1. Using the simple interest formula, compute the amount of interest due from the date of the loan to the date of the partial payment.
Step 2. Subtract the interest from Step 1 from the partial payment. This pays the interest to date.
Step 3. Subtract the balance of the partial payment, after Step 2, from the original principal of the loan. This gives the new adjusted principal.
Step 4. If another partial payment is made, repeat Steps 1, 2, and 3, using the adjusted principal and the number of days since the last partial payment.
Step 5. After all partial payments have been credited to the loan, the maturity value is computed by adding the interest since the last partial payment to the adjusted principal.

EXAMPLE

Ivan Figueroa borrowed $10,000 at 9% interest for 120 days. After 30 days, Ivan made a partial payment of $2,000. After another 40 days, he made a second partial payment of $3,000. What is the final amount due on the loan?

SOLUTION STRATEGY

Step 1. Compute the interest from the date of the loan to the partial payment. In this problem, the first partial payment was made on day 30.

$$I = PRT$$
$$I = 10,000 \times .09 \times \frac{30}{360} = 75$$
$$\text{Interest} = \$75.00$$

Step-by-Step Approach

After the text explanation, the math sequence of each performance objective is illustrated using a step-by-step approach that is easy for the student to follow and remember. These "step" elements are easily distinguishable by their design layout for ease in looking them up while working problems or reviewing material.

Examples with Solution Strategies

Following each step-by-step sequence is an example problem with corresponding solution strategy. The Example and Solution Strategy provides both a worked-out solution and example with explanations, notes to the students, and calculator sequences for difficult computations.

Try-It Exercises

Following each Example and Solution Strategy is a Try-It Exercise, which provides a chance for students to try the math procedure they have just learned. The worked-out solutions to these Try-It Exercises follow each chapter's summary chart. The solutions provide students with *immediate feedback* as to their understanding of the material and their ability to solve related math problems.

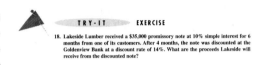

TRY-IT EXERCISE

18. Lakeside Lumber received a $35,000 promissory note at 10% simple interest for 6 months from one of its customers. After 4 months, the note was discounted at the Goldenview Bank at a discount rate of 14%. What are the proceeds Lakeside will receive from the discounted note?

Section Review Exercises

One of the most important features of this textbook is the Section Review Exercises, a comprehensive set of twenty-five to fifty numeric and word problems at the end of each section. These exercises allow the student to review manageable amounts of material from only two or three performance objectives as they read the chapter, rather than having to wait until the entire chapter has been covered. Section Review Exercises allow the instructor to assign homework or class practice problems without having to complete the entire chapter.

REVIEW EXERCISES CHAPTER 10—SECTION III

Calculate the bank discount and proceeds for the following simple discount notes (use the ordinary interest method, 360 days, when applicable):

	Face Value	Discount Rate	Term	Bank Discount	Proceeds
1.	$4,500	13%	6 months	$292.50	$4,207.50
2.	$235	11.3%	50 days	$3.69	$231.31
3.	$1,850	12½%	1 year	$231.25	$1,618.75

CHAPTER 10 ■ SIMPLE INTEREST AND PROMISSORY NOTES

FORMULAS

$$\text{Interest} = \text{Principal} \times \text{Rate} \times \text{Time}$$
$$\text{Exact time} = \frac{\text{Number of days of a loan}}{365}$$
$$\text{Ordinary time} = \frac{\text{Number of days of a loan}}{360}$$

Formula Recap Chart

Located before chapter summary charts, this list reviews all the important formulas used in the chapter. This recap is useful to the student as a quick reference for doing homework or reviewing for a test.

Chapter Summary Chart

This extensive chart provides a comprehensive page-referenced review of each performance objective in the chapter. It contains a review of the important concepts, steps, and formulas for every topic, with a new illustrative example and worked-out solution for each topic. It is an invaluable tool for the student to use in learning and reviewing the chapter material or studying for an exam.

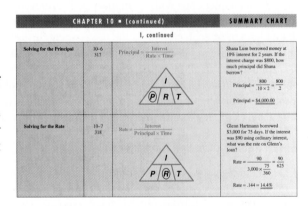

CHAPTER 10 ■ (continued)			SUMMARY CHART

I, continued

| Solving for the Principal | 10-6 317 | $\text{Principal} = \dfrac{\text{Interest}}{\text{Rate} \times \text{Time}}$ | Shana Lum borrowed money at 10% interest for 2 years. If the interest charge was $800, how much principal did Shana borrow? |

$$\text{Principal} = \frac{800}{.10 \times 2} = \frac{800}{.2}$$
$$\text{Principal} = \$4,000.00$$

| Solving for the Rate | 10-7 318 | $\text{Rate} = \dfrac{\text{Interest}}{\text{Principal} \times \text{Time}}$ | Glenn Hartmann borrowed $3,000 for 75 days. If the interest was $90 using ordinary interest, what was the rate on Glenn's loan? |

$$\text{Rate} = \frac{90}{3,000 \times \frac{75}{360}} = \frac{90}{625}$$
$$\text{Rate} = .144 = 14.4\%$$

Try-It Exercise Solutions

These step-by-step worked-out solutions to all of the Try-It Exercises in the chapter provide students with immediate feedback on their progress. The solutions are located after the Summary Chart in each chapter.

Assessment Test

This section provides comprehensive set of exercises. As with the Section Review Exercises, these are business-realistic in nature and are designed to promote critical-thinking and problem-solving ability. Many of these problems have multiple parts that build on previous answers and previously learned material.

Using the exact interest method (365 days) find the amount of interest on the following loans:

	Principal	Rate	Time	Exact Interest
1.	$15,000	13%	120 days	$641.10
2.	$1,700	$12\frac{1}{2}$%	33 days	$19.21

Using the ordinary interest method (360 days) find the amount of interest on the following loans:

	Principal	Rate	Time	Ordinary Interest
3.	$20,600	12%	98 days	$672.93
4.	$286,000	$13\frac{1}{2}$%	224 days	$24,024.00

Name_____

Class_____

ANSWERS

1.	$641.10
2.	$19.21
3.	$672.93
4.	$24,024.00
5.	$24,648.00
6.	$129,015.72

BUSINESS DECISION
Borrowing to Take Advantage of a Cash Discount

35. You are the accountant for Leather City, a retail furniture store. Recently an order of sofas and chairs was received from a manufacturer with terms of 3/15, n/45. The order amounted to $230,000, and Leather City can borrow money at 13% ordinary interest.

a. How much can be saved by borrowing the funds for 30 days in order to take advantage of the cash discount? (Remember, Leather City only has to borrow the net amount due, after the cash discount is taken.)

Cash discount = 230,000 × .03 = $6,900

Amount needed = 230,000 − 6,900 = $223,100

$I = PRT = 223,100 \times .13 \times \frac{30}{360} = \$2,416.92$

Savings = Discount − Interest = 6,900 − 2,416.92 = $4,483.08

b. What would you recommend?

Recommendation: Savings of almost $4,500 is significant—Borrow the money

Business Decision Exercise

The final problem in each Assessment Test is a problem describing an actual business scenario. This is a challenge-level problem designed to test students' ability to apply critical-thinking and problem-solving skills to realistic business situations.

Grading Panels

The grading panels are found in the margins of the Assessment Tests. These answer blanks are for students to use in answering each question and instructors to use in grading student work. The grading panel is set up in a vertical list format, allowing the instructor to place an answer template next to it for easy evaluation and grading. The pages of the book are also perforated for easy removal and grading.

Name_____

Class_____

ANSWERS

1.	$641.10
2.	$19.21
3.	$672.93
4.	$24,024.00
5.	$24,648.00
6.	$129,015.72

Business Math Times

Each chapter ends with a newspaper-style feature called "The Business Math Times." This engaging page features articles related to mathematics and business, information about career options, amusing quotes and trivia, and challenging brainteasers.

Collaborative Learning Activities

Located in Appendix A of the book, the Collaborative Learning Activities provide valuable opportunities to reinforce the concept of teamwork and polish presentation skills. Activities range from interviews to research, with emphasis on the application of mathematical concepts to real-world situations.

Answers to Odd-Numbered Problems

This appendix contains answers to the odd-numbered questions in the text. This feature allows students to easily check their progress on class assignments or homework.

Supplements to accompany *Contemporary Mathematics*

The learning package provided with *Contemporary Mathematics* was specifically designed to meet the needs of instructors facing a variety of teaching conditions and to enhance students' experience of the subject. We have attempted to address both the traditional and the innovative classroom environment by providing an array of quality, fundamental, and technologically advanced items, to bring a contemporary, real-world feel to the study of basic business mathematics.

The Dryden Press may provide complimentary instructional aids and supplements or supplement packages to those adopters qualified under our adoption policy. Please contact your sales representative for more information. If as an adopter or potential user you receive supplements you do not need, please return them to your sales representative or send them to:

Attn: Returns Department
Troy Warehouse
465 South Lincoln Drive
Troy, MO 63379

For the Instructor:

Annotated Instructor's Edition

This valuable teaching aid includes annotated solutions for all problems and exercises. These annotations appear in blue for clarity and ease of duplication. References to teaching and solution transparencies are highlighted by an icon in the margin.

Instructor's Resource Database

This innovative tool allows instructors to customize their teaching notes for class. Every chapter contains a general chapter outline and teaching suggestions, ideas, and problem-solving hints based on the author's 30 years of teaching experience, and those suggestions from our class testers and reviewers. There is also a section on using "The Business Math Times" that appears at the end of each chapter and various ways to utilize the "Collaborative Learning Activities." Finally, there are numerous suggestions and instructions for using the MathCue.Business software and the PowerPoint electronic transparencies, incorporating video into the classroom, and how students might use the interactive student tutorial.

Transparency Acetate Package

Available in acetate form are over 100 two- and four-color teaching transparencies derived from figures, exhibits, and Try-It Exercises in the text. These provide an easy display format to reinforce important concepts. Also provided are over 250 solutions transparencies keyed to the review exercises in each chapter. These are also indicated by an icon in the Annotated Instructor's Edition.

Testing Resources

This valuable resource provides additional testing items for instructors' reference in four distinct formats. The test bank contains over 800 problems, ranging from vocabulary reviews and matching to drill and word problems. Each chapter has a variety of tests already created for easy duplication and distribution. The test items are also available in computerized format, allowing instructors to select problems at random by level of difficulty or type, customize or add test questions, and create multiple versions of the same test. This resource is available in DOS, Mac, or Windows formats. The RequesTest phone-in testing service is also available to adopters. Individual tests can be ordered by question number via fax, mail, phone, or e-mail. Finally, Dryden can provide instructors with software to install their own on-line testing program, allowing tests to be administered over network or individual terminals. This program allows instructors to grade and store results, providing greater flexibility and convenience.

The MathCue.Business software also allows the instructor or student to create a limitless number of questions and problems algorithmically derived from any given problem in *Contemporary Mathematics*.

Electronic Transparencies

These PowerPoint overheads have been prepared with the assistance of the author to provide a powerful visual teaching tool for the classroom. There are approximately 1,000 screens, demonstrating a variety of problems and concepts from the text. Instructors may adapt or add screens to customize their lectures.

For the Student:

Student Resource Manual

This supplement is available as a recommended support item for students. It contains "Look It Up" material—reproductions of tables, charts, and formulas—from the book for easy reference during tests or comprehensive reviews. It also contains extensive information on business measurements, the metric system, and international applications, including currency conversions and import/export issues. Over 300 additional review exercises cover each chapter in the main text, providing another source of practice problems. This manual can be ordered for a minimal cost through your bookstore as a stand-alone or shrinkwrapped item with the text.

Interactive Student Tutorial

This interactive CD-ROM–based tutorial can be used by the student alone or by the instructor in class to demonstrate the applicability of business mathematics to real-world situations. Using video, audio, and animation, the user is asked to view and define a situation, identify the math problem, and convert the scenario into numerical form. The student is then guided through the Brechner step-by-step process to solve the problem.

MATHCUE.BUSINESS SOFTWARE

MathCue.Business is a new software package specifically created by George Bergeman to accompany *Contemporary Mathematics for Business and Consumers*. A Windows-based product, it is an easy-to-use, powerful learning and assessment tool.

Math Cue.Business has two primary modes plus a help module:

- In **tutorial-practice mode,** the software presents problems, evaluates answers, and gives immediate feedback. Each problem is accompanied by a step-by-step solution and, if necessary, students may ask for help starting a problem.

  In addition, the help module provides a comprehensive review of terms, equations, and formulas. This module features a searchable index and pop-up definitions.

- In **test mode,** problem answers and results are given only when students finish the entire session. When testing is completed, students may compare their answers to the correct answers and examine the solutions to any problems that they missed.

Both tutorial-practice and test mode include these key features:

- Algorithms randomly generate large numbers of carefully designed problems keyed to performance objectives in the text.

- Sessions are easily customized to include problems from one or more performance objectives. This unique feature allows instructors and students to construct highly targeted, multi-section tutorial sessions, practice tests, tests, and retests.

- Result summaries provide a detailed record of a student's session. Results are broken out by performance objective so that both instructors and students can determine areas of strength and pinpoint and correct areas of weakness.

Contemporary Mathematics for Business and Consumers benefited from the valuable input of instructors throughout the country. I would especially like to thank those who responded to our questions about how they teach business math, reviewed various parts of the manuscript, and allowed this book to be tested by their classes:

Christine F. Belles, Macomb Community College
Elizabeth Domenico, Gaston College
J.D. Dulgeroff, San Bernadino Valley Community College
Acie B. Earl, Black Hawk Community College
Rene Garcia, Miami-Dade Community College, Wolfson Campus
Patricia Gardner, San Bernadino Valley College
Cecil Green, Riverside Community College
Stephen W. Griffin, Tarrant County Junior College, South Campus
James Grigsby, Lake Sumter Community College
Paul Grutsis, San Bernadino Valley College
Giselle Halpern, El Camino Community College
Phil C. Kopriva, San Francisco Community College District
Paul H. Martin, Aims Community College
Jack L. Nelson, Ferris State University
Wayne A. Paper, Hawkeye Institute of Technology
Barbara Rosenthal, Miami-Dade Community College, Wolfson Campus
Ben Sadler, Miami-Dade Community College, Wolfson Campus
Amy Shinoki, Kapiolani Community College
David D. Stringer, DeAnza College
Daniel F. Symancyk, Anne Arundel Community College
Charles Webb, Miami-Dade Community College, Wolfson Campus
Gregory J. Worosz, Schoolcraft College

I would like to extend personal thanks to the many academic and business information contributors who helped me develop the textbook:

Bob Albrecht
John Anderson
Vince Arenas
Marcie Bader
Robert Barton
Ed Blakemore
Martha Cavalaris
Patricia Conroy
Ralph Covert
Nancy De La Vega
Elliott Denner
Ivan Figueroa
Mario Font
Butch Gemin
Blanca Gonzalez
Lionel Howard

Scott Isenberg
Al Kahn
Hazel Kates
Joseph Kreutle
Kimberly Lipscomb
Jane Mangrum
Jim McHugh
Rolando Montoya
Joseph Moutran
Cheryl Robinson
Brian Rochlin
Howard Schoninger
Richard Waldman
Joseph Walzer
Kathryn Warren

Also, I would like to thank the corporate and government organizations that I used as examples and sources of information in preparing and developing this book:

Arthur Andersen & Company
Barnett Banks, Inc.
Board of Governors, Federal Reserve System
Bureau of Labor Statistics
Citicorp Financial Services
Dow Jones, Inc., *The Wall Street Journal*
Federal Express
Harcourt General, Inc.
Internal Revenue Service
Knight-Ridder, Inc., *The Miami Herald*
MasterCard International

Popular Bank of Florida
Reebok, Inc.
Smith Barney Shearson
State of Florida, Department of Revenue
Time, Inc., *Fortune Magazine*
Toys "R" Us, Inc.
Transamerica Life Companies
U.S. Department of Commerce
U.S. Department of Housing and Urban Development
U.S. Government Printing Office, *Statistical Abstract of the United States*
Wal-Mart, Inc.
Walt Disney Company
Winn-Dixie Stores, Inc.

I extend my deepest gratitude to the accuracy checkers who will ensure the success of this book: Susan Adkison, Cheryl Isham, Josephine Pettis, Dave Williams, and Tricia Zingone.

I offer my heartfelt thanks to George Bergeman for developing a sensational software package and for his high-voltage enthusiasm. I would like to thank Nancy Sheridan for her hard work on the test bank.

Finally, I want to thank my dedicated colleagues at The Dryden Press: my acquisitions editor, Lyn Maize, for her energy and support; product manager, Nick Agnew, for his marvelous insights and professionalism; developmental editor, Traci Keller, who has been there for me since word one; project editor, Cheryl Hauser, the magician who can fit square pegs into round holes; designer, Linda Wooton, for a wonderfully smooth and effective layout; picture & literary rights editor, Adele Krause, for always knowing where to look; and production managers, Erin Gregg and Eddie Dawson, for keeping all the wheels turning in the same direction.

Robert A. Brechner

ABOUT THE AUTHOR

Robert A. Brechner is Professor, School of Business, at Miami-Dade Community College. For the past 30 years he has taught Business Math, Principles of Business, Marketing, Advertising, Public Relations, Marketing Research, Management, and Finance. He has been Adjunct Professor at Florida Atlantic University, Boca Raton, and International Fine Arts College, Miami, and recently served as Adjunct Professor at Florida International University School of Journalism and Mass Communications. He consults widely with industrial companies and has published the following books: *Annuities and Sinking Funds* (Prentice Hall, 1990); *Guidelines for the New Manager* (The Dryden Press, 1991); and *A Little Math with Your Business* (The Dryden Press, 1993). Professor Brechner is a member of the National Council of Teachers of Mathematics and the Florida Association of Community Colleges.

Chapter 21 • Business Statistics and Data Presentation   701

Chapter 1

A Review of Basic Operations

THE DECIMAL NUMBER SYSTEM: WHOLE NUMBERS

Numbers are one of the primary tools used in business. The ability to read, comprehend, and manipulate numbers is an essential part of the everyday activity in today's complex business world. It is very important that business students become competent in dealing with numbers. We shall begin our study of business mathematics with whole numbers and their basic operations—addition, subtraction, multiplication, and division. The material in this chapter is based on the assumption that you have a basic working knowledge of these operations. Our goal is to review these fundamentals and build accuracy and speed. This arithmetic review will set the groundwork for our study of fractions, decimals, and percents. Most business math applications involve calculations using these components.

The number system most widely used in the world today is known as the Hindu-Arabic, or **decimal number system.** This system is far superior to any other for today's complex business calculations. It derives its name from the Latin words *decimus,* meaning tenth, and *decem,* meaning ten. The decimal system is based on tens, with the starting point marked by a dot known as the **decimal point.** The decimal system utilizes the ten familiar Hindu-Arabic symbols or digits:

$$0, 1, 2, 3, 4, 5, 6, 7, 8, 9$$

1-1 Reading and Writing Whole Numbers in Numerical and Word Form

The major advantage of our decimal system over previous systems is that the position of a digit to the left or right of the decimal point affects its value. This enables us to write any number with only the ten single-digit numbers, 0 through 9. For this reason, we have given names to the places or positions. In this chapter we will work with places to the left of the decimal point, **whole numbers.** The next two chapters will be concerned with the places to the right of the decimal point, fractions and decimals.

When whole numbers are written, a decimal point is understood to be located on the right of the number. For example, the number **27** is actually

27.

● **decimal number system**

A system utilizing the ten Hindu-Arabic symbols, 0 through 9. In this place-value system, the position of a digit to the left or right of the decimal point affects its value.

● **decimal point**

A dot written in a decimal number to indicate where the place values change from whole numbers to decimals.

● **whole number**

Any number, 0 or greater, that does not contain a decimal or fraction. Whole numbers are found to the left of the decimal point. Also known as an integer. For example, 6, 25, and 300 are whole numbers.

The Hindu-Arabic, or decimal number system, is based on an ancient system of counting.

The decimal point is not displayed until we write a decimal number or dollars and cents, such as 27.25 inches or $27.25.

Exhibit 1-1 illustrates the first 15 places, and five groups, of the decimal number system. Note that our system is made up of groups of three places, separated by commas, each with their own name. Whole numbers start at the understood decimal point and increase in value from right to left. Each group contains the same three places: one, ten, and hundred. Note that each place increases by a factor of "times 10." The group names are units, thousands, millions, billions, and trillions.

STEPS FOR READING AND WRITING WHOLE NUMBERS:

Step 1. Beginning at the right side of the number, insert a comma every three digits to mark the groups.

Step 2. Beginning from left to right, name the digits and the groups. The units group and groups that have all zeros are not named.

Step 3. When writing whole numbers in word form, the numbers from 21 to 99 are hyphenated. For example, 83 would be written eighty-three.

Note: The word "and" should *not* be used in reading or writing whole numbers. It represents the decimal point, and will be covered in Chapter 3.

EXAMPLES

Read and write the following whole numbers in numerical and word form:

a. 14296   **b.** 560
c. 2294857   **d.** 184910
e. 3004959001   **f.** 24000064

SOLUTION STRATEGY

Following the steps above, we insert the commas to mark the groups, then read and write the numbers from left to right.

	Number	Numerical Form	Word Form
a.	14296	14,296	fourteen thousand, two hundred ninety-six
b.	560	560	five hundred sixty
c.	2294857	2,294,857	two million, two hundred ninety-four thousand, eight hundred fifty-seven
d.	184910	184,910	one hundred eighty-four thousand, nine hundred ten
e.	3004959001	3,004,959,001	three billion, four million, nine hundred fifty-nine thousand, one
f.	24000064	24,000,064	twenty-four million, sixty-four

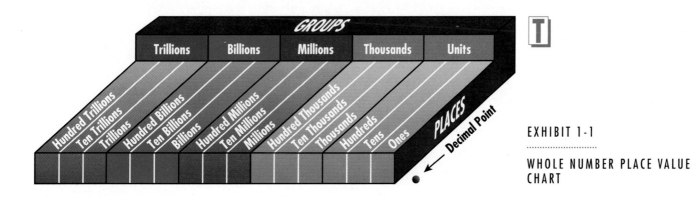

EXHIBIT 1-1

WHOLE NUMBER PLACE VALUE CHART

Read and write the following whole numbers in numerical and word form:

1. 49588   **2.** 804   **3.** 1928837   **4.** 900015

5. 6847365911   **6.** 2000300007

Check your answers with the solutions on page 22.

1-2 Rounding Whole Numbers to a Specified Place Value

● **rounded numbers**

Numbers that are approximations or estimates of exact numbers. For example, 50 is the rounded number of the exact number 49.

● **estimate**

To calculate approximately the amount or value of something. The number 50 would be an estimate of 49.

● **rounding all the way**

A process of rounding numbers to the first digit. Used to prework a problem to an estimated answer. For example, 2,865 rounded all the way is 3,000.

In many business applications, an approximation of an exact number may be more desirable to use than the number itself. Approximations, or **rounded numbers,** are easier to refer to and remember. For example, if a grocery store carries 9,858 items on its shelves, you would probably say that it carries 10,000 items. If you drive 1,593 miles, you would say that the trip is 1,600 miles. Another rounding application in business involves money. If your company has profits of $1,302,201, you might refer to this exact amount by the rounded number $1,300,000. Money amounts are usually rounded to the nearest cent, although they could also be rounded to the nearest dollar or to any other place. The Internal Revenue Service, for example, requires that monetary amounts reported on income tax forms be rounded to the nearest dollar.

Rounded numbers are frequently used to **estimate** an answer to a problem, before working that problem. Estimation approximates the exact answer. By knowing an estimate of an answer in advance, you will be able to catch many math errors. When using estimation to prework a problem, you can generally round off to the first digit, which is called **rounding all the way.**

Once you have rounded to the first digit, perform the indicated math procedure. This can often be done quickly, and will give you a ballpark or general idea of what the actual answer is. In the example below, the estimated answer of 26,000 is a good indicator of the actual answer.

Original Calculation	Estimated Solution (rounding all the way)	Actual Solution
19,549 + 6,489	20,000 + 6,000 26,000	19,549 + 6,489 26,038

If you say you traveled 3,000 miles from Boston to Los Angeles, you would be rounding the actual mileage of 2,979.

If, for example, you had mistakenly added for a total of 23,038 instead of 26,038, your estimate would have immediately indicated that something was wrong.

STEPS FOR ROUNDING WHOLE NUMBERS TO A SPECIFIED PLACE VALUE:

Step 1. Determine the place to which the number is to be rounded.

Step 2a. If the digit to the right of the place being rounded is 5 or more, increase the digit in that place by 1.

Step 2b. If the digit to the right of the place being rounded is 4 or less, do not change the digit in the place being rounded.

Step 3. Change all digits to the right of the place being rounded to zeros.

EXAMPLES

Round the following numbers to the indicated place:

a. 1,867 to tens
b. 760 to hundreds
c. 129,338 to thousands
d. 293,847 to hundred thousands
e. 97,078,838,576 to billions
f. 85,600,061 all the way

SOLUTION STRATEGY

Following the steps above, locate the place to be rounded, use the digit to the right of that place to determine whether to round up or leave it as is, then change all digits to the right of the place being rounded to zeros.

	Place Indicated	Rounded Number
a. 1,867 to tens	1,867	1,870
b. 760 to hundreds	760	800
c. 129,338 to thousands	129,338	129,000
d. 293,847 to hundred thousands	293,847	300,000
e. 97,078,838,576 to billions	97,078,838,576	97,000,000,000
f. 85,600,061 all the way	85,600,061	90,000,000

 TRY-IT **EXERCISES**

Round the following numbers to the indicated place:

7. 51,667 to hundreds

8. 23,441 to tens

9. 175,445,980 to ten thousands

10. 59,561 all the way

11. 14,657,000,138 to billions

12. 8,009,070,436 to ten millions

Check your answers with the solutions on page 22.

Read and write the following whole numbers in numerical and word form:

Number	Numerical Form	Word Form
1. 22938	22,938	Twenty-two thousand, nine hundred thirty-eight
2. 1573	1,573	One thousand, five hundred seventy-three
3. 184	184	One hundred eighty-four
4. 984773	984,773	Nine hundred eighty-four thousand, seven hundred seventy-three
5. 2433590	2,433,590	Two million, four hundred thirty-three thousand, five hundred ninety
6. 49081472	49,081,472	Forty-nine million, eighty-one thousand, four hundred seventy-two

Write the following whole numbers in numerical form:

7. One hundred eighty-three thousand, six hundred twenty-two   183,622

8. Two million, forty-three thousand, twelve   2,043,012

9. One thousand, nine hundred thirty-six   1,936

Match the following numbers in word form with the numbers in numerical form:

10. One hundred two thousand, four hundred seventy __b__   **a.** 11,270

11. One hundred twelve thousand, seven hundred forty-three __d__   **b.** 102,470

12. Twelve thousand, seven hundred forty-three __e__   **c.** 102,740

13. Eleven thousand, two hundred seventy __a__   **d.** 112,743

14. One hundred two thousand, seven hundred forty __c__   **e.** 12,743

Round the following numbers to the indicated place:

15. 1,757 to tens   1,760

16. 32,475 to thousands   32,000

17. 235,376 to hundreds   235,400

18. 559,443 to ten thousands   560,000

19. 8,488,710 to millions   8,000,000

20. 45,699 all the way   50,000

21. 1,325,669,226 to hundred millions   1,300,000,000

22. 23,755 all the way   20,000

23. 18,750,000,000 to billions   19,000,000,000

24. 860,002 to hundred thousands   900,000

Approximate the following exact numbers by rounding to an easier number:

Answers to questions 25–30 may vary. This is a good place to discuss how far numbers should be rounded.

25. 75,669—gallons of fuel   76,000

26. 1,205,860—population of a city   1,200,000

27. $45,329—net sales $45,300

28. 4,928—items in inventory   _____5,000_____

29. 22,610—employees in a company   _____22,600_____

30. $1,984,649,121—company profit   _____$2,000,000,000_____

ADDITION AND SUBTRACTION OF WHOLE NUMBERS

Addition and subtraction are the most basic mathematical operations. They are used in almost all business calculations. In business, amounts of things or dollars are often combined or added to determine the total. Likewise, subtraction is frequently used to determine an amount of something after it has been reduced in quantity. Typical examples might be a decrease in inventory, or a reduction of a bank account balance when writing checks. This section reviews the basics of addition and subtraction. With practice, it will help increase your accuracy and speed.

It is very important for businesspeople to be able to do the basic mathematical calculations by hand. In business, you may not always have a calculator when you need to do math. For now, put aside your calculator. Use only pencil and paper to compute the exercises in the next few sections. After this review chapter, you will be asked to use your calculators once again.

1-3 Adding Whole Numbers and Verifying Your Answers

Addition is the mathematical process of computing sets of numbers to find their sum, or total. The numbers being added are known as **addends,** and the result or answer of the addition is known as the **sum, total,** or **amount.** The "+" symbol represents addition and is called the **plus sign.**

$$
\begin{array}{rl}
1,932 & \text{addend} \\
2,928 & \text{addend} \\
+6,857 & \text{addend} \\
\hline
11,717 & \text{total}
\end{array}
$$

STEPS FOR ADDING WHOLE NUMBERS:

Step 1. Write the whole numbers in columns so that you line up the place values—units, tens, hundreds, thousands, and so on.

Step 2. Add the digits in each column, starting on the right with the units column.

Step 3. When the total in a column is greater than nine, write the units digit and carry the tens digit to the top of the next column to the left.

Verification and Shortcuts

Generally, when adding the digits in each column, we add from top to bottom. An easy and commonly used method of verifying your addition is to add the numbers again, but this time from bottom to top. By adding the digits in the *reverse* order, you will check your answer without making the same error twice.

For illustrative purposes, addition verification will be rewritten in reverse. In actuality, you don't have to rewrite the numbers, just add them from bottom to top. As mentioned earlier, speed and accuracy will be achieved with practice.

Once you become proficient at this process, you can speed up your addition by recognizing and combining two numbers that add up to 10, such as $1 + 9$, $2 + 8$, $6 + 4$, $5 + 5$, and so on. After you have mastered combining two numbers, try combining three numbers that add up to 10, such as $3 + 3 + 4$, $2 + 5 + 3$, $4 + 4 + 2$, and so on.

A Word about Word Problems

In business math, calculations are only a part of the story! Business math, most importantly, involves the ability to (a) understand and analyze the facts of business situations;

addition
The mathematical process of computing sets of numbers to find their sum or total.

addends
Any of a set of numbers being added in an addition problem. For example, 4 and 1 are the addends of the addition problem $4 + 1 = 5$.

sum, total, or amount
The result or answer of an addition problem. The number 5 is the sum or total of $4 + 1 = 5$.

plus sign
The symbol "+" representing addition.

(b) determine what information is given and what is missing; and (c) decide what strategy and procedure is required to solve for an answer. Business application word problems are an important part of each chapter's subject matter. As you progress through the course, your ability to analyze and solve these business situations will improve. Now, start slowly, and relax!

EXAMPLES

Add the following sets of whole numbers. Verify your answers by adding in reverse:

a.   40,562
      29,381
    + 60,095

b. 2,293 + 121 + 7,706 + 20 + 57,293 + 4

c. A furniture manufacturing company has 229 employees in the cutting department, 439 employees in the assembly department, and 360 in the finishing department. There are 57 warehouse workers, 23 salespeople, 4 bookkeepers, 12 secretaries, and 5 executives. How many people work for this company?

SOLUTION STRATEGY

a.

Step 1. Write the numbers in columns so that the place values line up. In this example they are already lined up.

```
    11 2
  40,562
  29,381
+ 60,095
 130,038
```

Verification:
```
    11 2
  60,095
  29,381
+ 40,562
 130,038
```

Step 2. Add the digits in each column, starting with the units column.

Units column: $2 + 1 + 5 = 8$ Enter the 8 under the units column.

Tens column: $6 + 8 + 9 = 23$ Enter the 3 under the tens column and carry the 2 to the hundreds column.

Hundreds column: $2 + 5 + 3 + 0 = 10$ Enter the 0 under the hundreds columns and carry the 1 to the thousands column.

Thousands column: $1 + 0 + 9 + 0 = 10$ Enter the 0 under the thousands column and carry the 1 to the ten thousands column.

Ten thousands column: $1 + 4 + 2 + 6 = 13$ Enter the 3 under the ten thousands column and the 1 under the hundred thousands column.

b.

Addition	Verification
11 21	1121
2,293	4
121	57,293
7,706	20
20	7,706
57,293	121
+ 4	+ 2,293
67,437 ←	67,437

c.

Addition	Verification
23	23
229	5
439	12
360	4
57	23
23	57
4	360
12	439
+ 5	+ 229
1,129 ←	1,129

TRY-IT   EXERCISES

Add the following sets of whole numbers and verify your answers:

13.   39,481
       5,594
    + 11,029

14. $6,948 + 330 + 7,946 + 89 + 5,583,991 + 7 + 18,606$

15. A restaurant served 183 meals on Monday, 228 meals on Tuesday, 281 meals on Wednesday, 545 meals on Thursday, and 438 meals on Friday. On the weekend they served 1,157 meals. How many total meals were served that week?

Check your answers with the solutions on page 22.

1-4 Subtracting Whole Numbers and Verifying Your Answers

Subtraction is the mathematical computation of taking away, or deducting, an amount from a given number. Subtraction is the opposite of addition. The original or top number is the **minuend,** the amount we are subtracting from the original number is the **subtrahend,** and the answer is the **remainder,** or **difference.** The "−" symbol represents subtraction and is called the **minus sign.** In subtraction, the answer or difference is usually a positive number. Sometimes, however, the subtrahend will be larger than the minuend, resulting in a negative number.

$$\begin{array}{r} 938,477 \\ -\ \ \ 4,482 \\ \hline 933,995 \end{array} \quad \begin{array}{l} \text{minuend} \\ \text{subtrahend} \\ \text{difference} \end{array}$$

> **STEPS FOR SUBTRACTING WHOLE NUMBERS:**
>
> **Step 1.** Write the whole numbers in columns so that the place values line up.
> **Step 2.** Starting with the units column, subtract the digits.
> **Step 3.** When a column can't be subtracted, you must "borrow" a digit from the column to the left of the one you are working in.
>
> Note: Since each place value increases by a factor of ten as we move from right to left (units, tens, hundreds, etc.), when we borrow a digit, we are actually borrowing a 10.

Verification

An easy and well-known method of verifying subtraction is to add the difference and the subtrahend. If you subtracted correctly, this total will equal the minuend.

Subtraction		**Verification**	
200	minuend	150	difference
− 50	subtrahend	+ 50	subtrahend
150	difference	200	minuend

EXAMPLES

Subtract the following whole numbers and verify your answers:

a. $\begin{array}{r} 4,968 \\ -\ \ 192 \end{array}$ **b.** $189,440 - 1,347$

c. On Monday morning, an appliance dealer had 165 microwave ovens in stock. During the week the store had a clearance sale and sold 71 of the ovens. How many ovens remain in stock for next week?

subtraction
The mathematical process of taking away, or deducting, an amount from a given number.

minuend
In subtraction, the original number. The amount from which another number, the subtrahend, is subtracted. For example, 5 is the minuend of the subtraction problem $5 - 1 = 4$.

subtrahend
The amount being taken or subtracted from the minuend. For example, 1 is the subtrahend of $5 - 1 = 4$.

difference or remainder
The number obtained when one number is subtracted from another. The answer or result of subtraction. For example, 4 is the difference or remainder of $5 - 1 = 4$.

minus sign
The symbol "−" representing subtraction.

a.

$$\overset{8}{4,\cancel{9}68} \leftarrow$$
$$\underline{-\ 192}$$
$$4,776$$

Verification:

$$\overset{1}{4,776}$$
$$\underline{+\ 192}$$
$$4,968$$

Step 1. Write the numbers in columns so that the place values are lined up. In this problem they are already lined up.

Step 2. Starting with the units column, subtract the digits.

Units column: $8 - 2 = 6$ Enter the 6 under the units column.

Tens column: $6 - 9$ can't be subtracted so we must borrow a digit, 10, from the hundreds column of the minuend. This reduces the 9 to an 8 and gives us a 10 to add to the 6, making it 16.

Now we can subtract 9 from 16 to get 7. Enter the 7 under the tens column.

Hundreds column: $8 - 1 = 7$. Enter the 7 under the hundreds column.

Thousands column: This column has no subtrahend, so just bring down the 4 from the minuend to the answer line.

b. Subtraction   Verification

$$\overset{33}{189,440} \qquad \overset{11}{188,093}$$
$$\underline{-\ \ \ 1,347} \qquad \underline{+\ \ 1,347}$$
$$188,093 \qquad 189,440$$

c. Subtraction   Verification

$$\overset{0}{165} \qquad \overset{1}{94}$$
$$\underline{-\ 71} \qquad \underline{+\ 71}$$
$$94 \qquad 165$$

TRY-IT   EXERCISES

Subtract the following whole numbers and verify your answers:

16. $98,117$
         $\underline{-\ 7,682}$

17. $12,395 - 5,589$

18. Don Robinson has \$4,589 in his checking account. If he writes a check for \$344, how much will be left in the account?

Check your answers with the solutions on page 22.

REVIEW EXERCISES   CHAPTER 1—SECTION II

Add the following numbers:

1.	**2.**	**3.**	**4.**	**5.**
45	548	339	2,359	733
27	229	1,236	8,511	401
+ 19	4,600	5,981	+ 14,006	1,808
91	+ 62,660	3,597	24,876	24,111
	68,037	+ 8,790		+ 10,595
		19,943		37,648

6. $2,339 + 118 + 3,650 + 8,770 + 81 + 6 = \underline{\ \ 14,964\ \ }$

$$2,339$$
$$118$$
$$3,650$$
$$8,770$$
$$81$$
$$\underline{+\quad\ \ 6}$$
$$14,964$$

7. $12,554 + 22,606 + 11,460 + 20,005 + 4,303 = \underline{\quad 70,928 \quad}$

$$
\begin{array}{r}
12,554 \\
22,606 \\
11,460 \\
20,005 \\
+ \quad 4,303 \\
\hline
70,928
\end{array}
$$

Estimate the following by rounding each number, then add to find the exact answer:

		Estimate	**Rounded Estimate**	**Exact Answer**
8.	288	300	6,800	6,694
	512	500		
	3,950	4,000		
	+ 1,944	+ 2,000		
	6,694	6,800		
9.	35,599	40,000	42,100	37,844
	2,116	2,000		
	+ 129	+ 100		
	37,844	42,100		
10.	318,459	300,000	600,000	601,864
	+ 283,405	+ 300,000		
	601,864	600,000		

11. A toy manufacturer makes 2,594 stuffed animals in January; 2,478 in February; and 1,863 in March.

    a. Round each number to the nearest hundred, and add to get an *estimate* of the production.

    $$
    \begin{array}{r}
    2,600 \\
    2,500 \\
    + 1,900 \\
    \hline
    7,000
    \end{array}
    $$

    b. What was the *exact* amount of production for the 3-month period?

    $$
    \begin{array}{r}
    2,594 \\
    2,478 \\
    + 1,863 \\
    \hline
    6,935
    \end{array}
    $$

12. While shopping, Alex Johnson purchases items for $3, $24, $13, $2, and $175. How much did he spend?

    $$
    \begin{array}{r}
    3 \\
    24 \\
    13 \\
    2 \\
    + 175 \\
    \hline
    \$217
    \end{array}
    $$ Total spent

13. The following chart shows the output of Dandy Dry Cleaners and Laundry for last week. Total each column to get the *daily totals*. Total each row to get the *total items* per clothing category. What is the week's *grand total?*

	Monday	Tuesday	Wednesday	Thursday	Friday		Total Items
Shirts	342	125	332	227	172		1,198
Slacks	298	267	111	198	97		971
Suits	66	85	121	207	142		621
Dresses	98	48	79	118	103		446
Daily						**Grand**	
Totals	804	525	643	750	514	**Total**	3,236

350
288
590
43
9
+ 4
1,284 Total acres

14. A farmer plants 350 acres of soybeans, 288 acres of corn, 590 acres of wheat, and 43 acres of assorted vegetables. In addition, the farm has 9 acres for grazing, and 4 acres for the barnyard and farmhouse. What is the total acreage of the farm?

15. ABC Office Machines pays its sales staff a salary of $575 per month, plus commissions. Last month Anita Covington earned commissions of $129, $216, $126, $353, and $228. What was Anita's total income for the month?

575
129
216
126
353
+ 228
$1,627 Total income

Subtract the following numbers:

16. 354
  − 48
   306

17. 5,596
  − 967
  4,629

18. 95,490
  − 73,500
  21,990

19. 339,002
  − 60,911
  278,091

20. 2,000,077
  − 87,801
  1,912,276

21. $185 minus $47
185
− 47
$138

22. 67,800 − 9,835
67,800
− 9,835
57,965

23. $308 less $169
308
− 169
$139

24. Subtract 264 from 1,893
1,893
− 264
1,629

25. 8,906,000 from 12,396,700
12,396,700
− 8,906,000
3,490,700

26. Tom Watson had $153 in his wallet this morning. During the day he spent $5 for breakfast, $43 on a pair of pants, and $29 on a shirt.

a. How much did he spend?
5
43
+ 29
$77 Spent

b. How much did Tom have left?
153
− 77
$76 Left

27. Last year Jan Hopkins earned $27,000. She paid $5,490 in income taxes and $1,290 for social security. How much did Jan have left after these deductions?

5,490
+ 1,290
$6,780 Deductions

27,000
− 6,780
$20,220 Left

28. The beginning inventory of a shoe store for August was 850 pairs of shoes. On the 9th, they received a shipment from the factory of 297 pairs. On the 23rd, another shipment of 188 pairs arrived. When inventory was taken at the end of the month, there were 754 pairs left. How many pairs of shoes were sold that month?

850 Beginning inventory
297 ⎤
+ 188 ⎦ Purchases
1,335 Total inventory

1,335 Total inventory
− 754 Ending inventory
581 Pairs sold

12 Chapter 1 / A Review of Basic Operations

29. An electrician starts the day with 650 feet of wire on his truck. In the morning he cuts off pieces 26, 78, 45, and 89 feet long. During lunch he goes to an electrical supply warehouse and buys another 250 feet of wire. In the afternoon he uses lengths of 75, 89, and 120 feet. How many feet of wire are still on the truck at the end of the day?

```
  26
  78                                      75
  45          650          412           89          662
+ 89        − 238        + 250         + 120        − 284
 238 Morning 412 Morning  662 Afternoon 284 Afternoon 378 Feet left
   feet used   feet left     start        feet used     end of day
```

30. A moving company's truck picks up loads of furniture weighing 5,500 pounds, 12,495 pounds, and 14,562 pounds. The truck weighs 11,480 pounds and the driver weighs 188 pounds. If a bridge has a weight limit of 42,500 pounds, is the truck within the weight limit to cross over the bridge?

```
   5,500
  12,495
  14,562
  11,480           44,225
+    188         − 42,500          No, truck is
  44,225 Pounds    1,725 Pounds over  overweight
    total weight        weight limit
```

MULTIPLICATION AND DIVISION OF WHOLE NUMBERS

Multiplication and division are the next two mathematical procedures used with whole numbers. Both are found in business as often as addition and subtraction. In reality, most business problems involve a combination of procedures. For example, invoices, which are a detailed list of goods and services sold by a company, require multiplication of items by the price per item, and then addition to reach a total. From the total, discounts are frequently subtracted, or transportation charges added. A working knowledge of all math fundamentals is essential for success in today's business world. A little extra time spent on these basics now will go a long way toward making the remainder of this course a much easier and richer learning experience.

1-5 Multiplying Whole Numbers and Verifying Your Answers

Multiplication of whole numbers is actually a shortcut method for addition. Let's see how this works. If a clothing store buys 12 pairs of jeans at $29 per pair, what is the total cost of the jeans? One way to solve this problem is to add $29 + $29 + . . . , 12 times. It's not hard to see how tedious this repeated addition becomes, especially with large numbers. Imagine a chain of stores such as The Limited ordering 2,500 pairs of jeans. Calculating the amount of this order by addition would be out of the question! By using multiplication, the total cost can be found in one step: $2,500 \times \$29 = \$72,500$.

Multiplication is the combination of two whole numbers in which the number of times one is represented is determined by the value of the other. These two whole numbers are known as factors. The number being multiplied is the **multiplicand,** and the number by which the multiplicand is multiplied is the **multiplier.** The answer to a multiplication problem is the **product.** Intermediate answers are called partial products.

```
    258    multiplicand or factor
×    43    multiplier or factor
    774    partial product 1
  10 32    partial product 2
 11,094    product
```

In mathematics, the **times sign**—represented by the symbols "×" and "•" and "()"—is used to indicate multiplication. For example, 12 times 18 can be expressed as

$$12 \times 18 \quad 12 \cdot 18 \quad (12)(18) \quad 12(18)$$

Note: The symbol • is *not* a decimal point.

● multiplication
The combination of two integers in which the number of times one is represented is determined by the value of the other.

● multiplicand
In multiplication, the number being multiplied. For example, 5 is the multiplicand of $5 \times 4 = 20$.

● multiplier
The number by which the multiplicand is multiplied. For example, 4 is the multiplier of $5 \times 4 = 20$.

● product
The answer or result of multiplication. The number 20 is the product of $5 \times 4 = 20$.

● times sign
The symbol "×" representing multiplication. Also represented by a dot "•" or parentheses "( )".

Step 1. Write the multiplication factors in columns so that the place values line up. Note: In multiplication the factors are interchangeable. For example, 15 times 5 gives the same product as 5 times 15. Multiplication is usually expressed with the larger factor on top as the multiplicand, and the smaller factor placed under it as the multiplier.

Step 2. Multiply each digit of the multiplier, starting with units, times the multiplicand. Each will yield a partial product whose units digit appears under the corresponding digit of the multiplier.

Step 3. Add the digits in each column of the partial products, starting on the right with the units column.

Multiplication Shortcuts

The following shortcuts can be used to make multiplication easier and faster:

1. When the multiplier has a 0 in one or more of its middle digits, there is no need to write a whole line of zeros as a partial product. Simply place a 0 in the next partial product row, directly below the 0 in the multiplier, and go on to the next digit in the multiplier. The next partial product will start on the same row, one place to the left of the 0, and directly below its corresponding digit in the multiplier. For example, consider 554 times 103.

$$
\begin{array}{r}
\textit{Long way:} \quad 554 \\
\times\ 103 \\
\hline
1\ 662 \\
0\ 00 \\
55\ 4 \quad\ \\
\hline
57{,}062
\end{array}
\qquad
\begin{array}{r}
\textit{Shortcut:} \quad 554 \\
\times\ 103 \\
\hline
1\ 662 \\
55\ 40 \\
\hline
57{,}062
\end{array}
$$

2. When multiplying any number times zero, the resulting product is *always* zero. For example,

$$573 \times 0 = 0 \qquad 0 \times 34 = 0 \qquad 1{,}254{,}779 \times 0 = 0$$

3. The product of any number multiplied by one is that number itself. For example,

$$1{,}844 \times 1 = 1{,}844 \qquad 500 \times 1 = 500 \qquad 1 \times 894 = 894$$

4. When a number is multiplied by 10, 100, 1,000, 10,000, 100,000, and so on, simply add the zeros of the multiplier to the end of that number. For example,

$$792 \times 100 = 792 + 00 = 79{,}200 \qquad 9{,}345 \times 1{,}000 = 9{,}345 + 000 = 9{,}345{,}000$$

5. When the multiplicand and/or the multiplier have zeros at the end, multiply the two numbers without the zeros, and then add that number of zeros to the product. For example,

$$
130 \times 90 = \quad
\begin{array}{r}
13 \\
\times\ 9 \\
\hline
117 + \underline{00} = 11{,}700
\end{array}
\qquad\qquad
5{,}800 \times 3{,}400 = \quad
\begin{array}{r}
58 \\
\times\ 34 \\
\hline
232 \\
1\ 74\quad \\
\hline
1{,}972 + \underline{0000} = 19{,}720{,}000
\end{array}
$$

Verifying Multiplication

In order to check your multiplication for accuracy, divide the product by the multiplier. If the multiplication was correct, this will yield the multiplicand. For example,

Multiplication	Verification	Multiplication	Verification
48		527	
× 7		× 18	
336	$336 \div 7 = 48$	4 216	
		5 27	
		9,486	$9{,}486 \div 18 = 527$

Multiply the following numbers and verify your answers by division:

a. 2,293
  × 45

b. 59,300
  × 180

c. 436 × 2,027

d. 877 × 1

e. 6,922 × 0

f. A new plastic parts molding machine produces 85 parts per minute. How many parts can this machine produce in an hour? If a company has 15 of these machines, and they run for 8 hours per day, what is the total output of parts per day?

SOLUTION STRATEGY

a.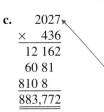
$$\begin{array}{r} 2{,}293 \\ \times\ \ \ 45 \\ \hline 11\ 465 \\ 91\ 72\ \ \\ \hline 103{,}185 \end{array}$$

This is a standard multiplication problem with two partial products. Always be sure to keep your columns lined up. The answer, 103,185, can be verified by division:
$103{,}185 \div 45 = 2{,}293$

b.
$$\begin{array}{r} 593 \\ \times\ \ 18 \\ \hline 4\ 744 \\ 5\ 93\ \ \\ \hline 10{,}674 + 000 = \underline{10{,}674{,}000} \end{array}$$

In this problem we remove the three zeros, multiply, and then add back the zeros.

c.
$$\begin{array}{r} 2027 \\ \times\ \ \ 436 \\ \hline 12\ 162 \\ 60\ 81\ \ \\ 810\ 8\ \ \ \\ \hline 883{,}772 \end{array}$$

This is another standard multiplication problem. Note that the larger number was made the multiplicand (top), and the smaller number became the multiplier. This makes the problem easier to work.
Verification: $883{,}772 \div 436 = 2{,}027$

d. $877 \times 1 = \underline{877}$

Remember, any number multiplied by one is that number.

e. $6{,}922 \times 0 = \underline{0}$

Remember, any number multiplied by zero is zero.

f. 85 parts per minute × 60 minutes per hour = 5,100 parts per hour

5,100 parts per hour × 15 machines = 76,500 parts per hour, all machines

76,500 parts per hour × 8 hours per day = $\underline{612{,}000}$ parts per day, total production

TRY-IT   EXERCISES

Multiply the following numbers and verify your answers:

19. 8,203
  × 508

20. 5,400
  × 250

21. 3,370
  × 4,002

22. 189 × 169

23. A typical plasterer can finish 150 square feet of interior wall per hour. If he works 6 hours per day, how many square feet can he finish? If a contractor hires 4 plasterers, how many feet can they finish in a 5-day week?

Check your answers with the solutions on page 22.

1-6 Dividing Whole Numbers and Verifying Your Answers

Just as multiplication is a shortcut for repeated addition, division is a shortcut for repeated subtraction. Let's say while shopping you want to know how many $5 items you can purchase with $45. You could get the answer by finding out how many times 5 can be subtracted from 45. You would begin by subtracting 5 from 45 to get 40; then subtracting 5 from 40 to get 35; 5 from 35 to get 30; and so on, until you got to zero. Quite tedious, but it does give you the answer, 9. By using division, we simply ask, how many $5 are contained in $45? By dividing 45 by 5 we get the answer in one step ($45 \div 5 = 9$). Since division is the opposite of multiplication, we can verify our answer by multiplying 5 times 9 to get 45.

Division of whole numbers is the process of determining how many times one number is contained within another number. The number being divided is called the **dividend,** the number doing the dividing is called the **divisor,** and the answer is known as the **quotient.** When the divisor has only one digit, as in 100 divided by 5, it is called short division. When the divisor has more than one digit, as in 100 divided by 10, it is known as long division.

The "$\div$" symbol represents division, and is known as the **division sign.** For example, $12 \div 4$ is read "12 divided by 4." Another way to show division is

$$\frac{12}{4}$$

This also reads "12 divided by 4." In order to actually solve the division, we use the sign $\overline{)}$. The problem is then written as $4\overline{)12}$. As in addition, subtraction, and multiplication, proper alignment of the digits is very important.

$$\frac{\text{Dividend}}{\text{Divisor}} = \text{Quotient} \qquad \text{Divisor}\overline{)\text{Dividend}}^{\text{Quotient}}$$

When the divisor divides evenly into the dividend, it is known as even division. When the divisor does not divide evenly into the dividend, the answer then becomes a quotient plus a **remainder.** The remainder is the amount left over after the division is completed. This is known as uneven division. In this chapter, a remainder of 3, for example, will be expressed as R 3. In Chapter 2, remainders will be expressed as fractions, and in Chapter 3, remainders will be expressed as decimals.

Verifying Division

To verify even division, multiply the quotient by the divisor. If the problem was worked correctly, this will yield the dividend. To verify uneven division, multiply the quotient by the divisor, and add the remainder to the product. If the problem was worked correctly, this will yield the dividend.

Even Division Illustrated

$$\frac{850 \ (\text{dividend})}{25 \ (\text{divisor})} = 34 \ (\text{quotient})$$

Verification: $34 \times 25 = 850$

Uneven Division Illustrated

$$\frac{850 \ (\text{dividend})}{20 \ (\text{divisor})} = 42 \ \text{R} \ 10 \ (\text{quotient})$$

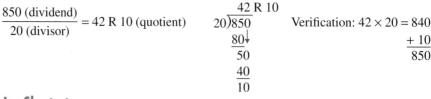

Verification: $42 \times 20 = 840$, $+ \ 10$, 850

Division Shortcut

When both the dividend and the divisor end in one or more zeros, you can remove an *equal* number of zeros from each and then divide. This gives the same answer with much less work. For example, 7,000 divided by 200 is the same as 70 divided by 2. Note: Although 7,000 has three zeros, you can't remove three zeros, since 200 has only two zeros.

$$\frac{7000}{200} = 35 \qquad \frac{70}{2} = 35$$

- **division**
  The mathematical process of determining how many times one number is contained within another number.

- **dividend**
  In division, the quantity being divided. For example, 20 is the dividend of $20 \div 5 = 4$.

- **divisor**
  The quantity by which another quantity, the dividend, is being divided. The number doing the dividing. For example, 5 is the divisor of $20 \div 5 = 4$.

- **quotient**
  The answer or result of division. The number 4 is the quotient of $20 \div 5 = 4$.

- **division sign**
  The symbol "$\div$" representing division.

- **remainder**
  In uneven division, the amount left over after the division is completed. For example, 2 is the remainder of $22 \div 5 = 4$, R2.

Field yield? If we know one acre yields 100 bales of hay and our field is five acres, we can use multiplication to determine the answer: $100 \times 5 = 500$ bales of hay.

STEPS FOR DIVIDING WHOLE NUMBERS:

Step 1. Determine the first group of digits in the dividend that the divisor will divide into at least once. This group will contain an equal or larger number of places than the divisor. Divide, and place the partial quotient over the last digit in that group.

Step 2. Multiply the partial quotient by the divisor. Place it under the first group of digits and subtract.

Step 3. From the dividend, bring down the next digit after the first group of digits.

Step 4. Repeat Steps 1, 2, and 3, until all of the digits in the dividend have been brought down.

EXAMPLES

Divide the following numbers and verify your answers:

a. $210 \div 7$

b. $185 \div 9$

c. $\dfrac{1,508}{6}$

d. $\dfrac{14,000}{3,500}$

e. An electrician has a roll of wire containing 650 feet. How many 8-foot pieces can be cut from this roll?

SOLUTION STRATEGY

a.
$$\begin{array}{r} 30 \\ 7\overline{)210} \\ \underline{21}\downarrow \\ 00 \end{array}$$

This is an example of even division. Note that there is no remainder.

Verification: $30 \times 7 = \underline{\underline{210}}$

b.
$$\begin{array}{r} 20 \text{ R } 5 \\ 9\overline{)185} \\ \underline{18}\downarrow \\ 5 \end{array}$$

This example illustrates uneven division. Note that there is a remainder.

Verification: $20 \times 9 = 180$

$$\begin{array}{r} + \ 5 \\ \hline 185 \end{array}$$

c.
$$\begin{array}{r} 251 \text{ R } 2 \\ 6\overline{)1508} \\ \underline{12} \\ 30 \\ \underline{30}\downarrow \\ 08 \\ \underline{6} \\ 2 \end{array}$$

This is another example of uneven division. Be sure to keep the digits properly lined up.

Verification: $251 \times 6 = 1,506$

$$\begin{array}{r} + \ \ 2 \\ \hline 1,508 \end{array}$$

d.
$$\begin{array}{r} 4 \\ 35\overline{)140} \\ \underline{140} \\ 0 \end{array}$$

In this example, we simplify the division by deleting 2 zeros from the dividend and the divisor.

Verification: $4 \times 35 = \underline{\underline{140}}$

e.
$$\begin{array}{r} 81 \text{ R } 2 \\ 8\overline{)650} \\ \underline{64}\downarrow \\ 10 \\ \underline{8} \\ 2 \end{array}$$

In this word problem, we want to know how many 8-foot pieces of wire are contained in a 650-foot roll. The dividend is 650 and the divisor is 8. The quotient, 81 R 2, means that 81 whole pieces of wire can be cut from the roll, with some left over, but not enough for another whole piece.

Verification: $81 \times 8 = 648$

$$\begin{array}{r} + \ 2 \\ \hline 650 \end{array}$$

TRY-IT EXERCISES

Divide the following numbers and verify your answers:

24. $910 \div 35$ **25.** $1,503 \div 160$ **26.** $\dfrac{3,358}{196}$ **27.** $\dfrac{175,000}{12,000}$

28. A factory has 39 production line workers, each making the same amount of money. If last week's total payroll amounted to $18,330, how much did each employee earn?

Check your answers with the solutions on page 22.

REVIEW EXERCISES CHAPTER 1—SECTION III

Multiply the following numbers and verify your answers:

1.	**2.**	**3.**	**4.**	**5.**
589	1,292	327	76,000	56,969
× 19	× 158	× 900	× 45	× 1,000
11,191	204,136	294,300	3,420,000	56,969,000

6. Multiply $4 times 501

501
× 4
$2,004

7. 23×570

570
× 23
13,110

8. What is 475 times 12?

475
× 12
5,700

Estimate the following by rounding each number, then multiply to get the exact answer:

		Estimate	Rounded Estimate	Exact Answer
9.	202	200		
	× 490	× 500	100,000	98,980
	98,980	100,000		
10.	515	500		
	× 180	× 200	100,000	92,700
	92,700	100,000		
11.	17	20		
	× 11	× 10	200	187
	187	200		

12. Sara Gomez earns $6 per hour. How much does Sara make in a 35-hour week?

35
× 6
210 Total earned

13. Bill Cunningham has a car that averages 19 miles per gallon. If the gas tank holds 21 gallons, how many miles can he travel on a tank of gas?

$$
\begin{array}{r}
21 \\
\times\ 19 \\
\hline
399\ \text{Miles}
\end{array}
$$

14. To earn extra money while attending college, you work as a cashier in a restaurant.

    a. Find the total bill for the following food order: 3 sirloin steak dinners at $12 each; 2 baked chicken specials at $7 each; 4 steak burger platters at $5 each; 2 extra salads at $2 each; 6 drinks at $1 each; and tax of $7.

$$
\begin{array}{lrcl}
\text{Steaks} & 3 \times 12 & = & 36 \\
\text{Chicken} & 2 \times\ \ 7 & = & 14 \\
\text{Burgers} & 4 \times\ \ 5 & = & 20 \\
\text{Salads} & 2 \times\ \ 2 & = & \ 4 \\
\text{Drinks} & 6 \times\ \ 1 & = & \ 6 \\
\text{Tax} & & + & \ 7 \\
\hline
& & & \$87\ \text{Total}
\end{array}
$$

    b. How much change will you give back if the check is paid with a $100 bill?

$$
\begin{array}{r}
100 \\
-\ \ 87 \\
\hline
\$13\ \text{Change}
\end{array}
$$

15. A model #35 press can print 620 posters per hour. Model #45 can print 1,035 posters per hour. If a publishing company has 3 model #35 presses and 5 model #45 presses, how many posters can be printed in a 10-hour day?

Model #35		Model #45		
620 Posters		1,035 Posters		18,600
× 3 Presses		× 5 Presses		+ 51,750
1,860 Per hour		5,175 Per hour		70,350 Total posters
× 10 Hours		× 10 Hours		per day
18,600 Per day		51,750 Per day		

Divide the following numbers:

16. $4{,}500 \div 35$

$$
\begin{array}{r}
128\ \text{R}\ 20 \\
35\overline{)47500} \\
\underline{35} \\
100 \\
\underline{70} \\
300 \\
\underline{280} \\
20
\end{array}
$$

17. $74{,}770 \div 5{,}700$

$$
\begin{array}{r}
13\ \text{R}\ 67 \\
570\overline{)7477} \\
\underline{570} \\
1777 \\
\underline{1710} \\
67
\end{array}
$$

18. $\dfrac{60{,}000}{250}$

$$
\begin{array}{r}
240 \\
25\overline{)6000} \\
\underline{50} \\
100 \\
\underline{100} \\
00
\end{array}
$$

19. $\dfrac{236{,}500{,}000}{4{,}300{,}000}$

$$
\begin{array}{r}
55 \\
43\overline{)2365} \\
\underline{215} \\
215 \\
\underline{215} \\
0
\end{array}
$$

Estimate the following by rounding each number to hundreds, then divide to get the exact answer:

		Estimate	Rounded Estimate	Exact Answer
20.	$890 \div 295$	$\dfrac{900}{300}$	3	3 R 5
21.	$1{,}499 \div 580$	$\dfrac{1{,}500}{600}$	2 R 300	2 R 339
22.	$57{,}800 \div 102$	$\dfrac{57{,}800}{100}$	578	566 R 68

23. A roofer has 50,640 square feet of roofing material. If the average roof requires 8,440 square feet of material, how many roofs can he cover?

$$\frac{50{,}640}{8{,}440} = \underline{\underline{6}} \text{ Roofs}$$

24. A calculator uses 8 circuit boards, each containing 450 parts. A company has 421,215 parts in stock.

   a. How many calculators can it manufacture?

$$\begin{array}{r} 450 \\ \times \quad 8 \\ \hline 3{,}600 \end{array} \text{ Parts per} \atop \text{calculator}$$

$$\frac{421{,}215}{3{,}600} = 117 \text{ R } 15 \qquad \underline{\underline{117}} \text{ Calculators}$$

   b. How many parts will be left?

$$\underline{\underline{15}} \text{ Parts left}$$

25. John Fernandez borrows $24,600 from the Friendly Bank and Trust Co. The interest charge amounts to $8,664. What equal monthly payments must John make in order to pay back the loan, with interest, in 36 months?

$$\begin{array}{r} 24{,}600 \\ + \quad 8{,}664 \\ \hline \$33{,}264 \end{array} \text{ Total payback}$$

$$\frac{33{,}264}{36} = \underline{\underline{\$924}} \text{ Per month}$$

CHAPTER 1 ▪ A REVIEW OF BASIC OPERATIONS   SUMMARY CHART

SECTION I   THE DECIMAL NUMBER SYSTEM: WHOLE NUMBERS

Topic	P/O, Page	Important Concepts	Illustrative Examples
Reading and Writing Whole Numbers in Numerical and Word Form	1–1 2	1. Insert the commas every three digits to mark the groups, beginning at the right side of the number. 2. From left to right, name the places and the groups. Groups that have all zeros are not named. 3. When writing whole numbers in word form, the numbers from 21 to 99 are hyphenated. Note: The word "and" should *not* be used in reading or writing whole numbers.	The number 15538 takes on the numerical form 15,538 and is read, "fifteen thousand, five hundred thirty-eight." The number 22939643 takes on the numerical form 22,939,643 and is read, "twenty-two million, nine hundred thirty-nine thousand, six hundred forty-three." The number 1000022 takes on the numerical value 1,000,022 and is read, "one million, twenty-two."
Rounding Whole Numbers to a Specified Place Value	1–2 4	1. Determine the place to which the number is to be rounded. 2a. If the digit to the right of the one being rounded is 5 or more, increase the digit in the place being rounded by 1. 2b. If the digit to the right of the one being rounded is 4 or less, do not change the digit in the place being rounded. 3. Change all digits to the right of the place being rounded to zeros.	1,449 rounded to tens = 1,450 255 rounded to hundreds = 300 345,391 rounded to thousands = 345,000 68,658,200 rounded to millions = 69,000,000 768,892 rounded all the way = 800,000

SECTION II　ADDITION AND SUBTRACTION OF WHOLE NUMBERS

Topic	P/O, Page	Important Concepts	Illustrative Examples
Adding Whole Numbers	1–3 7	1. Write the whole numbers in columns so that the place values line up. 2. Add the digits in each column, starting on the right with the units column. 3. When the total in a column is greater than nine, write the units digit and carry the tens digit to the top of the next column to the left. To verify addition, add the numbers in reverse, from bottom to top.	2 1 1 1,931　addend 2,928　addend + 5,857　addend 10,716　sum Verification: 2 1 1 5,857 2,928 + 1,931 10,716
Subtracting Whole Numbers	1–4 9	1. Write the whole numbers in columns so that the place values line up. 2. Starting with the units column, subtract the digits. 3. When a column can't be subtracted, borrow a digit from the column to the left of the one you are working in. To verify subtraction, add the difference and the subtrahend; this should equal the minuend.	34,557　minuend − 6,224　subtrahend 28,333　difference Verification: 28,333 + 6,224 34,557

SECTION III　MULTIPLICATION AND DIVISION OF WHOLE NUMBERS

Topic	P/O, Page	Important Concepts	Illustrative Examples
Multiplying Whole Numbers	1–5 13	1. Write the multiplication factors in columns so that the place values are lined up. 2. Multiply each digit of the multiplier, starting with units, times the multiplicand. Each will yield a partial product whose units digit appears under the corresponding digit of the multiplier. 3. Add the digits in each column of the partial products, starting on the right, with the units column. To verify multiplication, divide the product by the multiplier. If the multiplication is correct, this should yield the multiplicand.	258　multiplicand or factor × 43　multiplier or factor 774　partial product 1 10 32　partial product 2 11,094　product Verification: $\frac{11,094}{43} = 258$
Dividing Whole Numbers	1–6 16	1. The number being divided is the dividend. The number by which we are dividing is the divisor. The answer is known as the quotient. Divisor$\overline{)}$Dividend, Quotient 2. If the divisor does not divide evenly into the dividend, the quotient will have a remainder. To verify division, multiply the divisor by the quotient and add the remainder. If the division is correct, this will yield the dividend.	Divide six hundred fifty by twenty-seven. $650 \div 27 = \frac{650}{27} =$ 24 R 2 27)650 54 110 108 2 Verification: $27 \times 24 = 648 + 2 = 650$

Numerical Form	**Word Form**
1. 49,588	Forty-nine thousand, five hundred eighty-eight
2. 804	Eight hundred four
3. 1,928,837	One million, nine hundred twenty-eight thousand, eight hundred thirty-seven
4. 900,015	Nine hundred thousand, fifteen
5. 6,847,365,911	Six billion, eight hundred forty-seven million, three hundred sixty-five thousand, nine hundred eleven
6. 2,000,300,007	Two billion, three hundred thousand, seven

7. 51,7̲00 **8.** 23,44̲0 **9.** 175,45̲0,000 **10.** 6̲0,000 **11.** 15̲,000,000,000 **12.** 8,01̲0,000,000

13.
$$
\begin{array}{r}
39,481 \\
5,594 \\
+\ 11,029 \\
\hline
56,104
\end{array}
\qquad Verify:\quad
\begin{array}{r}
11,029 \\
5,594 \\
+\ 39,481 \\
\hline
56,104
\end{array}
$$

14.
$$
\begin{array}{r}
6,948 \\
330 \\
7,946 \\
89 \\
5,583,991 \\
7 \\
+\ 18,606 \\
\hline
5,617,917
\end{array}
\qquad Verify:\quad
\begin{array}{r}
18,606 \\
7 \\
5,583,991 \\
89 \\
7,946 \\
330 \\
+\ 6,948 \\
\hline
5,617,917
\end{array}
$$

15.
$$
\begin{array}{r}
183 \\
228 \\
281 \\
545 \\
438 \\
+\ 1,157 \\
\hline
2,832 \text{ meals}
\end{array}
\qquad Verify:\quad
\begin{array}{r}
1,157 \\
438 \\
545 \\
281 \\
228 \\
+\ 183 \\
\hline
2,832 \text{ meals}
\end{array}
$$

16.
$$
\begin{array}{r}
98,117 \\
-\ 7,682 \\
\hline
90,435
\end{array}
\quad Verify:\quad
\begin{array}{r}
90,435 \\
+\ 7,682 \\
\hline
98,117
\end{array}
$$

17.
$$
\begin{array}{r}
12,395 \\
-\ 5,589 \\
\hline
6,806
\end{array}
\quad Verify:\quad
\begin{array}{r}
6,806 \\
+\ 5,589 \\
\hline
12,395
\end{array}
$$

18.
$$
\begin{array}{r}
\$4,589 \\
-\ 344 \\
\hline
\$4,245 \text{ left in account}
\end{array}
\quad Verify:\quad
\begin{array}{r}
\$4,245 \\
+\ 344 \\
\hline
\$4,589
\end{array}
$$

19.
$$
\begin{array}{r}
8,203 \\
\times\ 508 \\
\hline
65\ 624 \\
4\ 101\ 50 \\
\hline
4,167,124
\end{array}
$$
Verify:
$$
\frac{4,167,124}{508} = 8,203
$$

20.
$$
\begin{array}{r}
5,400 \\
\times\ 250 \\
\hline
270\ 000 \\
1\ 080\ 00 \\
\hline
1,350,000
\end{array}
$$
Verify:
$$
\frac{1,350,000}{250} = 5,400
$$

21.
$$
\begin{array}{r}
3,370 \\
\times\ 4,002 \\
\hline
6\ 740 \\
13\ 480\ 00 \\
\hline
13,486,740
\end{array}
$$
Verify:
$$
\frac{13,486,740}{4,002} = 3,370
$$

22. 189×169
$$
\begin{array}{r}
189 \\
\times\ 169 \\
\hline
1\ 701 \\
11\ 34 \\
18\ 9 \\
\hline
31,941
\end{array}
$$
Verify:
$$
\frac{31,941}{169} = 189
$$

23.
$$
\begin{array}{r}
150 \\
\times\ 6 \\
\hline
900 \text{ sq. ft. per day}
\end{array}
\qquad
\begin{array}{r}
900 \\
\times\ 4 \text{ plasterers} \\
\hline
3,600 \text{ sq. ft. per day}
\end{array}
\qquad
\begin{array}{r}
3,600 \\
\times\ 5 \text{ days} \\
\hline
18,000 \text{ sq. ft. in 5 days}
\end{array}
$$

24.
$$
\begin{array}{r}
26 \\
35{\overline{)910}} \\
70 \\
\hline
210 \\
210 \\
\hline
0
\end{array}
$$
Verify:
$26 \times 35 = 910$

25.
$$
\begin{array}{r}
9 \text{ R63} \\
160{\overline{)1,503}} \\
1\ 440 \\
\hline
63
\end{array}
$$
Verify:
$160 \times 9 = 1,440$
$$
\begin{array}{r}
+\ 63 \\
\hline
1,503
\end{array}
$$

26.
$$
\begin{array}{r}
17 \text{ R26} \\
196{\overline{)3,358}} \\
196 \\
\hline
1\ 398 \\
1\ 372 \\
\hline
26
\end{array}
$$
Verify:
$196 \times 17 = 3,332$
$$
\begin{array}{r}
+\ 26 \\
\hline
3,358
\end{array}
$$

27.
$$
\begin{array}{r}
14 \text{ R7} \\
12{\overline{)175}} \\
12 \\
\hline
55 \\
48 \\
\hline
7
\end{array}
$$
Verify:
$12 \times 14 = 168$
$$
\begin{array}{r}
+\ 7 \\
\hline
175
\end{array}
$$

28. $\dfrac{18,330}{39} = \$470$ per employee
$$
\begin{array}{r}
470 \\
39{\overline{)18,330}} \\
15\ 6 \\
\hline
2\ 73 \\
2\ 73 \\
\hline
0
\end{array}
$$
Verify: $39 \times 470 = 18,330$

Name_____

Class_____

Read and write the following whole numbers in numerical and word form:

Number	Numerical Form	Word Form
1. 200049	200,049	Two hundred thousand, forty-nine
2. 52308411	52,308,411	Fifty-two million, three hundred eight thousand, four hundred eleven

Write the following whole numbers in numerical form:

3. Three hundred sixteen thousand, two hundred twenty-nine   316,229

4. Four million, five hundred sixty thousand   4,560,000

Round the following numbers to the indicated place:

5. 18,334 to hundreds   18,300

6. 3,545,687 all the way   4,000,000

7. 256,733 to ten thousands   260,000

Perform the indicated operation for the following:

8.
```
   1,860
     429
     133
 + 1,009
   3,431
```

9.
```
   927
 - 828
    99
```

10.
```
    207
 ×  106
   1242
   2070
 21,942
```

11.
```
      44 R 28
 42)1876
    168
    196
    168
     28
```

12.
```
   3,505
 ×   290
  315450
    7010
 1,016,450
```

13.
```
    6,800
      919
      201
 + 14,338
   22,258
```

14. $150,000 \div 188$
```
       797 R 164
 188)150000
     1316
     1840
     1692
     1480
     1316
      164
```

15. $1,205 - 491$
```
   1205
 -  491
    714
```

16. The following chart shows Melody Music Shop's product sales for last week. Use addition and subtraction to fill in the blank spaces. What is the week's grand total?

	Monday	Tuesday	Wednesday	Thursday	Friday	Saturday	Total Units
Records	82	56	68	57	72	92	427
Tapes	29	69	61	58	82	75	374
CDs	96	103	71	108	112	159	649
Daily Totals	207	228	200	223	266	326 **Grand Total**	1,450

17. You are the bookkeeper for Melody Music, in problem 16. If records sell for $9 each, tapes sell for $6 each, and CDs sell for $13 each, what was the total dollar sales for last week?

Records	Tapes	CDs	
427	374	649	3,843
× 9	× 6	× 13	2,244
$3,843	$2,244	$8,437	+ 8,437
			$14,524 Total sales

ANSWERS

1. 200,049 Two hundred thousand, forty-nine
2. 52,308,411 Fifty-two million, three hundred eight thousand, four hundred eleven
3. 316,229
4. 4,560,000
5. 18,300
6. 4,000,000
7. 260,000
8. 3,431
9. 99
10. 21,942
11. 44 R 28
12. 1,016,450
13. 22,258
14. 797 R 164
15. 714
16. 1,450
17. $14,524 Total sales

ANSWERS

18. _____$104 Per acre_____

19. a. _____19 Boats_____

  b. _____25 Boats_____

20. _____$520 Per week_____

21. a. _____$11,340 Total cost_____

  b. _____$36 Per stockholder_____

22. _____$4,325 Per month_____

18. A 1,600-acre farm was sold for a total of $235,000. If the house and equipment are worth $68,600 and the land represents the balance, what was the price paid per acre for the land?

235,000 Total
− 68,600 House and equipment
166,400 Land

$\dfrac{166,400}{1,600} = \$104$ Per acre

19. A summer camp has budgeted $85,500 for a new fleet of sailboats. The boat selected is a deluxe model costing $4,500.

  a. How many boats can be purchased by the camp?

$\dfrac{85,500}{4,500} = 19$ Boats

  b. If instead a standard model were chosen costing $3,420, how many boats could be purchased?

$\dfrac{85,500}{3,420} = 25$ Boats

20. Jeffrey Miller makes a salary of $23,440 per year plus a commission of $300 per month. What is his weekly income? (There are 52 weeks in a year.)

300
× 12
$3,600 Commission

23,440
+ 3,600
$27,040 Total salary

$\dfrac{27,040}{52} = \$520$ Per week

21. You are in charge of putting together the annual stockholder's luncheon for your company. The meal will cost $13 per person; entertainment will cost $2,100; facility rental is $880; invitations and annual report printing costs are $2,636; and other expenses come to $1,629. Calculate the costs, if 315 stockholders plan to attend.

  a. What is the total cost of the affair?

315
× 13
4,095 Meals

4,095
2,100
880
2,636
+ 1,629
$11,340 Total cost

  b. What is the cost per stockholder?

$\dfrac{11,340}{315} = \$36$ Per stockholder

22. Century Bank requires mortgage loan applicants to have a gross monthly income of five times the amount of their monthly payment. How much monthly income must Jennifer Adams have in order to qualify for a payment of $865?

865
× 5
$4,325 Per month

23. Nina Sanders had $868 in her checking account on April 1. During the month she wrote checks for $15, $123, $88, $276, and $34. She also deposited $45, $190, and $436. What is the balance in Nina's checking account at the end of April?

Checks	Deposits	868 Balance April 1
15	45	− 536
123	190	332
88	+ 436	+ 671
276	$671	$1,003 Balance April 30
+ 34		
$536		

24. Last week, the *More Joy,* a commercial fishing boat, brought in 360 pounds of tuna, 225 pounds of halibut, and 570 pounds of snapper. At the dock, the catch was sold to Atlantic Seafood Wholesalers. The tuna brought $3 per pound; the halibut, $4 per pound; and the snapper, $5 per pound. If fuel and crew expenses amounted to $1,644, how much profit did Captain Bob make on this trip?

Tuna	Halibut	Snapper	1,080
360	225	570	900
× 3	× 4	× 5	+ 2,850
$1,080	$900	$2,850	4,830 Total sales
			− 1,644 Expenses
			$3,186 Profit

25. Samuel Charles bought 2,000 shares of stock at $62 per share. Six months later he sold the 2,000 shares at $87 per share. If the total stockbroker's commission was $740, how much profit did he make on this transaction?

Buy	Sell	174,000
2,000	2,000	− 124,000
× 62	× 87	50,000
$124,000	$174,000	− 740 Commission
		$49,260 Profit

26. A construction job was estimated to cost $24,890,000. If the actual cost was $32,009,770, by how much was the job over budget?

32,009,770
− 24,890,000
$7,119,770 Over budget

27. The Nelson Coal Mining Company produces 40 tons of ore in an 8-hour shift. The mine operates continuously—3 shifts per day, 7 days per week. How many tons of ore can be extracted in 6 weeks?

40 Tons	120	840
× 3 Shifts	× 7 Days	× 6 Weeks
120 Per day	840 Per week	5,040 Total in 6 weeks

28. The Wilson Corporation purchased a new building for $165,000. After a down payment of $45,600, the balance was paid in equal monthly payments, with no interest.

a. If the loan was paid off in 2 years, how much were the monthly payments?

165,000	12 Months	$\frac{119,400}{24} = \$4,975$ Per month
− 45,600	× 2 Years	
$119,400 Amount financed	24 Months	

b. If the loan was paid off in 5 years, how much *less* were the monthly payments?

12 Months	$\frac{119,400}{60} = \$1,990$ Per month	4,975
× 5 Years		− 1,990
60 Months		$2,985 Less if paid in 5 years

Name_____

Class_____

ANSWERS

29. _____15 Tons per trailer_____

30. ____$4,500 Profit last week____

31. a. ___Living room: 345 sq. ft.___

_____Dining room: 216 sq. ft._____

_____Kitchen: 99 sq. ft._____

_____Study: 120 sq. ft._____

b. _____780 Total sq. feet_____

c. ___$2,559 Total cost of tile___

d. ___$4,119 Total cost of job___

e. _____Yes_____

29. A flatbed railroad car weighs 150 tons empty and 420 tons loaded with 18 trailers. How many tons does each trailer weigh?

420 Total
− 150 Railroad car
270 Weight
    of trailers

$\frac{270}{18} = 15$ Tons per trailer

30. Star-Bright Security charges $14 per hour for security guards. The guards are paid $8 per hour. If Star-Bright has 30 guards, each working a 25-hour week, how much profit did the company make last week?

14
− 8
$6 Profit per guard
    per hour

30 Guards
× 6 Profit per guard
$180 Total profit per hour
× 25 Hours last week
$4,500 Profit last week

 ### BUSINESS DECISION
Estimating a Tile Job

31. You are the owner of The Tile Galleria. Chuck and Jill have asked you to give them an estimate for tiling 4 rooms of their house. The living room is 15 feet × 23 feet; the dining room is 12 feet × 18 feet; the kitchen is 9 feet × 11 feet; and the study is 10 feet × 12 feet.

a. How many square feet of tile are required for each room? (Multiply the length times the width.)

Living Room	Dining Room	Kitchen	Study
23	18	11	12
× 15	× 12	× 9	× 10
345 sq.ft.	216 sq.ft.	99 sq.ft.	120 sq.ft.

b. What is the total number of square feet to be tiled?

345
216
99
+ 120
780 Total sq. feet

c. If the tile for the kitchen and study costs $4 per square foot, and the tile for the living and dining rooms costs $3 per square foot, what is the total cost of the tile?

99 Kitchen
+ 120 Study
219 sq.ft.
× 4 Price
$876

345 Living Room
+ 216 Dining Room
561 sq.ft.
× 3 Price
$1,683

876
+ 1,683
$2,559 Total cost
    of tile

d. If your company charges $2 per square foot for installation, what is the total cost of the tile job?

780 sq.ft.
× 2 Price
$1,560 Installation
    charge

1,560
+ 2,559
$4,119 Total cost
    of job

e. If Chuck and Jill have saved $4,500 for the tile job, have they saved enough money? If not, how much more do they need?

4,500 Saved
− 4,119 Cost
$381 Extra

Yes

All the Math That's Fit to Learn

The Business Math Times

Volume I   **A Review of Basic Operations**   One Dollar

Overcoming Anxiety in Business Math

Math! It makes throats lumpy, stomachs queasy, and palms sweaty. Each year, in thousands of math classes around the country, it transforms otherwise excellent students into a state of absolute anxiety.

What can you do? To begin with, understand that math isn't just a course you have to take in school and then not deal with any more. On the contrary, math skills, particularly in business, are an integral part of what it takes to build a successful career.

Even as a consumer, today's complex marketplace requires some business math skills in order to function in an informed and prudent manner. Remember, "Caveat Emptor!"…"Let the buyer beware!"

Make the commitment; learn it now!

Now that we've agreed on the commitment, here are a few pointers to help you reduce your anxiety and learn a new skill, mathematics:

* The mind is like a parachute, it functions better open. Keep an open mind about math, you may even learn to like it!
* Not everybody learns at the same speed. It may take you a little longer—so what!—as long as it's before the next test.
* Once you gain knowledge, no one can take it from you. It's yours for life. That makes it pretty valuable.
* Everybody makes mistakes. Use them as a learning opportunity, not as failure.
* Be prepared! This will definitely help reduce your anxiety level.
* Attendance is very important. A missed class is hard to make up.
* Do all of your homework and be ready for each class.
* Ask questions about things you didn't understand.
* Be willing to try alternative strategies in solving problems.
* Woodrow Wilson said, "I not only use all the brains that I have, but all that I can borrow." Study with a friend; test each other.
* Relax!

Brainteaser

According to legend, Euclid, a Greek mathematician in the third century B.C., was the author of the following:

A mule and a donkey were carrying sacks of grain to market. The mule exclaimed, "Wow, is this load heavy!" The donkey replied, "What are you complaining about? If you gave me one of your sacks, I would have twice as many as you. If I gave you one of mine, we would have equal amounts."

How many sacks was each animal carrying? Mule_____ Donkey_____

SOURCE: Gyles Brandeth, *Classic Puzzles* (New York: Harper & Row, 1985), p. 1. Reprinted with permission.

DON'T BE NERVOUS... ROUNDED OFF TO THE NEAREST MILLION, THERE'S NO ONE HERE!

All About Money

A Dollar Frayed Is a Dollar Recycled

Paper money, like the mortals who spend it, doesn't last. After 18 months, $1 bills are too frayed for general circulation. A $5 is around for just two years. And 20 greenbacks?…three to four years. The feds dispose of 7,000 tons of worn-out bills annually, and it costs big bucks to shred bills, pack them into bricks, then dump them in landfills.

Several Southern California companies have a novel use for all that spent cash: recycle it into everything from stationery to fiberboard used in walls during construction. You can see pieces of dollars in the white fiberboard made by Gridcore Systems International in Carlsbad. Terra Roofing in Fontana makes roof shingles, while others produce fireplace logs—for buyers with money to burn.

SOURCE: Scott LaFee, "Up Front," *Business Week*—America Online July 25, 1994.

College Education Not Included

According to a government study done by the Agriculture Department's Family Economics Research Group, the average cost of raising a child from birth to age eighteen—in 1992 dollars—was $128,670, not including college.

SOURCE: Dean D. Dauphinais, and Kathleen Droste. *Astounding Averages!* Visible Ink Press, a division of Gale Research Inc., 1995, p. 6.

Fractions

Performance Objectives

UNDERSTANDING AND WORKING WITH FRACTIONS

Fractions are a mathematical way of expressing a part of a whole thing. This concept is used quite commonly in business. We may look at sales for $\frac{1}{2}$ the year, or reduce prices by $\frac{1}{4}$ for a sale. A share of stock may go up $2\frac{5}{8}$ points, or you might want to cut $5\frac{3}{4}$ yards of fabric from a roll of material. Just like whole numbers, fractions can be added, subtracted, multiplied, divided, and even combined with whole numbers. This chapter will introduce you to the various types of fractions, and show you how they are used in the business world.

2-1 Distinguishing between the Various Types of Fractions

Technically, fractions express the relationship between two numbers, set up as a division. The **numerator** is the number on the top of the fraction. It represents the dividend in the division. The **denominator** is the bottom number of the fraction. It represents the divisor. The numerator and the denominator are separated by a horizontal or slanted line, known as the **division line.** This line means "divided by." For example, the fraction 2/3, or $\frac{2}{3}$, read as "two-thirds," means 2 divided by 3, or 2 ÷ 3.

Remember, fractions express parts of a whole unit. The unit may be dollars, feet, ounces, or anything. The denominator describes how many total parts are in the unit. The numerator represents how many of the total parts we are describing or referring to. For example, a pizza (the whole unit) is divided into 8 slices (total equal parts, denominator). As a fraction, the whole pizza would be represented as $\frac{8}{8}$. If 5 of the slices were eaten (parts referred to, numerator), what fraction represents the part that was eaten? The answer would be the fraction $\frac{5}{8}$, read "five-eighths." On the other hand, since 5 slices were eaten out of a total of 8, 3 slices, or $\frac{3}{8}$, of the pizza is left. Fractions such as $\frac{3}{8}$ and $\frac{5}{8}$, in which the numerator is smaller than the denominator, represent less than a whole unit, and are known as **common, or proper fractions.** Some examples of proper fractions would be

$$\frac{3}{16} \quad \text{three-sixteenths} \qquad \frac{1}{4} \quad \text{one-fourth} \qquad \frac{9}{32} \quad \text{nine-thirty-seconds}$$

When a fraction's denominator is equal to or less than the numerator, it represents one whole unit or more, and is known as an **improper fraction.** Some examples of improper fractions are

$$\frac{9}{9} \quad \text{nine-ninths} \qquad \frac{15}{11} \quad \text{fifteen-elevenths} \qquad \frac{19}{7} \quad \text{nineteen-sevenths}$$

A number that combines a whole number with a proper fraction is known as a **mixed number.** Some examples of mixed numbers are

$$3\frac{1}{8} \quad \text{three and one-eighth} \qquad 7\frac{11}{16} \quad \text{seven and eleven-sixteenths}$$

$$46\frac{51}{60} \quad \text{forty-six and fifty-one-sixtieths}$$

EXAMPLES

For each of the following, identify the type of fraction, and write it in word form:

a. $\dfrac{45}{16}$ **b.** $14\dfrac{2}{5}$ **c.** $\dfrac{11}{12}$

● **fractions**

A mathematical way of expressing a part of a whole thing. For example, $\frac{1}{4}$ is a fraction expressing 1 part out of a total of 4 parts.

● **numerator**

The number on top of the division line of a fraction. It represents the dividend in the division. In the fraction $\frac{1}{4}$, 1 is the numerator.

● **denominator**

The number on the bottom of the division line of a fraction. It represents the divisor in the division. In the fraction $\frac{1}{4}$, 4 is the denominator.

● **division line**

The horizontal or slanted line separating the numerator from the denominator. The symbol representing "divided by" in a fraction. In the fraction $\frac{1}{4}$, the line between the 1 and the 4 is the division line.

● **common or proper fraction**

A fraction in which the numerator is smaller than the denominator. Represents less than a whole unit. The fraction $\frac{1}{4}$ is a common or proper fraction.

● **improper fraction**

A fraction in which the denominator is equal to or less than the numerator. Represents one whole unit or more. The fraction $\frac{4}{1}$ is an improper fraction.

● **mixed number**

A number that combines a whole number with a proper fraction. The fraction $10\frac{1}{4}$ is a mixed number.

a. $\frac{45}{16}$ This is an <u>improper fraction</u> because the denominator, 16, is less than the numerator, 45. In word form we say, "<u>forty-five-sixteenths</u>." It could also be read as "45 divided by 16," or "45 over 16."

b. $14\frac{2}{5}$ This is a <u>mixed number</u> because it combines the whole number 14 with the fraction $\frac{2}{5}$. In word form this is read, "<u>fourteen and two-fifths</u>."

c. $\frac{11}{12}$ This is a <u>common or proper fraction</u>, because the numerator, 11, is less than the denominator, 12. This fraction is read, "<u>eleven-twelfths</u>." It could also be read, "11 over 12" or "11 divided by 12."

Construction workers must accurately measure and calculate various lengths of building materials using fractions.

TRY-IT   **EXERCISES**

For each of the following, identify the type of fraction, and write it in word form:

1. $76\frac{3}{4}$ **2.** $\frac{3}{5}$ **3.** $\frac{18}{18}$ **4.** $\frac{33}{8}$

Check your answers with the solutions on page 54.

2-2 Converting Improper Fractions to Whole or Mixed Numbers

It often becomes necessary to change or convert an improper fraction into a whole or mixed number. For example, final answers cannot be left as improper fractions; they must be converted.

> **STEPS FOR CONVERTING IMPROPER FRACTIONS TO WHOLE OR MIXED NUMBERS:**
>
> **Step 1.** Divide the numerator of the improper fraction by the denominator.
> **Step 2a.** If there is no remainder, the improper fraction becomes a whole number.
> **Step 2b.** If there is a remainder, write the whole number and then write the fraction as
>
> $$\text{Whole number} \; \frac{\text{Remainder}}{\text{Divisor}}$$

EXAMPLES

Convert the following improper fractions to whole or mixed numbers:

a. $\frac{30}{5}$ **b.** $\frac{9}{2}$

a. $\frac{30}{5} = \underline{\underline{6}}$ When we divide the numerator, 30, by the denominator, 5, we get the whole number 6. There is no remainder.

b. $\dfrac{9}{2} = 2\overline{)9} = 4\dfrac{1}{2}$

This improper fraction divides 4 times with a remainder of 1, therefore it will become a mixed number. In this case, the 4 is the whole number. The remainder, 1, becomes the numerator of the new fraction; and the divisor, 2, becomes the denominator.

TRY-IT   EXERCISES

Convert the following improper fractions to whole or mixed numbers:

5. $\dfrac{8}{3}$ **6.** $\dfrac{25}{4}$ **7.** $\dfrac{39}{3}$

Check your answers with the solutions on page 54.

2-3 Converting Mixed Numbers to Improper Fractions

> **STEPS FOR CONVERTING A MIXED NUMBER TO AN IMPROPER FRACTION:**
>
> **Step 1.** Multiply the denominator by the whole number.
> **Step 2.** Add the numerator to the product from step 1.
> **Step 3.** Place the total from step 2 as the "new" numerator.
> **Step 4.** Place the original denominator as the "new" denominator.

EXAMPLES

Convert the following mixed numbers to improper fractions:

a. $5\dfrac{2}{3}$ **b.** $9\dfrac{5}{6}$

SOLUTION STRATEGY

a. $5\dfrac{2}{3} = \dfrac{17}{3}$

In this example, we multiply the denominator, 3, by the whole number, 5, and add the numerator, 2, to get 17 ($3 \times 5 = 15 + 2 = 17$). We then place the 17 over the original denominator, 3.

b. $9\dfrac{5}{6} = \dfrac{59}{6}$

In this example, we multiply the denominator, 6, by the whole number, 9, and add the numerator, 5, to get 59 ($6 \times 9 = 54 + 5 = 59$). We then place the 59 over the original denominator, 6.

TRY-IT   EXERCISES

Convert the following mixed numbers to improper fractions:

8. $2\dfrac{3}{4}$ **9.** $9\dfrac{1}{5}$ **10.** $22\dfrac{5}{8}$

Check your answers with the solutions on page 54.

2-4 Reducing Fractions to Lowest Terms

When working with fractions, it is often necessary to reduce them to lowest terms. For example, when the final answer to a math problem contains a fraction, it is common practice to reduce that fraction to its lowest terms. Thus, you would express an answer of $\frac{4}{8}$ as $\frac{1}{2}$, or $\frac{6}{9}$ as $\frac{2}{3}$. Fractions may be reduced to lower terms or raised to higher terms without changing the value of the fraction.

Reducing a fraction means finding whole numbers, called common divisors or common factors, that divide evenly into both the numerator and denominator of the fraction. For example, the fraction $\frac{24}{48}$ can be reduced to $\frac{12}{24}$, by the common divisor 2. The new fraction, $\frac{12}{24}$, can be further reduced to $\frac{4}{8}$ by the common divisor 3, and to $\frac{1}{2}$, by the common divisor 4. When a fraction has been reduced to the point where there are no common divisors left, other than 1, it is said to be **reduced to lowest terms.**

The largest number that is a common divisor of a fraction is known as the **greatest common divisor.** It reduces the fraction to lowest terms in one step. In the example of $\frac{24}{48}$ above, we could have used 24, the greatest common divisor, to reduce the fraction to $\frac{1}{2}$.

a. Reducing Fractions by Inspection

Reducing fractions by inspection or observation is often a trial-and-error procedure. Sometimes a fraction's common divisors are obvious; other times they are more difficult to determine. The following rules of divisibility may be helpful:

Rules of Divisibility

A Number Is Divisible By	Conditions
2	If the last digit is 0, 2, 4, 6, or 8.
3	If the sum of the digits is divisible by 3.
4	If the last two digits are divisible by 4.
5	If the last digit is 0 or 5.
6	If the number is divisible by 2 and 3, or if it is even and the sum of the digits is divisible by 3.
8	If the last three digits are divisible by 8.
9	If the sum of the digits is divisible by 9.
10	If the last digit is 0.

• reduce to lowest terms

The process of dividing whole numbers, known as common divisors or common factors, into both the numerator and denominator of a fraction. Used for expressing fractions as final answers. For example, $\frac{5}{20}$ reduces to $\frac{1}{4}$ by the common divisor, 5.

• greatest common divisor

The largest number that is a common divisor of a fraction. Used to reduce a fraction to lowest terms in one step. For example, 5 is the greatest common divisor of $\frac{5}{20}$.

EXAMPLE

Use observation and the rules of divisibility to reduce $\frac{48}{54}$ to lowest terms.

SOLUTION STRATEGY

$$\frac{48}{54} = \frac{48 \div 2}{54 \div 2} = \frac{24}{27}$$

Since the last digit of the numerator is 8, and the last digit of the denominator is 4, they are both divisible by 2.

$$\frac{24}{27} = \frac{24 \div 3}{27 \div 3} = \frac{8}{9}$$

Since the sum of the digits of the numerator, $2 + 4$, and the denominator, $2 + 7$, are both divisible by 3, the fraction is divisible by 3.

$$\frac{48}{54} = \frac{8}{9}$$

Since no numbers other than 1 divide evenly into the new fraction $\frac{8}{9}$, it is now reduced to lowest terms.

When buying gas, the price per gallon is frequently quoted as a fraction. The price of 120⁹ is read as "120 and 9/10ths."

b. Reducing Fractions by the Greatest Common Divisor Method

The best method for reducing a fraction to lowest terms is to divide the numerator and the denominator by the greatest common divisor, since this accomplishes the task in one step. When the greatest common divisor is not obvious to you, use the following steps to determine it:

STEPS FOR DETERMINING THE GREATEST COMMON DIVISOR OF A FRACTION:

Step 1. Divide the numerator of the fraction into the denominator.

Step 2. Take the remainder from Step 1 and divide it into the divisor from Step 1.

Step 3. Repeat this division process until the remainder is either 0 or 1.

■ If the remainder is 0, the last divisor is the greatest common divisor.

■ If the remainder is 1, the fraction cannot be reduced, and is therefore in lowest terms.

EXAMPLE

Reduce the fraction $\frac{63}{231}$ by finding the greatest common divisor.

SOLUTION STRATEGY

$$\begin{array}{r} 3 \\ 63\overline{)231} \\ 189 \\ \hline 42 \end{array}$$

Divide the numerator, 63, into the denominator, 231. This leaves a remainder of 42.

$$\begin{array}{r} 1 \\ 42\overline{)63} \\ 42 \\ \hline 21 \end{array}$$

Next, divide the remainder, 42, into the previous divisor, 63. This leaves a remainder of 21.

$$\begin{array}{r} 2 \\ 21\overline{)42} \\ 42 \\ \hline 0 \end{array}$$

Then, divide the remainder, 21, into the previous divisor, 42. Because this leaves a remainder of 0, the last divisor, 21, is the greatest common divisor of the original fraction.

$$\frac{63 \div 21}{231 \div 21} = \frac{3}{11}$$

By dividing both the numerator and the denominator by the greatest common divisor, 21, we get the fraction, $\frac{3}{11}$, which is the original fraction reduced to lowest terms.

TRY-IT **EXERCISES**

Reduce the following fractions to lowest terms:

11. $\frac{30}{55}$ **12.** $\frac{72}{148}$ **13.** $\frac{270}{810}$ **14.** $\frac{175}{232}$

Check your answers with the solutions on page 54.

2-5 Raising Fractions to Higher Terms

Raising a fraction to higher terms is a procedure sometimes needed in addition and subtraction. It is the opposite of reducing fractions to lower terms. In reducing, we used common divisors; in raising fractions we use common multiples. To **raise to higher terms,** simply multiply the numerator and denominator of a fraction by a **common multiple.**

For example, if we want to raise the fraction $\frac{3}{4}$ by a factor of 7, multiply the numerator and the denominator by 7. This procedure raises the fraction to $\frac{21}{28}$.

$$\frac{3 \times 7}{4 \times 7} = \frac{21}{28}$$

It is important to remember that the value of the fraction has not changed by raising it; we have simply divided the "whole" into more parts. Therefore $\frac{3}{4}$ has the same value as $\frac{21}{28}$. The fraction $\frac{7}{7}$, which we used as the common multiple, reduces to 1 ($7 \div 7 = 1$). Because the common multiple equals 1, multiplying it by a fraction does not change the value of that fraction.

● **raise to higher terms**

The process of multiplying whole numbers, known as common multiples, by the numerator and denominator of a fraction. Sometimes needed in addition and subtraction of fractions. For example, $\frac{5}{20}$ is the fraction $\frac{1}{4}$ raised to higher terms, 20ths, by the common multiple, 5.

● **common multiples**

Whole numbers used to raise fractions to higher terms. The common multiple 5 raises the fraction $\frac{1}{4}$ to $\frac{5}{20}$.

Understanding and Working with Fractions 33

In fractions, remember the denominator indicates how many total parts make up the whole, while the numerator indicates how many of those parts we are describing.

STEPS FOR RAISING A FRACTION TO A NEW DENOMINATOR:

Step 1. Divide the original denominator into the new denominator. The resulting quotient is the common multiple that raises the fraction.

Step 2. Multiply the numerator and the denominator of the original fraction by the common multiple.

EXAMPLES

Convert the following fractions to higher terms, as indicated:

a. $\frac{2}{3}$ to fifteenths

b. $\frac{3}{5}$ to fortieths

SOLUTION STRATEGY

a. $\frac{2}{3} = \frac{?}{15}$

In this example, we are raising the fraction $\frac{2}{3}$ to the denominator 15.

$15 \div 3 = 5$

Divide the original denominator, 3, into 15. This yields the common multiple, 5.

$\frac{2 \times 5}{3 \times 5} = \frac{10}{15}$

Now, multiply both the numerator and denominator by the common multiple, 5.

b. $\frac{3}{5} = \frac{?}{40}$

Here, the indicated denominator is 40.

$40 \div 5 = 8$

Dividing 5 into 40, we get the common multiple, 8.

$\frac{3 \times 8}{5 \times 8} = \frac{24}{40}$

Now raise the fraction by multiplying the numerator, 3, and the denominator, 5, by 8.

TRY-IT EXERCISES

Convert the following fractions to higher terms, as indicated:

15. $\frac{7}{8}$ to sixty-fourths

16. $\frac{3}{7}$ to thirty-fifths

Check your answers with the solutions on page 54.

 REVIEW EXERCISES CHAPTER 2—SECTION I

For each of the following, identify the type of fraction, and write it in word form:

1. $23\frac{4}{5}$

Mixed
Twenty-three and four-fifths

2. $\frac{12}{12}$

Improper
Twelve-twelfths

3. $\frac{15}{9}$

Improper
Fifteen-ninths

4. $\frac{7}{16}$

Proper
Seven-sixteenths

5. $2\frac{1}{8}$

Mixed
Two and one-eighth

Convert the following improper fractions to whole or mixed numbers:

6. $\dfrac{26}{8} = 3\dfrac{2}{8} = 3\dfrac{1}{4}$

7. $\dfrac{20}{6} = 3\dfrac{2}{6} = 3\dfrac{1}{3}$

8. $\dfrac{92}{16} = 5\dfrac{12}{16} = 5\dfrac{3}{4}$

9. $\dfrac{64}{15} = 4\dfrac{4}{15}$

10. $\dfrac{88}{11} = 8$

11. $\dfrac{33}{31} = 1\dfrac{2}{31}$

Convert the following mixed numbers to improper fractions:

12. $6\dfrac{1}{2} = \dfrac{13}{2}$

$(6 \times 2 = 12 + 1 = 13)$

13. $11\dfrac{4}{5} = \dfrac{59}{5}$

$(11 \times 5 = 55 + 4 = 59)$

14. $25\dfrac{2}{3} = \dfrac{77}{3}$

$(25 \times 3 = 75 + 2 = 77)$

15. $18\dfrac{5}{8} = \dfrac{149}{8}$

$(18 \times 8 = 144 + 5 = 149)$

16. $1\dfrac{5}{9} = \dfrac{14}{9}$

$(1 \times 9 = 9 + 5 = 14)$

17. $250\dfrac{1}{4} = \dfrac{1,001}{4}$

$(250 \times 4 = 1,000 + 1 = 1,001)$

Use inspection or the greatest common divisor to reduce the following fractions to their lowest terms:

18. $\dfrac{21}{35}$

$\dfrac{21 \div 7}{35 \div 7} = \dfrac{3}{5}$

19. $\dfrac{9}{12}$

$\dfrac{9 \div 3}{12 \div 3} = \dfrac{3}{4}$

20. $\dfrac{18}{48}$

$\dfrac{18 \div 6}{48 \div 6} = \dfrac{3}{8}$

21. $\dfrac{216}{920}$

$\dfrac{216 \div 8}{920 \div 8} = \dfrac{27}{115}$

22. $\dfrac{27}{36}$

$\dfrac{27 \div 9}{36 \div 9} = \dfrac{3}{4}$

23. $\dfrac{14}{112}$

$\dfrac{14 \div 14}{112 \div 14} = \dfrac{1}{8}$

24. $\dfrac{9}{42}$

$\dfrac{9 \div 3}{42 \div 3} = \dfrac{3}{14}$

25. $\dfrac{95}{325}$

$\dfrac{95 \div 5}{325 \div 5} = \dfrac{19}{65}$

26. $\dfrac{8}{23}$

$\dfrac{8}{23} = $ Lowest terms

27. $\dfrac{78}{96}$

$\dfrac{78 \div 6}{96 \div 6} = \dfrac{13}{16}$

28. $\dfrac{30}{150}$

$\dfrac{30 \div 30}{150 \div 30} = \dfrac{1}{5}$

29. $\dfrac{85}{306}$

$\dfrac{85 \div 17}{306 \div 17} = \dfrac{5}{18}$

Convert the following fractions to higher terms, as indicated:

30. $\dfrac{2}{3}$ to twenty-sevenths

$\dfrac{2}{3} = \dfrac{18}{27} \quad \left(\begin{array}{l} 27 \div 3 = 9 \\ 9 \times 2 = 18 \end{array} \right)$

31. $\dfrac{3}{4}$ to forty-eighths

$\dfrac{3}{4} = \dfrac{36}{48} \quad \left(\begin{array}{l} 48 \div 4 = 12 \\ 12 \times 3 = 36 \end{array} \right)$

32. $\dfrac{7}{8}$ to eightieths

$\dfrac{7}{8} = \dfrac{70}{80} \quad \left(\begin{array}{l} 80 \div 8 = 10 \\ 10 \times 7 = 70 \end{array} \right)$

33. $\dfrac{11}{16}$ to sixty-fourths

$\dfrac{11}{16} = \dfrac{44}{64} \quad \left(\begin{array}{l} 64 \div 16 = 4 \\ 4 \times 11 = 44 \end{array} \right)$

34. $\dfrac{1}{5}$ to hundredths

$\dfrac{1}{5} = \dfrac{20}{100} \quad \left(\begin{array}{l} 100 \div 5 = 20 \\ 20 \times 1 = 20 \end{array} \right)$

35. $\dfrac{3}{7}$ to ninety-eighths

$\dfrac{3}{7} = \dfrac{42}{98} \quad \left(\begin{array}{l} 98 \div 7 = 14 \\ 14 \times 3 = 42 \end{array} \right)$

36. $\dfrac{3}{5} = \dfrac{}{25}$

$\dfrac{3}{5} = \dfrac{15}{25} \quad \left(\begin{array}{l} 25 \div 5 = 5 \\ 5 \times 3 = 15 \end{array} \right)$

37. $\dfrac{5}{8} = \dfrac{}{64}$

$\dfrac{5}{8} = \dfrac{40}{64} \quad \left(\begin{array}{l} 64 \div 8 = 8 \\ 8 \times 5 = 40 \end{array} \right)$

38. $\dfrac{5}{6} = \dfrac{}{360}$

$\dfrac{5}{6} = \dfrac{300}{360} \quad \left(\begin{array}{l} 360 \div 6 = 60 \\ 60 \times 5 = 300 \end{array} \right)$

39. $\dfrac{9}{13} = \dfrac{}{182}$

$\dfrac{9}{13} = \dfrac{126}{182} \quad \left(\begin{array}{l} 182 \div 13 = 14 \\ 14 \times 9 = 126 \end{array} \right)$

40. $\dfrac{23}{24} = \dfrac{}{96}$

$\dfrac{23}{24} = \dfrac{\underline{92}}{96}$ $\left(\begin{array}{c} 96 \div 24 = 4 \\ 4 \times 23 = 92 \end{array}\right)$

41. $\dfrac{2}{9} = \dfrac{}{72}$

$\dfrac{2}{9} = \dfrac{\underline{16}}{72}$ $\left(\begin{array}{c} 72 \div 9 = 8 \\ 8 \times 2 = 16 \end{array}\right)$

42. $\dfrac{3}{8} = \dfrac{}{4,000}$

$\dfrac{3}{8} = \dfrac{\underline{1,500}}{4,000}$ $\left(\begin{array}{c} 4000 \div 8 = 500 \\ 500 \times 3 = 1500 \end{array}\right)$

43. A wedding cake was cut into 40 slices. If 24 of the slices were eaten, what fraction represents the eaten portion of the cake? Reduce your answer to lowest terms.

$\dfrac{24}{40} = \dfrac{3}{\underline{5}}$ Was eaten

44. In last year's Indianapolis 500 car race, 11 of the 33 starters were still running at the end. What fraction represents the portion of the total cars that dropped out of the race?

$\begin{array}{r} 33 \text{ Total} \\ -\,11 \text{ Running} \\ \hline 22 \text{ Dropped out} \end{array}$ $\dfrac{22}{33} = \dfrac{2}{\underline{3}}$ Dropped out

SECTION II

ADDITION AND SUBTRACTION OF FRACTIONS

Adding and subtracting fractions occurs frequently in business. Quite often, we must combine or subtract quantities expressed as fractions. In order to add or subtract fractions, the denominators must be the same. If they are not, we must find a common multiple, or **common denominator,** of all the denominators in the problem. The most efficient common denominator to use is the **least common denominator,** or **LCD.** By using the LCD you avoid raising fractions to terms higher than necessary.

2-6 Determining the Least Common Denominator (LCD) of Two or More Fractions

Finding least common denominators, or LCDs, involves a series of divisions using prime numbers. A **prime number** is a whole number divisible only by itself and 1. Some examples of prime numbers are

$$2, 3, 5, 7, 11, 13, 17, 19, 23, 29, 31, \text{ and so on}$$

STEPS FOR FINDING THE LEAST COMMON DENOMINATOR OF TWO OR MORE FRACTIONS:

Step 1. Write all the denominators in a row.

Step 2. Find the smallest prime number that divides evenly into any of the denominators. Write that prime number to the left of the row, and divide. Place all quotients and undivided numbers in the next row down.

Step 3. Repeat this process until the new row contains all ones.

Step 4. Multiply all the prime numbers on the left together to get the LCD of the fractions.

EXAMPLE

Find the least common denominator of the fractions $\dfrac{3}{4}, \dfrac{1}{5}, \dfrac{4}{9},$ **and** $\dfrac{5}{6}.$

SOLUTION STRATEGY

The following chart shows our solution. Note that the first row contains the original denominators. The first prime number, 2, divides evenly into the 4 and the 6. The quotients, 2 and 3, and the nondivisible numbers, 5 and 9, are brought down to the next row.

- **common denominator**
  A common multiple of all the denominators in an addition or subtraction of fractions problem. A common denominator of the fractions $\frac{1}{4} + \frac{3}{5}$ is 40.

- **least common denominator (LCD)**
  The smallest and, therefore, most efficient common denominator in addition or subtraction of fractions. Avoids raising the fraction to terms higher than necessary. The least common denominator of the fractions $\frac{1}{4} + \frac{3}{5}$ is 20.

- **prime number**
  A whole number divisible only by itself and 1. For example, 2, 3, 5, 7, and 11 are prime numbers.

The same procedure is repeated with the prime numbers 2, 3, 3, and 5. When the bottom row becomes all ones, we multiply all the prime numbers to get the LCD, 180.

Prime Number	Denominators			
2	4	5	9	6
2	2	5	9	3
3	1	5	9	3
3	1	5	3	1
5	1	5	1	1
	1	1	1	1

$$2 \times 2 \times 3 \times 3 \times 5 = \underline{\underline{180}} = \text{LCD}$$

TRY-IT   **EXERCISE**

17. **Find the least common denominator of** $\dfrac{3}{8}$, $\dfrac{4}{5}$, $\dfrac{4}{15}$, **and** $\dfrac{11}{12}$.

Check your answer with the solution on page 54.

2-7 Adding Fractions and Mixed Numbers

Now that you have learned to convert fractions to higher and lower terms, and find least common denominators, you are ready to add and subtract fractions. We shall learn to add and subtract fractions with the same denominator, fractions with different denominators, and mixed numbers.

Adding Fractions with the Same Denominator

Proper fractions that have the same denominator are known as **like fractions.**

> **STEPS FOR ADDING LIKE FRACTIONS:**
>
> **Step 1.** Add all the numerators and place the total over the original denominator.
> **Step 2.** If the result is a proper fraction, reduce it to lowest terms.
> **Step 3.** If the result is an improper fraction, convert it to a whole or a mixed number.

● **like fractions**
Proper fractions that have the same denominator. For example, $\frac{1}{4}$ and $\frac{3}{4}$ are like fractions.

EXAMPLE

Add $\dfrac{4}{15} + \dfrac{2}{15}$

SOLUTION STRATEGY

$$\frac{4}{15} + \frac{2}{15} = \frac{4+2}{15} = \frac{6}{15} = \underline{\underline{\frac{2}{5}}}$$

Since these are like fractions, we simply add the numerators, $4 + 2$, and place the total, 6, over the original denominator, 15. This gives us the fraction $\frac{6}{15}$, which reduces by 3 to $\frac{2}{5}$.

Add and reduce to lowest terms:

18. $\dfrac{3}{25} + \dfrac{9}{25} + \dfrac{8}{25}$

Check your answer with the solution on page 54.

Adding Fractions with Different Denominators

● **unlike fractions**

Proper fractions that have different denominators. Must be converted to like fractions before adding or subtracting. For example, $\frac{1}{4}$ and $\frac{1}{3}$ are unlike fractions.

Proper fractions that have different denominators are known as **unlike fractions.** Unlike fractions must first be converted to like fractions before they can be added.

> **STEPS FOR ADDING UNLIKE FRACTIONS:**
>
> **Step 1.** Find the least common denominator of the unlike fractions.
> **Step 2.** Raise all fractions to the terms of the LCD, making them like fractions.
> **Step 3.** Follow the same procedure used for adding like fractions.

EXAMPLE

Add $\dfrac{3}{8} + \dfrac{5}{7} + \dfrac{1}{2}$

SOLUTION STRATEGY

Prime Number	Denominator		
2	8	7	2
2	4	7	1
2	2	7	1
7	1	7	1
	1	1	1

$2 \times 2 \times 2 \times 7 = 56$

These are unlike fractions and must be converted to obtain the same denominator.

First, find the LCD, 56.

$$\dfrac{3}{8} = \dfrac{21}{56}$$
$$\dfrac{5}{7} = \dfrac{40}{56}$$
$$+\ \dfrac{1}{2} = \dfrac{28}{56}$$
$$\overline{\dfrac{89}{56} = 1\dfrac{33}{56}}$$

Next raise each fraction to fifty-sixths.

Then add the fractions and convert the answer, an improper fraction, to a mixed number.

Add and reduce to lowest terms:

19. $\dfrac{1}{6} + \dfrac{3}{5} + \dfrac{2}{3}$

Check your answer with the solution on page 54.

STEPS FOR ADDING MIXED NUMBERS:

Step 1. Add the fractional parts. If the sum is an improper fraction, convert it to a mixed number.

Step 2. Add the whole numbers.

Step 3. Add the fraction from Step 1 to the whole number from Step 2.

Step 4. Reduce the sum to lowest terms.

EXAMPLE

Add $15\dfrac{3}{4} + 18\dfrac{5}{8}$

SOLUTION STRATEGY

$$15\dfrac{3}{4} = 15\dfrac{6}{8}$$
$$+18\dfrac{5}{8} = 18\dfrac{5}{8}$$
$$\overline{\phantom{+18\dfrac{5}{8}=}33\dfrac{11}{8} = 33 + 1\dfrac{3}{8} = 34\dfrac{3}{8}}$$

First add the fractional parts, using 8 as the LCD. Since $\dfrac{11}{8}$ is an improper fraction, convert it to the mixed number, $1\dfrac{3}{8}$.

Next add the whole numbers, $15 + 18 = 33$. Then add the fraction and the whole number to get the answer, $34\dfrac{3}{8}$.

T R Y - I T   EXERCISE

Add and reduce to lowest terms:

20. $45\dfrac{1}{4} + 16\dfrac{5}{9} + \dfrac{1}{3}$

Check your answer with the solution on page 54.

2-8 Subtracting Fractions and Mixed Numbers

In addition, we add the numerators of like fractions. In subtraction, we subtract the numerators of like fractions. If the fractions have different denominators, first raise the fractions to the terms of the least common denominator, then subtract.

STEPS FOR SUBTRACTING LIKE FRACTIONS:

Step 1. Subtract the numerators and place the difference over the original denominator.

Step 2. Reduce the fraction to lowest terms.

EXAMPLE

Subtract $\dfrac{9}{16} - \dfrac{5}{16}$

$$\begin{array}{r} \dfrac{9}{16} \\[2mm] -\dfrac{5}{16} \\[2mm] \hline \dfrac{4}{16} = \dfrac{1}{4} \end{array}$$

In this example, the denominators are the same so we simply subtract the numerators, 9 − 5, and place the difference, 4, over the original denominator, 16. Then reduce the fraction $\frac{4}{16}$ to lowest terms, $\frac{1}{4}$.

TRY-IT **EXERCISE**

Subtract and reduce to lowest terms:

21. $\dfrac{11}{25} - \dfrac{6}{25}$

Check your answer with the solution on page 54.

Subtracting Fractions with Different Denominators

Unlike fractions must first be converted to like fractions before they can be subtracted.

STEPS FOR SUBTRACTING UNLIKE FRACTIONS:

Step 1. Find the least common denominator.

Step 2. Raise each fraction to the denominator of the LCD.

Step 3. Follow the same procedure used to subtract like fractions.

EXAMPLE

Subtract $\dfrac{7}{9} - \dfrac{1}{2}$

SOLUTION STRATEGY

$$\begin{array}{r} \dfrac{7}{9} = \dfrac{14}{18} \\[2mm] -\dfrac{1}{2} = \dfrac{9}{18} \\[2mm] \hline \dfrac{5}{18} \end{array}$$

In this example, we must first find the least common denominator. By inspection we can see that the LCD is 18.

Next raise both fractions to eighteenths. Now subtract the numerators, 14 − 9, and place the difference, 5, over the common denominator, 18. Since it cannot be reduced, $\frac{5}{18}$ is the final answer.

TRY-IT **EXERCISE**

Subtract and reduce to lowest terms:

22. $\dfrac{5}{12} - \dfrac{2}{9}$

Check your answer with the solution on page 54.

STEPS FOR SUBTRACTING MIXED NUMBERS:

Step 1. If the fractions of the mixed numbers have the same denominator, subtract them and reduce to lowest terms.

Step 2. If the fractions don't have the same denominator, raise them to the denominator of the LCD, and subtract.

Step 3. Subtract the whole numbers.

Step 4. Add the difference of the whole numbers and the difference of the fractions.

Note: When the numerator of the fraction in the minuend is less than the numerator of the fraction in the subtrahend, we must *borrow* one whole unit from the whole number of the minuend. This will be in the form of the LCD/LCD, and is added to the fraction of the minuend.

EXAMPLES

Subtract: **a.** $15\frac{2}{3} - 9\frac{1}{5}$ **b.** $7\frac{1}{8} - 2\frac{3}{4}$

SOLUTION STRATEGY

a.

$$15\frac{2}{3} = 15\frac{10}{15}$$
$$- 9\frac{1}{5} = -9\frac{3}{15}$$
$$\overline{\qquad 6\frac{7}{15}}$$

In this example raise the fractions to fifteenths; LCD = $5 \times 3 = 15$.

Then subtract the fractions to get $\frac{7}{15}$.

Now subtract the whole numbers, $15 - 9$, to get the whole number 6.

By combining the 6 and the $\frac{7}{15}$, we get the final answer, $6\frac{7}{15}$.

b.

$$7\frac{1}{8} = 7\frac{1}{8} = 6\frac{8}{8} + \frac{1}{8} = 6\frac{9}{8}$$
$$-2\frac{3}{4} = -2\frac{6}{8} = \qquad\qquad -2\frac{6}{8}$$
$$\overline{\qquad\qquad\qquad\qquad 4\frac{3}{8}}$$

In this example, after raising $\frac{3}{4}$ to $\frac{6}{8}$, we find that we cannot subtract $\frac{6}{8}$ from $\frac{1}{8}$. We must *borrow* one whole unit, $\frac{8}{8}$, from the whole number, 7, making it a 6 ($8 \div 8 = 1$).

By adding $\frac{8}{8}$ to $\frac{1}{8}$, we get $\frac{9}{8}$.

Now we can subtract $\frac{9}{8} - \frac{6}{8}$, to get $\frac{3}{8}$.

We now subtract the whole numbers, $6 - 2 = 4$. By combining the whole number, 4, and the fraction, $\frac{3}{8}$, we get the final answer, $4\frac{3}{8}$.

TRY-IT   EXERCISES

Subtract the following mixed numbers and reduce to lowest terms:

23. $6\frac{3}{4} - 4\frac{2}{3}$ **24.** $25\frac{2}{9} - 11\frac{5}{6}$

Check your answers with the solutions on page 54.

Find the least common denominator for the following groups of fractions:

1. $\dfrac{4}{5}, \dfrac{2}{3}, \dfrac{8}{15}$

$\begin{array}{l|ccc} 3 & 5 & 3 & 15 \\ 5 & 5 & 1 & 5 \\ \hline & 1 & 1 & 1 \end{array}$

$3 \times 5 = \underline{\underline{15}}$ LCD

2. $\dfrac{1}{3}, \dfrac{4}{9}, \dfrac{3}{4}$

$\begin{array}{l|ccc} 3 & 3 & 9 & 4 \\ 2 & 1 & 3 & 4 \\ 3 & 1 & 3 & 2 \\ 2 & 1 & 1 & 2 \\ \hline & 1 & 1 & 1 \end{array}$

$3 \times 2 \times 3 \times 2 = \underline{\underline{36}}$ LCD

3. $\dfrac{5}{6}, \dfrac{11}{12}, \dfrac{1}{4}, \dfrac{1}{2}$

$\begin{array}{l|cccc} 2 & 6 & 12 & 4 & 2 \\ 2 & 3 & 6 & 2 & 1 \\ 3 & 3 & 3 & 1 & 1 \\ \hline & 1 & 1 & 1 & 1 \end{array}$

$2 \times 2 \times 3 = \underline{\underline{12}}$ LCD

4. $\dfrac{1}{6}, \dfrac{19}{24}, \dfrac{2}{3}, \dfrac{3}{5}$

$\begin{array}{l|cccc} 2 & 6 & 24 & 3 & 5 \\ 2 & 3 & 12 & 3 & 5 \\ 2 & 3 & 6 & 3 & 5 \\ 3 & 3 & 3 & 3 & 5 \\ 5 & 1 & 1 & 1 & 5 \\ \hline & 1 & 1 & 1 & 1 \end{array}$

$2 \times 2 \times 2 \times 3 \times 5 = \underline{\underline{120}}$ LCD

5. $\dfrac{21}{25}, \dfrac{9}{60}, \dfrac{7}{20}, \dfrac{1}{3}$

$\begin{array}{l|cccc} 2 & 25 & 60 & 20 & 3 \\ 2 & 25 & 30 & 10 & 3 \\ 3 & 25 & 15 & 5 & 3 \\ 5 & 25 & 5 & 5 & 1 \\ 5 & 5 & 1 & 1 & 1 \\ \hline & 1 & 1 & 1 & 1 \end{array}$

$2 \times 2 \times 3 \times 5 \times 5 = \underline{\underline{300}}$ LCD

6. $\dfrac{5}{12}, \dfrac{9}{14}, \dfrac{2}{3}, \dfrac{7}{10}$

$\begin{array}{l|cccc} 2 & 12 & 14 & 3 & 10 \\ 2 & 6 & 7 & 3 & 5 \\ 3 & 3 & 7 & 3 & 5 \\ 5 & 1 & 7 & 1 & 5 \\ 7 & 1 & 7 & 1 & 1 \\ \hline & 1 & 1 & 1 & 1 \end{array}$

$2 \times 2 \times 3 \times 5 \times 7 = \underline{\underline{420}}$ LCD

Add the following fractions, and reduce to lowest terms:

7. $\dfrac{5}{6} + \dfrac{1}{2}$

$\begin{array}{r} \frac{5}{6} \\ +\frac{3}{6} \\ \hline \frac{8}{6} = 1\frac{2}{6} = 1\frac{1}{3} \end{array}$

8. $\dfrac{2}{3} + \dfrac{3}{4}$

$\begin{array}{r} \frac{8}{12} \\ +\frac{9}{12} \\ \hline \frac{17}{12} = 1\frac{5}{12} \end{array}$

9. $\dfrac{5}{8} + \dfrac{13}{16}$

$\begin{array}{r} \frac{10}{16} \\ +\frac{13}{16} \\ \hline \frac{23}{16} = 1\frac{7}{16} \end{array}$

10. $\dfrac{9}{32} + \dfrac{29}{32}$

$\dfrac{9+29}{32} = \dfrac{38}{32} = 1\dfrac{6}{32} = 1\dfrac{3}{16}$

11. $\dfrac{1}{2} + \dfrac{4}{5} + \dfrac{7}{20}$

$\begin{array}{r} \frac{10}{20} \\ \frac{16}{20} \\ +\frac{7}{20} \\ \hline \frac{33}{20} = 1\frac{13}{20} \end{array}$

12. $\dfrac{3}{4} + \dfrac{7}{8} + \dfrac{5}{16}$

$\begin{array}{r} \frac{12}{16} \\ \frac{14}{16} \\ +\frac{5}{16} \\ \hline \frac{31}{16} = 1\frac{15}{16} \end{array}$

13. $\dfrac{11}{12} + \dfrac{3}{5} + \dfrac{19}{30}$

$\begin{array}{r} \frac{55}{60} \\ \frac{36}{60} \\ +\frac{38}{60} \\ \hline \frac{129}{60} = 2\frac{9}{60} = 2\frac{3}{20} \end{array}$

14. $5\dfrac{4}{7} + \dfrac{2}{3}$

$\begin{array}{r} 5\frac{12}{21} \\ +\frac{14}{21} \\ \hline 5\frac{26}{21} = 5 + 1\frac{5}{21} = 6\frac{5}{21} \end{array}$

15. $7\dfrac{1}{2} + 2\dfrac{7}{8} + 1\dfrac{1}{6}$

$\begin{array}{r} 7\frac{12}{24} \\ 2\frac{21}{24} \\ +1\frac{4}{24} \\ \hline 10\frac{37}{24} = 10 + 1\frac{13}{24} = 11\frac{13}{24} \end{array}$

16. $13\dfrac{5}{9} + 45\dfrac{1}{3} + 9\dfrac{7}{27}$

$\begin{array}{r} 13\frac{15}{27} \\ 45\frac{9}{27} \\ +9\frac{7}{27} \\ \hline 67\frac{31}{27} = 67 + 1\frac{4}{27} = 68\frac{4}{27} \end{array}$

17. Michael Stone walked $3\frac{1}{2}$ miles on Monday, $2\frac{4}{5}$ miles on Tuesday, and $4\frac{1}{8}$ miles on Wednesday. What is Michael's total mileage for the three days?

$\begin{array}{lrr} \text{Monday} & 3\frac{1}{2} = & 3\frac{20}{40} \\ \text{Tuesday} & 2\frac{4}{5} = & 2\frac{32}{40} \\ \text{Wednesday} & 4\frac{1}{8} = + & 4\frac{5}{40} \\ \hline & & 9\frac{57}{40} = 9 + 1\frac{17}{40} = 10\frac{17}{40} \text{ Total miles} \end{array}$

18. A manufacturer shipped three packages to San Francisco weighing $45\frac{1}{5}$, $126\frac{3}{4}$, and $88\frac{3}{8}$ pounds. What was the total weight of the shipment?

$\begin{array}{rr} 45\frac{1}{5} = & 45\frac{8}{40} \\ 126\frac{3}{4} = & 126\frac{30}{40} \\ +\ 88\frac{3}{8} = + & 88\frac{15}{40} \\ \hline & 259\frac{53}{40} = 259 + 1\frac{13}{40} = 260\frac{13}{40} \text{ Pounds} \end{array}$

19. Consolidated International stock opened this morning at $40\frac{3}{4}$ points per share. During the day the stock went up by $2\frac{3}{8}$ points. What was the points per share at the end of the day?

$\begin{array}{rr} 40\frac{3}{4} = & 40\frac{6}{8} \\ +\ 2\frac{3}{8} = + & 2\frac{3}{8} \\ \hline & 42\frac{9}{8} = 42 + 1\frac{1}{8} = 43\frac{1}{8} \text{ Points} \end{array}$

20. A coffee manufacturer purchased $12\frac{1}{2}$ tons of coffee beans in January, $15\frac{4}{5}$ tons in February, and $34\frac{7}{10}$ tons in March. What was the total weight of the purchases?

$\begin{array}{lrr} \text{January} & 12\frac{1}{2} = & 12\frac{5}{10} \\ \text{February} & 15\frac{4}{5} = & 15\frac{8}{10} \\ \text{March} & +\ 34\frac{7}{10} = + & 34\frac{7}{10} \\ \hline & & 61\frac{20}{10} = 61 + 2 = 63 \text{ Tons} \end{array}$

Subtract the following fractions, and reduce to lowest terms:

21. $\dfrac{5}{6} - \dfrac{1}{6}$ $= \dfrac{4}{6} = \underline{\underline{\dfrac{2}{3}}}$

22. $\dfrac{4}{7} - \dfrac{1}{8}$ $= \dfrac{32}{56} - \dfrac{7}{56} = \underline{\underline{\dfrac{25}{56}}}$

23. $\dfrac{2}{3} - \dfrac{1}{18}$ $= \dfrac{12}{18} - \dfrac{1}{18} = \underline{\underline{\dfrac{11}{18}}}$

24. $\dfrac{3}{4} - \dfrac{9}{16}$ $= \dfrac{12}{16} - \dfrac{9}{16} = \underline{\underline{\dfrac{3}{16}}}$

25. $12\dfrac{3}{5} - 4\dfrac{1}{3}$

$= 12\dfrac{9}{15} - 4\dfrac{5}{15} = \underline{\underline{8\dfrac{4}{15}}}$

26. $8\dfrac{1}{4} - 5\dfrac{2}{3}$

$= 8\dfrac{3}{12} - 5\dfrac{8}{12} = 7\dfrac{15}{12} - 5\dfrac{8}{12} = \underline{\underline{2\dfrac{7}{12}}}$

27. $28\dfrac{4}{9} - 1\dfrac{4}{5}$

$= 28\dfrac{20}{45} - 1\dfrac{36}{45} = 27\dfrac{65}{45} - 1\dfrac{36}{45} = \underline{\underline{26\dfrac{29}{45}}}$

28. $8\dfrac{11}{12} - 8\dfrac{3}{8}$ $= 8\dfrac{22}{24} - 8\dfrac{9}{24} = \underline{\underline{\dfrac{13}{24}}}$

29. Bill North sold $18\dfrac{4}{5}$ of his $54\dfrac{2}{3}$ acres of land. How many acres does Bill have left?

$$54\dfrac{2}{3} = \quad 54\dfrac{10}{15} = \quad 53\dfrac{25}{15}$$
$$-18\dfrac{4}{5} = -18\dfrac{12}{15} = -18\dfrac{12}{15}$$
$$\overline{\qquad\qquad\qquad\qquad 35\dfrac{13}{15}} \text{ Acres left}$$

30. A water tank weighs $1,877\dfrac{5}{8}$ pounds full, and $343\dfrac{1}{4}$ pounds empty. How many pounds of water does the tank hold?

$$1,877\dfrac{5}{8} = 1,877\dfrac{5}{8}$$
$$-343\dfrac{1}{4} = -343\dfrac{2}{8}$$
$$\overline{\qquad\qquad 1,534\dfrac{3}{8}} \text{ Pounds of water}$$

31. A roll of flexible tubing is 136 feet long. Dave Wilson cut lengths of $7\dfrac{2}{3}$, $16\dfrac{1}{5}$, and $21\dfrac{1}{2}$ feet from the roll.

a. How many feet did he cut?

$$7\dfrac{2}{3} = \quad 7\dfrac{20}{30}$$
$$16\dfrac{1}{5} = \quad 16\dfrac{6}{30}$$
$$+21\dfrac{1}{2} = +21\dfrac{15}{30}$$
$$\overline{\qquad\qquad 44\dfrac{41}{30} = 45\dfrac{11}{30}} \text{ Feet cut}$$

b. How much tubing is left on the roll?

$$136 \quad = 135\dfrac{30}{30}$$
$$-45\dfrac{11}{30} = -45\dfrac{11}{30}$$
$$\overline{\qquad\qquad 90\dfrac{19}{30}} \text{ Feet left on roll}$$

32. Last week, Stillwell Pharmaceutical, Inc., stock dropped from $16\dfrac{1}{2}$ points per share to $12\dfrac{7}{8}$ points per share. By how much did the stock fall?

$$16\dfrac{1}{2} = \quad 16\dfrac{4}{8} = \quad 15\dfrac{12}{8}$$
$$-12\dfrac{7}{8} = -12\dfrac{7}{8} = -12\dfrac{7}{8}$$
$$\overline{\qquad\qquad\qquad 3\dfrac{5}{8}} \text{ Points stock fell}$$

33. An electric sanding machine reduced a table top from $\dfrac{5}{8}$ inches to $\dfrac{5}{16}$ inches thick. How much of the wood was sanded off?

$$\dfrac{5}{8} = \quad \dfrac{10}{16}$$
$$-\dfrac{5}{16} = -\dfrac{5}{16}$$
$$\overline{\qquad\quad \dfrac{5}{16}} \text{ Inch sanded off}$$

MULTIPLICATION AND DIVISION OF FRACTIONS

In addition and subtraction we were concerned with common denominators; however, in multiplication and division common denominators are not required. This simplifies the process considerably.

2-9 Multiplying Fractions and Mixed Numbers

STEPS FOR MULTIPLYING FRACTIONS:

Step 1. Multiply all the numerators to form the new numerator.

Step 2. Multiply all the denominators to form the new denominator.

Step 3. If necessary, reduce the answer to lowest terms.

● **cancellation**

When multiplying fractions, cancellation is the process of finding a common factor that divides evenly into at least one numerator and one denominator. A useful shortcut that simplifies multiplication and often leaves the answer in lowest terms. The common factor 2 can be used to cancel $\frac{1}{4} \times \frac{6}{7}$ to $\frac{1}{2} \times \frac{3}{7}$.

A procedure known as **cancellation** can serve as a useful shortcut when multiplying fractions. Cancellation simplifies the numbers with which we are dealing, and often leaves the answer in lowest terms.

STEPS FOR APPLYING CANCELLATION:

Step 1. Find a common factor that divides evenly into at least one of the denominators and one of the numerators.

Step 2. Divide that common factor into the denominator and numerator, thereby reducing it.

Step 3. Repeat this process until there are no more common factors.

Step 4. Multiply the fractions as before.

EXAMPLES

Multiply the following fractions:

a. $\dfrac{5}{7} \times \dfrac{3}{4}$ **b.** $\dfrac{2}{3} \times \dfrac{7}{8}$

SOLUTION STRATEGY

a. $\dfrac{5}{7} \times \dfrac{3}{4}$

In this example, there are no common factors between the numerators and the denominators, therefore we cannot use cancellation.

$\dfrac{5 \times 3}{7 \times 4} = \dfrac{15}{28}$

Multiply the numerators, 5×3, to form the new numerator, 15; and multiply the denominators, 7×4, to form the new denominator, 28. This fraction does not reduce.

b. $\dfrac{2}{3} \times \dfrac{7}{8}$

In this example, the 2 in the numerator and the 8 in the denominator have the common factor of 2.

$\dfrac{\overset{1}{2}}{3} \times \dfrac{7}{\underset{4}{8}} =$

Dividing each by the common factor reduces the 2 to a 1, and the 8 to a 4.

$\dfrac{1 \times 7}{3 \times 4} = \dfrac{7}{12}$

Now multiply the simplified numbers; 1×7 forms the numerator, 7, and 3×4 forms the denominator, 12. The resulting product is $\frac{7}{12}$.

Multiply and reduce to lowest terms:

25. $\dfrac{12}{21} \times \dfrac{7}{8}$

Check your answer with the solution on page 54.

Multiplying Mixed Numbers

STEPS FOR MULTIPLYING MIXED NUMBERS:

Step 1. Convert all mixed numbers to improper fractions.

Step 2. Multiply as before, using cancellation wherever possible.

Step 3. If the answer is an improper fraction, convert it to a whole or mixed number.

Step 4. Reduce to lowest terms.

    Note: When multiplying fractions by whole numbers, change the whole numbers to fractions by placing them over 1. For example, the whole number 9 becomes the fraction $\frac{9}{1}$.

EXAMPLES

Multiply: **a.** $3\dfrac{3}{4} \times 5\dfrac{1}{2}$ **b.** $12\dfrac{5}{6} \times 4$

SOLUTION STRATEGY

a. $3\dfrac{3}{4} \times 5\dfrac{1}{2}$

     $\dfrac{15}{4} \times \dfrac{11}{2}$

In this example, convert the mixed numbers to improper fractions; $3\frac{3}{4}$ becomes $\frac{15}{4}$, and $5\frac{1}{2}$ becomes $\frac{11}{2}$.

     $\dfrac{15 \times 11}{4 \times 2} = \dfrac{165}{8} = 20\dfrac{5}{8}$

After multiplying the numerators together and the denominators together, we get the improper fraction $\frac{165}{8}$, which converts to the mixed number $20\frac{5}{8}$.

b. $12\dfrac{5}{6} \times 4$

This example demonstrates a mixed number multiplied by a whole number.

     $\dfrac{77}{6} \times \dfrac{4}{1}$

The mixed number $12\frac{5}{6}$ converts to the improper fraction $\frac{77}{6}$. The whole number, 4, expressed as a fraction, becomes $\frac{4}{1}$.

     $\dfrac{77}{\cancel{6}_{3}} \times \dfrac{\cancel{4}^{2}}{1}$

Before multiplying, cancel the 4 in the numerator and the 6 in the denominator by the common factor, 2.

     $\dfrac{77 \times 2}{3 \times 1} = \dfrac{154}{3} = 51\dfrac{1}{3}$

After multiplying, convert the improper fraction $\frac{154}{3}$ to the mixed number $51\frac{1}{3}$.

Multiply and reduce to lowest terms.

26. $8\frac{2}{5} \times 6\frac{1}{4}$

27. $45 \times \frac{4}{9} \times 2\frac{1}{4}$

Check your answers with the solutions on page 54.

2-10 Dividing Fractions and Mixed Numbers

In division of fractions, it is important to identify which fraction is the dividend, and which is the divisor. In whole numbers, we found that a problem such as $12 \div 5$ is read, "12 divided by 5." The 12 therefore is the dividend and the 5 is the divisor. Fractions work in the same way. The number *after* the "÷" sign is the divisor. In the problem $\frac{3}{4} \div \frac{2}{3}$, for example, $\frac{3}{4}$ is the dividend and $\frac{2}{3}$ is the divisor.

$$\text{Dividend} \div \text{Divisor} = \frac{\text{Dividend}}{\text{Divisor}} = \text{Divisor} \overline{)\text{Dividend}}$$

● **invert**

To turn upside down. For example, $\frac{1}{4}$ inverted becomes $\frac{4}{1}$. In division of fractions, the divisor is inverted.

● **reciprocals**

Numbers whose product is 1. Inverted numbers are also known as reciprocals of each other. The fractions $\frac{1}{4}$ and $\frac{4}{1}$ are reciprocals since $\frac{1}{4} \times \frac{4}{1} = 1$.

Division of fractions requires that we **invert** the divisor. To invert means to turn upside down. By inverting a fraction, the numerator becomes the denominator, and the denominator becomes the numerator. For example, the fraction $\frac{5}{12}$ becomes $\frac{12}{5}$ when inverted. The inverted fraction is also known as a **reciprocal.** Therefore $\frac{5}{12}$ and $\frac{12}{5}$ are reciprocals of each other.

As in multiplication, division requires that mixed numbers be converted to improper fractions.

STEPS FOR DIVIDING FRACTIONS:

Step 1. Identify the fraction that is the divisor, and invert.

Step 2. Change the "divided by" sign, ÷, to a "multiplied by" sign, ×.

Step 3. Multiply the fractions.

Step 4. Reduce the answer to lowest terms.

EXAMPLES

Divide the following fractions:

a. $\frac{4}{5} \div \frac{2}{3}$

b. $6\frac{3}{8} \div 2\frac{1}{2}$

c. $12\frac{1}{6} \div 3$

SOLUTION STRATEGY

a. $\frac{4}{5} \div \frac{2}{3} = \frac{4}{5} \times \frac{3}{2}$

In this example, invert the divisor, $\frac{2}{3}$, to form its reciprocal, $\frac{3}{2}$, and change the sign from "÷" to "×."

$\overset{2}{\frac{4}{5}} \times \frac{3}{\underset{1}{2}} = \frac{6}{5} = 1\frac{1}{5}$

Now multiply in the usual manner. Note that the 4 in the numerator and the 2 in the denominator can be reduced by the common factor, 2. The answer, $\frac{6}{5}$, is an improper fraction and must be converted to the mixed number $1\frac{1}{5}$.

b. $6\dfrac{3}{8} \div 2\dfrac{1}{2} = \dfrac{51}{8} \div \dfrac{5}{2}$

First, convert the mixed numbers to the improper fractions $\frac{51}{8}$ and $\frac{5}{2}$, and state them again as a division.

$$\dfrac{51}{8} \times \dfrac{2}{5}$$

Next invert the divisor, $\frac{5}{2}$, to its reciprocal, $\frac{2}{5}$, and change the sign from "÷" to "×."

$$\dfrac{51}{\overset{}{\underset{4}{8}}} \times \dfrac{\overset{1}{2}}{5} = \dfrac{51}{20} = 2\dfrac{11}{20}$$

Now multiply in the usual way. Note that the 2 in the numerator and the 8 in the denominator can be reduced by the common factor, 2. The answer, $\frac{51}{20}$, is an improper fraction, and must be converted to the mixed number $2\frac{11}{20}$.

c. $12\dfrac{1}{6} \div 3 = \dfrac{73}{6} \div \dfrac{3}{1}$

In this example, we have a mixed number that must be converted to the improper fraction, $\frac{73}{6}$, and a whole number, 3, that converts to $\frac{3}{1}$.

$$\dfrac{73}{6} \times \dfrac{1}{3}$$

The fraction $\frac{3}{1}$ is the divisor, and must be inverted to its reciprocal, $\frac{1}{3}$. The sign is changed from "÷" to "×."

$$\dfrac{73}{6} \times \dfrac{1}{3} = \dfrac{73}{18} = 4\dfrac{1}{18}$$

The answer is the improper fraction $\frac{73}{18}$, which converts to the mixed number $4\frac{1}{18}$.

TRY-IT   EXERCISES

Divide the following fractions and mixed numbers:

28. $\dfrac{14}{25} \div \dfrac{4}{5}$

29. $11\dfrac{3}{16} \div 8\dfrac{2}{3}$

30. $18 \div 5\dfrac{3}{5}$

Check your answers with the solutions on page 55.

REVIEW EXERCISES   CHAPTER 2—SECTION III

Multiply the following fractions and reduce to lowest terms. Use cancellation whenever possible:

1. $\dfrac{2}{3} \times \dfrac{4}{5} = \dfrac{8}{15}$

2. $\dfrac{5}{6} \times \dfrac{1}{4} = \dfrac{5}{24}$

3. $\dfrac{1}{2} \times \dfrac{\overset{2}{4}}{\underset{1}{9}} = \dfrac{2}{9}$

4. $\dfrac{\overset{1}{7}}{\underset{2}{8}} \times \dfrac{1}{3} \times \dfrac{\overset{1}{4}}{\underset{1}{7}} = \dfrac{1}{6}$

5. $\dfrac{\overset{2}{16}}{19} \times \dfrac{5}{8} = \dfrac{10}{19}$

6. $\dfrac{25}{51} \times \dfrac{2}{\underset{1}{5}} = \dfrac{10}{51}$

7. $\dfrac{\overset{1}{8}}{\underset{1}{11}} \times \dfrac{\overset{3}{33}}{\underset{5}{40}} \times 4 = \dfrac{12}{5} = 2\dfrac{2}{5}$

8. $\dfrac{2}{3} \times \dfrac{2}{3} \times \overset{2}{6} = \dfrac{8}{3} = 2\dfrac{2}{3}$

9. $8\dfrac{1}{5} \times 2\dfrac{2}{3}$
$= \dfrac{41}{5} \times \dfrac{8}{3} = \dfrac{328}{15} = 21\dfrac{13}{15}$

10. $\dfrac{1}{2} \times \dfrac{\overset{1}{2}}{3} \times \dfrac{\overset{1}{4}}{5} \times \dfrac{\overset{1}{3}}{4} \times \overset{1}{5} = \dfrac{1}{1} = 1$

11. $\dfrac{1}{5} \times \dfrac{1}{5} \times \dfrac{1}{5} = \dfrac{1}{125}$

12. $\dfrac{2}{3} \times 5\dfrac{4}{5} \times 9$
$\dfrac{2}{\underset{1}{3}} \times \dfrac{29}{5} \times \dfrac{\overset{3}{9}}{1} = \dfrac{174}{5} = 34\dfrac{4}{5}$

13. A recent market research survey showed that $\frac{3}{8}$ of the people interviewed preferred decaffeinated coffee over regular.

   a. What fraction of the people preferred regular coffee?

   $\dfrac{8}{8} - \dfrac{3}{8} = \dfrac{5}{8}$ Preferred regular

b. If 4,400 people were interviewed, how many preferred regular coffee?

$$\frac{\overset{550}{\cancel{4,400}}}{1} \times \frac{5}{\cancel{8}} = \frac{2,750}{1} = \underline{\underline{2,750}} \text{ People preferred regular}$$

14. Fred Wilson earns $1\frac{3}{5}$ times as much as Stan Freeman. If Stan earns \$375 per week, how much does Fred earn per week?

$$\$375 \times 1\frac{3}{5} = \frac{\overset{75}{\cancel{375}}}{1} \times \frac{8}{\cancel{5}} = \underline{\underline{\$600}} \text{ Earned by Fred}$$

15. A driveway requires $9\frac{1}{2}$ truckloads of gravel. If the truck holds $4\frac{5}{8}$ cubic yards of gravel, how many total cubic yards of gravel are used for the driveway?

$$9\frac{1}{2} \times 4\frac{5}{8} = \frac{19}{2} \times \frac{37}{8} = \frac{703}{16} = \underline{\underline{43\frac{15}{16}}} \text{ Yards of gravel}$$

16. Molly borrowed \$4,200 from the bank. If she has already repaid $\frac{3}{7}$ of the loan, what is the remaining balance owed to the bank?

$$\frac{\overset{600}{\cancel{4,200}}}{1} \times \frac{3}{\cancel{7}} = \frac{1,800}{1} = \$1,800 \text{ Already paid}$$

$$\begin{array}{r} 4,200 \text{ Total} \\ -\ 1,800 \\ \hline \underline{\$2,400} \text{ Still owed} \end{array}$$

17. Mel Johnson works $36\frac{4}{5}$ hours per week for 3 weeks on Project 1, and $27\frac{2}{3}$ hours per week for $7\frac{1}{2}$ weeks on Project 2. What is the total number of hours spent on both projects?

$$\text{Project 1} = 36\frac{4}{5} \times 3 = \frac{184}{5} \times \frac{3}{1} = \frac{552}{5} = 110\frac{2}{5} \text{ Hours}$$

$$\text{Project 2} = 27\frac{2}{3} \times 7\frac{1}{2} = \frac{83}{\cancel{3}} \times \frac{\overset{5}{\cancel{15}}}{2} = \frac{415}{2} = 207\frac{1}{2} \text{ Hours}$$

$$\begin{array}{r} 110\frac{2}{5} = \quad 110\frac{4}{10} \\ +\ 207\frac{1}{2} = +\ 207\frac{5}{10} \\ \hline 317\frac{9}{10} \text{ Total hours} \end{array}$$

18. Three partners share a business. Sam owns $\frac{3}{8}$, Anita owns $\frac{2}{5}$, and David owns the rest. If the profits this year are \$150,000, how much does each partner receive?

Sam $\$150,000 \times \frac{3}{8} = \frac{\overset{18,750}{\cancel{150,000}}}{1} \times \frac{3}{\cancel{8}} = \frac{56,250}{1} = \underline{\underline{\$56,250}}$

Anita $\$150,000 \times \frac{2}{5} = \frac{\overset{30,000}{\cancel{150,000}}}{1} \times \frac{2}{\cancel{5}} = \frac{60,000}{1} = \underline{\underline{\$60,000}}$

David
$$\begin{array}{r} 56,250 \\ +\ 60,000 \\ \hline 116,250 \end{array} \qquad \begin{array}{r} 150,000 \\ -\ 116,250 \\ \hline \underline{\$33,750} \end{array}$$

Divide the following fractions and reduce to lowest terms:

19. $\dfrac{5}{6} \div \dfrac{3}{8}$

$$= \frac{5}{\cancel{6}} \times \frac{\overset{4}{\cancel{8}}}{3} = \frac{20}{9} = \underline{\underline{2\frac{2}{9}}}$$

20. $\dfrac{7}{10} \div \dfrac{1}{5}$

$$= \frac{7}{\cancel{10}} \times \frac{\cancel{5}}{1} = \frac{7}{2} = \underline{\underline{3\frac{1}{2}}}$$

21. $\dfrac{2}{3} \div \dfrac{5}{8}$

$$= \frac{2}{3} \times \frac{8}{5} = \frac{16}{15} = \underline{\underline{1\frac{1}{15}}}$$

22. $7 \div \dfrac{4}{5}$

$$= \frac{7}{1} \times \frac{5}{4} = \frac{35}{4} = \underline{\underline{8\frac{3}{4}}}$$

23. $\dfrac{1}{3} \div \dfrac{5}{6}$

$$= \frac{1}{\cancel{3}} \times \frac{\overset{2}{\cancel{6}}}{5} = \underline{\underline{\frac{2}{5}}}$$

24. $\dfrac{9}{16} \div \dfrac{9}{16}$

$$= \frac{\cancel{9}}{\cancel{16}} \times \frac{\cancel{16}}{\cancel{9}} = \frac{1}{1} = \underline{\underline{1}}$$

25. $4\dfrac{4}{5} \div \dfrac{7}{8}$

$$= \frac{24}{5} \times \frac{8}{7} = \frac{192}{35} = \underline{\underline{5\frac{17}{35}}}$$

26. $21\dfrac{1}{2} \div 5\dfrac{2}{3}$

$$= \frac{43}{2} \times \frac{3}{17} = \frac{129}{34} = \underline{\underline{3\frac{27}{34}}}$$

27. $18 \div \dfrac{18}{19}$

$$= \dfrac{\cancel{18}}{1} \times \dfrac{19}{\cancel{18}} = \dfrac{19}{1} = \underline{\underline{19}}$$

28. $12 \div 1\dfrac{3}{5}$

$$= \dfrac{\cancel{12}}{1} \times \dfrac{5}{\cancel{8}} = \dfrac{15}{2} = 7\dfrac{1}{2}$$

29. $\dfrac{15}{60} \div \dfrac{7}{10}$

$$= \dfrac{15}{\cancel{60}} \times \dfrac{\cancel{10}}{7} = \dfrac{15}{42} = \dfrac{5}{14}$$

30. $1\dfrac{1}{5} \div 10$

$$= \dfrac{\cancel{6}}{5} \times \dfrac{1}{\cancel{10}} = \dfrac{3}{25}$$

31. Dream Homes, Inc., a builder of custom homes, owns $126\dfrac{1}{2}$ acres of undeveloped land. If the property is divided into $2\dfrac{3}{4}$-acre pieces, how many homesites can be developed?

$$126\dfrac{1}{2} \div 2\dfrac{3}{4} = \dfrac{253}{2} \div \dfrac{11}{4} = \dfrac{\overset{23}{\cancel{253}}}{\underset{\cdot 1}{\cancel{2}}} \times \dfrac{\overset{2}{\cancel{4}}}{\underset{1}{\cancel{11}}} = \dfrac{46}{1} = \underline{\underline{46}} \text{ Homesites}$$

32. An automobile travels 365 miles on $16\dfrac{2}{3}$ gallons of gasoline.

a. How many miles per gallon does the car get on the trip?

$$365 \div 16\dfrac{2}{3} = \dfrac{365}{1} \div \dfrac{50}{3} = \dfrac{\overset{73}{\cancel{365}}}{1} \times \dfrac{3}{\underset{10}{\cancel{50}}} = \dfrac{219}{10} = 21\dfrac{9}{10} \text{ Miles per gallon}$$

b. How many gallons would be required for the car to travel 876 miles?

$$876 \div 21\dfrac{9}{10} = \dfrac{876}{1} \div \dfrac{219}{10} = \dfrac{\overset{4}{\cancel{876}}}{1} \times \dfrac{10}{\underset{1}{\cancel{219}}} = \dfrac{40}{1} = \underline{\underline{40}} \text{ Gallons}$$

33. Spencer's Department Store purchases 600 straw baskets from a wholesaler.

a. In the first week, $\dfrac{2}{5}$ of the baskets are sold. How many are sold?

$$\dfrac{\overset{120}{\cancel{600}}}{1} \times \dfrac{2}{\underset{1}{\cancel{5}}} = \dfrac{240}{1} = \underline{\underline{240}} \text{ Baskets sold first week}$$

b. By the third week, only $\dfrac{3}{20}$ remain. How many baskets are left?

$$\dfrac{\overset{30}{\cancel{600}}}{1} \times \dfrac{3}{\underset{1}{\cancel{20}}} = \dfrac{90}{1} = \underline{\underline{90}} \text{ Baskets left third week}$$

34. A hardware supply company buys nails in bulk from the manufacturer, and packs them into $2\dfrac{4}{5}$-pound boxes. How many boxes can be filled from 518 pounds of nails?

$$518 \div 2\dfrac{4}{5} = \dfrac{518}{1} \div \dfrac{14}{5} = \dfrac{\overset{37}{\cancel{518}}}{1} \times \dfrac{5}{\underset{1}{\cancel{14}}} = \dfrac{185}{1} = \underline{\underline{185}} \text{ Boxes}$$

35. The chef at the Sizzling Steakhouse has 140 pounds of sirloin steak on hand for Saturday night. If each portion is $10\dfrac{1}{2}$ ounces, how many sirloin steak dinners can be served? Round to the nearest whole dinner. (There are 16 ounces in a pound.)

$$\begin{array}{r} 140 \text{ lbs} \\ \times\ \ 16 \text{ oz} \\ \hline 2,240 \text{ Total ounces} \end{array}$$

$$2,240 \div 10\dfrac{1}{2} = \dfrac{2,240}{1} \div \dfrac{21}{2} = \dfrac{\overset{320}{\cancel{2,240}}}{1} \times \dfrac{2}{\underset{3}{\cancel{21}}} = \dfrac{640}{3} = 213\dfrac{1}{3} = \underline{\underline{213}} \text{ Dinners}$$

36. Engineers at Alamo Electronics use special silver wire to manufacture fuzzy logic circuit boards. The wire comes in 840-foot rolls that cost $1,200 each. Each board requires $4\frac{1}{5}$ feet of wire.

a. How many circuit boards can be made from each roll?

$$840 \div 4\frac{1}{5} = \frac{840}{1} \div \frac{21}{5} = \frac{\overset{40}{\cancel{840}}}{1} \times \frac{5}{\cancel{21}} = \frac{200}{1} = \underline{\underline{200}} \text{ Circuit boards}$$
$$1$$

b. What is the cost of wire per circuit board?

$1,200 \div 200 = \underline{\underline{\$6}}$ Each

37. Southern Reflective Signs makes speed limit signs for the state department of transportation. By law, these signs must be displayed every $\frac{5}{8}$ of a mile. How many signs will be required on a new highway that is $34\frac{3}{8}$ miles long?

$$34\frac{3}{8} \div \frac{5}{8} = \frac{275}{8} \div \frac{5}{8} = \frac{\overset{55}{\cancel{275}}}{\underset{1}{\cancel{8}}} \times \frac{\overset{1}{\cancel{8}}}{\underset{1}{\cancel{5}}} = \underline{\underline{55}} \text{ Signs}$$

CHAPTER 2 ▪ FRACTIONS		**SUMMARY CHART**

SECTION I UNDERSTANDING AND WORKING WITH FRACTIONS

Topic	P/O, Page	Important Concepts	Illustrative Examples
Distinguishing between the Various Types of Fractions	2–1 29	Common or proper fraction: A fraction representing less than a whole unit, where the numerator is less than the denominator. Improper fraction: A fraction representing one whole unit or more, where the denominator is equal to or less than the numerator. Mixed number: A number that combines a whole number with a proper fraction.	Proper $\frac{4}{7}, \frac{2}{3}, \frac{93}{124}$ Improper $\frac{5}{4}, \frac{7}{7}, \frac{88}{51}, \frac{796}{212}, \frac{1,200}{1,200}$ Mixed $12\frac{2}{5}, 4\frac{5}{9}, 78\frac{52}{63}$
Converting Improper Fractions to Whole or Mixed Numbers	2–2 30	1. Divide the numerator of the improper fraction by the denominator. 2a. If there is no remainder, the improper fraction becomes a whole number. 2b. If there is a remainder, write the whole number and then write the fraction as: Whole number $\dfrac{\text{Remainder}}{\text{Divisor}}$	$\frac{68}{4} = 17$ $\frac{127}{20} = 6\frac{7}{20}$
Converting Mixed Numbers to Improper Fractions	2–3 31	1. Multiply the denominator by the whole number. 2. Add the numerator to the product from Step 1. 3. Place the total from Step 2 as the new numerator. 4. Place the original denominator as the new denominator.	$15\frac{3}{4} = \frac{(15 \times 4) + 3}{4} = \frac{63}{4}$

I, continued

Topic	P/O, Page	Important Concepts	Illustrative Examples
Reducing Fractions to Lowest Terms by Inspection	2–4a 32	Reducing a fraction means finding whole numbers, called common divisors or common factors, that divide evenly into both the numerator and denominator of the fraction. When a fraction has been reduced to the point where there are no common divisors left other than 1, it is said to be reduced to lowest terms.	$\frac{24}{120} = \frac{24 \div 3}{120 \div 3} = \frac{8}{40} =$ $\frac{8}{40} = \frac{8 \div 2}{40 \div 2} = \frac{4}{20} =$ $\frac{4}{20} = \frac{4 \div 4}{20 \div 4} = \frac{1}{5}$
Finding the Greatest Common Divisor (Reducing Shortcut)	2–4b 32	The largest number that is a common divisor of a fraction is known as the greatest common divisor. It reduces the fraction to lowest terms in one step. To find the GCD: 1. Divide the numerator of the fraction into the denominator. 2. Take the remainder from Step 1 and divide it into the divisor from Step 1. 3. Repeat this division process until the remainder is either 0 or 1. If the remainder is 0, the last divisor is the greatest common divisor. If the remainder is 1, the fraction cannot be reduced, and is therefore in lowest terms.	What greatest common divisor will reduce the fraction $\frac{48}{72}$? $\begin{array}{r} 1 \\ 48\overline{)72} \\ 48 \\ \overline{24} \end{array}$ $\begin{array}{r} 2 \\ 24\overline{)48} \\ 48 \\ \overline{0} \end{array}$ The greatest common divisor is 24.
Raising Fractions to Higher Terms	2–5 33	To raise a fraction to a new denominator: 1. Divide the original denominator into the new denominator. The resulting quotient is the common multiple that raises the fraction. 2. Multiply the numerator and the denominator of the original fraction by the common multiple.	Raise $\frac{5}{8}$ to forty-eighths: $\frac{5}{8} = \frac{?}{48}$ $48 \div 8 = 6$ $\frac{5 \times 6}{8 \times 6} = \frac{30}{48}$

SECTION II   ADDITION AND SUBTRACTION OF FRACTIONS

Topic	P/O, Page	Important Concepts	Illustrative Examples
Understanding Prime Numbers	2–6 36	A prime number is a whole number greater than 1 that is divisible only by 1 and itself. Prime numbers are used to find the least common denominator.	Examples of prime numbers: 2, 3, 5, 7, 11, 13, 17, 19, 23, 29
Determining the Least Common Denominator (LCD) of Two or More Fractions	2–6 36	1. Write all the denominators in a row. 2. Find the smallest prime number that divides evenly into any of the denominators. Write that prime number to the left of the row, and divide. Place all quotients and undivided numbers in the next row down. 3. Repeat this process until the new row contains all ones. 4. Multiply all the prime numbers on the left together, to get the LCD of the fractions.	Find the LCD of $\frac{2}{9}$, $\frac{5}{6}$, $\frac{1}{4}$, and $\frac{4}{5}$. **Prime Number Denominators** 3 | 9 6 4 5 2 | 3 2 4 5 2 | 3 1 2 5 3 | 3 1 1 5 5 | 1 1 1 5 | 1 1 1 1 $LCD = 3 \times 2 \times 2 \times 3 \times 5 = 180$

II, continued

Topic	P/O, Page	Important Concepts	Illustrative Examples
Adding Like Fractions	2–7 37	1. Add all the numerators and place the total over the original denominator. 2. If the result is a proper fraction, reduce it to lowest terms. 3. If the result is an improper fraction, convert it to a whole or a mixed number.	Add $\frac{8}{9}$, $\frac{4}{9}$, and $\frac{1}{9}$ $\frac{8+4+1}{9} = \frac{13}{9} = 1\frac{4}{9}$
Adding Unlike Fractions	2–7 38	1. Find the least common denominator of the unlike fractions. 2. Raise each fraction to the terms of the LCD, thereby making them like fractions. 3. Add the like fractions.	Add $\frac{2}{3} + \frac{5}{7}$ $LCD = 3 \times 7 = 21$ $\frac{2 \times 7}{21} + \frac{5 \times 3}{21} = \frac{14+15}{21} =$ $\frac{29}{21} = 1\frac{8}{21}$
Adding Mixed Numbers	2–7 39	1. Add the whole numbers. 2. Add the fractions and reduce to lowest terms. If they are improper, convert to whole or mixed numbers. 3. Add the whole numbers from Step 1 and the fractions from Step 2 to get the total.	Add $3\frac{3}{4} + 4\frac{1}{8}$ $3 + 4 = 7$ $\frac{3}{4} + \frac{1}{8} = \frac{(3 \times 2)+1}{8} = \frac{7}{8}$ $7 + \frac{7}{8} = 7\frac{7}{8}$
Subtracting Like Fractions	2–8 39	1. Subtract the numerators and place the difference over the original denominator. 2. Reduce the fraction to lowest terms.	Subtract $\frac{11}{12} - \frac{5}{12}$ $\frac{11-5}{12} = \frac{6}{12} = \frac{1}{2}$
Subtracting Unlike Fractions	2–8 40	1. Find the least common denominator. 2. Raise each fraction to the denominator of the LCD. 3. Subtract the like fractions.	Subtract $\frac{7}{8} - \frac{2}{3}$ $LCD = 8 \times 3 = 24$ $\frac{21}{24} - \frac{16}{24} = \frac{5}{24}$
Subtracting Mixed Numbers	2–8 41	1. If the fractions of the mixed numbers have the same denominator, subtract them and reduce to lowest terms. 2. If the fractions don't have the same denominator, raise them to the denominator of the LCD, and subtract. 3. Subtract the whole numbers. 4. Add the difference of the whole numbers and the difference of the fractions.	Subtract $15\frac{5}{8} - 12\frac{1}{2}$ $15\frac{5}{8} = \quad 15\frac{5}{8}$ $-12\frac{1}{2} = -12\frac{4}{8}$ $\qquad\quad = \quad 3\frac{1}{8}$

II, continued

Topic	P/O, Page	Important Concepts	Illustrative Examples
Subtracting Mixed Numbers, Using Borrowing	2–8 41	When the numerator of the fraction in the minuend is less than the numerator of the fraction in the subtrahend, we must borrow one whole unit from the whole number of the minuend. This will be in the form of the LCD/LCD, and is added to the fraction of the minuend. Now, subtract as before.	Subtract $6\frac{1}{7} - 2\frac{5}{7}$ $$6\frac{1}{7} = 5\frac{7}{7} + \frac{1}{7} = 5\frac{8}{7}$$ $$-2\frac{5}{7} \qquad -2\frac{5}{7}$$ $$= 3\frac{3}{7}$$

SECTION III   MULTIPLICATION AND DIVISION OF FRACTIONS

Topic	P/O, Page	Important Concepts	Illustrative Examples
Multiplying Fractions	2–9 44	1. Multipy all the numerators to form the new numerator. 2. Multiply all the denominators to form the new denominator. 3. If necessary, reduce the answer to lowest terms.	Multiply $\frac{5}{8} \times \frac{2}{3}$ $$\frac{5}{8} \times \frac{2}{3} = \frac{10}{24} = \frac{5}{12}$$
Multiplying Fractions, Using Cancellation	2–9 44	Cancellation simplifies the numbers, and leaves the answer in lowest terms. 1. Find a common factor which divides evenly into at least one of the denominators and one of the numerators. 2. Divide that common factor into the denominator and the numerator, thereby reducing it. 3. Repeat this process until there are no more common factors. 4. Multiply the fractions. The resulting product will be in lowest terms.	Use cancellation to solve the multiplication problem above: Cancellation Method: $$\frac{5}{8} \times \frac{2}{3} = \frac{5}{\overset{}{\underset{4}{8}}} \times \frac{\overset{1}{2}}{3} = \frac{5}{12}$$
Multiplying Mixed Numbers	2–9 45	1. Convert all mixed numbers to improper fractions. 2. Multiply, using cancellation wherever possible. 3. If the answer is an improper fraction, convert it to a whole or mixed number. 4. Reduce to lowest terms. Note: When multiplying fractions by whole numbers, change the whole numbers to fractions by placing them over 1.	Multiply $3\frac{1}{2} \times 2\frac{3}{8}$ $$3\frac{1}{2} = \frac{7}{2} \qquad 2\frac{3}{8} = \frac{19}{8}$$ $$\frac{7}{2} \times \frac{19}{8} = \frac{133}{16} = 8\frac{5}{16}$$
Dividing Fractions and Mixed Numbers	2–10 46	Division of fractions requires that we invert the divisor, or turn it upside down. The inverted fraction is also known as a reciprocal. Dividing fractions: 1. Convert all mixed numbers to improper fractions. 2. Identify the fraction that is the divisor, and invert it. 3. Change ÷ to ×. 4. Multiply the fractions. 5. Reduce the answer to lowest terms.	Divide $\frac{11}{12} \div \frac{2}{3}$ $\frac{11}{12}$ is the dividend $\frac{2}{3}$ is the divisor $$\frac{11}{12} \div \frac{2}{3} = \frac{11}{12} \times \frac{3}{2}$$ $$\frac{11}{\underset{4}{12}} \times \frac{\overset{1}{3}}{2} = \frac{11}{8} = 1\frac{3}{8}$$

1. Mixed fraction   Seventy-six and three-fourths
2. Common or proper fraction   Three-fifths
3. Improper fraction   Eighteen-eighteenths
4. Improper fraction   Thirty-three-eighths

5. $8 \div 3 = 2\dfrac{2}{3}$

6. $25 \div 4 = 6\dfrac{1}{4}$

7. $39 \div 3 = 13$

8. $\dfrac{11}{4}$ ◄

$(2 \times 4 = 8 + 3 = 11)$

9. $\dfrac{46}{5}$ ◄

$(9 \times 5 = 45 + 1 = 46)$

10. $\dfrac{181}{8}$ ◄

$(22 \times 8 = 176 + 5 = 181)$

11. $\dfrac{30 \div 5}{55 \div 5} = \dfrac{6}{11}$

$$
\begin{array}{r}
1 \\
30\overline{)55} \\
30 \\
\hline
25
\end{array}
$$

$$
\begin{array}{r}
1 \\
25\overline{)30} \\
25 \\
\hline
5
\end{array}
$$

$$
\begin{array}{r}
5 \\
5\overline{)25} \\
25 \\
\hline
0
\end{array}
$$

12. $\dfrac{72 \div 4}{148 \div 4} = \dfrac{18}{37}$

$$
\begin{array}{r}
2 \\
72\overline{)148} \\
144 \\
\hline
4
\end{array}
$$

$$
\begin{array}{r}
18 \\
4\overline{)72} \\
72 \\
\hline
0
\end{array}
$$

13. $\dfrac{270 \div 270}{810 \div 270} = \dfrac{1}{3}$

$$
\begin{array}{r}
3 \\
270\overline{)810} \\
810 \\
\hline
0
\end{array}
$$

14. At lowest terms

$$
\begin{array}{r}
1 \\
175\overline{)232} \\
175 \\
\hline
57
\end{array}
$$

$$
\begin{array}{r}
3 \\
57\overline{)175} \\
171 \\
\hline
4
\end{array}
$$

$$
\begin{array}{r}
14 \\
4\overline{)57} \\
4 \\
\hline
17 \\
16 \\
\hline
1
\end{array}
$$

15. $\dfrac{7 \times 8}{8 \times 8} = \dfrac{56}{64}$ $(64 \div 8 = 8)$

16. $\dfrac{3 \times 5}{7 \times 5} = \dfrac{15}{35}$ $(35 \div 7 = 5)$

17.
$$
\begin{array}{c|cccc}
2 & 8 & 5 & 15 & 12 \\
2 & 4 & 5 & 15 & 6 \\
2 & 2 & 5 & 15 & 3 \\
3 & 1 & 5 & 15 & 3 \\
5 & 1 & 5 & 5 & 1 \\
\hline
 & 1 & 1 & 1 & 1
\end{array}
$$
$2 \times 2 \times 2 \times 3 \times 5 = 120 = $ LCD

18. $\dfrac{3}{25} + \dfrac{9}{25} + \dfrac{8}{25} = \dfrac{3 + 9 + 8}{25} = \dfrac{20}{25} = \dfrac{4}{5}$

19.
$$
\begin{aligned}
\dfrac{1}{6} &= \dfrac{5}{30} \\
\dfrac{3}{5} &= \dfrac{18}{30} \\
+\dfrac{2}{3} &= +\dfrac{20}{30} \\
\hline
&\ \ \dfrac{43}{30} = 1\dfrac{13}{30}
\end{aligned}
$$

20.
$$
\begin{aligned}
45\dfrac{1}{4} &= 45\dfrac{9}{36} \\
16\dfrac{5}{9} &= 16\dfrac{20}{36} \\
+\ \dfrac{1}{3} &= +\ \dfrac{12}{36} \\
\hline
&61\dfrac{41}{36} = 61 + 1\dfrac{5}{36} = 62\dfrac{5}{36}
\end{aligned}
$$

21.
$$
\begin{aligned}
&\dfrac{11}{25} \\
-&\dfrac{6}{25} \\
\hline
&\dfrac{5}{25} = \dfrac{1}{5}
\end{aligned}
$$

22.
$$
\begin{aligned}
\dfrac{5}{12} &= \dfrac{15}{36} \\
-\dfrac{2}{9} &= -\dfrac{8}{36} \\
\hline
&\dfrac{7}{36}
\end{aligned}
$$

23.
$$
\begin{aligned}
6\dfrac{3}{4} &= 6\dfrac{9}{12} \\
-4\dfrac{2}{3} &= -4\dfrac{8}{12} \\
\hline
&2\dfrac{1}{12}
\end{aligned}
$$

24.
$$
\begin{aligned}
25\dfrac{2}{9} &= 25\dfrac{4}{18} = 24\dfrac{18}{18} + \dfrac{4}{18} = 24\dfrac{22}{18} \\
-11\dfrac{5}{6} &= -11\dfrac{15}{18} = \underline{\hspace{2cm}} \quad -11\dfrac{15}{18} \\
\hline
&\hspace{7cm} 13\dfrac{7}{18}
\end{aligned}
$$

25. $\dfrac{\overset{1}{\cancel{12}}}{\underset{3}{\cancel{21}}} \times \dfrac{\overset{1}{\cancel{7}}}{\underset{2}{\cancel{8}}} = \dfrac{1}{2}$

26. $8\dfrac{2}{5} \times 6\dfrac{1}{4} = \dfrac{\overset{21}{\cancel{42}}}{\cancel{5}_1} \times \dfrac{\overset{5}{\cancel{25}}}{\cancel{4}_2} = \dfrac{105}{2} = 52\dfrac{1}{2}$

27. $45 \times \dfrac{4}{9} \times 2\dfrac{1}{4} = \dfrac{45}{1} \times \dfrac{\overset{1}{\cancel{4}}}{\cancel{9}_1} \times \dfrac{\overset{1}{\cancel{9}}}{\cancel{4}_1} = \dfrac{45}{1} = 45$

28. $\dfrac{14}{25} \div \dfrac{4}{5} = \dfrac{\overset{7}{\cancel{14}}}{\underset{5}{\cancel{25}}} \times \dfrac{\overset{1}{\cancel{5}}}{\underset{2}{\cancel{4}}} = \dfrac{7}{10}$

29. $11\dfrac{3}{16} \div 8\dfrac{2}{3} = \dfrac{179}{16} \div \dfrac{26}{3} = \dfrac{179}{16} \times \dfrac{3}{26} = \dfrac{537}{416} = 1\dfrac{121}{416}$

30. $18 \div 5\dfrac{3}{5} = \dfrac{18}{1} \div \dfrac{28}{5} = \dfrac{\overset{9}{\cancel{18}}}{1} \times \dfrac{5}{\underset{14}{\cancel{28}}} = \dfrac{45}{14} = 3\dfrac{3}{14}$

Name_____

Class_____

ANSWERS

1. Improper fraction / Eighteen-elevenths

2. Mixed fraction / Four and one-sixth

3. Proper fraction / Thirteen-sixteenths

4. $6\frac{1}{3}$

5. 25

6. $\frac{51}{4}$

7. $\frac{86}{9}$

8. $\frac{8}{9}$

9. $\frac{2}{5}$

10. $\frac{20}{25}$

11. $\frac{18}{78}$

12. 60

13. $\frac{25}{36}$

14. $1\frac{3}{4}$

15. $5\frac{1}{3}$

16. $\frac{5}{24}$

17. $4\frac{3}{10}$

18. $4\frac{8}{9}$

19. $13\frac{1}{3}$

20. $15\frac{3}{10}$

Identify the type of fraction and write it in word form:

1. $\dfrac{18}{11}$

Improper fraction
Eighteen-elevenths

2. $4\dfrac{1}{6}$

Mixed fraction
Four and one-sixth

3. $\dfrac{13}{16}$

Proper fraction
Thirteen-sixteenths

Convert to whole or mixed numbers:

4. $\dfrac{57}{9} = 6\dfrac{3}{9} = 6\underline{\underline{\dfrac{1}{3}}}$

5. $\dfrac{125}{5} = \underline{\underline{25}}$

Convert to improper fractions:

6. $12\dfrac{3}{4} = \underline{\underline{\dfrac{51}{4}}}$

$(12 \times 4 = 48 + 3 = 51)$

7. $9\dfrac{5}{9} = \underline{\underline{\dfrac{86}{9}}}$

$(9 \times 9 = 81 + 5 = 86)$

Reduce to lowest terms:

8. $\dfrac{96}{108} = \dfrac{96 \div 12}{108 \div 12} = \underline{\underline{\dfrac{8}{9}}}$

$96\overline{)108}$ $12\overline{)96}$
$\underline{96}$ $\underline{96}$
$\dfrac{1}{12}$ $\dfrac{8}{0}$

9. $\dfrac{26}{65} = \dfrac{26 \div 13}{65 \div 13} = \underline{\underline{\dfrac{2}{5}}}$

$26\overline{)65}$ $13\overline{)26}$
$\underline{52}$ $\underline{26}$
$\dfrac{2}{13}$ $\dfrac{1}{0}$

Convert to higher terms, as indicated:

10. $\dfrac{4}{5}$ to twenty-fifths $\dfrac{4}{5} = \underline{\underline{\dfrac{20}{25}}}$

$\begin{pmatrix} 25 \div 5 = 5 \\ 5 \times 4 = 20 \end{pmatrix}$

11. $\dfrac{3}{13} = \dfrac{}{78}$ $\dfrac{3}{13} = \underline{\underline{\dfrac{18}{78}}}$

$\begin{pmatrix} 78 \div 13 = 6 \\ 3 \times 6 = 18 \end{pmatrix}$

Find the least common denominator for the following fractions:

12. $\dfrac{3}{4}, \dfrac{19}{20}, \dfrac{1}{6}, \dfrac{3}{5}, \dfrac{8}{15}$

$\begin{array}{c|ccccc} 2 & 4 & 20 & 6 & 5 & 15 \\ 2 & 2 & 10 & 3 & 5 & 15 \\ 3 & 1 & 5 & 3 & 5 & 15 \\ 5 & 1 & 5 & 1 & 5 & 5 \\ & 1 & 1 & 1 & 1 & 1 \end{array}$

$2 \times 2 \times 3 \times 5 = \underline{\underline{60}}$ LCD

Solve the following problems and reduce to lowest terms:

13. $\dfrac{3}{4} - \dfrac{1}{18}$

$\begin{array}{r} \frac{27}{36} \\ -\frac{2}{36} \\ \hline \frac{25}{36} \end{array}$

14. $\dfrac{2}{3} + \dfrac{1}{6} + \dfrac{11}{12}$

$\begin{array}{r} \frac{8}{12} \\ \frac{2}{12} \\ +\frac{11}{12} \\ \hline \frac{21}{12} = 1\frac{9}{12} = 1\frac{3}{4} \end{array}$

15. $\dfrac{2}{3} \div \dfrac{1}{8} = \dfrac{2}{3} \times \dfrac{8}{1} = \dfrac{16}{3} = 5\frac{1}{3}$

16. $\dfrac{5}{6} \times \dfrac{1}{4} = \underline{\underline{\dfrac{5}{24}}}$

17. $\dfrac{2}{5} \times 5\dfrac{3}{8} \times 2$

$= \dfrac{\overset{1}{\cancel{2}}}{5} \times \dfrac{43}{\underset{4}{\cancel{8}}} \times \dfrac{2}{1} = \dfrac{86}{20} = 4\dfrac{6}{20} = 4\dfrac{3}{10}$

18. $6\dfrac{5}{6} - \dfrac{17}{18}$

$\begin{array}{r} 6\frac{15}{18} = \quad 5\frac{18}{18} + \frac{15}{18} = \quad 5\frac{33}{18} \\ -\frac{17}{18} = \quad -\frac{17}{18} = \quad -\frac{17}{18} \\ \hline 5\frac{16}{18} = 5\frac{8}{9} \end{array}$

19. $4\dfrac{1}{2} + 5\dfrac{5}{6} + 3$

$\begin{array}{r} 4\frac{3}{6} \\ 5\frac{5}{6} \\ +3 \\ \hline 12\frac{8}{6} = 13\frac{2}{6} = 13\frac{1}{3} \end{array}$

20. $25\dfrac{1}{2} \div 1\dfrac{2}{3}$

$= \dfrac{51}{2} \div \dfrac{5}{3} = \dfrac{51}{2} \times \dfrac{3}{5} = \dfrac{153}{10} = 15\frac{3}{10}$

21. The Number Crunchers, an accounting firm, has 161 employees. If $\frac{3}{7}$ of them are Certified Public Accountants, how many CPAs are there?

$$161 \times \frac{3}{7} = \frac{\overset{23}{\cancel{161}}}{1} \times \frac{3}{\cancel{7}} = \frac{69}{1} = \underline{\underline{69}} \text{ CPAs}$$

22. Northeastern Coal mined $6\frac{2}{3}$ tons on Monday, $7\frac{3}{4}$ tons on Tuesday, and $4\frac{1}{2}$ tons on Wednesday. If the goal is to mine 25 tons this week, how many more tons must be mined?

$$6\frac{2}{3} = 6\frac{8}{12}$$
$$7\frac{3}{4} = 7\frac{9}{12}$$
$$+4\frac{1}{2} = +4\frac{6}{12}$$
$$17\frac{23}{12} = 18\frac{11}{12} \text{ Tons mined}$$

$$25 = 24\frac{12}{12}$$
$$-18\frac{11}{12} = -18\frac{11}{12}$$
$$6\frac{1}{12} \text{ Tons remaining}$$

23. A blueprint of a house has a scale of 1 inch equals $4\frac{1}{2}$ feet. If the living room wall measures $5\frac{1}{4}$ inches on the drawing, what is the actual length of the wall?

$$4\frac{1}{2} \times 5\frac{1}{4} = \frac{9}{2} \times \frac{21}{4} = \frac{189}{8} = 23\frac{5}{8} \text{ Feet}$$

24. On a canned fruit assembly line, a large container holds 255 gallons of fruit salad.

a. If each can holds $\frac{5}{12}$ of a gallon, how many cans does the container fill?

$$255 \div \frac{5}{12} = \frac{\overset{51}{\cancel{255}}}{1} \times \frac{12}{\cancel{5}} = \frac{612}{1} = \underline{\underline{612}} \text{ Cans per container}$$

b. If the process uses $2\frac{3}{4}$ containers per hour, how many cans are packed in an 8-hour day?

$$2\frac{3}{4} \times 8 = \frac{11}{\cancel{4}} \times \frac{\overset{2}{\cancel{8}}}{1} = \frac{22}{1} = 22 \text{ Containers per 8 hour day}$$

$$\begin{array}{r} 612 \text{ Cans} \\ \times \quad 22 \text{ Containers} \\ \hline 13{,}464 \text{ Cans per day} \end{array}$$

25. A developer owns 3 lots measuring $1\frac{2}{3}$ acres each, 4 lots measuring $2\frac{1}{2}$ acres each, and 1 lot measuring $3\frac{3}{8}$ acres.

a. What is the total acreage owned by the developer?

$$3 \times 1\frac{2}{3} = 5 \qquad 4 \times 2\frac{1}{2} = 10 \qquad 1 \times 3\frac{3}{8} = 3\frac{3}{8}$$

$$5 + 10 + 3\frac{3}{8} = 18\frac{3}{38} \text{ Total acres}$$

b. If each acre is worth $10,000, what is the total value of the properties?

$$\$10{,}000 \times 18\frac{3}{8} = \frac{\overset{1{,}250}{\cancel{10{,}000}}}{1} \times \frac{147}{\cancel{8}} = \frac{183{,}750}{1} = \underline{\underline{\$183{,}750}} \text{ Total value}$$

26. A manufacturer has been using glass jars weighing $11\frac{2}{3}$ ounces each. If the company switches to plastic jars, each weighing $7\frac{3}{4}$ ounces, how many ounces would be saved per 48-jar carton?

$$11\frac{2}{3} = 11\frac{8}{12} = 10\frac{20}{12}$$
$$-7\frac{3}{4} = -7\frac{9}{12} = -7\frac{9}{12}$$
$$3\frac{11}{12} \text{ Ounces saved per jar}$$

$$3\frac{11}{12} \times 48 = \frac{47}{\cancel{12}} \times \frac{\overset{4}{\cancel{48}}}{1} = \frac{188}{1} = \underline{\underline{188}} \text{ Ounces saved per carton}$$

Name_____

Class_____

ANSWERS

21. _____ 69 CPAs _____

22. _____ $6\frac{1}{12}$ Tons remaining _____

23. _____ $23\frac{5}{8}$ Feet _____

24. a. _____ 612 Cans per container _____

b. _____ 13,464 Cans per day _____

25. a. _____ $18\frac{3}{8}$ Total acres _____

b. _____ $183,750 Total value _____

26. _____ 188 Ounces saved per carton

Name_____

Class_____

ANSWERS

27. ___$3,325 Lost on investment___

28. a. ___$180 Sale price___

   b. ___$144 Final selling price___

29. ___Pasta: 15 Ounces___

   ___Garlic: 4 Tablespoons___

   Onion: $3\frac{1}{8}$ Cups

   Cheese: $6\frac{1}{4}$ Tablespoons

27. Vera Johnson bought stock for $\$113\frac{3}{8}$ and sold it for $\$96\frac{3}{4}$. If Vera had 200 shares, how much money did she lose on this investment?

$$113\frac{3}{8} = \quad 113\frac{3}{8} = \quad 112\frac{11}{8}$$
$$-\ 96\frac{3}{4} = -\ 96\frac{6}{8} = -\ 96\frac{6}{8}$$
$$\overline{\qquad\qquad\qquad\qquad 16\frac{5}{8}} \text{ Points lost per share}$$

$$16\frac{5}{8} \times 200 = \frac{133}{\cancel{8}} \times \frac{\overset{25}{\cancel{200}}}{1} = \frac{3,325}{1} = \$3,325 \text{ Lost on investment}$$

28. During a Spring clearance sale, JCPenney advertised $\frac{1}{4}$ off the list price of Model II microwave ovens, and an additional $\frac{1}{5}$ off the sale price for ovens that are scratched or dented.

a. If the list price of a Model II is $240, what is the sale price?

$$\frac{\overset{60}{\cancel{240}}}{1} \times \frac{1}{\cancel{4}} = \frac{60}{1} = \$60 \text{ Off}$$

$$\begin{array}{r} 240 \text{ List price} \\ -\ 60 \text{ Discount} \\ \hline \$180 \text{ Sale price} \end{array}$$

b. What is the price of a scratched one?

$$\$180 \times \frac{1}{5} = \frac{\overset{36}{\cancel{180}}}{1} \times \frac{1}{\cancel{5}} = \frac{36}{1} = \$36 \text{ Additional discount}$$

$$\begin{array}{r} 180 \text{ Sale price} \\ -\ 36 \text{ Discount} \\ \hline \$144 \text{ Final selling price} \end{array}$$

29. Among other ingredients, a recipe for linguini with red sauce calls for the following: 24 ounces linguini pasta, $6\frac{2}{5}$ tablespoons minced garlic, 5 cups fresh tomatoes, and 10 tablespoons parmesan cheese. If this recipe serves 8 people, recalculate the quantities to serve 5 people.

Pasta:

$$\frac{\overset{3}{\cancel{24}}}{1} \times \frac{5}{\cancel{8}} = \frac{15}{1} = \underline{\underline{15}} \text{ Ounces}$$

Garlic:

$$6\frac{2}{5} \times \frac{5}{8} = \frac{\overset{4}{\cancel{32}}}{\cancel{5}} \times \frac{\overset{1}{\cancel{5}}}{\cancel{8}} = \frac{4}{1} = \underline{\underline{4}} \text{ Tablespoons}$$

Tomatoes:

$$\frac{5}{1} \times \frac{5}{8} = \frac{25}{8} = 3\frac{1}{8} \text{ Cups}$$

Cheese:

$$\frac{\overset{5}{\cancel{10}}}{1} \times \frac{5}{\cancel{8}} = \frac{25}{4} = 6\frac{1}{4} \text{ Tablespoons}$$

30. A house has 4,400 square feet. The bedrooms occupy $\frac{2}{5}$ of the space, the living and dining rooms occupy $\frac{1}{4}$ of the space, the garage represents $\frac{1}{10}$ of the space, and the balance is split evenly between 3 bathrooms and the kitchen.

a. How many square feet are in the kitchen?

$$\frac{2}{5} = \frac{8}{20}$$
$$\frac{1}{4} = \frac{5}{20}$$
$$+\frac{1}{10} = +\frac{2}{20}$$
$$\frac{15}{20} = \frac{3}{4} \text{ Space for bedroom, living room, garage}$$

$$\frac{4}{4} \text{ Whole house}$$
$$-\frac{3}{4}$$
$$\frac{1}{4} \text{ Balance of space 3 baths and kitchen}$$

$$\overset{1,100}{\frac{\cancel{4,400}}{1}} \times \frac{1}{\cancel{4}} = \frac{1,100}{1} = \frac{1,100 \text{ sq. ft 3 Baths}}{\text{and kitchen}}$$

$$\frac{1,100}{4} = \underline{\underline{275}} \text{ sq. ft each bath and kitchen}$$

b. If the owner wants to increase the size of the garage by $\frac{1}{8}$, how many square feet will the new garage have?

$$\overset{440}{\frac{\cancel{4,400}}{1}} \times \frac{1}{\cancel{10}} = 440 \text{ sq. ft. garage}$$
$$\underset{1}{}$$

$$\overset{55}{\frac{\cancel{440}}{1}} \times \frac{1}{\cancel{8}} = + \frac{55 \text{ sq. ft. additional}}{495 \text{ sq. ft. larger garage}}$$
$$\underset{1}{}$$

![icon] **BUSINESS DECISION**
Al's Custom Tailor Shop

31. Al Weinberger, a custom tailor, buys fabric in rolls containing 171 yards each. Pants require $2\frac{3}{4}$ yards of material, vests require $\frac{7}{8}$ of a yard, and jackets take $3\frac{1}{2}$ yards.

a. How many yards of material are required for each complete suit?

$$2\frac{3}{4} = 2\frac{6}{8}$$
$$\frac{7}{8} = \frac{7}{8}$$
$$+3\frac{1}{2} = +3\frac{4}{8}$$
$$5\frac{17}{8} = \underline{\underline{7\frac{1}{8}}} \text{ Yards per suit}$$

b. How many suits can Al make from each roll?

$$171 \div 7\frac{1}{8} = \frac{171}{1} \times \frac{57}{8} = \frac{\overset{3}{\cancel{171}}}{1} \div \frac{8}{\cancel{57}} = \underline{\underline{24}} \text{ Suits per roll}$$
$$\underset{1}{}$$

c. If each roll of 100% wool material costs $1,800, what is the cost of material per suit?

$1,800 \div 24 = \underline{\underline{\$75}}$ Cost of material per suit

d. If Al adds labor and overhead charges of $290 per suit, and profit of $100 per suit, how much should he charge for a custom-made suit?

$$\begin{array}{l} 75 \text{ Material} \\ 290 \text{ Labor and overhead} \\ + \ 100 \text{ Profit} \\ \hline \$465 \text{ Price per suit} \end{array}$$

Name_____

Class_____

Copyright © 1997 by Harcourt Brace & Company. All rights reserved.

ANSWERS

30. a. _____ 275 sq. ft each bath and kitchen

b. _____ 495 sq. ft. larger garage

31. a. _____ $7\frac{1}{8}$ Yards per suit

b. _____ 24 Suits per roll

c. _____ $75 Cost of material per suit

d. _____ $465 Price per suit

| All the Math That's Fit to Learn | # The Business Math Times |

Volume II   **Fractions**   One Dollar

All about Money

U.S. Paper Money Has Enjoyed a Colorful, Ever-Changing History

Money is one of the most important inventions of humankind. Without it a complex, modern economy based on the division of labor and the consequent widespread exchange of goods and services would be impossible.

The government's recent decision to redesign paper money marks the first substantial change in the nation's currency since the 1920s. Details about the new bills will appear in future issues of *The Business Math Times*.

Before the current-style bills entered circulation in July 1929, paper money was more than an inch longer, half an inch taller, and was subject to frequent design and color changes. Over the years, a sitting president, Christopher Columbus, a dog, and bare-breasted women have appeared on U.S. paper money.

And while green and black have always predominated, other colors have been used. Some late-19th century bills are so colorful they are known to collectors as Technicolor bills.

The federal government first issued paper money in 1775— in the name of the United Colonies— as a way to finance the Revolution. Backed by neither gold nor silver and issued by a financially weak nation, Continental Currency fell in value to near worthlessness by 1779, when the last bills were printed.

From 1780 to the Civil War, several state banks and thousands of private banks issued their own paper money. These bills were as good as the banks that issued them, meaning that most of the bills were worthless.

Pressed by rising war costs and decreasing tax revenue, the federal government again turned to the printing press during the Civil War. Many of the early notes paid interest at 5 to 7.3 percent a year. Some even had a table on the back showing their value at various times.

SOURCE: *Columbus Dispatch* (September 28, 1995), p. IC.

Did You Know?

A **complex fraction** is one in which the numerator or the denominator, or both, are fractions.

Examples: $\dfrac{\frac{2}{3}}{6}$, $\dfrac{9}{\frac{3}{4}}$, $\dfrac{\frac{7}{8}}{\frac{1}{4}}$

Can you solve them?

(Answers: $\frac{1}{9}$, 12, $3\frac{1}{2}$)

Did You Know?

Two can live as cheaply as one—for half the time!

Etymology Anyone?

If you were a king in the old days you would expect to be rich.

In fact, our word *rich* evolved from *rex,* Latin for *king.*

In ancient Rome, the temple to the goddess Juno was used for the production of coins. Juno's surname was *moneta!* This gave us two words we still use today, *money* and *mint.*

Although money cannot buy happiness, our word *wealth* is from *wela,* Anglo-Saxon for *happiness* and *well-being.*

The Romans always added a column of numbers from the bottom, putting the total at the top! This explains why we still say "to add up."

The Romans called the total of addition problems *res summa* (the highest thing). Later this was shortened to *summa,* which is why we call addition answers *sums.*

The *equal sign,* two parallel lines (=), was invented in the 16th century by Robert Recorde. He stated, "Nothing can be more equal than parallel lines!"

Most people know that two tens equal twenty. In Old English it was *twegentia,* based on *twa* (two) and *tia* (ten), that is, two tens, which is how we come by the word twenty.

SOURCE: Atchison, *Word for Word.*

Brainteaser

A snail is taking a walk and falls into a 30-foot well. Each day he climbs up 3 feet. Each night while he's sleeping he slides down 2 feet. How many days will it take the snail to get out of the well?

SOURCE: James Fixx, *Games for the Super Intelligent* (New York: Doubleday, 1972).

Answers to Last Issue's Brainteaser
Mule 5, Donkey 7

Chapter 3

Decimals

Performance Objectives

SECTION I UNDERSTANDING DECIMAL NUMBERS

SECTION II DECIMAL NUMBERS AND THE FUNDAMENTAL PROCESSES

SECTION III CONVERSION OF DECIMALS TO FRACTIONS AND FRACTIONS TO DECIMALS

UNDERSTANDING DECIMAL NUMBERS

In Chapter 1, we learned that the position of the digits in our number system affects their value. In whole numbers, we dealt with the positions or places to the left of the decimal point. In decimal numbers, we will deal with the places to the right of the decimal point. These places express values that are less than whole numbers.

Just as with fractions, decimals are a way of expressing *parts* of a whole thing. Decimals are used extensively in business applications. Transactions involving dollars and cents are decimals. Percents, an integral part of business, use decimals in their calculation, and frequently fractions are written in decimal form to accommodate digital displays, such as in calculators and other digital readouts. In this chapter you will learn to read, write, and work problems involving all types of decimal numbers.

3-1 Reading and Writing Decimal Numbers in Numerical and Word Form

● **decimal numbers, or decimals**
Amounts less than whole, or less than one. For example, .44 is a decimal number.

● **decimal point**
A dot written in a decimal number to indicate where the place values change from whole numbers to decimal numbers.

● **mixed decimals**
Decimals written in conjunction with whole numbers. For example, 2.44 is a mixed decimal.

By definition, **decimal numbers,** or **decimals,** are amounts less than whole, or less than one. They are preceded by a dot known as the **decimal point,** and are written .31 or 0.31, for example. The zero is used to ensure that the decimal point is not missed. Often, decimals are written in conjunction with whole numbers. These are known as **mixed decimals.** In mixed decimals, the decimal point separates the whole numbers from the decimal, such as 4.31.

The place value chart, shown in Exhibit 3-1, expands the whole number chart from Chapter 1 to include the places representing decimals. In decimals, the value of each place, starting at the decimal point and moving from left to right, decreases by a factor of 10. The names of the places on the decimal side end in *ths;* they are tenths, hundredths, thousandths, ten-thousandths, hundred-thousandths, and millionths.

To read or write decimal numbers in words, you must read or write the decimal part as if it were a whole number, then name the place value of the last digit on the right. For example, .0594 would be read as "five hundred ninety-four ten-thousandths."

Dollars and cents are expressed as decimals. The numbers to the left of the decimal represent whole dollars; the numbers to the right represent parts of a dollar, or cents.

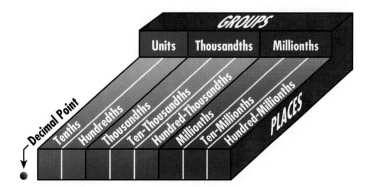

In reading and writing mixed decimals, the decimal point should be read as "and." For example, 81.205 would be read as "eighty-one and two hundred five thousandths." If the decimal has a fraction at the end, simply read them together, using the place value of the last digit of the decimal. For example, $.12\frac{1}{2}$ would be read as "twelve and one-half hundredths."

When a dollar sign ($) precedes a number, the whole number value represents dollars and the decimal value represents cents. The decimal point is read as "and." For example, $146.79 would be read as "one hundred forty-six dollars and seventy-nine cents."

EXAMPLES

Read and write the following numbers in word form:

a. .18   **b.** .0391   **c.** .00127   **d.** 34.892   **e.** 1,299.008   **f.** $.328\frac{2}{3}$

Write the following decimal numbers in numerical form:

g. Three hundred seventy-two ten-thousandths
h. Sixteen thousand and forty-one hundredths
i. Twenty-five and sixty-three and one-half thousandths

SOLUTION STRATEGY

a. .18

Strategy: In this example, write the number eighteen. Since the last digit, 8, is in the hundredths place, the decimal would be written:

Eighteen hundredths

b. .0391

Strategy: Write the number three hundred ninety-one. The last digit, 1, is in the ten-thousandths place, therefore the decimal would be written:

Three hundred ninety-one ten-thousandths

c. .00127

Strategy: Write the number one hundred twenty-seven. The last digit, 7, is in the hundred-thousandths place, therefore the decimal would be written:

One hundred twenty-seven hundred-thousandths

d. 34.892

Strategy: This example is a mixed decimal. First, write the whole number, thirty-four. The decimal point is represented by the word "and." Now write the decimal part as the number, eight hundred ninety-two. The last digit, 2, is in the thousandths place, therefore the mixed decimal is written:

Thirty-four and eight hundred ninety-two thousandths

e. 1,299.008

Strategy: This example is also a mixed decimal. Start by writing the whole number, one thousand, two hundred ninety-nine. Write "and" for the decimal point, and write the number eight. Since the last digit, 8, is in the thousandths place, the mixed decimal is written:

<u>One thousand, two hundred ninety-nine and eight thousandths</u>

f. $.328\frac{2}{3}$

Strategy: This decimal has a fraction at the end. Start by writing the number, three hundred twenty eight. Write "and," then write the fraction, two-thirds. Since the last digit of the decimal, 8, is in the thousandths place, it is written:

<u>Three hundred twenty-eight and two-thirds thousandths</u>

g. Three hundred seventy-two ten-thousandths

Strategy: Write three hundred seventy-two in numerical form. Place the last digit, 2, in the ten-thousandths place. Since ten thousand has four zeros, this is four places to the right of the decimal point. Note that we have to add a zero in the tenths place in order for the last digit, 2, to be in the ten-thousandths place.

<u>.0372</u>

h. Sixteen thousand and forty-one hundredths

Strategy: Write the whole number sixteen thousand. Place the decimal point for the word "and." Write the number forty-one, and place the last digit, 1, in the hundredths place. Note that hundred has two zeros, therefore the hundredths place is two places to the right of the decimal point.

<u>16,000.41</u>

i. Twenty-five and sixty-three and one-half thousandths

Strategy: Write the whole number twenty-five. Place the decimal point for the word "and." Write the number sixty-three, and place the fraction one-half after it. Write the last digit, 3, in the thousandths place, three places to the right of the decimal point.

<u>$25.063\frac{1}{2}$</u>

TRY-IT   EXERCISES

Read and write the following decimal numbers in word form:

1. .64   **2.** .492   **3.** .10019   **4.** 579.0004   **5.** 26.708   **6.** $.33\frac{1}{3}$

Write the following words in numerical form:

7. Two hundred seventy-two and ninety-four hundred-thousandths

8. Eleven and three and one-quarter thousandths

Check your answers with the solutions on page 81.

3-2 Rounding Decimal Numbers to a Specified Place Value

Rounding decimals is important in business because frequently numbers contain many more decimal places than necessary. For money amounts, we round to the nearest cent, or hundredth place. For other business applications, we usually do not go beyond thousandths as a final answer.

Rounding decimal numbers is much like rounding whole numbers. In whole numbers, after rounding, we substitute zeros for the remaining spaces to the right of the rounded digit to preserve the place value of the number. In rounding decimals, we do not add zeros, just drop the rest of the digits.

STEPS TO ROUND DECIMALS TO A SPECIFIED PLACE VALUE:

Step 1. Determine the place to which the decimal is to be rounded.

Step 2a. If the digit to the right of the one being rounded is 5 or more, increase the digit in the place being rounded by 1.

Step 2b. If the digit to the right of the one being rounded is 4 or less, do not change the digit in the place being rounded.

Step 3. Delete all digits to the right of the one being rounded.

EXAMPLES

Round the following numbers to the indicated place:

a. .0292 to hundredths **b.** .33945 to thousandths **c.** 36.798 to tenths
d. 177.0212782 to hundred-thousandths **e.** $46.976 to cents **f.** $66.622 to dollars

SOLUTION STRATEGY

	Decimal Number	Indicated Place	Rounded Number
a.	.0292	.0292	.03
b.	.33945	.33945	.339
c.	36.798	36.798	36.8
d.	177.0212782	177.0212782	177.02128
e.	$46.976	$46.976	$46.98
f.	$66.622	$66.622	$67

TRY-IT   EXERCISES

Round the following numbers to the indicated place:

9. 5.78892 to thousandths **10.** .004522 to ten-thousandths **11.** $345.8791 to cents

12. 76.03324 to hundredths **13.** $766.43 to dollars **14.** 34,956.1229 to tenths

Check your answers with the solutions on page 81.

Write the following decimal numbers in word form:

1. .21

Twenty-one hundredths

2. 3.76

Three and seventy-six hundredths

3. .092

Ninety-two thousandths

4. 14.659

Fourteen and six hundred fifty-nine thousandths

5. 98,045.045

Ninety-eight thousand, forty-five and forty-five thousandths

6. .000033

Thirty-three millionths

7. .00938

Nine hundred thirty-eight hundred-thousandths

8. $36.99\frac{2}{3}$

Thirty-six and ninety-nine and two-thirds hundredths

9. $.00057\frac{1}{2}$

Fifty-seven and one half hundred-thousandths

10. $2,885.59

Two thousand, eight hundred eighty-five dollars and fifty-nine cents

Write the following decimal numbers in numerical form:

11. Eight-tenths

.8

12. Twenty-nine thousandths

.029

13. Sixty-seven thousand, three hundred nine and four hundredths

67,309.04

14. Eleven hundred fifty-four dollars and thirty-four cents

$1,154.34

15. One hundred eighty-three thousand and one hundred eighty-three ten-thousandths

183,000.0183

Round the following numbers to the indicated place:

16. .448557 to hundredths

$0.4\underline{4}8557 = 0.45$

17. 123.0069 to thousandths

$123.00\underline{6}9 = 123.007$

18. .9229388 to ten-thousandths

$0.922\underline{9}388 = 0.9229$

19. .0100393 to hundred-thousandths

$0.0100\underline{3}93 = 0.01004$

20. $688.75 to dollars

$$68\underline{8}.75 = 689.00

21. $14.59582 to cents

$$14.5\underline{9}582 = 14.60

22. 88.964 to tenths

$88.\underline{9}64 = 89.0$

23. 43.0056 to hundredths

$43.0\underline{0}56 = 43.01$

24. 1.344 to hundredths

$1.3\underline{4}4 = 1.34$

25. 45.80901 to whole numbers

$4\underline{5}.80901 = 46$

SECTION II

DECIMAL NUMBERS AND THE FUNDAMENTAL PROCESSES

In business, working with decimals is an everyday occurrence. As you shall see, performing the fundamental processes of addition, subtraction, multiplication, and division on decimal numbers is very much like performing them on whole numbers. As before, the alignment of the numbers is very important. The difference is in the handling and placement of the decimal point.

3-3 Adding and Subtracting Decimals

In adding and subtracting decimals we follow the same procedure as we did with whole numbers. As before, be sure that you line up all the place values, including the decimal points. The decimal point in the answer will appear in the same position (column) as in the problem. When all the numbers have been lined up, you may add zeros to the right of the decimal numbers that do not have enough places. This will not change the value of the number.

$$
\begin{array}{r}
.2500 \\
.4703 \\
+21.6530 \\
\hline
22.3733
\end{array}
$$

EXAMPLES

a. Add 45.3922 + .0019 + 2.9 + 1,877.332   **b.** Add $37.89 + $2.76

c. Subtract 87.06 − 35.2   **d.** Subtract $67.54 from $5,400

SOLUTION STRATEGY

These examples are solved by lining up the decimal points, then performing the indicated operation as if they were whole numbers.

a.
$$
\begin{array}{r}
45.3922 \\
.0019 \\
2.9000 \\
+1,877.3320 \\
\hline
1,925.6261
\end{array}
$$

b.
$$
\begin{array}{r}
\$37.89 \\
+ \ 2.76 \\
\hline
40.65
\end{array}
$$

c.
$$
\begin{array}{r}
87.06 \\
-35.20 \\
\hline
51.86
\end{array}
$$

d.
$$
\begin{array}{r}
\$5,400.00 \\
- \ \ \ 67.54 \\
\hline
5,332.46
\end{array}
$$

   **TRY-IT**   **EXERCISES**

Perform the indicated operation:

15. 35.7008 + 311.2 + 84,557.54   **16.** $65.79 + $154.33

17. Subtract 57.009 from 186.7   **18.** $79.80 minus $34.61

Check your answers with the solutions on page 81.

3-4 Multiplying Decimals

Decimals are multiplied in the same way as whole numbers, except we must now deal with placing the decimal point in the answer. The rule is that there must be as many decimal places in the product as there are total decimal places in the multiplier and the multiplicand. This may require adding zeros to the product.

EXAMPLE

Multiply 125.4 by 3.12.

SOLUTION STRATEGY

$$
\begin{array}{rl}
125.4 & \text{1 decimal place} \\
\times\ \ 3.12 & \text{2 decimal places} \\
\hline
2508 & \\
1254\ \ & \\
3762\ \ \ \ & \\
\hline
391.248 & \text{3 decimal places}
\end{array}
$$

EXAMPLE

To illustrate a situation where we must add zeros to the product, multiply .0004 × 6.3.

SOLUTION STRATEGY

$$
\begin{array}{rl}
6.3 & \text{1 decimal place} \\
\times\ .0004 & \text{4 decimal places} \\
\hline
.00252 & \text{5 decimal places}
\end{array}
$$

Here, we had to add 2 zeros to the left of the product to make 5 decimal places.

 Multiplication Shortcut   Whenever you are multiplying a decimal by a power of 10, such as 10, 100, 1,000, 10,000, etc., count the number of zeros in the multiplier and move the decimal point in the multiplicand the same number of places to the right. If necessary, add zeros to the product to provide the required places.

EXAMPLES

To illustrate the shortcut, multiply 138.57 by 10, 100, 1,000, and 10,000.

SOLUTION STRATEGY

$138.57 \times 10 = 1,385.7$ Decimal moved 1 place to the right

$138.57 \times 100 = 13,857.$ Decimal moved 2 places to the right

$138.57 \times 1,000 = 138,570.$ Decimal moved 3 places to the right—1 zero added

$138.57 \times 10,000 = 1,385,700.$ Decimal moved 4 places to the right—2 zeros added

Multiply the following decimals:

| 19. | 876.66
× .045 | 20. | 4,955.8
× 2.9 | 21. | $65.79
× 558 | 22. | .00232 by 1,000 |

Check your answers with the solutions on page 81.

3-5 Dividing Decimals

In division of decimals, be aware of the decimal points. The basic rule is that you cannot divide with a decimal in the divisor. If there is a decimal, you must convert it to a whole number before dividing.

STEPS FOR DIVIDING DECIMALS IF THE DIVISOR IS A WHOLE NUMBER:

Step 1. Place the decimal point in the quotient directly above the decimal point in the dividend.

Step 2. Divide the numbers.

EXAMPLE

Divide: 8.50 ÷ 25

SOLUTION STRATEGY

$$8.50 \div 25 = 25 \overline{)8.50}$$
$$\begin{array}{r} .34 \\ \underline{75} \\ 100 \\ \underline{100} \\ 0 \end{array}$$

In this example, the divisor, 25, is a whole number, so we place the decimal point in the quotient directly above the decimal point in the dividend, and then divide. The answer is .34.

STEPS FOR DIVIDING DECIMALS IF THE DIVISOR IS A DECIMAL NUMBER

Step 1. Move the decimal point in the divisor to the right until it becomes a whole number.

Step 2. Move the decimal point in the dividend the same number of places as you moved it in the divisor. It may be necessary to add zeros to the right of the dividend if there are not enough places.

Step 3. Place the decimal point in the quotient directly above the decimal point in the dividend.

Step 4. Divide the numbers.

Note: All answers involving money should be rounded to the nearest cent. This means dividing until the quotient has a thousandths place, and then rounding back to hundredths. For example, $45.671 = $45.67 or $102.879 = $102.88.

Divide: 358.75 ÷ 17.5

$358.75 ÷ 17.5 =$

$17.5)\overline{358.75}$

In this example, the divisor, 17.5, is a decimal with one place. To make it a whole number, move the decimal point one place to the right. Now move the decimal point in the dividend one place to the right.

$175)\overline{3587.5}$

Then place the decimal point in the quotient above the decimal point in the dividend.

$$
\begin{array}{r}
20.5 \\
175)\overline{3587.5} \\
\underline{350} \\
87\ 5 \\
\underline{87\ 5} \\
0
\end{array}
$$

Now divide the numbers. The answer is <u>20.5</u>.

Division Shortcut   Whenever you divide a decimal by a power of 10, such as 10, 100, 1,000, 10,000, etc., count the number of zeros in the divisor and move the decimal point in the dividend the same number of places to the left. It may be necessary to add zeros to provide the required places.

EXAMPLES

To illustrate this shortcut, divide 43.78 by 10, 100, 1,000, and 10,000.

$43.78 ÷ 10 = 4.378$	Decimal moved 1 place to the left
$43.78 ÷ 100 = .4378$	Decimal moved 2 places to the left
$43.78 ÷ 1,000 = .04378$	Decimal moved 3 places to the left—1 zero added
$43.78 ÷ 10,000 = .004378$	Decimal moved 4 places to the left—2 zeros added

TRY-IT   **EXERCISES**

Divide the following decimals:

23. $716.8 ÷ 16$ **24.** $21.336 ÷ .007$ **25.** $\$3,191.18 ÷ 42.1$ **26.** $2.03992 ÷ 1,000$

Check your answers with the solutions on page 81.

   REVIEW EXERCISES   CHAPTER 3—SECTION II

Perform the indicated operation for the following:

1. $2.03 + 56.003$

$$
\begin{array}{r}
2.030 \\
+\ 56.003 \\
\hline
58.033
\end{array}
$$

2. $.006 + 12.33$

$$
\begin{array}{r}
.006 \\
+\ 12.330 \\
\hline
12.336
\end{array}
$$

3. $24.66 + $19.72 + $.89

$$\begin{array}{r} \$24.66 \\ 19.72 \\ + \quad .89 \\ \hline \$45.27 \end{array}$$

4. 54.669 + 121.3393 + 7.4

$$\begin{array}{r} 54.6690 \\ 121.3393 \\ + \quad 7.4000 \\ \hline 183.4083 \end{array}$$

5. .000494 + 45.776 + 16.008 + 91

$$\begin{array}{r} .000494 \\ 45.776000 \\ 16.008000 \\ + 91.000000 \\ \hline 152.784494 \end{array}$$

6. 495.09 − 51.05

$$\begin{array}{r} 495.09 \\ - \quad 51.05 \\ \hline 444.04 \end{array}$$

7. 58.043 − 41.694

$$\begin{array}{r} 58.043 \\ - 41.694 \\ \hline 16.349 \end{array}$$

8. $70.55 − $12.79

$$\begin{array}{r} \$70.55 \\ - 12.79 \\ \hline \$57.76 \end{array}$$

9. $1.71 − $.84

$$\begin{array}{r} \$1.71 \\ - \quad .84 \\ \hline \$ \ .87 \end{array}$$

10. 28.90922 − 16.41

$$\begin{array}{r} 28.90922 \\ - 16.41000 \\ \hline 12.49922 \end{array}$$

11. The Fancy Fruit Company shipped 218 pounds of strawberries, 186.9 pounds of cherries, and 374.85 pounds of apples to a customer. What was the total weight of the order?

$$\begin{array}{l} 218.00 \ \text{Strawberries} \\ 186.90 \ \text{Cherries} \\ + \ 374.85 \ \text{Apples} \\ \hline 779.75 \ \text{Total weight} \end{array}$$

12. Todd Gulliver wants to build a fence around his property. If the dimensions of the land are 145.66 feet, 97.1 feet, 164.09 feet, and 103.6 feet, what will be the total length of the fence?

$$\begin{array}{l} 145.66 \\ 97.10 \\ 164.09 \\ + \ 103.60 \\ \hline 510.45 \ \text{Total feet} \end{array}$$

13. While at the mall, Maria Gomez spends $46.50 for a blouse, $39.88 for a skirt, and $51.99 for a pair of shoes. What is the total amount of Maria's purchases?

$$\begin{array}{l} \$46.50 \ \text{Blouse} \\ 39.88 \ \text{Skirt} \\ + \ 51.99 \ \text{Shoes} \\ \hline \$138.37 \ \text{Total purchase} \end{array}$$

14. On a recent trip, Edward Spencer filled up his gas tank four times with the following quantities of gasoline: 23.4 gallons, 19.67 gallons, 21.008 gallons, and 16.404 gallons. How many gallons did Edward use?

$$\begin{array}{l} 23.400 \\ 19.670 \\ 21.008 \\ + \ 16.404 \\ \hline 80.482 \ \text{Total gallons} \end{array}$$

15. Last week, Carley Hopkins ran a 5-kilometer race in 26.696 minutes. This week she ran a race in 24.003 minutes. What is the difference in Carley's times?

$$\begin{array}{l} 26.696 \\ - \ 24.003 \\ \hline 2.693 \ \text{Minutes difference} \end{array}$$

16. Before dieting, John Richards weighed 188.75 pounds. After three weeks, he weighed 179.46. How much weight did John lose?

$$\begin{array}{l} 188.75 \\ - \ 179.46 \\ \hline 9.29 \ \text{Pounds lost} \end{array}$$

17. In a manufacturing process, three pieces of wood are glued together. In thickness, they measure .65 inch, .0591 inch, and 1.6 inches.

    a. What is the total thickness of the pieces?

          0.6500
          0.0591
      + 1.6000
        2.3091 Inches total thickness

    b. If these pieces are fit into a space measuring 3.94 inches, how much room is left for other parts?

          3.9400
      − 2.3091
        1.6309 Inches left over

18. On Monday an electrician used 184.66 feet of wire; on Tuesday he used 121.03 feet.

    a. How many total feet did he use?

        184.66 Ft. Monday
      + 121.03 Ft. Tuesday
       305.69 Total feet used

    b. If he started with a roll 445 feet in length, how much wire remains on the roll?

        445.00
      − 305.69
       139.31 Feet remain on roll

19. Sandy's checking account had a starting balance of $1,850.37. During the week, Sandy wrote checks for $131.57, $533.19, $51.50, and $8.70. He also made deposits of $422.17 and $88.66. What is the new balance of the checking account?

$131.57	$422.17	$1,850.37 Start
533.19	+ 88.66	− 724.96 Checks
51.50	$510.83 Total deposits	1,125.41
+ 8.70		+ 510.83 Deposits
$724.96 Total checks		$1,636.24 New balance

20. A milk tanker truck weighs 57,699 pounds empty. After filling up at the dairy, the truck weighed 64,707.2 pounds.

    a. How many pounds of milk did the truck pick up?

        64,707.2 Full weight
      − 57,699.0 Empty weight
        7,008.2 Pounds of milk picked up

    b. At the end of the day the truck weighed 59,202.9 pounds. How much milk did the truck deliver?

        64,707.2 Full
      − 59,202.9 End of day
        5,504.3 Pounds delivered

Multiply the following decimals:

21. 45.77
$\times$ 12
549.24

22. 494.09
$\times$ .81
400.2129

23. 2.311
$\times$ 3.2
7.3952

24. 112.005
$\times$ 10,000
1,120,050.

25. .00202
$\times$ 24
.04848

26. 15.032 × 1.008
15.032
$\times$ 1.008
15.152256

27. 45.0079 × 1,000
45.0079
$\times$ 1000
45,007.9

28. .3309 × 100,000
.3309
$\times$ 100,000
33,090.

Divide the following decimals, rounding to hundredths where necessary:

29. 24.6 ÷ 19
= 1.294 = 1.29

30. .593 ÷ 8.6
= .068 = .07

31. 18.69 ÷ 1,000
= .018 = .02

32. $24.50 ÷ 9
= 2.722 = $2.72

33. 72)266.4
3.7
72)266.4 = 3.7

34. 23.18)139.08
6.0
2318)13908.0 = 6.0

35. .04)62.2
1555
4)6220 = 1,555

36. 4.6)1000
217.391
46)10000.000 = 217.39

37. The Williams Company purchases 23 fax machines for its office staff. Each of the machines costs $345.50. What is the total cost of the machines?

$345.50
$\times$ 23
$7,946.50 Total cost

38. A developer is building 13 homes at one time. Each roof measures 45.7 feet by 68.55 feet.

a. What is the total square feet per roof? (Multiply length by width.)

68.55
$\times$ 45.7
3,132.735 Sq. ft. per roof

b. What is the total square feet of roof for the entire project?

3,132.735
$\times$ 13
40,725.555 Total sq. ft. entire project

c. If the roofing company charges $4.15 per square foot, what is the total cost of the roofs?

40,725.555 Total sq. ft.
$\times$ $4.15 Cost per sq. ft.
$169,011.05 Total cost

39. a. What is the cost of a dress requiring 3.63 yards of material, if the material is $12.59 per yard?

3.63 Yards
$\times$ $12.59 Cost per yard
$45.70 Cost per dress

b. How much is saved on the dress if material costing $9.45 per yard is used instead?

$12.59   3.14
− 9.45   × 3.63
$3.14 Savings per yard $11.40 Savings per dress

40. A vegetable wholesaler sold 1,168.07 pounds of potatoes, 1,246.11 pounds of lettuce, and 1,217.82 pounds of onions on Monday.

a. What is the total pounds the wholesaler sold?

1,168.07 Potatoes
1,246.11 Lettuce
+1,217.82 Onions
3,632.00 Total pounds

b. If the wholesaler had 8 customers on Monday, what was the average pounds per sale?

$$\frac{3,632}{8} = 454 \text{ Pounds per customer}$$

41. Randy Blake has a car with a gas tank that holds 19.48 gallons. If the car averages 16.22 miles per gallon, how many miles can Randy drive on a tank?

19.48 Gallons
× 16.22 Miles per gallon
315.9656 = 316 Miles per tank

42. Danny Elliott purchases 153.6 square yards of carpeting on sale for $13.70 per yard.

a. What is the cost of the carpet?

153.6 Sq. yds.
× $13.70 Per yard
$2,104.32 Cost of carpet

b. Normally, this carpeting sells for $19.69 per yard. How much does Danny save by purchasing during the sale?

$19.69 Regular price   153.6 Sq. yds
− 13.70 Sale price   × $5.99 Savings per yard
5.99 Savings per yard $920.06 Total savings

43. Lillian Gilbert started the day with $65.78 in her purse. During the day she spent $13.58 at the bookstore; $34.62 at the supermarket; and $11.86 at the dry cleaner. On the way home, she cashed a check for $40.00.

a. How much cash did Lillian have that evening?

$13.58 Bookstore $65.78 Start
 34.62 Supermarket   − 60.06 Spent
+ 11.86 Dry cleaners   5.72
$60.06 Total spending   + 40.00 Cashed check
                        $45.72 Cash at end of day

b. If her spending budget was $50.00 per day, was she over or under budget for the day? By how much?

$60.06 Total spending
− 50.00 Daily budget
$10.06 Over budget

44. Jim Fowler bought a car at Grove Auto Sales for $14,566.90. The sticker price was $17,047.88.

a. How much did Jim save from the sticker price?

$17,047.88 Sticker price
− 14,566.90 Sale price
$2,480.98 Saved

b. The tax was $957.70, and the registration and license plate cost $65.40. What is the total cost of the car?

$14,566.90 Price of car
957.70 Tax
+ 65.40 Registration and license plate
$15,590 Total cost

c. If Jim makes a down payment of $4,550 and gets an interest-free car loan from Grove, what will the equal monthly payments be for 48 months?

$15,590 Total cost
− 4,550 Down payment
$11,040 Amount financed

$$\frac{\$11,040}{48} = \$230 \text{ Monthly payment}$$

45. Boxes of candy are 5.77 inches high.

a. How many boxes can be stacked in a container 86.55 inches high?

$$\frac{86.55}{5.77} = 15 \text{ Boxes}$$

b. If each box weighs 1.4 pounds, and the container weighs 6 pounds, what is the total weight of a filled container?

15 Boxes
× 1.4 Pounds per box
21 Pounds—Boxes
+ 6 Pounds—Container
27 Pounds—Total weight

c. If freight charges to Toledo, Ohio, are $1.48 per pound, what is the total cost to ship the container?

27 Pounds
× $1.48 Freight per pound
$39.96 Freight to Toledo

SECTION III

CONVERSION OF DECIMALS TO FRACTIONS AND FRACTIONS TO DECIMALS

Changing a number from decimal form to its fractional equivalent, or changing a number in fractional form to its decimal equivalent, is quite common in the business world. For example, a builder or an architect may use fractions when dealing with the measurements of a project, but convert to decimals when calculating the cost of materials.

3-6 Converting Decimals to Fractions

Keep in mind that decimals are another way of writing fractions whose denominators are powers of 10 (10, 100, 1,000). When you are converting a mixed decimal, the whole number is added to the new fraction, resulting in a mixed fraction.

STEPS FOR CONVERTING DECIMALS TO THEIR FRACTIONAL EQUIVALENT:

Step 1. Write the decimal as a fraction by making the decimal number, without the decimal point, the numerator.

Step 2. The denominator is 1 followed by as many zeros as there are decimal places in the original decimal number.

Step 3. Reduce the fraction to lowest terms.

EXAMPLES

Convert the following decimals to their fractional equivalent, reducing where possible:

a. .64   **b.** .125   **c.** .0457   **d.** 17.31

SOLUTION STRATEGY

a. $.64 = \dfrac{64}{100} = \dfrac{16}{25}$

In this example, 64 becomes the numerator. Since there are two decimal places, the denominator is 1 with two zeros. Then reduce the fraction.

b. $.125 = \dfrac{125}{1000} = \dfrac{1}{8}$

Once again, the decimal becomes the numerator, 125. This decimal has three places, therefore the denominator will be 1 followed by three zeros. The resulting fraction is then reduced to lowest terms.

c. $.0457 = \dfrac{457}{10,000}$

This fraction does not reduce.

d. $17.31 = 17 + \dfrac{31}{100} = 17\dfrac{31}{100}$

This mixed decimal results in a mixed fraction. It cannot be reduced.

T R Y - I T   EXERCISES

Convert the following decimals to their fractional equivalent, reducing where possible:

27. .875   **28.** 23.076   **29.** .0004   **30.** 84.75

Check your answers with the solutions on page 81.

3-7 Converting Fractions to Decimals

In Chapter 2, we learned that fractions are actually a way of expressing a division, with the line separating the numerator and the denominator representing "divided by."

$$\frac{\text{Numerator (dividend)}}{\text{Denominator (divisor)}} \longrightarrow \text{Denominator}\overline{)\text{Numerator}}$$

In business, decimal numbers are usually rounded to three places (thousandths) or less. When expressing money, round to the nearest hundredth, or cent.

STEPS FOR CONVERTING FRACTIONS TO DECIMALS:

Step 1. Divide the numerator by the denominator.

Step 2. Add a decimal point and zeros, as necessary, to the numerator (dividend).

EXAMPLES

Convert the following fractions to their decimal equivalents, rounding to hundredths:

a. $\dfrac{3}{5}$　　　**b.** $\dfrac{1}{3}$　　　**c.** $\dfrac{23}{9}$　　　**d.** $15\dfrac{3}{8}$

SOLUTION STRATEGY

a. $\dfrac{3}{5} = 5\overline{)3.0}^{\,.6} = \underline{\underline{.6}}$

In this example, the numerator, 3, becomes the dividend, with a decimal point and zero added. The denominator, 5, becomes the divisor.

b. $\dfrac{1}{3} = 3\overline{)1.0000}^{\,.3333} = \underline{\underline{.33}}$

In this example, the division is uneven, and goes on and on, so we round the quotient to hundredths.

c. $\dfrac{23}{9} = 9\overline{)23.00000}^{\,2.55555} = \underline{\underline{2.56}}$

Improper fractions result in mixed decimals. Note that the quotient was rounded because of an endlessly repeating decimal.

d. $15\dfrac{3}{8} = 15 + 8\overline{)3.000}^{\,.375}$

$\qquad = \underline{\underline{15.38}}$

This example contains a whole number. Remember to add it to the resulting decimal.

TRY-IT EXERCISES

Convert the following fractions to their decimal equivalents, rounding to hundredths where necessary:

31. $\dfrac{4}{5}$　　　**32.** $84\dfrac{2}{3}$　　　**33.** $\$6\dfrac{3}{4}$　　　**34.** $\dfrac{5}{2}$　　　**35.** $\dfrac{5}{8}$

Check your answers with the solutions on page 81.

 REVIEW EXERCISES　CHAPTER 3—SECTION III　

Convert the following decimals to fractions and reduce to lowest terms:

1. .125　　　**2.** 4.75　　　**3.** .008　　　**4.** 93.0625　　　**5.** 14.82

$= \dfrac{125}{1,000} = \underline{\underline{\dfrac{1}{8}}}$　$= 4\dfrac{75}{100} = 4\underline{\underline{\dfrac{3}{4}}}$　$= \dfrac{8}{1,000} = \underline{\underline{\dfrac{1}{125}}}$　$= 93\dfrac{625}{10,000} = 93\underline{\underline{\dfrac{1}{16}}}$　$= 14\dfrac{82}{100} = 14\underline{\underline{\dfrac{41}{50}}}$

Convert the following fractions to decimals, rounding the quotients to hundredths:

6. $\dfrac{9}{16}$　　　**7.** $5\dfrac{2}{3}$　　　**8.** $24\dfrac{1}{8}$　　　**9.** $\dfrac{55}{45}$　　　**10.** $\dfrac{3}{5}$

$= .5625 = \underline{\underline{.56}}$　$= 5.666 = \underline{\underline{5.67}}$　$= 24.125 = \underline{\underline{24.13}}$　$= 1\dfrac{10}{45} = 1.222 = \underline{\underline{1.22}}$　$= \underline{\underline{.6}}$

For the following numbers, perform the indicated operation:

11. $34.55 + 14.08 + 9\frac{4}{5}$

$$
\begin{array}{r}
34.55 \\
14.08 \\
+\ 9.80 \\
\hline
58.43
\end{array}
$$

12. $565.809 - 224\frac{3}{4}$

$$
\begin{array}{r}
565.809 \\
-\ 224.750 \\
\hline
341.059
\end{array}
$$

13. $12\frac{1}{2} \div 2.5$

$12.5 \div 2.5 = \underline{\underline{5}}$

14. $\$35.88 \times 21\frac{1}{4}$

$$
\begin{array}{r}
\$35.88 \\
\times\ 21.25 \\
\hline
\$762.45
\end{array}
$$

15. a. How many 8-slice pizzas must you purchase in order to feed 24 women, who eat $2\frac{1}{8}$ slices each, and 20 men, who eat $3\frac{3}{4}$ slices each? (Round to the nearest whole pizza.)

Women $24 \times 2.125 = 51$ Slices

Men $20 \times 3.75 = 75$ Slices

$$
\begin{array}{r}
51 \\
+\ 75 \\
\hline
126 \text{ Total slices}
\end{array}
$$

$\dfrac{126}{8} = 15.75 = \underline{\underline{16}}$ Pizzas

b. If each pizza costs $11.89, what is the total cost?

$$
\begin{array}{l}
16 \text{ Pizzas} \\
\underline{\times\ \$11.89} \text{ Cost per pizza} \\
\$190.24 \text{ Total cost}
\end{array}
$$

16. Janice buys $4\frac{3}{5}$ pounds of potatoes at $.75 per pound. What is the cost of the potatoes?

$4\dfrac{3}{5} \times .75 =$

$$
\begin{array}{l}
4.6 \text{ Pounds of potatoes} \\
\underline{\times\ .75} \text{ Price per pound} \\
\$3.45 \text{ Total cost}
\end{array}
$$

17. a. What is the cost of 5,000 shares of stock selling at $12\frac{7}{8}$ per share?

$5000 \times \$12\dfrac{7}{8} =$

$$
\begin{array}{l}
5{,}000 \text{ Shares} \\
\underline{\times\ 12.875} \text{ Price per share} \\
\$64{,}375 \text{ Total cost of shares}
\end{array}
$$

b. If the broker's commission is $\frac{1}{25}$ of the value of the stock, what is the amount of the commission?

$64375 \times \dfrac{1}{25} =$

$$
\begin{array}{l}
64{,}375 \text{ Cost of shares} \\
\underline{\times\ \ \ \ .04} \text{ Broker's portion} \\
\$2{,}575 \text{ Total cost of shares}
\end{array}
$$

c. What is the total cost of the transaction?

$$
\begin{array}{l}
64{,}375 \text{ Cost of shares} \\
\underline{+\ 2{,}575} \text{ Broker's commission} \\
\$66{,}950 \text{ Total cost of transaction}
\end{array}
$$

18. You are the purchasing manager for a company that uses specially treated photo paper. The yellow paper cost $.07\frac{1}{5}$ per sheet and the blue paper costs $.05\frac{3}{8}$ per sheet. If you order 15,000 yellow sheets and 26,800 blue sheets, what is the total cost of the order?

Yellow

$$
\begin{array}{l}
15{,}000 \text{ Sheets} \\
\underline{\times\ \ \ .072} \text{ Price per sheet} \\
\$1{,}080 \text{ Cost—yellow}
\end{array}
$$

Blue

$$
\begin{array}{l}
26{,}800 \text{ Sheets} \\
\underline{\times\ .05375} \text{ Price per sheet} \\
\$1{,}440.50 \text{ Cost—blue}
\end{array}
$$

$$
\begin{array}{l}
\$1{,}080.00 \text{ Cost—yellow} \\
\underline{+\ 1{,}440.50} \text{ Cost—blue} \\
\$2{,}520.50 \text{ Total cost}
\end{array}
$$

19. Magic City taxicabs charge $1.20 for the first $\frac{1}{4}$ of a mile, and $.35 for each additional $\frac{1}{4}$ of a mile. What is the cost of a trip from the airport to downtown, a distance of $8\frac{3}{4}$ miles?

$.35 Cost per $\frac{1}{4}$ mile	$1.40 Per mile
$\times \quad 4$ $\frac{1}{4}$'s Per mile	$\times \quad 8.5$ Miles left after first $\frac{1}{4}$
$1.40 Cost per mile	$11.90
	$+ \quad 1.20$ First $\frac{1}{4}$ mile
	$13.10 Cost from airport

CHAPTER 3 ■ DECIMALS   SUMMARY CHART

SECTION I   UNDERSTANDING DECIMAL NUMBERS

Topic	P/O, Page	Important Concepts	Illustrative Examples
Writing Decimals in Word and Numerical Form	3–1 62	In decimals, the value of each place, starting at the decimal point and moving from left to right, decreases by a factor of 10. The names of the places end in *ths;* they are tenths, hundredths, thousandths, ten-thousandths, hundred-thousandths, and millionths. 1. To write decimal numbers in words, write the decimal part as a whole number, then add the place value of the last digit on the right. 2. When writing mixed decimals, the decimal point should be read as "and." 3. If the decimal ends in a fraction, read them together, using the place value of the last digit of the decimal. 4. When a dollar sign ($) precedes a number, the whole number value represents dollars, the decimal value represents cents, and the decimal point is read as "and."	*Decimal Numbers* .0691 is six hundred ninety-one ten-thousandths Twenty-one ten-thousandths is .0021 *Mixed Decimals* 51.305 is fifty-one and three hundred five thousandths Eighteen and thirty-six thousandths is 18.036 *Decimals with Fractions* $.22\frac{1}{2}$ is twenty-two and one-half hundredths Seventeen and one-half hundredths is $.17\frac{1}{2}$ *Dollars and Cents* $946.73 is nine hundred forty-six dollars and seventy-three cents Six dollars and twelve cents is $6.12
Rounding off Decimal Numbers to a Specified Place Value	3–2 65	1. Determine the place to which the decimal is to be rounded. 2a. If the digit to the right of the one being rounded is 5 or more, increase the digit in the place being rounded by 1. 2b. If the digit to the right of the one being rounded is 4 or less, do not change the digit in the place being rounded. 3. Delete all digits to the right of the one being rounded.	.645 rounded to hundredths is .65 42.5596 rounded to tenths is 42.6 .00291 rounded to thousandths is .003 $75.888 rounded to cents is $75.89

SECTION II   DECIMAL NUMBERS AND THE FUNDAMENTAL PROCESSES

Topic	P/O, Page	Important Concepts	Illustrative Examples
Adding and Subtracting Decimals	3–3 67	1. Line up all the place values, including the decimal points. 2. The decimal point in the answer will appear in the same position (column) as in the problem. 3. You may add zeros to the right of the decimal numbers that do not have enough places.	Addition: 2,821.049 12.500 + 143.008 2,976.557 Subtraction: 194.1207 − 45.3400 148.7807

II, continued

Topic	P/O, Page	Important Concepts	Illustrative Examples
Multiplying Decimals	3–4 67	1. Multiply the numbers as if they are whole numbers, disregarding the decimal points. 2. Total the number of decimal places in the multiplier and the multiplicand. 3. Insert the decimal point in the product, giving it the same number of decimal places as the total from Step 2. 4. If necessary, place zeros to the left of the product to provide the correct number of digits. Note: If the situation involves money, answers should be rounded to the nearest cent.	Multiply 224.5 by 4.53 $\quad$ 224.5$\quad$ 1 decimal place $\times\quad$ 4.53$\quad$ 2 decimal places $\quad\overline{6\,735}$ $\quad$ 112 25 $\quad\underline{898\,0}$ 1,016.985$\quad$ 3 decimal places
Multiplication Shortcut: Powers of 10	3–4 68	When multiplying a decimal times a power of 10 (such as 10, 100, 1,000, 10,000, etc.): 1. Count the number of zeros in the multiplier and move the decimal point in the multiplicand the same number of places to the right. 2. If necessary, add zeros to the product to provide the required places.	$.064 \times 10\quad = .64\quad$ 1 place $.064 \times 100\quad = 6.4\quad$ 2 places $.064 \times 1,000\quad = 64\quad$ 3 places $.064 \times 10,000 = 640\quad$ 4 places $.064 \times 100,000 = 6,400\quad$ 5 places
Dividing Decimals	3–5 69	*If the divisor is a whole number* 1. Place the decimal point in the quotient directly above the decimal point in the dividend. 2. Divide the numbers. *If the divisor is a decimal number* 1. Move the decimal point in the divisor to the right until it becomes a whole number. 2. Move the decimal point in the dividend the same number of places you moved it in the divisor. It may be necessary to add zeros to the right of the dividend if there are not enough places. 3. Place the decimal point in the quotient directly above the decimal point in the dividend. 4. Divide the numbers. Note: All answers involving money should be rounded to the nearest cent.	Divide: $9.5 \div 25$ $\quad\quad\;\;.38$ $25\overline{)9.50}$ $\quad\;\underline{75}$ $\quad\;200$ $\quad\;\underline{200}$ $\quad\quad\;0$ Divide: $14.3 \div 2.2$ $2.2\overline{)14.3}$ $\quad\quad\;6.5$ $22\overline{)143.0}$ $\quad\;\underline{132}$ $\quad\;110$ $\quad\;\underline{110}$ $\quad\quad\;0$
Division Shortcut: Powers of 10	3–5 70	When dividing a decimal by a power of 10 (10, 100, 1,000, 10,000, etc.): 1. Count the number of zeros in the divisor, and move the decimal point in the dividend the same number of places to the left. 2. It may be necessary to add zeros to provide the required number of decimal places.	$21.69 \div 10\quad = 2.169\quad$ 1 place $21.69 \div 100\quad = .2169\quad$ 2 places $21.69 \div 1,000 = .02169\quad$ 3 places $21.69 \div 10,000 = .002169\quad$ 4 places

SECTION III CONVERSION OF DECIMALS TO FRACTIONS AND FRACTIONS TO DECIMALS

Topic	P/O, Page	Important Concepts	Illustrative Examples
Converting Decimals to Fractions	3–6 76	1. Write the decimal as a fraction by making the decimal number, without the decimal point, the numerator. 2. The denominator is "1" followed by as many zeros as there are decimal places in the original decimal number. 3. Reduce the fraction to lowest terms.	$.88 = \dfrac{88}{100} = \dfrac{22}{25}$ $5.57 = 5 + \dfrac{57}{100} = 5\dfrac{57}{100}$
Converting Fractions to Decimals	3–7 76	1. Divide the numerator by the denominator. 2. Add a decimal point and zeros, as necessary, to the numerator.	$\dfrac{4}{5} = 5\overline{)4.0}\ ^{.8}$ $\dfrac{22}{4} = 4\overline{)22.0}\ ^{5.5}$

TRY-IT EXERCISE SOLUTIONS

1. Sixty-four hundredths
2. Four hundred ninety-two thousandths
3. Ten thousand nineteen hundred-thousandths
4. Five hundred seventy-nine and four ten-thousandths
5. Twenty-six and seven hundred eight thousandths
6. Thirty-three and one-third hundredths
7. 272.00094
8. $11.003\frac{1}{4}$

9. $5.78\underset{=}{8}92 = 5.789$
10. $.004\underset{=}{5}22 = .0045$
11. $\$345.8\underset{=}{7}91 = \$345.88$

12. $76.03\underset{=}{3}24 = 76.03$
13. $\$766.\underset{=}{4}3 = \$766.00$
14. $34,956.1\underset{=}{2}29 = 34,956.1$

15.
$$
\begin{array}{r}
35.7008 \\
311.2000 \\
+84,557.5400 \\
\hline
84,904.4408
\end{array}
$$

16.
$$
\begin{array}{r}
\$\ 65.79 \\
+154.33 \\
\hline
\$220.12
\end{array}
$$

17.
$$
\begin{array}{r}
186.700 \\
-\ 57.009 \\
\hline
129.691
\end{array}
$$

18.
$$
\begin{array}{r}
\$79.80 \\
-34.61 \\
\hline
\$45.19
\end{array}
$$

19.
$$
\begin{array}{r}
876.66 \\
\times\ .045 \\
\hline
4\ 38330 \\
35\ 0664 \\
\hline
39.44970
\end{array}
$$

20.
$$
\begin{array}{r}
4,955.8 \\
\times\ 2.9 \\
\hline
4\ 460\ 22 \\
9\ 911\ 6 \\
\hline
14,371.82
\end{array}
$$

21.
$$
\begin{array}{r}
\$65.79 \\
\times\ 558 \\
\hline
526\ 32 \\
3\ 289\ 5 \\
32\ 895 \\
\hline
36,710.82
\end{array}
$$

22. $.00232 \times 1,000 = 2.32$
Move decimal 3 places to the right

23.
$$
\begin{array}{r}
44.8 \\
16\overline{)716.8} \\
64 \\
\hline
76 \\
64 \\
\hline
12\ 8 \\
12\ 8 \\
\hline
0
\end{array}
$$

24.
$$
\begin{array}{r}
3048 \\
7\overline{)21336} \\
21 \\
\hline
33 \\
28 \\
\hline
56 \\
56 \\
\hline
0
\end{array}
$$

25.
$$
\begin{array}{r}
75.8 \\
421\overline{)31911.8} \\
2947 \\
\hline
2441 \\
2105 \\
\hline
336\ 8 \\
336\ 8 \\
\hline
0
\end{array}
$$

26. $2.03992 \div 1,000 = .00203992$
Move decimal 3 places to the left

27. $\dfrac{875}{1000} = \dfrac{7}{8}$
28. $23\dfrac{76}{1000} = 23\dfrac{19}{250}$
29. $\dfrac{4}{10000} = \dfrac{1}{2500}$
30. $84\dfrac{75}{100} = 84\dfrac{3}{4}$

31. $\dfrac{4}{5} = .8$
$$
\begin{array}{r}
.8 \\
5\overline{)4.0} \\
4\ 0 \\
\hline
0
\end{array}
$$

32. $84\dfrac{2}{3} = 84.67$
$$
\begin{array}{r}
.666 \\
84 + 3\overline{)2.000} \\
18 \\
\hline
20 \\
18 \\
\hline
20 \\
18 \\
\hline
2
\end{array}
$$

33. $\$6\dfrac{3}{4} = \$6.75$
$$
\begin{array}{r}
.75 \\
6 + 4\overline{)3.00} \\
2\ 8 \\
\hline
20 \\
20 \\
\hline
0
\end{array}
$$

34. $\dfrac{5}{2} = 2.5$
$$
\begin{array}{r}
2.5 \\
2\overline{)5.0} \\
4 \\
\hline
1\ 0 \\
1\ 0 \\
\hline
0
\end{array}
$$

35. $\dfrac{5}{8} = 0.63$
$$
\begin{array}{r}
.625 \\
8\overline{)5.000} \\
4\ 8 \\
\hline
20 \\
16 \\
\hline
40 \\
40 \\
\hline
0
\end{array}
$$

Name_____

Class_____

ANSWERS

1. _____Sixty-one hundredths_____

2. Thirty-four and five hundred eighty-one thousandths

3. One hundred nineteen dollars and eighty-five cents

4. _Nine and three-sevenths hundredths_

5. Four hundred ninety-five ten-thousandths

6. _____.0967_____

7. _____5.014_____

8. _____843.2_____

9. _____$16.57_____

10. _____.45_____

11. _____99.070_____

12. _____$128.00_____

13. _____4.7_____

14. _____51.198_____

15. _____$37.19_____

16. _____473.8241_____

17. _____7.7056_____

18. _____$92.83_____

19. _____.736_____

20. _____221.1_____

21. _____.000192_____

22. _____99,120._____

23. _____.4_____

24. _____.00793_____

25. _____$20.06_____

Write the following decimal numbers in word form:

1. .61

Sixty-one hundredths

2. 34.581

Thirty-four and five hundred eighty-one thousandths

3. $119.85

One hundred nineteen dollars and eighty-five cents

4. $.09\frac{3}{7}$

Nine and three-sevenths hundredths

5. .0495

Four hundred ninety-five ten-thousandths

Write the following decimal numbers in numerical form:

6. Nine hundred sixty-seven ten-thousandths

.0967

7. Five and fourteen thousandths

5.014

8. Eight hundred forty-three and two tenths

843.2

9. Sixteen dollars and fifty-seven cents

$16.57

Round the following numbers to the indicated place:

10. .44857 to hundredths

.44857 = .45

11. 995.06966 to thousandths

99.06966 = 99.070

12. $127.94 to dollars

$127.94 = $128.00

13. 4.6935 to tenths

4.6935 = 4.7

Perform the indicated operation for the following:

14. 6.03 + 45.168

6.030
+ 45.168
51.198

15. $1.58 + $15.63 + $19.81 + $.17

$1.58
15.63
19.81
+ .17
$37.19

16. .0031 + 69.271 + 193.55 + 211

.0031
69.2710
193.5500
+ 211.0000
473.8241

17. 23.0556 − 15.35

23.0556
− 15.3500
7.7056

18. $95.67 − $2.84

$95.67
− 2.84
$92.83

19. .802 − .066

.802
− .066
.736

20. 14.74
× 15
221.1

21. .008
× .024
.000192

22. .9912 × 100,000
99,120.

23. .503 ÷ 1.2575 = .4

24. 79.3 ÷ 10,000 = .00793

25. $150.48 ÷ 7.5
= 20.064 = $20.06

Convert the following decimals to fractions and reduce to lowest terms:

26. $12.035 = 12\frac{35}{100} = 12\frac{7}{20}$

27. $.0441 = \frac{441}{10,000}$

Convert the following fractions to decimals. Round the quotients to hundredths.

28. $\frac{8}{29} = .275 = \underline{.28}$

29. $3\frac{1}{9} = 3.111 = \underline{3.11}$

30. $\frac{95}{42} = 2.261 = \underline{2.26}$

31. Paul Clinton went shopping for a stereo. He purchased an AM-FM tuner for $335.79, a control amplifier for $435.67, and a CD player for $287.99. He also bought 2 CDs for $11.88 each and 3 CDs for $14.88 each. What was the total of Paul's purchase?

```
$335.79 Tuner          $11.88      $14.88
 435.67 Amplifier      ×    2      ×    3
 287.99 CD Player       $23.76      $44.64
  23.76 CDs
+ 44.64 CDs
$1,127.85 Total cost of stereo
```

32. Mike's Bikes has a 22-inch off-road racer on sale this month for $239.95. If the original price of the bike was $315.10, how much would a customer save buying it on sale?

```
 $315.10 Original price
− 239.95 Sale price
  $75.15 Savings
```

33. Stan and Myra Jordan both work for the Caliper Company. Stan earns $17.75 per hour as a technician and Myra earns $19.50 per hour as a research analyst. Last week Stan worked 43.22 hours and Myra worked 37.6 hours. What was their combined total earnings for the week?

```
      Stan              Myra
$17.75 Hourly rate   $19.50       $767.16 Stan
× 43.22 Hours        × 37.6     + 733.20 Myra
$767.16              $733.20    $1,500.36 Total
```

34. A ream of paper contains 500 sheets and costs $7.50. What is the cost per sheet?

$$\frac{\$7.50 \text{ Cost per ream}}{500 \text{ Sheets}} = \$.015 \text{ Per sheet}$$

35. Richard Bush bought 600 shares of stock at $34\frac{7}{8}$. Three months later he sold the shares for $26\frac{1}{2}$. How much did Richard lose on this investment?

```
      Buy                     Sell
   600 Shares              600 Shares          $20,925 Buy
× $34.875 Price per share  × $26.5 Price per share  − 15,900 Sell
  $20,925 Buy price        $15,900 Sell price      $5,025 Loss
```

36. Great Impressions, a printing company, charges $.066 per page for color brochures.

  a. What is the cost of 10,000 copies of a 4-page brochure?

```
  10,000 Copies
×      4 Pages
  40,000 Total pages
×   .066 Price per page
  $2,640 Total cost—Great Impressions
```

Name_____

Class_____

ANSWERS

26. $12\frac{7}{20}$

27. $\frac{441}{10,000}$

28. .28

29. 3.11

30. 2.26

31. $1,127.85

32. $75.15

33. $1,500.36

34. $.015

35. $5,025

36. a. $2,640

ANSWERS

b. _____$200_____

37. _____$21,773.77_____

38. a. _____$18.75_____

b. _____$166,380_____

c. _____$830,130_____

39. a. _____23_____

b. _____$41.17_____

b. If Payless Printers will do the job for $.061, how much can be saved by using them to print the brochure?

    40,000 Pages $2,640
×   .061 Price per page   − 2,440
    $2,440 Total cost—Payless $200 Savings

37. Jim Massey owes the Mountain City Bank $34,880.41 for his home mortgage. If he makes monthly payments of $546.11 for two years, what is the balance remaining on Jim's loan?

    $546.11 Monthly payment   34,880.41 Amount owed
×   24 Months   − 13,106.64 Total payments
$13,106.64 Total of payments $21,773.77 Balance remaining

38. The Enchanted Island Theme Park took in $663,750 in June on ticket sales.

    a. If 35,400 people attended the park, what was the average price per ticket?

$$\frac{\$663,750 \text{ Total revenue}}{35,400 \text{ People}} = \$18.75 \text{ Average price per ticket}$$

    b. If, on the average, each person spent $4.70 on food, how much did the park make on food?

        35,400 People
× $4.70 Average food sales
$166,380 Total food sales

    c. What was the total revenue for the tickets and the food?

        $663.750 Total ticket sales
+ 166,380 Total food sales
   $830,130 Total revenue

39. As the food manager for a local charity, you are planning a fund-raising pasta party. Spaghetti sells for $1.79 per 16-ounce box.

    a. If the average adult serving is $5\frac{3}{4}$ ounces, and the average child eats $3\frac{1}{2}$ ounces, how many boxes will you have to purchase in order to serve 36 adults and 46 children?

      36 Adults   46 Children   207 $\frac{368}{16} = 23$ Boxes of
× 5.75 Ounces per adult × 3.5 Ounces per child + 161   pasta
   207 Ounces   161 Ounces   368 Total ounces

    b. What is the total cost of the spaghetti?

        23 Boxes
× 1.79 Cost per box
$41.17 Total cost

40. Bill Brammer wanted to make some money at a flea market. He purchased 55 small orchids from a nursery for a total of $233.75, 3 bags of potting soil for $2.75 each, and 55 ceramic pots at $4.60 each. After planting the orchids in the pots, Bill sold each plant for $15.50 at the next flea market.

a. What was his total cost per potted plant?

$$\begin{array}{cc} \$2.75 \text{ Per bag} \\ \times \quad 3 \text{ Bags} \\ \hline \$8.25 \text{ Total cost soil} \end{array} \qquad \begin{array}{c} \$4.60 \text{ Per pot} \\ \times \quad 55 \text{ Pots} \\ \hline \$253 \text{ Total cost pots} \end{array} \qquad \begin{array}{c} \$233.75 \text{ Plants} \\ 8.25 \text{ Soil} \\ + \ 253.00 \text{ Pots} \\ \hline \$495 \text{ Total cost} \end{array} \qquad \begin{array}{c} \$495 \text{ Total cost} \\ 55 \ \text{ Plants} \\ \hline = \underline{\$9.00} \text{ per plant} \end{array}$$

b. How much profit did Bill make on this venture?

$$\begin{array}{l} \$15.50 \text{ Selling price per plant} \\ \times \quad\quad 55 \text{ Plants} \\ \hline \$852.50 \text{ Total revenue} \\ - \ 495.00 \text{ Total cost} \\ \hline \underline{\$357.50} \text{ Total profit} \end{array}$$

 ## BUSINESS DECISION
Pepsi, Please!

41. Randy Keller owns a PepsiCo vending truck that holds 360 quarts of soda. Last Saturday at a carnival, Randy sold out completely. He sells a 10-ounce Pepsi for $1.25. There are 16 ounces in a pint, and 2 pints in a quart.

a. How many drinks did he serve?

$$\begin{array}{l} 360 \text{ Quarts} \\ \times \quad 2 \\ \hline 720 \text{ Pints} \\ \times \quad 16 \\ \hline 11{,}520 \text{ Ounces} \end{array} \qquad \dfrac{11{,}520 \ \text{Total ounces}}{10 \ \text{ Ounces per drink}} = \underline{1{,}152} \text{ Drinks served}$$

b. How much money did he take in for the day?

$$\begin{array}{l} 1{,}152 \text{ Drinks served} \\ \times \ 1.25 \text{ Per drink} \\ \hline \underline{\$1{,}440} \text{ Revenue for the day} \end{array}$$

c. For the next carnival, Randy is considering switching to either a 12-ounce drink for $1.65 or a 16-ounce drink for $1.95. As his business advisor, what size do you recommend, assuming each would be a sellout?

$$\dfrac{11{,}520 \ \text{Total ounces}}{12 \ \text{ Ounces per drink}} = \begin{array}{l} 960 \text{ Drinks} \\ \times \ 1.65 \text{ Per drink} \\ \hline \$1{,}584 \text{ Revenue} \end{array}$$

$$\dfrac{11{,}520 \ \text{Total ounces}}{16 \ \text{ Ounces per drink}} = \begin{array}{l} 720 \text{ Drinks} \\ \times \ 1.95 \text{ Per drink} \\ \hline \$1{,}404 \text{ Revenue} \end{array}$$

<u>12-ounce size</u> is the best deal.

Name_____

Class_____

ANSWERS

40. a. _____ $9.00 _____

b. _____ $357.50 _____

41. a. _____ 1,152 _____

b. _____ $1,440 _____

c. _____ 12-ounce size _____

All the Math That's Fit to Learn

The Business Math Times

Volume III   **Decimals**   One Dollar

What the Heck Is ENIAC!

On February 14, 1946, the age of bits and bytes was born when the first all-electronic digital computer, ENIAC (Electronic Numerical Integrator And Computer), was introduced to the world in a special ceremony at the University of Pennsylvania's Moore School of Electrical Engineering.

ENIAC was developed for the United States Army during World War II under the code name Project PX. It was a U-shaped black metal behemoth that weighed 30 tons; used nearly 18,000 vacuum tubes, 6,000 switches, 10,000 capacitors, 70,000 resistors, and 1,500 relays; stood 10 feet tall; and occupied 1,800 square feel in a room by itself.

And it was fast. ENIAC could calculate the angle that a gun must be aimed to hit a target—the reason it was developed—in 30 seconds. By comparison, such a calculation would take an hour using the other most powerful mechanical device available at the time.

Today, a pentium-powered laptop measures about 8-by-12 inches,

and weighs 6 pounds. A 150MHz Pentium microprocessor is capable of calculating 300 million additions per second, compared with ENIAC's 5,000. That makes the Pentium 60,000 times faster than ENIAC, and ENIAC was 1,000 times faster than any calculating machine before it.

Moore's Law, a rule of thumb in the computer industry, first coined in the 1960s, states that the power of a computer chip will double every 18 months. "We'll be at one million times faster than ENIAC by the year 2002 if Moore's Law continues to hold true, which it always has," said Professor Mitchell Marcus, chairman of Moore's Computer and Information Science Department.

SOURCE: From Robert E. Calem, "New York Times on the Web" (www.nytimes.com), February 14, 1996.

Photo Finish

Did you know that fractions and decimals are used in all forms of racing to express the time difference between the competitors? For example, in the 1995 Winston Select Nascar race at Talladega, Alabama, Mark Martin's Ford beat Dale Earnhardt's Chevrolet by only eighteen hundredths (.18) of a second—and that's after 500 miles! In the 1992 Indianapolis 500, Al Unser, Jr., beat Scott Goodyear by only forty-three thousandths (.043) of a second, the closest finish in the history of the race.

Calculating Things!

Did you know that the first calculating machine was invented in 1850. This forerunner of today's computers was invented by Charles Babbage in 1823.

Do you know what an abacus is? How about a slide rule? Check it out. Tell the class, and demonstrate how they are used.

Holiday Numbers!

Match the holiday with the average number of greeting cards sold for that holiday.

1. Valentine's Day   A.   40 million
2. Easter   B. 101 million
3. Christmas   C. 150 million
4. Thanksgiving   D. 165 million
5. Mother's Day   E.   1.0 billion
6. Father's Day   F.   2.3 billion

(Answers: 1E, 2D, 3F, 4A, 5C, 6B)

SOURCE: Dean D. Dauphinais, and Kathleen Droste. *Astounding Averages!* Visible Ink Press, a division of Gale Research Inc., 1995, p. 141.

Brainteaser

What mathematical symbol can you put between the number one and the number two, in order to yield a new number, larger than one, but less than two?

Answer to Last Issue's Brainteaser

28 days. The snail would advance one foot per day (3 feet up, 2 feet down) for the first 27 days. On the 28th day, the snail would climb up 3 feet and be out.

WHAP!

BLAIR

THE INVENTION OF THE DECIMAL POINT

Chapter 4

Checking Accounts

Performance Objectives

SECTION I UNDERSTANDING AND USING CHECKING ACCOUNTS

SECTION II BANK STATEMENT RECONCILIATION

UNDERSTANDING AND USING CHECKING ACCOUNTS

Checking accounts are one of the most useful and common banking services available today. Well over 90 percent of all business transactions involve the use of checks. Most businesses and individuals use checking accounts to purchase goods and pay bills, because checks are convenient to use, are safer than cash, and provide an accurate record of the transactions.

Checking accounts are offered by banks, savings and loan institutions, and credit unions. For the purpose of this chapter, the word "bank" will be used to represent any of these institutions. Recently, decreased government regulation has increased the competition among banking institutions, and as a consequence, a variety of new services and options have been offered to the banking customer. Some checking accounts even pay interest on the balances maintained in the account.

Although checking account options, charges, and restrictions are too numerous and varied to list here, before opening a checking account, a business or individual should shop for those that best fit their financial needs. Some important things to consider are monthly service charges, check printing charges, minimum balance requirements, interest paid on the account, availability of automated teller machines (ATMs) and electronic funds transfer (EFT), overdraft privileges, and for businesses, services such as note collection and payroll assistance. Bank customers may also be offered free traveler's checks, free safe-deposit boxes, and even credit cards and loans at preferred rates.

4-1 Opening a Checking Account and Understanding How the Various Forms Are Used

● **signature card**

A card signed by all persons authorized to sign checks on the account. Used by the bank to verify the authenticity of the signatures on checks.

After you have chosen a bank, the account is usually opened by a new accounts officer or clerk. The customer is assigned an account number and is given a **signature card** that is filled out and signed by all persons authorized to sign checks on the account. The bank uses the signature card to verify the authenticity of the signature on your checks. Exhibit 4-1 is an example of a signature card.

Automatic teller machines are one of the many services that banks provide.

After the initial paperwork has been completed, the customer will place an amount of money into the account as an opening balance. Funds added to a checking account are known as **deposits.** The bank will then give the **depositor** a checkbook containing checks and deposit slips.

Checks, or **drafts,** are negotiable instruments ordering the bank to pay money from the checking account to the name written on the check. The person or business named on the check to receive the money is known as the **payee.** The person or business issuing the check is known as the **payor.**

Checks are available in many sizes, colors, and designs; however, they all contain the same fundamental elements. Exhibit 4-2 shows a check with the major parts labeled. Look at this illustration carefully, and familiarize yourself with the various parts of the check.

Deposit slips or deposit tickets are printed forms with the depositor's name, address, account number, and space for the details of the deposit. Deposit slips are used to record money, both cash and checks, being *added* to the checking account. They are presented to the bank teller along with the items to be deposited. When a deposit is completed, the depositor receives a copy of the deposit slip as a receipt, or proof of the transaction. The deposit should also be recorded by the depositor on the current check stub, or in the check register. Exhibit 4-3 is an example of a deposit slip.

---

deposits
Funds added to a checking account.

depositor
A person who deposits money in a checking account.

check or draft
A written order to a bank by a depositor to pay the amount specified on the check from funds on deposit in a checking account.

payee
The person or business named on the check to receive the money.

payor
The person or business issuing the check.

deposit slip
Printed forms with the depositor's name, address, account number, and space for the details of the deposit. Used to record money, both cash and checks, being added to the checking account.

Grove Isle Bank

ACCOUNT NAME _____

ACCOUNT #: _____
RELATED ACCTS.: _____

SIGNATURES - THE UNDERSIGNED AGREE(S) TO THE TERMS STATED ON THE FRONT AND BACK OF THIS FORM, AND THE SEPARATE DISCLOSURE FORM, AND ACKNOWLEDGE(S) RECEIPT OF A COPY OF EACH ON TODAY'S DATE.

Name #1 _____ Title _____

X _____

Name #2 _____ Title _____

X _____

Name _____ Title _____

X _____

Name _____ Title _____

X _____

Ofc. Code: _____
Cycle Code: _____ Class Code: _____
Stmt. Address: _____
_____
Street Address (if Diff.): _____
_____
SS #: _____
Fed ID #: _____
Date: _____
Home Phone: _____
Business Phone: _____
Initial Deposit: $ _____
☐ Cash ☐ Check/Source _____
Req. Signers _____
Media Source _____
Referral Source _____

COMMERCIAL ACCOUNTS
☐ Corporation ☐ Non-Profit
☐ Partnership ☐ Estate
☐ Organization ☐ Guardianship (Restrict.)
☐ Sole Prop. ☐ Escrow
☐ Other _____

ACCOUNT TYPE
☐ Personal Checking ☐ Savings Account
☐ Business Checking ☐ Money Market Account
☐ Now Account ☐ Certificate of Deposit
☐ Super Now Account ☐ IRA ☐ SDB ☐ ATM

OTHER TERMS, EXPLANATIONS, OTHER SERVICES, ETC.
BY SIGNING ABOVE I hereby acknowledge receipt of the bank disclosure statement with the terms and conditions of **Pan American Bank,** Electronic Funds Transfer Services, Funds Availability Disclosure and a copy of the Depositors Contract. I also authorize the Bank to request a credit report from any credit agency and to check employment history.

IDENTIFICATION for Signer #1 SS# _____
Date of Birth _____ Employer_____
Driver's License # _____ Occupation _____
Other I.D. _____ Passport # _____

IDENTIFICATION for Signer #2 SS# _____
Date of Birth _____ Employer_____
Driver's License # _____ Occupation _____
Other I.D. _____ Passport # _____

ACCOUNT OPENED BY: _____ ☐ NEW ACCOUNT ☐ REVISED/EXISTING
APPROVED BY: _____ OFFICER CODE: _____ DATE: _____
Chex Systems: _____

EXHIBIT 4-1

SIGNATURE CARD

EXHIBIT 4-2

CHECK

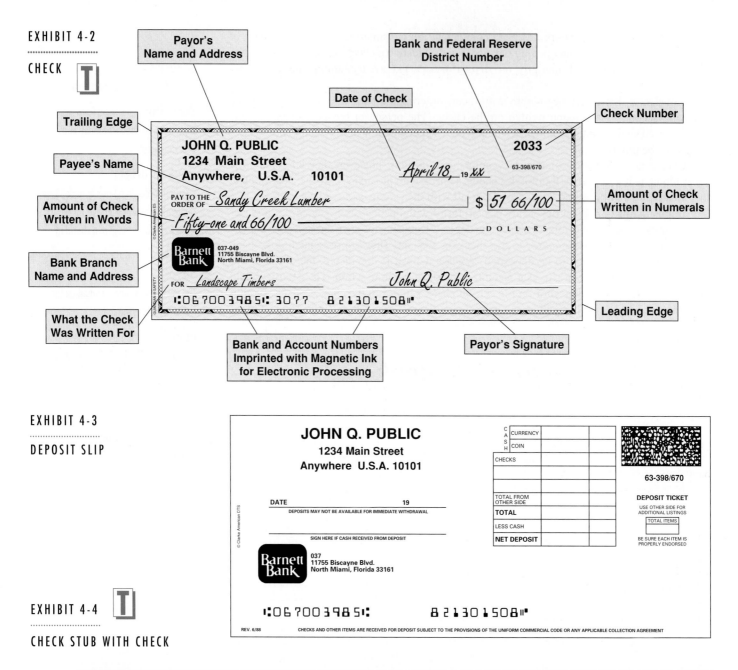

Payor's Name and Address

Bank and Federal Reserve District Number

Date of Check

Check Number

Trailing Edge

Payee's Name

Amount of Check Written in Words

Bank Branch Name and Address

What the Check Was Written For

Bank and Account Numbers Imprinted with Magnetic Ink for Electronic Processing

Payor's Signature

Leading Edge

Amount of Check Written in Numerals

EXHIBIT 4-3

DEPOSIT SLIP

EXHIBIT 4-4

CHECK STUB WITH CHECK

check stub

A bound part of the checkbook, attached by perforation to checks. Used to keep track of the checks written, deposits, and current account balance of a checking account.

Either **check stubs** or a **check register** can be used to keep track of the checks written, the deposits added, and the current account balance. It is very important to keep these records accurate and up to date. This will prevent the embarrassing error of writing checks with insufficient funds in the account.

Check stubs, with checks attached by perforation, are usually a bound part of the checkbook. A sample check stub with a check is shown in Exhibit 4-4. Note that the check number

		PLEASE BE SURE TO **DEDUCT** ANY BANK CHARGES THAT APPLY TO YOUR ACCOUNT.							
CHECK NUMBER	DATE	DESCRIPTION OF TRANSACTION	AMOUNT OF PAYMENT OR WITHDRAWAL (–)		✓	AMOUNT OF DEPOSIT OR INTEREST (+)		BALANCE FORWARD	
		To							
		For						Bal.	
		To							
		For						Bal.	
		To							
		For						Bal.	
		To							
		For						Bal.	
		To							
		For						Bal.	
		To							
		For						Bal.	

EXHIBIT 4-5

······························

CHECK REGISTER

is preprinted on both the check and the attached stub. Each stub is used to record the issuing of its corresponding check and any deposits made on that date.

Check registers are the alternative method for keeping track of checking account activity. They are a separate booklet of forms, rather than stubs attached to each check. A sample check register is shown in Exhibit 4-5. Note that space is provided for all the pertinent information required to keep an accurate and up-to-date running balance of the account.

● **check register**
A separate booklet of blank forms used to keep track of all checking account activity. An alternative to the check stub.

4-2 Writing Checks in Proper Form

When a checking account is opened, you will choose the color and style of your checks. The bank will then order custom-printed checks with your name, address, and account number identifications. The bank will provide you with some blank checks and deposit slips to use until your printed ones arrive.

Checks should be typed or neatly written in ink. There are six parts to be filled in when writing a check.

STEPS FOR WRITING CHECKS IN PROPER FORM:

Step 1. Enter the *date* of the check in the space provided.

Step 2. Enter the name of the person or business to whom the check is written, the payee, in the space labeled "*pay to the order of.*"

Step 3. Enter the amount of the check, in numerical form, in the space with the dollar sign, $. The dollar amount should be written close to the $ sign so additional digits cannot be added. The cents should be written as xx/100.

Step 4. Enter the amount of the check, this time written in word form, on the next line down, labeled *dollars*. As before, the cents should be written as xx/100. A horizontal, wavy line is then written to the end of the line.

Step 5. The space labeled *memo* is used to write the purpose of the check. Although it is optional, it's a good idea to use this space so you won't forget why the check was written.

Step 6. The space in the lower right-hand corner of the check is for the signature. It should be written exactly as it is on the signature card.

EXAMPLE

Write a check for Bill Pearson to the Fifth Avenue Flower Shop, for a ceramic planter, in the amount of $83.73, on June 7, 19xx.

SOLUTION STRATEGY

Here is the check for Bill Pearson, written in proper form. Note that the amount, $83.73, is written $83 73/100, and the name is signed as it is printed on the check.

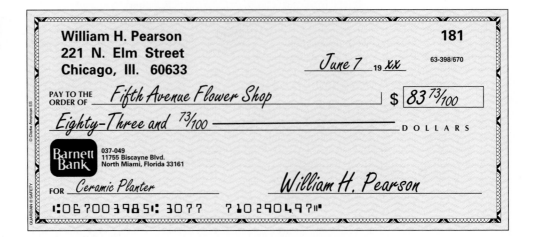

TRY-IT EXERCISE

1. **Use the following blank to write a check for Anne Marie Richards to Snappy Photo Service for developing 4 rolls of film in the amount of $41.88 on April 27.**

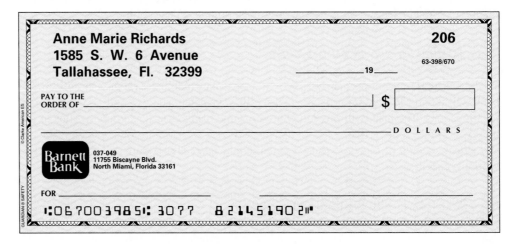

Check your answer with the solution on page 110.

4-3 Endorsing Checks Using Blank, Restrictive, and Full Endorsements

● **endorsement**

The signature and instructions on the back of a check instructing the bank on what to do with that check.

● **blank endorsement**

An endorsement used when the payee wants to cash a check.

● **restrictive endorsement**

An endorsement used when the payee wants to deposit a check into his or her account.

● **full endorsement**

An endorsement used when the payee wants to transfer a check to another party.

When you receive a check, you may either cash it, deposit it into your account, or transfer it to another party. The **endorsement** on the back of the check instructs the bank what to do. Federal regulations require that specific areas of the reverse side of checks be designated for the payee and bank endorsements. Your endorsement should be written within the $1\frac{1}{2}$-inch space at the trailing edge of the check, as shown in Exhibit 4-6. The space is usually labeled "ENDORSE HERE."

There are three types of endorsements with which you should become familiar: blank endorsements, restrictive endorsements, and full endorsements, which are shown in Exhibits 4-7, 4-8, and 4-9.

A **blank endorsement** is used when you want to cash the check. You, as the payee, simply sign your name exactly as it appears on the front of the check. Once you have endorsed a check in this manner, anyone who has possession of the check can cash it. For this reason, you should use blank endorsements cautiously.

A **restrictive endorsement** is used when you want to deposit the check into your account. In this case, you endorse the check "for deposit only," sign your name as it appears on the front, and write your account number.

A **full endorsement** is used when you want to transfer the check to another party. In this case, you endorse the check "pay to the order of," write the name of the person or business to whom the check is being transferred, and sign your name and account number.

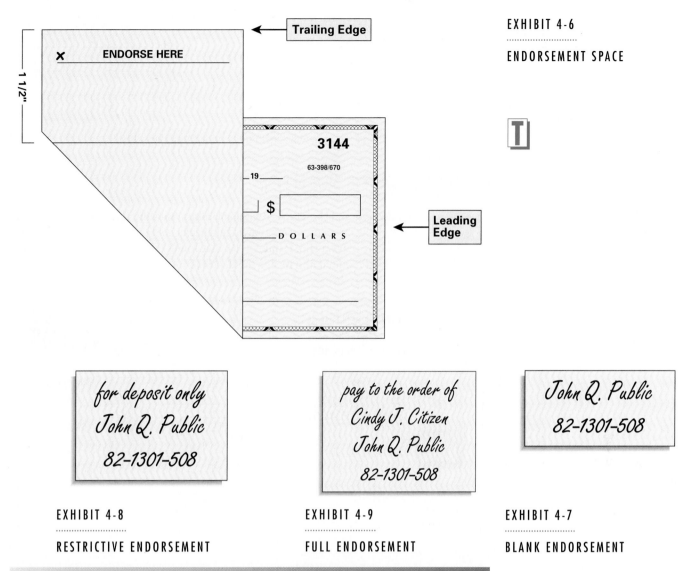

Trailing Edge

ENDORSE HERE

1 1/2"

Leading Edge

3144

63-398/670

19_____

$

D O L L A R S

EXHIBIT 4-6

ENDORSEMENT SPACE

for deposit only
John Q. Public
82-1301-508

EXHIBIT 4-8

RESTRICTIVE ENDORSEMENT

pay to the order of
Cindy J. Citizen
John Q. Public
82-1301-508

EXHIBIT 4-9

FULL ENDORSEMENT

John Q. Public
82-1301-508

EXHIBIT 4-7

BLANK ENDORSEMENT

EXAMPLES

You have just received a check. Your account number is #2922-22-33-4. Write the following endorsements and identify what type they are:

a. Allowing you to cash the check.
b. Allowing you to deposit the check into your checking account.
c. Allowing the check to be transferred to your partner Sam Johnson.

SOLUTION STRATEGY

a. Blank Endorsement
Your Signature
2922-22-33-4

b. Restrictive Endorsement
for deposit only
Your Signature
2922-22-33-4

c. Full Endorsement
pay to the order of
Sam Johnson
Your Signature
2922-22-33-4

TRY-IT   EXERCISES

You have just received a check. Your account number is #696-339-1028. Write the following endorsements in the space provided and identify what type they are:

2. Allowing the check to be transferred to your friend Roz Reitman.
3. Allowing you to cash the check.
4. Allowing you to deposit the check in your checking account.

2. _____
_____
_____
_____

3. _____
_____
_____
_____

4. _____
_____
_____
_____

Check your answers with the solutions on page 110.

4-4 Preparing Deposit Slips in Proper Form

Deposit slips are filled out and presented to the bank along with the funds being deposited. They are dated and list the currency, coins, individual checks, and the total amount of the deposit. Note on the sample deposit slip, Exhibit 4-10, that John Q. Public took $100.00 in cash out of the deposit, which required him to sign the deposit slip.

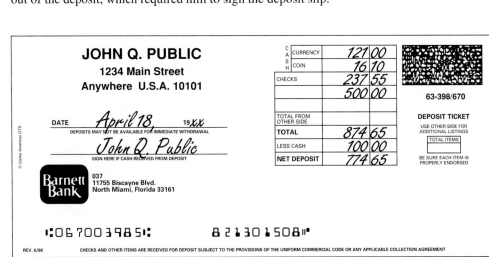

EXHIBIT 4-10

COMPLETED DEPOSIT SLIP

EXAMPLE

Prepare a deposit slip for Rob Donaldson, based on the following information:

a. Date: June 4, 19xx
b. $127 in currency
c. $3.47 in coins
d. A check for $358.89 and a check for $121.68

SOLUTION STRATEGY

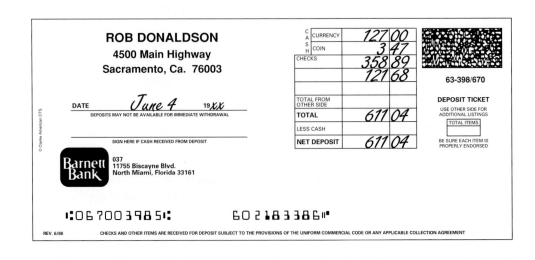

5. Fill out the deposit slip for Dawson Electronics, based on the following information:

a. Date: November 11, 19xx
b. $3,549 in currency
c. 67 quarters, 22 dimes, and 14 nickels
d. A check for $411.92, and a check for $2,119.56

DAWSON ELECTRONICS
12155 Miller Road
New Orleans, La. 54933

C A S H	CURRENCY		
	COIN		
CHECKS			

63-398/670

DATE _____ 19 _____

DEPOSITS MAY NOT BE AVAILABLE FOR IMMEDIATE WITHDRAWAL

TOTAL FROM OTHER SIDE		
TOTAL		
LESS CASH		
NET DEPOSIT		

DEPOSIT TICKET

USE OTHER SIDE FOR
ADDITIONAL LISTINGS

TOTAL ITEMS

BE SURE EACH ITEM IS
PROPERLY ENDORSED

SIGN HERE IF CASH RECEIVED FROM DEPOSIT

Barnett Bank
037
11755 Biscayne Blvd.
North Miami, Florida 33161

⑆067003985⑆   536101902⑈

REV. 6/88   CHECKS AND OTHER ITEMS ARE RECEIVED FOR DEPOSIT SUBJECT TO THE PROVISIONS OF THE UNIFORM COMMERCIAL CODE OR ANY APPLICABLE COLLECTION AGREEMENT

Check your answer with the solution on page 111.

4-5 Using Check Stubs or Checkbook Registers to Record Account Transactions

In part 4-1 we learned that some people use check stubs to keep records, and some use check registers. Exhibit 4-11 shows a check and its corresponding stub properly filled out. Note that the check number is printed on the stub. The stub is used to record the amount of the check, the date, the payee, and the purpose of the check. In addition, the stub also records the balance forwarded from the last stub, deposits made since the previous check, and the new balance of the account, after deducting the current check and any other charges.

Check registers record the same information as the stub, but in a different format. Exhibit 4-12 shows a check register properly filled out. The starting balance is located in the upper right-hand corner. In keeping a check register, it is your option to write it single spaced, or double spaced. Remember, in reality you would use *either* the check stub or the checkbook register.

EXHIBIT 4-11

CHECK WITH FILLED-OUT STUB

IF TAX DEDUCTIBLE CHECK HERE ☐	$ _183.12_		
3078			
May 26 19 _xx_			
TO _Circuit City_			
FOR _Stereo_			
		DOLLARS	CENTS
BAL. FWD.		1240	89
DEPOSIT		300	00
DEPOSIT			
TOTAL		1540	89
THIS ITEM		183	12
SUB-TOTAL		1357	77
OTHER DEDUCT. (IF ANY)			
BAL. FWD.		1357	77

BARRY COOPER   **3078**
299 Williams Road
Dallas, Tx. 95583   _May 26_ 19 _xx_   63-398/670

PAY TO THE ORDER OF _____ _Circuit City_ _____ $ _183 ¹²/100_

One Hundred Eighty Three and ¹²/100 _____ D O L L A R S

Barnett Bank
037-049
11755 Biscayne Blvd.
North Miami, Florida 33161

FOR _Stereo_   _Barry Cooper_

⑆067003985⑆ 3078 536768792⑈

EXHIBIT 4-12

FILLED-OUT CHECK REGISTER

PLEASE BE SURE TO **DEDUCT** ANY BANK CHARGES THAT APPLY TO YOUR ACCOUNT.								
CHECK NUMBER	DATE	DESCRIPTION OF TRANSACTION	AMOUNT OF PAYMENT OR WITHDRAWAL (−)		✓	AMOUNT OF DEPOSIT OR INTEREST (+)	BALANCE FORWARD	
							560	00
450	1/6	To Mastercard	34	60			525	40
		For					Bal.	
451	1/8	To State Farm Insurance	166	25			359	15
		For					Bal.	
	1/12	To Deposit				340 00	699	15
		For					Bal.	
452	1/13	To Walgreens	15	50			683	65
		For					Bal.	
	1/15	To Deposit				88 62	772	27
		For					Bal.	
	1/17	To ATM–Withdrawal	100	00			672	27
		For					Bal.	
453	1/21	To Time-Life Books	24	15			648	12
		For						

EXAMPLE

From the following information, complete the two check stubs and the check register in proper form:

a. Starting balance $1,454.21.

b. January 14, 19xx, check #056 issued to Paints & Pails Hardware for a ladder in the amount of $69.97.

c. January 19, 19xx, deposit of $345.00.

d. February 1, 19xx, check #057 issued to Northern Power & Light for electricity bill, in the amount of $171.55.

SOLUTION STRATEGY

Below are the properly completed stubs and register. Note that the checks were subtracted from the balance and the deposits were added to the balance.

	056		
IF TAX DEDUCTIBLE CHECK HERE ☐	$ 69.97		
Jan. 14 19 xx			
TO Paints & Pails			
FOR ladder			
		DOLLARS	CENTS
BAL. FWD.		1454	21
DEPOSIT			
DEPOSIT			
TOTAL		1454	21
THIS ITEM		69	97
SUB-TOTAL		1384	24
OTHER DEDUCT. (IF ANY)			
BAL. FWD.		1384	24

	057		
IF TAX DEDUCTIBLE CHECK HERE ☐	$ 171.55		
Feb. 1 19 xx			
TO Northern P & L			
FOR electricity bill			
		DOLLARS	CENTS
BAL. FWD.		1384	24
DEPOSIT		345	00
DEPOSIT			
TOTAL		1729	24
THIS ITEM		171	55
SUB-TOTAL		1557	69
OTHER DEDUCT. (IF ANY)			
BAL. FWD.		1557	69

PLEASE BE SURE TO **DEDUCT** ANY BANK CHARGES THAT APPLY TO YOUR ACCOUNT.								
CHECK NUMBER	DATE	DESCRIPTION OF TRANSACTION	AMOUNT OF PAYMENT OR WITHDRAWAL (−)		✓	AMOUNT OF DEPOSIT OR INTEREST (+)	BALANCE FORWARD	
							1454	21
056	1/14	To Paints & Pails Hdw.	69	97			1384	24
		For					Bal.	
	1/19	To Deposit				345 00	1729	24
		For					Bal.	
057	2/1	To Northern Power	171	55			1557	69
		For					Bal.	
		To						
		For					Bal.	

TRY-IT EXERCISE

6. From the following information, complete the two check stubs and the check register in proper form:

a. Starting balance $887.45.

b. March 12, 19xx, check #137 issued to Nathan & David Hair Stylists for a permanent and manicure in the amount of $55.75.

c. March 16, 19xx, deposits of $125.40 and $221.35.

d. March 19, 19xx, check #138 issued to Complete Auto Service for car repairs in the amount of $459.88.

IF TAX DEDUCTIBLE CHECK HERE ☐ $ _____		
137		
_____ 19 ____		
TO _____		
FOR		
	DOLLARS	CENTS
BAL. FWD.		
DEPOSIT		
DEPOSIT		
TOTAL		
THIS ITEM		
SUB-TOTAL		
OTHER DEDUCT. (IF ANY)		
BAL. FWD.		

IF TAX DEDUCTIBLE CHECK HERE ☐ $ _____		
138		
_____ 19 ____		
TO _____		
FOR		
	DOLLARS	CENTS
BAL. FWD.		
DEPOSIT		
DEPOSIT		
TOTAL		
THIS ITEM		
SUB-TOTAL		
OTHER DEDUCT. (IF ANY)		
BAL. FWD.		

PLEASE BE SURE TO **DEDUCT** ANY BANK CHARGES THAT APPLY TO YOUR ACCOUNT.

CHECK NUMBER	DATE	DESCRIPTION OF TRANSACTION	AMOUNT OF PAYMENT OR WITHDRAWAL (–)	✓	AMOUNT OF DEPOSIT OR INTEREST (+)	BALANCE FORWARD	
		To					
		For				Bal.	
		To					
		For				Bal.	
		To					
		For				Bal.	
		To					
		For				Bal.	
		To					
		For				Bal.	
		To					
		For				Bal.	

Check your answers with the solutions on page 111.

REVIEW EXERCISES CHAPTER 4—SECTION I

You are the owner of the Ultimate Care Car Wash. Using the blanks provided on page 98, write out the following checks, in proper form:

1. Check #2550, September 14, 19xx, in the amount of $345.54, to the Silky Soap Company, for 300 gallons of liquid soap.

```
┌─────────────────────────────────────────────────────────────┐
│  ULTIMATE CARE CAR WASH                              2550     │
│     214 Collings Blvd.                                        │
│     Durham, N.C.  76955          Sept. 14  19 xx   63-398/670 │
│                                                               │
│  PAY TO THE                                                   │
│  ORDER OF ___ Silky Soap Company _____ $ │345 54/100│        │
│                                                               │
│  Three Hundred Forty-Five and 54/100 _____ D O L L A R S     │
│                                                               │
│  ┌────────┐ 037-049                                           │
│  │Barnett │ 11755 Biscayne Blvd.                              │
│  │ Bank   │ North Miami, Florida 33161                        │
│  └────────┘                                                   │
│  FOR ___ 300 gals. Soap _____   Your Signature               │
│  ⑈067003985⑆ 3077   967011204⑈                                │
└─────────────────────────────────────────────────────────────┘
```

2. Check #2551, September 20, 19xx, in the amount of $68.95, to the Tidy Towel Service, for 6 dozen wash rags.

```
┌─────────────────────────────────────────────────────────────┐
│  ULTIMATE CARE CAR WASH                              2551     │
│     214 Collings Blvd.                                        │
│     Durham, N.C.  76955          Sept. 20  19 xx   63-398/670 │
│                                                               │
│  PAY TO THE                                                   │
│  ORDER OF ___ Tidy Towel Service _____ $ │68 95/100│         │
│                                                               │
│  Sixty-Eight and 95/100 _____ D O L L A R S                  │
│                                                               │
│  ┌────────┐ 037-049                                           │
│  │Barnett │ 11755 Biscayne Blvd.                              │
│  │ Bank   │ North Miami, Florida 33161                        │
│  └────────┘                                                   │
│  FOR ___ Wash Rags _____   Your Signature                    │
│  ⑈067003985⑆ 3077   967011204⑈                                │
└─────────────────────────────────────────────────────────────┘
```

3. Check #2552, September 23, 19xx, in the amount of $644.30, to the Arch Creek Valley Water Dept., for August service.

```
┌─────────────────────────────────────────────────────────────┐
│  ULTIMATE CARE CAR WASH                              2552     │
│     214 Collings Blvd.                                        │
│     Durham, N.C.  76955          Sept. 23  19 xx   63-398/670 │
│                                                               │
│  PAY TO THE                                                   │
│  ORDER OF ___ Arch Creek Valley Water Dept. ___ $ │644 30/100││
│                                                               │
│  Six Hundred Forty-Four and 30/100 _____ D O L L A R S       │
│                                                               │
│  ┌────────┐ 037-049                                           │
│  │Barnett │ 11755 Biscayne Blvd.                              │
│  │ Bank   │ North Miami, Florida 33161                        │
│  └────────┘                                                   │
│  FOR ___ August Service _____   Your Signature               │
│  ⑈067003985⑆ 3077   821301508⑈                                │
└─────────────────────────────────────────────────────────────┘
```

You have just received a check. Your account number is #099-506-8. Write the following endorsements in the space provided on the next page, and identify what type they are:

4. Allowing you to deposit the check into your account.

5. Allowing you to cash the check.

6. Allowing you to transfer the check to your friend David Sporn.

4. *for deposit only*

Your Signature

099–506–8

_____

Restrictive Endorsement

5. *Your Signature*

099–506–8

_____

_____

Blank Endorsement

6. *Pay to the order of*

David Sporn

Your Signature

099–506–8

Full Endorsement

7. Properly fill out the deposit slip for The Williamson Corp., based on the following information:

    a. Date: July 9, 19xx.
    b. $1,680 in currency.
    c. $62.25 in coins.
    d. Checks in the amount of $2,455.94; $4,338.79; and $1,461.69.

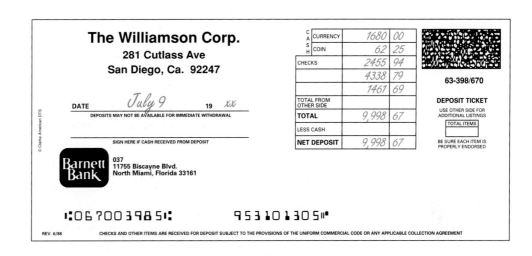

8. Properly fill out the deposit slip for Sally Randall, based on the following information:

    a. Date: December 18, 19xx.
    b. A check for $651.03.
    c. $150 cash withdrawal.

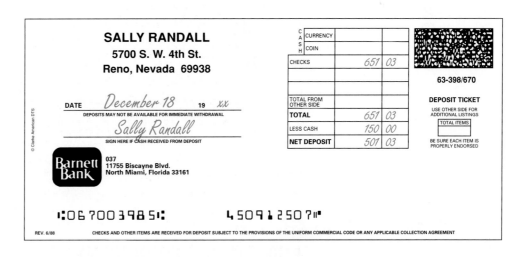

9. From the following information, complete the three check stubs, in proper form:

    a. Starting balance $265.73.
    b. February 12, 19xx, check #439, in the amount of $175.05, to The Biloxie Bank, for a car payment.
    c. February 15, deposit of $377.10.
    d. February 18, check #440, in the amount of $149.88, to Fitness Equipment Co., for a set of dumbbells.

e. February 22, deposit of $570.00.

f. February 27, check #441, in the amount of $23.40, to Royalty Cleaners, for dry cleaning a shirt.

IF TAX DEDUCTIBLE CHECK HERE ☐	$ 175.05
439	
February 12 19 xx	
TO	Biloxie Bank
FOR	Car Payment
	DOLLARS	CENTS
BAL. FWD.	265	73
DEPOSIT		
DEPOSIT		
TOTAL	265	73
THIS ITEM	175	05
SUB-TOTAL	90	68
OTHER DEDUCT. (IF ANY)		
BAL. FWD.	90	68

IF TAX DEDUCTIBLE CHECK HERE ☐	$ 149.88
440	
February 18 19 xx	
TO	Fitness Equipment Co.
FOR	Dumbells
	DOLLARS	CENTS
BAL. FWD.	90	68
DEPOSIT 2/15	377	10
DEPOSIT		
TOTAL	467	78
THIS ITEM	149	88
SUB-TOTAL	317	90
OTHER DEDUCT. (IF ANY)		
BAL. FWD.	317	90

IF TAX DEDUCTIBLE CHECK HERE ☐	$ 23.40
441	
February 27 19 xx	
TO	Royalty Cleaners
FOR	Dry Cleaning
	DOLLARS	CENTS
BAL. FWD.	317	90
DEPOSIT 2/22	570	00
DEPOSIT		
TOTAL	887	90
THIS ITEM	23	40
SUB-TOTAL	864	50
OTHER DEDUCT. (IF ANY)		
BAL. FWD.	864	50

10. From the following information, complete the checkbook register below:

a. Starting balance, $479.20.

b. April 7, 19xx, Deposit, $766.90.

c. April 14, 19xx, check #1207, in the amount of $45.65, to Mario's Supermarket, for groceries.

d. April 16, ATM withdrawal, $125.00.

e. April 17, check #1208, in the amount of $870.00, to Howard Properties, Inc., for rent.

f. April 21, 19xx, Deposit, $1,350.00.

g. April 27, check #1209, in the amount of $864.40, to Elegant Decor, for a dining room set.

PLEASE BE SURE TO **DEDUCT** ANY BANK CHARGES THAT APPLY TO YOUR ACCOUNT.								
CHECK NUMBER	DATE	DESCRIPTION OF TRANSACTION	AMOUNT OF PAYMENT OR WITHDRAWAL (–)	✓	AMOUNT OF DEPOSIT OR INTEREST (+)		BALANCE FORWARD	
							479	20
	4/7	To Deposit			766	90	1246	10
		For				Bal.		
1207	4/14	To Mario's Market	45	65			1200	45
		For				Bal.		
	4/16	To ATM Withdrawal	125	00			1075	45
		For				Bal.		
1208	4/17	To Howard Properties	870	00			205	45
		For				Bal.		
	4/21	To Deposit			1350	00	1555	45
		For				Bal.		
1209	4/27	To Elegant Decor	864	40			691	05
		For				Bal.		

SECTION II

BANK STATEMENT RECONCILIATION

● **canceled checks**

Checks that have been paid out of the account; usually sent back to the account holder each month along with the bank statement.

Each month the bank sends to the account holder a record of all checking account activity known as the bank statement, or statement of account. In addition, most banks send back the checks that have been paid out of the account. These are known as **canceled checks.** Banks that don't send the canceled checks with the statements retain them at the bank for a period of time and then copy them on microfilm for future reference. When a depositor needs a canceled check as proof of payment, for example, the bank will send a copy of it for a small service charge.

4-6 Understanding the Bank Statement

Bank statements vary widely in style from bank to bank, however most contain essentially the same information. Exhibit 4-13 is an example of a typical bank statement. Note that it shows the balance brought forward from the last statement; the deposits and credits that have been added to the account during the month; the checks and debits that have been subtracted from the account during the month; any service charges assessed to the account; and the current or ending balance.

  Credits are additions to the account, such as interest earned, notes collected, and electronic fund transfers of direct deposit payroll checks. **Debits** are subtractions from the account, such as automatic teller machine (ATM) withdrawals, monthly service charges, check printing charges, nonsufficient fund (NSF) fees, and returned items. A **nonsufficient fund (NSF) fee** is a fee charged by the bank when a check is written without sufficient funds in the account to cover the amount of that check. **Returned items** are checks from others that you deposited into your account, but were returned to your bank unpaid because the person or business issuing the check had insufficient funds in its account to cover the check. Banks normally charge a **returned item fee** when this occurs.

● **bank statement**
A monthly summary of the activities in a checking account, including debits, credits, and beginning and ending balance. Sent by the bank to the account holder.

● **credits**
Additions to a checking account, such as deposits and interest earned.

● **debits**
Subtractions from a checking account, such as service charges.

● **nonsufficient fund (NSF) fees**
A fee charged by the bank when a check is written without sufficient funds in the account to cover the amount of that check.

● **returned item**
A check that you deposited into your account, but was returned to your bank unpaid because the person or business issuing the check had insufficient funds in its account to cover the check.

● **returned item fee**
A fee charged to your checking account when a check you deposit becomes a returned item.

037-049
11755 Biscayne Blvd.
North Miami, Florida 33161

STATEMENT DATE
11-2-19xx

John Q. Public
1234 Main St.
Anywhere, U.S.A. 10101

CHECKING ACCOUNT SUMMARY
10-1-19xx THRU 10-31-19xx

ACCOUNT NUMBER
82-1301-508

Previous Balance	Deposits & Credits Number Total		Checks & Debits Number Total		Current Balance
775.20	3	3,228.11	7	2,857.80	1,145.51

CHECKING ACCOUNT TRANSACTIONS

DATE	AMOUNT	DESCRIPTION	BALANCE
10-2	125.00	Check #445	650.20
10-4	357.18	Deposit	1,007.38
10-7	884.22	Check #446	123.16
10-13	1,409.30	EFT Payroll Deposit	1,532.46
10-15	12.95	Check #447	1,519.51
10-16	326.11	Check #448	1,193.40
10-22	200.00	ATM Withdrawal	993.40
10-25	1,461.63	Deposit	2,455.03
10-27	1,294.52	Check #449	1,160.51
10-31	15.00	Service Charge	1,145.51

T

EXHIBIT 4-13

·····························

BANK STATEMENT

● **bank statement reconciliation**
The process of adjusting the bank and checkbook balances to reflect the actual current balance of the checking account.

● **outstanding checks**
Checks that have been written, but have not yet reached the bank, and therefore do not appear on the current bank statement.

● **deposits in transit**
Deposits made close to the statement date, or by mail, which do not clear in time to appear on the current bank statement.

● **adjusted checkbook balance**
The checkbook balance minus service charges and other debits; plus interest earned and other credits.

● **adjusted bank balance**
The bank balance minus outstanding checks; plus deposits in transit.

When the statement arrives from the bank each month, the depositor must compare the bank balance with the balance shown in the checkbook. Usually, the balances are not the same because during the month some account activity has taken place without being recorded by the bank, and other activities have occurred without being recorded in the checkbook. The process of adjusting the bank and checkbook balances to reflect the actual current balance is known as **bank statement reconciliation.** When we use the word "checkbook" in this chapter, we are actually referring to the records kept by the depositor on the check stubs or in the checkbook register.

Before a statement can be reconciled, you must identify and total all the checks that have been written, but have not yet reached the bank. These are known as **outstanding checks.** Outstanding checks are found by comparing and checking off each check in the checkbook with those shown on the statement. Any checks not appearing on the statement are outstanding checks.

Sometimes deposits are made close to the statement date, or by mail, and don't clear the bank in time to appear on the current statement. These are known as **deposits in transit.** Just like outstanding checks, deposits in transit must be identified and totaled. Once again, this is done by comparing and checking off the checkbook records with the deposits shown on the bank statement.

A bank statement is reconciled when the **adjusted checkbook balance** is equal to the **adjusted bank balance.** Most bank statements have a form on the back to use in reconciling the account. Exhibit 4-14 is an example of such a form, and will be used in this chapter.

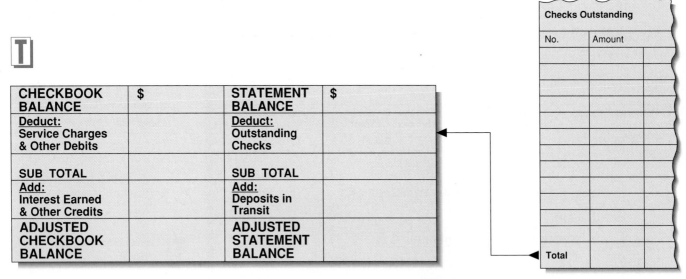

EXHIBIT 4-14

BANK STATEMENT
RECONCILIATION FORM

STEPS FOR PREPARING A BANK STATEMENT RECONCILIATION:

Step 1. Calculate the adjusted checkbook balance:

a. Look over the bank statement and find any charges or debits, such as service charges, NSF fees, or returned items, which have not been recorded in the checkbook, and *subtract* them from the checkbook balance to get a subtotal.

b. Locate any credits on the statement not recorded in the checkbook, such as interest earned or notes collected, and *add* them to the subtotal from the above step.

continued

(continued)

Step 2. Calculate the adjusted bank balance:

    a. Locate all outstanding checks and *subtract* them from the statement balance to get a subtotal.

    b. Locate all of the deposits in transit and *add* them to the subtotal from the above step.

Step 3. Compare the adjusted balances:

    a. If they are equal, the statement has been reconciled.

    b. If they are *not* equal, an error exists that must be found and corrected. The error is either in the checkbook or on the bank statement.

EXAMPLE

Prepare a bank reconciliation for Winston Hill from the following bank statement and checkbook records:

Grove Isle Bank

STATEMENT DATE
8-2-19xx

WINSTON HILL
1190 Cherry Lane
Baltimore, Md. 93958

CHECKING ACCOUNT SUMMARY
7-1-19xx THRU 7-31-19xx

ACCOUNT NUMBER
82-1301-508

| Previous Balance | Deposits & Credits | | Checks & Debits | | Current Balance |
	Number	Total	Number	Total	
1,233.40	3	2,445.80	7	2,158.92	1,520.28

CHECKING ACCOUNT TRANSACTIONS

DATE	AMOUNT	DESCRIPTION	BALANCE
7-3	450.30	Check #1209	783.10
7-6	500.00	Deposit	1,283.10
7-10	47.75	Check #1210	1,235.35
7-13	1,300.00	EFT Payroll Deposit	2,535.35
7-15	312.79	Check #1212	2,222.56
7-17	547.22	Check #1214	1,675.34
7-22	350.00	ATM Withdrawal	1,325.34
7-24	645.80	Deposit	1,971.14
7-28	430.86	Check #1215	1,540.28
7-30	20.00	Service Charge	1,520.28

CHECK NUMBER	DATE	DESCRIPTION OF TRANSACTION	AMOUNT OF PAYMENT OR WITHDRAWAL (−)	✓	AMOUNT OF DEPOSIT OR INTEREST (+)	BALANCE FORWARD
						1233 40
1209	7/1	To Stillwell Supply Co.	450 30			783 10
		For				Bal.
	7/6	To Deposit			500 00	1283 10
		For				Bal.
1210	7/8	To Food Spot	47 75			1235 35
		For				Bal.
1211	7/10	To Delta Airlines	342 10			893 25
		For				Bal.
	7/13	To Payroll Deposit			1300 00	2193 25
		For				Bal.
1212	7/13	To Hyatt Hotel	312 79			1880 46
		For				Bal.
1213	7/15	To Wall Street Journal	75 00			1805 46
		For				Bal.
1214	7/15	To Builder's Depot	547 22			1258 24
		For				Bal.
	7/21	To ATM Withdrawal	350 00			908 24
		For				Bal.
	7/24	To Deposit			645 80	1554 04
		For				Bal.
1215	7/25	To Williams Roofing	430 86			1123 18
		For				Bal.
	7/31	To Deposit			550 00	1673 18
		For				Bal.
		To				
		For				Bal.

SOLUTION STRATEGY

Below is the properly completed reconciliation form. Note that the adjusted checkbook balance equals the adjusted bank statement balance. The balances are now reconciled. After some practice, the format will become familiar to you, and you should no longer need the form.

CHECKBOOK BALANCE	$ 1,673.18	STATEMENT BALANCE	$ 1,520.28
Deduct: Service Charges & Other Debits	20.00	Deduct: Outstanding Checks	417.10
SUB TOTAL	1,653.18	SUB TOTAL	1,103.18
Add: Interest Earned & Other Credits		Add: Deposits in Transit	550.00
ADJUSTED CHECKBOOK BALANCE	1,653.18	ADJUSTED STATEMENT BALANCE	1,653.18

Reconciled Balances

Checks Outstanding

No.	Amount
1211	342 10
1213	75 00
Total	417 10

7. Using the form provided, reconcile the following bank statement and checkbook records for Penny Hart:

Grove Isle Bank

STATEMENT DATE
4-3-19xx

PENNY HART
4121 Pinetree Rd.
Bangor, Ma. 76910

CHECKING ACCOUNT SUMMARY
3-1-19xx THRU 3-31-19xx

ACCOUNT NUMBER
097440

Previous Balance	Deposits & Credits Number	Deposits & Credits Total	Checks & Debits Number	Checks & Debits Total	Current Balance
625.40	3	1,790.00	8	690.00	1,725.40

CHECKING ACCOUNT TRANSACTIONS

DATE	AMOUNT	DESCRIPTION	BALANCE
3-3	34.77	Check #338	590.63
3-6	750.00	Payroll- EFT Deposit	1,340.63
3-10	247.05	Check #340	1,093.58
3-13	390.00	Deposit	1,483.58
3-15	66.30	Check #342	1,417.28
3-17	112.18	Check #343	1,305.10
3-22	150.00	ATM Withdrawal	1,155.10
3-24	650.00	Deposit	1,805.10
3-28	50.00	Check #345	1,755.10
3-30	17.70	Check printing charge	1,737.40
3-31	12.00	Service charge	1,725.40

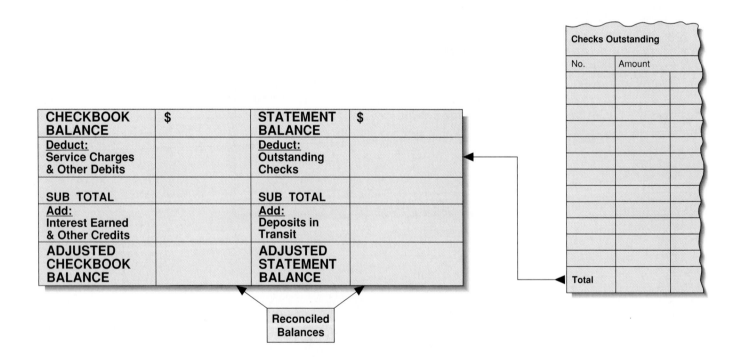

CHECK NUMBER	DATE	DESCRIPTION OF TRANSACTION	AMOUNT OF PAYMENT OR WITHDRAWAL (−)	✓	AMOUNT OF DEPOSIT OR INTEREST (+)	BALANCE FORWARD 625	40
		PLEASE BE SURE TO **DEDUCT** ANY BANK CHARGES THAT APPLY TO YOUR ACCOUNT.					
338	3/2	To Naples Pet Shop	34	77			590	63
		For				Bal.	
	3/5	To Deposit			750	00	1340	63
		For				Bal.	
339	3/5	To Alison Company	19	83			1320	80
		For				Bal.	
340	3/9	To Silver Software	247	05			1073	75
		For				Bal.	
	3/12	To Deposit			390	00	1463	75
		For				Bal.	
341	3/12	To The Book Shelf	57	50			1406	25
		For				Bal.	
342	3/13	To Wal-Mart	66	30			1339	95
		For				Bal.	
343	3/15	To S.E. Office Supply	112	18			1227	77
		For				Bal.	
	3/22	To ATM Withdrawal	150	00			1077	77
		For				Bal.	
	3/24	To Deposit			650	00	1727	77
		For				Bal.	
344	3/24	To Flower Decor, Inc.	119	32			1608	45
		For				Bal.	
345	3/28	To Cablevision, Inc.	50	00			1558	45
		For				Bal.	
	3/30	To Deposit			240	23	1798	68
		For				Bal.	

		Checks Outstanding	
		No.	Amount	
CHECKBOOK BALANCE	$	**STATEMENT BALANCE**	$		
Deduct: Service Charges & Other Debits		**Deduct:** Outstanding Checks			
SUB TOTAL		**SUB TOTAL**			
Add: Interest Earned & Other Credits		**Add:** Deposits in Transit			
ADJUSTED CHECKBOOK BALANCE		**ADJUSTED STATEMENT BALANCE**		**Total**	

Reconciled Balances

Check your answers with the solutions on page 111.

1. On April 3, Skeeter King received her bank statement, showing a balance of $1,637.93. Her checkbook showed a balance of $1,493.90. Outstanding checks were $224.15, $327.80, $88.10, $122.42, and $202.67. There was an $8.00 service charge, and the deposits in transit amounted to $813.11. Use the form below to reconcile Skeeter's account.

Checks Outstanding	
No.	Amount
	224 15
	327 80
	88 10
	122 42
	202 67
Total	965 14

CHECKBOOK BALANCE	$ 1,493.90	STATEMENT BALANCE	$ 1,637.93
Deduct: Service Charges & Other Debits	8.00	Deduct: Outstanding Checks	965.14
SUB TOTAL	1,485.90	SUB TOTAL	672.79
Add: Interest Earned & Other Credits	—	Add: Deposits in Transit	813.11
ADJUSTED CHECKBOOK BALANCE	1,485.90	ADJUSTED STATEMENT BALANCE	1,485.90

Reconciled Balances

2. Bob Albrecht received his bank statement on July 5, showing a balance of $2,663.31. His checkbook had a balance of $1,931.83. The statement showed a service charge of $15.80 and a note collected by the bank for Bob, in the amount of $200.00. (A note collected is a payment owed to Bob by someone who makes that payment directly to Bob's bank account.) The deposits in transit totaled $314.12, and the outstanding checks were for $182.00, $261.40, and $418.00. Use the form below to reconcile Bob's account.

Checks Outstanding	
No.	Amount
	182 00
	261 40
	418 00
Total	861 40

CHECKBOOK BALANCE	$ 1,931.83	STATEMENT BALANCE	$ 2,663.31
Deduct: Service Charges & Other Debits	15.80	Deduct: Outstanding Checks	861.40
SUB TOTAL	1,916.03	SUB TOTAL	1,801.91
Add: Interest Earned & Other Credits	200.00	Add: Deposits in Transit	314.12
ADJUSTED CHECKBOOK BALANCE	2,116.03	ADJUSTED STATEMENT BALANCE	2,116.03

Reconciled Balances

3. On December 2, Marcy Diaz received her bank statement showing a balance of $358.97. Her checkbook showed a balance of $479.39. There was a check printing charge of $13.95, and interest earned was $6.40. The outstanding checks were for $22.97, $80.36, $19.80, $4.50. The deposits in transit totaled $240.50. Use the form below to reconcile Marcy's account.

CHECKBOOK BALANCE	$ 479.39	STATEMENT BALANCE	$ 358.97
Deduct: Service Charges & Other Debits	13.95	Deduct: Outstanding Checks	127.63
SUB TOTAL	465.44	SUB TOTAL	231.34
Add: Interest Earned & Other Credits	6.40	Add: Deposits in Transit	240.50
ADJUSTED CHECKBOOK BALANCE	471.84	ADJUSTED STATEMENT BALANCE	471.84

Reconciled Balances

Checks Outstanding

No.	Amount
	22 97
	80 36
	19 80
	4 50
Total	127 63

CHAPTER 4 ■ CHECKING ACCOUNTS   SUMMARY CHART

SECTION I   UNDERSTANDING AND USING CHECKING ACCOUNTS

Topic	P/O, Page	Important Concepts	Illustrative Examples
Checks	4–1 88	Checks, or drafts, are negotiable instruments ordering the bank to pay money from the checking account to the name written on the check.	See Check, with Parts Labeled Exhibit 4-2, p. 90
	4–2 91	The person or business named on the check to receive the money is known as the payee. The person or business issuing the check is known as the payor.	
Deposit Slips	4–1 89	Deposit slips or deposit tickets are printed forms with the depositor's name, address, account number, and space for the details of the deposit.	See Deposit Slip Exhibit 4-3, p. 90
		Deposit slips are used to record money, both cash and checks, being added to the checking account. They are presented to the bank teller along with the items to be deposited.	
		When a deposit is completed, the depositor receives a copy of the deposit slip as a receipt, or proof of the transaction.	See Completed Deposit Slip Exhibit 4-10, p. 94

Topic	P/O, Page	Important Concepts	Illustrative Examples
Check Stubs	4–1 90 4–5 95	Check stubs, with checks attached by perforation, are a bound part of the checkbook. The check number is preprinted on both the check and the attached stub. Each stub is used to record the issuing of its corresponding check, and any deposits made on that date.	See Check Stub with Check Exhibit 4-4, p. 90
Check Registers	4–1 90 4–5 95	Check registers are the alternative method for keeping track of checking account activities. They are a separate booklet of forms, rather than stubs attached to each check. Space is provided for all the pertinent information required to keep an accurate and up-to-date running balance of the account.	See Check Register Exhibit 4-5, p. 91
Endorsements	4–3 92	When you receive a check, you may either cash it, deposit it in your account, or transfer it to another party. The endorsement on the back of the check instructs the bank on what to do. Your endorsement should be written within the $1\frac{1}{2}$-inch space at the trailing edge of the check.	See Endorsement Space Exhibit 4-6, p. 93
Blank Endorsement	4–3 92	A blank endorsement is used when you want to cash the check. You, as the payee, simply sign your name exactly as it appears on the front of the check. Once you have endorsed a check in this manner, anyone who has possession of the check can cash it.	See Blank Endorsement Exhibit 4-7, p. 93 *John Q. Public 82-1301-508*
Restrictive Endorsement	4–3 92	A restrictive endorsement is used when you want to deposit the check into your account. In this case, you endorse the check "for deposit only," sign your name as it appears on the front, and write your account number.	See Restrictive Endorsement Exhibit 4-8, p. 93 *for deposit only John Q. Public 82-1301-508*
Full Endorsement	4–3 92	A full endorsement is used when you want to transfer the check to another party. In this case, you endorse the check "pay to the order of," write the name of the person or business to whom the check is being transferred, and sign your name and account number.	See Full Endorsement Exhibit 4-9, p. 93 *pay to the order of Cindy J. Citizen John Q. Public 82-1301-508*

SECTION II BANK STATEMENT RECONCILIATION

Topic	P/O, Page	Important Concepts	Illustrative Examples
Bank Statements	4–6 101	Bank statements are a recap of the checking account activity for the month. They show the balance brought forward from the last statement, the deposits and credits which have been added to the account during the month, the checks and debits which have been subtracted from the account during the month, service charges assessed to the account, and the current or ending balance.	See Bank Statement Exhibit 4-13, p.101
Bank Statement Reconciliation	4–7 102	1. Calculate the adjusted checkbook balance: a. Subtract any debits or charges such as service charges, NSF fees, or returned items from the checkbook balance to get a subtotal. b. Locate any credits on the statement, not recorded in the checkbook, such as interest earned or notes collected, and add them to the subtotal above. 2. Calculate the adjusted bank balance: a. Locate all outstanding checks and subtract them from the statement balance to get a subtotal. b. Locate all of the deposits in transit and add them to the subtotal above. 3. Compare the adjusted balances: a. If they are equal, the statement has been reconciled. b. If they are *not* equal, an error exists which must be found and corrected. The error is either in the checkbook or on the bank statement.	See Blank Reconciliation Form Exhibit 4-14, p.102

TRY-IT EXERCISE ▶ SOLUTIONS

1.

Anne Marie Richards   **206**
1585 S. W. 6 Avenue
Tallahassee, Fl. 32399   *April 27* 19 *xx*   63-398/670

PAY TO THE ORDER OF *Snappy Photo Service* $ *41 88/100*

Forty-one and 88/100 —————————— D O L L A R S

Barnett Bank   037-049 11755 Biscayne Blvd. North Miami, Florida 33161

FOR *Film Developing*   *Anne Marie Richards*

⑆067003985⑆ 3077 82145190 2⑈

2. *Pay to the order of*	**3.** *Your Signature*	**4.** *for deposit only*
Roz Reitman	*696-339-1028*	*Your Signature*
Your Signature		*696-339-1028*
696-339-1028		
Full Endorsement	Blank Endorsement	Restrictive Endorsement

5.

DAWSON ELECTRONICS
12155 Miller Road
New Orleans, La. 54933

DATE _November 11_ 19 XX
DEPOSITS MAY NOT BE AVAILABLE FOR IMMEDIATE WITHDRAWAL

SIGN HERE IF CASH RECEIVED FROM DEPOSIT

Barnett Bank
037
11755 Biscayne Blvd.
North Miami, Florida 33161

1:06 700 3985 1: 53610 190 211

REV. 6/88   CHECKS AND OTHER ITEMS ARE RECEIVED FOR DEPOSIT SUBJECT TO THE PROVISIONS OF THE UNIFORM COMMERCIAL CODE OR ANY APPLICABLE COLLECTION AGREEMENT

C A S H	CURRENCY	3549	00
	COIN	19	65
CHECKS		411	92
		2119	56
TOTAL FROM OTHER SIDE			
TOTAL		6100	13
LESS CASH			
NET DEPOSIT		6100	13

63-398/670

DEPOSIT TICKET
USE OTHER SIDE FOR ADDITIONAL LISTINGS
TOTAL ITEMS
BE SURE EACH ITEM IS PROPERLY ENDORSED

6.

IF TAX DEDUCTIBLE CHECK HERE ☐	$ 55.75
137	
March 12 19 XX	
TO Nathan & David	
FOR perm & manicure	

	DOLLARS	CENTS
BAL. FWD.	887	45
DEPOSIT		
DEPOSIT		
TOTAL	887	45
THIS ITEM	55	75
SUB-TOTAL	831	70
OTHER DEDUCT. (IF ANY)		
BAL. FWD.	831	70

IF TAX DEDUCTIBLE CHECK HERE ☐	$ 459.88
138	
March 19 19 XX	
TO Complete Auto Service	
FOR Car repair	

	DOLLARS	CENTS
BAL. FWD.	831	70
DEPOSIT 3/16	125	40
DEPOSIT 3/16	221	35
TOTAL	1178	45
THIS ITEM	459	88
SUB-TOTAL	718	57
OTHER DEDUCT. (IF ANY)		
BAL. FWD.	718	57

PLEASE BE SURE TO **DEDUCT** ANY BANK CHARGES THAT APPLY TO YOUR ACCOUNT.

CHECK NUMBER	DATE	DESCRIPTION OF TRANSACTION	AMOUNT OF PAYMENT OR WITHDRAWAL (−)	✓	AMOUNT OF DEPOSIT OR INTEREST (+)	BALANCE FORWARD	
						887	45
137	3/12	To Nathan & David Hair Stylists	55	75			831	70
		For				Bal.		
	3/16	To Deposit			125	40	957	10
		For				Bal.		
	3/16	To Deposit			221	35	1178	45
		For				Bal.		
138	3/19	To Complete Auto Service	459	88			718	57
		For				Bal.		

7.

CHECKBOOK BALANCE	$ 1,798.68	STATEMENT BALANCE	$ 1,725.40
Deduct: Service Charges & Other Debits	29.70	Deduct: Outstanding Checks	196.65
SUB TOTAL	1,768.98	SUB TOTAL	1,528.75
Add: Interest Earned & Other Credits		Add: Deposits in Transit	240.23
ADJUSTED CHECKBOOK BALANCE	1,768.98	ADJUSTED STATEMENT BALANCE	1,768.98

Reconciled Balances

Checks Outstanding

No.	Amount	
339	19	83
341	57	50
344	119	32
Total	196	65

1. As the purchasing manager for Fuzzy Logic Industries, write a check dated April 29, 19xx, in the amount of $24,556.00, to Outback Electronics, Inc., for circuit boards.

FUZZY LOGIC INDUSTRIES   **081**
12221 Keystone Blvd
Greenville, S.C. 84851   *April 29* 19 *xx*   63-398/670

PAY TO THE
ORDER OF _____ *Outback Electronics, Inc.* _____ $ *24,556 xx/100*

Twenty-Four Thousand Five Hundred Fifty-Six and xx/100 — D O L L A R S

037-049
11755 Biscayne Blvd.
North Miami, Florida 33161

FOR _____ *Circuit Boards* _____   *Your Signature* _____

⑆06700398 5⑆ 3081   731021807⑈

2. You have just received a check. Your account number is #9299-144-006. Write the following endorsements in the space provided below, and identify what type they are:
   a. Allowing the check to be transferred to Expo, Inc.
   b. Allowing you to cash the check.
   c. Allowing you to deposit the check into your account.

   a. *Pay to the order of*   **b.** *Your Signature*   **c.** *for deposit only*

   Expo, Inc.   *9299-144-006*   *Your Signature*

   Your Signature   *9299-144-006*

   9299-144-006

   Full Endorsement   Blank Endorsement   Restrictive Endorsement

3. As cashier for the Country Kitchen Cafe, it is your responsibility to make the daily deposits. Complete the deposit slip below, based on the following information:
   a. Date: January 20, 19xx.
   b. Checks totaling $344.20.
   c. Currency of $547.00.
   d. Coins: 125 quarters, 67 dimes, 88 nickels, and 224 pennies.

COUNTRY KITCHEN CAFE
1470 Fleetwood St.
Madison, Wisconson 22930

DATE *January 20* 19 *xx*
DEPOSITS MAY NOT BE AVAILABLE FOR IMMEDIATE WITHDRAWAL

SIGN HERE IF CASH RECEIVED FROM DEPOSIT

Grove Isle Bank

CASH	CURRENCY	547	00
	COIN	44	59
CHECKS		344	20
TOTAL FROM OTHER SIDE			
TOTAL		935	79
LESS CASH			
NET DEPOSIT		935	79

63-398/670

DEPOSIT TICKET
USE OTHER SIDE FOR
ADDITIONAL LISTINGS

TOTAL ITEMS

BE SURE EACH ITEM IS
PROPERLY ENDORSED

⑆06700398 5⑆   730451408⑈

REV. 6/88   CHECKS AND OTHER ITEMS ARE RECEIVED FOR DEPOSIT SUBJECT TO THE PROVISIONS OF THE UNIFORM COMMERCIAL CODE OR ANY APPLICABLE COLLECTION AGREEMENT

4. From the following information, complete the two check stubs and the check register below:

   a. Starting balance: $463.30.
   b. April 15, 19xx, check #450, issued to the Keystone Market, for groceries, in the amount of $67.78.
   c. April 17, ATM withdrawal, $250.
   d. April 19, deposit of $125.45.
   e. April 20, deposit of $320.00.
   f. April 27, check #451, in the amount of $123.10, to Ace Appliance, Inc., for refrigerator repair.

IF TAX DEDUCTIBLE CHECK HERE ☐	$ 67.78
450	
April 15 ____ 19 xx	
TO Keystone Market	
FOR Groceries	

	DOLLARS	CENTS
BAL. FWD.	463	30
DEPOSIT		
DEPOSIT		
TOTAL	463	30
THIS ITEM	67	78
SUB-TOTAL	395	52
OTHER DEDUCT. (IF ANY) 4/17	ATM 250	00
BAL. FWD.	145	52

IF TAX DEDUCTIBLE CHECK HERE ☐	$ 123.10
451	
April 27 ____ 19 xx	
TO Ace Appliance	
FOR Ref. Repair	

	DOLLARS	CENTS
BAL. FWD.	145	52
DEPOSIT 4/19	125	45
DEPOSIT 4/20	320	00
TOTAL	590	97
THIS ITEM	123	10
SUB-TOTAL	467	87
OTHER DEDUCT. (IF ANY)		
BAL. FWD.	467	87

PLEASE BE SURE TO **DEDUCT** ANY BANK CHARGES THAT APPLY TO YOUR ACCOUNT.

CHECK NUMBER	DATE	DESCRIPTION OF TRANSACTION	AMOUNT OF PAYMENT OR WITHDRAWAL (−)	✓	AMOUNT OF DEPOSIT OR INTEREST (+)	BALANCE FORWARD
						463 30
450	4/15	To Keystone Market	67 78			395 52
		For			Bal.	
	4/17	To ATM Withdrawal	250 00			145 52
		For			Bal.	
	4/19	To Deposit			125 45	270 97
		For			Bal.	
	4/20	To Deposit			320 00	590 97
		For			Bal.	
451	4/27	To Ace Appliance	123 10			467 87
		For			Bal.	
		To				
		For			Bal.	

5. On October 1, Ellen Wynn received her bank statement showing a balance of $440.22. Her checkbook records indicate a balance of $338.97. There was a service charge for the month of $14.40 on the statement. The outstanding checks were for $47.10, $110.15, $19.80, and $64.10. The deposits in transit totaled $125.50. Use the form on the following page to reconcile Ellen's checking account.

CHECKBOOK BALANCE	$ 338.97	STATEMENT BALANCE	$ 440.22
Deduct: Service Charges & Other Debits	14.40	Deduct: Outstanding Checks	241.15
SUB TOTAL	324.57	SUB TOTAL	199.07
Add: Interest Earned & Other Credits	—	Add: Deposits in Transit	125.50
ADJUSTED CHECKBOOK BALANCE	324.57	ADJUSTED STATEMENT BALANCE	324.57

Reconciled Balances

Checks Outstanding

No.	Amount
	47 10
	110 15
	19 80
	64 10
Total	241 15

6. Prepare a bank reconciliation for Keith Mack, from the following checkbook records and bank statement.

PLEASE BE SURE TO **DEDUCT** ANY BANK CHARGES THAT APPLY TO YOUR ACCOUNT.

CHECK NUMBER	DATE	DESCRIPTION OF TRANSACTION	AMOUNT OF PAYMENT OR WITHDRAWAL (−)	✓	AMOUNT OF DEPOSIT OR INTEREST (+)	BALANCE FORWARD
						879 36
801	10/1	To Technique Photo Lab	236 77			642 59
		For			Bal.	
	10/6	To Deposit			450 75	1,093 34
		For			Bal.	
802	10/8	To L.L. Bean	47 20			1,046 14
		For			Bal.	
803	10/10	To Sam Newman	75 89			970 25
		For			Bal.	
	10/13	To Deposit			880 34	1,850 59
		For			Bal.	
804	10/13	To Sheraton Hotel	109 00			1,741 59
		For			Bal.	
805	10/15	To American Express	507 82			1,233 77
		For			Bal.	
	10/20	To ATM Withdrawal	120 00			1,113 77
		For			Bal.	
	10/24	To Deposit			623 50	1,737 27
		For			Bal.	
	10/27	To Deposit			208 40	1,945 67
		For			Bal.	
806	10/28	To K-Mart	48 25			1,897 42
		For			Bal.	
		To				
		For			Bal.	
		To				
		For			Bal.	

Grove Isle Bank

Keith Mack
1127 Pineapple Place
Honolulu, Hawaii 96825

CHECKING ACCOUNT SUMMARY
10-1-19xx THRU 10-31-19xx

ACCOUNT NUMBER
449-56-7792

Previous Balance	Deposits & Credits Number	Deposits & Credits Total	Checks & Debits Number	Checks & Debits Total	Current Balance
879.36	3	1,954.59	7	1,347.83	1,486.12

CHECKING ACCOUNT TRANSACTIONS

DATE	AMOUNT	DESCRIPTION	BALANCE
10-3	236.77	Check #801	642.59
10-6	450.75	Deposit	1,093.34
10-10	324.70	Returned Item	768.64
10-13	880.34	EFT Payroll Deposit	1,648.98
10-15	75.89	Check #803	1,573.09
10-17	507.82	Check #805	1,065.27
10-22	120.00	ATM Withdrawal	945.27
10-24	623.50	Deposit	1,568.77
10-28	48.25	Check #806	1,520.52
10-30	34.40	Check printing charge	1,486.12

Checks Outstanding

No.	Amount	
802	47	20
804	109	00
Total	156	20

CHECKBOOK BALANCE	$ 1,897.42	STATEMENT BALANCE	$ 1,486.12
Deduct: Service Charges & Other Debits	359.10	Deduct: Outstanding Checks	156.20
SUB TOTAL	1,538.32	SUB TOTAL	1,329.92
Add: Interest Earned & Other Credits	—	Add: Deposits in Transit	208.40
ADJUSTED CHECKBOOK BALANCE	1,538.32	ADJUSTED STATEMENT BALANCE	1,538.32

Reconciled Balances

7. You are looking for a bank in which to open a checking account for your new part-time business. You estimate that in the first year you will be writing 30 checks per month and will make 3 balance inquiries per month. Your minimum daily balance is estimated to be $700 for the first six months and $1,200 for the next six months.

Use the following information to solve the problem.

Bank	Monthly Fees and Conditions
Intercontinental Bank	$15.00 with $1,000 min. daily balance -or- $25.00 under $1,000 min. daily balance
City National Bank	$4.50 plus $.50 per check over 10 checks monthly $1.00 per balance inquiry
Bank of America	$6 plus $.25 per check $2.00 per balance inquiry
First Union Bank	$9 plus $.15 per check $1.50 per balance inquiry

a. Calculate the cost of doing business with each bank for a year.

Intercontinental Bank: 6 Months at $25.00 = $150.00
                        6 Months at $15.00 = $90.00
                                              $240.00

City National Bank: Monthly service charge $4.50
                      20 Checks at $.50   = $10.00
                      3 Balance inquiries at $1.00 = $3.00
                                                     $17.50
                                              × 12 Months
                                                    $210.00

Bank of America: Monthly service charge $6.00
                   30 Checks at $.25   = $7.50
                   3 Balance inquiries at $2.00 = $6.00
                                                  $19.50
                                           × 12 Months
                                                 $234.00

First Union Bank: Monthly service charge $9.00
                    30 Checks at $.15   = $4.50
                    3 Balance inquiries at $1.50 = $4.50
                                                   $18.00
                                            × 12 Months
                                                  $216.00

b. Which bank should you choose for your checking account?

City National Bank is best choice.

All the Math That's Fit to Learn

The Business Math Times

Volume IV | **Checking Accounts** | One Dollar

Career Track:
Bank Teller

Most bank customers have contact with tellers. Tellers generally handle a wide range of banking transactions, such as cashing checks, accepting deposits and loan payments, and processing withdrawals. They sell savings bonds, accept payment for customers' utility bills, receive deposits for special accounts, keep records and perform the necessary paperwork for customer loans.

In hiring tellers, banks seek people who enjoy public contact and have good numerical, clerical, and communication skills. Tellers must feel comfortable handling large amounts of cash and working with computers and video terminals.

In general, banks prefer applicants who have had high school courses in mathematics, accounting, bookkeeping, economics, and public speaking. New tellers, espe-

"That's the service charge we charge you for not having any service charges last month."

Did You Know!

According to *Fortune* magazine, the top 5 commercial banks in the United States are

BANK	REVENUES ($MILLIONS)	EMPLOYEES
1. Citicorp	31,690	85,300
2. BankAmerica Corp.	20,386	95,288
3. Nationsbank Corp.	16,298	58,322
4. Chemical Banking Corp.	14,884	39,078
5. J.P. Morgan & Co.	11,915	17,055

SOURCE: *Fortune*, April 29, 1996, p. F-45, F-46.

---

cially at larger banks, receive at least one week of formal classroom training followed by several weeks of on-the-job training where tellers observe experienced workers before doing the work themselves.

Advancement opportunities are good for well-trained, motivated employees. Experienced tellers may advance to head teller, customer service representative, or new accounts clerk. Outstanding tellers who have had some college or specialized training offered by the banking industry may be promoted to a managerial position.

SOURCE: U.S. Department of Labor (America Online Career Center, March 1996). *Occupational Outlook Handbook*

Brainteaser

You are a bank teller for the Last National Bank of Greenback. A customer has come to your window to make a very large deposit of one dollar bills. You can count bills at the rate of one bill per second. Without taking lunch, how long will it take you to count a deposit of one billion one-dollar bills?

Answer to Last Issue's Brainteaser
Decimal point   1.2

Bank Robbery!

Did you know:

- A bank in Wisconsin is charging its customers 40 cents for accidentally punching in the wrong PIN number and $15 for depositing an empty envelope in the automatic teller machine!

- Some banks mark up actual costs by nearly 1,000% for checks and deposits returned for insufficient funds.

- One banker told Congress recently that a bounced check costs his bank $2.00, but the bank charges customers $20.00 for a bounced check "as a deterrent."

SOURCE: *Bankcard Holders of America Newsletter*, July/August 1994, Salem, Virginia.

Check Writing Tip!

Tax advisers warn not to write "IRS" when filling out a tax check. If your check falls into the hands of a crook, "IRS" may be changed to "MRS." followed by someone's name. Instead, write "Internal Revenue Service."

SOURCE: *The Miami Herald* (April 6, 1995), p. 3K.

Chapter 5

Using Equations to Solve Business Problems

Performance Objectives

SECTION I SOLVING BASIC EQUATIONS

5-1 Understanding the concept, terminology, and rules of equations. (p. 119)

5-2 Solving equations for the unknown and proving the solution. (p. 120)

5-3 Writing expressions and equations from written statements. (p. 126)

SECTION II USING EQUATIONS TO SOLVE BUSINESS-RELATED WORD PROBLEMS

5-4 Setting up and solving business-related word problems using equations. (p. 129)

5-5 Understanding and solving ratio and proportion problems. (p. 134)

SOLVING BASIC EQUATIONS

One of the primary objectives of business mathematics is to describe business situations and solve business problems. Many business problems requiring a mathematical solution have been converted to formulas used to solve those problems. A **formula** is a mathematical statement describing a real-world situation in which letters represent number quantities. A typical example of a formula follows:

Business Situation: Revenue less expenses equals profit
Mathematical Formula: Revenue − Expenses = Profit

or

$$R - E = P$$

By knowing the numerical value of any two of the three parts, we can use the formula to determine the unknown part. Formulas are a way of standardizing repetitive business situations. They are used in almost every aspect of business activity and are an essential tool for the businessperson. Later in the book, we shall see formulas applied to topics such as markup and markdown, percents, interest rates, financial ratios, inventory, depreciation, and many more.

As valuable and widespread as formulas are, they cannot anticipate all business situations. Today, businesspeople must have the ability to analyze the facts of a situation and devise custom-made formulas to solve business problems. These formulas are actually mathematical equations.

In this important chapter you will learn to write and solve equations. At first, some of the concepts may seem a bit strange. Equations use letters of the alphabet as well as numbers. Don't be intimidated! After some practice, you will be able to write and solve equations comfortably.

5-1 Understanding the Concept, Terminology, and Rules of Equations

In English, we write by using words to form complete thoughts known as sentences. Equations convert written sentences describing business situations into mathematical sentences. When the statement contains an equal sign, =, it is an **equation.** If it does not contain an equal sign, it is simply an **expression.** Equations express business problems in their simplest form. There are no adjectives or words of embellishment, just the facts.

$$S + 12 \text{ is an } expression \qquad S + 12 = 20 \text{ is an } equation$$

An equation is a mathematical statement using numbers, letters, and symbols to express a relationship of equality. Equations have an expression on the left side and an expression on the right side, connected by an equal sign.

Letters of the alphabet are used to represent unknown quantities in equations, and are called **variables.** In the equation, above, S is the variable, or the **unknown.** The 12 and the 20 are the **knowns,** or **constants.** Variables and constants are also known as the **terms** of the equation. The plus sign and the equal sign separate the terms, and describe the relationship between them.

To **solve an equation** means to find the numerical value of the unknown. From our equation $S + 12 = 20$, what value of S would make the equation true? Is it 6? No, 6 plus 12 is 18, and 18 does not equal 20. Is it 10? No, 10 plus 12 is 22, and 22 does not equal 20. How about 8? Yes, 8 plus 12 does equal 20.

$$S + 12 = 20$$
$$8 + 12 = 20$$
$$20 = 20$$

formula
A mathematical representation of a fact, rule, principle, or other logical relation in which letters represent number quantities. An example is the simple interest formula, I = PRT, where interest equals principal times rate times time.

equation
A mathematical statement expressing a relationship of equality; usually written as a series of symbols that are separated into left and right sides and joined by an equal sign. $X + 7 = 10$ is an equation.

expression
A mathematical operation or a quantity stated in symbolic form, not containing an equal sign. $X + 7$ is an expression.

variables (unknowns)
The part of an equation that is not given. In equations, the unknowns are variables (letters of the alphabet), that are quantities having no fixed value. In the equation $X + 7 = 10$, X is the unknown or variable.

constants (knowns)
The portion or parts of an equation that are given. In equations, the knowns are constants (numbers), that are quantities having a fixed value. In the equation $X + 7 = 10$, 7 and 10 are the knowns or constants.

terms
The knowns (constants) and unknowns (variables) of an equation. In the equation $X + 7 = 10$, X, 7, and 10 are the terms.

solve an equation
The process of finding the numerical value of the unknown in an equation.

Today, managers must have the ability to analyze the facts of a business problem and devise custom-made formulas to solve them.

 solution, or root

The numerical value of the unknown that makes the equation true. In the equation $X + 7 = 10$, for example, 3 is the solution, since $3 + 7 = 10$.

● **coefficient**

A number or quantity placed before another quantity, indicating multiplication. For example, 4 is the coefficient in the expression $4C$. This indicates 4 multiplied by C.

● **transpose**

To bring a term from one side of an equation to the other, with corresponding change of sign.

EXHIBIT 5-1 **T**

EQUATIONS—A QUESTION OF BALANCE

By substituting 8 for the variable, *S*, we have found the value of the unknown that satisfies the equation and makes it true: 20 equals 20. The numerical value of the variable that makes the equation true, in this case 8, is known as the **solution,** or **root,** of the equation.

5-2 Solving Equations for the Unknown and Proving the Solution

In solving equations, we use the same basic operations we used in arithmetic: addition, subtraction, multiplication, and division. The meanings of the signs +, −, ×, and ÷ are still the same. Equations have a few new designations, however, that we must learn.

Multiplication of 5 times *Y*, for example, may be written as

$$5 \times Y$$
$$5 \cdot Y$$
$$5(Y)$$
$$5Y$$

The number 5 in the term $5Y$ is known as the **coefficient** of the term. In cases where there is no numerical coefficient written, such as *W*, the coefficient is understood to be a 1. Therefore, $1W = W$.

Division in equations is indicated by the fraction bar, just as in Chapter 2. For example, the term 5 divided by *Y* would be written as

$$\frac{5}{Y}$$

In order to solve equations we must move or transpose all the unknowns or variables to one side and isolate all the knowns on the other side. To **transpose** means to transfer a term from one side of the equation to the other. It is customary for the unknowns to be on the left side and the knowns to be on the right side, such as $X = 7$.

It is important to remember that an equation is a statement of equality. The left side must always be equal to the right side. Think of an equation as a balance or scale with the equal sign in the center. In order to keep the equation balanced or equal, whatever operation we do to one side, we must do to the other side. If we add 6 to the left side, we must add 6 to the right side. If we divide the left side by 21, we must divide the right side by 21. Exhibit 5-1 illustrates the idea of balancing equations.

The procedure for moving terms from one side of the equation to the other involves the use of inverse or opposite operations. To solve for the unknown value, apply the opposite operation to both sides of the equation. These are as follows:

Operation Indicated	Opposite Operation
Addition ⟶	Subtraction
Subtraction ⟶	Addition
Multiplication ⟶	Division
Division ⟶	Multiplication

The examples on the following pages will illustrate how the opposite or inverse operations work.

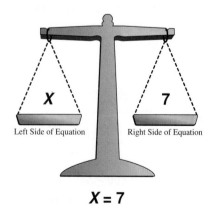

$$X = 7$$

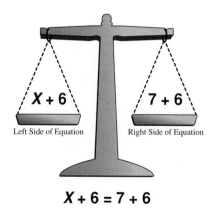

$$X + 6 = 7 + 6$$

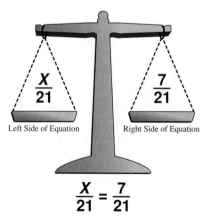

$$\frac{X}{21} = \frac{7}{21}$$

SOURCE: Jeffrey Slater, *Practical Business Math Procedures,* Fourth Edition (Burr Ridge, Ill.: Irwin, 1994), p. 117. © 1994.

EXAMPLE

Solve the equation $X + 4 = 15$ and prove the solution.

SOLUTION STRATEGY

The equation $X + 4 = 15$ indicates addition (+4). To solve for X, apply the opposite operation, subtraction. Subtract 4 from each side.

$$
\begin{array}{rcr}
X + 4 = & & 15 \\
- 4 & & -4 \\
\hline
X \quad = & & 11
\end{array}
$$

$$\underline{X = 11}$$

Proof: The solution can easily be proven by substituting our answer (11) for the letter or letters in the original equation. If the left and right sides are equal, the equation is true and the solution is correct.

$$
\begin{array}{rcl}
X + 4 & = & 15 \\
11 + 4 & = & 15 \\
15 & = & 15
\end{array}
$$

EXAMPLE

Solve the equation $H - 20 = 44$ and prove the solution.

SOLUTION STRATEGY

The equation $H - 20 = 44$ indicates subtraction (−20). To solve for H, apply the opposite operation, addition. Add 20 to each side of the equation.

$$
\begin{array}{rcr}
H - 20 = & & 44 \\
+ 20 & & + 20 \\
\hline
H \quad = & & 64
\end{array}
$$

$$\underline{H = 64}$$

Proof: Substitute 64 for H:

$$
\begin{array}{rcl}
H - 20 & = & 44 \\
64 - 20 & = & 44 \\
44 & = & 44
\end{array}
$$

TRY-IT   EXERCISES

Solve the following equations for the unknown and prove your solutions:

1. $W + 10 = 25$ **2.** $A - 8 = 40$ **3.** $Q + 30 = 100$ **4.** $L - 3 = 7$

Check your answers with the solutions on page 143.

EXAMPLE

Solve the equation $9T = 36$ and prove the solution.

SOLUTION STRATEGY

The equation $9T = 36$ indicates multiplication. $9T$ means 9 times T. To solve for T, apply the opposite operation. Divide both sides of the equation by 9.

$$9T = 36$$

$$\frac{\cancel{9}T}{\cancel{9}} = \frac{36}{9}$$

$$\underline{\underline{T = 4}}$$

Proof:

$$9T = 36$$

$$9(4) = 36$$

$$\underline{\underline{36 = 36}}$$

EXAMPLE

Solve the equation $\frac{M}{5} = 4$ and prove the solution.

SOLUTION STRATEGY

The equation $\frac{M}{5} = 4$ indicates division. To solve for M, do the opposite operation. Multiply both sides of the equation by 5.

$$(5)\frac{M}{5} = 4(5)$$

$$\underline{\underline{M = 20}}$$

Proof:

$$\frac{M}{5} = 4$$

$$\frac{20}{5} = 4$$

$$\underline{\underline{4 = 4}}$$

TRY-IT   EXERCISES

Solve the following equations for the unknown and prove your solutions:

5. $15L = 75$ **6.** $\frac{Z}{8} = 2$ **7.** $16F = 80$ **8.** $\frac{C}{9} = 9$

Check your answers with the solutions on page 143.

Multiple Operation Rule: **To solve equations with more than one operation, perform the addition and subtraction first, then the multiplication and division.**

EXAMPLE

Solve the equation $7R - 5 = 51$ and prove the solution.

SOLUTION STRATEGY

The equation $7R - 5 = 51$ indicates subtraction and multiplication. Following the rule for multiple operations, begin by adding 5 to each side of the equation.

$$\begin{array}{r} 7R - 5 = 51 \\ \underline{+ 5 \quad +5} \\ 7R \quad\; = 56 \end{array}$$

$$7R = 56$$

Next, divide both sides of the equation by 7.

$$\frac{7R}{7} = \frac{56}{7}$$

$$\underline{\underline{R = 8}}$$

Proof:

$$7R - 5 = 51$$
$$7(8) - 5 = 51$$
$$56 - 5 = 51$$
$$\underline{\underline{51 = 51}}$$

EXAMPLE

Solve the equation $\frac{X}{2} + 20 = 34$ and prove the solution.

SOLUTION STRATEGY

The equation $\frac{X}{2} + 20 = 34$ indicates addition and division. Following the rule for multiple operations, begin by subtracting 20 from each side.

$$\frac{X}{2} + 20 = 34$$
$$\underline{\quad -20 \quad -20}$$
$$\frac{X}{2} \quad = 14$$

$$\frac{X}{2} = 14$$

Next, multiply each side by 2.

$$(2)\frac{X}{2} = 14(2)$$

$$\underline{\underline{X = 28}}$$

Proof:

$$\frac{X}{2} + 20 = 34$$

$$\frac{28}{2} + 20 = 34$$

$$14 + 20 = 34$$

$$\underline{\underline{34 = 34}}$$

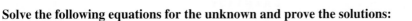

TRY-IT   EXERCISES

Solve the following equations for the unknown and prove the solutions:

9. $12N + 14 = 50$ **10.** $3W - 4 = 26$ **11.** $\frac{F}{3} - 6 = 2$ **12.** $\frac{Z}{5} + 15 = 24$

Check your answers with the solutions on page 143.

Frequently, parentheses are used in equations. They contain a number just outside the left-hand parentheses known as the coefficient, and two or more terms inside the parentheses. An example is $5(3X + 6)$.

Parentheses Rule: **In solving equations, parentheses must be removed before any other operations are performed. To remove parentheses, multiply the coefficient by each term inside the parentheses.**

To apply this rule to the example above,

$$5(3X + 6) =$$
$$5(3X) + 5(6) =$$
$$15X + 30 =$$

In equations, when terms with like signs are multiplied, the result is a positive and contains a plus sign. For example, $+5(+4) = +20$; and $-5(-4) = +20$. When terms with unlike signs are multiplied, the result is a negative and contains a minus sign. For example, $+5(-4) = -20$.

EXAMPLE

Solve the equation $8(2K - 4) = 48$ and prove the solution.

SOLUTION STRATEGY

Since this equation contains parentheses, we must begin there. Following the rule for removing parentheses, multiply the coefficient, 8, by each term inside the parentheses.

$$8(2K - 4) = 48$$
$$8(2K) - 8(4) = 48$$
$$16K - 32 = 48$$

Now solve the equation as before, by isolating the unknown, K, on the left side of the equal sign. Remember, add and subtract first, then multiply and divide.

$$
\begin{array}{rcl}
16K - 32 & = & 48 \\
+ 32 & & +32 \\
\hline
16K & = & 80
\end{array}
$$

$$16K = 80$$
$$\frac{16K}{16} = \frac{80}{16}$$
$$\underline{\underline{K = 5}}$$

Proof:

$$8(2K - 4) = 48$$
$$8(2\{\,5\,\} - 4) = 48$$
$$8(10 - 4) = 48$$
$$8(6) = 48$$
$$\underline{\underline{48 = 48}}$$

TRY-IT   EXERCISES

Solve the following equations for the unknown and prove the solutions:

13. $4(5G + 6) = 64$ **14.** $6(3H - 5) = 42$

Check your answers with the solutions on page 144.

When equations contain unknowns that appear two or more times, they must be combined.

> **STEPS FOR COMBINING MULTIPLE UNKNOWNS:**
>
> **Step 1.** In order to combine unknowns, they must be on the same side of the equation. If they are not, move them all to the same side.
>
> $$5X = 12 + 2X$$
> $$5X - 2X = 12$$
>
> **Step 2.** Once the unknowns are on the same side of the equation, add or subtract their coefficients as indicated:
>
> $$5X - 2X = 12$$
> $$3X = 12$$

EXAMPLE

Solve the equation $4C + 7 - C = 25 - 6C$ and prove the solution.

SOLUTION STRATEGY

To solve this equation, we begin by combining the two terms on the left side that contain C: $4C - C = 3C$. This leaves

$$3C + 7 = 25 - 6C$$

Next move the $-6C$ to the left side by adding $+6C$ to both sides of the equation.

$$3C + 7 = 25 - 6C$$
$$\underline{+6C \qquad\quad +6C}$$
$$9C + 7 = 25$$

Now that all the terms containing the unknown, C, have been combined, we can solve the equation.

$$9C + 7 = 25$$
$$\underline{-7 \quad\;\; -7}$$
$$9C = 18$$
$$\frac{9C}{9} = \frac{18}{9}$$
$$\underline{\underline{C = 2}}$$

Proof:

$$4C + 7 - C = 25 - 6C$$
$$4(2) + 7 - 2 = 25 - 6(2)$$
$$8 + 7 - 2 = 25 - 12$$
$$\underline{\underline{13 = 13}}$$

TRY-IT   **EXERCISES**

Solve the following equations for the unknown and prove the solutions:

15. $X + 3 = 18 - 4X$ **16.** $9S + 8 - S = 2(2S + 8)$

Check your answers with the solutions on page 144.

5-3 Writing Expressions and Equations from Written Statements

Expressions and equations are created from written statements by identifying the unknowns and the knowns and determining the mathematical relationship between them. The variables are assigned letters of the alphabet. The letter X is commonly used to represent the unknown. The relationship between the knowns and the unknowns involves either addition, subtraction, multiplication, or division; or a combination of two or more of these.

Key words and phrases indicate the mathematical relationship between the terms. The verb, or action word, represents the equal sign. If the written statement has a verb, the statement is an equation. The following chart should be helpful in writing expressions and equations from written statements.

> ### Key Words and Phrases for Creating Equations
> **Equal Sign:**
> is, are, was, equals, gives, giving, leaves, leaving, makes, denotes
> **Addition:**
> added to, totals, the sum of, plus, more than, increased by, greater than, and
> **Subtraction:**
> less, less than, minus, difference between, decreased by, reduced by
> **Multiplication:**
> of, times, product of, multiplied by, twice, double, triple, at, @
> **Division:**
> divide, divided by, the average of, divided into, the quotient of

Creating expressions and equations takes time and practice. Read the statement carefully, and identify the key words and phrases. Most of the time a second or third reading is necessary. Underlining the key terms also helps to analyze the information and clarify the problem.

EXAMPLES

For the following statements, underline the key words and translate into *expressions:*

a. A number increased by 18

b. 19 times W

c. 12 less than S

d. $\dfrac{2}{3}$ of Y

e. 9 more than two times R

f. 4 times the sum of X and 8

SOLUTION STRATEGY

	Key Words	Expression
a.	A number <u>increased by</u> 18	$N + 18$
b.	19 <u>times</u> W	$19W$
c.	12 <u>less than</u> S	$S - 12$
d.	$\dfrac{2}{3}$ <u>of</u> Y	$\dfrac{2}{3}Y$
e.	9 <u>more than</u> two <u>times</u> R	$2R + 9$
f.	4 <u>times</u> the <u>sum of</u> X <u>and</u> 8	$4(X + 8)$

TRY-IT   EXERCISES

For the following statements, underline the key words and translate into *expressions:*

17. The sum of twice E and 9

18. 6 times N divided by Z

19. 8 less than half of F

20. $45.75 more than the product of X and Y

21. The difference of Q and 44

22. R times A times B

Check your answers with the solutions on page 144.

EXAMPLES

For the following statements, underline the key words and translate into *equations:*

a. A number decreased by 14 is 23
b. 8 less than $3D$ leaves 19
c. A number totals 4 times the quantity of V and N
d. The cost of X lbs at $3 per lb is $12
e. Cost is the product of price and quantity
f. The sum of liabilities and capital is assets

SOLUTION STRATEGY

Key Words	Equation
a. A number <u>decreased by</u> 14 <u>is</u> 23	$X - 14 = 23$
b. 8 <u>less than</u> $3D$ <u>leaves</u> 19	$3D - 8 = 19$
c. A number <u>totals</u> 4 <u>times</u> the quantity of V <u>and</u> N	$X = 4(V + N)$
d. The cost <u>of</u> X lbs at $3 per lb <u>is</u> $12	$3X = 12$
e. Cost <u>is</u> the <u>product of</u> price and quantity	$C = PQ$
f. The <u>sum of</u> liabilities <u>and</u> capital <u>is</u> assets	$L + C = A$

TRY-IT EXERCISES

For the following statements, underline the key words and translate into *equations:*

23. What number increased by 32 yields 125?

24. 21 less than twice C gives 9.

25. 5 more than 6 times a number, plus 3 times that number, is 25.

26. The cost of G gallons at $1.33 per gallon equals $34.40.

27. The area of a rectangle is the length times the width.

28. Challenge: What number less 12 is the average of *A*, *B*, and *C?*

Check your answers with the solutions on page 144.

S **REVIEW EXERCISES** CHAPTER 5—SECTION I

Complete worked-out solutions for exercises 1–17 appear in appendix following the index.

Solve the following equations for the unknown and prove your solutions:

1. $B + 11 = 24$
$B = \underline{\underline{13}}$

2. $C - 16 = 5$
$C = \underline{\underline{21}}$

3. $S + 35 = 125$
$S = \underline{\underline{90}}$

4. $M - 58 = 12$
$M = \underline{\underline{70}}$

5. $21K = 63$
$K = \underline{\underline{3}}$

6. $\dfrac{Z}{3} = 45$
$Z = \underline{\underline{135}}$

7. $50Y = 375$
$Y = 7\dfrac{1}{2}$

8. $\dfrac{L}{5} = 8$
$L = \underline{\underline{40}}$

9. $6G + 5 = 29$
$G = \underline{\underline{4}}$

10. $\dfrac{D}{3} - 5 = 15$
$D = \underline{\underline{60}}$

11. $25A - 11 = 64$
$A = \underline{\underline{3}}$

12. $\dfrac{R}{5} + 33 = 84$
$R = \underline{\underline{255}}$

13. $3(4X + 5) = 63$
$X = \underline{\underline{4}}$

14. $C + 5 = 26 - 2C$
$C = \underline{\underline{7}}$

15. $12(2D - 4) = 72$
$D = \underline{\underline{5}}$

16. $14V + 5 - 5V = 4(V + 5)$
$V = \underline{\underline{3}}$

17. $Q + 20 = 3(9 - 2Q)$
$Q = \underline{\underline{1}}$

For the following statements, underline the key words and translate into *expressions:*

18. 5 <u>times</u> *G* <u>divided by</u> *R*
$\dfrac{5G}{R}$

19. The <u>sum of</u> 5 <u>times</u> *F* <u>and</u> 33
$5F + 33$

20. 6 <u>less than</u> one-fourth <u>of</u> *C*
$\dfrac{1}{4}C - 6$

21. 550 <u>more than</u> the <u>product of</u> *H* and *P*
$HP + 550$

22. *T* <u>times</u> *B* <u>times</u> 9
$9TB$

23. The <u>difference</u> of 8*Y* and 128
$8Y - 128$

24. 7 <u>times</u> the <u>quantity</u> of *X* <u>plus</u> 7
$7(X + 7)$

25. 40 <u>more than</u> $\dfrac{3}{4}$ <u>of</u> *B*
$\dfrac{3}{4}B + 40$

For the following statements, underline the key words and translate into *equations:*

26. A number <u>increased by</u> 24 <u>is</u> 35.
$X + 24 = 35$

27. A number <u>totals</u> 5 <u>times</u> *B* <u>and</u> *C.*
$X = 5B + C$

28. 12 <u>less than</u> 4*G* <u><u>leaves</u></u> 33.
$$4G - 12 = 33$$

29. The cost of *R* at \$5.75 each <u><u>is</u></u> \$28.75.
$$\$5.75R = \$28.75$$

30. Cost per person <u><u>is</u></u> the total cost <u>divided by</u> the number of persons.
$$C = \dfrac{T}{N}$$

31. 4 <u>more than</u> 5 <u>times</u> a number, <u>plus</u> 2 <u>times</u> that number, <u><u>is</u></u> that number <u>increased by</u> 40.
$$5X + 4 + 2X = X + 40$$

USING EQUATIONS TO SOLVE BUSINESS-RELATED WORD PROBLEMS

In business, most of the math encountered is in the form of business-situation word problems. Variables such as profits, production units, inventory, employees, money, customers, and interest rates are constantly interacting mathematically. Your boss won't ask you simply to add, subtract, multiply, or divide, but will ask for information requiring you to perform these functions in a business context. Business students must be able to analyze a business situation requiring math, set up the situation in a mathematical expression or equation, and work it out to a correct solution.

5-4 Setting Up and Solving Business-Related Word Problems Using Equations

In Section I of this chapter we learned to create and solve equations from written statements. Let's see how to apply these skills in business situations. You will learn a logical procedure for setting up and solving business-related word problems. Some problems have more than one way to arrive at an answer. The key, once again, is not to be intimidated. Learning to solve word problems requires practice and the more you do it, the easier it will become and the more comfortable you will feel with it.

Just as signs on the highway help you locate your final destination, equations make it easier to find your way through a business problem.

Now let's see how this works. The following examples illustrate several common business situations and their solutions.

EXAMPLE

On Tuesday, the Jiffy Car Wash took in $360 less in wash business than in wax business. If the total sales for the day were $920, what were the sales for each service?

SOLUTION STRATEGY

Reasoning: Wax sales <u>plus</u> wash sales <u>equal</u> the total sales, $920.

$$\text{Let } X = \$ \text{ amount of wax sales}$$
$$\text{Let } X - 360 = \$ \text{ amount of wash sales}$$

$$X + X - 360 = \quad 920$$
$$\underline{\quad\quad +\,360 \quad +\,360}$$
$$X + X \quad\quad = 1{,}280$$
$$2X = 1{,}280$$
$$\frac{\cancel{2}X}{\cancel{2}} = \frac{1{,}280}{2}$$
$$X = 640 \qquad \underline{\text{wax sales} = \$640}$$
$$X - 360 = 640 - 360 = 280 \qquad \underline{\text{wash sales} = \$280}$$

Proof:

$$X + X - 360 = 920$$
$$640 + 640 - 360 = 920$$
$$\underline{920 = 920}$$

T R Y - I T   E X E R C I S E

29. Jose and Bob are salesmen for TV Giant Warehouse. Last week Jose sold 12 less televisions than Bob. Together they sold 44. How many TV sets did each sell?

Check your answer with the solution on page 144.

EXAMPLE

Johnson Equipment, Inc., spends $\frac{1}{4}$ of total revenue on payroll expenses. If last week's payroll amounted to $5,000, what was the revenue for the week?

SOLUTION STRATEGY

Reasoning: $\frac{1}{4}$ of revenue is the week's payroll, $5,000.

$$\text{Let } R = \text{revenue for the week}$$

$$\frac{1}{4}R = 5,000$$

$$(4)\frac{1}{4}R = 5,000(4)$$

$$R = 20,000 \quad \underline{\text{Revenue for the week} = \$20,000}$$

Proof:

$$\frac{1}{4}R = 5,000$$

$$\frac{1}{4}(20,000) = 5,000$$

$$\underline{5,000 = 5,000}$$

TRY-IT EXERCISE

30. One-third of the checking accounts at the Liberty National Bank are for corporations. If 2,500 accounts are for corporations, how many total checking accounts does the bank have?

Check your answer with the solution on page 144.

EXAMPLE

The Harrison Company has 25 shareholders. If management decides to split the $80,000 net profit equally among the shareholders, how much will each investor receive?

SOLUTION STRATEGY

Reasoning: Profit per shareholder is the net profit, $80,000, divided by the number of shareholders.

$$\text{Let } P = \text{Profit per shareholder}$$

$$P = \frac{80,000}{25}$$

$$P = 3,200 \quad \underline{\text{Profit per shareholder} = \$3,200}$$

Proof:

$$P = \frac{80,000}{25}$$

$$3,200 = \frac{80,000}{25}$$

$$\underline{3,200 = 3,200}$$

31. Southwest Supply Company fills an order for 58 cartons of merchandise weighing a total of 7,482 pounds. What is the weight per carton?

Check your answer with the solution on page 145.

EXAMPLE

Sounds Good, Inc., a stereo shop, sold 144 CD players last week. If 5 times as many single CD models sold as carousel models, how many of each were sold?

SOLUTION STRATEGY

Reasoning: Carousel models <u>plus</u> single CD models <u>equals</u> total CD players sold, 144.

$$\text{Let } X = \text{carousel models}$$
$$\text{Let } 5X = \text{single CD models}$$

$$X + 5X = 144$$
$$6X = 144$$
$$\frac{6X}{6} = \frac{144}{6}$$
$$X = 24 \qquad \qquad \underline{\text{carousel models sold} = 24}$$
$$5X = 5(24) = 120 \qquad \underline{\text{single CD models sold} = 120}$$

Proof:

$$X + 5X = 144$$
$$24 + 5(24) = 144$$
$$24 + 120 = 144$$
$$\underline{144 = 144}$$

32. The Centerville Department Store sells three times as much in soft goods, such as clothing and linens, as it sells in hard goods, such as furniture and appliances. If total store sales on Saturday were $180,000, how much of each category was sold?

Check your answer with the solution on page 145.

Yesterday, the Bay City recycling van picked up a total of 4,500 pounds of material. If newspaper weighed 3 times as much as aluminum cans, and aluminum weighed twice as much as glass, what was the weight of each material?

SOLUTION STRATEGY

Reasoning: Glass <u>plus</u> aluminum <u>plus</u> newspaper <u>amounts to</u> the total material, 4,500 pounds.

Hint: Let the least (smallest) element equal X. That way the larger ones will be multiples of X. By doing this, you avoid having fractions in your equation.

$$\text{Let } X = \text{pounds of glass}$$
$$\text{Let } 2X = \text{pounds of aluminum}$$
$$\text{Let } 3(2X) = \text{pounds of newspaper}$$

$$X + 2X + 3(2X) = 4{,}500$$
$$X + 2X + 6X = 4{,}500$$
$$9X = 4{,}500$$
$$\frac{9X}{9} = \frac{4500}{9}$$

$$X = 500 \quad \underline{\text{glass collected} = 500 \text{ pounds}}$$
$$2X = 2(500) = 1{,}000 \quad \underline{\text{aluminum collected} = 1{,}000 \text{ pounds}}$$
$$3(2X) = 3(1{,}000) = 3{,}000 \quad \underline{\text{newspaper collected} = 3{,}000 \text{ pounds}}$$

Proof:

$$X + 2X + 3(2X) = 4{,}500$$
$$500 + 2(500) + 3(2\{500\}) = 4{,}500$$
$$500 + 1{,}000 + 3{,}000 = 4{,}500$$
$$\underline{4{,}500 = 4{,}500}$$

TRY-IT EXERCISE

33. At Contempo Furniture, 520 items were sold last week. They sold twice as many sofas as chairs, and four times as many chairs as tables. How many were sold of each product?

Check your answer with the solution on page 145.

Cluckers' Chicken Restaurant sells whole chicken dinners for $12.00 and half chicken dinners for $8.00. Yesterday they sold a total of 400 dinners and took in $4,200. How many of each size dinner were sold? What were the dollar sales of each size dinner?

SOLUTION STRATEGY

Reasoning: The <u>sum of</u> the price <u>multiplied by</u> the quantity of each item <u>is</u> total sales, $4,200.

Hint: This type of problem requires that we multiply the price of each item by the quantity. We know that a total of 400 dinners were sold, therefore,

Let X = quantity of whole chicken dinners

Let $400 - X$ = quantity of half chicken dinners

Note: By letting X equal the more expensive item, we avoid dealing with negative numbers.

Price times quantity of whole chicken dinners = $\$12X$

Price times quantity of half chicken dinners = $\$8(400 - X)$

$$12X + 8(400 - X) = 4{,}200$$
$$12X + 3{,}200 - 8X = 4{,}200$$
$$4X + 3{,}200 = 4{,}200$$
$$\underline{-3{,}200 \quad -3{,}200}$$
$$4X = 1{,}000$$
$$\frac{4X}{4} = \frac{1{,}000}{4}$$
$$X = 250 \qquad \underline{\text{Quantity of whole chicken dinners} = 250}$$

$400 - X = 400 - 250 = 150$ \quad \underline{Quantity of half chicken dinners = 150}

Proof:

$$12X + 8(400 - X) = 4{,}200$$
$$12(250) + 8(400 - 250) = 4{,}200$$
$$3{,}000 + 8(150) = 4{,}200$$
$$3{,}000 + 1{,}200 = 4{,}200$$
$$\underline{4{,}200 = 4{,}200}$$

Now that we have calculated the quantity sold of each size dinner, we can find the dollar sales:

Reasoning: Dollar sales <u>are</u> the price per dinner <u>multiplied by</u> the quantity sold.

Let S = dollar sales

Whole chicken dinners: \quad $S = \$12(250) = \underline{\$3{,}000 \text{ in sales}}$

Half chicken dinners: \quad $S = \$8(150) = \underline{\$1{,}200 \text{ in sales}}$

TRY-IT \qquad EXERCISE

34. **PowerKing sells a regular car battery for $70 and a heavy-duty model for $110. If they sold 40 batteries yesterday for a total of $3,400, how many of each type battery were sold? What were the dollar sales of each?**

Check your answer with the solution on page 145.

5-5 Understanding and Solving Ratio and Proportion Problems

ratio

A fraction that describes a comparison of two numbers or quantities. For example, 5 cats for every 3 dogs would be a ratio of 5 to 3, written as 5:3.

Many business problems and situations are expressed as ratios. A **ratio** is a fraction that describes a comparison of two numbers or quantities. In business, numbers often take on much more meaning when compared with other numbers in the form of a ratio.

For example, a factory has an output of 40 units per hour. Is this good or bad? If we also know that the industry average is 20 units per hour, we can set up a ratio of our factory, 40, compared to the industry average, 20.

$$\frac{\text{Factory}}{\text{Industry}} = \frac{40}{20} = 40 : 20 \quad \text{Expressed verbally, we say, "40 to 20"}$$

Since ratios are fractions, we can reduce our fraction, and state that our factory output is 2 to 1 over the industry average. If the industry average changed to 40, the ratio would be $\frac{40}{40}$ or 1 to 1. Had the industry average been 80, the ratio would be $\frac{40}{80}$ or 1 to 2.

Ratios can compare anything: money, weights, measures, output, or people. The units don't have to be the same. If we can buy 9 ounces of shampoo for $2.00, this is actually a ratio of ounces to dollars, or 9 : 2.

A **proportion** is a statement showing that two ratios are equal. Proportions are equations, with "as" being the equal sign. For example, we could say, "9 is to 2 as 18 is to 4."

$$\frac{9}{2} = \frac{18}{4} \quad \text{or} \quad 9 : 2 = 18 : 4$$

This means that if we can buy 9 ounces for $2.00, we can buy 18 ounces for $4.00. Proportions with three knowns and one unknown become a very useful business tool. For example, if we can buy 9 ounces for $2.00, how many ounces can we buy for $7.00? This proportion, 9 is to 2 as X is to 7, would be written as

$$\frac{9 \text{ ounces}}{\$2.00} = \frac{X \text{ ounces}}{\$7.00} \quad \text{or} \quad 9 : 2 = X : 7$$

● **proportion**

A statement showing that two ratios are equal. For example, 9 is to 3 as 3 is to 1, written $9:3 = 3:1$.

STEPS FOR SOLVING PROPORTION PROBLEMS USING CROSS-MULTIPLICATION

Step 1. Let X represent the unknown quantity.

Step 2. Set up the equation with one ratio (expressed as a fraction) on each side of the equal sign.

Step 3. Multiply the numerator of the first ratio by the denominator of the second and place the product to the left of the equal sign.

Step 4. Multiply the denominator of the first ratio by the numerator of the second and place the product to the right of the equal sign.

Step 5. Solve the equation for X.

EXAMPLE

If a car can travel 350 miles on 16 gallons of fuel, how many gallons would be required to complete a trip of 875 miles?

SOLUTION STRATEGY

This business situation can be solved using a proportion. The equation reads "350 miles is to 16 gallons as 875 miles is to X gallons."

$$\frac{350}{16} = \frac{875}{X}$$

Using cross-multiplication to solve the equation:

$350X = 16(875)$

$350X = 14,000$

$\quad X = 40 \qquad$ <u>40 gallons</u> of fuel are required for the car to travel 875 miles.

TRY-IT   **EXERCISE**

35. **If Wilbur earns $87.50 for 7 hours of work, how much can he expect to earn in a 35-hour week?**

Check your answer with the solution on page 146.

Set up and solve equations for the following business situations:

1. Kathy and Karen work in a boutique. During a sale, Kathy sold 8 less dresses than Karen. If together they sold 86 dresses, how many did each sell?

Karen $= X$ $X + X - 8 = 86$ $\dfrac{2X}{2} = \dfrac{94}{2}$

Kathy $= X - 8$ $2X - 8 = 86$

$\underline{ +8 \quad +8}$ $X = \underline{47}$ Karen's sales

$2X \quad = 94$ $X - 8 = 47 - 8 = \underline{39}$ Kathy's sales

2. One-fifth of the employees of Consolidated Widget Corporation work in the Midwest region. If the company employs 252 workers in that region, what is the total number of employees working for Consolidated?

Total employees $= X$ $\dfrac{1}{5}X = 252$

$$(5)\dfrac{1}{5}X = 252(5)$$

$$X = \underline{1260} \text{ Total employees}$$

3. Glacier Clear Water, Inc., received an order for 456 gallon jugs of water. If Glacier packs the gallons in cartons containing 4 jugs each, how many cartons will be required to fill the order?

Cartons required $= X$ $4X = 456$

$$\dfrac{4X}{4} = \dfrac{456}{4}$$

$$X = \underline{114} \text{ Cartons}$$

4. A bookstore sells 4 times as many in paperback books as in hardcover books. If last month's sales totaled \$124,300, how much was sold of each type book?

Hardcover $= X$ $X + 4X = 124,300$ $X = \underline{\$24,860}$ Hardcovers

Paperback $= 4X$ $5X = 124,300$ $4X = \underline{\$99,440}$ Paperbacks

$$\dfrac{5X}{5} = \dfrac{124,300}{5}$$

5. A new production machine can make 5 more than twice the production per hour of the old machine. If the new machine can produce 41 units per hour, how many does the old machine produce?

Old machine $= X$ $2X + 5 = 41$

New machine $= 2X + 5$ $2X = 36$

$$X = \underline{18} \text{ Old machine}$$

6. The Toy Box, a retail toy chain, placed a seasonal order for stuffed animals from a distributor. Large animals cost \$20.00 and small ones cost \$14.00.

a. If the total cost of the order was \$7,320 for 450 pieces, how many of each size were ordered?

Large size $= X$ $20X + 14(450 - X) = 7,320$

Small size $= 450 - X$ $20X + 6,300 - 14X = 7,320$

$$6X = 1,020$$

$$X = \underline{170} \text{ Large size}$$

$$450 - X = \underline{280} \text{ Small size}$$

b. What was the dollar amount of each size ordered?

Large size $= \$20(170) = \underline{\$3,400}$

Small size $= \$14(280) = \underline{\$3,920}$

7. Robbins and Bryant invested $89,600 in a business. If Bryant invested three times as much as Robbins, how much did each invest?

Robbins = X $X + 3X = 89,600$ $X = \underline{\$22,400}$ Robbins' investment
Bryant = $3X$ $4X = 89,600$ $3X = \underline{\$67,200}$ Bryant's investment
$\dfrac{4X}{4} = \dfrac{89,600}{4}$

8. An estate is to be distributed among the wife, 3 children, and 2 grandchildren. The children will each receive three times as much as each grandchild, and the wife will receive four times as much as each child. If the estate amounted to $115,000, how much will each person receive?

Grandchild = X $2X + 3(3X) + 4(3X) = 115,000$ $X = \underline{\$5,000}$ = Each grandchild's share
Child = $3X$ $2X + 9X + 12X = 115,000$ $3X = \underline{\$15,000}$ = Each child's share
Wife = $4(3X)$ $\dfrac{23X}{23} = \dfrac{115,000}{23}$ $4(3X) = \underline{\$60,000}$ = Wife's share

9. A retailer found that last week 7 less than three-fourths of its sales transactions were paid for by charge cards. If 209 transactions were charged, how many total transactions took place?

Total transactions = X $\dfrac{3}{4}X - 7 = 209$
Charge cards = $\dfrac{3}{4}X - 7$
$\dfrac{3}{4}X = 216$
$X = \underline{288}$ Total transactions

10. The deluxe model of an oven costs $46 more than twice the cost of the standard model. If together they cost $1,234, what is the cost of each model?

Standard oven = X $X + 2X + 46 = 1,234$
Deluxe oven = $2X + 46$ $3X + 46 = 1,234$
$3X = 1,188$
$X = \underline{\$396}$ Cost of standard oven
$2X + 46 = \underline{\$838}$ Cost of deluxe oven

11. The Computer Outlet sells standard keyboards for $84.00 and extended keyboards for $105.00. Last week the store sold three times as many standard keyboards as extended. If total keyboard sales were $4,998, how many of each type were sold?

Extended keyboards = X $105X + 84(3X) = 4,998$
Standard keyboards = $3X$ $105X + 252X = 4,998$
$357X = 4,998$
$X = \underline{14}$ Extended keyboards
$3X = \underline{42}$ Standard keyboards

12. The Michigan plant of a manufacturing company is 4 times as old as the Ohio plant. If the difference in the ages of the two plants is 9 years, what is the age of each?

Ohio plant = X $4X - X = 9$
Michigan plant = $4X$ $3X = 9$
$X = \underline{3}$ Age of Ohio plant
$4X = \underline{12}$ Age of Michigan plant

13. The Bakery Center sells oatmeal cookies for $1.30 per pound and peanut butter cookies for $1.60 per pound.

a. If total cookie sales last week amounted to 530 pounds, valued at $755, how many pounds of each type of cookie were sold?

Peanut butter = X $1.60X + 1.30(530 - X) = 755$ $X = \underline{220}$ Pounds of peanut butter cookies
Oatmeal = $530 - X$ $1.60X + 689 - 1.30X = 755$ $530 - X = \underline{310}$ Pounds of oatmeal cookies
$.30X + 689 = 755$
$.30X = 66$

b. What dollar amount of each type was sold?

$1.60(220) = $352 Sales of peanut butter cookies
$1.30(310) = $403 Sales of oatmeal cookies

14. One-ninth of a company's sales are made in New England. If New England sales amount to $600,000, what are the total sales of the company?

Total sales = X $\frac{1}{9}X = 600,000$

New England sales = $\frac{1}{9}X$ $X = $5,400,000$ Total sales

15. If a 48-piece set of stainless steel flatware costs $124.80, what is the cost per piece?

Cost per piece = X $48X = 124.80$ $X = \frac{124.80}{48}$

$\frac{48X}{48} = \frac{124.80}{48}$ $X = 2.60 Cost per piece

16. What is the total cost to ship an order weighing 1,860 pounds, if the breakdown is $.04 per pound for packing, $.02 per pound for insurance, $.13 per pound for transportation, and $132.40 for the crate?

Total cost = X $X = .04(1,860) + .02(1,860) + .13(1,860) + 132.40$

$X = 74.40 + 37.20 + 241.80 + 132.40$

$X = 485.80 Total cost to ship order

Use ratio and proportion to solve the following business situations:

17. If the interest on a $4,600 loan is $370, what would be the interest on a loan of $9,660?

$\frac{4,600}{370} = \frac{9,660}{X}$ $4,600X = 370(9,660)$

$4,600X = 3,574,200$

$X = 777 Interest on $9,660 loan

18. At Friendly Fruit Distributors, Inc., the ratio of fruits to vegetables sold is 5 to 3. If 1,848 pounds of vegetables are sold, how many pounds of fruit are sold?

$\frac{5}{3} = \frac{X}{1,848}$ $3X = 5(1,848)$

$3X = 9,240$

$X = 3,080$ Pounds of fruit

19. If auto insurance costs $6.52 monthly per $1,000 of coverage, what is the cost to insure a car valued at $17,500?

$\frac{6.52}{1,000} = \frac{X}{17,500}$ $1,000X = 6.52(17,500)$

$1,000X = 114,100$

$X = 114.10 Cost of insurance

20. A recipe calls for 3 eggs for every $12\frac{1}{2}$ ounces of bread crumbs. If a dinner party requires $87\frac{1}{2}$ ounces of bread crumbs, how many eggs should be used?

$\frac{3}{12\frac{1}{2}} = \frac{X}{87\frac{1}{2}}$ $12\frac{1}{2}X = 3(87\frac{1}{2})$

$12\frac{1}{2}X = 262\frac{1}{2}$

$X = 21$ Eggs needed for recipe

21. An architect uses a scale of $\frac{3}{4}$ inch to represent 1 foot on a blueprint for a building. If the east wall of the building is 36 feet long, how long will the line be on the blueprint?

$$\frac{\frac{3}{4}}{1} = \frac{X}{36} \qquad X = \frac{3}{4}(36)$$

$$X = \underline{27} \text{ Inches on blueprint}$$

22. If a car goes 48 miles per hour at 3,300 rpm (revolutions per minute) of the engine, how fast will it go at 4,000 rpm in the same gear?

$$\frac{48}{3,300} = \frac{X}{4,000} \qquad \begin{aligned} 3,300X &= 48(4,000) \\ 3,300X &= 192,000 \end{aligned}$$

$$X = \underline{58.2} \text{ Miles per hour at 4,000 RPM}$$

23. KwikPrint has a press that can print 5,800 sheets per hour. How many sheets can be printed during a $3\frac{1}{4}$-hour run?

$$\frac{5,800}{1} = \frac{X}{3\frac{1}{4}} \qquad X = 5,800(3\frac{1}{4})$$

$$X = \underline{18,850} \text{ Sheets printed in } 3\frac{1}{4} \text{ hours}$$

24. A local airport handles passenger to cargo traffic in a ratio of 8 to 5. If 45 cargo planes landed yesterday, how many passenger flights came in?

$$\frac{8}{5} = \frac{X}{45} \qquad \begin{aligned} 5X &= 8(45) \\ 5X &= 360 \end{aligned}$$

$$X = \underline{72} \text{ Passenger flights}$$

25. Eighty ounces of Happy Lawn fertilizer covers 1,250 square feet of lawn.

a. How many ounces would be required to cover a 4,000-square-foot lawn?

$$\frac{80}{1,250} = \frac{X}{4,000} \qquad \begin{aligned} 1,250X &= 80(4,000) \\ 1,250X &= 320,000 \end{aligned}$$

$$X = \underline{256} \text{ Ounces needed to cover 4,000 sq. ft.}$$

b. If Happy Lawn costs $1.19 for a 32-ounce bag, what is the total cost to fertilize the lawn?

$$\frac{1.19}{32} = \frac{X}{256} \qquad \begin{aligned} 32X &= 1.19(256) \\ 32X &= 304.64 \end{aligned}$$

$$X = \underline{\$9.52} \text{ Total cost}$$

CHAPTER 5 ■ USING EQUATIONS		SUMMARY CHART

SECTION I SOLVING BASIC EQUATIONS

Topic	P/O, Page	Important Concepts	Illustrative Examples
Solving Equations Using Inverse or Opposite Operations	5–2 120	In order to solve equations we must move or transpose all the unknowns to one side, and isolate all the knowns on the other side. It is customary for the unknowns to be on the left side and the knowns to be on the right side, such as $X = 33$. To solve for the unknown value, apply an inverse or opposite operation to both sides of the equation.	Solve the equation $R + 7 = 12$ The equation indicates addition, therefore, use the opposite operation: subtract 7 from both sides: $R + 7 = 12$ $\underline{-7 = -7}$ $R \quad = 5 \qquad \underline{R = 5}$

I, continued

Topic	P/O, Page	Important Concepts	Illustrative Examples
		Operation—Opposite Addition → Subtraction Subtraction → Addition Multiplication → Division Division → Multiplication	Solve the equation $W - 4 = 30$. The equation indicates subtraction, therefore, use the opposite operation: add 4 to both sides: $\begin{aligned} W - 4 &= 30 \\ +4 \quad &+4 \\ \hline W &= 34 \end{aligned}$ $\quad W = 34$ Solve the equation $3G = 18$. The equation indicates multiplication, therefore, use the opposite operation: divide both sides by 3: $\dfrac{3G}{3} = \dfrac{18}{3}$ $\quad G = 6$ Solve the equation $\dfrac{T}{5} = 9$. The equation indicates division, therefore, use the opposite operation: multiply both sides by 5: $(5)\dfrac{T}{5} = 9(5)$ $\qquad T = 45$
Solving Equations Containing Multiple Operations	5–2 122	Multiple Operation Rule: To solve equations with more than one operation, perform the addition and subtraction first, then do the multiplication and division.	Solve the equation $5X - 4 = 51$ $\begin{aligned} 5X - 4 &= 51 \\ +4 \quad &+4 \\ \hline 5X &= 55 \end{aligned}$ $\dfrac{5X}{5} = \dfrac{55}{5}$ $\quad X = 11$
Solving Equations Containing Parentheses	5–2 124	To remove parentheses, multiply the coefficient by each term inside the parentheses. Sign Rules: When like signs are multiplied, the result is positive. For example, $5(5) = 25$, and $-5(-5) = 25$. When unlike signs are multiplied, the result is negative. For example, $5(-5) = -25$.	Solve the equation $3(4S - 5) = 9$. To remove the parentheses, multiply the coefficient, 3, by both terms inside the parentheses: $\begin{aligned} 3(4S - 5) &= 9 \\ 3(4S) - 3(5) &= 9 \\ 12S - 15 &= 9 \\ 12S &= 24 \quad S = 2 \end{aligned}$

I, continued

Topic	P/O, Page	Important Concepts	Illustrative Examples
Solving Equations by Combining Unknowns	5–2 125	To combine unknowns in an equation, add or subtract their coefficients. If the unknowns are on opposite sides of the equal sign, first move them all to one side.	Solve the equation $3B + 5 - B = 7$ $3B + 5 - B = 7$ $2B + 5 = 7$ $2B = 2 \qquad B = 1$
Writing Expressions and Equations from Written Statements	5–3 126	Expressions and equations are created from written statements by identifying the unknowns and the knowns, and determining the mathematical relationship between them. The variables are assigned letters of the alphabet. The relationship between the knowns and the unknowns involve addition, subtraction, multiplication, division, or a combination of two or more. Key words indicate what relationship exists between the terms (see chart, page 126). If the written statement has a verb, the statement is an equation.	A number <u>increased by</u> 44 $X + 44$ 6 <u>more than</u> 3 <u>times</u> U $3U + 6$ 3 <u>times</u> the <u>sum of</u> C <u>and</u> 9 $3(C + 9)$ 7 <u>less than</u> 4 <u>times</u> M <u>leaves</u> 55 $4M - 7 = 55$ 2 <u>less than</u> 5 <u>times</u> a number, <u>plus</u> 9 <u>times</u> that number, <u>is</u> 88 $5X - 2 + 9X = 88$

SECTION II   USING EQUATIONS TO SOLVE BUSINESS-RELATED WORD PROBLEMS

Topic	P/O, Page	Important Concepts	Illustrative Examples
Solving Business-Related Equations	5–4 129	Example 1: Mary and Beth sell furniture at Futura Designs. Last week Mary sold 8 less recliner chairs than Beth. Together they sold 30. How many chairs did each sell?	Solution: *Reasoning:* Beth's sales <u>plus</u> Mary's sales <u>equal</u> total sales, 30 Let X = Beth's sales Let $X - 8$ = Mary's sales $X + X - 8 = 30$ $2X - 8 = 30$ $2X = 38$ $X = 19$ chairs = Beth's sales $X - 8 = 11$ chairs = Mary's sales
Solving Business-Related Equations	5–4 131	Example 2: One-fourth of the employees at Atlantic Distributors work in the accounting division. If there are 45 workers in this division, how many people work for Atlantic?	Solution: *Reasoning:* $\frac{1}{4}$ of the total employees <u>are</u> in accounting, 45. Let X = total employees Let $\frac{1}{4}X$ = accounting employees $\frac{1}{4}X = 45$ $(4)\frac{1}{4}X = 45(4)$ $X = 180$ = Total employees

II, continued

Topic	P/O, Page	Important Concepts	Illustrative Examples
Solving Business-Related Equations	5–4 131	Example 3: Longhorn Industries, a small manufacturing company, made a profit of $315,000 last year. If the 9 investors decide to evenly split this profit, how much will each receive?	Solution: *Reasoning:* Each investor's share is the total profit divided by the number of investors. Let X = each investor's share $X = \dfrac{315,000}{9}$ $X = \$35,000$ = investor's share
Solving Business-Related Equations	5–4 132	Example 4: The Pet Carnival sells 4 times as much in cat supplies as in fish supplies. If total sales last week were $6,800, how much of each category was sold?	Solution: *Reasoning:* Fish supplies plus cat supplies equals total, $6,800. Let X = fish supplies Let $4X$ = cat supplies $X + 4X = 6,800$ $5X = 6,800$ $X = \$1,360$ = fish supplies $4X = \$5,440$ = cat supplies
Solving Business-Related Equations	5–4 133	Example 5: The Image, a men's clothing store, sells suits for $275 and sport coats for $180. Yesterday they made 20 sales, for a total of $4,360. a. How many suits and how many sport coats were sold? b. What were the dollar sales of each?	Solution a: *Reasoning:* The sum of the price multiplied by the quantity of each item is the total sales, $4,360. Let X = suit sales Let $20 - X$ = sport coat sales $275X + 180(20 - X) = 4,360$ $275X + 3,600 - 180X = 4,360$ $95X + 3,600 = 4,360$ $95X = 760$ $X = 8$ = number of suits sold $(20 - X) = 12$ = sport coats sold Solution b: 8 suits × $275 each = $2,200 12 coats × $180 each = $2,160
Solving Business Problems Using Ratio and Proportion	5–5 134	A ratio is a fraction that describes a comparison of two numbers or quantities. A proportion is a statement showing that two ratios are equal. Proportions are equations with "as" being the equal sign, and "is to" being the division bar.	Example 1: 12 is to 42 as 6 is to X $\dfrac{12}{42} = \dfrac{6}{X}$ $12X = 42(6)$

II, continued

Topic	P/O, Page	Important Concepts	Illustrative Examples
		Proportion problems are solved by cross-multiplication: 1. Let X represent the unknown quantity. 2. Set up the equation with one ratio on each side of the equal sign. 3. Multiply the numerator of the first ratio by the denominator of the second and place the product to the left of the equal sign. 4. Multiply the denominator of the first ratio by the numerator of the second and place the product to the right of the equal sign. 5. Solve the equation for X.	$12X = 252$ $\underline{X = 21}$ Example 2: If Larry works 6 hours for $150.00, how much can he expect to earn in a 42-hour week? $\dfrac{6}{150} = \dfrac{42}{X}$ $6X = 150(42)$ $6X = 6{,}300$ $\underline{X = \$1{,}050} =$ Larry's salary for 42 hours work

TRY-IT EXERCISE   SOLUTIONS

1. $W + 10 = 25$ *Proof:*
$$\begin{aligned} W + 10 &= 25 \\ -10 \quad &-10 \\ \hline W \quad &= 15 \\ \underline{W} &= \underline{15} \end{aligned}$$
$W + 10 = 25$
$\boxed{15} + 10 = 25$
$\underline{25 = 25}$

2. $A - 8 = 40$ *Proof:*
$$\begin{aligned} A - 8 &= 40 \\ +8 \quad &+8 \\ \hline A \quad &= 48 \\ \underline{A} &= \underline{48} \end{aligned}$$
$A - 8 = 40$
$\boxed{48} - 8 = 40$
$\underline{40 = 40}$

3. $Q + 30 = 100$ *Proof:*
$$\begin{aligned} Q + 30 &= 100 \\ -30 \quad &-30 \\ \hline Q \quad &= 70 \\ \underline{Q} &= \underline{70} \end{aligned}$$
$Q + 30 = 100$
$\boxed{70} + 30 = 100$
$\underline{100 = 100}$

4. $L - 3 = 7$ *Proof:*
$$\begin{aligned} L - 3 &= 7 \\ +3 \quad &+3 \\ \hline L \quad &= 10 \\ \underline{L} &= \underline{10} \end{aligned}$$
$L - 3 = 7$
$\boxed{10} - 3 = 7$
$\underline{7 = 7}$

5. $15L = 75$ *Proof:*
$$\dfrac{15L}{15} = \dfrac{75}{15}$$
$$\underline{L = 5}$$
$15L = 75$
$15(\boxed{5}) = 75$
$\underline{75 = 75}$

6. $\dfrac{Z}{8} = 2$ *Proof:*
$$(8)\dfrac{Z}{8} = 2(8)$$
$$\underline{Z = 16}$$
$\dfrac{Z}{8} = 2$
$\dfrac{\boxed{16}}{8} = 2$
$\underline{2 = 2}$

7. $16F = 80$ *Proof:*
$$\dfrac{16F}{16} = \dfrac{80}{16}$$
$$\underline{\underline{F = 5}}$$
$16F = 80$
$16(\boxed{5}) = 80$
$\underline{80 = 80}$

8. $\dfrac{C}{9} = 9$ *Proof:*
$$(9)\dfrac{C}{9} = 9(9)$$
$$\underline{C = 81}$$
$\dfrac{C}{9} = 9$
$\dfrac{\boxed{81}}{9} = 9$
$\underline{9 = 9}$

9. $12N + 14 = 50$ *Proof:*
$$\begin{aligned} 12N + 14 &= 50 \\ -14 \quad &-14 \\ \hline 12N \quad &= 36 \end{aligned}$$
$$\dfrac{12N}{12} = \dfrac{36}{12}$$
$$\underline{N = 3}$$
$12N + 14 = 50$
$12(\boxed{3}) + 14 = 50$
$36 + 14 = 50$
$\underline{50 = 50}$

10. $3W - 4 = 26$ *Proof:*
$$\begin{aligned} 3W - 4 &= 26 \\ +4 \quad &+4 \\ \hline 3W \quad &= 30 \end{aligned}$$
$$\dfrac{3W}{3} = \dfrac{30}{3}$$
$$\underline{W = 10}$$
$3W - 4 = 26$
$3(\boxed{10}) - 4 = 26$
$30 - 4 = 26$
$\underline{26 = 26}$

11. $\dfrac{F}{3} - 6 = 2$ *Proof:*
$$\begin{aligned} \dfrac{F}{3} - 6 &= 2 \\ +6 \quad &+6 \\ \hline \dfrac{F}{3} \quad &= 8 \end{aligned}$$
$$(3)\dfrac{F}{3} = 8(3)$$
$$\underline{F = 24}$$
$\dfrac{F}{3} - 6 = 2$
$\dfrac{\boxed{24}}{3} - 6 = 2$
$8 - 6 = 2$
$\underline{2 = 2}$

12. $\dfrac{Z}{5} + 15 = 24$ *Proof:*
$$\begin{aligned} \dfrac{Z}{5} + 15 &= 24 \\ -15 \quad &-15 \\ \hline \dfrac{Z}{5} \quad &= 9 \end{aligned}$$
$$(5)\dfrac{Z}{5} = 9(5)$$
$$\underline{Z = 45}$$
$\dfrac{Z}{5} + 15 = 24$
$\dfrac{\boxed{45}}{5} + 15 = 24$
$9 + 15 = 24$
$\underline{24 = 24}$

13. $4(5G + 6) = 64$ *Proof:*

$20G + 24 = 64$ $4(5G + 6) = 64$

$20G + 24 = 64$ $4(5\{2\} + 6) = 64$

$\underline{\quad -24 \quad -24 \quad}$ $4(10 + 6) = 64$

$20G \quad = 40$ $4(16) = 64$

$\dfrac{20G}{20} = \dfrac{40}{20}$ $\underline{64 = 64}$

$\underline{G = 2}$

14. $6(3H - 5) = 42$ *Proof:*

$18H - 30 = 42$ $6(3H - 5) = 42$

$18H - 30 = 42$ $6(3\{4\} - 5) = 42$

$\underline{\quad +30 \quad +30}$ $6(12 - 5) = 42$

$18H \quad = 72$ $6(7) = 42$

$\dfrac{18H}{18} = \dfrac{72}{18}$ $\underline{42 = 42}$

$\underline{H = 4}$

15. $X + 3 = 18 - 4X$ *Proof:*

$X + 3 = 18 - 4X$ $X + 3 = 18 - 4X$

$\underline{+4X \qquad\qquad +4X}$ $3 + 3 = 18 - 4(3)$

$5X + 3 = 18$ $6 = 18 - 12$

$5X + 3 = 18$ $\underline{6 = 6}$

$\underline{\quad -3 \quad -3 \quad}$

$5X \quad = 15$

$\dfrac{5X}{5} = \dfrac{15}{5}$

$\underline{X = 3}$

16. $9S + 8 - S = 2(2S + 8)$ *Proof:*

$9S + 8 - S = 4S + 16$ $9S + 8 - S = 2(2S + 8)$

$8S + 8 = 4S + 16$ $9(2) + 8 - 2 = 2(2\{2\} + 8)$

$8S + 8 = 4S + 16$ $18 + 8 - 2 = 2(4 + 8)$

$\underline{-4S \qquad -4S}$ $24 = 2(12)$

$4S + 8 = \qquad +16$ $\underline{24 = 24}$

$4S + 8 = 16$

$\underline{\quad -8 \quad -8 \quad}$

$4S \quad = 8$

$\dfrac{4S}{4} = \dfrac{8}{4}$

$\underline{S = 2}$

17. The <u>sum of</u> twice E <u>and</u> 9

$$2E + 9$$

18. 6 <u>times</u> N <u>divided by</u> Z

$$\frac{6N}{Z}$$

19. 8 <u>less than</u> half <u>of</u> F

$$\frac{1}{2}F - 8$$

20. \$45.75 <u>more than</u> the <u>product of</u> X and Y

$$XY + \$45.75$$

21. The <u>difference of</u> Q and 44

$$Q - 44$$

22. R <u>times</u> A <u>times</u> B

$$RAB$$

23. What number <u>increased by</u> 32 <u>yields</u> 125?

$$X + 32 = 125$$

24. 21 <u>less than</u> twice C <u>gives</u> 9.

$$2C - 21 = 9$$

25. 5 <u>more than</u> 6 <u>times</u> a number, <u>plus</u> 3 <u>times</u> that number, <u>is</u> 25.

$$6X + 5 + 3X = 25$$

26. The cost of G gallons <u>at</u> \$1.33 per gallon <u>equals</u> \$34.40.

$$\$1.33G = \$34.40$$

27. The area of a rectangle <u>is</u> the length <u>times</u> the width.

$$A = LW$$

28. What number <u>less</u> 12 <u>is</u> the average of A, B, and C?

$$X - 12 = \frac{A + B + C}{3}$$

29. *Reasoning:* Jose's sales <u>and</u> Bob's sales <u>equal</u> total sales, 44.

Let $X =$ Bob's sales

Let $X - 12 =$ Jose's sales

$X + X - 12 = 44$

$2X - 12 = 44$

$2X = 56$

$\dfrac{2X}{2} = \dfrac{56}{2}$

$X = 28$ <u>Bob's sales = 28 sets</u>   *Proof:*

$X - 12 = 28 - 12 = 16$ <u>Jose's sales = 16 sets</u> $X + X - 12 = 44$

     $28 + 28 - 12 = 44$

     $\underline{44 = 44}$

30. *Reasoning:* $\dfrac{1}{3}$ <u>of</u> the total checking accounts <u>are</u> corporations, 2,500.

Let $C =$ total checking accounts

$\dfrac{1}{3}C = 2,500$

$(3)\dfrac{1}{3}C = 2,500(3)$

$C = 7,500$

<u>Total checking accounts = 7,500</u>

Proof:

$\dfrac{1}{3}C = 2,500$

$\dfrac{1}{3}(7,500) = 2,500$

$\underline{2,500 = 2,500}$

31. *Reasoning:* Weight per carton <u>equals</u> the total weight <u>divided by</u> the number of cartons.

Let W = weight per carton

$$W = \frac{7{,}482}{58}$$

Proof:

$$W = \frac{7{,}482}{58}$$

$$W = 129$$

$$129 = \frac{7{,}482}{58}$$

<u>Weight per carton = 129 pounds</u>

$$\underline{129 = 129}$$

32. *Reasoning:* Soft goods <u>plus</u> hard goods <u>equals</u> total store sales, \$180,000.

Let X = hard goods

Let $3X$ = soft goods

$X + 3X = \$180{,}000$

$4X = 180{,}000$

Proof:

$$X + 3X = 180{,}000$$

$$\frac{4X}{4} = \frac{180{,}000}{4}$$

$$(45{,}000) + 3(45{,}000) = 180{,}000$$

$X = 45{,}000$ <u>hard goods = \$45,000</u> $45{,}000 + 135{,}000 = 180{,}000$

$3X = 3(45{,}000) = 135{,}000$ <u>soft goods = \$135,000</u> $\underline{180{,}000 = 180{,}000}$

33. *Reasoning:* Tables <u>plus</u> chairs <u>plus</u> sofas <u>equals</u> total items sold, 520.

Let X = tables

Let $4X$ = chairs

Let $2(4X)$ = sofas

$X + 4X + 2(4X) = 520$

$X + 4X + 8X = 520$

$13X = 520$

$$\frac{13X}{13} = \frac{520}{13}$$

$X = 40$ <u>tables sold = 40</u>

$4X = 4(40) = 160$ <u>chairs sold = 160</u>

$2(4X) = 2(4\{40\}) = 2(160) = 320$ <u>sofas sold = 320</u>

Proof:

$$X + 4X + 2(4X) = 520$$

$$(40) + 4(40) + 2(4\{40\}) = 520$$

$$40 + 160 + 2(160) = 520$$

$$40 + 160 + 320 = 520$$

$$\underline{520 = 520}$$

34. *Reasoning:* The <u>sum of</u> the price of each item <u>multiplied by</u> the quantity of each item <u>is</u> the total sales, \$3,400.
Remember: Let X equal the more expensive item, thereby avoiding negative numbers.

Let X = Quantity of heavy duty batteries

Let $40 - X$ = Quantity of regular batteries

Price times quantity of heavy duty batteries = $\$110X$

Price times quantity of regular batteries = $\$70(40 - X)$

$110X + 70(40 - X) = 3{,}400$

$110X + 2{,}800 - 70X = 3{,}400$

$40X + 2{,}800 = 3{,}400$

$40X = 600$

$$\frac{40X}{40} = \frac{600}{40}$$

$X = 15$ <u>Quantity of heavy duty batteries = 15</u>

$40 - X = 40 - 15 = 25$ <u>Quantity of regular batteries = 25</u>

Proof:

$$110X + 70(40 - X) = 3{,}400$$

$$110(15) + 70(40 - 15) = 3{,}400$$

$$1{,}650 + 70(25) = 3{,}400$$

$$1{,}650 + 1{,}750 = 3{,}400$$

$$\underline{3{,}400 = 3{,}400}$$

Now that we have calculated the quantity of each size battery, we can find the dollar sales:
Reasoning: Dollar sales <u>are</u> the price per battery <u>multiplied by</u> the quantity sold.

Let S = dollar sales

Heavy duty battery: $S = \$110(15) = \underline{\$1{,}650 \text{ in sales}}$

Regular battery: $S = \$70(25) = \underline{\$1{,}750 \text{ in sales}}$

35.

$$\frac{87.50}{7} = \frac{X}{35}$$

$$7X = 87.50(35)$$

$$7X = 3{,}062.50$$

$$\frac{7X}{7} = \frac{3{,}062.50}{7}$$

$$X = 437.50$$ Wilbur would earn $437.50 for 35 hours of work.

Proof:

$$\frac{87.50}{7} = \frac{X}{35}$$

$$\frac{87.50}{7} = \frac{437.50}{35}$$

$$12.50 = 12.50$$

Name_____

Class_____

Solve the following equations for the unknown, and prove your solutions:

1. $T + 45 = 110$
$T = \underline{65}$

2. $G - 24 = 75$
$G = \underline{99}$

3. $11K = 165$
$K = \underline{15}$

4. $3(2C - 5) = 45$
$C = \underline{10}$

5. $8X - 15 = 49$
$X = \underline{8}$

6. $\dfrac{S}{7} = 12$
$S = \underline{84}$

7. $B + 5 = 61 - 6B$
$B = \underline{8}$

8. $\dfrac{N}{4} - 7 = 8$
$N = \underline{60}$

9. $4(3X + 8) = 212$
$X = \underline{15}$

For the following statements, underline the key words and translate into *expressions*:

10. 15 <u>less than</u> <u>one-ninth</u> <u>of</u> P
$\dfrac{1}{9}P - 15$

11. The <u>difference</u> of $4R$ and 108
$4R - 108$

12. 3 <u>times</u> the <u>quantity</u> of H <u>minus</u> 233
$3(H - 233)$

13. 24 <u>more than</u> the <u>product of</u> Z and W
$ZW + 24$

For the following statements, underline the key words and translate into *equations*:

14. A number <u>decreased by</u> 4 <u>is</u> 25
$X - 4 = 25$

15. A number <u>totals</u> 4 <u>times</u> C <u>and</u> L
$X = 4C + L$

16. The cost of Q <u>at</u> $4.55 each <u>is</u> $76.21
$\$4.55Q = \$76.21$

17. 14 <u>less than</u> $3F$ <u>leaves</u> 38
$3F - 14 = 38$

18. 2 <u>more than</u> 6 <u>times</u> a number, <u>plus</u> 7 <u>times</u> that number, <u>is</u> that number <u>decreased by</u> 39
$6X + 2 + 7X = X - 39$

Set up and solve equations for each of the following business situations:

19. At a recent boat show, Atlas Marine sold 5 more boats than Blue Water Marine. If together they sold 33 boats, how many were sold by each company?
$X = $ Blue Water Marine $X + X + 5 = 33$
$X + 5 = $ Atlas Marine $2X + 5 = 33$
                           $2X = 28$
                        $X = \underline{14}$ Boats sold by Blue Water
                $X + 5 = \underline{19}$ Boats sold by Atlas Marine

20. One-seventh of the customers responding to a survey at Walton's Department Store were not satisfied with the merchandise selection. If 145 customers were not satisfied, how many customers responded to the survey?
$X = $ Total customers

$\dfrac{1}{7}X = 145$

$(7)\dfrac{1}{7}X = 145(7)$

$X = \underline{1,015} = $ Total customers

ANSWERS

1. _____ $T = 65$ _____
2. _____ $G = 99$ _____
3. _____ $K = 15$ _____
4. _____ $C = 10$ _____
5. _____ $X = 8$ _____
6. _____ $S = 84$ _____
7. _____ $B = 8$ _____
8. _____ $N = 60$ _____
9. _____ $X = 15$ _____
10. _____ $\dfrac{1}{9}P - 15$ _____
11. _____ $4R - 108$ _____
12. _____ $3(H - 233)$ _____
13. _____ $ZW + 24$ _____
14. _____ $X - 4 = 25$ _____
15. _____ $X = 4C + L$ _____
16. _____ $\$4.55Q = \$76.21$ _____
17. _____ $3F - 14 = 38$ _____
18. _____ $6X + 2 + 7X = X - 39$ _____
19. _____ Blue Water: 14 _____
       Atlas Marine: 19
20. _____ 1,015 _____

Complete worked out solutions for questions 1–9 appear in the appendix following the index.

ANSWERS

21. _____$55_____

22. _____$8,000 Muffins_____

_____$36,000 Donuts_____

23. _____95_____

24. a. _____225 Long_____

_____150 Short_____

b. _____$6,412.50_____

_____$3,450.00_____

25. _____$1.15_____

26. _____$60,000_____

_____$135,000_____

21. The Phone Booth, a telephone store, ordered 3 dozen cordless phones from the manufacturer. If the total order amounted to $1,980.00, what was the cost of each phone?

X = Cost per phone

$36X = 1,980$

$\dfrac{36X}{36} = \dfrac{1,980}{36}$

$X = \dfrac{1,980}{36}$

$X = \underline{\$55}$ Cost per phone

22. The Donut Hole sells $4\frac{1}{2}$ times as much in donuts as muffins. If total sales were $44,000 for May, what dollar amount of each was sold?

X = Muffins

$4\frac{1}{2}X$ = Donuts

$X + 4\frac{1}{2}X = 44,000$

$5\frac{1}{2}X = 44,000$

$X = \underline{\$8,000}$ Muffin sales

$4\frac{1}{2}X = \underline{\$36,000}$ Donut sales

23. For the same amount of light, a regular light bulb uses 20 watts less than twice the power of an energy-saver light bulb. If the regular bulb uses 170 watts, how much does the energy-saver bulb use?

X = Energy-saver bulb

$2X - 20$ = Regular bulb

$2X - 20 = 170$

$2X = 190$

$X = \underline{95}$ Watts for energy-saver bulb

24. A men's shop ordered short-sleeve shirts for $23 each and long-sleeve shirts for $28.50 each from a manufacturer.

   a. If the total order amounted to $9,862.50 for 375 shirts, how many of each were ordered?

X = Long-sleeve shirts

$375 - X$ = Short-sleeve shirts

$28.50X + 23(375 - X) = 9,862.50$

$28.50X + 8,625 - 23X = 9,862.50$

$5.50X + 8,625 = 9,862.50$

$5.50X = 1,237.50$

$X = \underline{225}$ Long-sleeve shirts

$375 - X = \underline{150}$ Short-sleeve shirts

   b. What was the dollar amount of each type of shirt ordered?

$\$28.50(225) = \underline{\$6,412.50}$ Amount long-sleeve

$\$23(150) = \underline{\$3,450.00}$ Amount short-sleeve

25. Handy Hardware is offering a 140-piece mechanics tool set plus a $65 tool chest for $226. What is the cost per tool?

X = Cost per tool

$140X + 65 = 226$

$140X = 161$

$X = \underline{\$1.15}$ Cost per tool

26. Denski and Schwartz invested $195,000 in a business venture. If Schwartz invested $2\frac{1}{4}$ times as much as Denski, how much did each invest?

X = Denski

$2\frac{1}{4}X$ = Schwartz

$X + 2\frac{1}{4}X = 195,000$

$3\frac{1}{4}X = 195,000$

$X = \underline{\$60,000}$ Denski's share

$2\frac{1}{4}X = \underline{\$135,000}$ Schwartz's share

27. A Hägen-Dazs ice cream shop sells sundaes for $3.60 and banana splits for $4.25. The shop sells 4 times as many sundaes as banana splits.

    a. If total sales amount to $3,730.00, how many of each dish are sold?

$$X = \text{Banana splits} \qquad 4.25X + 3.60(4X) = 3,730$$
$$4X = \text{Sundaes} \qquad\qquad 4.25X + 14.40X = 3,730$$
$$18.65X = 3,730$$
$$X = \underline{200} \text{ Banana splits sold}$$
$$4X = \underline{\underline{800}} \text{ Sundaes sold}$$

    b. What are the dollar sales of each?

$$\$4.25(200) = \underline{\$850} \text{ Sales of banana splits}$$
$$\$3.60(800) = \underline{\$2,880} \text{ Sales of sundaes}$$

28. What is the total cost to ship an order weighing 420 pounds if the breakdown is $.18 per pound for packing, $.12 per pound for insurance, $.37 per pound for transportation, and $148.60 for the shipping crate?

$$X = \text{Total cost of shipping}$$
$$X = .18(420) + .12(420) + .37(420) + 148.60$$
$$X = 75.60 + 50.40 + 155.40 + 148.60$$
$$X = \underline{\$430.00} \text{ Total shipping cost}$$

Use ratio and proportion to solve the following business situations:

29. At The Sports Authority, the inventory ratio of equipment to clothing is 8 to 5. If the clothing inventory amounts to $65,000, what is the amount of the equipment inventory?

$$\frac{8}{5} = \frac{X}{65,000} \qquad 5X = 8(65,000)$$
$$5X = 520,000$$
$$X = \underline{\$104,000} \text{ Equipment inventory}$$

30. If the interest on a $6,000 loan is $400, what would be the interest on a loan of $2,250?

$$\frac{6,000}{400} = \frac{2,250}{X} \qquad 6,000X = 400(2,250)$$
$$6,000X = 900,000$$
$$X = \underline{\$150} = \text{Interest}$$

31. If property insurance costs $.75 per $100 of coverage, how much will it cost Albright Enterprises to insure a building and equipment worth $182,000?

$$\frac{.75}{100} = \frac{X}{182,000} \qquad 100X = .75(182,000)$$
$$100X = 136,500$$
$$X = \underline{\$1,365} \text{ Insurance premium}$$

32. A recipe calls for $1\frac{1}{2}$ tablespoons of minced garlic for every $\frac{1}{4}$ pound of pasta. How much garlic would be required for $2\frac{1}{2}$ pounds of pasta?

$$\frac{1\frac{1}{2}}{\frac{1}{4}} = \frac{X}{2\frac{1}{2}} \qquad \begin{aligned} .25X &= 1.5(2.5) \\ .25X &= 3.75 \\ X &= \underline{15} \text{ Tablespoons garlic} \end{aligned}$$

33. A contractor is using a blueprint for a shopping center with a scale of 1.25 inches equals 4 feet. If a concrete slab is 18.75 inches on the blueprint, how many feet long is the slab?

$$\frac{1.25}{4} = \frac{18.75}{X} \qquad \begin{aligned} 1.25X &= 4(18.75) \\ 1.25X &= 75 \\ X &= \underline{60} \text{ Feet} \end{aligned}$$

Name_____

Class_____

ANSWERS

27. a.   Banana splits 200

       Sundaes 800

  b.   Banana splits $850

       Sundaes $2,880

28. $430.00

29. $104,000

30. $150

31. $1,365

32.   15

33.   60

ANSWERS

34. a. _____News: 12_____

_____Advertising: 36_____

b. _____Retail: 20_____

_____National: 12_____

_____Classified: 4_____

BUSINESS DECISION
Managing The Chronicle

34. You have just been hired as managing editor of *The Daily Chronicle,* a not-very-successful newspaper. In the past, *The Chronicle* contained one-half advertising and one-half news stories. Current industry research indicates a newspaper must have three times as much advertising as news stories in order to make money. In addition, the advertising must be divided in the following ratio: 5 to 3 to 1, retail advertising to national advertising to classified advertising. *The Chronicle* is typically 48 pages in length.

a. How many pages should be advertising and how many should be news stories?

X = News story pages
$3X$ = Advertising pages
$X + 3X = 48$
$4X = 48$
$X = \underline{\underline{12}}$ = Pages of news
$3X = \underline{\underline{36}}$ = Pages of advertising

b. Based on the industry ratios, how should the pages be divided among the three types of advertising?

Situation: Distribute 36 pages of advertising in the ratio of 5 to 3 to 1 (Retail + National + Classified).

Strategy: A ratio of 5:3:1 has 9 total parts (5 + 3 + 1).

Create a fraction for each variable with the total parts as the denominator. Next, multiply each fraction by the total number of advertising pages, 36.

$\dfrac{5}{9}$ = Retail advertising $\quad$ $\dfrac{5}{9}(36) = \underline{\underline{20}}$ Pages retail

$\dfrac{3}{9}$ = National advertising $\quad$ $\dfrac{3}{9}(36) = \underline{\underline{12}}$ Pages national

$\dfrac{1}{9}$ = Classified advertising $\quad$ $\dfrac{1}{9}(36) = \underline{\underline{4}}$ Pages classified

All the Math That's Fit to Learn

The Business Math Times

Volume V   **Using Equations to Solve Business Problems**   One Dollar

The Ultimate Homework Assignment

Fermat's Last Theorem

More than 350 years ago, a French mathematician, Pierre de Fermat, wrote a deceptively simple theorem in the margins of a math book, adding that he had created a "truly marvelous" proof of it but lacked space to show the worked-out theory.

Fermat claimed that equations of the form $X^2 + Y^2 = Z^2$ (the Pythagorean theorem) have no positive whole number solutions when the exponent is greater than 2. He died without ever offering his proof, and mathematicians have been trying ever since to prove "Fermat's Last Theorem."

In 1993 a professor at Princeton University, Dr. Andrew Wiles, claimed to have proven the theorem. Working feverishly and in secret—and without a computer—for seven years in his attic, Wiles apparently proved Fermat's theorem using math unheard of in Fermat's day. His solution filled 200 pages.

Although, to this day, scholars are not totally in agreement over Wiles' claim, the general consensus in the scientific community is that Wiles' revised proof is, in fact, "definitive!"

SOURCES: Gina Kolata, "350-Year-Old Math Mystery Finally Adds Up," *Miami Herald*, July 1, 1993: 1G. Kristin Leutwyler, "Finessing Fermat Again," *Scientific American*, February 1995: 16.

WITH VITAMIN X

ALGEBITS

AN EQUATION IN EVERY MOUTHFUL

BLAIR

Tips for Taking Math Tests

Before the Test

- Know exactly what material will be covered on the test and pace your study schedule accordingly.
- Get a restful night's sleep—don't study all night!
- Get up earlier than usual on test day to review your notes.
- Have a positive mental attitude about doing well on the test.
- Bring all necessary materials—calculator, 2–3 pencils, erasers, paper, ruler, etc.

During the Test

- Listen carefully to all verbal instructions. If you have any questions, or don't understand something, ask for clarification.
- If you feel nervous, close your eyes and take a few deep breaths.
- Read all written directions carefully.
- If there is an answer sheet, make sure you are putting your answers in the proper place. Use a note card or your finger to help you stay in the right spot.
- Budget your time. Spend the most time on those portions of the test that are worth the most points. Don't spend too much time on any one problem.
- Skip questions you don't know and come back to them at the end. Place a check by the questions you must return to.
- Be sure your answers are logical. On multiple choice tests, eliminate the answers that you know can't be right, and work from there.
- If time permits, double check your answers.

After the Test

- If you did well, reward yourself.
- If you didn't do so well, reward yourself for trying and learn from your mistakes.

SOURCE: Judith A. Muscha and Gary Robert Muscha, The Math Teacher's Book of Lists, Prentice Hall, 1995, pp. 55–56.

Did You Know?

As long ago as 2000 B.C., the Babylonians and the Egyptians posed problems that used algebra for their solution. For example, in the Rhind papyrus, dating from about 1650 B.C., problem 24 asks for the value of "heap" if heap and a seventh of heap is 19. In modern terminology and notation, this problem could be formulated as "What number plus a seventh of that number is 19?" $X + \frac{1}{7}X = 19$

SOURCES: "Word for Word" syndicated column, March 20, 1993; and Grolier Encyclopedia (CD-ROM), Grolier Electronic Publishing, Inc., 1992.

Brainteaser

The Sweetie Pie Bakery sold 100 apple pies in 5 days. Each day they sold 6 more than the day before. How many pies were sold on the first day? (Use your knowledge of equations to solve this one.)

SOURCE: Adapted from James Fixx, *Games for the Super Intelligent* (New York: Doubleday, 1972).

Answer to Last Issue's Brainteaser

31.7 Years

1 minute = $1 x 60 = $60

1 hour = $60 x 60 = $3,600

1 day = $3,600 x 24 = $86,400

1 year = $86,400 x 365 = $31,536,000

$$\frac{1,000,000,000}{31,536,000} = 31.7 \text{ years}$$

Chapter 6

Percents and their Applications in Business

Performance Objectives

UNDERSTANDING AND CONVERTING PERCENTS

It takes only a glance at the business section of a newspaper or an annual report of a company to see how extensively percents are applied in business. Percents are the primary way of measuring change among business variables. For example, a business might report "revenue is up 6% this year" or "expenses have been cut by 2.3% this month." Interest rates, commissions, and many taxes are expressed in percent form. You may have heard phrases like these: "Sunnyside Bank charged 12% on the loan," "A real estate broker made 5% commission on the sale of the property," or "The state charges a $6\frac{1}{2}$% sales tax." Even price changes are frequently advertised as percents, "Sears Dishwasher Sale—All Models, 25% off!"

To this point, we have learned that fractions and decimals are two ways of representing parts of a whole. Percents are another way of expressing quantity with relation to a whole. **Percent** means *per hundred* or *parts per hundred,* and is represented by the **percent sign, %.** Percents are numbers equal to a fraction with a denominator of 100. Five percent, for example, means 5 parts out of 100, and may be written in the following ways:

$$5 \text{ percent} \quad 5\% \quad 5 \text{ hundredths} \quad \frac{5}{100} \quad .05$$

Before performing any mathematical calculations with percents, they must be converted to either decimals or fractions. Although this function is performed automatically by the percent key on a calculator, Section I of this chapter covers the procedures for making these conversions manually. Sections II and III introduce you to some very important applications of percents in business.

Percents are a way of expressing quantity with relation to a whole. For example, a supermarket chain might report "produce sales represent 15% of total sales."

● **percent**
A way of representing the parts of a whole. Percent means *per hundred* or *parts per hundred.*

● **percent sign**
The symbol, %, used to represent percents. For example, one percent would be written 1%.

6-1 Converting Percents to Decimals and Decimals to Percents

Since percents are numbers expressed as parts per 100, the percent sign, %, means multiplication by $\frac{1}{100}$. Therefore, 25% means

$$25\% = 25 \times \frac{1}{100} = \frac{25}{100} = .25$$

STEPS FOR CONVERTING A PERCENT TO A DECIMAL:

Step 1. Remove the percent sign.

Step 2. Move the decimal point two places to the left. Remember, if there is no decimal point, it is understood to be to the right of the digit in the ones place (2 = 2.).

Step 3. If the percent is a fraction, such as $\frac{3}{8}$%, or a mixed number, such as $4\frac{3}{4}$%, first change the fraction to a decimal, then follow Steps 1 and 2 above.

$$\frac{3}{8}\% = .375\% = .00375 \qquad 4\frac{3}{4}\% = 4.75\% = .0475$$

Step 4. If the percent is a fraction such as $\frac{2}{3}$%, which converts to a repeating decimal, .66666, round the decimal to hundredths, .67, then follow Steps 1 and 2 above.

$$\frac{2}{3}\% = .67\% = .0067$$

Convert the following percents to decimals:

a. 44%   **b.** 233%   **c.** 56.4%   **d.** .68%   **e.** $18\frac{1}{4}$%   **f.** $\frac{1}{8}$%   **g.** $9\frac{1}{3}$%

SOLUTION STRATEGY

Remove the percent sign and move the decimal point two places to the left:

a. $44\% = \underline{\underline{.44}}$ **b.** $233\% = \underline{\underline{2.33}}$ **c.** $56.4\% = \underline{\underline{.564}}$ **d.** $.68\% = \underline{\underline{.0068}}$

e. $18\frac{1}{4}\% = 18.25\% = \underline{\underline{.1825}}$ **f.** $\frac{1}{8}\% = .125\% = \underline{\underline{.00125}}$ **g.** $9\frac{1}{3}\% = 9.33 = \underline{\underline{.0933}}$

TRY-IT   EXERCISES

Convert the following percents to decimals:

1. 27%   **2.** 472%   **3.** 93.7%   **4.** .81%   **5.** $12\frac{3}{4}$%   **6.** $\frac{7}{8}$%

Check your answers with the solutions on page 177.

STEPS FOR CONVERTING A DECIMAL OR WHOLE NUMBER TO A PERCENT:

Step 1. Move the decimal point two places to the right.

Step 2. Add a percent sign to the number.

Step 3. If there are fractions involved, such as $\frac{3}{4}$, convert them to decimals first, then proceed with Steps 1 and 2 above.

$$\frac{3}{4} = .75 = 75\%$$

Convert the following decimals or whole numbers to percents:

a. .5   **b.** 3.7   **c.** .044   **d.** $.09\frac{3}{5}$ **e.** 7   **f.** $6\frac{1}{2}$

SOLUTION STRATEGY

Move the decimal point two places to the right and add a percent sign.

a. $.5 = \underline{50\%}$ **b.** $3.7 = \underline{370\%}$ **c.** $.044 = \underline{4.4\%}$

d. $.09\frac{3}{5} = .096 = \underline{9.6\%}$ **e.** $7 = \underline{700\%}$ **f.** $6\frac{1}{2} = 6.5 = \underline{650\%}$

T R Y - I T **EXERCISES**

Convert the following decimals or whole numbers to percents:

7. .8 **8.** 1.4 **9.** .0023 **10.** .016$\frac{2}{5}$ **11.** 19 **12.** .57$\frac{2}{3}$

Check your answers with the solutions on page 177.

6-2 Converting Percents to Fractions and Fractions to Percents

STEPS FOR CONVERTING A PERCENT TO A FRACTION:

Step 1. Remove the percent sign.

Step 2. (*If the percent is a whole number*) Write a fraction with the percent as the numerator and 100 as the denominator. If that fraction is improper, change it to a mixed number. Reduce the fraction to lowest terms.

or

Step 2. (*If the percent is a fraction*) Multiply the number by $\frac{1}{100}$ and reduce to lowest terms.

or

Step 2. (*If the percent is a decimal*) Convert it to a fraction and multiply by $\frac{1}{100}$. Reduce to lowest terms.

EXAMPLES

Convert the following percents to reduced fractions, mixed numbers, or whole numbers:

a. 3% **b.** 57% **c.** $2\frac{1}{2}$% **d.** 150% **e.** 4.5% **f.** 600%

SOLUTION STRATEGY

a. $3\% = \dfrac{3}{100}$ **b.** $57\% = \dfrac{57}{100}$ **c.** $2\frac{1}{2}\% = \dfrac{5}{2} \times \dfrac{1}{100} = \dfrac{5}{200} = \dfrac{1}{40}$

d. $150\% = \dfrac{150}{100} = 1\dfrac{50}{100} = 1\dfrac{1}{2}$ **e.** $4.5\% = 4\frac{1}{2}\% = \dfrac{9}{2} \times \dfrac{1}{100} = \dfrac{9}{200}$ **f.** $600\% = \dfrac{600}{100} = 6$

T R Y - I T **EXERCISES**

Convert the following percents to reduced fractions, mixed numbers, or whole numbers:

13. 9% **14.** 23% **15.** 75% **16.** 225% **17.** 8.7% **18.** 1,000%

Check your answers with the solutions on page 177.

STEPS FOR CONVERTING FRACTIONS OR MIXED NUMBERS TO PERCENTS:

Step 1. Change the fraction to a decimal by dividing the numerator by the denominator.

Step 2. Move the decimal point two places to the right.

Step 3. Write a percent sign after the number.

EXAMPLES

Convert the following fractions or mixed numbers to percents:

a. $\dfrac{1}{10}$ **b.** $\dfrac{69}{100}$ **c.** $\dfrac{15}{4}$ **d.** $4\dfrac{3}{8}$ **e.** $\dfrac{18}{25}$ **f.** $13\dfrac{1}{2}$

SOLUTION STRATEGY

Change the fractions to decimals by dividing the denominator into the numerator, then move the decimal point two places to the right and add a percent sign.

a. $\dfrac{1}{10} = .10 = \underline{\underline{10\%}}$ **b.** $\dfrac{69}{100} = .69 = \underline{\underline{69\%}}$ **c.** $\dfrac{15}{4} = 3\dfrac{3}{4} = 3.75 = \underline{\underline{375\%}}$

d. $4\dfrac{3}{8} = 4.375 = \underline{\underline{437.5\%}}$ **e.** $\dfrac{18}{25} = .72 = \underline{\underline{72\%}}$ **f.** $13\dfrac{1}{2} = 13.5 = \underline{\underline{1350\%}}$

TRY-IT   EXERCISES

Convert the following fractions or mixed numbers to percents:

19. $\dfrac{1}{5}$ **20.** $\dfrac{70}{200}$ **21.** $\dfrac{23}{5}$ **22.** $6\dfrac{9}{10}$ **23.** $\dfrac{45}{54}$ **24.** $140\dfrac{1}{8}$

Check your answers with the solutions on pages 177–178.

 REVIEW EXERCISES   CHAPTER 6—SECTION I

Convert the following percents to decimals:

1. 28%   **2.** 76%   **3.** 13.4%   **4.** 121%   **5.** 42.68%

   $\underline{\underline{.28}}$ $\underline{\underline{.76}}$ $\underline{\underline{.134}}$ $\underline{\underline{1.21}}$ $\underline{\underline{.4268}}$

6. $6\dfrac{1}{2}\%$ **7.** .02%   **8.** $\dfrac{3}{5}\%$ **9.** $125\dfrac{1}{6}\%$ **10.** 2,000%

  $6.5\% = \underline{\underline{.065}}$ $\underline{\underline{.0002}}$ $.6\% = \underline{\underline{.006}}$ $125.17\% = \underline{\underline{1.2517}}$ $\underline{\underline{20.0}}$

Convert the following decimals or whole numbers to percents:

11. 3.5   **12.** .11   **13.** 46   **14.** $.34\dfrac{1}{2}$ **15.** .00935

  $\underline{\underline{350\%}}$ $\underline{\underline{11\%}}$ $\underline{\underline{4600\%}}$ $.345 = \underline{\underline{34.5\%}}$ $\underline{\underline{.935\%}}$

16. $.9\frac{3}{4}$

$.975 = \underline{\underline{97.5\%}}$

17. 164

$\underline{\underline{16,400\%}}$

18. .04

$\underline{\underline{4\%}}$

19. 5.33

$\underline{\underline{533\%}}$

20. $1.15\frac{5}{8}$

$1.15625 = \underline{\underline{115.625\%}}$

Convert the following percents to reduced fractions, mixed numbers, or whole numbers:

21. 5%

$\frac{5}{100} = \underline{\underline{\frac{1}{20}}}$

22. 75%

$\frac{75}{100} = \underline{\underline{\frac{3}{4}}}$

23. 89%

$\underline{\underline{\frac{89}{100}}}$

24. 230%

$\frac{230}{100} = 2\frac{30}{100} = \underline{\underline{2\frac{3}{10}}}$

25. 38%

$\frac{38}{100} = \underline{\underline{\frac{19}{50}}}$

26. 37.5%

$37\frac{1}{2} \times \frac{1}{100} = \frac{75}{2} \times \frac{1}{100} = \frac{75}{200} = \underline{\underline{\frac{3}{8}}}$

27. $62\frac{1}{2}\%$

$62\frac{1}{2} \times \frac{1}{100} = \frac{125}{2} \times \frac{1}{100} = \frac{125}{200} = \underline{\underline{\frac{5}{8}}}$

28. 450%

$\frac{450}{100} = 4\frac{50}{100} = \underline{\underline{4\frac{1}{2}}}$

29. 125%

$\frac{125}{100} = 1\frac{25}{100} = \underline{\underline{1\frac{1}{4}}}$

30. .8%

$\frac{8}{10} \times \frac{1}{100} = \frac{8}{1000} = \underline{\underline{\frac{1}{125}}}$

Convert the following fractions or mixed numbers to percents:

31. $\frac{3}{4}$

$.75 = \underline{\underline{75\%}}$

32. $\frac{1}{8}$

$.125 = \underline{\underline{12.5\%}}$

33. $\frac{12}{5}$

$2\frac{2}{5} = 2.4 = \underline{\underline{240\%}}$

34. $6\frac{3}{10}$

$6.3 = \underline{\underline{630\%}}$

35. $\frac{125}{100}$

$1\frac{1}{4} = 1.25 = \underline{\underline{125\%}}$

36. $\frac{78}{24}$

$3.25 = \underline{\underline{325\%}}$

37. $\frac{3}{16}$

$.1875 = \underline{\underline{18.75\%}}$

38. $4\frac{1}{5}$

$4.2 = \underline{\underline{420\%}}$

39. $\frac{35}{100}$

$.35 = \underline{\underline{35\%}}$

40. $\frac{375}{1,000}$

$.375 = \underline{\underline{37.5\%}}$

SECTION II

USING THE PERCENTAGE FORMULA TO SOLVE BUSINESS PROBLEMS

Now that we have learned to manipulate percents, let's look at some of their practical applications in business. Percent problems involve the use of equations known as the percentage formulas. These formulas have three variables: the **base**, the **portion**, and the **rate**. In business situations, two of the variables will be given, and are the knowns; one of the variables will be the unknown.

Once the variables have been properly identified, the equations are quite simple to solve. The variables have the following characteristics, which should be used to help identify them:

BASE: The base is the number that represents 100%, or the whole thing. It is the starting point, the beginning, or total value of something. The base is often preceded by the word "of" in the written statement of the situation because it is multiplied by the rate.

PORTION: The portion is the number that represents a part of the base. The portion is always in the same terms as the base. For example, if the base is dollars, the portion is dollars; if the base is people, the portion is people; if the base is production units, the portion will be production units. The portion often has a unique characteristic that is being measured or compared to the base. For example, if the base is the total number of cars in a parking lot, the portion could be the part of the total cars that are convertibles (the unique characteristic).

RATE: The rate is easily identified. It is the variable with the % sign or the word *percent*. It defines what part the portion is of the base. If the rate is under 100%, the portion is less than the base. If the rate is 100%, the portion is equal to the base. If the rate is over 100%, the portion is greater than the base.

● **base**
The variable of the percentage formula that represents 100%, or the whole thing.

● **portion**
The variable of the percentage formula that represents a part of the base.

● **rate**
The variable of the percentage formula that defines how much or what part the portion is of the base. The rate is the variable with the percent sign.

The following percentage formulas are used to solve percent problems:

$$\text{Portion} = \text{Rate} \times \text{Base} \qquad P = R \times B$$

$$\text{Rate} = \frac{\text{Portion}}{\text{Base}} \qquad R = \frac{P}{B}$$

$$\text{Base} = \frac{\text{Portion}}{\text{Rate}} \qquad B = \frac{P}{R}$$

STEPS FOR SOLVING PERCENTAGE PROBLEMS:

Step 1. Identify the two knowns and the unknown.

Step 2. Choose the formula that solves for that unknown.

Step 3. Solve the equation by substituting the known values for the letters in the formula.

Hint: By remembering the one basic formula, $P = R \times B$, you can derive the other two using your knowledge of solving equations from Chapter 5. Since multiplication is indicated, we isolate the unknown by performing the inverse or opposite operation, division.

To solve for rate, R, divide both sides of the equation by B:

$$P = R \times B \;\rightarrow\; \frac{P}{B} = \frac{R \times \cancel{B}}{\cancel{B}} \;\rightarrow\; \frac{P}{B} = R$$

To solve for base, B, divide both sides of the equation by R:

$$P = R \times B \;\rightarrow\; \frac{P}{R} = \frac{\cancel{R} \times B}{\cancel{R}} \;\rightarrow\; \frac{P}{R} = B$$

Another method for remembering the percentage formulas is by using the Magic Triangle.

The Magic Triangle

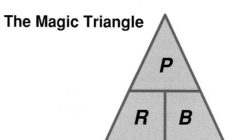

The triangle is divided into three sections, representing the portion, rate, and base. By circling or covering the letter in the triangle that corresponds to the unknown of the problem, the triangle will "magically" reveal the correct formula to use.

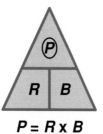

$$P = R \times B$$

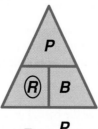

$$R = \frac{P}{B}$$

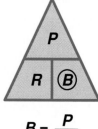

$$B = \frac{P}{R}$$

$$P = R \times B$$

6-3 Solving for the Portion

Remember, the portion is a part of the whole, and will always be in the same terms as the base. It is found by multiplying the rate times the base: $P = R \times B$. The following examples will demonstrate solving for the portion.

EXAMPLE

What is the portion if the base is $400 and the rate is 12%?

SOLUTION STRATEGY

In this basic problem, simply substitute the known numbers for the letters in the formula, portion = rate × base. In this problem, 12% is the rate, and $400 is the base. Don't forget to convert the percent (rate) to a decimal by deleting the % sign and moving the decimal point two places to the left (12% = .12).

$$P = R \times B$$
$$P = 12\% \times 400 = .12 \times 400 = 48$$
$$\underline{\text{Portion} = \$48}$$

EXAMPLE

What number is 43.5% of 250?

SOLUTION STRATEGY

In this problem, the rate is easily identified as the term with the % sign. The base, or whole amount, is preceded by the word "of." We use the formula, portion = rate × base, substituting the knowns for the letters that represent them.

$$P = R \times B$$
$$P = 43.5\% \times 250 = .435 \times 250 = 108.75$$
$$\underline{\text{Portion} = 108.75}$$

EXAMPLE

An electronics firm made 6,000 radios last week. If 2% of them were defective, how many defective radios were produced?

SOLUTION STRATEGY

To solve this problem, we must first identify the variables. Because 2% has the percent sign, it is the rate. The terms are radios; the total number of radios (6,000) is the base. The unique characteristic of the portion, the unknown, is that they were defective.

$$P = R \times B$$
$$P = 2\% \times 6,000 = .02 \times 6,000 = 120$$
$$\underline{\text{Portion} = 120 = \text{Number of defective radios last week}}$$

TRY-IT   EXERCISES

Solve the following for the portion:

25. What is the portion if the base is 980 and the rate is 55%?

26. What number is 72% of 3,200?

27. A company has 1,250 employees. 16% constitute the sales staff. How many employees are in sales?

28. If Sunshine Savings & Loan requires a 15% down payment on a mortgage loan, what is the down payment needed to finance a $148,500 home?

Check your answers with the solutions on page 178.

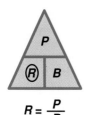

$$R = \frac{P}{B}$$

6-4 Solving for the Rate

The rate is the variable that describes what part of the base is represented by the portion. It is *always* the term with the percent sign. When solving for the rate, your answer will be a decimal. Be sure to convert the decimal to a percent by moving the decimal point two places to the right and adding a percent sign. We use the formula

$$\text{Rate} = \frac{\text{Portion}}{\text{Base}} \text{ or } R = \frac{P}{B}$$

The following examples demonstrate solving for the rate.

EXAMPLE

What is the rate if the base is 160 and the portion is 40?

SOLUTION STRATEGY

In this basic problem, we simply substitute the known numbers for the letters in the formula.

$$\text{Rate} = \frac{\text{Portion}}{\text{Base}}$$

$$R = \frac{P}{B}$$

$$R = \frac{40}{160} = .25 = 25\%$$

$$\underline{\text{Rate} = 25\%}$$

EXAMPLE

What percent of 700 is 56?

SOLUTION STRATEGY

This problem asks what percent, indicating that the rate is the unknown. The 700 is preceded by the word "of" and is therefore the base. The 56 is part of the base and is therefore the portion. Once again we use the formula $R = P \div B$ substituting the knowns for the letters that represent them.

$$R = \frac{P}{B}$$

$$R = \frac{56}{700} = .08 = 8\%$$

$$\underline{\text{Rate} = 8\%}$$

A retail chain of pet shops placed an order for 560 fish tanks. If only 490 tanks were delivered, what percent of the order was received?

SOLUTION STRATEGY

The first step in solving this problem is to identify the variables. The statement asks what percent, therefore, the rate is the unknown. Because 560 is the total order, it is the base; 490 is a part of the total and is therefore the portion. Note that the base and the portion are in the same terms, fish tanks; the unique characteristic of the portion is that 490 tanks *were delivered*.

$$R = \frac{P}{B}$$

$$R = \frac{490}{560} = .875 = 87.5\%$$

$$\underline{\text{Rate} = 87.5\% = \text{Percent of the order received}}$$

TRY-IT EXERCISES

Solve the following for the rate, rounding to tenths when necessary:

29. What is the rate if the base is 21 and the portion is 9?

30. 67 is what percent of 142?

31. A contract called for 18,000 square feet of tile to be installed in a shopping mall. In the first week 5,400 feet of tile was completed. What percent of the job has been completed?

32. During a recent sale, Image Makers, a boutique, sold $5,518 in men's business suits. If total sales amounted to $8,900, what percent of the sales were suits?

Check your answers with the solutions on page 178.

6-5 Solving for the Base

In order to solve business situations in which the whole or total amount is the unknown, we use the formula

$$\text{Base} = \frac{\text{Portion}}{\text{Rate}} \text{ or } B = \frac{P}{R}$$

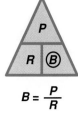

$$B = \frac{P}{R}$$

The following examples illustrate solving for the base.

EXAMPLE

What is the base if the rate is 21% and the portion is 58.8?

SOLUTION STRATEGY

In this basic problem, we simply substitute the known values for the letters in the formula. Remember, the rate must be converted from a percent to a decimal.

$$B = \frac{P}{R}$$

$$B = \frac{58.8}{21\%} = \frac{58.8}{.21} = 280$$

$$\underline{Base = 280}$$

EXAMPLE

75 is 15% of what number?

SOLUTION STRATEGY

Remember, the base is usually identified as the value preceded by "of" in the statement. In this case, that value is the unknown. Because 15 has the percent sign, it is the rate and 75 is the part of the whole, or the portion.

$$B = \frac{P}{R}$$

$$B = \frac{75}{15\%} = \frac{75}{.15} = 500$$

$$\underline{Base = 500}$$

EXAMPLE

Sidekicks, an athletic shoe store chain, reports that 28% of total sales are from Nike products. If last week's Nike sales were $15,400, what is the total amount of sales for the week?

SOLUTION STRATEGY

In this problem, the total amount of sales, the base, is the unknown. Because 28% has the percent sign, it is the rate, and $15,400 is the portion. Note again, the portion is in the same terms as the base, dollar sales; however, the unique characteristic is that the portion represents Nike sales.

$$B = \frac{P}{R}$$

$$B = \frac{15,400}{28\%} = \frac{15,400}{.28} = 55,000$$

$$\underline{Base = \$55,000 = \text{Total sales for the week}}$$

TRY-IT   EXERCISES

Solve the following for the base, rounding answers to hundredths or the nearest cent when necessary:

33. What is the base if the rate is 40% and the portion is 690?

34. $550 is 88% of what amount?

35. In a machine shop, 35% of the motor repairs are for broken shafts. If 126 motors had broken shafts last month, how many total motors were repaired?

36. At Office Depot, 75% of the copy paper sold is letter size. If 3,420 reams of letter size were sold, how many total reams of copy paper were sold?

Check your answers with the solutions on page 178.

REVIEW EXERCISES   CHAPTER 6—SECTION II

Solve the following for the portion, rounding to hundredths when necessary:

1. 15% of 380 is _____

$P = R \times B = .15 \times 380 = \underline{57}$

2. 3.6% of 1,800 is _____

$P = R \times B = .036 \times 1800 = \underline{64.8}$

3. 200% of 45 is _____

$P = R \times B = 2 \times 45 = \underline{90}$

4. $5\frac{1}{2}$% of $600 is _____

$P = R \times B = .055 \times 600 = \underline{33}$

5. What is the portion if the base is 450 and the rate is 19%?

$P = R \times B = .19 \times 450 = \underline{85.5}$

6. What is the portion if the base is 1,650 and the rate is 150%?

$P = R \times B = 1.5 \times 1,650 = \underline{2,475}$

7. What number is 35.2% of 184?

$P = R \times B = .352 \times 184 = \underline{64.77}$

8. What number is .8% of 500?

$P = R \times B = .008 \times 500 = \underline{4}$

9. What number is $15\frac{4}{5}$% of 360?

$P = R \times B = .158 \times 360 = \underline{56.88}$

10. What number is 258% of 2,500?

$P = R \times B = 2.58 \times 2,500 = \underline{6,450}$

Solve the following for the rate, rounding to a tenth percent when necessary:

11. 40 is _____ % of 125

$R = \dfrac{P}{B} = \dfrac{40}{125} = .32 = \underline{32\%}$

12. _____ % of 50 is 23

$R = \dfrac{P}{B} = \dfrac{23}{50} = .46 = \underline{46\%}$

13. 600 is _____ % of 240

$R = \dfrac{P}{B} = \dfrac{600}{240} = 2.5 = \underline{250\%}$

14. What is the rate if the base is 288 and the portion is 50?

$R = \dfrac{P}{B} = \dfrac{50}{288} = .1736 = \underline{17.4\%}$

15. What is the rate if the portion is 21.6 and the base is 160?

$R = \dfrac{P}{B} = \dfrac{21.6}{160} = .135 = \underline{13.5\%}$

16. What is the rate if the base is $3,450 and the portion is $290?

$R = \dfrac{P}{B} = \dfrac{290}{3,450} = .0840 = \underline{8.4\%}$

17. What percent of 77 is 23?

$R = \dfrac{P}{B} = \dfrac{23}{77} = .2987 = \underline{29.9\%}$

18. What percent of 1,600 is 1,900?

$R = \dfrac{P}{B} = \dfrac{1900}{1600} = 1.1875 = \underline{118.8\%}$

19. 68 is what percent of 262?

$$R = \frac{P}{B} = \frac{68}{262} = .2595 = \underline{\underline{26\%}}$$

20. $7.80 is what percent of $58.60?

$$R = \frac{P}{B} = \frac{7.80}{58.60} = .1331 = \underline{\underline{13.3\%}}$$

Solve the following for the base, rounding to hundredths when necessary:

21. 69 is 15% of _____

$$B = \frac{P}{R} = \frac{69}{.15} = \underline{\underline{460}}$$

22. 360 is 150% of _____

$$B = \frac{P}{R} = \frac{360}{1.5} = \underline{\underline{240}}$$

23. 6.45 is $18\frac{1}{2}$% of _____

$$B = \frac{P}{R} = \frac{6.45}{.185} = \underline{\underline{34.86}}$$

24. What is the base if the rate is 16.8% and the portion is 451?

$$B = \frac{P}{R} = \frac{451}{.168} = \underline{\underline{2684.52}}$$

25. What is the base if the portion is 10 and the rate is $2\frac{3}{4}$%?

$$B = \frac{P}{R} = \frac{10}{.0275} = \underline{\underline{363.64}}$$

26. What is the base if the portion is $4,530 and the rate is 35%?

$$B = \frac{P}{R} = \frac{45}{.35} = \underline{\underline{\$128.57}}$$

27. 60 is 15% of what number?

$$B = \frac{P}{R} = \frac{60}{.15} = \underline{\underline{400}}$$

28. 160 is 130% of what number?

$$B = \frac{P}{R} = \frac{160}{1.3} = \underline{\underline{123.08}}$$

29. $46.50 is $86\frac{2}{3}$% of what number?

$$B = \frac{P}{R} = \frac{46.50}{.8667} = \underline{\underline{\$53.65}}$$

30. .55 is 21.4% of what number?

$$B = \frac{P}{R} = \frac{.55}{.214} = \underline{\underline{2.57}}$$

Solve the following word problems for the portion, rate, or base:

31. Iva Foster owns 37% of a boutique. If the total worth of the business is $160,000, how much is Iva's share?

$$P = R \times B = .37 \times 160,000 = \underline{\underline{\$59,200}}$$

32. What is the sales tax rate in a state where the tax on a purchase of $464.00 is $25.52?

$$R = \frac{P}{B} = \frac{25.52}{464} = .055 = \underline{\underline{5.5\%}}$$

33. A local newspaper reports that 28% of its advertising is for department stores. If department store advertising amounts to $46,200, what is the total advertising revenue of the newspaper?

$$B = \frac{P}{R} = \frac{46,200}{.28} = \underline{\underline{\$165,000}}$$

34. A Chevrolet assembly line produced 1,650 cars on Tuesday. If 759 of the cars were convertibles, what percent of the production was convertibles?

$$R = \frac{P}{B} = \frac{759}{1650} = \underline{\underline{46\%}}$$

35. If Eddie Dawson, a real estate agent, earned $6\frac{1}{2}$% commission on the sale of property valued at $210,000, how much was Eddie's commission?

$P = R \times B = .065 \times 210,000 = \underline{\$13,650}$

36. Thirty percent of the inventory of a Nine West shoe store is in high heels. If the store has 846 pairs of high heels in stock, how many total pairs of shoes are in the inventory?

$B = \dfrac{P}{R} = \dfrac{846}{.3} = \underline{\underline{2,820}}$

37. In a state with sales tax of $3\frac{1}{4}$%, what is the tax on a purchase of $4,380?

$P = R \times B = .0325 \times 4,380 = \underline{\$142.35}$

38. Friendly Ford advertised a down payment of $1,200 on a Mustang valued at $14,700. What is the percent of the down payment? Round to a tenth percent.

$R = \dfrac{P}{B} = \dfrac{1,200}{14,700} = .0816 = \underline{\underline{8.2\%}}$

39. Carmel Highland, a sales associate for a large company, successfully makes the sale on 40% of her presentations. If she made 25 presentations last week, how many sales did she make?

$P = R \times B = .4 \times 25 = \underline{10}$

40. A quality control process finds 17.2 defects for every 8,600 units of production. What percent of the production is defective?

$R = \dfrac{P}{B} = \dfrac{17.2}{8,600} = .002 = \underline{.2\%}$

41. The Muffin Company employs 68 part-time workers. If this represents 4% of the total work force, how many people work for the company?

$B = \dfrac{P}{R} = \dfrac{68}{.04} = \underline{\underline{1,700}}$

42. Twenty-six percent of the clerical workers responding to a survey used WordPerfect as their primary word-processing software. If 1,900 people were interviewed, how many used WordPerfect?

$P = R \times B = .26 \times 1,900 = \underline{\underline{494}}$

43. A corporation earned $457,800 last year. If their tax rate is $13\frac{3}{8}\%$, how much tax was paid?

$P = R \times B = .13375 \times 457,800 = \underline{\$61,230.75}$

44. In June, the New York Yankees won 15 games and lost 9. What percent of the games did they win? (Hint: Use total games played as the base.)

Total games = Base = 24

$R = \dfrac{P}{B} = \dfrac{15}{24} = .625 = \underline{62.5\%}$

45. At a recent banquet, a caterer served 152 chicken dinners, 133 steak dinners, and 95 fish dinners. What percent of the total meals served was each type of dinner? (Hint: Use total meals served as the base.)

Total meals = Base = 380

Steak: $R = \dfrac{P}{B} = \dfrac{133}{380} = .35 = \underline{\underline{35\%}}$

Chicken: $R = \dfrac{P}{B} = \dfrac{152}{380} = .4 = \underline{\underline{40\%}}$ Fish: $R = \dfrac{P}{B} = \dfrac{95}{380} = .25 = \underline{\underline{25\%}}$

SECTION III

SOLVING OTHER BUSINESS PROBLEMS INVOLVING PERCENTS

In addition to the basic percentage formulas, percents are used in many other ways in business. Measuring increases and decreases, comparing results from one year to another, and reporting economic activity and trends are just a few of these applications.

The ability of managers to make correct decisions is fundamental to success in business. These decisions require accurate and up-to-date information. Measuring percent changes in business activity is an important source of this information. Percents often describe a situation in a more informative way than simply the raw data alone.

For example, a company reports a profit of $50,000 for the year. Although the number $50,000 is correct, it doesn't give a perspective of whether that amount of profit is good or bad. A comparison to last year's figures, using percents, might reveal that profits are up 45% over last year, or profits are down 66.8%. Significant news!

Predicting the probability of an event occurring is often expressed as a percent. For example, a weather forecast might include "a 50% chance of snow tonight."

6-6 Determining Rate of Increase or Decrease

In calculating the rate of increase or decrease of something, we use the same percentage formula concepts as before. Rate of change means percent change, therefore the *rate* is the unknown. Once again we will use the formula $R = P \div B$. Rate of change situations contain an original amount of something, which either increases or decreases to a new amount.

In solving these problems, the original amount is always the base. The difference between the original and the new is the portion. The unknown is the rate, which describes the percent change between the two amounts.

STEPS FOR DETERMINING THE RATE OF INCREASE OR DECREASE:

Step 1. Identify the original and the new amounts, and find the difference between them.

Step 2. Using the rate formula, $R = P \div B$, substitute the difference from Step 1 for the portion, and the original amount for the base.

Step 3. Solve the equation for R. Remember, your answer will be in decimal form, which must be converted to a percent.

The following examples illustrate how this procedure is applied.

EXAMPLE

If a number increases from 60 to 75, what is the rate of increase?

SOLUTION STRATEGY

In this basic situation, a number changes from 60 to 75, and we are looking for the percent change; in this case it is an increase. The original amount is 60; the new amount is 75.

The portion is the difference between the amounts, $75 - 60 = 15$, and the base is the original amount, 60. We now substitute these values into the formula,

$$R = \frac{P}{B} = \frac{15}{60} = .25 = 25\%$$

Rate of increase = 25%

EXAMPLE

A number decreased from 120 to 80. What is the percent decrease?

SOLUTION STRATEGY

This problem illustrates a number decreasing in value. The unknown is the rate of decrease. We identify the original amount as 120, and the new amount as 80.

The difference between them is the portion: $120 - 80 = 40$. The original amount, 120, is the base. Now apply the formula:

$$R = \frac{P}{B} = \frac{40}{120} = .333 = 33.3\%$$

Rate of decrease = 33.3%

EXAMPLE

Last year a company had a work force of 360 employees. This year there are 504 employees. What is the rate of change in the number of employees?

The key to solving this problem is to properly identify the variables. The problem asks "what is the rate," therefore, the rate is the unknown. The original amount, 360 employees, is the base. The difference between the two amounts, $504 - 360 = 144$, is the portion. We now apply the rate formula:

$$R = \frac{P}{B} = \frac{144}{360} = .4 = 40\%$$

<u>Rate of increase in employees = 40%</u>

EXAMPLE

A retail store had revenue of \$122,300 in May and \$103,955 in June. What is the percent change in revenue from May to June?

SOLUTION STRATEGY

In this problem, the rate of change, the unknown, is a decrease. The original amount, \$122,300, is the base. The difference between the two amounts, $\$122,300 - \$103,955 = \$18,345$, is the portion. We apply the rate formula:

$$R = \frac{P}{B} = \frac{18,345}{122,300} = .15 = 15\%$$

<u>Rate of decrease in revenue = 15%</u>

TRY-IT   EXERCISES

Solve the following problems for the rate of increase or decrease, rounding to a tenth percent when necessary:

37. If a number increases from 650 to 948, what is the rate of increase?

38. If a number decreases from 21 to 15, what is the rate of decrease?

39. When Leonardo Mendez was promoted from supervisor to manager he received a salary increase from \$450 to \$540 per week. What was the percent change in his salary?

40. You are the production manager for the Emory Corporation. After starting a quality control program on the production line, defects per day dropped from 60 to 12. Top management was very pleased with your results, but wanted to know what percent decrease this change represented. Calculate the percent change in defects.

Check your answers with the solutions on page 178.

6-7 Determining Amounts in Increase or Decrease Situations

Finding the New Amount after a Percent Change

Sometimes the original amount of something and the rate of change will be known and the new amount, after the change, will be the unknown. For example, if a store sold $5,000 in merchandise on Tuesday, and 8% more on Wednesday, what are Wednesday's sales?

Keep in mind that the original amount, or beginning point, is always the base, and represents 100%. Because the new amount is the total of the original amount, 100%, and the amount of increase, 8%, the rate of the new amount is 108% (100% + 8%). If the rate of change had been a decrease instead of an increase, the rate would have been 8% less than the base, or 92% (100% − 8%).

The unknown in this situation, the new amount, is the portion; therefore, we use the formula, Portion = Rate × Base.

STEPS FOR DETERMINING THE NEW AMOUNT AFTER A PERCENT CHANGE:

Step 1. In the formula, Portion = Rate × Base, substitute the original amount, or starting point, for the base.

Step 2a. If the rate of change is an increase, add that rate to 100% to determine the rate.

Step 2b. If the rate of change is a decrease, subtract that rate from 100% to determine the rate.

Step 3. Solve the equation for the portion.

The following examples illustrate how these problems are solved.

EXAMPLE

An insurance company estimated that the number of claims on homeowner's insurance would increase by 15%. If the company received 1,240 claims last year, how many can it expect this year?

SOLUTION STRATEGY

Last year's claims, the original amount, is the base. Because the rate of change is an increase, we find the rate by adding that change to 100% (100% + 15% = 115%). Now substitute these values in the portion formula.

$$P = R \times B$$
$$P = 115\% \times 1,240 = 1.15 \times 1,240 = 1,426$$

Portion = 1,426 = Number of homeowner's claims expected this year

---

EXAMPLE

Scotty's Drive-in Restaurant sold 25% less milk shakes this week than last week. If they sold 380 shakes last week, how many did they sell this week?

SOLUTION STRATEGY

Because this situation represents a percent decrease, the rate is determined by subtracting the rate of decrease from 100% (100% − 25% = 75%). As usual, the base is the original amount.

$$P = R \times B$$
$$P = 75\% \times 380 = .75 \times 380 = 285$$

Portion = 285 = Number of milk shakes sold this week

Solve the following business situations for the new amount, after a percent change:

41. A small company had an IBM computer with a 160 megabyte hard drive. If it was replaced with a new model containing 30% more capacity, how many megabytes would the new hard drive have?

42. A delivery truck covers 20% less miles per week during the winter snow season. If the truck averages 650 miles per week during the summer, how many miles can be expected per week during the winter?

Check your answers with the solutions on page 178.

Finding the Original Amount before a Percent Change

In another business situation involving percent change, the new amount is known and the original amount, the base, is unknown. For example, a car dealer sold 42 cars today. If this represents a 20% increase from yesterday, how many cars were sold yesterday? Solving for the original amount is a base problem, therefore we use the formula:

$$\text{Base} = \frac{\text{Portion}}{\text{Rate}}$$

STEPS FOR DETERMINING THE ORIGINAL AMOUNT BEFORE A PERCENT CHANGE:

Step 1. In the formula, Base = Portion ÷ Rate, substitute the new amount for the portion.

Step 2a. If the rate of change is an increase, add that rate to 100% to determine the rate.

Step 2b. If the rate of change is a decrease, subtract that rate from 100% to determine the rate.

Step 3. Solve the equation for the base.

The following examples illustrate how these problems are solved.

EXAMPLE

A company found that after an advertising campaign, business in April increased 12% over March. If April sales were $53,760, how much were the sales in March?

SOLUTION STRATEGY

April's sales, the new amount, is the portion. Since the rate of change is an increase, we find the rate by adding that change to 100%. 100% + 12% = 112%.

$$B = \frac{P}{R}$$

$$B = \frac{53,760}{112\%} = \frac{53,760}{1.12} = 48,000$$

$$\underline{\text{Base} = \$48,000 = \text{March sales}}$$

EXAMPLE

At Circuit City the price of a Sony VCR dropped by 15% to $425. What was the original price?

SOLUTION STRATEGY

Because this situation represents a percent decrease, the rate is determined by subtracting the rate of decrease from 100%. 100% − 15% = 85%. The portion is the new amount, $425. The original price, the base, is the unknown. Using the formula for the base,

$$B = \frac{P}{R}$$

$$B = \frac{425}{85\%} = \frac{425}{.85} = 500$$

Base = $500 = Original price of VCR

TRY-IT EXERCISES

Solve the following business situations for the original amount, before a percent change:

43. A harvester can cover 90 acres per day with a new direct-drive system. If this represents an increase of 20% over the conventional chain-drive system, how many acres per day were covered with the old chain-drive?

44. The water level in a large holding tank decreased to 12 feet. If it is down 40% from last week, what was last week's level?

Check your answers with the solutions on page 178.

6-8 Understanding and Solving Problems Involving Percentage Points

Percentage points are another way of expressing a change from an original amount to a new amount, without using a percent sign. When percentage points are used, it is assumed that the base amount, 100%, stays constant. For example, if a company's market share increased from 40 to 44 percent of a total market, this is expressed as an increase of 4 percentage points.

The actual percent change in business, however, is calculated using the formula:

$$\text{Rate of change} = \frac{\text{Change in percentage points}}{\text{Original amount of percentage points}}$$

In this illustration, the change in percentage points is 4, and the original amount of percentage points is 40, therefore,

$$\text{Rate of change} = \frac{4}{40} = .10 = 10\% \text{ increase in business}$$

> **percentage points**
> A way of expressing a change from an original amount to a new amount, without using a percent sign.

Note: This procedure is actually an application of the rate formula, Rate = Portion ÷ Base, with the change in percentage points as the portion, and the original percentage points as the base.

EXAMPLE

When a competitor built a better mouse trap, a company's market share dropped from 55 to 44 percent of the total market, a drop of 11 percentage points. What percent decrease in business did this represent?

SOLUTION STRATEGY

In this problem, the change in percentage points is 11, and the original market share is 55. Using the formula to find rate of change:

$$\text{Rate of change} = \frac{\text{Change in percentage points}}{\text{Original amount of percentage points}}$$

$$\text{Rate of change} = \frac{11}{55} = .2 = 20\%$$

$$\underline{\text{Rate of change} = 20\% = \text{Decrease in market share}}$$

TRY-IT EXERCISE

45. Prior to an election, a political research firm announced that a candidate for mayor had gained 8 percentage points in the polls this month, from 20 to 28 percent of the total registered voters. What is the candidate's actual percent increase in voters?

Check your answer with the solution on page 178.

REVIEW EXERCISES CHAPTER 6—SECTION III

Solve the following increase or decrease problems for the unknown, rounding decimals to hundredths and percents to the nearest tenth:

1. If a number increases from 320 to 440, what is the rate of increase?
Portion = Increase = 440 − 320 = 120
Base = Original number = 320
$R = \dfrac{P}{B} = \dfrac{120}{320} = .375 = \underline{\underline{37.5\%}}$

2. If a number decreases from 56 to 49, what is the rate of decrease?
Portion = Decrease = 56 − 49 = 7
Base = Original number = 56
$R = \dfrac{P}{B} = \dfrac{7}{56} = .125 = \underline{\underline{12.5\%}}$

3. What is the rate of change if the price of an item rises from $123.00 to $154.00?
Portion = Increase = 154 − 123 = 31
Base = Original number = 123
$R = \dfrac{P}{B} = \dfrac{31}{123} = .252 = \underline{\underline{25.2\%}}$

4. What is the rate of change if the number of employees in a company decreases from 133 to 89?
Portion = Decrease = 133 − 89 = 44
Base = Original number = 133
$R = \dfrac{P}{B} = \dfrac{44}{133} = .3308 = \underline{\underline{33.1\%}}$

5. 50 increased by 20% = _____
Rate = 100% + 20% = 120%
Base = Original number = 50
$P = R \times B = 1.2 \times 50 = \underline{60}$

6. 750 increased by 60% = _____
Rate = 100% + 60% = 160%
Base = Original number = 750
$P = R \times B = 1.6 \times 750 = \underline{1,200}$

7. 25 decreased by 40% = _____
Rate = 100% − 40% = 60%
Base = Original number = 25
$P = R \times B = .6 \times 25 = \underline{15}$

8. 3,400 decreased by 18.2% = _____
Rate = 100% − 18.2% = 81.8%
Base = Original number = 3,400
$P = R \times B = .818 \times 3400 = \underline{2,781.2}$

9. 2,500 increased by 300% = _____

Rate = 100% + 300% = 400%
Base = Original number = 2,500
$P = R \times B = 4 \times 2500 = \underline{10,000}$

10. $46 decreased by $10\frac{1}{2}$% = _____

Rate = 100% − 10.5% = 89.5%
Base = Original number = $46.00
$P = R \times B = .895 \times 46 = \underline{\$41.17}$

11. A plumbing supply wholesaler sold 2,390 feet of $\frac{5}{8}$-inch galvanized pipe in April. If 2,558 feet were sold in May, what is the percent increase in pipe footage sales?
Portion = Increase = 2,558 − 2,390 = 168
Base = Original number = 2,390
$$R = \frac{P}{B} = \frac{168}{2390} = .070 = \underline{7\%}$$

12. At a Safeway Supermarket the price of yellow onions dropped from $.59 per pound to $.45 per pound.

a. What is the percent decrease in the price of onions?
Portion = Decrease = $.59 − $.45 = $.14
Base = Original number = $.59
$$R = \frac{P}{B} = \frac{.14}{.59} = .2372 = \underline{23.7\%}$$

b. Tomatoes are expected to undergo the same percent decrease in price. If they currently sell for $1.09 per pound, what will be the new price of tomatoes?
Rate = 100% − 23.7% = 76.3%
Base = Original number = $1.09
$P = R \times B = .763 \times 1.09 = \underline{\$.83}$

13. At a Sports Authority store 850 tennis rackets were sold last season.

a. If business is predicted to be 30% higher this season, how many rackets should be ordered from the distributor?
Rate = 100% + 30% = 130%
Base = Original number = 850
$P = R \times B = 1.3 \times 850 = \underline{1,105}$ Rackets

b. If racket sales break down into 40% graphite and 60% wood, how many of each type should be ordered?

Graphite	Wood
Rate = 40%	Rate = 60%
Base = 1,105	Base = 1,105
$P = R \times B = .4 \times 1,105 = \underline{442}$ Rackets	$P = R \times B = .6 \times 1,105 = \underline{663}$ Rackets

14. A Toyota dealership sold 112 cars this month. If that is 40% better than last month, how many cars were sold last month?
Rate = 100% + 40% = 140%
Portion = 112
$$B = \frac{P}{R} = \frac{112}{1.4} = \underline{80} \text{ Cars}$$

15. The Mario Andretti Racing Team increased the horsepower of an engine from 340 to 440 by converting to fuel injection. What was the percent increase in horsepower?

Portion = 440 − 340 = 100

Base = Original number = 340

$$R = \frac{P}{B} = \frac{100}{340} = .2941 = \underline{\underline{29.4\%}}$$

16. The second shift of a factory produced 17,010 units. If this was $5\frac{1}{2}\%$ less than shift 1, how many units were produced on the first shift?

Rate = $100\% - 5\frac{1}{2}\% = 94\frac{1}{2}\%$

Portion = 17,010

$$B = \frac{P}{R} = \frac{17{,}010}{.945} = \underline{\underline{18{,}000}}$$

17. Housing prices in Denver have increased 37.5% over the price of homes five years ago.

a. If $80,000 was the average price of a house five years ago, what is the average price of a house today?

Rate = 100% + 37.5% = 137.5%

Base = $80,000

$P = R \times B = 1.375 \times 80{,}000 = \underline{\underline{\$110{,}000}}$

b. Economists predict that next year housing prices will drop by 4%. Based on your answer from part a, what will the average price of a house be next year?

Rate = 100% − 4% = 96%

Base = $110,000

$P = R \times B = .96 \times 110{,}000 = \underline{\underline{\$105{,}600}}$

18. After a vigorous promotion campaign, Kellogg's Frosted Flakes increased its market share from 5.4% to 8.1%, a rise of 2.7 percentage points. What percent increase in sales does this represent?

Portion = 2.7

Base = 5.4

$$R = \frac{P}{B} = \frac{2.7}{5.4} = .5 = \underline{\underline{50\%}}$$

19. In July, the price of a share of Apex Corporation stock decreased from $45\frac{1}{8}$ to $39\frac{3}{4}$.

a. What percent decrease does this represent?

Portion = $45\frac{1}{8} - 39\frac{3}{4} = 5\frac{3}{8}$

Base = Original number = $45\frac{1}{8}$

$$R = \frac{P}{B} = \frac{5.375}{45.125} = .1191 = \underline{\underline{11.9\%}}$$

b. In August, the stock rose 50%. What is the new price per share?

Rate = 100% + 50% = 150%

Base = $39\frac{3}{4}$

$P = R \times B = 1.5 \times 39.75 = \underline{\underline{\$59.625}}$

20. Recent economic reports indicate that unemployment in Summerville dropped from 8.8% to 6.8% in the last quarter, a decrease of 2 percentage points. What percent decrease does this represent?

Portion = 2

Base = 8.8

$$R = \frac{P}{B} = \frac{2}{8.8} = .2272 = \underline{\underline{22.7\%}}$$

FORMULAS

Portion = Rate × Base

Rate = Portion ÷ Base

Base = Portion ÷ Rate

CHAPTER 6 ■ PERCENTS			SUMMARY CHART

SECTION I UNDERSTANDING AND CONVERTING PERCENTS

Topic	P/O, Page	Important Concepts	Illustrative Examples
Converting a Percent to a Decimal	6–1 153	1. Remove the percent sign. 2. Move the decimal point two places to the left. 3. If the percent is a fraction, such as $\frac{4}{5}\%$, or a mixed number, such as $9\frac{1}{2}\%$, first change the fraction part to a decimal, then follow Steps 1 and 2.	$28\% = .28$ $159\% = 1.59$ $.37\% = .0037$ $\frac{4}{5}\% = .8\% = .008$ $9\frac{1}{2}\% = 9.5\% = .095$
Converting a Decimal or Whole Number to a Percent	6–1 154	1. Move the decimal point two places to the right. 2. Add a percent sign to the number. 3. If there are fractions involved, convert them to decimals first, then proceed with Steps 1 and 2.	$.8 = 80\%$ $2.9 = 290\%$ $.075 = 7.5\%$ $3 = 300\%$ $\frac{1}{2} = .5 = 50\%$
Converting a Percent to a Fraction	6–2 155	1. Remove the percent sign. 2. (If the percent is a whole number) Write a fraction with the percent as the numerator and 100 as the denominator. Reduce to lowest terms. or 2. (If the percent is a fraction) Multiply the number by $\frac{1}{100}$ and reduce to lowest terms. or 2. (If the percent is a decimal) Convert it to a fraction and multiply by $\frac{1}{100}$. Reduce to lowest terms.	$7\% = \frac{7}{100}$ $60\% = \frac{60}{100} = \frac{3}{5}$ $400\% = \frac{400}{100} = 4$ $2.1\% = 2\frac{1}{10}\% = \frac{21}{10} \times \frac{1}{100} = \frac{21}{1{,}000}$ $5\frac{3}{4}\% = \frac{23}{4} \times \frac{1}{100} = \frac{23}{400}$
Converting Fractions or Mixed Numbers to Percents	6–2 156	1. Change the fraction to a decimal by dividing the numerator by the denominator. 2. Move the decimal point two places to the right. 3. Write a percent sign after the number.	$\frac{1}{8} = .125 = 12.5\%$ $\frac{16}{3} = 5.333 = 533.3\%$ $12\frac{3}{4} = 12.75 = 1{,}275\%$

SECTION II   USING THE PERCENTAGE FORMULA TO SOLVE BUSINESS PROBLEMS

Topic	P/O, Page	Important Concepts	Illustrative Examples
Solving for the Portion	6–3 158	The portion is the number that represents a part of the base. To solve for portion use the formula: $$Portion = Rate \times Base$$	15% of a company's employees got raises this year. If 1,800 people work for the company, how many got raises? $$P = .15 \times 1,800 = 270$$ <u>270 employees got raises this year</u>
Solving for the Rate	6–4 160	The rate is the variable that describes what part of the base is represented by the portion. It is always the term with the percent sign. To solve for rate use the formula: $$Rate = \frac{Portion}{Base}$$	28 out of 32 of a company's warehouses passed safety inspection. What percent of the warehouses passed? $$Rate = \frac{28}{32} = .875 = 87.5\%$$ <u>87.5% passed inspection</u>
Solving for the Base	6–5 161	Base is the variable that represents 100%, the starting point, or the whole thing. To solve for base use the formula: $$Base = \frac{Portion}{Rate}$$	34.3% of a company's sales are from customers west of the Mississippi River. If those sales last year were $154,350, what are the company's total sales? $$Base = \frac{154,350}{.343} = \$450,000$$ <u>Total sales = $450,000</u>

SECTION III   SOLVING OTHER BUSINESS PROBLEMS INVOLVING PERCENTS

Topic	P/O, Page	Important Concepts	Illustrative Examples
Determining Rate of Increase or Decrease	6–6 167	1. Identify the original and the new amounts, and find the difference between them. 2. Using the rate formula, $R = P \div B$, substitute the difference from Step 1 for the portion, and the original amount for the base. 3. Solve the equation for R.	A price rises from $45 to $71. What is the rate of increase? $$Portion = 71 - 45 = 26$$ $$Rate = \frac{P}{B} = \frac{26}{45} = .577 = \underline{\underline{57.7\%}}$$ What is the rate of decrease from 152 to 34? $$Portion = 152 - 34 = 118$$ $$Rate = \frac{P}{B} = \frac{118}{152} = .776 = \underline{\underline{77.6\%}}$$

III, continued

Topic	P/O, Page	Important Concepts	Illustrative Examples
Determining New Amount after a Percent Change	6–7 169	Solving for the new amount is a portion problem, therefore we use the formula: Portion = Rate × Base 1. Substitute the original amount for the base. 2a. If the rate of change is an increase, add that rate to 100%. 2b. If the rate of change is a decrease, subtract that rate from 100%.	A company projects a 24% increase in sales for next year. If sales this year were $172,500, what sales can be expected next year? Rate = 100% + 24% = 124% $P = R \times B = 1.24 \times 172,500$ $P = 213,900$ <u>Projected sales = $213,900</u>
Determining Original Amount before a Percent Change	6–7 170	Solving for the original amount is a base problem, therefore we use the formula: $$\text{Base} = \frac{\text{Portion}}{\text{Rate}}$$ 1. Substitute the new amount for the portion. 2a. If the rate of change is an increase, add that rate to 100%. 2b. If the rate of change is a decrease, subtract that rate from 100%.	If an item was marked down by 30% to $16.80, what was the original price? Portion = 100% − 30% = 70% $$\text{Base} = \frac{P}{R} = \frac{16.80}{.7} = 24$$ <u>Original price = $24.00</u>
Solving Problems Involving Percentage Points	6–8 171	Percentage points are another way of expressing a change from an original amount to a new amount, without using the percent sign. When percentage points are used, it is assumed that the base amount, 100%, stays constant. The actual percent change in business, however, is calculated using the formula: $$\% \text{ Change} = \frac{\text{Change in percentage points}}{\text{Original percentage points}}$$	After an intensive advertising campaign, a company's market share increased from 21 to 27 percent, an increase of 6 percentage points. What percent increase in business does this represent? $$\% \text{ change} = \frac{6}{21} = .2857 = 28.6\%$$ <u>% increase in business = 28.6%</u>

TRY-IT EXERCISE   SOLUTIONS

1. $27\% = \underline{.27}$ **2.** $472\% = \underline{4.72}$ **3.** $93.7\% = \underline{.937}$ **4.** $.81\% = \underline{.0081}$

5. $12\frac{3}{4}\% = 12.75\% = \underline{.1275}$ **6.** $\frac{7}{8}\% = .875\% = \underline{.00875}$ **7.** $.8 = \underline{80\%}$ **8.** $1.4 = \underline{140\%}$

9. $.0023 = \underline{.23\%}$ **10.** $.016\frac{2}{5} = 1.6\frac{2}{5}\% = \underline{1.64\%}$ **11.** $19 = \underline{1,900\%}$ **12.** $.57\frac{2}{3} = 57\frac{2}{3}\% = \underline{57.67\%}$

13. $9\% = \underline{\frac{9}{100}}$ **14.** $23\% = \underline{\frac{23}{100}}$ **15.** $75\% = \frac{75}{100} = \underline{\frac{3}{4}}$ **16.** $225\% = \frac{225}{100} = 2\frac{25}{100} = \underline{2\frac{1}{4}}$

17. $8.7\% = 8\frac{7}{10}\% = \frac{87}{10} \times \frac{1}{100} = \underline{\frac{87}{1,000}}$ **18.** $1,000\% = \frac{1,000}{100} = \underline{10}$ **19.** $\frac{1}{5} = .2 = \underline{20\%}$

20. $\dfrac{70}{200} = .35 = \underline{\underline{35\%}}$ **21.** $\dfrac{23}{5} = 4\dfrac{3}{5} = 4.6 = \underline{\underline{460\%}}$ **22.** $6\dfrac{9}{10} = 6.9 = \underline{\underline{690\%}}$ **23.** $\dfrac{45}{54} = .8333 = \underline{\underline{83.3\%}}$

24. $140\dfrac{1}{8} = 140.125 = \underline{\underline{14{,}012.5\%}}$ **25.** $P = R \times B = .55 \times 980 = \underline{\underline{539}}$ **26.** $P = R \times B = .72 \times 3{,}200 = \underline{\underline{2{,}304}}$

27. $P = R \times B = .16 \times 1{,}250 = \underline{\underline{200}}$ salespeople   **28.** $P = R \times B = .15 \times 148{,}500 = \underline{\underline{\$22{,}275}}$ down payment

29. $R = \dfrac{P}{B} = \dfrac{9}{21} = .4285 = \underline{\underline{42.9\%}}$ **30.** $R = \dfrac{P}{B} = \dfrac{67}{142} = .4718 = \underline{\underline{47.2\%}}$ **31.** $R = \dfrac{P}{B} = \dfrac{5{,}400}{18{,}000} = .3 = \underline{\underline{30\%}}$ of job completed

32. $R = \dfrac{P}{B} = \dfrac{5{,}518}{8{,}900} = .62 = \underline{\underline{62\%}}$ suits   **33.** $B = \dfrac{P}{R} = \dfrac{690}{.4} = \underline{\underline{1{,}725}}$ **34.** $B = \dfrac{P}{R} = \dfrac{550}{.88} = \underline{\underline{\$625}}$

35. $B = \dfrac{P}{R} = \dfrac{126}{.35} = \underline{\underline{360}}$ motors   **36.** $B = \dfrac{P}{R} = \dfrac{3{,}420}{.75} = \underline{\underline{4{,}560}}$ reams of paper

37. Portion = Increase = $948 - 650 = 298$

Base = Original number = 650

$R = \dfrac{P}{B} = \dfrac{298}{650} = .4584 = \underline{\underline{45.8\%}}$ increase

38. Portion = Decrease = $21 - 15 = 6$

Base = Original number = 21

$R = \dfrac{P}{B} = \dfrac{6}{21} = .2857 = \underline{\underline{28.6\%}}$ decrease

39. Portion = Increase = $\$540 - \$450 = \$90$

Base = Original number = $450

$R = \dfrac{P}{B} = \dfrac{90}{450} = .2 = \underline{\underline{20\%}}$ increase

40. Portion = Decrease = $60 - 12 = 48$

Base = Original number = 60

$R = \dfrac{P}{B} = \dfrac{48}{60} = .8 = \underline{\underline{80\%}}$ decrease

41. Rate = $100\% + 30\% = 130\%$

$P = R \times B = 1.3 \times 160 = \underline{\underline{208}}$ megabytes

42. Rate = $100\% - 20\% = 80\%$

$P = R \times B = .8 \times 650 = \underline{\underline{520}}$ miles per week

43. Rate = $100\% + 20\% = 120\%$

$B = \dfrac{P}{R} = \dfrac{90}{1.2} = \underline{\underline{75}}$ acres per day

44. Rate = $100\% - 40\% = 60\%$

$B = \dfrac{P}{R} = \dfrac{12}{.6} = \underline{\underline{20}}$ feet

45. $R = \dfrac{P}{B} = \dfrac{8}{20} = .4 = \underline{\underline{40\%}}$ increase in voters

Name_____

Class_____

Convert the following percents to decimals:

1. 88%

.88

2. $3\frac{3}{4}\%$

$3.75\% = .0375$

3. 59.68%

.5968

4. 422%

4.22

5. $\frac{9}{16}\%$

$.5625 = .005625$

Convert the following decimals or whole numbers to percents:

6. 12.6

1,260%

7. .681

68.1%

8. 53

5,300%

9. $24\frac{4}{5}$

$24.8 = 2,480\%$

10. .0929

9.29%

Convert the following percents to reduced fractions, mixed numbers, or whole numbers:

11. 19%

$\frac{19}{100}$

12. 217%

$\frac{217}{100} = 2\frac{17}{100}$

13. 7.44%

$7\frac{44}{100} \times \frac{1}{100} = \frac{744}{100} \times \frac{1}{100}$

$= \frac{744}{10,000} = \frac{93}{1250}$

14. 126%

$\frac{126}{100} = 1\frac{26}{100}$

$= 1\frac{13}{50}$

15. $25\frac{2}{5}\%$

$25\frac{2}{5} \times \frac{1}{100}$

$= \frac{127}{5} \times \frac{1}{100} = \frac{127}{500}$

Convert each of the following fractions or mixed numbers to percents:

16. $\frac{4}{5}$

$.8 = 80\%$

17. $\frac{5}{9}$

$.5556 = 55.56\%$

18. $\frac{33}{4}$

$8\frac{1}{4} = 8.25 = 825\%$

19. $56\frac{3}{10}$

$56.3 = 5,630\%$

20. $\frac{745}{100}$

$7\frac{45}{100}$

$= 7.45 = 745\%$

Solve the following for the portion, rate, or base, rounding decimals to hundredths and percents to the nearest tenth when necessary:

21. 24% of 1,700 =

$P = R \times B = .24 \times 1700$

$= 408$

22. 56 is _____ % of 125

$R = \frac{P}{B} = \frac{56}{125} = .448 = 44.8\%$

23. 91 is 88% of _____

$B = \frac{P}{R} = \frac{91}{.88} = 103.41$

24. What number is 45% of 680?

$P = R \times B = .45 \times 680 = 306$

25. $233.91 is what percent of $129.95?

$R = \frac{P}{B} = \frac{233.91}{129.95} = 1.8 = 180\%$

26. 315 is 126% of _____

$B = \frac{P}{R} = \frac{315}{1.26} = 250$

27. 60 increased by 15% = _____

$R = 100\% + 15\% = 115\%$

$P = R \times B = 1.15 \times 60 = 69$

28. If a number increases from 47 to 70.5, what is the rate of increase?

Portion = Increase = 70.5 − 47 = 23.5

$R = \frac{P}{B} = \frac{23.5}{47} = .5 = 50\%$

29. What is the base if the portion is 444 and the rate is 15%?

$B = \frac{P}{R} = \frac{444}{.15} = 2,960$

ANSWERS

1. _____ .88 _____
2. _____ .0375 _____
3. _____ .5968 _____
4. _____ 4.22 _____
5. _____ .005625 _____
6. _____ 1,260% _____
7. _____ 68.1% _____
8. _____ 5,300% _____
9. _____ 2,480% _____
10. _____ 9.29% _____
11. _____ $\frac{19}{100}$ _____
12. _____ $2\frac{17}{100}$ _____
13. _____ $\frac{93}{1250}$ _____
14. _____ $1\frac{13}{50}$ _____
15. _____ $\frac{127}{500}$ _____
16. _____ 80% _____
17. _____ 55.56% _____
18. _____ 825% _____
19. _____ 5,630% _____
20. _____ 745% _____
21. _____ 408 _____
22. _____ 44.8% _____
23. _____ 103.41 _____
24. _____ 306 _____
25. _____ 180% _____
26. _____ 250 _____
27. _____ 69 _____
28. _____ 50% _____
29. _____ 2,960 _____

ANSWERS

30. _____114.75_____

31. _____1,492_____

32. _____2,660_____

33. _____$122.48_____

34. _____73.1%_____

35. _____50%_____

36. a. _____$72,000_____

b. _____$.24_____

c. _____25%_____

30. What is the portion if the base is 900 and the rate is $12\frac{3}{4}\%$?

$P = R \times B = .1275 \times 900 = \underline{114.75}$

31. What is 100% of 1,492?

$P = R \times B = 1.0 \times 1,492 = \underline{1,492}$

32. 7,000 decreased by 62% = _____

Rate $= 100\% - 62\% = 38\%$

$P = R \times B = .38 \times 7000 = \underline{2,660}$

Solve the following word problems for the unknown, rounding decimals to hundredths and percents to the nearest tenth when necessary:

33. An ad for JCPenney read, "This week only, all merchandise 35% off!" If a television set normally sells for $349.95, what is the amount of the savings?

$P = R \times B = .35 \times \$349.95 = \underline{\$122.48}$ Savings

34. If 453 runners out of 620 completed a marathon, what percent of the runners finished the race?

$R = \dfrac{P}{B} = \dfrac{453}{620} = \underline{73.1\%}$ Finished the race

35. A letter carrier can deliver mail to 112 homes per hour by walking and 168 homes per hour by driving. By what percent is productivity increased by driving?

Portion = Increase $= 168 - 112 = 56$

$R = \dfrac{P}{B} = \dfrac{56}{112} = .5 = \underline{50\%}$ Increase in productivity

36. Last year Blue Ribbon's corporate jet required $23,040 in maintenance and repairs.

a. If this represents 32% of the total operating costs of the airplane, what was the total cost to fly the plane for the year?

$B = \dfrac{P}{R} = \dfrac{23040}{.32} = \underline{\$72,000}$ Total cost

b. If the plane flew 300,000 miles last year, what is the cost per mile to operate the plane?

Cost per mile $= \dfrac{\text{Total cost}}{\text{Total miles}} = \dfrac{72,000}{300,000} = \underline{\$.24}$ Per mile

c. Hamilton Leasing offered a deal whereby they would operate the plane for Blue Ribbon for only $.18 per mile. What is the percent decrease in operating expense per mile being offered by Hamilton?

Portion = Decrease $= .24 - .18 = .06$

$R = \dfrac{P}{B} = \dfrac{.06}{.24} = \underline{25\%}$ Savings per mile

37. Last year the Lopez Corporation had sales of $343,500. If this year's sales are forecast to be $415,700, what is the percent increase in sales?

Portion = Increase = 415,700 − 343,500 = 72,200

$$R = \frac{P}{B} = \frac{72,200}{343,500} = .21 = \underline{21\%} \text{ Increase}$$

38. After a 15% pay raise, Georgia Salisbury now earns $27,600. What was her salary before the raise?

$$B = \frac{P}{R} = \frac{\$27,600}{115\%} = \frac{27,600}{1.15} = \underline{\$24,000}$$

39. A freight container weighed 360 percent of its empty weight when it was full.

a. If the full weight was 1,800 pounds, what was the weight of the empty container?

$$B = \frac{P}{R} = \frac{1800}{3.6} = \underline{500} \text{ Pounds empty}$$

b. What percent of the total loaded weight of the container was the merchandise?

Portion = 1800 − 500 = 1300 Pounds

$$R = \frac{1300}{1800} = .722 = \underline{72.2\%}$$

40. Three out of every seven sales transactions in a department store are on credit cards. What percent of the transactions are *not* credit card sales?

Credit card transactions: $R = \dfrac{P}{B} = \dfrac{3}{7} = .429 = 42.9\%$

Non-credit transactions: $100\% - 42.9\% = \underline{57.1\%}$

41. A pre-election survey shows that an independent presidential candidate has increased his popularity from 26.5 percent to 31.3 percent of the electorate, an increase of 4.8 percentage points. What percent does this increase represent?

$$R = \frac{P}{B} = \frac{4.8}{26.5} = .181 = \underline{18.1\%} \text{ Increase}$$

42. By what percent is a 100-watt light bulb brighter than a 60-watt bulb?

Portion = Increase = 100 − 60 = 40 Watts

$$R = \frac{P}{B} = \frac{40}{60} = .667 = \underline{66.7\%} \text{ Brighter}$$

43. Eddie Dawson, an ice cream vendor, pays $17.50 for a five-gallon container of premium ice cream. From this quantity, he sells 80 scoops at $.90 per scoop. If he sold smaller scoops, he could sell 98 scoops from the same container, however he could only charge $.80 per scoop. As his accountant, you are asked the following questions:

a. If he switches to the smaller scoops, by how much will his profit per container go up or down? (Profit = Sales − Expenses.)

Large $.90	$72.00	Small $.80	$78.40	$60.90	
× 80	−17.50	× 98	−17.50	$54.50	
$72.00	$54.50 Profit	$78.40	$60.90 Profit	$6.40 Profit increase using small scoops	

Name _____

Class _____

ANSWERS

37. _____ 21% _____

38. _____ $24,000 _____

39. a. _____ 500 _____

b. _____ 72.2% _____

40. _____ 57.1% _____

41. _____ 18.1% _____

42. _____ 66.7% _____

43. a. _____ $6.40 Increase _____

Name_____

Class_____

ANSWERS

b. _____11.7% Increase_____

44. _____$40,583.33_____

45. a. _____70%_____

b. _____$7,965,000_____

c. _____Owned 59.3%_____

_____Leased 40.7%_____

46. a. _____7%_____

_____20.1%_____

_____28.5%_____

_____24.6%_____

_____19.9%_____

b. _____$318,292.50_____

b. By what percent will the profit change?

$$R = \frac{P}{B} = \frac{6.40}{54.50}$$
$$= \underline{\underline{11.7\%}}\ \text{Increase}$$

44. An insurance adjuster found that 12% of a shipment was damaged in transit. If the damaged goods amounted to $4,870, what was the total value of the shipment?

$$B = \frac{P}{R} = \frac{4,870}{.12} = \underline{\underline{\$40,583.33}}\ \text{Total shipment}$$

45. A state had 1,350,000 registered vehicles last year.

a. If 405,000 are leased, what percent of the total vehicles are *owned*?

1,350,000 − 405,000 = 945,000 Owned vehicles

$$R = \frac{P}{B} = \frac{945,000}{1,350,000} = \underline{\underline{70\%}}\ \text{Of vehicles are owned}$$

b. If the state charges each owned vehicle a $5 highway tax per year and each leased vehicle an $8 highway tax per year, how much highway tax was collected last year?

Owned = 945,000 × $5 = $4,725,000
Leased = 405,000 × $8 = $3,240,000
   $7,965,000 Total highway tax

c. What is the percent breakdown of owned and leased vehicles' dollar contribution as a percent of the total highway tax fund?

$$\text{Owned:}\ R = \frac{P}{B} = \frac{4,725,000}{7,965,000} = \underline{\underline{59.3\%}}$$

$$\text{Leased:}\ R = \frac{P}{B} = \frac{3,240,000}{7,965,000} = \underline{\underline{40.7\%}}$$

46. Tom Hall, a contractor, built a warehouse complex for the following costs: land, $12,000; concrete and steel work, $34,500; plumbing and electrical, $48,990; general carpentry and roof, $42,340; and all other expenses, $34,220.

a. What percent of the total cost is represented by each category of expenses?

Base = Total expenses = $172,050

$$\text{Land:}\ R = \frac{P}{B} = \frac{12,000}{172,050} = \underline{\underline{7\%}}$$

$$\text{Concrete and steel:}\ R = \frac{P}{B} = \frac{34,500}{172,050} = \underline{\underline{20.1\%}}$$

$$\text{Plumbing and electrical:}\ R = \frac{P}{B} = \frac{48,990}{172,050} = \underline{\underline{28.5\%}}$$

$$\text{Carpentry and roof:}\ R = \frac{P}{B} = \frac{42,340}{172,050} = \underline{\underline{24.6\%}}$$

$$\text{Other expenses:}\ R = \frac{P}{B} = \frac{34,220}{172,050} = \underline{\underline{19.9\%}}$$

*Note: Total = 100.1% Due to rounding

b. When the project was completed, Tom sold the entire complex for 185% of its cost. What was the selling price of the complex?

$$P = R \times B = 1.85 \times \$172,050 = \underline{\underline{\$318,292.50}}\ \text{Selling price}$$

BUSINESS DECISION
Allocating the Expenses at Burger King

Name_____

Class_____

47. Cheryl Hauser owns three Burger King locations with the following number of seats in each: airport, 340 seats; downtown, 218 seats; and suburban, 164 seats.

a. If the liability insurance premium is $5,400 per year, how much of that premium should be allocated to each of the restaurants, based on percent of total seating capacity? (Round each percent to tenths.)

Total seats = Base = 722

Airport: $R = \dfrac{P}{B} = \dfrac{340}{722} = 47.1\%$ $.471 \times \$5,400 = \underline{\$2,543.40}$

Downtown: $R = \dfrac{P}{B} = \dfrac{218}{722} = 30.2\%$ $.302 \times \$5,400 = \underline{\$1,630.80}$

Suburban: $R = \dfrac{P}{B} = \dfrac{164}{722} = 22.7\%$ $.227 \times \$5,400 = \underline{\$1,225.80}$

b. If the restaurant chain opens a fourth location at the beach, with 150 seats, and the total insurance premium increases by 17%, what is the new allocation of insurance premiums among the four locations?

New base = 722 + 150 = 872 Seats

New insurance premium = 5,400 × 1.17 = $6,318

Airport: $R = \dfrac{P}{B} = \dfrac{340}{872} = 39\%$ $.39 \times \$6,318 = \underline{\$2,464.02}$

Downtown: $R = \dfrac{P}{B} = \dfrac{218}{872} = 25\%$ $.25 \times \$6,318 = \underline{\$1,579.50}$

Suburban: $R = \dfrac{P}{B} = \dfrac{164}{872} = 18.8\%$ $.188 \times \$6,318 = \underline{\$1,187.78}$

Beach: $R = \dfrac{P}{B} = \dfrac{150}{872} = 17.2\%$ $.172 \times \$6,318 = \underline{\$1,086.70}$

ANSWERS

47. a. _____ Airport: $2,543.40 _____

_____ Downtown: $1,630.80 _____

_____ Suburban: $1,225.80 _____

b. _____ Airport: $2,464.02 _____

_____ Downtown: $1,579.50 _____

_____ Suburban: $1,187,78 _____

_____ Beach: $1,086,70 _____

All the Math That's Fit to Learn

The Business Math Times

| Volume VI | **Percents and Their Applications in Business** | One Dollar |

When "Close Enough" Isn't

People often say, "It's close enough, it's only a small percentage!" But is it? What would constitute an ambitious but realistic error—or conversely, success—rate? How about 99%? A 99% success rate would be a great batting average but a pretty crummy surgical success rate. Each day in the United States, 67,000 Americans undergo surgery. A 99% success rate would mean that 670 of those surgeries would not be successful. Assuming a six-day surgical work week, that comes to 4,020 failures a week and 210,000 a year. Not very good!

What if the performance standard were set at 99.9% by some everyday organizations? This one-tenth of one percent failure rate would result in some startling numbers:

- 2 million documents would be lost by the IRS this year.
- 22,000 checks would be deducted from the wrong bank accounts in the next hour.
- 12 babies would be given to the wrong parents each day.
- 2,488,200 books would be shipped in the next year with the wrong cover.
- 18,322 pieces of mail would be mishandled in the next hour.
- 114,500 mismatched pairs of shoes would be shipped this year.
- 20,000 incorrect drug prescriptions would be written in the next 12 months.
- 315 entries in Webster's Third New International Dictionary of the English Language (unabridged) would be misspelled.
- 91 pacemaker operations would be performed incorrectly this year.

SOURCE: Ron Zemke, Editor, "When 'Close Enough' Isn't," *The Service Edge*, November 1991, p. 8. From Lakewood Publications, a subsidiary of Maclean Hunter Publishing Company.

Tomorrow's Jobs

The Changing American Work Force

Let's take a look at some current and projected figures relating to the composition of the U.S. labor force. According to the U.S. Bureau of the Census, the labor force comprises all civilians, 16 years and older, who are employed for pay or profit.

U.S. workers will be an increasingly diverse group as we begin the new century. In 1994, women comprised 45.9% of the labor force. By 2005, their numbers are expected to grow to 47.7%. Also by 2005, African-Americans are expected to be 11.6% of the work force, an increase of 1% from 1994, while Hispanics will constitute 11.0%, an increase of almost 2% over 1994.

CIVILIAN LABOR FORCE (MILLIONS)	1990	1994	2000*	2005*
Total	124.8	131.0	141.8	150.5
Male	68.2	70.8	75.3	78.7
Female	56.6	60.2	66.6	71.8

* projected

In recent years, the level of educational attainment of the labor force has risen dramatically. In 1994, 27.3% of all workers aged 25 and over had a bachelor's degree or higher, while only 11% did not have a high school diploma. The trend toward higher educational attainment is expected to continue.

The Changing American Work Place

The fastest growing occupational groups will be executive, administrative, and managerial; professional specialty; and technicians and related support occupations. These groups generally require the highest levels of education and skill, and will make up an increasing proportion of new jobs.

The more than 15 million jobs that will be added to the U.S. economy by 2005 will not be evenly distributed across major industrial and occupational groups. The long-term shift from goods-producing to service producing employment is expected to continue. Industries such as transportation, communications, and utilities; retail and wholesale trade; health, business and educational services; government; and finance, insurance, and real estate are expected to account for over 90% of job growth.

SOURCE: *Occupational Outlook Handbook*, 1994–1995 Edition, U.S. Department of Labor; and *Statistical Abstract of the United States*, 1995, Bureau of Labor Statistics.

Brainteaser

Ninety-nine girls and one boy are in a business math class. How many girls must leave the room so that the percentage of girls becomes 98 percent?

SOURCE: *Mathematics Teacher* Magazine (December 1996).

Answer to Last Issue's Brainteaser
8 Apple Pies

Let X = pies sold on the first day

X + (X + 6) + (X + 12) + (X + 18) + (X + 24) = 100

5X + 60 = 100   5X = 40

X = 8

Chapter 7

Invoices, Trade and Cash Discounts

Performance Objectives

SECTION I THE INVOICE

SECTION II TRADE DISCOUNTS—SINGLE

SECTION III TRADE DISCOUNTS—SERIES

SECTION IV CASH DISCOUNTS AND TERMS OF SALE

THE INVOICE

● **invoice**

A document detailing a sales transaction, containing a list of goods shipped or services rendered, with an account of all costs.

In business, merchandise is bought and sold many times as it passes from the manufacturer through wholesalers and retailers to the final consumer. Bills of sale or **invoices** are business documents used to keep track of these sales and purchases. From the seller's point of view they are sales invoices; from the buyer's point of view they are purchase invoices, or purchase orders.

Invoices are a comprehensive record of a sales transaction. They show what merchandise or services have been sold, to whom, in what quantities, at what price, and under what conditions and terms. They vary in style and format from company to company, but most contain essentially the same information. Invoices are used extensively in business and it is important to be able to read and understand them. In this chapter you will become familiar with how businesses use invoices and the math applications that relate to them.

7-1 Reading and Understanding the Parts of an Invoice

Exhibit 7-1 shows a typical format used in business for an invoice. The important parts have been labeled and are explained in Exhibit 7-2. Some of the terms have page references, which direct you to the sections in this chapter that further explain those terms and their business math applications. Exhibit 7-2 also presents some of the most commonly used invoice abbreviations. These pertain to merchandise quantities and measurements.

EXHIBIT 7-1

....

TYPICAL INVOICE FORMAT

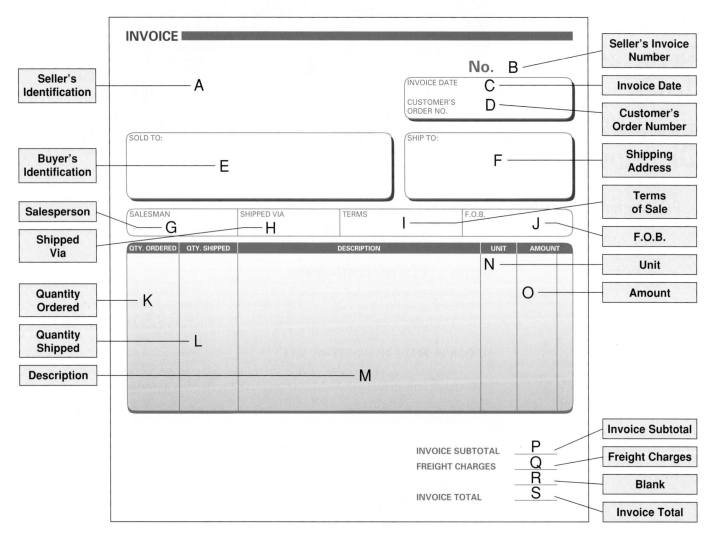

Invoices are a detailed record of inventory merchandise purchased and sold.

With some practice, these terms and abbreviations will become familiar to you. Take some time to look them over, before you continue reading.

Freight Terminology

Two frequently used freight terms that you should become familiar with are **F.O.B. shipping point** and **F.O.B. destination. F.O.B.** means "free on board" or "freight on board." These terms define who pays the freight charges and when the title (ownership) of the goods is transferred from the seller to the buyer. Ownership becomes important when insurance claims

● **F.O.B. shipping point**
The buyer pays all transportation charges from the vendor's location.

● **F.O.B. destination**
The seller pays all transportation charges to the buyer's store or warehouse.

● **F.O.B.**
Term used in quoting shipping charges meaning "free on board" or "freight on board."

EXHIBIT 7-2

INVOICE TERMINOLOGY AND ABBREVIATIONS

INVOICE TERMINOLOGY

A **Seller's Identification**—Name, address, and logo or corporate symbol of the seller

B **Seller's Invoice Number**—Seller's identification number of the transaction

C **Invoice Date**—Date the invoice was written

D **Customer's Order Number**—Buyer's identification number of the transaction

E **Buyer's Identification**—Name and mailing address of the buyer

F **Shipping Address**—Address where merchandise will be shipped

G **Salesperson**—Name of salesperson credited with the sale

H **Shipped Via**—Name of freight company handling the shipment

I **Terms**—Terms of Sale—Section detailing date of payment and cash discount (p. 206)

J **F.O.B.**—"Free on Board"—Section detailing who pays the freight charges (p. 187–188)

K **Quantity Ordered**—Number of units ordered

L **Quantity Shipped**—Number of units shipped

M **Description**—Detailed description of the merchandise, including model numbers

N **Unit**—Price per unit of merchandise

O **Amount**—Extended total—Quantity in units times the unit price for each line (p. 190)

P **Invoice Subtotal**—Total of the "amount" column—Merchandise total (p. 190)

Q **Freight Charges**—Shipping charges—Cost to physically transport the merchandise from the seller to the buyer (p. 188)

R **Blank Line**—Line used for other charges, such as insurance or handling

S **Invoice Total**—Total amount of the invoice—Includes merchandise plus all other charges (p. 190)

INVOICE ABBREVIATIONS

ea.	each	pr.	pair	in.	inch	oz	ounce
dz. or doz.	dozen	dm. or drm.	drum	ft	foot	g or gr	gram
gr. or gro.	gross	bbl.	barre	yd	yard	kg	kilogram
bx.	box	sk.	sack	mm	millimeter	pt	pint
cs.	case	@	at	cm	centimeter	qt	quart
ct. or crt.	crate	C.	100 items	m	meter	gal	gallon
ctn. or cart.	carton	M.	1,000 items	lb	pound	cwt	hundred weight

must be filed due to problems in shipment. Freight terms, like terms of sale, are a negotiable issue between the seller and the buyer.

F.O.B. Shipping Point   When the terms are F.O.B. shipping point, the freight charges are paid by the buyer. The merchandise title is transferred to the buyer at the manufacturer's factory, or at a shipping point such as a railroad freight yard or air freight terminal. From this point the buyer is responsible for the merchandise.

F.O.B. Destination   When the shipping terms are F.O.B. destination, the seller is responsible for the shipping charges to the destination. The destination is usually the buyer's store or warehouse.

Sometimes the freight terms are stated as F.O.B. with the name of a city. For example, if the seller is in Ft. Worth and the buyer is in New York, F.O.B. Ft. Worth means the title is transferred in Ft. Worth, and the buyer pays the shipping charges from Ft. Worth to New York. If the terms are F.O.B. New York, the seller pays the shipping charges to New York and then the title is transferred to the buyer. Exhibit 7.3 illustrates these transactions.

Freight Terminology

Seller's Factory

Buyer's Warehouse

Title Transfer

Title Transfer

F.O.B. Shipping Point
F.O.B. Fort Worth

F.O.B. Destination
F.O.B. New York

EXHIBIT 7-3

FREIGHT TERMINOLOGY

EXAMPLE

From the following Whole Grain invoice, identify the indicated parts.

a. Seller   _____

b. Invoice number   _____

c. Invoice date   _____

d. Cust. order #   _____

e. Buyer   _____

f. Terms of sale   _____

g. Shipping address   _____

h. Salesman   _____

i. Shipped via   _____

j. Insurance   _____

k. Freight charges   _____

l. Invoice Subtotal   _____

m. Unit price—Fruit and Nut Flakes   _____

n. Invoice Total   _____

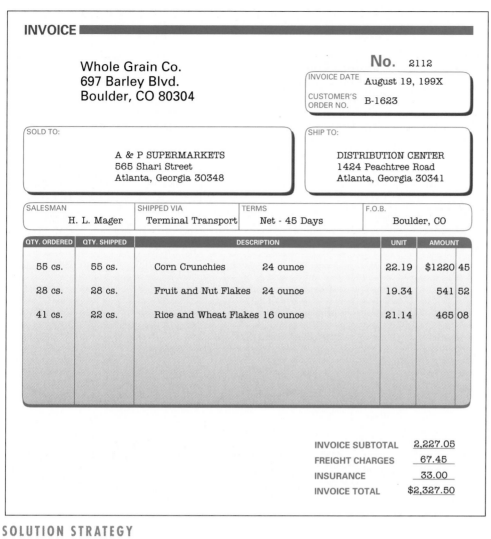

INVOICE

Whole Grain Co.
697 Barley Blvd.
Boulder, CO 80304

No. 2112

INVOICE DATE: August 19, 199X
CUSTOMER'S ORDER NO.: B-1623

SOLD TO:
A & P SUPERMARKETS
565 Shari Street
Atlanta, Georgia 30348

SHIP TO:
DISTRIBUTION CENTER
1424 Peachtree Road
Atlanta, Georgia 30341

SALESMAN	SHIPPED VIA	TERMS	F.O.B.
H. L. Mager	Terminal Transport	Net - 45 Days	Boulder, CO

QTY. ORDERED	QTY. SHIPPED	DESCRIPTION		UNIT	AMOUNT
55 cs.	55 cs.	Corn Crunchies	24 ounce	22.19	$1220 45
28 cs.	28 cs.	Fruit and Nut Flakes	24 ounce	19.34	541 52
41 cs.	22 cs.	Rice and Wheat Flakes	16 ounce	21.14	465 08

INVOICE SUBTOTAL 2,227.05
FREIGHT CHARGES 67.45
INSURANCE 33.00
INVOICE TOTAL $2,327.50

SOLUTION STRATEGY

a. Seller — Whole Grain
b. Invoice number — 2112
c. Invoice date — August 19
d. Cust. order # — B-1623
e. Buyer — A & P
f. Terms of sale — Net 45 Days
g. Shipping address — 1424 Peachtree Rd
h. Salesman — H. L. Mager
i. Shipped via — Terminal Transport
j. Insurance — $33.00
k. Freight charges — $67.45
l. Invoice Subtotal — $2,227.05
m. Unit price—Fruit and Nut Flakes — $19.34
n. Invoice Total — $2,327.50

TRY-IT EXERCISE

1. From the following FotoFair invoice, identify the indicated parts:

a. Buyer _____
b. Invoice number _____
c. Invoice date _____
d. Amount—Model 55 _____
e. Seller _____
f. Terms of sale _____
g. Shipping address _____
h. Salesman _____
i. Shipped via _____
j. F.O.B. _____
k. Freight charges _____
l. Invoice Subtotal _____
m. Unit price—Model 75 _____
n. Invoice Total _____

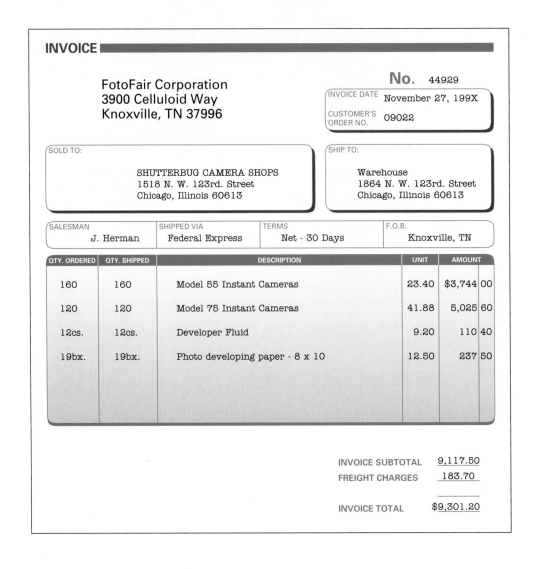

INVOICE

FotoFair Corporation
3900 Celluloid Way
Knoxville, TN 37996

No. 44929

INVOICE DATE November 27, 199X

CUSTOMER'S ORDER NO. 09022

SOLD TO:

SHUTTERBUG CAMERA SHOPS
1518 N. W. 123rd. Street
Chicago, Illinois 60613

SHIP TO:

Warehouse
1864 N. W. 123rd. Street
Chicago, Illinois 60613

SALESMAN	SHIPPED VIA	TERMS	F.O.B.
J. Herman	Federal Express	Net - 30 Days	Knoxville, TN

QTY. ORDERED	QTY. SHIPPED	DESCRIPTION	UNIT	AMOUNT
160	160	Model 55 Instant Cameras	23.40	$3,744 00
120	120	Model 75 Instant Cameras	41.88	5,025 60
12cs.	12cs.	Developer Fluid	9.20	110 40
19bx.	19bx.	Photo developing paper - 8 x 10	12.50	237 50

INVOICE SUBTOTAL	9,117.50
FREIGHT CHARGES	183.70
INVOICE TOTAL	$9,301.20

Check your answers with the solutions on page 219.

7-2 Extending and Totaling an Invoice

Extending an invoice is the process of computing the value in the Total or Amount column for each line of the invoice. This number represents the total dollar amount of each type of merchandise or service being purchased. The **invoice subtotal** is the amount of all items on the invoice before shipping and handling charges, insurance, and other adjustments, such as discounts, returns, and credits. The **invoice total** is the final amount due from the buyer to the seller.

● **invoice subtotal**

The amount of all merchandise or services on the invoice before adjustments.

● **invoice total**

The final amount due from the buyer to the seller.

STEPS TO EXTEND AND TOTAL AN INVOICE:

Step 1. For each line of the invoice, multiply the number of items by the cost per item.

Extended total = Number of items × Cost per item

Step 2. Add all extended totals to get the invoice subtotal.

Step 3. Calculate the invoice total by adding the shipping charges and insurance to the subtotal and taking into account any other adjustments that may be involved in the transaction.

From the following invoice, extend each line to the total column and calculate the invoice subtotal and total.

Stock #	Quantity	Unit	Merchandise Description	Unit Price	Total
4334	17	ea.	15" B & W Monitors	$244.00	_____
1217	8	ea.	13" Color Monitors	525.80	_____
2192	2	doz.	Connecting Cables	24.50	_____
5606	1	box	15" Anti-Glare Filters	365.90	_____
				Invoice Subtotal	
				Shipping Charges	$244.75
				Invoice Total	_____

SOLUTION STRATEGY

					Total
B & W Monitors	17	×	$244.00	=	$4,148.00
Color Monitors	8	×	525.80	=	4,206.40
Connecting Cables	2	×	24.50	=	49.00
Anti-Glare Filters	1	×	365.90	=	365.90
			Invoice Subtotal		$8,769.30
			Shipping Charges	+	244.75
			Invoice Total		$9,014.05

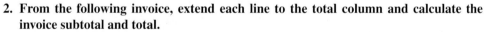

TRY-IT EXERCISE

2. From the following invoice, extend each line to the total column and calculate the invoice subtotal and total.

Stock #	Quantity	Unit	Merchandise Description	Unit Price	Total
R443	125	ea.	Food Processors	$ 89.00	_____
B776	24	ea.	Microwave Ovens	225.40	_____
Z133	6	doz.	12" Mixers	54.12	_____
Z163	1	bx.	Mixer Covers	166.30	_____
				Invoice Subtotal	
				Shipping Charges	$194.20
				Invoice Total	_____

Check your answers with the solutions on page 219.

REVIEW EXERCISES   CHAPTER 7—SECTION I

What word is represented by each of the following abbreviations?

1. bx.   Box   2. pt   Pint   3. drm.   Drum   4. kg   Kilogram

5. gro.   Gross   6. oz   Ounce   7. M.   Thousand   8. cwt   Hundredweight

Using the Frasier invoice below, extend each line to the amount column and calculate the subtotal and total. Then answer Questions 9–22. (Note: Although 26 boxes of 2-inch reflective tape were ordered, only 11 boxes were shipped. Charge only for the boxes shipped.)

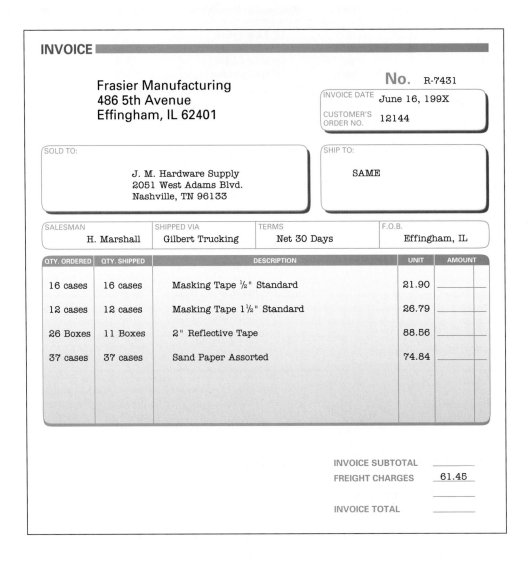

INVOICE

Frasier Manufacturing
486 5th Avenue
Effingham, IL 62401

No. R-7431

INVOICE DATE June 16, 199X

CUSTOMER'S ORDER NO. 12144

SOLD TO:

J. M. Hardware Supply
2051 West Adams Blvd.
Nashville, TN 96133

SHIP TO:

SAME

SALESMAN	SHIPPED VIA	TERMS	F.O.B.
H. Marshall	Gilbert Trucking	Net 30 Days	Effingham, IL

QTY. ORDERED	QTY. SHIPPED	DESCRIPTION	UNIT	AMOUNT
16 cases	16 cases	Masking Tape ½" Standard	21.90	
12 cases	12 cases	Masking Tape 1½" Standard	26.79	
26 Boxes	11 Boxes	2" Reflective Tape	88.56	
37 cases	37 cases	Sand Paper Assorted	74.84	

INVOICE SUBTOTAL _____

FREIGHT CHARGES   61.45

INVOICE TOTAL _____

21.   ½" Tape $350.40

    1½" Tape   321.48

    2" Tape   974.16

    Sand paper 2,769.08

    Subtotal $4,415.12

22.   Subtotal $4,415.12

    Freight   61.45

    Total $4,476.57

9. Seller — Frasier Manufacturing

11. Invoice date — June 16, 199x

13. Buyer — J.M. Hardware Supply

15. Shipping address — 2051 W. Adams Blvd. Nashville, TN 96133

17. Shipped via — Gilbert Trucking

19. Freight charges — $61.45

21. Invoice subtotal — $4,415.12

10. Invoice number — R-7431

12. Cust. order # — 12144

14. Terms of sale — Net 30 days

16. Salesman — H. Marshall

18. Insurance — None listed

20. Unit price—2" Tape — $88.56

22. Invoice total — $4,476.57

SECTION II

TRADE DISCOUNTS—SINGLE

The path merchandise travels as it moves from the manufacturer through wholesalers and retailers to the ultimate consumer is known as a channel of distribution or trade channel. The businesses that form these channels are said to be "in the trade." In today's complex economy, a number of different trade channels are used to move goods and services efficiently.

Trade discounts are reductions from the manufacturer's suggested **list price.** They are given to businesses at various levels of the trade channel for the performance of marketing functions. These functions may include activities such as selling, advertising, storage, service, and display.

Manufacturers print catalogs showcasing their merchandise. Often, these catalogs contain the manufacturer's suggested list or retail prices. Businesses in the trade receive price sheets from the manufacturer listing the trade discounts, in percent form, associated with each item in the catalog. By issuing updated price sheets of trade discounts, manufacturers have the flexibility of changing the prices of their merchandise without the expense of reprinting the entire catalog.

Trade discounts are sometimes quoted as a single discount and sometimes as a series or chain of discounts. The number of discounts is dependent on the extent of the marketing services performed by the channel member.

7-3 Calculating the Amount of a Single Trade Discount

The amount of a single trade discount is calculated by multiplying the list price by the trade discount percent.

Trade discount amount = List price × Trade discount percent

EXAMPLE

What is the amount of the trade discount on merchandise with a list price of $2,800 and a trade discount of 45%?

SOLUTION STRATEGY

Trade discount amount = List price × Trade discount percent
Trade discount amount = 2,800 × .45 = $1,260

TRY-IT   EXERCISE

3. **A retail gift shop buys merchandise with a list price of $7,600 from a wholesaler of novelty items and toys. The wholesaler extends a 30% trade discount to the retailer. What is the amount of the trade discount?**

Check your answer with the solution on page 219.

7-4 Calculating Net Price Using the Net Price Factor, Complement Method

The **net price** is the amount a business actually pays for the merchandise after the discount has been deducted. It may be calculated by subtracting the amount of the trade discount from the list price.

Net price = List price – Trade discount amount

Frequently, merchants are more interested in knowing the net price of an item than the amount of the trade discount. In that case, the net price can be calculated directly from the list price without first finding the amount of the discount.

The list price of an item is considered to be 100%. If, for example, the trade discount on an item is 40% of the list price, the net price will be 60%, because the two must equal 100%. This 60%, the complement of the trade discount percent (100% − 40%), is the portion of the list price that *is* paid. Known as the **net price factor,** it is usually written in decimal form.

● **net price factor**
The percent of the list price a business pays for merchandise. It is the multiplier used to calculate the net price.

STEPS TO CALCULATE NET PRICE USING THE NET PRICE FACTOR:

Step 1. Calculate the net price factor, complement of the trade discount percent:

$$\text{Net price factor} = 100\% - \text{Trade discount percent}$$

Step 2. Calculate the net price:

$$\text{Net price} = \text{List price} \times \text{Net price factor}$$

Note: This procedure can be combined into one step by the formula:

$$\text{Net price} = \text{List price} (100\% - \text{Trade discount percent})$$

EXAMPLE

Calculate the net price of merchandise listing for \$900 less a trade discount of 45%.

SOLUTION STRATEGY

Net price = List price (100% − Trade discount percent)
Net price = 900 (100% − 45%)
Net price = 900 (.55) = $\underline{\$495}$

TRY-IT   **EXERCISE**

4. **A hardware store bought merchandise listing for \$2,100 with a single trade discount of 35%. What is the net price of the hardware order?**

Check your answer with the solution on page 219.

7-5 Calculating Trade Discount Rate When List Price and Net Price Are Known

The trade discount rate can be calculated by using the now-familiar percentage formula, Rate = Portion ÷ Base. For this application, the amount of the trade discount is the portion, or numerator, and the list price is the base, or denominator.

$$\text{Trade discount rate} = \frac{\text{Amount of trade discount}}{\text{List price}}$$

STEPS FOR CALCULATING TRADE DISCOUNT RATE:

Step 1. Calculate the amount of the trade discount:

$$\text{Trade discount amount} = \text{List price} - \text{Net price}$$

continued

(continued)

> **Step 2.** Calculate the trade discount rate:
>
> $$\text{Trade discount rate} = \frac{\text{Amount of trade discount}}{\text{List price}}$$

EXAMPLE

Oxford Manufacturing sells tools to American Hardware & Garden Supply. In a recent transaction, the list price of an order was $47,750, and the net price of the order was $32,100. Calculate the amount of the trade discount? What was the trade discount rate. Round your answer to the nearest tenth percent.

SOLUTION STRATEGY

Trade discount amount = List price − Net price

Trade discount amount = 47,750 − 32,100 = $15,650

$$\text{Trade discount rate} = \frac{\text{Amount of trade discount}}{\text{List price}}$$

$$\text{Trade discount rate} = \frac{15,650}{47,750} = .3277 = 32.8\%$$

TRY-IT   EXERCISE

5. **Proline Sporting Goods recently sold tennis rackets listing for $109,500 to The Sports Authority. The net price of the order was $63,300. What was the amount of the trade discount? What was the trade discount rate? Round your answer to the nearest tenth percent.**

Check your answer with the solution on page 219.

REVIEW EXERCISES   CHAPTER 7—SECTION II

Calculate the following trade discounts. Round all answers to the nearest cent.

	List Price	Trade Discount Rate	Trade Discount		Trade Discount = List Price × Trade Discount Rate
1.	$860.00	30%	$258.00		Trade discount = $860.00 × .30 = $258.00
2.	125.50	12%	$15.06		Trade discount = $125.50 × .12 = $15.06
3.	41.75	19%	$7.93		Trade discount = $41.75 × .19 = $7.93
4.	499.00	8%	$39.92		Trade discount = $499.00 × .08 = $39.92
5.	88.25	50%	$44.13		Trade discount = $88.25 × .5 = $44.13

Calculate the following trade discounts and net prices to the nearest cent.

	List Price	Trade Discount Rate	Trade Discount	Net Price	Trade Discount	Net Price
6.	$286.00	25%	$71.50	$214.50	$286.00 × .25 = $71.50	$286.00 − 71.50 = $214.50
7.	134.79	40%	$53.92	$80.87	$134.79 × .4 = $53.92	$134.79 − 53.92 = $80.87
8.	21.29	18%	$3.83	$17.46	$21.29 × .18 = $3.83	$21.29 − 3.83 = $17.46
9.	959.00	55%	$527.45	$431.55	$959.00 × .55 = $527.45	$959.00 − 527.45 = $431.55

Calculate the following net price factors and net prices using the complement method. Round all answers to the nearest cent.

Complete, worked out solutions for exercises 10–16 appear in the appendix following the index.

	List Price	Trade Discount Rate	Net Price Factor	Net Price
10.	$3,499.00	37%	63%	$2,204.37
11.	565.33	24%	76%	$429.65
12.	1,244.25	45.8%	54.2%	$674.38
13.	4.60	$12\frac{3}{4}\%$	87.25%	$4.01

Calculate the following trade discounts and trade discount rates. Round answers to the nearest tenth percent.

	List Price	Trade Discount	Trade Discount Rate	Net Price
14.	$4,500.00	$935.00	20.8%	$3,565.00
15.	345.50	$120.50	34.9%	225.00
16.	2.89	$.74	25.6%	2.15

17. Find the amount of the trade discount on a television set that has a list price of $799.95 less a trade discount of 30%.

Trade discount = List price × Trade discount rate
Trade discount = $799.95 × .30 = $239.99

18. Find the amount of the trade discount on a set of fine china that lists for $345.70 less 55%.

Trade discount = $345.70 × .55 = $190.14

19. What is the amount of the trade discount offered to a hardware store for merchandise purchased at a total list price of $7,800 less a trade discount of 25%?

Trade discount = $7,800.00 × .25 = $1,950.00

20. Kalaidoscope for Kids, a chain of clothing stores, purchased merchandise with a total list price of $25,450 from Sandy Sport, a manufacturer. The order has a trade discount of 34%.

a. What is the amount of the trade discount?

Trade discount = $25,450.00 × .34 = $8,653.00

b. What is the net amount Kalaidoscope owes Sandy Sport for the merchandise?

Net price = $25,450.00 − 8,653.00 = $16,797.00

21. Bay Street Market ordered 12 cases of soup with a list price of $18.90 per case, and 8 cases of baked beans with a list price of $33.50 per case. The wholesaler offered a 39% trade discount to Bay Street Market.

a. What is the total extended list price of the order?

$18.90 × 12 =   226.80
$33.50 ×   8 = +268.00
Total extended list price = $494.80

b. What is the total amount of the trade discount on this order?

Trade discount = $494.80 × .39 = $192.97

c. What is the total net amount Bay Street Market owes the wholesaler for the order?

Net Amount = $494.80 − 192.97 = $301.83

22. An item with a trade discount of 41% has a list price of $289.50. What is the net price?

Net price factor = 100 − 41 = 59%
Net price   = $289.50 × .59 = $170.81

23. Gilbert Miranda, owner of Innovations Hair Boutique, places an order for beauty supplies from a wholesaler. The list price of the order is $2,800. If the vendor offers Gilbert a trade discount of 46%, what is the net price of the order?

Net price factor = 100 − 46 = 54%
Net price   = $2,800.00 × .54 = $1,512.00

24. A watch has a list price of $889.00 and can be bought by Sterling Jewelers for a net price of $545.75.

a. What is the amount of the trade discount?

Trade discount amount = $889.00 − 545.75 = $343.25

b. What is the trade discount rate?

$$\text{Trade discount rate} = \frac{343.25}{889.00} = .3861 = 38.6\%$$

25. You are the buyer for the housewares department of a large department store. A number of vendors in your area carry similar lines of merchandise. On sets of microwavable serving bowls, Kitchen Magic offers a list price of $400 per dozen, less a 38% trade discount. Pro-Chef offers a similar set for a list price of $425, less a 45% trade discount.

a. Which vendor is offering the lower net price?

Kitchen Magic	Pro-Chef
$400.00 × (1.00 − .38)	425.00 × (1.00 − .45)
400.00 × .62 = 248.00	425.00 × .55 = 233.75
Net price per dozen = $248.00	Net price per dozen = $233.75

Pro-Chef has a lower price.

b. If you order 500 dozen sets of the bowls, how much money will be saved using the lower-priced vendor?

$$500 \times 248.00 = 124,000.00$$
$$500 \times 233.75 = 116,875.00$$
$$124,000.00 - 116,875.00 = \underline{\$7,125.00} \text{ Savings}$$

TRADE DISCOUNTS—SERIES

● **chain, or series, trade discount**

Term used when a vendor offers a buyer more than one trade discount.

Trade discounts are frequently offered by manufacturers to wholesalers and retailers in a series of two or more, known as **chain** or **series trade discounts.** For example, a series of 25% and 10% is verbally stated as "25 and 10." It is written 25/10. A three-discount series is written 25/10/5.

Multiple discounts are given for many reasons. Some of the more common ones follow:

Position or Level in the Channel of Distribution   A manufacturer might sell to a retailer at 30% trade discount, whereas a wholesaler in the same channel might be quoted a 30% and a 15% trade discount.

Volume Buying   Many manufacturers and wholesalers grant an extra discount for buying a large volume of merchandise. For example, any purchase over 5,000 units at one time may earn an extra 7% trade discount. Retailers with many stores or those with large storage capacity can enjoy a considerable savings (additional trade discounts) by purchasing in large quantities.

Advertising and Display   Additional discounts are often given to retailers and wholesalers who heavily advertise and aggressively promote a manufacturer's line of merchandise.

Competition   Competitive pressures often cause extra trade discounts to be offered. In certain industries, such as household products and consumer electronics, price wars are not an uncommon occurrence.

7-6 Calculating Net Price and Trade Discount Amount Using a Series of Trade Discounts

Finding net price with a series of trade discounts is accomplished by taking each trade discount, one at a time, from the succeeding net price until all discounts have been deducted. Note, you *cannot* simply add the trade discounts together. They must be calculated individually, unless we use the net price factor method—a handy shortcut. Trade discounts can be taken in any order, although they are usually listed and calculated in descending order.

For illustrative purposes, let's begin with an example of how to calculate a series of trade discounts one at a time; then we shall try the shortcut method.

EXAMPLE

Calculate the net price and trade discount amount for merchandise with a list price of $2,000 less trade discounts of 30/20/15.

SOLUTION STRATEGY

$$
\begin{array}{cccccc}
\$2,000 & \$2,000 & \$1,400 & \$1,400 & \$1,120 & \$1,120 \\
\times\ .30 & -\ \ 600 & \times\ .20 & -\ \ 280 & \times\ .15 & -\ \ 168 \\
\hline
\$600 & \$1,400 & \$280 & \$1,120 & \$168 & \underline{\$952} = \text{Net price}
\end{array}
$$

Trade discount amount = List price − Net price

Trade discount amount = $2,000 - 952 = \underline{\$1,048}$

6. Northwest Publishers sold an order of books to The Bookworm, Inc., a chain of book-stores. The list price of the order was $25,000. The Bookworm buys in volume from Northwest. They also prominently display and heavily advertise Northwest's books. Northwest, in turn, gives The Bookworm a series of trade discounts, amounting to 35/20/10. Calculate the net price of the order and the amount of the trade discount.

Check your answers with the solutions on page 219.

7-7 Calculating the Net Price of a Series of Trade Discounts Using the Net Price Factor, Complement Method

As a shortcut, the net price can be calculated directly from the list price, bypassing the trade discount, by using the net price factor as before. Remember, the net price factor is the complement of the trade discount percent. With a series of discounts, we must find the complement of each trade discount in order to calculate the net price factor of the series.

The net price factor indicates to buyers what percent of the list price they actually *do* pay. For example, if the net price factor of a series of discounts is calculated to be .665, this means that the buyer is paying 66.5% of the list price.

STEPS TO CALCULATE NET PRICE OF A SERIES OF DISCOUNTS USING THE NET PRICE FACTOR:

Step 1. Find the complement of the trade discounts in the series by subtracting each from 100% and converting them to decimal form.

Step 2. Calculate the net price factor of the series by multiplying all the decimals together.

Step 3. Calculate the net price by multiplying the list price by the net price factor:

$$\text{Net price} = \text{List price} \times \text{Net price factor}$$

EXAMPLE

The Crystal Gallery purchased merchandise from a manufacturer in Italy with a list price of $37,000 less trade discounts of 40/25/10. Calculate the net price factor and the net price of the order.

SOLUTION STRATEGY

Step 1. Subtract each trade discount from 100% and convert to decimals.

$$
\begin{array}{ccc}
100\% & 100\% & 100\% \\
-\ 40\% & -\ 25\% & -\ 10\% \\
\hline
60\% = .6 & 75\% = .75 & 90\% = .9
\end{array}
$$

Step 2. Multiply all the complements together to get the net price factor.

Net price factor = .6 × .75 × .9
Net price factor = .405

Step 3.   Net price = List price × Net price factor
Net price = 37,000 × .405
Net price = $14,985

7. Something's Fishy, a pet shop, always gets a 30/20/12 series of trade discounts from the Clearview Fish Tank Company. In June, the shop ordered merchandise with a list price of $3,500. In September they placed an additional order listing for $5,800.

a. What is the net price factor for the series of trade discounts?

b. What is the net price of the merchandise purchased in June?

c. What is the net price of the merchandise purchased in September?

Check your answers with the solutions on page 220.

7-8 Calculating the Amount of a Trade Discount Using a Single Equivalent Discount

● **single equivalent discount**
A single trade discount that equates to all the discounts in a series or chain.

Sometimes retailers and wholesalers want to know the one single discount rate that equates to a series of trade discounts. This is known as the **single equivalent discount.** We have already learned that the trade discounts *cannot* simply be added together.

Here is the logic: The list price of the merchandise is 100%. If the net price factor is the part of the list price that is paid, then 100% minus the net price factor is the part of the list price that *is* the trade discount. The single equivalent discount, therefore, is the complement of the net price factor (100% − Net price factor percent).

STEPS TO CALCULATE THE SINGLE EQUIVALENT DISCOUNT AND THE AMOUNT OF A TRADE DISCOUNT:

Step 1. Calculate the net price factor as before, by subtracting each trade discount from 100% and multiplying them all together in decimal form.

Step 2. Calculate the single equivalent discount by subtracting the net price factor in decimal form from 1.

$$\text{Single equivalent discount} = 1 - \text{Net price factor}$$

Step 3. Find the amount of the trade discount by multiplying the list price by the single equivalent discount.

$$\text{Trade discount amount} = \text{List price} \times \text{Single equivalent discount}$$

EXAMPLE

Calculate the single equivalent discount and amount of the trade discount on merchandise listing for $10,000, less trade discounts of 30/10/5.

SOLUTION STRATEGY

Step 1. Calculate the net price factor:

$$\begin{array}{ccccc} 100\% & & 100\% & & 100\% \\ -\ 30\% & & -\ 10\% & & -\ 5\% \\ \hline .70 & \times & .90 & \times & .95 \end{array} = .5985 = \text{Net price factor}$$

Step 2. Calculate the single equivalent discount:

Single equivalent discount = 1 − Net price factor

Single equivalent discount = 1− .5985 = .4015

Note: 40.15% is the single equivalent discount of the series 30%, 10%, and 5%.

Step 3. Calculate the trade discount amount:

Trade discount amount = List price × Single equivalent discount

Trade discount amount = $10,000 × .4015 = $4,015

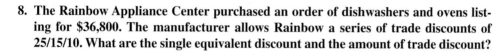 **TRY-IT** **EXERCISE**

8. **The Rainbow Appliance Center purchased an order of dishwashers and ovens listing for $36,800. The manufacturer allows Rainbow a series of trade discounts of 25/15/10. What are the single equivalent discount and the amount of trade discount?**

Check your answers with the solutions on page 220.

REVIEW EXERCISES   CHAPTER 7—SECTION III

Calculate the following net price factors and net prices. For convenience, round net price factors to five decimal places when necessary:

	List Price	Trade Discount Rates	Net Price Factor	Net Price
1.	$360.00	12/10	.792	$285.12
2.	425.80	18/15/5	.66215	$281.94
3.	81.75	20/10/10	.648	$ 52.97
4.	979.20	15/10/5	.72675	$711.63
5.	7.25	25/15/10½	.57056	$ 4.14
6.	.39	20/9/8	.66976	$ .26

1. Net price factor = 100% 100%
     −12% −10%
     .88 × .90 = .792
   Net price = 360.00 × .792 = $285.12
2. Net price factor = .82 × .85 × .95 = .66215
   Net price = 425.80 × .66215 = $281.94
3. Net price factor = .80 × .90 × .90 = .648
   Net price = 81.75 × .648 = $52.97
4. Net price factor = .85 × .90 × .95 = .72675
   Net price = 979.20 × .72675 = $711.63
5. Net price factor = .75 × .85 × .895 = .57056
   Net price = 7.25 × .57056 = $4.14
6. Net price factor = .80 × .91 × .92 = .66976
   Net price = .39 × .66976 = $.26

Calculate the following net price factors and single equivalent discounts.

	Trade Discount Rates	Net Price Factor	Single Equivalent Discount
7.	15/10	.765	.235
8.	20/15/12	.5984	.4016
9.	25/15/7	.59288	.40712
10.	30/5/5	.63175	.36825
11.	35/15/7.5	.51106	.48894

Net Price Factor		Single Equivalent Discount	
.85 × .90	= .765	1.00 − .765	= .235
.80 × .85 × .88	= .5984	1.00 − .5984	= .4016
.75 × .85 × .93	= .59288	1.00 − .59288	= .40712
.70 × .95 × .95	= .63175	1.00 − .63175	= .36825
.65 × .85 × .925	= .51106	1.00 − .51106	= .48894

Complete the following table. Round net price factors to five decimal place when necessary.

Complete, worked out solutions for exercises 12–17 appear in the appendix following the index.

	List Price	Trade Discount Rates	Net Price Factor	Single Equivalent Discount	Trade Discount	Net Price
12.	$7,800.00	15/5/5	.76713	= .23287	$1,816.39	$5,983.61
13.	1,200.00	20/15/7	.6324	= .3676	$441.12	$758.88
14.	560.70	25/15/5	.60563	= .39437	$221.12	$339.58
15.	883.50	18/12/9	.65666	= .34334	$303.34	$580.16
16.	4.89	12/10/10	.7128	= .2872	$1.40	$3.49
17.	2,874.95	30/20/5.5	.5292	= .4708	$1,353.53	$1,521.42

18. What is the net price factor of a 25/10 series of trade discounts?

$25/10 = .75 \times .90$

Net price factor $= \underline{\underline{0.675}}$

19. What is the net price factor of a 35/15/10 series of discounts?

$35/15/10 = .65 \times .85 \times .90$

Net price factor $= \underline{\underline{0.49725}}$

20. Toy Town orders toys, games, and videos with a list price of $10,300 less trade discounts of 25/15/12.

a. What is the net price factor?

Net price factor $= .75 \times .85 \times .88 = \underline{\underline{0.561}}$

b. What is the net price of the order?

Net price $= 10,300.00 \times .561 = \underline{\underline{\$5,778.30}}$

21. Contempo Designs places an order for furniture listing for $90,500 less trade discounts of 25/20.

a. What is the net price factor?

Net price factor $= .75 \times .80 = \underline{\underline{.6}}$

b. What is the net price of the order?

Net price $= 90,500.00 \times .6 = \underline{\underline{\$54,300.00}}$

22. If a supplier offers you trade discounts with a net price factor of .5788, what is the single equivalent discount?

Single equivalent discount = $1.00 - .5788 = \underline{\underline{.4212}}$

23. A vendor offers trade discounts of 25/15/10.

    a. What is the net price factor?

        Net price factor = $.75 \times .85 \times .90 = \underline{\underline{.57375}}$

    b. What is the single equivalent discount?

        Single equivalent discount = $1.00 - .57375 = \underline{\underline{.42625}}$

24. An order of lightbulbs listing for $9,500 has trade discounts of 25/13/8.

    a. What is the net price factor?

        Net price factor = $.75 \times .87 \times .92 = \underline{\underline{.6003}}$

    b. What is the single equivalent discount?

        Single equivalent discount = $1.00 - .6003 = \underline{\underline{.3997}}$

    c. What is the amount of the trade discount?

        Trade discount = $9,500.00 \times .3997 = \underline{\underline{\$3,797.15}}$

    d. What is the net price of the order?

        Net price = $9,500.00 \times .6003 = \underline{\underline{\$5,702.85}}$

25. Shari's Boutique is offered a line of blouses that list for $700 per dozen from a clothing manufacturer. They are offering trade discounts of 35/25/5.

    a. What is the net price per dozen Shari will pay for the blouses?

        $.65 \times .75 \times .95 = .46313 \times 700.00 = \underline{\underline{\$324.19}}$ Per dozen

b. What is the single equivalent discount of this deal?

Single equivalent discount = 1.00 − .46313 = .53687

26. The Speedy Auto Service Center can buy auto parts from Southeast Auto Supply at a series discount of 20/15/5 and from Northwest Auto Supply for 25/10/8.

a. Which auto parts supplier offers a better deal to Speedy?

Southeast	Northwest
.80 × .85 × .95 = 0.646	.75 × .90 × .92 = .621
Single equivalent discount = 1.00 − .646	Single equivalent discount = 1.00 − .621
= .354	= .379
Northwest offers better discount.	

b. If Speedy orders $15,000 in parts at list price per month, how much will they save in a year by choosing the lower-priced supplier?

Southeast	Northwest	
		9,690.00
$15,000.00 × .646	$15,000.00 × .621	− 9,315.00
= $9,690.00	= $9,315.00	$375.00 × 12 = $4,500.00 Savings per year

27. A TV manufacturer offers wholesalers a series discount of 35/20/20 and retailers a series discount of 35/20. A television set has a list price of $560.

a. What is the price the wholesaler pays?

.65 × .80 × .80 = 0.416
$560.00 × .416 = $232.96

b. What is the price to the retailer?

.65 × .80 = .52
$560 × .52 = $291.20

28. Taylor Pharmacy buys merchandise from B. G. Distributors with a series discount of 35/15/7.

a. What is the single equivalent discount?

.65 × .85 × .93 = .51383
1.00 − .51383 = .48617

b. What is the amount of the trade discount on an order with a list price of $5,700?

$5,700.00 × .48617 = $2,771.17

29. Tasty Food Distributors received the following items at a discount of 25/20/10: 18 cases of marinara sauce listing at $26.80 per case and 45 cases of tomato sauce listing at $22.50 per case.

a. What is the total list price of this order?

$26.80 × 18 = $ 482.40
$22.50 × 45 = $1,012.50
Total list price $1,494.90

b. What is the amount of the trade discount?

$$.75 \times .80 \times .90 = \quad .54 \quad \text{Net price factor}$$
$$1.00 - .54 = \quad .46 \quad \text{Single equivalent discount}$$
$$1494.90 \times .46 = \underline{\$687.65} \quad \text{Trade discount}$$

c. What is the net price of the order?

$$\text{Net price} = \$1,494.90 \times .54 = \underline{\$807.25}$$

30. Shopper's Mart purchased the following items. Calculate the extended total after the trade discounts for each line, the invoice subtotal, and the invoice total:

Quantity	Unit	Merchandise	Unit List	Trade Discounts	Extended Total
150	ea.	Blenders	$ 59.95	20/15/15	5,197.67
400	ea.	Toasters	39.88	20/10/10	10,336.90
18	doz.	Coffee Mills	244.30	30/9/7	2,605.06
12	doz.	Juicers	460.00	25/10/5	3,539.70
				Invoice subtotal	21,679.33
				Extra $5\frac{1}{2}$% volume discount on total order	− 1,192.36
				Invoice total	20,486.97

Blenders $150 \times 59.95 \times .578 = \$ \ 5,197.67$

Toasters $400 \times 39.88 \times .648 = \$10,336.90$

Coffee mills $18 \times 244.30 \times .59241 = \$ \ 2,605.06$

Juicers $12 \times 460 \times .64125 = \$ \ 3,539.70$

CASH DISCOUNTS AND TERMS OF SALE

As merchandise physically arrives at the buyer's back door, the invoice ordinarily arrives by mail through the front door. What happens next? The invoice has a section entitled **terms of sale.** The terms of sale are the details of when the invoice must be paid and whether any additional discounts will be offered.

Commonly, manufacturers allow wholesalers and retailers 30 days or even longer to pay the bill. In certain industries this time period is as much as 60 or 90 days. This is known as the **credit period.** This gives the buyer time to unpack and check the order, and more importantly, begin selling the merchandise. This credit period clearly gives the wholesaler and retailer an advantage. They can generate revenue by selling merchandise that they haven't paid for yet.

To encourage them to pay the bill earlier than the **net date,** or **due date,** sellers frequently offer buyers an optional extra discount, over and above the trade discounts. This is known as a **cash discount.** Cash discounts are an extra few percent offered as an incentive for early payment of the invoice, usually within 10 to 15 days after the **invoice date.** This is known as the **cash discount period.** The last date for a buyer to take advantage of a cash discount is known as the **discount date.**

The Importance of Cash Discounts

Both buyers and sellers benefit from cash discounts. Sellers get their money much sooner, which improves their cash flow, while buyers get an additional discount, which lowers their merchandise cost, thereby raising their margin or gross profit.

Cash discounts generally range from an extra one percent to five percent off the net price of the merchandise. One to five percent may not seem like a significant discount, but it is. Let's say that an invoice is due in 30 days, however a distributor would like payment sooner. They might offer the retailer a cash discount of 2% if the bill is paid within 10 days rather than 30 days. If the retailer chooses to take the cash discount, he must pay the bill by the 10th day after the date of the invoice. Note that this is *20 days* earlier than the due date. The retailer is therefore receiving a 2% discount for paying the bill 20 days early.

● **terms of sale**
The details of when an invoice must be paid, and if a cash discount is being offered.

● **credit period**
The time period that the seller allows the buyer to pay an invoice.

● **net date, due date**
The last day of the credit period.

● **cash discount**
An extra discount offered by the seller as an incentive for early payment of an invoice.

● **invoice date**
The date an invoice is written. The beginning of the discount and credit periods when ordinary dating is used.

● **cash discount period**
The time period in which a buyer can take advantage of the cash discount.

● **discount date**
The last day of the discount period.

The logic: There are 18.25 20-day periods in a year (365 days divided by 20 days). By multiplying the 2% discount by the 18.25 periods, we see that on a yearly basis, 2% cash discounts can *theoretically* amount to 36.5%. Very significant!

Cash discounts are so important to a wholesaler's or retailer's profit picture that frequently they borrow the money to take advantage of the cash discount. This business math application will be covered in Chapter 10.

7-9 Calculating Cash Discounts and Net Amount Due

● **net amount**
The amount of money due from the buyer to the seller.

Cash discounts are offered in the terms of sale. A transaction with no cash discount would have terms of sale of net 30, for example. This means the **net amount** of the invoice is due in 30 days. If a cash discount is offered, the terms of sale would be written as 2/10, n/30. This means a 2% cash discount may be taken if the invoice is paid within 10 days; if not, the net amount is due in 30 days.

The following illustration shows a time line of the discount period and credit period on an invoice, dated October 15. The 2/10, n/30 terms of sale stipulate a cash discount if the bill is paid within 10 days. If not, the balance is due in 30 days. As you can see, the cash discount period runs for 10 days from the invoice date, October 15 to October 25. The credit period, 30 days, extends from the invoice date through November 14.

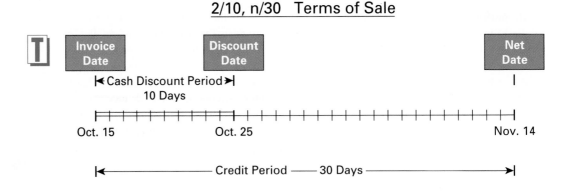

Sometimes two cash discounts are offered, such as 3/15, 1/25, n/60. This means a 3% cash discount is offered if the invoice is paid within 15 days, a 1% cash discount if the invoice is paid within 25 days, with the net amount due in 60 days.

Cash discounts cannot be taken on freight charges or returned goods, only on the net price of the merchandise. If freight charges are included in the amount of an invoice, they must be subtracted before taking the cash discount. After the cash discount has been deducted, the freight charges are added back to get the invoice total.

If arriving merchandise is damaged or is not what was ordered, those goods will be returned to the vendor. The amount of the returned goods must also be subtracted from the amount of the invoice. They are no longer a part of the transaction.

STEPS TO CALCULATE CASH DISCOUNT AND NET AMOUNT DUE:

Step 1. Calculate the amount of the cash discount by multiplying the cash discount percent by the net price of the merchandise:

$$\text{Cash discount} = \text{Net price} \times \text{Cash discount percent}$$

Step 2. Calculate the net amount due by subtracting the amount of the cash discount from the net price:

$$\text{Net amount due} = \text{Net price} - \text{Cash discount}$$

Note: As with trade discounts, buyers are frequently more interested in the net amount due than the amount of the discount. When that's the case, we can simplify the calculation by using the complement method to determine the net amount due.

$$\text{Net amount due} = \text{Net price} \ (100\% - \text{Cash discount percent})$$

EXAMPLE

A retailer buys merchandise from a supplier with an invoice amount of $16,000. The terms of sale are 2/10, n/30. What is the amount of the cash discount? What is the net amount due on this order if the bill is paid by the 10th day?

SOLUTION STRATEGY

$$\text{Cash discount} = \text{Net price} \times \text{Cash discount percent}$$
$$\text{Cash discount} = 16,000 \times .02 = \underline{\$320}$$

$$\text{Net amount due} = \text{Net price} - \text{Cash discount}$$
$$\text{Net amount due} = 16,000 - 320 = \underline{\$15,680}$$

TRY-IT   EXERCISE

9. Melody Music ordered cassette tapes and compact discs from a supplier with a net price of $8,300, and terms of sale of 3/15, n/45. What is the amount of the cash discount? What is the net amount due if the bill is paid by the 15th day?

Check your answers with the solutions on page 220.

7-10 Calculating Net Amount Due, with Credit Given for Partial Payment

Sometimes buyers don't have all the money needed to take advantage of the cash discount. Manufacturers and suppliers usually allow them to pay part of the invoice by the discount date, and the balance by the end of the credit period. These **partial payments** earn partial cash discount credit. In this situation, we must calculate how much **partial payment credit** is given.

Here's how it works. Assume a cash discount of 4/15, n/45 is offered to a retailer. A 4% cash discount means that the retailer will pay 96% of the bill (100% − 4%) and receive 100% credit. Another way to look at it is that every $.96 paid toward the invoice earns $1.00 credit. We must determine how many $.96s are in the partial payment. This will tell us how many $1.00s of credit we receive.

● **partial payment**
When a portion of the invoice is paid within the discount period.

● **partial payment credit**
The amount of the invoice paid off by the partial payment.

STEPS TO CALCULATE PARTIAL PAYMENT CREDIT AND NET AMOUNT DUE:

Step 1. Calculate the amount of credit given for a partial payment by dividing the partial payment by the complement of the cash discount percent:

$$\text{Partial payment credit} = \frac{\text{Partial payment}}{100\% - \text{Cash discount percent}}$$

Step 2. Calculate the net amount due by subtracting the partial payment credit from the net price:

$$\text{Net amount due} = \text{Net price} - \text{Partial payment credit}$$

EXAMPLE

Happy Feet, a chain of children's shoe stores, receives an invoice from a tennis shoe manufacturer on September 3, with terms of 3/20, n/60. The net price of the order is $36,700. Happy Feet wants to send a partial payment of $10,000 by the discount date, and the balance on the net date. How much credit does Happy Feet get for the partial payment? What is the remaining net amount due to the manufacturer?

SOLUTION STRATEGY

$$\text{Partial payment credit} = \frac{\text{Partial payment}}{100\% - \text{Cash discount percent}}$$

$$\text{Partial payment credit} = \frac{10,000}{100\% - 3\%} = \frac{10,000}{.97} = \underline{\underline{\$10,309.28}}$$

$$\text{Net amount due} = \text{Net price} - \text{Partial payment credit}$$

$$\text{Net amount due} = \$36,700.00 - \$10,309.28 = \underline{\underline{\$26,390.72}}$$

TRY-IT   EXERCISE

10. Major League Sports Center purchases $45,300 from Atlas Sporting Goods on May 5. Atlas allows 4/15, n/45. If Major League sends a partial payment of $20,000 on the discount date, how much credit will be given for the partial payment? What is the net amount still due on the order?

Check your answers with the solutions on page 220.

7-11 Determining Discount Date and Net Date Using Various Dating Methods

In order to determine future dates, we must know how many days are in each month of the year. Aside from using a calendar, one commonly used memory device is this poem:

> Thirty days has September,
> April, June, and November,
> All the rest have thirty-one,
> Except February, which has twenty-eight.

In leap years, February has 29 days. Leap years fall every four years. An easy way to remember leap year is that it always occurs in the year of a presidential election: 1996, 2000, 2004, 2008. Note: these are the only years evenly divisible by 4.

Terms of Sale—Dating Methods

Ordinary Dating **Ordinary dating** is when the discount period and the credit period start on the date of the invoice. It is the most common method of dating the terms of sale. The last day to take advantage of the cash discount, the discount date, is found by adding the number of days in the discount period to the date of the invoice. For example, in order to receive a cash discount, an invoice dated November 8 with terms of 2/10, n/30 should be paid no later than November 18 (November 8 + 10 days). The last day to pay the invoice, the net date, is found by adding the number of days in the credit period to the invoice date. With terms of 2/10, n/30, the net date would be December 8 (November 8 + 30 days). If the buyer does not pay the bill by the net date, the seller may impose a penalty charge for late payment.

EXAMPLE

Robinson's Pharmacy receives an invoice from Sterling Drug Wholesalers for merchandise on August 19. The terms of sale are 3/10, n/45. If Robinson's elects to take the cash discount, what is the discount date? If Robinson's does not take the cash discount, what is the last day to pay the bill?

SOLUTION STRATEGY

Find the discount date by adding the number of days in the discount period to the date of the invoice.

$$\text{Discount date} = \text{August } 19 + 10 \text{ days} = \underline{\text{August } 29}$$

If the discount is not taken, find the net date by adding the number of days in the credit period to the invoice date.

$$\text{August } 19 + 45 \text{ days} = \begin{array}{l} 12 \text{ days left in August } (31-19) \\ +30 \text{ days in September} \\ \underline{+\ 3 \text{ days in October}} \\ 45 \text{ days} \end{array}$$

The net date, the 45th day, is <u>October 3</u>

TRY-IT   EXERCISE

11. Southwest Printing buys ink and paper from a supplier with an invoice date of June 11. If the terms of sale are 4/10, n/60, what is the discount date and what is the net date of the invoice?

Check your answers with the solutions on page 220.

EOM or Proximo Dating **EOM dating** or end-of-month dating means that the terms of sale start *after* the end of the month of the invoice. Another name for this dating method is **proximo,** or **prox.** Proximo means "in the following month." For example, 2/10 EOM, or 2/10 proximo, means that a 2% cash discount will be allowed if the bill is paid 10 days after the *end of the month* of the invoice. This is the case for any invoice dated from the 1st to the 25th of a month. If an invoice is dated the 26th of the month or later, the terms of sale begin *after* the end of the *following* month. Unless otherwise specified, the net amount is due *20 days* after the discount date.

a. **What are the discount date and the net date of an invoice dated March 3, with terms of 3/15 EOM?**

b. **What are the discount date and the net date of an invoice dated March 27, with terms of 3/15 EOM?**

SOLUTION STRATEGY

a. Because the invoice date is between the 1st and the 25th of the month, March 3, the discount date on terms of 3/15 EOM would be 15 days *after* the end of the month of the invoice. The net date will be 20 days later.

$$\text{Discount date} = 15 \text{ days after the end of March} = \underline{\text{April 15}}$$

$$\text{Net date} = \text{April } 15 + 20 \text{ days} = \underline{\text{May 5}}$$

b. Because the invoice date is after the 26th of the month, March 27, the discount date on terms of 3/15 EOM would be 15 days *after* the end of the month *following* the invoice month. The net date will be 20 days later.

$$\text{Discount date} = 15 \text{ days after the end of April} = \underline{\text{May 15}}$$

$$\text{Net date} = \text{May } 15 + 20 \text{ days} = \underline{\text{June 4}}$$

T R Y - I T   EXERCISE

12. a. **What are the discount date and the net date of an invoice dated November 18, with terms of 3/15 EOM?**

b. **What are the discount date and the net date of an invoice dated November 27, with terms of 3/15 EOM?**

Check your answers with the solutions on page 220.

● **ROG dating**

Receipt of goods dating. Terms of sale begin on the date the goods are received by the buyer.

ROG Dating Receipt of goods or **ROG dating** is a common method used when shipping times are long, such as with special or custom orders. When ROG dating is used, the terms of sale begin the day the goods are received at the buyer's location. With this method, the buyer doesn't have to pay for the merchandise before it arrives. An example would be 2/10 ROG. As usual, the net date is 20 days after the discount date.

What are the discount date and the net date for an invoice dated June 23, if the shipment arrives on August 16, and the terms are 3/15 ROG?

SOLUTION STRATEGY

In this case, the discount period starts on August 16, the date the shipment arrives. The net date will be 20 days after the discount date.

$$\text{Discount date} = \text{August } 16 + 15 \text{ days} = \underline{\text{August } 31}$$

$$\text{Net date} = \text{August } 31 + 20 \text{ days} = \underline{\text{September } 20}$$

TRY-IT   EXERCISE

13. **What are the discount date and the net date of an invoice dated October 11, if the shipment arrives on December 29, and the terms are 2/20 ROG?**

Check your answers with the solutions on page 220.

Extra Dating   The last dating method commonly used in business today is called **Extra, Ex, or X dating.** With this dating method, the seller offers an extra discount period to the buyer as an incentive for purchasing slow-moving or out-of-season merchandise, such as Christmas goods in July or bathing suits in January. An example would be 3/10, 60 extra. This means the buyer gets a 3% cash discount in 10 days plus 60 *extra* days, or a total of 70 days. Once again, unless otherwise specified, the net date is 20 days after the discount date.

● **extra, ex, or x dating**
The buyer receives an extra discount period as an incentive to purchase slow-moving or out-of-season merchandise.

EXAMPLE

What are the discount date and the net date of an invoice dated February 9, with terms of 3/15, 40 Extra?

SOLUTION STRATEGY

These terms, 3/15, 40 Extra, give the retailer 55 days (15 + 40) from February 9 to take the cash discount. The net date will be 20 days after the discount date.

$$\text{Discount date} = \text{February } 9 + 55 \text{ days} = \underline{\text{April } 5}$$

$$\text{Net date} = \text{April } 5 + 20 \text{ days} = \underline{\text{April } 25}$$

TRY-IT   EXERCISE

14. **What are the discount date and the net date of an invoice dated February 22, with terms of 4/20, 60 Extra?**

Check your answers with the solutions on page 220.

REVIEW EXERCISES   CHAPTER 7—SECTION IV

Calculate the cash discount and the net amount due for each of the following transactions:

	Amount of Invoice	Terms of Sale	Cash Discount	Net Amount Due
1.	$15,800.00	3/15, n/30	$474.00	$15,326.00
2.	12,660.00	2/10, n/45	$253.20	$12,406.80

Complete, worked out solutions for exercises 1–2 appear in the appendix following the index.

Complete, worked out solutions for exercises 3–9 appear in the appendix following the index.

3.	2,421.00	4/10, n/30	$96.84	$2,324.16
4.	6,940.20	2/10, n/30	$138.80	$6,801.40
5.	9,121.44	$3\frac{1}{2}$/15, n/60	$319.25	$8,802.19

For the following transactions, calculate the credit given for the partial payment, and the net amount due on the invoice:

	Amount of Invoice	Terms of Sale	Partial Payment	Credit for Partial Payment	Net Amount Due
6.	$8,303.00	2/10, n/30	$2,500	$2,551.02	$5,751.98
7.	1,344.60	3/10, n/45	460	$474.23	$870.37
8.	5,998.20	4/15, n/60	3,200	$3,333.33	$2,664.87
9.	7,232.08	$4\frac{1}{2}$/20, n/45	5,500	$5,759.16	$1,472.92

Using the ordinary dating method, calculate the discount date and the net date for the following transactions:

	Date of Invoice	Terms of Sale	Discount Date(s)	Net Date
10.	November 4	2/10, n/45	Nov. 14	Dec. 19
11.	April 23	3/15, n/60	May 8	June 22
12.	August 11	3/20, n/45	Aug. 31	Sept. 25
13.	January 29	2/10, 1/20, n/60	2% 1% Feb. 8, Feb. 18	Mar. 30
14.	July 8	4/25, n/90	Aug. 2	Oct. 6

Using the EOM, ROG, and Extra dating methods, calculate the discount date and the net date for the following transactions. Unless otherwise specified, the net date is 20 days after the discount date:

	Date of Invoice	Terms of Sale	Discount Date	Net Date
15.	December 5	2/10, EOM	Jan. 10	Jan. 30
16.	June 27	3/15, EOM	Aug. 15	Sept. 4
17.	September 1	3/20, ROG		
		Rec'd Oct. 3	Oct. 23	Nov. 12
18.	February 11	2/10, 60 Extra	Apr. 22	May 12
19.	May 18	4/25, EOM	June 25	July 15
20.	October 26	2/10, ROG		
		Rec'd Nov. 27	Dec. 7	Dec. 27

21. The Mayfield Company received an invoice from a vendor on April 12 in the amount of $1,420.00. The terms of sale were 2/15, n/45. The invoice included freight charges of $108. The vendor sent $250 in merchandise that was not ordered. These goods will be returned by Mayfield. (Remember, no discounts on freight or returned goods.)

    a. What are the discount date and the net date?

        Discount date
        April 12 + 15 days = April 27
        Net date
        April 12 + 45 days = May 27

    b. What is the amount of the cash discount?

        Cash discount $1,420.00 − $108.00 − $250.00 = $1,062.00
        $1,062.00 × .02 = $21.24

    c. What is the net amount due?

        $1,062.00 − $21.24 = $1,040.76
                    +   108.00 Freight
        Net amount due $1,148.76

22. An invoice is dated August 29 with terms of 4/15 EOM.

    a. What is the discount date?

       October 15

    b. What is the net date?

       October 15 + 20 days = November 4

23. An invoice dated January 15 has terms of 3/20 ROG. The goods are delayed in shipment and arrive on March 2.

    a. What is the discount date?

       March 22

    b. What is the net date?

       March 22 + 20 days = April 11

24. What payment should be made on an invoice in the amount of $3,400 dated August 7, if the terms of sale are 3/15, 2/30, n/45, and the bill is paid on:

    a. August 19?

       August 7 to August 19 = 12 days   This is within 3% discount period.

          $3,400.00 × .03   = $102.00

       $3,400.00 − $102.00   = $3,298.00 on August 19

    b. September 3?

       August 7 to September 3 = 27 days   This is within 2% discount period.

          $3,400.00 × .02   = $68.00

       $3,400.00 − $68.00   = $3,332.00 on September 3

25. City Cellular purchased $28,900 in portable phones and beepers on April 25. The terms of sale were 4/20, 3/30, n/60. Freight terms were F.O.B. destination. Returned goods amounted to $650.

    a. What is the net amount due if City Cellular sends the manufacturer a partial payment of $5,000 on May 20?

       April 25 to May 20 = 25 days   This is within 3% discount period.

          $28,900.00 − $650.00 = $28,250.00 Invoice less returns

       Partial payment credit = $\dfrac{5,000.00}{.97}$ = $5,154.64

          $28,250.00 − $5,154.64 = $23,095.36 Net due

    b. What is the net date?

       April 25 + 60 days = June 24

       Net date = June 24

c. If the manufacturer charges a $4\frac{1}{2}$% late fee, how much would City Cellular owe if they didn't pay the balance by the net date?

Net due on net date = $23,095.36

$23,095.36 \times .045 = \$1,039.29$ Late fee

$+\quad 1,039.29$

$\underline{\$24,134.65}$ Net due after net date

Answer Questions 26–30 from the information on the following invoice:

TARGET
ELECTRONIC WHOLESALERS
1979 N.E. 123 Street
Jacksonville, Florida 33181

Sold to: StereoMaster Stores
117 Peachtree Street
Atlanta, Georgia 43113

Invoice Date: June 28, 199X

Terms of Sale: 3/15,n/30 ROG

Quantity	Stock #	Description	Unit Price	Amount
50	4811V	AM-FM Stereo Receivers	$297.50	$14,875.00
25	511CX	CD Players-8 bit	132.28	3,307.00
40	6146M	VCR-Super VHS	658.12	26,324.80
20	1031A	D.A.T. Recorders	591.00	11,820.00

Merchandise Total	$56,326.80
Insurance & Freight charges	$1,150.00
Invoice Total	$57,476.80

AM-FM Stereo Receivers $50 \times \$297.50 = \$14,875.00$
CD Players $25 \times \$132.28 = \quad 3,307.00$
VCR-Super VHS $40 \times \$658.12 = 26,324.80$
D.A.T. Recorders $20 \times \$591.00 = 11,820.00$
Merchandise total $\underline{\$56,326.80}$
Insurance + freight $\underline{1,150.00}$
Invoice total $\underline{\$57,476.80}$

26. Extend each line and calculate the merchandise total and the total amount of the invoice, using the space provided on the invoice.   See invoice above.

27. What is the discount date and the net date if the shipment arrived on July 16?

Discount date = July 16 + 15 days = $\underline{\text{July 31}}$
Net date = July 16 + 30 days = $\underline{\text{August 15}}$

28. While in transit, 5 CD players and 4 D.A.T. recorders were damaged and will be returned. What is the amount of the returned merchandise? What is the revised invoice total?

CD players $5 \times \$132.28 = \quad\$661.40$
D.A.T. recorders $4 \times \$591.00 = +\quad 2364.00$
Returned merchandise = $\underline{\$3,025.40}$
Revised invoice total = $\$57,476.80 - \$3,025.40 = \underline{\$54,451.40}$

29. What are the amount of the cash discount and the net amount due if the discount is taken?

$57,476.80$ Total
$-\quad 3,025.40$ Returns
$\underline{-\quad 1,150.00}$ Insurance and freight
$\$53,301.40 \times .03 = \underline{\$1,599.04}$ Cash discount

$53,301.40$ Merchandise
$-1,599.04$ Cash discount
$\underline{+1,150.00}$ Insurance and freight
$\$52,852.36$ Net amount due

30. If StereoMaster sends in a partial payment of $20,000 within the discount period, what is the net balance still due?

Partial payment credit = $\dfrac{20,000}{.97} = \$20,618.56$

Net balance = $\$52,852.36 - 20,618.56 = \underline{\$32,233.80}$

FORMULAS

The Invoice

Extended total = Number of items × Cost per item

Trade Discounts—Single

Trade discount amount = List price × Trade discount percent

Net price = List price − Trade discount amount

Net price = List price (100% − Trade discount percent)

$$\text{Trade discount rate} = \frac{\text{Amount of trade discount}}{\text{List Price}}$$

Trade Discounts—Series

Net price = List price × Net price factor

Single equivalent discount = 1 − Net price factor

Trade discount amount = List price × Single equivalent discount

Cash Discounts and Terms of Sale

Net amount due = Net price (100% − Cash discount percent)

$$\text{Partial payment credit} = \frac{\text{Partial payment}}{100\% - \text{Cash discount percent}}$$

Net amount due = Net price − Partial payment credit

CHAPTER 7 ■ INVOICES, TRADE AND CASH DISCOUNTS	SUMMARY CHART

SECTION I   THE INVOICE

Topic	P/O, Page	Important Concepts	Illustrative Examples
Reading and Understanding the Parts of an Invoice	7–1 186	Refer to Exhibits 7-1, 7-2, and 7-3.	
Extending and Totaling an Invoice	7–2 190	Extended amount = Number of items × Cost per item Invoice subtotal = Total of extended amount column Invoice total = Invoice subtotal + Other charges	The Great Subversion, a sandwich shop, ordered 25 lbs. of ham at $3.69 per pound, and 22 lbs. of cheese at $4.25 per pound. There is a $7.50 delivery charge. Extend each item and find the invoice subtotal and invoice total. 25 × 3.69 = 92.25 ham 22 × 4.25 = 93.50 cheese 185.75 subtotal + 7.50 delivery $193.25 invoice total

SECTION II   TRADE DISCOUNTS—SINGLE

Topic	P/O, Page	Important Concepts	Illustrative Examples
Calculating the Amount of a Single Trade Discount	7–3 193	Trade discounts are reductions from the manufacturer's list price given to businesses in the trade for the performance of various marketing functions. **Trade discount amount = List price × Trade discount percent**	The Sunglass King ordered merchandise from a manufacturer with a list price of $12,700. Since they are in the trade Sunglass King gets a 35% trade discount. What is the amount of the trade discount? Trade disc = 12,700 × .35 = $\underline{\$4,445}$
Calculating Net Price Using the Net Price Factor, Complement Method	7–4 193	**Net price factor = 100% – Trade discount percent** **Net price = List price (100% – Trade discount%)**	From the previous problem, use the net price factor to find the net price of the order for Sunglass King. Net price = 12,700 (100% − 35%) Net price = 12,700 × .65 = $\underline{\$8,255}$
Calculating Trade Discount Rate When List Price and Net Price Are Known	7–5 194	$\text{Trade discount rate} = \dfrac{\text{Amount of trade discount}}{\text{List price}}$	Cycle World Bike Shop orders merchandise listing for $5,300 from Schwinn. They receive a $2,110 trade discount. What is the trade discount rate? $\text{Trade disc rate} = \dfrac{2,110}{5,300} = \underline{39.8\%}$

SECTION III   TRADE DISCOUNTS—SERIES

Topic	P/O, Page	Important Concepts	Illustrative Examples
Calculating Net Price and Trade Discount Amount Using a Series of Trade Discounts	7–6 198	Net price is found by taking each trade discount in the series from the succeeding net price until all discounts have been deducted. **Trade discount = List price – Net price**	An invoice with merchandise listing for $4,700 was entitled to trade discounts of 20% and 15%. What is the net price and the amount of the trade discount? 4,700 × .20 = 940 4,700 − 940 = 3,760 3,760 × .15 = 564 3,760 − 564 = $\underline{\$3,196}$ Net price Trade discount = 4,700 − 3,196 = $\underline{\$1,504}$
Calculating Net Price of a Series of Trade Discounts Using the Net Price Factor, Complement Method	7–7 199	Net price factor is found by subtracting each trade discount from 100% (complement) and multiplying these complements together. **Net price = List price × Net price factor**	Use the net price factor method to verify your answer to the previous problem. 100% 100% −20% −15% .80 × .85 = .68 Net price factor Net price = 4,700 × .68 = $\underline{\$3,196}$

III, continued

Topic	P/O, Page	Important Concepts	Illustrative Examples
Calculating the Amount of a Trade Discount Using a Single Equivalent Discount	7–8 200	Single equivalent discount = $\quad$ 1 – Net price factor Trade discount = $\quad$ List price × Single equivalent discount	What is the single equivalent discount in the previous problem? Use this to verify your trade discount answer. Single equivalent discount = 1 – .68 = .32 Trade discount = 4,700 × .32 $\quad$ = $1,504

SECTION IV   CASH DISCOUNTS AND TERMS OF SALE

Topic	P/O, Page	Important Concepts	Illustrative Examples
Calculating Cash Discount and Net Amount Due	7–9 206	Terms of sale are the details of when an invoice must be paid, and if a cash discount is offered. Cash discount is an extra discount offered by the seller as an incentive for early payment of an invoice. Cash discount = $\quad$ Net price × Cash discount percent Net amount due = $\quad$ Net price – Cash discount	Wilbur's Auto Parts orders merchandise for $1,800 including $100 in freight charges. They get a 3% cash discount. What is the amount of the cash discount and the net amount due? 1,800 – 100 = 1,700 Net price Cash discount = 1,700 × .03 $\quad$ = $51 1,700 – 51 = 1,649 $\quad$ + 100 $\quad$ Freight $\quad$ $1,749 $\quad$ Net amount due
Calculating Net Amount Due with Credit Given for Partial Payment	7–10 207	Partial payment credit $= \dfrac{\text{Partial payment}}{100\% - \text{Cash discount percent}}$ Net amount due = $\quad$ Net price – Partial payment credit	Fancy Fashions makes a partial payment of $3,000 on an invoice of $7,900. The terms of sale are 3/15, n/30. What is the amount of the partial payment credit, and how much does Fancy Fashions still owe on the invoice? Part pmt credit $= \dfrac{3000}{100\% - 3\%}$ $\quad = $3,092.78$ Net amount due = $\quad$ 7,900.00 $\quad$ – 3,092.78 $\quad$ $4,807.22
Determining Discount Date and Net Date Using Various Dating Methods	7–11 208	Discount date: last date to take advantage of a cash discount. Net date: last date to pay an invoice without incurring a penalty charge.	

IV, continued

Topic	P/O, Page	Important Concepts	Illustrative Examples
Ordinary Dating	7–11 209	Ordinary dating: discount period and the credit period start on the date of the invoice.	Sam's Jewelers receives an invoice for merchandise on March 12 with terms of 3/15, n/30. What are the discount date and the net date? Disc date = March 12 + 15 days = March 27 Net date = March 12 + 30 days = April 11
EOM or Proximo Dating Method	7–11 209	EOM means end of month. It is a dating method in which the terms of sale start *after* the end of the month of the invoice. If the invoice is dated after the 25th of the month, the terms of sale start *after* the end of the *following* month. Unless otherwise specified, the net date is *20 days* after the discount date. · *Proximo* or prox. is another name for EOM dating. It means in the following month.	Superior Cleaning Service buys supplies with terms of sale of 2/10, EOM. What are the discount date and the net date if the invoice date is: a. May 5? b. May 27? a. May 5 invoice terms start *after* the end of May: Discount date = June 10 Net date = June 10 + 20 days = June 30 b. May 27 invoice terms start *after* the end of the *following* month, June: Discount date = July 10 Net date = July 10 + 20 days = July 30
ROG Dating Method	7–11 210	ROG means receipt of goods. It is a dating method in which the terms of sale begin on the date the goods are received rather than the invoice date. This is used to accommodate long shipping times. Unless otherwise specified, the net date is *20 days* after the discount date.	An invoice dated August 24 has terms of 3/10 ROG. If the merchandise arrives on October 1, what are the discount date and the net date? Disc date = October 1 + 10 days = October 11 Net date = October 11 + 20 days = October 31

IV, continued

Topic	P/O, Page	Important Concepts	Illustrative Examples
Extra Dating Method	7–11 211	Extra, Ex, or X is a dating method in which the buyer receives an extra period of time before the terms of sale begin. Vendors use extra dating as an incentive to entice buyers to purchase out-of-season or slow-moving merchandise. Unless otherwise specified, the net date is *20 days* after the discount date.	The Lacy Linen Shop buys merchandise from a vendor with terms of 3/15, 60 Extra. The invoice is dated December 11. What are the discount date and the net date? Disc date = December 11 + 75 days = February 24 Net date = February 24 + 20 = March 16

TRY-IT EXERCISE SOLUTIONS

1. a. Shutterbug Camera Shops **b.** 44929
   c. November 27, 199x **d.** $3,744.00
   e. FotoFair **f.** Net—30 Days
   g. 1864 N.W. 123rd St. Chicago, Ill. 60613 **h.** J. Herman
   i. Federal Express **j.** Knoxville, TN
   k. $183.70 **l.** $9,117.50
   m. $41.88 **n.** $9,301.20

2.

Stock #	Quantity	Unit	Merchandise Description	Unit Price	Total
R443	125	ea.	Food Processors	$ 89.00	$11,125.00
B776	24	ea.	Microwave Ovens	225.40	5,409.60
Z133	6	doz.	12" Mixers	54.12	324.72
Z163	1	bx.	Mixer Covers	166.30	166.30
				Invoice Subtotal	17,025.62
				Shipping Charges	194.20
				Invoice Total	$17,219.82

3. Trade discount amount = List price × Trade discount percent
Trade discount amount = 7,600 × .30 = $2,280.00

4. Net price = List price (100% − Trade discount percent)
Net price = 2,100 (100% − .35)
Net price = 2,100 × .65 = $1,365.00

5. Trade discount amount = List price − Net price
Trade discount amount = 109,500 − 63,300 = $46,200

$$\text{Trade discount rate} = \frac{\text{Amount of trade discount}}{\text{List price}} = \frac{46,200}{109,500} = 42.2\%$$

6.

25,000	25,000	16,250	16,250	13,000	13,000
× .35	− 8,750	× .20	− 3,250	× .10	− 1,300
8,750	16,250	3,250	13,000	1,300	$11,700 = Net price

Trade discount amount = 25,000 − 11,700 = $13,300

7. a.

$$\begin{array}{ccc} 100\% & 100\% & 100\% \\ \underline{-\ 30\%} & \underline{-\ 20\%} & \underline{-\ 12\%} \\ .7 \quad \times & .8 \quad \times & .88 \quad = \underline{.4928} = \text{Net price factor} \end{array}$$

b. Net price = List price × Net price factor
Net price = 3,500 × .4928 = $\underline{\$1,724.80}$

c. Net price = List price × Net price factor
Net price = 5,800 × .4928 = $\underline{\$2,858.24}$

8.

$$\begin{array}{ccc} 100\% & 100\% & 100\% \\ \underline{-\ 25\%} & \underline{-\ 15\%} & \underline{-\ 10\%} \\ .75 \quad \times & .85 \quad \times & .9 \quad = .57375 = .5738 \text{ Net price factor} \end{array}$$

Single equivalent discount = 1 − Net price factor
Single equivalent discount = 1 − .5738 = $\underline{.4262}$

Trade discount amount = List price × Single equivalent discount
Trade discount amount = 36,800.00 × .4262 = $\underline{\$15,684.16}$

9. Cash discount = Net price × Cash discount percent
Cash discount = 8,300.00 × .03 = $\underline{\$249.00}$

Net amount due = Net price − Cash discount
Net amount due = 8,300.00 − 249.00 = $\underline{\$8,051.00}$

10. Partial payment credit = $\dfrac{\text{Partial payment}}{100\% - \text{Cash discount percent}}$

Partial payment credit = $\dfrac{20,000.00}{100\% - 4\%} = \dfrac{20,000.00}{.96} = \underline{\$20,833.33}$

Net amount due = Net price − Partial payment credit
Net amount due = 45,300.00 − 20,833.33 = $\underline{\$24,466.67}$

11. Discount date = June 11 + 10 days = $\underline{\text{June 21}}$

Net date = June 11 + 60 days

$$\begin{array}{l} 30 \text{ Days in June} \\ \underline{-11} \text{ Discount date} \\ 19 \text{ June} \\ 31 \text{ July} \\ \underline{10 \text{ Aug}} \longrightarrow \underline{\text{August 10}} \\ 60 \text{ days} \end{array}$$

12. a. Discount date = 15 days after end of November = $\underline{\text{December 15}}$

Net date = December 15 + 20 days = $\underline{\text{January 4}}$

b. Discount date = 15 days after end of December = $\underline{\text{January 15}}$

Net date = January 15 + 20 days = $\underline{\text{February 4}}$

13. Discount date = December 29 + 20 days = $\underline{\text{January 18}}$

Net date = January 18 + 20 days = $\underline{\text{February 7}}$

14. Discount date = February 22 + 80 days = $\underline{\text{May 13}}$

Net date = May 13 + 20 days = $\underline{\text{June 2}}$

Name_____

Class_____

Answer the following questions based on the Sunshine Patio Furniture invoice below:

1. Who is the vendor?
Sunshine Patio Furniture Manufacturers

2. What is the date of the invoice?
November 2

3. What is the stock # of rockers?
4387

4. What does dz. mean?
dozen

5. What is the unit price of lounge covers?
$46.55

6. What is the destination city?
Raleigh, NC

7. What is the extended total for chaise lounges with no armrest?
20 × $127.90 = $2,558.00

8. Who pays the freight if the terms are F.O.B. shipping point?
The Buyer, Patio Magic Stores

9. What is the invoice subtotal?

10. What is the invoice total?

ANSWERS

1. Sunshine Patio Furniture Manufacturers

2. November 2

3. 4387

4. dozen

5. $46.55

6. Raleigh, NC

7. $2,558.00

8. The Buyer, Patio Magic Stores

9. $11,562.45

10. $12,164.95

9.　　40 × $169.00 = $6,760.00
　　　20 × $127.90 = $2,558.00
　　　24 × $ 87.70 = $2,104.80
　　　　3 × $ 46.55 = $　139.65
　Invoice subtotal　$11,562.45

10.　　　　　　$11,562.45
　　　　　　　　　$125.00
　　　　　　+　$477.50
　Invoice total $12,164.95

Sunshine
Patio Furniture Manufacturers
1930 Main Street
Ft. Worth, Texas

SOLD TO: **Patio Magic Stores**
                3386 Fifth Avenue
                Raleigh, N.C.

DATE: November 2

INVOICE #   **B-112743**

TERMS OF SALE: Net 30 days   **SHIPPING INFO: Fed-Ex Freight**

STOCK #	QUANTITY	UNIT	MERCHANDISE DESCRIPTION	UNIT PRICE	TOTAL
1455	40	ea.	Chaise Lounges with armrest	$169.00	$6,760.00
1475	20	ea.	Chaise Lounges—no armrest	127.90	2,558.00
4387	24	ea.	Rocker Chairs	87.70	2,104.80
8100	3	dz.	Plastic Lounge Covers	46.55	139.65

                       INVOICE SUBTOTAL: $11,562.45
                       Packing and Handling: $125.00
                       Shipping charges: 477.50

                       INVOICE TOTAL: $12,164.95

ANSWERS

11. _____$1,485.00_____

12. a. _____$203.99_____

b. _____$475.96_____

13. _____33.76%_____

14. a. _____$1,083.00_____

b. _____$1,292.00_____

15. _____Fancy Footwear_____

16. a. _____0.57375_____

11. E-Z Shop Grocery Store receives an invoice for the purchase of merchandise with a list price of $5,500. Because they are in the trade, E-Z Shop gets a 27% trade discount. What is the amount of the trade discount?

Trade discount = $5,500.00 × .27 = $1,485.00

12. Natureland Garden Supply buys lawnmowers that list for $679.95 less a 30% trade discount.

a. What is the amount of the trade discount?

Trade discount = $679.95 × .30 = $203.99

b. What is the net price of each lawnmower?

Net price = $679.95 − $203.99 = $475.96

13. Billy's BBQ Restaurant places an order with a meat and poultry supplier listing for $1,250. They receive a trade discount of $422 on the order. What is the trade discount rate on this transaction?

Trade discount rate = $\dfrac{\$422.00}{1,250.00}$ = .3376 = 33.76%

14. Exotic Gardens Florist Shop purchases an order of imported roses with a list price of $2,375 less trade discounts of 15/20/20.

a. What is the amount of the trade discount?

.85 × .80 × .80 = 0.544   1.00 − 0.544 = .456

Trade discount = $2,375.00 × .456 = $1,083.00

b. What is the net amount of the order?

Net price of order = $2,375.00 − $1,083.00 = $1,292.00

15. First String Sports can purchase sneakers for $450 per dozen less trade discounts of 14/12 from Ideal Shoes. Fancy Footwear is offering the same sneakers for $435 less trade discounts of 18/6. Which supplier offers a lower net price?

Ideal Shoes	Fancy Footwear
.86 × .88 = .7568	.82 × .94 = .7708
450.00 × .7568 = $340.56	435.00 × .7708 = $335.30

Fancy Footwear offers a lower price.

16. a. What is the net price factor for trade discounts of 25/15/10?

Net price factor = .75 × .85 × .90 = 0.57375

b. Use that net price factor to find the net price of a couch listing for $800.

Net price of couch = $800.00 × .57375 = $459.00

17. a. What is the net price factor of the trade discount series 20/15/11?

Net price factor = .80 × .85 × .89 = 0.6052

b. What is the single equivalent discount?

Single equivalent discount = 1.00 − 0.6052 = .3948

18. The Empress Carpet Company orders merchandise for $17,700, including $550 in freight charges, from The Apex Carpet Mill on May 4. Carpets valued at $1,390 will be returned because they are damaged. The terms of sale are 2/10, n/30 ROG. The shipment arrives on May 26, and Empress wants to take advantage of the cash discount.

a. By what date must they pay the invoice?

May 26 + 10 = June 5

b. As the bookkeeper for Empress, how much will you send to Apex?

$17,700.00
 −   550.00 Freight
 − 1,390.00 Returns
 $15,760.00 Amount subject to discount

$15,760.00 × .98 = $15,444.80
                    + 550.00 Freight
Total amount due $15,994.80

19. Blue Ribbon Laundry receives an invoice for detergent dated April 9 with terms of 3/15, n/30.

a. What is the discount date?

April 9 + 15 = April 24

b. What is the net date?

April 9 + 30 = May 9

c. If the invoice terms are changed to 3/15 EOM, what is the new discount date?

May 15

ANSWERS

b.	$459.00
17. a.	0.6052
b.	.3948
18. a.	June 5
b.	$15,994.80
19. a.	April 24
b.	May 9
c.	May 15

d. What is the new net date?

May 15 + 20 = <u>June 4</u>

20. Ned's Sheds purchases building materials from Grove Lumber for $3,700 with terms of 4/15, n/30. The invoice is dated October 17. Ned decides to send in a $2,000 partial payment.

a. By what date must the partial payment be sent to take advantage of the cash discount?

Discount date = October 17 + 15 = <u>November 1</u>

b. What is the net date?

Net date = October 17 + 30 = <u>November 16</u>

c. If partial payment was sent by the discount date, what is the balance still due on the order?

$$\text{Partial payment credit} = \frac{\$2,000.00}{.96} = \$2,083.33$$

$$\begin{array}{r} \$3,700.00 \\ -2,083.33 \\ \hline \end{array}$$
Balance due = <u>$1,616.67</u>

 BUSINESS DECISION
The Busy Executive

21. You are a salesperson for Victory Lane Wholesale Auto Parts. You have just taken a phone order from one of your best customers, Champion Motors. Because you were quite busy when the call came in, you recorded the details of the order on a notepad. Before the order can be processed, you must transfer your notes to an invoice, extend each line, and calculate the total. Use the invoice form on the next page.

Phone Order Notes

- The invoice date is April 4, 199X.
- The customer order no. is 443B.
- Champion Motors' warehouse is located at 7011 N.W. 4th Avenue, Columbus, Ohio, 70409.
- Terms of sale—3/15, n/45.
- The order will be filled by D. Watson.
- The goods will be shipped by truck.
- Champion Motors' home office is located next to the warehouse at 7013 N.W. 4th Avenue.
- Champion ordered 44 car batteries, stock #394, listing for $69.95 each; and 24 truck batteries, stock #395, listing for $89.95 each. These items get trade discounts of 20/15.
- Champion also ordered 36 cases of 10W/30 motor oil, stock #838-W, listing for $11.97 per case; and 48 cases of 10W/40 super-oil, stock #1621S, listing for $14.97 per case. These items get trade discounts of 20/20/12.
- The freight charges for the order amount to $67.50.
- Insurance charges amount to $27.68.

INVOICE

**Victory Lane
Wholesale Auto Parts
422 Riverfront Road
Cincinnatti, Ohio 78002**

Invoice #

Invoice Date: April 4, 199X

Sold To: Champion Motors
7013 N.W. 4th Ave
Columbus, Ohio 70409

Ship To: Champion Motors
7011 N.W. 4th Ave
Columbus, Ohio 70409

Customer Order No.		Salesperson	Ship Via	Terms of Sale	Filled By
443B			Truck	3/15, n/45	D. Watson

Quantity Ordered	Stock Number	Description	Unit List Price	Trade Discounts	Extended Amount
44	#394	Car Batteries	$69.95	20/15	$2,092.90
24	#395	Truck Batteries	$89.95	20/15	1,467.98
36 Cases	#838-W	10W 30 Motor Oil	$11.97	20/20/12	242.69
48 Cases	#1621-S	10W 40 Super Oil	$14.97	20/20/12	404.69

Invoice Subtotal	$4,208.26
Shipping charges	67.50
Insurance	27.68
Invoice Total	$4,303.44

Golden Arches Everywhere

Did you know that each day over 18 million people eat at McDonald's restaurants, the largest food service organization in the world. Since the Big Mac sandwich was invented in 1967, over 18 billion have been sold.

Most American children recognize Ronald McDonald by age 2. For many of them, McDonald's is their first restaurant experience. However, the "superheavy users," as McDonald's calls them, are males in their mid-teens to early 30s. They come back at least twice a week, and account for 75% of the company's business.

In 1995, McDonald's rang up almost $30 billion in worldwide sales, up 15% from 1994, and up from $18.8 billion in 1990. Over half of those customers never got out of their vehicles.

There are currently about 11,500 McDonald's restaurants in the United States, and about 7,000 in 89 other countries. Three new restaurants open each day. In addition, McDonald's food is served on United Airlines flights.

Chairman and chief executive officer, Michael R. Quinlan describes the company mission: "Someday we are all meant to be no more than a four-minute walk or drive from McDonald's."

SOURCE: 1995 Annual Report, McDonald's Corporation.

OVER 456 x 10²¹ SOLD

FLY-IN WINDOW

Career Track:

Restaurant and Food Service Managers

Nature of the Work

Food service managers have many responsibilities Efficient and profitable operations require that managers select and appropriately price interesting menu items, efficiently use food and other supplies, and recruit, train, and supervise adequate numbers of workers.

Additional managerial duties include supervising the kitchen and the dining room; resolving customer complaints about food quality or service; and maintaining records of payroll and the costs of supplies and equipment purchased.

Working Conditions

Restaurant and food service managers are often the first to arrive in the morning and the last to leave at night. Since evenings and weekends are popular dining periods, night and weekend work is common. Many managers work 50 hours or more per week.

Job Outlook

Employment of restaurant and food service managers is expected to increase much faster than the average for all occupations through the year 2005. Population growth, rising personal incomes, and increased leisure time will continue to produce growth in the number of meals consumed outside the home. To meet the demand for prepared food, more restaurants will be built, and more managers will be employed to supervise them.

SOURCE: *Occupational Outlook Handbook*, U.S. Department of Labor, 1994-95 Edition.

Now That's A Lot of Dough!

Did you know that according to the National Association of Pizza Operators, Americans as a whole consume an average of 90 acres of pizza a day?

According to a study done by Domino's Pizza, colleges with less than 10,000 students order 12% more pizza than larger institutions and freshman dorm students order 15% more than upperclassmen.

SOURCE: Dean D. Dauphinais and Kathleen Droste, *Astounding Averages*! Visible Ink Press, 1995; 38, 39. Visible Ink Press is a division of Gale Research Inc.

TOP 10 FAST FOOD CHAINS (U.S.)

Rank	Chain	Revenue (millions)
1	McDonald's	$23,587
2	KFC	7,100
3	Burger King	6,700
4	Pizza Hut	6,300
5	Wendy's	3,924
6	Taco Bell	3,720
7	Hardee's	3,550
8	Dairy Queen	2,400
9	Subway	2,200
9	Domino's Pizza	2,200

SOURCE: Russell Ash, *The Top 10 of Everything*, 1996. (New York: Dorling Kindersley, 1995); 192.

Brainteaser

As the merchandise manager for a department store, decide which is a more favorable deal from one of your vendors: a discount of 20% followed by an increase of 20%, or an increase of 20% followed by a discount of 20%?

SOURCE: *Mathematics Teacher* Magazine (February 1984).

Answer to Last Issue's Brainteaser

50 Girls

$$99 - 50 = 49, \frac{49}{50} = .98 = 98\%$$

Chapter 8

Markup and Markdown

Performance Objectives

MARKUP BASED ON COST

Determining an appropriate selling price for a company's goods or services is an extremely important function in business. The price must be attractive to potential customers, yet sufficient to cover expenses and provide the company with a reasonable profit.

In business, expenses are separated into two major categories. The first is the **cost of goods sold.** To a manufacturer, this expense would be the cost of production; to a wholesaler or retailer, the expense is the price paid to a manufacturer or distributor for the merchandise. The second category includes all the other expenses required to operate the business, such as salaries, rent, utilities, taxes, insurance, advertising, maintenance, and so on. These expenses are known as **operating expenses,** overhead expenses, or simply **overhead.**

The amount added to the cost of an item to cover the operating expenses and profit is known as the **markup, markon,** or **margin.** It is the difference between the cost and the selling price of an item. Markup is applied at all levels of the marketing channels of distribution. This chapter deals with the business math applications involved in the pricing of goods and services.

8-1 Understanding and Using the Basic Retailing Equation to Find Cost, Amount of Markup, and Selling Price of an Item

The fundamental principle upon which business operates is to sell goods and services for a price high enough to cover all expenses and provide the owners with a reasonable profit. The formula that describes this principle is known as the **basic retailing equation.** The equation states that the selling price of an item is equal to the cost plus the markup.

$$\text{Selling price} = \text{Cost} + \text{Markup}$$

Using the abbreviations *C* for cost, *M* for markup, and *SP* for selling price, the formula is written as

$$SP = C + M$$

To illustrate, if a camera costs a retailer $60, and a $50 markup is added to cover operating expenses and profit, the selling price of the camera would be $110.

$$\$60 \text{ (cost)} + \$50 \text{ (markup)} = \$110 \text{ (selling price)}$$

In Chapter 5, we learned that equations are solved by isolating the unknown on one side and the knowns on the other. Using this theory, when the amount of markup is the unknown, the equation can be rewritten as

$$\text{Markup} = \text{Selling price} - \text{Cost} \qquad M = SP - C$$

When the cost is the unknown, the equation becomes

$$\text{Cost} = \text{Selling price} - \text{Markup} \qquad C = SP - M$$

The following examples illustrate how these formulas are used to determine the dollar amount of cost, markup, and selling price.

Sidebar definitions

● **cost of goods sold**

The cost of the merchandise sold during an operating period. One of two major expense categories of a business.

● **operating expenses, or overhead**

All business expenses, other than cost of merchandise, required to operate a business, such as payroll, rent, utilities, and insurance.

● **markup, markon, margin**

The amount added to the cost of an item to cover the operating expenses and profit. It is the difference between the cost and the selling price.

● **basic retailing equation**

The selling price of an item is equal to the cost plus the markup.

According to the basic retailing equation, the selling price of merchandise is equal to the cost plus the markup.

EXAMPLE

A card shop pays $8.00 for a picture frame. If a markup of $6.50 is added, what is the selling price of the frame?

SOLUTION STRATEGY

Because selling price is the unknown variable, we use the formula $SP = C + M$ as follows:

$$SP = C + M$$
$$SP = 8.00 + 6.50 = 14.50$$

Selling price = $\underline{\$14.50}$

EXAMPLE

The Electronic Warehouse buys printing calculators from Taiwan for $22.50 each. If they are sold for $39.95, what is the amount of the markup?

SOLUTION STRATEGY

Since the markup is the unknown variable, we use the formula $M = SP - C$ as follows:

$$M = SP - C$$
$$M = 39.95 - 22.50 = 17.45$$

Markup = $\underline{\$17.45}$

EXAMPLE

Food Fair Supermarkets sell Corn Crunchies for $3.29 per box. If the markup on this item is $2.12, how much did the store pay for the cereal?

SOLUTION STRATEGY

Since the cost is the unknown variable in this problem, we use the formula $C = SP - M$.

$$C = SP - M$$
$$C = 3.29 - 2.12 = 1.17$$

Cost = $\underline{\$1.17}$

TRY-IT EXERCISES

For each of the following, use the basic retailing equation to solve for the unknown:

1. Ceramic planters cost the manufacturer $6.80 per unit to produce. If a markup of $9.40 each is added to the cost, what is the selling price per planter?

2. The SuperSport sells a dozen golf balls for $28.50. If the distributor was paid $16.75, what is the amount of the markup?

3. After a wholesaler adds a markup of $75.00 to a television set, it is sold to a retail store for $290.00. What is the wholesaler's cost?

Check your answers with the solutions on page 254.

8-2 Calculating Percent Markup Based on Cost

In addition to being expressed in dollar amounts, markup is frequently expressed as a percent. There are two ways of representing markup as a percent: based on cost and based on selling price. Manufacturers and most wholesalers use cost as the base in calculating the percent markup since cost figures are readily available to them. When markup is based on cost, the cost is 100%, and the markup is expressed as a percent of that cost. Retailers, on the other hand, use selling price figures as the base of most calculations, including percent markup. In retailing, the selling price represents 100%, and the markup is expressed as a percent of that selling price.

In Chapter 6, we used the percentage formula, Portion = Rate × Base. To review these variables, portion is a *part* of a whole amount, base is the *whole amount,* and the rate, as a percent, describes what part the portion is of the base. When we calculate markup as a percent, we are actually solving a rate problem, using the formula: Rate = Portion ÷ Base.

When the markup is based on cost, the percent markup is the rate, the dollar amount of markup is the portion, and the cost, representing 100%, is the base. The answer will describe what percent the markup is of the cost, therefore it is called percent **markup based on cost.** We use the formula:

● **markup based on cost**
When cost is 100%, and the markup is expressed as a percent of that cost.

$$\text{Percent markup based on cost (rate)} = \frac{\text{Markup (portion)}}{\text{Cost (base)}} \quad \text{or} \quad \%M_{\text{COST}} = \frac{M}{C}$$

EXAMPLE

A manufacturer produces stainless steel sinks at a cost of $56.00 each. If the sinks are sold to distributors for $89.60 each, what are the amount of the markup and the percent markup based on cost?

SOLUTION STRATEGY

$$M = SP - C$$
$$M = 89.60 - 56.00 = 33.60$$

$$\text{Markup} = \underline{\$33.60}$$

$$\%M_{\text{COST}} = \frac{M}{C}$$

$$\%M_{\text{COST}} = \frac{33.60}{56.00} = .6$$

$$\text{Percent markup based on cost} = \underline{\underline{60\%}}$$

TRY-IT   **EXERCISE**

4. A wholesaler buys lamps for $45 and sells them for $63. What is the amount of the markup and the percent markup based on cost?

Check your answers with the solutions on page 254.

8-3 Calculating Selling Price When Cost and Percent Markup Based on Cost Are Known

From the basic retailing equation, we know that the selling price is equal to the cost plus the markup. When the markup is based on cost, the cost equals 100%, and the selling price equals 100% plus the percent markup. If, for example, the percent markup is 30%, then

$$\text{Selling price} = \text{Cost} + \text{Markup}$$
$$\text{Selling price} = 100\% + 30\%$$
$$\text{Selling price} = 130\% \text{ of the cost}$$

Since "of" means multiply, we multiply the cost by (100% plus the percent markup)

$$\text{Selling price} = \text{Cost}(100\% + \text{Percent markup based on cost})$$
$$SP = C(100\% + \%M_{COST})$$

EXAMPLE

A watch costs $50.00 to produce. If the manufacturer wants a 70% markup based on cost, what should be the selling price of the watch?

SOLUTION STRATEGY

$$SP = C(100\% + \%M_{COST})$$
$$SP = 50.00(100\% + 70\%)$$
$$SP = 50.00(170\%) = 50.00(1.7) = 85$$

Selling price = $85.00

TRY-IT   EXERCISE

5. **Capital Appliances buys toasters for $38.00. If a 65% markup based on cost is desired, what should be the selling price of the toaster?**

Check your answer with the solution on page 254.

8-4 Calculating Cost When Selling Price and Percent Markup Based on Cost Are Known

To calculate cost when selling price and percent markup on cost are known, let's use our knowledge of solving equations from Chapter 5. Since we are dealing with the same three variables from the last section, simply solve the equation $SP = C(100\% + \%M_{COST})$ for the cost. Cost, the unknown, is isolated to one side of the equation by dividing both sides by (100% + Percent markup).

$$\text{Cost} = \frac{\text{Selling price}}{100\% + \text{Percent markup on cost}} \qquad C = \frac{SP}{100\% + \%M_{COST}}$$

EXAMPLE

A clothing wholesaler sells a blouse for **$66.00**. If a **50% markup based on cost** is used, what is the cost of the blouse?

SOLUTION STRATEGY

$$\text{Cost} = \frac{\text{Selling price}}{100\% + \text{Percent markup on cost}}$$

$$\text{Cost} = \frac{66.00}{100\% + 50\%} = \frac{66.00}{150\%} = \frac{66.00}{1.5} = 44.00$$

$$\text{Cost} = \underline{\$44.00}$$

TRY-IT EXERCISE

6. An appliance manufacturer sells automatic coffee makers to distributors for **$39.00**. If a **30% markup based on cost** is used, how much did it cost to manufacture the coffee maker?

Check your answer with the solution on page 254.

REVIEW EXERCISES CHAPTER 8—SECTION I

For the following items, calculate the missing information, rounding dollars to the nearest cent and percents to the nearest tenth percent:

Complete, worked out solutions for exercises 1–10 appear in the appendix following the index.

Item	Cost	Amount of Markup	Selling Price	Percent Markup Based on Cost
1. television set	$161.50	$138.45	$299.95	85.7%
2. bookcase	$32.40	$21.50	$53.90	66.4%
3. automobile	$6,944.80	$5,400.00	$12,344.80	77.8%
4. dress	$75.00	$60.00	$135.00	80%
5. vacuum cleaner	$156.22	$93.73	$249.95	60%
6. hat	$46.25	$50.00	$96.25	108.1%
7. computer	$1,350.00	$2,149.00	$3,499.00	159.2%
8. treadmill	$1,455.00	$880.00	$2,335.00	60.5%
9. 1 lb potatoes	$.58	$.75	$1.33	130%
10. wallet	$25.69	$19.26	$44.95	75%

Solve the following word problems, rounding dollars to the nearest cent and percents to the nearest tenth:

11. Alarm clocks cost the manufacturer $56.10 per unit to produce. If a markup of $29.80 is added to the cost, what is the selling price per clock?

$SP = C + M = 56.10 + 29.80 = \underline{\$85.90}$

12. The Image Boutique sells dress shirts for $22.88. If the cost per shirt is $15.50, what is the amount of the markup?

$M = SP - C = 22.88 - 15.50 = \underline{\$7.38}$

13. After a wholesaler adds a markup of $125.00 to a stereo, it is sold for $320.00. What is the cost of the stereo?

$C = SP - M = 320.00 - 125.00 = \underline{\underline{\$195.00}}$

14. A distributor buys light bulbs for $3.66 per dozen and sells them for $5.90.

  a. What is the amount of the markup?

  $M = SP - C = 5.90 - 3.66 = \underline{\underline{\$2.24}}$

  b. What is the percent markup based on cost?

  $\%M_C = \dfrac{M}{C} = \dfrac{2.24}{3.66} = .6120 = \underline{\underline{61.2\%}}$

15. The Holiday Card Shop purchased stationery for $2.44 per box. A $1.75 markup is added to the stationery.

  a. What is the selling price?

  $SP = C + M = 2.44 + 1.75 = \underline{\underline{\$4.19}}$

  b. What is the percent markup based on cost?

  $\%M_C = \dfrac{M}{C} = \dfrac{1.75}{2.44} = .7172 = \underline{\underline{71.7\%}}$

16. The Electronic Warehouse adds a $4.60 markup to calculators and sells them for $9.95.

  a. What is the cost of the calculators?

  $C = SP - M = 9.95 - 4.60 = \underline{\underline{\$5.35}}$

  b. What is the percent markup based on cost?

  $\%M_C = \dfrac{M}{C} = \dfrac{4.60}{5.35} = .8598 = \underline{\underline{86\%}}$

17. The Green Thumb Garden Shop purchases automatic lawn sprinklers for $12.50 from the manufacturer. If a 75% markup based on cost is added, at what retail price should the sprinklers be marked?

$SP = C(100\% + \%M_C) = 12.50(100\% + 75\%) = 12.50(1.75) = \underline{\underline{\$21.88}}$

18. Golden Auto Supply purchases water pumps from the distributor for $35.40 each. If Golden adds a 120% markup based on cost, at what retail price should the pumps be sold?

$$SP = C(100\% + \%M_C) = 35.40(100\% + 120\%) = 35.40(2.2) = \underline{\$77.88}$$

19. A department store sells refrigerators at retail for $875.88. If a 50% markup based on cost is added, what is the cost of the refrigerator?

$$C = \frac{SP}{100\% + \%M_C} = \frac{875.88}{100\% + 50\%} = \frac{875.88}{1.5} = \underline{\$583.92}$$

20. What is the cost of a printer that sells at retail for $1,750, with a 70% markup based on cost?

$$C = \frac{SP}{100\% + \%M_C} = \frac{1,750.00}{100\% + 70\%} = \frac{1,750.00}{1.7} = \underline{\$1,029.41}$$

21. a. What is the amount of markup on this Panasonic microwave oven, if the cost is $103.70?

$$M = SP - C$$
$$M = \$168.88 - \$103.70$$
$$M = \underline{\$65.18}$$

Panasonic

AS LOW AS $10 A MONTH

NN-6523

• 1.2 cu. ft.
• 900 watts
• English/Spanish
• Pop Corn
• Convenience Food

168^{88}

b. What is the percent markup based on cost?

$$\%M_C = \frac{M}{C} = \frac{65.18}{103.70} = .6285 = \underline{62.9\%}$$

MAYTAG

Dishwasher

• Three Wash Levels
• 2 Push Buttons
• Water Heater

AS LOW AS $12 A MONTH

DWU8250

399^{88}

22. If the Maytag dishwasher is marked up by $140.88,

a. What is the cost?

$$C = SP - M$$
$$C = \$399.88 - \$140.88 = \underline{\$259.00}$$

b. What is the percent markup based on cost?

$$\%M_C = \frac{\$140.88}{259.00} = .5439 = \underline{54.4\%}$$

23. What is the cost of this General Electric refrigerator, if the markup is 70% based on the cost?

$$C = \frac{SP}{100\% + \%M_C} = \frac{\$548.88}{100\% + 70\%}$$

$$C = \frac{548.88}{1.7} = \underline{\underline{\$322.87}}$$

SECTION II

MARKUP BASED ON SELLING PRICE

In Section I, we calculated markup as a percentage of the cost of an item. The cost was the base and represented 100%. As noted, this method is primarily used by manufacturers and wholesalers. In this section, the markup will be calculated as a percentage of the selling price; therefore, the selling price will be the base and represent 100%. This practice is used by most retailers, because most retail records and statistics are kept in sales dollars.

8-5 Calculating Percent Markup Based on Selling Price

The calculation of percent **markup based on selling price** is the same as that for percent markup based on cost, except the base (the denominator) changes from cost to selling price. Remember, finding percent markup is a rate problem, using the now familiar percentage formula, Rate = Portion ÷ Base.

For this application of the formula, the percent markup based on selling price is the rate, the amount of the markup is the portion, and the selling price is the base. The formula is

$$\text{Percent markup based on selling price (rate)} = \frac{\text{Markup (portion)}}{\text{Selling price (base)}} \quad \text{or} \quad \%M_{SP} = \frac{M}{SP}$$

● **markup based on selling price**
When selling price is 100%, and the markup is expressed as a percent of that selling price.

EXAMPLE

American Hardware & Garden Supply purchases electric drills for $60.00 each. If it sells the drills for $125, what is the amount of the markup, and what is the percent markup based on selling price?

SOLUTION STRATEGY

$$M = SP - C$$
$$M = 125 - 60 = 65$$

$$\text{Markup} = \underline{\underline{\$65.00}}$$

$$\%M_{SP} = \frac{M}{SP}$$

$$\%M_{SP} = \frac{65}{125} = .52$$

$$\text{Percent markup based on selling price} = \underline{52\%}$$

7. **Playtime Toys buys bicycles from the distributor for $94.50 each. If the bikes sell for $157.50, what is the amount of the markup and what is the percent markup based on selling price?**

Check your answers with the solutions on page 254.

8-6 Calculating Selling Price When Cost and Percent Markup Based on Selling Price Are Known

When the percent markup is based on selling price, remember that the selling price is the base, and represents 100%. This means the percent cost plus the percent markup must equal 100%. If, for example, the markup is 25% of the selling price, the cost must be 75% of the selling price,

$$\text{Cost} + \text{Markup} = \text{Selling price}$$
$$75\% + 25\% = 100\%$$

Since the percent markup is known, the percent cost will always be the complement, or,

% Cost = (100% − Percent markup based on selling price)

Since the selling price is the base, we can solve for the selling price using the percentage formula, Base = Portion ÷ Rate, where the cost is the portion, and the percent cost or (100% − Percent markup on selling price) is the rate.

$$\text{Selling price} = \frac{\text{Cost}}{100\% - \text{Percent markup on selling price}} \quad \text{or} \quad SP = \frac{C}{100\% - \%M_{SP}}$$

EXAMPLE

Stylistic Furniture purchases wall units from the manufacturer for $550. If the store policy is to mark up all merchandise 60% based on the selling price, what is the retail selling price of the wall units?

SOLUTION STRATEGY

$$SP = \frac{C}{100\% - \%M_{SP}}$$

$$SP = \frac{550}{100\% - 60\%} = \frac{550}{40\%} = 1,375$$

$$\text{Selling price} = \underline{\$1,375}$$

8. **Grand Prix Menswear buys suits for $169.00 from the manufacturer. If a 35% markup based on selling price is the objective, what should be the selling price of the suit?**

Check your answer with the solution on page 254.

8-7 Calculating Cost When Selling Price and Percent Markup Based on Selling Price Are Known

Often, retailers know how much their customers are willing to pay for an item. The following procedure is used to determine the most a store can pay for an item, and still get the intended markup.

In order to calculate the cost of an item when the selling price and percent markup based on selling price are known, we use a variation of the formula used in the last section. To solve for cost, we must isolate cost on one side of the equation by multiplying both sides of the equation by (100% − Percent markup). This yields the equation for cost

$$\text{Cost} = \text{Selling price}(100\% - \text{Percent markup on selling price})$$

$$C = SP(100\% - \%M_{SP})$$

EXAMPLE

A buyer for a chain of boutiques is looking for a line of dresses to retail for $120. If a 40% markup based on selling price is the objective, what is the most the buyer can pay for these dresses and still get the intended markup?

SOLUTION STRATEGY

$$C = SP(100\% - \%M_{SP})$$
$$C = 120(100\% - 40\%) = 120(.6) = 72$$

$$\text{Cost} = \underline{\$72.00}$$

TRY-IT **EXERCISE**

9. **What is the most a gift shop buyer can pay for a clock if he wants a 55% markup based on selling price, and expects to sell the clock for $79 at retail?**

Check your answer with the solution on page 254.

8-8 Converting Percent Markup Based on Cost to Percent Markup Based on Selling Price, and Vice Versa

Converting Percent Markup Based on Cost to Percent Markup Based on Selling Price

When percent markup is based on cost, it can be converted to percent markup based on selling price by using the following formula:

$$\text{Percent markup based on selling price} = \frac{\text{Percent markup based on cost}}{100\% + \text{Percent markup based on cost}}$$

Note: For any given item, the percent markup based on selling price is always lower than the corresponding percent markup based on cost, because the selling price is always greater than the cost. When using the percentage formula, the greater the base, the lower the rate.

EXAMPLE

If a bookcase is marked up 60% based on cost, what is the corresponding percent markup based on selling price?

$$\text{Percent markup based on selling price} = \frac{\text{Percent markup based on cost}}{100\% + \text{Percent markup based on cost}}$$

$$\text{Percent markup based on selling price} = \frac{60\%}{100\% + 60\%} = \frac{.6}{1.6} = .375$$

Percent markup based on selling price = <u>37.5%</u>

TRY-IT   EXERCISE

10. **A photocopier is marked up 50% based on cost. What is the corresponding percent markup based on selling price?**

Check your answer with the solution on page 254.

Converting Percent Markup Based on Selling Price to Percent Markup Based on Cost

When percent markup is based on selling price, it can be converted to percent markup based on cost by the formula:

$$\text{Percent markup based on cost} = \frac{\text{Percent markup based on selling price}}{100\% - \text{Percent markup based on selling price}}$$

EXAMPLE

A Sony stereo is marked up 25% based on selling price at Circuit City. What is the corresponding percent markup based on cost? Round your answer to the nearest tenth percent.

SOLUTION STRATEGY

$$\text{Percent markup based on cost} = \frac{\text{Percent markup based on selling price}}{100\% - \text{Percent markup based on selling price}}$$

$$\text{Percent markup based on cost} = \frac{25\%}{100\% - 25\%} = \frac{.25}{.75} = .3333$$

Percent markup based on cost = <u>33.3%</u>

TRY-IT   EXERCISE

11. **A video game is marked up 75% based on selling price at Playtime Toys. What is the corresponding percent markup based on cost? Round your answer to the nearest tenth percent.**

Check your answer with the solution on page 254.

$\boxed{S}$

For the following items, calculate the missing information, rounding dollars to the nearest cent and percents to the nearest tenth:

Item	Cost	Amount of Markup	Selling Price	Percent Markup Based on Cost	Percent Markup Based on Selling Price
1. sink	$65.00	$50.00	$115.00		43.5%
2. textbook	$34.44	$17.06	$51.50		33.1%
3. telephone	$75.00	$61.36	$136.36		45%
4. bicycle	$53.40	$80.10	$133.50		60%
5. magazine				60%	37.5%
6. flashlight				53.8%	35%
7. doll house	$71.25	$94.74	$165.99	133%	57.1%
8. 1 qt. milk	$1.18	$.79	$1.97	66.9%	40.1%
9. truck	$15,449.00	$9,468.74	$24,917.74	61.3%	38%
10. sofa	$584.55	$714.45	$1,299.00	122.2%	55%
11. fan				150%	60%
12. drill				88.7%	47%

Complete, worked out solutions for exercises 1–12 appear in the appendix following the index.

Solve the following word problems, rounding dollars to the nearest cent and percents to the nearest tenth:

13. A computer has a cost of $540 and a selling price of $875.

   a. What is the amount of the markup?

   $$M = SP - C = 875.00 - 540.00 = \underline{\$335.00}$$

   b. What is the percent markup based on selling price?

   $$\%M_{SP} = \frac{M}{SP} = \frac{335.00}{875.00} = .3828 = \underline{38.3\%}$$

14. A distributor purchases tractors at a cost of $6,500 and sells them for $8,995.

   a. What is the amount of the markup?

   $$M = SP - C = 8,995.00 - 6,500.00 = \underline{\$2,495.00}$$

   b. What is the percent markup based on selling price?

   $$\%M_{SP} = \frac{M}{SP} = \frac{2,495.00}{8,995.00} = .2773 = \underline{27.7\%}$$

15. Waterbed City purchases beds from the manufacturer for $212.35. If the store policy is to mark up all merchandise 42% based on selling price, what is the retail selling price of the beds?

   $$SP = \frac{C}{100\% - \%M_{SP}} = \frac{212.35}{100\% - 42\%} = \frac{212.35}{.58} = \underline{\$366.12}$$

16. Cindy's Sundries purchases color film for $2.67 per roll. If Cindy's policy is to mark up all film 30% based on selling price, what is the retail selling price per roll?

$$SP = \frac{C}{100\% - \%M_{SP}} = \frac{2.67}{100\% - 30\%} = \frac{2.67}{.7} = \underline{\underline{\$3.81}}$$

17. A book retails for $36.75. If the markup is 28% based on selling price, what is the cost of the book?

$$C = SP(100\% - \%M_{SP}) = 36.75(100\% - 28\%) = 36.75(.72) = \underline{\underline{\$26.46}}$$

18. A buyer for a shoe store chain is looking for a line of men's shoes to retail for $79.95. If the objective is a 55% markup based on selling price, what is the most that the buyer can pay for the shoes to still get the desired markup?

$$C = SP(100\% - \%M_{SP}) = 79.95(100\% - 55\%) = 79.95(.45) = \underline{\underline{\$35.98}}$$

19. If the markup on a washing machine is 43% based on selling price, what is the corresponding percent markup based on cost?

$$\%M_C = \frac{\%M_{SP}}{100\% - \%M_{SP}} = \frac{43\%}{100\% - 43\%} = \frac{.43}{.57} = .7543 = \underline{\underline{75.4\%}}$$

20. If the markup on an oven is 200% based on cost, what is the corresponding percent markup based on selling price?

$$\%M_{SP} = \frac{\%M_C}{100\% + \%M_C} = \frac{200\%}{100\% + 200\%} = \frac{2}{3} = .6666 = \underline{\underline{66.7\%}}$$

21. A pillow has a cost of $21.50 and a selling price of $51.99.

    a. What is the amount of markup on the pillow?

$$M = SP - C = 51.99 - 21.50 = \underline{\underline{\$30.49}}$$

    b. What is the percent markup based on cost?

$$\%M_C = \frac{M}{C} = \frac{30.49}{21.50} = 1.4181 = \underline{\underline{141.8\%}}$$

    c. What is the corresponding percent markup based on selling price?

$$\%M_{SP} = \frac{M}{SP} = \frac{30.49}{51.99} = .5864 = \underline{\underline{58.6\%}}$$

22. What is the cost and amount of markup for each brand of anti-freeze, if the markup based on selling price is 60%?

SALE 3^{99}

a. Shellzone:
$$C = SP(100\% - \%M_{SP}) = 3.33(.4) = \underline{\$1.33}$$
$$M = SP - C = 3.33 - 1.33 = \underline{\$2.00}$$

b. Texaco:
$$C = SP(100\% - \%M_{SP}) = 3.99(.4) = \underline{\$1.60}$$
$$M = SP - C = 3.99 - 1.60 = \underline{\$2.39}$$

c. Prestone:
$$C = SP(100\% - \%M_{SP}) = 4.99(.4) = \underline{\$2.00}$$
$$M = SP - C = 4.99 - 2.00 = \underline{\$2.99}$$

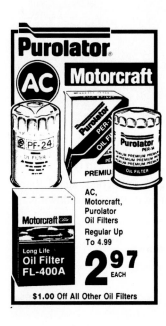

23. The cost of each oil filter is $1.09.

a. What is the percent markup based on selling price?
$$M = SP - C = 2.97 - 1.09 = 1.88$$
$$\%M_{SP} = \frac{M}{SP} = \frac{1.88}{2.97} = .6329 = \underline{\underline{63.3\%}}$$

b. What is the corresponding percent markup based on cost?
$$\%M_C = \frac{M}{C} = \frac{1.88}{1.09} = 1.7247 = \underline{\underline{172.5\%}}$$

MARKDOWNS, MULTIPLE OPERATIONS, AND PERISHABLE GOODS

The original selling price of merchandise usually represents only a temporary situation, based on customer and competitor reaction to that price. A price reduction from the original selling price of merchandise is known as a **markdown.** Markdowns are frequently used in retailing because of errors in initial pricing or merchandise selection. For example, the original price may have been set too high, or the buyer ordered the wrong styles, sizes, or quantities of merchandise.

Most markdowns should not be regarded as losses, but as sales promotion opportunities, used to increase sales and profits. When a sale has been concluded, raising prices back to the original selling price is known as a **markdown cancellation.** This section deals with the mathematics of markdowns, a series of markups and markdowns, and the pricing of perishable merchandise.

● **markdown**
A price reduction from the original selling price of merchandise.

● **markdown cancellation**
Raising prices back to the original selling price after a sale is over.

8-9 Determining the Amount of Markdown and the Markdown Percent

A markdown is a reduction from the original selling price of an item to a new **sale price.** In order to determine the amount of a markdown, we use the formula,

Amount of markdown = Original selling price – Sale price

● **sale price**
The promotional price of merchandise, after a markdown.

Markdowns are considered sales promotion opportunities, used to increase sales and profits.

For example, if a sweater was originally marked at $89.95 and then was sale priced at $59.95, the amount of the markdown would be $30.00 ($89.95 − $59.95 = $30.00).

In order to find the markdown percent, we use the percentage formula once again, Rate = Portion ÷ Base, where the markdown percent is the rate, the amount of the markdown is the portion, and the original selling price is the base:

$$\text{Markdown percent} = \frac{\text{Amount of markdown}}{\text{Original selling price}}$$

EXAMPLE

A lamp that originally sold for $60 was marked down and sold for $48. What are the amount of the markdown and the markdown percent?

SOLUTION STRATEGY

Amount of markdown = Original selling price − Sale price

Amount of markdown = 60 − 48 = 12

Amount of markdown = $12.00

$$\text{Markdown percent} = \frac{\text{Amount of markdown}}{\text{Original selling price}} = \frac{12}{60} = .2$$

Markdown percent = 20%

TRY-IT   EXERCISE

12. An FM radio that originally sold for $75 was marked down and sold for $56. What are the amount of the markdown and the markdown percent? Round your answer to the nearest tenth percent.

Check your answers with the solutions on page 254.

8-10 Determining the Sale Price after a Markdown and the Original Price before a Markdown

Determining Sale Price after a Markdown

In markdown calculations, the original selling price is the base, or 100%. After a markdown is subtracted from that price, the new price represents (100% − Markdown percent) *of* the original price. For example, if a chair is marked down 30%, the sale price would be 70% (100% − 30%) of the original price.

To find the new sale price after a markdown, we use the familiar percentage formula, Portion = Rate × Base, where the sale price is the portion, the original price is the base, and (100% − Markdown percent) is the rate.

Sale price = Original selling price(100% − Markdown percent)

EXAMPLE

A men's shop originally sold a line of ties for $55 each. If the manager decides to mark them down 40% for a clearance sale, what is the sale price of a tie?

SOLUTION STRATEGY

Remember, if the markdown is 40%, the sale price must be 60% (100% − 40%) *of* the original price.

Sale price = Original selling price (100% − Markdown percent)
Sale price = $55(100% − 40%) = 55(.6) = 33

Sale price = $33

TRY-IT   EXERCISE

13. **A lumber yard originally sold paneling for $27.50 per sheet. When the stock was almost depleted, the price was marked down 60% to make room for incoming merchandise. What was the sale price per sheet of paneling?**

Check your answer with the solution on page 254.

Finding the Original Price before a Markdown

To find the original selling price before a markdown, we use the sale price formula solved for the original selling price. The original selling price is isolated to one side by dividing both sides of the equation by (100% − Markdown percent). Note: This is actually the percentage formula, Base = Portion ÷ Rate, with the original selling price as the base.

$$\text{Original selling price} = \frac{\text{Sale price}}{100\% - \text{Markdown percent}}$$

EXAMPLE

What was the original selling price of Rollerblades, currently on sale for $99 after a 25% markdown?

SOLUTION STRATEGY

Reasoning: $99 = 75\%(100\% - 25\%)$ *of* the original price. Solve for the original price.

$$\text{Original selling price} = \frac{\text{Sale price}}{100\% - \text{Markdown percent}} = \frac{99}{100\% - 25\%} = \frac{99}{.75} = 132$$

Original selling price = $\underline{\$132}$

TRY-IT　　**EXERCISE**

14. **What was the original selling price of a briefcase, currently on sale for $79 after a 35% markdown? Round your answer to the nearest cent.**

Check your answer with the solution on page 254.

8-11 Computing the Final Selling Price after a Series of Markups and Markdowns

● **staple goods**
Products, considered basic and routinely purchased, that do not undergo seasonal fluctuations in sales, such as food, tools, and furniture.

● **seasonal goods**
Products that undergo seasonal fluctuations in sales, such as fashion apparel and holiday merchandise.

Products that do not undergo seasonal fluctuations in sales, such as food, tools, tires, and furniture, are known as **staple goods.** These products are usually marked up once and perhaps marked down occasionally, on sale. **Seasonal goods,** such as men's and women's fashion items, snow shovels, bathing suits, and holiday merchandise, may undergo many markups and markdowns during their selling season. Merchants must continually adjust prices as the season progresses. Getting caught with an excessive amount of out-of-season inventory can ruin an otherwise bright profit picture. Christmas decorations in January or snow tires in June are virtually useless profit-wise!

In a series of markups and markdowns, each calculation is based on the previous selling price.

EXAMPLE

In March, a boutique purchased designer bathing suits for $50 each. The original markup was 60% based on the selling price. In May, the shop took a 25% markdown by having a sale. After three weeks, the sale was over and all merchandise was marked up 15%. By July, many of the bathing suits were still in stock, so the shop took a 30% markdown to stimulate sales. At the end of August, the balance of the bathing suits were put on clearance sale, with a final markdown of another 25%. What was the final selling price of the bathing suits? Round your answer to the nearest cent.

SOLUTION STRATEGY

When solving a series of markups and markdowns, remember that each should be based on the previous selling price. Use the formulas presented in this chapter, and take each step one at a time.

Step 1. Find the original selling price, with markup based on the selling price:

$$\text{Selling price} = \frac{\text{Cost}}{100\% - \text{Percent markup}} = \frac{50}{100\% - 60\%} = \frac{50}{.4} = 125$$

Original selling price = $\underline{\$125}$

Step 2. Calculate the 25% markdown in May:

Sale price = Original selling price (100% − Markdown percent)
Sale price = 125(100% − 25%) = 125(.75) = 93.75

Sale price = $93.75

Step 3. Calculate the after-sale 15% markup:
Remember, the base is the previous selling price, $93.75.

Selling price = Sale price (100% + Percent markup)
Selling price = 93.75(100% + 15%) = 93.75(1.15) = 107.81

Selling price = $107.81

Step 4. Calculate the July 30% markdown:

Sale price = Previous selling price (100% − Markdown percent)
Sale price = 107.81 (100% − 30%) = 107.81(.7) = 75.47

Sale price = $75.47

Step 5. Calculate the final 25% markdown:

Sale price = Previous selling price (100% − Markdown percent)
Sale price = 75.47(100% − 25%) = 75.47(.75) = 56.60

Final sale price = $56.60

TRY-IT   EXERCISE

15. In September, a tire shop in Chicago purchased snow tires from a distributor for $48.50 each. The original markup was 55% based on the selling price. In November, the tires were marked down 30% and put on sale. In December, they were marked up 20%. In February, the tires were again on sale at 30% off, and in March were cleared out with a final 25% markdown. What was the final selling price of the tires? Round your answer to the nearest cent.

Check your answer with the solution on page 254.

8-12 Calculating the Selling Price of Perishable Goods

Out-of-season merchandise still has some value, whereas **perishable goods** (such as fruits, vegetables, flowers, and dairy products) have a certain shelf life and then no value at all. In order for sellers of this type of merchandise to achieve their intended markups, the selling price must be based on the quantity of products sold at the original price. The quantity sold is calculated as total items less spoilage. For example, if a tomato vendor anticipates a 20% spoilage rate, the selling price of the tomatoes should be calculated based on 80% of the original stock. In order to calculate the selling price of perishables, use the formula,

$$\text{Selling price of perishables} = \frac{\text{Total expected selling price}}{\text{Total quantity} - \text{Anticipated spoilage}}$$

● **perishable goods**
Products that have a certain shelf life, and then no value at all, such as fruits, vegetables, flowers, and dairy products.

EXAMPLE

The Farmer's Market buys 1,500 pounds of fresh peaches at a cost of $.60 a pound. If a 15% spoilage rate is anticipated, at what price per pound should the peaches be sold in order to achieve a 50% markup based on selling price? Round your answer to the nearest cent.

SOLUTION STRATEGY

Step 1. Find the total expected selling price: The total expected selling price is found by applying the selling price formula, $SP = C \div (100\% - \%M_{SP})$. The cost will be the total pounds times the price per pound, $1,500 \times \$.60 = \$900$.

$$SP = \frac{\text{Cost}}{100\% - \%M_{SP}} = \frac{900}{100\% - 50\%} = \frac{900}{.5} = 1,800$$

Total expected selling price = $\underline{\$1,800}$

Step 2. Find the anticipated spoilage: To find the amount of anticipated spoilage, use the formula,

$$\text{Anticipated spoilage} = \text{Total quantity} \times \text{Spoilage rate}$$
$$\text{Anticipated spoilage} = 1,500 \times 15\% = 1,500(.15) = 225$$

Anticipated spoilage = $\underline{225 \text{ pounds}}$

Step 3. Calculate the selling price of the perishables:

$$\text{Selling price of perishables} = \frac{\text{Total expected selling price}}{\text{Total quantity} - \text{Anticipated spoilage}}$$
$$\text{Selling price} = \frac{\$1,800}{1,500 - 225} = \frac{\$1,800}{1,275} = 1.4117$$

Selling price of peaches = $\underline{\$1.41 \text{ per pound}}$

TRY-IT   EXERCISE

16. Exotic Gardens, a chain of flower shops, purchases 800 dozen roses for Valentine's Day at a cost of $6.50 per dozen. If a 10% spoilage rate is anticipated, at what price per dozen should the roses be sold in order to achieve a 60% markup based on selling price? Round your answer to the nearest cent.

Check your answer with the solution on page 254.

 REVIEW EXERCISES   CHAPTER 8—SECTION III

For the following items, calculate the missing information, rounding dollars to the nearest cent and percents to the nearest tenth:

Complete, worked out solutions for exercises 1–10 appear in the appendix following the index.

Item	Original Selling Price	Amount of Markdown	Sale Price	Markdown Percent
1. fish tank	$189.95	$28.50	$161.45	15%
2. sneakers	$53.88	$16.38	$37.50	30.4%
3. cantaloupe	$1.68	$.39	$1.29	23.2%
4. CD player	$264.95	$79.48	$185.47	30%

5. 1 yd carpet	$41.10	$16.44	$24.66	40%
6. suitcase	$68.00	$16.01	$51.99	23.5%
7. chess set	$115.77	$35.50	$80.27	30.7%
8. necklace	$390.00	$155.00	$235.00	39.7%
9. copier	$1,599.88	$559.96	$1,039.92	35%
10. pen	$21.20	$5.30	$15.90	25%

Solve the following word problems, rounding dollars to the nearest cent and percents to the nearest tenth:

11. A cellular phone that originally sold for $235.75 was marked down and sold for $189.95.

  a. What is the amount of the markdown?

    MD = Original price − Sale price = 235.75 − 189.95 = <u>$45.80</u>

  b. What is the markdown percent?

$$MD\% = \frac{MD}{\text{Original price}} = \frac{45.80}{235.75} = .1942 = \underline{\underline{19.4\%}}$$

12. A set of glasses that originally sold for $34.88 was marked down by $12.11.

  a. What is the sale price?

    Sale price = Original price − MD = 34.88 − 12.11 = <u>$22.77</u>

  b. What is the markdown percent?

$$MD\% = \frac{MD}{\text{Original price}} = \frac{12.11}{34.88} = .3471 = \underline{\underline{34.7\%}}$$

13. Office Headquarters, a retail store, originally sold file cabinets for $68.50. If they were put on sale at a markdown of 35%, what is the sale price?

Sale price = Original price(100% − $MD\%$) = 68.50(100% − 35%) = 68.50(.65) = <u>$44.53</u>

14. Home Library, a book store, sold dictionaries for $75.00. If they were put on clearance sale at 60% off, what is the sale price?

Sale price = Original price(100% − $MD\%$) = 75.00(100% − 60%) = 75.00(.4) = <u>$30.00</u>

15. What was the original selling price of a typewriter, currently on sale for $154.99 after a 38% markdown?

$$\text{Original price} = \frac{\text{Sale price}}{100\% - MD\%} = \frac{154.99}{100\% - 38\%} = \frac{154.99}{.62} = \underline{\underline{\$249.98}}$$

16. A lamp is on sale for $63.25, after a markdown of 45%. What was the original selling price of the lamp?

$$\text{Original price} = \frac{\text{Sale price}}{100\% - MD\%} = \frac{63.25}{100\% - 45\%} = \frac{63.25}{.55} = \underline{\underline{\$115.00}}$$

17. In February, Golf World, a retail shop, purchased golf clubs for $453.50 per set. The original markup was 35% based on selling price. In April, the shop took a 20% markdown by having a special sale. After two weeks, the sale was over and the clubs were marked up 10%. In June, it offered a storewide sale of 15% off all merchandise, and in September, a final 10% markdown was taken on the clubs. What was the final selling price of the golf clubs?

$$SP = \frac{C}{100\% - \%M_{SP}} = \frac{453.50}{100\% - 35\%} = \frac{453.50}{.65} = \$697.69$$

Markdown #1:   Original price$(100\% - MD\%) = 697.69(.8) = \$558.15$
10% Markup: $558.15(1.10) = \$613.97$
Markdown #2: $613.97(.85) = \$521.87$
Final Markdown: $521.87(.9) = \underline{\underline{\$469.68}}$

18. The Farmer's Market purchases 460 pounds of sweet potatoes at $.76 per pound. If a 10% spoilage rate is anticipated, at what price per pound should the sweet potatoes be sold in order to achieve a 35% markup based on selling price?

Total cost = 460 pounds @ $.76 = $349.60

$$\text{Expected selling price} = \frac{C}{100\% - \%M_{SP}} = \frac{349.60}{.65} = \$537.85$$

$$SP \text{ perishable} = \frac{\text{Expected } SP}{\text{Total quantity} - \text{Spoilage}} = \frac{537.85}{460 - 46} = \frac{537.85}{414} = \underline{\underline{\$1.30 \text{ Per pound}}}$$

19. A microwave oven cost The Electronic Warehouse $141.30 and was initially marked up by 55% based on selling price. In the next few months the item was marked down 20%, marked up 15%, marked down 10%, and marked down a final 10%. What was the final selling price of the microwave oven?

$$SP = \frac{C}{100\% - \%M_{SP}} = \frac{141.30}{100\% - 55\%} = \frac{141.30}{.45} = \$314$$

Markdown #1:   Original price$(100\% - MD\%) = 314(.8) = \$251.20$
15% Markup: $251.20(1.15) = \$288.88$
Markdown #2: $288.88(.9) = \$259.99$
Final markdown: $259.99(.9) = \underline{\underline{\$233.99}}$

20. The Goldenflake Bakery makes 200 cherry cheesecakes at a cost of $2.45 each. If a spoilage rate of 5% is anticipated, at what price should the cakes be sold in order to achieve a 40% markup based on cost?

Total cost = 200 Cheesecakes @ $2.45 = $490.00
Expected selling price = $C(100\% + M_C) = 490(1.4) = \$686.00$

$$SP \text{ perishable} = \frac{\text{Expected } SP}{\text{Total quantity} - \text{Spoilage}} = \frac{686.00}{200 - 10} = \frac{686.00}{190} = \underline{\underline{\$3.61 \text{ Per cheesecake}}}$$

Answer Questions 21–23 based on the following advertisements.

JVC® AM/FM STEREO RADIO/CASSETTE/CD
PLAYER and RECORDER with REMOTE CONTROL
- Super-Bass Horn • COMPU PLAY
- Clock/timer • Front-load CD tray
- Digital tuner
  Model #RC-QS11

REG. $249.99
Sale! $179⁹⁹

JVC® PORTABLE AM/FM STEREO RADIO/
CASSETTE/CD PLAYER and RECORDER
- Multi-Bass Horn • 30-station preset
- Synchro start record/hi-speed edit
- Digital tuner
  Model #PC-X105

REG. $299.99
Sale! $199⁹⁹

21. What is the amount of markdown on each stereo?

Markdown = Original price − Sale price

$MD = \$249.99 - \$179.99 = \underline{\underline{\$70.00}}$

$MD = \$299.99 - \$199.99 = \underline{\underline{\$100.00}}$

22. What is the markdown percent for each?

$$\%MD = \frac{MD}{\text{Original price}}$$

$$\%MD = \frac{70.00}{249.99} = .28 = \underline{\underline{28\%}} \qquad \%MD = \frac{100.00}{299.99} = .3333 = \underline{\underline{33.3\%}}$$

23. If an extra 15% off was given on each stereo as a final clearance, what would be the new sale price of each?

"Sale" price = Original price(100% − MD%)

"Sale" price = $\$179.99 \times .85 = \underline{\underline{\$152.99}}$

"Sale" price = $\$199.99 \times .85 = \underline{\underline{\$169.99}}$

CHAPTER 8 ■ MARKUP AND MARKDOWN

FORMULAS

Selling price = Cost + Markup

Cost = Selling price − Markup

Markup = Selling price − Cost

$$\textbf{Percent markup}_{\textbf{COST}} = \frac{\textbf{Markup}}{\textbf{Cost}}$$

$$\textbf{Percent markup}_{\textbf{SP}} = \frac{\textbf{Markup}}{\textbf{Selling price}}$$

Selling price = Cost(100% + %Markup$_{\text{COST}}$)

$$\textbf{Cost} = \frac{\textbf{Selling price}}{\textbf{100\% + \%Markup}_{\textbf{COST}}}$$

$$\textbf{Selling price} = \frac{\textbf{Cost}}{\textbf{100\% − \%Markup}_{\textbf{SP}}}$$

Cost = Selling price(100% − %Markup$_{\text{SP}}$)

$$\textbf{\%Markup}_{\textbf{SP}} = \frac{\textbf{\%Markup}_{\textbf{COST}}}{\textbf{100\% + \%Markup}_{\textbf{COST}}}$$

$$\textbf{\%Markup}_{\textbf{COST}} = \frac{\textbf{\%Markup}_{\textbf{SP}}}{\textbf{100\% − \%Markup}_{\textbf{SP}}}$$

Markdown = Original price − Sale price

Sale price = Original price − Markdown

Original price = Sale price + Markdown

$$\textbf{Markdown\%} = \frac{\textbf{Markdown}}{\textbf{Original price}}$$

Sale price = Original price(100% − Markdown%)

$$\textbf{Original price} = \frac{\textbf{Sale price}}{\textbf{100\% − Markdown\%}}$$

$$\textbf{Selling price}_{\textbf{Perishables}} = \frac{\textbf{Expected selling price}}{\textbf{Total quantity − Spoilage}}$$

SECTION I   MARKUP BASED ON COST

Topic	P/O, Page	Important Concepts	Illustrative Examples
Using the Basic Retailing Equation	8–1 228	The basic retailing equation can be applied to solve for selling price *(SP)*, cost *(C)*, and amount of markup *(M)*. Selling price = Cost + Markup $SP = C + M$ Cost = Selling price − Markup $C = SP - M$ Markup = Selling price − Cost $M = SP - C$	1. What is the selling price of a lamp that costs $86.00 and has a $55.99 markup? $SP = 86.00 + 55.99$ Selling price = $141.99 2. What is the cost of a radio that sells for $125.50 and has a $37.29 markup? $C = 125.50 - 37.29$ Cost = $88.21 3. What is the markup on a set of dishes costing $53.54 and selling for $89.95? $M = 89.95 - 53.54$ Markup = $36.41
Calculating Percent Markup Based on Cost	8–2 230	$\% \text{Markup}_{\text{COST}} = \dfrac{\text{Markup}}{\text{Cost}}$ $\%M_{\text{COST}} = \dfrac{M}{C}$	A calculator costs $25.00. If the markup is $10.00, what is the percent markup based on cost? $\%M_{\text{COST}} = \dfrac{10.00}{25.00} = .4$ $\%M_{\text{COST}} = 40\%$
Calculating Selling Price	8–3 231	Selling price = Cost (100% + %Markup$_{\text{COST}}$) $SP = C(100\% + \%M_{\text{COST}})$	A fax machine costs $260 to manufacture. What should be the selling price if a 60% markup based on cost is desired? $SP = 260(100\% + 60\%)$ $SP = 260(1.6) = 416$ Selling price = $416.00
Calculating Cost	8–4 231	$\text{Cost} = \dfrac{\text{Selling price}}{100\% + \text{Markup}_{\text{COST}}}$ $C = \dfrac{SP}{100\% + \%M_{\text{COST}}}$	What is the cost of a chair with a selling price of $250 and a 45% markup based on cost? $C = \dfrac{250}{100\% + 45\%} = \dfrac{250}{1.45}$ Cost = $172.41

SECTION II   MARKUP BASED ON SELLING PRICE

Topic	P/O, Page	Important Concepts	Illustrative Examples
Calculating Percent Markup Based on Selling Price	8–5 235	$\%\text{Markup}_{SP} = \dfrac{\text{Markup}}{\text{Selling price}}$ $\%M_{SP} = \dfrac{M}{SP}$	What is the percent markup on the selling price of a Xerox copier with a selling price of $400.00 and a markup of $188.00? $\%M_{SP} = \dfrac{188.00}{400.00} = .47$ $\%M_{SP} = \underline{47\%}$
Calculating Selling Price	8–6 236	$\text{Selling price} = \dfrac{\text{Cost}}{100\% - \%\text{Markup}_{SP}}$ $SP = \dfrac{C}{100\% - \%M_{SP}}$	What is the selling price of a quart of milk with a cost of $1.19 and a 43% markup based on selling price? $SP = \dfrac{1.19}{100\% - 43\%} = \dfrac{1.19}{.57}$ $SP = \underline{\$2.09}$
Calculating Cost	8–7 237	$\text{Cost} = \text{Selling price}\,(100\% - \%\text{Markup}_{SP})$ $C = SP(100\% - \%M_{SP})$	What is the most a hardware store can pay for a drill if it will have a selling price of $65.50 and a 45% markup based on selling price? $C = 65.50(100\% - 45\%)$ $C = 65.50(.55)$ $\text{Cost} = \underline{\$36.03}$
Converting Percent Markup Based on Cost to Percent Markup Based on Selling Price	8–8 237	$\%\text{Markup}_{SP} = \dfrac{\%\text{Markup}_{COST}}{100\% + \%\text{Markup}_{COST}}$ $\%M_{SP} = \dfrac{\%M_{COST}}{100\% + \%M_{COST}}$	If a hair dryer is marked up 70% based on cost, what is the corresponding percent markup based on selling price? $\%M_{SP} = \dfrac{70\%}{100\% + 70\%} = \dfrac{.7}{1.7}$ $\%M_{SP} = \underline{.4118 = 41.2\%}$
Converting Percent Markup Based on Selling Price to Percent Markup Based on Cost	8–8 238	$\%\text{Markup}_{COST} = \dfrac{\%\text{Markup}_{SP}}{100\% - \%\text{Markup}_{SP}}$ $\%M_{COST} = \dfrac{\%M_{SP}}{100\% - \%M_{SP}}$	If a toaster is marked up 35% based on selling price, what is the corresponding percent markup based on cost? $\%M_{COST} = \dfrac{35\%}{100\% - 35\%} = \dfrac{.35}{.65}$ $\%M_{COST} = \underline{.5384 = 53.8\%}$

SECTION III   MARKDOWNS, MULTIPLE OPERATIONS, AND PERISHABLE GOODS

Topic	P/O, Page	Important Concepts	Illustrative Examples
Calculating Markdown and Markdown Percent	8–9 241	Markdown = Original price − Sale price $MD = \text{Orig} - \text{Sale}$ $\text{Markdown \%} = \dfrac{\text{Markdown}}{\text{Original price}}$ $MD\% = \dfrac{MD}{\text{Orig}}$	Calculate the amount of markdown and the markdown percent of a television set that originally sold for $425.00 and was then put on sale for $299.95. $MD = 425.00 - 299.95$ Markdown = $\underline{\$125.05}$ $MD\% = \dfrac{125.05}{425.00} = .2942$ Markdown % = $\underline{29.4\%}$
Determining the Sale Price after a Markdown	8–10 243	Sale price = Original price (100% − Markdown %) $\text{Sale} = \text{Orig}\,(100\% - MD\%)$	What is the sale price of a computer that originally sold for $2,500.00 and was then marked down by 35%? Sale = 2,500(100% − 35%) Sale = 2,500(.65) = 1,625 Sale price = $\underline{\$1,625.00}$
Determining the Original Selling Price before a Markdown	8–10 243	$\text{Original price} = \dfrac{\text{Sale price}}{100\% - \text{Markdown\%}}$ $\text{Orig} = \dfrac{\text{Sale}}{100\% - MD\%}$	What is the original selling price of an exercise bicycle, currently on sale at Sears for $235.88 after a 30% markdown? $\text{Orig} = \dfrac{235.88}{100\% - 30\%} = \dfrac{235.88}{.7}$ Original price = $\underline{\$336.97}$
Computing the Final Selling Price after a Series of Markups and Markdowns	8–11 244	To solve for the final selling price after a series of markups and markdowns, calculate each step based on the previous selling price.	Compute is the final selling price of an umbrella costing $27.50, with the following seasonal activity: a. Initial markup, 40% on cost b. 20% markdown c. 15% markdown d. 10% markup e. Final clearance, 25% markdown a. Initial 40% markup: $SP = C(100\% + \%M_{COST})$ $SP = 27.50(100\% + 40\%)$ $SP = 27.50(1.4) = 38.50$ Original price = $\underline{\$38.50}$

III, continued

Topic	P/O, Page	Important Concepts	Illustrative Examples
			b. 20% markdown: Sale = Orig $(100\% - MD\%)$ Sale = 38.50$(100\% - 20\%)$ Sale = 38.50$(.8)$ Sale price = $\underline{\$30.80}$ c. 15% markdown: Sale = Orig $(100\% - MD\%)$ Sale = 30.80$(100\% - 15\%)$ Sale = 30.80$(.85)$ Sale price = $\underline{\$26.18}$ d. 10% markup: SP = sale price $(100\% + M\%)$ SP = 26.18$(100\% + 10\%)$ SP = 26.18(1.10) Selling price = $\underline{\$28.80}$ e. Final 25% markdown: Sale = Orig $(100\% - MD\%)$ Sale = 28.80$(100\% - 25\%)$ Sale = 28.80$(.75)$ Final selling price = $\underline{\$21.60}$
Calculating the Selling Price of Perishable Goods	8–12 245	Selling price$_{\text{Perishables}}$ = $$\frac{\text{Expected selling price}}{\text{Total quantity} - \text{Spoilage}}$$ $$SP_{\text{perish}} = \frac{\text{Exp } SP}{\text{Quan} - \text{Spoil}}$$	A grocery store purchases 250 pounds of apples from a wholesaler for $.67 per pound. If a 10% spoilage rate is anticipated, what selling price per pound will yield a 45% markup based on cost? Total Cost = 250 lb @ .67 = \$167.50 Exp $SP = C(100\% + M_{\text{COST}})$ Exp SP = 167.50$(100\% + 45\%)$ Exp SP = 167.50(1.45) = \$242.88 $$SP_{\text{perish}} = \frac{242.88}{250 - 25} = \frac{242.88}{225}$$ SP_{perish} = $\underline{\$1.08 \text{ per lb}}$

1. $SP = C + M = 6.80 + 9.40 = \underline{\underline{\$16.20}}$

2. $M = SP - C = 28.50 - 16.75 = \underline{\underline{\$11.75}}$

3. $C = SP - M = 290.00 - 75.00 = \underline{\underline{\$215.00}}$

4. $M = SP - C = 63.00 - 45.00 = \underline{\underline{\$18.00}}$

$\%M_{\text{COST}} = \dfrac{M}{C} = \dfrac{18.00}{45.00} = .4 = \underline{\underline{40\%}}$

5. $SP = C(100\% + \%M_{\text{COST}}) = 38.00\,(100\% + 65\%) = 38.00(1.65) = \underline{\underline{\$62.70}}$

6. $C = \dfrac{SP}{100\% + \%M_{\text{COST}}} = \dfrac{39.00}{100\% + 30\%} = \dfrac{39.00}{1.3} = \underline{\underline{\$30.00}}$

7. $M = SP - C = 157.50 - 94.50 = \underline{\underline{\$63.00}}$

$\%M_{SP} = \dfrac{M}{SP} = \dfrac{63.00}{157.50} = .40 = \underline{\underline{40\%}}$

8. $SP = \dfrac{C}{100\% - \%M_{SP}} = \dfrac{169.00}{100\% - 35\%} = \dfrac{169.00}{.65} = \underline{\underline{\$260.00}}$

9. $C = SP(100\% - \%M_{SP}) = 79.00(100\% - 55\%) = 79.00(.45) = \underline{\underline{\$35.55}}$

10. $\%M_{SP} = \dfrac{\%M_{\text{COST}}}{100\% + \%M_{\text{COST}}} = \dfrac{50\%}{100\% + 50\%} = \dfrac{.5}{1.5} = .333 = \underline{\underline{33.3\%}}$

11. $\%M_{\text{COST}} = \dfrac{\%M_{SP}}{100\% - \%M_{SP}} = \dfrac{75\%}{100\% - 75\%} = \dfrac{.75}{.25} = 3 = \underline{\underline{300\%}}$

12. $MD = \text{Original price} - \text{Sale price} = 75.00 - 56.00 = \underline{\underline{\$19.00}}$

$MD\% = \dfrac{MD}{\text{Original price}} = \dfrac{19.00}{75.00} = .2533 = \underline{\underline{25.3\%}}$

13. Sale price $= \text{Original price}\,(100\% - MD\%) = 27.50(100\% - 60\%) = 27.50(.4) = \underline{\underline{\$11.00}}$

14. Original price $= \dfrac{\text{Sale price}}{100\% - MD\%} = \dfrac{79.00}{100\% - 35\%} = \dfrac{79.00}{.65} = \underline{\underline{\$121.54}}$

15. $SP = \dfrac{C}{100\% - \%M_{SP}} = \dfrac{48.50}{100\% - 55\%} = \dfrac{48.50}{.45} = \$107.78$

Markdown #1: Original price$(100\% - MD\%) = 107.78(.7) = \$75.45$

20% markup: $75.45(100\% + 20\%) = 75.45(1.2) = \$90.54$

Markdown #2: Original price$(100\% - MD\%) = 90.54(.7) = \$63.38$

Final markdown: Original price$(100\% - MD\%) = 63.38(.75) = \underline{\underline{\$47.54}}$

16. Total cost $= 800$ dozen @ $\$6.50 = \$5,200.00$

Expected selling price $= \dfrac{C}{100\% - \%M_{SP}} = \dfrac{5,200.00}{100\% - 60\%} = \dfrac{5200}{.4} = \$13,000$

$SP_{\text{perish}} = \dfrac{\text{Expected } SP}{\text{Total quantity} - \text{Spoilage}} = \dfrac{13,000.00}{800 - 80} = \dfrac{13,000.00}{720} = \underline{\underline{\$18.06 \text{ per doz.}}}$

Name_____

Class_____

Solve the following word problems, rounding dollars to the nearest cent and percents to the nearest tenth:

ANSWERS

1. Vacuum cleaners cost the manufacturer $83.22 to produce. If a markup of $69.38 is added to the cost, what is the selling price per unit?

   $SP = C + M = 83.22 + 69.38 = \underline{\$152.60}$

<table>
<tr><td>1.</td><td>$152.60</td></tr>
<tr><td>2.</td><td>$133.34</td></tr>
<tr><td>3.</td><td>$18.58</td></tr>
<tr><td>4. a.</td><td>$5.55</td></tr>
<tr><td>b.</td><td>48.9%</td></tr>
<tr><td>c.</td><td>32.8%</td></tr>
<tr><td>5. a.</td><td>$81.50</td></tr>
</table>

2. Modernage Furniture sells desks for $346.00. If the desks cost $212.66, what is the amount of the markup?

   $M = SP - C = 346.00 - 212.66 = \underline{\$133.34}$

3. After Southwest Food Wholesalers adds a markup of $15.40 to a case of tomato sauce, it sells for $33.98. What is the wholesaler's cost per case?

   $C = SP - M = 33.98 - 15.40 = \underline{\$18.58}$

4. The Bookworm buys textbooks for $11.35 and sells them for $16.90.

   a. What is the amount of the markup?

   $M = SP - C = 16.90 - 11.35 = \underline{\$5.55}$

   b. What is the percent markup based on cost?

   $\%M_C = \dfrac{M}{C} = \dfrac{5.55}{11.35} = .4889 = \underline{48.9\%}$

   c. What is the percent markup based on selling price?

   $\%M_{SP} = \dfrac{M}{SP} = \dfrac{5.55}{16.90} = .3284 = \underline{32.8\%}$

5. Cody's Western Wear purchases shirts for $47.50 each. A $34.00 markup is added to the shirts.

   a. What is the selling price?

   $SP = C + M = 47.50 + 34.00 = \underline{\$81.50}$

ANSWERS

b. _____71.6%_____

c. _____41.7%_____

6. _____$39.84_____

7. _____$15.95_____

8. a. _____100%_____

b. _____54.5%_____

9. a. _____$32.55_____

b. _____26.6%_____

b. What is the percent markup based on cost?

$$\%M_C = \frac{M}{C} = \frac{34.00}{47.50} = .7157 = \underline{\underline{71.6\%}}$$

c. What is the percent markup based on selling price?

$$\%M_{SP} = \frac{M}{SP} = \frac{34.00}{81.50} = .4171 = \underline{\underline{41.7\%}}$$

6. Lacy's purchases imported perfume for $24.30 per ounce. If the store policy is to mark up all merchandise in that department 39% based on selling price, what is the retail selling price of the perfume?

$$SP = \frac{C}{100\% - \%M_{SP}} = \frac{24.30}{100\% - 39\%} = \frac{24.30}{.61} = \underline{\underline{\$39.84}}$$

7. The Carpet Gallery is looking for a new line of nylon carpeting to retail at $39.88 per square yard. If management wants a 60% markup based on selling price, what is the most that can be paid for the carpeting to still get the desired markup?

$$C = SP(100\% - \%M_{SP}) = 39.88(100\% - 60\%) = 39.88(.4) = \underline{\underline{\$15.95}}$$

8. a. If the markup on a vacuum cleaner is 50% based on selling price, what is the corresponding percent markup based on cost?

$$\%M_C = \frac{\%M_{SP}}{100\% - \%M_{SP}} = \frac{50\%}{100\% - 50\%} = \frac{.5}{.5} = \underline{\underline{100\%}}$$

b. If the markup on a VCR is 120% based on cost, what is the corresponding percent markup based on selling price?

$$\%M_{SP} = \frac{\%M_C}{100\% + \%M_C} = \frac{120\%}{100\% + 120\%} = \frac{1.2}{2.2} = .5454 = \underline{\underline{54.5\%}}$$

9. A hammock that originally sold for $122.50 at Outdoor World was marked down and sold for $89.95.

a. What is the amount of the markdown?

$$MD = \text{Original price} - \text{Sale price} = 122.50 - 89.95 = \underline{\underline{\$32.55}}$$

b. What is the markdown percent?

$$MD\% = \frac{MD}{\text{Original price}} = \frac{32.55}{122.50} = .2657 = \underline{\underline{26.6\%}}$$

10. A three-day cruise on the Bahamas Fiesta originally selling for $988 was marked down by $210 at the end of the season.

   a. What is the sale price of the cruise?

     Sale price = Original price − MD = 988.00 − 210.00 = $\underline{\$778.00}$

   b. What is the markdown percent?

$$MD\% = \frac{MD}{\text{Original price}} = \frac{210.00}{998.00} = .2125 = \underline{\underline{21.3\%}}$$

11. TV City originally sold 12-inch portables for $277. If they are put on sale at a markdown of 22%, what is the sale price of the TV sets?

   Sale price = Original price$(100\% − MD\%)$ = 277$(100\% − 22\%)$ = 277$(.78)$ = $\underline{\underline{\$216.06}}$

12. What was the original selling price of a computer, currently on sale for $2,484.00 after a 20% markdown?

$$\text{Original price} = \frac{\text{Sale price}}{100\% − MD\%} = \frac{2,484.00}{100\% − 20\%} = \frac{2,484.00}{.8} = \underline{\underline{\$3,105.00}}$$

13. Patio World brought in a line of inflatable plastic swimming pools for the summer season. The cost of the pools was $120 each. The store has a policy of initially marking up merchandise in the toy department 50% based on selling price. As the summer progressed, the pools were marked down 25%, marked up 15%, marked down 20%, and cleared out in October at a final 25%-off sale. What was the final selling price of the pools?

$$SP = \frac{C}{100\% − \%M_{SP}} = \frac{120.00}{100\% − 50\%} = \frac{120.00}{.5} = \$240.00$$

Markdown #1:   Original price$(100\% − MD\%)$ = 240$(.75)$ = $180.00
15% Markup: 180$(100\% − \%M)$ = 180(1.15) = $207.00
Markdown #2:   207$(.8)$ = $165.60
Final markdown: 165.60$(.75)$ = $\underline{\underline{\$124.20}}$

14. The Epicure Market prepares fresh gourmet entrees each day. On Wednesday, 80 baked chicken dinners were made at a cost of $3.50 each. A 10% rate of spoilage is anticipated.

   a. At what price should the dinners be sold in order to achieve a 60% markup based on selling price?

     Total cost = 80 Dinners @ $3.50 = $280.00

$$\text{Expected } SP = \frac{C}{100\% − \%M_{SP}} = \frac{280.00}{100\% − 60\%} = \frac{280.00}{.4} = \$700.00$$

$$SP \text{ Perishables} = \frac{\text{Expected } SP}{\text{Total quantity − Spoilage}} = \frac{700}{80 − 8} = \frac{700}{72} = \underline{\underline{\$9.72}}$$

   b. If Epicure offers a $1.00-off coupon in a newspaper advertisement, what markdown percent does the coupon represent?

$$MD\% = \frac{MD}{\text{Original price}} = \frac{1.00}{9.72} = .1028 = \underline{\underline{10.3\%}}$$

Name_____

Class_____

ANSWERS

10. a. _____ $778.00 _____

   b. _____ 21.3% _____

11. _____ $216.06 _____

12. _____ $3,105.00 _____

13. _____ $124.20 _____

14. a. _____ $9.72 _____

   b. _____ 10.3% _____

15. a. What is the markdown percent for a single-room carpet cleaning?

$$MD = \frac{\text{Original}}{\text{price}} - \frac{\text{Sale}}{\text{price}}$$

$$MD = 24.99 - 14.00 = 10.99$$

$$MD\% = \frac{MD}{\text{Original price}}$$

$$= \frac{10.99}{24.99} = .4397 = \underline{44\%}$$

b. What is the markdown percent for a 6-area carpet cleaning?

$$MD = 149.99 - 79.00 = \$70.99$$

$$MD\% = \frac{70.99}{149.99} = .4732 = \underline{47.3\%}$$

16. a. What is the original selling price of the carpeting, before the "40% Blowout Sale"?

$$\text{Original price} = \frac{\text{Sale price}}{100\% - MD\%} = \frac{12.99}{100\% - 40\%} = \frac{12.99}{.6} = \underline{\$21.65}$$

b. How much did Harry Rich pay for the carpeting from the manufacturer, if the initial markup was 150% based on cost?

$$C = \frac{SP}{100\% + \%M_C} = \frac{21.65}{100\% + 150\%} = \frac{21.65}{2.5} = \underline{\$8.66}$$

BUSINESS DECISION
Price versus Volume

Name_____

Class_____

17. You are the manager of The Shutterbug Camera Shop. The shop sells 12 FX model cameras per week at a retail price of $449.95 each. Recently you put the FX model on sale for $379.95. At the sale price, 15 cameras per week were sold.

ANSWERS

  a. What is the amount of the markdown and the markdown percent?

MD = Original price − Sale price = 449.95 − 379.95 = $70.00

$$MD\% = \frac{MD}{\text{Original price}} = \frac{70.00}{449.95} = .1555 = \underline{15.6\%}$$

17. a. _____$70.00_____

             _____15.6%_____

  b. What is the percent increase in number of cameras sold each week during the sale?

Increase in sales = 15 − 12 = 3 More cameras per week

$$\% \text{ Increase} = \frac{3}{12} = .25 = \underline{25\%}$$

b. _____25%_____

c. _____$3,898.05_____

d. _____Yes._____

  c. How much more revenue will be earned every three months (13 weeks) by permanently selling the FX model at the lower price?

Revenue before markdown: $449.95 \times 12 = \$5,399.40$ Per week

Revenue after markdown: $379.95 \times 15 = \$5,699.25$ Per week

Increase = 5,699.25 − 5,399.40 = 299.85 × 13 wks = $\underline{\$3,898.05}$

  d. As manager of the store, would you recommend this permanent price reduction?

Yes.

All the Math That's Fit to Learn

The Business Math Times

| Volume VIII | **Markup and Markdown** | One Dollar |

Career Track:

Retail Sales Worker

Nature of the Work

Sales workers are employed by many types of retailers to assist customers in the selection and purchase of merchandise in hundreds of categories. Whether selling clothing, electronic equipment, building supplies or automobiles, a salesperson's primary job is to interest customers in the merchandise and complete the sale.

Working Conditions

The Monday through Friday, 9-to-5 work week is the exception rather than the rule in retailing. Most salespersons can expect to work during some evening and weekend hours and longer than normal hours may be scheduled during Christmas and other peak selling periods.

Job Outlook and Earnings

Employment of retail sales workers is expected to increase about as fast as the average for all workers through the year 2005 due to anticipated growth in retail sales. There will continue to be opportunities for part-time workers and strong demand for temporary workers during peak selling periods.

The starting wage for many part-time retail sales positions is about $4.25 to $5.00 per hour. In areas where employers have difficulty attracting and retaining workers, wages are much higher.

SOURCE: *Occupational Outlook Handbook*, U.S. Department of Labor, 1994–95 Edition.

TOP 5 GENERAL MERCHANDISERS IN THE UNITED STATES

Rank	Company	Revenue (millions)	Employees
1	Wal-Mart Stores	$93,627	675,000
2	Sears Roebuck	35,181	275,000
3	Kmart	34,654	250,000
4	Dayton Hudson	23,516	214,000
5	JCPenney	21,419	205,000

SOURCE: *Fortune*, May 15, 1995: F-53.

TOP 5 SHOPPING MALLS IN THE UNITED STATES

Rank	Mall	Gross Leasable Area (sq ft)
1	Del Amo Fashion Center Torrence, California	3,000,000
2	South Coast Plaza/Crystal Court Costa Mesa, California	2,918,236
3	Mall of America Bloomington, Minnesota	2,472,500
4	Lakewood Center Mall Lakewood, California	2,390,000
5	Roosevelt Field Mall Garden City, New York	2,300,000

SOURCE: Russell Ash, *The Top Ten of Everything*, 1996. (New York: Dorling Kindersley, 1995), p. 171.

TOP 5 FOOD AND DRUG STORES IN THE UNITED STATES

Rank	Company	Revenue (millions)	Employees
1	Kroger	$23,938	200,00
2	American Stores	18,309	121,000
3	Safeway	16,398	113,000
4	Albertson's	12,585	80,000
5	Winn-Dixie Stores	11,788	123,000

SOURCE: *Fortune*, May 15, 1995: F-51.

Brainteaser

A bicycle, originally priced under $100, was on sale at a 25% discount. When the original price, a whole number of dollars, was discounted, the discounted price was also a whole number of dollars. What is the largest possible number of dollars in the original price of the bicycle?

SOURCE: *Mathematics Teacher* Magazine (September 1986).

Answer to Last Issue's Brainteaser

They are exactly the same. Each of these gives a final price of 96% of the original price.

Chapter 9

Payroll

Performance Objectives

SECTION I EMPLOYEE'S GROSS EARNINGS AND INCENTIVE PAY PLANS

9-1 Prorating annual salary on the basis of weekly, biweekly, semimonthly, and monthly pay periods. (p. 262)

9-2 Calculating gross pay by hourly wages, including regular and overtime rates. (p. 263)

9-3 Calculating gross pay by straight and differential piecework schedules. (p. 264)

9-4 Calculating gross pay by straight and incremental commission, salary plus commission, and drawing accounts. (p. 266)

SECTION II EMPLOYEE'S PAYROLL DEDUCTIONS

9-5 Computing FICA taxes, both social security and Medicare, withheld from an employee's paycheck. (p. 272)

9-6 Determining an employee's federal income tax withholding (FIT) by the wage bracket table method. (p. 273)

9-7 Calculating an employee's federal income tax withholding (FIT) by the percentage method. (p. 277)

SECTION III EMPLOYER'S PAYROLL EXPENSES AND RECORD KEEPING RESPONSIBILITIES

9-8 Computing FICA tax for employers and self-employment tax for self-employed persons. (p. 282)

9-9 Computing the amount of state unemployment taxes (SUTA) and federal unemployment taxes (FUTA). (p. 283)

9-10 Calculating employer's fringe benefit expenses. (p. 284)

9-11 Understanding Internal Revenue Service payroll forms. (p. 286)

SECTION I

EMPLOYEE'S GROSS EARNINGS AND INCENTIVE PAY PLANS

Because payroll is frequently a company's largest operating expense, efficient payroll preparation and record keeping are extremely important functions in any business operation. Although today most businesses have their payroll function computerized, it is important for businesspeople to understand the processes and procedures involved.

Employers are responsible for paying employees for services rendered to the company over a period of time. In addition, the company is responsible for withholding certain taxes and other deductions from an employee's paycheck and depositing those taxes with the Internal Revenue Service (IRS), through authorized financial institutions. Other deductions, such as insurance premiums and charitable contributions, are also disbursed by the employer to the appropriate place.

In business, the term **gross pay** or **gross earnings** means the *total* amount of earnings due an employee for work performed before payroll deductions are withheld. The **net pay, net earnings,** or **take-home pay** is the actual amount of the employee's paycheck after all payroll deductions have been withheld. This concept is easily visualized by the formula:

Net pay = Gross pay − Total deductions

This chapter deals with the business math involved in payroll management: the computation of employee gross earnings, calculating withholding taxes and other deductions, and the associated governmental deposits, regulations, and record keeping requirements.

● **gross pay, or gross earnings**
Total amount of earnings due an employee for work performed before payroll deductions are withheld.

● **net pay, or net earnings, or take-home pay**
The actual amount of the employee's paycheck after all payroll deductions have been withheld.

● **salary**
A fixed gross amount of pay, equally distributed over periodic payments, without regard to the number of hours worked.

9-1 Prorating Annual Salary on the Basis of Weekly, Biweekly, Semimonthly, and Monthly Pay Periods

Employee compensation takes on many forms in the business world. Nonunion employees, who usually hold managerial, administrative, or professional positions, are paid a salary. A **salary** is a fixed gross amount of pay, equally distributed over periodic payments, without regard to the number of hours worked. Salaries are usually expressed as an annual, or yearly, amount. For example, a corporate accountant might receive an annual salary of $50,000.

Although salaries may be stated as annual amounts, they are usually distributed to employees on a more timely basis. A once-a-year paycheck would be a real trick to manage! Employees are most commonly paid in one of the following ways:

Weekly	52 paychecks per year	Annual salary ÷ 52
Biweekly	26 paychecks per year	Annual salary ÷ 26
Semimonthly	24 paychecks per year	Annual salary ÷ 24
Monthly	12 paychecks per year	Annual salary ÷ 12

EXAMPLE

What is the weekly, biweekly, semimonthly, and monthly amount of gross pay for a corporate accountant with an annual salary of $50,000?

SOLUTION STRATEGY

Employee stock option plans are a form of voluntary payroll deduction.

The amount of gross pay per period is determined by dividing the annual salary by the number of pay periods per year.

$$\text{Weekly pay} = \frac{50{,}000}{52} = \underline{\underline{\$961.54}}$$

$$\text{Biweekly pay} = \frac{50{,}000}{26} = \underline{\underline{\$1{,}923.08}}$$

$$\text{Semimonthly pay} = \frac{50{,}000}{24} = \underline{\underline{\$2{,}083.33}}$$

$$\text{Monthly pay} = \frac{50{,}000}{12} = \underline{\underline{\$4{,}166.67}}$$

TRY-IT   **EXERCISE**

1. **An executive of a large manufacturing company earns a gross annual salary of $43,500. What is the weekly, biweekly, semimonthly, and monthly pay for this employee?**

Check your answers with the solutions on page 297.

9-2 Calculating Gross Pay by Hourly Wages, Including Regular and Overtime Rates

Wages are earnings for routine or manual work, usually based on the number of hours worked. An **hourly wage** or **hourly rate** is the amount an employee is paid for each hour worked. The hourly wage is the most frequently used pay method and is designed to compensate employees for the amount of time spent on the job. The Fair Labor Standards Act of 1938, a federal law, specifies that a standard work week is 40 hours, and **overtime,** amounting to at least $1\frac{1}{2}$ times the hourly rate, must be paid for all hours worked over 40 hours per week. Paying an employee $1\frac{1}{2}$ times the hourly rate is known as **time-and-a-half.**

Many companies have taken overtime a step further than required by compensating employees at time-and-a-half for all hours over 8 hours per day instead of 40 hours per week. Another common payroll benefit is when companies pay **double time,** twice the hourly rate, for holidays, midnight shifts, and weekend hours.

- **wages**
  Earnings for routine or manual work, usually based on the number of hours worked.

- **hourly wage, or hourly rate**
  The amount an employee is paid for each hour worked.

- **overtime**
  According to federal law, the amount an employee is paid for each hour worked over 40 hours per week.

- **time-and-a-half**
  Overtime rate amounting to one and a half times the hourly rate.

- **double time**
  Overtime rate usually paid for holidays, midnight shifts, and weekend hours, amounting to twice the hourly rate.

> **STEPS TO CALCULATE AN EMPLOYEE'S GROSS PAY BY HOURLY WAGES:**
>
> **Step 1.** Calculate an employee's regular gross pay for working 40 hours or less:
>
> **Regular pay = Hourly rate × Number of regular hours worked**
>
> **Step 2.** Calculate an employee's overtime rate by multiplying the hourly rate by the overtime factor, either 1.5 for time-and-a-half, or 2 for double time.
>
> **Overtime rate = Hourly rate × Overtime factor**
>
> **Step 3.** Calculate an employee's overtime pay (over 40 hours):
>
> **Overtime pay = Overtime rate × Number of overtime hours worked**
>
> **Step 4.** Calculate total gross pay:
>
> **Total gross pay = Regular pay + Overtime pay**

Tina Allen earns $8.00 per hour as a checker on an assembly line. If her overtime rate is time-and-a-half, what is Tina's total gross pay for working 46 hours last week?

SOLUTION STRATEGY

To find Tina's total gross pay, compute her regular pay plus overtime pay.

$$\text{Regular pay} = \text{Hourly rate} \times \text{Number of hours worked}$$
$$\text{Regular pay} = 8.00 \times 40 = \underline{\$320.00}$$

$$\text{Time-and-a-half overtime rate} = \text{Hourly rate} \times \text{Overtime factor}$$
$$\text{Time-and-a-half overtime rate} = 8.00 \times 1.5 = \$12.00$$
$$\text{Time-and-a-half pay} = \text{Overtime rate} \times \text{Hours worked}$$
$$\text{Time-and-a-half pay} = 12.00 \times 6 = \underline{\$72.00}$$

$$\text{Total gross pay} = \text{Regular pay} + \text{Time-and-a-half pay}$$
$$\text{Total gross pay} = 320.00 + 72.00 = \underline{\$392.00}$$

TRY-IT   EXERCISE

2. **David Wiechmann works as a delivery truck driver for $6.50 per hour, with time-and-a-half for overtime and double time on Sundays. What is David's total gross pay for last week if he worked 45 hours on Monday through Saturday, plus a 4-hour shift on Sunday?**

Check your answer with the solution on page 297.

9-3 Calculating Gross Pay by Straight and Differential Piecework Schedules

● **piecework**

Pay rate schedule based on an employee's production output, not hours worked.

● **straight piecework plan**

Pay per unit of output, regardless of output quantity.

● **differential piecework plan**

Greater incentive method of compensation than straight piecework, where pay per unit increases as output goes up.

A **piecework** pay rate schedule is not based on time but on production output. The incentive is that the more units the worker produces, the more money he or she makes. A **straight piecework plan** is where the worker receives a certain amount of pay per unit of output, regardless of output quantity. A **differential piecework plan** gives workers a greater incentive to increase output, since the rate per unit increases as output goes up. For example, a straight piecework plan might pay $3.15 per unit, whereas a differential plan might pay $3.05 for the first 50 units produced, $3.45 for units 51–100, and $3.90 for any units over 100.

STEPS TO CALCULATE GROSS PAY BY PIECEWORK:

Straight Piecework:
Step 1. Total gross pay under a straight piecework schedule is calculated by multiplying the number of pieces or output units by the rate per unit.

$$\textbf{Total gross pay} = \textbf{Output quantity} \times \textbf{Rate per unit}$$

Differential Piecework:
Step 1. Multiply the number of output units at each level by the rate per unit at that level.
Step 2. Find the total gross pay by adding the total from each level.

EXAMPLE

Kim Evans works on a hat assembly line. Kim gets paid at a straight piecework rate of $.35 per hat. What is Kim's total gross pay for last week if she produced 1,655 hats?

SOLUTION STRATEGY

Total gross pay = Output quantity × Rate per unit
Total gross pay = 1,655 × .35 = $579.25

TRY-IT   EXERCISE

3. **Ben Sadler works at a tire manufacturing plant. He is on a straight piecework rate of $.41 per tire. What is Ben's total gross pay for last week if he produced 950 tires?**

Check your answer with the solution on page 297.

EXAMPLE

Michelle Sala assembled 190 watches last week. Calculate her total gross pay based on the following differential piecework schedule:

Pay Level	Watches Assembled	Rate per Watch
1	1–100	$2.45
2	101–150	$2.75
3	Over 150	$3.10

SOLUTION STRATEGY

To find Michelle's total gross earnings, we calculate her earnings at each level of the pay schedule and add the totals. In this case, Michelle will be paid for all of level 1, all of level 2, and for 40 watches at level 3 (190 − 150).

Level pay = Output × Rate per piece
Level 1 = 100 × 2.45 = $245.00
Level 2 = 50 × 2.75 = $137.50
Level 3 = 40 × 3.10 = $124.00
Total gross pay = Level 1 + Level 2 + Level 3
Total gross pay = 245.00 + 137.50 + 124.00 = $506.50

TRY-IT   EXERCISE

4. **You are the payroll manager for Royal Toys, Inc., a manufacturer of small plastic toys. Your workers are on a differential piecework schedule as follows:**

Pay Level	Toys Produced	Rate per Toy
1	1–300	$.68
2	301–500	$.79
3	501–750	$.86
4	Over 750	$.94

Calculate last week's total gross pay for the following employees:

Name	Toys Produced	Total Gross Pay
C. Gomez	515	_____
L. Clifford	199	_____
M. Maken	448	_____
B. Nathan	804	_____

Check your answers with the solutions on page 297.

9-4 Calculating Gross Pay by Straight and Incremental Commission, Salary Plus Commission, and Drawing Accounts

Straight and Incremental Commission

● **commission**

Percentage method of compensation primarily used to pay employees who sell a company's goods and services.

● **straight commission**

Commission based on a specified percentage of the sales volume attained by an employee.

● **incremental commission**

Greater incentive method of compensation than straight commission, whereby higher levels of sales earn increasing rates of commission.

Commission is a method of compensation primarily used to pay employees who sell a company's goods or services. **Straight commission** is based on a single specified percentage of the sales volume attained. For example, Delta Distributors pays its sales staff a commission of 8% on all sales. **Incremental commission** is much like the differential piecework rate, whereby higher levels of sales earn increasing rates of commission. An example would be 5% commission on all sales up to $70,000; 6% on sales over $70,000 and up to $120,000; and 7% commission on any sales over $120,000.

STEPS TO CALCULATE GROSS PAY BY COMMISSION:

Straight Commission:

Step 1. Total gross pay under a straight commission schedule is calculated by multiplying the total sales by the commission rate.

$$\text{Total gross pay} = \text{Total sales} \times \text{Commission rate}$$

Incremental Commission:

Step 1. Multiply the total sales at each level by the commission rate for that level.

Step 2. Find the total gross pay by adding the total from each level.

EXAMPLE

Allied Wholesalers pays its sales force a commission rate of 6% of all sales. What is the total gross pay for an employee who sold $113,500 last month?

SOLUTION STRATEGY

$$\text{Total gross pay} = \text{Total sales} \times \text{Commission rate}$$
$$\text{Total gross pay} = 113,500 \times .06 = \underline{\$6,810}$$

TRY-IT EXERCISE

5. Caroline Salkind sells for South Hills International, a manufacturer of women's clothing. Caroline is paid a straight commission of 2.4%. If her sales volume last month was $233,760, what is her total gross pay?

Check your answer with the solution on page 297.

EXAMPLE

A furniture manufacturer pays its sales representatives on the following incremental commission schedule:

Level	Sales Volume	Commission Rate
1	$1–$50,000	4%
2	$50,001–$150,000	5%
3	Over $150,000	6.5%

What is the total gross pay for a sales rep who sold $162,400 last month?

SOLUTION STRATEGY

Using an incremental commission schedule, we find the pay for each level and then add the totals from each level. In this problem, the sales rep will be paid for all of level 1, all of level 2, and for $12,400 of level 3 ($162,400 − $150,000).

Level pay = Sales per level × Commission rate
Level 1 pay = 50,000 × .04 = $2,000.00
Level 2 pay = 100,000 × .05 = $5,000.00
Level 3 pay = 12,400 × .065 = $806.00
Total gross pay = Level 1 + Level 2 + Level 3
Total gross pay = 2,000.00 + 5,000.00 + 806.00 = $7,806.00

TRY-IT EXERCISE

6. Roger Fine sells copiers for Sharp Business Products. He is on an incremental commission schedule of 1.7% of sales up to $100,000 and 2.5% on sales over $100,000. What is Roger's total gross pay for last month if his sales volume was $184,600?

Check your answer with the solution on page 297.

Salary Plus Commission

A variation of straight and incremental commission pay schedules is the **salary plus commission,** whereby the employee is paid a guaranteed salary plus a commission on sales over a certain specified amount. To calculate the total gross pay, find the amount of commission and add it to the salary.

● **salary plus commission**
A guaranteed salary plus a commission on sales over a certain specified amount.

Angus McDonald works on a pay schedule of **$1,500 per month salary plus a 3% commission on all sales over $40,000. If he sold $60,000 last month, what is Angus's total gross pay?**

SOLUTION STRATEGY

To solve for Angus's total gross pay, add his monthly salary to his commission for the month.

Commission = Commission rate × Sales subject to commission

Commission = 3%(60,000 − 40,000)

Commission = .03 × 20,000 = $600

Total gross pay = Salary + Commission

Total gross pay = $1,500 + $600 = $2,100

TRY-IT EXERCISE

7. **Ronnie Jerome is a salesperson for Continental Supply, Inc. He is paid a salary of $1,400 per month plus a commission of 4% on all sales over $20,000. If Ronnie sold $45,000 last month, what was his total gross earnings?**

Check your answer with the solution on page 298.

Draw against Commission

In certain industries and at certain times of the year, sales fluctuate significantly. In order to provide salespeople on commission with at least some income during slack periods of sales, a drawing account is used. A **drawing account,** or **draw against commission,** is a commission paid in advance of sales and later deducted from the commissions earned. If a period goes by where the salesperson does not earn enough commission to cover the draw, the unpaid balance carries over to the next period.

● **drawing account, or draw against commission**

Commission paid in advance of sales and later deducted from the commission earned.

EXAMPLE

Charlie Sparkle is a salesperson for a company that pays 8% commission on all sales and gives Charlie a $1,500 per month draw against commission. If Charlie receives his draw at the beginning of the month and then sells $58,000 during the month, how much commission is owed to Charlie?

SOLUTION STRATEGY

To find the amount of commission owed to Charlie, find the total amount of commission he earned and subtract $1,500, the amount of his draw against commission.

Commission = Total sales × Commission rate

Commission = $58,000 × 8% = $4,640

Commission owed = Commission − Amount of draw

Commission owed = 4,640 − 1,500 = $3,140

TRY-IT EXERCISE

8. Jessica Wyatt sells for Panorama Products, Inc. She is on a 3.5% straight commission with a $2,000 drawing account. If she is paid the draw at the beginning of the month and then sells $120,000 during the month, how much commission is owed to Jessica?

Check your answer with the solution on page 298.

REVIEW EXERCISES   CHAPTER 9—SECTION I

Calculate the gross earnings per pay period for the following pay schedules:

	Annual Salary	Monthly	Semimonthly	Biweekly	Weekly
1.	$15,000.00	1,250.00	625.00	576.92	288.46
2.	$44,200.00	3,683.33	1,841.67	1,700.00	850.00
3.	$100,000.00	8,333.33	4,166.67	3,846.15	1,923.08
4.	21,600.00	$1,800.00	900.00	830.77	415.38
5.	34,800.00	2,900.00	$1,450.00	1,338.46	669.23
6.	22,750.00	1,895.83	947.92	$875.00	437.50
7.	17,420.00	1,451.67	725.83	670.00	$335.00

8. Lana Cargile has gross earnings of $1,600 semimonthly. If her company switches pay schedules from semimonthly to biweekly, what are Lana's new gross earnings?

$1,600.00 \times 24 = 38,400.00$ Annual salary

$\dfrac{38,400.00}{26} = \underline{1,476.92}$ Biweekly salary

9. The president and founder of a large corporation earns a salary of $2,000,000 per year. What are the gross earnings of this executive on a monthly pay schedule?

$\dfrac{2,000,000.00}{12} = \underline{\$166,666.67}$ Per month

10. Michele Tomiak works 40 hours per week. At the rate of $7.60 per hour, what are her gross weekly earnings?

$\$7.60 \times 40 = \underline{\$304.00}$

11. Val Mebust works for a company that pays time-and-a-half for all hours worked over 40. If she earns $8.70 per hour, what are her gross weekly earnings for a 51-hour week?

$\$8.70 \times 40 = 348.00$	$(51 - 40 = 11$ Hours OT)	Reg.	348.00
$\$8.70 \times 1.5 = 13.05$ Overtime rate		OT	+ 143.55
$\$13.05 \times 11 = 143.55$			$\underline{\$491.55}$

12. Alan Barnett earns $6.25 per hour for regular time up to 40 hours, time-and-a-half for overtime, and double time for the midnight shift. Last week Alan worked 58 hours, including 6 on the midnight shift. What are his gross earnings?

58 Hours total	Reg 40 × 6.25 = 250.00
− 40 Reg	OT 12 × 9.38 = 112.56
18 OT	DT 6 × 12.50 = 75.00
− 6 Double time (6.25 × 2 = 12.50)	$437.56
12 Time-and-a-half (6.25 × 1.5 = 9.38)	

As the payroll manager for International Systems, Inc., it is your task to complete the following weekly payroll record. The company pays overtime for all hours worked over 40 at the rate of time-and-a-half (round all overtime rates to the nearest cent):

	Employee	M	T	W	T	F	S	S	Hourly Rate	Total Hours	Overtime Hours	Regular Pay	Overtime Pay	Total Pay
13.	Williams	7	8	5	8	8	0	0	$5.70	36	0	205.20		205.20
14.	Tanner	6	5	9	8	10	7	0	$9.50	45	5	380.00	71.25	451.25
15.	Gomez	8	6	11	7	12	0	4	$7.25	48	8	290.00	87.04	377.04
16.	Wells	9	7	7	7	9	0	8	$14.75	47	7	590.00	154.91	744.91

17. Rosa Sanchez assembles circuit boards for United Electronics. She is paid a straight piecework rate of $6.50 per board. If she assembled 88 units last week, what were her gross earnings?

6.50 × 88 = $572.00

18. Keith Andrews works for a company that manufactures small appliances. Keith is paid $2.00 for each toaster, $4.60 for each microwave oven, and $1.55 for each food blender he assembles. If Keith produced 56 toasters, 31 microwave ovens, and 79 blenders, what were his total weekly gross earnings?

Toaster	56 × 2.00 = 112.00
Microwave	31 × 4.60 = 142.60
Blender	79 × 1.55 = 122.45
	$377.05

You are the payroll manager for the Glitzy Garment Company, a manufacturer of women's apparel. Your workers are paid per garment sewn on a differential piecework schedule as follows:

Pay Level	Garments Produced	Rate per Garment
1	1–50	$3.60
2	51–100	$4.25
3	101–150	$4.50
4	Over 150	$5.10

Calculate last week's total gross pay for each of the following employees:

	Employee	Garments Produced	Total Gross Pay
19.	Johnston, C.	109	$433.00
20.	Barber, W.	83	$320.25
21.	Lynn, K.	174	$739.90

Complete, worked out solutions for exercises 19–21 appear in the appendix following the index.

22. What is the total gross pay for a salesperson on a straight commission of 4.7% if her sales volume is $123,200?

123,200.00 × .047 = $5,790.40

23. What is the total gross pay for a salesperson on an incremental commission schedule of 1.2% of sales up to $200,000 and 1.5% on sales over $200,000, if last month's sales volume was $284,300?

$$200,000.00 \times .012 = 2,400.00$$
$$\underline{84,300.00} \times .015 = \underline{1,264.50}$$
$$284,300.00 \qquad \underline{\$3,664.50}$$

24. John Carey is a salesman for a company that pays a salary of $770 per month plus a commission of $8\frac{1}{2}\%$ of all sales over $10,000. If John sold $25,880 last month, what was his total gross pay?

$$25,880.00$$
$$\underline{-10,000.00}$$
$$15,880.00 \times .085 = 1,349.80$$
$$\underline{+770.00} \text{ Base salary}$$
$$\underline{\$2,119.80}$$

25. Ross Perez is a salesman for General Industries. He is paid a 2.8% straight commission with a $1,200 drawing account. If he receives the draw at the beginning of the month and then sells $162,000 during the month, how much commission is owed to Ross?

$$162,000.00 \times .028 = 4,536.00$$
$$\underline{-1,200.00} \text{ Received}$$
$$\underline{\$3,336.00}$$

26. Caroline Huber works for Lacy's selling clothing. She is on a salary of $140 per week plus a commission of 7% of her sales. Last week Caroline sold 19 dresses at $79.95 each, 26 skirts at $24.75 each, and 17 jackets at $51.50 each. What were her total gross earnings for the week?

$$19 \times 79.95 = 1,519.05 \qquad\qquad 3,038.05$$
$$26 \times 24.75 = 643.50 \qquad\qquad \underline{\times .07}$$
$$17 \times 51.50 = \underline{875.50} \qquad\qquad 212.66 \text{ Commission}$$
$$3,038.05 \text{ Total sales} \quad \underline{+140.00} \text{ Salary}$$
$$\underline{\$352.66} \text{ Total gross earnings}$$

27. Bob Tessman is a waiter in a restaurant that pays a salary of $22 per day. He also averages tips of 18% of his total gross food orders. Last week Bob worked 6 days and had total food orders of $2,766.50. What was his total gross pay for the week?

$$6 \times 22.00 = 132.00 \text{ Salary}$$
$$2,766.50 \times .18 + \underline{497.97} \text{ Commission}$$
$$\underline{\$629.97} \text{ Total gross earnings}$$

EMPLOYEE'S PAYROLL DEDUCTIONS

"Hey! What happened to my paycheck?" This is the typical reaction of employees upon seeing their paychecks for the first time after a raise or a promotion. As we shall see, gross pay is by no means the amount of money that the employee takes home.

Employers, by federal law, are required to deduct or withhold certain funds, known as **deductions** or **withholdings,** from an employee's paycheck. Employee payroll deductions fall into two categories: mandatory and voluntary. The three major **mandatory deductions** most workers in the United States are subject to are social security, Medicare, and federal income tax. Other mandatory deductions, found only in some states, are state income tax and state disability insurance.

In addition to the mandatory deductions, employees may also choose to have **voluntary deductions** taken out of their paycheck. Some examples include payments for life or health insurance premiums, union or professional organization dues, credit union savings deposits or loan payments, stock or bond purchases, and charitable contributions.

● **deductions, or withholdings**
Funds withheld from an employee's paycheck.

● **mandatory deductions**
Deductions withheld from an employee's paycheck by law: social security, Medicare, and federal income tax.

● **voluntary deductions**
Deductions withheld from an employee's paycheck by request of the employee, such as insurance premiums, dues, loan payments, and charitable contributions.

After all the deductions have been subtracted from the employee's gross earnings, the remaining amount is known as net or take-home pay.

$$\text{Net pay} = \text{Gross pay} - \text{Total deductions}$$

9-5 Computing FICA Taxes, Both Social Security and Medicare, Withheld from an Employee's Paycheck

● **Federal Insurance Contribution Act (FICA)**

Federal legislation, enacted in 1937 during the Great Depression, to provide retirement funds and hospital insurance for retired and disabled workers. Today, FICA is divided into two categories, social security and Medicare.

● **wage base**

The amount of earnings up to which an employee must pay social security tax.

● **social security tax (OASDI)**

Old Age, Survivors, and Disability Insurance—a federal tax, based on a percentage of a worker's income up to a specified limit or wage base, for the purpose of providing monthly benefits to retired and disabled workers and to the families of deceased workers.

● **Medicare tax**

A federal tax used to provide health care benefits and hospital insurance to retired and disabled workers.

In 1937 during the Great Depression, Congress enacted legislation known as the **Federal Insurance Contribution Act (FICA)** with the purpose of providing monthly benefits to retired and disabled workers and to the families of deceased workers. This social security tax, which is assessed to virtually every worker in the United States, is based on a certain percent of the worker's income up to a specified limit or **wage base** per year. When the tax began in 1937, the tax rate was 1% up to a wage base of $3,000. At that time, the maximum a worker could be taxed per year for social security was $30.00 (3,000 × .01).

Today, the FICA tax is divided into two categories. **Social security tax** (OASDI, which stands for Old Age, Survivors, and Disability Insurance) is a retirement plan, and **Medicare tax** is for health care and hospital insurance. The social security tax rate and wage base change almost every year. For the most current information, consult the Internal Revenue Service, *Circular E: Employer's Tax Guide*. As of this writing, the following rates and wage base are in effect for the FICA tax and should be used for all problems in this chapter:

	Tax Rate	Wage Base
Social Security (OASDI)	6.2%	$62,700
Medicare	1.45%	no limit

When an employee has reached the wage base for the year, he or she is no longer subject to the tax. The maximum social security tax per year is currently $3,887.40 (62,700 × .062). There is no limit on the amount of Medicare tax. The 1.45% is in effect regardless of how much an employee earns.

EXAMPLE

What are the withholdings for social security and Medicare for an employee with gross earnings of $650 per week?

SOLUTION STRATEGY

To find the withholdings we apply the tax rates for social security (6.2%) and Medicare (1.45%) to the gross earnings for the week:

$$\text{Social security tax} = \text{Gross earnings} \times 6.2\%$$
$$\text{Social security tax} = 650 \times .062 = \underline{\$40.30}$$
$$\text{Medicare tax} = \text{Gross earnings} \times 1.45\%$$
$$\text{Medicare tax} = 650 \times .0145 = 9.425 = \underline{\$9.43}$$

TRY-IT EXERCISE

9. **What are the withholdings for social security and Medicare for an employee with gross earnings of $5,000 per month?**

Check your answers with the solutions on page 298.

Mandatory payroll deductions include social security, Medicare, and federal income tax.

Reaching the Wage Base Limit

At that point during the year when an employee's paycheck puts his or her year-to-date (YTD) earnings over the wage base for social security, the tax is applied only to the portion of the check below the limit.

EXAMPLE

Tricia Zingone has earned $60,000 so far this year. Her next paycheck, $5,000, will put her earnings over the wage base limit for social security. What is the amount of Tricia's social security deduction for that paycheck?

SOLUTION STRATEGY

In order to calculate Tricia's social security deduction, first determine how much more she must earn to reach the wage base of $62,700.

Earnings subject to tax = Wage base − Year-to-date earnings

Earnings subject to tax = 62,700 − 60,000 = $2,700

Social security tax = Earnings subject to tax × 6.2%

Social security tax = $2,700 × .062 = $167.40

TRY-IT EXERCISE

10. **Peter Massar has year-to-date earnings of $57,800. If his next paycheck is for $6,000, what is the amount of his social security deduction?**

Check your answer with the solution on page 298.

9-6 Determining an Employee's Federal Income Tax Withholding (FIT) by the Wage Bracket Table Method

In addition to social security and Medicare tax withholdings, an employer is also responsible, by federal law, for withholding an appropriate amount of **federal income tax (FIT)** from each employee's paycheck. This graduated tax allows the government a steady flow of tax revenues throughout the year. Self-employed persons must send quarterly tax payments based on estimated earnings to the Internal Revenue Service.

The amount of income tax withheld from an employee's paycheck is determined by his or her amount of gross earnings, marital status, and the number of **withholding allowances** or **exemptions** claimed. Employees are allowed one exemption for themselves, one for their spouse if the spouse does not work, and one for each dependent child or elderly parent living with the taxpayer but not working.

Each employee is required to complete a form called W-4, Employee's Withholding Allowance Certificate, shown in Exhibit 9-1. The information provided on this form is used by the employer in calculating the amount of income tax withheld from the paycheck.

One method of calculating the income tax withheld is by using the **wage bracket tables,** found in *Circular E: Employer's Tax Guide.* This publication contains a complete set of tables for both single and married people, covering weekly, biweekly, semimonthly, monthly, and even daily pay periods. The wage bracket method is used primarily by companies whose payroll is done manually, without the aid of a computer.

Exhibit 9-2 shows a portion of the wage bracket tables for Married Persons—Weekly Payroll Period and Exhibit 9-3 shows a portion of the wage bracket table for Single Persons—Monthly Payroll Period. Use these tables to solve wage bracket problems in this chapter.

● **federal income tax (FIT)**
A graduated tax, based on gross earnings, marital status, and number of exemptions, that is paid by all workers earning over a certain amount of money in the United States.

● **withholding allowance, or exemption**
An amount that reduces an employee's taxable income. Employees are allowed one exemption for themselves, one for their spouse if the spouse does not work, and one for each dependent child or elderly parent living with the taxpayer, but not working.

● **wage bracket tables**
IRS tables used to determine the amount of income tax that must be withheld from an employee's gross earnings each pay period.

Form **W-4**	**Employee's Withholding Allowance Certificate**	OMB No. 1545-0010
Department of the Treasury Internal Revenue Service	▶ **For Privacy Act and Paperwork Reduction Act Notice, see reverse.**	**19**

1 Type or print your first name and middle initial	Last name	2 Your social security number

Home address (number and street or rural route)	3 ☐ Single ☐ Married ☐ Married, but withhold at higher Single rate. **Note:** *If married, but legally separated, or spouse is a nonresident alien, check the Single box.*
City or town, state, and ZIP code	4 If your last name differs from that on your social security card, check here and call 1-800-772-1213 for more information . ▶ ☐

5 Total number of allowances you are claiming (from line G above or from the Worksheets on back if they apply) **5** ☐

6 Additional amount, if any, you want deducted from each paycheck . . . . **6** $ ☐

7 I claim exemption from withholding and I certify that I meet **ALL** of the following conditions for exemption:
- Last year I had a right to a refund of **ALL** Federal income tax withheld because I had **NO** tax liability; **AND**
- This year I expect a refund of **ALL** Federal income tax withheld because I expect to have **NO** tax liability; **AND**
- This year if my income exceeds $600 and includes nonwage income, another person cannot claim me as a dependent.

If you meet all of the above conditions, enter the year effective and "EXEMPT" here . . ▶ **7** | 19

8 Are you a full-time student? (**Note:** *Full-time students are not automatically exempt.*) . . . . **8** ☐ Yes ☐ No

Under penalties of perjury, I certify that I am entitled to the number of withholding allowances claimed on this certificate or entitled to claim exempt status.

Employee's signature ▶ _____ Date ▶ _____ , 19

9 Employer's name and address (Employer: Complete 9 and 11 only if sending to the IRS)	10 Office code (optional)	11 Employer identification number

Cat. No. 10220Q

EXHIBIT 9-1

EMPLOYEE W-4 FORM

STEPS TO FIND THE INCOME TAX WITHHELD USING THE WAGE BRACKET TABLE:

Step 1. Based on the employee's marital status and period of payment, find the corresponding table (Exhibit 9-2 or 9-3).

Step 2. Note that the two left-hand columns, labeled "At least" and "But less than," are the wage brackets. Scan down these columns until you find the bracket containing the gross pay of the employee.

Step 3. Scan across the row of that wage bracket to the intersection of the column containing the number of withholding allowances claimed by the employee.

Step 4. The number in that column, on the wage bracket row, is the amount of tax withheld.

EXAMPLE

Use the wage bracket tables to determine the amount of income tax withheld from the monthly paycheck of Cherie Norvell, a single employee, claiming three withholding allowances, and earning $2,675 per month.

SOLUTION STRATEGY

To find Cherie Norvell's monthly income tax withholding, choose the table for Single Persons—Monthly Payroll Period, Exhibit 9.3. Scanning down the "At least" and "But less than" columns, we find the wage bracket containing Cherie's earnings: "At least 2,640—But less than 2,680."

Next, scan across that row from left to right to the "3" withholding allowances column. The number at that intersection, $271, is the tax to be withheld from Cherie's paycheck.

MARRIED Persons—WEEKLY Payroll Period
(For Wages Paid in 1996)

If the wages are—		And the number of withholding allowances claimed is—										
At least	But less than	0	1	2	3	4	5	6	7	8	9	10
		The amount of income tax to be withheld is—										
$740	$750	93	86	79	71	64	56	49	42	34	27	20
750	760	95	87	80	73	65	58	51	43	36	29	21
760	770	96	89	82	74	67	59	52	45	37	30	23
770	780	98	90	83	76	68	61	54	46	39	32	24
780	790	99	92	85	77	70	62	55	48	40	33	26
790	800	101	93	86	79	71	64	57	49	42	35	27
800	810	102	95	88	80	73	65	58	51	43	36	29
810	820	104	96	89	82	74	67	60	52	45	38	30
820	830	105	98	91	83	76	68	61	54	46	39	32
830	840	107	99	92	85	77	70	63	55	48	41	33
840	850	108	101	94	86	79	71	64	57	49	42	35
850	860	110	102	95	88	80	73	66	58	51	44	36
860	870	113	104	97	89	82	74	67	60	52	45	38
870	880	116	105	98	91	83	76	69	61	54	47	39
880	890	119	107	100	92	85	77	70	63	55	48	41
890	900	121	108	101	94	86	79	72	64	57	50	42
900	910	124	111	103	95	88	80	73	66	58	51	44
910	920	127	113	104	97	89	82	75	67	60	53	45
920	930	130	116	106	98	91	83	76	69	61	54	47
930	940	133	119	107	100	92	85	78	70	63	56	48
940	950	135	122	109	101	94	86	79	72	64	57	50
950	960	138	125	111	103	95	88	81	73	66	59	51
960	970	141	127	114	104	97	89	82	75	67	60	53
970	980	144	130	116	106	98	91	84	76	69	62	54
980	990	147	133	119	107	100	92	85	78	70	63	56
990	1,000	149	136	122	109	101	94	87	79	72	65	57
1,000	1,010	152	139	125	111	103	95	88	81	73	66	59
1,010	1,020	155	141	128	114	104	97	90	82	75	68	60
1,020	1,030	158	144	130	117	106	98	91	84	76	69	62
1,030	1,040	161	147	133	119	107	100	93	85	78	71	63
1,040	1,050	163	150	136	122	109	101	94	87	79	72	65
1,050	1,060	166	153	139	125	111	103	96	88	81	74	66
1,060	1,070	169	155	142	128	114	104	97	90	82	75	68
1,070	1,080	172	158	144	131	117	106	99	91	84	77	69
1,080	1,090	175	161	147	133	120	107	100	93	85	78	71
1,090	1,100	177	164	150	136	123	109	102	94	87	80	72
1,100	1,110	180	167	153	139	125	112	103	96	88	81	74
1,110	1,120	183	169	156	142	128	114	105	97	90	83	75
1,120	1,130	186	172	158	145	131	117	106	99	91	84	77
1,130	1,140	189	175	161	147	134	120	108	100	93	86	78
1,140	1,150	191	178	164	150	137	123	109	102	94	87	80
1,150	1,160	194	181	167	153	139	126	112	103	96	89	81
1,160	1,170	197	183	170	156	142	128	115	105	97	90	83
1,170	1,180	200	186	172	159	145	131	117	106	99	92	84
1,180	1,190	203	189	175	161	148	134	120	108	100	93	86
1,190	1,200	205	192	178	164	151	137	123	109	102	95	87
1,200	1,210	208	195	181	167	153	140	126	112	103	96	89
1,210	1,220	211	197	184	170	156	142	129	115	105	98	90
1,220	1,230	214	200	186	173	159	145	131	118	106	99	92
1,230	1,240	217	203	189	175	162	148	134	121	108	101	93
1,240	1,250	219	206	192	178	165	151	137	123	110	102	95
1,250	1,260	222	209	195	181	167	154	140	126	112	104	96
1,260	1,270	225	211	198	184	170	156	143	129	115	105	98
1,270	1,280	228	214	200	187	173	159	145	132	118	107	99
1,280	1,290	231	217	203	189	176	162	148	135	121	108	101
1,290	1,300	233	220	206	192	179	165	151	137	124	110	102
1,300	1,310	236	223	209	195	181	168	154	140	126	113	104
1,310	1,320	239	225	212	198	184	170	157	143	129	115	105
1,320	1,330	242	228	214	201	187	173	159	146	132	118	107
1,330	1,340	245	231	217	203	190	176	162	149	135	121	108
1,340	1,350	247	234	220	206	193	179	165	151	138	124	110
1,350	1,360	250	237	223	209	195	182	168	154	140	127	113
1,360	1,370	253	239	226	212	198	184	171	157	143	129	116
1,370	1,380	256	242	228	215	201	187	173	160	146	132	119
1,380	1,390	259	245	231	217	204	190	176	163	149	135	121

$1,390 and over   Use Table 1(b) for a **MARRIED person** on page 34. Also see the instructions on page 32.

EXHIBIT 9-2

PAYROLL DEDUCTIONS—
MARRIED, PAID WEEKLY

If the wages are—		And the number of withholding allowances claimed is—										
At least	But less than	0	1	2	3	4	5	6	7	8	9	10
		The amount of income tax to be withheld is—										
$2,440	$2,480	380	321	272	241	209	177	145	113	81	49	17
2,480	2,520	391	332	278	247	215	183	151	119	87	55	23
2,520	2,560	403	343	284	253	221	189	157	125	93	61	29
2,560	2,600	414	354	295	259	227	195	163	131	99	67	35
2,600	2,640	425	366	306	265	233	201	169	137	105	73	41
2,640	2,680	436	377	317	271	239	207	175	143	111	79	47
2,680	2,720	447	388	328	277	245	213	181	149	117	85	53
2,720	2,760	459	399	340	283	251	219	187	155	123	91	59
2,760	2,800	470	410	351	291	257	225	193	161	129	97	65
2,800	2,840	481	422	362	303	263	231	199	167	135	103	71
2,840	2,880	492	433	373	314	269	237	205	173	141	109	77
2,880	2,920	503	444	384	325	275	243	211	179	147	115	83
2,920	2,960	515	455	396	336	281	249	217	185	153	121	89
2,960	3,000	526	466	407	347	288	255	223	191	159	127	95
3,000	3,040	537	478	418	359	299	261	229	197	165	133	101
3,040	3,080	548	489	429	370	310	267	235	203	171	139	107
3,080	3,120	559	500	440	381	321	273	241	209	177	145	113
3,120	3,160	571	511	452	392	333	279	247	215	183	151	119
3,160	3,200	582	522	463	403	344	285	253	221	189	157	125
3,200	3,240	593	534	474	415	355	296	259	227	195	163	131
3,240	3,280	604	545	485	426	366	307	265	233	201	169	137
3,280	3,320	615	556	496	437	377	318	271	239	207	175	143
3,320	3,360	627	567	508	448	389	329	277	245	213	181	149
3,360	3,400	638	578	519	459	400	340	283	251	219	187	155
3,400	3,440	649	590	530	471	411	352	292	257	225	193	161
3,440	3,480	660	601	541	482	422	363	303	263	231	199	167
3,480	3,520	671	612	552	493	433	374	314	269	237	205	173
3,520	3,560	683	623	564	504	445	385	326	275	243	211	179
3,560	3,600	694	634	575	515	456	396	337	281	249	217	185
3,600	3,640	705	646	586	527	467	408	348	289	255	223	191
3,640	3,680	716	657	597	538	478	419	359	300	261	229	197
3,680	3,720	727	668	608	549	489	430	370	311	267	235	203
3,720	3,760	739	679	620	560	501	441	382	322	273	241	209
3,760	3,800	750	690	631	571	512	452	393	333	279	247	215
3,800	3,840	761	702	642	583	523	464	404	345	285	253	221
3,840	3,880	772	713	653	594	534	475	415	356	296	259	227
3,880	3,920	783	724	664	605	545	486	426	367	307	265	233
3,920	3,960	795	735	676	616	557	497	438	378	319	271	239
3,960	4,000	806	746	687	627	568	508	449	389	330	277	245
4,000	4,040	817	758	698	639	579	520	460	401	341	283	251
4,040	4,080	828	769	709	650	590	531	471	412	352	293	257
4,080	4,120	839	780	720	661	601	542	482	423	363	304	263
4,120	4,160	851	791	732	672	613	553	494	434	375	315	269
4,160	4,200	862	802	743	683	624	564	505	445	386	326	275
4,200	4,240	873	814	754	695	635	576	516	457	397	338	281
4,240	4,280	884	825	765	706	646	587	527	468	408	349	289
4,280	4,320	895	836	776	717	657	598	538	479	419	360	300
4,320	4,360	907	847	788	728	669	609	550	490	431	371	312
4,360	4,400	918	858	799	739	680	620	561	501	442	382	323
4,400	4,440	929	870	810	751	691	632	572	513	453	394	334
4,440	4,480	940	881	821	762	702	643	583	524	464	405	345
4,480	4,520	952	892	832	773	713	654	594	535	475	416	356
4,520	4,560	965	903	844	784	725	665	606	546	487	427	368
4,560	4,600	977	914	855	795	736	676	617	557	498	438	379
4,600	4,640	989	926	866	807	747	688	628	569	509	450	390
4,640	4,680	1,002	937	877	818	758	699	639	580	520	461	401
4,680	4,720	1,014	948	888	829	769	710	650	591	531	472	412
4,720	4,760	1,027	961	900	840	781	721	662	602	543	483	424
4,760	4,800	1,039	973	911	851	792	732	673	613	554	494	435
4,800	4,840	1,051	985	922	863	803	744	684	625	565	506	446
4,840	4,880	1,064	998	933	874	814	755	695	636	576	517	457
4,880	4,920	1,076	1,010	944	885	825	766	706	647	587	528	468
4,920	4,960	1,089	1,023	957	896	837	777	718	658	599	539	480
4,960	5,000	1,101	1,035	969	907	848	788	729	669	610	550	491
5,000	5,040	1,113	1,047	982	919	859	800	740	681	621	562	502

$5,040 and over   Use Table 4(a) for a **SINGLE person** on page 34. Also see the instructions on page 32.

EXHIBIT 9-3

PAYROLL DEDUCTIONS—
SINGLE, PAID MONTHLY

11. Using the wage bracket tables, what amount of income tax should be withheld from Shane Davis's weekly paycheck of $835 if he is married and claims two withholding allowances?

Check your answer with the solution on page 298.

9-7 Calculating an Employee's Federal Income Tax Withholding (FIT) by the Percentage Method

The **percentage method** for determining the amount of federal income tax withheld from an employee's paycheck is mostly used by companies whose payroll processing is on a computerized system. As before, the amount of tax withheld is based on the amount of gross earning, the marital status of the employee, and the number of withholding allowances claimed.

The percentage method of calculating federal income tax requires the use of two tables. The first is the Percentage Method—Amount for One Withholding Allowance Table, Exhibit 9-4. This table shows the dollar amount of one withholding allowance, for the various payroll periods. The second, Exhibit 9-5, is the Rate Tables for Percentage Method of Withholding.

● **percentage method**
An alternate method to the wage bracket tables, used to calculate the amount of an employee's federal income tax withholding.

STEPS TO CALCULATE THE INCOME TAX WITHHELD USING THE PERCENTAGE METHOD:

Step 1. Using the proper payroll period, multiply one withholding allowance, Exhibit 9-4, by the number of allowances claimed by the employee.

Step 2. Subtract that amount from the employee's gross earnings to find the wages subject to federal income tax.

Step 3. From Exhibit 9-5, locate the proper segment (Table 1, 2, 3, or 4) corresponding to the employee's payroll period. Within that segment, use the *left* side (a) for single employees and the *right* side (b) for married employees.

Step 4. Locate the "Over—" and "But not over—" brackets containing the employee's taxable wages from Step 2. The tax is listed to the right as a percent or a dollar amount and a percent.

Payroll Period	One Withholding Allowance
Weekly	$ 49.04
Biweekly	98.08
Semimonthly	106.25
Monthly.............................	212.50
Quarterly	637.50
Semiannually	1,275.00
Annually.............................	2,550.00
Daily or miscellaneous (each day of the payroll period)	9.81

EXHIBIT 9-4
....
PERCENTAGE METHOD
WITHHOLDING ALLOWANCES

Tables for Percentage Method of Withholding
(For Wages Paid in 1996)

TABLE 1—WEEKLY Payroll Period

(a) SINGLE person (including head of household)—

If the amount of wages (after subtracting withholding allowances) is:

The amount of income tax to withhold is:

Not over $50 . . . . . $0

Over—	But not over—		of excess over—
$50	—$489 . .	15%	—$50
$489	—$1,033 . .	$65.85 plus 28%	—$489
$1,033	—$2,361 . .	$218.17 plus 31%	—$1,033
$2,361	—$5,100 . .	$629.85 plus 36%	—$2,361
$5,100 .	. . . . .	$1,615.89 plus 39.6%	—$5,100

(b) MARRIED person—

If the amount of wages (after subtracting withholding allowances) is:

The amount of income tax to withhold is:

Not over $124 . . . . . $0

Over—	But not over—		of excess over—
$124	—$851 . .	15%	—$124
$851	—$1,725 . .	$109.05 plus 28%	—$851
$1,725	—$2,920 . .	$353.77 plus 31%	—$1,725
$2,920	—$5,152 . .	$724.22 plus 36%	—$2,920
$5,152 .	. . . . .	$1,527.74 plus 39.6%	—$5,152

TABLE 2—BIWEEKLY Payroll Period

(a) SINGLE person (including head of household)—

If the amount of wages (after subtracting withholding allowances) is:

The amount of income tax to withhold is:

Not over $101 . . . . $0

Over—	But not over—		of excess over—
$101	—$979 . .	15%	—$101
$979	—$2,066 . .	$131.70 plus 28%	—$979
$2,066	—$4,721 . .	$436.06 plus 31%	—$2,066
$4,721	—$10,200 . .	$1,259.11 plus 36%	—$4,721
$10,200	. . . . . .	$3,231.55 plus 39.6%	—$10,200

(b) MARRIED person—

If the amount of wages (after subtracting withholding allowances) is:

The amount of income tax to withhold is:

Not over $247 . . . . $0

Over—	But not over—		of excess over—
$247	—$1,702 . .	15%	—$247
$1,702	—$3,449 . .	$218.25 plus 28%	—$1,702
$3,449	—$5,840 . .	$707.41 plus 31%	—$3,449
$5,840	—$10,304 . .	$1,448.62 plus 36%	—$5,840
$10,304 .	. . . . .	$3,055.66 plus 39.6%	—$10,304

TABLE 3—SEMIMONTHLY Payroll Period

(a) SINGLE person (including head of household)—

If the amount of wages (after subtracting withholding allowances) is:

The amount of income tax to withhold is:

Not over $109 . . . . $0

Over—	But not over—		of excess over—
$109	—$1,060 . .	15%	—$109
$1,060	—$2,239 . .	$142.65 plus 28%	—$1,060
$2,239	—$5,115 . .	$472.77 plus 31%	—$2,239
$5,115	—$11,050 . .	$1,364.33 plus 36%	—$5,115
$11,050	. . . . . .	$3,500.93 plus 39.6%	—$11,050

(b) MARRIED person—

If the amount of wages (after subtracting withholding allowances) is:

The amount of income tax to withhold is:

Not over $268 . . . . $0

Over—	But not over—		of excess over—
$268	—$1,844 . .	15%	—$268
$1,844	—$3,736 . .	$236.40 plus 28%	—$1,844
$3,736	—$6,327 . .	$766.16 plus 31%	—$3,736
$6,327	—$11,163 . .	$1,569.37 plus 36%	—$6,327
$11,163 .	. . . . .	$3,310.33 plus 39.6%	—$11,163

TABLE 4—MONTHLY Payroll Period

(a) SINGLE person (including head of household)—

If the amount of wages (after subtracting withholding allowances) is:

The amount of income tax to withhold is:

Not over $219 . . . . $0

Over—	But not over—		of excess over—
$219	—$2,121 . .	15%	—$219
$2,121	—$4,477 . .	$285.30 plus 28%	—$2,121
$4,477	—$10,229 . .	$944.98 plus 31%	—$4,477
$10,229	—$22,100 . .	$2,728.10 plus 36%	—$10,229
$22,100	. . . . . .	$7,001.66 plus 39.6%	—$22,100

(b) MARRIED person—

If the amount of wages (after subtracting withholding allowances) is:

The amount of income tax to withhold is:

Not over $535 . . . . $0

Over—	But not over—		of excess over—
$535	—$3,688 . .	15%	—$535
$3,688	—$7,473 . .	$472.95 plus 28%	—$3,688
$7,473	—$12,654 . .	$1,532.75 plus 31%	—$7,473
$12,654	—$22,325 . .	$3,138.86 plus 36%	—$12,654
$22,325 .	. . . . .	$6,620.42 plus 39.6%	—$22,325

EXHIBIT 9-5

....

TABLES FOR PERCENTAGE
METHOD OF WITHHOLDING

Nathalie Cunningham is a manager for Harcourt Wholesalers. She is single and is paid $600 weekly. She claims two withholding allowances. Using the percentage method, calculate the amount of tax withheld from her weekly paycheck.

SOLUTION STRATEGY

From Exhibit 9-4, the amount of one withholding allowance for an employee paid weekly is $49.04. Next, multiply this amount by the number of allowances claimed, two.

$$\$49.04 \times 2 = \underline{\$98.08}$$

Subtract that amount from the gross wages to get taxable income.

$$\$600.00 - \$98.08 = \underline{\$501.92}$$

From Exhibit 9-5 find the tax withheld from Nathalie's paycheck in Table 1(a), Weekly payroll period, Single person. Nathalie's taxable wages of $501.92 fall in the category Over $489, But not over $1,033. The tax, therefore, is $65.85 plus 28% of the excess over $489.

$$Tax = 65.85 + 28\%(501.92 - 489.00)$$
$$Tax = 65.85 + .28(12.92)$$
$$Tax = 65.85 + 3.62 = \underline{\$69.47}$$

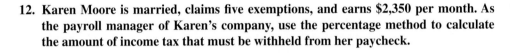

TRY-IT   **EXERCISE**

12. Karen Moore is married, claims five exemptions, and earns $2,350 per month. As the payroll manager of Karen's company, use the percentage method to calculate the amount of income tax that must be withheld from her paycheck.

Check your answer with the solution on page 298.

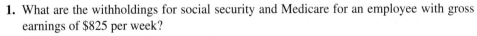

REVIEW EXERCISES   CHAPTER 9—SECTION II

Solve the following problems using 6.2%, up to $62,700, for social security tax, and 1.45%, no wage limit, for Medicare tax:

1. What are the withholdings for social security and Medicare for an employee with gross earnings of $825 per week?

   825.00 × .062   = <u>51.15</u> Social security
   825.00 × .0145 = <u>11.96</u> Medicare

2. What are the withholdings for social security and Medicare for an employee with gross earnings of $1,400.00 paid semimonthly?

   1,400.00 × .062   = <u>86.80</u> Social security
   1,400.00 × .0145 = <u>20.30</u> Medicare

3. Paul Yelverton is an executive with Federal Distributors. His gross earnings are $6,000 per month.

   a. What are the withholdings for social security and Medicare for Paul in his January paycheck?

   $6,000.00 \times .062 = \underline{\$372.00}$ Social security (January)

   $6,000.00 \times .0145 = \underline{\$87.00}$ Medicare (January)

   b. In what month will Paul's salary reach the social security wage base limit?

   $\dfrac{62,700}{6,000} = 10.45$ 10 Full months, plus a portion of the 11th month (<u>November</u>)

   c. What are the social security and Medicare tax withholdings for Paul in the month named in part b?

   $62,700$ Wage limit social security

   $- 60,000$ $(6,000 \times 10)$ Salary reached in October

   $\overline{\$2,700}$ Wage subject to social security in November

   $2,700 \times .062 = \underline{\$167.40}$ Social security in November

   $6,000 \times .0145 = \underline{\$87.00}$ Medicare in November

4. Gloria Lewin has biweekly gross earnings of $1,750. What are her total social security and Medicare tax withholdings for a whole year?

   $1,750.00 \times 26 = 45,500.00$ Annual salary

   $45,500.00 \times .062 = \underline{2,821.00}$ Annual social security deduction

   $45,500.00 \times .0145 = \underline{659.75}$ Annual Medicare deduction

As payroll manager for Andretti Enterprises, it is your task to calculate the monthly social security and Medicare withholdings for the following employees:

Employee	Year-to-Date Earnings	Current Month	Social Security	Medicare
5. Chad, J.	$23,446	$3,422	212.16	49.62
6. Graham, C.	$14,800	$1,540	95.48	22.33
7. Potter, R.	$59,330	$4,700	208.94	68.15
8. Andretti, K.	$145,000	$12,450	0	180.53

Use Exhibits 9-2 and 9-3 to solve the following problems:

9. How much income tax should be withheld from the paycheck of a married employee earning $1,075 per week and claiming four withholding allowances?

   <u>$117</u>

10. How much income tax should be withheld from the paycheck of a single employee earning $3,185 per month and claiming zero withholding allowances?

   <u>$582</u>

11. Earl Campbell is single, claims one withholding allowance, and earns $2,670 per month. Calculate the amount of Earl's paycheck after his employer withholds social security, Medicare, and federal income tax.

$$2,670.00 \times .062 = 165.54$$
$$2,670.00 \times .0145 = 38.72$$
$$\text{Federal income tax} = \underline{377.00}$$
$$\$581.26 \text{ Total deductions}$$
$$2,670.00 - 581.26 = \$\underline{2,088.74} \text{ Paycheck}$$

Use the wage bracket method of income tax calculation to complete the following payroll roster:

Employee	Marital Status	Withholding Allowances	Pay Period	Gross Earnings	Income Tax Withholding
12. Milton, A.	S	3	Monthly	$4,633	$807.00
13. Wallace, P.	M	5	Weekly	$937	$85.00
14. Blount, S.	M	4	Weekly	$1,172	$145.00
15. Cairns, K.	S	1	Monthly	$3,128	$511.00

Use the percentage method of income tax calculation to complete the following payroll roster:

Employee	Marital Status	Withholding Allowances	Pay Period	Gross Earnings	Income Tax Withholding
16. Needle, B.	M	2	Weekly	$594	$55.79
17. White, W.	S	0	Semimonthly	$1,127	$161.41
18. Benator, B.	S	1	Monthly	$4,150	$793.92
19. Ismart, D.	M	4	Biweekly	$1,849	$181.45

Complete, worked out solutions to exercises 16–19 appear in the appendix following the index.

20. Stuart Spector is married, claims four withholding allowances, and earns $3,600 per month. In addition to social security, Medicare, and income tax, Stuart pays 2.3% state income tax, $\frac{1}{2}$% for state disability insurance (both based on gross earnings), $23.74 for term life insurance, $122.14 to the credit union, and $40 to the United Way. As payroll manager for Stuart's company, what is his net take-home pay per month?

F.I.T. $212.50 \times 4 = 850.00$
$3,600.00 - 850.00 = 2,750.00$
$2,750.00 - 535.00 = 2,215.00 \times .15 = \$332.25$
Social security $3,600 \times .062 = 223.20$
Medicare $3,600 \times .0145 = 52.20$
State income tax $3,600 \times .023 = 82.80$
State disability $3,600 \times .005 = 18.00$
Other deductions $23.74 + 122.14 + 40.00 = \underline{185.88}$
$\$894.33$

$3,600.00$ Gross pay
$-\quad\underline{894.33}$ Total deductions
$\$\underline{2,705.67}$ Net take-home pay

EMPLOYER'S PAYROLL EXPENSES AND RECORD KEEPING RESPONSIBILITIES

To this point we have discussed payroll deductions from the employee's point of view. Now let's take a look at the payroll expenses and record keeping responsibilities of the employer. According to the Fair Labor Standards Act, employers are required to maintain complete and up-to-date earnings records for each employee. These records are a quarterly (every 13 weeks) summary of an employee's gross earnings and payroll deductions.

Employers are responsible for the payment of four payroll taxes: social security, Medicare, state unemployment tax (SUTA), and federal unemployment tax (FUTA). In addition, most employers are responsible for a variety of **fringe benefits** that are offered to their employees. These are benefits over and above an employee's normal earnings and can be a significant expense to the employer. Some typical examples are retirement plans, stock option plans, holiday leave, sick days, health and dental insurance, and tuition reimbursement. This section deals with the calculation of these employer taxes and other payroll expenses.

● **fringe benefits**
Employer provided benefits and service packages, over and above an employee's paycheck, such as pension funds, paid vacations, sick leave, and health insurance.

Paid vacation time is one of the many fringe benefits offered by employers today.

9-8 Computing FICA Tax for Employers and Self-Employment Tax for Self-Employed Persons

Employer's FICA Tax

Employers are required to *match* all FICA tax payments, both social security and Medicare, made by each employee. For example, if a company withheld a total of $23,000 in FICA taxes from its employee paychecks this month, the company would be responsible for a matching share of $23,000.

EXAMPLE

A company has 25 employees, each with gross earnings of $250 per week. What are the total social security and Medicare taxes that should be withheld from the employee paychecks, and what is the employer's share of FICA for the first quarter of the year?

SOLUTION STRATEGY

To solve for the total FICA tax due quarterly from the employees and the employer, first calculate the tax due per employee per week, multiply by 25 to find the total weekly FICA for all employees, then multiply by 13 weeks to find the total quarterly amount withheld from all employees. The employer's share will be an equal amount.

Social security tax = Gross earnings × 6.2% = 250 × .062 = $15.50

Medicare tax = Gross earnings × 1.45% = 250 × .0145 = $3.63

Total FICA tax per employee per week = $15.50 + $3.63 = $19.13

Total FICA tax per week = FICA tax per employee × 25 employees
Total FICA tax per week = 19.13 × 25 = $478.25

Total FICA tax per quarter = Total FICA tax per week × 13 weeks
Total FICA tax per quarter = 478.25 × 13 = 6,217.25

Total FICA tax per quarter—Employee's share = $6,217.25

Total FICA tax per quarter—Employer's share = $6,217.25

13. A company has 18 employees, 12 with gross earnings of $350 per week and 6 with gross earnings of $425 per week. What are the employee's share and the employer's share of the social security and Medicare tax for the first quarter of the year?

Check your answers with the solutions on page 298.

Self-Employment Tax

Self-employed persons are responsible for social security and Medicare taxes at twice the rate deducted for employees. Technically they are the employee and the employer, and therefore must pay both shares. For a self-employed person, the social security and Medicare tax rates are twice the normal rates, as follows:

	Tax Rate	Wage Base
Social Security	12.4% (6.2% × 2)	$62,700
Medicare	2.9% (1.45% × 2)	No limit

EXAMPLE

What are the social security and Medicare taxes due on gross earnings of $3,560 per month for a self-employed person?

SOLUTION STRATEGY

To find the amount of tax due, apply the self-employed tax rates to the gross earnings.

Social security tax = Gross earnings × Tax rate = $3,560 × 12.4%
Social security tax = 3,560 × .124 = $441.44

Medicare tax = Gross earnings × Tax rate = $3,560 × 2.9%
Medicare tax = 3,560 × .029 = $103.24

TRY-IT   **EXERCISE**

14. Linda Miller, a self-employed commercial artist, had total gross earnings of $60,000 last year. What is the amount of the social security and Medicare taxes that Linda was required to send the IRS each quarter?

Check your answers with the solutions on page 298.

9-9 Computing the Amount of State Unemployment Taxes (SUTA) and Federal Unemployment Taxes (FUTA)

The **Federal Unemployment Tax Act (FUTA),** together with state unemployment systems, provides for payments of unemployment compensation to workers who have lost their jobs. Most employers are responsible for both a federal and a state unemployment tax. These taxes are paid by the employer, not deducted from an employee's paycheck.

At the time of this writing, the FUTA tax was 6.2% of the first $7,000 of wages paid to each employee during the year. Generally, an employer can take a credit against the FUTA tax

● **Federal Unemployment Tax Act (FUTA)**

A federal tax that is paid by employers for each employee, to provide unemployment compensation to workers who have lost their jobs.

State Unemployment Tax Act (SUTA)

A state tax that is paid by employers for each employee, to provide unemployment compensation to workers who have lost their jobs.

for amounts paid into state unemployment funds. These state taxes are commonly known as the **State Unemployment Tax Act (SUTA).** This credit cannot be more than 5.4% of the first $7,000 of employees' taxable wages.

SUTA tax rates vary from state to state according to the employment record of the company. These merit-rating systems, found in many states, provide significant SUTA tax savings to companies with good employment records, companies with relatively few firings and layoffs.

For companies with full and timely payments to the state unemployment system, the FUTA tax rate is .8% (6.2% FUTA rate − 5.4% SUTA credit).

EXAMPLE

Continental Industries, Inc., had a total payroll of $50,000 last month. Continental pays a SUTA tax rate of 5.4%, and a FUTA rate of 6.2% less the SUTA credit. If none of the employees had reached the $7,000 wage base, what is the amount of SUTA and FUTA tax the company must pay?

SOLUTION STRATEGY

To calculate the SUTA and FUTA taxes, apply the appropriate tax rates to the gross earnings subject to the tax, in this case, all the gross earnings.

$$\text{SUTA tax} = \text{Gross earnings} \times 5.4\%$$
$$\text{SUTA tax} = 50,000 \times .054 = \underline{\$2,700}$$

The FUTA tax rate will be .8%. Remember, it is actually 6.2% less the 5.4% credit.

$$\text{FUTA tax} = \text{Gross earnings} \times .8\%$$
$$\text{FUTA tax} = 50,000 \times .008 = \underline{\$400}$$

TRY-IT   EXERCISE

15. **Weston Service Corporation had a total payroll of $10,000 last month. Weston pays a SUTA tax rate of 5.4% and a FUTA rate of 6.2% less the SUTA credit. If none of the employees had reached the $7,000 wage base, what is the amount of SUTA and FUTA tax the company must pay?**

Check your answers with the solutions on page 298.

9-10 Calculating Employer's Fringe Benefit Expenses

In addition to compensating employees with a paycheck, most companies today offer employee fringe benefit and services packages. These packages include a wide variety of benefits such as pension plans, paid vacations and sick leave, day-care centers, tuition assistance, and health insurance. Corporate executives may receive benefits such as company cars, first-class airline travel, and country club memberships. At the executive level of business, these benefits are known as **perquisites** or **perks.**

Over the past decade, employee benefits have become increasingly important to workers. They have grown in size to the point where today total benefits may cost a company as much as 40 to 50 percent of payroll. Frequently employees are given a *menu* of fringe benefits to choose from, up to a specified dollar amount. These plans are known as **cafeteria-style,** or **flexible benefit programs.**

perquisites, or perks

Executive-level fringe benefits such as first-class airline travel, company cars, and country club membership.

cafeteria-style or flexible benefit program

A plan whereby employees are given a menu of fringe benefits to choose from, up to a specified dollar amount.

> **STEPS TO CALCULATE EMPLOYER'S FRINGE BENEFITS EXPENSE:**
>
> **Step 1.** If the fringe benefit is a percent of gross payroll, multiply that percent by the amount of the gross payroll. If the fringe benefit is a dollar amount per employee, multiply that amount by the number of employees.
>
> *(continued)*

(continued)

Step 2. Find the total fringe benefits by adding all of the individual fringe benefit amounts.

Step 3. Calculate the fringe benefit percent by using the percentage formula, Rate = Portion ÷ Base, with total fringe benefits as the portion and gross payroll as the base.

$$\text{Fringe benefit percent} = \frac{\text{Total fringe benefits}}{\text{Gross payroll}}$$

EXAMPLE

In addition to its gross payroll of $150,000 per month, General Distributors, Inc., with 75 employees pays 7% of payroll to a retirement fund, 9% for health insurance, and $25 per employee for a stock purchase plan.

a. What are the company's monthly fringe benefit expenses?

b. What percent of payroll does this represent?

SOLUTION STRATEGY

a. To solve for monthly fringe benefits, compute the amount of each benefit, then add them to find the total.

Retirement fund expense = Gross payroll × 7%
Retirement fund expense = 150,000 × .07 = $10,500

Health insurance expense = Gross payroll × 9%
Health insurance expense = 150,000 × .09 = $13,500

Stock plan expense = Number of employees × $25
Stock plan expense = 75 × 25 = $1,875

Total fringe benefits = Retirement + Health + Stock
Total fringe benefits = 10,500 + 13,500 + 1,875 = $25,875

b. $$\text{Fringe benefit percent} = \frac{\text{Total fringe benefits}}{\text{Gross payroll}} = \frac{25,875}{150,000} = .1725 = \underline{\underline{17.25\%}}$$

TRY-IT   EXERCISE

16. Consolidated Enterprises employs 250 workers with a gross payroll of $123,400 per week. Fringe benefits are 5% of gross payroll for sick days and holiday leave, 8% for health insurance, and $12.40 per employee for dental insurance.

   a. What is the total weekly cost of fringe benefits for Consolidated?

   b. What percent of payroll does this represent?

   c. What is the cost of these fringe benefits to the company for a year?

Check your answers with the solutions on page 298.

9-11 Understanding Internal Revenue Service Payroll Forms
Form 1040-ES   Estimated Quarterly Tax Voucher for Self-Employed Persons

Earlier we learned that self-employed persons must pay the self-employment tax, the equivalent of the employer's and employee's share of social security and Medicare tax. In addition, those who are self-employed are required to pay quarterly federal income tax on their gross earnings. When earnings are listed on an annual basis, divide the annual earnings by 4 to get quarterly earnings.

$$\text{Quarterly earnings} = \frac{\text{Estimated annual earnings}}{4 \text{ (quarters)}}$$

Exhibit 9-6 illustrates the Internal Revenue Service Form 1040-ES. Note that it requires the taxpayer's name, address, social security number, amount of payment, and the current date.

EXAMPLE

Diana Farrell is a self-employed marketing consultant. Her estimated annual earnings this year are $80,000. Her social security tax rate is 12.4% up to the wage base, Medicare is 2.9%, and her estimated federal income tax rate is 24%. How much quarterly estimate tax must Diana send to the IRS each quarter?

SOLUTION STRATEGY

$$\text{Quarterly earnings} = \frac{\text{Estimated annual earnings}}{4 \text{ (quarters)}} = \frac{80,000}{4} = \$20,000$$

Note: In the first three quarters of the year Diana's quarterly tax will be equal. In the fourth quarter, her wages will reach the social security wage base. In that quarter she will pay less taxes.

First, Second, and Third Quarters:

Social security = $20,000 \times 12.4\%$ = $\underline{\$2,480}$

Medicare = $20,000 \times 2.9\%$ = $\underline{\$580}$

Income tax = $20,000 \times 24\%$ = $\underline{\$4,800}$

Quarterly tax (first 3 quarters) = $2,480 + 580 + 4,800 = \underline{\$7,860}$

Fourth Quarter:

Wages subject to social security = $61,200 - 60,000 = 1,200$

Social security = $1,200 \times 12.4\%$ = $\underline{\$148.80}$

Medicare = $20,000 \times 2.9\%$ = $\underline{\$580}$

Income Tax = $20,000 \times 24\%$ = $\underline{\$4,800}$

Quarterly tax (fourth quarter) = $148.80 + 580 + 4,800 = \underline{\$5,528.80}$

EXHIBIT 9-6

....

ESTIMATED TAX PAYMENT
VOUCHER

Form **1040-ES**			
Department of the Treasury Internal Revenue Service	**Payment– Voucher 1**		OMB No. 1545-0087

Return this voucher with check or money order payable to the **"Internal Revenue Service."** Please write your social security number and "1992 Form 1040-ES" on your check or money order. Please do not send cash. Enclose, but do not staple or attach, your payment with this voucher. File only if you are making a payment of estimated tax.

Calendar year—Due April 15,

Amount of payment	Please type or print	Your first name and initial	Your last name	Your social security number
		If joint payment, complete for spouse		
		Spouse's first name and initial	Spouse's last name	Spouse's social security number
$.............		Address (number, street, and apt. no.)		
		City, state, and ZIP code		

For Paperwork Reduction Act Notice, see instructions on page 1.

17. **Traci Keller is a self-employed freelance editor and project director for a large publishing company. Her annual salary this year is estimated to be $100,000, with a federal income tax rate of 20%. What is the amount of tax that Traci must send to the IRS each quarter?**

Check your answer with the solution on page 299.

Form 8109   Federal Tax Deposit Coupon

After employers withhold social security, Medicare, and income taxes from employee paychecks, these funds must be combined with the employer's share of FICA and deposited in an authorized financial institution or a Federal Reserve Bank or branch in the employer's area. These deposits must be made monthly if the total taxes withheld for the previous year were less than $50,000, and semiweekly if the taxes withheld last year amounted to more than $50,000. For new employers with no taxes withheld last year the deposits are made monthly.

Form 8109, Exhibit 9-7, is used as a *deposit slip* to accompany these deposits. The form requires the name and address of the employer; the amount of the deposit; the type of tax, which in this case is known as 941; and the tax period.

Form 941   Employer's Quarterly Federal Tax Return

Employers are required to file Form 941, Employer's Quarterly Tax Return, by the end of the month following each quarter to inform the IRS of the total amount of social security, Medicare, and income tax withheld from employee paychecks during the quarter, and the amount of the employer's share of social security and Medicare taxes. Form 941 appears in Exhibit 9-8.

Note that Line 1 shows number of employees; Line 3 shows the total income tax withheld from employee's wages; Line 8 shows total social security and Medicare taxes; and Line 11 shows total taxes. If the total deposits for the quarter, Line 14, are over $500 and deposited on time, then Line 15, balance due, will be zero.

EXHIBIT 9-7

....

FEDERAL TAX DEPOSIT COUPON

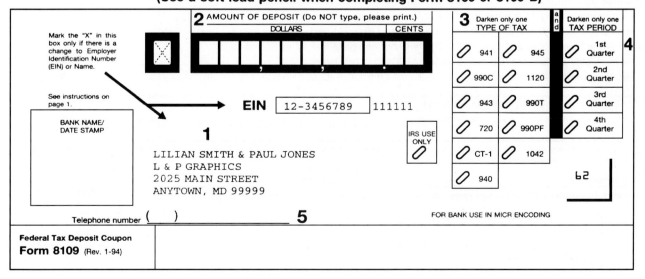

Form **941**
(Rev. April 1994)
Department of the Treasury
Internal Revenue Service

4141

Employer's Quarterly Federal Tax Return

▶ **See separate instructions for information on completing this return.**

Please type or print.

OMB No. 1545-0029

Enter state code for state in which deposits made (see page 2 of instructions). ▶ ☐

Name (as distinguished from trade name)	Date quarter ended
Trade name, if any	Employer identification number
Address (number and street)	City, state, and ZIP code

| T |
| FF |
| FD |
| FP |
| I |
| T |

If address is different from prior return, check here ▶ ☐

IRS Use

| 1 1 1 1 1 1 1 1 1 1 | 2 | 3 3 3 3 3 3 | 4 4 4 |
| 5 5 5 | 6 | 7 | 8 8 8 8 8 8 | 9 9 9 | 10 10 10 10 10 10 10 10 10 10 |

If you do not have to file returns in the future, check here ▶ ☐ and enter date final wages paid ▶

If you are a seasonal employer, see **Seasonal employers** on page 2 and check here (see instructions) ▶ ☐

1	Number of employees (except household) employed in the pay period that includes March 12th ▶		
2	Total wages and tips subject to withholding, plus other compensation	**2**	
3	Total income tax withheld from wages, tips, and sick pay	**3**	
4	Adjustment of withheld income tax for preceding quarters of calendar year	**4**	
5	Adjusted total of income tax withheld (line 3 as adjusted by line 4—see instructions)	**5**	
6a	Taxable social security wages . . . . . . $ × 12.4% (.124) =	**6a**	
b	Taxable social security tips . . . . . . $ × 12.4% (.124) =	**6b**	
7	Taxable Medicare wages and tips . . . . $ × 2.9% (.029) =	**7**	
8	Total social security and Medicare taxes (add lines 6a, 6b, and 7). Check here if wages are not subject to social security and/or Medicare tax . . . . ▶ ☐	**8**	
9	Adjustment of social security and Medicare taxes (see instructions for required explanation) Sick Pay $_____ ± Fractions of Cents $_____ ± Other $_____ =	**9**	
10	Adjusted total of social security and Medicare taxes (line 8 as adjusted by line 9—see instructions)	**10**	
11	**Total taxes** (add lines 5 and 10)	**11**	
12	Advance earned income credit (EIC) payments made to employees, if any	**12**	
13	Net taxes (subtract line 12 from line 11). **This should equal line 17, column (d) below** (or line D of Schedule B (Form 941))	**13**	
14	Total deposits for quarter, including overpayment applied from a prior quarter	**14**	
15	**Balance due** (subtract line 14 from line 13). Pay to Internal Revenue Service	**15**	
16	**Overpayment,** if line 14 is more than line 13, enter excess here ▶ $_____		

and check if to be: ☐ Applied to next return **OR** ☐ Refunded.

● **All filers:** If line 13 is less than $500, you need not complete line 17 or Schedule B.

● **Semiweekly depositors:** Complete Schedule B and check here . . . . ▶ ☐

● **Monthly depositors:** Complete line 17, columns (a) through (d) and check here . . . . ▶ ☐

17	**Monthly Summary of Federal Tax Liability.**		
(a) First month liability	**(b)** Second month liability	**(c)** Third month liability	**(d)** Total liability for quarter

Sign Here

Under penalties of perjury, I declare that I have examined this return, including accompanying schedules and statements, and to the best of my knowledge and belief, it is true, correct, and complete.

Signature ▶

Print Your Name and Title ▶

Date ▶

For Paperwork Reduction Act Notice, see page 1 of separate instructions. Cat. No. 17001Z Form **941** (Rev. 4-94)

EXHIBIT 9-8

EMPLOYER'S QUARTERLY TAX RETURN

Form **940-EZ**		**Employer's Annual Federal Unemployment (FUTA) Tax Return**	OMB No. 1545-1110

Department of the Treasury
Internal Revenue Service

19

	T	
	FF	
	FD	
	FP	
	I	
	T	

If incorrect, make any necessary changes. ▶

Name (as distinguished from trade name)

Trade name, if any

Address and ZIP code

Calendar year

Employer identification number

Follow the chart under **Who May Use Form 940-EZ** on page 2. If you cannot use Form 940-EZ, you must use Form 940 instead.

A Enter the amount of contributions paid to your state unemployment fund. (See instructions for line A on page 4.) ▶ $ ....

B (1) Enter the name of the state where you have to pay contributions . . . . . . ▶ ....

   (2) Enter your state reporting number as shown on state unemployment tax return. ▶

If you will not have to file returns in the future, check here (see **Who Must File**, on page 2) **complete, and sign the return** . . . . . ▶ ☐

If this is an Amended Return check here . . . . ▶ ☐

Part I   **Taxable Wages and FUTA Tax**

1	Total payments (including payments shown on lines 2 and 3) during the calendar year for services of employees	**1**	

Amount paid

2 Exempt payments. (Explain all exempt payments, attaching additional sheets if necessary.) ▶ ....

    2

3 Payments for services of more than $7,000. Enter only amounts over the first $7,000 paid to each employee. Do not include any exempt payments from line 2. Do not use your state wage limitation. The $7,000 amount is the Federal wage base. Your state wage base may be different . . . .

    3

4	Total exempt payments (add lines 2 and 3)	**4**	
5	**Total taxable wages** (subtract line 4 from line 1) . . . . ▶	**5**	
6	**FUTA tax.** Multiply the wages on line 5 by .008 and enter here. (If the result is over $100, also complete Part II.)	**6**	
7	Total FUTA tax deposited for the year, including any overpayment applied from a prior year (from your records)	**7**	
8	**Amount you owe** (subtract line 7 from line 6). This should be $100 or less. Pay to "Internal Revenue Service" ▶	**8**	
9	**Overpayment** (subtract line 6 from line 7). Check if it is to be: ☐ **Applied to next return,** or ☐ **Refunded.** ▶	**9**	

Part II   **Record of Quarterly Federal Unemployment Tax Liability** (Do not include state liability.) Complete only if line 6 is over $100.

Quarter	First (Jan. 1 – Mar. 31)	Second (Apr. 1 – June 30)	Third (July 1 – Sept. 30)	Fourth (Oct. 1 – Dec. 31)	Total for year
Liability for quarter					

Under penalties of perjury, I declare that I have examined this return, including accompanying schedules and statements, and, to the best of my knowledge and belief, it is true, correct, and complete, and that no part of any payment made to a state unemployment fund claimed as a credit was, or is to be, deducted from the payments to employees.

Signature ▶   Title (Owner, etc.) ▶   Date ▶

Cat. No. 10983G   Form **940-EZ**

EXHIBIT 9-9

EMPLOYER'S ANNUAL FUTA RETURN

Form 940-EZ   **Employer's Annual Federal Unemployment (FUTA) Tax Return**

Employers are required to file a FUTA tax return each year. Exhibit 9-9 is an example of such a return. Note that the wages over $7,000, the wage base, Line 3, are subtracted from the total wages, Line 1, to get total taxable wages, Line 5. Also note, as we learned in this chapter, the FUTA tax rate is .8%, or .008 (Line 6).

REVIEW EXERCISES   CHAPTER 9—SECTION III

T

1. Universal Systems, Inc., has 40 employees on the assembly line, each with gross earnings of $325 per week.

  a. What is the total social security and Medicare taxes that should be withheld from the employee paychecks each week?

    $325.00 \times 40 = 13,000.00$ Gross per week

    $13,000.00 \times .062 = \underline{\$806.00}$ Total social security

    $13,000.00 \times .0145 = \underline{\$188.50}$ Total Medicare

b. What is the employer's share of these taxes for the first quarter of the year?

$806.00 \times 13 = \underline{10,478.00}$ Social security for 1st quarter

$188.50 \times 13 = \underline{2,450.50}$ Medicare for 1st quarter

2. VIP Industries has 24 employees, 15 with gross earnings of $345 per week, and 9 with gross earnings of $385 per week. What is the total social security and Medicare tax that the company must send to the Internal Revenue Service for the first quarter of the year?

$345.00 \times 15 = 5,175.00$

$385.00 \times 9\ \ = 3,465.00$

　　　　$8,640.00$ Total gross weekly earnings

$8,640.00 \times .062\ \ = 535.68 \times 2 = 1,071.36$

$8,640.00 \times .0145 = 125.28 \times 2 = \underline{\quad 250.56}$

　　　　　　　　　　　　$1,321.92$

$1,321.92 \times 13 = \underline{\$17,184.96}$ Total social security plus Medicare sent to government in 1st quarter

3. What are the social security and Medicare taxes due on gross earnings of $2,800 per month for a self-employed person?

$2,800.00 \times 12.4\%$

$2,800.00 \times\ \ 2.9\%$

$2,800.00 \times .124 = \underline{\$347.20}$ Social security

$2,800.00 \times .029 = \underline{\ \$81.20}$ Medicare

4. Alan Cunningham is a self-employed painter. Last year he had total gross earnings of $38,700. How much must Alan send to the IRS for his quarterly social security and Medicare payments?

$38,700.00 \div 4 = 9,675.00$ Income per quarter

$9,675.00 \times .124 = \underline{\$1,199.70}$ Social security per quarter

$9,675.00 \times .029 = \underline{\$\ \ \ 280.58}$ Medicare per quarter

5. Bill Ronald earns $21,450 annually as a line supervisor for Blossom Manufacturers.

a. If the SUTA tax rate is 5.4% of the first $7,000 earned in a year, how much SUTA tax must Blossom pay each year for Bill?

$7,000.00 \times 5.4\%$

$7,000.00 \times .054 = \underline{\$378.00}$ SUTA annually

b. If the FUTA tax rate is 6.2% of the first $7,000 earned in a year minus the SUTA tax paid, how much FUTA tax must the company pay each year for Bill?

$7,000.00 \times .008 = \underline{\$56.00}$ FUTA annually

6. Sheila Berger worked part time last year as a cashier in a supermarket. Her total gross earnings were $6,443.00.

a. How much SUTA tax must the supermarket pay to the state for Sheila?

$6,443.00 \times .054 = \underline{\$347.92}$ SUTA annually

b. How much FUTA tax must be paid for her?

$6,443.00 \times .008 = \underline{\$51.54}$ FUTA annually

7. Riteway Roofing Company has three installers. Larry earns $355 per week, Curly earns $460 per week, and Moe earns $585 per week. The company's SUTA rate is 5.4%, and the FUTA rate is 6.2% minus the SUTA. As usual, these taxes are paid on the first $7,000 of each employee's earnings.

a. How much SUTA and FUTA tax does Riteway owe for the first quarter of the year?

Larry = 355 × 13 = $4,615.00   Larry = 4,615.00 × .054 = $249.21 SUTA   Larry = 4,615.00 × .008 = $36.92 FUTA
Curly = 460 × 13 = $5,980.00   Curly = 5,980.00 × .054 = $322.92 SUTA   Curly = 5,980.00 × .008 = $47.84 FUTA
Moe = 585 × 13 = $7,000.00   Moe = 7,000.00 × .054 = $378.00 SUTA   Moe = 7,000.00 × .008 = $56.00 FUTA
                                              $950.13 Total SUTA   140.76 Total FUTA

b. How much SUTA and FUTA tax does Riteway owe for the second quarter of the year?

Larry = 7,000.00 − 4,615.00 = 2,385.00   2,385.00 × .054 = 128.79   2,385.00 × .008 = 19.08
Curly = 7,000.00 − 5,980.00 = 1,020.00   1,020.00 × .054 = 55.08   1,020.00 × .008 = 8.16
Moe = 0 $183.87 SUTA $27.24 FUTA

8. Metro Industries employs 166 workers and has a gross payroll of $154,330 per week. Fringe benefits are $4\frac{1}{2}$% of gross payroll for sick days and maternity leave, 7.4% for health insurance, 3.1% for the retirement fund, and $26.70 per employee for a stock purchase plan.

a. What is the total weekly cost of fringe benefits for the company?

154,330.00 × .045 = 6,944.85 Sick days
154,330.00 × .074 = 11,420.42 Insurance
154,330.00 × .031 = 4,784.23 Retirement
26.70 × 166   = 4,432.20 Stock purchase
                     27,581.70 Total fringe benefit costs per week

b. What percent of payroll does this represent?

$$R = \frac{P}{B} = R = \frac{27,581.70}{154,330.00} = 0.1787$$
$$= 17.9\%$$

c. What is the company's annual cost of fringe benefits?

27,581.70 × 52 = $1,434,248.40 Annual cost of fringe benefits

9. Robert Spence, a self-employed attorney, has an estimated gross salary of $300,000 this year. His social security tax rate is 12.4% up to the wage base, Medicare is 2.9%, and his estimated federal income tax rate is 24%.

a. How much quarterly estimate tax must Robert send to the IRS for each quarter?

$$\frac{300,000.00}{4} = 75,000 \text{ Per quarter}$$

75,000 × .24 = 18,000.00 Income tax   18,000.00 Income tax
62,700 × .124 = 7,774.80 Social security   2,175.00 Medicare
75,000 × .029 = 2,175.00 Medicare $20,175.00 2nd, 3rd, 4th quarters
                $27,949.80 1st quarter

b. What form should he use?

Form 1040-ES, *Estimated Quarterly Tax Voucher for Self-Employed Persons*

10. You are the payroll manager for Biltmore International, Inc.

    a. According to IRS deposit rules, if your company's tax liability last year was $70,000, when are the deposits due?

    Semiweekly

    b. What form should accompany these deposits?

    Form 8109, *Federal Tax Deposit Coupon*

    c. How often must you file a tax return for Biltmore?

    Quarterly

    d. What IRS form should you use for this purpose?

    Form 941, *Employer's Quarterly Federal Tax Return*

CHAPTER 9 ■ PAYROLL

FORMULAS

Hourly Wages

Regular pay = Hourly rate × Hours worked

Overtime rate = Hourly rate × Overtime factor

Overtime pay = Overtime rate × Hours worked

Total gross pay = Regular pay + Overtime pay

Piecework

Total gross pay = Output quantity × Rate per unit

Commission

Total gross pay = Total sales × Commission rate

Payroll Deductions

Total deductions = Social security + Medicare + Income Tax + Voluntary deductions

Net pay = Gross pay − Total deductions

Fringe Benefits

$$\text{Fringe benefit percent} = \frac{\text{Total fringe benefits}}{\text{Gross payroll}}$$

Estimated Quarterly Tax

$$\text{Quarterly earnings} = \frac{\text{Estimated annual earnings}}{4 \text{ (quarters)}}$$

SECTION I   EMPLOYEE'S GROSS EARNINGS AND INCENTIVE PAY PLANS

Topic	P/O, Page	Important Concepts	Illustrative Examples
Prorating Annual Salary to Various Pay Periods	9–1 262	Salaried employees are most commonly paid based on one of the following pay schedules: *Weekly:* 52 paychecks per year Annual salary ÷ 52 *Biweekly:* 26 paychecks per year Annual salary ÷ 26 *Semimonthly:* 24 paychecks per year Annual salary ÷ 24 *Monthly:* 12 paychecks per year Annual salary ÷ 12	What are the gross earnings of an employee with an annual salary of $40,000 based on weekly, biweekly, semimonthly, and monthly pay schedules? Weekly $= \dfrac{40,000}{52} = \$769.23$ Biweekly $= \dfrac{40,000}{26} = \$1,538.46$ Semimonthly $=$ $\dfrac{40,000}{24} = \$1,666.67$ Monthly $= \dfrac{40,000}{12} = \$3,333.33$

Calculating Gross Pay by Regular Hourly Wages and Overtime	9–2 263	An hourly wage is the amount an employee is paid for each hour worked.
		 Regular time specifies that a standard work week is 40 hours.
		 Overtime amounting to at least time-and-a-half must be paid for all hours over 40. Some employers pay double time for weekend, holiday, and midnight shifts.
		
		 Regular pay =
		     Hourly rate × Hours worked
		
		 Overtime rate =
		     Hourly × Overtime factor
		
		 Overtime pay =
		     Overtime rate × Overtime hours
		
		 Total gross pay =
		     Regular pay + Overtime pay
			Sandi Yee earns $9.50 per hour as a supervisor in a plant. If her overtime rate is time-and-a-half and holidays are double time, what is Sandi's total gross pay for working 49 hours last week, including 4 holiday hours?
			
			 Regular pay =
			     $9.50 \times 40 = \$380.00$
			 Time-and-a-half rate =
			     $9.50 \times 1.5 = \$14.25$
			 Time-and-a-half pay =
			     $14.25 \times 5 = \$71.25$
			 Double time rate =
			     $9.50 \times 2 = \$19.00$
			 Double time pay =
			     $19.00 \times 4 = \$76.00$
			 Total gross pay =
			 $380.00 + 71.25 + 76.00 = \$527.25$

Calculating Straight and Differential Piecework Wages	9–3 264	A piecework pay rate schedule is based on production output, not time. Straight piecework pays the worker a certain amount of pay per unit, regardless of quantity. In differential piecework the rate per unit increases as output quantity goes up.
		
		 Total gross pay =
		     Output quantity × Rate per unit
			A factory pays its workers $2.50 per unit of production. What is the gross pay of a worker producing 233 units?
			
			 Gross pay =
			     $233 \times 2.50 = \$582.50$
			
			 A factory pays its production workers $.54 per unit up to 5,000 units and $.67 per unit above 5,000 units. What is the gross pay of an employee who produces 6,500 units?
			
			 $5,000 \times .54 = 2,700$
			 $+\ 1,500 \times .67 = \underline{1,005}$
			 Total gross pay = $\underline{\$3,705}$

I, continued

Topic	P/O, Page	Important Concepts	Illustrative Examples
Calculating Straight and Incremental Commission	9–4 266	Commission is a method of compensation primarily used to pay employees selling goods and services. Straight commission is based on a single specified percentage of the sales volume attained. Incremental commission, like differential piecework, is where various levels of sales earn increasing rates of commission. Total gross pay = Total sales × Commission rate	A company pays 4% straight commission on all sales. What is the gross pay of an employee who sells $135,000? Gross pay = $135,000 \times .04 = \underline{\$5,400.00}$ A company pays incremental commissions of 3.5% on sales up to $100,000 and 4.5% on all sales over $100,000. What is the gross pay of an employee selling $164,000? $100,000 \times .035 = 3,500.00$ $\underline{+\ 64,000 \times .045 = 2,880.00}$ Gross pay = $\underline{\$6,380.00}$
Calculating Salary Plus Commissions	9–4 267	Salary plus commission is a pay schedule whereby the employee receives a guaranteed salary in addition to a commission on sales over a certain specified amount.	An employee is paid a salary of $350 per week plus a 2% commission on sales over $8,000. If Jeff sold $13,400 last week, how much did he earn? $350 + 2\% (13,400 - 8,000)$ $350 + .02 \times 5,400$ $350 + 108 = \underline{\$458.00}$
Computing Gross Earnings with Drawing Accounts	9–4 268	A drawing account, or draw against commission, is a commission paid in advance of sales and later deducted from the commission earned.	Jim Hall sells for a company that pays $6\frac{1}{2}\%$ commission with a $600 per month drawing account. If Jim takes the draw and then sells $16,400 in goods, how much commission is he owed? $(16,400 \times .065) - 600$ $1,066 - 600 = \underline{\$466.00}$

SECTION II   EMPLOYEE'S PAYROLL DEDUCTIONS

Computing FICA Taxes, Both Social Security and Medicare	9–5 272	FICA taxes are divided into two categories: social security and Medicare. When employees reach the wage base for the year, they are no longer subject to the tax. <table><tr><td></td><td>Tax Rate</td><td>Wage Base</td></tr><tr><td>**Social Security**</td><td>6.2%</td><td>$62,700</td></tr><tr><td>**Medicare**</td><td>1.45%</td><td>no limit</td></tr></table>	What are the FICA tax withholdings for social security and Medicare for an employee with gross earnings of $760 per week? Social security = $\$760 \times 6.2\% = \underline{\$47.12}$ Medicare = $\$760 \times 1.45\% = \underline{\$11.02}$

Topic	P/O, Page	Important Concepts	Illustrative Examples
Determining Federal Income Tax (FIT) Using Wage Bracket Tables	9–6 273	1. Based on marital status and payroll period, choose either Exhibit 9-2 or 9-3. 2. Scan down the left-hand columns until you find the bracket containing the gross pay of the employee. 3. Scan across the row of that wage bracket to the intersection of that employee's "withholding allowances claimed" column. 4. The number in that column, on the wage bracket row, is the amount of withholding tax.	What amount of income tax should be withheld from the monthly paycheck of a single employee claiming two withholding allowances and earning $3,495 per month? Use Exhibit 9-3. Scan down the wage brackets to $3,480—$3,520. Scan across to "2" withholding allowances to find the tax, $552.
Calculating Federal Income Tax Using Percentage Method	9–7 277	1. Multiply one withholding allowance, in Exhibit 9-4, by the number of allowances the employee claims. 2. Subtract that amount from the employee's gross earnings to find the income subject to income tax. 3. Determine the amount of tax withheld from the appropriate section of Exhibit 9-5.	Carol Starkey is single, earns $645 per week, and claims three withholding allowances. Calculate the amount of tax withheld from Carol's weekly paycheck. From Exhibit 9-4: $49.04 × 3 = $147.12 Taxable income = $645.00 − $147.12 = $497.88 From Exhibit 9-5: Withholding tax = $65.85 + 28% (497.88 − 489.00) 65.85 + .28 (8.88) 65.85 + 2.49 = $68.34

SECTION III   EMPLOYER'S PAYROLL EXPENSES AND RECORD KEEPING RESPONSIBILITIES

Topic	P/O, Page	Important Concepts	Illustrative Examples
Computing FICA Tax for Employers	9–8 282	Employers are required to match all FICA tax payments made by each employee.	Last month a company withheld a total of $3,400 in FICA taxes from employee paychecks. What is the company's FICA liability? The company is responsible for a matching amount withheld from the employees, $3,400.
Calculating Self-Employment Tax	9–8 283	Self-employed persons are responsible for social security and Medicare taxes at twice the rate deducted for employees. Technically, they are the employee and the employer, therefore they must pay both shares, as follows: *Social Security* 12.4% (6.2% × 2), wage base $62,700 *Medicare* 2.9% (1.45% × 2), no limit	What are the social security and Medicare taxes due on gross earnings of $4,260 per month for a self-employed person? *Social security* Gross earnings × 12.4% = 4,260 × .124 = $528.24 *Medicare* Gross earnings × 2.9% = 4,260 × .029 = 123.54

III, continued

Topic	P/O, Page	Important Concepts	Illustrative Examples
Calculating State Unemployment Tax (SUTA) and Federal Unemployment Tax (FUTA)	9–9 283	SUTA and FUTA taxes provide for unemployment compensation to workers who have lost their jobs. These taxes are paid by the employer. The SUTA tax rate is 5.4% of the first $7,000 of earnings per year by each employee. The FUTA tax rate is 6.2% of the first $7,000 minus the SUTA tax paid (6.2% − 5.4% = .8%).	Chang Enterprises had a total payroll of $40,000 last month. If none of the employees have reached the $7,000 wage base, what is the amount of SUTA and FUTA tax due? $$\text{SUTA} = 40{,}000 \times 5.4\% = \underline{\$2{,}160}$$ $$\text{FUTA} = 40{,}000 \times .8\% = \underline{\$320}$$
Calculating Employer's Fringe Benefit Expenses	9–10 284	In addition to compensating employees with a paycheck, most companies offer benefit packages that may include pensions, paid sick days, tuition assistance, and health insurance. Fringe benefits represent a significant expense to employers. $$\text{Fringe benefit percent} = \frac{\text{Total fringe benefits}}{\text{Gross payroll}}$$	Northern Industries employs 48 workers and has a monthly gross payroll of $120,000. In addition the company pays 6.8% to a pension fund, 8.7% for health insurance, and $30 per employee for a stock purchase plan. What are Northern's monthly fringe benefit expenses? What percent of payroll does this represent? $$120{,}000 \times 6.8\% = \quad 8{,}160$$ $$120{,}000 \times 8.7\% = \quad 10{,}440$$ $$48 \times \$30 = \underline{+\,1{,}440}$$ Total fringe benefits $\underline{\$20{,}040}$ $$\text{Fringe ben.\%} = \frac{20{,}040}{120{,}000} = \underline{16.7\%}$$
Filing Form 1040-ES— Quarterly Estimate Tax for Self-Employed	9–11 286	Each quarter, self-employed persons must send to the IRS Form 1040-ES along with a tax payment for social security, Medicare, and income tax. $$\text{Quarterly earnings} = \frac{\text{Annual earnings}}{4 \text{ (quarters)}}$$	Jane Perez is self-employed as a decorator. She estimates her annual earnings this year to be $44,000. On what quarterly earnings should her taxes be based? $$\text{Qtly earnings} = \frac{44{,}000}{4} = \underline{\$11{,}000}$$
Filing Form 8109— Federal Tax Deposit Coupon	9–11 287	Form 8109 is used as a deposit slip when employers send social security, Medicare, and income tax payments to the IRS. Deposits must be made monthly if last year's deposits were less than $50,000, and semiweekly if last year's deposits were more than $50,000.	Last year a restaurant deposited $72,000 with the IRS for employee withholdings. How often must deposits be made this year? Since last year's amount was over $50,000, deposits must be made <u>semiweekly</u> this year.

III, continued

Topic	P/O, Page	Important Concepts	Illustrative Examples
Filing Form 941— Employer's Quarterly Tax Return	9–11 288	IRS Form 941 is filed quarterly by employers to report: 1. Amount of employee FICA tax withheld from gross earnings. 2. Employer's share of FICA. 3. Amount of federal income tax withheld from employees' gross earnings.	The Appleton Corp. withheld $5,360 in FICA taxes and $12,920 in federal income tax from its employees' gross earnings in the first quarter. How much should be reported on Form 941? Employees' FICA $5,360 Employer's share 5,360 Income tax + 12,920 Total deposits for Qtr. $23,640

TRY-IT EXERCISE   SOLUTIONS

1. Weekly pay $= \dfrac{\text{Annual salary}}{52} = \dfrac{43,500}{52} = \underline{\$836.54}$

Biweekly pay $= \dfrac{\text{Annual salary}}{26} = \dfrac{43,500}{26} = \underline{\$1,673.08}$

Semimonthly pay $= \dfrac{\text{Annual salary}}{24} = \underline{\$1,812.50}$

Monthly pay $= \dfrac{\text{Annual salary}}{12} = \underline{\$3,625.00}$

2. Regular pay = Hourly rate × Number of hours worked
Regular pay = 6.50 × 40 = $\underline{\$260}$

Time-and-a-half rate = Hourly rate × Overtime factor
Time-and-a-half rate = 6.50 × 1.5 = $9.75

Time-and-a-half pay = Rate × Hours worked
Time-and-a-half pay = 9.75 × 5 = $\underline{\$48.75}$

Double time rate = Hourly rate × Overtime factor
Double time rate = 6.50 × 2 = $13.00

Double time pay = Rate × Hours worked
Double time pay = 13.00 × 4 = $\underline{\$52.00}$

Total gross pay = Regular pay + Overtime pay
Total gross pay = 260.00 + 48.75 + 52.00 = $\underline{\$360.75}$

3. Total gross pay = Output quantity × Rate per unit
Total gross pay = 950 × .41 = $\underline{\$389.50}$

4. Level pay = Output × Rate per piece

Gomez: 300 × .68 = $204.00
           200 × .79 =   158.00
            15 × .86 = +   12.90
                      $374.90 Total gross pay

Clifford: 199 × .68 = $135.32 Total gross pay

Maken: 300 × .68 = $204.00
           148 × .79 = + 116.92
                      $320.92 Total gross pay

Nathan: 300 × .68 = $204.00
           200 × .79 =   158.00
           250 × .86 =   215.00
            54 × .94 = +   50.76
                      $627.76 Total gross pay

5. Total gross pay = Total sales × Commission rate
Total gross pay = 233,760 × .024 = $\underline{\$5,610.24}$

6. Level pay = Sales per level × Commission rate
Level pay = 100,000 × .017 = $1,700.00
           84,600 × .025 = + 2,115.00
                      $3,815.00

7. Commission = Commission rate × Sales subject to commission
   Commission = 4%(45,000 − 20,000)
   Commission = .04 × 25,000 = $1,000

   Total gross pay = Salary + Commission
   Total gross pay = 1,400 + 1,000 = $2,400

8. Commission = Total sales × Commission rate
   Commission = 120,000 × 3.5% = $4,200

   Commission owed = Commission − Amount of draw
   Commission owed = 4,200 − 2,000 = $2,200

9. Social security tax = Gross earnings × 6.2%
   Social security tax = 5,000 × .062 = $310

   Medicare tax = Gross earnings × 1.45%
   Medicare tax = 5,000 x .0145 = $72.50

10. Earnings subject to tax = Wage base − Year-to-date earnings
    Earnings subject to tax = 62,700 − 57,800 = $4,900

    Social security tax = Earnings subject to tax × 6.2%
    Social security tax = 4,900 × .062 = $303.80

11. From Exhibit 9-2
    $835 Weekly, married, 2 Allowances = $92.00

12. From Exhibit 9-4
    1 withholding allowance = $212.50
                            ×   5 Exemptions claimed
                                    $1,062.50

    Taxable income = Gross pay − Withholding allowance
    Taxable income = 2,350.00 − 1,062.50 = $1,287.50

    From Exhibit 9-5, Table 4(b)
    Category $535 to $3,688
    Tax = 15% of amount over $535.00
         $1,287.50 $752.50
       −   535.00   ×   .15
          $752.50 $112.88 = Tax withholding

13. *12 employees at $350:*
    Social security = 350 × .062 × 12 = $260.40
    Medicare   = 350 × .0145 × 12 = +   60.90
                                          321.30 per week
                                     ×   13 weeks
                                         $4,176.90

    6 employees at $425:
    Social security = 425 × .062 × 6 = $158.10
    Medicare   = 425 × .0145 × 6 = +   36.98
                                        $195.08 per week
                                   ×   13 weeks
                                       $2,536.04

    18 employees' share = $4,176.90 + $2,536.04 = $6,712.94

    Employer's share = Same as employees' = $6,712.94

14. Quarterly earnings = $\frac{\text{Annual earnings}}{4} = \frac{60,000}{4} = \$15,000$

    Social security = Gross earnings × Tax rate
    Social security = 15,000 × .124 = $1,860

    Medicare tax = Gross earnings × Tax rate
    Medicare tax = 15,000 × .029 = $435

15. SUTA tax = Gross earnings × 5.4%
    SUTA tax = 10,000 × .054 = $540

    FUTA tax = Gross earnings × .8%
    FUTA tax = 10,000 × .008 = $80

16. a. Fringe benefits
       Sick days = Gross payroll × 5%
       Sick days = 123,400 × .05 = $6,170

       Health ins = Gross payroll × 8%
       Health ins = 123,400 × .08 = $9,872

       Dental ins = Number of employees × 12.40
       Dental ins = 250 × 12.40 = $3,100

       Total fringe benefits = 6,170 + 9,872 + 3,100 = $19,142

    b. Fringe benefit percent = $\dfrac{\text{Total fringe benefits}}{\text{Gross payroll}}$

       Fringe benefit percent = $\dfrac{19,142}{123,400} = .155 = 15.5\%$

    c. Yearly fringe benefits = Weekly total × 52
       Yearly fringe benefits = 19,142 x 52 = $995,384

17. Quarterly earnings $= \dfrac{\text{Annual earnings}}{4}$

Quarterly earnings $= \dfrac{100,000}{4} = \$25,000$

1st quarter: Social security $= 25,000 \times .124 = \$3,100.00$
Medicare $= 25,000 \times .029 = 725.00$
Income tax $= 25,000 \times .20 = + 5,000.00$
$\underline{\$8,825.00}$ Estimate tax

2nd quarter: Social security was same as 1st quarter

3rd quarter: Social security limit reached

Wage base − year-to-date earnings = Wages subject to social security
$62,700 − 50,000 = \$12,700$ subject to social security

Social security $= 12,700 \times .124 = \$1,574.00$
Medicare $= 25,000 \times .029 = 725.00$
Income tax $= 25,000 \times .20 = + 5,000.00$
$\underline{\$7,299.80}$

4th quarter: No social security
Medicare $= 25,000 \times .029 = \$725.00$
Income tax $= 25,000 \times .20 = + 5,000.00$
$\underline{\$5,725.00}$

Name_____

Class_____

ANSWERS

1. a. _____ $67,200.00 _____

   b. _____ $2,584.62 _____

2. _____ $322.00 _____

3. _____ $491.76 _____

4. _____ $656.25 _____

5. _____ $32,275.00 _____

6. _____ $9,656.40 _____

1. Jorge Kevin earns $2,800 semimonthly as a congressional aide for a senator in the state legislature.

  a. How much are his annual gross earnings?

    $2,800.00 \times 24 = \underline{\$67,200.00}$

  b. If the senator switches pay schedules from semimonthly to biweekly, what will Jorge's new gross earnings be per payroll period?

    $67,200.00 \div 26 = \underline{\$2,584.62}$ Biweekly

2. Hazel Kates works 40 hours per week. At the rate of $8.05 per hour, what are her gross weekly earnings?

  $8.05 \times 40 = \underline{\$322.00}$ Per week

3. Reagann Keller earns $7.45 per hour for regular time up to 40 hours, time-and-a-half for overtime, and double time for the midnight shift. If Reagann worked 56 hours last week, including four on the midnight shift, how much are her gross earnings?

  $7.45 \times 1.5 = 11.18$ OT $40 \times 7.45 = 298.00$
  $7.45 \times 2 \ \ = 14.90$ DT $12 \times 11.18 = 134.16$
                                 $4 \ \times 14.90 = \underline{\ \ \ 59.60}$
                                       $\underline{\$491.76}$ Gross earnings for week

4. Tiffany Francis assembles electric fans for the Hunter Corporation. She is paid on a differential piecework rate of $2.70 per fan for the first 160 fans and $3.25 for each fan over 160. If she assembled 229 units last week, how much were her gross earnings?

  $160 \times \$2.70 = \$432.00$
  $\underline{\ 69} \times \$3.25 = \underline{\$224.25}$
  229 $\underline{\$656.25}$

5. Brian Gonzalez is the official scorekeeper for a professional baseball team. He earns $140 per home game and $195 for each away game. The regular season is 162 games, evenly split between home and away. Last season Brian's team also made the playoffs and got into the World Series. The playoffs were an extra 12 games (5 at home and 7 away), paying an additional $75 each over and above his regular game pay. The 6 World Series games (3 home and 3 away) paid an additional $120 each over and above his playoff game pay. Calculate Brian's total earnings last season.

  140×81 $= 11,340.00$ Home
  195×81 $= 15,795.00$ Away
  $(140.00 + 75.00) \times 5 \ =$ $1,075.00$ Home playoff
  $(195.00 + 75.00) \times 7 \ =$ $1,890.00$ Away playoff
  $(215.00 + 120.00) \times 3 =$ $1,005.00$ World Series home
  $(270.00 + 120.00) \times 3 =$ $\underline{\ 1,170.00}$ World Series away
                            $\underline{\$32,275.00}$ Total earnings

6. What is the total gross pay for a salesperson on a straight commission of 7.8% if his sales volume is $123,800?

  $123,800.00 \times .078 = \underline{\$9,656.40}$

7. What is the total gross pay for a salesperson on an incremental commission schedule of 4.3% of sales up to $50,000 and 5.3% on sales over $50,000 if last month's sales volume was $71,700?

$$50,000.00 \times .043 = 2,150.00$$
$$+ \; 21,700.00 \times .053 = \underline{1,150.10}$$
$$\overline{71,700.00} \qquad \underline{\$3,300.10} \text{ Total commission}$$

8. Joan Brenner works in the telemarketing division for a company that pays a salary of $735 per month plus a commission of $3\frac{1}{2}\%$ of all sales over $15,500. If Joan sold $45,900 last month, what was her total gross pay?

$$45,900.00 \qquad 30,400.00 \times .035 \quad = \quad 1,064.00$$
$$- \; 15,500.00 \qquad 1,064.00 + 735.00 = \underline{\$1,799.00} \text{ Total gross pay}$$
$$\overline{30,400.00}$$

9. Elaine Cottey is on a 2.1% straight commission with a $700 drawing account. If she is paid the draw at the beginning of the month and then sells $142,100 during the month, how much commission is owed to Elaine?

$$142,100.00 \times .021 = 2,984.10 \text{ Commission}$$
$$- \quad 700.00 \text{ Drawing account}$$
$$\underline{\$2,284.10} \text{ Commission owed}$$

10. Dennis Morgan is the first mate on a charter fishing boat. He is paid a salary of $40.00 per day. He also averages tips amounting to 12% of the $475 daily charter rate. Last month during a fishing tournament Dennis worked 22 days. What were his total gross earnings for the month?

$$475.00 \qquad 10,450.00 \times .12 = 1,254.00 \text{ Tips}$$
$$\underline{\times \; 22} \qquad 40.00 \times 22 \qquad = \underline{\;\; 880.00} \text{ Salary}$$
$$\overline{10,450.00} \qquad \qquad \qquad \underline{\$2,134.00} \text{ Total gross pay}$$

Solve the following problems, using 6.2% up to $62,700 for social security withholding, and 1.45% for Medicare:

11. What are the withholdings for social security and Medicare for an employee with gross earnings of $725 per week?

$$725.00 \times .062 \; = \underline{\$44.95} \text{ Social security}$$
$$725.00 \times .0145 = \underline{\$10.51} \text{ Medicare}$$

12. Craig Gagstetter is an executive with Metro Distributors. His gross earnings are $7,750 per month.

   a. What are the withholdings for social security and Medicare for Craig's January paycheck?

$$7,750.00 \times .062 \; = \underline{\$480.50} \text{ Social security}$$
$$7,750.00 \times .0145 = \underline{\$112.38} \text{ Medicare}$$

   b. In what month will his salary reach the social security wage base limit?

$$\frac{62,700}{7,750} = 8.1 \quad \text{8 Full months, plus a portion of the 9th month } \underline{\text{(September)}}$$

ANSWERS

7.	$3,300.10
8.	$1,799.00
9.	$2,284.10
10.	$2,134.00
11.	$44.95 Social security
	$10.51 Medicare
12. a.	$480.50 Social security
	$112.38 Medicare
b.	September

ANSWERS

c. _____$43.40_____

_____$112.38_____

13. _____$97.00_____

14. _____$940.00_____

15. a. _____$1,704.54_____

b. _____$1,783.82_____

c. _____$2,029.79_____

16. _____$2,516.21_____

c. What are the social security and Medicare tax withholdings for Craig in the month named in part b?

$8 \times 7,750$ $= \$62,000$ Year-to-date earnings
$62,700 - 62,000 = \$700$ Subject to social security
$700.00 \times .062 = \underline{\$43.40}$ Social security (September)
$7,750.00 \times .0145 = \underline{\$112.38}$ Medicare (September)

Use the *wage bracket method* to solve the following problems:

13. How much income tax should be withheld from the paycheck of a married employee earning $910 per week and claiming three withholding allowances?

$\underline{\$97.00}$

14. How much income tax should be withheld from the paycheck of a single employee earning $4,458 per month and claiming zero withholding allowances?

$\underline{\$940.00}$

Use the *percentage method* to solve the following:

15. Larry Alison is single, claims one withholding allowance, and earns $2,120 per month.

a. What is the amount of Larry's paycheck after his employer withholds social security, Medicare, and income tax?

$2,120.00 - 212.50 = 1,907.50$ $1,688.50 \times 15\% = \$253.28$ Income tax
$1,907.50 - 219.00 = 1,688.50$ $2,120.00 \times .062 = 131.44$ Social security
$2,120.00 \times .0145 = \underline{30.74}$ Medicare
$\$415.46$ Total deductions

$2,120.00 - 415.46 = \underline{\$1,704.54}$ Net pay

b. If Larry gets married and changes to two withholding allowances, what will be the new amount of his paycheck?

$212.50 \times 2 = 425.00$ $1,160 \times 15\% = \$174.00$ Income tax
$2,120.00 - 425.00 = 1,695.00$ 131.44 Social security
$1,695.00 - 535.00 = 1,160$ $\underline{30.74}$ Medicare
$\$336.18$ Total deductions

$2,120.00 - 336.18 = \underline{\$1,783.82}$ Net pay

c. If he then gets a 15% raise, what is the new amount of his paycheck?

$2,120.00 \times 115\% = \$2,438.00$ New salary $1,478.00 \times 15\% = \$221.70$ Income tax
$2,438.00 - 425.00 = 2,013.00$ $2,438.00 \times .062 = 151.16$ Social security
$2,013.00 - 535.00 = 1,478.00$ $2,438.00 \times .0145 = \underline{35.35}$ Medicare
$\$408.21$ Total deductions

$2,438.00 - 408.21 = \underline{\$2,029.79}$ Net pay

16. Molly Allscheid is married, claims five withholding allowances, and earns $3,200 per month. In addition to social security, Medicare, and FIT, Molly pays 2.1% state income tax, $\frac{1}{2}\%$ for state disability insurance (both based on gross income), $43.11 for life insurance, and $72.30 to the credit union. As payroll manager for Molly's company, calculate her net take-home pay per month.

212.50×5 $= 1,062.50$ $1,602.50 \times 15\% = \$240.38$ Income tax
$3,200.00 - 1,062.50 = 2,137.50$ $3,200.00 \times .062 = 198.40$ Social security
$2,137.50 - 535.00 = 1,602.50$ $3,200.00 \times .0145 = 46.40$ Medicare
$3,200.00 \times .021 = 67.20$ State income tax
$3,200.00 \times .005 = 16.00$ Disability insurance
43.11 Life insurance
$\underline{72.30}$ Credit union
$3,200.00 - 683.79 = \underline{\$2,516.21}$ Net pay $\$683.79$ Total deductions

17. The Hastings Corporation has 83 employees on the assembly line, each with gross earnings of $329 per week.

    a. What are the total social security and Medicare taxes that should be withheld from the employee paychecks each week?

        329.00   27,307.00 × .062 = $1,693.03 Social security

        <u>× 83</u>   27,307.00 × .0145 = $395.95 Medicare

       27,307.00

    b. What is the total social security and Medicare that Hastings should send to the IRS for the first quarter of the year?

        1,693.03 × 13× 2 = $44,018.79 Social security

        395.95 × 13× 2 = $10,294.70 Medicare

18. John Sulzycki is a self-employed mechanic. Last year he had total gross earnings of $44,260. What are John's quarterly social security and Medicare payments due the IRS?

$$\frac{44,260}{4} = 11,065.00 \text{ Quarterly earnings}$$

    11,065.00 × .124 = $1,372.06 Social security

    11,065.00 × .029 = $320.89 Medicare

19. David Hirsch earns $28,330 annually as a supervisor for The International Bank.

    a. If the SUTA tax rate is 5.4% of the first $7,000 earned in a year, how much SUTA tax must the bank pay each year for David?

        7,000.00 × .054 = $378.00 SUTA per year

    b. If the FUTA tax rate is 6.2% of the first $7,000 earned in a year minus the SUTA tax paid, how much FUTA tax must the bank pay each year for David?

        7,000.00 × .008 = $56

20. Global Travel has three employees: Sanders earns $422 per week, Wilcox earns $510 per week, and Jenkins earns $695 per week. The company's SUTA tax rate is 5.4%, and the FUTA rate is 6.2% minus the SUTA. As usual, these taxes are paid on the first $7,000 of each employee's earnings.

    a. How much SUTA and FUTA tax does the company owe on these employees for the first quarter of the year?

        422.00 × 13 = 5,486.00   Sanders   5,486.00   19,116.00 × .054 = $1,032.26 SUTA

        510.00 × 13 = 6,630.00   Wilcox   6,630.00   19,116.00 × .008 = $152.93 FUTA

        695.00 × 13 = 9,035.00   Jenkins   <u>7,000.00</u> (Limit)

                                    19,116.00

    b. How much SUTA and FUTA tax does Global owe for the second quarter of the year?

        7,000.00 − 5,486.00 = 1,514.00

        7,000.00 − 6,630.00 = <u>370.00</u>

                     1,884.00 Taxable

        1,884.00 × .054 = $101.74 SUTA

        1,884.00 × .008 = $15.07 FUTA

ANSWERS

17. a. _____ $1,693.03   395.95

    b. _____ $44,018.78 Social security

         $10,294.70 Medicare

18. _____ $1,372.06 Social security

         $320.89 Medicare

19. a. _____ $378.00

    b. _____ $56.00

20. a. _____ $1,032.26 SUTA

         $152.93 FUTA

    b. _____ $101.74 SUTA

         $15.07 FUTA

21. Flamingo Developers employs 150 workers and has a gross payroll of $282,100 per week. Fringe benefits are $6\frac{1}{2}$% of gross payroll for sick days and holiday leave, 9.1% for health and hospital insurance, 4.6% for the retirement fund, and $10.70 per employee for a stock purchase plan.

a. What is the total weekly cost of fringe benefits for the company?

$282,100.00 \times .065 = 18,336.50$ Sick days
$282,100.00 \times .091 = 25,671.10$ Health plan
$282,100.00 \times .046 = 12,976.60$ Retirement
$150 \times 10.70 \qquad = \underline{1,605.00}$ Stock purchase
$\qquad\qquad\qquad\quad \underline{$58,589.20}$ Total cost of benefits per week

b. What percent of payroll does this represent?

$$R = \frac{P}{B} = R = \frac{58,589.20}{282,100.00} = .2076 = \underline{20.8\%} \text{ of payroll}$$

c. What is the company's annual cost of fringe benefits?

$58,589.20 \times 52 = \underline{$3,046,638.40}$ Cost of benefits per year

22. Pat Ayres is self-employed with an annual salary of $66,520. Her social security tax rate is 12.4%, Medicare is 2.9%, and her estimated federal income tax rate is 14%.

a. How much quarterly estimate tax must Pat send to the IRS each quarter?

$\dfrac{66,520}{4} = 16,630.00$ Salary per quarter

$16,630.00 \times .124 = 2,062.12$ Social security
$16,630.00 \times .029 = 482.27$ Medicare
$16,630.00 \times .14 = \underline{2,328.20}$ Income tax
$\qquad\qquad\qquad \underline{$4,872.59}*$ Quarterly estimated tax

$16,630.00 \times 3 = 49,890.00$
$62,700.00 - 49,890.00 = 12,810.00$
$1,2810.00 \times .124 = \underline{$1,588.44}$ Social security, 4th quarter

*Note: Social security limit reached in 4th quarter

b. What form should she use?

Form 1040-ES, *Estimated Quarterly Tax Voucher for Self-Employed Persons*

BUSINESS DECISION
The Bride, the Groom, and the Taxman

23. Two of your friends, John and Carmen, have been living together for a year. John earns $3,000 per month as the manager of a Blockbuster Music Store. Carmen is a sophomore at college and is not currently working. They plan to marry, but cannot decide whether to get married now or wait a year or two.

After studying the payroll chapter in your business math class, you inform John that married couples generally pay less income taxes, and that if they got married now instead of waiting he would have less income tax withheld from his paychecks. John's current tax filing status is single, one exemption. If he and Carmen got married he could file as married, two exemptions. Use the percentage method and Exhibits 10-4 and 10-5 to calculate the following:

a. How much income tax is withheld from John's paycheck each month now?

Single

$3,000 - 212.50 = \$2,787.50$
$285.30 + 28\%(2,787.50 - 2,121)$
$285.30 + 28\%(666.50)$
$285.30 + 186.62 = \underline{\$471.92}$ Income tax withheld

b. How much income tax would be withheld from John's check if he and Carmen got married?

Married

$212.50 \times 2 = 425$
$3,000 - 425 = 2,575$
$2,575 - 535 = 2,040 \times .15 = \underline{\$306.00}$ Income tax withheld

c. Assuming Carmen has three more years of full-time college before going to work, and John expects a 10% raise in one year and a 15% raise the year after, what is the total 3-year tax advantage of their getting married now?

Year 2   10% Raise—$3,000 \times 110\% = \$3,300$ New salary

Single	Married
$3,300 - 212.50 = 3,087.50$	$212.50 \times 2 = 425$
$285.30 + 28\%(3,087.50 - 2,121)$	$3,300 - 425 = 2,875$
$285.30 + 28\%(966.50)$	$2,875 - 535 = 2,340 \times .15 = \$351.00$
$285.30 + 270.62 = \$555.92$	

Year 3   15% Raise—$3,300 \times 115\% = \$3,795$ New salary

Single	Married
$3,795 - 212.50 = \$3,582.50$	$212.50 \times 2 = 425$
$285.30 + 28\%(3,582.50 - 2,121)$	$3,795 - 425 = 3,370$
$285.30 + 28\%(1,461.50)$	$3,370 - 535 = 2,835 \times .15 = \$425.25$
$285.30 + 409.22 = \$694.52$	

Single

Year 1	$471.92 \times 12 =$	5,663.04
Year 2	$555.92 \times 12 =$	6,671.04
Year 3	$694.52 \times 12 =$	8,334.24

$\$20,668.32$ Total 3-year withholding

Married

Year 1	$306.00 \times 12 =$	3,672.00
Year 2	$351.00 \times 12 =$	4,212.00
Year 3	$425.25 \times 12 =$	5,103.00

$\$12,987.00$ Total 3-year withholding

$20,668.32 - 12,987.00 = \underline{\$7,681.32}$ Total 3-year savings if married

All the Math That's Fit to Learn

The Business Math Times

Volume IX — Payroll — One Dollar

U.S. Currency Gets a High-Tech Face-Lift

The new features of the $100 bill are among some first major changes to the nation's currency in over 66 years. Beginning with the $100 Federal Reserve note in 1996, the United States Treasury Department is issuing newly redesigned currency.

The mint has plans to introduce new $50, $20, $10, $5 and $1 bills before the turn of the century—one denomination every eight to twelve months. The $100 bill was chosen first because it is a favorite of foreign, professional forgers. The change also reflects the new threat from today's sophisticated computers, color copiers, digital scanners, and laser printers.

A total of $400 billion in U.S. currency is in circulation worldwide, with about 66 percent in foreign countries. Before the new changes, which were 10 years in development, the "greenback" was among the least sophisticated currencies in terms of anti-counterfeiting technology.

According to the Treasury, there will be no recall of any U.S. currency. Old bills will remain legal tender as long as they are in circulation. As they wear out, they'll be replaced with redesigned bills.

Let's take a closer look at what's new about your money:

Top 10 Employers in the U.S.

Employer	Employees
1 General Motors	709,000
2 Wal-Mart Stores	675,000
3 PepsiCo	480,000
4 Ford Motor	360,000
5 United Parcel Service	337,00
6 AT&T	299,300
7 Sears Roebuck	275,000
8 IBM	252,215
9 Kmart	250,000
10 Columbia/HCA Healthcare	240,000

SOURCE: *Fortune,* May 15, 1995, p. F-30.

Did You Know?

Henry Ford shocked his follow capitalists by more than doubling the daily wage of most of his workers in 1914, eleven years after he had established his first automobile factory.

He knew what he was doing. The buying power of his workers was increased, and their raised consumption stimulated buying elsewhere. Ford called it the "wage motive."

SOURCE: Isaac Asimov, *Isaac Asimov's Book of Facts,* (Mamaroneck, NY: Hastings House, 1992).

Brainteaser

A painter agrees to work under the condition that he is paid $55.00 every day he works and he must pay $66.00 every day he does not work. At the end of 30 days, he has earned $924.00. How many days did he work?

SOURCE: *Mathematics Teacher* Magazine, (October 1986).

Answer to Last Issue's Brainteaser
$96.00

Since 25 percent is equivalent to $\frac{1}{4}$, you are looking for the largest multiple of 4 that is less than 100.

WHAT'S NEW ABOUT YOUR MONEY

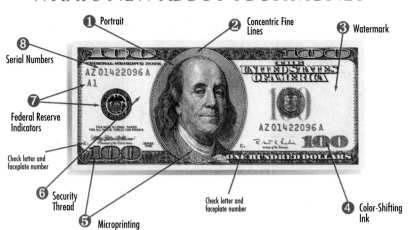

1 Portrait
2 Concentric Fine Lines
3 Watermark
8 Serial Numbers
7 Federal Reserve Indicators
Check letter and faceplate number
6 Security Thread
5 Microprinting
Check letter and faceplate number
4 Color-Shifting Ink

1. Portrait The enlarged, off-center, portrait of Benjamin Franklin is easier to recognize, while the added detail is harder to duplicate.

2. Concentric Fine Lines The fine lines printed behind the portrait are difficult to replicate.

3. Watermark A watermark depicting Benjamin Franklin is visible from both sides when held up to a light.

4. Color-Shifting Ink The number in the lower right corner on the front of the note looks green when viewed straight on, but appears black when viewed at an angle.

5. Microprinting On the front of the note, "USA 100" is printed within the number in the lower left corner and "United States of America" is on Benjamin Franklin's coat.

6. Security Thread A polymer thread is embedded vertically in the paper and indicates, by its unique position, the note's denomination. The words "USA 100" on the thread can be seen from both sides of the note when held up to a bright light. Additionally, the thread glows red when held under an ultraviolet light.

7. Federal Reserve Indicators A new universal seal represents the entire Federal Reserve System. A letter and number beneath the left serial number identifies the issuing Federal Reserve Bank.

8. Serial Numbers An additional letter is added to the serial number. The unique combination of eleven numbers and letters appears twice on the front of the note.

SOURCE: Adapted from Treasury Department Brochure. Federal Reserve Bank of Atlanta, Financial Update Bulletin.

Chapter 10

Simple Interest and Promissory Notes

Performance Objectives

UNDERSTANDING AND COMPUTING SIMPLE INTEREST

The practice of borrowing and lending money dates back in history for thousands of years. Today, institutions such as banks, savings and loans, and credit unions are specifically in business to borrow and lend money. They constitute a significant portion of the service sector of the American economy.

Interest is the rental fee charged by a lender to a business or individual for the use of money. The amount of interest charged is determined by three factors: the amount of money being borrowed or invested, known as the **principal;** the percent of interest charged on the money per year, known as the **rate;** and the length of time of the loan, known as **time.** The manner in which the interest is computed is an additional factor that influences the amount of interest. The two most commonly used methods in business today for computing interest are simple and compound.

Simple interest means that the interest is calculated *only once* for the entire time period of the loan. At the end of the time period the borrower repays the principal plus the interest. Simple interest loans are usually made for short periods of time, such as a few days, weeks, or months. **Compound interest** means that the interest is calculated *more than once* during the time period of the loan. When compound interest is applied to a loan, each succeeding time period accumulates interest on the previous interest, in addition to interest on the principal. Compound interest loans are generally for time periods of a year or longer.

This chapter will discuss the concepts of simple interest; simple discount, which is a variation of a simple interest loan; and promissory notes. Chapter 11 will cover the concepts and calculations related to compound interest and present value.

10-1 Computing Simple Interest for Loans with Terms of Years or Months

Simple interest is calculated by using a formula known as the simple interest formula. It is stated as

$$\text{Interest} = \text{Principal} \times \text{Rate} \times \text{Time}$$
$$I = PRT$$

interest

The price or rental fee charged by a lender to a borrower for the use of money.

principal

A sum of money, either invested or borrowed, upon which interest is calculated.

rate

The percent that is charged or earned for the use of money per year.

time

Length of time, expressed in days, months, or years, of an investment or loan.

simple interest

Interest calculated solely on the principal amount borrowed or invested. It is calculated only *once* for the entire time period of the loan.

compound interest

Interest, calculated at regular intervals, on the principal and previously earned interest. Covered in Chapter 11.

Banking institutions all over the world are in business specifically to borrow and lend money.

When applying the simple interest formula keep in mind two important rules. First, the rate must be converted from a percent to a decimal; second, the time must be expressed in years, or fractions of a year. For time periods of a year or longer, simply use the number of years as the time factor, converting fractional parts to decimals. For example, the time factor for a two-year loan is 2, three years is 3, $1\frac{1}{2}$ years is 1.5, $4\frac{3}{4}$ years is 4.75, and so on.

When the time period of a loan is for a specified number of months, express the time factor as a fraction of a year. This is done by making the number of months the numerator, and 12 months (1 year) the denominator. A loan for 1 month would have a time factor of $\frac{1}{12}$, a loan for 2 months would have a factor of $\frac{2}{12}$ or $\frac{1}{6}$, a 5-month loan would use $\frac{5}{12}$ as the factor, and a loan for 18 months would use $\frac{18}{12}$ or $1\frac{1}{2}$, written as 1.5.

EXAMPLE

What is the amount of interest for a loan of $8,000, at 9% interest, for one year?

SOLUTION STRATEGY

To solve this problem, we apply the simple interest formula,

$$\text{Interest} = \text{Principal} \times \text{Rate} \times \text{Time}$$
$$\text{Interest} = 8,000 \times 9\% \times 1$$
$$\text{Interest} = 8,000 \times .09 \times 1$$
$$\text{Interest} = \underline{\underline{\$720}}$$

EXAMPLE

What is the amount of interest for a loan of $16,500, at $12\frac{1}{2}$% interest, for 7 months?

SOLUTION STRATEGY

In this example, the rate is converted to .125, and the time factor is expressed as a fraction of a year, $\frac{7}{12}$.

$$\text{Interest} = \text{Principal} \times \text{Rate} \times \text{Time}$$
$$\text{Interest} = 16,500 \times .125 \times \frac{7}{12}$$
$$\text{Interest} = \underline{\underline{\$1,203.13}}$$

Calculator Sequence: 16500 $\boxed{\times}$ .125 $\boxed{\times}$ 7 $\boxed{\div}$ 12 $\boxed{=}$ $\underline{\underline{\$1,203.13}}$

 TRY-IT   **EXERCISES**

Find the amount of interest on each of the following loans:

	Principal	Rate	Time
1.	$4,000	7%	$2\frac{1}{4}$ years
2.	$45,000	$9\frac{3}{4}$%	3 months
3.	$130,000	10.4%	42 months

Check your answers with the solutions on page 335.

10-2 Calculating Simple Interest for Loans with Terms of Days Using the Exact Interest and Ordinary Interest Methods

In actuality, there are two different methods for calculating the time factor, *T,* when applying the simple interest formula. Because time must be expressed in years, loans whose terms are given in days must be made into a fractional part of a year. This is accomplished by dividing the days of a loan by the number of days in a year.

Exact Interest

● **exact interest**

Interest calculation method using 365 days (366 in leap year) as the time factor denominator.

The first method for calculating the time factor is known as **exact interest.** Exact interest uses *365 days* as the time factor denominator. This method is used by government agencies, the Federal Reserve Bank, and most credit unions.

$$\text{Time} = \frac{\text{Number of days of a loan}}{365}$$

Ordinary Interest

● **ordinary interest, or banker's rule**

Interest calculation method using 360 days as the time factor denominator.

The second method for calculating the time factor is known as **ordinary interest.** Ordinary interest uses *360 days* as the denominator of the time factor. This method dates back to the time before electronic calculators and computers. In the past, when calculating the time factor manually, a denominator of 360 was easier to use than 365.

Regardless of today's electronic sophistication, banks and most other lending institutions still use ordinary interest since it yields a somewhat higher amount of interest than the exact interest method. Over the years, ordinary interest has become known as the **banker's rule.**

$$\text{Time} = \frac{\text{Number of days of a loan}}{360}$$

EXAMPLE

Using the exact interest method, what is the amount of interest on a loan of $4,000, at 7% interest, for 88 days?

SOLUTION STRATEGY

Since we are looking for exact interest, we will use 365 days as the denominator of the time factor in the simple interest formula:

$$\text{Interest} = \text{Principal} \times \text{Rate} \times \text{Time}$$
$$\text{Interest} = 4,000 \times .07 \times \frac{88}{365}$$
$$\text{Interest} = 67.506849$$
$$\text{Interest} = \underline{\$67.51}$$

Calculator Sequence: 4000 [×] .07 [×] 88 [÷] 365 [=] $\underline{\$67.51}$

EXAMPLE

Using the ordinary interest method, what is the amount of interest on a loan of $19,500, at 12% interest, for 160 days?

SOLUTION STRATEGY

Since we are looking for ordinary interest, we will use 360 days as the denominator of the time factor in the simple interest formula:

$$\text{Interest} = \text{Principal} \times \text{Rate} \times \text{Time}$$

$$\text{Interest} = 19{,}500 \times .12 \times \frac{160}{360}$$

$$\text{Interest} = \underline{\$1{,}040.00}$$

Calculator Sequence: 19500 ⊠ .12 ⊠ 160 ÷ 360 = $\underline{\$1{,}040.00}$

TRY-IT   EXERCISES

4. **Sandra Miller goes to the bank and borrows \$15,000, at $9\frac{1}{2}\%$, for 250 days. If the bank uses the ordinary interest method, how much interest will Sandra have to pay?**

5. **David Hall goes to a credit union and borrows \$23,000, at 8%, for 119 days. If the credit union calculates interest by the exact interest method, what is the amount of interest on the loan?**

Check your answers with the solutions on page 335.

10-3 Calculating the Maturity Value of a Loan

When the time period of a loan is over, the loan is said to mature. At that time, the borrower repays the original principal plus the interest. The total payback of principal and interest is known as the **maturity value** of a loan. Once the interest has been calculated, the maturity value can be found by using the formula:

● maturity value
The total payback of principal and interest of an investment or loan.

$$\text{Maturity value} = \text{Principal} + \text{Interest}$$
$$MV = P + I$$

For example, if a loan for \$50,000 had interest of \$8,600, the maturity value would be found by adding the principal and the interest: $50{,}000 + 8{,}600 = \$58{,}600$.

Maturity value can also be calculated directly, without first calculating the interest, by using the following formula:

$$\text{Maturity value} = \text{Principal} (1 + \text{Rate} \times \text{Time})$$
$$MV = P(1 + RT)$$

Note: When using this formula, always multiply the rate and time first, then add the 1.

EXAMPLE

What is the maturity value of a loan for \$25,000, at 11%, for $2\frac{1}{2}$ years?

SOLUTION STRATEGY

Because this example asks for the maturity value, not the amount of interest, we shall use the formula for finding maturity value directly, $MV = P(1 + RT)$. Remember to multiply the rate and time first, then add the 1. Note that the time, $2\frac{1}{2}$ years, should be converted to the decimal equivalent 2.5 for ease in calculation.

$$\text{Maturity value} = \text{Principal} (1 + \text{Rate} \times \text{Time})$$
$$\text{Maturity value} = 25,000(1 + .11 \times 2.5)$$
$$\text{Maturity value} = 25,000(1 + .275)$$
$$\text{Maturity value} = 25,000(1.275)$$
$$\text{Maturity value} = \underline{\$31,875}$$

TRY-IT EXERCISES

6. **What is the amount of interest and the maturity value of a loan for \$15,400, at $6\frac{1}{2}$ % simple interest, for 24 months? (Use the formula $MV = P + I$.)**

7. **Precision Air Taxi Service borrowed \$450,000, at 8% simple interest, for 9 months, to purchase a new airplane. Use the formula $MV = P(1 + RT)$ to find the maturity value of the loan.**

Check your answers with the solutions on page 335.

10-4 Calculating the Number of Days of a Loan

● **loan date**
The first day of a loan.

● **due date, or maturity date**
The last day of a loan.

The first day of a loan is known as the **loan date** and the last day is known as the **due date** or **maturity date.** When these dates are known, the number of days of the loan can be calculated by using the days in each month chart and the steps that follow:

Days in Each Month

28 Days	30 Days	31 Days
February (29 leap year)	April June September November	January March May July August October December

STEPS FOR DETERMINING THE NUMBER OF DAYS OF A LOAN:

Step 1. Determine the number of days remaining in the first month by subtracting the loan date from the number of days in that month.

Step 2. List the number of days for each succeeding whole month.

Step 3. List the number of loan days in the last month.

Step 4. Add the days from Steps 1, 2, and 3.

EXAMPLE

Val Alger borrowed money from the Capital Bank on August 18 and repaid the loan on November 27. For how many days was this loan?

SOLUTION STRATEGY

The number of days from August 18 to November 27 would be calculated as follows:

Step 1. Days remaining in first month   Aug   31

                               Aug −18

                                   13 → August   13 days

Step 2. Days in succeeding whole months ⟶ September   30 days

                                      ↗ October   31 days

Step 3. Days of loan in last month ⟶ November   +27 days

Step 4. Add the days   Total 101 days

TRY-IT   EXERCISES

8. A loan was made on April 4 and had a due date of July 18. What is the number of days of the loan?

9. Iain MacDonald borrowed $3,500 on June 15, at 11% interest. If the loan was due on October 9, what was the amount of interest on Iain's loan using the exact interest method?

Check your answers with the solutions on page 335.

10-5 Determining the Maturity Date of a Loan

When the loan date and number of days of the loan are known, the maturity date can be found as follows:

> **STEPS FOR DETERMINING THE MATURITY DATE OF A LOAN:**
>
> **Step 1.** Find the number of days remaining in the first month by subtracting the loan date from the number of days in that month.
>
> **Step 2.** Subtract the days remaining in the first month (Step 1) from the number of days of the loan.
>
> **Step 3.** Continue subtracting the number of days in each succeeding whole month, until you reach a month where the difference is less than the total days in that month. At that point, the maturity date will be the day of that month that corresponds to the difference.

EXAMPLE

What is the maturity date of a loan that was taken out on April 14, for 85 days?

SOLUTION STRATEGY

Step 1. Days remaining in first month   30   Days in April

                                        −14   Loan date April 14

                Days remaining in April   16

Step 2. Subtract remaining days in first month
from days of the loan

85	Days of the loan
−16	Days remaining in April
Difference 69	

Step 3. Subtract succeeding whole months

69	Difference
−31	Days in May
Difference 38	
38	Difference
−30	Days in June
Difference 8	

At this point, the difference, 8, is less than the number of days in the next month, July, therefore the maturity date is <u>July 8</u>.

TRY-IT   EXERCISES

10. What is the maturity date of a loan taken out on September 9, for 125 days?

11. On October 21, Sally Kafka went to the Republic Bank and took out a loan for $9,000, at 10% ordinary interest, for 80 days. What is the maturity value and maturity date of this loan?

Check your answers with the solutions on page 335.

REVIEW EXERCISES   CHAPTER 10—SECTION I

Find the amount of interest on each of the following loans:

Complete, worked out solutions to exercises 1–12 appear in the appendix following the index.

	Principal	Rate	Time	Interest
1.	$5,000	8%	2 years	$800.00
2.	$75,000	$10\frac{3}{4}\%$	6 months	$4,031.25
3.	$100,000	12.7%	18 months	$19,050.00
4.	$80,000	15%	$3\frac{1}{2}$ years	$42,000.00
5.	$6,440	$5\frac{1}{2}\%$	7 months	$206.62
6.	$13,200	9.2%	$4\frac{3}{4}$ years	$5,768.40

Use the exact interest method (365 days) and the ordinary interest method (360 days) to compare the amount of interest for the following loans:

	Principal	Rate	Time	Exact Interest	Ordinary Interest
7.	$45,000	13%	100 days	$1,602.74	$1,625.00
8.	$184,500	$15\frac{1}{2}\%$	58 days	$4,544.26	$4,607.38
9.	$32,400	8.6%	241 days	$1,839.79	$1,865.34
10.	$7,230	9%	18 days	$32.09	$32.54
11.	$900	$10\frac{1}{4}\%$	60 days	$15.16	$15.38
12.	$100,000	10%	1 day	$27.40	$27.78

13.	$2,500	12%	74 days	$60.82	$61.67
14.	$350	14.1%	230 days	$31.10	$31.53
15.	$50,490	$9\frac{1}{4}\%$	69 days	$882.88	$895.15
16.	$486,000	$13\frac{1}{2}\%$	127 days	$22,828.68	$23,145.75

Complete, worked out solutions for exercises 13–33 appear in the appendix following the index.

Find the amount of interest and the maturity value of the following loans (use the formula $MV = P + I$ to find the maturity values):

	Principal	Rate	Time	Interest	Maturity Value
17.	$54,000	11.9%	2 years	$12,852.00	$66,852.00
18.	$125,000	$12\frac{1}{2}\%$	5 months	$6,510.42	$131,510.42
19.	$33,750	8.4%	10 months	$2,362.50	$36,112.50
20.	$91,000	$9\frac{1}{4}\%$	$2\frac{1}{2}$ years	$21,043.75	$112,043.75

Find the maturity value of the following loans (use $MV = P(1 + RT)$ to find the maturity values):

	Principal	Rate	Time	Maturity Value
21.	$1,500	9%	2 years	$1,770.00
22.	$18,620	$10\frac{1}{2}\%$	30 months	$23,507.75
23.	$1,000,000	11%	3 years	$1,330,000.00
24.	$750,000	13.35%	11 months	$841,781.25

From the following information, determine the number of days of each loan:

	Loan Date	Due Date	Number of Days
25.	September 5	December 12	98
26.	June 27	October 15	110
27.	January 23	November 8	289
28.	March 9	July 30	143

From the following information, determine the maturity date of each loan:

	Loan Date	Time of Loan	Maturity Date
29.	October 19	45 days	December 3
30.	February 5	110 days	May 26
31.	May 26	29 days	June 24
32.	July 21	200 days	February 6
33.	December 6	79 days	February 23

Solve the following word problems:

34. On April 12, Jeri Lynn Cullison borrowed $5,000 from her credit union at 9%, for 80 days. The credit union uses the ordinary interest method.

  a. What is the amount of interest on the loan?

  $$I = PRT = 5,000 \times .09 \times \frac{80}{360} = \underline{\$100.00}$$

  b. What is the maturity value of the loan?

  $$MV = P + I = 5,000 + 100 = \underline{\$5,100.00}$$

c. What is the maturity date of the loan?

$$
\begin{array}{r}
30 \\
-\ 12 \\
\hline
18\ \text{Days}
\end{array}
\qquad
\begin{array}{l}
18\ \text{Apr} \\
61\ \text{May-June} \\
+\ \ 1\ \text{July} \longrightarrow \underline{\text{July 1}} \\
\hline
80\ \text{Days}
\end{array}
$$

35. What is the maturity value of a $60,000 loan, for 100 days, at 12.2% interest, using the exact interest method?

$$MV = P(1 + RT) = 60,000\left(1 + .122 \times \frac{100}{365}\right) = \underline{\$62,005.48}$$

36. Playtime Toys borrowed $350,000 at 9% interest on July 19, for 120 days.

a. If the bank uses the ordinary interest method, what is the amount of interest on the loan?

$$I = PRT = 350,000 \times .09 \times \frac{120}{360} = \underline{\$10,500.00}$$

b. What is the maturity date?

$$
\begin{array}{r}
31 \\
-\ 19 \\
\hline
12\ \text{Days}
\end{array}
\qquad
\begin{array}{l}
12\ \text{July} \\
92\ \text{Aug-Oct} \\
+\ 16\ \text{Nov} \longrightarrow \underline{\text{November 16}} \\
\hline
120\ \text{Days}
\end{array}
$$

37. Bo Brady missed an income tax payment of $9,000. The Internal Revenue Service charges a 13% simple interest penalty calculated by the exact interest method. If the tax was due on April 15 but was paid on August 19, what is the amount of the penalty charge?

$$
\begin{array}{r}
30 \\
-\ 15 \\
\hline
15\ \text{Days}
\end{array}
\qquad
\begin{array}{l}
15\ \text{Apr} \\
92\ \text{May-July} \\
+\ 19\ \text{Aug} \\
\hline
126\ \text{Days}
\end{array}
\qquad
I = PRT = 9,000 \times .13 \times \frac{126}{365} = \underline{\$403.89}
$$

38. FastTrack Electronics needs to borrow $3,000,000, for 90 days, to purchase a large order of transistors from the manufacturer. If the interest rate for such loans is currently 11%, how much can FastTrack save by finding a lending institution that uses the exact interest method rather than the ordinary interest method?

Ordinary: $I = PRT = 3,000,000 \times .11 \times \dfrac{90}{360} = \underline{\$82,500.00}$

Exact: $\quad I = PRT = 3,000,000 \times .11 \times \dfrac{90}{365} = \underline{\$81,369.86}$

$$\underline{\$1,130.14}\ \text{Savings}$$

SECTION II

USING THE SIMPLE INTEREST FORMULA

In Section I we used the simple interest formula, $I = PRT$, to solve for the interest. Frequently in business, however, the principal, rate, or time might be the unknown factor. Remember from Chapter 5 that an equation can be solved for any of the variables by isolating that variable to one side of the equation. In this section, we will convert the simple interest formula to equations that solve for each of the other variable factors.

If you find this procedure difficult or hard to remember, use the Magic Triangle, as we did in Chapter 6, to calculate the portion, rate, and base. Remember, to use the Magic Triangle, cover the variable you are solving for and the new formula will "magically" appear!

Magic Triangle
Simple Interest Formula

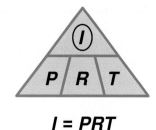

$$I = PRT$$

10-6 Solving for the Principal

When using the simple interest formula to solve for principal, P, we isolate the P on one side of the equation by dividing both sides of the equation by RT. This yields the new equation:

$$\text{Principal} = \frac{\text{Interest}}{\text{Rate} \times \text{Time}} \qquad P = \frac{I}{RT}$$

We can also find the formula in the Magic Triangle by covering the unknown variable, P, as follows:

Magic Triangle
Solving for Principal

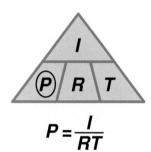

$$P = \frac{I}{RT}$$

EXAMPLE

A bank loaned a business money at 8% interest for 90 days. If the amount of interest was $4,000, use the ordinary interest method to find the amount of principal borrowed.

SOLUTION STRATEGY

To solve for the principal, we use the formula $P = \dfrac{I}{RT}$.

$P = \dfrac{I}{RT}$ Substitute the known variables into the equation.

$P = \dfrac{4,000}{.08 \times \dfrac{90}{360}}$ Calculate the denominator first.
Calculator sequence: .08 $\boxed{\times}$ 90 $\boxed{\div}$ 360 $\boxed{\text{M+}}$

$P = \dfrac{4,000}{.02}$ Next, divide the numerator by the denominator.
Calculator sequence: 4000 $\boxed{\div}$ $\boxed{\text{MR}}$ $\boxed{=}$ 200,000

Principal = $200,000   The company borrowed $200,000 from the bank.

Note: This formula provides a good opportunity to use your calculator's memory key. Use $\boxed{\text{M+}}$ to store a number in memory. Use $\boxed{\text{MR}}$ to retrieve that number.

12. **Walzer Industries borrowed money at 9% interest for 125 days. If the interest charge was $560, use the ordinary interest method to calculate the amount of principal of the loan.**

Check your answer with the solution on page 335.

10-7 Solving for the Rate

When solving the simple formula for rate, the answer will be a decimal that must be converted to a percent. In business, interest rates are always expressed as a percent.

When the rate is the unknown variable, we isolate the R on one side of the equation by dividing both sides of the equation by PT. This yields the new equation:

$$\text{Rate} = \frac{\text{Interest}}{\text{Principal} \times \text{Time}} \qquad R = \frac{I}{PT}$$

We can also find the formula in the Magic Triangle by covering the unknown variable, R, as follows:

Magic Triangle
Solving for Rate

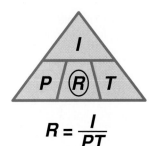

$$R = \frac{I}{PT}$$

EXAMPLE

What is the rate of interest on a loan of $5,000, for 125 days, if the amount of interest is $166, using the ordinary interest method? Round your answer to the nearest hundredth percent.

SOLUTION STRATEGY

To solve for the rate, we use the formula, $R = \dfrac{I}{PT}$.

$R = \dfrac{I}{PT}$ Substitute the known variables into the equation.

$R = \dfrac{166}{5,000 \times \dfrac{125}{360}}$ Calculate the denominator first.

Calculator sequence: 5000 ⨯ 125 ÷ 360 **M+**

$R = \dfrac{166}{1736.1111}$ Next, divide the numerator by the denominator.
Note: Don't round the denominator.
Calculator sequence: 166 ÷ **MR** = .095616

$R = .095616$ Round the answer to the nearest hundredth percent.

Rate = 9.56%   The bank charged 9.56% interest.

TRY-IT **EXERCISE**

13. **What is the rate of interest on a loan of $25,000, for 245 days, if the amount of interest is $1,960, using the ordinary interest method? Round your answer to the nearest hundredth percent.**

Check your answer with the solution on page 335.

10-8 Solving for the Time

When solving the simple interest formula for time, a whole number in the answer represents years and a decimal represents a portion of a year. The decimal should be converted to days by multiplying it by 360 for ordinary interest or by 365 for exact interest.

For example, an answer of 3 means 3 years. An answer of 3.23 means 3 years and .23 of the next year. Assuming ordinary interest, multiply the decimal portion of the answer, .23, by 360. This gives 82.8, which represents the number of days. The total time of the loan would be 3 years and 83 days. Note: Any fraction of a day is always rounded up to the next higher day, even if it is less than .5. Lending institutions always consider any part of a day to be a full day. For example, 25.1 days would round up to 26 days.

When using the simple interest formula to solve for time, T, we isolate the T on one side of the equation by dividing both sides of the equation by PR. This yields the new equation:

$$\text{Time} = \frac{\text{Interest}}{\text{Principal} \times \text{Rate}} \qquad T = \frac{I}{PR}$$

We can also find the formula in the Magic Triangle by covering the unknown variable, T, as follows:

Magic Triangle
Solving for Time

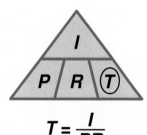

$$T = \frac{I}{PR}$$

EXAMPLE

What would be the time period of a loan for $7,600, at 11% ordinary interest, if the amount of interest is $290?

SOLUTION STRATEGY

To solve for the time, we use the formula $T = \dfrac{I}{PR}$.

$T = \dfrac{I}{PR}$ Substitute the known variables into the equation.

$T = \dfrac{290}{7,600 \times .11}$ Calculate the denominator first.
Calculator sequence: 7600 ⨯ .11 M+

$T = \dfrac{290}{836}$ Next, divide the numerator by the denominator.
Calculator sequence: 290 ÷ MR = .3468899

Using the Simple Interest Formula   319

$T = .3468899$ years — Since the answer is a decimal, the time is less than one year. Using ordinary interest, we multiply the entire decimal by 360 to find the number of days of the loan.

$T = .3468899 \times 360$ — Remember, don't round off; use the entire decimal.

Time = 124.8 or <u>125 days</u>

T R Y - I T   E X E R C I S E

14. What is the time period of a loan for \$15,000, at 9.5% ordinary interest, if the amount of interest is \$650?

Check your answer with the solution on page 335.

10-9 Calculating Loans Involving Partial Payments before Maturity

Frequently, businesses and individuals who have borrowed money for a specified length of time find that they want to save some interest by making one or more partial payments on the loan before the maturity date. The most commonly used method for this calculation is known as the **U.S. rule.** The rule states that when a partial payment is made on a loan, the payment is first used to pay off the accumulated interest to date, and the balance is used to reduce the principal. In this application, the ordinary interest method (360 days) will be used for all calculations.

● **U.S. rule**

Method for distributing early partial payments of a loan, whereby the payment is first used to pay off the accumulated interest to date, with the balance used to reduce the principal.

> **STEPS FOR CALCULATING MATURITY VALUE OF A LOAN AFTER ONE OR MORE PARTIAL PAYMENTS:**
>
> **Step 1.** Using the simple interest formula, compute the amount of interest due from the date of the loan to the date of the partial payment.
>
> **Step 2.** Subtract the interest from Step 1 from the partial payment. This pays the interest to date.
>
> **Step 3.** Subtract the balance of the partial payment, after Step 2, from the original principal of the loan. This gives the new adjusted principal.
>
> **Step 4.** If another partial payment is made, repeat Steps 1, 2, and 3, using the adjusted principal and the number of days since the last partial payment.
>
> **Step 5.** After all partial payments have been credited to the loan, the maturity value is computed by adding the interest since the last partial payment to the adjusted principal.

EXAMPLE

Ivan Figueroa borrowed \$10,000 at 9% interest for 120 days. After 30 days, Ivan made a partial payment of \$2,000. After another 40 days, he made a second partial payment of \$3,000. What is the final amount due on the loan?

SOLUTION STRATEGY

Step 1. Compute the interest from the date of the loan to the partial payment. In this problem, the first partial payment was made on day 30.

$$I = PRT$$

$$I = 10,000 \times .09 \times \frac{30}{360} = 75$$

Interest = \$75.00

Step 2. Subtract the interest from the partial payment.

$2,000   partial payment
−   75   accumulated interest
$1,925   amount of partial payment left to reduce the principal

Step 3. Reduce the principal.

$10,000   original principal
−   1,925   amount of partial payment used to reduce principal
$8,075   new adjusted principal

Step 4. A second partial payment of $3,000 was made 40 days later. We now repeat Steps 1, 2, and 3, to properly credit the second partial payment. Remember, use the new adjusted principal and 40 days for this calculation.

Step 1.

$$I = PRT$$

$$I = \$8,075 \times .09 \times \frac{40}{360}$$

$$I = \$80.75 \quad \text{accumulated interest since last partial payment}$$

Step 2.

$3,000.00   partial payment
−   80.75   accumulated interest
$2,919.25   amount of partial payment left to reduce the principal

Step 3.

$8,075.00   principal
− 2,919.25   amount of partial payment used to reduce principal
$5,155.75   new adjusted principal

Step 5. Once all partial payments have been credited, we find the maturity value of the loan by calculating the interest due from the last partial payment to the maturity date, and adding it to the last adjusted principal. Note: The last partial payment was made on day 70 of the loan (30 + 40 = 70). Therefore, 50 days remain on the loan (120 − 70 = 50 days).

$$I = PRT$$

$$I = \$5,155.75 \times .09 \times \frac{50}{360}$$

$$I = \$64.45 \quad \text{interest from last partial payment to maturity date}$$

Maturity Value = Principal + Interest
Maturity Value = $5,155.75 + $64.45
Maturity Value = $5,220.20

TRY-IT   **EXERCISE**

15. **Jessica Gormley borrowed $15,000 at 12% ordinary interest for 100 days. On day 20 of the loan she made a partial payment of $4,000. On day 60 she made another partial payment of $5,000. What is the final amount due on the loan?**

Check your answer with the solution on page 335.

Compute the principal for the following loans (use ordinary interest when time is stated in days):

Complete, worked out solutions to exercises 1–20 appear in the appendix following the index.

	Principal	Rate	Time	Interest
1.	$1,250	12%	2 years	$300
2.	$5,000	9%	$1\frac{1}{2}$ years	$675
3.	$50,000	8%	9 months	$3,000
4.	$200,000	10.7%	90 days	$5,350
5.	$12,000	13.1%	210 days	$917

Compute the rate for the following loans (round answers to the nearest tenth percent; use ordinary interest when time is stated in days):

	Principal	Rate	Time	Interest
6.	$5,000	8%	3 years	$1,200
7.	$1,800	14%	5 months	$105
8.	$48,000	9.1%	60 days	$728
9.	$4,600	12.8%	168 days	$275
10.	$125,000	7.5%	2 years	$18,750

Use the ordinary interest method to compute the time for the following loans (round answers to the next higher day, when necessary):

	Principal	Rate	Time	Interest
11.	$18,000	12%	158 Days	$948
12.	$7,900	10.4%	100 Days	$228
13.	$4,500	$9\frac{3}{4}$%	308 Days	$375
14.	$25,000	8.9%	2 Years	$4,450
15.	$680	15%	180 Days	$51

Calculate the missing information for the following loans (round percents to the nearest tenth and days to the next higher day, when necessary):

	Principal	Rate	Time	Interest Method	Interest	Maturity Value
16.	$16,000	13%	132 Days	Ordinary	$760	$16,760.00
17.	$13,063.16	9.5%	100 days	Exact	$340	$13,403.16
18.	$3,600	14.3%	160 days	Exact	$225	$3,825.00
19.	$25,500	$11\frac{1}{4}$%	300 days	Ordinary	$2,390.63	$27,890.63
20.	$55,000	10.4%	256 Days	Exact	$4,000	$59,000

Solve the following word problems:

21. Williamson Motors, a Chevrolet dealership, borrowed $225,000 on April 16 to purchase a shipment of new cars. The interest rate was 9.3% using the ordinary interest method. The amount of interest was $9,600.

   a. For how many days was the loan?

   $$T = \frac{I}{PR} = \frac{9,600}{225,000 \times .093} = .4587814$$
   $$\underline{\times 360}$$
   $$166 \text{ Days}$$

   b. What was the maturity date of the loan?

   30
   − 16
   ‾‾‾‾
   14 Apr
   123 May-Aug
   + 29 Sept ——► September 29
   ‾‾‾‾‾‾‾
   166 Days

22. Ed Sandow took out a loan for \$3,500 at the Fortune Bank for 270 days. If the bank uses the ordinary interest method, what rate of interest was charged if the amount of interest was \$269? Round your answer to the nearest tenth percent.

$$R = \frac{I}{PT} = \frac{269}{3,500 \times \frac{270}{360}} = \underline{10.2\%}$$

23. Kathleen Abraham borrowed money to buy a car at 13.5% simple interest from her credit union. If the loan was repaid in 2 years and the amount of interest was \$2,700, how much did Kathleen borrow?

$$P = \frac{I}{RT} = \frac{2,700}{.135 \times 2} = \underline{\$10,000.00}$$

24. What is the maturity date of a loan for \$5,000, at 15% exact interest, taken out on June 3? The amount of interest on the loan was \$150.

$$T = \frac{I}{PR} = \frac{150}{5,000 \times .15} = \begin{array}{r} .2 \\ \times 365 \\ \hline 73 \text{ Days} \end{array}$$

June 3 + 73 days = $\underline{\text{August 15}}$

25. What rate of interest was charged on an ordinary interest loan for \$135,000, if the interest was \$4,400, and the time period was from January 16 to April 27? Round your answer to the nearest tenth percent.

$$
\begin{array}{r}
31 \\
- 16 \\
\hline
15 \text{ Days}
\end{array}
\quad
\begin{array}{l}
15 \text{ Jan} \\
59 \text{ Feb-Mar} \\
+ 27 \text{ Apr} \\
\hline
101 \text{ Days}
\end{array}
\qquad
R = \frac{I}{PT} = \frac{4,400}{135,000 \times \frac{101}{360}} = \underline{11.6\%}
$$

26. Rossen Garcia deposited \$8,000 in a savings account paying 6.25% simple interest. How long will it take for her investment to amount to \$10,000?

$$T = \frac{I}{PR} = \frac{2,000}{8,000 \times .0625} = \underline{4 \text{ Years}}$$

27. Matt Anderson borrowed \$10,000 at 12% ordinary interest, for 60 days. On day 20 of the loan Matt made a partial payment of \$4,000. What is the new maturity value of the loan?

$$I = PRT = 10,000 \times .12 \times \frac{20}{360} = \$66.67$$

$$
\begin{array}{ll}
4,000.00 \text{ Pd} & 10,000.00 \\
- 66.67 \text{ Int} & - 3,933.33 \\
\hline
\$3,933.33 & \$6,066.67 \text{ Adjusted balance}
\end{array}
$$

$$MV = P(1 + RT) = 6,066.67\left(1 + .12 \times \frac{40}{360}\right) = \underline{\$6,147.56}$$

28. Standard Plumbing Supplies borrowed \$60,000 on March 15 for 90 days. The rate was 13% using the ordinary interest method. On day 25 of the loan Standard made a partial payment of \$16,000, and on day 55 of the loan Standard made a second partial payment of \$12,000.

a. What is the new maturity value of the loan?

$$I = PRT = 60,000 \times .13 \times \frac{25}{360} = \$541.67$$

$$
\begin{array}{lll}
\$16,000.00 \text{ Pd} & \$60,000.00 & 55 \\
- 541.67 \text{ Int} & - 15,458.33 & - 25 \\
\hline
\$15,458.33 & \$44,541.67 \text{ Adj Bal} & 30 \text{ Days}
\end{array}
$$

$$I = PRT = 44,541.67 \times .13 \times \frac{30}{360} = \$482.53$$

$$
\begin{array}{lll}
\$12,000.00 \text{ Pd} & \$44,541.67 & 90 \\
- 482.53 \text{ Int} & - 11,517.47 & - 55 \\
\hline
\$11,517.47 & \$33,024.20 \text{ Adj Bal} & 35 \text{ Days left}
\end{array}
$$

$$MV = P(1 + RT) = 33,024.20\left(1 + .13 \times \frac{35}{360}\right) = \underline{\$33,441.59}$$

b. What is the maturity date of the loan?

$$\begin{array}{r} 31 \\ -\ 15 \\ \hline 16\ \text{Days} \end{array}$$

$$\begin{array}{l} 16\ \text{Mar} \\ 61\ \text{Apr-May} \\ +\ 13\ \text{June} \longrightarrow \text{June 13} \\ \hline 90\ \text{Days} \end{array}$$

29. a. How many years will it take $5,000 invested at 8% simple interest to double to $10,000?

$$T = \frac{I}{PR} = \frac{5,000}{5,000 \times .08} = \underline{\underline{12.5\ \text{Years}}}$$

b. How long will it take if the interest rate is increased to 10%?

$$T = \frac{I}{PR} = \frac{5,000}{5,000 \times .1} = \underline{\underline{10\ \text{Years}}}$$

SECTION III

UNDERSTANDING PROMISSORY NOTES AND DISCOUNTING

● **promissory note**

A debt instrument in which one party agrees to repay money to another, within a specified period of time. Promissory notes may be noninterest-bearing, at no interest, or interest-bearing, at a specified rate of interest.

Technically, the document that states the details of a loan, and is signed by the borrower, is known as a **promissory note**. *Promissory* means it is a promise to pay the principal back to the lender on a certain date. *Note* means that the document is a negotiable instrument, and can be transferred or sold to others not involved in the original loan. Much like a check, with proper endorsement by the payee, the note can be transferred to another person, company, or lending institution.

Promissory notes are either noninterest-bearing or interest-bearing. When a note is noninterest-bearing, the maturity value equals the principal, since there is no interest being charged. With interest-bearing notes, the maturity value equals the principal plus the interest.

Exhibit 10-1 is an example of a typical promissory note with its parts labeled. Notice the similarity between a note and a check. A list explaining the labels follows.

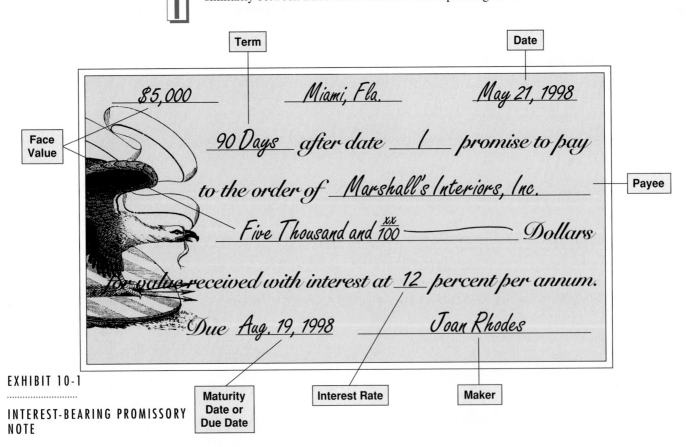

EXHIBIT 10-1

················

INTEREST-BEARING PROMISSORY NOTE

Maker: The person or company borrowing the money and issuing the note.

Payee: The person or institution lending the money and receiving the payment.

Term: The time period of the note, usually stated in days.

Date: The date that the note is issued.

Face Value or Principal: The amount of money borrowed.

Interest Rate: The annual rate of interest being charged.

Maturity Date or Due Date: The date when maturity value is due the payee.

10-10 Calculating Bank Discount and Proceeds for Simple Discount Notes

To this point, we have been dealing with simple interest notes where the interest was added to the principal to determine the maturity value. Another way of lending money is to deduct the interest from the principal at the beginning of the loan, and give the borrower the difference. These are known as **simple discount notes.** When this method is used, the amount of interest charged is known as the **bank discount,** and the amount that the borrower receives is known as the **proceeds.** When the term of the note is over, the borrower will repay the entire principal or face value of the note as the maturity value.

    For example, Julie goes to a bank and signs a simple interest note for $5,000. If the interest charge amounts to $500, she will receive $5,000 at the beginning of the note and repay $5,500 upon maturity of the note. If the bank used a simple discount note for Julie's loan, the bank discount (interest) would be deducted from the face value (principal). Julie's proceeds on the loan would be $4,500 and upon maturity she would pay $5,000.

Bank Discount

Because bank discount is the same as interest, we use the formula $I = PRT$ as before, substituting bank discount for interest, face value for principal, and discount rate for interest rate:

$$\textbf{Bank discount} = \textbf{Face value} \times \textbf{Discount rate} \times \textbf{Time}$$

Proceeds

The proceeds of a note are calculated using the following formula:

$$\textbf{Proceeds} = \textbf{Face value} - \textbf{Bank discount}$$

- **simple discount note**
  Promissory note in which the interest is deducted from the principal at the beginning of the loan.

- **bank discount**
  The amount of interest charged (deducted from principal) on a discounted promissory note.

- **proceeds**
  The amount of money that the borrower receives at the time a discounted note is made.

EXAMPLE

What are the bank discount and proceeds of a $7,000 note at a 14% discount rate, for 9 months?

SOLUTION STRATEGY

Bank discount = Face value × Discount rate × Time

$$\text{Bank discount} = \$7,000 \times .14 \times \frac{9}{12}$$

Bank discount = $\underline{\$735}$

Proceeds = Face value − Bank discount

Proceeds = $7,000 − $735

Proceeds = $\underline{\$6,265}$

16. **Daryl Fox signed a $20,000 simple discount promissory note at the Manhattan International Bank. The discount rate is 13%, and the term of the note is 11 months. What is the amount of the bank discount, and what are Daryl's proceeds on the loan?**

Check your answers with the solutions on page 335.

10-11 Calculating True or Effective Rate of Interest for a Simple Discount Note

In a simple interest note, the borrower receives the full face value, whereas with a simple discount note the borrower receives only the proceeds. Because the proceeds are less than the face value, the stated discount rate is not the true or actual interest rate of the note. To protect the consumer, the United States Congress has passed legislation requiring all lending institutions to quote the **true** or **effective interest rate** for all loans. Effective interest rate is calculated by substituting the bank discount for interest, and the proceeds for principal, in the rate formula,

● **true, or effective interest rate**
The actual interest rate charged on a discounted note. Takes into account the fact that the borrower does not receive the full amount of the principal.

$$\text{Effective interest rate} = \frac{\text{Bank discount}}{\text{Proceeds} \times \text{Time}}$$

EXAMPLE

What is the effective interest rate of a simple discount note for $10,000, at a bank discount rate of 14%, for a period of 3 months? (Round to the nearest tenth percent.)

SOLUTION STRATEGY

To find the effective interest rate, we must first calculate the amount of the bank discount and the proceeds of the note, then substitute these numbers in the effective interest rate formula.

Step 1. Bank Discount

$$\text{Bank discount} = \text{Face value} \times \text{Discount rate} \times \text{Time}$$

$$\text{Bank discount} = 10,000 \times .14 \times \frac{3}{12}$$

$$\text{Bank discount} = \underline{\$350}$$

Step 2. Proceeds

$$\text{Proceeds} = \text{Face value} - \text{Bank discount}$$

$$\text{Proceeds} = 10,000 - 350$$

$$\text{Proceeds} = \underline{\$9,650}$$

Step 3. Effective Interest Rate

$$\text{Effective interest rate} = \frac{\text{Bank discount}}{\text{Proceeds} \times \text{Time}}$$

$$\text{Effective interest rate} = \frac{350}{9,650 \times \frac{3}{12}}$$

$$\text{Effective interest rate} = \frac{350}{2,412.50}$$

$$\text{Effective interest rate} = .14507 \text{ or } \underline{14.5\%}$$

TRY-IT   **EXERCISE**

17. **What is the effective interest rate of a simple discount note for $40,000, at a bank discount rate of 11%, for a period of 9 months? Round your answer to hundredths.**

Check your answer with the solution on page 335.

10-12 Discounting Notes before Maturity

Frequently in business, companies extend credit to their customers by accepting short-term promissory notes as payment for goods or services. These notes are simple interest and are usually for less than one year. Prior to the maturity date of these notes, the payee (lender) may take the note to a bank and sell it. This is a convenient way for a company or individual to cash in a note at any time before maturity. This process is known as **discounting a note.**

When a note is discounted at a bank, the original payee receives the proceeds of the discounted note, and the bank (the new payee) receives the maturity value of the note when it matures. The time period used to calculate the proceeds is from the date the note is discounted to the maturity date. This is known as the **discount period.**

Exhibit 10-2 illustrates the time-line for a 90-day simple interest note discounted on the 60th day.

● **discounting a note**
A process whereby a company or individual can cash in or sell a promissory note, at a discount, at any time before maturity.

● **discount period**
The time period between the date a note is discounted and the maturity date. Used to calculate the proceeds of a discounted note.

STEPS FOR DISCOUNTING A NOTE BEFORE MATURITY:

Step 1. Calculate the maturity value of the note. If the original note was noninterest-bearing, the maturity value will be the same as the face value. If the original note was interest-bearing, the maturity value should be calculated as usual:

Maturity value = Principal (1 + Rate × Time)

Step 2. Determine the number of days or months of the discount period. The discount period is used as the numerator of the time in Step 3.

Step 3. Calculate the amount of the bank discount using the formula:

Bank discount = Maturity value × Discount rate × Time

Step 4. Calculate the proceeds of the note using the formula:

Proceeds = Maturity value − Bank discount

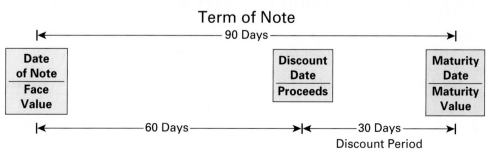

Term of Note

EXHIBIT 10-2

TIME-LINE FOR DISCOUNTED NOTE

Bradley Distributors received a $15,000 promissory note for 5 months at 12% simple interest from one of its customers. After 3 months, Bradley needed cash so it discounted the note at the InterAmerican Bank at a discount rate of 14%. What are the proceeds Bradley will receive from the discounted note?

SOLUTION STRATEGY

Step 1. Calculate the maturity value of the original note:

$$\text{Maturity value} = \text{Principal} \ (1 + \text{Rate} \times \text{Time})$$

$$\text{Maturity value} = 15,000 \ (1 + .12 \times \frac{5}{12})$$

$$\text{Maturity value} = 15,000 \ (1 + .05) = 15,000(1.05)$$

$$\text{Maturity value} = \underline{\$15,750}$$

Step 2. Find the months or days of the discount period:
In this example, the note was discounted after 3 months of a 5-month note, therefore the discount period is <u>2 months</u> (5 months − 3 months = 2 months).

Step 3. Calculate the amount of the bank discount:

$$\text{Bank discount} = \text{Maturity value} \times \text{Discount rate} \times \text{Time}$$

$$\text{Bank discount} = \$15,750 \times .14 \times \frac{2}{12}$$

$$\text{Bank discount} = \underline{\$367.50}$$

Step 4. Calculate the proceeds of the discounted note:

$$\text{Proceeds} = \text{Maturity value} - \text{Bank discount}$$

$$\text{Proceeds} = \$15,750.00 - \$367.50$$

$$\text{Proceeds} = \underline{\$15,382.50}$$

TRY-IT EXERCISE

18. Lakeside Lumber received a $35,000 promissory note at 10% simple interest for 6 months from one of its customers. After 4 months, the note was discounted at the Goldenview Bank at a discount rate of 14%. What are the proceeds Lakeside will receive from the discounted note?

Check your answer with the solution on page 336.

 REVIEW EXERCISES CHAPTER 10—SECTION III

Calculate the bank discount and proceeds for the following simple discount notes (use the ordinary interest method, 360 days, when applicable):

	Face Value	Discount Rate	Term	Bank Discount	Proceeds
1.	$4,500	13%	6 months	$292.50	$4,207.50
2.	$235	11.3%	50 days	$3.69	$231.31
3.	$1,850	$12\frac{1}{2}\%$	1 year	$231.25	$1,618.75

Complete, worked out solutions to exercises 1–3 appear in the appendix following the index.

4. $35,000   9.65%   11 months $3,096.04 $31,903.96   Complete, worked out solutions to ex-

5. $7,800 $8\frac{1}{4}\%$ 130 days $232.38 $7,567.62   ercises 4–18 appear in the appendix following the index.

Using ordinary interest, 360 days, calculate the missing information for the following simple discount notes:

	Face Value	Discount Rate	Date of Note	Term	Maturity Date	Bank Discount	Proceeds
6.	$16,800	10%	June 3	80 days	Aug 22	$373.33	$16,426.67
7.	$5,000	14.7%	April 16	84 Days	July 9	$171.50	$4,828.50
8.	$800	12.1%	Sept. 3	109 days	Dec 21	$29.31	$770.69
9.	$1,300	$9\frac{1}{2}\%$	Aug. 19	100 Days	Nov. 27	$34.31	$1,265.69
10.	$75,000	15%	May 7	53 days	June 29	$1,656.25	$73,343.75

Using ordinary interest, 360 days, calculate the bank discount, proceeds, and effective rate for the following simple discount notes (round effective rate to the nearest hundredth percent):

	Face Value	Discount Rate	Term	Bank Discount	Proceeds	Effective Rate
11.	$2,700	14%	126 days	$132.30	$2,567.70	14.72%
12.	$6,505	10.39%	73 days	$137.05	$6,367.95	10.61%
13.	$3,800	$14\frac{1}{2}\%$	140 days	$214.28	$3,585.72	15.37%
14.	$95,000	9.7%	45 days	$1,151.88	$93,848.12	9.82%
15.	$57,500	$12\frac{3}{4}\%$	230 days	$4,683.85	$52,816.15	13.88%

The following interest-bearing promissory notes were discounted at a bank by the payee before maturity. Use the ordinary interest method, 360 days, to calculate the missing information:

	Face Value	Interest Rate	Date of Note	Term of Note	Maturity Date	Maturity Value	Date of Discount	Discount Period	Discount Rate	Proceeds
16.	$2,500	12%	Mar. 4	70 days	May 13	$2,558.33	Apr. 15	28 Days	13%	$2,532.46
17.	$4,000	10.4%	Dec. 12	50 days	Jan 31	$4,057.78	Jan. 19	12 Days	15%	$4,037.49
18.	$850	$13\frac{1}{2}\%$	June 7	125 days	Oct 10	$889.84	Sept. 3	37 Days	16.5%	$874.75

Use the ordinary interest method, 360 days, to solve the following word problems:

19. Lisa Figueroa signed a $24,000 simple discount promissory note at the Central Bank. The discount rate is 14%, and the note was made on February 19, for 50 days.

a. What proceeds will Lisa receive on the note?

$$\text{Bank discount} = FV \times R \times T = 24,000 \times .14 \times \frac{50}{360} = \$466.67$$

$$\text{Proceeds} = FV - \text{Discount} = 24,000.00 - 466.67 = \underline{\$23,533.33}$$

b. What is the maturity date of the note?

$$\begin{array}{r} \text{Maturity} \\ \text{date} \end{array} = \begin{array}{r} 28 \\ -19 \\ \hline 9 \text{ Days} \end{array} \quad \begin{array}{l} 9 \text{ Feb} \\ 31 \text{ Mar} \\ +10 \text{ Apr} \longrightarrow \underline{\text{April 10}} \\ \hline 50 \text{ Days} \end{array}$$

20. Jeff Relue signed a $10,000 simple discount promissory note at a bank discount rate of 13%. If the term of the note was 125 days, what was the effective rate of interest of the note? Round your answer to the nearest hundredth percent.

$$\text{Bank discount} = FV \times R \times T = 10,000 \times .13 \times \frac{125}{360} = \$451.39$$

$$\text{Proceeds} = FV - \text{Discount} = 10,000.00 - 451.39 = 9,548.61$$

$$\begin{array}{r} \text{Effective} \\ \text{rate} \end{array} = \frac{\text{Discount}}{\text{Proceeds} \times \text{Time}} = \frac{451.39}{9,548.61 \times \frac{125}{360}} = \underline{13.61\%}$$

21. Berkshire Manufacturing received a $40,000 promissory note at 12% simple interest for 95 days from one of its customers. After 70 days Berkshire discounted the note at the Weston Hills Bank at a discount rate of 15%. The note was made on September 12.

a. What is the maturity date of the note?

$$\begin{array}{ll} \text{Maturity} \\ \text{date} \end{array} = \begin{array}{r} 30 \\ -\,12 \\ \hline 18 \text{ Days} \end{array} \quad \begin{array}{l} 18 \text{ Sept} \\ 61 \text{ Oct-Nov} \\ +\,16 \text{ Dec} \\ \hline 95 \text{ Days} \end{array} \longrightarrow \underline{\underline{\text{December 16}}}$$

b. What is the maturity value of the note?

$$MV = FV(1 + RT) = 40{,}000\left(1 + .12 \times \frac{95}{360}\right) = \underline{\underline{\$41{,}266.67}}$$

c. What is the discount date of the note?

$$\begin{array}{ll} \text{Discount} \\ \text{date} \end{array} = \begin{array}{r} 30 \\ -\,12 \\ \hline 18 \text{ Days} \end{array} \quad \begin{array}{l} 18 \text{ Sept} \\ 31 \text{ Oct} \\ +\,21 \text{ Nov} \\ \hline 70 \text{ Days} \end{array} \longrightarrow \underline{\underline{\text{November 21}}}$$

d. What proceeds will Berkshire receive after discounting the note?

$$\text{Bank discount} = MV \times R \times T = 41{,}266.67 \times .15 \times \frac{25}{360} = \$429.86$$

$$\text{Proceeds} = MV - \text{disc} = 41{,}266.67 - 429.86 = \underline{\underline{\$40{,}836.81}}$$

CHAPTER 10 ■ SIMPLE INTEREST AND PROMISSORY NOTES

FORMULAS

Interest = Principal × Rate × Time

$$\textbf{Exact time} = \frac{\textbf{Number of days of a loan}}{\textbf{365}}$$

$$\textbf{Ordinary time} = \frac{\textbf{Number of days of a loan}}{\textbf{360}}$$

Maturity value = Principal + Interest

Maturity value = Principal (1 + Rate × Time)

$$\textbf{Principal} = \frac{\textbf{Interest}}{\textbf{Rate} \times \textbf{Time}}$$

$$\textbf{Rate} = \frac{\textbf{Interest}}{\textbf{Principal} \times \textbf{Time}}$$

$$\textbf{Time} = \frac{\textbf{Interest}}{\textbf{Principal} \times \textbf{Rate}}$$

Bank discount = Face value × Discount rate × Time

Proceeds = Face value − Bank discount

$$\textbf{Effective interest rate} = \frac{\textbf{Bank discount}}{\textbf{Proceeds} \times \textbf{Time}}$$

SECTION I   UNDERSTANDING AND COMPUTING SIMPLE INTEREST

Topic	P/O, Page	Important Concepts	Illustrative Examples
Computing Simple Interest for Loans With Terms of Years or Months	10–1 308	Simple interest is calculated by using the formula, $I = PRT$. **Interest = Principal × Rate × Time** Note: Time is always expressed in years or fractions of a year.	What is the amount of interest for a loan of $20,000, at 12% simple interest, for 9 months? $$I = 20,000 \times .12 \times \frac{9}{12}$$ Interest = $\underline{\$1,800.00}$
Calculating Interest for Loans with Terms of Days by the Exact Interest Method	10–2 310	Exact interest uses *365 days* as the time factor denominator. $$\text{Time} = \frac{\text{Number of days of a loan}}{365}$$	Using the exact interest method, what is the amount of interest on a loan of $5,000, at 8%, for 95 days? $$I = PRT$$ $$I = 5,000 \times .08 \times \frac{95}{365}$$ Interest = $\underline{\$104.11}$
Calculating Interest for Loans with Terms of Days by the Ordinary Interest Method	10–2 310	Ordinary interest uses *360 days* as the time factor denominator. $$\text{Time} = \frac{\text{Number of days of a loan}}{360}$$	Using the ordinary interest method, what is the amount of interest on a loan of $8,000, at 9%, for 120 days? $$I = PRT$$ $$I = 8,000 \times .09 \times \frac{120}{360}$$ Interest = $\underline{\$240.00}$
Calculating the Maturity Value of a Loan	10–3 311	When the time period of a loan is over, the loan is said to mature. The total payback of principal and interest is known as the maturity value of a loan. **Maturity value = Principal + Interest** **Maturity value = Principal (1 + Rate × Time)**	What is the maturity value of a loan for $50,000, at 12% interest, for 3 years? $$MV = 50,000(1 + .12 \times 3)$$ $$MV = 50,000(1.36)$$ Maturity Value = $\underline{\$68,000.00}$
Calculating the Number of Days of a Loan	10–4 312	1. Determine the number of days remaining in the first month by subtracting the loan date from the number of days in that month. 2. List the number of days for each succeeding whole month. 3. List the number of loan days in the last month. 4. Add the days from Steps 1, 2, and 3.	John Corwin borrowed money from the Republic Bank on May 5 and repaid the loan on August 19. For how many days was this loan? May 31 −May 5 $\underline{\hphantom{-}}$ 26 days in May 61 June–July +19 August $\underline{\hphantom{+}}$ 106 Days

I, continued

Topic	P/O, Page	Important Concepts	Illustrative Examples
Determining the Maturity Date of a Loan	10–5 313	**1.** Determine the number of days remaining in the first month. **2.** Subtract days from Step 1 from number of days in the loan. **3.** Subtract days in each succeeding whole month until you reach a month where the difference is less than the days in that month. The maturity date will be the day of that month that corresponds to the difference.	What is the maturity date of a loan taken out on June 9 for 100 days? $$\begin{array}{r} \text{June } 30 \\ \underline{\text{June} - 9} \\ 21 \text{ days in June} \end{array}$$ $$\begin{array}{r} 100 \text{ days of the loan} \\ \underline{-\ 21} \text{ days in June} \\ 79 \end{array}$$ $$\begin{array}{r} \underline{-31} \text{ days in July} \\ 48 \end{array}$$ $$\begin{array}{r} \underline{-31} \text{ days in August} \\ 17 \end{array}$$ At this point, the difference, 17, is less than the days in September, therefore the maturity date is <u>September 17.</u>

SECTION II   USING THE SIMPLE INTEREST FORMULA

Solving for the Principal	10–6 317	$$\text{Principal} = \frac{\text{Interest}}{\text{Rate} \times \text{Time}}$$ $\triangle$ I / ⓟ R T	Shana Lum borrowed money at 10% interest for 2 years. If the interest charge was $800, how much principal did Shana borrow? $$\text{Principal} = \frac{800}{.10 \times 2} = \frac{800}{.2}$$ $$\text{Principal} = \underline{\$4,000.00}$$
Solving for the Rate	10–7 318	$$\text{Rate} = \frac{\text{Interest}}{\text{Principal} \times \text{Time}}$$ $\triangle$ I / P ⓡ T	Glenn Hartmann borrowed $3,000 for 75 days. If the interest was $90 using ordinary interest, what was the rate on Glenn's loan? $$\text{Rate} = \frac{90}{3,000 \times \dfrac{75}{360}} = \frac{90}{625}$$ $$\text{Rate} = .144 = \underline{14.4\%}$$

II, continued

Topic	P/O, Page	Important Concepts	Illustrative Examples
Solving for the Time	10–8 319	When solving for time, whole numbers are years, and decimals are multiplied by 360 or 365 to get days. Any fraction of a day should be rounded up to the next higher day, since lending institutions consider any portion of a day to be another day. $$\text{Time} = \frac{\text{Interest}}{\text{Principal} \times \text{Rate}}$$ Triangle diagram with I on top, P, R, T below.	What is the time period of a loan for $20,000 at 9% ordinary interest if the amount of interest is $1,000? $$\text{Time} = \frac{1{,}000}{20{,}000 \times .09} = \frac{1{,}000}{1{,}800}$$ Time = .5555555 $\times$ 360 199.99 = <u>200 days</u>
Calculating Loans Involving Partial Payments before Maturity	10–9 320	1. Compute the interest due from the date of loan to the date of partial payment. 2. Subtract the interest (Step 1) from the partial payment. 3. The balance of the partial payment is used to reduce the principal. 4. Maturity value is computed by adding the interest since the last partial payment to the adjusted principal.	Larry Mager borrowed $7,000 at 10% ordinary interest for 120 days. After 90 days Larry made a partial payment of $3,000. What is the new maturity value of the loan? $I = PRT$ $$I = 7{,}000 \times .10 \times \frac{90}{360} = \$175$$ $3,000 partial payment −175 accumulated interest $2,825 reduces principal $7,000 original principal −2,825 $4,175 adjusted principal Days remaining = 120 − 90 = 30 $I = PRT$ $$I = 4{,}175 \times .10 \times \frac{30}{360} = \$34.79$$ Maturity value = $P + I$ MV = 4,175.00 + 34.79 Maturity value = <u>$4,209.79</u>

SECTION III   UNDERSTANDING PROMISSORY NOTES AND DISCOUNTING

Topic	P/O, Page	Important Concepts	Illustrative Examples
Calculating Bank Discount and Proceeds for a Simple Discount Note	10–10 325	With discounting, the interest, known as the bank discount, is deducted from the face value of the loan. The borrower gets the difference, known as the proceeds. Bank discount = Face value × Discount rate × Time Proceeds = Face value – Bank discount	What are the bank discount and proceeds of a $10,000 note, discounted at 12% for 6 months? $\text{Bank disc} = 10{,}000 \times .12 \times \dfrac{6}{12}$ Bank disc = $600 Proceeds = $10{,}000 - 600 = \underline{\$9{,}400}$
Calculating True or Effective Rate of Interest for a Simple Discount Note	10–11 326	Since the proceeds are less than the face value of a loan, the true or effective interest rate is higher than the stated bank discount rate. $\text{Effective rate} = \dfrac{\text{Bank discount}}{\text{Proceeds} \times \text{Time}}$	What is the effective rate of a simple discount note for $20,000, at a bank discount of 15%, for a period of 9 months? Bank disc = $FV \times R \times T$ $\text{Bank disc} = 20{,}000 \times .15 \times \dfrac{9}{12}$ Bank disc = $2,250 Proceeds = Face Value – Discount Proceeds = $20{,}000 - 2{,}250$ Proceeds = $17,750 $\text{Effective rate} = \dfrac{2{,}250}{17{,}750 \times \dfrac{9}{12}}$ Effective rate = $\underline{16.9\%}$
Discounting Notes before Maturity	10–12 327	Frequently companies extend credit to their customers by accepting short-term promissory notes as payment for goods or services. These notes can be cashed in early by discounting them at a bank and receiving the proceeds. 1. Calculate the maturity value $MV = P(1 + RT)$ 2. Determine the discount period. 3. Calculate the bank discount. Bank discount = $MV \times R \times T$ 4. Calculate the proceeds. Proceeds = MV – Discount	Dixie Food Wholesalers received a $100,000 promissory note for 6 months, at 11% interest, from SuperSaver Supermarkets. If Dixie discounts the note after 4 months at a discount rate of 15%, what proceeds will they receive? $MV = 100{,}000(1 + .11 \times \dfrac{6}{12})$ $MV = \$105{,}500$ Discount period = 2 months (6–4) $\text{Bank disc} = 105{,}500 \times .15 \times \dfrac{2}{12}$ Bank disc = $2,637.50 Proceeds = $105{,}500.00 - 2{,}637.50$ Proceeds = $\underline{\$102{,}862.50}$

1. $I = PRT = 4,000 \times .07 \times 2.25 = \underline{\underline{\$630.00}}$

2. $I = PRT = 45,000 \times .0975 \times \dfrac{3}{12} = \underline{\underline{\$1,096.88}}$

3. $I = PRT = 130,000 \times .104 \times \dfrac{42}{12} = \underline{\underline{\$47,320.00}}$

4. $I = PRT = 15,000 \times .095 \times \dfrac{250}{360} = \underline{\underline{\$989.58}}$

5. $I = PRT = 23,000 \times .08 \times \dfrac{119}{365} = \underline{\underline{\$599.89}}$

6. $I = PRT = 15,400 \times .065 \times \dfrac{24}{12} = \underline{\underline{\$2,002.00}}$

$MV = P + I = 15,400 + 2,002 = \underline{\underline{\$17,402.00}}$

7. $MV = P(1 + RT) = 450,000(1 + .08 \times \dfrac{9}{12}) = \underline{\underline{\$477,000.00}}$

8.
$$\begin{array}{r} \text{Days of} \\ \text{loan} \end{array} = \begin{array}{r} 30 \\ -\ 4 \\ \hline 26 \text{ days} \end{array} \nearrow \begin{array}{rl} 26 & \text{April} \\ 61 & \text{May–June} \\ +18 & \text{July} \\ \hline 105 & \text{days} \end{array}$$

9.
$$\begin{array}{r} \text{Days of} \\ \text{loan} \end{array} = \begin{array}{r} 30 \\ -15 \\ \hline 15 \text{ days} \end{array} \nearrow \begin{array}{rl} 15 & \text{June} \\ 92 & \text{July–Sept.} \\ +\ 9 & \text{Oct.} \\ \hline 116 & \text{days} \end{array}$$

$I = PRT = 3,500 \times .11 \times \dfrac{116}{365} = \underline{\underline{\$122.36}}$

10.
$$\begin{array}{r} \text{Maturity} \\ \text{date} \end{array} = \begin{array}{r} 30 \\ -\ 9 \\ \hline 21 \text{ days} \end{array} \nearrow \begin{array}{rl} 21 & \text{Sept.} \\ 92 & \text{Oct.–Dec.} \\ +12 & \text{Jan.} \longrightarrow \underline{\underline{\text{January 12}}} \\ \hline 125 & \text{days} \end{array}$$

11. $MV = P(1 + RT) = 9,000(1 + .10 \times \dfrac{80}{360}) = \underline{\underline{\$9,200.00}}$

$$\begin{array}{r} \text{Maturity} \\ \text{date} \end{array} = \begin{array}{r} 31 \\ -21 \\ \hline 10 \text{ days} \end{array} \nearrow \begin{array}{rl} 10 & \text{Oct.} \\ 61 & \text{Nov.–Dec.} \\ +\ 9 & \text{Jan.} \longrightarrow \underline{\underline{\text{January 9}}} \\ \hline 80 & \text{days} \end{array}$$

12. $P = \dfrac{I}{RT} = \dfrac{560}{.09 \times \dfrac{125}{360}} = \underline{\underline{\$17,920.00}}$

13. $R = \dfrac{I}{PT} = \dfrac{1,960}{25,000 \times \dfrac{245}{360}} = \underline{\underline{11.52\%}}$

14. $T = \dfrac{I}{PR} = \dfrac{650}{15,000 \times .095} = .4561404$
$\times\ \ \ 360$
$164.2 = \underline{\underline{165 \text{ days}}}$

15. $I = PRT = 15,000 \times .12 \times \dfrac{20}{360} = \$100$ \qquad 1st Part pay = 20 days

$$\begin{array}{rl} 4,000 & \text{pmt} \\ -\ 100 & \text{int} \\ \hline 3,900 & \end{array} \qquad \begin{array}{l} 15,000 \\ -\ 3,900 \\ \hline 11,100 \text{ Adj. Prin.} \end{array}$$

$I = PRT = 11,100 \times .12 \times \dfrac{40}{360} = \$148$ \qquad 2nd Part pay = 40 days (60–20)

$$\begin{array}{rl} 5,000 & \text{pmt} \\ -\ 148 & \text{int} \\ \hline 4,852 & \end{array} \qquad \begin{array}{l} 11,100 \\ -\ 4,852 \\ \hline 6,248 \text{ Adj. Prin.} \end{array} \qquad \text{Days remaining} = 40\ (100\text{–}60)$$

$I = PRT = 6,248 \times .12 \times \dfrac{40}{360} = \$83.31$

Final due $= P + I = 6,248.00 + 83.31 = \underline{\underline{\$6,331.31}}$

16. Bank discount $= FV \times R \times T = 20,000 \times .13 \times \dfrac{11}{12} = \underline{\underline{\$2,383.33}}$

Proceeds $= FV - \text{Disc} = 20,000 - 2,383.33 = \underline{\underline{\$17,616.67}}$

17. Bank discount $= FV \times R \times T = 40,000 \times .11 \times \dfrac{9}{12} = \$3,300.00$

Proceeds $= FV - \text{Disc} = 40,000 - 3,300 = \$36,700.00$

Effective rate $= \dfrac{\text{Bank discount}}{\text{Proceeds} \times \text{Time}} = \dfrac{3,300}{36,700 \times \dfrac{9}{12}} = \underline{\underline{11.99\%}}$

18. $MV = P(1 + RT) = 35,000(1 + .10 \times \dfrac{6}{12}) = \$36,750$

Discount period $= \begin{array}{r} 6 \text{ months} \\ -\ 4 \text{ months} \\ \hline 2 \text{ months} \end{array}$

Bank discount $= MV \times R \times T = 36,750 \times .14 \times \dfrac{2}{12} = \$857.50$

Proceeds $= MV - \text{Disc} = \$36,750.00 - 857.50 = \underline{\$35,892.50}$

Using the exact interest method (365 days) find the amount of interest on the following loans:

	Principal	Rate	Time	Exact Interest
1.	$15,000	13%	120 days	$641.10
2.	$1,700	$12\frac{1}{2}\%$	33 days	$19.21

Using the ordinary interest method (360 days) find the amount of interest on the following loans:

	Principal	Rate	Time	Ordinary Interest
3.	$20,600	12%	98 days	$672.93
4.	$286,000	$13\frac{1}{2}\%$	224 days	$24,024.00

What is the maturity value of the following loans (use $MV = P(1 + RT)$ to find the maturity values):

	Principal	Rate	Time	Maturity Value
5.	$15,800	14%	4 years	$24,648.00
6.	$120,740	$11\frac{3}{4}\%$	7 months	$129,015.72

From the following information, determine the number of days of each loan:

	Loan Date	Due Date	Number of Days
7.	April 16	August 1	107
8.	October 20	December 18	59

From the following information, determine the maturity date of each loan:

	Loan Date	Time Loan	Maturity Date
9.	November 30	55 days	Jan 24
10.	May 15	111 days	Sept 3

Compute the principal for the following loans (round answers to the nearest cent):

	Principal	Rate	Time	Interest
11.	$11,666.67	12%	2 years	$2,800
12.	$67,428.57	$10\frac{1}{2}\%$	10 months	$5,900

Compute the rate for the following loans (round answers to the nearest tenth percent):

	Principal	Rate	Time	Interest
13.	$2,200	9.1%	4 years	$800
14.	$50,000	12%	9 months	$4,500

Use the ordinary interest method to compute the time for the following loans (round answers to the next higher day, when necessary):

	Principal	Rate	Time	Interest
15.	$13,500	13%	72 days	$350
16.	$7,900	10.4%	274 days	$625

Name_____

Class_____

ANSWERS

1. _____$641.10_____
2. _____$19.21_____
3. _____$672.93_____
4. _____$24,024.00_____
5. _____$24,648.00_____
6. _____$129,015.72_____
7. _____107_____
8. _____59_____
9. _____Jan 24_____
10. _____Sept 3_____
11. _____$11,666.67_____
12. _____$67,428.57_____
13. _____9.1%_____
14. _____12%_____
15. _____72 days_____
16. _____274 days_____

Complete, worked out solutions to questions 1–16 appear in the appendix following the index.

Name_____

Class_____

17. _____190 days_____

_____$13,960.00_____

18. _____$40,265.62_____

_____$42,055.62_____

19. _____15.2%_____

_____$2,795.00_____

20. _____131 days_____

_____$2,365.28_____

_____$47,634.72_____

21. _____Jan 20_____

_____$20,088.54_____

_____$854,911.46_____

22. _____$393.75_____

_____$22,106.25_____

_____10.69%_____

23. _____$10,544.72_____

_____$279,455.28_____

_____12.35%_____

24. _____Apr 5_____

_____$8,202.89_____

_____35 days_____

_____$8,083.26_____

25. _____Aug 25_____

_____$5,642.31_____

_____34 days_____

_____$5,569.30_____

26. a. _____$227.95_____

b. _____$4,227.95_____

c. _____October 30_____

Calculate the missing information for the following loans (round percents to the nearest tenth, and days to the next higher day, when necessary):

	Principal	Rate	Time	Interest Method	Interest	Maturity Value
17.	$13,000	14%	190 days	Ordinary	$960	$13,960.00
18.	$40,265.62	12.2%	133 days	Exact	$1,790	$42,055.62
19.	$2,500	15.2%	280 days	Ordinary	$295	$2,795.00

Using ordinary interest, calculate the missing information for the following simple discount notes:

	Face Value	Discount Rate	Date of Note	Term	Maturity Date	Bank Discount	Proceeds
20.	$50,000	13%	Apr. 5	131 days	Aug. 14	$2,365.28	$47,634.72
21.	$875,000	$9\frac{1}{2}$%	Oct. 25	87 days	Jan 20	$20,088.54	$854,911.46

Using ordinary interest (360 days) calculate the bank discount, proceeds, and effective rate for the following simple discount notes (round effective rate to the nearest hundredth percent):

	Face Value	Discount Rate	Term	Bank Discount	Proceeds	Effective Rate
22.	$22,500	$10\frac{1}{2}$%	60 days	$393.75	$22,106.25	10.69%
23.	$290,000	11.9%	110 days	$10,544.72	$279,455.28	12.35%

The following interest-bearing promissory notes were discounted at a bank by the payee before maturity. Use the ordinary interest method (360 days) to solve for the missing information:

	Face Value	Interest Rate	Date of Note	Term of Note	Maturity Date	Maturity Value	Date Note Discounted	Discount Period	Discount Rate	Proceeds
24.	$8,000	11%	Jan. 12	83 days	Apr 5	$8,202.89	Mar. 1	35 days	15%	$8,083.26
25.	$5,500	$13\frac{1}{2}$%	June 17	69 days	Aug 25	$5,642.31	July 22	34 days	13.7%	$5,569.30

Solve the following word problems:

26. On May 23, Debra Hoover borrowed $4,000 from the Summerville Credit Union at 13%, for 160 days. The credit union uses the exact interest method.

a. What was the amount of interest on the loan?

$$I = PRT = 4,000 \times .13 \times \frac{160}{365} = \underline{\$227.95}$$

b. What was the maturity value of the loan?

$$MV = P + I = 4,000.00 + 227.95 = \underline{\$4,227.95}$$

c. What is the maturity date of the loan?

$$\text{Maturity date} = \begin{array}{r} 31 \\ -23 \\ \hline 8 \text{ Days} \end{array}$$

8 May
122 June-Sept
+ 30 Oct ⟶ October 30
160 Days

Complete, worked out solutions to questions 17–25 appear in the appendix following the index.

27. Robert Romero missed an income tax payment of $2,600. The Internal Revenue Service charges a 15% simple interest penalty calculated by the exact interest method. If the tax was due on April 15 but was paid on July 17, what is the amount of the penalty charge?

$$\begin{array}{r} 30 \\ -\ 15 \\ \hline 15 \text{ Days} \end{array} \qquad \begin{array}{l} 15 \text{ Apr} \\ 61 \text{ May-June} \\ +\ 17 \text{ July} \\ \hline 93 \text{ Days} \end{array}$$

$$I = PRT = 2,600 \times .15 \times \frac{93}{365} = \underline{\$99.37}$$

28. Sam Duque borrowed money to buy furniture from his credit union at 13.2% simple interest. If the loan was repaid in $2\frac{1}{2}$ years and the amount of interest was $1,320, how much did Sam borrow?

$$P = \frac{I}{RT} = \frac{1,320}{.132 \times 2.5} = \underline{\$4,000.00}$$

29. Jeff Lukenbill took out a loan for $5,880 at the Northern Trust Bank for 110 days. The bank uses the ordinary method for calculating interest. What rate of interest was charged if the amount of interest was $275? Round to the nearest tenth percent.

$$R = \frac{I}{PT} = \frac{275}{5,880 \times \dfrac{110}{360}} = \underline{15.3\%}$$

30. Kipp Murray deposited $2,000 in a savings account paying 6% ordinary interest. How long will it take for her investment to amount to $2,600?

$$T = \frac{I}{PR} = \frac{600}{2,000 \times .06} = \underline{5 \text{ Years}}$$

31. Adele Krause borrowed $16,000 at 14% ordinary interest, for 88 days. On day 30 of the loan she made a partial payment of $7,000. What is the new maturity value of the loan?

$$I = PRT = 16,000 \times .14 \times \frac{30}{360} = \$186.67 \qquad\qquad I = PRT = 9,186.67 \times .14 \times \frac{58}{360} = \$207.21$$

$$\begin{array}{ll} \begin{array}{r} 7,000.00 \text{ Paid} \\ -\ 186.67 \text{ Interest} \\ \hline \$6,813.33 \end{array} & \begin{array}{r} 16,000.00 \\ -\ 6,813.33 \\ \hline \$9,186.67 \text{ Adjusted} \\ \text{balance} \end{array} \quad \begin{array}{r} 88 \\ -\ 30 \\ \hline 58 \text{ Days} \\ \text{remaining} \end{array} \end{array} \qquad MV = P + I = 9,186.67 + 207.21 = \underline{\$9,393.88}$$

32. Samson Industries borrowed $40,000 on April 6, for 66 days. The rate was 14% using the ordinary interest method. On day 25 of the loan Samson made a partial payment of $15,000, and on day 45 of the loan Samson made a second partial payment of $10,000.

a. What is the new maturity value of the loan?

$$I = PRT = 40,000 \times .14 \times \frac{25}{360} = \$388.89 \qquad I = PRT = 25,388.89 \times .14 \times \frac{20}{360} = \$197.47 \qquad I = PRT = 15,586.36 \times .14 \times \frac{21}{360} = \$127.29$$

$$\begin{array}{lll} \begin{array}{r} 15,000.00 \text{ Paid} \\ -\ 388.89 \text{ Interest} \\ \hline \$14,611.11 \end{array} & \begin{array}{r} 40,000.00 \\ -\ 14,611.11 \\ \hline \$25,388.89 \text{ Adjusted} \\ \text{balance} \end{array} & \begin{array}{r} 10,000.00 \text{ Paid} \\ -\ 197.47 \text{ Interest} \\ \hline \$9,802.53 \end{array} \quad \begin{array}{r} 25,388.89 \\ -\ 9,802.53 \\ \hline \$15,586.36 \text{ Adjusted} \\ \text{balance} \end{array} \end{array}$$

$$MV = P + I = 15,586.36 + 127.29 = \underline{\$15,713.65}$$

b. What is the maturity date of the loan?

$$\text{Maturity date} = \begin{array}{r} 30 \\ -\ 6 \\ \hline 24 \text{ Days} \end{array} \quad \begin{array}{l} 24 \text{ Apr} \\ 31 \text{ May} \\ +\ 11 \text{ June} \longrightarrow \underline{\text{June 11}} \\ \hline 66 \text{ Days} \end{array}$$

Name_____

Class_____

ANSWERS

27. _____ $99.37 _____

28. _____ $4,000.00 _____

29. _____ 15.3% _____

30. _____ 5 Years _____

31. _____ $9,393.88 _____

32. a. _____ $15,713.65 _____

  b. _____ June 11 _____

ANSWERS

33. a. _____$28,970.83_____

b. _____November 12_____

c. _____13.46%_____

34. a. _____May 20_____

b. _____$71,400.00_____

c. _____April 10_____

d. _____$70,249.67_____

33. Dave Gondry signed a $30,000 simple discount promissory note at the Plantation Bank. The discount rate was 13%, and the note was made on August 9, for 95 days.

a. What proceeds will Dave receive on the note?

$$\frac{\text{Bank}}{\text{discount}} = FV \times R \times T = 30,000 \times .13 \times \frac{95}{360} = \$1,029.17$$

$$\text{Proceeds} = FV - \text{Discount} = 30,000.00 - 1,029.17 = \underline{\$28,970.83}$$

b. What is the maturity date of the note?

$$\frac{\text{Maturity}}{\text{date}} = \begin{array}{r} 31 \\ -\ 9 \\ \hline 22 \text{ Days} \end{array} \nearrow \begin{array}{l} 22 \text{ Aug} \\ 61 \text{ Sept-Oct} \\ + 12 \text{ Nov} \longrightarrow \underline{\text{November 12}} \\ \hline 95 \text{ Days} \end{array}$$

c. What is the effective rate of interest of the note? Round the answer to the nearest hundredth percent.

$$\frac{\text{Effective}}{\text{rate}} = \frac{\text{Discount}}{\text{Proceeds} \times \text{Time}} = \frac{1,029.17}{28,970.83 \times \dfrac{95}{360}} = \underline{13.46\%}$$

34. Schoninger Publishing, Inc., received a $70,000 promissory note at 12% ordinary interest for 60 days from one of its customers. After 20 days, Schoninger discounted the note at the Bank of Keystone Point at a discount rate of 14.5%. The note was made on March 21.

a. What is the maturity date of the note?

$$\frac{\text{Maturity}}{\text{date}} = \begin{array}{r} 31 \\ -21 \\ \hline 10 \text{ Days} \end{array} \nearrow \begin{array}{l} 10 \text{ Mar} \\ 30 \text{ Apr} \\ + 20 \text{ May} \longrightarrow \underline{\text{May 20}} \\ \hline 60 \text{ Days} \end{array}$$

b. What is the maturity value of the note?

$$MV = FV(1 + RT) = 70,000\left(1 + .12 \times \frac{60}{360}\right) = \underline{\$71,400.00}$$

c. What is the discount date of the note?

$$\frac{\text{Discount}}{\text{date}} = \begin{array}{r} 31 \\ -21 \\ \hline 10 \text{ Days} \end{array} \nearrow \begin{array}{l} 10 \text{ Mar} \\ + 10 \text{ Apr} \longrightarrow \underline{\text{April 10}} \\ \hline 20 \text{ Days} \end{array}$$

d. What proceeds will Schoninger receive after discounting the note?

$$\frac{\text{Bank}}{\text{discount}} = MV \times R \times T = 71,400 \times .145 \times \frac{40}{360} = \$1,150.33$$

$$\text{Proceeds} = MV - \text{disc} = 71,400.00 - 1,150.33 = \underline{\$70,249.67}$$

BUSINESS DECISION
Borrowing to Take Advantage of a Cash Discount

Name_____

Class_____

35. You are the accountant for Leather City, a retail furniture store. Recently an order of sofas and chairs was received from a manufacturer with terms of 3/15, n/45. The order amounted to $230,000, and Leather City can borrow money at 13% ordinary interest.

ANSWERS

35. a. _____ $4,483.08 _____

    b. ____ Borrow the money ____

  a. How much can be saved by borrowing the funds for 30 days in order to take advantage of the cash discount? (Remember, Leather City only has to borrow the net amount due, after the cash discount is taken.)

    Cash discount = 230,000 × .03 = $6,900

    Amount needed = 230,000 − 6,900 = $223,100

$$I = PRT = 223,100 \times .13 \times \frac{30}{360} = \$2,416.92$$

    Savings = Discount − Interest = 6,900 − 2,416.92 = $4,483.08

  b. What would you recommend?

    Recommendation: Savings of almost $4,500 is significant—Borrow the money

All the Math That's Fit to Learn	# The Business Math Times

Volume X — Simple Interest and Promisssory Notes — **One Dollar**

Your Next Car: Leasing vs. Buying

Over the past 10 years, enticed by low monthly payments and heavy promotional campaigns, hundreds of thousands of would-be car buyers have opted instead to lease their cars. In 1988, 7% of all new cars on the road were leased. By 1991, the figure had jumped to 15%. Leasing today accounts for over 35% of all new car transactions.

Consumers are generally familiar with car buying strategies, but when it comes to leasing, it's a whole new ball game, with different terminology and different rules. It's easy for consumers to be taken advantage of if they don't know what they are doing. At first glance, leasing a car may be a tempting proposition: little or no down payment, lower monthly payments than buying, and generally more car for the money. Remember, however, at the end of the lease you own nothing. With a purchase, although the payments are higher, in the end you have equity, you own the car.

With leasing, car prices and other charges are negotiable, just as with purchases. Don't just look at the monthly payments. Speak with a few competitive dealers and compare what they are offering.

Federal law requires the lessor to disclose all up-front costs and other details of the lease. Be sure to ask about the security deposit, capitalized cost reduction (down payment), rate or money factor (equivalent to the annual percentage rate if you took a car loan), sales taxes, title fees, license fees, bank fees, and insurance.

Be sure that the annual mileage limit is appropriate for the amount of driving you do. Most leases allow 12,000 to 15,000 miles per year. If you go beyond that limit, you may be charged as much as 25 cents per mile. That can get very expensive. If you drive far less than the lease's limit, you will, in effect, be paying for miles you never drove.

Don't be pressured. Don't let them tell you that someone else is about to make a deal on the same car, or that it's the last one available at that price. The less anxious you are, the better your bargaining position.

SOURCES: Adapted from Bankcard Holders of America—Pamphlet #15, "The Year of the Lease," *The Washington Post*, June 17, 1987; *Consumer Reports*, America Online, April 1995; and Kapoor et al., *Personal Finance*, Second Edition, Burr Ridge, IL: Irwin, 1991, p.57.

Prepaying a Loan

Did you know that if you have a simple interest loan, any payment over the required monthly installment will be applied directly to reduce the principal? If however your loan is not simple interest, paying off your loan early will not necessarily reduce your interest payments. Check with the lender to be sure.

Before signing, be sure there are no prepayment penalties in the contract. You don't always have a choice, but it can't hurt to ask.

GUESS THE NUMBER OF MARBLES AND WIN A CAR!!

BLAIR

Motor Vehicle Facts and Figures

Did you know?

In the United States there are approximately
- 150 million autos and taxis
- 42 million trucks
- 4 million motorcycles
- 175 million licensed drivers

Automobiles average:
- 11,100 miles per year
- 21.64 miles per gallon

Average cost of owning and operating an automobile:
- $ .451 per mile—total
- $ .060 per mile—gas and oil
- $ .024 per mile—maintenance
- $ .009 per mile—tires
- $724 per year—insurance
- $183 per year—license and registration
- $2,883 per year—depreciation
- $696 per year—finance charge

SOURCE: *Statistical Abstract of the United States*, 1995 Edition, U.S. Federal Highway Administration, American Automobile Manufacturers Association.

Brainteaser

A collector of cars and motorcycles was asked, "How many of each do you have?" The collector replied, "I have 30 motors and 100 tires." From this information, can you calculate the number of cars and the number of motorcycles?

SOURCE: James Fixx, *Games for the Super Intelligent* (New York: Doubleday, 1972).

Answer to Last Issue's Brainteaser

24 Days — Let X = days worked, and $(30 - X)$ = days not worked
Solve the equation:
$55X - 66(30 - X) = 924$

Chapter 11

Compound Interest and Present Value

Performance Objectives

SECTION I COMPOUND INTEREST—THE TIME VALUE OF MONEY

SECTION II PRESENT VALUE

COMPOUND INTEREST—THE TIME VALUE OF MONEY

● **compound interest**

Interest that is applied a number of times during the term of a loan or investment. Interest paid on principal and previously earned interest.

In Chapter 10 we studied simple interest, where the formula $I = PRT$ was applied once during the term of a loan or investment to find the amount of interest. In business, another common way of calculating interest is by a method known as *compounding,* or **compound interest,** in which the interest calculation is applied a number of times during the term of the loan or investment.

Compound interest yields considerably higher interest than simple interest because the investor is earning interest on the interest. Compounding is used by banks and other lending institutions to calculate interest for savings accounts and certificates of deposit (CDs). It is also used by the U.S. government for savings bonds.

With compound interest, the interest earned for each period is reinvested or added to the previous principal before the next calculation or compounding. The previous principal plus interest then becomes the new principal for the next period. For example, $100 invested at 8% interest is worth $108 after the first year ($100 principal + $8 interest). If the interest is not withdrawn, the interest for the next period will be calculated based on $108 principal. As this compounding process repeats itself each period, the principal keeps growing by the amount of the previous interest. As the number of compounding periods increases, the amount of interest earned grows dramatically, especially when compared to simple interest, as illustrated in Exhibit 11-1.

● **the time value of money**

The idea that money "now," or in the present, is worth more than money in the future, because it can be invested and earn interest as time goes by.

This chapter introduces you to an all important business concept, **the time value of money.** Consider this: if you were owed $1,000, would you rather have it now or one year

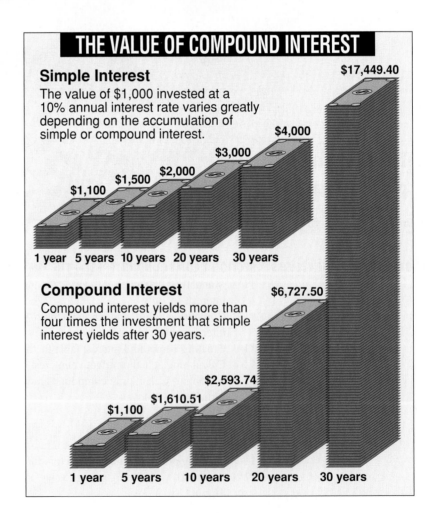

EXHIBIT 11-1

....

THE TIME VALUE OF MONEY

Many different types of investments are based on compound interest.

from now? If you answered "now," you already have a feeling for the concept. Money "now," or in the *present,* is worth more than money in the *future,* because it can be invested and earn interest as time goes by.

In this chapter you will learn to calculate the **compound amount (future value)** of an investment at compound interest, when the **present amount (present value)** is known. You will also learn to calculate the present value that must be deposited now, at compound interest, to yield a known future amount. See Exhibit 11-2.

11-1 Manually Calculating Compound Amount (Future Value) and Compound Interest

Compounding divides the time of a loan or investment into compounding periods or simply periods. In order to manually calculate the compound amount or future value of an investment, we must compound or calculate the interest as many times as there are compounding periods, at the interest rate per period.

For example, an investment made for 5 years at 12% compounded annually (once per year) would have 5 compounding periods (5 years × 1 period per year), each at 12%. If the same investment was compounded semiannually (two times per year), there would be 10 compounding periods (5 years × 2 periods per year), each at 6% (12% annual rate ÷ 2 periods per year).

● **compound amount, or future value (FV)**

The total amount of principal and accumulated interest at the end of a loan or investment.

● **present amount, or present value (PV)**

An amount of money that must be deposited today, at compound interest, in order to provide a specified lump sum of money in the future.

EXHIBIT 11-2

PRESENT VALUE AND FUTURE VALUE AT COMPOUND INTEREST

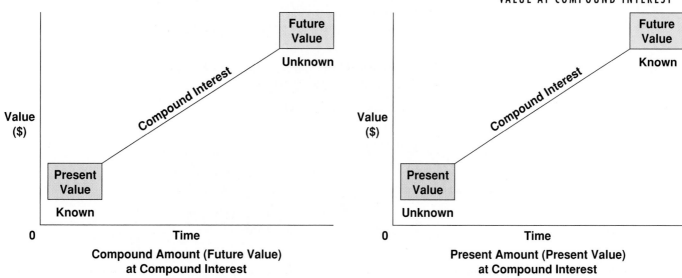

The amount of compound interest is calculated by subtracting the principal from the compound amount.

$$\text{Compound interest} = \text{Compound amount} - \text{Principal}$$

EXAMPLE

Bob Ochs invested $5,000 in a passbook savings account at 10% interest, compounded annually, for 2 years. Manually calculate the compound amount of the investment and the total amount of compound interest Bob earned.

SOLUTION STRATEGY

To solve this compound interest problem manually, we must apply the simple interest formula twice, because there are two compounding periods (2 years × 1 period per year). Note how the interest from the first period is reinvested or added to the original principal to earn interest in the second period.

Original principal	$5,000.00	
Interest—period 1	+ 500.00	$(I = PRT = 5,000.00 \times .10 \times 1)$
Principal—period 2	5,500.00	
Interest—period 2	+ 550.00	$(I = PRT = 5,500.00 \times .10 \times 1)$
Compound Amount	$6,050.00	
Compound Amount	$6,050.00	
Principal	− 5,000.00	
Compound Interest Earned	$1,050.00	

EXAMPLE

Manually recalculate the compound amount and compound interest from the previous example using semiannual compounding (two times per year). How much more interest would Bob earn if the bank offered semiannual compounding?

SOLUTION STRATEGY

To solve this compound interest problem, we must apply the simple interest formula 4 times, because there are four compounding periods (2 years × 2 periods per year). Note that the time factor is now $\frac{6}{12}$ or $\frac{1}{2}$, because semiannual compounding means every six months.

Original principal	$5,000.00	
Interest—period 1	+ 250.00	$(I = PRT = 5,000.00 \times .10 \times \frac{1}{2})$
Principal—period 2	5,250.00	
Interest—period 2	+ 262.50	$(I = PRT = 5,250.00 \times .10 \times \frac{1}{2})$
Principal—period 3	5,512.50	
Interest—period 3	+ 275.63	$(I = PRT = 5,512.50 \times .10 \times \frac{1}{2})$
Principal—period 4	5,788.13	
Interest—period 4	+ 289.41	$(I = PRT = 5,788.13 \times .10 \times \frac{1}{2})$
Compound Amount	$6,077.54	
Compound Amount	$6,077.54	
Principal	−5,000.00	
Compound Interest	$1,077.54	

For the same investment variables, semiannual compounding yields $27.54 more than annual compounding:

Interest with semiannual compounding	$1,077.54
Interest with annual compounding	−$1,050.00
	$27.54

TRY-IT EXERCISE

1. Blanca Gonzalez invested $10,000 at 12% interest, compounded semiannually, for 3 years. Manually calculate the compound amount and the compound interest of Blanca's investment.

Check your answer with the solution on page 363.

11-2 Computing Compound Amount (Future Value) and Compound Interest Using Compound Interest Tables

You don't have to work many compound interest problems manually, particularly those with numerous compounding periods, before you start wishing for an easier way! In actuality, there are two other methods for solving compound interest problems. The first uses a compound interest formula and the second uses compound interest tables.

The compound interest formula, $A = P(1 + i)^n$, contains an exponent and therefore requires the use of a calculator with an exponential function key. The use of the compound interest formula will be covered in Part 12-5.

A compound interest table, like Table 11-1 on page 348, is a useful set of factors that represents the future value of $1.00 at various interest rates for a number of compounding periods. Because these factors are based on one dollar, the future value of other principal amounts is found by multiplying the appropriate table factor by the number of dollars of principal.

Compound amount (future value) = Table factor × Principal

In order to use the compound interest tables, we must know the number of compounding periods and the interest rate per period. The following chart shows the various compounding options and the corresponding number of periods per year. Note: The greater the number of compounding periods per year, the higher the interest earned on the investment. With today's sophisticated computers, interest can actually be calculated on a continuous basis—that is, up to the minute. In competitive markets, many banks offer continuous compounding as an incentive to attract new deposits.

Interest Compounded		Compounding Periods per Year
Annually	Every year	1
Semiannually	Every 6 months	2
Quarterly	Every 3 months	4
Monthly	Every month	12
Daily	Every day	365
Continuously		Infinite

To find the number of compounding periods of an investment, multiply the number of years by the number of periods per year.

Compounding periods = Years × Periods per year

To find the interest rate per period, divide the annual or nominal rate by the number of periods per year.

$$\text{Interest rate per period} = \frac{\text{Nominal rate}}{\text{Periods per year}}$$

TABLE 11-1

COMPOUND INTEREST TABLE (FUTURE VALUE OF $1 AT COMPOUND INTEREST)

Periods	$\frac{1}{2}$%	1%	$1\frac{1}{2}$%	2%	3%	4%	5%	6%	7%	8%	Periods
1	1.00500	1.01000	1.01500	1.02000	1.03000	1.04000	1.05000	1.06000	1.07000	1.08000	1
2	1.01003	1.02010	1.03023	1.04040	1.06090	1.08160	1.10250	1.12360	1.14490	1.16640	2
3	1.01508	1.03030	1.04568	1.06121	1.09273	1.12486	1.15763	1.19102	1.22504	1.25971	3
4	1.02015	1.04060	1.06136	1.08243	1.12551	1.16986	1.21551	1.26248	1.31080	1.36049	4
5	1.02525	1.05101	1.07728	1.10408	1.15927	1.21665	1.27628	1.33823	1.40255	1.46933	5
6	1.03038	1.06152	1.09344	1.12616	1.19405	1.26532	1.34010	1.41852	1.50073	1.58687	6
7	1.03553	1.07214	1.10984	1.14869	1.22987	1.31593	1.40710	1.50363	1.60578	1.71382	7
8	1.04071	1.08286	1.12649	1.17166	1.26677	1.36857	1.47746	1.59385	1.71819	1.85093	8
9	1.04591	1.09369	1.14339	1.19509	1.30477	1.42331	1.55133	1.68948	1.83846	1.99900	9
10	1.05114	1.10462	1.16054	1.21899	1.34392	1.48024	1.62889	1.79085	1.96715	2.15892	10
11	1.05640	1.11567	1.17795	1.24337	1.38423	1.53945	1.71034	1.89830	2.10485	2.33164	11
12	1.06168	1.12683	1.19562	1.26824	1.42576	1.60103	1.79586	2.01220	2.25219	2.51817	12
13	1.06699	1.13809	1.21355	1.29361	1.46853	1.66507	1.88565	2.13293	2.40985	2.71962	13
14	1.07232	1.14947	1.23176	1.31948	1.51259	1.73168	1.97993	2.26090	2.57853	2.93719	14
15	1.07768	1.16097	1.25023	1.34587	1.55797	1.80094	2.07893	2.39656	2.75903	3.17217	15
16	1.08307	1.17258	1.26899	1.37279	1.60471	1.87298	2.18287	2.54035	2.95216	3.42594	16
17	1.08849	1.18430	1.28802	1.40024	1.65285	1.94790	2.29202	2.69277	3.15882	3.70002	17
18	1.09393	1.19615	1.30734	1.42825	1.70243	2.02582	2.40662	2.85434	3.37993	3.99602	18
19	1.09940	1.20811	1.32695	1.45681	1.75351	2.10685	2.52695	3.02560	3.61653	4.31570	19
20	1.10490	1.22019	1.34686	1.48595	1.80611	2.19112	2.65330	3.20714	3.86968	4.66096	20
21	1.11042	1.23239	1.36706	1.51567	1.86029	2.27877	2.78596	3.39956	4.14056	5.03383	21
22	1.11597	1.24472	1.38756	1.54598	1.91610	2.36992	2.92526	3.60354	4.43040	5.43654	22
23	1.12155	1.25716	1.40838	1.57690	1.97359	2.46472	3.07152	3.81975	4.74053	5.87146	23
24	1.12716	1.26973	1.42950	1.60844	2.03279	2.56330	3.22510	4.04893	5.07237	6.34118	24
25	1.13280	1.28243	1.45095	1.64061	2.09378	2.66584	3.38635	4.29187	5.42743	6.84848	25

Periods	9%	10%	11%	12%	13%	14%	15%	16%	17%	18%	Periods
1	1.09000	1.10000	1.11000	1.12000	1.13000	1.14000	1.15000	1.16000	1.17000	1.18000	1
2	1.18810	1.21000	1.23210	1.25440	1.27690	1.29960	1.32250	1.34560	1.36890	1.39240	2
3	1.29503	1.33100	1.36763	1.40493	1.44290	1.48154	1.52088	1.56090	1.60161	1.64303	3
4	1.41158	1.46410	1.51807	1.57352	1.63047	1.68896	1.74901	1.81064	1.87389	1.93878	4
5	1.53862	1.61051	1.68506	1.76234	1.84244	1.92541	2.01136	2.10034	2.19245	2.28776	5
6	1.67710	1.77156	1.87041	1.97382	2.08195	2.19497	2.31306	2.43640	2.56516	2.69955	6
7	1.82804	1.94872	2.07616	2.21068	2.35261	2.50227	2.66002	2.82622	3.00124	3.18547	7
8	1.99256	2.14359	2.30454	2.47596	2.65844	2.85259	3.05902	3.27841	3.51145	3.75886	8
9	2.17189	2.35795	2.55804	2.77308	3.00404	3.25195	3.51788	3.80296	4.10840	4.43545	9
10	2.36736	2.59374	2.83942	3.10585	3.39457	3.70722	4.04556	4.41144	4.80683	5.23384	10
11	2.58043	2.85312	3.15176	3.47855	3.83586	4.22623	4.65239	5.11726	5.62399	6.17593	11
12	2.81266	3.13843	3.49845	3.89598	4.33452	4.81790	5.35025	5.93603	6.58007	7.28759	12
13	3.06580	3.45227	3.88328	4.36349	4.89801	5.49241	6.15279	6.88579	7.69868	8.59936	13
14	3.34173	3.79750	4.31044	4.88711	5.53475	6.26135	7.07571	7.98752	9.00745	10.14724	14
15	3.64248	4.17725	4.78459	5.47357	6.25427	7.13794	8.13706	9.26552	10.53872	11.97375	15
16	3.97031	4.59497	5.31089	6.13039	7.06733	8.13725	9.35762	10.74800	12.33030	14.12902	16
17	4.32763	5.05447	5.89509	6.86604	7.98608	9.27646	10.76126	12.46768	14.42646	16.67225	17
18	4.71712	5.55992	6.54355	7.68997	9.02427	10.57517	12.37545	14.46251	16.87895	19.67325	18
19	5.14166	6.11591	7.26334	8.61276	10.19742	12.05569	14.23177	16.77652	19.74838	23.21444	19
20	5.60441	6.72750	8.06231	9.64629	11.52309	13.74349	16.36654	19.46076	23.10560	27.39303	20
21	6.10881	7.40025	8.94917	10.80385	13.02109	15.66758	18.82152	22.57448	27.03355	32.32378	21
22	6.65860	8.14027	9.93357	12.10031	14.71383	17.86104	21.64475	26.18640	31.62925	38.14206	22
23	7.25787	8.95430	11.02627	13.55235	16.62663	20.36158	24.89146	30.37622	37.00623	45.00763	23
24	7.91108	9.84973	12.23916	15.17863	18.78809	23.21221	28.62518	35.23642	43.29729	53.10901	24
25	8.62308	10.83471	13.58546	17.00006	21.23054	26.46192	32.91895	40.87424	50.65783	62.66863	25

STEPS FOR USING COMPOUND INTEREST TABLES:

Step 1. Scan across the top row to find the interest rate per period.

Step 2. Look down that column to the row corresponding to the number of periods.

Step 3. The table factor at the intersection of the rate per period column and the number of periods row is the future value of $1.00 at compound interest. Multiply the table factor by the principal to determine the compound amount.

Compound amount = Table factor × Principal

EXAMPLE

Barry Potter invested $1,200, at 8% interest compounded quarterly, for 5 years. Use Table 11-1 to find the compound amount of Barry's investment. What is the amount of the compound interest?

SOLUTION STRATEGY

To solve this compound interest problem, we must first find the interest rate per period and the number of compounding periods.

$$\text{Interest rate per period} = \frac{\text{Nominal rate}}{\text{Periods per year}}$$

$$\text{Interest rate per period} = \frac{8\%}{4} = 2\%$$

$$\text{Compounding periods} = \text{Years} \times \text{Periods per year}$$

$$\text{Compounding periods} = 5 \times 4 = 20$$

Now find the table factor by scanning across the top row of the compound interest table to 2%, and down the 2% column to 20 periods. The table factor at that intersection is 1.48595. The compound amount is found by multiplying the table factor by the principal:

$$\text{Compound amount} = \text{Table factor} \times \text{Principal}$$

$$\text{Compound amount} = 1.48595 \times 1,200 = \underline{\$1,783.14}$$

The amount of interest is found by subtracting the principal from the compound amount.

$$\text{Compound interest} = \text{Compound amount} - \text{Principal}$$

$$\text{Compound interest} = 1,783.14 - 1,200.00 = \underline{\$583.14}$$

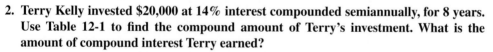

TRY-IT   **EXERCISE**

2. **Terry Kelly invested $20,000 at 14% interest compounded semiannually, for 8 years. Use Table 12-1 to find the compound amount of Terry's investment. What is the amount of compound interest Terry earned?**

Check your answers with the solutions on page 363.

11-3 Creating Compound Interest Table Factors for Periods beyond the Table

When the number of periods of an investment is greater than the number of periods provided by the compound interest table, you can compute a new table factor by multiplying the factors for any two periods that add up to the number of periods required. For example, at a given interest rate, the table factor for 40 periods would be the product of the table factors for 10 and 30 periods, 15 and 25, or any other combination that adds up to 40.

STEPS FOR CREATING NEW COMPOUND INTEREST TABLE FACTORS:

Step 1. For the stated interest rate per period, find any two table factors whose periods add up to the number of periods required.

Step 2. Multiply the two table factors from Step 1 to form the new factor.

Step 3. Round the new factor to five decimal places.

EXAMPLE

Calculate a new table factor and find the compound amount of $10,000 invested at 12% compounded monthly, for 3 years.

SOLUTION STRATEGY

This investment requires a table factor for 36 periods (12 periods per year for 3 years). Because Table 11-1 only provides factors up to 25 periods, we must create one using the steps above.

Step 1. At 12% interest compounded monthly, the rate per period is 1%. Because we are looking for 36 periods, we shall use the factors for 16 and 20 periods, at 1%.

Table factor for 16 periods, 1% = 1.17258
Table factor for 20 periods, 1% = 1.22019

Step 2. Multiply the factors for 16 and 20 periods:

1.17258 × 1.22019 = 1.43077039

Step 3. Round to five decimal places:

The new table factor for 36 periods is <u>1.43077</u>.

The compound amount of the $10,000 investment is

Compound amount = Table factor × Principal
Compound amount = 1.43077 × 10,000 = <u>$14,307.70</u>

TRY-IT   EXERCISE

3. **Herb Licon invests $3,500 at 16% interest compounded quarterly, for 7 years. Calculate a new table factor and find the compound amount of Herb's investment.**

Check your answer with the solution on page 363.

11-4 Calculating Actual or Effective Interest Rate

● **annual or nominal rate**
The advertised or stated interest rate of an investment or loan. The rate used to calculate the compound interest.

In describing investments and loans, the advertised or stated interest rate is known as the **annual** or **nominal rate.** It is also the rate used to calculate the compound interest. Consider, however, what happens to an investment of $100 at 12% nominal interest.

Compounding	Interest Earned
Annually	$12.00
Semiannually	$12.36
Quarterly	$12.55
Monthly	$12.68

● **actual or effective rate**
The real or true rate of return on an investment. It is the total compound interest earned in one year divided by the principal. The more compounding periods per year, the higher the effective rate.

As we learned in Part 11-2, the greater the number of compounding periods per year, the higher the amount of interest earned. Although the nominal interest rate is 12%, with monthly compounding the $100 earns more than 12%. This is why many investment offers today advertise daily or continuous compounding. How much are these investments really earning?

The **actual** or **effective rate** reflects the real rate of return on an investment. Effective interest rate is calculated by finding the total compound interest earned in one year, and dividing by the principal. Note: This is actually the simple interest formula solved for rate from Chapter 10, $R = I \div PT$, where T is equal to 1.

$$\text{Effective interest rate} = \frac{\text{Total compound interest earned in one year}}{\text{Principal}}$$

From the $100 investment example above, the effective rate is the same as the nominal rate when interest is compounded annually; however, it jumps to 12.36% when the compounding is changed to semiannually and to 12.68% when compounded monthly.

EXAMPLE

What is the compound amount, compound interest, and effective rate of $4,000 invested for one year at 8%, compounded semiannually?

SOLUTION STRATEGY

First we must find the total compound interest earned in one year. We can find the compound amount using the factor for 4%, 2 periods, from Table 11-1.

Compound amount = Table factor × Principal

Compound amount = 1.08160 × 4,000 = $4,326.40

Compound interest = Compound amount − Principal

Compound interest = 4,326.40 − 4,000 = $326.40

$$\text{Effective interest rate} = \frac{\text{Total compound interest earned in one year}}{\text{Principal}}$$

$$\text{Effective interest rate} = \frac{326.40}{4,000.00} = 8.16\%$$

TRY-IT   EXERCISE

4. Robert McCabe invested $7,000 in a certificate of deposit for one year, at 6% interest, compounded quarterly. What is the compound amount, compound interest, and effective rate of Robert's investment? (Round the effective rate to the nearest hundredth percent.)

Check your answers with the solution on page 363.

11-5 (Optional) Calculating Compound Amount (Future Value) Using the Compound Interest Formula

If your calculator has an exponential function key, y^x, you can calculate the compound amount of an investment using the compound interest formula.

The compound interest formula states:

$$A = P(1 + i)^n$$

where

A = Compound amount

P = Principal

i = Interest rate per period (expressed as a decimal)

n = Total compounding periods (years × periods per year)

Step 1. Add the 1 and the interest rate per period, i.

Step 2. Raise the sum from Step 1 to the nth power, using the y^x key on your calculator.

Step 3. Multiply the principal, P, by the answer from Step 2.

Calculator Sequence: 1 $+$ i y^x n $\times$ P $=$ A

EXAMPLE

Use the compound interest formula to calculate the compound amount of $5,000 invested at 10% interest compounded semiannually, for 3 years.

SOLUTION STRATEGY

This problem is solved by substituting the investment information into the compound interest formula. It is important to solve the formula in the sequence of steps as outlined above. Note that the rate per period, i, is 5% (10% ÷ 2 periods per year). The total number of periods, the exponent n, is 6 (3 years times 2 periods per year).

$$A = P(1 + i)^n$$
$$A = 5{,}000(1 + .05)^6$$
$$A = 5{,}000(1.05)^6$$
$$A = 5{,}000(1.3400956) = 6{,}700.4782 = \underline{\$6{,}700.48}$$

Calculator Sequence: 1 $+$ .05 y^x 6 $\times$ 5000 $=$ $\underline{6{,}700.4782}$

TRY-IT   EXERCISE

5. **Use the compound interest formula to calculate the compound amount of $3,000 invested at 8% interest compounded quarterly, for 5 years.**

Check your answer with the solution on page 363.

 REVIEW EXERCISES CHAPTER 11—SECTION I

For the following investments, find the total number of compounding periods and the interest rate per period:

Complete, worked out solutions to exercises 1–7 appear in the appendix following the index.

	Term of Investment	Nominal (Annual) Rate	Interest Compounded	Compounding Periods	Rate per Period
1.	3 years	13%	annually	3	13%
2.	5 years	16%	quarterly	20	4%
3.	12 years	8%	semiannually	24	4%
4.	6 years	18%	monthly	72	1.5%
5.	4 years	14%	quarterly	16	3.5%
6.	9 years	10.5%	semiannually	18	5.25%
7.	9 months	12%	quarterly	3	3%

Manually calculate the compound amount and compound interest for the following investments:

	Principal	Term of Investment	Nominal Rate	Interest Compounded	Compound Amount	Compound Interest
8.	$4,000	2 years	10%	annually	$4,840	$840
9.	$10,000	1 year	12%	quarterly	$11,255.09	$1,255.09
10.	$8,000	3 years	8%	semiannually	$10,122.55	$2,122.55

Complete, worked out solutions to exercises 8–26 appear in the appendix following the index.

Using Table 11-1, calculate the compound amount and compound interest for the following investments:

	Principal	Term of Investment	Nominal Rate	Interest Compounded	Compound Amount	Compound Interest
11.	$7,000	4 years	13%	annually	$11,413.29	$4,413.29
12.	$11,000	6 years	14%	semiannually	$24,774.09	$13,774.09
13.	$5,300	3 years	8%	quarterly	$6,721.67	$1,421.67
14.	$67,000	2 years	18%	monthly	$95,776.50	$28,776.50
15.	$25,000	15 years	11%	annually	$119,614.75	$94,614.75
16.	$400	2 years	6%	monthly	$450.86	$50.86
17.	$8,800	$12\frac{1}{2}$ years	10%	semiannually	$29,799.88	$20,999.88

The following investments require table factors for periods beyond the table. Create the new table factor, rounded to five places, and calculate the compound amount for each:

	Principal	Term of Investment	Nominal Rate	Interest Compounded	New Table Factor	Compound Amount
18.	$13,000	3 years	12%	monthly	1.43077	$18,600.01
19.	$19,000	29 years	9%	annually	12.17216	$231,271.04
20.	$34,700	11 years	16%	quarterly	5.61652	$194,893.24
21.	$10,000	40 years	13%	annually	132.78160	$1,327,816.00
22.	$1,000	16 years	14%	semiannually	8.71525	$8,715.25

For the following investments, compute the amount of compound interest earned in one year and the effective interest rate:

	Principal	Nominal Rate	Interest Compounded	Compound Interest Earned in One year	Effective Rate
23.	$5,000	10%	semiannually	$512.50	10.25%
24.	$2,000	13%	annually	$260.00	13%
25.	$36,000	12%	monthly	$4,565.88	12.68%
26.	$1,000	8%	quarterly	$82.43	8.24%

Solve the following word problems using either Table 11-1 or the optional compound interest formula, $A = P(1 + i)^n$:

27. Nina Horne invested $3,000 at the Independent Bank, at 6% interest compounded quarterly.

    a. What is the effective rate of this investment?

    $1\frac{1}{2}$%, 4 Periods

    Compound amount = $1.06136 \times 3,000 = \$3,184.08$
    Compound interest = $3,184.08 - 3,000.00 = \$184.08$
    Effective rate = $\dfrac{184.08}{3,000.00} = \underline{\underline{6.14\%}}$

    b. What will Nina's investment be worth after 6 years?

    $1\frac{1}{2}$%, 24 Periods
    Compound amount = $1,42950 \times 3,000 = \underline{\$4,288.50}$

28. As a savings plan for college, the Chongs deposited $10,000 in an account paying 8% compounded annually when their son Masahiro was born. How much will the account be worth when Masahiro is 18 years old?

8%, 18 Periods

Compound amount = 3.99602 × 10,000 = $39,960.20

29. Southeastern Supply, Inc., deposited $500,000 in an account earning 12% compounded monthly. This account is intended to pay for the construction of a new warehouse. How much will be available for the project in $2\frac{1}{2}$ years?

Table factor required = 1%, 30 periods

1%, 15 Periods: 1.16097
1%, 15 Periods: × 1.16097
     30 Periods   1.3478513 = 1.34785 "New" factor

Compound amount = 1.34785 × 500,000 = $673,925.00

30. The First National Bank is offering savings accounts at 8% interest, compounded quarterly; the Second National Bank is offering 9% compounded annually. If you had $5,000 to invest for 6 years, which bank would you choose?

First National:
2%, 24 Periods
Compound amount = 1.60844 × 5,000 = $8,042.20
Second National:
9%, 6 Periods
Compound amount = 1.67710 × 5,000 = $8,385.50 ← Better deal

SECTION II
PRESENT VALUE

In Section I we learned how to find a future value when the present value was known. Let's take a look at the reverse situation, also commonly found in business. When a future value (an amount needed in the future) is known, the present value is the amount that must be invested today in order to accumulate with compound interest to that future value. For example, if a corporation wants $100,000 in 5 years (future value—known) to replace its fleet of trucks, what amount must be invested today (present value—unknown) at 8% compounded quarterly to achieve this goal? See Exhibit 11-3.

11-6 Calculating the Present Value of a Future Amount Using Present Value Tables

Just as there are compound interest tables to aid in the calculation of compound amounts, present value tables help calculate the present value of a known future amount. Table 11-2, page 355, is such a table. Note that it is similar to the compound interest table in that the table factors are based on various interest rates per period, for many periods.

Notice also that the table factors for compound interest (Table 11-1) are all greater than one, because the compound amount is larger than the original investment; whereas for present value (Table 11-2) all the factors are less than one, because the original investment (present value) is less than the compound amount. Keeping this in mind should help you choose the correct table to use when solving compound interest and present value problems.

EXHIBIT 11-3
....

PRESENT VALUE TO FUTURE
VALUE

TABLE 11-2

PRESENT VALUE TABLE (PRESENT VALUE OF $1 AT COMPOUND INTEREST)

Periods	$\frac{1}{2}$%	1%	$1\frac{1}{2}$%	2%	3%	4%	5%	6%	7%	8%	Periods
1	0.99502	0.99010	0.98522	0.98039	0.97087	0.96154	0.95238	0.94340	0.93458	0.92593	1
2	0.99007	0.98030	0.97066	0.96117	0.94260	0.92456	0.90703	0.89000	0.87344	0.85734	2
3	0.98515	0.97059	0.95632	0.94232	0.91514	0.88900	0.86384	0.83962	0.81630	0.79383	3
4	0.98025	0.96098	0.94218	0.92385	0.88849	0.85480	0.82270	0.79209	0.76290	0.73503	4
5	0.97537	0.95147	0.92826	0.90573	0.86261	0.82193	0.78353	0.74726	0.71299	0.68058	5
6	0.97052	0.94205	0.9l454	0.88797	0.83748	0.79031	0.74622	0.70496	0.66634	0.63017	6
7	0.96569	0.93272	0.90103	0.87056	0.81309	0.75992	0.71068	0.66506	0.62275	0.58349	7
8	0.96089	0.92348	0.88771	0.85349	0.78941	0.73069	0.67684	0.62741	0.58201	0.54027	8
9	0.95610	0.91434	0.87459	0.83676	0.76642	0.70259	0.64461	0.59190	0.54393	0.50025	9
10	0.95135	0.90529	0.86167	0.82035	0.74409	0.67556	0.61391	0.55839	0.50835	0.46319	10
11	0.94661	0.89632	0.84893	0.80426	0.72242	0.64958	0.58468	0.52679	0.47509	0.42888	11
12	0.94191	0.88745	0.83639	0.78849	0.70138	0.62460	0.55684	0.49697	0.44401	0.39711	12
13	0.93722	0.87866	0.82403	0.77303	0.68095	0.60057	0.53032	0.46884	0.41496	0.36770	13
14	0.93256	0.86996	0.81185	0.75788	0.66112	0.57748	0.50507	0.44230	0.38782	0.34046	14
15	0.92792	0.86135	0.79985	0.74301	0.64186	0.55526	0.48102	0.41727	0.36245	0.31524	15
16	0.92330	0.85282	0.78803	0.72845	0.62317	0.53391	0.45811	0.39365	0.33873	0.29189	16
17	0.91871	0.84438	0.77639	0.71416	0.60502	0.51337	0.43630	0.37136	0.31657	0.27027	17
18	0.91414	0.83602	0.76491	0.70016	0.58739	0.49363	0.41552	0.35034	0.29586	0.25025	18
19	0.90959	0.82774	0.75361	0.68643	0.57029	0.47464	0.39573	0.33051	0.27651	0.23171	19
20	0.90506	0.81954	0.74247	0.67297	0.55368	0.45639	0.37689	0.31180	0.25842	0.21455	20
21	0.90056	0.81143	0.73150	0.65978	0.53755	0.43883	0.35894	0.29416	0.24151	0.19866	21
22	0.89608	0.80340	0.72069	0.64684	0.52189	0.42196	0.34185	0.27751	0.22571	0.18394	22
23	0.89162	0.79544	0.71004	0.63416	0.50669	0.40573	0.32557	0.26180	0.21095	0.17032	23
24	0.88719	0.78757	0.69954	0.62172	0.49193	0.39012	0.31007	0.24698	0.19715	0.15770	24
25	0.88277	0.77977	0.68921	0.60953	0.47761	0.37512	0.29530	0.23300	0.18425	0.14602	25

Periods	9%	10%	11%	12%	13%	14%	15%	16%	17%	18%	Periods
1	0.91743	0.90909	0.90090	0.89286	0.88496	0.87719	0.86957	0.86207	0.85470	0.84746	1
2	0.84168	0.82645	0.81162	0.79719	0.78315	0.76947	0.75614	0.74316	0.73051	0.71818	2
3	0.77218	0.75131	0.73119	0.71178	0.69305	0.67497	0.65752	0.64066	0.62437	0.60863	3
4	0.70843	0.68301	0.65873	0.63552	0.61332	0.59208	0.57175	0.55229	0.53365	0.51579	4
5	0.64993	0.62092	0.59345	0.56743	0.54276	0.51937	0.49718	0.47611	0.45611	0.43711	5
6	0.59627	0.56447	0.53464	0.50663	0.48032	0.45559	0.43233	0.41044	0.38984	0.37043	6
7	0.54703	0.51316	0.48166	0.45235	0.42506	0.39964	0.37594	0.35383	0.33320	0.31393	7
8	0.50187	0.46651	0.43393	0.40388	0.37616	0.35056	0.32690	0.30503	0.28478	0.26604	8
9	0.46043	0.42410	0.39092	0.36061	0.33288	0.30751	0.28426	0.26295	0.24340	0.22546	9
10	0.42241	0.38554	0.35218	0.32197	0.29459	0.26974	0.24718	0.22668	0.20804	0.19106	10
11	0.38753	0.35049	0.31728	0.28748	0.26070	0.23662	0.21494	0.19542	0.17781	0.16192	11
12	0.35553	0.31863	0.28584	0.25668	0.23071	0.20756	0.18691	0.16846	0.15197	0.13722	12
13	0.32618	0.28966	0.25751	0.22917	0.20416	0.18207	0.16253	0.14523	0.12989	0.11629	13
14	0.29925	0.26333	0.23199	0.20462	0.18068	0.15971	0.14133	0.12520	0.11102	0.09855	14
15	0.27454	0.23939	0.20900	0.18270	0.15989	0.14010	0.12289	0.10793	0.09489	0.08352	15
16	0.25187	0.21763	0.18829	0.16312	0.14150	0.12289	0.10686	0.09304	0.08110	0.07078	16
17	0.23107	0.19784	0.16963	0.14564	0.12522	0.10780	0.09293	0.08021	0.06932	0.05998	17
18	0.21199	0.17986	0.15282	0.13004	0.11081	0.09456	0.08081	0.06914	0.05925	0.05083	18
19	0.19449	0.16351	0.13768	0.11611	0.09806	0.08295	0.07027	0.05961	0.05064	0.04308	19
20	0.17843	0.14864	0.12403	0.10367	0.08678	0.07276	0.06110	0.05139	0.04328	0.03651	20
21	0.16370	0.13513	0.11174	0.09256	0.07680	0.06383	0.05313	0.04430	0.03699	0.03094	21
22	0.15018	0.12285	0.10067	0.08264	0.06796	0.05599	0.04620	0.03819	0.03162	0.02622	22
23	0.13778	0.11168	0.09069	0.07379	0.06014	0.04911	0.04017	0.03292	0.02702	0.02222	23
24	0.12640	0.10153	0.08170	0.06588	0.05323	0.04308	0.03493	0.02838	0.02310	0.01883	24
25	0.11597	0.09230	0.07361	0.05882	0.04710	0.03779	0.03038	0.02447	0.01974	0.01596	25

STEPS FOR USING PRESENT VALUE TABLES:

Step 1. Scan across the top row to find the interest rate per period.

Step 2. Look down that column to the row corresponding to the number of periods.

Step 3. The table factor found at the intersection of the rate per period column and the number of periods row is the present value of $1.00 at compound interest. Multiply the table factor by the compound amount to determine the present value:

Present value = Table factor × Compound amount (future value)

Sheryl Nelson wants $5,000 in 8 years. Use Table 11-2 to find how much Sheryl must invest now at 6% interest compounded semiannually in order to have $5,000, 8 years from now.

SOLUTION STRATEGY

To solve this present value problem, we shall use 3% per period (6% nominal rate divided by 2 periods per year) and 16 periods (8 years times 2 periods per year).

Step 1. Scan across the top row of the present value table to 3%.

Step 2. Look down that column to the row corresponding to 16 periods.

Step 3. Find the table factor at the intersection of Steps 1 and 2, and multiply it by the compound amount to find the present value. Table factor = .62317.

$$\text{Present value} = \text{Table factor} \times \text{Compound amount}$$
$$\text{Present value} = .62317 \times 5,000 = \underline{\$3,115.85}$$

TRY-IT   EXERCISE

6. Baron von Keller III wants to renovate his castle in Germany in 3 years. He estimates the cost to be $300,000. Use Table 11-2 to find how much the Baron must invest now at 8% interest compounded quarterly, in order to have $300,000, 3 years from now.

Check your answer with the solution on page 363.

11-7 Creating Present Value Table Factors for Periods beyond the Table

Just as with the compound interest tables, there may be times when the number of periods of an investment or loan is greater than the number of periods provided by the present value tables. When this occurs, you can create a new table factor by multiplying the table factors for any two periods that add up to the number of periods required.

For example, at a given interest rate, the table factor for 35 periods would be the product of the table factors for 15 and 20 periods, or 10 and 25 periods, or any other combination that adds up to 35.

STEPS FOR CREATING NEW TABLE FACTORS:

Step 1. For the stated interest rate per period, find any two table factors whose periods add up to the number of periods required.

Step 2. Multiply the two table factors from Step 1 to form the new factor.

Step 3. Round the new factor to five decimal places.

EXAMPLE

Calculate a new table factor and find the present value of $2,000, if the interest rate is 12% compounded quarterly, for 8 years.

SOLUTION STRATEGY

This investment requires a table factor for 32 periods, 4 periods per year for 8 years. Because Table 11-2 only provides factors up to 25 periods, we must create one using the steps above.

Step 1. At 12% interest compounded quarterly, the rate per period is 3%. Because we are looking for 32 periods, we shall use the factors for 12 and 20 periods, at 3%.

Table factor for 12 periods, 3% = .70138

Table factor for 20 periods, 3% = .55368

Step 2. Multiply the factors for 12 and 20 periods:

.70138 × .55368 = .3883401

Step 3. Rounding to five decimal places, the new table factor for 32 periods is .38834. The present value of the $2,000 investment is

Present value = Table factor × Compound amount

Present value = .38834 × 2,000 = $776.68

 TRY-IT **EXERCISE**

7. **Calculate a new table factor and find the present value of $8,500, if the interest rate is 6% compounded quarterly, for 10 years.**

Check your answer with the solution on page 363.

11-8 (Optional) Calculating Present Value of a Future Amount Using the Present Value Formula

If your calculator has an exponential function key, y^x, you can calculate the present value of an investment using the present value formula.

The present value formula states:

$$PV = \frac{A}{(1+i)^n}$$

where

 PV = **Present value**

 A = **Compound amount**

 i = **Interest rate per period (expressed as a decimal)**

 n = **Total compounding periods (years × periods per year)**

STEPS FOR SOLVING THE PRESENT VALUE FORMULA:

Step 1. Add the 1 and the interest rate per period, i.

Step 2. Raise the sum from Step 1 to the nth power, using the y^x key on your calculator.

Step 3. Divide the compound amount, A, by the answer from Step 2.

Calculator Sequence: 1 ＋ i y^x n ＝ M+ A ÷ MR ＝ PV

EXAMPLE

Use the present value formula to calculate the present value of $3,000, if the interest rate is 16% compounded quarterly, for 6 years.

SOLUTION STRATEGY

This problem is solved by substituting the investment information into the present value formula. It is important to solve the formula in the sequence of steps as outlined. Note the rate per period, *i*, is 4% (16% ÷ 4 periods per year). The total number of periods, the exponent *n*, is 24 (6 years times 4 periods per year).

$$\text{Present value} = \frac{A}{(1+i)^n}$$

$$\text{Present value} = \frac{3,000}{(1+.04)^{24}}$$

$$\text{Present value} = \frac{3,000}{(1.04)^{24}}$$

$$\text{Present value} = \frac{3,000}{2.5633041} = \underline{\$1,170.36}$$

Calculator Sequence: 1 ⊞ .04 y^x 24 ⊜ M+ 3000 ÷ MR ⊜ $\underline{\$1,170.36}$

TRY-IT EXERCISE

8. **Barry and Linda Cannata want to accumulate $30,000, 17 years from now, as a college fund for their baby daughter, Vanessa. Use the present value formula to calculate how much they must invest now, at an interest rate of 8% compounded semiannually, in order to have $30,000 in 17 years.**

Check your answer with the solution on page 363.

S REVIEW EXERCISES   CHAPTER 11—SECTION II

For the following investments, calculate the present value (principal) and the compound interest. Use Table 11-2 (round your answers to the nearest cent):

Complete, worked out solutions to exercises 1–10 appear in the appendix following the index.

	Compound Amount	Term of Investment	Nominal Rate	Interest Compounded	Present Value	Compound Interest
1.	$6,000	3 years	9%	annually	$4,633.08	$1,366.92
2.	$24,000	6 years	14%	semiannually	$10,656.24	$13,343.76
3.	$650	5 years	8%	quarterly	$437.43	$212.57
4.	$2,000	12 years	6%	semiannually	$983.86	$1,016.14
5.	$50,000	25 years	11%	annually	$3,680.50	$46,319.50
6.	$14,500	18 months	10%	semiannually	$12,525.68	$1,974.32
7.	$9,800	4 years	12%	quarterly	$6,107.07	$3,692.93
8.	$100,000	10 years	9%	annually	$42,241.00	$57,759.00
9.	$250	1 year	18%	monthly	$209.10	$40.90
10.	$4,000	27 months	8%	quarterly	$3,347.04	$652.96

358   Chapter 11 / Compound Interest and Present Value

The following investments require table factors for periods beyond the table. Create the new table factor and calculate the present value for each:

	Principal	Term of Investment	Nominal Rate	Interest Compounded	New Table Factor	Present Value
11.	$12,000	10 years	16%	quarterly	.20829	$2,499.48
12.	$33,000	38 years	7%	annually	.07646	$2523.18
13.	$1,400	12 years	12%	quarterly	.24200	$338.80
14.	$1,000	45 years	13%	annually	.00409	$4.09
15.	$110,000	17 years	8%	semiannually	.26356	$28,991.60

Complete, worked out solutions to exercises 11–15 appear in the appendix following the index.

Solve the following word problems using either Table 11-2 or the optional present value formula:

$$PV = \frac{A}{(1 + i)^n}$$

16. How much must be invested today at 6% compounded quarterly to have $8,000 in 3 years?

$1\frac{1}{2}\%$, 12 Periods

Present value = .83639 × 8,000 = $6,691.12

17. Lisa Rittby is planning a vacation in Europe in 4 years, after graduation. She estimates that she will need $3,500 for the trip.

    a. If her bank is offering 4-year certificates of deposit with 8% interest compounded quarterly, how much must Lisa invest now in order to have the money for the trip?

    2%, 16 Periods

    Present value = .72845 × 3,500 = $2,549.58

    b. How much compound interest will be earned on the investment?

    Compound interest = 3,500.00 – 2,549.58 = $950.42

18. Sunshine Homes, a real estate development company, is planning to build 5 custom homes, each costing $125,000, in $2\frac{1}{2}$ years. The Bank of Aventura pays 6% interest compounded semiannually. How much should the company invest now, in order to have sufficient funds to build the homes in the future?

3%, 5 Periods

Amount needed = 125,000 × 5 = $625,000

Present value = .86261 × 625,000 = $539,131.25

19. Dimitry Alexander estimates he will need $25,000 to set up a law office in 7 years, when he graduates from law school.

    a. How much must Dimitry invest now at 12% interest compounded quarterly in order to achieve his goal?

    Table factor required 3%, 28 Periods

    3%, 20 Periods: .55368

    3%, 8 Periods: ×.78941

        28 Periods   .4370805 = .43708 "New" factor 3%, 28 Periods

    Present value .43708 × 25,000 = $10,927.00

b. How much compound interest will he earn on the investment?

Compound interest = 25,000.00 − 10,927.00 = $14,073.00

20. American Airlines intends to pay off a $20,000,000 bond issue that comes due in 4 years. How much must the company set aside now, at 6% interest compounded monthly, in order to accumulate the required amount of money?

Table factor required = .5%, 48 Periods

.5%, 24 Periods: .88719

.5%, 24 Periods: × .88719

.7871061 = .78711 "New" factor .5%, 48 Periods

Present value .78711 × 20,000,000 = $15,742,200.00

> # CHAPTER 11 ■ COMPOUND INTEREST & PRESENT VALUE
>
> ## FORMULAS
>
> Compound interest = Compound amount − Principal
>
> Compounding periods = Years × Periods per year
>
> $$\text{Interest rate per period} = \frac{\text{Nominal rate}}{\text{Periods per year}}$$
>
> Compound amount = Table factor × Principal
>
> $$\text{Effective rate} = \frac{\text{Total interest earned in 1st year}}{\text{Principal}}$$
>
> Compound amount = Principal$(1 + \text{interest})^{\text{periods}}$
>
> Present value = Table factor × Compound amount
>
> $$\text{Present value} = \frac{\text{Compound amount}}{(1 + \text{interest})^{\text{periods}}}$$

CHAPTER 11 ■ COMPOUND INTEREST	SUMMARY CHART

SECTION I   COMPOUND INTEREST—THE TIME VALUE OF MONEY

Topic	P/O, Page	Important Concepts	Illustrative Examples
Manually Calculating Compound Amount (Future Value)	11–1 345	In compound interest the interest is applied a number of times during the term of an investment. Compound interest yields considerably higher interest than simple interest because the investor is earning interest on the interest. Interest can be compounded annually, semiannually, quarterly, monthly, daily, and continuously. 1. Determine number of compounding periods (years × periods per year). 2. Apply the simple interest formula, $I = PRT$, as many times as there are compounding periods, adding interest to principal before each succeeding calculation.	Manually calculate the compound amount of a $1,000 investment at 8% interest compounded annually for 2 years. Original principal 1,000.00 Interest—period 1 + 80.00 Principal—period 2 1,080.00 Interest—period 2 + 86.40 Compound Amount $1,166.40

I, continued

Topic	P/O, Page	Important Concepts	Illustrative Examples
Calculating Amount of Compound Interest	11–1 346	Amount of compound interest is calculated by subtracting the original principal from the compound amount. Compound interest = Compound amount – Principal	What is the amount of compound interest earned in the problem above? $1,166.40 – $1,000 = <u>$166.40</u>
Computing Compound Amount (Future Value) Using the Compound Interest Tables	11–2 347	1. Scan across the top row of Table 11-1 to find the interest rate per period. 2. Look down that column to the row corresponding to the number of compounding periods. 3. The table factor found at the intersection of the rate per period column and the periods row is the future value of $1.00 at compound interest. Compound amount = Table factor × Principal	Use Table 11-1 to find the compound amount of an investment of $2,000, at 12% interest compounded quarterly, for 6 years. Rate = 3% per period (12% ÷ 4) Periods = 24 (6 years × 4) Table factor = 2.03279 Compound amount = 2.03279 × 2,000 = <u>$4,065.58</u>
Creating Compound Interest Table Factors for Periods beyond the Table	11–3 349	1. For the stated interest rate per period, find any two table factors whose periods add up to the number of periods required. 2. Multiply the two table factors from Step 1 to form the new factor. 3. Round the new factor to five decimal places.	Create a new table factor for 5% interest for 35 periods. Multiply the 5% factors for 20 and 15 periods from Table 12-1, since 20 + 15 = 35. Factor 5%, 20 periods = 2.65330 Factor 5%, 15 periods = 2.07893 New table factor = 2.65330 × 2.07893 = 5.5160249 New factor, rounded = <u>5.51602</u>
Calculating Actual or Effective Interest Rate	11–4 350	To calculate effective rate, divide total compound interest earned in one year by the principal. Effective rate = $\dfrac{\text{One year compound interest}}{\text{Principal}}$	What is the effective rate of $5,000 invested for one year at 12% compounded monthly? From Table 11-1, we use the table factor for 12 periods, 1%, to find the compound amount: 1.12683 × 5,000 = 5,634.15 Interest = Cmp amt – Principal Int = 5,634.15 – 5,000 = 634.15 Effective rate = $\dfrac{634.15}{5,000}$ = <u>12.68%</u>

I, continued

Topic	P/O, Page	Important Concepts	Illustrative Examples
(Optional) Calculating Compound Amount (Future Value) Using the Compound Interest Formula	11–5 351	In addition to the compound interest tables, another method for calculating compound amount is by the compound interest formula. $$A = P(1 + i)^n$$ where A = Compound amount P = Principal i = Interest rate per period (decimal form) n = Number of compounding periods	What is the compound amount of $3,000 invested at 8% interest compounded quarterly for 10 years? $A = P(1 + i)^n$ $A = 3,000(1 + .02)^{40}$ $A = 3,000(1.02)^{40}$ $A = 3,000(2.2080396)$ $A = \underline{\$6,624.12}$

SECTION II PRESENT VALUE

Calculating the Present Value of a Future Amount Using the Present Value Tables	11–6 354	When the future value, an amount needed in the future, is known, the present value is the amount that must be invested today in order to accumulate, with compound interest, to that future value. 1. Scan across the top row of Table 11-2 to find the rate per period. 2. Look down that column to the row corresponding to the number of periods. 3. The table factor found at the intersection of the rate per period column and the periods row is the present value of $1.00 at compound interest. Present value = Table factor × Compound amount	How much must be invested now at 10% interest compounded semiannually, in order to have $8,000, 9 years from now? Rate = 5% (10% ÷ 2) Periods = 18 (9 years × 2) Table factor = .41552 Present value = .41552 × 8,000 Present value = $\underline{\$3,324.16}$
Creating Present Value Table Factors for Periods beyond the Table	11–7 356	1. For the stated rate per period, find any two table factors whose periods add up to the number of periods required. 2. Multiply the two table factors from Step 1 for the new factor. 3. Round the new factor to five decimal places.	Create a new table factor for 6% interest for 41 periods. Multiply the 6% factors for 21 and 20 periods from Table 11-2, since 21 + 20 = 41. Factor 6%, 21 periods = .29416 Factor 6%, 20 periods = .31180 New table factor = .29416 × .31180 = .0917191 New factor, rounded = $\underline{.09172}$
(Optional) Calculating Present Value of a Future Amount Using the Present Value Formula	11–8 357	If your calculator has an exponential function key, y^x, you can calculate the present value of an investment using the present value formula. $$PV = \frac{A}{(1 + i)^n}$$ where PV = Present value A = Compound amount i = Interest rate per period (decimal form) n = Total compounding periods	How much must be invested now in order to have $12,000 in 10 years, if the interest rate is 12% compounded quarterly? Present value = $\dfrac{12,000}{(1 + .03)^{40}}$ $PV = \dfrac{12,000}{(1.03)^{40}} = \dfrac{12,000}{3.2620378}$ Present value = $\underline{\$3,678.68}$

1.

10,000.00	Original principal
600.00	$(I = PRT = 10{,}000 \times .12 \times \frac{1}{2} = 600)$
10,600.00	Principal period 2
636.00	$(I = PRT = 10{,}600 \times .12 \times \frac{1}{2} = 636)$
11,236.00	Principal period 3
674.16	$(I = PRT = 11{,}236 \times .12 \times \frac{1}{2} = 674.16)$
11,910.16	Principal period 4
714.61	$(I = PRT = 11{,}910.16 \times .12 \times \frac{1}{2} = 714.61)$
12,624.77	Principal period 5
757.49	$(I = PRT = 12{,}624.77 \times .12 \times \frac{1}{2} = 757.49)$
13,382.26	Principal period 6
802.94	$(I = PRT = 13{,}382.26 \times .12 \times \frac{1}{2} = 802.94)$
$14,185.20	Compound amount

Compound interest = 14,185.20 − 10,000.00 = $4,185.20

2. 7%, 16 periods

Compound amount = Table factor × Principal

Compound amount = 2.95216 × 20,000 = $59,043.20

Compound interest = Compound amount − Principal

Compound interest = 59,043.20 − 20,000.00 = $39,043.20

3. Table factor required = 4%, 28 periods

4%, 14 periods: 1.73168

4%, 14 periods: × 1.73168

28 periods   2.9987156 = 2.99872 new factor
          4%, 28 periods

Compound amount = 2.99872 × 3,500 = $10,495.52

4. $1\frac{1}{2}$%, 4 periods

Compound amount = 1.06136 × 7,000 = $7,429.52

Compound interest = 7,429.52 − 7,000.00 = $429.52

$$\text{Effective rate} = \frac{1 \text{ yr int}}{\text{Principal}} = \frac{429.52}{7{,}000.00} = 6.14\%$$

5. $A = P(1 + i)^n$ $P = \$3{,}000$

$$i = \frac{8\%}{4} = .02$$

$$n = 5 \times 4 = 20$$

$A = 3{,}000(1 + .02)^{20}$

$A = 3{,}000(1.02)^{20}$

$A = 3{,}000(1.4859474)$

$A = \$4{,}457.84$

6. 2%, 12 periods

Present value = Table factor × Compound amount

Present value = .78849 × 300,000 = $236,547.00

7. Table factor required = $1\frac{1}{2}$%, 40 periods

$1\frac{1}{2}$%, 20 periods: .74247

$1\frac{1}{2}$%, 20 periods: × .74247

40 periods = .5512617 = .55126 new factor
          $1\frac{1}{2}$%, 40 periods

Present value = .55126 × 8,500 = $4,685.71

8. $PV = \dfrac{A}{(1 + i)^n}$ $A = 30{,}000$

$$i = \frac{8\%}{2} = .04$$

$$n = 17 \times 2 = 34$$

$$PV = \frac{30{,}000}{(1 + .04)^{34}}$$

$$PV = \frac{30{,}000}{(1.04)^{34}}$$

$$PV = \frac{30{,}000}{3.7943163} = \$7{,}906.56$$

ANSWERS

1. _____$31,530.66_____

_____$17,530.66_____

2. _____$10,370.82_____

_____$2,670.82_____

3. _____$3,586.86_____

_____$586.86_____

4. _____$305,060.28_____

_____$263,060.28_____

5. _____5.61652_____

_____$112,330.40_____

6. _____1.27049_____

_____$12,704.90_____

7. _____$1,078.06_____

_____12.68%_____

8. _____$82,430.00_____

_____8.24%_____

9. _____$6,930.00_____

_____$143,070.00_____

10. _____$14,259.80_____

_____$5,740.20_____

11. _____$658.35_____

_____$241.65_____

12. _____$4,981.52_____

_____$518.48_____

13. _____.62027_____

_____$806.35_____

14. _____.08720_____

_____$8,720.00_____

15. _____$81,392.40_____

_____$45,392.00_____

Completed, worked out solutions for
questions 1–14 appear in the appendix
following the index.

Using Table 11-1, calculate the compound amount and compound interest for the
following investments:

	Principal	Term of Investment	Nominal Rate	Interest Compounded	Compound Amount	Compound Interest
1.	$14,000	6 years	14%	semiannually	$31,530.66	$17,530.66
2.	$7,700	5 years	6%	quarterly	$10,370.82	$2,670.82
3.	$3,000	1 year	18%	monthly	$3,586.86	$586.86
4.	$42,000	19 years	11%	annually	$305,060.28	$263,060.28

The following investments require table factors for periods beyond the table. Create the
new table factor and calculate the compound amount for each:

	Principal	Term of Investment	Nominal Rate	Interest Compounded	New Table Factor	Compound Amount
5.	$20,000	11 years	16%	quarterly	5.61652	$112,330.40
6.	$10,000	4 years	6%	monthly	1.27049	$12,704.90

For the following investments, compute the amount of compound interest earned in one
year and the effective interest rate (round effective rate to the nearest hundredth
percent):

	Principal	Nominal Rate	Interest Compounded	Compound Interest Earned in 1 Year	Effective Rate
7.	$8,500	12%	monthly	$1,078.06	12.68%
8.	$1,000,000	8%	quarterly	$82,430.00	8.24%

Calculate the present value (principal) and the compound interest for the following
investments. Use Table 11-2 (round answers to the nearest cent):

	Compound Amount	Term of Investment	Nominal Rate	Interest Compounded	Present Value	Compound Interest
9.	$150,000	22 years	15%	annually	$6,930.00	$143,070.00
10.	$20,000	30 months	14%	semiannually	$14,259.80	$5,740.20
11.	$900	$1\frac{3}{4}$ years	18%	monthly	$658.35	$241.65
12.	$5,500	15 months	8%	quarterly	$4,981.52	$518.48

The following investments require table factors for periods beyond the table. Create the
new table factor and the present value for each:

	Principal	Term of Investment	Nominal Rate	Interest Compounded	New Table Factor	Present Value
13.	$1,300	4 years	12%	monthly	.62027	$806.35
14.	$100,000	50 years	5%	annually	.08720	$8,720.00

Solve the following word problems using either Tables 11-1 and 11-2 or the optional
compound interest and present value formulas. When necessary, create new table
factors (round dollars to the nearest cent and percents to the nearest hundredth):

15. What is the compound amount and compound interest of $36,000 invested at 12% com-
pounded semiannually for 7 years?
6%, 14 Periods
Compound amount = 2.26090 × 36,000 = $81,392.40
Compound interest = 81,392.40 − 36,000.00 = $45,392.40

16. What is the present value of $73,000 in 11 years if the interest rate is 8% compounded semiannually?

4%, 22 Periods

Present value = .42196 × 73,000 = $30,803.08

17. What is the compound amount and compound interest of $15,000 invested at 6% compounded quarterly for 27 months?

$1\frac{1}{2}$%, 9 Periods

Compound amount = 1.14339 × 15,000 = $17,150.85

Compound interest = 17,150.85 − 15,000.00 = $2,150.85

18. What is the effective rate of a $10,000 investment, for one year, at 12% interest compounded monthly?

1%, 12 Periods

Compound amount = 1.12683 × 10,000 = $11,268.30

1 yr. interest = 11,268.30 − 10,000 = $1,268.30

Effective rate = $\dfrac{1 \text{ yr. interest}}{\text{Principal}}$ = $\dfrac{1,268.30}{10,000.00}$ = 12.68%

19. Geoff and Audrey Coll want to save $50,000 in $5\frac{1}{2}$ years to redecorate their house. If the Bank of Kendall is paying 8% interest compounded quarterly, how much must they deposit now in order to have the money for the project?

2%, 22 Periods

Present value = .64684 × 50,000 = $32,342.00

20. What is the present value of $100,000 in 3 years if the interest rate is 6% compounded monthly?

Table value required .5%, 36 Periods

.5%, 18 Periods: .91414

.5%, 18 Periods: × .91414

    36 Periods   .8356519 = .83565

Present value = .83565 × 100,000 = $83,565.00

21. Tracy Morse invested $8,800 at the Worthington Credit Union at 12% interest compounded quarterly.

a. What is the effective rate of this investment?

3%, 4 Periods

Compound amount = 1.12551 × 8,800 = $9,904.49

1 yr. interest = 9,904.49 − 8,800.00 = $1,104.49

Effective rate = $\dfrac{1 \text{ yr. interest}}{\text{Principal}}$ = $\dfrac{1,104.49}{8,800.00}$ = 12.55%

b. What will Tracy's investment be worth after 6 years?

3%, 24 Periods

Compound amount = 2.03279 × 8,800 = $17,888.55

22. Swifty Delivery Service uses vans costing $13,800 each. How much will the company have to invest today in order to accumulate enough money to buy 6 new vans at the end of 4 years? Swifty's bank is currently paying 12% interest compounded quarterly.

Amount needed = 13,800 × 6 = $82,800

3%, 16 Periods

Present value = .62317 × 82,800 = $51,598.48

Name_____

Class_____

ANSWERS

16. _____$30,803.08_____

17. _____$17,150.85_____

_____$2,150.85_____

18. _____12.68%_____

19. _____$32,342.00_____

20. _____$83,565.00_____

21. a. _____12.55%_____

b. _____$17,888.55_____

22. _____$51,598.48_____

ANSWERS

23. _____$48,545.40_____

24. a. ____249,235.11 Sq. ft.____

b. ____240,582.38 Sq. ft.____

____Build after $3\frac{1}{2}$ years____

25. a. _____$1,414,750.00_____

b. _____$1,425,000 now_____

23. While rummaging through the attic, you discover a savings account left to you by your rich uncle David. When you were 5 years old, he invested $20,000 in your name, at 6% interest compounded semiannually. If you are now 20 years old, how much is the account worth?

Table value needed = 3%, 30 Periods

3%, 15 Periods: 1.55797
3%, <u>15</u> Periods: × 1.55797
     30 Periods   2.4272705 = 2.42727 "New" factor 3%, 30 periods

Compound amount = 2.42727 × 20,000 = <u>$48,545.40</u>

24. General Manufacturing, Inc., is planning to expand its production facility in a few years. New plant construction costs are estimated to be $4.50 per square foot. The company invests $850,000 today at 8% interest compounded quarterly.

a. How many square feet of new facility could be built after $3\frac{1}{2}$ years?

2%, 14 Periods

Compound amount = 1.31948 × 850,000 = $1,121,558.00

$$\text{sq ft} = \frac{1,121,558}{4.50} = \underline{249,235.11 \text{ Sq. ft.}}$$

b. If the company waits 5 years, but construction costs increase to $5.25 per square foot, how many square feet could be built? What do you recommend?

2%, 20 Periods

Compound amount = 1.48595 × 850,000 = $1,263,057.50

$$\text{sq ft} = \frac{1,263,057.50}{5.25} = \underline{240,582.38 \text{ Sq. ft.}}$$

Recommend: Build after $3\frac{1}{2}$ years

 BUSINESS DECISION
Pay Me Now, Pay Me Later

25. You are the owner of an apartment building that is being offered for sale for $1,500,000. You receive an offer from a prospective buyer who wants to pay you $500,000 now, $500,000 in six months, and $500,000 in one year.

a. What is the actual present value of this offer under the time value of money concept, considering you can earn 12% interest compounded monthly on your money?

Present value of $500,000 in 6 months 1%, 6 Periods $500,000.00 Now
Present value = .94205 × 500,000 = $471,025.00   471,025.00 6 Months
                                                    + 443,725.00 12 Months
Present value of $500,000 in 1 year 1%, 12 Periods $1,414,750.00 Present value of offer
Present value = .88745 × 500,000 = $443,725.00

b. If another buyer offers to pay you $1,425,000 cash now, which is a better deal?

<u>$1,425,000.00 Cash now is a better deal</u>

Putting Your Money to Work!

Checking Accounts

In Chapter 4, we learned about checking accounts. The money left in checking accounts is known as **demand deposits,** since it can be withdrawn "on demand," without advance notice. Over the years, these basic, no-frills accounts have lost popularity since they do not pay interest on the depositor's money.

Today, banks offer checking accounts that do pay interest. These accounts, commonly called **NOW accounts** (negotiable order of withdrawal), allow unlimited check writing, but require minimum balances ranging from a few hundred dollars to a few thousand dollars.

Another popular form of deposit account is known as a **money market account.** These pay even higher interest rates than NOW accounts, but have check writing limitations.

Savings Accounts

One common form of savings account is called a **passbook savings account.** These are a safe place to keep money; however the interest rates paid are not very competitive and there are no check writing privileges.

"IT'S THE ARCHITECT'S FIRST SKYSCRAPER. SOMEONE TOLD HIM IT'S TRADITIONAL TO LEAVE OUT THE THIRTEENTH FLOOR."

BLAIR

Another form of time deposit, **certificates of deposit (CDs),** pay higher interest than passbook savings accounts. These are notes issued by commercial banks or other financial institutions that guarantee a depositor a predetermined rate of interest for a specified period of time.

The latest offering in the certificate of deposit category of investments is known as the **bump-up CD.** These have rates that rise at least once during the term of the deposit and you can add up to 100% of your initial deposit whenever you like.

SOURCES: Adapted from "CDs That Try a Little Harder," *Business Week*, September 5, 1994, "How to Pick Up Sexier CDs" *Business Week*, Feburary 13, 1995.

The Rule of 72

Did you know there is an easy method for calculating how long it takes an amount of money to double in value at compound interest? Simply divide the number 72 by the interest rate. The result is the number of years it takes to double in value.

$$\text{Years to double} = \frac{72}{\text{Compound interest rate}}$$

For example, if you invested money at 6% compound interest, it would take 12 years ($\frac{72}{6} = 12$) to double your money. If you were able to find an investment that paid 9% interest, you could double your money in 8 years ($\frac{72}{6} = 8$).

Triskaidekaphobia

Did you know that triskaidekaphobia is a fear of the number 13? Most commonly, people with this phobia may have a fear of Friday the 13th, or living or working on the 13th floor of a building.

I'll Take Manhattan— The "Magic" of Compound Interest

In 1626, Peter Minuit, a Dutchman, is said to have purchased Manhattan Island from the Native Americans for the equivalent of $24 in trade goods and trinkets. At first, this might seem like an incredibly low price. But wait! Let's put the time value of money to work.

A. Using the compound interest formula from this chapter, if the Native Amerians had invested the $24 at 6% annual interest, by 1996, 370 years later, how much would their $24 be worth?

B. If they could have invested the money at 8% annual interest, rather than 6, how much would their $24 be worth?

The solution appears in the next issue of The Business Math Times on page 399.

Brainteaser

If a digital clock is the only light in an otherwise totally dark room, at what time will the room be the darkest? Brightest?

SOURCE: *Mathematics Teacher* Magazine (May 1996), p.404.

Answer to Last Issue's Brainteaser
20 cars and 10 motorcycles

Let C = number of cars and M = number of motorcycles

$$C + M = 30$$
$$4C + 2M = 100$$
$$M = 30 - C$$
$$4C + 2(30 - C) = 100$$
$$4C + 60 - 2C = 100$$
$$2C = 40$$
$$C = 20 \quad M = 10$$

Chapter 12

Annuities

Performance Objectives

SECTION I FUTURE VALUE OF AN ANNUITY: ORDINARY AND ANNUITY DUE

SECTION II PRESENT VALUE OF AN ANNUITY

SECTION III SINKING FUNDS AND AMORTIZATION

FUTURE VALUE OF AN ANNUITY: ORDINARY AND ANNUITY DUE

The concepts relating to compound interest in Chapter 11 were mainly concerned with lump sum investments or payments. Frequently in business, situations involve a series of equal periodic payments or receipts, rather than lump sums. These are known as annuities. An **annuity** is the payment or receipt of *equal* cash amounts per period for a specified amount of time. Some common applications are insurance and retirement plan premiums and payouts; loan payments; or savings plans for future events such as starting a business, going to college, or purchasing expensive items like real estate or business equipment.

In this chapter you will learn to calculate the future value of an annuity, the amount accumulated at compound interest from a series of equal periodic payments. You will also learn to calculate the present value of an annuity, the amount that must be deposited now at compound interest to yield a series of equal periodic payments. Exhibit 12-1 graphically shows the difference between a future value annuity and a present value annuity.

All of the problems in this chapter will be of the type known as **simple annuities.** This means that the number of compounding periods per year coincides with the number of annuity payments per year. For example, if the annuity payments are monthly, the interest is compounded monthly; if the annuity payments are made every six months, the interest is compounded semiannually. **Complex annuities** are those in which the annuity payments and compounding periods do not coincide.

As with compound interest, annuity problems can be solved manually, by tables, and by formulas. Manual computation is useful for illustrative purposes; however, it is too tedious for problem solving because it requires a calculation for each period. The table method is the easiest and most widely used, and shall be the basis for this chapter's exercises. As in Chapter 11, there are formulas to solve annuity problems, however they require calculators with the exponential function key, y^x, and the change-of-sign key, $+/-$. These optional performance objectives are for students with business or financial calculators.

12-1 Calculating the Future Value of an Ordinary Annuity Using Tables

Annuities are categorized into annuities certain and contingent annuities. **Annuities certain** are those that have a specified number of periods, such as $200 per month for 5 years, or $500 semiannually for 10 years. **Contingent annuities** are based on an uncertain time period, such as a retirement plan that is payable only for the lifetime of the retiree. This chapter will be concerned only with annuities certain.

• annuity
Payment or receipt of equal amounts of money per period for a specified amount of time.

• simple annuity
Annuity in which the number of compounding periods per year coincides with the number of annuity payments per year.

• complex annuity
Annuity in which the annuity payments and compounding periods do not coincide.

• annuities certain
Annuities that have a specified number of time periods.

• contingent annuities
Annuities based on an uncertain time period, such as the life of a person.

EXHIBIT 12-1

TIME LINE ILLUSTRATING PRESENT AND FUTURE VALUE OF ANNUITIES

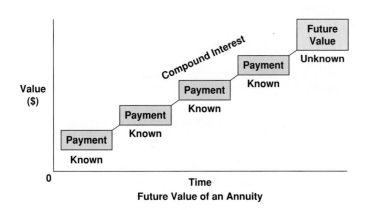

Future Value of an Annuity

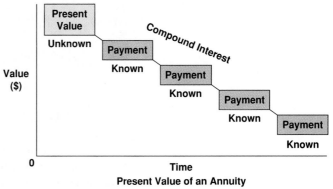

Present Value of an Annuity

● ordinary annuity
Annuity that is paid or received at the end of each time period.

● annuity due
Annuity that is paid or received at the beginning of each time period.

● future value of an annuity
The total amount of the annuity payments and the accumulated interest on those payments. Also known as the amount of an annuity.

When the annuity payment is made at the end of each period it is known as an **ordinary annuity.** When the payment is made at the beginning of each period, it is called an **annuity due.** A salary paid at the end of each month is an example of an ordinary annuity. A mortgage payment or rent paid at the beginning of each month is an example of an annuity due.

The **future value of an annuity** is also known as the amount of an annuity. It is the total of the annuity payments plus the accumulated compound interest on those payments.

For illustrative purposes, consider the following example, calculated manually.

EXAMPLE

What is the future value of an ordinary annuity of $10,000 per year, for 4 years, at 6% interest compounded annually?

SOLUTION STRATEGY

Because this is an ordinary annuity, the payment is made at the *end* of each period, in this case years. Each interest calculation uses $I = PRT$, with $R = .06$, and $T = 1$ year.

Time	Balance	
Beginning of period 1	0	
	+ 10,000.00	First annuity payment (end of period 1)
End of period 1	10,000.00	
Beginning of period 2	10,000.00	
	600.00	Interest earned, period 2 $(10,000,00 \times .06 \times 1)$
	+ 10,000.00	Second annuity payment (end of period 2)
End of period 2	20,600.00	
Beginning of period 3	20,600.00	
	1,236.00	Interest earned, period 3 $(20,600.00 \times .06 \times 1)$
	+ 10,000.00	Third annuity payment (end of period 3)
End of period 3	31,836.00	
Beginning of period 4	31,836.00	
	1,910.16	Interest earned, period 4 $(31,836.00 \times .06 \times 1)$
	+ 10,000.00	Fourth annuity payment (end of period 4)
End of period 4	$43,746.16	Future value of the ordinary annuity

As you can see, working annuity problems this way is quite tedious. An annuity of ten years, with payments made monthly, would require 120 calculations. As with compound interest, we shall use tables to calculate the future value (amount) of an annuity. Note that the steps for using annuity tables are similar to those used with the compound interest tables.

STEPS FOR CALCULATING FUTURE VALUE (AMOUNT) OF AN ORDINARY ANNUITY:

Step 1. Calculate the interest rate per period for the annuity (nominal rate ÷ periods per year).

Step 2. Determine the number of periods of the annuity (years × periods per year).

Step 3. From Table 12-1, locate the ordinary annuity table factor at the intersection of the rate column and the periods row.

Step 4. Calculate the future value of the ordinary annuity using the formula:

$$\frac{\text{Future value}}{\text{(ordinary annuity)}} = \frac{\text{Ordinary annuity}}{\text{table factor}} \times \frac{\text{Annuity}}{\text{payment}}$$

EXAMPLE

Yvette Rubio deposited $3,000 at the *end* of each year for 8 years in her savings account. If her bank paid 5% interest compounded annually, use Table 12-1 to find the future value of Yvette's account.

SOLUTION STRATEGY

Step 1. The rate period is 5% (5% ÷ 1 period per year).
Step 2. The number of periods is 8 (8 years × 1 period per year).
Step 3. From Table 12-1, the table factor for 5%, 8 periods is 9.54911.
Step 4. Future value = Table factor × Annuity payment

Future value = $9.54911 \times 3,000 = \underline{\$28,647.33}$

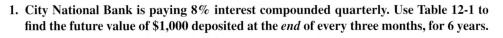

TRY-IT EXERCISE

1. **City National Bank is paying 8% interest compounded quarterly. Use Table 12-1 to find the future value of $1,000 deposited at the *end* of every three months, for 6 years.**

Check your answer with the solution on page 394.

12-2 Calculating the Future Value of an Annuity Due Using Tables

Once again, for illustrative purposes, let's manually calculate the future value of the annuity from Section 12-1, page 370. This time, however, it will be an annuity due.

EXAMPLE

What is the amount of an annuity due of $10,000 per year, for 4 years, at 6% interest compounded annually?

SOLUTION STRATEGY

Because this is an annuity due, the payment is made at the *beginning* of each period. Each interest calculation uses $I = PRT$, with $R = .06$, and $T = 1$ year.

Time	Balance	
Beginning of period 1	10,000.00	First annuity payment (beginning of period 1)
	+ 600.00	Interest earned, period 1 (10,000.00 × .06 × 1)
End of period 1	10,600.00	
Beginning of period 2	10,600.00	
	10,000.00	Second annuity payment (beginning of period 2)
	+ 1,236.00	Interest earned, period 2 (20,600.00 × .06 × 1)
End of period 2	21,836.00	
Beginning of period 3	21,836.00	
	10,000.00	Third annuity payment (beginning of period 3)
	+ 1,910.16	Interest earned, period 3 (31,836.00 × .06 × 1)
End of period 3	33,746.16	
Beginning of period 4	33,746.16	
	10,000.00	Fourth annuity payment (beginning of period 4)
	+ 2,624.76	Interest earned, period 4 (43,746.16 × .06 × 1)
End of period 4	$46,370.92	

TABLE 12-1 [T]

FUTURE VALUE (AMOUNT) OF AN ORDINARY ANNUITY OF $1.00

Periods	$\frac{1}{2}$%	1%	$1\frac{1}{2}$%	2%	3%	4%	5%	6%	7%	8%	Periods
1	1.00000	1.00000	1.00000	1.00000	1.00000	1.00000	1.00000	1.00000	1.00000	1.00000	1
2	2.00500	2.01000	2.01500	2.02000	2.03000	2.04000	2.05000	2.06000	2.07000	2.08000	2
3	3.01502	3.03010	3.04522	3.06040	3.09090	3.12160	3.15250	3.18360	3.21490	3.24640	3
4	4.03010	4.06040	4.09090	4.12161	4.18363	4.24646	4.31013	4.37462	4.43994	4.50611	4
5	5.05025	5.10101	5.15227	5.20404	5.30914	5.41632	5.52563	5.63709	5.75074	5.86660	5
6	6.07550	6.15202	6.22955	6.30812	6.46841	6.63298	6.80191	6.97532	7.15329	7.33593	6
7	7.10588	7.21354	7.32299	7.43428	7.66246	7.89829	8.14201	8.39384	8.65402	8.92280	7
8	8.14141	8.28567	8.43284	8.58297	8.89234	9.21423	9.54911	9.89747	10.25980	10.63663	8
9	9.18212	9.36853	9.55933	9.75463	10.15911	10.58280	11.02656	11.49132	11.97799	12.48756	9
10	10.22803	10.46221	10.70272	10.94972	11.46388	12.00611	12.57789	13.18079	13.81645	14.48656	10
11	11.27917	11.56683	11.86326	12.16872	12.80780	13.48635	14.20679	14.97164	15.78360	16.64549	11
12	12.33556	12.68250	13.04121	13.41209	14.19203	15.02581	15.91713	16.86994	17.88845	18.97713	12
13	13.39724	13.80933	14.23683	14.68033	15.61779	16.62684	17.71298	18.88214	20.14064	21.49530	13
14	14.46423	14.94742	15.45038	15.97394	17.08632	18.29191	19.59863	21.01507	22.55049	24.21492	14
15	15.53655	16.09690	16.68214	17.29342	18.59891	20.02359	21.57856	23.27597	25.12902	27.15211	15
16	16.61423	17.25786	17.93237	18.63929	20.15688	21.82453	23.65749	25.67253	27.88805	30.32428	16
17	17.69730	18.43044	19.20136	20.01207	21.76159	23.69751	25.84037	28.21288	30.84022	33.75023	17
18	18.78579	19.61475	20.48938	21.41231	23.41444	25.64541	28.13238	30.90565	33.99903	37.45024	18
19	19.87972	20.81090	21.79672	22.84056	25.11687	27.67123	30.53900	33.75999	37.37896	41.44626	19
20	20.97912	22.01900	23.12367	24.29737	26.87037	29.77808	33.06595	36.78559	40.99549	45.76196	20
21	22.08401	23.23919	24.47052	25.78332	28.67649	31.96920	35.71925	39.99273	44.86518	50.42292	21
22	23.19443	24.47159	25.83758	27.29898	30.53678	34.24797	38.50521	43.39229	49.00574	55.45676	22
23	24.31040	25.71630	27.22514	28.84496	32.45288	36.61789	41.43048	46.99583	53.43614	60.89330	23
24	25.43196	26.97346	28.63352	30.42186	34.42647	39.08260	44.50200	50.81558	58.17667	66.76476	24
25	26.55912	28.24320	30.06302	32.03030	36.45926	41.64591	47.72710	54.86451	63.24904	73.10594	25
26	27.69191	29.52563	31.51397	33.67091	38.55304	44.31174	51.11345	59.15638	68.67647	79.95442	26
27	28.83037	30.82089	32.98668	35.34432	40.70963	47.08421	54.66913	63.70577	74.48382	87.35077	27
28	29.97452	32.12910	34.48148	37.05121	42.93092	49.96758	58.40258	68.52811	80.69769	95.33883	28
29	31.12439	33.45039	35.99870	38.79223	45.21885	52.96629	62.32271	73.63980	87.34653	103.96594	29
30	32.28002	34.78489	37.53868	40.56808	47.57542	56.08494	66.43885	79.05819	94.46079	113.28321	30
31	33.44142	36.13274	39.10176	42.37944	50.00268	59.32834	70.76079	84.80168	102.07304	123.34587	31
32	34.60862	37.49407	40.68829	44.22703	52.50276	62.70147	75.29883	90.88978	110.21815	134.21354	32
33	35.78167	38.86901	42.29861	46.11157	55.07784	66.20953	80.06377	97.34316	118.93343	145.95062	33
34	36.96058	40.25770	43.93309	48.03380	57.73018	69.85791	85.06696	104.18375	128.25876	158.62667	34
35	38.14538	41.66028	45.59209	49.99448	60.46208	73.65222	90.32031	111.43478	138.23688	172.31680	35
36	39.33610	43.07688	47.27597	51.99437	63.27594	77.59831	95.83632	119.12087	148.91346	187.10215	36

Note that the interest earned with an annuity due is higher than that of an ordinary annuity, because the annuity due starts earning interest from the *beginning* of the first period, not the *end*. Future values of annuities due table factors are calculated using the same table as ordinary annuities (Table 12-1), with some modifications in the steps.

STEPS FOR CALCULATING FUTURE VALUE (AMOUNT) OF AN ANNUITY DUE:

Step 1. Calculate the number of periods of the annuity (years × periods per year), and add 1 period to the total.

Step 2. Calculate the interest rate per period (nominal rate ÷ periods per year).

Step 3. From Table 12-1, locate the table factor at the intersection of the rate column and the periods row.

Step 4. Subtract 1.00000 from the ordinary annuity table factor to get the annuity due table factor.

Step 5. Calculate the future value of the annuity due by the formula:

Future value (annuity due) = Annuity due table factor × Annuity payment

Periods	9%	10%	11%	12%	13%	14%	15%	16%	17%	18%	Periods
1	1.00000	1.00000	1.00000	1.00000	1.00000	1.00000	1.00000	1.00000	1.00000	1.00000	1
2	2.09000	2.10000	2.11000	2.12000	2.13000	2.14000	2.15000	2.16000	2.17000	2.18000	2
3	3.27810	3.31000	3.34210	3.37440	3.40690	3.43960	3.47250	3.50560	3.53890	3.57240	3
4	4.57313	4.64100	4.70973	4.77933	4.84980	4.92114	4.99338	5.06650	5.14051	5.21543	4
5	5.98471	6.10510	6.22780	6.35285	6.48027	6.61010	6.74238	6.87714	7.01440	7.15421	5
6	7.52333	7.71561	7.91286	8.11519	8.32271	8.53552	8.75374	8.97748	9.20685	9.44197	6
7	9.20043	9.48717	9.78327	10.08901	10.40466	10.73049	11.06680	11.41387	11.77201	12.14152	7
8	11.02847	11.43589	11.85943	12.29969	12.75726	13.23276	13.72682	14.24009	14.77325	15.32700	8
9	13.02104	13.57948	14.16397	14.77566	15.41571	16.08535	16.78584	17.51851	18.28471	19.08585	9
10	15.19293	15.93742	16.72201	17.54874	18.41975	19.33730	20.30372	21.32147	22.39311	23.52131	10
11	17.56029	18.53117	19.56143	20.65458	21.81432	23.04452	24.34928	25.73290	27.19994	28.75514	11
12	20.14072	21.38428	22.71319	24.13313	25.65018	27.27075	29.00167	30.85017	32.82393	34.93107	12
13	22.95338	24.52271	26.21164	28.02911	29.98470	32.08865	34.35192	36.78620	39.40399	42.21866	13
14	26.01919	27.97498	30.09492	32.39260	34.88271	37.58107	40.50471	43.67199	47.10267	50.81802	14
15	29.36092	31.77248	34.40536	37.27971	40.41746	43.84241	47.58041	51.65951	56.11013	60.96527	15
16	33.00340	35.94973	39.18995	42.75328	46.67173	50.98035	55.71747	60.92503	66.64885	72.93901	16
17	36.97370	40.54470	44.50084	48.88367	53.73906	59.11760	65.07509	71.67303	78.97915	87.06804	17
18	41.30134	45.59917	50.39594	55.74971	61.72514	68.39407	75.83636	84.14072	93.40561	103.74028	18
19	46.01846	51.15909	56.93949	63.43968	70.74941	78.96923	88.21181	98.60323	110.28456	123.41353	19
20	51.16012	57.27500	64.20283	72.05244	80.94683	91.02493	102.44358	115.37975	130.03294	146.62797	20
21	56.76453	64.00250	72.26514	81.69874	92.46992	104.76842	118.81012	134.84051	153.13854	174.02100	21
22	62.87334	71.40275	81.21431	92.50258	105.49101	120.43600	137.63164	157.41499	180.17209	206.34479	22
23	69.53194	79.54302	91.14788	104.60289	120.20484	138.29704	159.27638	183.60138	211.80134	244.48685	23
24	76.78981	88.49733	102.17415	118.15524	136.83147	158.65862	184.16784	213.97761	248.80757	289.49448	24
25	84.70090	98.34706	114.41331	133.33387	155.61956	181.87083	212.79302	249.21402	292.10486	342.60349	25
26	93.32398	109.18177	127.99877	150.33393	176.85010	208.33274	245.71197	290.08827	342.76268	405.27211	26
27	102.72313	121.09994	143.07864	169.37401	200.84061	238.49933	283.56877	337.50239	402.03234	479.22109	27
28	112.96822	134.20994	159.81729	190.69889	227.94989	272.88923	327.10408	392.50277	471.37783	566.48089	28
29	124.13536	148.63093	178.39719	214.58275	258.58338	312.09373	377.16969	456.30322	552.51207	669.44745	29
30	136.30754	164.49402	199.02088	241.33268	293.19922	356.78685	434.74515	530.31173	647.43912	790.94799	30
31	149.57522	181.94342	221.91317	271.29261	332.31511	407.73701	500.95692	616.16161	758.50377	934.31863	31
32	164.03699	201.13777	247.32362	304.84772	376.51608	465.82019	577.10046	715.74746	888.44941	1103.49598	32
33	179.80032	222.25154	275.52922	342.42945	426.46317	532.03501	664.66552	831.26706	1040.48581	1303.12526	33
34	196.98234	245.47670	306.83744	384.52098	482.90338	607.51991	765.36535	965.26979	1218.36839	1538.68781	34
35	215.71075	271.02437	341.58955	431.66350	546.68082	693.57270	881.17016	1120.71295	1426.49102	1816.65161	35
36	236.12472	299.12681	380.16441	484.46312	618.74933	791.67288	1014.34568	1301.02703	1669.99450	2144.64890	36

EXAMPLE

Scott Timian deposited $60 at the *beginning* of each month, for 2 years, at his credit union. If the interest rate was 12% compounded monthly, use Table 12-1 to calculate the future value of Scott's account.

SOLUTION STRATEGY

Step 1. Number of periods of the annuity due is 24 (2×12) + 1 for a total of 25.

Step 2. Interest rate per period is 1% (12% ÷ 12).

Step 3. The ordinary annuity table factor at the intersection of the rate column and the periods row is 28.24320.

Step 4. Subtract 1.00000 from table factor:

$$\begin{array}{ll} 28.24320 & \text{ordinary annuity table factor} \\ \underline{-\ 1.00000} & \\ 27.24320 & \text{annuity due table factor} \end{array}$$

Step 5. Future value = Annuity due table factor × Annuity payment

Future value = 27.24320 × 60 = $\underline{\$1,634.59}$

2. **Atlanta Savings & Loan is paying 6% interest compounded quarterly. Use Table 12-1 to calculate the future value of $1,000, deposited at the *beginning* of every 3 months, for 5 years.**

Check your answer with the solution on page 394.

12-3 (Optional) Calculating the Future Value of an Ordinary Annuity and an Annuity Due by Formula

Students with financial, business, or scientific calculators may use the following formulas to solve for the future value of an ordinary annuity and the future value of an annuity due. Note that the annuity due formula is the same as the ordinary annuity formula except it is multiplied by $(1 + i)$. This is to account for the fact that with an annuity due each payment earns interest for one additional period, because payments are made at the beginning of each period, not the end.

Future value of an ordinary annuity

$$FV = Pmt \times \frac{(1 + i)^n - 1}{i}$$

Future value of an annuity due

$$FV = Pmt \times \frac{(1 + i)^n - 1}{i} \times (1 + i)$$

where

FV = Future Value

Pmt = annuity payment

i = interest rate per period (nominal rate ÷ periods per year)

n = number of periods (years × periods per year)

Ordinary Annuity

Calculator Sequence: 1 [+] i [=] [y^x] n [−] 1 [÷] i [×] Pmt [=] $FV_{\text{ordinary annuity}}$

Annuity Due

Calculator Sequence: 1 [+] i [=] [×] $FV_{\text{ordinary annuity}}$ [=] $FV_{\text{annuity due}}$

EXAMPLES

a. **What is the future value of an ordinary annuity of $100 per month, for 3 years, at 12% interest compounded monthly?**

b. **What is the future value of this investment if it is an annuity due?**

SOLUTION STRATEGY

a. For this future value of an ordinary annuity problem we shall use $i = 1\%$ ($12\% \div 12$), and $n = 36$ periods (3 years × 12 periods per year).

$$FV = Pmt \times \frac{(1 + i)^n - 1}{i}$$

$$FV = 100 \times \frac{(1 + .01)^{36} - 1}{.01}$$

$$FV = 100 \times \frac{(1.01)^{36} - 1}{.01}$$

$$FV = 100 \times \frac{1.4307688 - 1}{.01}$$

$$FV = 100 \times \frac{.4307688}{.01}$$

$$FV = 100 \times 43.07688 = \underline{\$4,307.69}$$

Calculator Sequence: 1 ➕ .01 ═ y^x 36 ➖ 1 ➗ .01 ✖ 100 ═ $\underline{\$4,307.69}$

b. To solve the problem as an annuity due, rather than an ordinary annuity, multiply $(1 + i)$, for one extra compounding period, by the future value of the ordinary annuity.

$$FV_{\text{annuity due}} = (1 + i) \times FV_{\text{ordinary annuity}}$$
$$FV_{\text{annuity due}} = (1 + .01) \times 4,307.69$$
$$FV_{\text{annuity due}} = (1.01) \times 4,307.69 = \underline{\$4,350.77}$$

Calculator Sequence: 1 ➕ .01 ═ ✖ 4,307.69 ═ $\underline{\$4,350.77}$

TRY-IT   EXERCISE

3. Ruth Rominger invested $250 at the *end* of every 3-month period, for 5 years, at 8% interest compounded quarterly.

   a. How much is Ruth's investment worth after 5 years?

   b. If Ruth would have invested the money at the *beginning* of each 3-month period, rather than at the end, how much would be in the account?

Check your answers with the solutions on page 394.

REVIEW EXERCISES   CHAPTER 12—SECTION I

Use Table 12-1 to calculate the future value of the following ordinary annuities:

	Annuity Payment	Payment Frequency	Time Period	Nominal Rate	Interest Compounded	Future Value of the Annuity
1.	$1,000	every 3 months	4 years	8%	quarterly	$18,639.29
2.	$2,500	every 6 months	5 years	10%	semiannually	$31,444.73
3.	$10,000	every year	10 years	9%	annually	$151,929.30
4.	$200	every month	2 years	12%	monthly	$5,394.69
5.	$1,500	every 3 months	7 years	16%	quarterly	$74,951.37

Use Table 12-1 to calculate the future value of the following annuities due:

	Annuity Payment	Payment Frequency	Time Period	Nominal Rate	Interest Compounded	Future Value of the Annuity
6.	$400	every 6 months	12 years	10%	semiannually	$18,690.84
7.	$1,000	every 3 months	3 years	8%	quarterly	$13,680.33
8.	$50	every month	$2\frac{1}{2}$ years	18%	monthly	$1,905.09
9.	$2,000	every year	25 years	5%	annually	$100,226.90
10.	$4,400	every 6 months	8 years	6%	semiannually	$91,351.00

Solve the following word problems using Table 12-1:

11. Grove Isle Savings & Loan is paying 6% interest compounded monthly. How much will $100 deposited at the *end* of each month be worth after two years?

    $R = \frac{1}{2}\%$ $P = 24$ $F = 25.43196$
    Annuity $= 25.43196 \times 100 = \underline{\$2,543.20}$

12. Emory Distributors, Inc., deposits $5,000 at the *beginning* of each 3-month period for 6 years in an account paying 8% interest compounded quarterly.

    a. How much will be in the account at the end of the 6-year period?
       $R = 2\%$ $P = 24 + 1 = 25$ $F = 32.03030 - 1.00000$
       Annuity $= 31.03030 \times 5,000 = \underline{\$155,151.50}$

    b. What is the total amount of interest earned in this account?
       Total investment $= 5000.00 \times 24 = 120,000.00$
       Interest earned $= 155,151.50 - 120,000.00 = \underline{\$35,151.50}$

13. Kassy Morgan is planning for her retirement. She deposits $3,000 at the *beginning* of each year into an account paying 5% interest compounded annually.

    a. How much would the account be worth after 10 years?
       $R = 5\%$ $P = 10 + 1 = 11$ $F = 14.20679 - 1.00000$
       $3,000.00 \times 13.20679 = \underline{\$39,620.37}$

    b. How much would the account be worth after 20 years?
       $R = 5\%$ $P = 20 + 1 = 21$ $F = 35.71925 - 1.00000$
       $3,000.00 \times 34.71925 = \underline{\$104,157.75}$

    c. When Kassy retires, in 30 years, what will be the total worth of the account?
       $R = 5\%$ $P = 30 + 1 = 31$ $F = 70.76079 - 1.00000$
       $3,000.00 \times 69.76079 = \underline{\$209,282.37}$

    d. If Kassy found a bank that paid 6% interest compounded annually, rather than 5%, how much more would she have in the account after 30 years?
       $R = 5\%$ $P = 30 + 1 = 31$ $F = 84.80168 - 1.00000$
       $3,000.00 \times 83.80168 = \underline{\$251,405.04}$

       $251,405.04 - 209,282.37 = \underline{\$42,122.67}$ More

14. When Pablo Magadan was born, his parents began depositing $500 at the *beginning* of every year into an annuity to save for his college education. If the account paid 7% interest compounded annually for the first ten years, and then dropped to 5% for the next

8 years, how much is the account worth now that Pablo is 18 years old and is ready for college?

Amount 500.00 $R = 7\%$ $P = 10 + 1 = 11$ $F = 15.78360 - 1.00000$

$500.00 \times 14.78360 = \$7,391.80$ First 10 years

Amount 500.00 $R = 5\%$ $P = 8 + 1 = 9$ $F = 11.02656 - 1.00000$

$500.00 \times 10.02656 = 5,013.28$ Next 8 years

$\$7,391.80 + \$5,013.28 = \underline{\$12,405.08}$ After 18 years

15. The Nails and Pails Hardware Store has been in business for a few years and is doing very well. The owner has decided to save for a future expansion to a second location. He invests $1,000 at the *end* of every month at 12% interest compounded monthly.

a. How much will be available for the second store after $2\frac{1}{2}$ years?

$R = 1\%$ $P = 30$ $F = 34.78489$

$1,000.00 \times 34.78489 = \underline{\$34,784.89}$

b. (Optional) Use the formula for an ordinary annuity to calculate how much would be in the account if the owner of Nails and Pails saved for 5 years.

$R = 1\%$ $P = 60$

$FV = 1,000 \dfrac{(1 + .01)^{60} - 1}{.01} = \underline{\$81,669.67}$ Ordinary annuity

c. (Optional) Use the formula for an annuity due to calculate how much would be in the account after 5 years if it had been an annuity due.

$FV = (1 + .01) \times 81,669.67 = \underline{\$82,486.37}$ Annuity due

PRESENT VALUE OF AN ANNUITY

In Section I of this chapter we learned to calculate the future value of annuities. These business situations require that a series of equal payments be made into an account, such as a savings account; it starts with nothing, and accumulates at compound interest to a future amount. Now consider the opposite situation. What if we wanted an account from which we could withdraw a series of equal payments over a period of time? This business situation requires that a lump sum amount be deposited at compound interest at the beginning of the period to yield the annuity payments. The lump sum required at the beginning is known as the **present value of an annuity.**

Let's look at a business situation using this type of annuity. A company owes $10,000 interest to bondholders at the end of each month for the next 3 years. The company decides to set up an account with a lump sum deposit now, which at compound interest will yield the $10,000 monthly payments for 3 years. After 3 years the debt will have been paid, and the account will be zero.

Just as in Section I, present value annuities can be ordinary, whereby withdrawals from the account are made at the end of each period, or annuity due, in which the withdrawals are made at the beginning. As with future value annuities, we shall use tables to calculate the present value of an annuity. Once again, in addition to tables, present value annuities can be solved by using formulas requiring a calculator with a y^x key.

● **present value of an annuity**
Lump sum amount of money that must be deposited today in order to provide a specified series of equal payments (annuity) in the future.

12-4 Calculating the Present Value of an Ordinary Annuity Using Tables

Table 12-2, Present Value of an Ordinary Annuity, will be used to calculate the lump sum required to be deposited now to yield the annuity payment.

TABLE 12-2

PRESENT VALUE (AMOUNT) OF AN ORDINARY ANNUITY OF $1.00

Periods	$\frac{1}{2}$%	1%	$1\frac{1}{2}$%	2%	3%	4%	5%	6%	7%	8%	Periods
1	0.99502	0.99010	0.98522	0.98039	0.97087	0.96154	0.95238	0.94340	0.93458	0.92593	1
2	1.98510	1.97040	1.95588	1.94156	1.91347	1.88609	1.85941	1.83339	1.80802	1.78326	2
3	2.97025	2.94099	2.91220	2.88388	2.82861	2.77509	2.72325	2.67301	2.62432	2.57710	3
4	3.95050	3.90197	3.85438	3.80773	3.71710	3.62990	3.54595	3.46511	3.38721	3.31213	4
5	4.92587	4.85343	4.78264	4.71346	4.57971	4.45182	4.32948	4.21236	4.10020	3.99271	5
6	5.89638	5.79548	5.69719	5.60143	5.41719	5.24214	5.07569	4.91732	4.76654	4.62288	6
7	6.86207	6.72819	6.59821	6.47199	6.23028	6.00205	5.78637	5.58238	5.38929	5.20637	7
8	7.82296	7.65168	7.48593	7.32548	7.01969	6.73274	6.46321	6.20979	5.97130	5.74664	8
9	8.77906	8.56602	8.36052	8.16224	7.78611	7.43533	7.10782	6.80169	6.51523	6.24689	9
10	9.73041	9.47130	9.22218	8.98259	8.53020	8.11090	7.72173	7.36009	7.02358	6.71008	10
11	10.67703	10.36763	10.07112	9.78685	9.25262	8.76048	8.30641	7.88687	7.49867	7.13896	11
12	11.61893	11.25508	10.90751	10.57534	9.95400	9.38507	8.86325	8.38384	7.94269	7.53608	12
13	12.55615	12.13374	11.73153	11.34837	10.63496	9.98565	9.39357	8.85268	8.35765	7.90378	13
14	13.48871	13.00370	12.54338	12.10625	11.29607	10.56312	9.89864	9.29498	8.74547	8.24424	14
15	14.41662	13.86505	13.34323	12.84926	11.93794	11.11839	10.37966	9.71225	9.10791	8.55948	15
16	15.33993	14.71787	14.13126	13.57771	12.56110	11.65230	10.83777	10.10590	9.44665	8.85137	16
17	16.25863	15.56225	14.90765	14.29187	13.16612	12.16567	11.27407	10.47726	9.76322	9.12164	17
18	17.17277	16.39827	15.67256	14.99203	13.75351	12.65930	11.68959	10.82760	10.05909	9.37189	18
19	18.08236	17.22601	16.42617	15.67846	14.32380	13.13394	12.08532	11.15812	10.33560	9.60360	19
20	18.98742	18.04555	17.16864	16.35143	14.87747	13.59033	12.46221	11.46992	10.59401	9.81815	20
21	19.88798	18.85698	17.90014	17.01121	15.41502	14.02916	12.82115	11.76408	10.83553	10.01680	21
22	20.78406	19.66038	18.62082	17.65805	15.93692	14.45112	13.16300	12.04158	11.06124	10.20074	22
23	21.67568	20.45582	19.33086	18.29220	16.44361	14.85684	13.48857	12.30338	11.27219	10.37106	23
24	22.56287	21.24339	20.03041	18.91393	16.93554	15.24696	13.79864	12.55036	11.46933	10.52876	24
25	23.44564	22.02316	20.71961	19.52346	17.41315	15.62208	14.09394	12.78336	11.65358	10.67478	25
26	24.32402	22.79520	21.39863	20.12104	17.87684	15.98277	14.37519	13.00317	11.82578	10.80998	26
27	25.19803	23.55961	22.06762	20.70690	18.32703	16.32959	14.64303	13.21053	11.98671	10.93516	27
28	26.06769	24.31644	22.72672	21.28127	18.76411	16.66306	14.89813	13.40616	12.13711	11.05108	28
29	26.93302	25.06579	23.37608	21.84438	19.18845	16.98371	15.14107	13.59072	12.27767	11.15841	29
30	27.79405	25.80771	24.01584	22.39646	19.60044	17.29203	15.37245	13.76483	12.40904	11.25778	30
31	28.65080	26.54229	24.64615	22.93770	20.00043	17.58849	15.59281	13.92909	12.53181	11.34980	31
32	29.50328	27.26959	25.26714	23.46833	20.38877	17.87355	15.80268	14.08404	12.64656	11.43500	32
33	30.35153	27.98969	25.87895	23.98856	20.76579	18.14765	16.00255	14.23023	12.75379	11.51389	33
34	31.19555	28.70267	26.48173	24.49859	21.13184	18.41120	16.19290	14.36814	12.85401	11.58693	34
35	32.03537	29.40858	27.07559	24.99862	21.48722	18.66461	16.37419	14.49825	12.94767	11.65457	35
36	32.87102	30.10751	27.66068	25.48884	21.83225	18.90828	16.54685	14.62099	13.03521	11.71719	36

STEPS FOR CALCULATING PRESENT VALUE OF AN ORDINARY ANNUITY:

Step 1. Calculate the interest rate per period for the annuity (nominal rate ÷ periods per year).

Step 2. Determine the number of periods of the annuity (years × periods per year).

Step 3. From Table 12-2, locate the present value table factor at the intersection of the rate column and the periods row.

Step 4. Calculate the present value of an ordinary annuity using the formula:

$$\frac{\text{Present value}}{\text{(ordinary annuity)}} = \frac{\text{Ordinary annuity}}{\text{table factor}} \times \frac{\text{Annuity}}{\text{payment}}$$

EXAMPLE

How much must be deposited now, at 9% compounded annually, to yield an annuity payment of $5,000 at the end of each year, for 10 years?

SOLUTION STRATEGY

Step 1. The rate per period is 9% (9% ÷ 1 period per year).

Step 2. The number of periods is 10 (10 years × 1 period per year).

Periods	9%	10%	11%	12%	13%	14%	15%	16%	17%	18%	Periods
1	0.91743	0.90909	0.90090	0.89286	0.88496	0.87719	0.86957	0.86207	0.85470	0.84746	1
2	1.75911	1.73554	1.71252	1.69005	1.66810	1.64666	1.62571	1.60523	1.58521	1.56564	2
3	2.53129	2.48685	2.44371	2.40183	2.36115	2.32163	2.28323	2.24589	2.20958	2.17427	3
4	3.23972	3.16987	3.10245	3.03735	2.97447	2.91371	2.85498	2.79818	2.74324	2.69006	4
5	3.88965	3.79079	3.69590	3.60478	3.51723	3.43308	3.35216	3.27429	3.19935	3.12717	5
6	4.48592	4.35526	4.23054	4.11141	3.99755	3.88867	3.78448	3.68474	3.58918	3.49760	6
7	5.03295	4.86842	4.71220	4.56376	4.42261	4.28830	4.16042	4.03857	3.92238	3.81153	7
8	5.53482	5.33493	5.14612	4.96764	4.79877	4.63886	4.48732	4.34359	4.20716	4.07757	8
9	5.99525	5.75902	5.53705	5.32825	5.13166	4.94637	4.77158	4.60654	4.45057	4.30302	9
10	6.41766	6.14457	5.88923	5.65022	5.42624	5.21612	5.01877	4.83323	4.65860	4.49409	10
11	6.80519	6.49506	6.20652	5.93770	5.68694	5.45273	5.23371	5.02864	4.83641	4.65601	11
12	7.16073	6.81369	6.49236	6.19437	5.91765	5.66029	5.42062	5.19711	4.98839	4.79322	12
13	7.48690	7.10336	6.74987	6.42355	6.12181	5.84236	5.58315	5.34233	5.11828	4.90951	13
14	7.78615	7.36669	6.98187	6.62817	6.30249	6.00207	5.72448	5.46753	5.22930	5.00806	14
15	8.06069	7.60608	7.19087	6.81086	6.46238	6.14217	5.84737	5.57546	5.32419	5.09158	15
16	8.31256	7.82371	7.37916	6.97399	6.60388	6.26506	5.95423	5.66850	5.40529	5.16235	16
17	8.54363	8.02155	7.54879	7.11963	6.72909	6.37286	6.04716	5.74870	5.47461	5.22233	17
18	8.75563	8.20141	7.70162	7.24967	6.83991	6.46742	6.12797	5.81785	5.53385	5.27316	18
19	8.95011	8.36492	7.83929	7.36578	6.93797	6.55037	6.19823	5.87746	5.58449	5.31624	19
20	9.12855	8.51356	7.96333	7.46944	7.02475	6.62313	6.25933	5.92884	5.62777	5.35275	20
21	9.29224	8.64869	8.07507	7.56200	7.10155	6.68696	6.31246	5.97314	5.66476	5.38368	21
22	9.44243	8.77154	8.17574	7.64465	7.16951	6.74294	6.35866	6.01133	5.69637	5.40990	22
23	9.58021	8.88322	8.26643	7.71843	7.22966	6.79206	6.39884	6.04425	5.72340	5.43212	23
24	9.70661	8.98474	8.34814	7.78432	7.28288	6.83514	6.43377	6.07263	5.74649	5.45095	24
25	9.82258	9.07704	8.42174	7.84314	7.32998	6.87293	6.46415	6.09709	5.76623	5.46691	25
26	9.92897	9.16095	8.48806	7.89566	7.37167	6.90608	6.49056	6.11818	5.78311	5.48043	26
27	10.02658	9.23722	8.54780	7.94255	7.40856	6.93515	6.51353	6.13636	5.79753	5.49189	27
28	10.11613	9.30657	8.60162	7.98442	7.44120	6.96066	6.53351	6.15204	5.80985	5.50160	28
29	10.19828	9.36961	8.65011	8.02181	7.47009	6.98304	6.55088	6.16555	5.82039	5.50983	29
30	10.27365	9.42691	8.69379	8.05518	7.49565	7.00266	6.56598	6.17720	5.82939	5.51681	30
31	10.34280	9.47901	8.73315	8.08499	7.51828	7.01988	6.57911	6.18724	5.83709	5.52272	31
32	10.40624	9.52638	8.76860	8.11159	7.53830	7.03498	6.59053	6.19590	5.84366	5.52773	32
33	10.46444	9.56943	8.80054	8.13535	7.55602	7.04823	6.60046	6.20336	5.84928	5.53197	33
34	10.51784	9.60857	8.82932	8.15656	7.57170	7.05985	6.60910	6.20979	5.85409	5.53557	34
35	10.56682	9.64416	8.85524	8.17550	7.58557	7.07005	6.61661	6.21534	5.85820	5.53862	35
36	10.61176	9.67651	8.87859	8.19241	7.59785	7.07899	6.62314	6.22012	5.86171	5.54120	36

Step 3. From Table 12-2, the table factor for 9%, 10 periods is 6.41766.

Step 4. Present value = Table factor × Annuity payment

Present value = 6.41766 × 5,000 = $32,088.30

TRY-IT   EXERCISE

4. The Coconut Grove Playhouse wants $20,000 at the end of each 6-month theater season for renovations and new stage and lighting equipment. How much must be deposited now, at 8% compounded semiannually, to yield this annuity payment for the next 6 years?

Check your answer with the solution on page 395.

12-5 Calculating the Present Value of an Annuity Due Using Tables

Present values of annuities due are calculated using the same table as ordinary annuities, with some modifications in the steps.

STEPS FOR CALCULATING PRESENT VALUE OF AN ANNUITY DUE:

Step 1. Calculate the number of periods of the annuity (years × periods per year), and *subtract* 1 period from the total.

Step 2. Calculate the interest rate per period (nominal rate ÷ periods per year).

Step 3. From Table 12-2 locate the table factor at the intersection of the rate column and the periods row.

Step 4. Add 1.00000 to the ordinary annuity table factor to get the annuity due table factor.

Step 5. Calculate the present value of an annuity due by the formula:

$$\frac{\text{Present value}}{\text{(annuity due)}} = \frac{\text{Annuity due}}{\text{table factor}} \times \frac{\text{Annuity}}{\text{payment}}$$

EXAMPLE

How much must be deposited now, at 10% compounded semiannually, to yield an annuity payment of \$2,000 at the beginning of each 6-month period, for 7 years?

SOLUTION STRATEGY

Step 1. The number of periods for the annuity due is 14 (7 years × 2 periods per year) less 1 period = 13.

Step 2. The rate per period is 5% (10% ÷ 2 periods per year).

Step 3. From Table 12-2, the ordinary annuity table factor for 5%, 13 periods is 9.39357.

Step 4. Add 1 to the table factor from Step 3 to get 10.39357, the annuity due table factor.

Step 5. Present value (annuity due) = Table factor × Annuity payment

Present value = 10.39357 × 2,000 = \$20,787.14

TRY-IT   EXERCISE

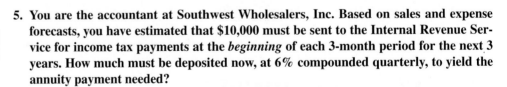

5. **You are the accountant at Southwest Wholesalers, Inc. Based on sales and expense forecasts, you have estimated that \$10,000 must be sent to the Internal Revenue Service for income tax payments at the *beginning* of each 3-month period for the next 3 years. How much must be deposited now, at 6% compounded quarterly, to yield the annuity payment needed?**

Check your answer with the solution on page 395.

12-6 (Optional) Calculating the Present Value of an Ordinary Annuity and an Annuity Due by Formula

Students with financial, business, or scientific calculators may use the following formulas to solve for the present value of an ordinary annuity and the present value of an annuity due.

Note that the annuity due formula is the same as the ordinary annuity formula, except it is multiplied by $(1 + i)$. This is to account for the fact that with an annuity due each payment earns interest for one additional period, because payments are made at the beginning of each period, not the end.

Present value of an ordinary annuity

$$PV = Pmt \times \frac{1 - (1 + i)^{-n}}{i}$$

Present value of an annuity due

$$PV = Pmt \times \frac{1 - (1 + i)^{-n}}{i} \times (1 + i)$$

where PV = Present Value (lump sum)
Pmt = annuity payment
i = interest rate per period (nominal rate ÷ periods per year)
n = number of periods (years × periods per year)

Ordinary Annuity
Calculator Sequence: 1 $\boxed{+}$ i $\boxed{=}$ $\boxed{y^x}$ n $\boxed{+/-}$ $\boxed{=}$ $\boxed{M+}$ 1 $\boxed{-}$ $\boxed{MR}$ $\boxed{÷}$ i $\boxed{\times}$
Pmt $\boxed{=}$ PV

Annuity Due
Calculator Sequence: 1 $\boxed{+}$ i $\boxed{=}$ $\boxed{\times}$ $PV_{\text{ordinary annuity}}$ $\boxed{=}$ $PV_{\text{annuity due}}$

EXAMPLES

a. What is the present value of an ordinary annuity of $100 per month, for 4 years, at 12% interest compounded monthly?
b. What is the present value of this investment if it is an annuity due?

SOLUTION STRATEGY

a. For this present value of an ordinary annuity problem we shall use $i = 1\%$ ($12\% \div 12$), and $n = 48$ periods (4 years × 12 periods per year).

$$PV = Pmt \times \frac{1 - (1 + i)^{-n}}{i}$$

$$PV = 100 \times \frac{1 - (1 + .01)^{-48}}{.01}$$

$$PV = 100 \times \frac{1 - (1.01)^{-48}}{.01}$$

$$PV = 100 \times \frac{1 - .6202604}{.01}$$

$$PV = 100 \times \frac{.3797396}{.01}$$

$$PV = 100 \times 37.97396 = \$3,797.40$$

Calculator Sequence:
1 $\boxed{+}$ .01 $\boxed{=}$ $\boxed{y^x}$ 48 $\boxed{+/-}$ $\boxed{=}$ $\boxed{M+}$ 1 $\boxed{-}$ $\boxed{MR}$ $\boxed{÷}$ .01 $\boxed{\times}$ 100 $\boxed{=}$ $\$3,797.40$

b. To solve the problem as an annuity due, rather than an ordinary annuity, multiply the present value of the ordinary annuity by $(1 + i)$, for one extra compounding period.

$$PV_{\text{annuity due}} = (1 + i) \times PV_{\text{ordinary annuity}}$$
$$PV_{\text{annuity due}} = (1 + .01) \times 3,797.40$$
$$PV_{\text{annuity due}} = (1.01) \times 3,797.40 = \$3,835.37$$

Calculator Sequence: 1 $\boxed{+}$ .01 $\boxed{=}$ $\boxed{\times}$ 3,797.40 $\boxed{=}$ $\$3,835.37$

6. Use the present value of an annuity formula to solve the following:

    a. Pat Rose wants $500 at the *end* of each 3-month period for the next 6 years. If Pat's bank is paying 8% interest compounded quarterly, how much must she deposit now in order to receive the desired ordinary annuity?

    b. If Pat wants the payments at the *beginning* of each 3-month period, rather than at the end, how much would she have to deposit?

Check your answers with the solutions on page 395.

REVIEW EXERCISES   CHAPTER 12—SECTION II

Use Table 12-2 to calculate the present value of the following ordinary annuities:

Complete, worked out solutions to exercises 1–10 appear in the appendix following the index.

	Annuity Payment	Payment Frequency	Time Period	Nominal Rate	Interest Compounded	Present Value of the Annuity
1.	$300	every 6 months	7 years	10%	semiannually	$2,969.59
2.	$2,000	every year	20 years	7%	annually	$21,188.02
3.	$1,600	every 3 months	6 years	12%	quarterly	$27,096.86
4.	$1,000	every month	$1\frac{3}{4}$ years	6%	monthly	$19,887.98
5.	$8,500	every 3 months	3 years	16%	quarterly	$79,773.10

Use Table 12-2 to calculate the present value of the following annuities due:

	Annuity Payment	Payment Frequency	Time Period	Nominal Rate	Interest Compounded	Present Value of the Annuity
6.	$1,400	every year	10 years	11%	annually	$9,151.87
7.	$1,300	every 3 months	4 years	12%	quarterly	$16,819.32
8.	$500	every month	$2\frac{1}{4}$ years	18%	monthly	$11,199.32
9.	$7,000	every 6 months	12 years	8%	semiannually	$110,997.88
10.	$4,000	every year	18 years	7%	annually	$43,052.88

Solve the following word problems using Table 12-2:

11. Transamerica Savings & Loan is paying 6% interest compounded monthly. How much must be deposited now in order to withdraw $400 at the end of each month for 2 years?

$$R = \tfrac{1}{2}\% \quad P = 24 \quad F = 22.56287$$
$$\text{Amount} = 400.00 \times 22.56287 = \underline{\$9,025.15}$$

12. Lisa Reid wants to receive $2,000 at the beginning of each year for the next ten years. How much should be deposited now at 6% compounded annually to accomplish this goal?

$$R = 6\% \quad P = 10 - 1 = 9 \quad F = 6.80169 + 1.00000$$
$$\text{Amount} = 2,000.00 \times 7.80169 = \underline{\$15,603.38}$$

13. As the chief accountant for the Worthington Corporation, you have estimated that the company must pay $100,000 income tax to the IRS at the end of each quarter this year. How much should be deposited now at 8% interest compounded quarterly in order to meet this tax obligation?

$R = 2\%$ $P = 4$ $F = 3.80773$

Amount $= 100,000.00 \times 3.80773 = \underline{\$380,773.00}$

14. Lucy Luckworth is the grand prize winner in a college tuition essay contest sponsored by a local scholarship fund. The winner receives $2,000 at the beginning of each year for the next four years. How much should be invested at 7% interest compounded annually in order to pay Lucy the prize?

$R = 7\%$ $P = 4 - 1 = 3$ $F = 2.62432 + 1.00000$

Amount $= 2,000.00 \times 3.62432 = \underline{\$7,248.64}$

15. Churchill Enterprises has been awarded an insurance settlement of $5,000 at the end of each 6-month period for the next 10 years.

   a. How much must the insurance company set aside now, at 6% interest compounded semiannually, in order to pay this obligation to Churchill?

   $R = 3\%$ $P = 20$ $F = 14.87747$

   Amount $= 5,000.00 \times 14.87747 = \underline{\$74,387.35}$

   b. (Optional) Use the present value of an ordinary annuity formula to calculate how much less the insurance company would have to invest now if the Churchill settlement was changed to $2,500 at the end of each 3-month period for 10 years, and the insurance company could earn 8% interest compounded quarterly.

   Interest 2% $P = 40$ Amount 2,500.00

   $PV = PMT \times \dfrac{1 - (1 + i)^{-n}}{i}$

   $PV = 2,500.00 \times \dfrac{1 - (1 + .02)^{-40}}{.02}$

   $PV = 2,500.00 \times \dfrac{1 - (1.02)^{-40}}{.02}$

   $2,500.00 \times 27.35547924 = \underline{\$68,388.70}$

   c. (Optional) Use the present value of an annuity due formula to calculate how much the insurance company would have to invest now if the Churchill settlement was paid at the beginning of each 3-month period rather than at the end.

   Interest $= 2\%$ $P = 40$ Amount 2,500.00

   PV annuity due $= (1 + i) \times PV$ ordinary annuity

   $PV = (1 + .02) \times 68,388.70$

   $\quad\quad = \underline{\$69,756.47}$

SECTION III

SINKING FUNDS AND AMORTIZATION

Sinking funds and amortization are two common applications of annuities. In the previous sections of this chapter, the amount of the annuity payment was known and you were asked to calculate the future or present value (lump sum) of the annuity. In this section, the future or present value of the annuity is known, and the amount of the payments will be calculated.

A sinking fund situation occurs when the future value of an annuity is known, and the payment required each period to amount to that future value is the unknown. **Sinking funds** are accounts used to set aside equal amounts of money at the end of each period, at compound interest, for the purpose of saving for a future obligation. Businesses use sinking funds to

● **sinking fund**
Account used to set aside equal amounts of money at the end of each period, at compound interest, for the purpose of saving for a future obligation.

amortization

A financial arrangement whereby a lump-sum obligation is incurred at compound interest now, such as a loan, and is paid off or liquidated by a series of equal periodic payments for a specified amount of time.

accumulate money for such things as new equipment, facility expansion, and other expensive items needed in the future. Another common use is to retire financial obligations such as bond issues that come due at a future date. Individuals can use sinking funds to save for a college education, a car, the down payment on a house, or a vacation.

Amortization is the opposite of a sinking fund. **Amortization** is a financial arrangement whereby a lump-sum obligation is incurred at compound interest now (present value) and is paid off or liquidated by a series of equal periodic payments for a specified amount of time. With amortization the amount of the loan or obligation is given, and the equal payments that will amortize or pay off the obligation must be calculated. Some business uses of amortization would be paying off loans or liquidating insurance or retirement funds.

Mortgages, which are real estate loans, are a common example of amortization. In this section you will learn how to calculate the amount of a mortgage payment as well as other loan payments. More detailed coverage of amortization, including the preparation of amortization schedules, is found in Chapter 15.

In this section you will learn to calculate the sinking fund payment required to save for a future amount, and the amortization payment required to liquidate a present amount. We shall assume that all annuities are ordinary, with payments made at the *end* of each period. As in previous sections, these problems can be calculated by tables and by formulas.

12-7 Calculating the Amount of a Sinking Fund Payment by Table

In a sinking fund, the future value is known; therefore, we shall use the future value of an annuity table (Table 12-1) to calculate the amount of the payment.

STEPS FOR CALCULATING THE AMOUNT OF A SINKING FUND PAYMENT:

Step 1. Using the appropriate rate per period and number of periods of the sinking fund, find the future value table factor from Table 12-1.

Step 2. Calculate the amount of the sinking fund payment by:

$$\text{Sinking fund payment} = \frac{\text{Future value of the sinking fund}}{\text{Future value table factor}}$$

Sinking funds enable businesses to plan for future purchases of expensive equipment.

What sinking fund payment is required at the end of each 6-month period, at 6% interest compounded semiannually, to amount to $12,000 in 4 years?

SOLUTION STRATEGY

Step 1. This sinking fund is for 8 periods (4 years × 2 periods per year) at 3% per period (6% ÷ 2 periods per year). From Table 12-1, 8 periods, 3% per period gives a future value table factor of 8.89234.

Step 2. $$\text{Sinking fund payment} = \frac{\text{Future value of the sinking fund}}{\text{Future value table factor}}$$

$$\text{Sinking fund payment} = \frac{12{,}000}{8.89234} = \underline{\underline{\$1{,}349.48}}$$

TRY-IT   EXERCISE

7. Nancy Hand wants to accumulate $8,000 in 5 years for a trip to Europe. If her bank is paying 12% interest compounded quarterly, how much must Nancy deposit at the end of each 3-month period to reach her desired goal?

Check your answer with the solution on page 395.

12-8 Calculating the Amount of an Amortization Payment by Table

Amortization is the process of paying off a financial obligation in a series of equal regular payments over a period of time. With amortization, the original amount of the loan or obligation is known (present value); therefore, we use the present value table (Table 12-2) to calculate the amount of the payment.

> **STEPS FOR CALCULATING THE AMOUNT OF AN AMORTIZATION PAYMENT:**
>
> **Step 1.** Using the appropriate rate per period and number of periods of the amortization, find the present value table factor from Table 12-2.
>
> **Step 2.** Calculate the amount of the amortization payment by the formula:
>
> $$\text{Amortization payment} = \frac{\text{Original amount of obligation}}{\text{Present value table factor}}$$

EXAMPLE

What amortization payments are required each month, at 12% interest, to pay off a $10,000 loan in 2 years?

SOLUTION STRATEGY

Step 1. This amortization is for 24 periods (2 years × 12 periods per year) at 1% per period (12% ÷ 12 periods per year). From Table 12-2, 24 periods, 1% per period gives a present value table factor of 21.24339.

Step 2. Amortization payment $= \dfrac{\text{Original amount of obligation}}{\text{Present value table}}$

$$\text{Amortization payment} = \frac{10{,}000}{21.24339} = \underline{\underline{\$470.73}}$$

TRY-IT   EXERCISE

8. **Captain Doug Black purchased a new fishing boat for $130,000. He made a $20,000 down payment, and financed the balance at his bank for 7 years. What amortization payments are required every 3 months, at 16% interest, to pay off the boat loan?**

Check your answer with the solution on page 395.

12-9 (Optional) Calculating Sinking Fund Payments by Formula

In addition to using Table 12-1, sinking fund payments are calculated by using the formula:

$$\text{Sinking fund payment} = FV \times \frac{i}{(1+i)^n - 1}$$

where

   $FV =$ **amount needed in the future**

   i = **interest rate per period (nominal rate ÷ periods per year)**

   n = **number of periods (years × periods per year)**

Calculator Sequence:

1 [+] i [=] [y^x] n [−] 1 [=] [M+] i [÷] [MR] [×] FV [=] Sinking fund payment

EXAMPLE

Consolidated Widget Corporation needs $100,000 in 5 years to pay off a bond issue. What sinking fund payment is required at the end of each month, at 12% interest compounded monthly, to meet this financial obligation?

SOLUTION STRATEGY

To solve this sinking fund problem we shall use 1% interest rate per period (12% ÷ 12), and 60 periods (5 years × 12 periods per year).

$$\text{Sinking fund payment} = \text{Future value} \times \frac{i}{(1+i)^n - 1}$$

$$\text{Sinking fund payment} = 100{,}000 \times \frac{.01}{(1+.01)^{60} - 1}$$

$$\text{Sinking fund payment} = 100{,}000 \times \frac{.01}{.8166967}$$

$$\text{Sinking fund payment} = 100{,}000 \times .0122444 = \underline{\underline{\$1{,}224.44}}$$

Calculator Sequence:

1 [+] .01 [=] [y^x] 60 [−] 1 [=] [M+] .01 [÷] [MR] [×] 100,000 = $\underline{\underline{\$1{,}224.44}}$

TRY-IT   EXERCISE

9. **What sinking fund payment is required at the end of each month, at 18% interest compounded monthly, to amount to $40,000 in 6 years?**

Check your answer with the solution on page 395.

12-10 (Optional) Calculating Amortization Payments by Formula

Amortization payments are calculated by using the formula

$$\text{Amortization payment} = PV \times \frac{i}{1 - (1 + i)^{-n}}$$

where

PV = amount of the loan or obligation

i = interest rate per period (nominal rate ÷ periods per year)

n = number of periods (years × periods per year)

Calculator Sequence:

1 $\boxed{+}$ i $\boxed{=}$ $\boxed{y^x}$ n $\boxed{+/-}$ $\boxed{=}$ $\boxed{M+}$ 1 $\boxed{-}$ $\boxed{MR}$ $\boxed{=}$ $\boxed{M+}$ i $\boxed{\div}$ $\boxed{MR}$ $\boxed{\times}$ PV $\boxed{=}$ Amortization payment

EXAMPLE

What amortization payment is required each month, at 18% interest, to pay off $5,000 in 3 years?

SOLUTION STRATEGY

To solve this amortization problem we shall use 1.5% interest rate per period (18% ÷ 12), and 36 periods (3 years × 12 periods per year).

$$\text{Amortization payment} = \text{Present value} \times \frac{i}{1 - (1 + i)^{-n}}$$

$$\text{Amortization payment} = 5,000 \times \frac{.015}{1 - (1 + .015)^{-36}}$$

$$\text{Amortization payment} = 5,000 \times \frac{.015}{.4149103}$$

$$\text{Amortization payment} = 5,000 \times .0361524 = \$180.76$$

Calculator Sequence:

1 $\boxed{+}$ .015 $\boxed{=}$ $\boxed{y^x}$ 36 $\boxed{+/-}$ $\boxed{=}$ $\boxed{M+}$ 1 $\boxed{-}$ $\boxed{MR}$ $\boxed{=}$ $\boxed{M+}$ .015 $\boxed{\div}$ $\boxed{MR}$ $\boxed{\times}$ 5,000 = $\underline{\$180.76}$

TRY-IT   EXERCISE

10. **Mountainview Manufacturing recently purchased a new computer system for $150,000. What amortization payment is required each month, at 12% interest, to pay off this obligation in 8 years?**

Check your answer with the solution on page 395.

For the following sinking funds, use Table 12-1 to calculate the amount of the periodic payments needed to amount to the financial objective (future value of the annuity):

	Sinking Fund Payment	Payment Frequency	Time Period	Nominal Rate	Interest Compounded	Future Value (Objective)
1.	$2,113.50	every 6 months	8 years	10%	semiannually	$50,000
2.	$9,608.29	every year	14 years	9%	annually	$250,000
3.	$55.82	every 3 months	5 years	12%	quarterly	$1,500
4.	$203.93	every month	$1\frac{1}{2}$ years	12%	monthly	$4,000
5.	$859.13	every 3 months	4 years	16%	quarterly	$18,750

You have just been hired as a loan officer at the Eagle National Bank. Your first assignment is to calculate the amount of the periodic payment required to amortize (pay off) the following loans being considered by the bank (use Table 12-2):

	Loan Payment	Payment Period	Term of Loan	Nominal Rate	Present Value (Amount of Loan)
6.	$4,189.52	every year	12 years	9%	$30,000
7.	$336.36	every 3 months	5 years	8%	$5,500
8.	$558.65	every month	$1\frac{3}{4}$ years	18%	$10,000
9.	$1,087.48	every 6 months	8 years	6%	$13,660
10.	$51.83	every month	1.5 years	12%	$850

11. Van Strength is planning a safari vacation in Africa in 4 years and will need $7,500 for the trip. Van decides to set up a sinking fund savings account for the vacation. He intends to make regular payments at the end of each 3-month period into the account that pays 6% interest compounded quarterly. What periodic sinking fund payment will allow Van to achieve his vacation goal?

$R = 1.5\%$ $P = 16$ $FV = 7,500.00$

Factor = 17.93237

$$\text{Payment} = \frac{7,500.00}{17.93237} = \underline{\$418.24}$$

12. Kelly Gibson bought a new Buick for $15,500. She made a $2,500 down payment and is financing the balance at the Mid-South Bank over a 3-year period at 12% interest. As her banker, calculate what equal monthly payments will be required by Kelly to amortize the car loan.

$R = 1\%$ $P = 36$ $PV = (15,500.00 - 2,500.00)$

Factor = 30.10751

$$\text{Payment} = \frac{13,000.00}{30.10751} = \underline{\$431.79}$$

13. Green Thumb Landscaping buys new lawn equipment every three years. It is estimated that $25,000 will be needed for the next purchase. The company sets up a sinking fund to save for this obligation.

a. What equal payments must be deposited every 6 months, if interest is 8% compounded semiannually?

$R = 4\%$ $P = 6$ $FV = 25,000.00$

Factor = 6.63298

$$\text{Payment} = \frac{25,000.00}{6.63298} = \underline{\$3,769.04}$$

b. What is the total amount of interest earned by the sinking fund?

$6 \times 3,769.04 = 22,614.24$

$25,000.00 - 22,614.24 = \underline{\$2,385.76}$

14. Alice Fox is ready to retire and has saved up $200,000 for that purpose. She wants to amortize (liquidate) that amount in a retirement fund so that she will receive equal annual payments over the next 25 years. At the end of the 25 years, there will be no funds left in the account. If the fund earns 12% interest, how much will Alice receive each year?

$R = 12\% \quad P = 25 \quad PV = 200,000.00$

Factor $= 7.84314$

Payment $= \dfrac{200,000.00}{7.84314} = \underline{\underline{\$25,499.99}}$

15. West Coast Manufacturing established a sinking fund to pay off a $10,000,000 bond issue that comes due in 8 years.

a. What equal payments must be deposited into the fund every 3 months at 6% interest compounded quarterly in order for West Coast to meet this financial obligation?

$R = 1\dfrac{1}{2}\% \quad P = 32 \quad PV = 10,000,000.00$

Factor $= 40.68829$

Payment $= \dfrac{10,000,000.00}{40.68829} = \underline{\underline{\$245,770.96}}$

b. What is the total amount of interest earned in this sinking fund account?

$245,770.96 \times 32 = 7,864,670.72$

$10,000,000.00 - 7,864,670.72$

Amount of interest $= \underline{\underline{\$2,135,329.28}}$

(Optional) Solve the following problems using the sinking fund or amortization formulas:

16. Rolando Montoya purchased a new home for $225,000 with a 20% down payment and the remainder amortized over a 15-year period, at 9% interest.

a. What is the amount of the house that was financed?

$225,000.00 \times .2 = 45,000.00$

Amount financed $= 225,000.00 - 45,000.00$

$ = \underline{\$180,000.00}$

b. What equal monthly payments are required to amortize this loan over 15 years?

$R = .75\% \quad P = 180 \quad \text{Present Value} = 180,000$

Amortization payment $= PV \times \dfrac{i}{1-(1+i)^{-n}} = 180,000 \times \dfrac{.0075}{1-(1+.0075)^{-180}} = \dfrac{.0075}{.73945057}$

$ = 180,000 \times .010142666$

Payment amount $= \underline{\$1,825.68}$

c. What equal monthly payments are required if Rolando decides to take a 20-year loan rather than a 15?

$R = .75\% \quad P = 240 \quad PV = 180,000$

Amortization payment $= PV \times \dfrac{i}{1-(1+i)^{-n}} = 180,000 \times \dfrac{.0075}{1-(1+.0075)^{-240}} = 180,000 \times \dfrac{.0075}{.833587155}$

$ = 180,000 \times .00899726$

Payment $= \underline{\$1,619.51}$

17. The Beach Club Hotel has a financial obligation of $1,000,000 due in 5 years. A sinking fund is established to meet this obligation at 12% interest compounded monthly.

a. What equal monthly sinking fund payments are required to accumulate the needed amount?

$R = 1\%$ $P = 60$ $FV = 1,000,000.00$

$$\text{Payment} = FV \times \frac{i}{(1 + i)^n - 1} = 1,000,000.00 \times \frac{.01}{.816696699} = \underline{\underline{\$12,244.45}}$$

$$\text{Payment} = 1,000,000.00 \times \frac{.01}{(1 + .01)^{60} - 1}$$

b. What is the total amount of interest earned in the account?

$60 \times 12,244.45 = 734,667.00$

$1,000,000.00 - 734,667.00$

Interest earned $= \underline{\underline{\$265,333.00}}$

CHAPTER 12 ■ ANNUITIES

FORMULAS

Future value (ordinary annuity) = **Ordinary annuity table factor** × **Annuity payment**

FV (ordinary annuity) = **Payment** $\times \dfrac{(1 + i)^n - 1}{i}$

Future value (annuity due) = **Annuity due table factor** × **Annuity payment**

FV (annuity due) = **Payment** $\times \dfrac{(1 + i)^n - 1}{i} \times (1 + i)$

Present value (ordinary annuity) = **Ordinary annuity table factor** × **Annuity payment**

PV (ordinary annuity) = **Payment** $\times \dfrac{1 - (1 + i)^{-n}}{i}$

Present value (annuity due) = **Annuity due table factor** × **Annuity payment**

PV (annuity due) = **Payment** $\times \dfrac{1 - (1 + i)^{-n}}{i} \times (1 + i)$

Sinking fund payment $= \dfrac{\text{Future value of the sinking fund}}{\text{Future value table factor}}$

Sinking fund payment = **Future value** $\times \dfrac{i}{(1 + i)^n - 1}$

Amortization payment $= \dfrac{\text{Original amount of obligation}}{\text{Present value table factor}}$

Amortization payment = **Present value** $\times \dfrac{i}{1 - (1 + i)^{-n}}$

| CHAPTER 12 ■ ANNUITIES | | | SUMMARY CHART |

SECTION I   FUTURE VALUE OF AN ANNUITY

Topic	P/O, Page	Important Concepts	Illustrative Examples
Calculating the Future Value of an Ordinary Annuity Using Tables	12–1 369	An annuity is the payment or receipt of *equal* cash amounts per period for a specified amount of time.	Calculate the future value of an ordinary annuity of $500 every 6 months for 5 years, at 12% interest compounded semiannually.

I, continued

Topic	P/O, Page	Important Concepts	Illustrative Examples
		1. Calculate the interest rate per period for the annuity (nominal rate ÷ periods per year). 2. Determine the number of periods of the annuity (years × periods per year). 3. From Table 12–1, locate the ordinary annuity table factor at the intersection of the rate column and the periods row. 4. Calculate the future value of an ordinary annuity by: Future value (ordinary annuity) = Table factor × Annuity payment	Rate per period = 6% (12% ÷ 2 periods per year) Periods = 10 (5 years × 2 periods per year) Table factor 6%, 10 periods = 13.18079 Future value = 13.18079 × 500 Future value = $6,590.40
Calculating the Future Value of an Annuity Due Using Tables	12–2 371	1. Calculate the number of periods of the annuity (years × periods per year), and add 1 period to the total. 2. Calculate the interest rate per period (nominal rate ÷ periods per year). 3. Locate the table factor at the intersection of the rate column and the periods row. 4. Subtract 1 from the ordinary annuity table factor to get the annuity due table factor. 5. Calculate the future value of an annuity due by: Future value (annuity due) = Table factor × Annuity payment	Calculate the future value of an annuity due to $100 per month, for 2 years, at 12% interest compounded monthly. Periods = 24 (2 × 12) + 1 for a total of 25 Rate per period = 1% (12% ÷ 12) Table factor 1%, 25 periods = 28.24320 28.24320 − 1 = 27.24320 Future value = 27.24320 × 100 Future value = $2,724.32
(Optional) Calculating the Future Value of an Ordinary Annuity and an Annuity Due by Formula	12–3 374	*Future Value: Ordinary Annuity* $FV = Pmt \times \dfrac{(1+i)^n - 1}{i}$ *Future Value: Annuity Due* $FV = Pmt \times \dfrac{(1+i)^n - 1}{i} \times (1+i)$ where FV = Future value Pmt = annuity payment i = interest rate per period (nominal rate ÷ periods per year) n = number of periods (years × periods per year)	a. What is the future value of an *ordinary annuity* of $200 per month for 4 years, at 12% interest compounded monthly? $FV = 200 \times \dfrac{(1+.01)^{48} - 1}{.01}$ $FV = 200 \times 61.222608$ $FV = \$12,244.52$ b. What is the future value of this investment if it was an *annuity due?* $FV = 12{,}244.52 \times (1+.01)$ $FV = 12{,}244.52 \times 1.01$ $FV = \$12,366.97$

SECTION II   PRESENT VALUE OF AN ANNUITY

Topic	P/O, Page	Important Concepts	Illustrative Examples
Calculating the Present Value of an Ordinary Annuity Using Tables	12–4 377	1. Calculate the interest rate per period for the annuity (nominal rate ÷ periods per year). 2. Determine the number of periods of the annuity (years × periods per year). 3. From Table 12–2, locate the present value table factor at the intersection of the rate column and the periods row. 4. Calculate the present value of an ordinary annuity by: **Present value (ordinary annuity) =** **Table factor × Annuity payment**	How much must be deposited now, at 5% compounded annually, to yield an annuity payment of $1,000 at the end of each year, for 11 years? Rate per period = 5% (5% ÷ 1 period per year) Number of periods = 11 (11 years × 1 period per year) Table factor 5%, 11 periods is 8.30641 Present value = 8.30641 × 1,000 Present value = $8,306.41
Calculating the Present Value of an Annuity Due Using Tables	12–5 380	1. Calculate the number of periods (years × periods per year), and subtract 1 from the total. 2. Calculate rate per period (nominal rate ÷ periods per year). 3. Locate the table factor at the intersection of the rate column and the periods row. 4. Add 1 to the ordinary annuity table factor to get the annuity due table factor. 5. Calculate the present value of an annuity due by: **Present value (annuity due) =** **Table factor × Annuity payment**	How much must be deposited now, at 8% compounded semiannually, to yield an annuity payment of $1,000 at the beginning of each 6-month period, for 5 years? Number of periods = 10 (5 × 2) less 1 period = 9 Rate per period = 4% (8% ÷ 2) Table factor 4%, 9 periods = 7.43533 7.43533 + 1 = 8.43533 Present value = 8.43533 × 1,000 Present value = $8,435.33
(Optional) Calculating the Present Value of an Ordinary Annuity and an Annuity Due by Formula	12–6 380	*Present Value: Ordinary Annuity* $PV = Pmt \times \dfrac{1 - (1+i)^{-n}}{i}$ *Present Value: Annuity Due* $PV = Pmt \times \dfrac{1 - (1+i)^{-n}}{i} \times (1+i)$	a. What is the present value of an ordinary annuity of $100 per month for 5 years, at 12% interest compounded monthly? $PV = 100 \times \dfrac{1 - (1+.01)^{-60}}{.01}$ $PV = 100 \times 44.955039$ $PV = \underline{\$4,495.50}$

II, continued

Topic	P/O, Page	Important Concepts	Illustrative Examples
		where PV = Present value Pmt = annuity payment i = interest rate per period (nominal rate ÷ periods per year) n = number of periods (years × periods per year)	b. What is the present value of this investment if it was an annuity due? $PV_{\text{annuity due}}$ = $PV_{\text{ordinary annuity}} \times (1 + i)$ $PV = 4{,}495.50 \times (1 + .01)$ $PV = 4{,}495.50 \times 1.01$ $PV = \underline{\$4{,}540.46}$

SECTION III   SINKING FUNDS AND AMORTIZATION

Topic	P/O, Page	Important Concepts	Illustrative Examples
Calculating the Amount of a Sinking Fund Payment by Table	12–7 384	Sinking funds are accounts used to set aside equal amounts of money at the end of each period, at compound interest, for the purpose of saving for a known future financial obligation. 1. Using the appropriate rate per period and number of periods, find the future value table factor from Table 12–1. 2. Calculate the amount of the sinking fund payment by: $\dfrac{\text{Sinking}}{\substack{\text{fund}\\\text{payment}}} = \dfrac{\text{Future value of sinking fund}}{\text{Future value table factor}}$	What sinking fund payment is required at the end of each 6-month period, at 10% interest compounded semiannually, to amount to $10,000 in 7 years? Number of periods = 14 (7 years × 2 periods per year) Rate per period = 5% (10% ÷ 2 periods per year) Table factor 14 periods, 5% = 19.59863 Payment = $\dfrac{10{,}000}{19.59863}$ Payment = $\underline{\$510.24}$
Calculating the Amount of an Amortization Payment by Table	12–8 385	Amortization is a financial arrangement whereby a lump-sum obligation is incurred now (present value) and is paid off or liquidated by a series of equal periodic payments for a specified amount of time. 1. Using the appropriate rate per period and number of periods of the amortization, find the present value table factor from Table 12–2. 2. Calculate the amount of the amortization payment by: $\dfrac{\text{Amortization}}{\text{payment}} = \dfrac{\text{Original amount obligation}}{\text{Present value table factor}}$	What amortization payments are required at the end of each month, at 18% interest to pay off a $15,000 loan in 3 years? Number of periods = 36 (3 years × 12 periods per year) Rate per period = 1.5% (18% ÷ 12 periods per year) Table factor 36 periods, 1.5% = 27.66068 Amort. payment = $\dfrac{15{,}000}{27.66068}$ Amortization payment = $\underline{\$542.29}$

III, continued

Topic	P/O, Page	Important Concepts	Illustrative Examples
(Optional) Calculating Sinking Fund Payments by Formula	12–9 386	Sinking fund payments can be calculated by using the following formula: $$Pmt = FV \times \frac{i}{(1+i)^n - 1}$$ where Pmt = sinking fund payment FV = future value, amount needed in the future i = interest rate per period (nominal rate ÷ periods per year) n = number of periods (years × periods per year)	What sinking fund payment is required at the end of each month, at 12% interest compounded monthly, to amount to $10,000 in 4 years? Rate per period = 1% (12% ÷ 12) Periods = 48 (4 × 12) $$Pmt = 10,000 \times \frac{.01}{(1+.01)^{48} - 1}$$ $$Pmt = 10,000 \times \frac{.01}{.6122261}$$ $Pmt = 10,000 \times .0163338$ Sinking fund payment = $\underline{\$163.34}$
(Optional) Calculating Amortization Payments by Formula	12–10 387	Amortization payments are calculated by using the following formula: $$Pmt = PV \times \frac{i}{1 - (1+i)^{-n}}$$ where Pmt = amortization payment PV = present value, amount of the loan or obligation i = interest rate per period (nominal rate ÷ periods per year) n = number of periods (years × periods per year)	What amortization payment is required each month, at 18% interest, to pay off $3,000 in 2 years? Rate = 1.5% (18% ÷ 12) Periods = 24 (2 × 12) $$Pmt = 3,000 \times \frac{.015}{1 - (1+.015)^{-24}}$$ $$Pmt = 3,000 \times \frac{.015}{.3004561}$$ $Pmt = 3,000 \times .0499241$ Amortization payment = $\underline{\$149.77}$

TRY-IT EXERCISE   SOLUTIONS

1. 2%, 24 periods
Future value = Table factor × Annuity payment
Future value = 30.42186 × 1,000 = $\underline{\$30,421.86}$

2. Periods = 20 (5 × 4) + 1 = 21
Rate = $\dfrac{6\%}{4} = 1\dfrac{1}{2}\%$
Table factor =   24.47052
          − 1.00000
          ─────────
           23.47052
Future value = Table factor × Annuity payment
Future value = 23.47052 × 1,000 = $\underline{\$23,470.52}$

3. a. 2%, 20 periods
$$FV = Pmt \times \frac{(1+i)^n - 1}{i}$$
$$FV = 250 \times \frac{(1+.02)^{20} - 1}{.02} = 250 \times \frac{(1.02)^{20} - 1}{.02}$$
$FV = 250 \times 24.297369 = \underline{\$6,074.34}$

b. $FV_{\text{annuity due}} = (1+i) \times FV_{\text{ordinary annuity}}$
$FV_{\text{annuity due}} = (1+.02)\,6,074.34 = \underline{\$6,195.83}$

4. 4%, 12 periods

Present value = Table factor × Annuity payment

Present value = 9.38507 × 20,000 = $\underline{\underline{\$187,701.40}}$

5. Periods = 12 (3 × 4) − 1 = 11

$$\text{Rate} = \frac{6\%}{4} = 1\frac{1}{2}\%$$

$$\text{Table factor} = \begin{array}{r} 10.07112 \\ + \ 1.00000 \\ \hline 11.07112 \end{array}$$

Present value = Table factor × Annuity payment

Present value = 11.07112 × 10,000 = $\underline{\underline{\$110,711.20}}$

6. a. 2%, 24 periods

$$PV = Pmt \times \frac{1 - (1 + i)^{-n}}{i}$$

$$PV = 500 \times \frac{1 - (1 + .02)^{-24}}{.02} = 500 \times \frac{1 - .6217215}{.02}$$

$$PV = 500 \times 18.913925 = \underline{\underline{\$9,456.96}}$$

b. $PV_{\text{annuity due}} = (1 + i) \times PV_{\text{ordinary annuity}}$

$PV_{\text{annuity due}} = (1 + .02) \times 9,456.96 = \underline{\underline{\$9,646.10}}$

7. 3%, 20 periods

$$\text{Sinking fund payment} = \frac{\text{Future value of sinking fund}}{\text{Future value table factor}}$$

$$\text{Sinking fund payment} = \frac{8,000}{26.87037} = \underline{\underline{\$297.73}}$$

8. 4%, 28 periods

$$\text{Amortization payment} = \frac{\text{Original amount of obligation}}{\text{Present value table factor}}$$

$$\text{Amortization payment} = \frac{110,000}{16.66306} = \underline{\underline{\$6,601.43}}$$

9. $1\frac{1}{2}\%$, 72 periods

$$\text{Sinking fund payment} = FV \times \frac{i}{(1 + i)^n - 1}$$

$$\text{Sinking fund payment} = 40,000 \times \frac{.015}{(1 + .015)^{72} - 1}$$

Sinking fund payment = 40,000 × .0078078 = $\underline{\underline{\$312.31}}$

10. 1%, 96 periods

$$\text{Amortization payment} = PV \times \frac{i}{1 - (1 + i)^{-n}}$$

$$\text{Amortization payment} = 150,000 \times \frac{.01}{1 - (1 + .01)^{-96}}$$

Amortization payment = 150,000 × .0162528 = $\underline{\underline{\$2,437.93}}$

Name_____

Class_____

Copyright © 1997 by Harcourt Brace & Company. All rights reserved.

ANSWERS

1. _____ $121,687.44
2. _____ $330,659.50
3. _____ $86,445.14
4. _____ $4,694.32
5. _____ $42,646.92
6. _____ $1,363,438.75
7. _____ $11,593.58
8. _____ $21,573.70
9. _____ $993.02
10. _____ $227.12
11. _____ $255.66
12. _____ $832.78
13. _____ $20,345.57
14. _____ $154,765.98

Complete, worked out solutions to exercises 1–11 appear in the appendix following the index.

Use Table 12-1 to calculate the future value of the following ordinary annuities:

	Annuity Payment	Payment Frequency	Time Period	Nominal Rate	Interest Compounded	Future Value of the Annuity
1.	$4,000	every 3 months	6 years	8%	quarterly	$121,687.44
2.	$10,000	every year	20 years	5%	annually	$330,659.50

Use Table 12-1 to calculate the future value of the following annuities due:

	Annuity Payment	Payment Frequency	Time Period	Nominal Rate	Interest Compounded	Future Value of the Annuity
3.	$1,850	every 6 months	12 years	10%	semiannually	$86,445.14
4.	$200	every month	$1\frac{3}{4}$ years	12%	monthly	$4,694.32

Use Table 12-2 to calculate the present value of the following ordinary annuities:

	Annuity Payment	Payment Frequency	Time Period	Nominal Rate	Interest Compounded	Present Value of the Annuity
5.	$6,000	every year	9 years	5%	annually	$42,646.92
6.	$125,000	every 3 months	3 years	6%	quarterly	$1,363,438.75

Use Table 12-2 to calculate the present value of the following annuities due:

	Annuity Payment	Payment Frequency	Time Period	Nominal Rate	Interest Compounded	Present Value of the Annuity
7.	$700	every month	$1\frac{1}{2}$ years	12%	monthly	$11,593.58
8.	$2,000	every 6 months	6 years	4%	semiannually	$21,573.70

Use Table 12-1 to calculate the amount of the periodic payments needed to amount to the financial objective (future value of the annuity) for the following sinking funds:

	Sinking Fund Payment	Payment Frequency	Time Period	Nominal Rate	Interest Compounded	Future Value (Objective)
9.	$993.02	every year	13 years	7%	annually	$20,000
10.	$227.12	every month	$2\frac{1}{4}$ years	12%	monthly	$7,000

Use Table 12-2 to calculate the amount of the periodic payment required to amortize (pay off) the following loans:

	Loan Payment	Payment Period	Term of Loan	Nominal Rate	Interest Compounded	Present Value (Amount of Loan)
11.	$255.66	every 3 months	8 years	8%	quarterly	$6,000
12.	$832.78	every month	$2\frac{1}{2}$ years	18%	monthly	$20,000

13. How much will $800 deposited at the *end* of each month into a savings account be worth after 2 years, at 6% interest compounded monthly?

$R = \frac{1}{2}\%$ $P = 24$ Amount = 800.00
FV ordinary annuity
Factor = 25.43196 × 800.00
FV = $20,345.57

14. How much will $3,500 deposited at the *beginning* of each 3-month period be worth after 7 years at 12% interest compounded quarterly?

$R = 3\%$ $P = 28 + 1 = 29$ Amount = 3,500.00
Factor = 45.21885 − 1.00000
     = 44.21885 × 3,500.00
FV of annuity due = $154,765.98

15. What amount must be deposited now in order to withdraw $200 at the *beginning* of each month for 3 years, if interest is 12% compounded monthly?

$R = 1\%$ $P = 36 - 1 = 35$ Amount $= 200.00$

Factor $= 29.40858 + 1.00000$

$\quad\quad\quad = 30.40858 \times 200.00$

PV annuity due $= \underline{\$6,081.72}$

16. How much must be deposited now in order to withdraw $4,000 at the *end* of each year for 20 years, if interest is 7% compounded annually?

$R = 7\%$ $P = 20$ Amount $= 4,000.00$

Factor $= 10.59401 \times 4,000.00$

PV ordinary annuity $= \underline{\$42,376.04}$

17. A sinking fund is established by Infinity, Inc., at 8% interest compounded semiannually to meet a financial obligation of $1,800,000 in 4 years.

a. What periodic sinking fund payment is required every 6 months to reach the company's goal?

$R = 4\%$ $P = 8$ $FV = 1,800,000.00$

Factor $= 9.21423$

$\text{Payment} = \dfrac{1,800,000.00}{9.21423} = \underline{\$195,350.02}$

b. How much greater would the payment be if the interest rate was 6% compounded semiannually, rather than 8%?

$R = 3\%$ $P = 8$ $FV = 1,800,000.00$

Factor $= 8.89234$

$\text{Payment} = \dfrac{1,800,000.00}{8.89234} = \begin{array}{r} 202,421.41 \\ -\ 195,350.02 \\ \hline \end{array}$

$\quad\quad\quad\quad\quad\quad\quad$ Greater by $\underline{\$7,071.39}$

18. The O'Neils buy a home for $120,500. After a 15% down payment, the balance is financed at 8% interest for 9 years.

a. What equal quarterly payments will be required to amortize this mortgage loan?

$120,500 \times .85 = \$102,425.00$ Amount financed

$R = 2\%$ $P = 36$ Obligation $= \$102,425.00$

Factor $= 25.48884$

$\text{Payment} = \dfrac{102,425.00}{25.48884} = \underline{\$4,018.43}$

b. What is the total amount of interest the O'Neils will pay on the loan?

$4,018.43 \times 36 = \$144,663.48$ Total paid in

$\quad\quad\quad\quad\quad \begin{array}{r} -\ 102,425.00 \text{ Amount borrowed} \\ \hline \underline{\$42,238.48} \text{ Total interest} \end{array}$

(Optional) Use formulas and a financial calculator to solve the following:

19. The Portland Bank is paying 9% interest compounded monthly.

a. If you deposit $100 at the beginning of each month into a savings plan, how much will it be worth in 10 years?

$R = .75\%$ $P = 120$ Amount $= 100.00$

FV of annuity due $= PMT \times \dfrac{(1 + i)^n - 1}{i} \times (1 + i)$

$\quad = 100.00 \times \dfrac{(1 + .0075)^{120} - 1}{.0075} \times (1 + .0075)$

$\quad = 100.00 \times \dfrac{1.451357078}{.0075} \times (1.0075)$

$\quad = 100.00 \times 194.9656342$

$\quad = \underline{\$19,496.56}$

ANSWERS

15.	$6,081.72
16.	$42,376.04
17. a.	$195,350.02
b.	$7,071.39
18. a.	$4,018.43
b.	$42,238.48
19. a.	$19,496.56

b. How much would the account be worth if the payments were made at the end of each month, rather than at the beginning?

$$FV \text{ of ordinary annuity} = PMT \times \frac{(1+i)^n - 1}{i}$$

$$= 100.00 \times \frac{(1+.0075)^{120} - 1}{.0075}$$

$$= 100.00 \times 193.5142771$$

$$= \underline{\$19,351.43}$$

20. The town of Bay Harbor is planning to buy 5 new police cars in 4 years. The cars are expected to cost $18,500 each.

a. What equal monthly payments must the city deposit into a sinking fund at 6% interest compounded monthly in order to achieve its goal?

$R = .5\%$ $P = 48$ $FV = 5 \times 18,500.00$
$= \$92,500.00$

$$= 92,500.00 \times .018485029$$
$$= \underline{\$1,709.87}$$

$$\text{Sinking fund payment} = FV \times \frac{i}{(1+i)^n - 1}$$

$$= 92,500.00 \times \frac{.005}{(1+.005)^{48} - 1}$$

b. What is the total amount of interest earned in the account?

$48 \times 1,709.87 = 82,073.76$

$$92,500.00$$
$$- 82,073.76$$
$$\text{Interest earned} = \underline{\$10,426.24}$$

21. Snow Mass Savings & Loan is offering mortgages at 9% interest. What monthly payments would be required to amortize a loan of $200,000 for 25 years?

$R = .75\%$ $P = 300$ $\text{Loan} = 200,000.00$

$$\text{Payment} = PV \times \frac{i}{1 - (1+i)^{-n}}$$

$$= 200,000.00 \times \frac{.0075}{1 - (1+.0075)^{-300}}$$

$$= 200,000.00 \times \frac{.0075}{.893712166}$$
$$= 200,000.00 \times .008391964$$
$$= \underline{\$1,678.39}$$

 BUSINESS DECISION
Don't Forget Inflation

22. You are the vice president of finance for Casablanca Enterprises, Inc., a manufacturer of office furniture. The company is planning a major plant expansion in 5 years. You have decided to start a sinking fund to accumulate the funds necessary for the project. Current bank rates are 8% compounded quarterly. It is estimated that $2,000,000 in today's dollars will be required; however, the inflation rate on construction costs and plant equipment is expected to average 5% per year, for the next 5 years.

a. Use the compound interest concept from Chapter 11 to determine how much will be required for the project, taking inflation into account.

From Table 11-1, future value at compound interest,
Rate = 5% Periods = 5 Factor = 1.27628

$$FV = 2,000,000.00 \times 1.27628 = \underline{\$2,552,560.00}$$

b. What sinking fund payments will be required at the end of every 3-month period to accumulate the necessary funds?

$R = 2\%$ $P = 20$ $FV = \$2,552,560.00$
Factor = 24.29737

$$\text{Payment} = \frac{FV}{\text{Factor}} = \frac{2,552,560.00}{24.29737} = \underline{\$105,054.99}$$

All the Math That's Fit to Learn

The Business Math Times

| Volume XII | **Annuities** | One Dollar |

Some Thoughts on Economics and Inflation

You know inflation is out of hand when piggy banks cost more than they hold.

An economist is a fortune teller with a job.

Inflation is when you never had anything, and now even that's gone.

Inflation is when half your salary goes for food and shelter and the other half does, too.

There's one consolation about inflation. The money you don't have isn't worth what is once was.

Economists are the only people who can make an abundant living without ever being right.

Inflation is when you're in the middle-income and upper-outgo bracket.

The paradox of economics: At a time when none of the economic theories are working, all the economists are.

Inflation is when you order a $25 steak, put it on your American Express card, and it fits.

New car buyer to a friend: "I never thought I'd ever spend that much money for anything that didn't have a doorbell on it."

SOURCE: Excerpted from Joe Griffith, *Speaker's Library of Business Stories, Anecdotes, and Humor.* Englewood Cliffs, NJ: Prentice Hall, 1990, pp. 95, 161, 162.

" IT'S ONLY A FLYSPOT, BUT IT BALANCED THE BUDGET. "

Numbers in the News

Just as sports scores tell us how our favorite teams are doing, economic indicators are a way to "keep score" of the U.S. economy. The following is a quick guide to some of the most influential economic statistics and how they affect our lives.

Consumer Price Index (CPI)

The consumer price index, also known as the cost-of-living index, measures the average prices of a "market basket" of goods and services that a typical family living in an urban area buys compared to the prices of those items purchased in a base year.

Producer Price Index (PPI)

The producer price index shows what is happening to prices paid by producers and wholesalers, which will eventually affect the prices of retail goods and services.

Gross Domestic Product (GDP)

Gross domestic product is the total market value of all finished products and services produced within the United States in a given year.

Unemployment Rate

A person is "unemployed" if they do not have a job, but want one. A nation's unemployment rate is the number of unemployed people divided by the total number of people in the labor force.

SOURCE: Concept adapted from *Consumer Reports,* August 1994.

You're in the Red!

Did you know that in 1900, the national debt averaged about $16.50 per person? In early 1996, it was approximately $18,800 per person, and over $51,000 per household.

SOURCE: *U.S. News & World Report,* February 1, 1993. U.S. Department of Commerce, 1996.

Up, Up, and Away!

A. If a stack of 1,000 thousand dollar bills ($1 million) is 4 inches thick, how high would the stack be if it was equal to $5 trillion, the national debt as of March 1996?

B. What is the current national debt? Where did you find out? How high would that stack be?

The solution appears in the next issue of *The Business Math Times* on page 443.

I'll Take Manhattan—Solution

A. At 6%, the $24 would be worth over $55 billion.
$24(1 + .06)^{370} = \$55,383,630,000$
B. At 8%, the $24 would be worth over $55 trillion.
$24(1 + .08)^{370} = \$55,847,120,000,000$

What a difference 2% can make! This is a dramatic example of the "time value of money."

Brainteaser

Election Day in the United States is always the first Tuesday after the first Monday in November. In any given year, what is the latest date that election day can occur?

Answer to Last Issue's Brainteaser

The room will be darkest at $1{:}11$ and brightest at $10{:}08$

Chapter 13

Consumer and Business Credit

Performance Objectives

OPEN-END CREDIT—CHARGE ACCOUNTS, CREDIT CARDS, AND LINES OF CREDIT

"Buy now, pay later" is a concept that has become an everyday part of the way individuals and businesses purchase goods and services. Merchants in all categories, and lending institutions alike, encourage us to just say "charge it!" Consumers are offered a wide variety of charge accounts with many extra services and incentives attached. Many businesses have charge accounts in the company name. These accounts may be used to facilitate employee travel and entertainment expenses, or just to fill up the company delivery truck with gasoline, without having to deal with cash. Exhibit 13-1 shows a sample credit card and its parts.

Lending and borrowing money comprise a huge portion of the U.S. economic system. Over the years, as the practice became more and more prevalent, the federal government enacted various legislation to protect the consumer from being misled about credit and finance charges. One of the most important and comprehensive pieces of legislation, known as Regulation Z, covers both installment and **open-end credit.**

Regulation Z of the Consumer Credit Protection Act, 1969, also known as the Truth in Lending Act, requires that the lender fully disclose to the customer, in writing, the cost of the credit, particularly the finance charge and the annual percentage rate. The **finance charge** is the dollar amount that is paid for the credit. The **annual percentage rate,** also known as the **APR,** is the effective or true annual interest rate being charged.

Under a similar law passed in 1993 known as Truth in Savings, the effective or true annual interest rate being *paid* on savings accounts and certificates of deposits (CDs) must be revealed to the depositor. This is known as the **annual percentage yield (APY).** Exhibit 13-2 is an example of a typical truth in lending disclosure statement.

The granting of credit involves a trust relationship between the borrower and the lender. The borrower promises to repay the loan, with interest, in one of many predetermined payment arrangements. Trust on the part of the lender is based on past lending experience with

open-end credit
A loan arrangement in which there is no set number of payments. As the balance of the loan is reduced, the borrower can renew the amount of the loan up to a pre-approved credit limit. A form of revolving credit.

finance charge
The dollar amount that is paid for credit. Total of installment payments for an item less the cost price of that item.

annual percentage rate (APR)
Effective or true annual interest rate being charged for credit. Must be revealed to borrowers under the Truth in Lending law.

annual percentage yield (APY)
Effective or true annual interest rate being paid on deposits in a savings account. Must be revealed to depositors under the Truth in Savings law.

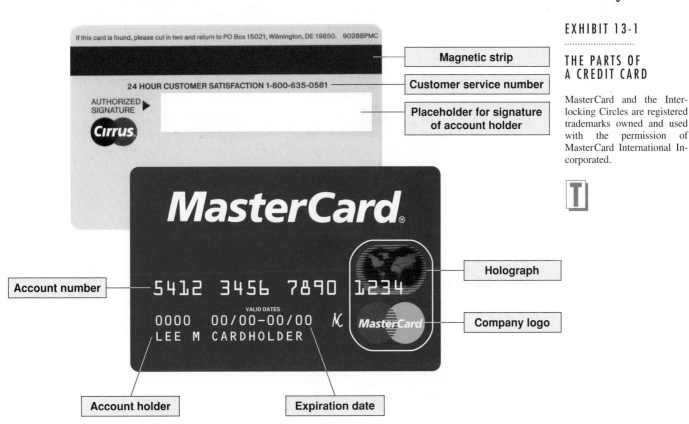

EXHIBIT 13-1

THE PARTS OF A CREDIT CARD

MasterCard and the Interlocking Circles are registered trademarks owned and used with the permission of MasterCard International Incorporated.

If this card is found, please cut in two and return to PO Box 15021, Wilmington, DE 19850. 90288PMC

24 HOUR CUSTOMER SATISFACTION 1-800-635-0581

AUTHORIZED SIGNATURE ▶

Cirrus

Magnetic strip

Customer service number

Placeholder for signature of account holder

MasterCard

Account number — 5412 3456 7890 1234

VALID DATES
0000 00/00–00/00
LEE M CARDHOLDER

Holograph

Company logo

Account holder

Expiration date

Toll Free Customer Service.
If you have a question or need special help, you have a direct line to our friendly, professional service representatives by calling toll free **1-800-323-6276.** Our representatives are available Monday through Friday. For your convenience and fastest response, call Tuesday through Friday. Please have your account number available.

Report a Lost or Stolen Card Immediately.
Representatives are available 24 hours a day, 7 days a week. Please telephone **1-800-342-6047.**

Billing Rights Summary.
In case of errors or questions about your bill:

If you think your bill is wrong, or if you need more information about a transaction on your bill, write us on a separate sheet of paper at the billing inquiry address listed on the front of your statement as soon as possible. We must hear from you no later than 60 days after we sent you the first bill on which the error or problem appeared. You can telephone us, but doing so will not preserve your rights.

In your letter, give us the following information:
- Your name and account number.
- The dollar amount of the suspected error.
- Describe the error and explain, if you can, why you believe there is an error. If you need more information, describe the item you are unsure about.

You do not have to pay any amount in question while we are investigating, but you are still obligated to pay the parts of your bill that are not in question. While we investigate your question, we cannot report you as delinquent or take any action to collect the amount you question.

Special Rule for Credit Card Purchases.
If you have a problem with the quality of goods and services that you purchased with a credit card, and you have tried in good faith to correct the problem with the merchant, you may not have to pay the remaining amount due on the goods or services. You have this protection only when the purchase price was more than $50 and the purchase was made in your home state or within 100 miles of your mailing address. (If we own or operate the merchant, or if we mailed you the advertisement for the property or services, all purchases are covered regardless of amount or location of purchase.)

The Calculation of your Finance Charge.
The balance upon which your Finance Charge is imposed is shown as the Average Daily Balance on your monthly billing statement. The balance each day (Daily Balance) consists of that portion of the Previous Balance shown on each current monthly statement to which is added cash advances and special checks from the date the loan is made and all purchases of goods and services, and from which is subtracted previously incurred Finance Charges and payments and credits as received. Unless we elect to use a later date, we add purchases to the balance as of the date of the purchase. Your Average

Daily Balance is then determined by dividing the sum of all Daily Balances in a billing period by the number of days in that period.

If there is no balance owed on your account at the beginning of the cycle, or if payments and credits equal or exceed that beginning balance, then a periodic Finance Charge is imposed only on cash advances. Appropriate adjustments will be made in the event of billing errors.

Your Daily Periodic Rate is determined by dividing the Annual Percentage Rate by 365 Days. The Finance Charge is computed by multiplying the Average Daily Balance by the Daily Periodic Rate, then multiplying the result by the number of days in the billing period. The Annual Percentage Rate, Average Daily Balance, and the Daily Periodic Rate are shown on the front of this statement.

Posting Payments.
Payments received at Bankcard Center, P.O. Box 1661, Jacksonville, FL 32231-0005, after 6 a.m. may not be credited until the following business day. Please allow 5-7 days for your payment to reach us. Payments by mail must be made by check or money order. Write your account number on the front of your check. There may be a delay of up to 5 days in posting payments made at a location other than the address listed above. The business days of the bank are Monday through Friday, excluding holidays.

Renewing Your Account.
If an Annual Membership Fee is shown on the front of this statement, you have 30 days from the date this statement was mailed (the "Interim Period") to avoid paying such charge or to have such charge re-credited to your account, if you elect to terminate credit availability under your account in the manner set forth below. You may use your Card(s) during the Interim Period without having to pay the Annual Membership Fee. To terminate credit availability under your account you must, prior to the expiration of the Interim Period, (i) give us written notice of cancellation of your account at the inquiry address indicated on the front of the statement, (ii) pay your outstanding account balance in full (not including the Annual Membership Fee) and (iii) cut in half and return to us any Card(s) which have been issued under your account. In connection with your account, the method of computing the balance for purchases is "Average Daily Balance (including new purchases)." There is a "Grace Period" for repayment of balances. You have until the payment due date shown on the front of this statement, which is not less than 25 days, to pay your new balance to avoid imposition of additional Finance Charges on purchases. You have no Grace Period in which to repay your balance for cash advances before a Finance Charge will be imposed. See front of this statement for additional information about (i) the Annual Percentage Rate applicable to your account and (ii) the Annual Membership applicable to your account.

Finance Charge Calculation

EXHIBIT 13-2

MASTERCARD—TRUTH IN LENDING DISCLOSURE STATEMENT

● **unsecured loan**

Loan that is backed simply by the borrower's "promise" to repay, without any tangible asset pledged as collateral. These loans carry more risk for the lender and therefore have higher interest rates than secured loans.

the borrower, the information provided on the credit application, and independent credit reports from credit bureaus. The degree and depth of lender investigation is directly proportional to the amount of money being borrowed. Exhibit 13-3 is an example of a typical credit application used to secure consumer credit.

For many consumers and almost all businesses, credit is a very important element of the financial plan. It allows borrowers the advantage of having an asset, and its use, before it is paid for. Credit should not be taken lightly nor used irresponsibly. Well-established credit and a good banking relationship should be long-term goals of businesses that plan to grow and prosper.

When loans are backed by a simple promise to repay, they are known as **unsecured loans.** Most open-end credit accounts are unsecured. Loans that are backed by tangible assets, such as car and boat loans and home mortgage loans, are known as **secured loans.** These loans are backed or secured by an asset that can be repossessed and sold by the lender if the

Apply now for the Ford Citibank Card. Call 1-800-374-7777, ext. 41.

FOLD, MOISTEN HERE, SEAL AND MAIL.
Have you included your ☐ Social Security Number ☐ Phone Numbers ☐ Signature?

PLEASE PRINT CLEARLY WITH A BLACK OR BLUE PEN — SECTIONS 1 THRU 7 MUST BE COMPLETED

1 YES! I want my Ford Citibank Card — Select One: MasterCard. ☐ Ford Citibank MasterCard. VISA ☐ Ford Citibank Visa* Card

PLEASE TELL US ABOUT YOURSELF

2 Please **Print** Your Full Name As You Wish It To Appear On The Card (First, Middle, Last) | Your Home Address, Number And Street | Apt. #
City Or Town | State | Zip Code | Years At Address | ☐ Own Home ☐ Rent ☐ Other ☐ Own Condo/Co-op ☐ Live w/Parents | Social Security Number – –
Date of Birth (Month/Day/Year) – – | Mother's Maiden Name | Home Phone Number And Area Code ( ) | Name Home Phone Is Listed Under | Are You A Permanent U.S. Resident? ☐ Yes ☐ No
Previous Home Address, Number And Street | City Or Town | State | Zip Code | Years There

ADDITIONAL STUDENT INFORMATION (Only current college or graduate students complete this section)

2A College Or Graduate School Name (Do not abbreviate) | Your Mailing Address at School | Apt. # | City Or Town
State | Zip Code | Your Phone Number And Area Code at School ( ) | Official School Zip Code | Name Your Phone Is Listed Under
Your Class: ☐ Fresh ☐ Soph ☐ Junior ☐ Senior ☐ Graduate ☐ Faculty/Staff ☐ Other | Graduation Date mo./yr. | Send Card And Billing Statement To: ☐ Home ☐ School

I M P O R T A N T
You must enclose in an envelope with this application a complete legible copy of your validated I.D. (or paid tuition bill) from a 4-year college or graduate school for the current semester.

PLEASE TELL US ABOUT YOUR JOB (Current Students: Job Not Required)

3 Business Name Or Employer At Current Job | Position | Years At Job | Employer Phone Number And Area Code ( )
Check Here If You Are: ☐ Retired ☐ Self-Employed | If Retired Or Self-Employed, Enter Bank Name | Bank Phone Number And Area Code ( ) | Bank Account Number

ABOUT YOUR INCOME

4 You need not include your spouse's income, alimony, child support, or maintenance payments paid to you if you are not relying on them to establish creditworthiness. Your total **yearly** income from all sources must be at least $12,000 to be considered for cardmembership. **(No student minimum.)**
Your Total Personal **Yearly** Income $ | Other **Yearly** Household Income $
Other **Yearly** Income Sources

IMPORTANT ACCOUNT INFORMATION

5 Please Check Those That Apply. Be Sure To Specify Institution/Bank Name
☐ Money Market/NOW Account — Institution Name:
☐ Checking Account — Institution Name:
☐ Savings Account — Institution Name:
☐ Visa/MasterCard ☐ Diners Club ☐ American Express ☐ Dept. Store/Sears ☐ Gasoline ☐ Other

WOULD YOU LIKE AN ADDITIONAL CARD AT NO CHARGE?

6 If Yes, **Print** The Full Name Of The User (First, Middle, Last) (Students: Does not apply)

PLEASE SIGN THIS AUTHORIZATION — Rev. 4/93

7 I certify that I have read and agree to all the Citibank credit terms and conditions of offer on other side. Please allow 30 days to process this application. | X Applicant's Signature | Date

17BHR 0135M LU15T 000B 1C70B 01359 5T0&& &&MJ

EXHIBIT 13-3

TYPICAL CREDIT APPLICATION

- **secured loan**
Loan that is backed by a tangible asset, such as a car, boat, or home, which can be repossessed and sold if the borrower fails to pay back the loan. These loans carry less risk for the lender and therefore have lower interest rates than unsecured loans.

borrower fails to comply with the rules of the loan. Secured loans will be covered in Section II of this chapter and in Chapter 14.

Revolving credit is the most popular type of open-end credit. Under this agreement, the consumer has a prearranged credit limit and two payment options. The first option is to use the account as a regular charge account, whereby the balance is paid off at the end of the month with no finance charge. The second option is to make a minimum payment or portion of the payment, but less than the full balance. This option leaves a carryover balance, which accrues finance charges using the simple interest formula,

$$\text{Interest} = \text{Principal} \times \text{Rate} \times \text{Time}$$

The name "revolving credit" comes from the fact that there is no set number of payments as with installment credit. The account revolves month-to-month, year-to-year—technically never being paid off as long as minimum monthly payments are made. Exhibits 13-4 and 13-5 illustrate a typical revolving credit charge slip and monthly statement.

- **revolving credit**
Loans made on a continuous basis and billed periodically. Borrower makes minimum monthly payments or more, and pays interest on the outstanding balance. A form of open-end credit extended by many retail stores and credit card companies.

Account Number — **BankCard**

Expiration Date | Approval Code | Type of Delayed Chg.
Account Holder | Check or Bill Number | Amt. of Delayed Chg.
Company/Service | Date of Charge | Revised Total

MERCHANDISE/SERVICES
TAXES
TIPS/MISC.
TOTAL
Dollars Cents

Signature
X

Merchandise and/or service purchased on this card shall not be resold or returned for cash refund.

Customer Copy

EXHIBIT 13-4

SAMPLE CHARGE SLIP

Statement of BankCard Account

Payable upon Receipt in U.S. Dollars with a check drawn on a bank located in the U.S. or a money order.
Please enter Corporate Account Number on all checks and correspondence.

☐ Check here if address or telephone number has changed. Please note changes on reverse side.

Account Number	Statement Closing Date	Total Amount Due
0000–657421–91226	04–02–95	$166.61

MAIL PAYMENT TO:

LINDA WILLIS
301 COMMERCE ST.
FT WORTH TX   76102

BANKCARD
P.O. BOX 631
DALLAS TX   73563-0001

Ilmlıldımlldmlldmdldlmllmdlmdllldlıldlmdl

Detach here and return upper portion with check or money order. Do not staple or fold.

Summary of BankCard Account

Retain this portion for your files.

Corporate Cardmember Name	Account Number	Statement Closing Date
LINDA WILLIS	0000–657421–91226	04–02–95

Previous Balance	New Charges	Other Debits	Payments Received	Other Credits	Balance Due
$174.84	$166.61	$.00	$174.84	$.00	$166.61

Reference Number	Item Number	Description of Monthly Activity			Charges	Credits
		PREVIOUS BALANCE			$174.84	
835078		PAYMENT RECEIVED – THANK YOU		03/19		$174.84
501065	1	WHATABURGER FOOD/BEVERAGE	FT. WORTH	TX 03/30/95	3.97	
501081	2	STEIN MART APPAREL/HOUSEWARES/ACC	FT. WORTH	TX 03/04/95	56.94	
501069	3	AMERICAN ARTIST PUBLICATIONS	MARION	OH 03/22/95	26.95	
501065	4	EXXON COMPANY USA FUEL/MISC	RED OAK	TX 02/20/95	13.30	
501071	5	TEXACO ISLE SALE	FORT WORTH	TX 03/05/95	16.00	
501079	6	TEXACO GASOLINE	FORT WORTH	TX 03/10/95	18.00	
501089	7	TEXACO ISLE SALE	FORT WORTH	TX 03/19/95	15.25	
501092	8	EXXON COMPANY USA FUEL/MISC	FORT WORTH	TX 03/29/95	16.20	
		TOTAL CHARGES AND CREDITS			$166.61	
		BALANCE DUE				$166.61

PAGE 1 OF 1

Payments or credits received after closing date above will appear on next month's statement.

FOR INQUIRIES ABOUT YOUR ACCOUNT, CALL TOLL-FREE 1-800-635-0581.

Rate Summary		Purchases	Advances
Number of days this Billing Period	30		
Balance Subject to Finance Charge		00.00	
Periodic Rate (Purchases-Monthly, Advances-Daily)		1.65000%	.05424%
Nominal Annual Percentage Rate		19.80%	19.80%
ANNUAL PERCENTAGE RATE		19.80%	19.80%

EXHIBIT 13-5

TYPICAL MONTHLY STATEMENT

Today there are two generally accepted methods for calculating the finance charge on a revolving charge account: the unpaid or previous month's balance method and the average daily balance method. In this section we shall learn to calculate both.

13-1 Calculating Finance Charge and New Balance by the Unpaid or Previous Month's Balance Method

Open-end credit transactions are divided into time periods known as **billing cycles.** These cycles are commonly between 28 and 31 days. At the end of a billing cycle a statement is sent to the account holder much like the one in Exhibit 13-5.

● **billing cycle**
Time period, usually 28 to 31 days, used in billing revolving credit accounts. Account statements are sent to the borrower after each billing cycle.

STEPS TO CALCULATE THE FINANCE CHARGE AND NEW BALANCE USING THE UNPAID BALANCE METHOD:

Step 1. Divide the annual percentage rate by 12 to find the monthly or periodic interest rate. (Round to the nearest hundredth percent when necessary.)

$$\text{Periodic rate} = \frac{\text{Annual percentage rate}}{12}$$

Step 2. Calculate the finance charge by multiplying the previous month's balance by the periodic interest rate from Step 1.

$$\text{Finance charge} = \text{Previous month's balance} \times \text{Periodic rate}$$

Step 3. Total all of the purchases and cash advances for the month.

Step 4. Total all of the payments and credits for the month.

Step 5. Use the following formula to determine the new balance:

$$\frac{\text{New}}{\text{balance}} = \frac{\text{Previous}}{\text{balance}} + \frac{\text{Finance}}{\text{charge}} + \frac{\text{Purchases and}}{\text{cash advances}} - \frac{\text{Payments and}}{\text{credits}}$$

EXAMPLE

John Fernandez has a revolving department store credit account, with an annual percentage rate of 18%. John's previous balance from last month is $322.40. During the month he purchased shirts for $65.60 and a drill for $43.25. He returned a tie for a credit of $22.95 and made a $50 payment. If the department store uses the unpaid balance method, what is the amount of the finance charge on the account and what is John's new balance?

SOLUTION STRATEGY

Step 1.
$$\text{Periodic rate} = \frac{\text{Annual percentage rate}}{12}$$
$$\text{Periodic rate} = \frac{18\%}{12} = 1.5\%$$

Step 2.
$$\text{Finance charge} = \text{Previous month's balance} \times \text{Periodic rate}$$
$$\text{Finance charge} = 322.40 \times .015$$
$$\text{Finance charge} = 4.836 = \underline{\$4.84}$$

Step 3. Total the purchases for the month:
$$\$65.60 + 43.25 = \$108.85$$

Step 4. Total the payments and credits for the month:
$$\$50.00 + \$22.95 = \$72.95$$

Step 5. Find the new balance for John's account using the formula:

$$\frac{\text{New}}{\text{balance}} = \frac{\text{Previous}}{\text{balance}} + \frac{\text{Finance}}{\text{charge}} + \frac{\text{Purchases and}}{\text{cash advances}} - \frac{\text{Payments and}}{\text{credits}}$$

$$\text{New balance} = \$322.40 + \$4.84 + \$108.85 - \$72.95$$

$$\text{New balance} = \underline{\$363.14}$$

TRY-IT EXERCISE

1. Lyn Maize has a BankCard account with an annual percentage rate of 15%. Her previous month's balance is $214.90. During the month of July Lyn's account showed the following activity:

Lyn Maize	**STATEMENT OF ACCOUNT**	
Account #097440	Billing cycle: July 1–31	
July 6	Royal Cleaners	$35.50
July 9	Payment	40.00
July 15	Budget Hardware	133.25
July 16	Casino Restaurant	41.10
July 21	Walgreens	29.00
July 27	Walgreens (credit)	9.12

How much is the finance charge for July, and what is Lyn's new balance?

Check your answers with the solutions on page 434.

13-2 Calculating Finance Charge and New Balance Using the Average Daily Balance Method

● average daily balance

In open-end credit, the most commonly used method for determining the account balance for a billing cycle. It is the total of the daily balances divided by the number of days in the cycle.

In business today, the method most widely used to calculate finance charge on a revolving credit account is known as the **average daily balance.** This method precisely tracks the activity in an account on a daily basis. Each day's balance of a billing cycle is totaled and then divided by the number of days in that cycle. This gives an average of all the daily balances.

For accounts in which many charges are made each month, the average daily balance method results in much higher interest than the unpaid balance method, because interest starts accruing on the day purchases are made or cash advances are taken.

STEPS TO CALCULATE THE FINANCE CHARGE USING THE AVERAGE DAILY BALANCE:

Step 1. Starting with the previous month's balance as the first unpaid balance, multiply each by the number of days that balance existed, until the next account transaction.

Step 2. At the end of the billing cycle, find the sum of all the daily balance figures.

Step 3. Find the average daily balance using the formula:

$$\text{Average daily balance} = \frac{\text{Sum of daily balances}}{\text{Days in billing cycle}}$$

Step 4. Calculate the finance charge by:

$$\text{Finance charge} = \text{Average daily balance} \times \text{Periodic rate}$$

Step 5. Compute the new balance as before using:

$$\frac{\text{New}}{\text{balance}} = \frac{\text{Previous}}{\text{balance}} + \frac{\text{Finance}}{\text{charge}} + \frac{\text{Purchases and}}{\text{cash advances}} - \frac{\text{Payments and}}{\text{credits}}$$

Todd Gomberg has a BankCard revolving credit account with a 15% annual percentage rate. The finance charge is calculated using the average daily balance method. The billing date is the first day of each month and the billing cycle is the number of days in that month. During the month of March Todd's account showed the following activity:

Todd Gomberg	**STATEMENT OF ACCOUNT**	
Account #1229-3390-0038	**Billing cycle: March 1–31**	

March 1	Previous month's balance	$215.60
March 7	Sports Authority	125.11
March 10	Exxon	23.25
March 12	Payment	75.00
March 17	Macy's (credit)	54.10
March 23	H.L. Mager, DDS	79.00
March 23	Exxon	19.43
March 24	Blockbuster Music	94.19

How much is the finance charge for March, and what is Todd's new balance?

SOLUTION STRATEGY

In order to find the average daily balance, we shall set up a chart that lists the activity in Todd's account by dates and number of days (Steps 1 and 2).

Dates	Number of Days	Activity/Amount		Unpaid Balance	Daily Balances (unpaid bal. × days)
March 1–6	6	Previous balance		$215.60	$1,293.60
March 7–9	3	Charge	+$125.11	340.71	1,022.13
March 10–11	2	Charge	+23.25	363.96	727.92
March 12–16	5	Payment	−75.00	288.96	1,444.80
March 17–22	6	Credit	−54.10	234.86	1,409.16
March 23	1	Charges	+79.00 +19.43	333.29	333.29
March 24–31	8	Charge	+94.19	427.48	3,419.84
	31 days in cycle				Total $9,650.74

Step 3.
$$\text{Average daily balance} = \frac{\text{Sum of daily balances}}{\text{Days in billing cycle}} = \frac{\$9,650.74}{31} = \$311.31$$

Step 4. The periodic rate is 1.25% (15% ÷ 12).

$$\text{Finance charge} = \text{Periodic rate} \times \text{Average daily balance}$$
$$\text{Finance charge} = .0125 \times 311.31 = \underline{\$3.89}$$

Step 5.
$$\frac{\text{New}}{\text{balance}} = \frac{\text{Previous}}{\text{balance}} + \frac{\text{Finance}}{\text{charge}} + \frac{\text{Purchases and}}{\text{cash advances}} - \frac{\text{Payments and}}{\text{credits}}$$

$$\frac{\text{New}}{\text{balance}} = \$215.60 + \$3.89 + \$340.98 - \$129.10$$

$$\frac{\text{New}}{\text{balance}} = \underline{\$431.37}$$

TRY-IT EXERCISE

2. Kathryn Warren has a BankCard revolving credit account with an 18% annual percentage rate. The finance charge is calculated using the average daily balance method. The billing date is the first day of each month and the billing cycle is the number of days in that month. During the month of August Kathryn's account showed the following activity:

Kathryn Warren   **STATEMENT OF ACCOUNT**

Account #2967-39460-0098   Billing cycle: August 1–31

August 1	Previous month's balance	$158.69
August 5	Nathan's Beauty Salon	55.00
August 11	Payment	100.00
August 15	Wal-Mart	43.22
August 17	Sunshine Auto Repair	54.10
August 20	Circuit City	224.50
August 26	Cash Advance	75.00

How much is the finance charge for August, and what is Kathryn's new balance?

Check your answers with the solutions on pages 434–435.

13-3 Calculating the Finance Charge and New Balance of Business and Personal Lines of Credit

A personal or business line of credit allows easy access to large amounts of money.

● **line of credit**
A pre-approved amount of open-end credit, based on borrower's ability to pay.

One of the most useful types of open-end credit is the business or personal **line of credit.** In this section we shall investigate the unsecured credit line, which is based on your own merit. In Chapter 14, we shall discuss the home equity line of credit, which is secured by a home or other piece of real estate property.

A line of credit is an important tool for on-going businesses and responsible individuals. For those who qualify, unsecured lines of credit generally range from $2,500 to $250,000. The amount is based on your ability to pay as well as your financial and credit history. This pre-approved borrowing power essentially gives you the opportunity to become your own private banker. Once the line has been established, you can borrow money by simply writing a check. Lines of credit usually have an annual usage fee of between $50 and $100, and most lenders also require that you update your financial information each year.

With credit lines, you only pay interest on the outstanding average daily balance of your loan. For most lines, the interest rate is variable and is based on, or indexed to, the prime rate. The **prime rate** is the lending rate at which the largest and most creditworthy corporations in the country borrow money from banks. The current prime rate is published daily in *The Wall Street Journal* as well as the business section of most newspapers, in a column entitled "Money Rates." Exhibit 13-6 shows examples of this column.

● **prime rate**
The lending rate at which the largest and most creditworthy corporations borrow money from banks. The interest rate of most lines of credit are tied to the movement of the prime rate.

A typical line of credit quotes interest as the prime rate plus a fixed percent, such as "prime + 3%" or "prime + 6.8%." Some lenders have a minimum rate regardless of the prime rate, such as "prime + 3%, minimum 10%." In this case, when the prime is above 7%, the rate varies up and down. When the prime falls below 7%, the minimum 10% rate applies. This guarantees the lender at least a 10% return on funds loaned. Generally, credit line rates are much lower than the interest charged on consumer loans or credit cards. See Exhibit 13-7.

MONEY RATES

Monday, November 28, 1994

The key U.S. and foreign annual interest rates below are a guide to general levels but don't always represent actual transactions.

PRIME RATE: 8½%. The base rate on corporate loans posted by at least 75% of the nation's 30 largest banks.

FEDERAL FUNDS: 5¾% high, 5 9/16% low, 5 11/16% near closing bid, 5¾% offered. Reserves traded among commercial banks for overnight use in amounts of $1 million or more. Source: Prebon Yamane (U.S.A.) Inc.

DISCOUNT RATE: 4¾%. The charge on loans to depository institutions by the Federal Reserve Banks.

CALL MONEY: 7¼%. The charge on loans to brokers on stock exchange collateral. Source: Dow Jones Telerate Inc.

COMMERCIAL PAPER placed directly by General Electric Capital Corp.: 5.50% 30 to 59 days; 5.75% 60 to 89 days; 5.78% 90 to 119 days; 5.87% 120 to 149 days; 5.95% 150 to 179 days; 6.03% 180 to 259 days; 6.23% 260 to 270 days.

COMMERCIAL PAPER: High-grade unsecured notes sold through dealers by major corporations: 5.60% 30 days; 5.85% 60 days; 5.91% 90 days.

CERTIFICATES OF DEPOSIT: 4.80% one month; 5.01% two months; 5.14% three months; 5.56% six months; 6.04% one year. Average of top rates paid by major New York banks on primary new issues of negotiable C.D.s, usually on amounts of $1 million and more. The minimum unit is $100,000. Typical rates in the secondary market: 5.60% one month; 5.95% three months; 6.40% six months.

BANKERS ACCEPTANCES: 5.55% 30 days; 5.78% 60 days; 5.82% 90 days; 5.87% 120 days; 5.96% 150 days; 6.08% 180 days. Offered rates of negotiable, bank-backed business credit instruments typically financing an import order.

LONDON LATE EURODOLLARS: 5⅝% - 5½% one month; 5⅞% - 5¾% two months; 6% - 5⅞% three months; 6⅛% - 6% four months; 6¼% - 6⅛% five months; 6⅜% - 6¼% six months.

LONDON INTERBANK OFFERED RATES (LIBOR): 5⅝% one month; 6% three months; 6 5/16% six months; 6 15/16% one year. The average of interbank offered rates for dollar deposits in the London market based on quotations at five major banks. Effective rate for contracts entered into two days from date appearing at top of this column.

FOREIGN PRIME RATES: Canada 7%; Germany 5.20%; Japan 3%; Switzerland 5.50%; Britain 5.75%. These rate indications aren't directly comparable; lending practices vary widely by location.

TREASURY BILLS: Results of the Monday, November 28, 1994, auction of short-term U.S. government bills, sold at a discount from face value in units of $10,000 to $1 million: 5.44% 13 weeks; 5.86% 26 weeks.

TREASURY BILLS: Results of the Monday, November 28, 1994, auction of short-term U.S. government bills, sold at a discount from face value in units of $10,000 to $1 million: 5.44%, 13 weeks; 5.86%, 26 weeks.

FEDERAL HOME LOAN MORTGAGE CORP. (Freddie Mac): Posted yields on 30-year mortgage commitments. Delivery within 30 days 9.21%, 60 days 9.29%, standard conventional fixed-rate mortgages; 6.375%, 2% rate capped one-year adjustable rate mortgages. Source: Dow Jones Telerate Inc.

FEDERAL NATIONAL MORTGAGE ASSOCIATION (Fannie Mae): Posted yields on 30 year mortgage commitments (priced at par) for delivery within 30 days 9.19%, 60 days 9.27%, standard conventional fixed rate-mortgages; 7.95%, 6/2 rate capped one-year adjustable rate mortgages. Source: Dow Jones Telerate Inc.

MERRILL LYNCH READY ASSETS TRUST: 4.60%. Annualized average rate of return after expenses for the past 30 days; not a forecast of future returns.

MONEY RATES

NEW YORK (AP) — Money rates for Wednesday as reported by Telerate Systems Inc:

Telerate interest rate index: 6.070
Prime Rate: 8.50
Discount Rate: 4.75
Broker call loan rate: 7.25
Federal funds market rate:
  High 5.875 Low 6.625 Last 5.625
Dealers commercial paper:
  30-180 days: 5.65-6.35
Commercial paper by finance company:
  30-270 days: 5.90-6.25
Bankers acceptances dealer indications:

30 days, 5.95		60 days, 5.95	
90 days, 6.03		120 days, 6.12	
150 days, 6.24		180 days, 6.33	

Certificates of Deposit Primary:

30 days, 4.53			
90 days, 4.85		180 days, 5.32	

Certificates of Deposit by dealer:

30 days, 5.97		60 days, 5.98	
90 days, 6.12		120 days, 6.26	
150 days, 6.38		180 days, 6.53	

Eurodollar rates:
  Overnight, 5.4375-5.5625
  1 month, 6.00-6.0625
  3 months, 6.1875-6.25
  6 months, 6.50-6.5625
  1 year, 7.1875-7.25
London Interbk Offered Rate:
  3 months, 6.0625
  6 months, 6.4375
  1 year, 7.125
Treasury Bill auction results:
  average discount rate:
  3-month as of Nov. 28: 5.44
  6-month as of Nov. 28: 5.86
Treasury Bill, annualized rate on weekly average basis, yield adjusted for constant maturity, 1-year, as of Nov. 28: 6.63
Treas. Billmarket rate,1-year: 6.47-6.45
Treas. Bondmarket rate,30-year: 8.00
Fannie Mae 30 year mortgage commitments:
  30 days, 9.26   60 days, 9.34
Fed Home Loan 11th District Cost of Funds:
  As of Oct. 31: 4.039
Money market fund:
Merrill Lynch Ready Assets:
  30 day average yield: 4.63
n.a. - not available.

EXHIBIT 13-6

MONEY RATES CHARTS

As before, the finance charge is calculated by multiplying the periodic interest rate by the average daily balance. This means that interest begins as soon as you write a check for a loan. Typically, the loan is paid back on a flexible schedule. In most cases, balances of $100 or less must be paid in full. Larger balances require minimum monthly payments of $100 or 2% of the outstanding balance, whichever is greater. As you repay, the line of credit renews itself. The new balance line of credit is calculated by

New Balance = Previous balance + Finance charge + Loans − Payments

EXAMPLE

Shari's Gift Shop has a $20,000 line of credit with The Executive National Bank. The annual percentage rate charged on the account is the current prime rate plus 4%. There is a minimum APR on the account of 10%. The starting balance on April 1 was $2,350. On April 9 Shari borrowed $1,500 to pay for a shipment of assorted gift items. On April 20 she made a $3,000 payment on the account. On April 26 another $2,500 was borrowed to pay for air conditioning repairs. The billing cycle for April has 30 days. If the current prime rate is 8%, what is the finance charge on the account, and what is Shari's new balance?

SOLUTION STRATEGY

To solve this problem we must find the annual percentage rate, the periodic rate, the average daily balance, the finance charge, and finally the new balance.

FORD CITIBANK CARD
c/o Citicorp Credit Services, Inc.
14700 Citicorp Drive
Hagerstown, Maryland 21749-9723

FOLD HERE ↑   ↑ FOLD HERE

Annual Fee	None first year; $20 thereafter
Grace Period for Purchases	20 to 25 days
Annual Percentage Rates	Currrently (April 1993) 15.4% for purchases; 19.8% for cash advances
Variable Rate Information	The annual percentage rate for purchases may vary each calendar quarter. We will calculate the variable rate by adding 9.4% to the rate disclosed as the U.S. Prime Rate reported in the "Money Rates" table of *The Wall Street Journal* on the third Tuesday of March, June, September and December of each year. This rate will not be lower than 12.9% or higher than 19.8%. However, if cardmember fail to keep all their Citibank accounts in good standing, the rate will increase to 19.8% on the full purchase balance.
Method of Computing the Balance for Purchases	Average Daily Balance (including new purchases)
Minumum Finance Charge	50¢
Transaction Fee for Cash Advances	At a financial institution, 2% of amount of advance but not less than $2 or more than $10. At an ATM, $1.75.
Last Payment Fee	$15; Over-the-Credit-Limit Fee: $10

←— *

Disclosure Box

The information about the costs of the card described in this application is accurate as of April 1993. This information may have changed after that date. To find out what may have changed, write to Citibank at P.O. Box 6116, Sioux Falls, SD 57117-6116. By signing this application, I authorize Citibank (South Dakota), N.A. ("you") to check my credit history, and I authorize any references listed to release information to you or any of your affiliates regarding my eligibility for the Citibank credit card and any renewal or future extension of credit. I certify that I am 18 years or older and that the information provided is accurate. If I am issued a card, I authorize you to exchange information about how I handle my account with Citibank affiliates, credit bureaus, and proper persons. If I request an authorized user to be added to my account, I understand that account information will also be reported to credit bureaus in the authorized user's name. I authorize your affiliates to perform certain customer service and payment processing functions for my Citibank credit card account. I also authorize you and your affiliates to periodically exchange information regarding any account I may have with you or your affiliates. I understand that if I use the card or authorize its use or do not cancel my account within 30 after I receive the card, the Citibank Agreement sent to me with the card will be binding. I verify that I have read and understand the disclosures above. ©1993 Citibank (South Dakota), N.A. **Member FDIC**.

EXHIBIT 13-7

....

CITIBANK RATE DISCLOSURE INDEXED TO PRIME RATE

Annual percentage rate: The annual percentage rate is prime plus 4%, with a minimum of 10%. Because the current prime is 8%, the APR on this line of credit is 12% (8% + 4%).

Periodic rate:

$$\text{Periodic rate} = \frac{\text{Annual percentage rate}}{12 \text{ months}} = \frac{12\%}{12} = 1\%$$

Average daily balance: From the information given, we construct the following chart showing the account activity.

Dates	Number of Days	Activity/Amount	Unpaid Balance	Daily Balances (unpaid balance × days)
April 1–8	8	Previous balance	$2,350.00	$18,800.00
April 9–19	11	Borrowed–$1,500	3,850.00	42,350.00
April 20–25	6	Payment–$3,000	850.00	5,100.00
April 26–30	5	Borrowed–$2,500	3,350.00	16,750.00
	30 days in cycle			Total $83,000.00

$$\text{Average daily balance} = \frac{\text{Sum of daily balances}}{\text{Days in billing cycle}} = \frac{83,000}{30} = \$2,766.67$$

Finance charge:

$$\text{Finance charge} = \text{Periodic rate} \times \text{Average daily balance}$$

$$\text{Finance charge} = .01 \times 2,766.67 = \underline{\$27.67}$$

New balance:

$$\text{New balance} = \frac{\text{Previous}}{\text{balance}} + \frac{\text{Finance}}{\text{charge}} + \frac{\text{Loan}}{\text{amounts}} - \text{Payments}$$

$$\text{New balance} = \$2,350.00 + \$27.67 + \$4,000.00 - \$3,000.00$$

$$\text{New balance} = \underline{\$3,377.67}$$

TRY-IT **EXERCISE**

3. V.I.P. Industries has a $75,000 line of credit with Citicorp Bank. The annual percentage rate is the current prime rate plus 4.5%. The balance on November 1 was $12,300. On November 7, V.I.P. borrowed $16,700 to pay for a shipment of merchandise, and on November 21, they borrowed another $8,800. On November 26, a $20,000 payment was made on the account. The billing cycle for November has 30 days. If the current prime rate is $8\frac{1}{2}\%$, what is the finance charge on the account, and what is V.I.P.'s new balance?

Check your answers with the solutions on page 435.

REVIEW EXERCISES CHAPTER 13—SECTION I

Calculate the missing information on the following revolving charge accounts. Interest is calculated on the unpaid or previous month's balance:

	Previous Balance	Annual Percentage Rate (APR)	Monthly Periodic Rate	Finance Charge	Purchases and Cash Advances	Payments and Credits	New Balance
1.	$167.88	18%	1.5%	$2.52	$215.50	$50.00	$335.90
2.	$35.00	12%	1%	.35	$186.40	$75.00	$146.75
3.	$455.12	21%	1.75%	7.96	$206.24	$125.00	$544.32
4.	$2,390.00	15%	$1\frac{1}{4}\%$	29.88	$1,233.38	$300.00	$3,353.26

5. Milton Alderfer has a BankCard account with an annual percentage rate of 12% calculated on the previous month's balance. From the Visa monthly statement below:

Milton Alderfer **STATEMENT OF ACCOUNT**

Account #2290-0090-4959 Billing cycle: September 1–30

September 1	Previous Month's Balance	$120.00
September 8	Toys R Us	65.52
September 11	Payment	70.00
September 14	Texaco Oil	23.25
September 22	Cash Advance	60.00
September 26	Kroger Supermarket	59.16

---

a. What is the amount of the finance charge?

$$\text{Finance charge} = 120.00 \times \frac{12\%}{12} = \underline{\$1.20}$$

b. What is Milton's new balance?

New balance = 120.00 + 1.20 + 207.93 − 70.00

$= \underline{\$259.13}$

Roberta Potter has a revolving charge account. The finance charge is calculated on the previous month's balance, and the annual percentage rate is 21%. Complete the following 5-month account activity table for Roberta:

A.P.R. = 21%   Periodic = 1.75

Month	Previous Month's Balance	Finance Charge	Purchases and Cash Advances	Payments and Credits	New Balance End of Month
6. March	$560.00	$9.80	$121.37	$55.00	$636.17
7. April	$636.17	$11.13	$46.45	$65.00	$628.75
8. May	$628.75	$11.00	$282.33	$105.00	$817.08
9. June	$817.08	$14.30	$253.38	$400.00	$684.76
10. July	$684.76	$11.98	$70.59	$100.00	$667.33

Complete, worked out solutions for exercises 11–13 appear in the appendix following the index.

11. Calculate the average daily balance for the month of October of an account with a previous month's balance of $140.00 and the following activity:

Average daily balance = $152.29

Date	Activity	Amount
October 3	Cash Advance	$50.00
October 7	Payment	$75.00
October 10	Purchase	$26.69
October 16	Credit	$40.00
October 25	Purchase	$122.70

12. Calculate the average daily balance for the month of February of an account with a previous month's balance of $69.50 and the following activity:

Average daily balance = $158.51

Date	Activity	Amount
February 6	Payment	$58.00
February 9	Purchase	$95.88
February 15	Purchase	$129.60
February 24	Credit	$21.15
February 27	Cash Advance	$100.00

13. Carolyn Salkind has a BankCard revolving credit account with a 15% annual percentage rate. The finance charge is calculated using the average daily balance method. The billing date is the first day of each month and the billing cycle is the number of days in that month. During the month of March Carolyn's account showed the following activity:

```
Carolyn Salkind        STATEMENT OF ACCOUNT

Account #2967-39460        Billing cycle: March 1–31


        March 1    Previous month's balance    $324.45
        March 5    A Nose for Clothes            156.79
        March 11   Payment                       150.00
        March 15   Office Depot                   45.60
        March 17   Delta Airlines                344.50
```

a. How much is the finance charge for March?

Finance charge = 551.10 × .0125
= $6.89

b. What is Carolyn's new balance?

New balance = 324.45 + 6.89 + 546.89 − 150.00
= $728.23

14. The First National Bank of Commerce offers a business line of credit that has an annual percentage rate of prime rate plus 5.4%, with a minimum of 11%. What is the APR if the prime rate is

a. 7%
$7 + 5.4$
$= \underline{12.4\%}$

b. 10.1%
$10.1 + 5.4$
$= \underline{15.5\%}$

c. 9.25%
$9.25 + 5.4$
$= \underline{14.65\%}$

d. $5\frac{3}{4}\%$
$5.75 + 5.4$
$= \underline{11.15\%}$

15. The Rocky Mountain Corporation has a $30,000 line of credit with NationsBank. The annual percentage rate is the current prime rate plus 4.7%. The balance on March 1 was $8,400. On March 6, Rocky Mountain borrowed $6,900 to pay for a shipment of supplies, and on March 17, they borrowed another $4,500 for equipment repairs. On March 24, a $10,000 payment was made on the account. The billing cycle for March has 31 days. The current prime rate is 9%.

a. What is the finance charge on the account?

Finance charge $= 13783.87 \times \dfrac{(9\% + 4.7\%)}{12}$

$= 13{,}783.87 \times 1.14\%$

$= \underline{\$157.14}$

Dates	# of Days	Activity	Unpaid Balance	Daily Balance
Mar 1–5	5	Previous balance	8,400.00	42,000.00
Mar 6–16	11	+ 6,900.00	15,300.00	168,300.00
Mar 17–23	7	+ 4,500.00	19,800.00	138,600.00
Mar 24–31	8	− 10,000.00	9,800.00	78,400.00
	31			$427,300.00

Average daily balance $= \dfrac{427{,}300.00}{31} = \$13{,}783.87$

b. What is Rocky Mountain's new balance?

New balance $= 8{,}400.00 + 157.14 + 11{,}400.00 - 10{,}000.00$

$= \underline{\$9{,}957.14}$

c. On April 1, how much credit does Rocky Mountain have left on the account?

Remaining credit $= 30{,}000.00 - 9{,}957.14$

$= \underline{\$20{,}042.86}$

CLOSED-END CREDIT—INSTALLMENT LOANS

Closed-end credit, in the form of installment loans, is used extensively today for the purchase of durable goods, such as cars, boats, electronic equipment, furniture, and appliances, as well as services, such as vacation trips and home improvements. **Installment loans** are lump-sum loans whereby the borrower repays the principal plus interest in a specified number of equal monthly payments. These loans generally range in time from 6 months to 10 years depending on what is being financed.

When homes and other real estate property are financed, the installment loans are known as **mortgages.** Mortgages may be for as long as 30 years on homes and even longer on commercial property such as office buildings or factories. These loans, along with home equity loans, will be discussed in Chapter 14.

Many installment loans are secured by the asset for which the loan was made. For example, when a bank makes a car loan for 3 years, the consumer gets the car to use and monthly payments to make, but the lender still owns the car. Only after the final payment is made on the loan does the lender turn over the title, or proof of ownership, to the borrower. An additional form of security for the lending institution is that borrowers are often asked to make a down payment as part of the loan arrangement.

A **down payment** is a percentage of the purchase price that the buyer must pay in a lump sum at the time of purchase. Down payments on installment loans vary by category of merchandise, and generally range from between 0% to 30% of the price of the item. Sometimes the amount of the down payment is based on the credit rating of the borrower. Usually, the better the credit, the less the down payment.

● **installment loan**
A loan made for a specified number of equal monthly payments. A form of closed-end credit used for purchasing durable goods such as cars, boats, and furniture or services such as vacations or home improvements.

● **mortgage**
Installment loans made for homes and other real estate property.

● **down payment**
A percentage of the purchase price that the buyer must pay in a lump sum at the time of purchase.

Until the loan on this boat is repaid, the lending institution is technically the owner.

As with open-credit, installment loan consumers are protected by Regulation Z of the Truth in Lending Law. Not only must lenders make full disclosure of the terms in the loan agreement, but advertisers of installment loans, such as car dealers and furniture stores, must by law disclose in the ad the following information:

1. The amount or percentage of the down payment.
2. The terms of the repayment of the loan.
3. The annual percentage rate.
4. The total payback over the life of the loan.

13-4 Calculating the Total Deferred Payment Price and the Amount of the Finance Charge of an Installment Loan

Let's take a look at some of the terminology of installment loans. When a consumer buys goods or services without any financing, the price paid is known as the **cash price** or **purchase price.** When financing is involved, the **amount financed** is found by subtracting the down payment from the cash or purchase price. Sometimes the down payment will be listed as a dollar amount, and other times it will be expressed as a percent of the purchase price.

Amount financed = Purchase price – Down payment

When the down payment is listed as a percent of the purchase price, it can be found by using:

Down payment = Purchase price × Down payment percent

A finance charge, including simple interest and any loan origination fees, is then added to the amount financed to give the total amount of installment payments.

Total amount of installment payments = Amount financed + Finance charge

The finance charge can be found by subtracting the amount financed from the total amount of installment payments.

Finance charge = Total amount of installment payments – Amount financed

When the amount of the monthly payments is known, the total amount of installment payments can be found by multiplying the monthly payment amount by the number of payments.

● **cash or purchase price**
The price paid for goods and services without the use of financing.

● **amount financed**
After the down payment, the amount of money that is borrowed to complete a sale.

$$\begin{array}{c}\text{Total amount of} \\ \text{installment payments}\end{array} = \begin{array}{c}\text{Monthly payment} \\ \text{amount}\end{array} \times \begin{array}{c}\text{Number of} \\ \text{monthly payments}\end{array}$$

The total deferred payment price is the sum of the total amount of installment payments plus the down payment. This represents the total out-of-pocket expenses incurred by the buyer for an installment purchase.

Total deferred payment price = Total of installment payments + Down payment

EXAMPLE

Joannie Herbert is interested in buying a computer. At Computers USA she picks out a computer and a printer for a total cash price of $2,550.00. The salesperson informs Joannie that if she qualifies for an installment loan she may pay 20% now, as a down payment, and finance the balance with payments of $110.00 per month, for 24 months.

a. What is the amount of the finance charge on this loan?
b. What is the total deferred payment price of Joannie's computer?

SOLUTION STRATEGY

a. Finance charge:

To calculate the finance charge on this loan we must first find the amount of the down payment, the amount financed, and the total amount of the installment payments.

Down payment = Purchase price × Down payment percent

Down payment = $2,550.00 × 20% = 2,550.00 × .2 = $510.00

Amount financed = Purchase price − Down payment

Amount financed = $2,550.00 − $510.00 = $2,040.00

$$\begin{array}{c}\text{Total amount of} \\ \text{installment payments}\end{array} = \begin{array}{c}\text{Monthly payment} \\ \text{amount}\end{array} \times \begin{array}{c}\text{Number of} \\ \text{monthly payments}\end{array}$$

Total amount of installment payments = 110.00 × 24 = $2,640.00

Finance charge = Total amount of installment payments − Amount financed

Finance charge = 2,640.00 − 2,040.00

Finance charge = $600.00

b. Total deferred payment price:

Total deferred payment price = Total of installment payments + Down payment
Total deferred payment price = $2,640.00 + $510.00

Total deferred payment price = $3,150.00

TRY-IT   EXERCISE

4. Fred Baldwin found a car he wanted to buy at Friendly Motors. He had the option of paying $12,500 in cash or financing the car with a 4-year installment loan. The loan required a 15% down payment and equal monthly payments of $309.90 for 48 months.

a. What is the finance charge on the loan?

b. What is the total deferred payment price of Fred's car?

Check your answers with the solutions on page 435.

13-5 Calculating the Amount of the Regular Monthly Payments of an Installment Loan by the Add-On Interest Method

● **add-on interest**

Popular method of calculating the interest on an installment loan. Found by adding the simple interest ($I = PRT$) to the amount financed.

One of the most common methods of calculating the finance charge on an installment loan is known as **add-on interest.** Add-on interest is essentially the simple interest that we studied in Chapter 10. The term gets its name from the fact that the simple interest is computed and then added on to the amount financed to get the total of installment payments. The interest or finance charge is computed using the simple interest formula:

$$\underset{(\textit{finance charge})}{\text{Interest}} = \underset{(\textit{amount financed})}{\text{Principal}} \times \text{Rate} \times \text{Time}$$

STEPS TO CALCULATE THE MONTHLY PAYMENT USING ADD-ON INTEREST:

Step 1. Calculate the amount to be financed by subtracting the down payment from the purchase price. Note: When the down payment is expressed as a percent, the amount financed can be found by the complement method, since the percent financed is 100% − the down payment percent:

Amount financed = Purchase price (100% − Down payment percent)

Step 2. Compute the add-on interest finance charge by using $I = PRT$.

Step 3. Find the total of installment payments by adding the finance charge to the amount financed.

Total of installment payments = Amount financed + Finance charge

Step 4. Find the regular monthly payments by dividing the total of installment payments by the number of months of the loan.

$$\text{Regular monthly payments} = \frac{\text{Total of installment payments}}{\text{Number of months of the loan}}$$

EXAMPLE

Nick Speckman bought a new boat with a 7% add-on interest installment loan from his credit union. The purchase price of the boat was $19,500.00. The credit union required a 20% down payment and equal monthly payments for 5 years (60 months). How much are Nick's monthly payments?

SOLUTION STRATEGY

Step 1. Amount financed = Purchase price (100% − Down payment percent)
Amount financed = $19,500.00 (100% − 20%) = 19,500.00 × .8
Amount financed = $15,600.00

Step 2.
$$\underset{(\textit{finance charge})}{\text{Interest}} = \underset{(\textit{amount financed})}{\text{Principal}} \times \text{Rate} \times \text{Time}$$
Finance charge = 15,600.00 × .07 × 5
Finance charge = $5,460.00

Step 3. Total of installment payments = Amount financed + Finance charge

Total of installment payments = 15,600.00 + 5,460.00

Total of installment payments = $21,060.00

Step 4. $$\text{Regular monthly payments} = \frac{\text{Total of installment payments}}{\text{Number of months of the loan}}$$

$$\text{Regular monthly payments} = \frac{\$21,060.00}{60}$$

$$\text{Regular monthly payments} = \underline{\$351.00}$$

T R Y - I T   E X E R C I S E

5. **Sylvia Ratner bought a bedroom set from Furniture City with a 6% add-on interest installment loan from her bank. The purchase price of the furniture was $1,500.00. The bank required a 10% down payment and equal monthly payments for 2 years. How much are Sylvia's monthly payments?**

Check your answer with the solution on page 435.

13-6 Calculating the Annual Percentage Rate of an Installment Loan by APR Tables and by Formula

As mentioned before, the add-on interest calculated for an installment loan is the same as on the simple interest promissory note we studied in Chapter 10. Although the interest is calculated the same way, the manner in which the loans are repaid is quite different. With promissory notes, the principal plus interest is repaid at the end of the loan period. The borrower has the use of the principal for the full time period of the loan. With an installment loan, the principal plus interest is repaid in equal regular payments. Each month in which a payment is made, the borrower has less and less use of the principal.

For this reason, the effective or true interest rate on an installment loan is considerably higher than the simple add-on rate. As we learned in Section I of this chapter, the effective or true annual interest rate being charged on open- and closed-end credit is known as the annual percentage rate, or APR. Under Regulation Z of the Truth in Lending Act, lenders are required to disclose the APR in the loan agreement and in all advertisements for products in which installment loans are offered.

The Federal Reserve Board has published annual percentage rate tables that can be used to find the APR of an installment loan. APR tables, like Table 13-1, have values representing the finance charge per $100 of the amount financed. In order to look up the APR of a loan, we must first calculate the finance charge per $100. Remember, under Regulation Z, finance charge includes not only the interest, but also other loan origination charges or fees.

STEPS TO FIND THE ANNUAL PERCENTAGE RATE OF AN INSTALLMENT LOAN USING APR TABLES:

Step 1. Calculate the finance charge per $100 by:

$$\textbf{Finance charge per } \$100 = \frac{\textbf{Finance charge} \times 100}{\textbf{Amount financed}}$$

Step 2. From Table 13-1, scan down the Number of Payments column to the number of payments for the loan in question.

Step 3. Scan to the right in that Number of Payments row to the table factor that most closely corresponds to the finance charge per $100 calculated in Step 1.

Step 4. Look to the top of the column containing the finance charge per $100 to find the APR of the loan.

TABLE 13-1 **T**

ANNUAL PERCENTAGE RATE (APR)
FINANCE CHARGE PER $100

ANNUAL PERCENTAGE RATE TABLE FOR MONTHLY PAYMENT PLANS
SEE INSTRUCTIONS FOR USE OF TABLES

FRB-103-M

NUMBER OF PAYMENTS	10.00%	10.25%	10.50%	10.75%	11.00%	11.25%	11.50%	11.75%	12.00%	12.25%	12.50%	12.75%	13.00%	13.25%	13.50%	13.75%
					(FINANCE CHARGE PER $100 OF AMOUNT FINANCED)											
1	0.83	0.85	0.87	0.90	0.92	0.94	0.96	0.98	1.00	1.02	1.04	1.06	1.08	1.10	1.12	1.15
2	1.25	1.28	1.31	1.35	1.38	1.41	1.44	1.47	1.50	1.53	1.57	1.60	1.63	1.66	1.69	1.72
3	1.67	1.71	1.76	1.80	1.84	1.88	1.92	1.96	2.01	2.05	2.09	2.13	2.17	2.22	2.26	2.30
4	2.09	2.14	2.20	2.25	2.30	2.35	2.41	2.46	2.51	2.57	2.62	2.67	2.72	2.78	2.83	2.88
5	2.51	2.58	2.64	2.70	2.77	2.83	2.89	2.96	3.02	3.08	3.15	3.21	3.27	3.34	3.40	3.46
6	2.94	3.01	3.08	3.16	3.23	3.31	3.38	3.45	3.53	3.60	3.68	3.75	3.83	3.90	3.97	4.05
7	3.36	3.45	3.53	3.62	3.70	3.78	3.87	3.95	4.04	4.12	4.21	4.29	4.38	4.47	4.55	4.64
8	3.79	3.88	3.98	4.07	4.17	4.26	4.36	4.46	4.55	4.65	4.74	4.84	4.94	5.03	5.13	5.22
9	4.21	4.32	4.43	4.53	4.64	4.75	4.85	4.96	5.07	5.17	5.28	5.39	5.49	5.60	5.71	5.82
10	4.64	4.76	4.88	4.99	5.11	5.23	5.35	5.46	5.58	5.70	5.82	5.94	6.05	6.17	6.29	6.41
11	5.07	5.20	5.33	5.45	5.58	5.71	5.84	5.97	6.10	6.23	6.36	6.49	6.62	6.75	6.88	7.01
12	5.50	5.64	5.78	5.92	6.06	6.20	6.34	6.48	6.62	6.76	6.90	7.04	7.18	7.32	7.46	7.60
13	5.93	6.08	6.23	6.38	6.53	6.68	6.84	6.99	7.14	7.29	7.44	7.59	7.75	7.90	8.05	8.20
14	6.36	6.52	6.69	6.85	7.01	7.17	7.34	7.50	7.66	7.82	7.99	8.15	8.31	8.48	8.64	8.81
15	6.80	6.97	7.14	7.32	7.49	7.66	7.84	8.01	8.19	8.36	8.53	8.71	8.88	9.06	9.23	9.41
16	7.23	7.41	7.60	7.78	7.97	8.15	8.34	8.53	8.71	8.90	9.08	9.27	9.46	9.64	9.83	10.02
17	7.67	7.86	8.06	8.25	8.45	8.65	8.84	9.04	9.24	9.44	9.63	9.83	10.03	10.23	10.43	10.63
18	8.10	8.31	8.52	8.73	8.93	9.14	9.35	9.56	9.77	9.98	10.19	10.40	10.61	10.82	11.03	11.24
19	8.54	8.76	8.98	9.20	9.42	9.64	9.86	10.08	10.30	10.52	10.74	10.96	11.18	11.41	11.63	11.85
20	8.98	9.21	9.44	9.67	9.90	10.13	10.37	10.60	10.83	11.06	11.30	11.53	11.76	12.00	12.23	12.46
21	9.42	9.66	9.90	10.15	10.39	10.63	10.88	11.12	11.36	11.61	11.85	12.10	12.34	12.59	12.84	13.08
22	9.86	10.12	10.37	10.62	10.88	11.13	11.39	11.64	11.90	12.16	12.41	12.67	12.93	13.19	13.44	13.70
23	10.30	10.57	10.84	11.10	11.37	11.63	11.90	12.17	12.44	12.71	12.97	13.24	13.51	13.78	14.05	14.32
24	10.75	11.02	11.30	11.58	11.86	12.14	12.42	12.70	12.98	13.26	13.54	13.82	14.10	14.38	14.66	14.95
25	11.19	11.48	11.77	12.06	12.35	12.64	12.93	13.22	13.52	13.81	14.10	14.40	14.69	14.98	15.28	15.57
26	11.64	11.94	12.24	12.54	12.85	13.15	13.45	13.75	14.06	14.36	14.67	14.97	15.28	15.59	15.89	16.20
27	12.09	12.40	12.71	13.03	13.34	13.66	13.97	14.29	14.60	14.92	15.24	15.56	15.87	16.19	16.51	16.83
28	12.53	12.86	13.18	13.51	13.84	14.16	14.49	14.82	15.15	15.48	15.81	16.14	16.47	16.80	17.13	17.46
29	12.98	13.32	13.66	14.00	14.33	14.67	15.01	15.35	15.70	16.04	16.38	16.72	17.07	17.41	17.75	18.10
30	13.43	13.78	14.13	14.48	14.83	15.19	15.54	15.89	16.24	16.60	16.95	17.31	17.66	18.02	18.38	18.74
31	13.89	14.25	14.61	14.97	15.33	15.70	16.06	16.43	16.79	17.16	17.53	17.90	18.27	18.63	19.00	19.38
32	14.34	14.71	15.09	15.46	15.84	16.21	16.59	16.97	17.35	17.73	18.11	18.49	18.87	19.25	19.63	20.02
33	14.79	15.18	15.57	15.95	16.34	16.73	17.12	17.51	17.90	18.29	18.69	19.08	19.47	19.87	20.26	20.66
34	15.25	15.65	16.05	16.44	16.85	17.25	17.65	18.05	18.46	18.86	19.27	19.67	20.08	20.49	20.90	21.31
35	15.70	16.11	16.53	16.94	17.35	17.77	18.18	18.60	19.01	19.43	19.85	20.27	20.69	21.11	21.53	21.95
36	16.16	16.58	17.01	17.43	17.86	18.29	18.71	19.14	19.57	20.00	20.43	20.87	21.30	21.73	22.17	22.60
37	16.62	17.06	17.49	17.93	18.37	18.81	19.25	19.69	20.13	20.58	21.02	21.46	21.91	22.36	22.81	23.25
38	17.08	17.53	17.98	18.43	18.88	19.33	19.78	20.24	20.69	21.15	21.61	22.07	22.52	22.99	23.45	23.91
39	17.54	18.00	18.46	18.93	19.39	19.86	20.32	20.79	21.26	21.73	22.20	22.67	23.14	23.61	24.09	24.56
40	18.00	18.48	18.95	19.43	19.90	20.38	20.86	21.34	21.82	22.30	22.79	23.27	23.76	24.25	24.73	25.22
41	18.47	18.95	19.44	19.93	20.42	20.91	21.40	21.89	22.39	22.88	23.38	23.88	24.38	24.88	25.38	25.88
42	18.93	19.43	19.93	20.43	20.93	21.44	21.94	22.45	22.96	23.47	23.98	24.49	25.00	25.51	26.03	26.55
43	19.40	19.91	20.42	20.94	21.45	21.97	22.49	23.01	23.53	24.05	24.57	25.10	25.62	26.15	26.68	27.21
44	19.86	20.39	20.91	21.44	21.97	22.50	23.03	23.57	24.10	24.64	25.17	25.71	26.25	26.79	27.33	27.88
45	20.33	20.87	21.41	21.95	22.49	23.03	23.58	24.12	24.67	25.22	25.77	26.32	26.88	27.43	27.99	28.55
46	20.80	21.35	21.90	22.46	23.01	23.57	24.13	24.69	25.25	25.81	26.37	26.94	27.51	28.08	28.65	29.22
47	21.27	21.83	22.40	22.97	23.53	24.10	24.68	25.25	25.82	26.40	26.98	27.56	28.14	28.72	29.31	29.89
48	21.74	22.32	22.90	23.48	24.06	24.64	25.23	25.81	26.40	26.99	27.58	28.18	28.77	29.37	29.97	30.57
49	22.21	22.80	23.39	23.99	24.58	25.18	25.78	26.38	26.98	27.59	28.19	28.80	29.41	30.02	30.63	31.24
50	22.69	23.29	23.89	24.50	25.11	25.72	26.33	26.95	27.56	28.18	28.80	29.42	30.04	30.67	31.29	31.92
51	23.16	23.78	24.40	25.02	25.64	26.26	26.89	27.52	28.15	28.78	29.41	30.05	30.68	31.32	31.96	32.60
52	23.64	24.27	24.90	25.53	26.17	26.81	27.45	28.09	28.73	29.38	30.02	30.67	31.32	31.98	32.63	33.29
53	24.11	24.76	25.40	26.05	26.70	27.35	28.00	28.66	29.32	29.98	30.64	31.30	31.97	32.63	33.30	33.97
54	24.59	25.25	25.91	26.57	27.23	27.90	28.56	29.23	29.91	30.58	31.25	31.93	32.61	33.29	33.98	34.66
55	25.07	25.74	26.41	27.09	27.77	28.44	29.13	29.81	30.50	31.18	31.87	32.56	33.26	33.95	34.65	35.35
56	25.55	26.23	26.92	27.61	28.30	28.99	29.69	30.39	31.09	31.79	32.49	33.20	33.91	34.62	35.33	36.04
57	26.03	26.73	27.43	28.13	28.84	29.54	30.25	30.97	31.68	32.39	33.11	33.83	34.56	35.28	36.01	36.74
58	26.51	27.23	27.94	28.66	29.37	30.10	30.82	31.55	32.27	33.00	33.74	34.47	35.21	35.95	36.69	37.43
59	27.00	27.72	28.45	29.18	29.91	30.65	31.39	32.13	32.87	33.61	34.36	35.11	35.86	36.62	37.37	38.13
60	27.48	28.22	28.96	29.71	30.45	31.20	31.96	32.71	33.47	34.23	34.99	35.75	36.52	37.29	38.06	38.83

continued

TABLE 13-1

ANNUAL PERCENTAGE RATE (APR)
FINANCE CHARGE PER $100

ANNUAL PERCENTAGE RATE TABLE FOR MONTHLY PAYMENT PLANS
SEE INSTRUCTIONS FOR USE OF TABLES

FRB-104-M

NUMBER OF PAYMENTS	14.00%	14.25%	14.50%	14.75%	15.00%	15.25%	15.50%	15.75%	16.00%	16.25%	16.50%	16.75%	17.00%	17.25%	17.50%	17.75%
	(FINANCE CHARGE PER $100 OF AMOUNT FINANCED)															
1	1.17	1.19	1.21	1.23	1.25	1.27	1.29	1.31	1.33	1.35	1.37	1.40	1.42	1.44	1.46	1.48
2	1.75	1.78	1.82	1.85	1.88	1.91	1.94	1.97	2.00	2.04	2.07	2.10	2.13	2.16	2.19	2.22
3	2.34	2.38	2.43	2.47	2.51	2.55	2.59	2.64	2.68	2.72	2.76	2.80	2.85	2.89	2.93	2.97
4	2.93	2.99	3.04	3.09	3.14	3.20	3.25	3.30	3.36	3.41	3.46	3.51	3.57	3.62	3.67	3.73
5	3.53	3.59	3.65	3.72	3.78	3.84	3.91	3.97	4.04	4.10	4.16	4.23	4.29	4.35	4.42	4.48
6	4.12	4.20	4.27	4.35	4.42	4.49	4.57	4.64	4.72	4.79	4.87	4.94	5.02	5.09	5.17	5.24
7	4.72	4.81	4.89	4.98	5.06	5.15	5.23	5.32	5.40	5.49	5.58	5.66	5.75	5.83	5.92	6.00
8	5.32	5.42	5.51	5.61	5.71	5.80	5.90	6.00	6.09	6.19	6.29	6.38	6.48	6.58	6.67	6.77
9	5.92	6.03	6.14	6.25	6.35	6.46	6.57	6.68	6.78	6.89	7.00	7.11	7.22	7.32	7.43	7.54
10	6.53	6.65	6.77	6.88	7.00	7.12	7.24	7.36	7.48	7.60	7.72	7.84	7.96	8.08	8.19	8.31
11	7.14	7.27	7.40	7.53	7.66	7.79	7.92	8.05	8.18	8.31	8.44	8.57	8.70	8.83	8.96	9.09
12	7.74	7.89	8.03	8.17	8.31	8.45	8.59	8.74	8.88	9.02	9.16	9.30	9.45	9.59	9.73	9.87
13	8.36	8.51	8.66	8.81	8.97	9.12	9.27	9.43	9.58	9.73	9.89	10.04	10.20	10.35	10.50	10.66
14	8.97	9.13	9.30	9.46	9.63	9.79	9.96	10.12	10.29	10.45	10.62	10.78	10.95	11.11	11.28	11.45
15	9.59	9.76	9.94	10.11	10.29	10.47	10.64	10.82	11.00	11.17	11.35	11.53	11.71	11.88	12.06	12.24
16	10.20	10.39	10.58	10.77	10.95	11.14	11.33	11.52	11.71	11.90	12.09	12.28	12.46	12.65	12.84	13.03
17	10.82	11.02	11.22	11.42	11.62	11.82	12.02	12.22	12.42	12.62	12.83	13.03	13.23	13.43	13.63	13.83
18	11.45	11.66	11.87	12.08	12.29	12.50	12.72	12.93	13.14	13.35	13.57	13.78	13.99	14.21	14.42	14.64
19	12.07	12.30	12.52	12.74	12.97	13.19	13.41	13.64	13.86	14.09	14.31	14.54	14.76	14.99	15.22	15.44
20	12.70	12.93	13.17	13.41	13.64	13.88	14.11	14.35	14.59	14.82	15.06	15.30	15.54	15.77	16.01	16.25
21	13.33	13.58	13.82	14.07	14.32	14.57	14.82	15.06	15.31	15.56	15.81	16.06	16.31	16.56	16.81	17.07
22	13.96	14.22	14.48	14.74	15.00	15.26	15.52	15.78	16.04	16.30	16.57	16.83	17.09	17.36	17.62	17.88
23	14.59	14.87	15.14	15.41	15.68	15.96	16.23	16.50	16.78	17.05	17.32	17.60	17.88	18.15	18.43	18.70
24	15.23	15.51	15.80	16.08	16.37	16.65	16.94	17.22	17.51	17.80	18.09	18.37	18.66	18.95	19.24	19.53
25	15.87	16.17	16.46	16.76	17.06	17.35	17.65	17.95	18.25	18.55	18.85	19.15	19.45	19.75	20.05	20.36
26	16.51	16.82	17.13	17.44	17.75	18.06	18.37	18.68	18.99	19.30	19.62	19.93	20.24	20.56	20.87	21.19
27	17.15	17.47	17.80	18.12	18.44	18.76	19.09	19.41	19.74	20.06	20.39	20.71	21.04	21.37	21.69	22.02
28	17.80	18.13	18.47	18.80	19.14	19.47	19.81	20.15	20.48	20.82	21.16	21.50	21.84	22.18	22.52	22.86
29	18.45	18.79	19.14	19.49	19.83	20.18	20.53	20.88	21.23	21.58	21.94	22.29	22.64	22.99	23.35	23.70
30	19.10	19.45	19.81	20.17	20.54	20.90	21.26	21.62	21.99	22.35	22.72	23.08	23.45	23.81	24.18	24.55
31	19.75	20.12	20.49	20.87	21.24	21.61	21.99	22.37	22.74	23.12	23.50	23.88	24.26	24.64	25.02	25.40
32	20.40	20.79	21.17	21.56	21.95	22.33	22.72	23.11	23.50	23.89	24.28	24.68	25.07	25.46	25.86	26.25
33	21.06	21.46	21.85	22.25	22.65	23.06	23.46	23.86	24.26	24.67	25.07	25.48	25.88	26.29	26.70	27.11
34	21.72	22.13	22.54	22.95	23.37	23.78	24.19	24.61	25.03	25.44	25.86	26.28	26.70	27.12	27.54	27.97
35	22.38	22.80	23.23	23.65	24.08	24.51	24.94	25.36	25.79	26.23	26.66	27.09	27.52	27.96	28.39	28.83
36	23.04	23.48	23.92	24.35	24.80	25.24	25.68	26.12	26.57	27.01	27.46	27.90	28.35	28.80	29.25	29.70
37	23.70	24.16	24.61	25.06	25.51	25.97	26.42	26.88	27.34	27.80	28.26	28.72	29.18	29.64	30.10	30.57
38	24.37	24.84	25.30	25.77	26.24	26.70	27.17	27.64	28.11	28.59	29.06	29.53	30.01	30.49	30.96	31.44
39	25.04	25.52	26.00	26.48	26.96	27.44	27.92	28.40	28.89	29.38	29.87	30.36	30.85	31.34	31.83	32.32
40	25.71	26.20	26.70	27.19	27.69	28.18	28.68	29.18	29.68	30.18	30.68	31.18	31.68	32.19	32.69	33.20
41	26.39	26.89	27.40	27.91	28.41	28.92	29.44	29.95	30.46	30.97	31.49	32.01	32.52	33.04	33.56	34.08
42	27.06	27.58	28.10	28.62	29.15	29.67	30.19	30.72	31.25	31.78	32.31	32.84	33.37	33.90	34.44	34.97
43	27.74	28.27	28.81	29.34	29.88	30.42	30.96	31.50	32.04	32.58	33.13	33.67	34.22	34.76	35.31	35.86
44	28.42	28.97	29.52	30.07	30.62	31.17	31.72	32.28	32.83	33.39	33.95	34.51	35.07	35.63	36.19	36.76
45	29.11	29.67	30.23	30.79	31.36	31.92	32.49	33.06	33.63	34.20	34.77	35.35	35.92	36.50	37.08	37.66
46	29.79	30.36	30.94	31.52	32.10	32.68	33.26	33.84	34.43	35.01	35.60	36.19	36.78	37.37	37.96	38.56
47	30.48	31.07	31.66	32.25	32.84	33.44	34.03	34.63	35.23	35.83	36.43	37.04	37.64	38.25	38.86	39.46
48	31.17	31.77	32.37	32.98	33.59	34.20	34.81	35.42	36.03	36.65	37.27	37.88	38.50	39.13	39.75	40.37
49	31.86	32.48	33.09	33.71	34.34	34.96	35.59	36.21	36.84	37.47	38.10	38.74	39.37	40.01	40.65	41.29
50	32.55	33.18	33.82	34.45	35.09	35.73	36.37	37.01	37.65	38.30	38.94	39.59	40.24	40.89	41.55	42.20
51	33.25	33.89	34.54	35.19	35.84	36.49	37.15	37.81	38.46	39.12	39.79	40.45	41.11	41.78	42.45	43.12
52	33.95	34.61	35.27	35.93	36.60	37.27	37.94	38.61	39.28	39.96	40.63	41.31	41.99	42.67	43.36	44.04
53	34.65	35.32	36.00	36.68	37.36	38.04	38.72	39.41	40.10	40.79	41.48	42.17	42.87	43.57	44.27	44.97
54	35.35	36.04	36.73	37.42	38.12	38.82	39.52	40.22	40.92	41.63	42.33	43.04	43.75	44.47	45.18	45.90
55	36.05	36.76	37.46	38.17	38.88	39.60	40.31	41.03	41.74	42.47	43.19	43.91	44.64	45.37	46.10	46.83
56	36.76	37.48	38.20	38.92	39.65	40.38	41.11	41.84	42.57	43.31	44.05	44.79	45.53	46.27	47.02	47.77
57	37.47	38.20	38.94	39.68	40.42	41.16	41.91	42.65	43.40	44.15	44.91	45.66	46.42	47.18	47.94	48.71
58	38.18	38.93	39.68	40.43	41.19	41.95	42.71	43.47	44.23	45.00	45.77	46.54	47.32	48.09	48.87	49.65
59	38.89	39.66	40.42	41.19	41.96	42.74	43.51	44.29	45.07	45.85	46.64	47.42	48.21	49.01	49.80	50.60
60	39.61	40.39	41.17	41.95	42.74	43.53	44.32	45.11	45.91	46.71	47.51	48.31	49.12	49.92	50.73	51.55

continued

TABLE 13-1

ANNUAL PERCENTAGE RATE (APR)
FINANCE CHARGE PER $100

NUMBER OF PAYMENTS	18.00%	18.25%	18.50%	18.75%	19.00%	19.25%	19.50%	19.75%	20.00%	20.25%	20.50%	20.75%	21.00%	21.25%	21.50%	21.75%
						(FINANCE CHARGE PER $100 OF AMOUNT FINANCED)										
1	1.50	1.52	1.54	1.56	1.58	1.60	1.62	1.65	1.67	1.69	1.71	1.73	1.75	1.77	1.79	1.81
2	2.26	2.29	2.32	2.35	2.38	2.41	2.44	2.48	2.51	2.54	2.57	2.60	2.63	2.66	2.70	2.73
3	3.01	3.06	3.10	3.14	3.18	3.23	3.27	3.31	3.35	3.39	3.44	3.48	3.52	3.56	3.60	3.65
4	3.78	3.83	3.88	3.94	3.99	4.04	4.10	4.15	4.20	4.25	4.31	4.36	4.41	4.47	4.52	4.57
5	4.54	4.61	4.67	4.74	4.80	4.86	4.93	4.99	5.06	5.12	5.18	5.25	5.31	5.37	5.44	5.50
6	5.32	5.39	5.46	5.54	5.61	5.69	5.76	5.84	5.91	5.99	6.06	6.14	6.21	6.29	6.36	6.44
7	6.09	6.18	6.26	6.35	6.43	6.52	6.60	6.69	6.78	6.86	6.95	7.04	7.12	7.21	7.29	7.38
8	6.87	6.96	7.06	7.16	7.26	7.35	7.45	7.55	7.64	7.74	7.84	7.94	8.03	8.13	8.23	8.33
9	7.65	7.76	7.87	7.97	8.08	8.19	8.30	8.41	8.52	8.63	8.73	8.84	8.95	9.06	9.17	9.28
10	8.43	8.55	8.67	8.79	8.91	9.03	9.15	9.27	9.39	9.51	9.63	9.75	9.88	10.00	10.12	10.24
11	9.22	9.35	9.49	9.62	9.75	9.88	10.01	10.14	10.28	10.41	10.54	10.67	10.80	10.94	11.07	11.20
12	10.02	10.16	10.30	10.44	10.59	10.73	10.87	11.02	11.16	11.31	11.45	11.59	11.74	11.88	12.02	12.17
13	10.81	10.97	11.12	11.28	11.43	11.59	11.74	11.90	12.05	12.21	12.36	12.52	12.67	12.83	12.99	13.14
14	11.61	11.78	11.95	12.11	12.28	12.45	12.61	12.78	12.95	13.11	13.28	13.45	13.62	13.79	13.95	14.12
15	12.42	12.59	12.77	12.95	13.13	13.31	13.49	13.67	13.85	14.03	14.21	14.39	14.57	14.75	14.93	15.11
16	13.22	13.41	13.60	13.80	13.99	14.18	14.37	14.56	14.75	14.94	15.13	15.33	15.52	15.71	15.90	16.10
17	14.04	14.24	14.44	14.64	14.85	15.05	15.25	15.46	15.66	15.86	16.07	16.27	16.48	16.68	16.89	17.09
18	14.85	15.07	15.28	15.49	15.71	15.93	16.14	16.36	16.57	16.79	17.01	17.22	17.44	17.66	17.88	18.09
19	15.67	15.90	16.12	16.35	16.58	16.81	17.03	17.26	17.49	17.72	17.95	18.18	18.41	18.64	18.87	19.10
20	16.49	16.73	16.97	17.21	17.45	17.69	17.93	18.17	18.41	18.66	18.90	19.14	19.38	19.63	19.87	20.11
21	17.32	17.57	17.82	18.07	18.33	18.58	18.83	19.09	19.34	19.60	19.85	20.11	20.36	20.62	20.87	21.13
22	18.15	18.41	18.68	18.94	19.21	19.47	19.74	20.01	20.27	20.54	20.81	21.08	21.34	21.61	21.88	22.15
23	18.98	19.26	19.54	19.81	20.09	20.37	20.65	20.93	21.21	21.49	21.77	22.05	22.33	22.61	22.90	23.18
24	19.82	20.11	20.40	20.69	20.98	21.27	21.56	21.86	22.15	22.44	22.74	23.03	23.33	23.62	23.92	24.21
25	20.66	20.96	21.27	21.57	21.87	22.18	22.48	22.79	23.10	23.40	23.71	24.02	24.32	24.63	24.94	25.25
26	21.50	21.82	22.14	22.45	22.77	23.09	23.41	23.73	24.04	24.36	24.68	25.01	25.33	25.65	25.97	26.29
27	22.35	22.68	23.01	23.34	23.67	24.00	24.33	24.67	25.00	25.33	25.67	26.00	26.34	26.67	27.01	27.34
28	23.20	23.55	23.89	24.23	24.58	24.92	25.27	25.61	25.96	26.30	26.65	27.00	27.35	27.70	28.05	28.40
29	24.06	24.41	24.77	25.13	25.49	25.84	26.20	26.56	26.92	27.28	27.64	28.00	28.37	28.73	29.09	29.46
30	24.92	25.29	25.66	26.03	26.40	26.77	27.14	27.52	27.89	28.26	28.64	29.01	29.39	29.77	30.14	30.52
31	25.78	26.16	26.55	26.93	27.32	27.70	28.09	28.47	28.86	29.25	29.64	30.03	30.42	30.81	31.20	31.59
32	26.65	27.04	27.44	27.84	28.24	28.64	29.04	29.44	29.84	30.24	30.64	31.05	31.45	31.85	32.26	32.67
33	27.52	27.93	28.34	28.75	29.16	29.57	29.99	30.40	30.82	31.23	31.65	32.07	32.49	32.91	33.33	33.75
34	28.39	28.81	29.24	29.66	30.09	30.52	30.95	31.37	31.80	32.23	32.67	33.10	33.53	33.96	34.40	34.83
35	29.27	29.71	30.14	30.58	31.02	31.47	31.91	32.35	32.79	33.24	33.68	34.13	34.58	35.03	35.47	35.92
36	30.15	30.60	31.05	31.51	31.96	32.42	32.87	33.33	33.79	34.25	34.71	35.17	35.63	36.09	36.56	37.02
37	31.03	31.50	31.97	32.43	32.90	33.37	33.84	34.32	34.79	35.26	35.74	36.21	36.69	37.16	37.64	38.12
38	31.92	32.40	32.88	33.37	33.85	34.33	34.82	35.30	35.79	36.28	36.77	37.26	37.75	38.24	38.73	39.23
39	32.81	33.31	33.80	34.30	34.80	35.30	35.80	36.30	36.80	37.30	37.81	38.31	38.82	39.32	39.83	40.34
40	33.71	34.22	34.73	35.24	35.75	36.26	36.78	37.29	37.81	38.33	38.85	39.37	39.89	40.41	40.93	41.46
41	34.61	35.13	35.66	36.18	36.71	37.24	37.77	38.30	38.83	39.36	39.89	40.43	40.96	41.50	42.04	42.58
42	35.51	36.05	36.59	37.13	37.67	38.21	38.76	39.30	39.85	40.40	40.95	41.50	42.05	42.60	43.15	43.71
43	36.42	36.97	37.52	38.08	38.63	39.19	39.75	40.31	40.87	41.44	42.00	42.57	43.13	43.70	44.27	44.84
44	37.33	37.89	38.46	39.03	39.60	40.18	40.75	41.33	41.90	42.48	43.06	43.64	44.22	44.81	45.39	45.98
45	38.24	38.82	39.41	39.99	40.58	41.17	41.75	42.35	42.94	43.53	44.13	44.72	45.32	45.92	46.52	47.12
46	39.16	39.75	40.35	40.95	41.55	42.16	42.76	43.37	43.98	44.58	45.20	45.81	46.42	47.03	47.65	48.27
47	40.08	40.69	41.30	41.92	42.54	43.15	43.77	44.40	45.02	45.64	46.27	46.90	47.53	48.16	48.79	49.42
48	41.00	41.63	42.26	42.89	43.52	44.15	44.79	45.43	46.07	46.71	47.35	47.99	48.64	49.28	49.93	50.58
49	41.93	42.57	43.22	43.86	44.51	45.16	45.81	46.46	47.12	47.77	48.43	49.09	49.75	50.41	51.08	51.74
50	42.86	43.52	44.18	44.84	45.50	46.17	46.83	47.50	48.17	48.84	49.52	50.19	50.87	51.55	52.23	52.91
51	43.79	44.47	45.14	45.82	46.50	47.18	47.86	48.55	49.23	49.92	50.61	51.30	51.99	52.69	53.38	54.08
52	44.73	45.42	46.11	46.80	47.50	48.20	48.89	49.59	50.30	51.00	51.71	52.41	53.12	53.83	54.55	55.26
53	45.67	46.38	47.08	47.79	48.50	49.22	49.93	50.65	51.37	52.09	52.81	53.53	54.26	54.98	55.71	56.44
54	46.62	47.34	48.06	48.79	49.51	50.24	50.97	51.70	52.44	53.17	53.91	54.65	55.39	56.14	56.88	57.63
55	47.57	48.30	49.04	49.78	50.52	51.27	52.02	52.76	53.52	54.27	55.02	55.78	56.54	57.30	58.06	58.82
56	48.52	49.27	50.03	50.78	51.54	52.30	53.06	53.83	54.60	55.37	56.14	56.91	57.68	58.46	59.24	60.02
57	49.47	50.24	51.01	51.79	52.56	53.34	54.12	54.90	55.68	56.47	57.25	58.04	58.84	59.63	60.43	61.22
58	50.43	51.22	52.00	52.79	53.58	54.38	55.17	55.97	56.77	57.57	58.38	59.18	59.99	60.80	61.62	62.43
59	51.39	52.20	53.00	53.80	54.61	55.42	56.23	57.05	57.87	58.68	59.51	60.33	61.15	61.98	62.81	63.64
60	52.36	53.18	54.00	54.82	55.64	56.47	57.30	58.13	58.96	59.80	60.64	61.48	62.32	63.17	64.01	64.86

Mike Hale purchased a used car for $7,000. He made a down payment of $1,000, and financed the remaining $6,000 for 36 months. With monthly payments of $200 each, the total finance charge on the loan was $1,200 ($200 × 36 = $7,200 - $6000 = $1,200). Use Table 13-1 to find what annual percentage rate was charged on Mike's automobile loan.

SOLUTION STRATEGY

Step 1.

$$\text{Finance charge per } \$100 = \frac{\text{Finance charge} \times 100}{\text{Amount financed}}$$

$$\text{Finance charge per } \$100 = \frac{1{,}200 \times 100}{6{,}000} = \frac{120{,}000}{6{,}000}$$

$$\text{Finance charge per } \$100 = \underline{\$20}$$

Step 2. Using Table 13-1 scan down the number of payments column to 36 payments.

Step 3. Scan to the right in that number of payments row until we find $20, the finance charge per $100.

Step 4. Looking to the top of the column containing the $20, we find the annual percentage rate for the loan to be 12.25%.

TRY-IT   EXERCISE

6. Joanne Chang purchased a living room set for $4,500 from Furniture City. She made a $500 down payment and financed the balance with an installment loan for 24 months. If Joanne's payments are $190 per month, what APR is she paying on the loan?

Check your answer with the solution on page 435.

Calculating APR by Formula

When APR tables are not available, the annual percentage rate can be closely approximated by the formula:

$$APR = \frac{72I}{3P(n+1) + I(n-1)}$$

where

I = finance charge on the loan

P = principal, or amount financed

n = number of months of the loan

EXAMPLE

Refer to the previous example. This time use the APR formula to find the annual percentage rate. How does it compare with the APR from the table?

SOLUTION STRATEGY

$$APR = \frac{72I}{3P(n+1) + I(n-1)}$$

$$APR = \frac{72(1{,}200)}{3(6{,}000)(36+1) + 1{,}200(36-1)} = \frac{86{,}400}{666{,}000 + 42{,}000} = \frac{86{,}400}{708{,}000}$$

$$APR = .1220338 = \underline{12.20\%}$$

In comparing the two answers, we can see that using the formula gives quite a close approximation of the actual APR table value of 12.25%.

TRY-IT — EXERCISE

7. **An installment loan for $2,200 is repaid with 18 monthly payments of $140.00 each. Use the APR formula to determine the annual percentage rate of the loan.**

Check your answer with the solution on page 435.

13-7 Calculating the Finance Charge and Monthly Payment of an Installment Loan Using the APR Tables

When the annual percentage rate and number of months of an installment loan are known, the APR tables can be used in reverse to find the amount of the finance charge. Once the finance charge is known, the monthly payment required to amortize the loan can be calculated as before.

STEPS TO FIND THE FINANCE CHARGE AND THE MONTHLY PAYMENT OF AN INSTALLMENT LOAN USING THE APR TABLES:

Step 1. Using the APR and the number of payments of the loan, locate the table factor at the intersection of the APR column and the number of payments row. This factor represents the finance charge per $100 financed.

Step 2. The total finance charge of the loan can be found by:

$$\text{Finance charge} = \frac{\text{Amount financed} \times \text{Table factor}}{100}$$

Step 3. The monthly payment can now be found by:

$$\text{Monthly payment} = \frac{\text{Amount financed} + \text{Finance charge}}{\text{Number of months of the loan}}$$

EXAMPLE

Southwest Motors uses The Morgan Bank to finance automobile and truck sales. This month Morgan Bank is offering up to 48-month installment loans with an APR of 15.5%. For qualified buyers, no down payment is required. If Bobby Knight wants to finance a new truck for $17,500, what are the finance charge and the amount of the monthly payment on Bobby's loan?

SOLUTION STRATEGY

Step 1. The table factor at the intersection of the 15.5% APR column and the 48 payments row is $\underline{\$34.81}$.

Step 2.

$$\text{Finance charge} = \frac{\text{Amount financed} \times \text{Table factor}}{100}$$

$$\text{Finance charge} = \frac{17,500 \times 34.81}{100} = \frac{609,175}{100}$$

$$\text{Finance charge} = \underline{\$6,091.75}$$

Step 3.

$$\text{Monthly payment} = \frac{\text{Amount financed} + \text{Finance charge}}{\text{Number of months of the loan}}$$

$$\text{Monthly payment} = \frac{17,500 + 6,091.75}{48} = \frac{23,591.75}{48}$$

$$\text{Monthly payment} = \underline{\$491.49}$$

TRY-IT　　　　**EXERCISE**

8. **Computer Warehouse uses a finance company that is offering up to 24-month install-ment loans with an APR of 13.25%. For qualified buyers, no down payment is re-quired. If Jorge Alonso wants to finance a computer and printer for $3,550, what are the finance charge and the amount of the monthly payment on Jorge's loan?**

Check your answers with the solutions on page 436.

13-8 Calculating the Finance Charge Rebate and the Amount of the Payoff When a Loan Is Paid Off Early, Using the Sum-of-the-Digits Method

Frequently, borrowers choose to repay installment loans before the full time period of the loan has elapsed. When loans are paid off early the borrower is entitled to a **finance charge rebate,** because the principal was not kept for the full amount of time on which the finance charge was calculated. At payoff, the lender must return or rebate any unearned portion of the finance charge to the borrower.

● **finance charge rebate**
The unearned portion of the finance charge that the lender returns to the borrower when an installment loan is paid off early.

Borrowers are sometimes entitled to a finance charge rebate when loans are paid off early.

A widely accepted method for calculating the finance charge rebate is known as the **sum-of-the-digits method.** This method is based on the assumption that the lender earns more interest in the early months of a loan, when the borrower has the use of much of the principal, than in the later months, when most of the principal has already been paid back.

When using this method, the finance charge is assumed to be divided in parts equal to the sum of the digits of the months of the loan. Since the sum of the digits of a 12-month loan is 78, the technique has become known as the **Rule of 78.**

$$\text{Sum of the digits of } 12 = 1 + 2 + 3 + 4 + 5 + 6 + 7 + 8 + 9 + 10 + 11 + 12 = 78$$

The amount of finance charge in any given month is represented by a fraction whose numerator is the number of payments remaining, and the denominator is the sum of the digits of the number of months in the loan.

For a 12-month loan, for example, the fraction of the finance charge in the first month would be $\frac{12}{78}$. The numerator is 12, because in the first month no payments have been made, therefore 12 payments remain. The denominator is 78 because the sum of the digits of 12 is 78. In the second month the lender earns $\frac{11}{78}$; in the third month, $\frac{10}{78}$. This decline continues until the last month when only $\frac{1}{78}$ remains. Exhibit 13-8 illustrates the distribution of a $1,000 finance charge using the sum-of-the-digits method.

This chart clearly demonstrates that the majority of the finance charge of an installment loan is incurred in the first half of the loan.

With the sum-of-the-digits method, a **rebate fraction** is established based on when a loan is paid off. The numerator of the rebate fraction is the sum-of-the-digits of the number of remaining payments and the denominator is the sum of the digits of the total number of payments.

$$\text{Rebate fraction} = \frac{\textbf{Sum of the digits of the number of remaining payments}}{\textbf{Sum of the digits of the total number of payments}}$$

Although the sum of the digits is easily calculated by addition, it can become quite tedious for loans of 24, 36, or 48 months. For this reason, we shall use the sum-of-the-digits formula to find the numerator and denominator of the rebate fraction. In the formula, n represents the number of months.

$$\text{Sum of the digits} = \frac{n(n + 1)}{2}$$

Month Number	Finance Charge Fraction	x	$1,000	Finance Charge
1	$\frac{12}{78}$	x	$1,000	$153.85
2	$\frac{11}{78}$	x	$1,000	$141.03
3	$\frac{10}{78}$	x	$1,000	$128.21
4	$\frac{9}{78}$	x	$1,000	$115.38
5	$\frac{8}{78}$	x	$1,000	$102.56
6	$\frac{7}{78}$	x	$1,000	$89.74
7	$\frac{6}{78}$	x	$1,000	$76.92
8	$\frac{5}{78}$	x	$1,000	$64.10
9	$\frac{4}{78}$	x	$1,000	$51.28
10	$\frac{3}{78}$	x	$1,000	$38.46
11	$\frac{2}{78}$	x	$1,000	$25.64
12	$\frac{1}{78}$	x	$1,000	$12.82

Step 1. Calculate the rebate fraction using the sum-of-the-digits formula for the numerator (number of remaining payments) and the denominator (total number of payments).

Step 2. Determine the finance charge rebate by:

Finance charge rebate = Rebate fraction × Total finance charge

Step 3. Find the loan payoff by:

$$\text{Loan payoff} = \left(\text{Payments remaining} \times \text{Payment amount}\right) - \text{Finance charge rebate}$$

EXAMPLE

Steve Gideon financed a $1,500 vacation with an installment loan for 12 months. The payments were $145 per month and the total finance charge was $240. After eight months Steve decided to pay off the loan. How much is the finance charge rebate and what is Steve's loan payoff?

SOLUTION STRATEGY

Step 1. *Rebate fraction*

Set up the rebate fraction using the sum-of-the-digits formula. Because Steve has already made 8 payments, he has 4 payments remaining (12 − 8 = 4).

The *numerator* will be the sum of the digits of the number of remaining payments, 4.

$$\text{Sum of the digits of } 4 = \frac{n(n + 1)}{2} = \frac{4(4 + 1)}{2} = \frac{4(5)}{2} = \frac{20}{2} = \underline{10}$$

The *denominator* will be the sum of the digits of the total number of payments, 12.

$$\text{Sum of the digits of } 12 = \frac{n(n + 1)}{2} = \frac{12(12 + 1)}{2} = \frac{12(13)}{2} = \frac{156}{2} = \underline{78}$$

The rebate fraction is therefore $\frac{10}{78}$.

Step 2. *Finance charge rebate*

$$\text{Finance charge rebate} = \text{Rebate fraction} \times \text{Total finance charge}$$
$$\text{Finance charge rebate} = \frac{10}{78} \times 240$$

$$\text{Finance charge rebate} = 30.7692 = \underline{\$30.77}$$

Step 3. *Loan payoff*

$$\text{Loan payoff} = (\text{Payments remaining} \times \text{Payment amount}) - \text{Finance charge rebate}$$
$$\text{Loan payoff} = (4 \times 145) - 30.77$$
$$\text{Loan payoff} = 580.00 - 30.77$$

$$\text{Loan payoff} = \underline{\$549.23}$$

T R Y - I T EXERCISE

9. **Beth Sheets financed a $4,000 automobile with an installment loan for 36 months. The payments were $141 per month and the total finance charge was $1,076. After**

twenty months Beth decided to pay off the loan. How much is the finance charge rebate and how much is Beth's loan payoff?

Check your answers with the solutions on page 436.

REVIEW EXERCISES CHAPTER 13—SECTION II

Calculate the amount financed, the finance charge, and the total deferred payment price for the following installment loans:

	Purchase (Cash) Price	Down Payment	Amount Financed	Monthly Payments	Number of Payments	Finance Charge	Total Deferred Payment Price
1.	$1,400	$350	$1,050.00	$68.00	24	$582.00	$1,982.00
2.	$3,500	20%	$2,800.00	$257.00	12	$284.00	$3,784.00
3.	$12,000	10%	$10,800.00	$375.00	36	$2,700.00	$14,700.00
4.	$2,900	0	$2,900.00	$187.69	18	$478.42	$3,378.42
5.	$8,750	15%	$7,437.50	$198.33	48	$2,082.34	$10,832.34

Calculate the amount financed, the finance charge, and the amount of the monthly payments for the following add-on interest loans:

	Purchase (Cash) Price	Down Payment	Amount Financed	Add-On Interest	Number of Payments	Finance Charge	Monthly Payment
6.	$788	10%	$709.20	8%	12	$56.74	$63.83
7.	$1,600	$250	$1,350.00	10%	24	$270.00	$67.50
8.	$4,000	15%	$3,400.00	$11\frac{1}{2}$%	30	$977.50	$145.92
9.	$17,450	$2,000	$15,450.00	14%	48	$8,652.00	$502.13
10.	$50,300	25%	$37,725.00	12.4%	60	$23,389.50	$1,018.58

Calculate the finance charge, finance charge per $100, and the annual percentage rate for the following installment loans using the APR tables, Table 13-1:

	Amount Financed	Number of Payments	Monthly Payment	Finance Charge	Finance Charge per $100	APR
11.	$2,300	24	$109.25	$322.00	$14.00	13%
12.	$14,000	36	$495.00	$3,820.00	$27.29	16.5%
13.	$1,860	18	$115.75	$223.50	$12.02	14.75%
14.	$35,000	60	$875.00	$17,500.00	$50.00	17.25%

Calculate the finance charge and the annual percentage rate for the following installment loans using the APR formula:

	Amount Financed	Number of Payments	Monthly Payment	Finance Charge	APR
15.	$500	12	$44.25	$31.00	11.25%
16.	$2,450	36	$90.52	$808.72	19.39%
17.	$13,000	48	$373.75	$4,940.00	16.6%
18.	$100,000	72	$2,055.50	$47,996.00	13.65%

Calculate the finance charge and the monthly payment for the following loans using the APR tables, Table 13-1:

	Amount Financed	Number of Payments	APR	Table Factor	Finance Charge	Monthly Payment
19.	$5,000	48	13.5%	29.97	$1,498.50	$135.39
20.	$7,500	36	12%	19.57	$1,467.75	$249.10
21.	$1,800	12	11.25%	6.20	$111.60	$159.30
22.	$900	18	$14\frac{3}{4}$%	12.08	$108.72	$56.04

Calculate the missing information for the following installment loans that are being paid off early:

	Number of Payments	Payments Made	Payments Remaining	Sum of Digits Payments Remaining	Sum of Digits Number of Payments	Rebate Fraction
23.	12	4	8	36	78	36/78
24.	36	22	14	105	666	105/666
25.	24	9	15	120	300	120/300
26.	60	40	20	210	1,830	210/1,830

You are the loan department supervisor for the Pacific National Bank. The following installment loans are being paid off early and it is your task to calculate the rebate fraction, the finance charge rebate, and the payoff for each loan:

	Amount Financed	Number of Payments	Monthly Payment	Payments Made	Rebate Fraction	Finance Charge Rebate	Loan Payoff
27.	$3,000	24	$162.50	9	120/300	$360.00	$2,077.50
28.	$1,600	18	$104.88	11	28/171	$47.13	$687.03
29.	$9,500	48	$267.00	36	78/1,176	$219.94	$2,984.06
30.	$4,800	36	$169.33	27	45/666	$87.56	$1,436.41

31. Delena Certo is interested in buying a dining room set for her home. At Furniture City she picks out a 7-piece set for a total cash price of $1,899.00. The salesperson informs her that if she qualifies for an installment loan, she may pay 10% now, as a down payment, and finance the balance with payments of $88.35 per month, for 24 months.

    a. What is the amount of the finance charge on this loan?

        Amount financed $= 1,899.00(100\% - 10\%)$

                     $= \$1,709.10$

        Total payments $= 88.35 \times 24 = 2,120.40$

        Finance charge $= 2,120.40 - 1,709.10$

                     $= \underline{\$411.30}$

    b. What is the total deferred payment price of the dining room set?

        Total deferred price $= 411.30 + 1,899.00$

                     $= \underline{\$2,310.30}$

32. Danny Denner found a car he wanted to buy at Spiffy Auto Sales. He had the option of paying $7,600 in cash or financing the car with a 2-year installment loan. The loan required a 20% down payment and equal monthly payments of $283.73.

    a. What is the finance charge on Danny's loan?

        Amount financed $= 7,600.00(100\% - 20\%)$

                     $= \$6,080.00$

        Total payments $= 283.73 \times 24$

                     $= \$6,809.52$

        Finance charge $= 6,809.52 - 6,080.00$

                     $= \underline{\$729.52}$

    b. What is the total deferred payment price of the car?

        Total deferred price $= 729.52 + 7,600.00$

                     $= \underline{\$8,329.52}$

33. Vince Arenas bought a new motorcycle with a 9% add-on interest installment loan from his credit union. The purchase price of the bike was $1,450.00. The credit union required a 15% down payment and equal monthly payments for 48 months. How much are Vince's monthly payments?

Amount financed = 1,450.00(100% − 15%)   Total payments   = 1,232.50 + 443.70
            = 1,232.50   = $1,676.20

$I = PRT$
$I = 1,232.50 \times .09 \times 4$ Monthly payment = $\dfrac{1,676.20}{48}$ = $34.92
$I = 443.70$

34. Sonya Cohen financed a trip to Europe with a 5% add-on interest installment loan from her bank. The total price of the trip was $1,500.00. The bank required equal monthly payments for 2 years. How much are Sonya's monthly payments?

Finance charge   = 1,500.00 × .05 × 2
            = $150.00
Total payments   = 150.00 + 1,500.00
            = $1,650.00
Monthly payment = $\dfrac{1,650.00}{24}$ = $68.75

35. Al Mosley purchased a car for $8,350. He made a down payment of $1,400, and financed the balance with monthly payments of $239.38 for 36 months.

   a. What is the amount of the finance charge on the loan?
   Amount financed = 8,350.00 − 1,400.00
               = $6,950.00
   Total payments   = 239.38 × 36
               = $8,617.68
   Finance charge   = 8,617.68 − 6,950.00
               = $1,667.68

   b. Use Table 13-1 to find what annual percentage rate was charged on Al's automobile loan.

   Table factor = $\dfrac{1,667.68 \times 100}{6,950.00}$ = 24.00

   APR = 14.5%

36. Suzanne Kennedy purchased a treadmill for $2,400 from Home Fitness, Inc. She made a $700 down payment and financed the balance with an installment loan for 48 months. If Suzanne's payments are $42.50 per month, use the APR formula to calculate what annual percentage rate she is paying on the loan.

Amount financed = 2,400.00 − 700.00 $\dfrac{72 \times 340.00}{(3 \times 1,700 \times 49) + (340 \times 47)} = \dfrac{24,480}{249,900 + 15,980} = \dfrac{24,480}{265,880}$
            = 1,700.00
Total payments   = 42.50 × 48   APR = 9.21%
            = $2,040.00
Finance charge   = 2,040.00 − 1,700.00
            = $340.00

37. The Electronic Warehouse uses The First American Bank to finance customer purchases. This month the bank is offering 24-month installment loans with an APR of 15.25%. For qualified buyers, no down payment is required. If Jim Lizotte wants to finance a complete stereo system for $1,300, use the APR tables to calculate the finance charge and the amount of the monthly payment on his loan.

Table factor for 15.25% for 24 months = 16.65   Monthly payment = $\dfrac{216.45 + 1,300.00}{24}$
Total finance charge = $\dfrac{1,300.00}{100} \times 16.65$ = $63.19
            = $216.45

38. At a recent boat show, MegaBank was offering boat loans for up to 5 years, with APRs of 13.5%. On new boats a 20% down payment was required. Neil Ramo wanted to finance a $55,000 boat for 5 years.

   a. What would be the finance charge on the loan?
   Amount financed = 55,000.00(100% − 20%)
               = $44,000.00
   Finance charge   = 44,000.00 × .135 × 5
               = $29,700.00

b. What would be the amount of the monthly payment?

$$\text{Monthly payment} = \frac{29{,}700.00 + 44{,}000.00}{60}$$
$$= \$1{,}228.33$$

39. Find the sum of the digits of $\text{Sum of digits} = \dfrac{n(n+1)}{2}$

   a. 24

$$\frac{24 \times 25}{2} = \underline{\underline{300}}$$

   b. 30

$$\frac{30 \times 31}{2} = \underline{\underline{465}}$$

40. a. What is the rebate fraction of a 36-month loan paid off after the 14th payment?

$$36 - 14 = 22 \qquad \frac{22 \times 23}{2} = 253 \qquad \text{Rebate fraction} = \underline{\underline{\frac{253}{666}}}$$
$$\frac{36 \times 37}{2} = 666$$

   b. What is the rebate fraction of a 42-month loan paid off after the 19th payment?

$$42 - 19 = 23 \qquad \frac{23 \times 24}{2} = 276 \qquad \text{Rebate fraction} = \underline{\underline{\frac{276}{903}}}$$
$$\frac{42 \times 43}{2} = 903$$

41. Jeff McNeeley financed a \$3,500 high definition TV set with an 8% add-on interest installment loan for 24 months. The loan required a 10% down payment.

   a. What is the amount of the finance charge on the loan?

$$\text{Amount financed} = 3{,}500.00(100\% - 10\%)$$
$$= \$3{,}150.00$$
$$\text{Finance charge} \quad = 3{,}150{,}00 \times .08 \times 2$$
$$= \underline{\underline{\$504.00}}$$

   b. How much are Jeff's monthly payments?

$$\text{Monthly payment} = 504.00 + 3{,}150.00$$
$$= \frac{3{,}654.00}{24}$$
$$= \underline{\underline{\$152.25}}$$

   c. What annual percentage rate is being charged on the loan?

$$\text{APR by formula} = \frac{72 \times 504.00}{(3 \times 3{,}150.00 \times 25) + (504 \times 23)}$$
$$= \frac{36{,}288.00}{236{,}250.00 + 11{,}592.00}$$
$$= \frac{36{,}288.00}{247{,}842.00}$$
$$= \underline{\underline{14.64\%}}$$

$$\text{APR by table} = \frac{504.00 \times 100}{3{,}150} = 16.00 \text{ Factor}$$

Table 13-1, 16.00, 24 periods = $\underline{\underline{14.75\%}}$

   d. If Jeff decides to pay off the loan after 16 months, what is his loan payoff?

$$24 - 16 = 8 \qquad \frac{8 \times 9}{2} = 36$$
$$\frac{24 \times 25}{2} = 300$$
$$\text{Rebate fraction} = \frac{36}{300}$$
$$\text{Rebate amount} = 504.00 \times \frac{36}{300} = \$60.48$$

$$\text{Payoff amount} = 8 \times 152.25$$
$$= 1{,}218.00 - 60.48$$
$$= \underline{\underline{\$1{,}157.52}}$$

FORMULAS

$$\text{Periodic rate} = \frac{\text{Annual percentage rate}}{12}$$

$$\text{Finance charge} = \text{Previous month's balance} \times \text{Periodic rate}$$

$$\text{Average daily balance} = \frac{\text{Sum of daily balances}}{\text{Days in billing cycle}}$$

$$\text{Finance charge} = \text{Average daily balance} \times \text{Periodic rate}$$

$$\frac{\text{New}}{\text{balance}} = \frac{\text{Previous}}{\text{balance}} + \frac{\text{Finance}}{\text{charge}} + \frac{\text{Purchases and}}{\text{cash advances}} = \frac{\text{Payments and}}{\text{credits}}$$

$$\text{Amount financed} = \text{Purchase price} - \text{Down payment}$$

$$\text{Down payment} = \text{Purchase price} \times \text{Down payment percent}$$

$$\text{Amount financed} = \text{Purchase price} \,(100\% - \text{Down payment percent})$$

$$\text{Total amount of installment payments} = \text{Amount financed} + \text{Finance charge}$$

$$\text{Finance charge} = \text{Total amount of installment payments} - \text{Amount financed}$$

$$\frac{\text{Total amount of}}{\text{installment payments}} = \frac{\text{Monthly payment}}{\text{amount}} \times \frac{\text{Number of}}{\text{monthly payments}}$$

$$\text{Total deferred payment price} = \text{Total of installment payments} + \text{Down payment}$$

$$\underset{(\textit{finance charge})}{\text{Interest}} = \underset{(\textit{amount financed})}{\text{Principal}} \times \text{Rate} \times \text{Time}$$

$$\text{Regular monthly payments} = \frac{\text{Total of installment payments}}{\text{Number of months of loan}}$$

$$\text{APR} = \frac{72I}{3\,P(n+1) + I(n-1)}$$

$$\text{Finance charge} = \frac{\text{Amount financed} \times \text{APR table factor}}{100}$$

$$\text{Sum of digits} = \frac{n(n+1)}{2}$$

$$\text{Rebate fraction} = \frac{\text{Sum of digits of remaining payments}}{\text{Sum of digits of total payment}}$$

$$\text{Finance charge rebate} = \text{Rebate fraction} \times \text{Total finance charge}$$

$$\text{Loan payoff} = (\text{Payments remaining} \times \text{Payment amount}) - \text{Finance charge rebate}$$

SECTION I   OPEN-END CREDIT—CHARGE ACCOUNTS, CREDIT CARDS, AND LINES OF CREDIT

Topic	P/O, Page	Important Concepts	Illustrative Examples
Calculating Finance Charge and New Balance Using Previous Month's Balance Method	13–1 405	1. Divide the annual percentage rate by 12 to find the monthly or periodic interest rate. 2. Calculate the finance charge by multiplying the previous month's balance by the periodic interest rate from Step 1. 3. Total all of the purchases and cash advances for the month. 4. Total all of the payments and credits for the month. 5. Use the following formula to determine the new balance: $\dfrac{\text{New}}{\text{bal.}} = \dfrac{\text{Prev}}{\text{bal.}} + \dfrac{\text{Fin}}{\text{chg}} + \dfrac{\text{Purch}}{\text{\& csh}} - \dfrac{\text{Pmts}}{\text{\& crd}}$	Calculate the finance charge and the new balance of an account with an annual percentage rate of 15%. Previous month's bal. = \$186.11 Purchases = \$365.77 Payments = \$200.00 Periodic rate $= \dfrac{15}{12} = 1.25\%$ Finance charge $= 186.11 \times .0125$ $= \underline{\$2.33}$ New balance = $186.11 + 2.33 + 365.77 - 200.00$ $= \underline{\$354.21}$
Calculating Finance Charge and New Balance Using the Average Daily Balance Method	13–2 406	1. Starting with the previous month's balance, multiply each by the number of days that balance existed, until the next account transaction. 2. At the end of the billing cycle, add all of the daily balances × days figures. 3. $\dfrac{\text{Average}}{\text{daily balance}} = \dfrac{\textbf{Sum of daily balances}}{\textbf{Number of days of billing cycle}}$ 4. $\dfrac{\text{Finance}}{\text{charge}} = \dfrac{\text{Periodic}}{\text{rate}} \times \dfrac{\text{Average daily}}{\text{balance}}$ 5. $\dfrac{\text{New}}{\text{bal.}} = \dfrac{\text{Prev}}{\text{bal.}} + \dfrac{\text{Fin}}{\text{chg}} + \dfrac{\text{Purch}}{\text{\& csh}} - \dfrac{\text{Pmts}}{\text{\& crd}}$	Calculate the finance charge and the new balance of an account with a periodic rate of 1%, a previous balance of \$132.26, and the following activity: May 5 Purchase \$45.60 May 9 Cash advance 100.00 May 15 Credit 65.70 May 23 Purchase 75.62 May 26 Payment 175.00 132.26×4 days = \$529.04 177.86×4 days = 711.44 277.86×6 days = 1,667.16 212.16×8 days = 1,697.28 287.78×3 days = 863.34 112.78×6 days = 676.68 31 days \$6,144.94 Average daily balance $= \dfrac{6{,}144.94}{31}$ $= \$198.22$ Finance charge $= 1\% \times 198.22$ $= \underline{\$1.98}$ New balance = $132.26 + 1.98 + 221.22 - 240.70$ $= \underline{\$114.76}$
Calculating the Finance Charge and New Balance of Business and Personal Lines of Credit	13–3 408	With business and personal lines of credit, the annual percentage rate is quoted as the current prime rate plus a fixed percent. Once the APR rate is determined, the finance charge and new balance are calculated as before, using the average daily balance method.	What are the finance charge and new balance of a line of credit with an APR of the current prime rate plus 4.6%? Previous balance = \$2,000 Average daily balance = \$3,200 Payments = \$1,500

I, continued

Topic	P/O, Page	Important Concepts	Illustrative Examples
		$\dfrac{\text{New}}{\text{bal.}} = \dfrac{\text{Previous}}{\text{balance}} + \dfrac{\text{Finance}}{\text{charge}} + \text{Loans} - \text{Payments}$	Loans = \$3,600 Current prime rate = 7% APR = 7% + 4.6% = 11.6% Periodic rate = $\dfrac{11.6}{12}$ = .97% Finance charge = 3,200 × .0097 = $\underline{\$31.04}$ New balance = 2,000 + 31.04 + 3,600 − 1,500 = $\underline{\underline{\$4,131.04}}$

SECTION II   CLOSED-END CREDIT—INSTALLMENT LOANS

Topic	P/O, Page	Important Concepts	Illustrative Examples
Calculating the Total Deferred Payment Price and the Amount of the Finance Charge of an Installment Loan	13–4 414	$\dfrac{\text{Finance}}{\text{charge}} = \dfrac{\text{Total amount of}}{\text{installment pmts}} - \dfrac{\text{Amount}}{\text{financed}}$ $\dfrac{\text{Total deferred}}{\text{payment price}} = \dfrac{\text{Total of}}{\text{installment}} + \dfrac{\text{Down}}{\text{payment}}$	Waterbed City sold a \$1,900 bedroom set to Tom Ash. Tom put down \$400 and financed the balance with an installation loan of 24 monthly payments of \$68.75 each. What are the finance charge and total deferred payment price of the bedroom set? Total amount of payments = \$68.75 × 24 = \$1,650 Finance charge = 1,650 − 1,500 = $\underline{\$150}$ Total deferred payment price = 1,650 + 400 = $\underline{\$2,050}$
Calculating the Regular Monthly Payment of a Loan by the Add-on Interest Method	13–5 416	1. Calculate the amount financed by subtracting the down payment from the purchase price. 2. Compute the add-on interest finance charge using $I = PRT$. 3. Find the total of the installment payments by adding the interest to the amount financed. 4. Calculate the monthly payment by dividing the total of the installment payments by the number of months of the loan.	Alice Walzer financed a new car with an 8% add-on interest loan. The purchase price of the car was \$13,540. The bank required a \$1,500 down payment and equal monthly payments for 48 months. How much are Alice's monthly payments? Amount financed = 13,540 − 1,500 = \$12,040 Interest = 12,040 × .08 × 4 = \$3,852.80 Total of installment payments = 12,040 + 3,852.80 = \$15,892.80 Monthly payment = $\dfrac{15,892.80}{48}$ = $\underline{\$331.10}$

II, continued

Topic	P/O, Page	Important Concepts	Illustrative Examples
Calculating the Annual Percentage Rate (APR) Using APR Tables	13–6 417	1. Calculate the finance charge per $100 by: $$\frac{\text{Finance charge} \times 100}{\text{Amount financed}}$$ 2. From Table 13–1, scan down the payments column to the number of payments of the loan. 3. Scan to the right in that row to the table factor that most closely corresponds to the finance charge per $100. 4. Look to the top of the column containing the finance charge per $100 to find the APR of the loan.	Juanita Cordero purchased a car for $8,000. She made a $1,500 down payment and financed the remaining $6,500 for 30 months. If Juanita's total finance charge is $1,858, what APR is she paying on the loan? Finance Charge per $100 = $$\frac{1,858 \times 100}{6,500} = \$28.58$$ From Table 13–1, scan down the payments column to 30. Then scan right to the table factor closest to 28.58, which is 28.64. The top of that column shows the APR to be 20.5%.
Calculating the Annual Percentage Rate (APR) Using the APR Formula	13–6 421	When APR tables are not available, the annual percentage rate can be approximated by the formula: $$APR = \frac{72I}{3P(n+1) + I(n-1)}$$ where I = finance charge on the loan P = principal; amount financed n = number of months of the loan	Using the APR formula, verify the annual percentage rate for Juanita's loan found in the table. APR = $$\frac{72(1,858)}{3(6,500)(30+1) + 1,858(30-1)}$$ $$= \frac{133776}{658382} = .2031 = 20.3\%$$
Calculating the Finance Charge and Monthly Payment of a Loan Using APR Tables	13–7 422	1. From Table 13–1, locate the table factor at the intersection of the APR and number of payments of the loan. This table factor is the finance charge per $100. 2. Total finance charge = $$\frac{\text{Amount financed} \times \text{Table factor}}{100}$$ 3. $$\text{Monthly payment} = \frac{\text{Amt. financed} + \text{Finance chg.}}{\text{Number of months of the loan}}$$	Contemporary Electronics uses the MegaBank to finance customer purchases. This month MegaBank is offering loans up to 36 months with an APR of 13.25%. For qualified buyers, no down payment is required. If John Black wants to purchase a $2,350 large-screen TV on a 36-month loan, what are the finance charge and monthly payment of the loan? From Table 13–1, the table factor for 36 payments, 13.25% = 21.73 Total finance charge = $$\frac{2,350 \times 21.73}{100} = \$510.66$$ Monthly payment = $$\frac{2,350 + 510.66}{36} = \$79.46$$

II, continued

Topic	P/O, Page	Important Concepts	Illustrative Examples
Calculating the Finance Charge Rebate and Payoff for Loans Paid Off Early, Using the Sum-of-the-Digits, or Rule of 78, Method	13–8 423	1. Calculate the rebate fraction using the sum-of-the-digits formula for the numerator (number of payments remaining) and the denominator (total number of payments). $$\text{Sum of digits} = \frac{n(n+1)}{2}$$ 2. Calculate the finance charge rebate by multiplying the rebate fraction by the total finance charge. 3. The payoff of the loan is found by multiplying the remaining number of payments by the payment amount, then subtracting the finance charge rebate.	Gene Curtis financed a $2,000 motorcycle with an installment loan for 24 months. The payments are $98.00 per month and the total finance charge is $352.00. After 18 months Gene decides to pay off the loan. How much is the finance charge rebate and what is the amount of the loan payoff? Rebate fraction = $$\frac{\text{Sum of digits of 6}}{\text{Sum of digits of 24}}$$ Sum Digits 6 = $\frac{6(7)}{2} = 21$ Sum Digits 24 = $\frac{24(25)}{2} = 300$ Rebate fraction = $\frac{21}{300}$ Finance charge rebate = $\frac{21}{300} \times 352 = \$24.64$ Loan Payoff = $(6 \times 98) - 24.64$ $= 588.00 - 24.64$ $= \$563.36$

TRY-IT EXERCISE   SOLUTIONS

1. Periodic rate = $\dfrac{\text{APR}}{12} = \dfrac{15\%}{12} = 1.25\%$

Finance charge = Previous balance × Periodic rate
Finance charge = $214.90 \times .0125 = \underline{\$2.69}$

New balance = Previous balance + Finance charge + Purchases & cash advance − Payment & credits
New balance = $214.90 + 2.69 + 238.85 - 49.12 = \underline{\$407.32}$

2. Periodic rate = $\dfrac{\text{APR}}{12} = \dfrac{18\%}{12} = 1.5\%$

Dates	Days	Activity/Amount		Unpaid Balance	Daily Balances
Aug. 1–4	4	Previous Balance	158.69	158.69	634.76
Aug. 5–10	6	Charge	55.00	213.69	1,282.14
Aug. 11–14	4	Payment	−100.00	113.69	454.76
Aug. 15–16	2	Charge	43.22	156.91	313.82
Aug. 17–19	3	Charge	54.10	211.01	633.03
Aug. 20–25	6	Charge	224.50	435.51	2,613.06
Aug. 26–31	6	Cash advance	75.00	510.51	3,063.06
	31				8,994.63

Average daily balance = $\dfrac{\text{Daily balances}}{\text{Days}} = \dfrac{8,994.63}{31} = \$290.15$

Finance charge = Average daily balance × Periodic rate
Finance charge = $290.15 × .015 = $4.35

New balance = Previous balance + Finance charge + Purchases & cash advance − Payments & credits
New balance = 158.69 + 4.35 + 451.82 − 100.00 = $514.86

3. APR = Prime rate + 4.5%
   APR = 8.5 + 4.5 = 13%

   Periodic rate = $\dfrac{13\%}{12}$ = 1.08%

Dates	Days	Activity/Amount		Unpaid Balance	Daily Balances
Nov. 1–6	6	Previous balance	12,300	12,300	73,800
Nov. 7–20	14	Loan	16,700	29,000	406,000
Nov. 21–25	5	Loan	8,800	37,800	189,000
Nov. 26–30	5	Payment	−20,000	17,800	89,000
	30				757,800

Average daily balance = $\dfrac{757,800}{30}$ = $25,260

Finance charge = 25,260 × .0108 = $272.81

New balance = Previous balance + Finance charge + Loan amounts − Payments
New balance = 12,300 + 272.81 + 25,500 − 20,000 = $18,072.81

4. **a.** Down payment = Purchase price × Down payment percent
   Down payment = 12,500 × .15 = $1,875.00

   Amount financed = Purchase price − Down payment
   Amount financed = 12,500 − 1,875 = $10,625.00

   Total amount of installment payments = Monthly payment × Number of payments
   Total amount of installment payments = 309.90 × 48 = $14,875.20

   Finance charge = Total amount of installment payments − Amount financed
   Finance charge = 14,875.20 − 10,625.00 = $4,250.20

   b. Total deferred payment price = Total amount of installment payments + Down payment
   Total deferred payment price = 14,875.20 + 1,875.00 = $16,750.20

5. Amount financed = Purchase price (100% − Down payment %)
   Amount financed = 1,500 × .9 = $1,350.00

   Finance charge = Amount financed × Rate × Time
   Finance charge = 1,350 × .06 × 2 = $162.00

   Total of installment payments = Amount financed + Finance charge
   Total of installment payments = 1,350.00 + 162.00 = $1,512.00

   Monthly payments = $\dfrac{\text{Total of installment payments}}{\text{Number of months of loan}}$

   Monthly payments = $\dfrac{1,512}{24}$ = $63.00

6. Amount financed = 4,500 − 500 = $4,000
   Total payments = 190 × 24 = 4,560
   Finance charge = 4,560 − 4,000 = $560.00

   Finance charge/100 = $\dfrac{\text{Finance charge} \times 100}{\text{Amount financed}}$ = $\dfrac{560 \times 100}{4,000}$ = $14.00

   From Table 13-1 APR for $14.00 = 13%

7. Total payments = 140 × 18 = 2,520
   Finance charge = 2,520 − 2,200 = $320.00

   APR = $\dfrac{72I}{3P(n+1) + I(n-1)}$

   APR = $\dfrac{72(320)}{3(2,200)(18+1) + 320(18-1)}$ = $\dfrac{23,040}{125,400 + 5,440}$

   APR = $\dfrac{23,040}{130,840}$ = .17609 = 17.6%

8. 13.25%, 24-month table factor = $14.38

Finance charge = $\dfrac{\text{Amount financed} \times \text{Table factor}}{100}$

Finance charge = $\dfrac{3{,}550.00 \times 14.38}{100} = \dfrac{51{,}049}{100} = \underline{\underline{\$510.49}}$

Monthly payment = $\dfrac{\text{Amount financed} + \text{Finance charge}}{\text{Number of months of loan}}$

Monthly payment = $\dfrac{3{,}550.00 + 510.49}{24} = \dfrac{4{,}060.49}{24}$

Monthly payment = $\underline{\underline{\$169.19}}$

9. 16 months remaining; total of 36 months.

Sum of digits 16 = $\dfrac{n(n+1)}{2} = \dfrac{16(16+1)}{2} = \dfrac{272}{2} = 136$

Sum of digits 36 = $\dfrac{n(n+1)}{2} = \dfrac{36(36+1)}{2} = \dfrac{1{,}332}{2} = 666$

Rebate fraction = $\dfrac{136}{666}$

Finance charge rebate = Rebate fraction $\times$ Total finance charge = $\dfrac{136}{666} \times 1{,}076$

Finance charge rebate = $\underline{\underline{\$219.72}}$

Loan payoff = (Payments remaining $\times$ Payment amount) $-$ Finance charge rebate
Loan payoff = $(16 \times 141.00) - 219.72 = 2{,}256.00 - 219.72$
Loan payoff = $\underline{\underline{\$2{,}036.28}}$

Name_____

Class_____

1. Kimberly Joy's revolving charge account has an annual percentage rate of 16%. The previous month's balance was $345.40. During the current month Kimberly's purchases and cash advances amounted to $215.39, and her payments and credits totaled $125.00.

ANSWERS

1. a. _____1.33%_____

   b. _____$4.59_____

   c. _____$440.38_____

2. a. _____$3.02_____

   b. _____$883.70_____

   a. What is the monthly periodic rate of the account?

$$\text{Periodic rate} = \frac{16\%}{12} = \underline{\underline{1.33\%}}$$

   b. What is the amount of the finance charge?

    $345.40 \times 1.33\% = \underline{\underline{\$4.59}}$

   c. What is Kimberly's new balance?

    New balance = $345.40 + 4.59 + 215.39 - 125.00$
                 $= \underline{\underline{\$440.38}}$

2. Joe Kreutle has a BankCard account with an annual percentage rate of 12% calculated on the previous month's balance. In April, the account had the following activity.

Joe Kreutle	STATEMENT OF ACCOUNT	
Account #9595-55-607	Billing cycle: April 1–30	
April 1	Previous Month's Balance	$301.98
April 8	Atlas Gym & Health Club	250.00
April 9	Payment	75.00
April 15	Lucky's Auto Repair	124.80
April 25	Cash Advance	100.00
April 28	Brandon's Menswear	178.90

   a. What is the amount of the finance charge?

    Periodic rate = $12\% \div 12 = 1\%$
    Finance charge = $301.98 \times 1\% = \underline{\underline{\$3.02}}$

   b. What is Joe's new balance?

    New balance = $301.98 + 3.02 + 653.70 - 75.00$
                 $= \underline{\underline{\$883.70}}$

Celia Grossman has a revolving charge account at Lacy's. The finance charge is calculated on the previous month's balance, and the annual percentage rate is 20%. Complete the following 3-month account activity table for Celia:

$$20\% \div 12 = 1.67\%$$

Month	Previous Month's Balance	Finance Charge	Purchases and Cash Advances	Payments and Credits	New Balance End of Month
3. December	$267.00	$4.46	$547.66	$95.00	$724.12
4. January	$724.12	$12.09	$213.43	$110.00	$839.64
5. February	$839.64	$14.02	$89.95	$84.00	$859.61

6. Calculate the average daily balance for the month of January of a charge account with a previous month's balance of $480.94 and the following activity:

Date	Activity	Amount
January 7	Cash Advance	$80.00
January 12	Payment	$125.00
January 18	Purchase	$97.64
January 24	Credit	$72.00
January 29	Purchase	$109.70
January 30	Purchase	$55.78

$$\text{Average daily balance} = \frac{15{,}640.76}{31} = \$504.54$$

7. Allan Levitt has a BankCard account with a 13% annual percentage rate calculated on the average daily balance. The billing date is the first day of each month and the billing cycle is the number of days in that month.

Allan Levitt

STATEMENT OF ACCOUNT

Account #4495-5607   Billing cycle: September 1– 30

September 1	Previous month's balance	$686.97
September 4	Lord & Taylor's	223.49
September 8	Payment	350.00
September 12	Office Depot	85.66
September 21	United Airlines (Credit)	200.00
September 24	Miller Paint and Body Shop	347.12
September 28	Ticketmasters	64.00

---

a. What is the average daily balance for September?

$$\text{Average daily balance} = \frac{20{,}842.71}{30} = \$694.76$$

b. How much is the finance charge for September?

$$\text{Periodic rate} = \frac{13\%}{12} = 1.08\%$$

$$\text{Finance charge} = 694.76 \times .0108 = \$7.50$$

c. What is Allan's new balance?

$$\text{New balance} = 686.97 + 7.50 + 720.27 - 550.00$$
$$= \$864.74$$

8. Precision Builders, Inc., has a $100,000 line of credit with the California National Bank. The annual percentage rate is the current prime rate plus $3\frac{1}{4}\%$. The balance on June 1 was $52,900. On June 8, Precision borrowed $30,600 to pay for a shipment of lumber and roofing materials and on June 18 borrowed another $12,300 for equipment repairs. On June 28, a $35,000 payment was made on the account. The billing cycle for June has 30 days. The current prime rate is $7\frac{3}{4}\%$.

a. What is the finance charge on the account?

Average daily balance $= \dfrac{\$2,345,700.00}{30} = \$78,190.00$

Periodic rate $= 7.75 + 3.25 = 11\%$

$11\% \div 12 = .917\%$

Finance charge for June $= \$78,190.00 \times .00917$

$\qquad\qquad = \underline{\$717.00}$

b. What is Precision's new balance?

New balance $= \$52,900.00 + \$42,900.00 + \$717.00 - \$35,000.00$

$\qquad\qquad = \underline{\$61,517.00}$

9. Irene McGuinness bought a motor home for a cash price of $29,200.00. She made a 15% down payment and financed the balance with payments of $579.00 per month for 60 months.

a. What is the amount of the finance charge on this loan?

Amount financed $= \$29,200.00 \times 85\% = \$24,820.00$

Total payments $= \$579.00 \times 60 = \$34,740.00$

Finance charge $= \$34,740.00 - \$24,820.00$

$\qquad\qquad = \underline{\$9,920.00}$

b. What is the total deferred payment price of the motor home?

Total deferred price $= \$9,920.00 + \$29,200.00 = \underline{\$39,120.00}$

10. Russ Rosabal bought a home exercise gym with a 9.3% add-on interest installment loan from his bank. The purchase price of the gym was $1,290.00. The bank required a 15% down payment and equal monthly payments for 24 months.

a. What is the total deferred payment price of the gym?

Amount financed $= \$1,290.00 \times 85\% = \$1,096.50$

Interest $= \$1,096.50 \times .093 \times 2 = \$203.95$

Total deferred price $= \$1,290.00 + \$203.95$

$\qquad\qquad = \underline{\$1,493.95}$

b. How much are Russ's monthly payments?

Total payments $= \$1,096.50 + \$203.95$

$\qquad\qquad = \$1,300.45$

Monthly payment $= \dfrac{1,300.45}{24} = \underline{\$54.19}$

11. Music City Recording Studio purchased a new 32-track recording console for $28,600. A down payment of $5,000 was made and the balance financed with monthly payments of $708.00 for 48 months.

a. What is the amount of the finance charge on the loan?

Amount financed $= \$28,600.00 - \$5,000.00 = \$23,600.00$

Total payments $= \$708.00 \times 48 = \$33,984.00$

Finance charge $= \$33,984.00 - \$23,600.00$

$\qquad\qquad = \underline{\$10,384.00}$

Name_____

Class_____

ANSWERS

8. a. _____ $717.00 _____

b. _____ $61,517.00 _____

9. a. _____ $9,920.00 _____

b. _____ $39,120.00 _____

10. a. _____ $1,493.95 _____

b. _____ $54.19 _____

11. a. _____ $10,384.00 _____

ANSWERS

b. _____19.25%_____

12. a. _____14.47%_____

b. _____14.5%_____

13. a. _____$66,300.00_____

b. _____$4,646.67_____

14. a. _____325/666_____

b. _____$634.38_____

15. a. _____$14,144.00_____

b. Use Table 13-1 to find what annual percentage rate was charged on the equipment loan.

$$\text{Factor} = \frac{10,384.00 \times 100}{23,600.00} = 44$$

APR = <u>19.25%</u>

12. A Pizza Palace franchise purchased a $7,590 pizza oven with a 36-month installment loan. The monthly payments are $261.44 per month.

a. Use the APR formula to calculate the annual percentage rate of the loan.

Total payments = 36 × 261.44 = $9,411.84
Interest = 9,411.84 − 7,590.00 = 1,821.84

$$\text{APR} = \frac{72 \times 1,821.84}{(3 \times 7,590.00 \times 37) + (1,821.84 \times 35)}$$

$$= \frac{131,172.48}{906,254.40} = 0.1447413$$

APR = <u>14.47%</u>

b. Use the APR tables to verify your answer from part a.

$$\text{Factor} = \frac{1,821.84 \times 100}{7,590.00} = 24.00$$

APR = <u>14.5%</u>

13. SkyHigh Aircraft Sales uses the Second National Bank to finance customer aircraft purchases. This month Second National is offering 60-month installment loans with an APR of 11.25%. A 15% down payment is required. The Caldwell Corporation president wants to finance the purchase of a company airplane for $250,000.

a. Use the APR tables to calculate the amount of the finance charge.

Table factor = 31.20
Amount financed = 250,000.00 × 85% = 212,500.00

$$\text{Finance charge} = \frac{212,500.00 \times 31.20}{100}$$

= <u>$66,300.00</u>

b. How much are the monthly payments on Caldwell's aircraft loan?

$$\text{Monthly payment} = \frac{66,300.00 + 212,500.00}{60}$$

= <u>$4,646.67</u>

14. a. What is the rebate fraction of a 36-month loan paid off after the 11th payment?

Total payments = 36
Payments remaining = 36 − 11 = 25

$$\frac{25 \times 26}{2} = 325 \qquad \frac{36 \times 37}{2} = 666$$

Rebate fraction = <u>325/666</u>

b. If the finance charge was $1,300, what is the amount of the finance charge rebate?

$$\text{Rebate amount} = 1,300.00 \times \frac{325}{666}$$

= <u>$634.38</u>

15. Blumenkranz Engineering financed a $68,000 circuit assembler with a $6\frac{1}{2}$% add-on interest installment loan for 48 months. The loan required a 20% down payment.

a. What is the amount of the finance charge on the loan?

Amount financed = 68,000.00 × 80%
= $54,400.00

Finance charge = 54,400.00 × .065 × 4
= <u>$14,144.00</u>

b. How much are the monthly payments?

$$\text{Monthly payments} = \frac{54,400.00 + 14,144.00}{48}$$
$$= \underline{\$1,428.00}$$

c. What annual percentage rate is being charged on the loan?

$$\text{Factor} = \frac{14,144.00 \times 100}{54,400.00} = 26.00$$
$$\text{APR} = \underline{11.75\%}$$

d. If Blumenkranz decides to pay off the loan after 22 months, what is the amount of the loan payoff?

Total months = 48
Remaining months = 48 − 22 = 26
Rebate fraction $\frac{351}{1,176}$

Rebate amount = $14,144.00 \times \frac{351}{1,176} = \$4,221.55$

Balance remaining = $26 \times 1,428.00 = \$37,128.00$
Payoff amount = $37,128.00 - 4,221.55$
$= \underline{\$32,906.45}$

16. Pam Singer found the following ad for a Mitsubishi Mirage in her local newspaper. Pam has asked for your help in calculating the following.

a. The amount financed.

Amount financed = 8,495.00 − 1,500.00
$= \underline{\$6,995.00}$

b. The amount of the finance charge.

Finance charge = $159.00 \times 60 = 9,540.00$
$= \$9,540.00 - 6,995.00$
$= \underline{\$2,545.00}$

c. The total deferred payments of the loan.

Total deferred price = 9,540.00 + 1,500.00
$= \underline{\$11,040.00}$

BRAND NEW **MITSUBISHI**

MIRAGE COUPE

AIR CONDITIONING, 5 Speed Transmission, Floor Mats, Radio Accomodation Package & More! Price includes Rebate. 60 Months, $1500 Down Plus Tax, Tag, Title With Approved Credit.

$8495

$159 PER MO.

d. The annual percentage rate of the loan.

$$\text{Factor} = \frac{2,545.00 \times 100}{6,995.00} = 36.38$$
$$\text{APR} = \underline{13.00\%}$$

Name_____

Class_____

ANSWERS

b. _____ $1,428.00 _____

c. _____ 11.75% _____

d. _____ $32,906.45 _____

16. a. _____ $6,995.00 _____

b. _____ $2,545.00 _____

c. _____ $11,040.00 _____

d. _____ 13.00% _____

ANSWERS

17. a. _____ 14.68% _____

b. _____ $51,480.00 _____

c. _____ $11,581.79 _____

18. a. _____ $55.18 _____

_____ $53.39 _____

b. _____ Gold by $1.79 _____

23 NOVA SPYDER

23 NOVA WAS $399 **NOW $379** per month*

SALE PRICE $29,000 - $6000 Down
120 Months

BUSINESS DECISION
Pick the Right Plastic!

17. You are a salesperson for Champion Boat Sales. Ray Lesikar, a customer, is interested in purchasing the 23 Nova in the ad and has asked you the following questions.

a. What is the APR of the loan? Use the formula to find the APR of the loan.

APR = 14.68%

b. What is the total deferred payment price of the boat?

Total deferred payment = 29,000.00 + 22,480.00
= $51,480.00

c. If the loan was paid off after 7 years, what is the payoff of the loan?

Total months = 120
Remaining months = 120 − 84 = 36
Rebate fraction = $\frac{666}{7,260}$

Rebate amount = 22,480.00 × $\frac{666}{7,260}$

= $2,062.21
Balance remaining = 36 × 379.00
= $13,644.00
Payoff amount = 13,644.00 − 2,062.21
= $11,581.79

18. On October 22 you plan to purchase a $2,000 computer using one of your two credit cards. The Silver Card charges 18% interest and calculates interest on the previous month's balance. The Gold Card charges 15% interest and calculates interest based on the average daily balance. Both cards have a $0 balance as of October 1.

Your plan is to make an $800 payment in November, an $800 payment in December, and pay off the remaining balance in January. All of your payments will be received and posted on the 10th of each month. No other charges will be made on the account.

a. Based on this information, calculate the interest charged by each card for this purchase.

Silver = $55.18
Gold = $53.39

b. Which card is the better deal and by how much?

Silver = 55.18
Gold = − 53.39
$1.79
Gold: Better deal by $1.79

All the Math That's Fit to Learn

The Business Math Times

Volume XIII — Consumer and Business Credit — One Dollar

Credit "Card Tricks"

Here are some of the latest tactics used by credit card companies in their quest to get your business and increase their profits.

- Promise that you qualify for a credit line of "up to" a high amount, say $10,000, then send you a card with a spending cap of only $1,000.
- Offer attractive "teaser" rates for a short period of time. After a few months, these rates often increase to over 18 percent.
- Encourage you to move all your other credit card balances to this card, although the teaser rate may only apply to purchases.
- Limit the total amount customers can charge on other cards. If customers overuse other cards, their account may be canceled, and the entire balance due immediately.
- Encourage cardholders to "skip a payment." This allows the card company to charge interest on top of interest.
- Raise the interest rate of cardholders who have a high balance but haven't been making enough new charges.
- Cancel the accounts of customers who don't use their cards much and who pay their bill in full each month.
- Require cardholders to sign away their rights to go to court if there is a dispute. These

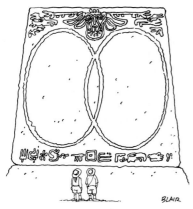

"Near as we can tell, it's a Mayan credit card."

issuers make you take your complaint to an arbitration board of their choice.

SOURCE: Adapted from "Credit Cards," *Consumer Reports* (America Online), January 1996.

Small Business Owners Say, "Charge It!"

Did you know small and mid-sized business owners frequently turn to credit cards to finance purchases when banks turn down their requests for loans? The smaller the company, the more likely it is to use a credit card as a financing tool.

The survey of 747 small and mid-sized businesses was conducted by business consultants Arthur Andersen's Enterprise Group and by National Small Business United, a business group. The study found that 45 percent of the business owners surveyed tried to get bank loans in the previous 12 months, and 26 percent were unsuccessful. Of those who could not obtain loans, 41 percent then financed purchases on their credit cards.

SOURCE: Reuters News Service, "Small Businesses: Charge It," *The Miami Herald*, July 27, 1994: 3C.

Up, Up, and Away!—Solution

The stack would be 315.65 miles high

4 inches = $1 million

12 inches = 1 foot = $3 million

1 mile = 5,280 feet x $3 million
= $15,840 million or
  $15.84 billion

$1 trillion = $\dfrac{1,000}{15.84}$ = 63.13 miles

5 x 63.13 = 315.65 miles

Mr. Plastic Fantastic

Did you know the largest collection of valid credit cards to date is one of 1,384 (all different) by Walter Cavanagh of Santa Clara, California? The cost of acquisition for "Mr. Plastic Fantastic" was zero, and he keeps them in the world's longest wallet—250 feet long, weighing 38 lbs., 4 oz. They are worth nearly $2 million in credit.

Cavanagh, who is a certified financial planner, has a credit philosophy which seems to be at odds with his mega-collection of plastic. He says the first thing he tells his clients is "Pay off your credit cards! And never charge on a credit card anything you can't pay off in six months or less."

SOURCES: Adapted from *The Guinness Book of Records,*1995 Edition, New York: Bantam Books, p. 504; "Bankcard Consumer News," Bankcard Holders of America, September/October 1994, p. 6.

Tax-Deductible Credit Card

Some banks are offering credit cards secured by the equity in your home. The advantage is that your credit card interest expense is reduced by the rate of income tax you pay; frivolous use could lead to catastrophic results, since the card debt is secured by your home.

Brainteaser

In what year was the first Super Bowl game played?
Clues: No digit is an 8.
The hundreds digit is 3 more than the tens digit.
The sum of the digits in the year is 23.

Answer to Last Issue's Brainteaser
November 8th
This occurs when November 1 falls on a Tuesday.

Chapter 14

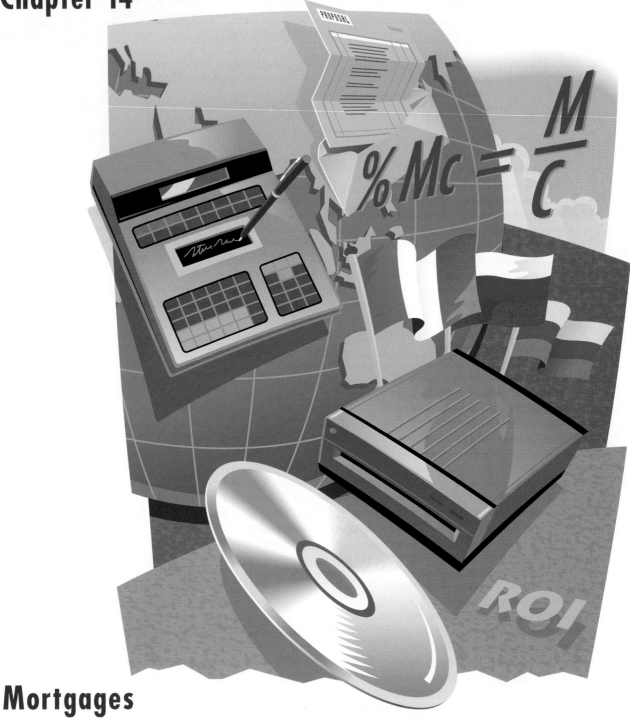

Mortgages

Performance Objectives

MORTGAGES—FIXED-RATE AND ADJUSTABLE-RATE

Real estate is defined as land, including the air above and the earth below, plus any permanent improvements to the land such as homes, apartment buildings, factories, hotels, shopping centers, or any other "real" property. Whether for commercial or residential property, practically all real estate transactions today involve some type of financing. The mortgage loan is the most popular method of financing real estate purchases.

A **mortgage** is any loan in which real property is used as security for a debt. During the term of the loan, the property becomes security or collateral for the lender, sufficient to ensure recovery of the amount loaned.

Mortgages today fall into one of three categories: FHA-insured, VA-guaranteed, and conventional. The National Housing Act of 1934 created the **Federal Housing Administration (FHA)** to encourage reluctant lenders to invest their money in the mortgage market, thereby stimulating the depressed construction industry. Today, the FHA is a government agency within the Department of Housing and Urban Development (HUD). The FHA insures private mortgage loans made by approved lenders.

In 1944, the Servicemen's Readjustment Act (GI Bill of Rights) was passed to help returning World War II veterans purchase homes. Special mortgages were established known as **Veterans Affairs (VA) mortgages** or **GI Loans.** Under this and subsequent legislation, the government guarantees payment of a mortgage loan made by a private lender to a veteran/buyer should the veteran default on the loan.

VA loans may be used by eligible veterans, surviving spouses, and active service members to buy, construct, or refinance homes, farm residences, or condominiums. Down payments by veterans are not required but are left to the discretion of lenders, whereas FHA and conventional loans require a down payment from all buyers.

Conventional loans are made by private lenders and generally have a higher interest rate than either FHA or VA loans. Most conventional lenders are restricted to loaning 80% of the appraised value of a property, thus requiring a 20% down payment. If the borrower agrees to pay the premium for **private mortgage insurance (PMI),** the conventional lender can lend up to 95% of the appraised value of the property.

real estate
Land, including any permanent improvements such as homes, apartment buildings, factories, hotels, shopping centers, or any other "real" structures.

mortgage
A loan in which real property is used as security for a debt.

Federal Housing Administration (FHA)
A government agency within the U.S. Department of Housing and Urban Development (HUD) that sets construction standards and insures residential mortgage loans made by approved lenders.

VA mortgage, or GI Loan
Long-term, low-down-payment home loans made by private lenders to eligible veterans, the payment of which is guaranteed by the Veterans Administration in the event of a default.

conventional loans
Real estate loans made by private lenders that are not FHA-insured or VA-guaranteed.

private mortgage insurance (PMI)
A special form of insurance primarily on mortgages for single-family homes, allowing the buyer to borrow more, by putting down a smaller down payment.

Mortgage loans are the most common form of loan made for real property purchases such as office buildings.

Copyright © 1997 by Harcourt Brace & Company. All rights reserved.

• adjustable-rate mortgage (ARM)

A mortgage loan in which the interest rate changes periodically, usually in relation to a predetermined economic index.

• mortgage discount points

Extra charge frequently added to the cost of a mortgage, allowing lenders to increase their yield without showing an increase in the mortgage interest rate.

• closing

A meeting at which the buyer and seller of real estate conclude all matters pertaining to the transaction. At the closing, the funds are transferred to the seller, and the ownership or title is transferred to the buyer.

Historically high interest rates in the early 1980s caused mortgage payments to skyrocket beyond the financial reach of the average home buyer. To revitalize the slumping mortgage industry, the **adjustable-rate mortgage (ARM)** was created. These are mortgage loans under which the interest rate is periodically adjusted to more closely coincide with changing economic conditions. ARMs are very attractive, particularly to first-time buyers, since a low, teaser rate may be offered for the first few years, and then adjusted upward to a higher rate later in the loan. Today, the adjustable-rate mortgage has become the most widely accepted option to the traditional 15- and 30-year fixed-rate mortgages.

Extra charges known as **mortgage discount points** are frequently added to the cost of a loan as a rate adjustment factor. This allows lenders to increase their yield without showing an increase in the mortgage interest rate. Each discount point is equal to 1% of the amount of the loan. Exhibit 14-1 illustrates a rates vs. points cost comparison of an $80,000 mortgage after 5 years.

Purchasing and financing a home is one of the major financial decisions a person will make in his or her lifetime. Substantial research should be done and much care should be taken in choosing the correct time to buy, the right property to buy, and the best financial arrangement.

In this section, you will learn to calculate the monthly payments of a mortgage loan and prepare a partial amortization schedule of that loan. You will also calculate the amount of property tax and insurance required as part of each monthly payment. In addition, you will learn about the **closing,** the all-important final step in a real estate transaction, and the calculation of the closing costs. Finally, you will learn about the important components of an adjustable-rate mortgage: the index, the lender's margin, the interest rate, and the cost caps.

14-1 Calculating the Monthly Payment and Total Interest Paid on a Fixed-Rate Mortgage

In Chapter 12, we learned that amortization is the process of paying off a financial obligation in a series of equal regular payments over a period of time. We calculated the amount of an amortization payment by using the present value of an annuity table or the optional amortization formula.

Because mortgages run for relatively long periods of time, we can also use a special present value table in which the periods are listed in years. The table factors represent the monthly payment required per $1,000 of debt to amortize a mortgage. The monthly payment includes mortgage interest and an amount to reduce the principal. See Table 14-1.

RATES VS. POINTS

When applying for a fixed-rate mortgage, you may have the choice of a lower rate or fewer points (assuming the seller doesn't pay the points). Which do you choose? The answer depends on how much cash you have on hand and how long you plan to live in your home.

Take these three examples below: After five years, the total cost of each of the three $80,000 mortgages is about the same. However, the lowest rate loan is nearly $322 a year cheaper than the highest rate mortgage, and so would be a better deal over a longer time period.

Rate/Points	Mo. payment	Points	Total cost
7.50/1	$545.74	$800	$33,544.40
7.00/2	$532.24	$1,600	$33,534.40
6.75/3	$518.88	$2,400	$33,532.80

With the highest rate, you would pay $545.74 monthly and owe one point, or $800, at closing. With the lowest rate, you would pay $518.88 monthly and put down three points or $2,400 at closing.

SOURCE: Personal Business, *Miami Herald*, September 27, 1993, p. 38. Copyright © Bank Rate Monitor,® North Palm Beach, FL 33408.

EXHIBIT 14-1

....

RATES VERSUS POINTS: COMPARISON OF $80,000 MORTGAGE AFTER 5 YEARS

Monthly Payments
(Necessary to amortize a loan of $1,000)

Interest Rate	5 Years	10 Years	15 Years	20 Years	25 Years	30 Years	35 Years	40 Years
5 %	18.88	10.61	7.91	6.60	5.85	5.37	5.05	4.83
5¼	18.99	10.73	8.04	6.74	6.00	5.53	5.21	4.99
5½	19.11	10.86	8.18	6.88	6.15	5.68	5.38	5.16
5¾	19.22	10.98	8.31	7.03	6.30	5.84	5.54	5.33
6	19.34	11.11	8.44	7.17	6.45	6.00	5.71	5.51
6¼	19.45	11.23	8.58	7.31	6.60	6.16	5.88	5.68
6½	19.57	11.36	8.72	7.46	6.76	6.33	6.05	5.86
6¾	19.69	11.49	8.85	7.61	6.91	6.49	6.22	6.04
7	19.81	11.62	8.99	7.76	7.07	6.66	6.39	6.22
7¼	19.92	11.75	9.13	7.91	7.23	6.83	6.57	6.40
7½	20.04	11.88	9.28	8.06	7.39	7.00	6.75	6.59
7¾	20.16	12.01	9.42	8.21	7.56	7.17	6.93	6.77
8	20.28	12.14	9.56	8.37	7.72	7.34	7.11	6.96
8¼	20.40	12.27	9.71	8.53	7.89	7.52	7.29	7.15
8½	20.52	12.40	9.85	8.68	8.06	7.69	7.47	7.34
8¾	20.64	12.54	10.00	8.84	8.23	7.87	7.66	7.53
9	20.76	12.67	10.15	9.00	8.40	8.05	7.84	7.72
9¼	20.88	12.81	10.30	9.16	8.57	8.23	8.03	7.91
9½	21.01	12.94	10.45	9.33	8.74	8.41	8.22	8.11
9¾	21.13	13.08	10.60	9.49	8.92	8.60	8.41	8.30
10	21.25	13.22	10.75	9.66	9.09	8.78	8.60	8.50
10¼	21.38	13.36	10.90	9.82	9.27	8.97	8.79	8.69
10½	21.50	13.50	11.06	9.99	9.45	9.15	8.99	8.89
10¾	21.62	13.64	11.21	10.16	9.63	9.34	9.18	9.09
11	21.75	13.78	11.37	10.33	9.81	9.53	9.37	9.29
11¼	21.87	13.92	11.53	10.50	9.99	9.72	9.57	9.49
11½	22.00	14.06	11.69	10.67	10.17	9.91	9.77	9.69
11¾	22.12	14.21	11.85	10.84	10.35	10.10	9.96	9.89
12	22.25	14.35	12.01	11.02	10.54	10.29	10.16	10.09
12¼	22.38	14.50	12.17	11.19	10.72	10.48	10.36	10.29
12½	22.50	14.64	12.33	11.37	10.91	10.68	10.56	10.49
12¾	22.63	14.79	12.49	11.54	11.10	10.87	10.76	10.70
13	22.76	14.94	12.66	11.72	11.28	11.07	10.96	10.90
13¼	22.89	15.08	12.82	11.90	11.47	11.26	11.16	11.10
13½	23.01	15.23	12.99	12.08	11.66	11.46	11.36	11.31
13¾	23.14	15.38	13.15	12.26	11.85	11.66	11.56	11.51
14	23.27	15.53	13.32	12.44	12.04	11.85	11.76	11.72

TABLE 14-1

AMORTIZATION TABLE OF MORTGAGE PRINCIPAL AND INTEREST PER $1,000

STEPS TO FIND THE MONTHLY MORTGAGE PAYMENT USING AN AMORTIZATION TABLE, AND TOTAL INTEREST:

Step 1. Find the number of $1,000s financed by:

$$\text{Number of \$1,000s financed} = \frac{\text{Amount financed}}{1,000}$$

Step 2. Using Table 14-1, locate the table factor, monthly payment per $1,000 financed, at the intersection of the number of years column and the interest rate row.

Step 3. Calculate the monthly payment by:

$$\text{Monthly payment} = \text{Number of \$1,000s financed} \times \text{Table factor}$$

Step 4. Find the total interest of the loan by:

$$\text{Total interest} = \left(\text{Monthly payment} \times \text{Number of payments}\right) - \text{Amount financed}$$

EXAMPLE

What is the monthly payment and total interest on a $50,000 mortgage at 8% for 30 years?

SOLUTION STRATEGY

Step 1. Number of $1,000s financed $= \dfrac{\text{Amount financed}}{1,000} = \dfrac{50,000}{1,000} = 50$

Step 2. Table factor for 8%, 30 years is 7.34.

Step 3. Monthly payment = Number of $1,000s financed × Table factor
Monthly payment = 50 × 7.34
Monthly payment = $\underline{\$367.00}$

Step 4. Total interest = (Monthly payment × Number of payments) − Amount financed
Total interest = (367 × 360) − 50,000
Total interest = 132,120 − 50,000
Total interest = $\underline{\$82,120}$

TRY-IT   **EXERCISE**

1. **What is the monthly payment and total interest on an $85,500 mortgage at 7% for 25 years?**

Check your answers with the solutions on page 466.

14-2 Preparing a Partial Amortization Schedule of a Mortgage

Mortgages used to purchase residential property generally require regular, equal payments. A portion of the payment is used to pay interest on the loan; the balance of the payment is used to reduce the principal. This type of mortgage is called a **level-payment plan** since the amount of the payment remains the same for the duration of the loan. The amount of the payment that is interest gradually decreases while the amount that reduces the debt gradually increases.

An **amortization schedule** is a chart that shows the status of the mortgage loan after each payment. The schedule illustrates month by month how much of the mortgage payment is interest and how much is left to reduce to principal. The schedule also shows the outstanding balance of the loan after each payment.

In reality, amortization schedules are quite long, because they show the loan status for each month. A 30-year mortgage, for example, would require a schedule with 360 lines (12 months × 30 years = 360 payments).

● **level-payment plan**

Mortgages with regular, equal payments over a specified period of time.

● **amortization schedule**

A chart that shows the month-by-month breakdown of each mortgage payment into interest and principal, and the outstanding balance of the loan.

STEPS TO CREATE AN AMORTIZATION SCHEDULE FOR A LOAN:

Step 1. Use Table 14-1 to calculate the amount of the monthly payment.

Step 2. Calculate the amount of interest for the current month using $I = PRT$, where P is the current outstanding balance of the loan, R is the annual interest rate, and T is $\frac{1}{12}$.

continued

continued

Step 3. Find the portion of the payment used to reduce principal by

Portion of payment reducing principal = Monthly payment – Interest

Step 4. Calculate the outstanding balance of the mortgage loan by

Outstanding balance = Previous balance – Portion of pmt. reducing principal

Step 5. Repeat Steps 2, 3, and 4 for each succeeding month and enter the values on a schedule labeled as follows:

| Payment Number | Monthly Payment | Monthly Interest | Portion Used to Reduce Principal | Loan Balance |

EXAMPLE

Prepare an amortization schedule for the first 3 months of the $50,000 mortgage at 8% for 30 years from the previous example. Remember, you have already calculated the monthly payment to be $367.00. (Step 1)

SOLUTION STRATEGY

Step 2.
> **MONTH 1:**
>
> Interest = Principal × Rate × Time
> Interest = $50,000 \times .08 \times \frac{1}{12}$
> Interest = $333.33

Step 3. Portion of payment reducing principal = Monthly payment – Interest
Portion of payment reducing principal = $367.00 – $333.33
Portion of payment reducing principal = $33.67

Step 4. Outstanding balance = Previous balance – Portion of payment reducing principal
Outstanding balance = 50,000 – 33.67
Outstanding balance after 1 payment = $49,966.33

Step 5. Repeat Steps 2, 3, and 4, for two more payments and enter the values on the schedule.
MONTH 2:

Interest = $49,966.33 \times .08 \times \frac{1}{12}$ = $333.11
(Note: Although very slightly, interest decreased.)
Portion reducing principal = 367.00 – 333.11 = $33.89
Outstanding balance after 2 payments = 49,966.33 – 33.89 = $49,932.44

MONTH 3:

Interest = $49,932.44 \times .08 \times \frac{1}{12}$ = $332.88
Portion reducing principal = 367.00 – 332.88 = $34.12
Outstanding balance after 3 payments = 49,932.44 – 34.12 = $49,898.32

Amortization Schedule
$50,000 Loan, 8%, 30 years

Payment Number	Monthly Payment	Monthly Interest	Portion Used to Reduce Principal	Loan Balance
0				$50,000.00
1	$367.00	$333.33	$33.67	$49,966.33
2	$367.00	$333.11	$33.89	$49,932.44
3	$367.00	$332.88	$34.12	$49,898.32

2. Prepare an amortization schedule of the first 4 payments of a $75,000 mortgage at 9% for 15 years. Use the amortization table to calculate the amount of the monthly payment.

Check your answers with the solutions on pages 466–467.

14-3 Calculating the Monthly PITI of a Mortgage Loan

● **PITI**

An abbreviation for the total amount of a mortgage payment; includes principal, interest, property taxes, and hazard insurance.

● **escrow account**

Bank account used by mortgage lenders for the safekeeping of the funds accumulating to pay next year's property taxes and hazard insurance.

In reality, mortgage payments include four elements: principal, interest, taxes, and insurance—thus the abbreviation **PITI.** VA, FHA, and most conventional loans require borrowers to pay $\frac{1}{12}$ of the estimated annual property taxes and hazard insurance with each month's mortgage payment. Each month the taxes and insurance portions of the payment are placed in a type of savings account for safekeeping known as an **escrow account.** Each year when the property taxes and hazard insurance premiums are due, the lender disburses those payments from the borrower's escrow account. During the next 12 months, the account again builds up to pay for the next year's taxes and insurance. Typically over the years of a mortgage, property taxes and insurance premiums rise. When this happens, the lender must increase the portion set aside in the escrow account by increasing the taxes and insurance parts of the monthly payment.

STEPS TO CALCULATE THE PITI OF A MORTGAGE:

Step 1. Calculate the principal and interest portion, PI, of the payment as before using the amortization table, Table 14-1.

Step 2. Calculate the monthly tax and insurance portion, TI:

$$\text{Monthly TI} = \frac{\text{Estimated property tax} + \text{Hazard insurance}}{12}$$

Step 3. Calculate the total monthly PITI:

$$\text{Monthly PITI} = \text{Monthly PI} + \text{Monthly TI}$$

EXAMPLE

Martha Cavalaris purchased a home with a mortgage of $87,500 at $7\frac{1}{2}$% for 30 years. The property taxes are $2,350.00 per year and the hazard insurance premium is $567.48. What is the monthly PITI payment of Martha's loan?

SOLUTION STRATEGY

Step 1. From the amortization table, Table 14-1, the factor for $7\frac{1}{2}$%, 30 years is 7.00. When we divide the amount of Martha's loan by 1,000 we get 87.5 as the number of 1,000s financed. The principal and interest portion, PI, is therefore $87.5 \times 7.00 = \underline{\$612.50}$.

Step 2. $\text{Monthly TI} = \dfrac{\text{Estimated property tax} + \text{Hazard Insurance}}{12}$

$\text{Monthly TI} = \dfrac{2,350.00 + 567.48}{12} = \dfrac{2,917.48}{12} = \underline{\$243.12}$

Step 3. Monthly PITI = PI + TI
   Monthly PITI = 612.50 + 243.12
   Monthly PITI = $855.62

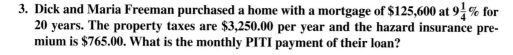

TRY-IT   **EXERCISE**

3. **Dick and Maria Freeman purchased a home with a mortgage of $125,600 at $9\frac{1}{4}$% for 20 years. The property taxes are $3,250.00 per year and the hazard insurance premium is $765.00. What is the monthly PITI payment of their loan?**

Check your answer with the solution on page 467.

14-4 Understanding Closing Costs and Calculating the Amount Due at Closing

The term closing, or settlement, is used to describe the final step in a real estate transaction. This is a meeting at which time documents are signed, the buyer pays the agreed purchase price, and the seller delivers the **title,** or right of ownership, to the buyer. The official document conveying ownership is known as the **deed.**

Closing costs are the expenses incurred in conjunction with the sale of real estate. In the typical real estate transaction, both the buyer and the seller are responsible for a number of costs that are paid for at the time of closing. The party obligated for paying a particular closing cost is often determined by local custom or by negotiation. Some closing costs are expressed as dollar amounts, while others are a percent of the amount financed or the amount of the purchase price.

At closing, the buyer is responsible for the purchase price (mortgage + down payment) plus closing costs. The amount received by the seller, after all expenses have been paid, is known as the proceeds.

The **settlement statement** or **closing statement** is a document, usually prepared by an attorney, that provides a detailed breakdown of the real estate transation. This document itemizes closing costs and indicates how they are allocated between the buyer and the seller. Exhibit 14-2 illustrates a typical real estate transaction settlement statement.

● **title, or deed**
The official document representing the right of ownership of real property.

● **closing costs**
Expenses incurred in conjunction with the sale of real estate, including loan origination fees, credit reports, appraisal fees, title search, title insurance, inspections, attorney's fees, recording fees, and broker's commission.

● **settlement or closing statement**
A document that provides a detailed accounting of payments, credits, and closing costs of a real estate transaction.

EXAMPLE

Rich and Linda Arrandt are purchasing a $180,000 home. The down payment is 25% and the balance will be financed with a 25-year fixed-rate mortgage at 10% and 2 discount points (each point is 1% of the amount financed). When Rich and Linda signed the sales contract they put down a deposit of $15,000, which will be credited to their down payment at the time of the closing. In addition they must pay the following expenses: credit report, $80; appraisal fee, $150; title insurance premium, $\frac{1}{2}$% of amount financed; title search, $200; and attorney's fees, $450.

a. Calculate the amount due from Rich and Linda at the closing.
b. If the sellers are responsible for the broker's commission, which is 6% of the purchase price; $900 in other closing costs; and the existing mortgage, with a balance of $50,000; what proceeds will they receive on the sale of the property?

A. Settlement Statement

U.S. Department of Housing and Urban Development   OMB No. 2502-0265

B. Type of Loan

1. ☐ FHA	2. ☐ FmHA	3. ☐ Conv. Unins.	6. File Number	7. Loan Number	8. Mortgage Insurance Case Number
4. ☐ VA	5. ☐ Conv. Ins.				

C. Note: This form is furnished to give you a statement of actual settlement costs. Amounts paid to and by the settlement agent are shown. Items marked "(p.o.c.)" were paid outside the closing; they are shown here for informational purposes and are not included in the totals.

D. Name and Address of Borrower	E. Name and Address of Seller	F. Name and Address of Lender

G. Property Location	H. Settlement Agent	
	Place of Settlement	I. Settlement Date

J. Summary of Borrower's Transaction		K. Summary of Seller's Transaction	
100. Gross Amount Due From Borrower		**400. Gross Amount Due To Seller**	
101. Contract sales price		401. Contract sales price	
102. Personal property		402. Personal property	
103. Settlement charges to borrower (line 1400)		403.	
104.		404.	
105.		405.	
Adjustments for items paid by seller in advance		*Adjustments for items paid by seller in advance*	
106. City/town taxes to		406. City/town taxes to	
107. County taxes to		407. County taxes to	
108. Assessments to		408. Assessments to	
109.		409.	
110.		410.	
111.		411.	
112.		412.	
120. Gross Amount Due From Borrower		**420. Gross Amount Due To Seller**	
200. Amounts Paid By Or In Behalf Of Borrower		**500. Reductions In Amount Due To Seller**	
201. Deposit or earnest money		501. Excess deposit (see instructions)	
202. Principal amount of new loan(s)		502. Settlement charges to seller (line 1400)	
203. Existing loan(s) taken subject to		503. Existing loan(s) taken subject to	
204.		504. Payoff of first mortgage loan	
205.		505. Payoff of second mortgage loan	
206.		506.	
207.		507.	
208.		508.	
209.		509.	
Adjustments for items unpaid by seller		*Adjustments for items unpaid by seller*	
210. City/town taxes to		510. City/town taxes to	
211. County taxes to		511. County taxes to	
212. Assessments to		512. Assessments to	
213.		513.	
214.		514.	
215.		515.	
216.		516.	
217.		517.	
218.		518.	
219.		519.	
220. Total Paid By/For Borrower		**520. Total Reduction Amount Due Seller**	
300. Cash At Settlement From/To Borrower		**600. Cash At Settlement To/From Seller**	
301. Gross Amount due from borrower (line 120)		601. Gross amount due to seller (line 420)	
302. Less amounts paid by/for borrower (line 220)	( )	602. Less reductions in amount due seller (line 520)	( )
303. Cash ☐ From ☐ To Borrower		603. Cash ☐ To ☐ From Seller	

Previous Edition is Obsolete

HUD-I(3-86)
RESPA, HB 4305.2

SOLUTION STRATEGY

a. Down payment = $180,000 \times 25\% = \$45,000$

Amount financed = $180,000 - 45,000 = \$135,000$

Closing Costs, Buyer

Discount points ($135,000 \times 2\%$)	$2,700
Down payment ($45,000 - 15,000$ deposit)	$30,000
Credit report	$80
Appraisal fee	$150
Title insurance ($135,000 \times \frac{1}{2}\%$)	$675
Title search	$200
Attorney's fees	$450
Due at closing	$34,255

b.

Proceeds, Seller

Sale price		$180,000
Less: Broker's commission:		
$180,000 \times 6\%$	$10,800	
Closing costs	$900	
Mortgage payoff	$50,000	
		− $61,700
Proceeds to seller:		$118,300

L. Settlement Charges

	@ % =	Paid From Borrowers Funds at Settlement	Paid From Seller's Funds at Settlement
700. Total Sales/Broker's Commission based on price $			
Division of Commission (line 700) as follows:			
701. $ to			
702. $ to			
703. Commission paid at Settlement			
704.			
800. Items Payable In Connection With Loan			
801. Loan Origination Fee %			
802. Loan Discount %			
803. Appraisal Fee to			
804. Credit Report to			
805. Lender's Inspection Fee			
806. Mortgage Insurance Application Fee to			
807. Assumption Fee			
808.			
809.			
810.			
811.			
900. Items Required By Lender To Be Paid In Advance			
901. Interest from to @ $ /day			
902. Mortgage Insurance Premium for months to			
903. Hazard Insurance Premium for years to			
904. years to			
905.			
1000. Reserves Deposited With Lender			
1001. Hazard insurance months @ $ per month			
1002. Mortgage insurance months @ $ per month			
1003. City property taxes months @ $ per month			
1004. County property taxes months @ $ per month			
1005. Annual assessments months @ $ per month			
1006. months @ $ per month			
1007. months @ $ per month			
1008. months @ $ per month			
1100. Title Charges			
1101. Settlement or closing fee to			
1102. Abstract or title search to			
1103. Title examination to			
1104. Title insurance binder to			
1105. Document preparation to			
1106. Notary fees to			
1107. Attorney's fees to			
(includes above items numbers:)			
1108. Title insurance to			
(includes above items numbers:)			
1109. Lender's coverage $			
1110. Owner's coverage $			
1111.			
1112.			
1113.			
1200. Government Recording and Transfer Charges			
1201. Recording fees: Deed $; Mortgage $;	Releases $		
1202. City/county tax/stamps: Deed $; Mortgage $			
1203. State tax/stamps: Deed $; Mortgage $			
1204.			
1205.			
1300. Additional Settlement Charges			
1301. Survey to			
1302. Pest inspection to			
1303.			
1304.			
1305.			
1400. Total Settlement Charges (enter on lines 103, Section J and 502, Section K)			

TRY-IT   EXERCISE

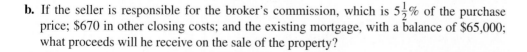

4. **Kathi Hanson is purchasing a townhouse for $120,000. The down payment is 20% and the balance will be financed with a 15-year fixed-rate mortgage at 9% and 3 discount points (each point is 1% of the amount financed). When Kathi signed the sales contract she put down a deposit of $10,000, which will be credited to her down payment at the time of the closing. In addition she must pay the following expenses: loan application fee, $100; condominium transfer fee, $190; title insurance premium, $\frac{3}{4}$% of amount financed; hazard insurance premium, $420; prepaid taxes, $310; and attorney's fees, $500.**

a. Calculate the amount due from Kathi at the closing.

b. If the seller is responsible for the broker's commission, which is $5\frac{1}{2}$% of the purchase price; $670 in other closing costs; and the existing mortgage, with a balance of $65,000; what proceeds will he receive on the sale of the property?

Check your answers with the solutions on page 467.

With a fixed-rate mortgage, the interest rate stays the same during the life of the loan. With an adjustable-rate mortgage (ARM), the interest rate changes periodically, usually in relation to an index, and payments may go up or down accordingly. In recent years, the ARM has become the most widely accepted alternative to the traditional 30-year fixed-rate mortgage.

The primary components of an ARM are the index, lender's margin, calculated interest rate, initial interest rate, and cost caps. With most ARMs, the interest rate and monthly payment change either every year, every three years, or every five years. The period between one rate change and the next is known as the **adjustment period.** A loan with an adjustment period of one year, for example, is called a one-year ARM.

Most lenders tie ARM interest rate changes to changes in an **index rate.** These indexes usually go up and down with the general movement of interest rates in the nation's economy. When the index goes up, so does the mortgage rate, resulting in higher monthly payments. When the index goes down, the mortgage rate may or may not go down.

In Chapter 13, we learned that the interest rates for lines of credit were tied to the prime rate. With ARMs, lenders base rates on a variety of indexes. Among the most common are the rates on short- and long-term Treasury securities and the regional or national average cost of money to savings and loan institutions.

To calculate the interest rate on an ARM, lenders add a few points called the **margin** or **spread** to the index rate. The amount of the margin can differ among lenders and can make a significant difference in the amount of interest paid over the life of a loan.

$$\text{Calculated interest rate} = \text{Index rate} + \text{Lender's margin}$$

The **calculated** or **initial interest rate** is usually the rate to which all future adjustments and caps apply, although this rate may be discounted by the lender during the first payment period in order to attract and qualify more potential borrowers. This low initial interest rate, sometimes known as a **teaser rate,** is one of the main appeals of the ARM; however, without some protection from rapidly rising interest rates, borrowers might be put in a position of not being able to afford the rising mortgage payments. To prevent this situation, standards have been established requiring limits or caps on increases.

Interest-rate caps place a limit on the amount the interest rate can increase. These may come in the form of **periodic caps,** which limit the increase from one adjustment period to

● adjustment period

The amount of time between one rate change and the next on an adjustable-rate mortgage; generally one, two, or three years.

● index rate

The economic index to which the interest rate on an adjustable-rate mortgage is tied.

● margin, or spread

The percentage points added to an index rate to get the interest rate of an adjustable-rate mortgage.

● calculated or initial interest rate

The interest rate of an adjustable-rate mortgage to which all future adjustments and caps apply.

● teaser rate

A discounted interest rate for the first adjustment period of an adjustable-rate mortgage that is below the current market rate of interest.

● interest-rate cap

Limit on the amount the interest rate can increase on an ARM.

● periodic cap

Limit on the amount the interest rate of an ARM can increase per adjustment period.

Adjustable-rate mortgages appeal to first-time home buyers, because the initial interest rate is usually low.

the next, and **overall caps,** which limit the increase over the life of the mortgage. The following formulas can be used to find the maximum interest rates of an ARM:

● **overall cap**

Limit on the amount the interest rate of an ARM can increase over the life of the loan.

$$\text{Maximum rate per adjustment period} = \text{Previous rate} + \text{Periodic cap}$$

$$\text{Maximum overall rate of ARM} = \text{Initial rate} + \text{Overall cap}$$

EXAMPLE

Tom Kairys bought a home with an adjustable-rate mortgage. The margin on the loan is 2.5% and the rate cap is 6% over the life of the loan.

a. If the current index rate is 4.9%, what is the calculated interest rate of the ARM?

b. What is the maximum overall rate of the loan?

SOLUTION STRATEGY

a. Because the loan interest rate is tied to an index, we use the formula

Calculated ARM interest rate = Index rate + Margin

Calculated ARM interest rate = 4.9% + 2.5%

Calculated ARM interest rate = <u>7.4%</u>

b.

Maximum overall rate = Calculated rate + Overall cap

Maximum overall rate = 7.4% + 6%

Maximum overall rate = <u>13.4%</u>

TRY-IT **EXERCISE**

5. Nadine Tracy bought a home with an adjustable-rate mortgage. The margin on the loan is 3.4% and the rate cap is 7% over the life of the loan. The current index rate is 3.2%.

a. What is the initial interest rate of the ARM?

b. What is the maximum overall rate of the loan?

Check your answers with the solutions on page 467.

REVIEW EXERCISES CHAPTER 14—SECTION I

Using Table 14-1 as needed, calculate the required information for the following mortgages:

	Amount Financed	Interest Rate	Term of Loan	Number of $1,000s Financed	Table Factor	Monthly Payment	Total Interest
1.	$80,000	9%	20 years	80	9.00	$720.00	$92,800.00
2.	$72,500	10%	30 years	72.5	8.78	$636.55	$156,658.00
3.	$130,900	$8\frac{1}{2}\%$	25 years	130.9	8.06	$1,055.05	$185,615.00
4.	$154,300	$9\frac{1}{4}\%$	15 years	154.3	10.30	$1,589.29	$131,772.20
5.	$96,800	$7\frac{3}{4}\%$	30 years	96.8	7.17	$694.06	$153,061.60

6. Sam Gore purchased a home with a $78,500 mortgage at 9% for 15 years. Calculate the monthly payment and prepare an amortization schedule for the first 4 months of Sam's loan.

Payment Number	Monthly Payment	Monthly Interest	Portion Used to Reduce Principal	Loan Balance
0				$78,500
1	$796.78	$588.75	$208.03	$78,291.97
2	$796.78	$587.19	$209.59	$78,082.38
3	$796.78	$585.62	$211.16	$77,871.22
4	$796.78	$584.03	$212.75	$77,658.47

Calculate the monthly principal and interest, PI, using Table 14-1, and the monthly PITI for the following mortgages:

Complete, worked out solutions to exercises 7–10 appear in the appendix following the index.

	Amount Financed	Interest Rate	Term of Loan	Monthly PI	Annual Property Tax	Annual Insurance	Monthly PITI
7.	$76,400	8%	20 years	$639.47	$1,317	$866	$821.39
8.	$128,800	10%	15 years	$1,384.60	$2,440	$1,215	$1,689.18
9.	$174,200	$7\frac{1}{4}\%$	30 years	$1,189.79	$3,505	$1,432	$1,601.21
10.	$250,000	$9\frac{1}{2}\%$	25 years	$2,185.00	$6,553	$2,196	$2,914.08

11. Deb Van Patten bought a home with an adjustable rate mortgage. The margin on the loan is 3.5% and the rate cap is 8% over the life of the loan.

    a. If the current index rate is 3.75%, what is the calculated interest rate of the ARM?

        Calculated interest rate of ARM   3.75
                                 + 3.50
                                 7.25%

    b. What is the maximum overall rate of Deb's loan?

        Maximum overall rate   7.25
                         + 8.00
                         15.25%

12. Christine Balmori purchased a condominium for $88,000. She made a 20% down payment and financed the balance with a 30-year, 9% fixed-rate mortgage.

    a. What is the amount of the monthly principal and interest portion, PI, of Christine's loan?

        Amount financed $= 88,000.00 \times 80\% = 70,400.00$

        Number of $1,000s financed $= \dfrac{70,400.00}{1,000} = 70.4$

        9%, 30 years Table factor
        Monthly PI $= 8.05 \times 70.4 = \$566.72$

    b. Construct an amortization schedule for the first 4 months of Christine's mortgage:

Payment Number	Monthly Payment	Monthly Interest	Portion Used to Reduce Principal	Loan Balance
0				$70,400.00
1	$566.72	$528.00	$38.72	$70,361.28
2	$566.72	$527.71	$39.01	$70,322.27
3	$566.72	$527.42	$39.30	$70,282.97
4	$566.72	$527.12	$39.60	$70,243.37

    c. If the annual property taxes are $1,650 and the hazard insurance premium is $780 per year, what is the total monthly PITI of Christine's loan?

        Taxes   =   1,650.00   PI   = 566.72
        Insurance = +   780.00   TI   = 202.50
                $2,430.00 \div 12 = \$202.50$ Monthly PITI $= \$769.22$

13. Joe Barrow is shopping for a 15-year mortgage for $150,000. Currently, the Fortune Bank is offering an $8\frac{1}{2}$% mortgage with 3 discount points; the Northern Trust Bank is offering a $8\frac{3}{4}$% mortgage with no points. Joe is unsure which mortgage is a better deal and has asked you to help him decide. (Remember, each discount point is equal to 1% of the amount financed.)

a. What is the total interest paid on each loan?

Fortune Bank

$8\frac{1}{2}$% for 15 years = $9.85 \times 150 = 1,477.50 \times 180$
$$\begin{align} \text{Total payment} &= 265,950.00 \\ \text{Amount financed} &= -150,000.00 \\ \text{Interest paid over life of loan} &= \underline{\$115,950.00} \end{align}$$

Northern Trust Bank

$8\frac{3}{4}$% for 15 years = $10.00 \times 150 = 1,500.00 \times 180$
$$\begin{align} \text{Total payment} &= 270,000.00 \\ \text{Amount financed} &= -150,000.00 \\ \text{Interest paid over life of loan} &= \underline{\$120,000.00} \end{align}$$

b. Taking into account the closing points, which bank is offering a better deal, and by how much?

Fortune Bank

$115,950.00 + 3\%$ of $150,000.00$
$115,950.00 + 4,500.00$

Interest + points = $\underline{\$120,450.00}$

Northern Trust Bank

Interest only = $\underline{\$120,000.00}$ $\underline{\$450.00}$ Less (Better deal)

14. Eduardo Padron is interested in a fixed-rate mortgage for $100,000. He is undecided whether to choose a 15- or 30-year mortgage. The current mortgage rate is 10% for the 15-year mortgage and 11% for the 30-year mortgage.

a. What are the monthly principal and interest payments for each loan?

100,000 10% for 15 years
$10.75 \times 100 = 1,075.00$
Monthly PI = $\underline{\$1,075.00}$

100,000 11% for 30 years
$9.53 \times 100 = 953.00$
Monthly PI = $\underline{\$953.00}$

b. What is the total amount of interest paid on each loan?

$15 \times 12 = 180 \times 1,075.00$
$$\begin{align} \text{Total payments} &= 193,500.00 \\ &\underline{-100,000.00} \\ \text{Total interest} \quad &\underline{\$93,500.00} \end{align}$$

$30 \times 12 = 360 \times 953.00$
$$\begin{align} \text{Total payments} &= 343,080.00 \\ &\underline{-100,000.00} \\ \text{Total interest} \quad &\underline{\$243,080.00} \end{align}$$

c. Overall, how much more interest is paid by choosing the 30-year mortgage?

$243,080.00 - 93,500.00 = 149,580.00$
30-year mortgage costs more by $\underline{\$149,580.00}$

15. Kam Fong is purchasing a $235,000 home. The down payment is 20% and the balance will be financed with a 15-year fixed-rate mortgage at $8\frac{3}{4}$% and $3\frac{1}{2}$ discount points. The annual property tax is $5,475 and the hazard insurance premium is $2,110. When Kam signed the original contract he put down a deposit of $5,000, which will be credited to his down payment at the time of closing. In addition, at the time of closing Kam must pay the following expenses:

Appraisal fee	$215.00
Credit report	$65.00
Roof inspection	$50.00
Mortgage insurance premium	$\frac{1}{2}$% of amount financed
Title search	$125.00
Attorney's fees	$680.00
Escrow fee	$210.00
Prepaid interest	$630.00

As Kam's real estate broker, he has asked you the following:

a. What is the total monthly PITI of the mortgage loan?

Amount financed $= 235,000 \times 80\%$
           $= \$188,000.00$

$8\frac{3}{4}\%$ for 15 years $= 10.00 \times 188$

PI $= \$1,880.00$

Tax	5,475.00
Insurance	2,110.00
	$\$7,585.00 \div 12 = \$632.08$

PI	1,880.00
TI +	632.08
	$\$2,512.08$ Monthly PITI

b. What is the total amount of interest that will be paid on the loan?

$15 \times 12 = 180 \times 1,880.00 = 338,400.00$
                       $-188,000.00$
Total interest paid on loan $\$150,400.00$

c. How much is due from Kam at the time of the closing?

Appraisal fee	$215.00	Escrow fee	210.00
Credit report	65.00	Prepaid int.	630.00
Roof Inspec.	50.00	Points	6,580.00 (188,000.00 × .035)
Mortgage Ins.	940.00 (188,000.00 × .005)	Down payment	+ 47,000.00 (235,000.00 × .2)
Title search	125.00		$56,495.00
Attorney's fees	680.00	Deposit	− 5,000.00
		Due at closing	$51,495.00

d. If your real estate office is entitled to a commission of $6\frac{1}{2}\%$ of the price of the home from the seller, how much commission is made on the sale?

$\$235,000.00 \times .065 = \underline{\$15,275.00}$

SECOND MORTGAGES— HOME EQUITY LOANS AND LINES OF CREDIT

home equity loan

A lump-sum second mortgage loan made on the available equity in a home.

home equity line

A revolving credit second mortgage loan made on the available equity in a home.

credit limit

A pre-approved limit on the amount of a home equity line of credit.

Home equity loans and home equity lines of credit are becoming more and more popular each year. By using the equity in a home, a borrower may qualify for a sizable amount of credit at an interest rate that is relatively low. In addition, under the tax law, the interest may be a tax deduction because the debt is secured by your home.

A **home equity loan** is a lump-sum second mortgage loan made on the available equity in your home. A **home equity line** is a form of revolving credit, also based on the available equity. Because the home is likely to be a consumer's largest asset, many homeowners use these loans and credit lines only for major expenditures such as debt consolidation, education, home improvements, business expansion, medical bills, or vacations.

With home equity lines of credit, the borrower will be approved for a specific amount of credit known as the **credit limit.** This is the maximum amount that can be borrowed at any one time on that line of credit.

Exhibit 14-3 illustrates some typical bank literature used to promote home equity loans. Note that with the tax deductibility advantage of these loans, a considerable amount of money can be saved on interest over installment loans or credit cards.

14-6 Calculating the Potential Amount of Credit Available to a Borrower

Most lenders set the credit limit on a home equity loan or line by taking a percentage of the appraised value of the home and subtracting the balance owed on the existing mortgage. In determining your actual credit limit, the lender also will consider your ability to repay by looking at your income, debts, and other financial obligations, as well as your credit history.

Does It Make Sense To Consolidate My Debt With A Home Equity Loan?

Product	Current Monthly Debts					Home Equity Loan To Refinance All Current Debt	
	Installment Loan	Credit Card #1	Credit Card #2	=	Total Of Current Debts	Home Equity Loan	Interest & Tax Savings
Remaining Amount Owed	$8,000	$3,000	$5,000	=	$16,000	$16,000	
Annual Percentage Rate	12.00%	18.00%	16.00%			10.50%	
Monthly Payment	$178	$76	$122	=	$376	$344	
Total Interest To Pay Off	$2,677	$1,571	$2,295	=	$6,544	$4,634	$1,920
Deductible Interest*	$0	$0	$0	=	$0	$4,634	
Total Tax Savings Over Term Of Loan	$0	$0	$0	=	$0	$1,298	$1,298
						Total Savings By Consolidating Debt	$3,218

For demonstration purposes only. Individual circumstances may vary. Tax savings based on 28% tax bracket.

Can A Home Equity Loan Save Me Money When I Buy A New Car?

Product	New Car Loan (5-year term)	VS.	Home Equity To Purchase A Car (5-year term)
Amount Borrowed	$12,000		$12,000
Annual Percentage Rate	11.37%		10.50%
Monthly Payment	$263		$258
Total Interest Paid	$3,788		$3,476
Deductible Interest*	$0		$3,476
Total Tax Savings Over Term Of Loan	$0		$973
Interest Savings Over Term Of Loan			$312
Total Savings			**$1,285**

For demonstration purposes only. Individual circumstances may vary.
Tax savings based on 28% tax bracket.
Barnett Bank

How Much Can I Save With A Home Equity Loan To Pay Off My Credit Cards?

Product	Credit Card Loan (5-year term)	VS.	Home Equity Loan To Pay Off Debt (5-year term)
Amount Borrowed	$5,000		$5,000
Annual Percentage Rate	18.50%		10.50%
Monthly Payment	$127		$107
Total Interest Paid	$2,618		$1,448
Deductible Interest*	$0		$1,448
Total Tax Savings Over Term Of Loan	$0		$405
Interest Savings Over Term Of Loan			$1,170
Total Savings			**$1,575**

For demonstration purposes only. Individual circumstances may vary.
Tax savings based on 28% tax bracket.

EXHIBIT 14-3

....

BANK LOAN PROMOTIONAL LITERATURE

STEPS TO CALCULATE THE POTENTIAL AMOUNT OF CREDIT AVAILABLE TO A BORROWER:

Step 1. Calculate the percentage of appraised value by:

Percentage of appraised value = Appraised value × Lender's percentage

Step 2. Find the potential amount of credit available by:

Potential credit = Percentage of appraised value − First mortgage balance

---

EXAMPLE

Miranda Lopez owns a home that was recently appraised for $115,700. The balance on her existing mortgage is $67,875. If her bank is willing to loan up to 75% of the appraised value, what is the potential amount of credit available to Miranda on a home equity loan?

SOLUTION STRATEGY

Step 1. Percentage of appraised value = Appraised value × Lender's percentage

Percentage of appraised value = 115,700 × .75

Percentage of appraised value = $86,775

Step 2. Potential credit = Percentage of appraised value − First mortgage balance

Potential credit = 86,775 − 67,875

Potential credit = $18,900

TRY-IT EXERCISE

6. **Norm Nuelle owns a home that was recently appraised for $92,900. The balance on his existing first mortgage is $32,440. If his credit union is willing to loan up to 80% of the appraised value, what is the potential amount of credit available to Norm on a home equity line of credit?**

Check your answer with the solution on page 467.

14-7 Calculating the Housing Expense Ratio and the Total Obligations Ratio of a Borrower

Mortgage lenders use ratios to determine if borrowers have the economic ability to repay the loan. FHA, VA, and conventional lenders all use monthly gross income as the base for calculating these **qualifying ratios.** Two important ratios used for this purpose are the **housing expense ratio** and the **total obligations ratio.** These ratios are expressed as percents and are calculated using the following formulas:

qualifying ratios
Ratios used by lenders to determine if borrowers have the economic ability to repay loans.

housing expense ratio
The ratio of a borrower's monthly housing expense (PITI) to monthly gross income.

total obligations ratio
The ratio of a borrower's total monthly financial obligations to monthly gross income.

$$\text{Housing expense ratio} = \frac{\text{Monthly housing expense (PITI)}}{\text{Monthly gross income}}$$

$$\text{Total obligations ratio} = \frac{\text{Total monthly financial obligations}}{\text{Monthly gross income}}$$

The mortgage business uses widely accepted guidelines for these ratios that should not be exceeded. The ratio guidelines are as follows:

Lending Ratio Guidelines Mortgage Type	Housing Expense Ratio	Total Obligations Ratio
FHA	29%	41%
Conventional	28%	36%

Note that the ratio formulas are an application of the percentage formula; the ratio is the rate, the PITI or total obligations are the portion, and the monthly gross income is the base. With this in mind, we are able to solve for any of the variables.

EXAMPLE

Tami Dreyfus earns a gross income of $2,490.00 per month. She has made application for a mortgage with a monthly PITI of $556.00. Tami has other financial obligations totaling $387.50 per month.

a. What is Tami's housing expense ratio?
b. What is Tami's total obligations ratio?
c. According to the lending ratio guidelines above, what type of mortgage would Tami qualify for, if any?

SOLUTION STRATEGY

a. $\text{Housing expense ratio} = \dfrac{\text{Monthly housing expense (PITI)}}{\text{Monthly gross income}}$

$$\text{Housing expense ratio} = \frac{556}{2,490}$$

$$\text{Housing expense ratio} = .2232 = \underline{\underline{22.3\%}}$$

b. $\text{Total obligations ratio} = \dfrac{\text{Total monthly financial obligations}}{\text{Monthly gross income}}$

$$\text{Total obligations ratio} = \frac{556 + 387.50}{2,490} = \frac{943.50}{2,490}$$

$$\text{Total obligations ratio} = .3789 = \underline{\underline{37.9\%}}$$

c. According to the lending ratio guidelines, Tami would qualify for an FHA mortgage but not a conventional mortgage; her total obligations ratio is 37.9%, which is above the limit for conventional mortgages.

TRY-IT   **EXERCISE**

7. **Howard Lockwood earns a gross income of $3,100.00 per month. He has made application for a mortgage with a monthly PITI of $669.00. Howard has other financial obligations totaling $375.00 per month.**

   a. What is Howard's housing expense ratio?

   b. What is Howard's total obligations ratio?

   c. According to the ratio guidelines, what type of mortgage would Howard qualify for, if any?

Check your answers with the solutions on page 468.

REVIEW EXERCISES   CHAPTER 14—SECTION II

For the following second mortgage applications, calculate the percentage of appraised value and the potential credit:

	Appraised Value	Lender's Percentage	Percentage of Appraised Value	Balance of First Mortgage	Potential Credit
1.	$118,700	75%	$89,025.00	$67,900	$21,125.00
2.	$89,400	65%	$58,110.00	$37,800	$20,310.00
3.	$141,200	80%	$112,960.00	$99,100	$13,860.02
4.	$324,600	75%	$243,450.00	$197,500	$45,950.02
5.	$98,000	65%	$63,700.00	$66,000	-0-

For the following mortgage applications, calculate the housing expense ratio and the total expense ratio:

Applicant	Monthly Gross Income	Monthly (PITI) Expense	Other Monthly Financial Obligations	Housing Expense Ratio	Total Obligations Ratio
6. Johnson	$2,000	$455	$380	22.75%	41.75%
7. Wilson	$3,700	$530	$360	14.32%	24.05%
8. Turnberry	$3,100	$705	$720	22.74%	45.97%
9. Gomez	$4,800	$1,250	$430	26.04%	35%
10. Black	$2,900	$644	$290	22.21%	32.21%

6.

Housing expense ratio $= \dfrac{\text{PITI}}{\text{monthly gross income}}$

Total obligations ratio $=$

$\dfrac{\text{Total monthly finance oblig.}}{\text{monthly gross income}}$

Housing expense ratio (HER) $=$

$\dfrac{455.00}{2000.00} = \underline{\underline{22.75\%}}$

Total obligations ratio (TOB) $=$

$\dfrac{455.00 + 380.00}{2,000.00} = \underline{\underline{41.75\%}}$

11. From the lending ratio guidelines on page 460:

　　a. Which of the applicants in questions 6–10 would *not* qualify for a conventional mortgage?

　　　6 and 8　Johnson and Turnberry

　　b. Which of the applicants in questions 6–10 would *not* qualify for any mortgage?

　　　6 and 8　Johnson and Turnberry

12. The Hamptons own a home that was recently appraised for $219,000. The balance on their existing first mortgage is $143,250. If their bank is willing to loan up to 65% of the appraised value, what is the potential amount of credit available to the Hamptons on a home equity loan?

　　$219,000.00 \times .65 =$　　　$142,350.00
　　　　　　　　　　　　　$- \$143,250.00$
　　　　　　　　　　　　　$- \$900.00$
　　Potential credit available $=$　　$\underline{\underline{0}}$

13. Pauline Mula is thinking about building an addition on her home. The home was recently appraised at $154,000 and the balance on her existing first mortgage is $88,600. If Pauline's bank is willing to loan 70% of the appraised value, does she have enough equity in the house to finance a $25,000 addition?

　　$154,000.00 \times .70 =$　　$107,800.00
　　　　　　　　　　　　　$- \$88,600.00$
　　Potential credit available $= \underline{\$19,200.00}$
　　No to the addition

14. Butch Porter earns a gross income of $4,890.00 per month. He has submitted an application for a mortgage with a monthly PITI of $1,259.00. Butch has other financial obligations totaling $654.50 per month.

　　a. What is his housing expense ratio?

　　　Housing expense ratio $= \dfrac{1,259.00}{4,890.00} = \underline{\underline{25.75\%}}$

　　b. What is his total obligations ratio?

　　　Total obligations ratio $= \dfrac{1,259.00 + 654.50}{4,890.00} = \underline{\underline{39.13\%}}$

c. According to the lending ratio guidelines on page 460, for what type of mortgage would Butch qualify, if any?

He qualifies for an FHA mortgage.

CHAPTER 14 ■ MORTGAGES

FORMULAS

Monthly payment = Number of $1,000s financed × Table 15-1 factor

Total interest = (Monthly payment × Number of payments) − Amount financed

$$\text{Monthly taxes and insurance (TI)} = \frac{\text{Estimated property tax + Hazard insurance}}{12}$$

Monthly PITI = Monthly PI + Monthly TI

ARM-Calculated interest rate = Index rate + Lender's margin

ARM-Maximum rate per adjustment period = Previous rate + Periodic cap

ARM-Maximum overall rate = Initial rate + Overall cap

Percentage of appraised value = Appraised value × Lender's percentage

Second mortgage potential credit = Percentage of appraised value − First mtg. balance

$$\text{Housing expense ratio} = \frac{\text{Monthly housing expense (PITI)}}{\text{Monthly gross income}}$$

$$\text{Total obligations ratio} = \frac{\text{Total monthly financial obligations}}{\text{Monthly gross income}}$$

CHAPTER 14 ■ MORTGAGES	SUMMARY CHART

SECTION I MORTGAGES: FIXED-RATE AND ADJUSTABLE-RATE

Topic	P/O, Page	Important Concepts	Illustrative Examples
Calculating the Monthly Payment and Total Interest Paid on a Fixed-Rate Mortgage	14–1 446	1. Find the number of $1,000s financed by: $$\text{Number of \$1,000s} = \frac{\text{Amount financed}}{1,000}$$ 2. From Table 14–1, locate the table factor, monthly payment per $1,000 financed, at the intersection of the number of years column and the interest rate row. 3. Calculate the monthly payment by: $$\text{Monthly payment} = \text{Number of 1,000s financed} \times \text{Table factor}$$ 4. Find the total interest of the loan by: $$\text{Total interest} = \left(\text{Monthly payments} \times \text{Number of payments} \right) - \text{Amount financed}$$	What is the monthly payment and total interest on a $100,000 mortgage at $9\frac{1}{2}\%$ for 30 years? Number of 1,000s = $$\frac{100,000}{1,000} = 100$$ Table factor: $9\frac{1}{2}\%$, 30 years = 8.41 Monthly payment $= 100 \times 8.41 = \underline{\$841.00}$ Total interest of the loan = $(841 \times 360) - 100,000 =$ $302,760 - 100,000 = \$202,760$

I, continued

Topic	P/O, Page	Important Concepts	Illustrative Examples
Preparing a Partial Amortization Schedule of a Mortgage	14–2 448	1. Calculate the monthly payment of the loan as before. 2. Calculate the amount of interest for the current month using $I = PRT$, where P is the current outstanding balance of the loan, R is the annual interest rate, and T is $\frac{1}{12}$. 3. Find the portion of the payment used to reduce principal by: $$\text{Portion of payment reducing principal} = \text{Monthly payment} - \text{Interest}$$ 4. Calculate outstanding balance of the loan by: $$\text{Outstanding balance} = \text{Previous balance} - \text{Portion of payment reducing principal}$$ 5. Repeat Steps 2, 3, and 4 for each succeeding month and enter the values on a schedule labeled appropriately.	Prepare an amortization schedule for the first month of a $70,000 mortgage at 9% for 20 years. Using Table 14–1, we find the monthly payment of the mortgage to be $630. *Month 1:* Interest = Principal × Rate × Time Interest = $70,000 \times .09 \times \frac{1}{12}$ Interest = $525.00 Portion of payment reducing principal $630.00 - 525.00 = $105.00 Outstanding balance after 1 payment = $70,000.00 - 105.00$ $= $69,895.00 An amortization schedule can now be prepared from this data.
Calculating the Monthly PITI of a Mortgage	14–3 450	In reality, mortgage payments include 4 elements: principal, interest, taxes, and insurance, thus the abbreviation PITI. *Monthly PITI of a mortgage:* 1. Calculate the principal and interest portion (PI) of the payment as before, using Table 14–1. 2. Calculate the monthly tax and insurance portion (TI) by: $$\text{Monthly TI} = \frac{\text{Estimated property tax} + \text{Hazard insurance}}{12}$$ 3. Calculate the total monthly PITI by: Monthly PITI = Monthly PI + Monthly TI	Betty Winn purchased a home for $97,500 with a mortgage at $8\frac{1}{2}\%$ for 15 years. The property taxes are $1,950 per year and the hazard insurance premium is $466. What is the monthly PITI payment of Betty's loan? Using a table factor of 9.85 from Table 14–1, we find the monthly PI for Betty's $8\frac{1}{2}\%$, 15-year mortgage to be $960.38. $$\text{Monthly TI} = \frac{1950 + 466}{12}$$ $$= \frac{2{,}416}{12} = $201.33$$ Monthly PITI = PI + TI $= 960.38 + 201.33$ $= $1161.71

I, continued

Topic	P/O, Page	Important Concepts	Illustrative Examples
Calculating the Amount Due at Closing	14–4 451	Closing costs are the expenses incurred in conjunction with the sale of real estate. Both buyer and seller are responsible for certain of these costs. The party responsible for paying a particular closing cost is often determined by local custom or by negotiation. Some closing costs are expressed as dollar amounts, while others are a percent of the amount financed or the amount of the purchase price. At closing, the buyer is responsible for the purchase price (mortgage + down payment) plus closing costs. The amount received by the seller after all expenses have been paid is known as the proceeds.	*Typical Closing Costs* *Buyer:* Attorney's fee, inspections, credit report, appraisal fee, hazard insurance premium, title exam and insurance premium, escrow fee, prepaid taxes and interest. *Seller:* Attorney's fee, broker's commission, survey expense, inspections, abstract of title, certificate of title, escrow fee, prepayment penalty–existing loan, documentary stamps.
Calculating the Interest Rate of an Adjustable-Rate Mortgage (ARM)	14–5 454	Use the following formulas to find the various components of an ARM: $\text{Calculated interest rate} = \text{Index rate} + \text{Lender's margin}$ $\text{Max rate per period} = \text{Previous rate} + \text{Periodic cap}$ $\text{Maximum overall rate of ARM} = \text{Initial rate} + \text{Overall cap}$	Jane Mangrum bought a home with an adjustable-rate mortgage. The margin on the loan is 3.5% and the rate cap is 8% over the life of the loan. If the current index rate is 3.6%, what is the calculated interest rate and the maximum overall rate of the loan? Calculated interest rate = $\quad 3.6\% + 3.5\% = \underline{7.1\%}$ Maximum overall rate = $\quad 7.1\% + 8\% = \underline{15.1\%}$

SECTION II SECOND MORTGAGES: HOME EQUITY LOANS AND LINES OF CREDIT

Topic	P/O, Page	Important Concepts	Illustrative Examples
Calculating the Potential Amount of Credit Available to a Borrower	14–6 458	Most lenders set the credit limit on a home equity loan or line by taking a percentage of the appraised value of the home and subtracting the balance owed on the existing first mortgage. In determining your actual credit limit, the lender also will consider your ability to repay by looking at your income, debts, and other financial obligations, as well as your credit history. *Potential amount of credit available to borrower:* 1. Calculate the percentage of appraised value by: $\text{Percentage of appraised value} = \text{Appraised value} \times \text{Lender's percentage}$ 2. Find the potential amount of credit available by: $\text{Potential credit} = \text{Percentage of appraised value} - \text{First mortgage debt}$	The Jacksons own a home that was recently appraised for $134,800. The balance on their existing first mortgage is $76,550. If their bank is willing to loan up to 70% of the appraised value, what is the potential amount of credit available to the Jacksons on a home equity loan? Percentage of appraised value = $\quad 134{,}800 \times .70 = \$94{,}360$ Potential credit = $94{,}360 - 76{,}550 = \underline{\$17{,}810}$

II, continued

Topic	P/O, Page	Important Concepts	Illustrative Examples
Calculating the Housing Expense Ratio and the Total Obligations Ratio of a Borrower	14–7 460	Mortgage lenders use ratios to determine if borrowers have the economic ability to repay the loan. Two important ratios used for this purpose are the housing expense ratio and the total obligations ratio. These ratios are expressed as percents, and are calculated using the following formulas: $$\text{Housing expense ratio} = \frac{\text{Monthly housing expense (PITI)}}{\text{Monthly gross income}}$$ $$\text{Total obligations ratio} = \frac{\text{Total monthly financial obligations}}{\text{Monthly gross income}}$$	Traci Kampai earns a gross income of $3,750.00 per month. She has made application for a mortgage with a monthly PITI of $956.00. Traci has other financial obligations totaling $447.00 per month. a. What is her housing expense ratio? b. What is her total obligations ratio? c. According to the ratio guidelines on page 558, for what type of mortgage would Traci qualify, if any? Housing exp. ratio = $$\frac{956}{3,750} = \underline{25.5\%}$$ Tot. oblig. ratio = $\dfrac{1,403}{3.750} = \underline{37.4\%}$ According to the ratio guidelines, Traci would qualify for an FHA mortgage but not a conventional mortgage; her total obligations ratio is 37.4%, which is above the limit for conventional mortgages.

TRY-IT EXERCISE   SOLUTIONS

1. $\text{Number of 1,000s financed} = \dfrac{\text{Amount financed}}{1,000}$

$\text{Number of 1,000s financed} = \dfrac{85,500}{1000} = 85.5$

Table factor 7%, 25 years = 7.07

Monthly payment = Number of 1,000s financed × Table factor
Monthly payment = 85.5 × 7.07 = $\underline{\$604.49}$

Total interest = (Monthly payment × Number of payments) − Amount financed
Total interest = (604.49 × 300) − 85,500
Total interest = 181,347 − 85,500 = $\underline{\$95,847}$

2. $\text{Number of 1,000s financed} = \dfrac{75,000}{1,000} = 75$

Table factor 9%, 15 years = 10.15
Monthly payment = 75 × 10.15 = 761.25
Month 1

$I = PRT = 75,000 \times .09 \times \frac{1}{12} = \$562.50$

Portion of payment reducing principal = 761.25 − 562.50 = $198.75
Outstanding balance = 75,000 − 198.75 = $74,801.25

Month 2

$$I = PRT = 74,801.25 \times .09 \times \tfrac{1}{12} = \$561.01$$

Portion of payment reducing principal = 761.25 − 561.01 = \$200.24
Outstanding balance = 74,801.25 − 200.24 = \$74,601.01

Month 3

$$I = PRT = 74,601.01 \times .09 \times \tfrac{1}{12} = \$559.51$$

Portion of payment reducing principal = 761.25 − 559.51 = \$201.74
Outstanding balance = 74,601.01 − 201.74 = \$74,399.27

Month 4

$$I = PRT = 74,399.27 \times .09 \times \tfrac{1}{12} = \$557.99$$

Portion of payment reducing principal = 761.25 − 557.99 = \$203.26
Outstanding balance = 74,399.27 − 203.26 = \$74,196.01

Amortization Schedule
\$75,000, 9%, 15 years

Payment Number	Monthly Payment	Monthly Interest	Portion Used to Reduce Principal	Loan Balance
0				\$75,000.00
1	\$761.25	\$562.50	\$198.75	\$74,801.25
2	\$761.25	\$561.01	\$200.24	\$74,601.01
3	\$761.25	\$559.51	\$201.74	\$74,399.27
4	\$761.25	\$557.99	\$203.26	\$74,196.01

3. Number of 1,000s = $\dfrac{125,600}{1000}$ = 125.6

Table factor $9\tfrac{1}{4}\%$, 20 years = 9.16

Monthly payment (PI) = 125.6 × 9.16 = \$1,150.50

Monthly TI = $\dfrac{\text{Property tax} + \text{Hazard insurance}}{12}$

Monthly TI = $\dfrac{3,250 + 765}{12} = \dfrac{4,015}{12}$ = \$334.58

Monthly PITI = PI + TI = 1,150.50 + 334.58 = $\underline{\$1,485.08}$

4. a. Down payment = 120,000 × 20% = \$24,000
Amount financed = 120,000 − 24,000 = \$96,000
Closing Costs, Buyer:
Discount points (96,000 × 3%) \$2,880.00
Down payment (24,000 − 10,000) . . .\$14,000.00
Application fee \$100.00
Condominium transfer fee \$190.00
Title insurance (96,000 × 3/4%) \$720.00
Hazard insurance \$420.00
Prepaid taxes \$310.00
Attorney's fees \$500.00
Due at closing: \$19,120.00

b. *Proceeds, Seller:*
Purchase price \$120,000.00
Less: Broker's commission
$120,000 \times 5\tfrac{1}{2}\%$ . . .\$6,600.00
Closing costs \$670.00
Mortgage payoff   \$65,000.00
−\$72,270.00
Proceeds to seller: \$47,730.00

5. a. Calculated ARM rate = Index rate + Margin
Calculated ARM rate = 3.2 + 3.4 = $\underline{6.6\%}$

b. Maximum overall rate = Calculated rate + Overall cap
Maximum overall rate = 6.6 + 7.0 = $\underline{13.6\%}$

6. Percentage of appraised value = Appraised value × Lender's percentage
Percentage of appraised value = 92,900 × 80% = \$74,320
Potential credit = Percentage of appraised value − First mtg. balance
Potential credit = 74,320 − 32,440 = $\underline{\$41,880.00}$

7. a. Housing expense ratio $= \dfrac{\text{Monthly housing expense (PITI)}}{\text{Monthly gross income}}$

Housing expense ratio $= \dfrac{669}{3100} = \underline{\underline{21.6\%}}$

b. Total obligations ratio $= \dfrac{\text{Total monthly financial obligations}}{\text{Monthly gross income}}$

Total obligations ratio $= \dfrac{669 + 375}{3,100} = \dfrac{1044}{3100} = \underline{\underline{33.7\%}}$

c. According to guidelines, Howard would qualify for both <u>FHA and conventional mortgages.</u>

You are one of the branch managers of the Fuji Bank. Today two loan applications were submitted to your office. Calculate the requested information for each loan:

	Amount Financed	Interest Rate	Term of Loan	Number of $1,000s Financed	Table Factor	Monthly Payment	Total Interest
1.	$134,900	$7\frac{3}{4}\%$	25 years	134.9	7.56	$1,019.84	$171,052.00
2.	$79,500	$8\frac{1}{4}\%$	20 years	79.5	8.53	$678.14	$83,253.60

3. Shirley Webster purchased a home with a $146,100 mortgage at $11\frac{1}{2}\%$ for 30 years. Calculate the monthly payment and prepare an amortization schedule for the first 3 months of Shirley's loan.

Payment Number	Monthly Payment	Monthly Interest	Portion Used to Reduce Principal	Loan Balance
0				$146,100
1	$1,447.85	$1,400.13	$47.72	$146,052.28
2	$1,447.85	$1,399.67	$48.18	$146,004.10
3	$1,447.85	$1,399.21	$48.64	$145,955.46

Calculate the monthly principal and interest using Table 14-1 and the monthly PITI for the following mortgages:

	Amount Financed	Interest Rate	Term of Loan	Monthly PI	Annual Property Tax	Annual Insurance	Monthly PITI
4.	$54,200	9%	25 years	$455.28	$719	$459	$553.45
5.	$132,100	$8\frac{3}{4}\%$	15 years	$1,321.00	$2,275	$1,033	$1,596.67

For the following second mortgage applications, calculate the percentage of appraised value and the potential credit:

	Appraised Value	Lender's Percentage	Percentage of Appraised Value	Amount of First Mortgage	Potential Credit
6.	$114,500	65%	$74,425.00	$77,900	0
7.	$51,500	80%	$41,200.00	$27,400	$13,800.00
8.	$81,200	70%	$56,840.00	$36,000	$20,840.00

For the following mortgage applications, calculate the housing expense ratio and the total expense ratio:

Applicant	Monthly Gross Income	Monthly (PITI) Expense	Other Monthly Financial Obligations	Housing Expense Ratio	Total Obligations Ratio
9. Morgan	$5,300	$1,288	$840	24.30%	40.15%
10. Willow	$3,750	$952	$329	25.39%	34.16%

11. As a loan officer using the lending ratio guidelines on page 460, what type of mortgage can you offer Morgan and Willow, from questions 9 and 10?

Morgan qualifies for FHA
Willow qualifies for FHA and Conventional

12. Chuck Pensinger bought a home with an adjustable rate mortgage. The margin on the loan is 3.9% and the rate cap is 6% over the life of the loan.

a. If the current index rate is 4.45%, what is the calculated interest rate of the ARM?

Calculated interest rate = 4.45% + 3.9%
= 8.35%

ANSWERS

1. _____ 134.9 _____
_____ 7.56 _____
_____ $1,019.84 _____
_____ $171,052.00 _____
2. _____ 79.5 _____
_____ 8.53 _____
_____ $678.14 _____
_____ $83,253.60 _____
3. ____ Month 1: $146,052.28 ____
____ Month 2: $146,004.10 ____
____ Month 3: $145,955.46 ____
4. _____ $455.28 _____
_____ $553.45 _____
5. _____ $1,321.00 _____
_____ $1,596.67 _____
6. _____ $74,425.00 _____
_____ 0 _____
7. _____ $41,200.00 _____
_____ $13,800.00 _____
8. _____ $56,840.00 _____
_____ $20,840.00 _____
9. _____ 24.3% _____
_____ 40.15% _____
10. _____ 25.39% _____
_____ 34.16% _____
11. _____ Morgan: FHA _____
____ Willow: FHA and Conventional ____
12. a. _____ 8.35% _____

Complete, worked out solutions to exercises 1–2, 4–10 appear in the appendix following the index.

b. What is the maximum overall rate of Chuck's loan?

Maximum overall rate = 8.35% + 6%

= 14.35%

13. Royal Properties purchased a 24-unit apartment building for $650,000. After a 20% down payment the balance was financed with a 20-year, $10\frac{1}{2}$% fixed-rate mortgage.

a. What is the amount of the monthly principal and interest portion of the loan?

Amount financed = 650,000.00 × 80% = $520,000.00
Number of $1,000s financed = 520
10.5%, 20 year table factor = 9.99
520 × 9.99 = $5,194.80 Monthly PI

b. Construct an amortization schedule for the first 2 months of Royal's mortgage:

Payment Number	Monthly Payment	Monthly Interest	Portion Used to Reduce Principal	Loan Balance
0				$520,000
1	$5,194.80	$4,550.00	$644.80	$519,355.20
2	$5,194.80	$4,544.36	$650.44	$518,704.76

c. If the annual property taxes are $9,177 and the hazard insurance premium is $2,253 per year, what is the total monthly PITI of the loan?

$$\text{Monthly PITI} = 5,194.80 + \frac{9,177.00 + 2,253.00}{12}$$

$$= \$6,147.30$$

d. If each apartment rents for $425 per month, how much income will Royal make per month after the PITI is paid on the building?

24 units × 425.00 = 10,200
− 6,147.30 PITI
Excess monthly income $4,052.70

14. Patty Powder purchased a ski lodge in Mountain Peak for $74,900. Her bank is willing to finance 70% of the purchase price. As part of the mortgage closing costs Patty had to pay $4\frac{1}{4}$ discount points. How much did this amount to?

74,900.00 × 70% = 52,430.00 × 4.25%
Points = $2,228.28

15. A Burger King franchisee is looking for a 20-year mortgage, with 90% financing, to purchase a new location costing $775,000. The Red River Bank is offering a $10\frac{1}{4}$% mortgage with $1\frac{1}{2}$ discount points; Sterling Savings and Loan is offering a 10% mortgage with 4 closing points. The franchisee is unsure which mortgage is a better deal and has asked for your help.

a. What is the total interest paid on each loan?

Red River Bank		Sterling Savings	
775,000.00 × 90% = $697,500.00		697,500.00 Amount of loan	
$10\frac{1}{4}$% 20 years = 9.82		10% 20 years = 9.66	
9.82 × 697.5	= 6,849.45 × 20 × 12	9.66 × 697.5	= 6,737.85 × 20 × 12
Total payments	= 1,643,868.00		= 1,617,084.00
Amount of loan	− 697,500.00	Amount of loan −	697,500.00
Total interest	= $946,368.00	Total interest	= $919,584.00

b. Taking into account the discount points, which lender is offering a better deal and by how much?

Red River Bank	Sterling Savings
Points = 1.5% × 697,500.00 = $10,462.50	Points = 4% × 697,500.00 = $27,900.00
Interest = 946,368.00	Interest = 919,584.00
Total cost = $956,830.50	Total cost = $947,484.00

956,830.50 − 947,484.00 = <u>Sterling</u> is better by <u>$9,346.50</u>

16. How much more total interest will be paid on a 30-year fixed-rate mortgage for $100,000 at 11% compared to a 15-year mortgage at $9\frac{1}{2}$%?

15 years	30 years	
100,000.00 at 9.5%	100,000.00 at 11%	
10.45 × 100 = 1,045.00	9.53 × 100 = 953.00	
15 × 12 × 1,045.00 = 188,100.00	30 × 12 × 953.00 = 343,080.00	243,080.00 − 88,100.00
− 100,000.00	− 100,000.00	
Interest = $88,100.00	Interest = $243,080.00	= $154,980.00 More on 30 years

17. The Waltons own a home that recently appraised for $161,400. The balance on their existing first mortgage is $115,200. If their bank is willing to loan up to 70% of the appraised value, what is the potential amount of credit available to the Waltons on a home equity line of credit?

161,400.00 × 70% = $112,980.00
Loan balance $115,200.00
Potential credit <u>0</u>

18. Nancy De LaVega is purchasing a $134,000 home. The down payment is 20% and the balance will be financed with a 20-year fixed-rate mortgage at $8\frac{3}{4}$% and 3 discount points. The annual property tax is $1,940 and the hazard insurance premium is $1,460. When Nancy signed the original sales contract she put down a deposit of $10,000, which will be credited to her down payment. In addition, at the time of closing she must pay the following expenses:

Appraisal fee	$165.00
Credit report	$75.00
Attorney's fees	$490.00
Roof inspection	$50.00
Mortgage insurance premium	1.2% of amount financed
Termite inspection	$88.00
Title search	$119.00
Documentary stamps	$\frac{1}{4}$% of amount financed

As Nancy's real estate agent, she has asked you the following:

a. What is the total monthly PITI of the mortgage loan?

$$\frac{134,000.00 \times 80\%}{1,000} = 107.2 \quad \text{\# of 1,000s}$$

107.2 × 8.84 = $947.65 = PI

$$\text{PITI} = 947.65 + \frac{1,940.00 + 1,460.00}{12} = \underline{\$1,230.98}$$

b. What is the total amount of interest that will be paid on the loan?

Total payments = 20 × 12 × 947.65
  = $227,436.00
Amount financed − $107,200.00
Total interest = $120,236.00

c. How much is due at the time of the closing?

Appraisal fee	165.00	Title search	119.00
Credit report	75.00	Doc stamps	268.00
Attorney's fees	490.00	Points	3,216.00 (107,200 × .03)
Roof inspection	50.00	Down payment	+ 26,800.00
Mortgage Ins.	1,286.40 (107,200 × .012)		32,557.40
Termite Ins.	88.00	Deposit	− 10,000.00
		Due at closing	$22,557.40

ANSWERS

b. <u>Sterling is better by $9,346.50</u>

16. <u>$154,980.00 More on 30 years</u>

17. _____0_____

18. a. _____$1,230.98_____

b. _____$120,236.00_____

c. _____$22,557.40_____

d. If the sellers are responsible for the 6% broker's commission, $900 in closing costs, and the existing first mortgage with a balance of $45,000, what proceeds will be received on the sale of the property?

Sale price	$134,000.00
Less: Closing costs –	900.00
Broker fees –	8,040.00 (134,000 × .06)
First mortgage –	45,000.00
Seller's proceeds	$80,060.00

19. Chuck Wells earns a gross income of $5,355.00 per month. He has submitted an application for a fixed-rate mortgage with a monthly PITI of $1,492.00. Chuck has other financial obligations totaling $625.00 per month.

a. What is his housing expense ratio?

$$\text{Housing expense ratio} = \frac{1,492.00}{5,355.00} = \underline{\underline{27.86\%}}$$

b. What is his total obligations ratio?

$$\text{Total obligations ratio} = \frac{1,492.00 + 625.00}{5,355.00} = \underline{\underline{39.53\%}}$$

c. According to the lending ratio guidelines on page 460, for what type of mortgage would Chuck qualify, if any?

FHA

 BUSINESS DECISION
What Size Mortgage Can You Qualify For?

20. You are applying for a conventional mortgage from the First National Bank. Your monthly gross income is $3,500, and the bank uses the 28% housing expense ratio guideline.

a. What is the highest PITI you can qualify for? Hint: Solve the housing expense ratio formula for PITI. (Remember, this is an application of the percentage formula, Portion = Rate × Base, where PITI is the portion, the expense ratio is the rate, and your monthly gross income is the base.)

$$P = B \times R$$
$$P = 3,500.00 \times 28\%$$
$$\text{PITI} = \underline{\underline{\$980.00}}$$

b. Based on your answer from part **a,** if you are applying for a 30-year, 9% mortgage, and the taxes and insurance portion of PITI is $175 per month, use Table 14-1 to calculate what size mortgage you qualify for. Hint: Subtract TI from PITI. Divide the PI by the appropriate table factor to determine how many $1,000s you qualify to borrow.

PI = 980 – 175 = 805.00   Mortgage can be $100,000.00 maximum

Factor = 8.05

$$\text{Number of \$1,000s} = \frac{805.00}{8.05} = 100$$

c. Based on your answer from part **b,** if you are planning on a 20% down payment, what is the most expensive house you can afford? Hint: Use the percentage formula again. The purchase price of the house is the base, the amount financed is the portion, and the percent financed is the rate.

$$B = \frac{P}{R} \qquad B = \frac{100,000.00}{80\%} = \$125,000.00$$

Maximum price of house = $125,000.00

Career Track:
Loan Officer

Nature of the Work

Loan officers usually specialize in commercial, consumer, or mortgage loans. Their primary duties are to prepare, analyze, and verify loan applications, make decisions regarding the extension of credit, and help borrowers fill out loan applications.

Loan officers must keep informed of changing rules and regulations in their industry as well as new financial priducts and services being offered. To meet their customers' needs, for example, banks and other lending institutions offer a variety of mortgage products.

Training, Other Qualifications, and Advancement

Most loan officer positions require a bachelor's degree in finance, economics, or a related field. Most employers also prefer applicants who are familiar with computers and their applications in banking. Many loan officers advance through the ranks in an

organization, acquiring several years of work experience in various other occupations, such as teller or customer service representative.

Job Outlook

Employment of loan officers is expected to grow faster than the average for all occupations through the year 2005. Growth in the variety and complexity of loans and the importance of loan officers to the success of banks and other lending institutions also should assure rapid employment growth. College graduates and those with banking or lending experience should have the best job prospects.

SOURCE: *Occupational Outlook Handbook*, 1994-95 Edition, U.S. Department of Labor.

"Quote...Unquote"

What we anticipate seldom occurs; what we least expected generally happens.
–Disraeli

A verbal agreement isn't worth the paper it's written on.
–Samuel Goldwyn

Bridge the Gap

Did you know, you don't necessarily have to sell your existing home before you purchase a new one? Many banks offer interim financing known as a bridge loan. These short-term loans allow you to borrow as much as 90 percent of the equity in your old house to complete the purchase of your new house.

If your existing home is expected to close quckly, one option is to choose a 90-day term bridge loan, which usually can be renewed for two additional 90-day periods, if you require more time. Some banks also offer a 180-day bridge loan with one renewal opportunity.

An interesting feature of the bridge loan is that you don't have two mortgage payments at the same time. The bridge loan allows you to pay "interest only" each month, until your old home is sold.

Brainteaser

As the manager of a 100-unit apartment building, you have been asked by the owner to install new numbers on each front door. If the apartments are numbered consecutively from 1 to 100, how many nines do you need?

SOURCE: James Fixx, *Games for the Super Intelligent,* New York: Doubleday, 1972

Answer to Last Issue's Brainteaser
1967

A Little Extra Saves A Lot!

Paying off your mortgage a little faster can save you thousands of dollars in interest and years of payments. One way of accomplishing this goal is to switch your current monthly payment mortgage to biweekly.

Normally, mortgage payments are made once a month, 12 times per year. A biweekly mortgage requires a payment every two weeks in an amount equal to one half the monthly payment. For example, if the monthly payment on a mortgage is $900, the biweekly payment would be $450. Since there are 52 weeks in a year, with a biweekly mortgage you make 26 half payments per year, or the equivalent of 13 full payments. Although it may not seem like much, this accelerated rate of payment pays off a 30-year mortgage in only 18 years.

A little extra each month can go a long way! Rather than a biweekly mortgage, you can accomplish the same result by sending in an additional $25, $50, or $100 with each regular monthly payment. Be sure to specify to the lender that this extra amount should be used to "reduce the prinicpal."

How well does this work? Let's say, for example, you have an $85,000 mortgage for 30 years, at 8 percent interest. By sending and extra $50 in principle each month, you would save over $38,000 in interest, and pay off the loan 83 months earlier. By sending $100 extra each month, you save over $58,000 in interest, and cut 130 months off the term of the loan.

Chapter 15

Financial Statements and Ratios

Performance Objectives

Financial statements are the periodic report cards of how a business is doing from a monetary perspective. After all, money is the primary way in which the score is kept in the competitive arena of business. These important statements are a summary of a company's financial data compiled from business activity over a period of time.

The four major financial statements used in business today are the balance sheet, the income statement, the owner's equity statement, and the cash flow statement. Together they tell a story about how a company has performed in the past and is likely to perform in the near future. In this chapter, we shall focus our attention on the preparation and analysis of the balance sheet and the income statement. At the end of each set of review exercises is a feature entitled The Annual Report. These are actual financial statements from the annual reports of well-known companies representing various industries. Here you will have an opportunity to examine some real-world statements and apply your own analytical skills.

Typically, a company's accounting department prepares financial statements quarterly for the purpose of management review and government reporting of income tax information. At the end of each year, the accounting department prepares annual financial statements in order to present the company's yearly financial position and performance. Public corporations, those whose stock can be bought and sold by the general investing public, are required by law to make their statements available to the stockholders and the financial community in the form of quarterly and annual reports. Since they are public information, condensed versions of these reports often appear in financial publications such as *The Wall Street Journal, Business Week, Forbes,* and *Fortune.*

Financial analysis is the assessment of a company's past, present, and anticipated future financial condition based on the information found on the financial statements. Financial ratios are the primary tool of this analysis. These ratios are a way of standardizing financial data so that they may be compared to ratios from previous operating periods of the same firm, or from other similar-size firms in the same industry.

Internally, owners and managers rely on this analysis to evaluate a company's financial strengths and weaknesses and to help make sound business decisions. From outside the firm, creditors and investors use financial statements and ratios to determine a company's creditworthiness or investment potential.

● **financial statements**
A series of accounting reports summarizing a company's financial data compiled from business activity over a period of time. The four most common are the balance sheet, the income statement, the owner's equity statement, and the cash flow statement.

● **financial analysis**
The assessment of a company's past, present, and anticipated future financial condition based on the information found on the financial statements.

● **balance sheet**
A financial statement illustrating the financial position of a company in terms of assets, liabilities, and owner's equity as of a certain date.

● **financial position**
The economic resources owned by a company and the claims against those resources at a specific point in time.

THE BALANCE SHEET

The **balance sheet** is the financial statement that lists a company's financial position on a certain date, usually at the end of a month, a quarter, or a year. In order to fully understand the balance sheet, we must first examine some basic accounting theory.

Financial position refers to the economic resources owned by a company and the claims against those resources at a specific point in time. *Equities* is another term for claims. Keep in mind that a firm's economic resources must always be equal to its equities. A business enterprise can therefore be pictured as an equation:

$$\text{Economic resources} = \text{Equities}$$

There are two types of equities: the rights of the **creditors** (those who are owed money by the business) and the rights of the owners. The rights of the creditors are known as **liabilities** and represent debts of the business. The rights of the owners are known as **owner's equity.** Owner's equity represents the resources invested in the business by the owners. Theoretically, owner's equity is what would be left over after all the liabilities were paid to the creditors. We can now enhance our equation:

$$\text{Economic resources} = \text{Liabilities} + \text{Owner's equity}$$

● **creditor**
One to whom money is owed.

● **liabilities**
Debts or obligations of a business resulting from past transactions that require the company to pay money, provide goods, or perform services in the future.

● **owner's equity**
The resources claimed by the owner against the assets of a business:
Owner's equity = Assets − Liabilities.
Also called proprietorship, capital, or net worth.

assets

Economic resources, such as cash, inventories, and land, buildings, and equipment owned by a business.

accounting equation

Algebraic expression of a company's financial position:

Assets = Liabilities + Owner's equity.

In accounting terminology the economic resources owned by a business are known as the **assets.** Our equation now becomes

$$\text{Assets} = \text{Liabilities} + \text{Owner's Equity}$$

This all-important equation is known as the **accounting equation.** The balance sheet is a visual presentation of this equation at a point in time. Some balance sheets display the assets on the left and the liabilities and owner's equity on the right. Another popular format lists the assets on the top and the liabilities and owner's equity below. Remember, on a balance sheet the assets must always be equal to the liabilities plus owner's equity.

T 15-1 Preparing a Balance Sheet

Let's begin by looking at an example of a typical balance sheet and then examining each section and its components more closely. A balance sheet for a corporation, Hypothetical Enterprises, Inc., follows. Carefully look over the statement. Next, read the descriptions of the Balance Sheet Components, pages 477–478, and the Steps to Prepare a Balance Sheet, page 478. Then follow the Example and attempt the Try-It Exercise.

Hypothetical Enterprises, Inc.
Balance Sheet
December 31, 199X

Assets

Current Assets		
Cash	$ 13,000	
Accounts Receivable	32,500	
Merchandise Inventory	50,600	
Prepaid Expenses	1,200	
Supplies	4,000	
Total Current Assets		$101,300
Property, Plant, and Equipment		
Land	40,000	
Buildings	125,000	
Machinery and Equipment	60,000	
Total Property, Plant, and Equipment		225,000
Investments and Other Assets		
Investments	10,000	
Intangible Assets	5,000	
Total Investments and Other Assets		15,000
Total Assets		$341,300

Liabilities and Owner's Equity

Current Liabilities		
Accounts Payable	$ 17,500	
Salaries Payable	5,400	
Taxes Payable	6,500	
Total Current Liabilities		$ 29,400
Long-Term Liabilities		
Mortgage Payable	115,000	
Debenture Bond	20,000	
Total Long-Term Liabilities		135,000
Total Liabilities		164,400
Stockholder's Equity		
Capital Stock	126,900	
Retained Earnings	50,000	
Total Stockholder's Equity		176,900
Total Liabilities and Stockholder's Equity		$341,300

A company's annual report is like a report card of how the company is doing financially.

Balance Sheet Components

Assets The asset section of a balance sheet is divided into three components: Current Assets; Property, Plant, and Equipment; and Investments and Other Assets.

Current Assets Assets that are cash or will be sold, used, or converted to cash within one year. The following are typical examples of current assets:

- Cash—Cash on hand in the form of bills, coins, checking accounts, and savings accounts.
- Marketable Securities—Investments in short-term securities that can be quickly converted to cash, such as stocks and bonds.
- Accounts Receivable—Money owed by customers to the firm for goods and services sold on credit.
- Notes Receivable—Money owed to the business involving promissory notes.
- Merchandise Inventory—The cost of goods a business has on hand for resale to its customers.
- Prepaid Expenses—Money paid in advance by the firm for benefits and services not yet received, such as prepaid insurance premiums or prepaid rent.
- Supplies—Cost of assets used in the day-to-day operation of the business. These might include office supplies such as paper, pencils, pens, and computer diskettes; or maintenance supplies, such as paper towels, soap, lubricants, light bulbs, batteries, etc.

Property, Plant, and Equipment Also known as fixed or long-term assets. These assets will be used by the firm in the operation of the business for a period of time longer than one year. Some examples follow:

- Land—The original purchase price of land owned by the company. Land is an asset that does not depreciate or lose its value over a period of time.
- Buildings—The cost of the buildings owned by the firm less the accumulated depreciation, or total loss in value, on those buildings since they were new. This is known as the book value of the buildings.
- Machinery and Equipment—The book value or original cost less accumulated depreciation of all machinery, fixtures, vehicles, and equipment used in the operation of a business.

Investments and Other Assets This category lists the firm's investments and all other assets.

- Investments—These are investments made by the firm and held for periods longer than a year.
- Other Assets—This catch-all category is for any assets not previously listed.
- Intangibles—Long-term assets that have no physical substance but have a value based on rights and privileges claimed by the owner. Some examples are copyrights, patents, royalties, and goodwill.

Liabilities The liabilities section of the balance sheet lists the current and long-term liabilities incurred by the company.

Current Liabilities Debts and financial obligations of the company that are due to be paid within one year. Some examples follow:

- Accounts payable—Debts owed by the firm to creditors for goods and services purchased with less than one year credit. These might include 30-, 60-, or 90-day terms of sale extended by suppliers and vendors.
- Notes payable—Debts owed by the firm involving promissory notes. An example would be a short-term loan from a bank.
- Salaries Payable—Compensation to employees that has been earned but not yet paid.
- Taxes Payable—Taxes owed by the firm but not yet paid by the date of the statement.

Long-Term Liabilities Debts and financial obligations of the company that are due to be paid in a year or more, or are to be paid out of noncurrent assets. Some examples follow:

- Mortgage Payable—The total obligation a firm owes for the long-term financing of land and buildings.
- Debenture Bonds—The total amount a firm owes on bonds at maturity to bondholders for money borrowed on the general credit of the company.

Equity That portion of a balance sheet representing an owner's worth or claim against the assets of the business. From the accounting equation, it is the difference between the total assets and the total liabilities.

Owner's Equity When a business is organized as a sole proprietorship or partnership, the equity section of the balance sheet is known as owner's equity. The ownership is labeled with the name of the owners or business and the word *capital.* Some examples follow:

■ John Smith, Capital

■ Handy Hardware Store, Capital.

Stockholder's Equity When the business is a corporation, the equity section of the balance sheet is known as stockholder's equity. The ownership is represented in two categories, capital stock and retained earnings.

■ Capital Stock—This represents money acquired by selling stock to investors who become stockholders. Capital stock is divided into preferred stock, which has preference over common stock regarding dividends, and common stock, representing the most basic rights to ownership of a corporation.

■ Retained Earnings—Profits from the operation of the business that have not been distributed to the stockholders in the form of dividends.

STEPS TO PREPARE A BALANCE SHEET:

Step 1. Centered at the top of the page, write the company name, type of statement, and date.

Step 2. In a section labeled ASSETS, list and total all of the Current Assets; Property, Plant, and Equipment; and Investments and Other Assets.

Step 3. Add the three components of the Assets section to get Total Assets.

Step 4. Double underline Total Assets.

Step 5. In a section labeled LIABILITIES AND OWNER'S EQUITY, list and total all Current Liabilities and Long-Term Liabilities.

Step 6. Add the two components of the Liabilities section to get Total Liabilities.

Step 7. List and total the Owner's or Stockholder's Equity.

Step 8. Add the Total Liabilities and Owner's Equity.

Step 9. Double underline Total Liabilities and Owner's Equity.

Note: In accordance with the accounting equation, check to be sure that:

$$\text{Assets} = \text{Liabilities} + \text{Owner's Equity}$$

EXAMPLE

Use the following financial information to prepare a balance sheet for Action Auto Parts, Inc., as of June 30, 1995: Cash, $3,400; accounts receivable, $5,600; merchandise inventory, $98,700; prepaid insurance, $455; supplies, $800; land and building, $147,000; fixtures, $8,600; delivery vehicles, $27,000; forklift, $7,000; goodwill, $10,000; accounts payable, $16,500; notes payable, $10,000; mortgage payable, $67,000; common stock, $185,055; and retained earnings, $30,000.

SOLUTION STRATEGY

The balance sheet for Action Auto Parts, Inc., follows. Note that the assets are equal to the liabilities plus stockholder's equity.

Action Auto Parts, Inc.
Balance Sheet
June 30, 1995

Assets

Current Assets

Cash	$ 3,400	
Accounts and Notes Receivable	5,600	
Merchandise Inventory	98,700	
Prepaid Insurance	455	
Supplies	800	
Total Current Assets		$108,955

Property, Plant, and Equipment

Land and Building	$147,000	
Fixtures	8,600	
Delivery Vehicles	27,000	
Forklift	7,000	
Total Property, Plant, and Equipment		189,600

Investments and Other Assets

Goodwill	10,000	
Total Investments and Other Assets		10,000
Total Assets		$308,555

Liabilities and Stockholder's Equity

Current Liabilities

Accounts Payable	$ 16,500	
Notes Payable`	10,000	
Total Current Liabilities		$ 26,500

Long-Term Liabilities

Mortgage Payable	67,000	
Total Long-Term Liabilities		67,000
Total Liabilities		93,500

Stockholder's Equity

Common Stock	185,055	
Retained Earnings	30,000	
Total Stockholder's Equity		215,055
Total Liabilities and Stockholder's Equity		$308,555

TRY-IT   EXERCISE

1. **Use the following financial information to prepare a balance sheet as of December 31, 1995, for Lee's Garage, a sole proprietorship, owned by Lee Sutherlin: Cash, $5,200; accounts receivable, $2,800; merchandise inventory, $2,700; prepaid salary, $235; supplies, $3,900; land, $35,000; building, $74,000; fixtures, $1,200; tow truck, $33,600; tools and equipment, $45,000; accounts payable, $6,800; notes payable, $17,600; taxes payable, $3,540; mortgage payable, $51,000; Lee Sutherlin, capital, $124,695.**

Check your balance sheet with the solution on page 513.

15-2 Preparing a Vertical Analysis of a Balance Sheet

vertical analysis

A percentage method of analyzing financial statements whereby each item on the statement is expressed as a percent of a base amount. On balance sheet analysis, the base is total assets; on income statement analysis, the base is net sales.

common-size balance sheet

A special form of balance sheet that lists only the vertical analysis percentages, not the dollar figures. All items are expressed as a percent of total assets.

Once the balance sheet has been prepared, a number of analytical procedures can be applied to the data in order to further evaluate a company's financial condition. One common method of analysis of a single financial statement is known as **vertical analysis.** In vertical analysis, each item on the balance sheet is expressed as a percent of total assets (total assets = 100%).

Once the vertical analysis has been completed, the figures show the relationship of each item on the balance sheet to total assets. For analysis purposes, these percents can then be compared to previous statements of the same company, to competitor's figures, or to published industry averages for similar-size companies.

A special form of balance sheet known as a common-size balance sheet is frequently used in financial analysis. **Common-size balance sheets** list only the vertical analysis percentages, not the dollar figures.

STEPS TO PREPARE A VERTICAL ANALYSIS OF A BALANCE SHEET:

Step 1. Use the percentage formula, Rate = Portion ÷ Base, to find the percentage of each item on the balance sheet. Use each individual item as the portion and total assets as the base.

Step 2. Round each answer to the nearest tenth percent. Note: a 0.1% differential may sometimes occur due to rounding.

Step 3. List the percent of each balance sheet item in a column to the right of the monetary amount.

EXAMPLE

Prepare a vertical analysis balance sheet for Hypothetical Enterprises, Inc., using the balance sheet found on page 476.

SOLUTION STRATEGY

Using the steps for vertical analysis, perform the following calculation for each balance sheet item and enter the results on the statement:

$$\frac{\text{Cash}}{\text{Total Assets}} = \frac{13,000}{341,300} = .038 = \underline{3.8\%}$$

Hypothetical Enterprises, Inc.
Balance Sheet
December 31, 199X

Assets

Current Assets		
Cash	$ 13,000	3.8
Accounts Receivable	32,500	9.5
Merchandise Inventory	50,600	14.8
Prepaid Expenses	1,200	0.4
Supplies	4,000	1.2
Total Current Assets	101,300	29.7
Property, Plant, and Equipment		
Land	40,000	11.7
Buildings	125,000	36.6
Machinery and Equipment	60,000	17.6
Total Property, Plant, and Equipment	225,000	65.9
Investments and Other Assets		
Investments	10,000	2.9
Intangible Assets	5,000	1.5
Total Investments and Other Assets	15,000	4.4
Total Assets	$341,300	100.0%

Liabilities and Owner's Equity

Current Liabilities		
Accounts Payable	$ 17,500	5.1
Salaries Payable	5,400	1.6
Taxes Payable	6,500	1.9
Total Current Liabilities	29,400	8.6
Long-Term Liabilities		
Mortgage Payable	115,000	33.7
Debenture Bond	20,000	5.9
Total Long-Term Liabilities	135,000	39.6
Total Liabilities	164,400	48.2
Stockholder's Equity		
Capital Stock	126,900	37.2
Retained Earnings	50,000	14.6
Total Stockholder's Equity	176,900	51.8
Total Liabilities and Stockholder's Equity	$341,300	100.0%

T R Y - I T   EXERCISE

2. Prepare a vertical analysis of the balance sheet for Action Auto Parts, Inc., on page 479.

Check your statement with the solution on page 514.

15-3 Preparing a Horizontal Analysis of a Balance Sheet

Frequently balance sheets are prepared with the data from the current year or operating period side-by-side with the figures from one or more previous periods. This type of presentation is known as a **comparative balance sheet** because the data from different periods can be readily compared. This information provides managers, creditors, and investors with important data concerning the progress of the company over a period of time, financial trends that may be developing, and the likelihood of future success.

Comparative balance sheets use horizontal analysis to measure the increases and decreases that have taken place in the financial data between two operating periods. In **horizontal analysis** each item of the current period is compared in dollars and percent with the corresponding item from a previous period.

● **comparative balance sheet**
Balance sheet prepared with the data from the current year or operating period side-by-side with the figures from one or more previous periods.

● **horizontal analysis**
Method of analyzing financial statements whereby each item of the current period is compared in dollars and percent with the corresponding item from a previous period.

STEPS TO PREPARE A HORIZONTAL ANALYSIS OF A BALANCE SHEET:

Step 1. Set up a comparative balance sheet format with the current period listed first and the previous period listed next.

Step 2. Label the next two columns:

Increase/Decrease	
Amount	Percent

Step 3. For each item on the balance sheet, calculate the dollar difference between the current and previous period and enter this figure in the Amount column. Enter all decreases in parentheses.

Step 4. Calculate the percent change (increase or decrease) using the percentage formula:

$$\text{Percent change (rate)} = \frac{\text{Amount of change, Step 3 (portion)}}{\text{Previous period amount (base)}}$$

Step 5. Enter the percent change, rounded to the nearest tenth percent, in the Percent column. Once again, enter all decreases in parentheses.

Using the comparative balance sheet for the Albrecht Construction Company, as of December 31, 1995 and 1996, prepare a horizontal analysis of this balance sheet for Mr. Albrecht.

Albrecht Construction Company
Comparative Balance Sheet
December 31, 1995 and 1996

Assets	1996	1995
Current Assets		
Cash	$ 3,500	$ 2,900
Accounts Receivable	12,450	7,680
Supplies	2,140	3,200
Total Current Assets	$ 18,090	$ 13,780
Property, Plant, and Equipment		
Land	$ 15,000	$ 15,000
Buildings	54,000	61,000
Machinery and Equipment	134,200	123,400
Total Property, Plant, and Equipment	$203,200	$199,400
Total Assets	$221,290	$213,180
Liabilities and Owner's Equity		
Current Liabilities		
Accounts Payable	$ 5,300	$ 4,100
Notes Payable	8,500	9,400
Total Current Liabilities	$ 13,800	$ 13,500
Long-Term Liabilities		
Mortgage Payable	$ 26,330	$ 28,500
Note Payable on Equipment (5-year)	10,250	11,430
Total Long-Term Liabilities	$ 36,580	$ 39,930
Total Liabilities	$ 50,380	$ 53,430
Owner's Equity		
Bob Albrecht, Capital	$170,910	$159,750
Total Liabilities and Owner's Equity	$221,290	$213,180

SOLUTION STRATEGY

Using the steps for horizontal analysis, perform the following operation on all balance sheet items and then enter the results on the statement.

Cash

$$1996 \text{ amount} - 1995 \text{ amount} = 3,500 - 2,900$$
$$= \$600 \text{ increase}$$

$$\text{Percent change} = \frac{\text{Amount of change}}{\text{Previous period amount}} = \frac{600}{2,900} = .20689 = \underline{20.7\%}$$

Albrecht Construction Company
Comparative Balance Sheet
December 31, 1995 and 1996

			Increase/Decrease	
Assets	1996	1995	Amount	Percent
Current Assets				
Cash	$ 3,500	$ 2,900	$ 600	20.7
Accounts Receivable	12,450	7,680	4,770	62.1
Supplies	2,140	3,200	(1,060)	(33.1)
Total Current Assets	$ 18,090	$ 13,780	4,310	31.3

Assets	1996	1995	Increase/Decrease Amount	Percent
Property, Plant, and Equipment				
Land	$ 15,000	$ 15,000	0	0
Buildings	54,000	61,000	(7,000)	(11.5)
Machinery and Equipment	134,200	123,400	10,800	8.8
Total Property, Plant, and Equipment	$203,200	$199,400	3,800	1.9
Total Assets	$221,290	$213,180	$ 8,110	3.8
Liabilities and Owner's Equity				
Current Liabilities				
Accounts Payable	$ 5,300	$ 4,100	$ 1,200	29.3
Notes Payable	8,500	9,400	(900)	(9.6)
Total Current Liabilities	$ 13,800	$ 13,500	300	2.2
Long-Term Liabilities				
Mortgage Payable	$ 26,330	$ 28,500	(2,170)	(7.6)
Note Payable on Equipment (5-year)	10,250	11,430	(1,180)	(10.3)
Total Long-Term Liabilities	$ 36,580	$ 39,930	(3,350)	(8.4)
Total Liabilities	$ 50,380	$ 53,430	(3,050)	(5.7)
Owner's Equity				
Bob Albrecht, Capital	$170,910	$159,750	11,160	7.0
Total Liabilities and Owner's Equity	$221,290	$213,180	$ 8,110	3.8

TRY-IT   **EXERCISE**

3. Complete the following comparative balance sheet with horizontal analysis for Figueroa Industries, Inc.

Figueroa Industries, Inc.
Comparative Balance Sheet
December 31, 1995 and 1996

Assets	1996	1995	Increase/Decrease Amount	Percent
Current Assets				
Cash	$ 8,700	$ 5,430	_____	_____
Accounts Receivable	23,110	18,450	_____	_____
Notes Receivable	2,900	3,400	_____	_____
Supplies	4,540	3,980	_____	_____
Total Current Assets	_____	_____	_____	_____
Property, Plant, and Equipment				
Land	$34,000	$34,000	_____	_____
Buildings	76,300	79,800	_____	_____
Machinery and Equipment	54,700	48,900	_____	_____
Total Property, Plant, and Equipment	_____	_____	_____	_____
Investments and Other Assets	54,230	48,810	_____	_____
Total Assets	_____	_____	_____	_____

Liabilities and Stockholder's Equity

Current Liabilities				
Accounts Payable	$15,330	$19,650	____	____
Salaries Payable	7,680	7,190	____	
Total Current Liabilities	____	____	____	____
Long-Term Liabilities				
Mortgage Payable	$53,010	$54,200	____	____
Note Payable (3-year)	32,400	33,560	____	
Total Long-Term Liabilities	____	____	____	____
Total Liabilities	____	____	____	____
Stockholder's Equity				
Figueroa Industries, Common Stock	____	____	____	____
Total Liabilities and Stockholder's Equity	____	____	____	____

Check your statement with the solution on page 514–515.

REVIEW EXERCISES CHAPTER 15—SECTION I

Calculate the following values according to the accounting equation:

	Assets	Liabilities	Owner's Equity
1.	$283,000	$121,400	$161,600
2.	$548,900	$335,900	$213,000
3.	$45,300	$29,000	$16,300

For the following balance sheet items, check the appropriate category:

	Current Asset	Fixed Asset	Current Liability	Long-Term Liability	Owner's Equity
4. Land		✓			
5. Supplies	✓				
6. Marketable Securities	✓				
7. Retained Earnings					✓
8. Buildings		✓			
9. Mortgage Payable				✓	
10. Cash	✓				
11. Notes Payable			✓		
12. Equipment		✓			
13. Note Receivable (3-month)	✓				
14. Prepaid Expenses	✓				
15. Merchandise Inventory	✓				
16. Common Stock					✓
17. Trucks		✓			
18. Debenture Bonds				✓	
19. Accounts Receivable	✓				
20. Salaries Payable			✓		
21. R. Smith, Capital					✓
22. Savings Account	✓				
23. Preferred Stock					✓
24. Note Payable (2-year)				✓	
25. Taxes Payable			✓		

Prepare the following statements on separate sheets of paper.

26. **a.** Use the following financial information to calculate the owner's equity and prepare a balance sheet with vertical analysis as of December 31, 1995, for Gary's Gifts, a sole proprietorship owned by Gary Robbins: current assets, $157,600; property, plant, and equipment, $42,000; investments and other assets, $35,700; current liabilities, $21,200; long-term liabilities, $53,400.

Gary's Gifts
Balance Sheet
December 31, 1995

b. The following financial information is for Gary's Gifts as of December 31, 1996: current assets, $175,300; property, plant, and equipment, $43,600; investments and other assets, $39,200; current liabilities, $27,700; long-term liabilities, $51,000.

Calculate the owner's equity for 1996 and prepare a comparative balance sheet with horizontal analysis for 1995 and 1996.

Gary's Gifts
Comparative Balance Sheet
December 31, 1995 and 1996

27. **a.** Use the following financial information to prepare a balance sheet with vertical analysis as of June 30, 1995, for Northern Industries, Inc.: cash, $44,300; accounts receivable, $127,600; merchandise inventory, $88,100; prepaid maintenance, $4,100; office supplies, $4,000; land, $154,000; building, $237,000; fixtures, $21,400; vehicles, $64,000; computers, $13,000; goodwill, $20,000; investments, $32,000; accounts payable, $55,700; salaries payable, $23,200; notes payable (6-month), $38,000; mortgage payable, $91,300; debenture bonds, $165,000; common stock, $350,000; and retained earnings, $86,300.

Northern Industries, Inc.
Balance Sheet
June 30, 1995

b. The following financial information is for Northern Industries as of June 30, 1996: cash, $40,200; accounts receivable, $131,400; merchandise inventory, $92,200; prepaid maintenance, $3,700; office supplies, $6,200; land, $154,000; building, $231,700; fixtures, $23,900; vehicles, $55,100; computers, $16,800; goodwill, $22,000; investments, $36,400; accounts payable, $51,800; salaries payable, $25,100; notes payable (6-month), $19,000; mortgage payable, $88,900; debenture bonds, $165,000; common stock, $350,000; and retained earnings, $113,800.

Prepare a comparative balance sheet with horizontal analysis for 1995 and 1996.

Northern Industries, Inc.
Comparative Balance Sheet
June 30, 1995 and 1996

The Annual Report

28. From the consolidated balance sheets for Wal-Mart on page 486, prepare a horizontal analysis of the Current Assets section comparing 1993 and 1994.

Consolidated Balance Sheets

Wal-Mart

(Amounts in thousands.)

January 31,	1994	1993
Assets		
Current Assets:		
Cash and cash equivalents	$ 20,115	$ 12,363
Receivables	689,987	524,555
Recoverable costs from sale/leaseback	208,236	312,016
Inventories:		
At replacement cost	11,483,119	9,779,981
Less LIFO reserve	469,413	511,672
LIFO	11,013,706	9,268,309
Prepaid expenses and other	182,558	80,347
Total Current Assets	12,114,602	10,197,590
Property, Plant, and Equipment, at Cost:		
Land	2,740,883	1,692,510
Buildings and improvements	6,818,479	4,641,009
Fixtures and equipment	3,980,674	3,417,230
Transportation equipment	259,537	111,151
	13,799,573	9,861,900
Less accumulated depreciation	2,172,808	1,607,623
Net property, plant, and equipment	11,626,765	8,254,277
Property under capital leases	2,058,588	1,986,104
Less accumulated amortization	509,987	447,500
Net property under capital leases	1,548,601	1,538,604
Other Assets and Deferred Charges	1,150,796	574,616
Total Assets	**$26,440,764**	**$20,565,087**
Liabilities and Shareholders' Equity		
Current Liabilities:		
Commercial paper	$ 1,575,029	$ 1,588,825
Accounts payable	4,103,878	3,873,331
Accrued liabilities	1,473,198	1,042,108
Accrued federal and state income taxes	183,031	190,620
Long-term debt due within one year	19,658	13,849
Obligations under capital leases due within one year	51,429	45,553
Total Current Liabilities	7,406,223	6,754,286
Long-Term Debt	6,155,894	3,072,835
Long-Term Obligations Under Capital Leases	1,804,300	1,772,152
Deferred Income Taxes	321,909	206,634
Shareholders' Equity:		
Preferred stock ($.10 par value; 100,000 shares authorized, none issued)		
Common stock ($.10 par value; 5,500,000 shares authorized, 2,298,769 and 2,299,638 issued and outstanding in 1994 and 1993, respectively)	229,877	229,964
Capital in excess of par value	535,639	526,647
Retained earnings	9,986,922	8,002,569
Total Shareholders' Equity	10,752,438	8,759,180
Total Liabilities and Shareholders' Equity	**$26,440,764**	**$20,565,087**

THE INCOME STATEMENT

The Bottom Line

When it's all said and done, the question is "how well did the business do?" The real score is found on the income statement. An **income statement** is a summary of the operations of a business over a period of time—usually a month, a quarter, or a year. In order for any business to exist it must have earnings and also expenses, either in the form of cash or credit. The income statement shows the **revenue** or earnings of the business from the sale of goods and services; the **expenses,** the costs incurred to generate that revenue; and the bottom line **profit** or **loss,** the difference between revenue and expenses.

For any operating period, when a company earns more than the expenses incurred there is a profit; when it incurs more expenses than it earns there is a loss. As with the balance sheet, a simple equation can be used to illustrate the structure of the statement.

$$\text{Profit (or Loss)} = \text{Revenue} - \text{Total Expenses}$$

where

Revenue = Earnings (either cash or credit) from sales during the period

Total expenses = Cost of goods sold + Operating expenses + Taxes

15-4 Preparing an Income Statement

Once again, let's begin by looking at a typical income statement. As before, we shall use Hypothetical Enterprises, Inc., to illustrate. Carefully look over the following income statement and then read the descriptions of each section and its components.

As with the balance sheet, don't try to memorize the parts of the statement. Your understanding will increase very quickly with some practice. After you have reviewed the Steps for Preparing an Income Statement, carefully follow the Example and Solution Strategy, then work the Try-It Exercise.

Hypothetical Enterprises, Inc.
Income Statement
For the year ended December 31, 199X

Revenue		
Gross sales	$923,444	
Less: Sales Returns and Allowances	22,875	
Sales Discounts	3,625	
Net Sales		$896,944
Cost of Goods Sold		
Merchandise Inventory, Jan. 1	220,350	
Net Purchases	337,400	
Freight In	12,350	
Goods Available for Sale	570,100	
Less: Merchandise Inventory, Dec. 31	88,560	
Cost of Goods Sold		481,540
Gross Margin		415,404
Operating Expenses		
Salaries and Benefits	152,600	
Rent and Utilities	35,778	
Advertising and Promotion	32,871	
Insurance	8,258	
General and Administrative Expenses	41,340	
Depreciation	19,890	
Miscellaneous Expenses	14,790	
Total Operating Expenses		305,527
Income before Taxes		109,877
Income Tax		18,609
Net Income		$ 91,268

● **income, operating, or profit and loss statement**
Financial statement summarizing the operations of a business over a period of time. Illustrates the amount of revenue earned, expenses incurred, and the resulting profit or loss:
Revenue − Expenses = Profit (or loss).

● **revenue**
The primary source of money, both cash and credit, flowing into the business from its customers for goods sold or services rendered over a period of time.

● **expenses**
Costs incurred by a business in the process of earning revenue.

● **profit or loss**
The difference between revenue earned and expenses incurred during an operating period. Profit when revenue is greater than expenses; loss when expenses are greater than revenue. Profit is also known as earnings or income.

Income Statement Components

Revenue The revenue section of the income statement represents the primary source of money, both cash and credit, flowing into the business from its customers for goods sold or services rendered.

Gross Sales
– Sales Returns and Allowances
– Sales Discounts
Net Sales

- Gross Sales—Total sales of goods and services achieved by the company during the operating period.
- Sales Returns and Allowances—Amount of merchandise returned for cash or credit by customers for various reasons.
- Sales Discounts—Cash discounts given to customers by the business as an incentive for early payment of an invoice. For example, 3/15, n/45, where there is a 3% extra discount if the invoice is paid within 15 days, rather than the net date, 45 days.
- Net Sales—Amount received after taking into consideration returned goods, allowances, and sales discounts.

Cost of Goods Sold The cost of goods sold section represents the cost to the business of the merchandise that was sold during the operating period.

Merchandise Inventory (Beginning)
+ Net Purchases
+ Freight In
Goods Available for Sale
– Merchandise Inventory (Ending)
Cost of Goods Sold

- Merchandise Inventory (beginning of operating period)—Total value of the goods in inventory at the beginning of the operating period.
- Net Purchases—Amount, at cost, of merchandise purchased during the period for resale to customers after deducting purchase returns and allowances and purchase discounts earned.
- Freight In—Total amount of the freight or transportation charges incurred for the net purchases.
- Goods Available for Sale—The total amount of the goods available to be sold during the operating period. It is the sum of beginning inventory, net purchases, and freight in.
- Merchandise Inventory (end of operating period)—Total value of the goods remaining in inventory at the end of the operating period.
- Cost of Goods Sold—Total value of the goods that were sold during the period. It is the difference between goods available for sale and the ending merchandise inventory.

Gross Margin Gross margin, also known as gross profit, represents the difference between net sales and cost of goods sold.

Net Sales
– Cost of Goods Sold
Gross Margin

Total Operating Expenses The sum of all the expenses incurred by the business during the operating period, except the cost of goods sold and taxes. Operating expenses differ from company to company. Some typical examples are salaries and benefits, sales commissions, rent and utilities, advertising and promotion, insurance, general and administrative expenses, depreciation, and miscellaneous expenses.

Income before Taxes This figure represents the money a company made before paying income tax. It is the difference between gross margin and total operating expenses.

Gross Margin
– Total Operating Expenses
Income before Taxes

Income Tax   This expense figure is the amount of income tax, both state and federal, that is paid by the business during the operating period.

Net Income, Net Profit (or Net Loss)   Literally the bottom line of the income statement. It is the difference between income before taxes and the income tax paid.

Income before Taxes
$\underline{\text{– Income Tax}}$
Net Income (Loss)

STEPS TO PREPARE AN INCOME STATEMENT:

Step 1. Centered at the top of the page, write the company name, type of statement, and period of time covered by the statement (example "Year ended Dec. 31, 1997" or "April 1997").

Step 2. In a two-column format, as illustrated on page 591, calculate:

A. *Net Sales*, using:

Gross Sales
– Sales Returns and Allowances
$\underline{\text{– Sales Discounts}}$
Net Sales

B. *Cost of Goods Sold,* using:

Merchandise Inventory (Beginning)
+ Net Purchases
$\underline{\text{+ Freight In}}$
Goods Available for Sale
$\underline{\text{– Merchandise Inventory (Ending)}}$
Cost of Goods Sold

C. *Gross Margin,* using:

Net Sales
$\underline{\text{– Cost of Goods Sold}}$
Gross Margin

D. *Total Operating Expenses*—Sum of all operating expenses

E. *Income before Taxes,* using:

Gross Margin
$\underline{\text{– Total Operating Expenses}}$
Income before Taxes

F. *Net Income,* using:

Income before Taxes
$\underline{\text{– Income Tax}}$
Net Income (Loss)

EXAMPLE

Use the following financial information to prepare an income statement for Action Auto Parts, Inc., for the year ended December 31, 1995: Gross sales, $458,400; sales returns and allowances, $13,200; sales discounts, $1,244; merchandise inventory, Jan. 1, 1995, $198,700; merchandise inventory, Dec. 31, 1995, $76,400; net purchases, $86,760; freight in, $875; salaries, $124,200; rent, $21,000; utilities, $1,780; advertising, $5,400; insurance, $2,340; administrative expenses, $14,500; miscellaneous expenses, $6,000; and income tax, $17,335.

The income statement for Action Auto Parts, Inc., follows.

Action Auto Parts, Inc.
Income Statement
For the year ended December 31, 1995

Revenue		
Gross Sales	$458,400	
Less: Sales Returns and Allowances	13,200	
Sales Discounts	1,244	
Net Sales		$443,956
Cost of Goods Sold		
Merchandise Inventory, Jan. 1	198,700	
Net Purchases	86,760	
Freight In	875	
Goods Available for Sale	286,335	
Less: Merchandise Inventory, Dec. 31	76,400	
Cost of Goods Sold		209,935
Gross Margin		234,021
Operating Expenses		
Salaries	124,200	
Rent	21,000	
Utilities	1,780	
Advertising	5,400	
Insurance	2,340	
Administrative Expenses	14,500	
Miscellaneous Expenses	6,000	
Total Operating Expenses		175,220
Income before Taxes		58,801
Income Tax		17,335
Net Income		$ 41,466

TRY-IT   EXERCISE

4. Use the following financial information to prepare an income statement for West-minster Manufacturing, Inc., for the year ended December 31, 1996: Gross sales, $1,356,000; sales returns and allowances, $93,100; sales discounts, $4,268; merchandise inventory, Jan. 1, 1996, $324,800; merchandise inventory, Dec. 31, 1996, $179,100; net purchases, $255,320; freight in, $3,911; salaries, $375,900; rent, $166,000; utilities, $7,730; advertising, $73,300; insurance, $22,940; administrative expenses, $84,500; miscellaneous expenses, $24,900; and income tax, $34,760.

Check your income statement with the solution on page 515.

15-5 Preparing a Vertical Analysis of an Income Statement

Vertical analysis can be applied to the income statement just as it was to the balance sheet. Each figure on the income statement is expressed as a percent of net sales (net sales = 100%). The resulting figures describe how net sales were distributed among the expenses and what percent was left as net profit. For analysis purposes, this information can then be compared to the figures from previous operating periods for the company, to competitor's figures, or to published industry averages for similar-size companies.

As with balance sheets, income statements with vertical analysis can be displayed in the format known as **common-size,** in which all figures on the statement appear as percentages.

STEPS TO PREPARE A VERTICAL ANALYSIS OF AN INCOME STATEMENT:

Step 1. Use the percentage formula, Rate = Portion ÷ Base, to find the rate of each item on the income statement. Use each individual item as the portion and net sales as the base.

Step 2. Round each answer to the nearest tenth percent. Note: a 0.1% differential may sometimes occur due to rounding.

Step 3. List the percentage of each statement item in a column to the right of the monetary amount.

EXAMPLE

Prepare a vertical analysis income statement for Hypothetical Enterprises, Inc., on page 487.

SOLUTION STRATEGY

Using the steps for vertical analysis, perform the following calculation for each income statement item and enter the results on the income statement as follows.

$$\frac{\text{Gross Sales}}{\text{Net Sales}} = \frac{923,444}{896,944} = 1.029 = \underline{103\%}$$

Hypothetical Enterprises, Inc.
Income Statement
For the year ended December 31, 199X

Revenue		
Gross Sales	$923,444	103.0
Less: Sales Returns and Allowances	22,875	2.6
Sales Discounts	3,625	.4
Net Sales	896,944	100.0%
Cost of Goods Sold		
Merchandise Inventory, Jan. 1	220,350	24.6
Net Purchases	337,400	37.6
Freight In	12,350	1.4
Goods Available for Sale	570,100	63.6
Less: Merchandise Inventory, Dec. 31	88,560	9.9
Cost of Goods Sold	481,540	53.7
Gross Margin	415,404	46.3
Operating Expenses		
Salaries and Benefits	152,600	17.0
Rent and Utilities	35,778	4.0
Advertising and Promotion	32,871	3.7
Insurance	8,258	.9
General and Administrative Expenses	41,340	4.6
Depreciation	19,890	2.2
Miscellaneous Expenses	14,790	1.6
Total Operating Expenses	305,527	34.1
Income before Taxes	109,877	12.3
Income Tax	18,609	2.1
Net Income	$ 91,268	10.2%

5. Prepare a vertical analysis of the income statement for Action Auto Parts, Inc., on page 490.

Check your statement with the solution on page 515.

15-6 Preparing a Horizontal Analysis of an Income Statement

As with the balance sheet, the income statement can be prepared in a format that compares the financial data of the business from one operating period to another. This horizontal analysis provides percent increase or decrease information for each item on the income statement. Information such as this provides a very useful progress report of the company. As before, the previous or original period figure is the base.

STEPS TO PREPARE A HORIZONTAL ANALYSIS OF AN INCOME STATEMENT:

Step 1. Set up a comparative income statement format with the current period listed first and the previous period listed next.

Step 2. Label the next two columns: $\dfrac{\text{Increase/Decrease}}{\text{Amount} \quad \text{Percent}}$

Step 3. For each item on the income statement, calculate the dollar difference between the current and previous period and enter this figure in the Amount column. Enter all decreases in parentheses.

Step 4. Calculate the percent change (increase or decrease) by the percentage formula:

$$\text{Percent change (rate)} = \frac{\text{Amount of change, Step 3 (portion)}}{\text{Previous period amount (base)}}$$

Step 5. Enter the percent change, rounded to the nearest tenth percent, in the Percent column. Once again, enter all decreases in parentheses.

EXAMPLE

A comparative income statement for Fisher Island Electronics, Inc., for the years 1995 and 1996, follows. Prepare a horizontal analysis of the statement for the company.

Fisher Island Electronics, Inc.
Comparative Income Statement
For the years ended December 31, 1995 and 1996

	1996	1995
Revenue		
Gross Sales	$623,247	$599,650
Less: Sales Returns and Allowances	8,550	9,470
Sales Discounts	3,400	1,233
Net Sales	611,297	588,947
Cost of Goods Sold		
Merchandise Inventory, Jan. 1	121,200	134,270
Purchases	154,630	111,208
Freight In	2,460	1,980
Goods Available for Sale	278,290	247,458
Less: Merchandise Inventory, Dec. 31	149,900	158,540
Cost of Goods Sold	128,390	88,918
Gross Margin	482,907	500,029

Operating Expenses		
Salaries and Benefits	165,300	161,200
Rent and Utilities	77,550	76,850
Depreciation	74,350	75,040
Insurance	4,560	3,900
Office Expenses	34,000	41,200
Warehouse Expenses	41,370	67,400
Total Operating Expenses	397,130	425,590
Income before Taxes	85,777	74,439
Income Tax	27,400	19,700
Net Income	$ 58,377	$ 54,739

SOLUTION STRATEGY

Using the steps for horizontal analysis, perform the following operation on all income statement items and then enter the results on the statement.

Gross Sales

$$1996 \text{ amount} - 1995 \text{ amount} = \text{Amount of change}$$
$$623,247 - 599,650 = \underline{\$23,597 \text{ increase}}$$

$$\text{Percent change} = \frac{\text{Amount of change}}{\text{Previous period amount}} = \frac{23,597}{599,650} = \underline{\underline{3.9\%}}$$

Fisher Island Electronics, Inc.
Comparative Income Statement
For the years ended December 31, 1995 and 1996

	1996	1995	Increase/Decrease Amount	Percent
Revenue				
Gross Sales	$623,247	$599,650	23,597	3.9
Less: Sales Returns and Allowances	8,550	9,470	(920)	(9.7)
Sales Discounts	3,400	1,233	2,167	176.0
Net Sales	611,297	588,947	22,350	3.8
Cost of Goods Sold				
Merchandise Inventory, Jan. 1	121,200	134,270	(13,070)	(9.7)
Purchases	154,630	111,208	43,422	39.0
Freight In	2,460	1,980	480	24.2
Goods Available for Sale	278,290	247,458	30,832	12.5
Less: Merchandise Inventory, Dec. 31	149,900	158,540	(8,640)	(5.4)
Cost of Goods Sold	128,390	88,918	39,472	44.4
Gross Margin	482,907	500,029	(17,122)	3.4
Operating Expenses				
Salaries and Benefits	165,300	161,200	4,100	2.5
Rent and Utilities	77,550	76,850	700	.9
Depreciation	74,350	75,040	(690)	(.9)
Insurance	4,560	3,900	660	16.9
Office Expenses	34,000	41,200	(7,200)	(17.5)
Warehouse Expenses	41,370	67,400	(26,030)	(38.6)
Total Operating Expenses	397,130	425,590	(28,460)	(6.7)
Income before Taxes	85,777	74,439	11,338	15.2
Income Tax	27,400	19,700	7,700	39.1
Net Income	$ 58,377	$ 54,739	$3,638	6.6

TRY-IT   EXERCISE

6. Complete the following comparative income statement with horizontal analysis for Winkler's Grocery Store, Inc.

Winkler's Grocery Store, Inc.
Comparative Income Statement
For the years ended December 31, 1995 and 1996

	1996	1995	Increase/Decrease Amount	Increase/Decrease Percent
Revenue				
Gross Sales	$1,223,000	$996,500	_____	_____
Less: Sales Returns and Allowances	121,340	99,600	_____	_____
Sales Discounts	63,120	51,237	_____	_____
Net Sales	_____	_____	_____	_____
Cost of Goods Sold				
Merchandise Inventory, Jan. 1	554,300	331,000	_____	_____
Purchases	360,190	271,128	_____	_____
Freight In	18,640	13,400	_____	_____
Goods Available for Sale	_____	_____	_____	_____
Less: Merchandise Inventory, Dec. 31	585,400	311,200	_____	_____
Cost of Goods Sold	_____	_____	_____	_____
Gross Margin	_____	_____	_____	_____
Operating Expenses				
Salaries and Benefits	215,200	121,800	_____	_____
Rent and Utilities	124,650	124,650	_____	_____
Depreciation	43,500	41,230	_____	_____
Insurance	24,970	23,800	_____	_____
Administrative Store Expenses	58,200	33,900	_____	_____
Warehouse Expenses	42,380	45,450	_____	_____
Total Operating Expenses	_____	_____	_____	_____
Income before Taxes	_____	_____	_____	_____
Income Tax	66,280	41,670	_____	_____
Net Income				

Check your statement with the solution on page 516.

REVIEW EXERCISES   CHAPTER 15—SECTION II

Calculate the missing information based on the format of the income statement:

	Net Sales	Cost of Goods Sold	Gross Margin	Operating Expenses	Net Profit
1.	$334,500	$132,300	$202,200	$108,000	$94,200
2.	$1,640,000	$880,000	$760,000	$354,780	$405,220
3.	$675,530	$257,000	$418,530	$334,160	$84,370

4. For the third quarter of 1995, Don Bailey Carpet Company had gross sales of $315,450; sales returns and allowances of $23,100; and sales discounts of $18,700. What were Bailey's net sales?

Gross sales $315,450
Less:
Sales returns + allowance   23,100
Sales discounts   18,700
Net sales $273,650

5. For the month of August, Wong's Imports, Inc., had the following financial information: merchandise inventory, August 1, $244,500; merchandise inventory, August 31, $193,440; gross purchases, $79,350; purchase returns and allowances, $8,700; and freight in, $970.

    a. What are Wong's goods available for sale?

Inventory (August 1)	$244,500
Net purchases	70,650
Freight in	+ 970
Goods available for sale =	$316,120

    b. What is the cost of goods sold for August?

Goods available for sale	$316,120
Inventory (August 31)	− $193,440
Cost of goods sold =	$122,680

    c. If net sales were $335,000, what was the gross margin for August?

Net sales	$335,000
Cost of goods sold −	$122,680
Gross margin =	$212,320

    d. If total operating expenses were $167,200, what was the net profit?

Gross margin	$212,320
Operating expenses −	$167,200
Net profit =	$45,120

Prepare the following statements on separate sheets of paper.

Financial statement solutions appear in the appendix following the index.

6. a. As the assistant accounting manager for Kwik-Mix Concrete, Inc., construct an income statement with vertical analysis for the first quarter of 1996 from the following information: gross sales, $240,000; sales discounts, $43,500; beginning inventory, Jan. 1, $86,400; ending inventory, March 31, $103,200; net purchases, $76,900; total operating expenses, $108,000; income tax, $14,550.

Kwik-Mix Concrete, Inc.
Income Statement
January 1 to March 31, 1996

    b. You have just received a report with the second quarter figures. Prepare a comparative income statement with horizontal analysis for the first and second quarter of 1996: gross sales, $297,000; sales discounts, $41,300; beginning inventory, April 1, $103,200; ending inventory, June 30, $96,580; net purchases, $84,320; total operating expenses, $126,700; income tax, $16,400.

Kwik-Mix Concrete, Inc.
Comparative Income Statement
First and Second Quarter, 1996

7. a. Use the following financial information to construct a 1996 income statement with vertical analysis for the Tasty Treats Food Wholesalers, Inc.: gross sales, $2,249,000; sales returns and allowances, $143,500; sales discounts, $54,290; merchandise inventory, Jan. 1, 1996, $875,330; merchandise inventory, Dec. 31, 1996, $716,090; net purchases, $546,920; freight in, $11,320; salaries, $319,800; rent, $213,100; depreciation, $51,200; utilities, $35,660; advertising, $249,600; insurance, $39,410; administrative expenses, $91,700; miscellaneous expenses, $107,500; and income tax, $38,450.

Tasty Treats Food Wholesalers, Inc.
Income Statement
1996

b. The following data represents Tasty Treats' operating results for 1997. Prepare a comparative income statement with horizontal analysis for 1996 and 1997: gross sales, $2,125,000; sales returns and allowances, $126,400; sales discounts, $73,380; merchandise inventory, Jan. 1, 1997, $716,090; merchandise inventory, Dec. 31, 1997, $584,550; net purchases, $482,620; freight in, $9,220; salaries, $340,900; rent, $215,000; depreciation, $56,300; utilities, $29,690; advertising, $217,300; insurance, $39,410; administrative expenses, $95,850; miscellaneous expenses, $102,500; and income tax, $44,530.

Tasty Treats Food Wholesalers, Inc.
Comparative Income Statement
1996 and 1997

The Annual Report

8. From the consolidated statement of income for the Walt Disney Company given below, prepare a horizontal analysis of the Revenues section comparing 1992 and 1993.

THE WALT DISNEY COMPANY

CONSOLIDATED STATEMENT OF INCOME

(IN MILLIONS, EXCEPT PER SHARE DATA)

YEAR ENDED SEPTEMBER 30	1993	1992	1991
REVENUES			
THEME PARKS AND RESORTS	$3,440.7	$3,306.9	$2,794.3
FILMED ENTERTAINMENT	3,673.4	3,115.2	2,593.7
CONSUMER PRODUCTS	1,415.1	1,081.9	724.0
	8,529.2	7,504.0	6,112.0
COSTS AND EXPENSES			
THEME PARKS AND RESORTS	2,693.8	2,662.9	2,247.7
FILMED ENTERTAINMENT	3,051.2	2,606.9	2,275.6
CONSUMER PRODUCTS	1,059.7	798.9	494.2
	6,804.7	6,068.7	5,017.5
OPERATING INCOME			
THEME PARKS AND RESORTS	746.9	644.0	546.6
FILMED ENTERTAINMENT	622.2	508.3	318.1
CONSUMER PRODUCTS	355.4	283.0	229.8
	1,724.5	1,435.3	1,094.5
CORPORATE ACTIVITIES			
GENERAL AND ADMINISTRATIVE EXPENSES	164.2	148.2	160.8
INTEREST EXPENSE	157.7	126.8	105.0
INVESTMENT AND INTEREST INCOME	(186.1)	(130.3)	(119.4)
	135.8	144.7	146.4
INCOME (LOSS) FROM INVESTMENT IN EURO DISNEY	(514.7)	11.2	63.8
INCOME BEFORE INCOME TAXES AND CUMULATIVE EFFECT OF			
ACCOUNTING CHANGES	1,074.0	1,301.8	1,011.9
INCOME TAXES	402.7	485.1	375.3
INCOME BEFORE CUMULATIVE EFFECT OF ACCOUNTING CHANGES	671.3	816.7	636.6
CUMULATIVE EFFECT OF ACCOUNTING CHANGES			
PRE-OPENING COSTS	(271.2)	–	–
POSTRETIREMENT BENEFITS	(130.3)	–	–
INCOME TAXES	30.0	–	–
NET INCOME	$ 299.8	$ 816.7	$ 636.6

FINANCIAL RATIOS AND TREND ANALYSIS

In addition to vertical and horizontal analysis of financial statements, managers, creditors, and investors also study comparisons among various components on the statements. These comparisons are expressed as ratios and are known as **financial ratios.** They can be compared to ratios from previous operating periods of the company or to published industry statistics for similar companies.

Basically, financial ratios represent an effort by analysts to standardize financial information, which in turn makes comparisons more meaningful. The fundamental purpose of ratio analysis is to indicate areas requiring further investigation. Think of them as signals indicating areas of potential strength or weakness of the firm. Frequently financial ratios have to be examined more closely to discover their true meaning. A high ratio, for example, might indicate that the numerator figure is too high or the denominator figure is too low.

Financial ratios fall into four major categories:

Liquidity ratios tell how well a company can pay off its short-term debts and meet unexpected needs for cash.

Efficiency ratios indicate how effectively a company utilizes its resources to generate sales.

Leverage ratios show how and to what degree a company has financed its assets.

Profitability ratios tell how much of each dollar of sales, assets, and stockholder's investment resulted in bottom-line net profit.

● **financial ratios**

A series of comparisons of financial statement components in ratio form used by analysts to evaluate the operating performance of a company.

15-7 Calculating Financial Ratios

As we learned in Chapter 5, a **ratio** is a comparison of one amount to another. A financial ratio is simply a ratio whose numerator and denominator are financial information taken from the balance sheet, income statement, or other important business data.

Ratios may be stated in a number of ways. For example, a ratio of credit sales, $40,000, to total sales, $100,000, in a retail store may be stated as:

a. Credit sales ratio is $\frac{40,000}{100,000}$, or 4 to 10, or 2 to 5 (written 2:5).

b. Credit sales are $\frac{4}{10}$, or 40% of total sales.

c. For every $1.00 of sales, $.40 is on credit.

● **ratio**

A comparison of one amount to another.

Managers analyze financial statement data to determine a business's strengths and weaknesses.

Conversely, the ratio of total sales, $100,000, to credit sales, $40,000, may be stated as:

a. Total sales ratio is $\frac{100,000}{40,000}$, or 10 to 4, or 2.5 to 1 (written 2.5:1).

b. Total sales are $\frac{10}{4}$, or 250% of credit sales.

c. For every $2.50 of sales, $1.00 is on credit.

To illustrate how ratios are used in financial analysis, let's apply this analysis to Hypothetical Enterprises, Inc., a company introduced in Sections I and II of this chapter.

EXAMPLE

Calculate the financial ratios for Hypothetical Enterprises, Inc., using the data from the financial statements presented on pages 476 and 487.

SOLUTION STRATEGY

Liquidity Ratios

● **liquidity ratios**

Financial ratios that tell how well a company can pay off its short-term debts and meet unexpected needs for cash.

Businesses must have enough cash on hand to pay their bills as they come due. The **liquidity ratios** examine the relationship between a firm's current assets and its maturing obligations. The amount of a firm's working capital and these ratios are good indicators of a firm's ability to pay its bills over the next few months. Short-term creditors pay particular attention to these figures.

● **working capital**

The difference between current assets and current liabilities at a point in time. Theoretically the amount of money left over if all the current liabilities were paid off by current assets.

The term **working capital** refers to the difference between current assets and current liabilities at a point in time. Theoretically, it is the amount of money that would be left over if all the current liabilities were paid off by current assets.

$$\text{Working capital} = \text{Current assets} - \text{Current liabilities}$$

● **current ratio, or working capital ratio**

The comparison of a firm's current assets to current liabilities.

Current ratio or working capital ratio is the comparison of a firm's current assets to current liabilities. This ratio indicates the amount of current assets available to pay off $1 of current debt. A current ratio of 2:1 or above is considered by banks and other lending institutions to be an acceptable ratio.

$$\text{Current ratio} = \frac{\text{Current assets}}{\text{Current liabilities}}$$

Hypothetical Enterprises, Inc.:

$$\text{Working capital} = 101,300 - 29,400 = \$71,900$$

$$\text{Current ratio} = \frac{101,300}{29,400} = 3.45 = 3.45{:}1$$

Analysis: This ratio shows that Hypothetical has $3.45 in current assets for each $1.00 it owes in current liabilities. A current ratio of 3.45:1 indicates that the company has more than sufficient means of covering short-term debt, and is therefore in a strong liquidity position.

● **acid test, or quick ratio**

A ratio that indicates a firm's ability to quickly liquidate assets to pay off current debt.

Acid test or quick ratio indicates a firm's ability to quickly liquidate assets to pay off current debt. This ratio recognizes that a firm's inventories are one of the least liquid current assets. Merchandise inventories and prepaid expenses are not part of quick assets since they are not readily convertible to cash. An acid test ratio of 1:1 or greater is considered to be acceptable.

$$\text{Quick assets} = \text{Cash} + \text{Marketable securities} + \text{Receivables}$$

$$\text{Acid test ratio} = \frac{\text{Quick assets}}{\text{Current liabilities}}$$

Hypothetical Enterprises, Inc. (note: Hypothetical has no marketable securities):

$$\text{Quick assets} = 13,000 + 32,500 = \underline{\$45,500}$$

$$\text{Acid test ratio} = \frac{45,500}{29,400} = 1.55 = \underline{\underline{1.55:1}}$$

Analysis: An acid test ratio of 1.55:1 also indicates a strong liquidity position. It means that Hypothetical has the ability to meet all short-term debt obligations immediately, if necessary.

Efficiency Ratios

Efficiency ratios provide the basis for determining how effectively the firm is using its resources to generate sales. A firm with $500,000 in assets producing $1,000,000 in sales is using its resources more efficiently than a firm producing the same sales with $2,000,000 invested in assets.

Average collection period indicates how quickly a firm's credit accounts are being collected and is a good measure of how efficiently a firm is managing its accounts receivable. Note: When credit sales figures are not available, net sales may be used instead.

$$\text{Average collection period} = \frac{\text{Accounts receivable}}{\text{Credit sales/365}}$$

Hypothetical Enterprises, Inc.:

$$\text{Average collection period} = \frac{32,500}{\dfrac{896,944}{365}} = 13.23 = \underline{\underline{13 \text{ days}}}$$

Analysis: This ratio tells us that, on the average, Hypothetical's credit customers take 13 days to pay their bills. Because most industries average between 30 and 60 days, the firm's 13-day collection period is quite favorable and shows considerable efficiency in handling credit accounts.

Inventory turnover is the number of times during an operating period that the average inventory was sold.

$$\text{Average inventory} = \frac{\text{Beginning inventory} + \text{Ending inventory}}{2}$$

$$\text{Inventory turnover} = \frac{\text{Cost of goods sold}}{\text{Average inventory}}$$

Hypothetical Enterprises, Inc.:

$$\text{Average inventory} = \frac{220,350 + 88,560}{2} = \underline{\$154,455}$$

$$\text{Inventory turnover} = \frac{481,540}{154,455} = 3.12 = \underline{\underline{3.1 \text{ times}}}$$

Analysis: Inventory turnover is one ratio that should be compared to the data from previous operating periods and to published industry averages for similar-sized firms in the same industry in order to draw any meaningful conclusions. When inventory turnover is below average, it may be a signal that the company is carrying too much inventory. Carrying excess inventory can lead to extra expenses, such as warehouse costs and insurance. It also ties up money that could be used more efficiently elsewhere.

Asset turnover ratio tells the number of dollars in sales the firm generates from each dollar it has invested in assets. This ratio is an important measure of a company's efficiency in managing its assets.

$$\text{Asset turnover ratio} = \frac{\text{Net sales}}{\text{Total assets}}$$

● **efficiency ratios**
Financial ratios that indicate how effectively a company utilizes its resources to generate sales.

● **average collection period**
Indicator of how quickly a firm's credit accounts are being collected. Expressed in days.

● **inventory turnover**
The number of times during an operating period that the average inventory was sold.

● **asset turnover ratio**
Ratio that tells the number of dollars in sales a firm generates from each dollar it has invested in assets.

Hypothetical Enterprises, Inc.:

$$\text{Asset turnover ratio} = \frac{896,944}{341,300} = 2.63 = \underline{\underline{2.63{:}1}}$$

Analysis: Asset turnover is another ratio best compared to those of previous operating periods and industry averages in order to reach any meaningful conclusions. Hypothetical's 2.63:1 ratio means that the company is generating $2.63 in sales for every $1.00 in assets.

Leverage Ratios

● **leverage ratios**
Financial ratios that show how and to what degree a company has financed its assets.

When firms borrow money to finance assets they are using financial leverage. Investors and creditors alike are particularly interested in the **leverage ratios** since the greater the leverage a firm has employed, the greater the risk of default on interest and principal payments. Situations such as this could lead the firm into eventual bankruptcy.

Debt-to-assets ratio measures to what degree the assets of the firm have been financed with borrowed funds, or leveraged. This ratio identifies the claim on assets by the creditors. It is commonly expressed as a percent.

● **debt-to-assets ratio**
Ratio that measures to what degree the assets of the firm have been financed with borrowed funds, or leveraged.

$$\textbf{Debt-to-assets ratio} = \frac{\textbf{Total liabilities}}{\textbf{Total assets}}$$

Hypothetical Enterprises, Inc.:

$$\text{Debt-to-assets ratio} = \frac{164,400}{341,300} = .4816 = \underline{\underline{48.2\%}}$$

Analysis: This ratio indicates that Hypothetical's creditors have claim to 48.2% of the company assets or, for each $1.00 of assets, the company owes $.48 to its creditors.

● **debt-to-equity ratio**
A ratio that compares the total debt of a firm to the owner's equity.

Debt-to-equity ratio is used as a safety-factor measure for potential creditors. The ratio compares the total debt of the firm to the owner's equity. It tells the amount of debt incurred by the company for each $1.00 of equity.

$$\textbf{Debt-to-equity ratio} = \frac{\textbf{Total liabilities}}{\textbf{Owner's equity}}$$

Hypothetical Enterprises, Inc.:

$$\text{Debt-to-equity ratio} = \frac{164,400}{176,900} = .929 = \underline{\underline{.93{:}1 \text{ or } 92.9\%}}$$

Analysis: This ratio indicates that for each $1.00 of owner's equity, Hypothetical has financed $.93 in assets. As the debt-to-equity ratio increases, so does the risk factor to potential creditors and investors. This ratio should be compared to previous periods and industry norms.

Profitability Ratios

● **profitability ratios**
Financial ratios that tell how much of each dollar of sales, assets, and owner's investment resulted in net profit.

The **profitability ratios** are important to anyone whose economic interests are tied to the long-range success of the firm. Investors expect a return on their investment in the form of dividends and stock price appreciation. Without adequate profits, firms quickly fall out of favor with current and future investors.

● **gross profit margin**
An assessment of how well the cost of goods sold category of expenses was controlled. Expressed as a percent of net sales.

Gross profit margin is an assessment of how well the cost of goods sold category of expenses was controlled. This measure particularly spotlights a firm's management of its purchasing and pricing functions. Gross profit margin is expressed as a percent of net sales.

$$\textbf{Gross profit margin} = \frac{\textbf{Gross profit}}{\textbf{Net sales}}$$

Hypothetical Enterprises, Inc.:

$$\text{Gross profit margin} = \frac{415,404}{896,944} = .463 = \underline{\underline{46.3\%}}$$

Analysis: Hypothetical's gross profit constitutes 46.3% of the company's sales, which means that for each $1.00 of sales, $.46 remains as gross margin. For a meaningful analysis, this ratio should be compared with previous operating periods and industry averages.

Net profit margin is an assessment of management's overall ability to control the cost of goods sold and the operating expenses of the firm. This ratio is the bottom-line score of a firm's profitability and is one of the most important and most frequently used. Net profit margin can be calculated either before or after income tax. As with gross profit margin, it is expressed as a percent.

$$\text{Net profit margin} = \frac{\text{Net income}}{\text{Net sales}}$$

Hypothetical Enterprises, Inc.:

$$\text{Net profit margin} = \frac{91,268}{896,944} = .1017 = 10.2\%$$

Analysis: This means that for each $1.00 of net sales, Hypothetical was able to generate $.10 in net profit. Most firms today have net profit margins between 1% and 8%, depending on the industry. Regardless of industry, Hypothetical's 10.2% net profit margin would be considered very profitable.

Return on investment is the amount of profit generated by the firm in relation to the amount invested by the owners. Abbreviated ROI, this ratio is commonly expressed as a percent.

$$\text{Return on investment} = \frac{\text{Net income}}{\text{Owner's equity}}$$

Hypothetical Enterprises, Inc.:

$$\text{Return on investment} = \frac{91,268}{176,900} = .5159 = 51.6\%$$

Analysis: This ratio indicates that Hypothetical generated $.52 in net profit for each $1.00 invested by the owners. Most investors would consider 51.6% an excellent return on their money.

TRY-IT   EXERCISE

7. **Use the balance sheet and income statement on pages 479 and 490 to calculate the financial ratios for Action Auto Parts, Inc.**

Check your answers with the solutions on page 516.

15-8 Preparing a Trend Analysis Chart and Graph of Financial Data

In Sections I and II of this chapter we used horizontal analysis to calculate and report the *amount* and *percent* change in various balance sheet and income statement items from one operating period to another. When these percentage changes are tracked for a number of successive periods it is known as **trend analysis.** Trend analysis introduces the element of time into financial analysis. Whereas data from one statement gives a firm's financial position at a given point in time, trend analysis provides a dynamic picture of the firm by showing its financial direction over a period of time.

• index numbers

Numbers used in trend analysis indicating changes in magnitude of financial data over a period of time. Calculated by setting a base period equal to 100% and calculating other periods in relation to the base period.

Index numbers are used in trend analysis to show the percentage change in various financial statement items. With index numbers, a base year is chosen and is equal to 100%. All other years' figures are measured as a percentage of the base year. Once again, we encounter the now familiar percentage formula, Rate = Portion ÷ Base. The index number should be expressed as a percent, rounded to the nearest tenth.

$$\text{Index number (rate)} = \frac{\text{Yearly amount (portion)}}{\text{Base year amount (base)}}$$

For example, if a company had sales of $50,000 in the base year and $60,000 in the index year, the index number would be 1.2 or 120% (60,000 ÷ 50,000). The index number means the sales for the index year were 1.2 times or 120% of the base year.

STEPS FOR PREPARING A TREND ANALYSIS:

Step 1. Choose a base year and let it equal 100%.

Step 2. Calculate the index number for each succeeding year using:

$$\text{Index number} = \frac{\text{Yearly amount}}{\text{Base year amount}}$$

Step 3. Round each index number to the nearest tenth percent.

EXAMPLE

From the following data, prepare a 5-year trend analysis of net sales, net income, and total assets for Hypothetical Enterprises, Inc.

Hypothetical Enterprises, Inc.
5-Year Selected Financial Data

	1995	1994	1993	1992	1991
Net Sales	896,944	881,325	790,430	855,690	825,100
Net Income	91,268	95,550	56,400	75,350	70,100
Total Assets	341,300	320,100	315,600	314,200	303,550

SOLUTION STRATEGY

To prepare the trend analysis we shall calculate the index number for each year using the percentage formula and then enter the figures in a trend analysis chart. The earliest year, 1991, will be the base year (100%). The first calculation, 1992 net sales index, is as follows:

$$\text{1992 net sales index number} = \frac{855,690}{825,100} = 1.037 = \underline{103.7\%}$$

Trend Analysis (in percentages)

	1995	1994	1993	1992	1991
Net Sales	108.7	106.8	95.8	103.7	100.0
Net Income	130.2	136.3	80.5	107.5	100.0
Total Assets	112.4	105.5	104.0	103.5	100.0

In addition to the chart form of presentation, trend analysis frequently uses graphs to visually present the financial data. Multiple-line graphs are a particularly good way of presenting comparative data. For even more meaningful analysis, company data can be graphed on the same coordinates as industry averages.

The multiple-line graph on page 503 illustrates Hypothetical's trend analysis figures in a multiple-line-graph format.

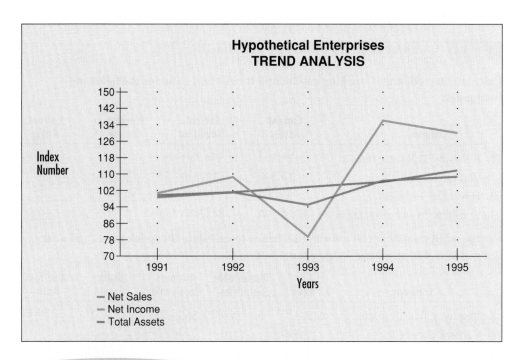

Hypothetical Enterprises
TREND ANALYSIS

Net Sales
Net Income
Total Assets

TRY-IT   **EXERCISE**

8. Prepare a trend analysis chart from the following financial data for the Scarborough Corporation and prepare a multiple-line graph of the net sales, total assets, and stockholder's equity.

Scarborough Corporation
5-Year Selected Financial Data

	1996	1995	1994	1993	1992
Net Sales	245,760	265,850	239,953	211,231	215,000
Total Assets	444,300	489,320	440,230	425,820	419,418
Stockholder's Equity	276,440	287,500	256,239	223,245	247,680

Scarborough Corporation
Trend Analysis Chart

	1996	1995	1994	1993	1992
Net Sales	_____	_____	_____	_____	_____
Total Assets	_____	_____	_____	_____	_____
Stockholder's Equity	_____	_____	_____	_____	_____

Check your answers with the solutions on page 517.

Calculate the amount of working capital and the current ratio for the following companies:

Company	Current Assets	Current Liabilities	Working Capital	Current Ratio
1. Roadway Trucking, Inc.	$125,490	$74,330	$51,160	1.69:1
2. Camera Corner, Inc.	14,540	19,700	$(5,160)	.74:1
3. Royal Dry Cleaners	3,600	1,250	$2,350	2.88:1
4. Computer Warehouse, Inc.	1,224,500	845,430	$379,070	1.45:1

Use the additional financial information below to calculate the quick assets and acid test ratio for the companies in Questions 1–4.

Company	Cash	Marketable Securities	Accounts Receivable	Quick Assets	Acid Test Ratio
5. Roadway Trucking, Inc.	$12,320	$30,000	$53,600	$95,920	1.29:1
6. Camera Corner, Inc.	2,690	0	4,330	$7,020	.36:1
7. Royal Dry Cleaners	1,180	0	985	$2,165	1.73:1
8. Computer Warehouse, Inc.	24,400	140,000	750,300	$914,700	1.08:1

9. Calculate the average collection period for Roadway Trucking, Inc., from Question 5 if the credit sales for the year amounted to $445,000.

$$\text{Average collection period} = \frac{\text{Accounts receivable}}{\dfrac{\text{Credit sales}}{365}}$$

$$\text{Average collection period} = \frac{53,600}{\dfrac{445,000}{365}} = \frac{53,600}{1,219} = \underline{44 \text{ Days}}$$

10. a. Calculate the average collection period for Computer Warehouse, Inc., from Question 8 if the credit sales for the year amounted to $8,550,000.

$$\text{Average collection period} = \frac{750,300}{\dfrac{8,550,000}{365}} = \frac{750,300}{23,425} = \underline{32 \text{ Days}}$$

b. If the industry average for similar firms is 48 days, evaluate the company's ratio.

Industry average $= 48$ Days
Computer warehouse average $= \underline{32}$ Days
Computer warehouse $= \underline{16 \text{ Days faster}}$ than competition

Calculate the average inventory and inventory turnover ratio for the following companies:

Company	Beginning Inventory	Ending Inventory	Average Inventory	Cost of Goods Sold	Inventory Turnover
11. The Bookworm	$121,400	$89,900	$105,650	$659,000	6.2
12. Eastern Wholesalers	856,430	944,380	$900,405	3,437,500	3.8
13. Alliance Corporation	90,125	58,770	$74,447.50	487,640	6.6
14. Walgreens Pharmacy	313,240	300,050	$306,645	4,356,470	14.2

15. Lakewood Enterprises had net sales of $1,354,600 last year. If the total assets of the company are $2,329,500, what is the asset turnover ratio?

$$\text{Asset turnover ratio} = \frac{\text{Net sales}}{\text{Total assets}}$$

$$= \frac{1,354,600}{2,329,500} = \underline{.58:1}$$

Calculate the amount of owner's equity and the two leverage ratios for the following companies:

Company	Total Assets	Total Liabilities	Owner's Equity	Debt to Assets Ratio	Debt to Equity Ratio
16. Big Ben Clock Company	$232,430	$115,320	$117,110	.5:1	.98:1
17. Far East Furniture	512,900	357,510	$155,390	.7:1	2.3:1
18. Magnum Industries	2,875,000	2,189,100	$685,900	.76:1	3.2:1

Calculate the gross and net profits and the two profit margins for the following companies:

Company	Net Sales	Cost of Goods Sold	Gross Profit	Operating Expenses	Net Profit	Gross Profit Margin	Net Profit Margin
19. Ace Manufacturing	$743,500	$489,560	$253,940	$175,410	$78,530	34.2%	10.6%
20. Europa Cafe	324,100	174,690	$149,410	99,200	$50,210	46.1%	15.5%
21. Pet Supermarket	316,735	203,655	$113,080	85,921	$27,159	35.7%	8.6%

Using the owner's equity information below, calculate the return on investment for the companies in Questions 19–21:

	Owner's Equity	Return on Investment
22. Ace Manufacturing	$434,210	18.1%
23. Europa Cafe	615,400	8.2%
24. Pet Supermarket	397,000	6.8%

25. Prepare a trend analysis chart from the following financial data for the King Tire Company.

King Tire Company
5-year Selected Financial Data

	1996	1995	1994	1993	1992
Net Sales	$238,339	$282,283	$239,448	$215,430	$221,800
Net Income	68,770	71,125	55,010	57,680	55,343
Total Assets	513,220	502,126	491,100	457,050	467,720
Stockholder's Equity	254,769	289,560	256,070	227,390	240,600

King Tire Company
Trend Analysis Chart

	1996	1995	1994	1993	1992
Net Sales	107.5	127.3	108.	97.1	100.0
Net Income	124.3	128.5	99.4	104.2	100.0
Total Assets	109.7	107.4	105.	97.7	100.0
Stockholder's Equity	105.9	120.3	106.4	94.5	100.0

The Annual Report

26. Use the financial information for Reebok on page 506 to answer **a** through **e**.

a. Calculate the asset turnover ratio for 1992 and 1993.

$$\text{Asset turnover ratio} = \frac{\text{Net Sales}}{\text{Total Assets}}$$

$$1992 = \frac{3,022,627}{1,345,346} = 2.25$$

$$1993 = \frac{2,893,900}{1,391,711} = 2.08$$

b. Calculate the net profit margin for 1991, 1992, and 1993.

$$\text{Net profit margin} = \frac{\text{Net Income}}{\text{Net Sales}}$$

$$1991 = \frac{234,711}{2,734,474} = 8.6\%$$

$$1992 = \frac{114,818}{3,022,627} = 3.8\%$$

$$1993 = \frac{223,415}{2,893,900} = 7.7\%$$

c. Calculate the return on investment for 1991, 1992, and 1993.

$$\text{Return on investment} = \frac{\text{Net Income}}{\text{Owner's Equity}} \qquad 1992 \quad = \frac{114{,}818}{838{,}656} = 13.7\%$$

$$1991 \quad = \frac{234{,}711}{823{,}537} = 28.5\% \qquad 1993 \quad = \frac{223{,}415}{846{,}617} = 26.4\%$$

d. Prepare a trend analysis *chart* of net sales and total assets for 1989 through 1993.

	1993	1992	1991	1990	1989
Net Sales	158.8	165.9	150.1	118.5	100
Total Assets	120.2	116.2	122.8	120.2	100

e. Extra Credit: Prepare a trend analysis *graph* for the information in part **d**.

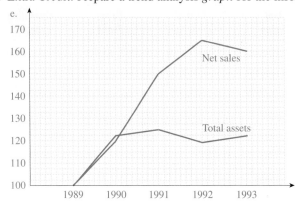

Selected Financial Data

Reebok International Ltd.

Amounts in thousands, except per share data

Year ended December 31	1993	1992	1991	1990	1989
Net sales	$2,893,900	$3,022,627	$2,734,474	$2,159,243	$1,822,092
Income before income taxes	363,247	257,964	389,886	294,835	290,779
Net income	223,415	114,818	234,711	176,606	174,998
Net income per common share	2.53	1.24	2.37	1.54	1.53
Cash dividends per common share	.30	.30	.30	.30	.30
Weighted average common and common equivalent shares outstanding	88,348	92,697	98,958	114,654	114,176

Balance Sheet Data

Amounts in thousands

December 31	1993	1992	1991	1990	1989
Working capital	$ 730,757	$ 682,342	$ 564,072	$ 705,303	$ 566,337
Total assets	1,391,711	1,345,346	1,422,283	1,392,076	1,157,793
Long-term debt	134,207	116,037	169,613	104,647	108,832
Stockholders' equity	846,617	838,656	823,537	996,729	844,296

FORMULAS

Liquidity Ratios

Working capital = Current assets − Current liabilities

$$\text{Current ratio} = \frac{\text{Current assets}}{\text{Current liabilities}}$$

Quick assets = Cash + Marketable securities + Receivables

$$\text{Acid test ratio} = \frac{\text{Quick assets}}{\text{Current liabilities}}$$

Efficiency Ratios

$$\text{Average collection period} = \frac{\text{Accounts receivable}}{\text{Credit sales}/365}$$

$$\text{Average inventory} = \frac{\text{Beginning inventory} + \text{Ending inventory}}{2}$$

$$\text{Inventory turnover} = \frac{\text{Cost of goods sold}}{\text{Average inventory}}$$

$$\text{Asset turnover ratio} = \frac{\text{Net sales}}{\text{Total assets}}$$

Leverage Ratios

$$\text{Debt-to-assets ratio} = \frac{\text{Total liabilities}}{\text{Total assets}}$$

$$\text{Debt-to-equity ratio} = \frac{\text{Total liabilities}}{\text{Owner's equity}}$$

Profitability Ratios

$$\text{Gross profit margin} = \frac{\text{Gross profit}}{\text{Net sales}}$$

$$\text{Net profit margin} = \frac{\text{Net income}}{\text{Net sales}}$$

$$\text{Return on investment} = \frac{\text{Net income}}{\text{Owner's equity}}$$

CHAPTER 15 ■ FINANCIAL STATEMENTS AND RATIOS — SUMMARY CHART

SECTION I   THE BALANCE SHEET

Topic	P/O, Page	Important Concepts	Illustrative Examples
Preparing a Balance Sheet	15–1 476	The balance sheet is a financial statement that shows a company's financial position on a certain date. It is based on the fundamental accounting equation: Assets = Liabilities + Owner's equity	*Land'n'Sea Exporters* Balance Sheet December 31, 1996 Assets Cash — $ 24,000 Receivables — 92,000 Inventory — 68,500 Supplies — 12,100 Total current assets — $196,600

I, continued

Topic	P/O, Page	Important Concepts	Illustrative Examples

		Balance sheet preparation:
		1. *List and total:*
		    Current assets
		    + Property, plant, and equipment
		    + Investments and other assets
		    Total assets
		2. *List and total:*
		    Current liabilities
		    + Long-term liabilities
		    Total liabilities
		3. *List and total:*
		    Owner's equity
		4. Add the Total liabilities and the Owner's equity. This total should equal the Total assets.
			Land and building $546,700
			Fixtures & equip. 88,400
			Vehicles 124,200
			   Total prop. & equip. $759,300
			     Total assets $955,900
			
			Liabilities & Owner's Equity
			
			Accounts payable $ 82,400
			Note payable (3-month) 31,300
			  Total current liab. $113,700
			Mortgage payable $213,400
			Note payable (2-year) 65,800
			  Total long-term liab. $279,200
			Total liabilities $392,900
			Owner's equity 563,000
			  Total liabilities
			  & owner's equity $955,900

Preparing a Vertical Analysis of a Balance Sheet	15–2
	480
		In vertical analysis, each item on the balance sheet is expressed as a percent of total assets.
		Vertical analysis preparation:
		1. Use the percentage formula,
		
		   Rate = Portion ÷ Base
		
		Use each balance sheet item as the portion and total assets as the base.
		2. Round each answer to the nearest tenth percent. Note: a 0.1% differential may occur due to rounding.
			Land'n'Sea Exporters
			Balance Sheet—Asset Section
			
			Cash $ 24,000 2.5
			Receivables 92,000 9.6
			Inventory 68,500 7.2
			Supplies 12,100 1.3
			Current assets $196,600 20.6
			Land & $546,700 57.2
			  building
			Fixtures & 88,400 9.2
			  equip.
			Vehicles 124,200 13.0
			Prop. & equip. $759,300 79.4
			Total assets $955,900 100.0

Preparing a Horizontal Analysis of a Comparative Balance Sheet	15–3
	481
		Comparative balance sheets display data from the current period side-by-side with the figures from one or more previous periods. In horizontal analysis each item of the current period is compared in dollars and percent with the corresponding item from the previous period.
		
		Horizontal analysis preparation:
		1. Set up a comparative balance sheet format with the current period listed first.
		2. Label the next two columns:
		    Increase/Decrease
		    Amount Percent
		3. For each item, calculate the dollar difference between the current and previous period and enter this figure in the amount column. Enter all decreases in parentheses.
			If the 1995 cash figure for Land'n'Sea Exporters was $21,300, the comparative balance sheet horizontal analysis would be listed as follows:
			
			Cash
			
			         Increase/Decrease
			1996 **1995** **Amount** **Percent**
			24,000 21,300 2,700 12.7
			
			$\dfrac{2,700}{21,300} = 12.7\%$

I, continued

Topic	P/O, Page	Important Concepts	Illustrative Examples
		4. Calculate the percent change using: $$\text{Percent change (rate)} = \frac{\text{Amount of change (portion)}}{\text{Previous period amount (base)}}$$ 5. Enter the percent change in the Percent column. Round to the nearest tenth percent. Enter all decreases in parentheses.	For a comprehensive example of a comparative balance sheet with horizontal analysis, see page xx, Albrecht Construction Company.

SECTION II   THE INCOME STATEMENT

Topic	P/O, Page	Important Concepts	Illustrative Examples
Preparing an Income Statement	15–4 487	An income statement is a summary of the operations of a business over a period of time. It is based on the equation: **Profit = Revenue – Total expenses** *Income Statement preparation:* 1. Label the top of the statement with the company name and period of time covered. 2. In a two-column format, calculate: a. *Net Sales,* using: Gross sales – Sales returns & allow. – Sales discounts Net sales b. *Cost of goods sold,* using: Beginning inventory + Net purchases + Freight in Goods available for sale – Ending inventory Cost of goods sold c. *Gross margin,* using: Net sales – Cost of goods sold Gross margin d. *Net income,* using: Gross margin – Total operating expenses Net income	*Land'n'Sea Exporters* Income Statement—1996 (000) Gross sales $435.3 Sales returns 11.1 Sales discounts 8.0 Net sales $416.2 Inventory, Jan. 1 124.2 Net purchases 165.8 Freight in 2.7 Goods available 292.7 Inventory, Dec. 31. 118.1 Cost of goods sold 174.6 Gross margin 241.6 Salaries 87.6 Rent & utilities 22.5 Other expenses 101.7 Total op. expenses 211.8 Net income $ 29.8

II, continued

Topic	P/O, Page	Important Concepts	Illustrative Examples
Preparing a Vertical Analysis of an Income Statement	15–5 490	In vertical analysis of an income statement, each figure is expressed as a percent of net sales. *Vertical analysis preparation:* 1. Use the percentage formula, Rate = Portion ÷ Base Use each income statement item as the portion and net sales as the base. 2. Round each answer to the nearest tenth percent. Note: a 0.1% differential may occur due to rounding.	*Land'n'Sea Exporters* Income Statement—1996 (000) Gross sales $435.3 104.6 Sales returns 11.1 2.7 Sales discounts 8.0 1.9 Net sales 416.2 100.0 Inventory, Jan. 1. 124.2 29.8 Net purchases 165.8 39.8 Freight in 2.7 .6 Goods available for sale 292.7 70.2 Inventory, Dec. 31. 118.1 28.4 Cost of goods sold 174.6 41.8 Gross margin 241.6 58.2 Salaries 87.6 21.0 Rent & utilities 22.5 5.4 Other expenses 101.7 24.4 Total op. expenses 211.8 50.8 Net income $ 29.8 7.4
Preparing a Horizontal Analysis of a Comparative Income Statement	15–6 492	In horizontal analysis of a comparative income statement, each item of the current period is compared in dollars and percent with the corresponding item from the previous period. *Horizontal analysis preparation:* 1. Set up a comparative income statement format with the current period listed first. 2. Label the next two columns: **Increase/Decrease** **Amount Percent** 3. For each item, calculate the dollar difference between the current and previous period and enter this figure in the amount column. Enter all decreases in parentheses. 4. Calculate the percent change using: Percent change (rate) = $\dfrac{\text{Amount of change (portion)}}{\text{Previous period amount (base)}}$ 5. Enter the percent change in the Percent column. Round to the nearest tenth percent. Enter all decreases in parentheses.	If the 1995 net income figure for Land'n'Sea Exporters was $23,100, the comparative income statement horizontal analysis would be listed as follows: Net Income |		Increase/Decrease	
1996	1995	Amount	Percent
28,800	23,100	5,700	24.7 | $\dfrac{5{,}700}{23{,}100} = 24.7\%$ For a comprehensive example of a comparative income statement with horizontal analysis, see page 493, Fisher Island Electronics, Inc.

SECTION III   FINANCIAL RATIOS AND TREND ANALYSIS

Topic	P/O, Page	Important Concepts	Illustrative Examples
Calculating Financial Ratios	15–7 497	Financial ratios are standardized comparisons of various items from the balance sheet and the income statement. When compared to ratios of previous operating periods and industry averages, they can be used as signals to analysts of potential strengths or weaknesses of the firm.	A company had net sales of $100,000 and net income of $10,000. Express this data as a ratio. $$\frac{100,000}{10,000} = 10$$ 1. The ratio of sales to income is 10 to 1, written 10:1. 2. Net income is $\frac{1}{10}$ or 10% of net sales. 3. For every $1.00 of net sales, the company generates $.10 in net income.
Liquidity Ratios	15–7 498	Liquidity ratios examine the relationship between a firm's current assets and its maturing obligation. They are a good indicator of a firm's ability to pay its bills over the next few months. $$\text{Current ratio} = \frac{\text{Current assets}}{\text{Current liabilities}}$$ $$\text{Acid test ratio} = \frac{\text{Cash} + \text{Marketable securities} + \text{Accounts receivable}}{\text{Current liabilities}}$$	Land'n'Sea Exporters Financial Ratios 1996 Current Ratio = $$\frac{196,600}{113,700} = 1.73 = \underline{1.73:1}$$ Acid Test Ratio = $$\frac{24,000 + 92,000}{113,700} = 1.02 = \underline{1.02:1}$$
Efficiency Ratios	15–7 499	Efficiency ratios provide the basis for determining how effectively a firm uses its resources to generate sales. $$\text{Average collection period} = \frac{\text{Accounts receivable}}{\text{Credit sales}/365}$$ $$\text{Inventory turnover} = \frac{\text{Cost of goods sold}}{\frac{\text{Beg inventory} + \text{End inventory}}{2}}$$ $$\text{Asset turnover ratio} = \frac{\text{Net sales}}{\text{Total assets}}$$	Credit sales for Land'n'Sea are 50% of net sales. Average collection period = $$\frac{92,000}{208,100/365} = \underline{161 \text{ days}}$$ Inventory turnover = $$\frac{174,600}{\frac{124,200 + 118.1}{2}} = \underline{1.44 \text{ times}}$$ Asset turnover ratio = $$\frac{416,200}{955,900} = .44 = \underline{.44:1}$$
Leverage Ratios	15–7 500	Leverage ratios provide information about the amount of money a company has borrowed to finance its assets. $$\text{Debt-to-assets ratio} = \frac{\text{Total liabilities}}{\text{Total assets}}$$	Debt-to-assets ratio = $$\frac{392,900}{955,900} = .411 = \underline{41.1\%}$$

III, continued

Topic	P/O, Page	Important Concepts	Illustrative Examples
		$$\text{Debt-to-equity ratio} = \frac{\text{Total liabilities}}{\text{Owner's equity}}$$	Debt-to-equity ratio = $$\frac{392,900}{563,000} = .698 = \underline{\underline{69.8\%}}$$
Profitability Ratios	15–7 500	Profitability ratios show a firm's ability to generate profits and provide its investors with a return on their investment. $$\text{Gross profit margin} = \frac{\text{Gross profit}}{\text{Net sales}}$$ $$\text{Net profit margin} = \frac{\text{Net income}}{\text{Net sales}}$$ $$\text{Return on investment} = \frac{\text{Net income}}{\text{Owner's equity}}$$	Gross profit margins = $$\frac{241,600}{416,200} = .580 = \underline{\underline{58.0\%}}$$ Net profit margin = $$\frac{29,800}{416,200} = .072 = \underline{\underline{7.2\%}}$$ Return on investment = $$\frac{29,800}{563,000} = .053 = \underline{\underline{5.3\%}}$$
Preparing Trend Analysis Charts and Graphs	15–8 501	Trend analysis is the process of tracking changes in financial statement items for three or more operating periods. Trend analysis figures can be displayed on a chart using index numbers, or more visually as a line graph or bar chart. *Trend analysis chart preparation:* 1. Choose a base year (usually the earliest year) and let it equal 100%. 2. Calculate the index number for each succeeding year using: $$\text{Index number (rate)} = \frac{\text{Yearly amount (portion)}}{\text{Base year amount (base)}}$$ 3. Round each index number to the nearest tenth percent. 4. *Optional:* Graph the index numbers or the raw data on a line graph.	Prepare a trend analysis chart for Land'n'Sea Exporters' net sales data. Land'n'Sea Exporters Net Sales (000) **1996 1995 1994 1993 1992** 416.2 401.6 365.4 388.3 375.1 For this trend analysis, we shall use 1992 as the base year, 100%. Each succeeding year's index number is calculated using the yearly amount as the portion and the 1992 amount as the base. For example, 1993 index number = $$\frac{388.3}{375.1} = 103.5$$ **1996 1995 1994 1993 1992** 111.0 107.1 97.4 103.5 100.0

1.

Lee's Garage
Balance Sheet
December 31, 1995

Assets

Current Assets

Cash	$ 5,200	
Accounts Receivable	2,800	
Merchandise Inventory	2,700	
Prepaid Salary	235	
Supplies	3,900	
Total Current Assets		$ 14,835

Property, Plant, and Equipment

Land	35,000	
Building	74,000	
Fixtures	1,200	
Tow Truck	33,600	
Tools and Equipment	45,000	
Total Property, Plant, and Equipment		188,800
Total Assets		$203,635

Liabilities and Owner's Equity

Current Liabilities

Accounts Payable	$ 6,800	
Notes Payable	17,600	
Taxes Payable	3,540	
Total Current Liabilities		$ 27,940

Long-Term Liabilities

Mortgage Payable	51,000	
Total Long-Term Liabilities		51,000

Owner's Equity

Lee Sutherlin, Capital	124,695	
Total Owner's Equity		124,695
Total Liabilities and Owner's Equity		$203,635

2.

Action Auto Parts, Inc.
Balance Sheet
June 30, 1995

Assets

Current Assets

Cash	$ 3,400	1.1
Accounts and Notes Receivable	5,600	1.8
Merchandise Inventory	98,700	32.0
Prepaid Insurance	455	.1
Supplies	800	.3
Total Current Assets	108,955	35.3

Property, Plant, and Equipment

Land and Building	147,000	47.6
Fixtures	8,600	2.8
Delivery Vehicles	27,000	8.8
Forklift	7,000	2.3
Total Property, Plant, and Equipment	189,600	61.5

Investments and Other Assets

Goodwill	10,000	3.2
Total Investments and Other Assets	10,000	3.2
Total Assets	$308,555	100%

Liabilities and Stockholder's Equity

Current Liabilities

Accounts Payable	$ 16,500	5.3
Notes Payable	10,000	3.2
Total Current Liabilities	26,500	8.6

Long-Term Liabilities

Mortgage Payable	67,000	21.7
Total Long-Term Liabilities	67,000	21.7
Total Liabilities	93,500	30.3

Stockholder's Equity

Common Stock	185,055	60.0
Retained Earnings	30,000	9.7
Total Stockholder's Equity	215,055	69.7
Total Liabilities and Stockholder's Equity	$308,555	100%

3.

Figueroa Industries, Inc.
Comparative Balance Sheet
December 31, 1995 and 1996

			Increase/Decrease	
Assets	1996	1995	Amount	Percent
Current Assets				
Cash	$ 8,700	$ 5,430	$3,270	60.2
Accounts Receivable	23,110	18,450	4,660	25.3
Notes Receivable	2,900	3,400	(500)	(14.7)
Supplies	4,540	3,980	560	14.1
Total Current Assets	39,250	31,260	7,990	25.6
Property, Plant, and Equipment				
Land	$ 34,000	$ 34,000	0	0
Buildings	76,300	79,800	(3,500)	(4.4)
Machinery and Equipment	54,700	48,900	5,800	11.9
Total Prop., Plant, and Equip.	165,000	162,700	2,300	1.4
Investments and Other Assets	54,230	49,810	4,420	8.9
Total Assets	258,480	243,770	14,710	6.0

Liabilities and Stockholder's Equity

Current Liabilities				
Accounts Payable	$ 15,330	$ 19,650	(4,320)	(22.0)
Salaries Payable	7,680	7,190	490	6.8
Total Current Liabilities	23,010	26,840	(3,830)	(14.3)
Long-Term Liabilities				
Mortgage Payable	$ 53,010	$ 54,200	(1,190)	(2.2)
Note Payable (3-year)	32,400	33,560	(1,160)	(3.5)
Total Long-Term Liabilities	85,410	87,760	(2,350)	(2.7)
Total Liabilities	108,420	114,600	(6,180)	(5.4)
Stockholder's Equity				
Figueroa Industries, Common Stock	150,060	129,170	20,890	16.2
Total Liabilities and Stockholder's Equity	258,480	243,770	14,710	6.0

4.

Westminster Manufacturing, Inc.
Income Statement
1996

Revenue		
Gross Sales	$1,356,000	
Less: Sales Returns and Allowances	93,100	
Sales Discounts	4,268	
Net Sales		1,258,632
Cost of Goods Sold		
Merchandise Inv., Jan. 1	324,800	
Net Purchases	255,320	
Freight In	3,911	
Goods Available for Sale	584,031	
Less: Merchandise Inv., Dec. 31	179,100	
Cost of Goods Sold		404,931
Gross Margin		853,701
Operating Expenses		
Salaries	375,900	
Rent	166,000	
Utilities	7,730	
Advertising	73,300	
Insurance	22,940	
Admin. Expenses	84,500	
Miscellaneous Expenses	24,900	
Total Operating Expenses		755,270
Income before Taxes		98,431
Income Tax		34,760
Net Income		$ 63,671

5.

Action Auto Parts, Inc.
Income Statement
For the year ended December 31, 1995

Revenue		
Gross Sales	$458,400	103.3
Less: Sales Returns and Allowances	13,200	3.0
Sales Discounts	1,244	.3
Net Sales	$443,956	100.0%
Cost of Goods Sold		
Merchandise Inventory, Jan. 1	198,700	44.8
Net Purchases	86,760	19.5
Freight In	875	.2
Goods Available for Sale	286,335	64.5
Less: Merchandise Inventory, Dec. 31	76,400	17.2
Cost of Goods Sold	209,935	47.3
Gross Margin	234,021	52.7
Operating Expenses		
Salaries	124,200	28.0
Rent	21,000	4.7
Utilities	1,780	.4
Advertising	5,400	1.2
Insurance	2,340	.5
Administrative Expenses	14,500	3.3
Miscellaneous Expenses	6,000	1.4
Total Operating Expenses	175,220	39.5
Income before Taxes	58,801	13.2
Income Tax	17,335	3.9
Net Income	$ 41,466	9.3

6.

Winkler's Grocery Store, Inc.
Comparative Income Statement
For the years ended December 31, 1995 and 1996

	1996	1995	Increase/Decrease Amount	Percent
Revenue				
Gross Sales	$1,223,000	$996,500	$226,500	22.7%
Less: Sales Returns and Allowances	121,340	99,600	21,740	21.8
Sales Discounts	63,120	51,237	11,883	23.2
Net Sales	1,038,540	845,663	192,877	22.8
Cost of Goods Sold				
Merchandise Inventory, Jan. 1	554,300	331,000	223,300	67.5
Purchases	360,190	271,128	89,062	32.8
Freight In	18,640	13,400	5,240	39.1
Goods Available for Sale	933,130	615,528	317,602	51.6
Less: Merchandise Inventory, Dec. 31	585,400	311,200	274,200	88.1
Cost of Goods Sold	347,730	304,328	43,402	14.3
Gross Margin	690,810	541,335	149,475	27.6
Operating Expenses				
Salaries and Benefits	215,200	121,800	93,400	76.7
Rent and Utilities	124,650	124,650	0	0
Depreciation	43,500	41,230	2,270	5.5
Insurance	24,970	23,800	1,170	4.9
Administrative Store Expenses	58,200	33,900	24,300	71.7
Warehouse Expenses	42,380	45,450	(3,070)	(6.8)
Total Operating Expenses	508,900	390,830	118,070	30.2
Income before Taxes	181,910	150,505	31,405	20.9
Income Tax	66,280	41,670	24,610	59.1
Net Income	$ 115,630	$108,835	$ 6,795	6.2

7. *Action Auto Parts—Financial Ratios 1995*

$$\text{Current ratio} = \frac{\text{Current assets}}{\text{Current liabilities}} = \frac{108,955}{26,500} = 4.11{:}1$$

$$\text{Acid test ratio} = \frac{\text{Cash + Marketable securities + Receivables}}{\text{Current liabilities}} = \frac{3,400 + 5,600}{26,500} = .34{:}1$$

$$\text{Average collection period} = \frac{\text{Accounts receivable}}{\text{Net sales/365}} = \frac{5,600}{443,956/365} = 4.6 \text{ days}$$

$$\text{Average inventory} = \frac{\text{Beginning inventory + Ending inventory}}{2} = \frac{198,700 + 76,400}{2} = \$137,550$$

$$\text{Inventory turnover} = \frac{\text{Cost of goods sold}}{\text{Average inventory}} = \frac{209,935}{137,550} = 1.5 \text{ times}$$

$$\text{Asset turnover ratio} = \frac{\text{Net sales}}{\text{Total assets}} = \frac{443,956}{308,555} = 1.44{:}1$$

$$\text{Debt-to-assets ratio} = \frac{\text{Total liabilities}}{\text{Total assets}} = \frac{93,500}{308,555} = .303 = 30.3\%$$

$$\text{Debt-to-equity ratio} = \frac{\text{Total liabilities}}{\text{Owner's equity}} = \frac{93,500}{215,055} = .435 = 43.5\%$$

$$\text{Gross profit margin} = \frac{\text{Gross profit}}{\text{Net sales}} = \frac{234,021}{443,956} = .527 = 52.7\%$$

$$\text{Net profit margin} = \frac{\text{Net income}}{\text{Net sales}} = \frac{41,466}{443,956} = .093 = 9.3\%$$

$$\text{Return on investment} = \frac{\text{Net income}}{\text{Owner's equity}} = \frac{41,466}{215,055} = .193 = 19.3\%$$

8.

Scarborough Corporation
Trend Analysis Chart

	1996	1995	1994	1993	1992
Net Sales	114.3	123.7	111.6	98.2	100.0
Total Assets	105.9	116.7	105.0	101.5	100.0
Stockholder's Equity	111.6	116.1	103.5	90.1	100.0

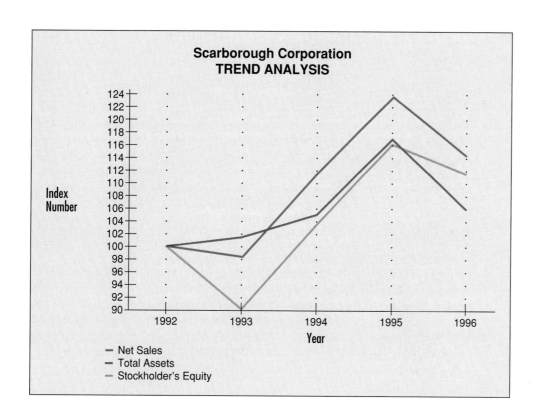

CHAPTER 15   **ASSESSMENT TEST**

Prepare the following statements on separate sheets of paper.

1. **a.** Use the following financial information to calculate the owner's equity and prepare a balance sheet with vertical analysis as of December 31, 1996, for Service Master Carpet Cleaning, a sole proprietorship owned by Al Mosley: Current assets, $132,500; property, plant, and equipment, $88,760; investments and other assets, $32,400; current liabilities, $51,150; long-term liabilities, $87,490.

Financial statement solutions appear in the appendix following the index.

Service Master Carpet Cleaning
Balance Sheet
As of December 31, 1996

b. The following financial information is for Service Master as of December 31, 1997. Calculate the owner's equity for 1997, and prepare a comparative balance sheet with horizontal analysis for 1996 and 1997: Current assets, $154,300; property, plant, and equipment, $124,650; investments and other assets, $20,000; current liabilities, $65,210; long-term liabilities, $83,800.

Service Master Carpet Cleaning
Comparative Balance Sheet
As of December 31, 1996 and 1997

2. **a.** Use the following financial information to prepare a balance sheet with vertical analysis as of October 31, 1996, for General Industries, Inc.: Cash, $45,260; accounts receivable, $267,580; merchandise inventory, $213,200; prepaid expenses, $13,400; supplies, $5,300; land, $87,600; building, $237,200; equipment, $85,630; vehicles, $54,700; computers, $31,100; investments, $53,100; accounts payable, $43,200; salaries payable, $16,500; notes payable (6-month), $102,400; mortgage payable, $124,300; notes payable (3-year), $200,000; common stock, $422,000; and retained earnings, $185,670.

General Industries, Inc.
Balance Sheet
As of October 31, 1996

b. The following financial information is for General Industries as of October 31, 1997. Prepare a comparative balance sheet with horizontal analysis for 1996 and 1997: Cash, $47,870; accounts receivable, $251,400; merchandise inventory, $223,290; prepaid expenses, $8,500; supplies, $6,430; land, $87,600; building, $234,500; equipment, $88,960; vehicles, $68,800; computers, $33,270; investments, $55,640; accounts payable, $48,700; salaries payable, $9,780; notes payable (6-month), $96,700; mortgage payable, $121,540; notes payable (3-year), $190,000; common stock, $450,000; and retained earnings, $189,540.

General Industries, Inc.
Consolidated Balance Sheet
As of October 31, 1996 and 1997

3. For the second quarter of 1997, the Quality Picture Frame Company had gross sales of $214,300, sales returns and allowances of $26,540, and sales discounts of $1,988. What were Quality's net sales?

Gross sales	$214,300
Sales returns	– 26,540
Sales discounts	– 1,988
Net sales =	$185,772

4. For the month of January, Premier Manufacturing, Inc., had the following financial information: merchandise inventory, January 1, $322,000; merchandise inventory, January 31, $316,400; gross purchases, $243,460; purchase returns and allowances, $26,880; and freight in, $3,430.

a. What are Premier's goods available for sale?

Inventory (January 1) $322,000
Net purchases $216,580
Freight in   + $3,430
Goods available for sale = $542,010

b. What is the cost of goods sold for January?

Goods available for sale $542,010
Inventory (January 31) – $316,400
Cost of goods sold January = $225,610

c. If net sales were $389,450 what was the gross margin for January?

Net sales $389,450
Cost of goods sold – $225,610
Gross margin = $163,840

d. If total operating expenses were $179,800, what was the net profit?

Gross margin $163,840
Operating expenses – $179,800
Net profit (loss) = ($15,960)

Name_____

Class_____

ANSWERS

4. a. _____ $542,010 _____

b. _____ $225,610 _____

c. _____ $163,840 _____

d. _____ ($15,960) _____

Financial statement solutions appear in the appendix following the index.

Prepare the following statements on separate sheets of paper.

5. a. From the following third quarter 1997 information for Abbey Road Restaurant Supply, construct an income statement with vertical analysis: Gross sales, $224,400; sales returns and allowances, $14,300; beginning inventory, July 1, $165,000; ending inventory, September 30, $143,320; net purchases, $76,500; total operating expenses, $68,600; income tax, $8,790.

Abbey Road Restaurant Supply
Income Statement
Third Quarter, 1997

b. The following financial information is for the fourth quarter of 1997 for Abbey Road Restaurant Supply. Prepare a comparative income statement with horizontal analysis for the third and fourth quarters: Gross sales, $218,200; sales returns and allowances, $9,500; beginning inventory, October 1, $143,320; ending inventory, December 31, $125,300; net purchases, $81,200; total operating expenses, $77,300; income tax, $11,340.

Abbey Road Restaurant Supply
Comparative Income Statement
Third and Fourth Quarters, 1997

6. a. Use the following financial information to construct a 1996 income statement with vertical analysis for Omega Optical, Inc.: Gross sales, $1,243,000; sales returns and allowances, $76,540; sales discounts, $21,300; merchandise inventory, Jan. 1, 1996, $654,410; merchandise inventory, Dec. 31, 1996, $413,200; net purchases, $318,000; freight in, $3,450; salaries, $92,350; rent, $83,100; depreciation, $87,700; utilities, $21,350; advertising, $130,440; insurance, $7,920; miscellaneous expenses, $105,900; and income tax, $18,580.

Omega Optical, Inc.
Income Statement
For the year ended December 31, 1996

ANSWERS

7. _____$653,300_____

8. _____2.49:1_____

9. _____1.02:1_____

10. _____117 Days_____

11. _____1.74 Times_____

12. _____.55:1_____

13. _____37.9%_____

14. _____61.1%_____

15. _____48.3%_____

16. _____4.8_____

17. _____4.2%_____

Financial statement solutions appear in the appendix following the index.

b. The following data represents Omega's operating results for 1997. Prepare a comparative income statement with horizontal analysis for 1996 and 1997: Gross sales, $1,286,500; sales returns and allowances, $78,950; sales discounts, $18,700; merchandise inventory, Jan. 1, 1997, $687,300; merchandise inventory, Dec. 31, 1997, $401,210; net purchases, $325,400; freight in, $3,980; salaries, $99,340; rent, $85,600; depreciation, $81,200; utilities, $21,340; advertising, $124,390; insurance, $8,700; miscellaneous expenses, $101,230; and income tax, $12,650.

Omega Optical, Inc.
Comparative Income Statement
For the years ended December 31, 1996 and 1997

As the accounting manager of Niagara Industries, Inc., you have been asked to calculate the following financial ratios for the company's 1997 annual report. Use the balance sheet and income statement for Niagara, on page 521:

7. Working capital:

$$\text{Working capital} = 1{,}093{,}000 - 439{,}700$$
$$= \underline{\underline{\$653{,}300}}$$

8. Current ratio:

$$\text{Current ratio} = \frac{1{,}093{,}000}{439{,}700} = \underline{\underline{2.49{:}1}}$$

9. Acid test ratio:

$$\text{Acid test ratio} = \frac{250{,}000 + 325{,}400 + 88{,}700}{653{,}300} = \underline{\underline{1.02{:}1}}$$

10. Average collection period (credit sales are 60% of net sales):

$$\text{Average collection period} = \frac{325{,}400}{\frac{(1{,}695{,}900 \times 60\%)}{365}} = \frac{325{,}400}{\frac{1{,}017{,}540}{365}} = \frac{325{,}400}{2{,}788} = 116.7 = \underline{\underline{117 \text{ Days}}}$$

11. Inventory turnover:

$$\text{Inventory turnover} = \frac{876{,}500}{\frac{767{,}800 + 239{,}300}{2}} = \frac{876{,}500}{503{,}550} = \underline{\underline{1.74 \text{ Times}}}$$

12. Asset turnover ratio:

$$\text{Asset turnover ratio} = \frac{1{,}695{,}900}{3{,}108{,}200} = \underline{\underline{.55{:}1}}$$

13. Debt-to-assets ratio:

$$\text{Debt to assets ratio} = \frac{1{,}178{,}500}{3{,}108{,}200} = \underline{\underline{37.9\%}}$$

14. Debt-to-equity ratio:

$$\text{Debt-to-equity ratio} = \frac{1{,}178{,}500}{1{,}929{,}700} = \underline{\underline{61.1\%}}$$

15. Gross profit margin:

$$\text{Gross profit margin} = \frac{819{,}400}{1{,}695{,}900} = \underline{\underline{48.3\%}}$$

16. Net profit margin:

$$\text{Net profit margin} = \frac{81{,}900}{1{,}695{,}900} = \underline{\underline{4.8\%}}$$

17. Return on investment:

$$\text{Return on investment} = \frac{81{,}900}{1{,}929{,}700} = \underline{\underline{4.2\%}}$$

Niagara Industries, Inc.
Balance Sheet
As of December 31, 1997

Assets

Cash	$250,000	
Accounts Receivable	325,400	
Merchandise Inventory	416,800	
Marketable Securities	88,700	
Supplies	12,100	
Total Current Assets		$1,093,000
Land and Building	1,147,000	
Fixtures and Equipment	868,200	
Total Property, Plant, and Equipment		2,015,200
Total Assets		$3,108,200

Liabilities and Owner's Equity

Accounts Payable	$286,500	
Notes Payable (6-month)	153,200	
Total Current Liabilities		$ 439,700
Mortgage Payable	325,700	
Notes Payable (4-year)	413,100	
Total Long-Term Liabilities		738,800
Total Liabilities		1,178,500
Owner's Equity		1,929,700
Total Liabilities and Owner's Equity		$3,108,200

Niagara Industries, Inc.
Income Statement, 1997

Net Sales		$1,695,900
Merchandise Inventory, Jan. 1	$ 767,800	
Net Purchases	314,900	
Freight In	33,100	
Goods Available for Sale	1,115,800	
Merchandise Inventory, Dec. 31	239,300	
Cost of Goods Sold		876,500
Gross Margin		819,400
Total Operating Expenses		702,300
Income before Taxes		117,100
Taxes		35,200
Net Income		$ 81,900

18. Prepare a trend analysis chart from the financial data listed below for ATM Systems, Inc.

ATM Systems, Inc.
4-year Selected Financial Data

	1997	1996	1995	1994
Net Sales	$898,700	$829,100	$836,200	$801,600
Net Income	96,300	92,100	94,400	89,700
Total Assets	2,334,000	2,311,000	2,148,700	1,998,900
Stockholder's Equity	615,000	586,000	597,200	550,400

ATM Systems, Inc.
Trend Analysis Chart

	1997	1996	1995	1994
Net Sales	112.1	103.4	104.3	100.0
Net Income	107.4	102.7	105.2	100.0
Total Assets	116.8	115.6	107.5	100.0
Stockholder's Equity	111.7	106.5	108.5	100.0

19. As part of the trend analysis for ATM Systems, Inc., prepare a multiple-line graph for the annual report comparing net sales and net income for the years 1994 through 1997.

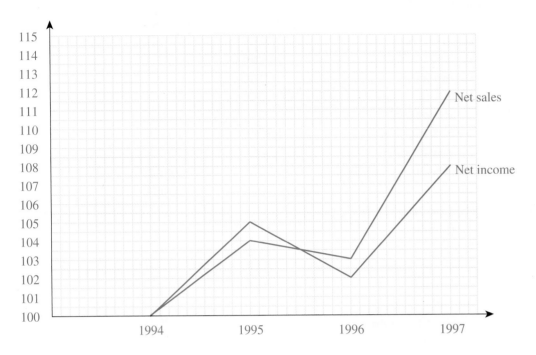

Worked-out solution to question 20 appears in the appendix following the index.

Annual Reports

20. From the consolidated statements of earnings for Toys"R"Us below, prepare a vertical analysis in the form of a common-size income statement (percentages only) for 1994.

TOYS"R"US, INC. AND SUBSIDIARIES

CONSOLIDATED STATEMENTS OF EARNINGS

(In thousands except per share information)

	January 29, 1994	January 30, 1993	Year Ended February 1, 1992
Net sales	$ 7,946,067	$ 7,169,290	$ 6,124,209
Costs and expenses:			
Cost of sales	5,494,766	4,968,555	4,286,639
Selling, advertising, general and administrative	1,497,011	1,342,262	1,153,576
Depreciation and amortization	133,370	119,034	100,701
Interest expense	72,283	69,134	57,885
Interest and other income	(24,116)	(18,719)	(13,521)
	7,173,314	6,480,266	5,585,280
Earnings before taxes on income	772,753	689,024	538,929
Taxes on income	289,800	251,500	199,400
Net earnings	$ 482,953	$ 437,524	$ 339,529
Earnings per share	$ 1.63	$ 1.47	$ 1.15

See notes to consolidated financial statements.

21. From the consolidated statements of earnings and balance sheets of Winn-Dixie Stores on page 524, prepare the following financial ratios for 1993 and 1994.

a. Current ratio

$$\text{Current ratio} = \frac{\text{Current assets}}{\text{Current liabilities}}$$

1993
$$\frac{1,413,200}{868,546} = 1.63:1$$

1994
$$\frac{1,361,184}{873,166} = 1.56:1$$

b. Acid test ratio (Note: Winn-Dixie has no marketable securities.)

$$\text{Acid test ratio} = \frac{\text{Cash} + \overset{\text{marketable}}{\text{securities}} + \overset{\text{Accounts}}{\text{receivable}}}{\text{Current liabilities}}$$

1993
$$\frac{107,784 + 162,590}{868,546} = .31:1$$

1994
$$\frac{31.451 + 171.834}{873,166} = .23:1$$

c. Asset turnover ratio

$$\text{Asset turnover ratio} = \frac{\text{Net sales}}{\text{Total assets}}$$

1993
$$\frac{10,831,535}{2,062,560} = 5.25:1$$

1994
$$\frac{11,082,169}{2,146,574} = 5.16:1$$

d. Debt-to-assets ratio

$$\text{Debt to assets ratio} = \frac{\text{Total liab.}}{\text{Total assets}}$$

1993
$$\frac{1,077,595}{2,062,560} = 52.2\%$$

1994
$$\frac{1,089,113}{2,146,574} = 50.7\%$$

e. Debt-to-equity ratio

$$\text{Debt to equity ratio} = \frac{\text{Total liab.}}{\text{Owner's equity}}$$

1993
$$\frac{1,077,595}{984,965} = 109.4\%$$

1994
$$\frac{1,089,113}{1,057.461} = 103\%$$

f. Net profit margin

$$\text{Net profit margin} = \frac{\text{Net income}}{\text{Net sales}}$$

1993
$$\frac{236,385}{10,831,535} = 2.18\%$$

1994
$$\frac{216,117}{11,082.169} = 1.95\%$$

g. Return on investment

$$\text{Return on investment} = \frac{\text{Net income}}{\text{Owner's equity}}$$

1993
$$\frac{236,385}{984,965} = 23.99\%$$

1994
$$\frac{216,117}{1,057.461} = 20.44\%$$

Name_____

Class_____

ANSWERS

21. a. _____ 1.63:1 _____

_____ 1.56:1 _____

b. _____ .31:1 _____

_____ .23:1 _____

c. _____ 5.25:1 _____

_____ 5.16:1 _____

d. _____ 52.2% _____

_____ 50.7% _____

e. _____ 109.4% _____

_____ 103% _____

f. _____ 2.18% _____

_____ 1.95% _____

g. _____ 23.99% _____

_____ 20.44% _____

◆ BUSINESS DECISION
Evaluating Financial Performance

22. a. Based on your calculations of the financial ratios for Winn-Dixie in the annual report in question 21 above, determine for each ratio whether the 1994 figure was better or worse than 1993.

Current ratio	1994 worse than 1993	Debt-to-equity ratio	1994 better than 1993
Acid test ratio	1994 worse than 1993	Net profit margin	1994 worse than 1993
Asset turnover ratio	1994 worse than 1993	Return on investment	1994 worse than 1993
Debt-to-assets ratio	1994 better than 1993		

b. How would you rate Winn-Dixie's financial performance from 1993 to 1994?

Winn-Dixie's financial performance from 1993 to 1994 was mixed.

The liquidity, efficiency, and profitability ratios were all slighty worse in 1994; however, none changed significantly. All of these ratios are still within acceptable limits.

The leverage ratios, debt-to-assets and debt-to-equity, were slightly better in 1994.

c. Based on the company's financial statements and the information in "Winn-Dixie at a Glance," page 525, what is your overall opinion of this company as a potential investment?

Student and even professional opinions will vary on this question.

Overall, based on the company's financial statements and the information in "Winn-Dixie at a Glance," the company is operating on a solid foundation. The financial position is quite solvent, and the return on investment is attractive at over 20 percent.

Although it is in a very competitive industry, the company has operated successfully for over 70 years. Management seems to be both expansion and automation oriented.

Consistent with managerial philosophy of the 1990s, there are programs in place concerning the environment as well as numerous community involvement activities.

Consolidated Statements of Earnings

Years Ended June 29, 1994 and June 30, 1993

	1994	1993*
	Amounts in thousands except per share data	
Net sales	$11,082,169	10,831,535
Cost of sales, including warehousing and delivery expenses	8,547,681	8,385,412
Gross profit on sales	2,534,488	2,446,123
Operating and administrative expenses	2,269,803	2,196,721
Operating income	264,685	249,402
Cash discounts and other income, net	98,085	132,398
	362,770	381,800
Interest expense	14,271	18,131
Earnings before income taxes	348,499	363,669
Income taxes	132,382	127,284
Net earnings	$ 216,117	236,385
Earnings per share	$ 2.90	3.11

Consolidated Balance Sheets

June 29, 1994 and June 30, 1993

Assets	1994	1993*
	Amounts in thousands	
Current assets:		
Cash and short-term investments	$ 31,451	107,784
Trade and other receivables, net	171,854	162,590
Associate stock loans	1,776	4,647
Merchandise inventories at lower of cost or market less LIFO reserve of $205,172,000 ($207,201,000 in 1993)	1,058,883	1,041,451
Prepaid expenses	97,220	96,728
Total current assets	1,361,184	1,413,200
Investments and other assets	37,587	15,043
Deferred income taxes	41,024	47,684
Net property, plant and equipment	706,779	586,633
	$ 2,146,574	2,062,560

Liabilities and Shareholders' Equity		
Current liabilities	$ 873,166	868,546
Obligations under capital leases	85,374	87,153
Defined benefit plan	22,852	19,454
Reserve for insurance claims and self-insurance	105,417	100,169
Other liabilities	2,304	2,273
Shareholders' equity	1,057,461	984,965
	$ 2,146,574	2,062,560

*53 weeks

Winn-Dixie Annual Report, 1994.

▲ Year Founded – 1925

▲ New York Stock Exchange Listing
(2/18/52) – **WIN**
- 51 consecutive annual
dividend increases,
a NYSE record

▲ Sales – $11,082,169,000
- 60 consecutive years of
sales increases
- Average annual sales per
store – $9,562,000
- Taxes per share – $3.50
- Earnings per share – $2.90
- Dividends per share – $1.44
(Present annual rate – $1.56)

▲ Number of Associates – 112,000

▲ Number of Stores – 1,159
- Total square footage –
40,685,000
- Average square footage
per store – 35,100
- Number of communities
served – 670

▲ Real Estate Development

	New	Enlarged/ Remodeled
1994	60	87
1995 (Projected)	70	100

▲ 22 Manufacturing Facilities
- Ice cream and milk bottling
- Coffee, tea and spices
- Detergents
- Meat processing
- Jams, jellies, peanut butter
and condiments
- Canned and bottled
carbonated beverages
- Egg processing
- Cheese products
- Crackers, cookies and
snacks
- Oleomargarine
- Frozen pizza
- Cottage cheese and yogurt
- Paper bags

▲ 16 Warehouse and Distribution Centers
- Items stocked – 26,200
- Tonnage– 5,911,000

▲ Trucking Fleet
- 1,250 tractors
- 2,100 trailers
- 1,400 drivers
- Delivered 6 million tons
of merchandise and
traveled 68 million miles

▲ Retail Automation
- Minicomputers are now in
all retail locations
- Computer-assisted
ordering
- Time and attendance
- Work planning
- Interviewing
- Electronic mail
- Electronic scale
monitoring
- Direct-delivery receiving
- In-store accounting

▲ Environmental Statement
- Recycling is important to
our environment and to
our Company. Last year,
we recycled more than
188,000 tons of paper and
cardboard.

▲ Major Contributions to Our
Community
- Winn-Dixie Stores
Foundation – $3.0 million
to hundreds of civic, youth,
service and educational
organizations across the
Sunbelt to recognize their
often unheralded accom-
plishments.
- Associate Matching Grants
Program – $1.8 million
- Winn-Dixie's Bowl for
Breath event raised over
$130,000 for the Cystic
Fibrosis Foundation in
Georgia
- Celebrity Baggers Day events
in four divisions generated
over $240,000 for the
American Cancer Society
- A total of 212,000 pounds
of food was collected
during Winn-Dixie's one
day food drive at North
Carolina's 1993 State Fair
- Winn-Dixie awarded Good
Citizenship Awards, along
with more than $3.2 million
in cash, product and equip-
ment contributions to local
charitable organizations.

▲ Total Stores – 1,159

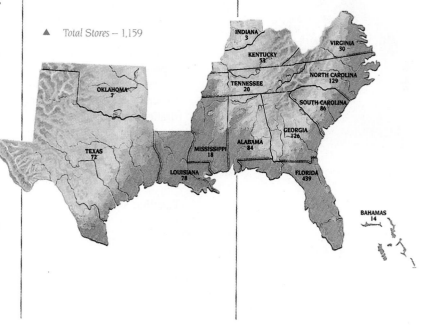

| All the Math That's Fit to Learn | # The Business Math Times |

Career Track:

Accountant

Nature of the Work

Managers require up-to-date financial information in order to make important decisions. Accountants prepare, analyze, and verify financial reports and taxes, and monitor information systems that furnish this information to managers in all business, industrial, and government organizations.

The premier achievement in public accounting is becoming a **Certified Public Accountant (CPA).** The CPA must fulfill certain state education and experience requirements and pass a rigorous examination.

Private or management accountants are responsible for

collecting, recording and analyzing the financial information of the companies for which they work. Private accountants also prepare financial reports for stockholders, creditors, regulatory agencies, and tax authorities.

Not-for-profit accountants work primarily for local, state, and federal governmental units and not-for-profit entities such as charities, hospitals, unions, colleges and universities, political parties, and religious organizations.

Training, Other Qualifications, and Advancement

Most public accounting and business firms require applicants to have at least a bachelor's degree in accounting or a related field. Some employers prefer those with a master's degree in accounting or a master's degree in business administration with a concentration in accounting.

Persons planning a career in accounting should have an aptitude for mathematics; be able to ana-

lyze, compare, and interpret facts and figures quickly; and make sound judgments. They must be able to clearly communicate the results of their work.

Job Outlook and Earnings

As the economy grows, the number of business establishments increases, requiring more accountants to set up their books, prepare their taxes, and provide management advice.

SOURCES: Adapted from *Occupational Outlook Handbook,* 1994-95 Edition, U.S. Department of Labor; and *Statistical Abstract of the United States,* 1995 Edition, U.S. Department of Commerce.

Brainteaser

A frog is standing 20 feet away from a wall. If each time it jumps it covers exactly half the distance left to the wall, how many jumps will it take the frog to reach the wall?

Answer to Last Issue's Brainteaser
20 Don't forget 90, 91, 92, 93...99!

THE "BIG SIX" ACCOUNTING FIRMS

Company/ Headquarters	Revenue (in billions)	Offices Countries	Employees	Major Clients
Arthur Andersen & Co. Geneva	8,000	358 74	72,722	American Express, Cadbury Schweppes, Chemical Bank, First Chicago, Inland Steel, KLM NYNEX
KPMG Peat Marwick Amsterdam	7,500	1,100 142	74,400	Aetna, BMW, Citicorp, General Mills, Gillette, Hasbro, Amsterdam Heineken, JCPenney, Kemper, Motorola, Nestlé, PepsiCo., Polaroid, Ryder, Xerox
Ernst & Young New York	6,867	670 130	68,452	Apple Computer, BankAmerica, Coca-Cola, Eli Lilly, Knight-Ridder, McDonald's, Mobil, Time Warner, USF&G, Wal-Mart
Coopers & Lybrand New York	6,200	755 130	70,500	American Brands, AT&T, Ford, Johnson & Johnson, The Limited, 3M, Philip Morris, Unilever
Deloitte, Touche, Tohmatsu, Intl. New York	5,950	680 124	59,000	Bank of New York, Boeing, Bridgestone, Chrysler, Dow Chemical, General Motors, Mitsubishi, Monsanto, Procter & Gamble, RJR Nabisco, Sears
Price Waterhouse London	4,460	434 118	52,699	Amoco, Anheuser-Busch, Campbell Soup, Chevron, DuPont, Eatman Kodak, Goodyear, IBM, Kellogg, Kmart, Nike, Walt Disney

SOURCES: Various corporate reports, 1995.

Chapter 16

Inventory

inventory

Goods that a company has in its possession at any given time. May be in the form of raw materials, partially finished goods, or goods available for sale.

merchandise inventory

Goods purchased by wholesalers and retailers for resale.

In business, the term **inventory** is used to describe the goods that a company has in its possession at any given time. For companies engaged in manufacturing activities, inventories are divided into raw materials (used to make other products), partially completed products (work in process), and finished goods (ready for sale to the trade).

Manufacturers sell their finished goods to wholesalers and retailers. These goods, purchased and held expressly for resale, are commonly known as **merchandise inventory.** For wholesalers and retailers, the primary source of revenue is from the sale of this merchandise. In terms of dollars, merchandise inventory is one of the largest and most important assets of a merchandising company. As an expense, the cost of goods sold is the largest deduction from sales in the determination of a company's profit, often larger than the total of operating or overhead expenses.

Interestingly, the merchandise inventory is the only account that is found on both the balance sheet and the income statement. The method used to determine the value of this inventory has a significant impact on a company's bottom-line results. In addition to appearing on the financial statements, the value of the merchandise inventory must also be determined for income tax purposes, insurance, and as a business indicator to management.

SECTION I

INVENTORY VALUATION

In order to place a value on a merchandise inventory, we must first know the quantity and the cost of the goods remaining at the end of an operating period. Merchandise held for sale must be physically counted at least once a year. Many businesses take inventory on a quarterly or even monthly basis. This is known as a **periodic inventory system,** since the physical inventory is counted periodically.

Today, more and more companies use computers to keep track of merchandise inventory on a continuous or perpetual basis. This is known as a **perpetual inventory system.** For each

periodic inventory system

Inventory system in which merchandise is physically counted at least once a year to determine the value of the goods available for sale.

perpetual inventory system

Inventory system in which goods available for sale are updated on a continuous basis by computer. Purchases by the company are added to inventory, while sales to customers are subtracted from inventory.

Merchandise inventory must be physically counted at least once a year in order to place a value on it.

merchandise category, the purchases made by the company are added to inventory, while the sales to customers are subtracted. These balances are known as **book inventories** of the items held for sale. As accurate as the perpetual system may be, it must be confirmed with an actual physical count at least once a year.

Taking inventory consists of physically counting, weighing, or measuring the items on hand; placing a price on each item; and multiplying the number of items by the price to determine the total cost. The counting part of taking inventory, although tedious, is not difficult. The pricing part, on the other hand, is an important and often controversial business decision. To this day, accountants have varying opinions on the subject of inventory valuation techniques.

The value placed on inventory has a significant effect on the net income of a company. Because net income is the basis of calculating federal income tax, accountants are frequently faced with the decision of whether to value inventory to reflect higher net profit to investors, or lower net profit to minimize income taxes.

In most industries, the prices paid by businesses for goods frequently change. A hardware store, for example, may buy a dozen light bulbs for $10.00 one month and $12.50 the next. A gasoline station may pay $.75 per gallon on Tuesday and $.69 on Thursday. When taking inventory, it is virtually impossible to determine what price items are left. This means that the *flow of goods* in and out of a business doesn't always match the *flow of costs* in and out of the business.

The one method of pricing inventory that actually matches the flow of costs to the flow of goods is known as the **specific identification method.** This method is feasible only when the variety of merchandise carried in stock and the volume of sales are relatively low, such as with automobiles or other expensive items. Each car, for example, has a specific vehicle identification number or serial number that makes inventory valuation quite accurate. A list of the actual vehicles in stock at any given time, and their corresponding costs, can easily be totaled to arrive at an inventory figure.

● **specific identification method**

Inventory valuation method in which each item in inventory is matched or coded with its actual cost. Feasible only for low-volume merchandise flow, such as automobiles, boats, or other expensive items.

In reality, most businesses have a wide variety of merchandise and find this method too expensive, because implementation would require sophisticated computer bar-coding systems. For this reason it is customary to use an assumption as to the flow of costs of merchandise in and out of the business. The three most common cost flow assumptions or inventory pricing methods are as follows:

1. *First in, first-out (FIFO):* Cost flow is in the order in which the costs were incurred.

2. *Last-in, first-out (LIFO):* Cost flow is in the reverse order in which the costs were incurred.

3. *Average cost:* Cost flow is an average of the costs incurred.

Although cost is the primary basis for the valuation of inventory, when market prices or current replacement costs fall below the actual cost of those in inventory, the company has incurred a loss. For example, let's say a computer retailer purchases a large quantity of CD-ROM drives at a cost of $200 each. A few months later, due to advances in technology, a faster model is introduced costing only $175 each. Under these market conditions, companies are permitted to choose a method for pricing inventory known as the lower-of-cost-or-market (LCM) rule.

All of the inventory valuation methods listed above are acceptable for both income tax reporting and a company's financial statements. As we shall see in this section, each of these methods has advantages and disadvantages. Economic conditions, such as whether merchandise prices are rising (inflation) or falling (deflation), play an important role in the decision of which method to adopt.

For income tax reporting, once a method has been chosen, the Internal Revenue Service requires that it be used consistently from one year to the next. Any changes in the method used for inventory valuation must be for a good reason and must be approved by the IRS.

16-1 Pricing Inventory Using the First-In, First-Out (FIFO) Method

The **first-in, first-out (FIFO) method,** assumes that the items you purchased *first* are the *first* items you sold. The items in inventory at the end of the year are matched with the costs of items of the same type that were most recently purchased. This method closely approximates the manner in which most businesses reduce their inventory, especially when the merchandise is perishable or subject to frequent style or model changes.

Essentially, this method involves taking physical inventory at the end of the year or accounting period and assigning cost in reverse order in which the purchases were received.

● **first-in, first-out (FIFO) method**

Inventory valuation method that assumes the items purchased by the company *first* are the *first* items to be sold. Items remaining in ending inventory at the end of an accounting period are therefore the most recently purchased.

FIFO

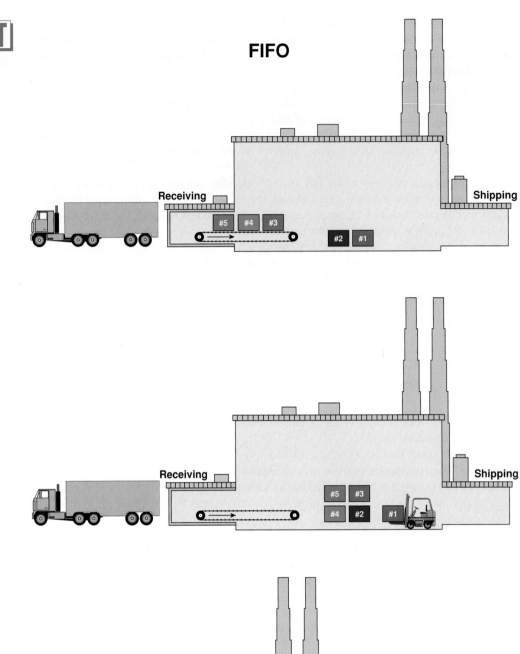

SOURCE: Adapted from Michael D. Tuttle, *Practical Business Math,* Sixth Edition (Dubuque, Iowa: William C. Brown, 1994), p. 293.

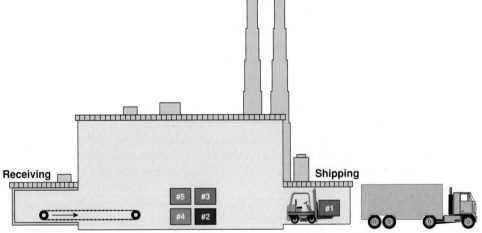

STEPS TO CALCULATE THE VALUE OF ENDING INVENTORY USING FIFO:

Step 1. List the number of units on hand at the end of the year and their corresponding costs, starting with the ending balance and working *backwards* through the incoming shipments.

Step 2. Multiply the number of units by the corresponding cost per unit for each purchase.

Step 3. Calculate the value of ending inventory by totaling the extensions from Step 2.

To illustrate the application of the FIFO method of inventory pricing, as well as the other methods in this section, we shall use the following annual inventory data for 12-inch clay pots at a Kmart Garden Center.

Kmart Garden Center

January 1	Beginning Inventory	400 units @ $5.00	$2,000
April 9	Purchase	200 units @ $6.00	1,200
July 19	Purchase	500 units @ $7.00	3,500
October 15	Purchase	300 units @ $8.00	2,400
December 8	Purchase	200 units @ $9.00	1,800
12-inch clay pots available for sale during the year		1,600	$10,900

EXAMPLE

When physical inventory of the 12-inch clay pots was taken on December 31, it was found that 700 remained in inventory. Using the FIFO method of inventory pricing, what is the dollar value of this ending inventory?

SOLUTION STRATEGY

With the assumption under FIFO that the inventory cost flow is made up of the *most recent* costs, the 700 clay pots in ending inventory would be valued as follows:

Step 1. Set up a table listing the 700 pots with costs in reverse order of acquisition.

> 200 units @ $9.00 from the December 8 purchase
> 300 units @ $8.00 from the October 15 purchase
> 200 units @ $7.00 from the July 19 purchase
> 700 Inventory, December 31

Steps 2 & 3. Next we extend each purchase, multiplying the number of units by the cost per unit, and find the total of the extensions.

Units	Cost/Unit	Total	
200	$9.00	$1,800	
300	8.00	2,400	
200	7.00	1,400	
700		$5,600	Ending inventory using FIFO

TRY-IT EXERCISE

1. **You are the merchandise manager of Video USA. The following data represents your records of the annual inventory figures for videotape rewinders.**

Video USA

January 1	Beginning Inventory	200 units @ $8.00	$1,600
May 14	Purchase	100 units @ $8.50	850
August 27	Purchase	250 units @ $9.00	2,250
November 18	Purchase	300 units @ $8.75	2,625
Videotape rewinders available for sale		850	$7,325

Using the FIFO method of inventory pricing, what is the dollar value of ending inventory if there were 380 rewinders on hand on December 31?

Check your answer with the solution on page 552.

16-2 Pricing Inventory Using the Last-In, First-Out (LIFO) Method

● **last-in, first-out (LIFO) method**

Inventory valuation method that assumes the items purchased by the company *last* are the *first* items to be sold. Items remaining in ending inventory at the end of an accounting period are therefore the oldest goods.

The **last-in, first-out (LIFO) method** assumes that the items you purchased *last* are sold or removed from inventory *first*. The items in inventory at the end of the year are matched with the cost of items of the same type that were purchased earliest. Therefore, items included in your ending inventory are considered to be those from the beginning inventory plus those acquired first from purchases.

This method involves taking physical inventory at the end of the year or accounting period and assigning cost in the same order in which the purchases were received.

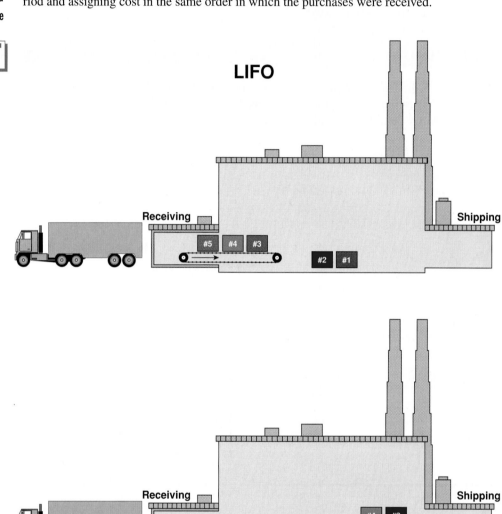

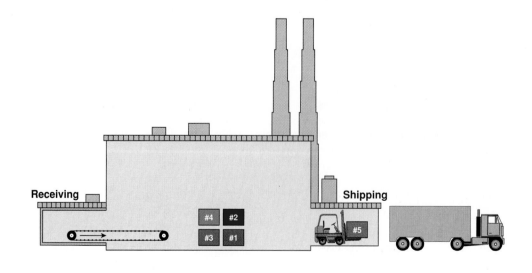

STEPS TO CALCULATE THE VALUE OF ENDING INVENTORY USING LIFO:

Step 1. List the number of units on hand at the end of the year and their corresponding costs starting with the beginning inventory and working *forward* through the incoming shipments.

Step 2. Multiply the number of units by the corresponding cost per unit for each purchase.

Step 3. Calculate the value of ending inventory by totaling the extensions from Step 2.

EXAMPLE

Let's return to the previous example about the 12-inch clay pots from Kmart, page 531. Once again, when physical inventory was taken on December 31, it was found that 700 remained in inventory. Using the LIFO method of inventory pricing, what is the dollar value of this ending inventory?

SOLUTION STRATEGY

With the assumption under LIFO that the inventory cost flow is made up of the *earliest* costs, the 700 clay pots in ending inventory would be valued as follows:

Step 1. Set up a table listing the 700 pots with costs in the order in which they were acquired.

> 400 units @ $5.00 from the January 1 beginning inventory
> 200 units @ $6.00 from the April 9 purchase
> 100 units @ $7.00 from the July 19 purchase
> 700 Inventory, December 31

Steps 2 & 3. Next we extend each purchase, multiplying the number of units by the cost per unit, and find the total of the extensions.

Units	Cost/Unit	Total	
400	$5.00	$2,000	
200	6.00	1,200	
100	7.00	700	
700		$3,900	Ending inventory using LIFO

TRY-IT   EXERCISE

2. **Let's return to Try-It Exercise 1, Video USA. Use the data from page 531 to calculate the dollar value of the 380 videotape rewinders in ending inventory using the LIFO method.**

Check your answer with the solution on page 552.

16-3 Pricing Inventory Using the Average Cost Method

The **average cost method,** also known as the **weighted average method,** assumes that the cost of each unit of inventory is the *average* cost of all goods available for sale during that accounting period. It is a weighted average because it takes into consideration not only the cost per unit in each purchase but also the number of units purchased at each cost.

● **average cost, or weighted average, method**
Inventory valuation method that assumes the cost of each unit of inventory is the *average* cost of all goods available for sale during that accounting period.

STEPS TO CALCULATE THE VALUE OF ENDING INVENTORY USING AVERAGE COST:

Step 1. Calculate the average cost per unit using the following formula:

$$\text{Average cost per unit} = \frac{\text{Cost of goods available for sale}}{\text{Total units available for sale}}$$

Step 2. Calculate the value of ending inventory by multiplying the number of units in ending inventory by the average cost per unit.

$$\text{Ending inventory} = \text{Units in ending inventory} \times \text{Average cost per unit}$$

EXAMPLE

Let's return once again to the example of the 12-inch clay pots from Kmart, page 531. Using the average cost method of inventory pricing, what is the dollar value of the 700 units on hand in ending inventory?

SOLUTION STRATEGY

Under the weighted average cost method, the 700 clay pots in ending inventory would be valued as follows:

Step 1. Calculate the average cost per unit:

$$\text{Average cost per unit} = \frac{\text{Cost of goods available for sale}}{\text{Total units available for sale}}$$

$$\text{Average cost per unit} = \frac{10,900}{1,600} = \$6.81$$

Step 2. Ending inventory = Units in ending inventory × Average cost per unit

$$\text{Ending inventory} = 700 \times 6.81 = \underline{\$4,767.00}$$

TRY-IT   EXERCISE

3. **Once again, let's use the Video USA example. This time use the data from page 531 to calculate the value of the 380 videotape rewinders in ending inventory using the average cost method.**

Check your answer with the solution on page 552.

16-4 Pricing Inventory Using the Lower-of-Cost-or-Market (LCM) Rule

● **lower-of-cost-or-market (LCM) rule**

Inventory valuation method whereby items in inventory are valued either at their actual cost or current replacement value, whichever is lower. This method is permitted under conditions of falling prices or merchandise obsolescence.

The three methods of pricing inventory discussed to this point—FIFO, LIFO, and weighted average—have been based on the cost of the merchandise. When the market price or current replacement price of an inventory item declines below the actual price paid for that item, companies are permitted to use a method known as the **lower-of-cost-or-market (LCM) rule.** This method takes into account such market conditions as severely falling prices, changing fashions or styles, or obsolescence of inventory items. The use of the LCM rule assumes that decreases in replacement costs will be accompanied by proportionate decreases in selling prices.

The lower-of-cost-or-market means comparing the market value (current replacement cost) of each item on hand with its cost, using the lower amount as its inventory value. Under ordinary circumstances, market value means the usual price paid, based on the volume of merchandise normally ordered by the firm.

STEPS TO CALCULATE THE VALUE OF ENDING INVENTORY USING THE LOWER-OF-COST-OR-MARKET RULE:

Step 1. Calculate the cost for each item in the inventory using one of the acceptable methods; FIFO, LIFO, or weighted average.

Step 2. Determine the market price or current replacement cost for each item.

Step 3. For each item, select the basis for valuation, cost or market, by choosing the lower figure.

Step 4. Calculate the total amount for each inventory item by multiplying the number of items by the valuation price chosen in Step 3.

Step 5. Calculate the total value of the inventory by adding all the figures in the Amount column.

EXAMPLE

The following data represent the inventory figures of the Exotica Boutique. Use the lower-of-cost-or-market rule to calculate (a) the extended amount for each item and (b) the total value of the inventory.

			Unit Price		Valuation	
Description		Quantity	Cost	Market	Basis	Amount
Blouses	Style #44	40	$27.50	$31.25	_____	_____
	Style #54	54	36.40	33.20	_____	_____
Slacks	Style #20	68	42.10	39.80	_____	_____
	Style #30	50	57.65	59.18	_____	_____
Jackets	Suede	30	141.50	130.05	_____	_____
	Wool	35	88.15	85.45	_____	_____
					Total Value of Inventory:	_____

SOLUTION STRATEGY

In this example, the cost and market price are given. We begin by choosing the lower of cost or market and then extending each item to the Amount column. For example, the Style #44 blouse will be valued at the cost, $27.50, because it is less than the market price, $31.25. The extension would be 40 × $27.50 = $1,100.00.

			Unit Price		Valuation	
Description		Quantity	Cost	Market	Basis	Amount
Blouses	Style #44	40	$27.50	$31.25	Cost	$1,100.00
	Style #54	54	36.40	33.20	Market	1,792.80
Slacks	Style #20	68	42.10	39.80	Market	2,706.40
	Style #30	50	57.65	59.18	Cost	2,882.50
Jackets	Suede	30	141.50	130.05	Market	3,901.50
	Wool	35	88.15	85.45	Market	2,990.75
					Total Value of Inventory:	$15,373.95

TRY-IT   **EXERCISE**

4. **Determine the value of the following inventory for Sandy's Gift Shop using the lower-of-cost-or-market rule.**

Description	Quantity	Cost	Market	Valuation Basis	Amount
		Unit Price			
Picture Frames	75	$ 9.50	$ 9.20	_____	_____
Ash Trays	120	26.30	27.15	_____	_____
16" Vases	88	42.40	39.70	_____	_____
12" Vases	64	23.65	21.40	_____	_____
Fruit Bowls	42	36.90	42.00	_____	_____
				Total Value of Inventory:	_____

Check your answers with the solutions on page 552.

REVIEW EXERCISES   CHAPTER 16—SECTION I

1. Calculate the total number of units available for sale and the cost of goods available for sale from the following inventory of oil filters for Action Auto Parts:

Action Auto Parts
Oil Filter Inventory

Date	Units Purchased	Cost per Unit	Total Cost
Beginning Inventory, Jan. 1	160	$1.45	232.00
Purchase, March 14	210	1.65	346.50
Purchase, May 25	190	1.52	288.80
Purchase, August 19	300	1.77	531.00
Purchase, October 24	250	1.60	400.00
Total units available	1,110	Cost of goods available for sale:	$1,798.30

2. When the merchandise manager of Action Auto Parts took physical inventory of the oil filters on December 31, it was found that 550 remained in inventory.

   a. What is the dollar value of the oil filter inventory using FIFO?

   550 remaining using FIFO

Units	Cost/Unit	Total
250	1.60	400.00
300	1.77	531.00
550		$931.00 FIFO

   b. What is the dollar value of the oil filter inventory using LIFO?

   550 remaining using LIFO

Units	Cost/Unit	Total
160	1.45	232.00
210	1.65	346.50
180	1.52	273.60
550		$852.10 LIFO

   c. What is the dollar value of the filters using the average cost method?

   Average cost = $\dfrac{\$1,798.30}{1,110}$ = $1.62 Each

   Total value = 550 × 1.62 = $891.00

3. The following data represents the inventory figures for 55-gallon fish tanks at Something's Fishy:

Something's Fishy
55-Gallon Fish Tanks Inventory

			Amount
January 1	Beginning Inventory	42 units @ $38.00	1,596.00
March 12	Purchase	80 units @ $36.50	2,920.00
July 19	Purchase	125 units @ $39.70	4,962.50
September 2	Purchase	75 units @ $41.75	3,131.25
	Fish tanks available for sale	322 Cost of tanks available for sale	$12,609.75

a. How many fish tanks did Something's Fishy have available for sale?

322

b. What is the total cost of the tanks available for sale?

$12,609.75

c. If physical inventory on December 31 was 88 tanks on hand, what is the value of those tanks using FIFO?

88 tanks using FIFO   75 @   41.75   = 3,131.25
                      13 @   39.70   =   516.10
                      88   Value of tanks $3,647.35

d. What is the value of the 88 tanks using LIFO?

88 tanks using LIFO   42 @   38.00   = 1,596.00
                      46 @   36.50   = 1,679.00
                      88   Value of tanks $3,275.00

e. What is the value of the 88 tanks using the average cost method?

$$\text{Average cost} = \frac{\$12,609.75}{322} = \$39.16 \text{ Each}$$

Total value = $88 \times 39.16 = $ $3,446.08

4. Determine the amount of the following inventory for True Value Hardware using the lower-of-cost-or-market rule:

True Value Hardware
Power Tool Inventory

Description	Quantity	Unit Price Cost	Unit Price Market	Valuation Basis	Amount
$\frac{3}{8}$" Drill	15	$25.60	$22.40	Market	$336.00
$\frac{1}{2}$" Drill	19	42.33	39.17	Market	744.23
7" Circle Saw	12	32.29	34.50	Cost	387.48
$\frac{3}{8}$" Router	8	55.30	54.22	Market	433.76
5" Rotary Sander	15	27.60	27.10	Market	406.50
9" Belt Sander	9	33.59	34.51	Cost	302.31
				Total value of inventory:	$2,610.28

INVENTORY ESTIMATION

In Section I of this chapter we learned to calculate the value of ending inventory by several methods using a physical count at the end of the accounting year. Most companies, however, require inventory figures more frequently than the once-a-year physical inventory. Monthly and quarterly financial statements, for example, may be prepared with inventory estimates, rather than expensive physical counts or perpetual inventory systems. In addition, when physical inventories are destroyed by fire or other disasters, estimates must be made for insurance claims purposes.

The two generally accepted methods for *estimating* the value of an inventory are the retail method and the gross profit method. For these methods to closely approximate the actual value of inventory, the markup rate for all items bought and sold by the company must be consistent. If they are not, the estimates should be calculated separately for each product category. For example, if a toy store gets a 30% markup on tricycles and 50% on bicycles, these categories should be calculated separately.

16-5 Estimating the Value of Ending Inventory Using the Retail Method

● **retail method**

Method of inventory estimation used by most retailers based on a comparison of goods available for sale at cost and at retail.

The **retail method** of inventory estimation is used by retail businesses of all types and sizes, from Wal-Mart and Sears to the corner grocery store. To use this method, the company must have certain figures in its accounting records, including the following:

a. *Beginning inventory* at cost price and at retail (selling price).

b. *Purchases* during the period at cost price and at retail.

c. *Net sales* for the period.

● **cost to retail price ratio, or cost ratio**

Ratio of goods available for sale at cost to the goods available for sale at retail. Used in the retail method of inventory estimation to represent the *cost* of each dollar of retail sales.

From these figures, the goods available for sale are determined at both cost and retail. We then calculate a ratio known as the **cost to retail price ratio,** or simply **cost ratio,** by the formula:

$$\text{Cost ratio} = \frac{\text{Goods available for sale at cost}}{\text{Goods available for sale at retail}}$$

This ratio represents the cost of each dollar of retail sales. For example, if the cost ratio for a company is .6 or 60%, this means that $.60 is the cost of each $1.00 of retail sales.

STEPS TO ESTIMATE THE VALUE OF ENDING INVENTORY USING THE RETAIL METHOD:

Step 1. List beginning inventory and purchases at both cost and retail.

Step 2. Add purchases to beginning inventory to determine goods available for sale at both cost and retail.

Beginning inventory
+ Purchases
_____
Goods available for sale

Step 3. Calculate the cost ratio:

$$\text{Cost ratio} = \frac{\text{Goods available for sale at cost}}{\text{Goods available for sale at retail}}$$

Step 4. Subtract net sales from goods available for sale at retail to get ending inventory at retail:

Goods available for sale at retail
− Net sales
_____
Ending inventory at retail

Step 5. Convert ending inventory at retail to ending inventory at cost by multiplying the ending inventory at retail by the cost ratio.

Ending inventory at cost = Ending inventory at retail × Cost ratio

Using the retail method, estimate the value of the ending inventory at cost on June 30, from the following information for Western Distributors, Inc.

Western Distributors, Inc.
Financial Highlights
June 1–June 30

	Cost	Retail
Beginning Inventory	$200,000	$400,000
Net Purchases (June)	150,000	300,000
Net Sales (June) $500,000		

SOLUTION STRATEGY

Steps 1 & 2. List the beginning inventory and purchases and calculate the goods available for sale.

	Cost	Retail
Beginning Inventory	$200,000	$400,000
+ Net Purchases (June)	+ 150,000	+ 300,000
Goods Available for Sale	$350,000	$700,000

Step 3. $\text{Cost ratio} = \dfrac{\text{Goods available for sale at cost}}{\text{Goods available for sale at retail}}$

$\text{Cost ratio} = \dfrac{350{,}000}{700{,}000} = .5 = 50\%$

Remember, this 50% figure means that $.50 was the cost of each $1.00 of retail sales.

Step 4. Next find ending inventory at retail:

Goods available for sale at retail		$700,000
– Net sales		– 500,000
Ending inventory at retail	=	$200,000

Step 5. Now convert the inventory at retail to inventory at cost using the cost ratio:

Ending inventory at cost = Ending inventory at retail × Cost ratio
Ending inventory at cost = 200,000 × .5 = $\underline{\$100{,}000}$

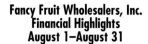

TRY-IT **EXERCISE**

5. Using the retail method, estimate the value of the ending inventory at cost on August 31, from the following information for Fancy Fruit Wholesalers, Inc.:

Fancy Fruit Wholesalers, Inc.
Financial Highlights
August 1–August 31

	Cost	Retail
Beginning Inventory	$600,000	$800,000
Net Purchases (August)	285,000	380,000
Net Sales (August) $744,000		

Check your answer with the solution on page 552.

16-6 Estimating the Value of Ending Inventory Using the Gross Profit Method

● **gross profit or gross margin method**

Method of inventory estimation using a company's gross margin percent to estimate the ending inventory. This method assumes that a company maintains approximately the same gross margin from year to year.

The **gross profit** or **gross margin method** uses a company's gross margin percent to estimate the ending inventory. This method assumes that a company maintains approximately the same gross margin from year to year. Inventories estimated in this manner are frequently used for interim reports and insurance claims; however, this method is not acceptable for inventory valuation on a company's annual financial statements.

From Chapter 15, remember that net sales is comprised of the cost of goods sold and gross margin.

$$\text{Net sales } (100\%) = \text{Cost of goods sold } (\%) + \text{Gross margin } (\%)$$

From this equation we see that when the gross margin percent is known, the cost of goods sold percent would be its complement, since together they equal net sales, which is 100%.

$$\text{Cost of goods sold percent} = 100\% - \text{Gross margin percent}$$

Knowing the cost of goods sold percent is the key to this calculation. We use this percent to find the cost of goods sold, which, when subtracted from goods available for sale, gives us the estimated ending inventory.

STEPS TO ESTIMATE THE VALUE OF ENDING INVENTORY USING THE GROSS PROFIT METHOD:

Step 1. Calculate the goods available for sale:

$$\frac{\begin{array}{l}\text{Beginning inventory}\\ + \text{Net purchases}\end{array}}{\text{Goods available for sale}}$$

Step 2. Find the estimated cost of goods sold by multiplying net sales by the cost of goods sold percent (complement of gross margin percent).

$$\text{Estimated cost of goods sold} = \text{Net sales } (100\% - \text{Gross margin } \%)$$

Step 3. Calculate the estimate of ending inventory by subtracting the estimated cost of goods sold from the goods available for sale.

$$\frac{\begin{array}{l}\text{Goods available for sale}\\ - \text{Estimated cost of goods sold}\end{array}}{\text{Estimated ending inventory}}$$

EXAMPLE

Wilbur Plumbing Supply, Inc., maintains a gross margin of 45% on all of its wholesale supplies. In April, Wilbur had a beginning inventory of $80,000, net purchases of $320,000, and net sales of $500,000. Use the gross profit method to estimate Wilbur's cost of ending inventory.

SOLUTION STRATEGY

Step 1.

Beginning inventory (April 1)	$ 80,000
+ Net purchases	320,000
Goods available for sale	$400,000

Step 2. Estimated cost of goods sold = Net sales (100% – Gross margin %)

Estimated cost of goods sold = $500,000 (100% – 45%) = $275,000

Step 3.

Goods available for sale	$400,000
– Estimated cost of goods sold	275,000
Estimated ending inventory (April 30)	$125,000

6. **European Beauty Supply, Inc., maintains a gross margin of 39% on all of its whole-sale beauty supplies. In November, the company had a beginning inventory of $137,000, net purchases of $220,000, and net sales of $410,000. Use the gross profit method to estimate the cost of ending inventory for November.**

Check your answer with the solution on page 552.

REVIEW EXERCISES CHAPTER 16—SECTION II

1. Using the retail method, estimate the value of the ending inventory at cost on September 30 from the following information for Contemporary Furniture Designs, Inc. Round the cost ratio to the nearest tenth percent.

Contemporary Furniture Designs, Inc.
September 1–September 30

	Cost	Retail
Beginning Inventory, Sept. 1	$150,000	$450,000
Purchases (September)	90,000	270,000
Net Sales (September) $395,000		

	Cost	Retail
Beginning inventory, Sept. 1	150,000	450,000
Purchases (September)	90,000	270,000
Goods available for sale	$240,000	$720,000

$$\text{Cost ratio} = \frac{240,000}{720,000} = 33.3\%$$

Goods available for sale at retail	720,000.00
Net sales	− 395,000.00
Ending inventory at retail	$325,000.00
Ending inventory at cost =	325,000.00 × 33.3%
	= $108,225.00

2. Precision Fitness Equipment, Inc., maintains a gross margin of 55% on all of its weight training products. In April, Precision had a beginning inventory of $146,000, net purchases of $208,000, and net sales of $437,000. Use the gross profit method to estimate the cost of ending inventory.

Beginning inventory	146,000.00
Net purchases	+ 208,000.00
Goods available	$354,000.00

Estimated cost of goods sold	437,000.00(100% − 55%)
	437,000.00 × .45
	= $196,650.00

Goods available for sale	354,000.00
Cost of goods sold	− 196,650.00
Estimated ending inventory	$157,350.00

3. The following data represents the inventory figures for Marathon Welding Supply, Inc. Using the retail method, estimate the value of the ending inventory at cost on January 31. Round the cost ratio to the nearest tenth percent.

Marathon Welding Supply, Inc.
January 1–January 31

	Cost	Retail
Beginning Inventory, Jan. 1	$50,000	$120,000
Purchases (January)	90,000	216,000
Net Sales (January) $188,000		

	Cost	Retail
Beginning inventory, Jan. 1	50,000.00	120,000.00
Purchases (January)	90,000.00	216,000.00
Goods available for sale	$140,000.00	$336,000.00

$$\text{Cost ratio} = \frac{140,000.00}{336,000.00} = 41.7\%$$

Goods available for sale at retail	336,000.00
Net sales	− 188,000.00
Ending inventory at retail	$148,000.00
Ending inventory at cost =	148,000.00 × .417
	= $61,716.00

4. You are the merchandise manager for the Carpet Boutique, Inc. On a Sunday in May you receive a phone call from the owner. He states that the entire building and contents were destroyed by fire. For the police report and the insurance claim, the owner has asked you to estimate the value of the lost inventory. Your records, which luckily were backed up on the hard drive of your home computer, indicate that at the time of the fire the net sales to date were $615,400 and the purchases were $232,600. The beginning inventory, on January 1, was $312,000. For the past three years the company has operated at a gross margin of 60%. Use the gross profit method to calculate your answer.

Beginning inventory	312,000.00	Est. cost of goods sold	615,400.00(100% − 60%)	Total goods available	544,600.00
Net purchases	+ 232,600.00		615,400.00 × .4	Est. cost of goods sold	− 246,160.00
Total goods available	$544,600.00		= $246,160.00	Est. ending inventory	$298,440.00

INVENTORY TURNOVER AND TARGETS

● **inventory or stock turnover**
The number of times during an operating period that the average dollar invested in merchandise inventory was theoretically sold out or turned over. May be calculated in retail dollars or in cost dollars.

In Chapter 16, we learned to use inventory turnover as one of the financial statement efficiency ratios. To review, **inventory turnover** or **stock turnover** is the number of times during an operating period that the average dollar invested in merchandise inventory was theoretically sold out or turned over.

Generally, the more expensive the item, the lower the turnover rate. For example, furniture and fine jewelry items might have a turnover rate of 3 or 4 times per year, while a grocery store might have a turnover of 15 or 20 times per year, or more. In this section, we shall revisit the concept of inventory turnover and learn to calculate it at retail and at cost.

Inventory turnover is an important business indicator, particularly when compared with the turnover rate from previous operating periods and with published industry statistics for similar-sized firms. Although a company must maintain inventory quantities large enough to meet the day-to-day demands of its operations, it is important to keep the amount invested in inventory to a minimum. In this section we shall also learn to calculate target inventories for companies based on published industry standards.

Regardless of the method used to determine inventory turnover, the procedure always involves dividing some measure of sales volume by a measure of the typical or average inventory. This **average inventory** is commonly found by adding the beginning and ending inventories of the operating period, and dividing by two.

● **average inventory**
An estimate of a company's typical inventory at any given time; calculated by dividing the total of all inventories taken during an operating period by the number of times inventory was taken.

$$\text{Average inventory} = \frac{\text{Beginning inventory} + \text{Ending inventory}}{2}$$

Inventory turnover rates are important business indicators.

Whenever possible, additional interim inventories should be used to increase the accuracy of the average inventory figure. For example, if a mid-year inventory was taken, this figure would be added to the beginning and ending inventories and the total divided by three. If monthly inventories were available, they would be added and the total divided by twelve.

16-7 Calculating Inventory Turnover Rate at Retail

When inventory turnover rate is calculated at retail, the measure of sales volume used is net sales. The average inventory is expressed in retail sales dollars by using the beginning and ending inventories at retail. The inventory turnover rate is expressed in number of *times* the inventory was sold out during the period.

STEPS TO CALCULATE INVENTORY TURNOVER RATE AT RETAIL:

Step 1. Calculate average inventory at retail:

$$\text{Average inventory}_{\text{at retail}} = \frac{\begin{array}{c}\text{Beginning} \\ \text{inventory} \\ \text{at retail}\end{array} + \begin{array}{c}\text{Ending} \\ \text{inventory} \\ \text{at retail}\end{array}}{2}$$

Step 2. Calculate the inventory turnover at retail:

$$\text{Inventory turnover}_{\text{at retail}} = \frac{\text{Net sales}}{\text{Average inventory at retail}}$$

EXAMPLE

International Copier had net sales of $650,900 for the year. If the beginning inventory at retail was $143,000 and the ending inventory at retail was $232,100, what are the average inventory at retail and the inventory turnover at retail, rounded to the nearest tenth?

SOLUTION STRATEGY

Step 1. $\text{Average inventory}_{\text{at retail}} = \dfrac{\text{Beginning inventory at retail} + \text{Ending inventory at retail}}{2}$

$\text{Average inventory}_{\text{at retail}} = \dfrac{143,000 + 232,100}{2} = \dfrac{375,100}{2} = \underline{\underline{\$187,550}}$

Step 2. $\text{Inventory turnover}_{\text{at retail}} = \dfrac{\text{Net sales}}{\text{Average inventory at retail}}$

$\text{Inventory turnover}_{\text{at retail}} = \dfrac{650,900}{187,550} = 3.47 = \underline{\underline{3.5 \text{ times}}}$

TRY-IT   EXERCISE

7. **Security Aluminum Windows, Inc., had net sales of $260,700 for the year. If the beginning inventory at retail was $65,100 and the ending inventory at retail was $52,800, what are (a) the average inventory and (b) the inventory turnover rounded to the nearest tenth?**

Check your answers with the solutions on page 553.

16-8 Calculating Inventory Turnover Rate at Cost

Frequently the inventory turnover rate of a company is expressed in terms of cost dollars rather than selling price or retail dollars. When this is the case, the cost of goods sold is used as the measure of sales volume and becomes the numerator in the formula. The denominator, average inventory, is calculated at cost.

STEPS TO CALCULATE INVENTORY TURNOVER RATE AT COST:

Step 1. Calculate the average inventory at cost:

$$\text{Average inventory }_{\text{at cost}} = \frac{\text{Beginning inventory at cost} + \text{Ending inventory at cost}}{2}$$

Step 2. Calculate the inventory turnover at cost:

$$\text{Inventory turnover }_{\text{at cost}} = \frac{\text{Cost of goods sold}}{\text{Average inventory at cost}}$$

EXAMPLE

Metro Hydraulics, Inc., had cost of goods sold of $416,200 for the year. If the beginning inventory at cost was $95,790 and the ending inventory at cost was $197,100, what are the average inventory at cost and the inventory turnover at cost, rounded to the nearest tenth?

SOLUTION STRATEGY

Step 1. $\text{Average inventory }_{\text{at cost}} = \dfrac{\text{Beginning inventory at cost} + \text{Ending inventory at cost}}{2}$

$\text{Average inventory }_{\text{at cost}} = \dfrac{95,790 + 197,100}{2} = \dfrac{292,890}{2} = \underline{\underline{\$146,445}}$

Step 2. $\text{Inventory turnover }_{\text{at cost}} = \dfrac{\text{Cost of goods sold}}{\text{Average inventory at cost}}$

$\text{Inventory turnover }_{\text{at cost}} = \dfrac{416,200}{146,445} = 2.84 = \underline{\underline{2.8 \text{ times}}}$

TRY-IT   EXERCISE

8. **E-Z Kwik Grocery Store had cost of goods sold of $756,400 for the year. If the beginning inventory at cost was $43,500 and the ending inventory at cost was $59,300, what are (a) the average inventory at cost and (b) the inventory turnover rounded to the nearest tenth?**

Check your answers with the solutions on page 553.

16-9 Calculating Target Inventories Based on Industry Standards

When inventory turnover is below average for a firm its size, it may be a signal that the company is carrying too much inventory. Carrying extra inventory can lead to extra expenses, such as warehousing costs and insurance. It also ties up money the company could use more efficiently elsewhere. In certain industries, some additional risks of large inventories would be losses due to price declines, obsolescence, or deterioration of the goods.

Trade associations and the federal government publish a wide variety of important industry statistics, ratios, and standards for every size company. When such inventory turnover figures are available, merchandise managers can use the following formulas to calculate the **target average inventory** required by their firm to achieve the published industry standards for a company with similar sales volume.

$$\text{Target average inventory}_{\text{at cost}} = \frac{\text{Cost of goods sold}}{\text{Published inventory turnover at cost}}$$

$$\text{Target average inventory}_{\text{at retail}} = \frac{\text{Net sales}}{\text{Published inventory turnover at retail}}$$

● **target average inventory**
Inventory standards published by trade associations and the federal government for companies of all sizes and in all industries. Used by managers as *targets* for the ideal amount of inventory to carry for maximum efficiency.

EXAMPLE

WorldWide Photo, Inc., a wholesale photo supply business, had cost of goods sold of $950,000 for the year. The beginning inventory at cost was $245,000 and the ending inventory at cost amounted to $285,000. According to the noted business research firm Dun & Bradstreet, the inventory turnover rate at cost for a photo business of this size is 5 times. (a) Calculate the average inventory and actual inventory turnover for World-Wide. (b) If the turnover is below 5 times, calculate the target average inventory needed by WorldWide to theoretically come up to industry standards.

SOLUTION STRATEGY

(a)

Step 1. $\text{Average inventory}_{\text{at cost}} = \dfrac{\text{Beginning inventory at cost} + \text{Ending inventory at cost}}{2}$

$\text{Average inventory}_{\text{at cost}} = \dfrac{245,000 + 285,000}{2} = \dfrac{530,000}{2} = \underline{\underline{\$265,000}}$

Step 2. $\text{Inventory turnover}_{\text{at cost}} = \dfrac{\text{Cost of goods sold}}{\text{Average inventory at cost}}$

$\text{Inventory turnover}_{\text{at cost}} = \dfrac{950,000}{265,000} = 3.58 = \underline{\underline{3.6 \text{ times}}}$

(b)

Step 3. The actual inventory turnover for WorldWide is *3.6 times* per year compared to the industry standard of 5 times. This indicates that the company is carrying too much inventory. Let's calculate the target average inventory WorldWide should carry to meet industry standards.

$\text{Target average inventory}_{\text{at cost}} = \dfrac{\text{Cost of goods sold}}{\text{Published inventory turnover at cost}}$

$\text{Target average inventory}_{\text{at cost}} = \dfrac{950,000}{5} = \underline{\underline{\$190,000}}$

The actual average inventory carried by WorldWide for the year was $265,000 compared with the target inventory of $190,000. This indicates that, at any given time, the inventory for WorldWide averaged about $75,000 higher than that of its competition.

TRY-IT   EXERCISE

9. Mobile Communications, Inc., had net sales of $2,650,000 for the year. The beginning inventory at retail was $495,000 and the ending inventory at retail amounted to $380,000. The inventory turnover at retail published as the standard for a business of this size is 7 times. (a) Calculate the average inventory and actual inventory

turnover for the company. (b) If the turnover is below 7 times, calculate the target average inventory needed to theoretically come up to industry standards.

Check your answers with the solutions on page 553.

Check your answers with the solutions on page 553.

S | REVIEW EXERCISES CHAPTER 16—SECTION III

Assuming that all net sales figures are at retail and all cost of goods sold figures are at cost, calculate the average inventory and inventory turnover for the following. If the actual turnover is below the published rate, calculate the target average inventory necessary to come up to industry standards:

	Net Sales	Cost of Goods Sold	Beginning Inventory	Ending Inventory	Average Inventory	Inventory Turnover	Published Rate	Target Average Inventory
1.	$500,000		$50,000	$70,000	$60,000.00	8.3	10.0	$50,000.00
2.		$335,000	48,000	56,000	$52,000.00	6.4	6.0	Above
3.		1,200,000	443,000	530,000	$486,500.00	2.5	3.5	$342,857.14
4.	4,570,000		854,000	650,300	$752,150.00	6.1	8.2	$557,317.07

5. Quality Brakes and Parts, Inc., had net sales of $145,900 for the year. The beginning inventory at retail was $24,000 and the ending inventory at retail was $32,900.

   a. What is the average inventory at retail?

   $$\text{Average inventory} = \frac{24{,}000 + 32{,}900}{2} = \$28{,}450.00$$

   b. What is the inventory turnover, rounded to the nearest tenth?

   $$\text{Inventory turnover} = \frac{145{,}900}{28{,}450} = 5.1 \text{ Times}$$

6. The Gourmet's Delight, a cooking equipment wholesaler, had cost of goods sold of $458,900 for the year. The beginning inventory at cost was $83,600 and the ending inventory at cost was $71,700.

   a. What is the average inventory at cost?

   $$\text{Average inventory} = \frac{83{,}600 + 71{,}700}{2} = \$77{,}650.00$$

   b. What is the inventory turnover, rounded to the nearest tenth?

   $$\text{Inventory turnover} = \frac{458{,}900}{77{,}650} = 5.9 \text{ Times}$$

7. Modern Molding Corporation had cost of goods sold for the year of $1,250,000. The beginning inventory at cost was $135,000 and the ending inventory at cost amounted to $190,900. The inventory turnover rate published as the industry standard for a business of this size is 9.5 times.

   a. Calculate the average inventory and actual inventory turnover rate for the company.

   $$\text{Average inventory} = \frac{135,000 + 190,900}{2} = \underline{\underline{\$162,950.00}}$$

   $$\text{Inventory turnover} = \frac{1,250,000}{162,950} = \underline{\underline{7.7 \text{ Times}}}$$

   b. If the turnover rate is below 9.5 times, calculate the target average inventory needed to theoretically come up to industry standards.

   $$\text{Target inventory} = \frac{1,250,000}{9.5} = \underline{\underline{\$131,578.95}}$$

8. Trophy Masters had net sales for the year of $145,000. The beginning inventory at retail was $36,000 and the ending inventory at retail amounted to $40,300. The inventory turnover rate published as the industry standard for a business of this size is 4.9 times.

   a. Calculate the average inventory and actual inventory turnover rate for the company.

   $$\text{Average inventory} = \frac{36,000 + 40,300}{2} = \underline{\underline{\$38,150.00}}$$

   $$\text{Inventory turnover} = \frac{145,000}{38,150} = \underline{\underline{3.8 \text{ Times}}}$$

   b. If the turnover rate is below 4.9 times, calculate the target average inventory needed to theoretically come up to industry standards.

   $$\text{Target inventory} = \frac{145,000}{4.9} = \underline{\underline{\$29,591.84}}$$

CHAPTER 16 ■ INVENTORY

FORMULAS

Inventory Valuation—Average Cost Method

$$\text{Average cost per unit} = \frac{\text{Cost of goods available for sale}}{\text{Total units available for sale}}$$

Ending inventory = Units in ending inventory × Average cost per unit

Inventory Estimation—Retail Method

$$\text{Cost ratio} = \frac{\text{Goods available for sale at cost}}{\text{Goods available for sale at retail}}$$

Estimated ending inventory at cost = Ending inventory at retail × Cost ratio

Inventory Estimation—Gross Profit Method

Estimated cost of goods sold = Net sales (100% − Gross margin %)

continued

Inventory Turnover—Retail

$$\text{Average inventory}_{\text{retail}} = \frac{\text{Beginning inventory}_{\text{retail}} + \text{Ending inventory}_{\text{retail}}}{2}$$

$$\text{Inventory turnover}_{\text{retail}} = \frac{\text{Net sales}}{\text{Average inventory}_{\text{retail}}}$$

Inventory Turnover—Cost

$$\text{Average inventory}_{\text{cost}} = \frac{\text{Beginning inventory}_{\text{cost}} + \text{Ending inventory}_{\text{cost}}}{2}$$

$$\text{Inventory turnover}_{\text{cost}} = \frac{\text{Cost of goods sold}}{\text{Average inventory}_{\text{cost}}}$$

Target Inventory

$$\text{Target average inventory}_{\text{cost}} = \frac{\text{Cost of goods sold}}{\text{Published inventory turnover}_{\text{cost}}}$$

$$\text{Target average inventory}_{\text{retail}} = \frac{\text{Net sales}}{\text{Published inventory turnover}_{\text{retail}}}$$

CHAPTER 16 ■ INVENTORY	SUMMARY CHART

SECTION I   INVENTORY VALUATION

Topic	P/O, Page	Important Concepts	Illustrative Examples
Pricing Inventory Using the First-In, First-Out (FIFO) Method	16–1 529	FIFO assumes that the items purchased first are the first items sold. The items in inventory at the end of the year are matched with the cost of items of the same type that were purchased most recently. *Inventory Pricing—FIFO:* 1, List the number of units on hand at the end of the year and their corresponding costs, starting with the ending balance and working *backwards* through the incoming shipments. 2. Multiply the number of units by the corresponding cost per unit for each purchase. 3. Calculate the value of ending inventory by totaling all the extensions from Step 2.	The following data represent the inventory figures for imported ceramic bowls at The Gift Express:

Date		Units	Cost per Unit
Jan. 1	Beg. Inv.	55	$12.30
Mar. 9	Purch.	60	13.50
Aug. 12	Purch.	45	13.90
Nov. 27	Purch.	75	14.25

On December 31, physical inventory revealed 130 bowls in stock. Calculate the value of the ending inventory using FIFO. With the assumption under FIFO that the inventory cost flow is made up of the most recent costs, the 130 bowls would be valued as follows:

Date	Units	Cost	Total
Nov. 27	75	@ 14.25	1,068.75
Aug. 12	45	@ 13.90	625.50
Mar. 9	10	@ 13.50	135.00
	130		$1,829.25

I, continued

Topic	P/O, Page	Important Concepts	Illustrative Examples
Pricing Inventory Using the Last-In, First-Out (LIFO) Method	16–2 532	LIFO assumes that the items purchased last are sold or removed from inventory first. The items in inventory at the end of the year are matched with the cost of the same type items purchased earliest. *Inventory Pricing—LIFO:* 1. List the number of units on hand at the end of the year and their corresponding costs, starting with the beginning inventory and working *forward* through the incoming shipments. 2. Multiply the number of units by the corresponding cost per unit for each purchase. 3. Calculate the value of ending inventory by totaling all the extensions from Step 2.	Using the data above for The Gift Express, calculate the value of the 130 bowls in ending inventory using LIFO. With the assumption under LIFO that the inventory cost flow is made up of the earliest costs, the 130 bowls would be valued as follows: **Date — Units — Cost — Total** Jan. 1 — 55 — @ 12.30 — 676.50 Mar. 9 — 60 — @ 13.50 — 810.00 Aug. 12 — 15 — @ 13.90 — 208.50 130 — $1,695.00
Pricing Inventory Using the Average Cost Method	16–3 533	The average cost method, also known as the weighted average method, assumes that the cost of each unit of inventory is the average cost of all goods available for sale during that accounting period. 1. Calculate the average cost per unit by: $$\text{Average cost} = \frac{\text{Cost of goods available for sale}}{\text{Total units available for sale}}$$ 2. Calculate the value of ending inventory by multiplying the number of units in ending inventory by the average cost per unit.	Using the average cost method of inventory pricing, what is the dollar value of the 130 bowls in ending inventory for The Gift Express? First we shall extend and sum each purchase to find the total units available and the total cost of those units available for sale. **Date — Units — Cost per Unit — Total** Jan. 1 — 55 — $12.30 — $676.50 Mar. 9 — 60 — 13.50 — 810.00 Aug. 12 — 45 — 13.90 — 625.50 Nov. 27 — 75 — 14.25 — 1,068.75 235 — $3,180.75 $\text{Av. cost} = \dfrac{3,180.75}{235} = \$13.54$ $\text{End. inv.} = 130 \times 13.54 = \underline{\$1,760.20}$
Pricing Inventory Using the Lower-of-Cost-or-Market (LCM) Rule	16–4 534	When the market price or current replacement price of an inventory item declines below the actual price paid for that item, a company is permitted to use the lower-of-cost-or-market rule. 1. Choose lower of cost or market as valuation basis. 2. Multiply the number of units by the valuation basis price. 3. Add the extended totals in the Amount column to get the value of ending inventory.	From the following inventory data for small, medium, and large lamps at The Gift Express, calculate the value of the ending inventory using the LCM rule.

Units	Unit Price Cost	Unit Price Market	Valuation Basis	Amount
small				
34	$40	$43	Cost	1,360
medium				
55	70	65	Market	3,575
large				
47	99	103	Cost	4,653
			Ending Inventory =	$9,588

SECTION II INVENTORY ESTIMATION

Topic	P/O, Page	Important Concepts	Illustrative Examples

Estimating the Value of Ending Inventory Using the Retail Method	16–5 538	When it is too costly or not feasible to take a physical inventory count, inventory can be estimated. The retail method, as the name implies, is used by retail operations of all sizes.
		
		1. List beginning inventory and purchases at both cost and retail.
		
		2. Add purchases to beginning inventory to determine goods available for sale.
		
		3. Calculate the cost ratio by:
		
		$$\text{Cost ratio} = \frac{\text{Goods available for sale at cost}}{\text{Goods available for sale at retail}}$$
		
		4. Calculate ending inventory at retail by subtracting net sales from goods available for sale at retail.
		
		5. Convert ending inventory at retail to ending inventory at cost by multiplying the ending inventory at retail by the cost ratio.
			Estimate the value of the ending inventory at cost on July 31 from the following information for Allstate Distributors, Inc.
			
			         Cost **Retail**
			Beg. Inv. $300,000 $450,000
			Net Purch. 100,000 150,000
			Net Sales $366,000
			
			         Cost **Retail**
			Beg. Inv. $300,000 $450,000
			Net Purch. +100,000 +150,000
			Goods Avail. $400,000 $600,000
			
			$$\text{Cost ratio} = \frac{400{,}000}{600{,}000} = .67$$
			
			Goods avail. at retail $600,000
			– Net sales – 366,000
			Ending inv. at retail = $234,000
			
			Ending inventory at cost = 234,000 × .67 = $156,780

Estimating the Value of Ending Inventory Using the Gross Profit Method	16–6 540	The gross profit or gross margin method uses a company's gross margin percent to estimate the ending inventory. This method assumes that a company maintains approximately the same gross margin from year to year.
		
		1. Calculate the goods available for sale.
		
		    Beginning inventory
		  + Net purchases
		    Goods available for sale
		
		2. Find the estimated cost of goods sold by multiplying net sales by the cost of goods sold percent (complement of gross margin percent).
		
		3. Calculate the estimate of ending inventory by:
		
		    Goods available for sale
		  – Estimated cost of goods sold
		    Estimated ending inventory
			The Stereo Connection maintains a gross margin of 60% on all speakers. In June, the beginning inventory was $95,000, net purchases were $350,600, and net sales were $615,000. What is the estimated cost of ending inventory using the gross profit method?
			
			Beginning inv. $95,000
			+ Net purchases + 350,600
			Goods available = $445,600
			
			Estimated cost of goods sold = Net sales (100% – Gr. margin %) = 615,000 (100% – 60%) = $246,000
			
			Goods available $445,600
			– Estimated CGS – 246,000
			Est. ending inv. = $199,600

SECTION III   INVENTORY TURNOVER AND TARGETS

Topic	P/O, Page	Important Concepts	Illustrative Examples
Calculating Inventory Turnover Rate at Retail	16–7 543	Inventory or stock turnover rate is the number of times during an operating period that the average inventory is sold out or turned over. Average inventory may be expressed either at retail or at cost. 1. Calculate the average inventory at retail by: $$\text{Average inventory} = \frac{\substack{\text{Beginning} \\ \text{inventory} \\ \text{at retail}} + \substack{\text{Ending} \\ \text{inventory} \\ \text{at retail}}}{2}$$ 2. Calculate the inventory turnover at retail by: $$\text{Inventory turnover} = \frac{\text{Net sales}}{\text{Average inventory at retail}}$$	Royal Rugs had net sales of $66,000 for the year. If the beginning inventory at retail was $24,400 and the ending inventory at retail was $19,600, what are the average inventory and the inventory turnover rate? Average inventory at retail = $$\frac{24,400 + 19,600}{2} = \underline{\underline{\$22,000}}$$ Inventory turnover at retail = $$\frac{66,000}{22,000} = \underline{\underline{3 \text{ times}}}$$
Calculating Inventory Turnover Rate at Cost	16–8 544	Inventory turnover may also be calculated at cost by using cost of goods sold and the average inventory at cost. 1. Calculate average inventory at cost by: $$\text{Average inventory} = \frac{\substack{\text{Beginning} \\ \text{inventory} \\ \text{at cost}} + \substack{\text{Ending} \\ \text{inventory} \\ \text{at cost}}}{2}$$ 2. Calculate the inventory turnover at cost by: $$\text{Inventory turnover} = \frac{\text{Cost of goods sold}}{\text{Average inventory at cost}}$$	Albrecht Enterprises had $426,000 in cost of goods sold. The beginning inventory at cost was $75,000 and the ending inventory at cost was $95,400. What are Albrecht's average inventory at cost and inventory turnover rate? Average inventory at cost = $$\frac{75,000 + 95,400}{2} = \underline{\underline{85,200}}$$ Inventory turnover at cost = $$\frac{426,000}{85,200} = \underline{\underline{5 \text{ times}}}$$
Calculating Target Average Inventories Based on Industry Standards	16–9 544	When inventory turnover is below average, based on published industry standards, it may be a signal that a company is carrying too much inventory. This can lead to extra expenses such as warehousing and insurance. The following formulas can be used to calculate target average inventories at cost or retail to theoretically achieve the published turnover rate. $$\substack{\text{Target} \\ \text{inventory} \\ \text{at cost}} = \frac{\text{Cost of goods sold}}{\text{Published rate at cost}}$$ $$\substack{\text{Target} \\ \text{inventory} \\ \text{at retail}} = \frac{\text{Net sales}}{\text{Published rate at retail}}$$	Eveready Distributing had cost of goods sold of $560,000 for the year. The beginning inventory at cost was $140,000 and the ending inventory was $180,000. The published rate for a firm this size is 4 times. Calculate the average inventory and turnover rate for Eveready. If the rate is below 4 times, calculate the target average inventory. Average inventory at cost = $$\frac{140,000 + 180,000}{2} = \underline{\underline{\$160,000}}$$ Inventory turnover at cost = $$\frac{560,000}{160,000} = \underline{\underline{3.5 \text{ times}}}$$ Target average inventory = $$\frac{560,000}{4} = \underline{\underline{\$140,000}}$$

1.

FIFO Inventory Valuation		
Units	**Cost/Unit**	**Total**
300	$8.75	$2,625
80	9.00	720
380		$3,345

2.

LIFO Inventory Valuation		
Units	**Cost/Unit**	**Total**
200	$8.00	$1,600
100	8.50	850
80	9.00	720
380		$3,170

3.

Average Cost Method

$$\text{Average cost/unit} = \frac{\text{Cost of goods available}}{\text{Total units available}} = \frac{7,325}{850} = \$8.62$$

Ending inventory = Units in inv × Av. cost/unit

Ending inventory = 380 × 8.62 = $3,275.60

4.

LCM Rule

Sandy's Gift Shop

Item	Quantity	Valuation/Basis	Price	Amount
Frames	75	Market	$ 9.20	$ 690.00
Ash trays	120	Cost	26.30	3,156.00
16" Vases	88	Market	39.70	3,493.60
12" Vases	64	Market	21.40	1,369.60
Bowls	42	Cost	36.90	1,549.80
				$10,259.00

5.

	Cost	Retail
Beginning Inventory	$600,000	$800,000
+ Net Purchases	+ 285,000	+ 380,000
Goods Available for Sale	$885,000	$1,180,000

$$\text{Cost ratio} = \frac{\text{Goods available}_{cost}}{\text{Goods available}_{retail}} = \frac{885,000}{1,180,000} = .75 = 75\%$$

Goods available_retail	1,180,000
− Net sales	− 744,000
Ending inventory _retail_	$436,000

Ending inventory _cost_ = Ending inventory _retail_ × Cost ratio

Ending inventory _cost_ = 436,000 × .75 = $327,000

6.

Beginning inventory	$137,000
+ Net purchases	+ 220,000
Goods available for sale	$357,000

Estimated cost of goods sold = Net sales (100% − Gross margin %)

Estimated cost of goods sold = 410,000 (100% − 39%)

Estimated cost of goods sold = 410,000 (.61) = $250,100

Goods available for sale	$357,000
− Estimated cost of goods sold	− 250,100
Estimated ending inventory	$106,900

7. a. $\text{Average inventory}_{retail} = \dfrac{\text{Beginning inventory}_{retail} + \text{Ending inventory}_{retail}}{2}$

$\text{Average inventory}_{retail} = \dfrac{65,100 + 52,800}{2} = \underline{\underline{\$58,950}}$

b. $\text{Inventory turnover}_{retail} = \dfrac{\text{Net sales}}{\text{Average inventory}_{retail}}$

$\text{Inventory turnover}_{retail} = \dfrac{260,700}{58,950} = \underline{\underline{4.4}}$

8. a. $\text{Average inventory}_{cost} = \dfrac{\text{Beginning inventory}_{cost} + \text{Ending inventory}_{cost}}{2}$

$\text{Average inventory}_{cost} = \dfrac{43,500 + 59,300}{2} = \underline{\underline{\$51,400}}$

b. $\text{Inventory turnover}_{cost} = \dfrac{\text{Cost of goods sold}}{\text{Average inventory}_{cost}}$

$\text{Inventory turnover}_{cost} = \dfrac{756,400}{51,400} = \underline{\underline{14.7}}$

9. a. $\text{Average inventory} = \dfrac{\text{Beginning inventory} + \text{Ending inventory}}{2}$

$\text{Average inventory} = \dfrac{495,000 + 380,000}{2} = \underline{\underline{\$437,500}}$

$\text{Inventory turnover} = \dfrac{\text{Net sales}}{\text{Average inventory}_{retail}} = \dfrac{2,650,000}{437,500} = \underline{\underline{6.1}}$

b. $\text{Target average inventory} = \dfrac{\text{Net sales}}{\text{Published turnover}}$

$\text{Target average inventory} = \dfrac{2,650,000}{7} = \underline{\underline{\$378,571.43}}$

1. Calculate the total number of units available for sale and the cost of goods available for sale from the following inventory of imported silk ties for Downtown Fashions, Inc.:

Date	Units Purchased	Cost per Unit	Total Cost
Beginning Inventory, January 1	59	$46.10	2,719.90
Purchase, March 29	75	43.50	3,262.50
Purchase, July 14	120	47.75	5,730.00
Purchase, October 12	95	50.00	4,750.00
Purchase, December 8	105	53.25	5,591.25

Total units available ___454___   Cost of goods available for sale: $22,053.65

2. As the manager of Downtown Fashions (Exercise 1), you took physical inventory of the ties on December 31 and found that 128 were still in stock.

a. What is the dollar value of the ending inventory using FIFO?

Value of 128 using FIFO   105 @ 53.25 = 5,591.25
          23 @ 50.00 = 1,150.00
          128       $6,741.25

b. What is the dollar value of the ending inventory using LIFO?

Value of 128 using LIFO   59 @ 46.10 = 2,719.90
          69 @ 43.50 = 3,001.50
          128       $5,721.40

c. What is the dollar value of the ending inventory using the average cost method?

Value of 128 using average cost

Average cost $= \dfrac{22,053.65}{454} = \$48.58$ Per unit

$128 \times 48.58 = \$6,218.24$

3. Determine the value of the following inventory for The Rainbow Tile Company using the lower-of-cost-or-market rule.

Description	Quantity in Square Feet	Unit Price Cost	Unit Price Market	Valuation Basis	Amount
Terracotta 12"	8,400	$4.55	$5.10	Cost	$38,220
Super Saltillo 16"	7,300	8.75	8.08	Market	58,984
Monocottura 10"	4,500	3.11	2.90	Market	13,050
Glazed Ceramic	6,200	4.50	5.25	Cost	27,900
Brick Pavers	12,700	3.25	3.15	Market	40,005

Total value of inventory: $178,159

4. Using the retail method, estimate the value of the ending inventory at cost on May 31 from the following information for Quality Shutters, Inc. Round the cost ratio to the nearest tenth percent.

Quality Shutters, Inc.
May 1–May 31

	Cost	Retail
Beginning Inventory, May 1	$145,600	$196,560
Purchases	79,000	106,650
Net Sales $210,800	$224,600	$303,210

$$\frac{\text{Goods available} - \text{Cost}}{\text{Goods available} - \text{Retail}} \quad \frac{224,600}{303,210} = 74.1\% \text{ Cost ratio}$$

Goods available for sale—Retail   303,210
　　　　　　　 − Net sales − 210,800   Ending inventory—Cost = $92,410 \times .741$
　　Ending inventory—Retail $92,410   　　　　　　　 = $68,475.81

5. On July 24, a tornado destroyed Midwest Wholesalers' main warehouse and all of its contents. Company records indicate that at the time of the tornado the net sales to date were $535,100 and the purchases were $422,900. The beginning inventory, on January 1, was $319,800. For the past three years the company has maintained a gross margin of 35%. Use the gross profit method to estimate the inventory loss for the insurance claim.

Beginning inventory	319,800	Goods available for sale	742,700
Net purchases	+ 422,900	Estimated cost of goods sold	− 347,815
Goods available for sale	$742,700		$394,885

$$\text{Estimated cost of goods sold} = 535,100(100\% - 35\%)$$
$$= 535,100 \times .65$$
$$= \$347,815$$

Assuming that all net sales figures are at retail and all cost of goods sold figures are at cost, calculate the average inventory and inventory turnover for Exercises 6–7. If the actual turnover is below the published rate, calculate the target average inventory necessary to come up to industry standards:

	Net Sales	Cost of Goods Sold	Beginning Inventory	Ending Inventory	Average Inventory	Inventory Turnover	Published Rate	Target Average Inventory
6.	$290,000		$88,000	$94,000	$91,000	3.2	4.4	$65,909.09
7.		$760,000	184,000	123,000	$153,500	5	6.8	$111,764.71

8. Midway Electronics had net sales of $435,900 for the year. The beginning inventory at retail was $187,600 and the ending inventory at retail was $158,800.

a. What is the average inventory at retail?

$$\text{Average inventory} = \frac{187,600 + 158,800}{2} = \$173,200$$

b. What is the inventory turnover rounded to the nearest tenth?

$$\text{Inventory turnover} = \frac{435,900}{173,200} = \underline{\underline{2.5 \text{ Times}}}$$

c. If the turnover rate for similar-sized competitors is 3.8 times, calculate the target average inventory needed to theoretically come up to industry standards.

$$\text{Target inventory} = \frac{435,900}{3.8} = \underline{\underline{\$114,710.53}}$$

ANSWERS

4.	$68,475.81
5.	$394,885
6.	$91,000
	3.2
	$65,909.09
7.	$153,500
	5
	$111,764.71
8. a.	$173,200
b.	2.5
c.	$114,710.53

9. The Fabric Warehouse had cost of goods sold for the year of $884,000. The beginning inventory at cost was $305,500 and the ending inventory at cost amounted to $414,200. The inventory turnover rate published as the industry standard for a business of this size is 5 times.

a. What is the average inventory at cost?

$$\text{Average inventory} = \frac{305,500 + 414,200}{2} = \underline{\$359,850}$$

b. What is the inventory turnover rounded to the nearest tenth?

$$\text{Inventory turnover} = \frac{884,000}{359,850} = \underline{2.5 \text{ Times}}$$

c. What is the target average inventory needed to theoretically come up to the industry standard?

$$\text{Target inventory} = \frac{884,000}{5} = \underline{\$176,800}$$

 BUSINESS DECISION
Inventory Valuation and the Bottom Line

10. You are the chief accountant of Dollar Time Industries, Inc. This morning, in anticipation of the upcoming annual stockholders meeting, the president of the company asked you to determine the effect of the FIFO, LIFO, and average inventory valuation methods on the company's income statement.

Beginning inventory, January 1, was 10,000 units at $5.00 each. Purchases during the year consisted of 15,000 units at $6.00 on April 15; 20,000 units at $7.00 on July 19; and 25,000 units at $8.00 on November 2.

a. If ending inventory on December 31 was 40,000 units, calculate the value of this inventory using the three valuation methods:

FIFO: $305,000   LIFO: $245,000   Average Cost: $274,400

Date	Number of Units	Price per Unit	Total Cost
Beginning inventory, Jan. 1	10,000	5.00	50,000
Purchase, April 15	15,000	6.00	90,000
Purchase, July 19	20,000	7.00	140,000
Purchase, November 2	25,000	8.00	200,000
Units for sale	70,000		$480,000

Value of 40,000 units using FIFO   25,000 @ 8.00 = 200,000
                                    15,000 @ 7.00 = 105,000
                                    40,000 $305,000

Value of 40,000 units using LIFO   10,000 @ 5.00 =   50,000
                                    15,000 @ 6.00 =   90,000
                                    15,000 @ 7.00 = 105,000
                                    40,000 $245,000

Value of 40,000 units using average cost

$$\frac{480,000}{70,000} = 6.86 \text{ Each}$$

$$40,000 \times 6.86 = \$274,400$$

b. Complete the comparative income statement for the year using the following information and the format below:

Net sales	30,000 units at $12 each
Operating expenses	$100,000
Income tax rate	30%

Dollar Time Industries, Inc.
Comparative Income Statement

	FIFO	LIFO	Average Cost
Net sales	$360,000	$360,000	$360,000
Beginning inventory	50,000	50,000	50,000
Purchases	430,000	430,000	430,000
Cost of goods available for sale	480,000	480,000	480,000
Ending inventory	305,000	245,000	274,400
Cost of goods sold	175,000	235,000	205,600
Gross profit	185,000	125,000	154,400
Operating expenses	100,000	100,000	100,000
Income before taxes	85,000	25,000	54,400
Income tax	25,500	7,500	16,320
Net income	$59,500	$17,500	$38,080

c. Which inventory method should be used if the objective is to pay the least amount of taxes?

LIFO method has the least amount of taxes

d. Which method should be used if the objective is to show the greatest amount of profit to the shareholders in the annual report?

FIFO method has the greatest profit

Name_____

Class_____

ANSWERS

b. _____ See table. _____

c. _____ LIFO method _____

d. _____ FIFO method _____

All the Math That's Fit to Learn

The Business Math Times

Volume XVI — Inventory — One Dollar

Career Track:

Stock Clerk

Nature of the Work

Stock clerks receive, unpack, check, store, and keep track of merchandise or materials. They keep records of items entering or leaving the stock room and report damaged or spoiled goods. They organize and, when necessary, mark items with identifying codes or prices so that inventories can be located quickly and easily.

Job Outlook and Related Occupations

Jobs for stock clerks are found in all parts of the country, but most of the work is in urban areas where stores, warehouses, and factories are concentrated. This occupations is very large and many job openings occur each year. Many jobs are entry level, and therefore many vacancies are created by normal career progression. Related occupations include shipping and receiving clerks, distributing clerks, routing clerks, stock supervisors, and cargo checkers.

"Quote...Unquote"

Everything is worth what its purchaser will pay for it.
–Publilius Syrus

Everyone who's ever taken a shower has an idea. It's the person who gets out of the shower, dries off and does something about it who makes a difference.
–Nolan Bushnell, founder, Atari

Ford Inventory and Assembly Changes	Savings per Vehicle	Savings per Year
Offering 3 types of carpeting rather than 9	$1.25	$9 million
Stocking 5 kinds of air filters rather than 18	$ .45	$3 million
Offering 1 type of cigarette lighter instead of 14	$ .16	$1 million
Using black screws instead of color-matched painted screws on Mustang side mirrors	$5.40	$740,000
Skipping the black paint inside Explorer ashtrays	$ .25	$100,000

SOURCES: Karen Schwartz, "Will You Miss Color-Matched Screws on a Car?" *Miami Herald,* March 31, 1996: 8F; and Nathaniel C. Nash, "Putting Porsche in the Pink," *New York Times,* Business Day section, January 20, 1996: 17.

Fewer Choices = More Profits

In business, sometimes very small and subtle changes can translate into millions of dollars in savings. A single minor adjustment can mean less time on an assembly line, reduced inventories, fewer workers to pay, and ultimately, more profit.

Lettuce Save. In 1992, Delta Airlines began leaving off the lettuce garnish from its airplane meals. Sound insignificant? Delta no longer needed to pay people to wash and trim the lettuce and place a single leaf on each meal tray. Savings? $1.5 million per year!

40% Faster Porsches. In 1992, Porsche began using Japanese techniques to improve the efficiency of its manufacturing process. By reducing the distance cars traveled on the assembly line from 455 yards to 119 yards and reducing the inventory of large parts from 8,490 to 1,600, manufacturing time was cut from 120 to 72 hours per car, a 40% time savings. In addition, these changes reduced the manufacturing flaws per car from 6 to 3.

Penny Pinch. Ford Motor Co. recently instituted some changes that amount to only cents per vehicle, but quickly added up to an estimated $11 billion in savings. A few examples are shown above.

People Inventory

Did you know, worldwide, an average of 9 babies are born every 2 seconds? The population grows by an average of 93 million people per year, 1.8 million people per week, 254,000 people per day, and 3 people every second.

SOURCE: Dean D. Dauphinais and Kathleen Droste. *Astounding Averages!* Visible Ink Press, a division of Gale Research Inc., 1995, p. 253.

Brainteaser

How much dirt is in a hole 15 feet long by 10 feet wide by 5 feet deep?

Answer to Last Issue's Brainteaser
The frog will **never** reach the wall.

Inventory Pie

According to a survey by the American Institute of Certified Public Accountants (AICPA) the following is the breakdown of inventory valuation methods used by the 600 largest U.S. companies.

SOURCE: Adapted from *Accounting Trends and Techniques,* 1995 Edition, AICPA, New York, NY.

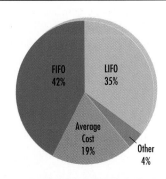

FIFO 42%
LIFO 35%
Average Cost 19%
Other 4%

Chapter 17

Depreciation

long-term or long-lived assets

Relatively fixed or permanent assets, such as land, buildings, tools, equipment, and vehicles, that companies acquire in the course of operating a business.

depreciation, or depreciation expense

The decrease in value from the original cost of a long-term asset over its useful life.

book value

The value of an asset at any given time. It is the original cost less the accumulated depreciation to that point.

total cost, or original basis

The total amount a company pays for an asset, including freight, handling, and setup charges.

residual, scrap, salvage, or trade-in value

The value of an asset at the time it is taken out of service.

useful life

The length of time an asset is expected to generate revenue.

In Chapter 15, we learned a firm's assets are divided into three categories: current assets; property, plant, and equipment; and investments and other assets. This chapter deals with the valuation of the **long-term** or **long-lived assets** of the firm: the property, plant, and equipment. Companies acquire these relatively fixed or permanent assets in the course of building and operating a business. Some examples of these assets would be land, buildings, equipment, machinery, vehicles, furniture, fixtures, and tools.

As time goes by, the usefulness or productivity of these assets, except land, decreases. Think of this decrease as a loss of revenue earning power. Accordingly, the cost of these assets is distributed over their useful life to coincide with the revenue earned. This cost write-off is known as **depreciation.** On the income statement, depreciation is listed under operating expenses as **depreciation expense.** On the balance sheet, it is used to determine the current **book value** of an asset, whereby:

$$\text{Book value} = \text{Original cost} - \text{Accumulated depreciation}$$

Assets depreciate for a number of reasons. They may physically wear out from use and deterioration or they may depreciate because they have become inadequate and obsolete. Four important factors must be taken into account in order to determine the amount of depreciation expense of an asset.

1. The **total cost,** or **original basis** of the asset. This amount includes such items as freight, handling, and set-up charges.
2. The asset's estimated **residual value** at the time that it is taken out of service. This is also known as **scrap value, salvage value,** or **trade-in value.**
3. An estimate of the **useful life** of the asset or the length of time it is expected to generate revenue. In order to be depreciated, an asset must have a life greater than one year.
4. The method of calculating depreciation must match the way in which the asset will depreciate. Some assets depreciate evenly over the years (straight-line depreciation), while others depreciate more quickly at first and then slow down in the later years (accelerated depreciation). Regardless of which method a company chooses, at the end of the useful life of an asset, the total amount of depreciation expense write-off will be the same.

This chapter will examine the various methods used to depreciate assets. In Section I, we will learn to calculate depreciation by the four traditional methods: straight-line; sum-of-the-years' digits; declining-balance; and units-of-production. Any of these methods may be used for financial statement reporting. However, once a method has been implemented, it cannot be changed.

Frequently, the amount of depreciation reported by a company on its financial statements will differ from the amount reported to the IRS for income tax purposes, because the IRS allows additional options for calculating depreciation expense. Today the most widely used method for tax purposes is known as the modified accelerated cost recovery system (MACRS). This method will be covered in Section II.

TRADITIONAL DEPRECIATION—METHODS USED FOR FINANCIAL STATEMENT REPORTING

Depreciation is most frequently based on time, how many years an asset is expected to last. Certain assets, however, are depreciated more accurately on the basis of some productivity measure such as units of output for production machinery, or mileage for vehicles, regardless of time. This section deals with both time- and productivity-based depreciation methods.

17-1 Calculating Depreciation by the Straight-Line Method

The **straight-line depreciation** method is by far the most widely used in business today. It provides for equal periodic charges to be written off over the estimated useful life of the asset.

Once the annual depreciation has been determined, we can set up a **depreciation schedule.** The depreciation schedule is a chart illustrating the depreciation activity of the asset for each year of its useful life. The chart shows the amount of depreciation each year, the accumulated depreciation to date, and the book value of the asset.

● **straight-line depreciation**
A method of depreciation that provides for equal periodic charges to be written off over the estimated useful life of an asset.

● **depreciation schedule**
Chart showing the depreciation activity (depreciation, accumulated depreciation, and book value) of an asset for each year of its useful life.

STEPS TO PREPARE A DEPRECIATION SCHEDULE BY THE STRAIGHT-LINE METHOD:

Step 1. Determine the total cost and salvage value of the asset.

Step 2. Subtract salvage value from total cost to find the total amount of depreciation.

$$\text{Total depreciation} = \text{Total cost} - \text{Salvage value}$$

Step 3. Calculate the annual amount of depreciation by dividing the total depreciation by the useful life of the asset.

$$\text{Annual depreciation} = \frac{\text{Total depreciation}}{\text{Estimated useful life (years)}}$$

Step 4. Set up the depreciation schedule in the form of a chart with the following headings:

End of Year	Annual Depreciation	Accumulated Depreciation	Book Value

Note: The starting book value is the original cost of the asset and the last book value is equal to the salvage value of the asset.

EXAMPLE

Barton Enterprises purchased a computer system for $9,000. Shipping charges were $125 and setup and programming amounted to $375. The system is expected to last four years and has a residual value of $1,500. If Barton elects to use the straight-line method of depreciation for the computer, calculate the total cost, total depreciation, and annual depreciation. Prepare a depreciation schedule for its useful life.

SOLUTION STRATEGY

Step 1.
Total cost = Cost + Freight + Setup expenses
Total cost = 9,000 + 125 + 375 = $9,500

Step 2.
Total depreciation = Total cost − Salvage value
Total depreciation = 9,500 − 1,500 = $8,000

Step 3.
$$\text{Annual depreciation} = \frac{\text{Total depreciation}}{\text{Estimated useful life (years)}}$$
$$\text{Annual depreciation} = \frac{8,000}{4} = \$2,000$$

Step 4.
Depreciation Schedule
Barton Enterprises, Computer System

End of Year	Annual Depreciation	Accumulated Depreciation	Book Value
			$9,500 (original cost)
1	$2,000	$2,000	7,500
2	2,000	4,000	5,500
3	2,000	6,000	3,500
4	2,000	8,000	1,500 (salvage value)

Expensive assets like this corporate jet are considered long-lived assets, the value of which depreciates over time.

1. **Holsum Bakery purchased a new bread oven for $125,000. Shipping charges were $1,150.00 and installation amounted to $750.00. The oven is expected to last five years and has a trade-in value of $5,000. If Holsum elects to use the straight-line method, calculate the total cost, total depreciation, and annual depreciation of the oven. Prepare a depreciation schedule for its useful life.**

Check your answers with the solutions on pages 578–579.

17-2 Calculating Depreciation by the Sum-of-the-Years' Digits Method

● **accelerated depreciation**

Depreciation methods that assume an asset depreciates more in the early years of its useful life than in the later years.

● **sum-of-the-years' digits**

A method of accelerated depreciation that allows an asset to depreciate the most during the first year, with decreasing amounts each year thereafter. Total depreciation is based on the total cost of an asset less its salvage value.

The sum-of-the-years' digits and the declining-balance methods of calculating depreciation are the two **accelerated depreciation** methods. These methods assume that an asset depreciates more in the early years of its useful life than in the later years. Under the sum-of-the-years' digits method, the yearly charge for depreciation declines steadily over the estimated useful life of the asset because a successively smaller fraction is applied each year to the total depreciation (total cost – salvage value).

This fraction is known as the **sum-of-the-years' digits** fraction. The denominator of the fraction is the sum of the digits of the estimated life of the asset. This number does not change. The numerator of the fraction is the number of years of useful life remaining. This number changes every year as the asset gets older and older. This sum-of-the-years' digits depreciation rate fraction can be expressed as

$$\text{SYD depreciation rate fraction} = \frac{\text{Years of useful life remaining}}{\text{Sum-of-the-digits of the useful life}}$$

The denominator (the sum of the years' digits) can be calculated by adding all the digits of the years, or by the following formula:

$$\text{SYD} = \frac{n(n+1)}{2}$$

where

n = **the number of years of useful life of the asset**

For example, let's compute the depreciation rate fractions for an asset that has a useful life of 4 years. The denominator, the sum of the digits of 4, is 10. This is calculated by $4 + 3 + 2 + 1 = 10$ or by the SYD formula, $4(4 + 1) \div 2 = 10$. Remember, the denominator does not change. The numerator of the fractions will be 4, 3, 2, and 1 for each succeeding year.

Year	Depreciation Rate Fraction	Depreciation Rate	
		Decimal	Percent
1	4/10	.40	40%
2	3/10	.30	30%
3	2/10	.20	20%
4	1/10	.10	10%

From this chart we can see that an asset with 4 years of useful life will depreciate $\frac{4}{10}$ or 40% in the first year, $\frac{3}{10}$ or 30% in the second year, and so on. The accelerated rate of 40% depreciation write-off in the first year gives the business a reduced tax advantage and therefore an incentive to invest in new equipment.

STEPS TO PREPARE A DEPRECIATION SCHEDULE USING THE SUM-OF-THE-YEARS' DIGITS METHOD:

Step 1. Find the total depreciation of the asset by:

$$\text{Total depreciation} = \text{Total cost} - \text{Salvage value}$$

Step 2. Calculate the SYD depreciation rate fraction for each year by:

$$\text{SYD depreciation rate fraction} = \frac{\text{Years of useful life remaining}}{\dfrac{n(n+1)}{2}}$$

Step 3. Calculate the depreciation for each year by multiplying the total depreciation by that year's depreciation rate fraction.

$$\text{Annual depreciation} = \text{Total depreciation} \times \text{Depreciation rate fraction}$$

Step 4. Set up a depreciation schedule in the form of a chart with the following headings:

End of Year	Total Depreciation	×	Depreciation Rate Fraction	=	Annual Depreciation	Accumulated Depreciation	Book Value

EXAMPLE

All City Wholesalers purchased a delivery truck for $35,000. The truck is expected to have a useful life of five years and a trade-in value of $5,000. Using the sum-of-the-years' digits method, prepare a depreciation schedule for All City.

SOLUTION STRATEGY

Following the steps for preparing a depreciation schedule using sum-of-the-years' digits:

Step 1.
$$\text{Total depreciation} = \text{Total cost} - \text{Salvage value}$$
$$\text{Total depreciation} = 35,000 - 5,000 = \underline{\$30,000}$$

Step 2. Year 1:
$$\text{SYD depreciation rate fraction} = \frac{\text{Years of useful life remaining}}{\dfrac{n(n+1)}{2}}$$

$$\text{SYD depreciation rate fraction} = \frac{5}{\dfrac{5(5+1)}{2}} = \frac{5}{15}$$

The depreciation rate fraction for year 1 is $\frac{5}{15}$. The depreciation fractions for the remaining years will have the same denominator, 15 (the sum of the digits of 5). Only the numerators will change, in descending order. The depreciation fractions for the remaining years are $\frac{4}{15}$, $\frac{3}{15}$, $\frac{2}{15}$, and $\frac{1}{15}$.

Note how accelerated this SYD method is: $\frac{5}{15}$, or $\frac{1}{3}$ of the asset (33.3%), is allowed to be written off in the first year. This is compared to only $\frac{1}{5}$ (20%) per year using the straight-line method.

Step 3.
$$\text{Annual depreciation} = \text{Total depreciation} \times \text{Depreciation rate fraction}$$

$$\text{Annual depreciation (year 1)} = 30,000 \times \tfrac{5}{15} = \underline{\$10,000}$$

$$\text{Annual depreciation (year 2)} = 30,000 \times \tfrac{4}{15} = \underline{\$8,000}$$

Continue this calculation for each of the remaining three years. Then prepare the schedule.

Step 4.

All City Wholesalers
SYD Depreciation Schedule
Delivery Truck

End of Year	Total Depreciation	×	Depreciation Rate Fraction	=	Annual Depreciation	Accumulated Depreciation	Book Value
							(new) $35,000
1	30,000	×	$\frac{5}{15}$	=	10,000	10,000	25,000
2	30,000	×	$\frac{4}{15}$	=	8,000	18,000	17,000
3	30,000	×	$\frac{3}{15}$	=	6,000	24,000	11,000
4	30,000	×	$\frac{2}{15}$	=	4,000	28,000	7,000
5	30,000	×	$\frac{1}{15}$	=	2,000	30,000	5,000

TRY-IT EXERCISE

2. **StyleCraft Furniture Manufacturers purchased new production-line machinery for a total of $44,500. The company expects this machinery to last six years and have a residual value of $2,500. Using the sum-of-the-years' digits method, prepare a depreciation schedule for StyleCraft.**

Check your answers with the solutions on page 579.

17-3 Calculating Depreciation by the Declining-Balance Method

● **declining-balance**

A method of accelerated depreciation that uses a multiple (125%, 150%, or 200%) of the straight-line rate to calculate depreciation. Further accelerated because depreciation is based on the original cost of the asset, with salvage value only being considered in the last year.

● **double-declining balance**

Name given to the declining-balance method of depreciation when the straight-line multiple is 200%.

The second widely accepted method of accelerated depreciation in business is known as the **declining-balance** method. This method uses a multiple of the straight-line rate to calculate depreciation. The most frequently used multiples are 1.25, 1.5, and 2. When 1.25 is used it is known as the 125% declining balance, when 1.5 is used it is known as the 150% declining balance. When 2 is the multiple, the method is known as the **double-declining balance.**

To calculate the declining-balance rate, we first determine the straight-line rate by dividing 1 by the number of years of useful life, then multiplying by the appropriate declining-balance multiple. For example, when using the double-declining balance, an asset with a useful life of 4 years would have a straight-line rate of 25% per year ($1 \div 4 = \frac{1}{4} = 25\%$). This rate is then multiplied by the declining-balance multiple, 2, to get 50%, the double-declining rate. The following formula should be used for this calculation:

$$\text{Declining-balance rate} = \frac{1}{\text{Useful life}} \times \text{Multiple}$$

To further accelerate the depreciation, this declining-balance rate is applied to the original total cost of the asset. Salvage value is not considered until the last year of depreciation. When preparing a depreciation schedule using the declining-balance method, the depreciation stops when the book value of the asset reaches the salvage value. By IRS regulations, the asset cannot be depreciated below the salvage value.

STEPS TO PREPARE A DEPRECIATION SCHEDULE USING THE DECLINING-BALANCE METHOD:

Step 1. Calculate the declining-balance rate by the formula:

$$\text{Declining-balance rate} = \frac{1}{\text{Useful life}} \times \text{Multiple}$$

Step 2. Calculate the depreciation for each year by applying the rate to each year's beginning book value, which is the ending book value of the previous year.

Depreciation for the year = Beginning book value × Declining-balance rate

Step 3. Calculate the ending book value for each year by subtracting the depreciation for the year from the beginning book value:

Ending book value = Beginning book value – Depreciation for the year

Step 4. When the ending book value equals the salvage value, the depreciation is complete.

Step 5. Set up a depreciation schedule in the form of a chart with the following headings:

End of Year	Beginning Book Value	Depreciation Rate	Depreciation for the Year	Accumulated Depreciation	Ending Book Value

EXAMPLE

Continental Shipping bought a forklift for $20,000. It is expected to have a five-year useful life and a trade-in value of $2,000. Prepare a depreciation schedule for this asset using the double-declining balance method.

SOLUTION STRATEGY

Step 1. $\text{Declining-balance rate} = \dfrac{1}{\text{Useful life}} \times \text{Multiple}$

$\text{Declining-balance rate} = \dfrac{1}{5} \times 2 = .20 \times 2 = .40 = \underline{40\%}$

Step 2. Depreciation for the year = Beginning book value × Declining-balance rate

Depreciation: Year 1 = 20,000 × .40 = $\underline{\$8,000}$

Step 3. Ending book value = Beginning book value – Depreciation for the year

Ending book value: Year 1 = 20,000 – 8,000 = $\underline{\$12,000}$

Repeat Steps 2 and 3 for years 2, 3, 4, and 5.

Step 4. In year 5, although the calculated depreciation is $1,036.80 (2,592 × .4), the allowable depreciation is limited to $592 (2,592 – 2,000), because the book value has reached the $2,000 salvage value. At this point, the depreciation is complete.

Step 5.

Continental Shipping, Inc.
Depreciation Schedule
5-year, double-declining balance

End of Year	Beginning Book Value	Depreciation Rate	Depreciation for the Year	Accumulated Depreciation	Ending Book Value
					(new) $20,000
1	20,000	40%	8,000	8,000	12,000
2	12,000	40%	4,800	12,800	7,200
3	7,200	40%	2,880	15,680	4,320
4	4,320	40%	1,728	17,408	2,592
5	2,592	40%	592*	18,000	2,000

*Maximum allowable to reach salvage value.

3. **Southwest Air Service bought a small commuter airplane for $386,000. It is expected to have a useful life of 4 years and a trade-in value of $70,000. Prepare a depreciation schedule for the airplane using the 150% declining-balance method.**

Check your answers with the solutions on page 579.

17-4 Calculating Depreciation by the Units-of-Production Method

● **units-of-production**

Depreciation method based on how much an asset is used, such as miles, hours, or units produced, rather than the passage of time.

When the useful life of an asset is more accurately defined in terms of how much it is used rather than the passage of time, we may use the **units-of-production** method to calculate depreciation. To apply this method, the life of the asset is expressed in productive capacity, such as miles driven, units produced, or hours used. Some examples of assets typically depreciated using this method would be cars, trucks, airplanes, production-line machinery, engines, pumps, and electronic equipment.

To calculate depreciation using this method, we begin by determining the depreciation per unit. This number is found by dividing the amount to be depreciated (cost − salvage value) by the estimated units of useful life:

$$\text{Depreciation per unit} = \frac{\text{Cost} - \text{Salvage value}}{\text{Units of useful life}}$$

For example, let's say that a hole-punching machine on a production line had a cost of $35,000 and a salvage value of $5,000. If we estimate that the machine had a useful life of 150,000 units of production, the depreciation per unit would be calculated as follows:

$$\text{Depreciation per unit} = \frac{\text{Cost} - \text{Salvage value}}{\text{Units of useful life}} = \frac{35,000 - 5,000}{150,000} = \frac{30,000}{150,000} = \underline{\$.20 \text{ per unit}}$$

Once we have determined the depreciation per unit, we can find the annual depreciation by multiplying the depreciation per unit by the number of units produced each year.

Annual depreciation = Depreciation per unit × Units produced

In the previous example, if the hole-punching machine produced 30,000 in a year, the annual depreciation for that year would be as follows:

Annual depreciation = Depreciation per unit × Units produced = .20 × 30,000 = $\underline{\$6,000}$

STEPS TO CALCULATE DEPRECIATION USING THE UNITS-OF-PRODUCTION METHOD:

Step 1. Determine the depreciation per unit using:

$$\text{Depreciation per unit} = \frac{\text{Cost} - \text{Salvage value}}{\text{Units of useful life}}$$

(Round to the nearest tenth of a cent when necessary.)

Step 2. Calculate the annual depreciation using:

Annual depreciation = Depreciation per unit × Units produced

Step 3. Set up the depreciation schedule in the form of a chart with the following headings:

End of Year	Depreciation per Unit	Units Produced	Annual Depreciation	Accumulated Depreciation	Book Value

Precision Printing purchased a new printing press for $8,500 with a salvage value of $500. For depreciation purposes, the press is expected to have a useful life of 5,000 hours. From the following estimate of hours of use, prepare a depreciation schedule for the printing press using the units-of-production method.

Year	Hours of Use
1	1,500
2	1,200
3	2,000
4	500

SOLUTION STRATEGY

Step 1.

$$\text{Depreciation per unit (hours)} = \frac{\text{Cost} - \text{Salvage value}}{\text{Hours of useful life}}$$

$$\text{Depreciation per unit} = \frac{8,500 - 500}{5,000} = \frac{8,000}{5,000} = \underline{\$1.60 \text{ per hour}}$$

Step 2.

$$\text{Annual depreciation} = \text{Depreciation per unit} \times \text{Units produced}$$

$$\text{Annual depreciation (year 1)} = 1.60 \times 1,500 = \underline{\$2,400}$$

$$\text{Annual depreciation (year 2)} = 1.60 \times 1,200 = \underline{\$1,920}$$

Continue this procedure for the remaining years.

Step 3.

Precision Printing, Inc.
Depreciation Schedule, Printing Press
Units-of-Production Method (5,000 hours)

End of Year	Depreciation per Hour	Hours Used	Annual Depreciation	Accumulated Depreciation	Book Value
				(new)	$8,500
1	$1.60	1,500	$2,400	$2,400	6,100
2	1.60	1,200	1,920	4,320	4,180
3	1.60	2,000	3,200	7,520	980
4	1.60	500	480*	8,000	500

*Maximum allowable to reach salvage value.

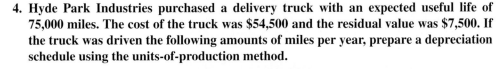

TRY-IT EXERCISE

4. Hyde Park Industries purchased a delivery truck with an expected useful life of 75,000 miles. The cost of the truck was $54,500 and the residual value was $7,500. If the truck was driven the following amounts of miles per year, prepare a depreciation schedule using the units-of-production method.

Year	Miles Driven
1	12,500
2	18,300
3	15,900
4	19,100
5	12,400

Check your answers with the solutions on pages 579–580.

Calculate the total cost, total depreciation, and annual depreciation for the following assets using the straight-line method:

	Cost	Freight Charges	Setup Charges	Total Cost	Salvage Value	Estimated Useful Life	Total Depreciation	Annual Depreciation
1.	$45,000	$150	$500	$45,650.00	$3,500	10 years	$42,150.00	$4,215.00
2.	$88,600	$625	$2,500	91,725.00	$9,000	7 years	82,725.00	11,817.86
3.	$158,200	$0	$1,800	160,000.00	$20,000	5 years	140,000.00	28,000.00
4.	$750,000	$0	$10,300	760,300.00	$70,000	15 years	690,300.00	46,020.00

5. The Fluffy Laundry purchased new washing machines and dryers for $57,000. Freight charges were $470 and installation amounted to $500. The machines are expected to last five years and have a residual value of $2,000. If Fluffy elects to use the straight-line method of depreciation, prepare a depreciation schedule for these machines.

Fluffy Laundry
Depreciation Schedule
Straight-line Method

End of Year	Annual Depreciation	Accumulated Depreciation	Book Value
(new)			$57,970.00
1	$11,194.00	$11,194.00	46,776.00
2	11,194.00	22,388.00	35,582.00
3	11,194.00	33,582.00	24,388.00
4	11,194.00	44,776.00	13,194.00
5	11,194.00	55,970.00	2,000.00

Total cost = 57,000.00 + 470.00 + 500.00 = $57,970.00

Total depreciation = 57,970.00 − 2,000.00 = 55,970.00

Annual depreciation = $\dfrac{55,970.00}{5}$ = 11,194.00

6. Carson Supply Company purchases warehouse shelving for $18,600. Freight charges were $370 and assembly and setup amounted to $575. The shelves are expected to last for 7 years and have a scrap value of $900. Using the straight-line method of depreciation:

   a. What is the annual depreciation expense of the shelving?

   Total cost = 18,600.00 + 370.00 + 575.00 = $19,545.00

   Total depreciation = 19,545.00 − 900.00 = $18,645.00

   Annual depreciation = $\dfrac{18,645.00}{7}$ = $2,663.57

   b. What is the accumulated depreciation after the third year?

   Accumulated depreciation after 3rd year = $2,663.57 × 3 = $7,990.71

   c. What is the book value of the shelving after the fifth year?

   Book value after 5th year = 19,545 − (2,663.57 × 5)
   = $6,227.15

Complete Exercises 7–9 as they relate to the sum-of-the-years' digits method of depreciation:

	Useful Life	Sum of the Years' Digits	Depreciation Rate Fraction		
			Year 1	Year 3	Year 5
7.	5 years	15	5/15	3/15	1/15
8.	7 years	28	7/28	5/28	3/28
9.	10 years	55	10/55	8/55	6/55

10. New Age Manufacturing, Inc., purchased production-line machinery for $445,000. It is expected to last for six years and have a trade-in value of $25,000. Using the sum-of-the-years' digits method, prepare a depreciation schedule for New Age.

New Age Manufacturing, Inc.
Machinery—SYD Depreciation Schedule

End of Year	Total Depreciation	Depreciation Rate Fraction	Annual Depreciation	Accumulated Depreciation	Book Value
				(new)	$445,000
1	$420,000	$\frac{6}{21}$	$120,000	$120,000	325,000
2	420,000	$\frac{5}{21}$	100,000	220,000	225,000
3	420,000	$\frac{4}{21}$	80,000	300,000	145,000
4	420,000	$\frac{3}{21}$	60,000	360,000	85,000
5	420,000	$\frac{2}{21}$	40,000	400,000	45,000
6	420,000	$\frac{1}{21}$	20,000	420,000	25,000

Original cost $445,000
Trade in value   − 25,000
Total depreciation $420,000

Complete Exercises 11–13 as they relate to the declining-balance method of depreciation:

	Years	Straight-Line Rate	Multiple	Declining-Balance Rate
11.	4	25%	125%	31.25%
12.	6	16.67%	200%	33.34%
13.	10	10%	150%	15%

14. Service America, Inc., bought a fleet of new cars for $180,000. The fleet is expected to have an eight-year useful life and a trade-in value of $35,000. Prepare a depreciation schedule using the 150% declining-balance method for the cars.

Service America, Inc.
Depreciation Schedule—Service Fleet
8-year, 150% declining-balance

End of Year	Beginning Book Value	Depreciation Rate	Depreciation for the Year	Accumulated Depreciation	Ending Book Value
				(new)	$180,000.00
1	$180,000.00	.1875	$33,750.00	$33,750.00	146,250.00
2	146,250.00	.1875	27,421.88	61,171.88	118,828.12
3	118,828.12	.1875	22,280.27	83,452.15	96,547.85
4	96,547.85	.1875	18,102.72	101,554.87	78,445.13
5	78,445.13	.1875	14,708.46	116,263.33	63,736.67
6	63,736.67	.1875	11,950.63	128,213.96	51,786.04
7	51,786.04	.1875	9,709.88	137,923.84	42,076.16
8	42,076.16	.1875	7,076.16*	145,000.00	35,000.00

Total depreciation = 180,000. − 35,000.
= $145,000.

*Maximum allowed to reach salvage value

Complete the following as they relate to the units-of-production method of depreciation (round to the nearest tenth of a cent when necessary):

	Asset	Cost	Salvage Value	Units of Useful Life	Depreciation per Unit
15.	pump	$15,000	$2,800	100,000 hours	$.122
16.	automobile	$27,400	$3,400	60,000 miles	.4
17.	assembly robot	$775,000	$25,000	3,000,000 units	.25

18. Millennium Manufacturing purchased a new stamping machine for $45,000 with a salvage value of $5,000. For depreciation purposes, the machine is expected to have a useful life of 250,000 units of production. Complete the following depreciation schedule using the units-of-production method:

Millennium Manufacturing, Inc.
Depreciation Schedule, Units-of-Production
Stamping Machine—250,000 Units

End of Year	Depreciation per Unit	Units Produced	Annual Depreciation	Accumulated Depreciation	Book Value
				(new)	$45,000.00
1	$0.16	50,000	$8,000.00	$8,000.00	37,000.00
2	0.16	70,000	11,200.00	19,200.00	25,800.00
3	0.16	45,000	7,200.00	26,400.00	18,600.00
4	0.16	66,000	10,560.00	36,960.00	8,040.00
5	0.16	30,000	3,040.00*	40,000.00	5,000.00

Total cost 45,000.00 − 5,000.00 = 40,000.00

Depreciation per unit = $\dfrac{40,000.00}{250,000}$ = $.16

*Maximum allowed to reach salvage value

SECTION II

ASSET COST RECOVERY SYSTEMS—IRS PRESCRIBED METHODS FOR INCOME TAX REPORTING

● **cost recovery allowance**
Term used under MACRS meaning the amount of depreciation of an asset that may be written off for tax purposes in a given year.

● **modified accelerated cost recovery system (MACRS)**
A 1986 modification of the property classes and the depreciation rates of the accelerated depreciation method; used for assets put into service after 1986.

● **general depreciation system (GDS)**
One of two MACRS depreciation systems. Most tangible depreciable property falls within the rules of the GDS, which permits the use of declining-balance depreciation and shorter recovery periods than the alternative depreciation system.

● **alternative depreciation system (ADS)**
One of two MACRS depreciation systems. Primarily for property used *outside* the United States during the year or for tax-exempt property. Uses straight-line depreciation and generally longer recovery periods than the GDS.

● **property class**
One of several time categories to which property is assigned under MACRS showing how many years are allowed for cost recovery.

● **cost recovery percentage**
An IRS-prescribed percentage that is multiplied by the original basis of an asset to determine the depreciation deduction for a given year. Based on property class and year of asset life.

Section I of this chapter described the depreciation methods used by businesses for the preparation of financial statements. For income tax purposes the Internal Revenue Service (IRS), through federal tax laws, prescribes how depreciation must be taken.

As part of the Economic Recovery Act of 1981, the IRS introduced a depreciation method known as the accelerated cost recovery system (ACRS), for tax purposes, which allows businesses to write off the cost of an asset more quickly than with traditional methods. The government designed the ACRS to stimulate a slumping economy by allowing businesses to write off the cost of an asset more quickly than with traditional methods, thus encouraging investment in new equipment and other capital assets. Essentially, this method discarded the concepts of estimated useful life and residual value. In their place it required that businesses compute a **cost recovery allowance.**

After the ACRS was modified by the Tax Equity and Fiscal Responsibility Act of 1982 and the Tax Reform Act of 1984, it was significantly overhauled by the Tax Reform Act of 1986. The resulting method was known as the **modified accelerated cost recovery system (MACRS).** This is the system we shall use to calculate depreciation for federal income tax purposes.

17-5 Calculating Depreciation Using the Modified Accelerated Cost Recovery System (MACRS)

According to the IRS, the modified accelerated cost recovery system (MACRS) is the name given to tax rules for getting back or recovering through depreciation deductions the cost of property used in a trade or business, or to produce income. These rules generally apply to tangible property placed in service *after 1986*. MACRS consists of two systems that determine how property is to be depreciated. The primary system is known as the **general depreciation system (GDS),** while the secondary system is called the **alternative depreciation system (ADS).**

Unless the ADS is specifically required by law, such as with tangible property used predominantly *outside* the United States during the year, the GDS should be used to calculate the depreciation deduction. The main difference between the two systems is that the GDS allows shorter recovery periods for each property class, and therefore greater write-offs each year.

Table 17-1 exhibits the eight main property classes, with some examples of assets included in each class under the GDS.

Once the **property class** for the asset has been identified, the amount of depreciation each year can be manually calculated or found by using percentage tables. As a general rule, the 3-, 5-, 7-, and 10-year property class assets are depreciated using the 200% declining-balance method; the 15- and 20-year classes use the 150% declining-balance method; and the 31.5- and 39-year classes use straight-line depreciation.

Because these calculations were already covered in Section I of this chapter, we shall focus on using one of the **cost recovery percentage** tables provided by the IRS. Table 17-2 is such a table.

3-Year Property	5-Year Property	7-Year Property
Over-the-road tractors	Automobiles and taxis	Office furniture and fixtures
Some horses and hogs	Buses and trucks	Railroad cars and engines
Special handling devices for the manufacture of food and beverages	Computers and peripherals	Commercial airplanes
Specialty tools used in the manufacture of motor vehicles	Office machinery	Equipment used in mining, petroleum drilling, and natural gas exploration
Specialty tools used in the manufacture of finished products made of plastic, rubber, glass, and metal	Research and experimental equipment	Equipment used in the manufacture of wood, pulp, and paper products
	Breeding or dairy cattle	Equipment used to manufacture aerospace products
	Sheep and goats	
	Airplanes (except those in commercial use)	
	Drilling and timber cutting equipment	
	Construction equipment	

10-Year Property	15-Year Property	20-Year Property
Vessels, barges, and tugs	Depreciable improvements made to land such as shrubbery, fences, roads, and bridges	Farm buildings
Single-purpose agricultural structures	Equipment used to manufacture cement	Railroad structures and improvements
Trees and vines bearing fruits or nuts	Gas utility pipelines	Communication cable and long-line systems
Equipment for grain, sugar, and vegetable oil products		Water utility plants and equipment

31.5-Year Property	39-Year Property
Placed into service before May 13, 1993:	*Placed into service after May 12, 1993:*
Nonresidential real estate	Nonresidential real estate
Office in the home	Office in the home

TABLE 17-1

MACRS PROPERTY CLASSES
GENERAL DEPRECIATION SYSTEM

Recovery Year	Depreciation Rate for Property Class					
	3-year	5-year	7-year	10-year	15-year	20-year
1	33.33%	20.00%	14.29%	10.00%	5.00%	3.750%
2	44.45	32.00	24.49	18.00	9.50	7.219
3	14.81	19.20	17.49	14.40	8.55	6.677
4	7.41	11.52	12.49	11.52	7.70	6.177
5		11.52	8.93	9.22	6.93	5.713
6		5.76	8.92	7.37	6.23	5.285
7			8.93	6.55	5.90	4.888
8			4.46	6.55	5.90	4.522
9				6.56	5.91	4.462
10				6.55	5.90	4.461
11				3.28	5.91	4.462
12					5.90	4.461
13					5.91	4.462
14					5.90	4.461
15					5.91	4.462
16					2.95	4.461
17						4.462
18						4.461
19						4.462
20						4.461
21						2.231

TABLE 17-2

COST RECOVERY
PERCENTAGE TABLE
MACRS

half-year convention

IRS rule under MACRS that assumes all property is placed in service or taken out of service at the midpoint of the year, regardless of the actual time.

Note that the number of recovery years is one greater than the property class. This is due to a rule known as the **half-year convention,** which assumes that the asset was placed in service in the middle of the first year and therefore begins depreciating at that point. Quarterly tables are listed in IRS Publication 534 for assets placed in service at other times of the year.

STEPS TO PREPARE A DEPRECIATION SCHEDULE USING MACRS:

Step 1. Use Table 17-1 to determine the property class for the asset in question.

Step 2. Multiply the cost recovery percentages for each year, from Table 17-2, by the original basis of the asset.

Depreciation deduction = Original basis (cost) × Cost recovery percentage

Step 3. Set up the depreciation schedule in the form of a chart with the following headings:

End of Year	Original Basis (cost)	Cost Recovery Percentage	Cost Recovery (depreciation)	Accumulated Depreciation	Book Value

---

EXAMPLE

Fantasy Tours purchased a new sightseeing bus for $185,000. Prepare a depreciation schedule for this new asset using MACRS.

SOLUTION STRATEGY

From Table 17-1, we find that buses are listed in the 5-year property class. Table 17-2 provides the percentages for each recovery year. Note once again, the extra year is to allow for the assumption that the asset was placed in service at mid-year.

Fantasy Tours, Inc.
MACRS Depreciation Schedule
Sightseeing Bus

End of Year	Original Basis (cost)	Cost Recovery Percentage	Cost Recovery (depreciation)	Accumulated Depreciation	Book Value
				(new)	$185,000
1	$185,000	20.00%	$37,000	$37,000	148,000
2	185,000	32.00	59,200	96,200	88,800
3	185,000	19.20	35,520	131,720	53,280
4	185,000	11.52	21,312	153,032	31,968
5	185,000	11.52	21,312	174,344	10,656
6	185,000	5.76	10,656	185,000	0

TRY-IT EXERCISE

5. **Allied Van Lines purchased an over-the-road tractor for $88,400. As the accountant for the company, you are asked to prepare a depreciation schedule for this new asset using MACRS.**

Check your answers with the solutions on page 580.

17-6 Calculating the Periodic Depletion Cost of Natural Resources

Just as depreciation is used to write off the useful life of plant assets such as trucks, equipment, and buildings, depletion is used to account for the consumption of natural resources such as coal, petroleum, timber, natural gas, and minerals. **Depletion** is the proportional allocation of the cost of natural resources to the units used up or depleted per accounting period. In accounting, natural resources are also known as **wasting assets,** since they are considered to be exhausted or to be used up as they are converted into inventory by mining, pumping, or cutting.

Depletion of natural resources is calculated in the same way as the units-of-production method of depreciation for plant assets. In order to calculate the depletion allocation, we must determine the following:

a. *Total cost of the natural resource package,* including the original purchase price, exploration expenses, and extraction or cutting expenses.

b. *Residual or salvage value* of the property after resources have been exhausted.

c. *Estimated total number of units* (tons, barrels, board feet) of resource available.

● **depletion**
The proportional allocation or write-off of the cost of natural resources to the units used up or depleted per accounting period. Calculated in the same way as units-of-production depreciation.

● **wasting assets**
An accounting term used to describe natural resources that are exhausted or used up as they are converted into inventory by mining, pumping, or cutting.

STEPS TO CALCULATE THE PERIODIC DEPLETION COST OF NATURAL RESOURCES:

Step 1. Compute the average depletion cost per unit by:

$$\text{Average depletion cost per unit} = \frac{\text{Total cost of resource} - \text{Residual value}}{\text{Estimated total units available}}$$

(Round to the nearest tenth of a cent when necessary.)

Step 2. Calculate the periodic depletion cost by:

$$\begin{array}{c}\text{Periodic} \\ \text{depletion} \\ \text{cost}\end{array} = \begin{array}{c}\text{Units produced in} \\ \text{current period}\end{array} \times \begin{array}{c}\text{Average depletion} \\ \text{cost per unit}\end{array}$$

EXAMPLE

Sunday Oil, Inc., purchased a parcel of land containing an estimated two million barrels of crude oil for $850,000. Two oil wells were drilled at a cost of $340,000. The residual value of the property and equipment is $50,000. Calculate the periodic depletion cost for the first year of operation if 325,000 barrels were extracted.

SOLUTION STRATEGY

Step 1. Average depletion cost per unit $= \dfrac{\text{Total cost of resource} - \text{Residual value}}{\text{Estimated total units available}}$

Average depletion cost per barrel $= \dfrac{(850,000 + 340,000) - 50,000}{2,000,000} = \$.57$ per barrel

Step 2. Periodic depletion cost = Units produced in current period × Average depl. cost per unit
Periodic depletion cost $= 325,000 \times .57 = \underline{\underline{\$185,250}}$

Natural resources are considered wasting assets, because they are used up when converted to inventory merchandise.

TRY-IT   EXERCISE

6. **Northwest Mining Company paid $5,330,000 for a parcel of land, including the mining rights. In addition, the company spent $900,000 on labor and equipment to prepare the site for mining operations. After mining is completed, it is estimated that the land and equipment would have a residual value of $400,000. Geologists estimated**

that the mine contains **7,000,000 tons of coal. If Northwest mined 1,500,000 tons of coal in the first year, what is the amount of the depletion cost?**

Check your answer with the solution on page 580.

1. Nationwide Nursing Services purchased a computer system for $24,300. What is the amount of the first year's depreciation using the modified accelerated cost recovery system?
   Computers are in the 5-year property class.
   First-year depreciation = 20%
   24,300 × .2 = $4,860.00

2. Atlantis Fantasy Company constructed roads and a bridge at AtlantisWorld in Orlando, Florida, at a cost of $15,000,000. Atlantis uses MACRS for tax purposes.

   a. What is the second year's depreciation expense?
      Roads and bridges are in the 15-year property class.
      Second year cost recovery percent = 9.50%
      MACRS, year 2 = 15,000,000 × 9.50%
      $\qquad$ = $1,425,000.00

   b. What is the ninth year's depreciation expense?
      Ninth year cost recovery percent = 5.91%
      MACRS, year 9 = 15,000,000 × 5.91%
      $\qquad$ = $886,500.00

3. Minute Maid Orange Groves planted fruit trees valued at $250,000.

   a. What is the property class for this asset under MACRS?
      10-year property

   b. What is the percentage for the sixth year of depreciation for this property?
      Sixth-year cost recovery percent = 7.37%

   c. What is the amount of the depreciation expense in the final year of write-off?
      Final year (eleventh year) depreciation =
      250,000.00 × 3.28% = $8,200.00

4. Island Hoppers Airways of Hawaii purchased a new commercial airplane for $2,400,000. As the accountant for the company, prepare a depreciation schedule for the asset using MACRS.
   Commercial airlines are in the 7-year property class.
   See the appendix following the index for schedule.

5. Lake Tahoe Timber Company purchased land containing an estimated 6,500,000 board feet of lumber for $3,700,000. The company invested another $300,000 to construct access roads and a company depot. The residual value of the property and equipment is estimated to be $880,000.

a. What is the average depletion cost per board foot of lumber?

Total cost of asset = 3,700,000 + 300,000 − 880,000

= $3,120,000

$$\text{Average depletion cost} = \frac{3,120,000}{6,500,000} = \underline{\underline{\$.48}}$$

b. If 782,000 board feet were cut in the second year of operation, what is the amount of the depletion cost for that year?

Second year depletion = 782,000 × .48 = $\underline{\$375,360}$

CHAPTER 17 ■ DEPRECIATION

FORMULAS

Straight-Line Method

Total cost = Cost + Freight + Setup expenses

Total depreciation = Total cost − Salvage value

$$\textbf{Annual depreciation} = \frac{\textbf{Total depreciation}}{\textbf{Estimated useful life (years)}}$$

Sum-of-the-Years' Digits Method

$$\textbf{SYD depreciation rate fraction} = \frac{\textbf{Years of useful life remaining}}{\dfrac{n(n+1)}{2}}$$

Annual depreciation = Total depreciation × Depreciation rate fraction

Declining-Balance Method

$$\textbf{Declining-balance rate} = \frac{1}{\textbf{Useful life}} \times \textbf{Multiple}$$

Beginning book value = Ending book value of the previous year

Ending book value = Beginning book value − Depreciation for the year

Units-of-Production Method

$$\textbf{Depreciation per unit} = \frac{\textbf{Cost − Salvage value}}{\textbf{Units of useful life}}$$

Annual depreciation = Depreciation per unit × Units produced

MACRS Depreciation

Depreciation deduction = Original basis × Cost recovery percentage

Natural Resource Depletion

$$\textbf{Average depletion cost per unit} = \frac{\textbf{Total cost of resource − Residual value}}{\textbf{Estimated total units available}}$$

$$\textbf{Periodic depletion cost} = \frac{\textbf{Units produced in}}{\textbf{current period}} \times \frac{\textbf{Average depletion}}{\textbf{cost per unit}}$$

SECTION I TRADITIONAL DEPRECIATION

Topic	P/O, Page	Important Concepts	Illustrative Examples
Calculating Depreciation by the Straight-Line Method	17–1 561	Straight-line depreciation provides for equal periodic charges to be written off over the estimated useful life of the asset. 1. Determine the total cost and residual value of the asset. 2. Subtract residual value from total cost to find the total amount of depreciation. Total depreciation = Total cost − Residual value 3. Calculate the annual depreciation by dividing the total depreciation by the useful life of the asset. $\text{Annual depreciation} = \dfrac{\text{Total depreciation}}{\text{Useful life of asset}}$ 4. Set up a depreciation schedule in the form of a chart.	The Diamond Bank purchased a closed-circuit television system for $45,000. Shipping charges were $325 and installation expenses amounted to $2,540. The system is expected to last five years and has a residual value of $3,500. Prepare a depreciation schedule for the system. Total cost = 45,000 + 325 + 2,540 = $47,865 Total depr. = 47,865 − 3,500 = $44,365 $\text{Annual depr.} = \dfrac{44,365}{5} = \$8,873$

Straight-line chart headers (Important Concepts column):

End of Year	Annual Depreciation	Accumulated Depreciation	Book Value

Illustrative Examples schedule:

End of Year	Annual Depr	Accum Depr	Book Value
		(new)	47,865
1	8,873	8,873	38,992
2	8,873	17,746	30,119
3	8,873	26,619	21,246
4	8,873	35,492	12,373
5	8,873	44,365	3,500

Topic	P/O, Page	Important Concepts	Illustrative Examples
Calculating Depreciation by the Sum-of-the-Years' Digits Method	17–2 562	The sum-of-the-years' digits method is one of the accelerated methods of calculating depreciation. 1. Find the total depreciation of the asset: Total depreciation = Total cost − Residual value 2. Calculate the SYD depreciation rate fraction for each year: $\text{Rate fraction} = \dfrac{\text{Years of life remaining}}{\dfrac{n(n+1)}{2}}$ 3. Calculate the depreciation for each year: Annual depreciation = Total depreciation × Depreciation rate fraction	Il Piccolo Cafe purchased new equipment for $45,000 with a four-year useful life and salvage value of $3,000. Using the sum-of-the-years' digits method, calculate the depreciation expense for year one and year three. Total depr. = 45,000 − 3,000 = 42,000 $\text{Rate fract. yr 1} = \dfrac{4}{\dfrac{4(4+1)}{2}} = \dfrac{4}{10}$ $\text{Depr. year 1} = 42,000 \times \dfrac{4}{10}$ = $16,800 $\text{Rate fract. year 3} = \dfrac{2}{\dfrac{4(4+1)}{2}} = \dfrac{2}{10}$ $\text{Depr. year 3} = 42,000 \times \dfrac{2}{10}$ = $8,400

I, continued

Topic	P/O, Page	Important Concepts	Illustrative Examples
Calculating Depreciation by the Declining-Balance Method	17–3 564	Declining-balance depreciation, the second accelerated method, uses a multiple of the straight-line rate, such as 125%, 150%, and 200%. Salvage value is not considered until the last year. 1. Calculate the declining-balance rate: $$\text{Declining-balance rate} = \frac{1}{\text{Useful life}} \times \text{Multiple}$$ 2. Calculate the depreciation for each year by applying the rate to each year's beginning book value. $$\text{Depreciation for year} = \text{Beginning book value} \times \text{Declining balance rate}$$ 3. Calculate the ending book value for each year by subtracting the depreciation for the year from the beginning book value. $$\text{Ending book value} = \text{Beginning book value} - \text{Depreciation for year}$$ 4. The depreciation is complete when the ending book value equals the salvage value.	The Fitness Factory purchased a treadmill for $5,000. It is expected to last four years and have a salvage value of $1,000. Use 150% declining-balance depreciation to calculate the book value after each year. $$\text{Decl. bal. rate} = \frac{1}{4} \times 1.5 = .375$$ *Year 1:* Depr. $= 5,000 \times .375 = 1,875$ Book value $=$ $\quad 5,000 - 1,875 = \underline{\$3,125}$ *Year 2:* Depr. $= 3,125 \times .375 = 1,172$ Book value $=$ $\quad 3,125 - 1,172 = \underline{\$1,953}$ *Year 3:* Depr. $= 1,953 \times .375 = 732$ Book value $=$ $\quad 1,953 - 732 = \underline{\$1,221}$ *Year 4:* Depr. $= 1,221 \times .375 = 458$ Book value $= 1,221 - 221 = \$1,000*$ *Note: In year 4 the calculated depreciation is $458. Because the book value of an asset cannot fall below the salvage value, the allowable depreciation is limited to $\underline{\$221}$ $(1,221 - 1,000 = 221)$.
Calculating Depreciation by the Units-of-Production Method	17–4 566	When the useful life of an asset is more accurately defined in terms of how much it is used, such as miles driven or units produced, we may apply the units-of-production method. 1. Determine the depreciation cost per unit using: $$\text{Depreciation per unit} = \frac{\text{Cost} - \text{Salvage value}}{\text{Units of useful life}}$$ 2. Calculate the depreciation for each year using: $$\text{Annual depreciation} = \text{Depreciation per unit} \times \text{Units produced}$$	Campbell purchased a new canning machine for one of its chicken soup production lines at a cost of $455,000. The machine has an expected useful life of 1,000,000 cans and a residual value of $25,000. In the first year the machine produced 120,000 cans. Calculate the depreciation on the machine for year 1. Depreciation per unit $=$ $$\frac{455,000 - 25,000}{1,000,000} = \$.43$$ Depreciation year 1 $=$ $\quad 120,000 \times .43 = \underline{\$51,600}$

SECTION II   ASSET COST RECOVERY SYSTEMS

Topic	P/O, Page	Important Concepts	Illustrative Examples
Calculating Depreciation Using the Modified Accelerated Cost Recovery System (MACRS)	17–5 570	MACRS is used for assets placed in service after 1986. This system uses property classes, Table 17-1, and recovery percentages, Table 17-2. 1. Use Table 17-1 to determine the property class for the asset in question. 2. Multiply the cost recovery percentages for each year, Table 17-2, by the original cost of the asset. Depreciation deduction = Original cost × Recovery percentage	Captain Morgan purchased a tug boat for $650,000. As his accountant, use MACRS to calculate the depreciation expense for the second and fifth year. Using Table 17-1, we find that tug boats are considered 10-year property. *MACRS Depreciation Expense:* *Year 2* $650,000 \times .18 = \underline{\$117,000}$ *Year 5* $650,000 \times .0922 = \underline{\$59,930}$
Calculating the Periodic Depletion Cost of Natural Resources	17–6 573	Depletion is the proportional allocation of natural resources to the units used up or depleted, per accounting period. Depletion is calculated in the same way as the units-of-production method of depreciation. 1. Compute the average depletion cost per unit: $\text{Average depletion/unit} = \dfrac{\text{Total cost} - \text{Salvage}}{\text{Total units available}}$ 2. Calculate the periodic depletion cost: Periodic depletion cost = Current units × Average depletion per unit	The Continental Mining Company purchased a parcel of land containing an estimated 800,000 tons of iron ore. The cost of the asset was $2,000,000. An additional $350,000 was spent to prepare the property for mining. The estimated residual value of the asset is $500,000. If the first year's output was 200,000 tons, what is the amount of the depletion allowance? Av. depl. per unit = $\dfrac{2,350,000 - 500,000}{800,000}$ $= \$2.31$ per ton Depletion cost: Year 1 = $200,000 \times 2.31 = \underline{\$462,000}$

TRY-IT EXERCISE   SOLUTIONS

1.   Total cost = Cost + Freight + Setup
       Total cost = 125,000 + 1,150 + 750 = $\underline{\$126,900}$

Total depreciation = Total cost − Salvage value
Total depreciation = 126,900 − 5,000 = $\underline{\$121,900}$

$\text{Annual depreciation} = \dfrac{\text{Total depreciation}}{\text{Estimated useful life}}$

$\text{Annual depreciation} = \dfrac{121,900}{5} = \underline{\$24,380}$

Holsum Bakery—Bread Oven

End of Year	Annual Depreciation	Accumulated Depreciation	Book Value
			$126,900 (cost)
1	$24,380	$24,380	102,520
2	24,380	48,760	78,140
3	24,380	73,140	53,760
4	24,380	97,520	29,380
5	24,380	121,900	5,000 (salvage value)

2.

$$\text{Total depreciation} = \text{Total cost} - \text{Salvage value}$$
$$\text{Total depreciation} = 44,500 - 2,500 = \underline{\$42,000}$$

$$\text{SYD depreciation rate fraction} = \frac{\text{Years of useful life remaining}}{\dfrac{n(n+1)}{2}}$$

$$\text{Rate fraction year 1} = \frac{6}{\dfrac{6(6+1)}{2}} = \frac{6}{\dfrac{42}{2}} = \frac{6}{21}$$

StyleCraft Furniture

End of Year	Total Depreciation	Rate Fraction	Annual Depreciation	Accumulated Depreciation	Book Value
					$44,500 (cost)
1	$42,000	$\frac{6}{21}$	$12,000	$12,000	32,500
2	42,000	$\frac{5}{21}$	10,000	22,000	22,500
3	42,000	$\frac{4}{21}$	8,000	30,000	14,500
4	42,000	$\frac{3}{21}$	6,000	36,000	8,500
5	42,000	$\frac{2}{21}$	4,000	40,000	4,500
6	42,000	$\frac{1}{21}$	2,000	42,000	2,500 (salvage value)

3. $\text{Declining-balance rate} = \dfrac{1}{\text{Useful life}} \times \text{Multiple}$

$\text{Declining-balance rate} = \dfrac{1}{4} \times 1.5 = .375$

Southwest Air Service

End of Year	Regular Book Value	Depreciation Rate	Depreciation for Year	Accumulated Depreciation	Ending Book Value
					$386,000 (new)
1	$386,000.00	.375	$144,750.00	$144,750.00	241,250.00
2	241,250.00	.375	90,468.75	235,218.75	150,781.25
3	150,781.25	.375	56,542.97	291,761.72	94,238.28
4	94,238.28	.375	24,238.28*	316,000.00	70,000.00 (salvage value)

*Maximum allowable to reach salvage value

4. $\text{Depreciation per unit} = \dfrac{\text{Cost} - \text{Salvage value}}{\text{Units of useful life}}$

$\text{Depreciation per unit} = \dfrac{54,500 - 7,500}{75,000} = \$.627/\text{mile}$

Hyde Park Industries

End of Year	Depreciation per Mile	Miles Used	Annual Depreciation	Accumulated Depreciation	Book Value
					$54,500 (new)
1	$.627	12,500	$7,837.50	$7,837.50	46,662.50
2	.627	18,300	11,474.10	19,311.60	35,188.40
3	.627	15,900	9,969.30	29,280.90	25,219.10
4	.627	19,100	11,975.70	41,256.60	13,243.40
5	.627	12,400	5,743.40*	47,000.00	7,500.00 (salvage value)

*Maximum allowable to reach salvage value

5. MACRS 3-Year Property

Allied Van Lines
Over-the-Road Tractor

End of Year	Original Basis	Cost Recovery Percentage	Cost Recovery	Accumulated Depreciation	Book Value
					(new) $88,400.00
1	$88,400.00	33.33%	$29,463.72	$29,463.72	58,936.28
2	88,400.00	44.45%	39,293.80	68,757.52	19,642.48
3	88,400.00	14.81%	13,092.04	81,849.56	6,550.44
4	88,400.00	7.41%	6,550.44	88,400.00	0

6. Average depletion cost/unit $= \dfrac{\text{Total cost} - \text{Residual value}}{\text{Estimated total units available}}$

Average depletion cost/unit $= \dfrac{(5,330,000 + 900,000) - 400,000}{7,000,000} = \dfrac{5,830,000}{7,000,000} = \$.833$

Periodic depletion cost = Units produced × Average depletion cost/unit

Periodic depletion cost (1st Year) $= 1,500,000 \times .833 = \underline{\underline{\$1,249,500}}$

Name_____

Class_____

Calculate the total cost, total depreciation, and annual depreciation for the following assets using the straight-line method:

	Cost	Freight Charges	Setup Charges	Total Cost	Salvage Value	Estimated Useful Life	Total Depreciation	Annual
1.	$5,600	$210	$54	$5,864.00	$600	6 years	$5,264.00	$877.33
2.	$16,900	$310	0	$17,210.00	$1,900	4 years	$15,310.00	$3,827.50

3. Modern Manufacturing, Inc., purchased new equipment totaling $648,000. Freight charges were $2,200 and installation amounted to $1,800. The equipment is expected to last 4 years and have a residual value of $33,000. If the company elects to use the straight-line method of depreciation, prepare a depreciation schedule for these assets.

Modern Manufacturing, Inc.
Depreciation Schedule
Straight-line Method

End of Year	Annual Depreciation	Accumulated Depreciation	Book Value
		(new)	$652,000
1	$154,750	$154,750	497,250
2	154,750	309,500	342,500
3	154,750	464,250	187,750
4	154,750	619,000	33,000

Complete the following as they relate to the sum-of-the-years' digits method of depreciation:

			Depreciation Rate Fraction		
	Useful life	Sum of the Years' Digits	Year 2	Year 4	Year 6
4.	7 years	28	$\frac{6}{28}$	$\frac{4}{28}$	$\frac{2}{28}$
5.	9 years	45	$\frac{8}{45}$	$\frac{6}{45}$	$\frac{4}{45}$

6. Appliance Masters purchased a service truck for $32,400. It has an estimated useful life of 3 years and a trade-in value of $3,100. Using the sum-of-the-years' digits method, prepare a depreciation schedule for the truck.

Appliance Masters
Service Truck, SYD—Depreciation Schedule

End of Year	Total Depreciation	Depreciation Rate Fraction	Annual Depreciation	Accumulated Depreciation	Book Value
				(new)	$32,400.00
1	$29,300	$\frac{3}{6}$	$14,650.00	$14,650.00	17,750.00
2	29,300	$\frac{2}{6}$	9,766.67	24,416.67	7,983.33
3	29,300	$\frac{1}{6}$	4,883.33	29,300.00	3,100.00

Complete the following as they relate to the declining-balance method of depreciation (round answers to thousandths where applicable):

	Years	Straight-Line Rate	Multiple	Declining-Balance Rate
7.	9	11.111%	125%	13.889%
8.	6	16.667%	200%	33.333%

ANSWERS

1. _____ $5,864.00

_____ $5,264.00

_____ $877.33

2. _____ $17,210.00

_____ $15,310.00

_____ $3,827.50

3. _____ See schedule.

4. _____ $\frac{28}{}$
_____ $\frac{6}{28}$
_____ $\frac{4}{28}$
_____ $\frac{2}{28}$

5. _____ $\frac{45}{}$
_____ $\frac{8}{45}$
_____ $\frac{6}{45}$
_____ $\frac{4}{45}$

6. _____ See schedule.

7. _____ 11.111%

_____ 13.889%

8. _____ 16.667%

_____ 33.333%

9. Academy Trophy bought a computerized engraving machine for $33,800. It is expected to have a six-year useful life and a trade-in value of $2,700. Prepare a depreciation schedule for the *first 3 years* using the 125% declining-balance method for the machine.

Academy Trophy
Depreciation Schedule
6-year, 125% declining-balance

End of Year	Beginning Book Value	Depreciation Rate	Depreciation for the Year	Accumulated Depreciation	Ending Book Value
				(new)	$33,800.00
1	$33,800.00	20.833	$7,041.55	$7,041.55	26,758.45
2	26,758.45	20.833	5,574.59	12,616.14	21,183.86
3	21,183.86	20.833	4,413.23	17,029.37	16,770.63

Complete the following as they relate to the units-of-production method of depreciation (round answers to the nearest tenth of a cent):

	Asset	Cost	Salvage Value	Units of Useful Life	Depreciation per Unit
10.	pump	$8,900	$250	500,000 gallons	$.017
11.	copier	3,900	0	160,000 copies	$.024

12. The Main Street Movie Theater purchased a new projector for $155,000 with a salvage value of $2,000. Delivery and installation amounted to $580. The projector is expected to have a useful life of 15,000 hours. Complete the following depreciation schedule for the *first 4 years* of operation using the units-of-production method:

Main Street Movie Theater
Depreciation Schedule, Units-of-Production
Projector—15,000 Hours

End of Year	Depreciation per Hour	Hours	Annual Depreciation	Accumulated Depreciation	Book Value
				(new)	$155,580.00
1	$10.24	2,300	$23,552.00	$23,552.00	132,028.00
2	10.24	1,890	19,353.60	42,905.60	112,674.40
3	10.24	2,160	22,118.40	65,024.00	90,556.00
4	10.24	2,530	25,907.20	90,931.20	64,648.80

12. Total depr. = 155,000 + 580 − 2,000
= $153,580

Depreciation per unit = $\dfrac{153,580}{15,000}$

$10.24 per unit

13. Custom Concrete Corporation purchased cement manufacturing equipment valued at $320,000. As the accountant for the company, prepare a depreciation schedule for the *first five years* of operation of this equipment using MACRS.

Custom Concrete, Inc.
Depreciation Schedule, MACRS
Cement Manufacturing Equipment

End of Year	Original Basis (cost)	Cost Recovery Percentage	Cost Recovery (depreciation)	Accumulated Depreciation	Book Value
				(new)	$320,000
1	$320,000	5	$16,000	$16,000	304,000
2	320,000	9.5	30,400	46,400	273,600
3	320,000	8.55	27,360	73,760	246,240
4	320,000	7.70	24,640	98,400	221,600
5	320,000	6.93	22,176	120,576	199,424

13. Cement manufacturing equip. depreciates over 15 yrs.

14. The Platinum Touch Mining Company paid $4,000,000 for a parcel of land, including the mining rights. In addition, the company spent $564,700 to prepare the site for mining operations. When mining is completed, it is estimated that the residual value of the asset will be $800,000. Scientists estimate that the site contains 150,000 ounces of platinum.

a. What is the average depletion cost per ounce?

Total depreciation = 4,000,000 + 564,700 − 800,000

$$= \$3,764,700$$

Average depletion per ounce $= \dfrac{3,764,700}{150,000} = \underline{\$25.098}$

b. If 12,200 ounces were mined in the first year of operation, what is the amount of the depletion cost?

Depletion first year = 25.098 × 12,200

$$= \underline{\underline{\$306,195.60}}$$

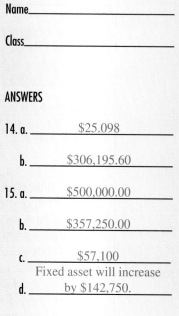

ANSWERS

14. a. _____ $25.098 _____

   b. _____ $306,195.60 _____

15. a. _____ $500,000.00 _____

   b. _____ $357,250.00 _____

   c. _____ $57,100 _____
       Fixed asset will increase

   d. _____ by $142,750. _____

◆ BUSINESS DECISION
A Dispute with the IRS

15. You are the accountant for the Carnival Corporation. Last year the company purchased a $2,500,000 corporate jet to be used for executive travel. To help offset the cost of the airplane, your company occasionally rents the jet to the executives of two other corporations when it is not in use by Carnival.

When the corporate tax return was filed this year, you began depreciating the jet using the MACRS. Today you received a letter from the Internal Revenue Service informing you that because your company occasionally rents the airplane to others, it is considered a commercial aircraft and must be depreciated as such. The corporate lawyers are considering to dispute this ruling with the IRS and have asked you the following:

a. How much depreciation did you claim this year?

Private planes depreciate over 5 years.
2,500,000.00 × 20% = $\underline{\$500,000.00}$

b. Under the new category, how much depreciation would be claimed?

Commercial planes depreciate over 7 years.
2,500,000.00 × 14.29% = $\underline{\$357,250.00}$

c. If the company is in the 40% income tax bracket, what effect will this change have on the amount of tax owed, assuming the company made a net profit this year?

Added income = 500,000 − 357,250 = $142,750
Added tax = 142,750 × 40% = $\underline{\$57,100}$

d. What effect will this change have on the company's balance sheet?

The fixed asset, an airplane, will increase by $142,750.

All the Math That's Fit to Learn

The Business Math Times

Volume XVII   **Depreciation**   One Dollar

CareerTrack:

Buyer

Nature of the Work

The primary function of buyers is to research and obtain the highest quality merchandise at the lowest possible price for their companies. The work generally involves determining which products or services are best, determining the suppliers, negotiating the lowest price, and awarding contracts that ensure the correct amount of the product or service is received at the appropriate time. In addition to their primary duties, many buyers assist in the planning and implementation of sales promotion programs.

Working with merchandising executives, they determine the nature of the sale and purchase accordingly. They also work with advertising personnel to choose the advertising media and create the ad campaign.

Training, Other Qualifications, and Advancement

Educational requirements tend to vary with the size of the organization. Large stores and distributors accept applicants who have completed associate or bachelor's degree programs from any field of study, but prefer individuals with a business background. Although training periods vary in length, most last several years.

"Here it is, Lewis! The Continental Divide!"

Persons who wish to become wholesale or retail buyers should be good at planning and decision making and have an interest in merchandising. They must be resourceful, have good judgement, and self-confidence.

Job Outlook

Mergers and consolidations of buying departments as well as increased use of computerized inventory control systems will tighten future demand. Persons who have a bachelor's degree in business should have the best chance of getting a job and advancing in the field.

SOURCE: *Occupational Outlook Handbook,* 1994-95 Edition, U.S. Department of Labor.

Upside Down!

Did you know that if you're not careful, you can be "upside down" in a loan? This means that the asset you financed, such as a car or a boat, is depreciating faster than the loan is being paid off. With new car purchases, for example, as soon as you drive away from the dealership, you have lost about 10 percent of the car's value to depreciation.

Being upside down means that your loan balance is greater than the current value of the asset you have financed. Amazingly, at that point you would have to pay money to get rid of it! To avoid this situation, you can:

- Purchase brands that hold their value better.
- Make a larger down payment.
- Finance for a shorter period of time.

Depreciation Domination

According to a survey by the American Institute of Certified Public Accountants (AICPA) the following is the breakdown of depreciation methods used by the 600 largest U.S. companies. From this illustration, it is clear that straight-line is by far the most commonly used depreciation method.

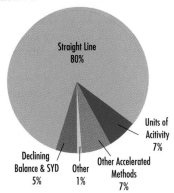

SOURCE: Adapted from *Accounting Trends and Techniques,* 1995 Edition, AICPA, New York, NY.

Beyond Depreciation

Did you know, an average of 10 million computers are discarded in America each year? At this rate, by 2005, a landfill space large enough to stack 15 Empire State Buildings end to end will be required to store them.

Brainteaser

If six boys can build six houses in six months and twelve girls can build twelve houses in twelve months, how many houses can twelve boys and twelve girls build in twelve months?

SOURCE: *Mathematics Teacher Magazine,* February 1987, used by permission.

Answer to Last Issue's Brainteaser

None There is no dirt in a hole!

Chapter 18

Taxes

Performance Objectives

taxation

The imposition of a mandatory levy or charge by a government unit to provide financing for public services.

Benjamin Franklin wrote that "nothing can be said to be certain except death and taxes." **Taxation** is the imposition of a mandatory levy on the citizens of a country by their government. According to Supreme Court Justice Oliver Wendell Holmes, Jr., "Taxes are the price we pay for living in a civilized society." In almost all countries, tax revenue is the major source of financing for publicly provided services. In a democracy, a majority of citizens or their representatives vote to impose taxes on themselves in order to finance, through the public sector, services on which they place value but that they believe cannot be adequately provided by market processes.

In addition to generating revenue to finance public services, taxation can be used for other objectives, such as income redistribution, economic stabilization, and the regulating of consumption of certain commodities or services. In this chapter we shall focus our attention on the three major categories of taxation: sales and excise tax, property tax, and individual and corporate income tax.

SECTION I
SALES AND EXCISE TAXES

sales tax

A tax based on the retail selling or rental price of tangible personal property, collected by the retailer at the time of purchase, and paid to the state or local government.

sales tax rate

Sales tax expressed in its most common form, as a percent of the retail price of an item.

A tax based on the retail selling or rental price of tangible personal property is called a **sales tax.** This tax may also be imposed on admission charges to places of amusement, sport, and recreation, as well as on certain services. Most states, currently 45, and many other taxing units such as cities, counties, and municipalities, levy or charge a tax on sales. Businesses that purchase merchandise for resale to others are normally exempt from this tax. Only final buyers pay sales tax. Many states allow a sales tax exemption for food, prescription drugs, household medicines, and other selected items.

The liability for the sales tax is incurred at the time the sale is made. Retail merchants act as agents, collecting sales taxes and periodically remitting them to the proper tax agency. The **sales tax rate** is expressed as a percent and varies from state to state. Currently, state tax rates range from 3% to 8%, while city and county rates add an additional .5% to 6%.

Revenue from taxes helps pay for many public services, such as the maintenance of highways and roads.

Another type of tax levied by federal, state, and local governments on certain products and services is known as an **excise tax.** This tax, which is paid in addition to the sales tax, is imposed on so-called luxury or nonessential items. Some typical examples would be motor vehicles (over $32,000), tires, alcoholic beverages, jewelry (except watches), gasoline, furs, firearms, certain recreational equipment and sporting goods, tobacco products, telecommunications services, airline and cruise ship transportation, and telephone service.

18-1 Determining Sales Tax Using Sales Tax Tables

Many state and local governments provide retailers with sales tax tables such as those in Exhibit 18-1. These tables are used by employees of businesses that do not have computer cash register systems that automatically compute the proper amount of sales tax.

STEPS TO DETERMINE SALES TAX DUE ON AN ITEM USING SALES TAX TABLES:

Step 1. Locate the taxable retail price in the Amount of Sale column.

Step 2. Scan to the right to locate the amount of tax due in the Tax column.

Note: Exhibit 18-1 is only a partial listing. Complete sales tax tables are available in most states from the Department of Revenue.

EXAMPLE

Kathy Antoine purchased a can of hair spray at Walgreens for $3.29. Use Exhibit 18-1 to determine the amount of sales tax on this item.

SOLUTION STRATEGY

Step 1. From Exhibit 18-1 we find that the retail price of the hair spray, $3.29, falls in the range of $3.24 to $3.38.

Step 2. Scanning to the right, we find the tax due on this item is $.22.

SALES TAX BRACKETS
ON ALL 6 1/2% TAXABLE TRANSACTIONS
(FLORIDA DEPT. OF REVENUE)

Amount of Sale		Tax	Amount of Sale		Tax
.10-	.15	.01	5.08-	5.23	.34
.16-	.30	.02	5.24-	5.38	.35
.31-	.46	.03	5.39-	5.53	.36
.47-	.61	.04	5.54-	5.69	.37
.62-	.76	.05	5.70-	5.84	.38
.77-	.92	.06	5.85-	6 09	.39
.93-	1.07	.07	6.10-	6.15	.40
1.08-	1.23	.08	6.16-	6.30	.41
1.24-	1.38	.09	6.31-	6.46	.42
1.39-	1.53	.10	6.47-	6.61	.43
1.54-	1.69	.11	6.62-	6.76	.44
1.70-	1.84	.12	6.77-	6.92	.45
1.85-	2.09	.13	6.93-	7.07	.46
2.10-	2.15	.14	7.08-	7.23	.47
2.16-	2.30	.15	7.24-	7.38	.48
2.31-	2.46	.16	7.39-	7.53	.49
2.47-	2.61	.17	7.54-	7.69	.50
2.62-	2.76	.18	7.70-	7.84	.51
2.77-	2.92	.19	7.85-	8.09	.52
2.93-	3.07	.20	8.10-	8.15	.53
3.08-	3.23	.21	8.16-	8.30	.54
3.24-	3.38	.22	8.31-	8.46	.55
3.39-	3.53	.23	8.47-	8.61	.56
3.54-	3.69	.24	8.62-	8.76	.57
3.70-	3.84	.25	8.77-	8.92	.58
3.85-	4.09	.26	8.93-	9.07	.59
4.10-	4.15	.27	9.08-	9.23	.60
4.16-	4.30	.28	9.24-	9.38	.61
4.31-	4.46	.29	9.39-	9.53	.62
4.47-	4.61	.30	9.54-	9.69	.63
4.62-	4.76	.31	9.70-	9.84	.64
4.77-	4.92	.32	9.85-	10.09	.65
4.93-	5.07	.33			

SALES TAX BRACKETS
ON ALL 6 1/2% TAXABLE TRANSACTIONS
(FLORIDA DEPT. OF REVENUE)

Amount of Sale		Tax	Amount of Sale		Tax
10.10-	10.15	.66	15.08-	15.23	.99
10.16-	10.30	.67	15.24-	15.38	1.00
10.31-	10.46	.68	15.39-	15.53	1.01
10.47-	10.61	.69	15.54-	15.69	1.02
10.62-	10.76	.70	15.70-	15.84	1.03
10.77-	10.92	.71	15.85-	16.09	1.04
10.93-	11.07	.72	16.10-	16.15	1.05
11.08-	11.23	.73	16.16-	16.30	1.06
11.24-	11.38	.74	16.31-	16.46	1.07
11.39-	11.53	.75	16.47-	16.61	1.08
11.54-	11.69	.76	16.62-	16.76	1.09
11.70-	11.84	.77	16.77-	16.92	1.10
11.85-	12.09	.78	16.93-	17.07	1.11
12.10-	12.15	.79	17.08-	17.23	1.12
12.16-	12.30	.80	17.24-	17.38	1.13
12.31-	12.46	.81	17.39-	17.53	1.14
12.47-	12.61	.82	17.54-	17.69	1.15
12.62-	12.76	.83	17.70-	17.84	1.16
12.77-	12.92	.84	17.85-	18.09	1.17
12.93	13.07	.85	18.10-	18.15	1.18
13.08-	13.23	.86	18.16-	18.30	1.19
13.24-	13.38	.87	18.31-	18.46	1.20
13.39-	13.53	.88	18.47-	18.61	1.21
13.54-	13.69	.89	18.62-	18.76	1.22
13.70-	13.84	.90	18.77-	18.92	1.23
13.85-	14.09	.91	18.93-	19.07	1.24
14.10-	14.15	.92	19.08-	19.23	1.25
14.16-	14.30	.93	19.24-	19.38	1.26
14.31-	14.46	.94	19.39-	19.53	1.27
14.47-	14.61	.95	19.54-	19.69	1.28
14.62-	14.76	.96	19.70-	19.84	1.29
14.77-	14.92	.97	19.85-	20.09	1.30
14.93-	15.07	.98			

[T]

EXHIBIT 18-1

SALES TAX BRACKETS

TRY-IT EXERCISE

1. Use Exhibit 18-1 to determine the amount of sales tax on an item with a retail price of $12.49.

Check your answer with the solution on page 618.

18-2 Calculating Sales Tax Using the Percent Method

When sales tax tables are not available, the percent method may be used to calculate the sales tax on an item or service. Other nontaxable charges, such as packing, delivery, handling, or setup, are added after the sales tax has been computed.

> **STEPS TO CALCULATE SALES TAX AND TOTAL PURCHASE PRICE USING THE PERCENT METHOD:**
>
> **Step 1.** Calculate the sales tax by multiplying the selling price of the good or service by the sales tax rate:
>
> $$\text{Sales tax} = \text{Selling price} \times \text{Sales tax rate}$$
>
> **Step 2.** Compute the total purchase price by adding the selling price, the sales tax, and any other additional charges.
>
> $$\text{Total purchase price} = \text{Selling price} + \text{Sales tax} + \text{Other charges}$$

EXAMPLE

Howard Lockwood purchased a riding lawnmower for $488.95 at a Wal-Mart store in Atlanta, Georgia. The store charges $25.00 for delivery and $15.00 for assembly. If the state sales tax in Georgia is 5%, and Atlanta has a 1.5% city tax, what is the amount of sales tax on the lawnmower and what is the total purchase price?

SOLUTION STRATEGY

In this example, the sales tax rate will be the total of the state and city taxes,

$$\text{Sales tax rate} = 5\% + 1.5\% = 6.5\%$$

Step 1. $\text{Sales tax} = \text{Selling price} \times \text{Sales tax rate}$
            $\text{Sales tax} = 488.95 \times .065 = \underline{\$31.78}$

Step 2. $\text{Total purchase price} = \text{Selling price} + \text{Sales tax} + \text{Other charges}$
            $\text{Total purchase price} = 488.95 + 31.78 + (25.00 + 15.00)$
            $\text{Total purchase price} = \underline{\$560.73}$

TRY-IT EXERCISE

2. Tony Segreto purchased a car for $18,600 at Friendly Ford in Boulder, Colorado. If the dealer preparation charges are $240 and the sales tax rate in Colorado is 8%, what is the amount of sales tax on the car and what is the total purchase price?

Check your answers with the solutions on page 618.

18-3 Calculating Selling Price and Amount of Sales Tax When Total Purchase Price Is Known

From time to time, merchants and customers may want to know the actual selling price of an item when the total purchase price, including sales tax, is known.

STEPS TO CALCULATE SELLING PRICE AND AMOUNT OF SALES TAX:

Step 1. Calculate the selling price of an item by dividing the total purchase price by 100% plus the sales tax rate:

$$\text{Selling price} = \frac{\text{Total purchase price}}{100\% + \text{Sales tax rate}}$$

Step 2. Determine the amount of sales tax by subtracting the selling price from the total purchase price:

$$\text{Sales tax} = \text{Total purchase price} - \text{Selling price}$$

EXAMPLE

Susan Marshall bought a television set for a total purchase price of $477. If her state has a 6% sales tax, what were the actual selling price of the TV and the amount of sales tax?

SOLUTION STRATEGY

Step 1.
$$\text{Selling price} = \frac{\text{Total purchase price}}{100\% + \text{Sales tax rate}}$$

$$\text{Selling price} = \frac{477}{100\% + 6\%} = \frac{477}{1.06} = \underline{\$450}$$

Step 2.
$$\text{Sales tax} = \text{Total purchase price} - \text{Selling price}$$
$$\text{Sales tax} = 477 - 450 = \underline{\$27.00}$$

TRY-IT   EXERCISE

3. At the end of a business day, the cash register at Gary's Gift Shop showed total sales, including sales tax, of $3,520.00. If the state and local sales taxes amounted to $8\frac{1}{2}\%$, what is the amount of Gary's actual sales? How much sales tax did he collect that day?

Check your answers with the solutions on page 618.

18-4 Calculating Excise Tax

As with the sales tax, an excise tax is usually expressed as a percentage of the purchase price. In certain cases, however, the excise tax may be expressed as a fixed amount per unit purchased, such as $5 per passenger on a cruise ship, or $.15 per gallon of gasoline.

When both sales tax and excise tax are imposed on merchandise at the retail level, the excise taxes are *not included* in the selling price when computing the sales tax. Each tax should be calculated independently on the actual selling price.

EXAMPLE

The round-trip airfare from Miami to New York is $379.00. If the federal excise tax on airline travel is 10% and the Florida state sales tax is 6%, what are the amounts of each tax and the total purchase price of the ticket?

SOLUTION STRATEGY

Step 1.

$$\text{Sales tax} = \text{Selling price} \times \text{Sales tax rate}$$
$$\text{Sales tax} = 379 \times .06 = \underline{\$22.74}$$

$$\text{Excise tax} = \text{Selling price} \times \text{Excise tax rate}$$
$$\text{Excise tax} = 379 \times .10 = \underline{\$37.90}$$

Step 2.

$$\text{Total purchase price} = \text{Selling price} + \text{Sales tax} + \text{Excise tax}$$
$$\text{Total purchase price} = 379.00 + 22.74 + 37.90 = \underline{\$439.64}$$

TRY-IT   EXERCISE

4. A bow and arrow set at The Sports Authority in Cincinnati, Ohio, has a retail price of $129.95. The sales tax in Ohio is 5% and the federal excise tax on this type of sporting goods is 11%. What is the amount of each tax, and what is the total purchase price of the bow and arrow set?

Check your answers with the solutions on page 618.

 REVIEW EXERCISES   CHAPTER 18—SECTION I

Use Exhibit 18-1 to determine the sales tax and calculate the total purchase price for the following items:

	Item	Selling Price	Sales Tax	Total Purchase Price
1.	flashlight	$8.95	$.59	$9.54
2.	candy	.79	.06	.85
3.	notebook	4.88	.32	5.20
4.	calculator	18.25	1.19	19.44

Calculate the missing information for the following purchases:

Item	Selling Price	Sales Tax Rate	Sales Tax	Excise Tax Rate	Excise Tax	Total Purchase Price
5. computer	$1,440.00	7%	$100.80	1.1%	$15.84	$1,556.64
6. sofa	$750.00	5	37.50	0	0	787.50
7. fishing rod	$219.95	$4\frac{1}{2}$	9.90	10	22.00	251.85
8. tire	$109.99	6	6.60	5	5.50	122.09
9. automobile	17,847.98	$5\frac{1}{4}$	937.02	0	0	$18,785.00
10. book	14.00	8	1.12	0	0	$15.12

11. Marlena Evans purchased a refrigerator at Sears for $899.90. The delivery charge was $20 and the ice maker hookup amounted to $55.00. The state sales tax is $6\frac{1}{2}$% and the city tax is 1.3%.

   a. What is the total amount of sales tax on the refrigerator?

   Total sales tax $= 899.90 \times (.065 + .013) = \underline{\$70.19}$

   b. What is the total purchase price?

   Total purchase price $= 899.90 + 70.19 + 20.00 + 55.00$
   $= \underline{\$1,045.09}$

12. Tony Demeara purchased supplies at Office Depot for a total purchase price of $46.71. The state has a 4% sales tax.

   a. What was the selling price of the supplies?

   Selling price $= \dfrac{46.71}{1.04} = \underline{\$44.91}$

   b. What was the amount of sales tax?

   Sales tax $= 46.71 - 44.91 = \underline{\$1.80}$

13. Last month, The Sweet Tooth Candy Shops had total sales, including sales tax, of $57,889.00. The stores are located in a state that has a sales tax of $5\frac{1}{2}$%. As the accountant for The Sweet Tooth, calculate:

   a. The amount of sales revenue for the shops last month.

   Sales revenue $= \dfrac{57,889.00}{1.055} = \underline{\$54,871.09}$

   b. The amount of sales taxes that must be sent to the state Department of Revenue.

   Sales tax $= 57,889.00 - 54,871.09 = \underline{\$3,017.91}$

14. Penny Lane purchased a diamond necklace for $17,400 at Kensington Jewelers. The state sales tax is 8% and the federal excise tax on this type of jewelry is 10% on amounts over $10,000.

   a. What is the amount of the sales tax?

   Sales tax = 17,400.00 × .08 = $1,392.00

   b. What is the amount of the federal excise tax?

   Excise tax = .10(17,400.00 − 10,000.00) = $740.00

   c. What is the total purchase price of the necklace?

   Total purchase price = 17,400.00 + 1,392.00 + $740.00
   = $19,532.00

15. The federal excise tax on commercial aviation fuel is 14.1 cents per gallon. If Universal Airlines used a total of 6,540,000 gallons of fuel last month, how much excise tax was paid?

   Excise tax = 6,540,000 × .141 = $922,140.00

PROPERTY TAX

- **ad valorem or property tax**
  A tax based on the assessed value of property, generally collected at the city or county level as the primary source of revenue for counties, municipalities, school districts, and special taxing districts.

- **real estate, or real property**
  Land, buildings, and all other permanent improvements situated thereon.

- **personal property**
  For ad valorem tax purposes, divided into tangible personal property such as business equipment, fixtures, and supplies and household goods such as clothing, furniture, and appliances.

- **assessed value**
  The value of property for tax purposes, generally a percentage of the fair market value.

- **fair market value**
  A value placed on property based on location, size, cost, replacement value, condition, and income derived from its use.

Most states have laws that provide for the annual assessment and collection of ad valorem taxes on real and personal property. **Ad valorem tax** means a tax based upon the assessed value of property. The term **property tax** is used interchangeably with the term ad valorem tax. Property taxes are assessed and collected at the county level as the primary source of revenue for counties, municipalities, school districts, and special taxing districts.

Real estate, or **real property** is defined as land, buildings, and all other permanent improvements situated thereon. Real estate is broadly classified based on land use and includes the following:

- Single-family and multifamily residential, condominiums, townhouses, and mobile homes
- Vacant residential and unimproved acreage
- Commercial and industrial land and improvements
- Agriculture

Personal property is divided into two categories for ad valorem tax purposes:

- Tangible personal property—such as business fixtures, supplies, and equipment and machinery for shop, plant, and farm.
- Household goods (exempt from property tax in most states)—apparel, furniture, appliances, and other items usually found in the home.

The value of property for tax purposes is known as the **assessed value.** In some states assessed value of the property is a specified percentage of the **fair market value,** while in other states it is fixed by law at 100%. Typical factors considered in determining the fair market value of a piece of property are location, size, cost, replacement value, condition, and income derived from its use.

The assessed value is determined each year by the **tax assessor** or **property appraiser.** Most states allow specific discounts for early payment of the tax and have serious penalties for delinquency. The Department of Revenue in each state has the responsibility of insuring that all property is assessed and taxes are collected in accordance with the law.

● **tax assessor, or property appraiser**
The city or county official designated to determine assessed values of property.

18-5 Calculating the Amount of Property Tax

On the basis of the fair market value, less all applicable exemptions, the property tax due is computed by applying the tax rates established by the taxing authorities within that area to the assessed value of the property.

Property tax = Assessed value of property × Tax rate

Property tax rates may be expressed in the following ways:

a. Decimal or percent of assessed value—.035 or 3.5%

b. Per $100 of assessed value—$3.50 per $100

c. Per $1,000 of assessed value—$35.00 per $1,000

d. Mills (one one-thousandth of a dollar)—35 mills

Let's look at the steps to calculate the property tax due when the same tax is expressed in each of the four different ways on a property with an assessed value of $250,000.

A. STEPS TO CALCULATE PROPERTY TAX WHEN THE TAX IS EXPRESSED AS A PERCENT:

Step 1. Convert the tax rate percent to a decimal by moving the decimal point 2 places to the left.

Step 2. Multiply the assessed value by the tax rate as a decimal.

Property tax = Assessed value × Tax rate

EXAMPLE A

Calculate the tax due on a property with an assessed value of $250,000. The tax rate is 7.88% of the assessed value.

SOLUTION STRATEGY

Step 1. Convert tax percent to decimal form: 7.88% = .0788.

Step 2.   Property tax = Assessed value × Tax rate
          Property tax = 250,000 × .0788 = $19,700

Property taxes are the primary source of income for most school districts.

    TRY-IT   **EXERCISE**

5a. Calculate the tax due on a property with an assessed value of $160,000. The property tax rate is 6.3%.

Check your answer with the solution on page 619.

Step 1. Divide the assessed value by $100 to determine the number of $100 the assessed value contains.

$$\text{Number of \$100} = \frac{\text{Assessed value}}{100}$$

Step 2. Calculate the property tax by multiplying the number of $100 times the tax per $100.

$$\text{Property tax} = \text{Number of \$100} \times \text{Tax per \$100}$$

EXAMPLE B

Calculate the tax due on a property with an assessed value of $250,000. The tax rate is $7.88 per $100 of assessed value.

SOLUTION STRATEGY

Step 1.

$$\text{Number of \$100} = \frac{\text{Assessed value}}{100} = \frac{250{,}000}{100} = 2{,}500$$

Step 2.

$$\text{Property tax} = \text{Number of \$100} \times \text{Tax per \$100}$$
$$\text{Property tax} = 2{,}500 \times 7.88 = \underline{\$19{,}700}$$

TRY-IT   EXERCISE

5b. Calculate the tax due on a property with an assessed value of $50,800. The property tax rate is $3.60 per $100 of assessed value.

Check your answer with the solution on page 619.

Step 1. Divide the assessed value by $1,000 to determine the number of $1,000 the assessed value contains.

$$\text{Number of \$1,000} = \frac{\text{Assessed value}}{1{,}000}$$

Step 2. Calculate the tax due by multiplying the number of $1,000 times the tax per $1,000.

$$\text{Property tax} = \text{Number of \$1,000} \times \text{Tax per \$1,000}$$

EXAMPLE C

Calculate the tax due on a property with an assessed value of $250,000. The tax rate is $78.80 per $1,000 of assessed value.

Step 1. $$\text{Number of } \$1{,}000 = \frac{\text{Assessed value}}{1{,}000} = \frac{250{,}000}{1{,}000} = 250$$

Step 2. Property tax = Number of $1,000 × Tax per $1,000
Property tax = 250 × 78.80 = $19,700

T R Y - I T   **EXERCISE**

5c. Calculate the tax due on a property with an assessed value of $325,400. The property tax rate is $88.16 per $1,000 of assessed value.

Check your answer with the solution on page 619.

D. STEPS TO CALCULATE PROPERTY TAX WHEN THE TAX IS EXPRESSED IN MILLS:

Step 1. Since mills means $\frac{1}{1000}$ (.001) of a dollar, convert tax rate in mills to tax rate in decimal form by multiplying mills times .001.

Tax rate in decimal form = Tax rate in mills × .001

Step 2. Calculate the tax due by multiplying the assessed value times the tax rate in decimal form:

Property tax = Assessed value × Tax rate in decimal form

EXAMPLE D

Calculate the tax due on a property with an assessed value of $250,000. The tax rate is 78.8 mills.

Step 1. Tax rate in decimal form = Tax rate in mills × .001
Tax rate in decimal form = 78.8 × .001 = .0788

Step 2. Property tax = Assessed value × Tax rate in decimal form
Property tax = 250,000 × .0788 = $19,700

T R Y - I T   **EXERCISE**

5d. Calculate the tax due on a property with an assessed value of $85,300. The property tax rate is 54.1 mills.

Check your answer with the solution on page 619.

18-6 Calculating Tax Rate Necessary in a Community to Meet Budgetary Demands

Each year local taxing units such as counties and cities must estimate the amount of tax dollars required to pay for all governmental services rendered. Typical examples include public schools, law enforcement, fire protection, hospitals, public parks and recreation, roads and highways, sanitation services, and many others. The tax rate necessary to meet these budgetary demands is determined by two factors: (1) the total taxes required, and (2) the total assessed value of the property in the taxing unit. The tax rate is computed by the following formula:

$$\text{Tax rate per dollar (decimal form)} = \frac{\text{Total taxes required}}{\text{Total assessed property value}}$$

As before, the tax rate may be expressed as a percent, per $100 of assessed value, per $1,000 of assessed value, or in mills.

STEPS TO COMPUTE TAX RATE:

Step 1. Calculate tax rate per dollar of assessed property value by dividing the total taxes required by the total assessed property value:

$$\text{Tax rate per dollar (decimal form)} = \frac{\text{Total taxes required}}{\text{Total assessed property value}}$$

Round your answer to ten-thousandths (4 decimal places). In most states, the rounding is always up, even if the next digit is less than 5.

Step 2. *To convert tax rate per dollar to:*

a. **percent,** move the decimal point 2 places to the right and add a percent sign;
b. **tax rate per $100,** multiply by 100;
c. **tax rate per $1,000,** multiply by 1,000;
d. **mills,** divide by .001.

EXAMPLE

The budget planners for Mountainview have determined that $5,700,000 will be needed to provide all government services for next year. If the total assessed property value in Mountainview is $68,000,000, what tax rate is required to meet these budgetary demands? Express your answer in each of the four ways.

SOLUTION STRATEGY

Step 1.

$$\text{Tax rate per dollar} = \frac{\text{Total tax required}}{\text{Total assessed property value}}$$

$$= \frac{5,700,000}{68,000,000} = .0838235 = \underline{\$.0839}$$

Hint: Drop an equal number of zeros from the numerator and denominator, so that large numbers can be entered into your calculator.

Step 2. **a.** To express tax rate as a percent, move the decimal point 2 places to the right, and add a percent sign. Tax rate = 8.39%.

b. Tax rate expressed per $100 = .0839 × 100 = $8.39.

c. Tax rate expressed per $1,000 = .0839 × 1,000 = $83.90.

d. Tax rate expressed in mills = $\dfrac{.0839}{.001}$ = 83.9 mills.

6. The budget planners for Century City have determined that $3,435,000 will be needed to provide governmental services for next year. The total assessed property value in Century City is $71,800,000. As the tax assessor, you have been asked by the city council to determine what tax rate will need to be imposed to meet these budgetary demands. Express your answer in each of the four ways.

Check your answers with the solutions on page 619.

REVIEW EXERCISES   CHAPTER 18—SECTION II

Calculate the assessed value and the property tax due on the following properties:

	Fair Market Value	Assessment Rate	Assessed Value	Property Tax Rate	Property Tax Due
1.	$76,000	100%	$76,000	3.44%	$2,614.40
2.	125,000	100	125,000	$1.30 per $100	1,625.00
3.	248,000	80	198,400	$25.90 per $1,000	5,138.56
4.	54,600	30	16,380	45.5 mills	745.29
5.	177,400	60	106,440	$2.13 per $100	2,267.17
6.	2,330,000	100	2,330,000	13.22 mills	30,802.60
7.	342,900	77	264,033	5.3%	13,993.75
8.	90,230	90	81,207	$12.50 per $1,000	1,015.09

Calculate the property tax rate required to meet the budgetary demands of the following communities:

	Community	Total Assessed Property Valuation	Total Taxes Required	Property Tax Rate			
				Percent	Per $100	Per $1,000	Mills
9.	Glendale	$657,000,000	$32,300,000	4.92	$4.92	$49.20	49.2
10.	Paxton	338,000,000	19,900,000	5.89	5.89	58.90	58.9
11.	Golden Isles	57,000,000	2,100,000	3.69	3.69	36.90	36.9
12.	Bayside	880,000,000	13,600,000	1.55	1.55	15.50	15.5

13. Stephanie Pawlak purchased a home with a market value of $125,000 in Cherokee Valley. The assessment rate in that county is 70% and the tax rate is 19.44 mills.

a. What is the assessed value of the Pawlak home?
   Assessed value = 125,000 × .70 = $87,500.00

b. What is the amount of property tax?
   Property tax = 19.44 × .001 × 87,500.00
             = $1,701.00

14. As the tax assessor for San Fernando County you have been informed that due to budgetary demands a tax increase will be necessary next year. The total market value of the property in the county is $600,000,000. Currently the assessment rate is 45% and the tax rate is 30 mills. The county commission increases the assessment rate to 55% and the tax rate to 35 mills.

    a. How much property tax was collected under the old rates?

        Old assessed value = $600,000,000 \times .45 = \$270,000,000$

        Total taxes at old rate = 30 mills $\times .001 = .03$

$$.03 \times 270,000,000$$
$$= \underline{\underline{\$8,100,000}}$$

    b. How much more tax revenue will be collected under the new rates?

        Total taxes at new rate = $600,000,000 \times .55 = \$330,000,000$

$$35 \text{ mills} \times .001 = .035$$
$$.035 \times 330,000,000 = \$11,550,000$$
$$11,550,000 - 8,100,000$$

      Under new rates $\underline{\underline{\$3,450,000}}$ More

15. Joe Aguilera owns a house with an assessed value of $185,400. The tax rate is $2.20 per $100 of assessed value.

    a. What is the amount of property tax?

$$\text{Property tax} = \frac{185,400}{100} \times 2.20 = \underline{\underline{\$4,078.80}}$$

    b. If the state offers a 4% discount for early payment, how much can Joe save by paying early?

        Discounted rate = $4,078.80(100\% - 4\%)$

$$4,078.80 \times 96\% = \$3,915.65$$
$$4,078.80 - 3,915.65 = \underline{\underline{\$163.15}} \text{ savings}$$

    c. If the state charges a mandatory $3\frac{1}{2}\%$ penalty for late payments, how much would the tax bill amount to if Joe paid late?

$$\text{Tax} + \text{late fee} = 4,078.80(100\% + 3\frac{1}{2}\%)$$
$$= \underline{\underline{\$4,221.56}}$$

SECTION III

INCOME TAX

"The Congress shall have power to lay and collect taxes on incomes, from whatever source derived. . . ." These are the words of the Sixteenth Amendment to the Constitution of the United States. Passed by Congress in 1909 and ratified in 1913, this amendment paved the way for the evolution of the federal income tax system as we know it today. Income taxes, both personal and corporate, compose the largest source of receipts for our federal government. In 1995, individuals paid over $545 billion in federal income taxes and corporations paid over $140 billion. In addition to the federal income tax, many state governments have also imposed income taxes on their citizens to finance government activities.

● income tax

A pay-as-you-go tax based on the amount of income of an individual or corporation.

Income tax is a pay-as-you-go tax. The tax is paid as you earn or receive income throughout the year. As we learned in Chapter 9, payment is accomplished through income tax withholdings made by employers on wages and salaries paid to employees, and quarterly estimate tax payments made by people earning substantial income other than wages and salaries, such as interest income and business profits.

For those individuals subject to personal income tax, a **tax return** must be filed on the appropriate IRS form before midnight on April 15th. The tax return pertains to income earned during the previous calendar year. As the income tax filing deadline approaches, taxpayers must begin the preparation of their tax returns. Although tax preparation services are available to help with this annual task, you still have to keep and organize the records necessary for the return. Keep in mind, even if someone else prepares your return, you are ultimately responsible for its accuracy!

Although the tax rules and forms change almost every year, the method for calculating the amount of income tax due remains generally the same. For the purpose of this chapter, we shall divide the task into two components: (a) calculating the taxable income; and (b) determining the amount of income tax due. The figures and tables used in this section reflect IRS requirements for tax year 1995. For the most recent tax information and tables, consult the instruction booklet that accompanies this year's income tax forms.

● **tax return**
The official Internal Revenue Service forms used to report and pay income tax for income earned during the previous calendar year.

18-7 Calculating Taxable Income for Individuals

Taxable income is the amount of income that tax rates are applied to in order to calculate the amount of tax owed for the year. Exhibit 18-2 is a schematic diagram of the procedure used to calculate taxable income. Look it over carefully, and then use the following steps to calculate taxable income.

● **taxable income**
The amount of income that tax rates are applied to in order to calculate the amount of tax owed for the year.

STEPS TO CALCULATE TAXABLE INCOME FOR INDIVIDUALS:

Step 1. Determine **total income** by adding all sources of taxable income.

Step 2. Calculate **adjusted gross income** by subtracting the sum of all adjustments to income from total income.

Step 3. Subtract the sum of the **itemized deductions** or the **standard deduction** (whichever is larger) from the adjusted gross income.

1995 Standard Deductions:

Single	$3,900
Married filing jointly or Qualifying widow(er)	6,550
Married, filing separately	3,275
Head of household	5,750
65 or older, and/or blind	See IRS instructions to find standard deduction

Step 4. *If adjusted gross income is $86,025 or less:*
Multiply $2,500 by the total number of exemptions claimed and subtract from the amount in Step 3. The result is **taxable income.**
If adjusted gross income is over $86,025:
See IRS instructions to find exemption amounts.

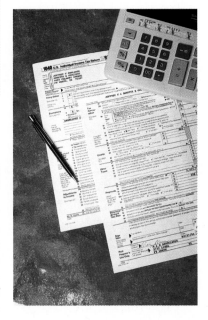

EXAMPLE

John and Sally Worthington are married and file a joint tax return. John is a manager and earned $43,500 last year. Sally worked as a secretary and earned $24,660. In addition, they earned $540 interest on their savings account. They each contributed $2,500 to a retirement account, and John paid alimony of $4,700 to his first wife. Itemized deductions amounted to $2,340 in real estate taxes, $4,590 in mortgage interest, $325 in charitable contributions, and $120 in unreimbursed employee expenses (above 2% of adjusted gross income). The Worthingtons claim three exemptions: one each for themselves and one for their dependent son Billy. From this information, calculate the Worthingtons' taxable income.

Federal income tax forms must be filed before midnight on April 15th.

Income	Wages, salaries, bonuses, commissions, tips, gratuities Interest and dividend income Rents, royalties, partnerships, S corporations, trusts Pensions and annuities Business income (or loss) Capital gain (or loss) from the sale or exchange of property Farm income Unemployment compensation, social security benefits Contest prizes, gambling winnings

Less

Adjustments to Income	Alimony payments Retirement fund payments—IRA, Keogh, 401K One-half of self-employment tax Self-employment health insurance Penalty on early withdrawal of savings

Equals

Adjusted Gross Income	Used in determining limits on certain itemized deductions, such as medical, dental, and employee expenses

Less

Deductions: Standard or Itemized	Medical and dental expenses (above 7.5% of adjusted gross income) Taxes paid: state and local income taxes; real estate taxes Home mortgage interest and points Charitable contributions Casualty and theft losses Moving expenses Unreimbursed employee expenses—union dues, job travel, education (above 2.0% of adjusted gross income)

and

Exemptions	Personal exemptions Dependents' exemptions

Equals

Taxable Income	Income on which the amount of income tax due is based. Used for Tax Table look-up and Tax Rate Schedule computation

EXHIBIT 18-2

....

PROCEDURE TO CALCULATE
TAXABLE INCOME

SOLUTION STRATEGY

Step 1. Total Income:

$43,500   John's income
+ 24,660   Sally's income
+___540   Interest from savings account
$68,700   Total income

Step 2. Adjusted Gross Income:

$68,700	Total income	$2,500	John's retirement payments
− 9,700	Deductions from total income	+ 2,500	Sally's retirement payments
$59,000	Adjusted gross income	+ 4,700	Alimony payments
		$9,700	Deductions from total income

Step 3. Deductions:

$2,340	Real estate taxes
+ 4,590	Mortgage interest
+ 325	Charitable contributions
+ 120	Unreimbursed employee expenses (above 2% of adjusted gross income)
$7,375	Total itemized deductions

Since the total itemized deductions, $7,375, is greater than the standard deduction for married filing jointly ($6,550) we shall use itemized deductions for John and Sally's tax return.

Step 4. Exemptions:
Since the Worthington's adjusted gross income is less than $86,025, multiply $2,500 by the number of exemptions, three:

$59,000	Adjusted gross income
− 7,375	Total itemized deductions
− 7,500	$2,500 × 3 exemptions
$44,125	Taxable income

TRY-IT **EXERCISE**

7. **Nick Mathews is single, claiming one exemption. He is a welder, earning $26,900 in wages per year. Last year he also earned $760 in cash dividends from his investment portfolio. Nick contributed $2,000 to his individual retirement account and lost $2,200 from the sale of 100 shares of Consolidated Widget stock. His itemized deductions amounted to medical expenses of $1,400 in excess of IRS exclusions; $1,920 in real estate taxes; $2,550 in mortgage interest; and $180 in charitable contributions. From this information, calculate Nick's taxable income.**

Check your answer with the solution on page 619.

18-8 Using the Tax Table to Determine Tax Liability

If taxable income is less than $100,000, the Tax Table must be used to figure the tax liability. When the taxable income is $100,000 or more, the Tax Rate Schedule for the appropriate filing status must be used. Exhibit 18-3 illustrates a portion of the 1995 **Tax Table** and Exhibit 18-4 shows the 1995 **Tax Rate Schedules.** The most current version of these may be found in "Instructions for Form 1040," published by the IRS.

● **Tax Table**
The IRS chart used to calculate the amount of income tax due for individuals with taxable income of under $100,000.

● **Tax Rate Schedules**
The IRS chart used to calculate the amount of income tax due for individuals with taxable income of $100,000 or more.

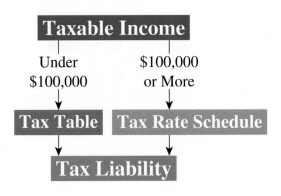

Taxable Income

Under $100,000 / $100,000 or More

Tax Table / Tax Rate Schedule

Tax Liability

23,000

At least	But less than	Single	Married filing jointly *	Married filing separately	Head of a household
23,000	23,050	3,454	3,454	3,912	3,454
23,050	23,100	3,461	3,461	3,926	3,461
23,100	23,150	3,469	3,469	3,940	3,469
23,150	23,200	3,476	3,476	3,954	3,476
23,200	23,250	3,484	3,484	3,968	3,484
23,250	23,300	3,491	3,491	3,982	3,491
23,300	23,350	3,499	3,499	3,996	3,499
23,350	23,400	3,510	3,506	4,010	3,506
23,400	23,450	3,524	3,514	4,024	3,514
23,450	23,500	3,538	3,521	4,038	3,521
23,500	23,550	3,552	3,529	4,052	3,529
23,550	23,600	3,566	3,536	4,066	3,536
23,600	23,650	3,580	3,544	4,080	3,544
23,650	23,700	3,594	3,551	4,094	3,551
23,700	23,750	3,608	3,559	4,108	3,559
23,750	23,800	3,622	3,566	4,122	3,566
23,800	23,850	3,636	3,574	4,136	3,574
23,850	23,900	3,650	3,581	4,150	3,581
23,900	23,950	3,664	3,589	4,164	3,589
23,950	24,000	3,678	3,596	4,178	3,596

24,000

At least	But less than	Single	Married filing jointly *	Married filing separately	Head of a household
24,000	24,050	3,692	3,604	4,192	3,604
24,050	24,100	3,706	3,611	4,206	3,611
24,100	24,150	3,720	3,619	4,220	3,619
24,150	24,200	3,734	3,626	4,234	3,626
24,200	24,250	3,748	3,634	4,248	3,634
24,250	24,300	3,762	3,641	4,262	3,641
24,300	24,350	3,776	3,649	4,276	3,649
24,350	24,400	3,790	3,656	4,290	3,656
24,400	24,450	3,804	3,664	4,304	3,664
24,450	24,500	3,818	3,671	4,318	3,671
24,500	24,550	3,832	3,679	4,332	3,679
24,550	24,600	3,846	3,686	4,346	3,686
24,600	24,650	3,860	3,694	4,360	3,694
24,650	24,700	3,874	3,701	4,374	3,701
24,700	24,750	3,888	3,709	4,388	3,709
24,750	24,800	3,902	3,716	4,402	3,716
24,800	24,850	3,916	3,724	4,416	3,724
24,850	24,900	3,930	3,731	4,430	3,731
24,900	24,950	3,944	3,739	4,444	3,739
24,950	25,000	3,958	3,746	4,458	3,746

25,000

At least	But less than	Single	Married filing jointly *	Married filing separately	Head of a household
25,000	25,050	3,972	3,754	4,472	3,754
25,050	25,100	3,986	3,761	4,486	3,761
25,100	25,150	4,000	3,769	4,500	3,769
25,150	25,200	4,014	3,776	4,514	3,776
25,200	25,250	4,028	3,784	4,528	3,784
25,250	25,300	4,042	3,791	4,542	3,791
25,300	25,350	4,056	3,799	4,556	3,799
25,350	25,400	4,070	3,806	4,570	3,806
25,400	25,450	4,084	3,814	4,584	3,814
25,450	25,500	4,098	3,821	4,598	3,821
25,500	25,550	4,112	3,829	4,612	3,829
25,550	25,600	4,126	3,836	4,626	3,836
25,600	25,650	4,140	3,844	4,640	3,844
25,650	25,700	4,154	3,851	4,654	3,851
25,700	25,750	4,168	3,859	4,668	3,859
25,750	25,800	4,182	3,866	4,682	3,866
25,800	25,850	4,196	3,874	4,696	3,874
25,850	25,900	4,210	3,881	4,710	3,881
25,900	25,950	4,224	3,889	4,724	3,889
25,950	26,000	4,238	3,896	4,738	3,896

26,000

At least	But less than	Single	Married filing jointly *	Married filing separately	Head of a household
26,000	26,050	4,252	3,904	4,752	3,904
26,050	26,100	4,266	3,911	4,766	3,911
26,100	26,150	4,280	3,919	4,780	3,919
26,150	26,200	4,294	3,926	4,794	3,926
26,200	26,250	4,308	3,934	4,808	3,934
26,250	26,300	4,322	3,941	4,822	3,941
26,300	26,350	4,336	3,949	4,836	3,949
26,350	26,400	4,350	3,956	4,850	3,956
26,400	26,450	4,364	3,964	4,864	3,964
26,450	26,500	4,378	3,971	4,878	3,971
26,500	26,550	4,392	3,979	4,892	3,979
26,550	26,600	4,406	3,986	4,906	3,986
26,600	26,650	4,420	3,994	4,920	3,994
26,650	26,700	4,434	4,001	4,934	4,001
26,700	26,750	4,448	4,009	4,948	4,009
26,750	26,800	4,462	4,016	4,962	4,016
26,800	26,850	4,476	4,024	4,976	4,024
26,850	26,900	4,490	4,031	4,990	4,031
26,900	26,950	4,504	4,039	5,004	4,039
26,950	27,000	4,518	4,046	5,018	4,046

27,000

At least	But less than	Single	Married filing jointly *	Married filing separately	Head of a household
27,000	27,050	4,532	4,054	5,032	4,054
27,050	27,100	4,546	4,061	5,046	4,061
27,100	27,150	4,560	4,069	5,060	4,069
27,150	27,200	4,574	4,076	5,074	4,076
27,200	27,250	4,588	4,084	5,088	4,084
27,250	27,300	4,602	4,091	5,102	4,091
27,300	27,350	4,616	4,099	5,116	4,099
27,350	27,400	4,630	4,106	5,130	4,106
27,400	27,450	4,644	4,114	5,144	4,114
27,450	27,500	4,658	4,121	5,158	4,121
27,500	27,550	4,672	4,129	5,172	4,129
27,550	27,600	4,686	4,136	5,186	4,136
27,600	27,650	4,700	4,144	5,200	4,144
27,650	27,700	4,714	4,151	5,214	4,151
27,700	27,750	4,728	4,159	5,228	4,159
27,750	27,800	4,742	4,166	5,242	4,166
27,800	27,850	4,756	4,174	5,256	4,174
27,850	27,900	4,770	4,181	5,270	4,181
27,900	27,950	4,784	4,189	5,284	4,189
27,950	28,000	4,798	4,196	5,298	4,196

28,000

At least	But less than	Single	Married filing jointly *	Married filing separately	Head of a household
28,000	28,050	4,812	4,204	5,312	4,204
28,050	28,100	4,826	4,211	5,326	4,211
28,100	28,150	4,840	4,219	5,340	4,219
28,150	28,200	4,854	4,226	5,354	4,226
28,200	28,250	4,868	4,234	5,368	4,234
28,250	28,300	4,882	4,241	5,382	4,241
28,300	28,350	4,896	4,249	5,396	4,249
28,350	28,400	4,910	4,256	5,410	4,256
28,400	28,450	4,924	4,264	5,424	4,264
28,450	28,500	4,938	4,271	5,438	4,271
28,500	28,550	4,952	4,279	5,452	4,279
28,550	28,600	4,966	4,286	5,466	4,286
28,600	28,650	4,980	4,294	5,480	4,294
28,650	28,700	4,994	4,301	5,494	4,301
28,700	28,750	5,008	4,309	5,508	4,309
28,750	28,800	5,022	4,316	5,522	4,316
28,800	28,850	5,036	4,324	5,536	4,324
28,850	28,900	5,050	4,331	5,550	4,331
28,900	28,950	5,064	4,339	5,564	4,339
28,950	29,000	5,078	4,346	5,578	4,346

29,000

At least	But less than	Single	Married filing jointly *	Married filing separately	Head of a household
29,000	29,050	5,092	4,354	5,592	4,354
29,050	29,100	5,106	4,361	5,606	4,361
29,100	29,150	5,120	4,369	5,620	4,369
29,150	29,200	5,134	4,376	5,634	4,376
29,200	29,250	5,148	4,384	5,648	4,384
29,250	29,300	5,162	4,391	5,662	4,391
29,300	29,350	5,176	4,399	5,676	4,399
29,350	29,400	5,190	4,406	5,690	4,406
29,400	29,450	5,204	4,414	5,704	4,414
29,450	29,500	5,218	4,421	5,718	4,421
29,500	29,550	5,232	4,429	5,732	4,429
29,550	29,600	5,246	4,436	5,746	4,436
29,600	29,650	5,260	4,444	5,760	4,444
29,650	29,700	5,274	4,451	5,774	4,451
29,700	29,750	5,288	4,459	5,788	4,459
29,750	29,800	5,302	4,466	5,802	4,466
29,800	29,850	5,316	4,474	5,816	4,474
29,850	29,900	5,330	4,481	5,830	4,481
29,900	29,950	5,344	4,489	5,844	4,489
29,950	30,000	5,358	4,496	5,858	4,496

30,000

At least	But less than	Single	Married filing jointly *	Married filing separately	Head of a household
30,000	30,050	5,372	4,504	5,872	4,504
30,050	30,100	5,386	4,511	5,886	4,511
30,100	30,150	5,400	4,519	5,900	4,519
30,150	30,200	5,414	4,526	5,914	4,526
30,200	30,250	5,428	4,534	5,928	4,534
30,250	30,300	5,442	4,541	5,942	4,541
30,300	30,350	5,456	4,549	5,956	4,549
30,350	30,400	5,470	4,556	5,970	4,556
30,400	30,450	5,484	4,564	5,984	4,564
30,450	30,500	5,498	4,571	5,998	4,571
30,500	30,550	5,512	4,579	6,012	4,579
30,550	30,600	5,526	4,586	6,026	4,586
30,600	30,650	5,540	4,594	6,040	4,594
30,650	30,700	5,554	4,601	6,054	4,601
30,700	30,750	5,568	4,609	6,068	4,609
30,750	30,800	5,582	4,616	6,082	4,616
30,800	30,850	5,596	4,624	6,096	4,624
30,850	30,900	5,610	4,631	6,110	4,631
30,900	30,950	5,624	4,639	6,124	4,639
30,950	31,000	5,638	4,646	6,138	4,646

31,000

At least	But less than	Single	Married filing jointly *	Married filing separately	Head of a household
31,000	31,050	5,652	4,654	6,152	4,654
31,050	31,100	5,666	4,661	6,166	4,661
31,100	31,150	5,680	4,669	6,180	4,669
31,150	31,200	5,694	4,676	6,194	4,676
31,200	31,250	5,708	4,684	6,208	4,684
31,250	31,300	5,722	4,691	6,222	4,695
31,300	31,350	5,736	4,699	6,236	4,709
31,350	31,400	5,750	4,706	6,250	4,723
31,400	31,450	5,764	4,714	6,264	4,737
31,450	31,500	5,778	4,721	6,278	4,751
31,500	31,550	5,792	4,729	6,292	4,765
31,550	31,600	5,806	4,736	6,306	4,779
31,600	31,650	5,820	4,744	6,320	4,793
31,650	31,700	5,834	4,751	6,334	4,807
31,700	31,750	5,848	4,759	6,348	4,821
31,750	31,800	5,862	4,766	6,362	4,835
31,800	31,850	5,876	4,774	6,376	4,849
31,850	31,900	5,890	4,781	6,390	4,863
31,900	31,950	5,904	4,789	6,404	4,877
31,950	32,000	5,918	4,796	6,418	4,891

* This column must also be used by a qualifying widow(er).

Continued on next page

EXHIBIT 18-3   TAX TABLE

32,000

At least	But less than	Single	Married filing jointly *	Married filing separately	Head of a household
			Your tax is—		
32,000	32,050	5,932	4,804	6,432	4,905
32,050	32,100	5,946	4,811	6,446	4,919
32,100	32,150	5,960	4,819	6,460	4,933
32,150	32,200	5,974	4,826	6,474	4,947
32,200	32,250	5,988	4,834	6,488	4,961
32,250	32,300	6,002	4,841	6,502	4,975
32,300	32,350	6,016	4,849	6,516	4,989
32,350	32,400	6,030	4,856	6,530	5,003
32,400	32,450	6,044	4,864	6,544	5,017
32,450	32,500	6,058	4,871	6,558	5,031
32,500	32,550	6,072	4,879	6,572	5,045
32,550	32,600	6,086	4,886	6,586	5,059
32,600	32,650	6,100	4,894	6,600	5,073
32,650	32,700	6,114	4,901	6,614	5,087
32,700	32,750	6,128	4,909	6,628	5,101
32,750	32,800	6,142	4,916	6,642	5,115
32,800	32,850	6,156	4,924	6,656	5,129
32,850	32,900	6,170	4,931	6,670	5,143
32,900	32,950	6,184	4,939	6,684	5,157
32,950	33,000	6,198	4,946	6,698	5,171

33,000

At least	But less than	Single	Married filing jointly *	Married filing separately	Head of a household
33,000	33,050	6,212	4,954	6,712	5,185
33,050	33,100	6,226	4,961	6,726	5,199
33,100	33,150	6,240	4,969	6,740	5,213
33,150	33,200	6,254	4,976	6,754	5,227
33,200	33,250	6,268	4,984	6,768	5,241
33,250	33,300	6,282	4,991	6,782	5,255
33,300	33,350	6,296	4,999	6,796	5,269
33,350	33,400	6,310	5,006	6,810	5,283
33,400	33,450	6,324	5,014	6,824	5,297
33,450	33,500	6,338	5,021	6,838	5,311
33,500	33,550	6,352	5,029	6,852	5,325
33,550	33,600	6,366	5,036	6,866	5,339
33,600	33,650	6,380	5,044	6,880	5,353
33,650	33,700	6,394	5,051	6,894	5,367
33,700	33,750	6,408	5,059	6,908	5,381
33,750	33,800	6,422	5,066	6,922	5,395
33,800	33,850	6,436	5,074	6,936	5,409
33,850	33,900	6,450	5,081	6,950	5,423
33,900	33,950	6,464	5,089	6,964	5,437
33,950	34,000	6,478	5,096	6,978	5,451

34,000

At least	But less than	Single	Married filing jointly *	Married filing separately	Head of a household
34,000	34,050	6,492	5,104	6,992	5,465
34,050	34,100	6,506	5,111	7,006	5,479
34,100	34,150	6,520	5,119	7,020	5,493
34,150	34,200	6,534	5,126	7,034	5,507
34,200	34,250	6,548	5,134	7,048	5,521
34,250	34,300	6,562	5,141	7,062	5,535
34,300	34,350	6,576	5,149	7,076	5,549
34,350	34,400	6,590	5,156	7,090	5,563
34,400	34,450	6,604	5,164	7,104	5,577
34,450	34,500	6,618	5,171	7,118	5,591
34,500	34,550	6,632	5,179	7,132	5,605
34,550	34,600	6,646	5,186	7,146	5,619
34,600	34,650	6,660	5,194	7,160	5,633
34,650	34,700	6,674	5,201	7,174	5,647
34,700	34,750	6,688	5,209	7,188	5,661
34,750	34,800	6,702	5,216	7,202	5,675
34,800	34,850	6,716	5,224	7,216	5,689
34,850	34,900	6,730	5,231	7,230	5,703
34,900	34,950	6,744	5,239	7,244	5,717
34,950	35,000	6,758	5,246	7,258	5,731

35,000

At least	But less than	Single	Married filing jointly *	Married filing separately	Head of a household
35,000	35,050	6,772	5,254	7,272	5,745
35,050	35,100	6,786	5,261	7,286	5,759
35,100	35,150	6,800	5,269	7,300	5,773
35,150	35,200	6,814	5,276	7,314	5,787
35,200	35,250	6,828	5,284	7,328	5,801
35,250	35,300	6,842	5,291	7,342	5,815
35,300	35,350	6,856	5,299	7,356	5,829
35,350	35,400	6,870	5,306	7,370	5,843
35,400	35,450	6,884	5,314	7,384	5,857
35,450	35,500	6,898	5,321	7,398	5,871
35,500	35,550	6,912	5,329	7,412	5,885
35,550	35,600	6,926	5,336	7,426	5,899
35,600	35,650	6,940	5,344	7,440	5,913
35,650	35,700	6,954	5,351	7,454	5,927
35,700	35,750	6,968	5,359	7,468	5,941
35,750	35,800	6,982	5,366	7,482	5,955
35,800	35,850	6,996	5,374	7,496	5,969
35,850	35,900	7,010	5,381	7,510	5,983
35,900	35,950	7,024	5,389	7,524	5,997
35,950	36,000	7,038	5,396	7,538	6,011

36,000

At least	But less than	Single	Married filing jointly *	Married filing separately	Head of a household
36,000	36,050	7,052	5,404	7,552	6,025
36,050	36,100	7,066	5,411	7,566	6,039
36,100	36,150	7,080	5,419	7,580	6,053
36,150	36,200	7,094	5,426	7,594	6,067
36,200	36,250	7,108	5,434	7,608	6,081
36,250	36,300	7,122	5,441	7,622	6,095
36,300	36,350	7,136	5,449	7,636	6,109
36,350	36,400	7,150	5,456	7,650	6,123
36,400	36,450	7,164	5,464	7,664	6,137
36,450	36,500	7,178	5,471	7,678	6,151
36,500	36,550	7,192	5,479	7,692	6,165
36,550	36,600	7,206	5,486	7,706	6,179
36,600	36,650	7,220	5,494	7,720	6,193
36,650	36,700	7,234	5,501	7,734	6,207
36,700	36,750	7,248	5,509	7,748	6,221
36,750	36,800	7,262	5,516	7,762	6,235
36,800	36,850	7,276	5,524	7,776	6,249
36,850	36,900	7,290	5,531	7,790	6,263
36,900	36,950	7,304	5,539	7,804	6,277
36,950	37,000	7,318	5,546	7,818	6,291

37,000

At least	But less than	Single	Married filing jointly *	Married filing separately	Head of a household
37,000	37,050	7,332	5,554	7,832	6,305
37,050	37,100	7,346	5,561	7,846	6,319
37,100	37,150	7,360	5,569	7,860	6,333
37,150	37,200	7,374	5,576	7,874	6,347
37,200	37,250	7,388	5,584	7,888	6,361
37,250	37,300	7,402	5,591	7,902	6,375
37,300	37,350	7,416	5,599	7,916	6,389
37,350	37,400	7,430	5,606	7,930	6,403
37,400	37,450	7,444	5,614	7,944	6,417
37,450	37,500	7,458	5,621	7,958	6,431
37,500	37,550	7,472	5,629	7,972	6,445
37,550	37,600	7,486	5,636	7,986	6,459
37,600	37,650	7,500	5,644	8,000	6,473
37,650	37,700	7,514	5,651	8,014	6,487
37,700	37,750	7,528	5,659	8,028	6,501
37,750	37,800	7,542	5,666	8,042	6,515
37,800	37,850	7,556	5,674	8,056	6,529
37,850	37,900	7,570	5,681	8,070	6,543
37,900	37,950	7,584	5,689	8,084	6,557
37,950	38,000	7,598	5,696	8,098	6,571

38,000

At least	But less than	Single	Married filing jointly *	Married filing separately	Head of a household
38,000	38,050	7,612	5,704	8,112	6,585
38,050	38,100	7,626	5,711	8,126	6,599
38,100	38,150	7,640	5,719	8,140	6,613
38,150	38,200	7,654	5,726	8,154	6,627
38,200	38,250	7,668	5,734	8,168	6,641
38,250	38,300	7,682	5,741	8,182	6,655
38,300	38,350	7,696	5,749	8,196	6,669
38,350	38,400	7,710	5,756	8,210	6,683
38,400	38,450	7,724	5,764	8,224	6,697
38,450	38,500	7,738	5,771	8,238	6,711
38,500	38,550	7,752	5,779	8,252	6,725
38,550	38,600	7,766	5,786	8,266	6,739
38,600	38,650	7,780	5,794	8,280	6,753
38,650	38,700	7,794	5,801	8,294	6,767
38,700	38,750	7,808	5,809	8,308	6,781
38,750	38,800	7,822	5,816	8,322	6,795
38,800	38,850	7,836	5,824	8,336	6,809
38,850	38,900	7,850	5,831	8,350	6,823
38,900	38,950	7,864	5,839	8,364	6,837
38,950	39,000	7,878	5,846	8,378	6,851

39,000

At least	But less than	Single	Married filing jointly *	Married filing separately	Head of a household
39,000	39,050	7,892	5,857	8,392	6,865
39,050	39,100	7,906	5,871	8,406	6,879
39,100	39,150	7,920	5,885	8,420	6,893
39,150	39,200	7,934	5,899	8,434	6,907
39,200	39,250	7,948	5,913	8,448	6,921
39,250	39,300	7,962	5,927	8,462	6,935
39,300	39,350	7,976	5,941	8,476	6,949
39,350	39,400	7,990	5,955	8,490	6,963
39,400	39,450	8,004	5,969	8,504	6,977
39,450	39,500	8,018	5,983	8,518	6,991
39,500	39,550	8,032	5,997	8,532	7,005
39,550	39,600	8,046	6,011	8,546	7,019
39,600	39,650	8,060	6,025	8,560	7,033
39,650	39,700	8,074	6,039	8,574	7,047
39,700	39,750	8,088	6,053	8,588	7,061
39,750	39,800	8,102	6,067	8,602	7,075
39,800	39,850	8,116	6,081	8,616	7,089
39,850	39,900	8,130	6,095	8,630	7,103
39,900	39,950	8,144	6,109	8,644	7,117
39,950	40,000	8,158	6,123	8,658	7,131

40,000

At least	But less than	Single	Married filing jointly *	Married filing separately	Head of a household
40,000	40,050	8,172	6,137	8,672	7,145
40,050	40,100	8,186	6,151	8,686	7,159
40,100	40,150	8,200	6,165	8,700	7,173
40,150	40,200	8,214	6,179	8,714	7,187
40,200	40,250	8,228	6,193	8,728	7,201
40,250	40,300	8,242	6,207	8,742	7,215
40,300	40,350	8,256	6,221	8,756	7,229
40,350	40,400	8,270	6,235	8,770	7,243
40,400	40,450	8,284	6,249	8,784	7,257
40,450	40,500	8,298	6,263	8,798	7,271
40,500	40,550	8,312	6,277	8,812	7,285
40,550	40,600	8,326	6,291	8,826	7,299
40,600	40,650	8,340	6,305	8,840	7,313
40,650	40,700	8,354	6,319	8,854	7,327
40,700	40,750	8,368	6,333	8,868	7,341
40,750	40,800	8,382	6,347	8,882	7,355
40,800	40,850	8,396	6,361	8,896	7,369
40,850	40,900	8,410	6,375	8,910	7,383
40,900	40,950	8,424	6,389	8,924	7,397
40,950	41,000	8,438	6,403	8,938	7,411

* This column must also be used by a qualifying widow(er).

Continued on next page

59,000 / 60,000 / 61,000

At least	But less than	Single	Married filing jointly *	Married filing separately	Head of a household
59,000	59,050	13,566	11,457	14,349	12,465
59,050	59,100	13,581	11,471	14,365	12,479
59,100	59,150	13,597	11,485	14,380	12,493
59,150	59,200	13,612	11,499	14,396	12,507
59,200	59,250	13,628	11,513	14,411	12,521
59,250	59,300	13,643	11,527	14,427	12,535
59,300	59,350	13,659	11,541	14,442	12,549
59,350	59,400	13,674	11,555	14,458	12,563
59,400	59,450	13,690	11,569	14,473	12,577
59,450	59,500	13,705	11,583	14,489	12,591
59,500	59,550	13,721	11,597	14,504	12,605
59,550	59,600	13,736	11,611	14,520	12,619
59,600	59,650	13,752	11,625	14,535	12,633
59,650	59,700	13,767	11,639	14,551	12,647
59,700	59,750	13,783	11,653	14,566	12,661
59,750	59,800	13,798	11,667	14,582	12,675
59,800	59,850	13,814	11,681	14,597	12,689
59,850	59,900	13,829	11,695	14,613	12,703
59,900	59,950	13,845	11,709	14,628	12,717
59,950	60,000	13,860	11,723	14,644	12,731
60,000	60,050	13,876	11,737	14,659	12,745
60,050	60,100	13,891	11,751	14,675	12,759
60,100	60,150	13,907	11,765	14,690	12,773
60,150	60,200	13,922	11,779	14,706	12,787
60,200	60,250	13,938	11,793	14,721	12,801
60,250	60,300	13,953	11,807	14,737	12,815
60,300	60,350	13,969	11,821	14,752	12,829
60,350	60,400	13,984	11,835	14,768	12,843
60,400	60,450	14,000	11,849	14,783	12,857
60,450	60,500	14,015	11,863	14,799	12,871
60,500	60,550	14,031	11,877	14,814	12,885
60,550	60,600	14,046	11,891	14,830	12,899
60,600	60,650	14,062	11,905	14,845	12,913
60,650	60,700	14,077	11,919	14,861	12,927
60,700	60,750	14,093	11,933	14,876	12,941
60,750	60,800	14,108	11,947	14,892	12,955
60,800	60,850	14,124	11,961	14,907	12,969
60,850	60,900	14,139	11,975	14,923	12,983
60,900	60,950	14,155	11,989	14,938	12,997
60,950	61,000	14,170	12,003	14,954	13,011
61,000	61,050	14,186	12,017	14,969	13,025
61,050	61,100	14,201	12,031	14,985	13,039
61,100	61,150	14,217	12,045	15,000	13,053
61,150	61,200	14,232	12,059	15,016	13,067
61,200	61,250	14,248	12,073	15,031	13,081
61,250	61,300	14,263	12,087	15,047	13,095
61,300	61,350	14,279	12,101	15,062	13,109
61,350	61,400	14,294	12,115	15,078	13,123
61,400	61,450	14,310	12,129	15,093	13,137
61,450	61,500	14,325	12,143	15,109	13,151
61,500	61,550	14,341	12,157	15,124	13,165
61,550	61,600	14,356	12,171	15,140	13,179
61,600	61,650	14,372	12,185	15,155	13,193
61,650	61,700	14,387	12,199	15,171	13,207
61,700	61,750	14,403	12,213	15,186	13,221
61,750	61,800	14,418	12,227	15,202	13,235
61,800	61,850	14,434	12,241	15,217	13,249
61,850	61,900	14,449	12,255	15,233	13,263
61,900	61,950	14,465	12,269	15,248	13,277
61,950	62,000	14,480	12,283	15,264	13,291

62,000 / 63,000 / 64,000

At least	But less than	Single	Married filing jointly *	Married filing separately	Head of a household
62,000	62,050	14,496	12,297	15,279	13,305
62,050	62,100	14,511	12,311	15,295	13,319
62,100	62,150	14,527	12,325	15,310	13,333
62,150	62,200	14,542	12,339	15,326	13,347
62,200	62,250	14,558	12,353	15,341	13,361
62,250	62,300	14,573	12,367	15,357	13,375
62,300	62,350	14,589	12,381	15,372	13,389
62,350	62,400	14,604	12,395	15,388	13,403
62,400	62,450	14,620	12,409	15,403	13,417
62,450	62,500	14,635	12,423	15,419	13,431
62,500	62,550	14,651	12,437	15,434	13,445
62,550	62,600	14,666	12,451	15,450	13,459
62,600	62,650	14,682	12,465	15,465	13,473
62,650	62,700	14,697	12,479	15,481	13,487
62,700	62,750	14,713	12,493	15,496	13,501
62,750	62,800	14,728	12,507	15,512	13,515
62,800	62,850	14,744	12,521	15,527	13,529
62,850	62,900	14,759	12,535	15,543	13,543
62,900	62,950	14,775	12,549	15,558	13,557
62,950	63,000	14,790	12,563	15,574	13,571
63,000	63,050	14,806	12,577	15,589	13,585
63,050	63,100	14,821	12,591	15,605	13,599
63,100	63,150	14,837	12,605	15,620	13,613
63,150	63,200	14,852	12,619	15,636	13,627
63,200	63,250	14,868	12,633	15,651	13,641
63,250	63,300	14,883	12,647	15,667	13,655
63,300	63,350	14,899	12,661	15,682	13,669
63,350	63,400	14,914	12,675	15,698	13,683
63,400	63,450	14,930	12,689	15,713	13,697
63,450	63,500	14,945	12,703	15,729	13,711
63,500	63,550	14,961	12,717	15,744	13,725
63,550	63,600	14,976	12,731	15,760	13,739
63,600	63,650	14,992	12,745	15,775	13,753
63,650	63,700	15,007	12,759	15,791	13,767
63,700	63,750	15,023	12,773	15,806	13,781
63,750	63,800	15,038	12,787	15,822	13,795
63,800	63,850	15,054	12,801	15,837	13,809
63,850	63,900	15,069	12,815	15,853	13,823
63,900	63,950	15,085	12,829	15,868	13,837
63,950	64,000	15,100	12,843	15,884	13,851
64,000	64,050	15,116	12,857	15,899	13,865
64,050	64,100	15,131	12,871	15,915	13,879
64,100	64,150	15,147	12,885	15,930	13,893
64,150	64,200	15,162	12,899	15,946	13,907
64,200	64,250	15,178	12,913	15,961	13,921
64,250	64,300	15,193	12,927	15,977	13,935
64,300	64,350	15,209	12,941	15,992	13,949
64,350	64,400	15,224	12,955	16,008	13,963
64,400	64,450	15,240	12,969	16,023	13,977
64,450	64,500	15,255	12,983	16,039	13,991
64,500	64,550	15,271	12,997	16,054	14,005
64,550	64,600	15,286	13,011	16,070	14,019
64,600	64,650	15,302	13,025	16,085	14,033
64,650	64,700	15,317	13,039	16,101	14,047
64,700	64,750	15,333	13,053	16,116	14,061
64,750	64,800	15,348	13,067	16,132	14,075
64,800	64,850	15,364	13,081	16,147	14,089
64,850	64,900	15,379	13,095	16,163	14,103
64,900	64,950	15,395	13,109	16,178	14,117
64,950	65,000	15,410	13,123	16,194	14,131

65,000 / 66,000 / 67,000

At least	But less than	Single	Married filing jointly *	Married filing separately	Head of a household
65,000	65,050	15,426	13,137	16,209	14,145
65,050	65,100	15,441	13,151	16,225	14,159
65,100	65,150	15,457	13,165	16,240	14,173
65,150	65,200	15,472	13,179	16,256	14,187
65,200	65,250	15,488	13,193	16,271	14,201
65,250	65,300	15,503	13,207	16,287	14,215
65,300	65,350	15,519	13,221	16,302	14,229
65,350	65,400	15,534	13,235	16,318	14,243
65,400	65,450	15,550	13,249	16,333	14,257
65,450	65,500	15,565	13,263	16,349	14,271
65,500	65,550	15,581	13,277	16,364	14,285
65,550	65,600	15,596	13,291	16,380	14,299
65,600	65,650	15,612	13,305	16,395	14,313
65,650	65,700	15,627	13,319	16,411	14,327
65,700	65,750	15,643	13,333	16,426	14,341
65,750	65,800	15,658	13,347	16,442	14,355
65,800	65,850	15,674	13,361	16,457	14,369
65,850	65,900	15,689	13,375	16,473	14,383
65,900	65,950	15,705	13,389	16,488	14,397
65,950	66,000	15,720	13,403	16,504	14,411
66,000	66,050	15,736	13,417	16,519	14,425
66,050	66,100	15,751	13,431	16,535	14,439
66,100	66,150	15,767	13,445	16,550	14,453
66,150	66,200	15,782	13,459	16,566	14,467
66,200	66,250	15,798	13,473	16,581	14,481
66,250	66,300	15,813	13,487	16,597	14,495
66,300	66,350	15,829	13,501	16,612	14,509
66,350	66,400	15,844	13,515	16,628	14,523
66,400	66,450	15,860	13,529	16,643	14,537
66,450	66,500	15,875	13,543	16,659	14,551
66,500	66,550	15,891	13,557	16,674	14,565
66,550	66,600	15,906	13,571	16,690	14,579
66,600	66,650	15,922	13,585	16,705	14,593
66,650	66,700	15,937	13,599	16,721	14,607
66,700	66,750	15,953	13,613	16,736	14,621
66,750	66,800	15,968	13,627	16,752	14,635
66,800	66,850	15,984	13,641	16,767	14,649
66,850	66,900	15,999	13,655	16,783	14,663
66,900	66,950	16,015	13,669	16,798	14,677
66,950	67,000	16,030	13,683	16,814	14,691
67,000	67,050	16,046	13,697	16,829	14,705
67,050	67,100	16,061	13,711	16,845	14,719
67,100	67,150	16,077	13,725	16,860	14,733
67,150	67,200	16,092	13,739	16,876	14,747
67,200	67,250	16,108	13,753	16,891	14,761
67,250	67,300	16,123	13,767	16,907	14,775
67,300	67,350	16,139	13,781	16,922	14,789
67,350	67,400	16,154	13,795	16,938	14,803
67,400	67,450	16,170	13,809	16,953	14,817
67,450	67,500	16,185	13,823	16,969	14,831
67,500	67,550	16,201	13,837	16,984	14,845
67,550	67,600	16,216	13,851	17,000	14,859
67,600	67,650	16,232	13,865	17,015	14,873
67,650	67,700	16,247	13,879	17,031	14,887
67,700	67,750	16,263	13,893	17,046	14,901
67,750	67,800	16,278	13,907	17,062	14,915
67,800	67,850	16,294	13,921	17,077	14,929
67,850	67,900	16,309	13,935	17,093	14,943
67,900	67,950	16,325	13,949	17,108	14,957
67,950	68,000	16,340	13,963	17,124	14,971

* This column must also be used by a qualifying widow(er).

Continued on next page

EXHIBIT 18-3 (continued)

Left panel

If line 37 (taxable income) is— At least	But less than	Single	Married filing jointly *	Married filing separately	Head of a household
68,000					
68,000	68,050	16,356	13,977	17,139	14,985
68,050	68,100	16,371	13,991	17,155	14,999
68,100	68,150	16,387	14,005	17,170	15,013
68,150	68,200	16,402	14,019	17,186	15,027
68,200	68,250	16,418	14,033	17,201	15,041
68,250	68,300	16,433	14,047	17,217	15,055
68,300	68,350	16,449	14,061	17,232	15,069
68,350	68,400	16,464	14,075	17,248	15,083
68,400	68,450	16,480	14,089	17,263	15,097
68,450	68,500	16,495	14,103	17,279	15,111
68,500	68,550	16,511	14,117	17,294	15,125
68,550	68,600	16,526	14,131	17,310	15,139
68,600	68,650	16,542	14,145	17,325	15,153
68,650	68,700	16,557	14,159	17,341	15,167
68,700	68,750	16,573	14,173	17,356	15,181
68,750	68,800	16,588	14,187	17,372	15,195
68,800	68,850	16,604	14,201	17,387	15,209
68,850	68,900	16,619	14,215	17,403	15,223
68,900	68,950	16,635	14,229	17,418	15,237
68,950	69,000	16,650	14,243	17,434	15,251
69,000					
69,000	69,050	16,666	14,257	17,449	15,265
69,050	69,100	16,681	14,271	17,465	15,279
69,100	69,150	16,697	14,285	17,480	15,293
69,150	69,200	16,712	14,299	17,496	15,307
69,200	69,250	16,728	14,313	17,511	15,321
69,250	69,300	16,743	14,327	17,527	15,335
69,300	69,350	16,759	14,341	17,542	15,349
69,350	69,400	16,774	14,355	17,558	15,363
69,400	69,450	16,790	14,369	17,573	15,377
69,450	69,500	16,805	14,383	17,589	15,391
69,500	69,550	16,821	14,397	17,604	15,405
69,550	69,600	16,836	14,411	17,620	15,419
69,600	69,650	16,852	14,425	17,635	15,433
69,650	69,700	16,867	14,439	17,651	15,447
69,700	69,750	16,883	14,453	17,666	15,461
69,750	69,800	16,898	14,467	17,682	15,475
69,800	69,850	16,914	14,481	17,697	15,489
69,850	69,900	16,929	14,495	17,713	15,503
69,900	69,950	16,945	14,509	17,728	15,517
69,950	70,000	16,960	14,523	17,744	15,531
70,000					
70,000	70,050	16,976	14,537	17,759	15,545
70,050	70,100	16,991	14,551	17,775	15,559
70,100	70,150	17,007	14,565	17,790	15,573
70,150	70,200	17,022	14,579	17,806	15,587
70,200	70,250	17,038	14,593	17,821	15,601
70,250	70,300	17,053	14,607	17,837	15,615
70,300	70,350	17,069	14,621	17,852	15,629
70,350	70,400	17,084	14,635	17,868	15,643
70,400	70,450	17,100	14,649	17,883	15,657
70,450	70,500	17,115	14,663	17,899	15,671
70,500	70,550	17,131	14,677	17,914	15,685
70,550	70,600	17,146	14,691	17,930	15,699
70,600	70,650	17,162	14,705	17,945	15,713
70,650	70,700	17,177	14,719	17,961	15,727
70,700	70,750	17,193	14,733	17,976	15,741
70,750	70,800	17,208	14,747	17,992	15,755
70,800	70,850	17,224	14,761	18,007	15,769
70,850	70,900	17,239	14,775	18,023	15,783
70,900	70,950	17,255	14,789	18,038	15,797
70,950	71,000	17,270	14,803	18,054	15,811

Middle panel

If line 37 (taxable income) is— At least	But less than	Single	Married filing jointly *	Married filing separately	Head of a household
71,000					
71,000	71,050	17,286	14,817	18,069	15,825
71,050	71,100	17,301	14,831	18,085	15,839
71,100	71,150	17,317	14,845	18,100	15,853
71,150	71,200	17,332	14,859	18,116	15,867
71,200	71,250	17,348	14,873	18,131	15,881
71,250	71,300	17,363	14,887	18,147	15,895
71,300	71,350	17,379	14,901	18,162	15,909
71,350	71,400	17,394	14,915	18,178	15,923
71,400	71,450	17,410	14,929	18,193	15,937
71,450	71,500	17,425	14,943	18,209	15,951
71,500	71,550	17,441	14,957	18,224	15,965
71,550	71,600	17,456	14,971	18,240	15,979
71,600	71,650	17,472	14,985	18,255	15,993
71,650	71,700	17,487	14,999	18,271	16,007
71,700	71,750	17,503	15,013	18,286	16,021
71,750	71,800	17,518	15,027	18,302	16,035
71,800	71,850	17,534	15,041	18,318	16,049
71,850	71,900	17,549	15,055	18,336	16,063
71,900	71,950	17,565	15,069	18,354	16,077
71,950	72,000	17,580	15,083	18,372	16,091
72,000					
72,000	72,050	17,596	15,097	18,390	16,105
72,050	72,100	17,611	15,111	18,408	16,119
72,100	72,150	17,627	15,125	18,426	16,133
72,150	72,200	17,642	15,139	18,444	16,147
72,200	72,250	17,658	15,153	18,462	16,161
72,250	72,300	17,673	15,167	18,480	16,175
72,300	72,350	17,689	15,181	18,498	16,189
72,350	72,400	17,704	15,195	18,516	16,203
72,400	72,450	17,720	15,209	18,534	16,217
72,450	72,500	17,735	15,223	18,552	16,231
72,500	72,550	17,751	15,237	18,570	16,245
72,550	72,600	17,766	15,251	18,588	16,259
72,600	72,650	17,782	15,265	18,606	16,273
72,650	72,700	17,797	15,279	18,624	16,287
72,700	72,750	17,813	15,293	18,642	16,301
72,750	72,800	17,828	15,307	18,660	16,315
72,800	72,850	17,844	15,321	18,678	16,329
72,850	72,900	17,859	15,335	18,696	16,343
72,900	72,950	17,875	15,349	18,714	16,357
72,950	73,000	17,890	15,363	18,732	16,371
73,000					
73,000	73,050	17,906	15,377	18,750	16,385
73,050	73,100	17,921	15,391	18,768	16,399
73,100	73,150	17,937	15,405	18,786	16,413
73,150	73,200	17,952	15,419	18,804	16,427
73,200	73,250	17,968	15,433	18,822	16,441
73,250	73,300	17,983	15,447	18,840	16,455
73,300	73,350	17,999	15,461	18,858	16,469
73,350	73,400	18,014	15,475	18,876	16,483
73,400	73,450	18,030	15,489	18,894	16,497
73,450	73,500	18,045	15,503	18,912	16,511
73,500	73,550	18,061	15,517	18,930	16,525
73,550	73,600	18,076	15,531	18,948	16,539
73,600	73,650	18,092	15,545	18,966	16,553
73,650	73,700	18,107	15,559	18,984	16,567
73,700	73,750	18,123	15,573	19,002	16,581
73,750	73,800	18,138	15,587	19,020	16,595
73,800	73,850	18,154	15,601	19,038	16,609
73,850	73,900	18,169	15,615	19,056	16,623
73,900	73,950	18,185	15,629	19,074	16,637
73,950	74,000	18,200	15,643	19,092	16,651

Right panel

If line 37 (taxable income) is— At least	But less than	Single	Married filing jointly *	Married filing separately	Head of a household
74,000					
74,000	74,050	18,216	15,657	19,110	16,665
74,050	74,100	18,231	15,671	19,128	16,679
74,100	74,150	18,247	15,685	19,146	16,693
74,150	74,200	18,262	15,699	19,164	16,707
74,200	74,250	18,278	15,713	19,182	16,721
74,250	74,300	18,293	15,727	19,200	16,735
74,300	74,350	18,309	15,741	19,218	16,749
74,350	74,400	18,324	15,755	19,236	16,763
74,400	74,450	18,340	15,769	19,254	16,777
74,450	74,500	18,355	15,783	19,272	16,791
74,500	74,550	18,371	15,797	19,290	16,805
74,550	74,600	18,386	15,811	19,308	16,819
74,600	74,650	18,402	15,825	19,326	16,833
74,650	74,700	18,417	15,839	19,344	16,847
74,700	74,750	18,433	15,853	19,362	16,861
74,750	74,800	18,448	15,867	19,380	16,875
74,800	74,850	18,464	15,881	19,398	16,889
74,850	74,900	18,479	15,895	19,416	16,903
74,900	74,950	18,495	15,909	19,434	16,917
74,950	75,000	18,510	15,923	19,452	16,931
75,000					
75,000	75,050	18,526	15,937	19,470	16,945
75,050	75,100	18,541	15,951	19,488	16,959
75,100	75,150	18,557	15,965	19,506	16,973
75,150	75,200	18,572	15,979	19,524	16,987
75,200	75,250	18,588	15,993	19,542	17,001
75,250	75,300	18,603	16,007	19,560	17,015
75,300	75,350	18,619	16,021	19,578	17,029
75,350	75,400	18,634	16,035	19,596	17,043
75,400	75,450	18,650	16,049	19,614	17,057
75,450	75,500	18,665	16,063	19,632	17,071
75,500	75,550	18,681	16,077	19,650	17,085
75,550	75,600	18,696	16,091	19,668	17,099
75,600	75,650	18,712	16,105	19,686	17,113
75,650	75,700	18,727	16,119	19,704	17,127
75,700	75,750	18,743	16,133	19,722	17,141
75,750	75,800	18,758	16,147	19,740	17,155
75,800	75,850	18,774	16,161	19,758	17,169
75,850	75,900	18,789	16,175	19,776	17,183
75,900	75,950	18,805	16,189	19,794	17,197
75,950	76,000	18,820	16,203	19,812	17,211
76,000					
76,000	76,050	18,836	16,217	19,830	17,225
76,050	76,100	18,851	16,231	19,848	17,239
76,100	76,150	18,867	16,245	19,866	17,253
76,150	76,200	18,882	16,259	19,884	17,267
76,200	76,250	18,898	16,273	19,902	17,281
76,250	76,300	18,913	16,287	19,920	17,295
76,300	76,350	18,929	16,301	19,938	17,309
76,350	76,400	18,944	16,315	19,956	17,323
76,400	76,450	18,960	16,329	19,974	17,337
76,450	76,500	18,975	16,343	19,992	17,351
76,500	76,550	18,991	16,357	20,010	17,365
76,550	76,600	19,006	16,371	20,028	17,379
76,600	76,650	19,022	16,385	20,046	17,393
76,650	76,700	19,037	16,399	20,064	17,407
76,700	76,750	19,053	16,413	20,082	17,421
76,750	76,800	19,068	16,427	20,100	17,435
76,800	76,850	19,084	16,441	20,118	17,449
76,850	76,900	19,099	16,455	20,136	17,463
76,900	76,950	19,115	16,469	20,154	17,477
76,950	77,000	19,130	16,483	20,172	17,491

* This column must also be used by a qualifying widow(er).

Continued on next page

1995 Tax Rate Schedules

Caution: Use **only** if your taxable income (Form 1040, line 37) is $100,000 or more. If less, use the **Tax Table.** Even though you cannot use the tax rate schedules below if your taxable income is less than $100,000, all levels of taxable income are shown so taxpayers can see the tax rate that applies to each level.

Schedule X—Use if your filing status is **Single**

If the amount on Form 1040, line 37, is: Over—	But not over—	Enter on Form 1040, line 38		of the amount over—
$0	$23,350	.... 15%		$0
23,350	56,550	$3,502.50 +	28%	23,350
56,550	117,950	12,798.50 +	31%	56,550
117,950	256,500	31,832.50 +	36%	117,950
256,500	....	81,710.50 +	39.6%	256,500

Schedule Y-1—Use if your filing status is **Married filing jointly** or **Qualifying widow(er)**

If the amount on Form 1040, line 37, is: Over—	But not over—	Enter on Form 1040, line 38		of the amount over—
$0	$39,000	.... 15%		$0
39,000	94,250	$5,850.00 +	28%	39,000
94,250	143,600	21,320.00 +	31%	94,250
143,600	256,500	36,618.50 +	36%	143,600
256,500	....	77,262.50 +	39.6%	256,500

Schedule Y-2—Use if your filing status is **Married filing separately**

If the amount on Form 1040, line 37, is: Over—	But not over—	Enter on Form 1040, line 38		of the amount over—
$0	$19,500	.... 15%		$0
19,500	47,125	$2,925.00 +	28%	19,500
47,125	71,800	10,660.00 +	31%	47,125
71,800	128,250	18,309.25 +	36%	71,800
128,250	....	38,631.25 +	39.6%	128,250

Schedule Z—Use if your filing status is **Head of household**

If the amount on Form 1040, line 37, is: Over—	But not over—	Enter on Form 1040, line 38		of the amount over—
$0	$31,250	.... 15%		$0
31,250	80,750	$4,687.50 +	28%	31,250
80,750	130,800	18,547.50 +	31%	80,750
130,800	256,500	34,063.00 +	36%	130,800
256,500	....	79,315.00 +	39.6%	256,500

EXHIBIT 18-4 TAX RATE SCHEDULES T

EXAMPLE

**Nathan Hemingway is single with taxable income of $37,440. Use the Tax Table, Exhibit
18-3, to calculate Nathan's tax liability.**

SOLUTION STRATEGY

Step 1. From the Tax Table, Exhibit 18-3, we read down the "If line 37 (taxable income) is —"
column to find Nathan's taxable income, $37,440, listed between 37,400 and 37,450.

Step 2. Scan across the "And you are—Single" column to locate Nathan's tax liability, $7,444.

TRY-IT   EXERCISE

**8. John Coleman and his wife, Louise, had taxable income last year amounting to
$32,113. The Colemans' filing status is married, filing jointly. Using the Tax Table, de-
termine their tax liability.**

Check your answer with the solution on page 619.

18-9 Using the Tax Rate Schedule to Determine Tax Liability

If taxable income is $100,000 or more, the appropriate Tax Rate Schedule must be used to
calculate the tax liability. Exhibit 18-4 contains the 1995 Tax Rate Schedules.

Maybelline Wiliams had taxable income last year of $121,334. For income tax purposes she files as married, filing separately. Use the appropriate Tax Rate Schedule to calculate her tax liability.

SOLUTION STRATEGY

Step 1. Since Maybelline files as married, filing separately, we shall use Tax Rate Schedule Y-2.

Step 2. Reading down the "If the amount on Form 1040, line 37, is:" column, we find Maybelline's taxable income in the range "Over $71,800, but not over $128,250."

Step 3.

121,334.00	Taxable income
− 71,800.00	Lower number of the range
49,534.00	

Step 4.

49,534.00	Result from Step 3
× .36	Tax rate for that range
$17,832.24	

Step 5.

17,832.24	Result from Step 4
+ 18,309.25	Dollar amount of tax indicated for that range
$36,141.49	Tax liability

TRY-IT   EXERCISE

9. Chuck Wells had taxable income of $109,706 last year. If he files as head of household, what is his tax liability?

Check your answer with the solution on page 619.

18-10 Calculating an Individual's Tax Refund or Amount of Tax Owed

Once the tax liability has been determined, we must consider the final three items in income tax preparation: tax credits, other taxes, and payments. The following formula is used to complete the tax preparation process. Note: When the result is a positive number, it is the amount of tax owed. When the result is a negative number, it indicates a tax overpayment by that amount. When an overpayment occurs, the taxpayer has the option of receiving a refund or applying the amount of the overpayment to next year's estimated tax.

Refund (−) or amount owed (+) = Tax liability − Credits + Other taxes − Payments

● tax credit

Dollar-for-dollar subtractions from an individual's or corporation's tax liability. Some examples for individuals would be the credit for child and dependent care expenses, the credit for the elderly or disabled, and the foreign tax credit.

Tax credits   Tax credits are a dollar-for-dollar subtraction from the tax liability. A **tax credit** of one dollar saves a full dollar in taxes, whereas a tax deduction of one dollar results in less than a dollar in tax savings (the amount depends on the tax rate). Some examples are credit for child and dependent care expenses; credit for the elderly or disabled; and the foreign tax credit.

Other taxes   In addition to the tax liability from the Tax Table or Tax Rate Schedules, other taxes may also be due. These taxes are added to the tax liability. Some examples would be self-employment taxes and Social Security and Medicare taxes on tip income.

Payments   This calculation involves subtracting payments such as employees' federal income tax withheld by employers, estimated tax payments made quarterly, excess Social Security and Medicare paid, and the Earned Income Credit (considered a payment). The Earned Income Credit is available to those taxpayers with a child and adjusted gross income of less than $23,050.

STEPS TO CALCULATE AN INDIVIDUAL'S TAX REFUND OR AMOUNT OF TAX OWED:

Step 1. Subtract total credits from the tax liability.

Step 2. Add total of other taxes to the tax liability to get total tax.

Step 3. If total payments are greater than total tax, a refund of the difference is due. If total payments are less than total tax, the difference is the tax owed.

EXAMPLE

After preparing her taxes for last year, Pat Reese determined that she had a tax liability of $5,326. In addition, she owed other taxes of $575. Because of her mother, Pat was entitled to a credit for the elderly of $1,412. If her employer withheld $510 from her paycheck each month, is Pat entitled to a refund or does she owe additional taxes? How much?

SOLUTION STRATEGY

Steps 1 & 2.

$5,326	Tax liability
− 1,412	Tax credits
+ 575	Other taxes
$4,489	Total tax owed

Step 3. Payments: Federal income tax withheld was $510 × 12 months = $6,120.

$6,120	Payments
− 4,489	Total tax
1,631	Overpayment

Since Pat's payments are greater than her total tax owed, she has made an overpayment by the amount of the difference, and is therefore entitled to a tax refund of $1,631.

TRY-IT   EXERCISE

10. **Lamar Walton had a tax liability of $14,600 last year. In addition, he owed other taxes of $2,336. He was entitled to a credit for child care of $668 and a foreign tax credit of $1,719. If Lamar's employer withheld $270 per week for 52 weeks, does Lamar qualify for a refund or owe more taxes? How much?**

Check your answer with the solution on page 619.

18-11 Calculating Corporate Income Tax and Net Income after Taxes

Just as with individuals, corporations are also taxable entities that must file tax returns and are taxed directly on their earnings. In Chapter 15, we learned to prepare a balance sheet and an income statement based on the operating figures of a company over a period of time. At the bottom of the income statement the net income before taxes was determined. Now let's use

● Corporate Tax Rate Schedule

The IRS chart used to calculate the amount of income tax due from corporations.

the 1995 **Corporate Tax Rate Schedule,** Exhibit 18-5 below, to figure the amount of corporate income tax due.

EXHIBIT 18-5

CORPORATE TAX RATE SCHEDULE

Tax Rate Schedule

If taxable income (line 30, Form 1120, or line 26, Form 1120-A) on page 1 is:

Over—	But not over—	Tax is:	Of the amount over—
$0	$50,000	15%	$0
50,000	75,000	**$7,500 + 25%**	50,000
75,000	100,000	**13,750 + 34%**	75,000
100,000	335,000	**22,250 + 39%**	100,000
335,000	10,000,000	**113,900 + 34%**	335,000
10,000,000	15,000,000	**3,400,000 + 35%**	10,000,000
15,000,000	18,333,333	**5,150,000 + 38%**	15,000,000
18,333,333	- - - - -	35%	0

STEPS TO CALCULATE CORPORATE INCOME TAX AND NET INCOME AFTER TAXES:

Step 1. Using the Corporate Tax Rate Schedule, read down the "Over—" and "But not over—" columns to find the range containing the taxable income of the corporation.

Step 2. Subtract the lower number of the range from the taxable income.

Step 3. Multiply the result from Step 2 by the tax rate listed for that range.

Step 4. Calculate the tax liability by adding the result from Step 3 to the dollar amount of tax indicated for that range.

Step 5. Calculate income after taxes by subtracting the tax liability from the net income before taxes.

EXAMPLE

The Strand Corporation had net income before taxes of $7,550,000. Use the Corporate Tax Rate Schedule to calculate the amount of income tax due. Also calculate the company's net income after taxes.

SOLUTION STRATEGY

Step 1. Strand's net income falls in the range 335,000 to 10,000,000.

Step 2.

7,550,000	Income before taxes
− 335,000	Lower number of the range
7,215,000	

Step 3.

7,215,000	Step 2 result
× .34	Tax rate for that range
2,453,100	

Step 4.

2,453,100	Result from Step 3
+ 113,900	Dollar amount of tax indicated for that range
$2,567,000	Tax liability

Step 5.

7,550,000	Income before taxes
− 2,567,000	Tax liability
$4,983,000	Net income after taxes

TRY-IT EXERCISE

11. The Bar BQ Barn had taxable income of $311,200 last year. Use the Corporate Tax Rate Schedule to calculate the amount of income tax due. Also, calculate the company's net income after taxes.

Check your answers with the solutions on page 619.

REVIEW EXERCISES CHAPTER 18—SECTION III

As a tax return preparer for The Walzer Tax & Accounting Service, you have been asked to calculate the missing information for eight of the firm's tax clients:

	Name	Filing Status (exemptions)	Income	Adjustments to Income	Adjusted Gross Income	Standard Deduction	Itemized Deductions	Exemption Allowance	Taxable Income
						(circle your choice)			
1.	Roman	Single (1)	$34,300	$2,120	$32,180	$3,900	($4,450)	2,500	$25,230
2.	Wilson	Married filing jointly (3)	48,472	1,244	$47,228	(6,550)	5,329	7,500	33,178
3.	Kirk	Qualifying widow (2)	45,670	1,760	43,910	(6,550)	3,870	5,000	32,360
4.	Bright	Single (2)	54,700	3,410	51,290	(3,900)	1,860	5,000	42,390
5.	Garcia	Married filing separately (2)	66,210	6,780	59,430	(3,275)	2,245	5,000	51,155
6.	Haines	Married filing jointly (5)	52,130	1,450	50,680	(6,550)	5,610	12,500	31,630
7.	Lee	Head of household (3)	88,600	4,080	84,520	5,750	(21,230)	7,500	55,790
8.	Montero	Married filing jointly (4)	38,246	696	37,550	6,550	(8,400)	10,000	19,150

9. Maria Barrios sells wholesale school supplies for Crayola Corporation. She is single, claiming three exemptions. For income tax purposes, she qualifies as a head of household. Last year she earned a total of $54,330 in salary and commission. She contributed $2,500 to her retirement plan and had the following itemized deductions: $1,231 in real estate taxes, $3,450 in mortgage interest, $2,000 in mortgage loan closing points, $420 in charitable contributions, and $3,392 in unreimbursed job expenses above the 2% adjusted gross income exclusion. From this information, calculate Maria's taxable income.

Total income =	54,300.00	Itemized deductions =	1,231.00	Exemptions = 2,500 × 3 = $7,500
Adjustments	−2,500.00		3,450.00	$51,800.00
Adjusted Gross income	$51,800.00		2,000.00	− 10,493.00 Itemized deductions
			420.00	− 7,500.00 Exemptions
			+3,392.00	$33,807.00 Taxable income
			$10,493.00	

Use the Tax Table, Exhibit 18-3, to calculate the tax liability for the following taxpayers earning under $100,000:

	Name	Filing Status	Taxable Income	Tax Liability
10.	Randall	Married, Separately	$27,665	$5,214.00
11.	Denner	Head of household	74,804	16,889.00
12.	Butler	Single	38,150	7,654.00
13.	Mesa	Married, Jointly	69,915	14,509.00

Use the Tax Rate Schedules, Exhibit 18-4, to calculate the tax liability for the following taxpayers earning $100,000 or above:

Name	Filing Status	Taxable Income	Tax Liability
14. Crenshaw	Married, Jointly	$121,430	$29,745.80
15. Brandon	Single	247,619	$78,513.34
16. Lowell	Head of household	185,188	$53,642.68
17. Perez	Married, Separately	334,515	$120,312.19

14. 121,430.00 − 94,250.00 = 27,180.00
   21,320.00 + 31% (27,180.00)
   21,320.00 + 8,425.80 = $29,745.80

15. 247,619.00 − 117,950.00 = 129,669.00
   31,832.50 + 36% (129,669.00)
   31,832.50 + 46,680.84 = $78,513.34

16. 185,188.00 − 130,800.00 = 54,388.00
   34,063.00 + 36%(54,388.00)
   34,063.00 + 19,579.68 = $53,642.68

17. 334,515.00 − 128,250.00 = 206,265.00
   38,631.25 + 39.6%(206,265.00)
   38,631.25 + 81,680.94 = $120,312.19

As a newly hired IRS trainee, you have been asked to calculate the amount of tax refund or tax owed for the following taxpayers:

Name	Tax Liability	Tax Credits	Other Taxes	Payments	Refund/Owe (circle one)	Amount
18. Grant	$5,320	$2,110	$325	$4,650	(Refund)/Owe	$1,115.00
19. Stonewall	3,229	750	0	3,130	(Refund)/Owe	651.00
20. Gonzalez	12,280	2,453	1,232	9,540	Refund/(Owe)	1,519.00
21. Youmans	6,498	1,221	885	7,600	(Refund)/Owe	1,438.00

22. Peter and Christina Anderson had combined income of $107,320 last year. For tax purposes the Andersons claim 4 exemptions and their filing status is married, filing jointly. They contributed $5,000 to their retirement plan and had total itemized deductions of $17,200. In addition, the Andersons had a tax credit for the disabled of $3,430. If their combined income tax withheld last year amounted to $12,887, calculate:

a. Adjusted gross income.
   107,320 Income
   − 5,000 Retirement plan
   $102,320 Adjusted gross income

b. Taxable income.
   $102,320 Adjusted gross income
   − 10,000 (4 × 2,500) Exemption allowance
   − 17,200 Itemized deductions
   $75,120 Taxable income

c. Tax liability.
   $15,965 Tax (tax table)
   − 3,430 Tax credit for disabled
   $12,535 Tax liability

d. Are the Andersons entitled to a refund or do they owe additional taxes? How much?
   $12,887 Tax withheld
   −12,535 Tax liability
   $352 Refund

Calculate the amount of corporate income tax due and the net income after taxes for the following corporations:

Name	Taxable Income	Tax Liability	Net Income after Taxes
23. Northwest Supply, Inc.	$88,955	$18,494.70	$70,460.30
24. Grambling Corp.	14,550,000	4,992,500.00	9,557,500.00
25. Kmart, Inc.	955,000,000	334,250,000.00	620,750,000.00

CHAPTER 18 ■ TAXES

FORMULAS

Sales and Excise Taxes

Sales tax = Selling price × Sales tax rate

Total purchase price = Selling price + Sales tax + Other charges

$$\text{Selling price} = \frac{\text{Total purchase price}}{100\% + \text{Sales tax rate}}$$

Sales tax = Total purchase price − Selling price

Excise tax = Selling price × Excise tax rate

Excise tax = Number of units × Excise tax per unit

Total purchase price = Selling price + Sales tax + Excise tax

Property Tax

a. Expressed as a Percent

Property tax = Assessed value of property × Tax rate

b. Expressed per $100 of Assessed Value

Property tax = Number of $100 of assessed value × Tax per $100

c. Expressed per $1,000 of Assessed Value

Property tax = Number of $1,000 of assessed value × Tax per $1,000

d. Expressed in Mills

Tax rate in decimal form = Tax rate in mills × .001

Property tax = Assessed value × Tax rate in decimal form

Community Tax Rate

$$\text{Tax rate per dollar (decimal form)} = \frac{\text{Total taxes required}}{\text{Total assessed property value}}$$

Income Tax

Refund (−) or amount owed (+) = Tax liability − Credits + Other taxes − Payments

---

CHAPTER 18 ■ TAXES	SUMMARY CHART

SECTION I   SALES AND EXCISE TAXES

Topic	P/O, Page	Important Concepts	Illustrative Examples
Determining Sales Tax Using Sales Tax Tables	18–1 587	Sales tax is a tax based on the total retail price of tangible personal property and certain services and admissions. Exhibit 18–1 is an example of a $6\frac{1}{2}\%$ sales tax table. *Sales tax tables* 1. Locate the taxable retail price in the Amount of Sale column. 2. Scan to the right to locate the amount of tax due in the Tax column.	Bill Gates purchased 3 rolls of film at The Shutterbug for a total of $16.23. The sales tax in that state is $6\frac{1}{2}\%$. Use Exhibit 18-1 to determine the amount of sales tax due on this sale. From Exhibit 18-1 we find that the retail price of the film, $16.23, falls in the range of $16.16 to $16.30. Scanning to the right, we find the tax due on this sale is $1.06.

I, continued

Topic	P/O, Page	Important Concepts	Illustrative Examples
Calculating Sales Tax Using the Percent Method	18–2 588	Sales tax is expressed as a percentage of the retail selling price. *Percent Method* 1. Calculate the sales tax by multiplying the retail selling price by the sales tax rate: Sales tax = Selling price × Sales tax rate 2. Compute total purchase price by adding the selling price, the sales tax, and any other additional charges: $\dfrac{\text{Total purchase}}{\text{price}} = \dfrac{\text{Selling}}{\text{price}} + \dfrac{\text{Sales}}{\text{tax}} + \dfrac{\text{Other}}{\text{charges}}$	Bob Rich purchased a barbecue grill for \$179.95 at JCPenney. The store charged \$12.00 for assembly. If the state sales tax is 4% and the city adds an additional $3\frac{1}{2}\%$, what is the amount of sales tax on the grill and what is Bob's total purchase price? Sales tax rate = $4 + 3\frac{1}{2} = 7\frac{1}{2}\%$ Sales tax = 179.95 × .075 = \$13.50 Total purchase price = 179.95 + 13.50 + 12.00 = \$205.45
Calculating Selling Price and Amount of Sales Tax When Total Purchase Price Is Known	18–3 589	When the total purchase price of an item or items, including sales tax, is known, actual selling price and amount of sales tax is calculated by: 1. Calculate the selling price of an item by dividing the total purchase price by 100% plus the sales tax rate: $\text{Selling price} = \dfrac{\text{Total purchase price}}{100\% + \text{Sales tax rate}}$ 2. Determine the amount of sales tax by subtracting the selling price from the total purchase price: Sales tax = Total purchase price − Selling price	At the end of the day, the cash register at Winkler's Knitting Salon showed total purchases, including sales tax, of \$2,251.83. If the sales tax rate in that state is 5%, calculate Winkler's actual sales revenue and sales tax collected. Sales revenue = $\dfrac{2{,}251.83}{1.05} = \$2{,}144.60$ Sales tax = 2,251.83 − 2,144.60 = \$107.23
Calculating Excise Tax	18–4 589	An excise tax is a tax levied by federal, state, and local governments on certain products and services deemed to be luxury or nonessential items. Excise tax is paid in addition to sales tax and is expressed as a percentage of the purchase price or as a fixed amount per unit purchased. *Percentage:* Excise tax = Selling price × Excise tax rate *Per Unit:* Excise tax = Units × Excise tax per unit	Larry Limbaugh purchased fishing equipment for \$244.00. The sales tax in his state is 4% and the federal excise tax on fishing equipment is 11%. What is the amount of each tax and the total purchase price of the equipment? Sales tax = 244.00 × .04 = \$9.76 Excise tax = 244.00 × .11 = \$26.84 Total purchase price = 244.00 + 9.76 + 26.84 = \$280.60

SECTION II PROPERTY TAX

Topic	P/O, Page	Important Concepts	Illustrative Examples
Calculating Property Tax Due with Tax Rate Expressed **a. As a Percent**	18–5a 593	A tax levied on the assessed value of real and certain personal property is known as property tax. *Expressed as a percent* 1. Convert the tax rate to a decimal. 2. Calculate property tax: **Property tax = Assessed value × Tax rate**	A house with an assessed value of $120,000 is subject to a property tax of 2.31%. What is the amount of property tax due? Property tax = 120,000 × .0231 = $2,772
b. Per $100 of Assessed Value	18–5b 594	*Per $100 of assessed value* 1. Calculate number of $100: $$\text{Number of \$100} = \frac{\text{Assessed value}}{100}$$ 2. Calculate property tax: **Property tax = Number of $100 × Tax per $100**	A house with an assessed value of $120,000 is subject to a property tax of $2.31 per $100 of assessed value. What is the amount of property tax due? Number of $100 = $$\frac{120,000}{100} = 1,200$$ Property tax = 1,200 × 2.31 = $2,772
c. Per $1,000 of Assessed Value	18–5c 594	*Per $1,000 of assessed value* 1. Calculate number of $1,000: $$\text{Number of \$1,000} = \frac{\text{Assessed value}}{1,000}$$ 2. Calculate property tax: **Property tax = Number of $1,000 × Tax per $1,000**	A house with an assessed value of $120,000 is subject to a property tax of $23.10 per $1,000 of assessed value. What is the amount of property tax due? Number of $1,000 = $$\frac{120,000}{1,000} = 120$$ Property tax = 120 × 23.10 = $2,772
d. In Mills	18–5d 595	*Expressed in mills* 1. Multiply tax rate in mills by .001 to get tax rate as a decimal: **Tax rate (decimal) = Tax rate in mills × .001** 2. Calculate property tax: **Property tax = Assessed value × Tax rate**	A house with an assessed value of $120,000 is subject to a property tax of 23.1 mills. What is the amount of property tax due? Tax rate (decimal) = 23.1 × .001 = .0231 Property tax = 120,000 × .0231 = $2,772
Calculating Tax Rate Necessary in a Community to Meet Budgetary Demands	18–6 596	1. Tax rate per dollar of assessed value = $$\frac{\text{Total taxes required}}{\text{Total assessed property value}}$$	A town requires $5,000,000 for its annual budget. If the total assessed property value of the town is $80,000,000, what property tax rate is needed to meet those demands? Express your answer in each of the four ways.

II, continued

Topic	P/O, Page	Important Concepts	Illustrative Examples
		2. To convert tax rate per dollar to: a. *Percent*—move the decimal point 2 places to the right and add a percent sign. b. *Tax rate per $100*—multiply by 100. c. *Tax rate per $1,000*—multiply by 1,000. d. *Mills—divide by .001.*	$\text{Tax rate} = \dfrac{5,000,000}{80,000,000} = .0625$ $\text{Percent} = \underline{6.25\%}$ Per $100 = $.0625 \times 100 = \underline{\$6.25 \text{ per } \$100}$ Per $1,000 = $.0625 \times 1,000 = \underline{\$62.50 \text{ per } \$1,000}$ $\text{Mills} = \dfrac{.0625}{.001} = \underline{62.5 \text{ mills}}$

SECTION III   INCOME TAX

Topic	P/O, Page	Important Concepts	Illustrative Examples
Computing Taxable Income for Individuals	18–7 599	Taxable income is the amount of income that tax rates are applied to in order to calculate the amount of tax owed for the year. Use Exhibit 18–2 and the following steps to compute taxable income. 1. Determine *gross income* by adding all sources of taxable income. 2. Calculate *adjusted gross income* by subtracting the sum of all adjustments to income from the gross income. 3. Subtract the sum of the *itemized deductions* or the *standard deduction* (whichever is larger) from the adjusted gross income. See Step 3, page 716, for standard deduction amounts. 4. If adjusted gross income is $86,025 or less, multiply $2,500 by the number of exemptions claimed and subtract from the amount in Step 3. The result is *taxable income.* For adjusted gross incomes over $86,025 see IRS instructions to find exemption amounts.	Richard and Cindy Greer are married. For income tax purposes they file jointly and claim 4 exemptions. Last year they earned a total of $45,460. They had adjustments to income of $3,241, and itemized deductions of $8,776. What is the amount of their taxable income? $45,460 Total income – 3,241 Adjustments to income $42,219 Adjusted gross income Since the itemized deductions are greater than the $6,550 allowed as the standard deduction for married, filing jointly, we shall use the itemized figure. The exemption allowance is 2,500 × 4 = $10,000. $42,219 Adjusted gross income – 8,776 Itemized deductions –10,000 Exemption allowance $23,443 Taxable income
Using the Tax Table to Determine Personal Income Tax Liability	18–8 601	If taxable income is under $100,000, the Tax Table must be used to figure the tax liability. Exhibit 18–3 illustrates a portion of the 1995 Tax Table. 1. Read down the "If line 37 (taxable income) is—" columns and find the line that includes the amount of taxable income. 2. Find the tax liability by scanning across to the "And you are—" column containing the appropriate filing status.	Laurenzo Picata files his taxes as a head of household. If his taxable income last year was $35,552, what was his tax liability? From Exhibit 18-3, we find Laurenzo's taxable income in the range 35,550 to 35,600. Scanning across to the Head of Household column, we find that Laurenzo's tax liability is $5,899.

III, continued

Topic	P/O, Page	Important Concepts	Illustrative Examples
Using the Tax Rate Schedule to Calculate Personal Income Tax Liability	18–9 607	When taxable income is $100,000 or more, the appropriate Tax Rate Schedule must be used to calculate the tax liability. Exhibit 18–4 contains the 1995 Tax Rate Schedules. 1. Locate the tax rate schedule corresponding to the appropriate filing status. 2. Read down the first column to find the range containing the taxable income. 3. Subtract the lower number of the range from the taxable income. 4. Multiply the result from Step 3 by the tax rate listed for that range. 5. Calculate tax liability by adding the result from Step 4 to the dollar amount of tax indicated for that range.	Albert Hall had taxable income last year of $145,000. For income tax purposes he files as married, filing separately. Use the appropriate Tax Rate Schedule to calculate his tax liability. *Step 1.* For Albert's filing status, we shall use Schedule Y-2. *Step 2.* His taxable income is in the last range, "128,250 to —" *Step 3.* $145,000 Taxable income −128,250 Lower number of range 16,750 *Step 4.* $16,750　Result from Step 3 × .396　Tax rate for that range 6,633 *Step 5.* $6,633.00　Result from Step 4 + 38,631.25　Dollar amount $45,264.25　Tax liability
Calculating Tax Refund or Income Tax Owed	18–10 608	To calculate the refund or tax owed, we must finally consider tax credits, other taxes, and payments. 1. Subtract total credits from the tax liability. 2. Add total of other taxes to the tax liability to get total tax. 3. If total payments are greater than total tax, a refund of the difference is due. If total payments are less than total tax, the difference is the tax owed.	After preparing his taxes, Gene Hamilton determined that he had a tax liability of $7,370. In addition, he owed other taxes of $1,225 and was entitled to a tax credit of $3,420. If Gene's employer withheld $445 each month for income tax, is Gene entitled to a refund or does he owe additional taxes? How much? $7,370　Tax liability − 3,420　Tax credits + 1,225　Other taxes $5,175　Total tax Payments = 445 × 12 = $5,340 $5,340　Payments − 5,175　Total tax $165　Tax refund due 　　　(may be applied to next year's taxes)

III, continued

Topic	P/O, Page	Important Concepts	Illustrative Examples
Calculating Corporate Income Tax and Net Income after Taxes	18–11 609	Corporate income tax is calculated using the Corporate Tax Rate Schedule, Exhibit 18–5. 1. Read down the "Over—" and "But not over—" columns to find the range containing the taxable income. 2. Subtract the lower number of the range from the taxable income. 3. Multiply the result from Step 2 by the tax rate listed for that range. 4. Calculate the tax liability by adding the result from Step 3 to the dollar amount of tax indicated for that range. 5. Calculate the net income after taxes by subtracting the tax liability from the taxable income. Net income after taxes = Income before tax – Tax liability	The Card Shop, Inc., had net income before taxes of $62,000. What is the amount of income tax due and the net income after taxes? *Step 1.* The taxable income falls in the range 50,000 to 75,000. *Step 2.* $62,000 Taxable income −50,000 Lower number of range 12,000 *Step 3.* $12,000 Result from Step 2 × .25 Tax rate for that range $3,000 *Step 4.* $3,000 Result from Step 3 + 7,500 Dollar amount $10,500 Tax liability *Step 5.* $62,000 Income before taxes − 10,500 Tax liability $51,500 Net income after taxes

TRY-IT EXERCISE   SOLUTIONS

1. From Exhibit 18-1, sales tax on $12.49 = $.82

2. Sales tax = Selling price × Sales tax rate
Sales tax = 18,600 × .08 = $1,488.00

Total purchase price = Selling price + Sales tax + Other charges
Total purchase price = 18,600 + 1,488 + 240 = $20,328.00

3. Selling price = $\dfrac{\text{Total purchase price}}{100\% + \text{Sales tax rate}}$

Selling price = $\dfrac{3,520.00}{100\% + 8\frac{1}{2}\%} = \dfrac{3,520.00}{1.085} = \$3,244.24$

Sales tax = Total purchase price − Selling price
Sales tax = 3,520.00 − 3,244.24 = $275.76

4. Sales tax = Selling price × Sales tax rate
Sales tax = 129.95 × .05 = $6.50

Excise tax = Selling price × Excise tax rate
Excise tax = 129.95 × .11 = $14.29

Total purchase price = Selling price + Sales tax + Excise tax
Total purchase price = 129.95 + 6.50 + 14.29 = $150.74

5. a. Tax rate $= 6.3\% = .063$
Property tax $=$ Assessed value $\times$ Tax rate
Property tax $= 160,000 \times .063 = \underline{\$10,080.00}$

b. Number of $\$100 = \dfrac{\text{Assessed value}}{100} = \dfrac{50,800}{100} = 508$
Property tax $=$ Number of $\$100 \times$ Tax per $\$100$
Property tax $= 508 \times 3.60 = \underline{\$1,828.80}$

c. Number of $\$1,000 = \dfrac{\text{Assessed value}}{1,000} = \dfrac{325,400}{1,000} = 325.4$
Property tax $=$ Number of $\$1,000 \times$ Tax per $\$1,000$
Property tax $= 325.4 \times 88.16 = \underline{\$28,687.26}$

d. Tax rate in decimal form $=$ Tax rate in mills $\times .001$
Tax rate in decimal form $= 54.1 \times .001 = .0541$

Property tax $=$ Assessed value $\times$ Tax rate in decimal form
Property tax $= 85,300 \times .0541 = \underline{\$4,614.73}$

6. Tax rate per dollar $= \dfrac{\text{Total tax required}}{\text{Total assessed property value}}$

Tax rate per dollar $= \dfrac{3,435,000}{71,800,000} = .0478412 = \underline{\$.0479}$

a. *Percent* $.0479 = \underline{4.79\%}$

b. *Per $100* $.0479 \times 100 = \underline{\$4.79}$

c. *Per $1000* $.0479 \times 1000 = \underline{\$47.90}$

d. *Mills* $\dfrac{.0479}{.001} = \underline{47.9 \text{ mills}}$

7.

$26,900	Wages
+ 760	Cash dividends
− 2,200	Sale of stock (loss)
$25,460	Total income

$25,460	Total income
− 2,000	Retirement contribution
$23,460	Adjusted gross income

$1,400	Medical expenses
1,920	Real estate taxes
2,550	Mortgage interest
180	Charitable contributions
$6,050	Itemized deductions

$23,460	Adjusted gross income
− 6,050	Itemized deductions
− 2,500	($2,500 × 1) exemptions
$14,910	Taxable income

8. Using Exhibit 18-3, Tax liability,
John and Louise Coleman $= \underline{\$4,819}$

9. Using Tax Rate Schedule Z, Exhibit 18-4

109,706	Taxable income
− 80,750	Lower number of range
$28,956	

28,956.00	
× .31	Tax rate for that range
8,976.36	Computed tax
+ 18,547.50	Dollar amount for that range
$27,523.86	Tax liability

10.

$14,600	Tax liability
+ 2,336	Other taxes
− 668	Child care credit
− 1,719	Foreign tax credit
$14,549	Total tax

Employer withheld $270 \times 52 = \$14,040$
Tax owed $=$ Total tax $-$ Payments
Tax owed $= 14,549 - 14,040 = \underline{\$509}$

11. Using Corporate Tax Rate Schedule, Exhibit 18-5:

$311,200	Income before taxes
− 100,000	Lower number of range
$211,200	

× .39	Tax rate
82,368	Computed tax
+ 22,250	Dollar amount for that range
$104,618	Tax liability

$311,200	Income before taxes
− 104,618	Tax liability
$206,582	Net income after tax

ANSWERS

1. ____$1.17____

____$19.05____

2. ____$.19____

____$3.09____

3. ____$6.62____

____$141.62____

4. ____$1.22____

____$1.02____

____$26.64____

5. ____$1,184.63____

____$755.00____

____$19,489.63____

6. ____$1,188.00____

____$89.10____

7. a. ____$25.42____

b. ____$471.30____

8. a. ____$15,459.02____

b. ____$1,043.48____

9. a. ____$3.83____

____$2,221.40____

Use Exhibit 18-1 to determine the sales tax and calculate the total purchase price for the following items:

Item	Selling Price	Sales Tax	Total Purchase Price
1. alarm clock	$17.88	$1.17	$19.05
2. magazine	2.90	.19	3.09

Calculate the missing information for the following purchases:

Item	Selling Price	Sales Tax Rate	Sales Tax	Excise Tax Rate	Excise Tax	Total Purchase Price
3. ceiling fan	$135.00	4.9%	$6.62	0	0	$141.62
4. cable TV bill	24.40	5	1.22	4.2	$1.02	26.64
5. fur coat	17,550	$6\frac{3}{4}$	1,184.63	10% (over $10,000)	755.00	19,489.63
6. scanner	1,188.00	$7\frac{1}{2}$	89.10	0	0	$1,277.10

7. Jim Rogers purchased a dishwasher at Sears for $345.88. The delivery charge was $25.00 and the installation amounted to $75.00. The state sales tax is $6\frac{1}{4}$% and the county tax is 1.1%.

   a. What is the total amount of sales tax on the dishwasher?

   Total tax = 345.88(6.25% + 1.1%) = $25.42

   b. What is the total purchase price?

   Total purchase price = 345.88 + 25.42 + 25.00 + 75.00
   $$= \$471.30$$

8. Last week Porch & Patio Furniture had total sales, including sales tax, of $16,502.50. The store is located in a state that has a sales tax of $6\frac{3}{4}$%. As the accountant for the store, calculate:

   a. The amount of sales revenue.

   $$\text{Sales revenue} = \frac{16{,}502.50}{100\% + 6.75\%} = \$15{,}459.02$$

   b. The amount of sales taxes that must be sent to the state Department of Revenue.

   Sales tax = 16,502.50 − 15,459.02 = $1,043.48

9. Transport Services, Inc., purchased 580 tires rated at 50 pounds each for its fleet of trucks. The tires had a retail price of $85.00 each. The sales tax is 4.5% and the federal excise tax is $.15 per pound.

   a. What are the amount of sales tax per tire and the total sales tax?

   Sales tax per tire = 85.00 × 4.5% = $3.83
   Total sales tax   = 3.83 × 580   = $2,221.40

b. What are the amount of federal excise tax per tire and the total excise tax?

Excise tax per tire = $50 \times .15$ = $\underline{\$7.50}$

Total excise tax = $7.50 \times 580 = \underline{\$4,350}$

c. What is the total purchase price of the tires?

Total purchase price = $85.00 \times 580 = 49,300$

$49,300 + 2,221.40 + 4,350.00$

$= \underline{\$55,871.40}$

Calculate the assessed value and the property tax due on the following properties:

	Fair Market Value	Assessment Rate	Assessed Value	Property Tax Rate	Property Tax Due
10.	$92,200	80%	$73,760	2.33%	$1,718.61
11.	74,430	70	52,101	$12.72 per $1,000	662.72
12.	2,450,900	100	2,450,900	$2.16 per $100	52,939.44
13.	165,230	50	82,615	28.98 mills	2,394.18

Calculate the property tax rate required to meet the budgetary demands of the following communities:

				Property Tax Rate			
Community	Total Assessed Property Valuation	Total Taxes Required	Percent	Per $100	Per $1,000	Mills
14. Cherry Hill	$860,000,000	$32,400,000	3.77	$3.77	$37.70	37.7
15. Mill Valley	438,000,000	7,200,000	1.64	1.64	16.40	16.4

16. The Valdes family is considering the purchase of a home. They have narrowed the choice down to a $162,000 home in Palm Springs and a $151,200 home in Weston. With regard to property taxes, Palm Springs has an assessment rate of 90% and a tax rate of 22.45 mills, while Weston has a 100% assessment rate and a tax rate of $2.60 per $100 of assessed value. Which house has the higher property tax, and by how much?

Palm Springs

$162,000 \times 90\% = 145,800(22.45 \times .001)$

$= \$3,273.21$

Weston is higher by $\underline{\$657.99}$

Weston

$151,200 \times 100\% = \dfrac{151,200}{100} \times 2.60$

$= \$3,931.20$

17. As the tax assessor for Golden County you have been informed that an additional $4,500,000 in taxes will be required next year for new street lighting and bridge repairs. If the total assessed value of the property in Golden County is $6,500,000,000, how much will this add to property taxes?

a. As a percent

Additional tax = $\dfrac{4,500,000}{6,500,000,000} = .00069 = \underline{0.07\%}$

b. Per $100 of assessed value

$\underline{\$.07 \text{ per } \$100}$

ANSWERS

b.	$7.50
	$4,350
c.	$55,871.40
10.	$73,760
	$1,718.61
11.	$52,101
	$662.72
12.	$2,450,900
	$52,939.44
13.	$82,615
	$2,394.18
14.	3.77
	$3.77
	$37.70
	37.7
15.	1.64
	$1.64
	$16.40
	16.4
16.	$657.99
17. a.	0.07%
b.	$.07 per $100

c. Per $1,000 of assessed value
   $.70 per $1000

d. In mills
   0.7 mills

Calculate the missing information for the following taxpayers:

Name	Filing Status (Exemptions)	Income	Adjustments to Income	Adjusted Gross Income	(circle your choice) Standard Deduction	Itemized Deductions	Exemption Allowance	Taxable Income
18. Albert	Single (1)	$34,900	$660	$34,240	$3,900	$3,980 (circled)	$2,500	$27,760
19. Stiber	Married filing jointly (3)	66,003	2,180	63,823	6,550 (circled)	3,199	7,500	49,773
20. Chong	Head of household (4)	38,100	2,450	35,650	5,750 (circled)	3,960	10,000	19,900

Use the Tax Table, Exhibit 18-3, or the Tax Rate Schedule, Exhibit 18-4, whichever is appropriate, to calculate the tax liability for the following taxpayers:

Name	Filing Status	Taxable Income	Tax Liability
21. Siemans	Head of household	$184,112	$53,255.32
22. Jones	Single	70,890	$17,239.00
23. Gomez	Married, Jointly	24,938	$3,739.00
24. Williams	Head of household	125,202	$32,327.62
25. Herbert	Married, Separately	213,280	$72,303.13
26. Cuesta	Single	38,216	$7,668.00

18. _____Taxable: $27,760_____

19. _____Taxable: $49,773_____

20. _____Taxable: $19,900_____

21. _____$53,255.32_____

22. _____$17,239_____

23. _____$3,739_____

24. _____$32,327.62_____

25. _____$72,303.13_____

26. _____$7,668_____

27. _____Owe, $228.00_____

28. _____Refund, $1,527.00_____

29. a. _____$33,650_____

b. _____$24,750_____

Calculate the amount of tax refund or tax owed for the following taxpayers:

Name	Tax Liability	Tax Credits	Other Taxes	Payments	(circle one) Refund/Owe	Amount
27. Brown	$6,540	$1,219	0	$5,093	Refund/Owe (Owe circled)	$228.00
28. Mager	25,112	7,650	2,211	21,200	Refund/Owe (Refund circled)	1,527.00

29. Sam Duque is the promotions director for Power 96, a local radio station. He is single and claims two exemptions. Last year Sam earned a salary of $2,450 per month from the station and received a $1,000 Christmas bonus. In addition, he earned royalties of $3,250 from a song he wrote, which was recorded and made popular by a famous musical group. Sam's itemized deductions amounted to $1,850 and he is entitled to a tax credit of $1,765. If the radio station withheld $325 per month for income tax, what is Sam's:

a. Adjusted gross income?
   $29,400 (2,450 × 12) Income
   + 1,000 Bonus
   + 3,250 Royalties
   $33,650 Adjusted gross income

b. Taxable income?
   33,650 Adjusted gross income
   − 3,900 Standard deduction
   − 5,000 (2,500 × 2) Exemption allowance
   $24,750 Taxable income

c. Tax liability?

$3.902 Tax (tax table)
− 1,765 Tax credit
$2,137 Tax liability

d. Is Sam entitled to a refund or does he owe additional taxes? How much?

$3.900 (325 × 12) Tax withheld
− 2,137
$1,763 Refund

30. You are the tax consultant for Macintosh Associates, Inc. If the company had taxable income of $875,500 last year, calculate:

a. Corporate tax liability.

Tax liability = 875,500
= 113,900 + 34%(875,500 − 335,000)
113,900 + 183,770
= $297,670

b. Net income after taxes.

Net income = 875,500 − 297,670
= $577,830

BUSINESS DECISION
The 90% Rule, Happy New Year!

31. Scott Stewart, a successful sales manager for a large company, earns a gross income of $6,000 per month. Scott is single, claims one exemption, and uses the standard deduction. Throughout last year, his company withheld $1,000 each month from his paycheck for federal income tax.

Today is January 4th. As Scott's accountant, you just informed him that although his tax return is due at the IRS by April 15, 90% of the income tax due for last year must be paid by January 15, or a penalty would be imposed.

a. Calculate the amount of tax Scott owes for the year.

$72,000 (6,000 × 12) Total income
− 3,900 Standard deduction
− 2,500 Exemption allowance
$65,600 Taxable income
Tax liability (tax table) = $15,612.00

b. Did his company withhold enough from each paycheck to cover the 90% requirement?

$1,000 × 12 = 12,000 Amount withheld
$15,612 × 90% = $14,050 Amount required
Not enough withheld

c. How much should Scott send the IRS by January 15 so he will not be penalized?

14,050 Amount required
− 12,000 Amount withheld
$2,050 Amount due

ANSWERS

c. _____ $2,137 _____

d. _____ $1,763 Refund _____

30. a. _____ $297,670 _____

b. _____ $577,830 _____

31. a. _____ $15,612.00 _____

b. _____ Not enough withheld _____

c. _____ $2,050 _____

ANSWERS

d. _____$90.99_____

e. _____$1,338.30_____

d. If Scott waits until April 15 to send the balance of his taxes to the IRS, how much will he be penalized, if the penalty is 18% per year, or 1.5% per month on the shortfall up to 90%? (Hint: Use the simple formula, $I = PRT$.)

January 15 to April 15 = 90 Days

$I = PRT$

$$I = 2,050 \times .18 \times \frac{90}{365}$$

$I = \underline{\$90.99}$ Penalty charge

e. If Scott gets a 10% raise, all other factors being the same, how much should he tell his payroll department to withhold from each month's paycheck so that 90% of the tax due will have been taken out?

$72,000 \times 110\% = \$79,200$

$79,200 New salary

  − 3,900

  − 2,500

$72,800 Taxable income

Tax liability (tax table) = $17,844

$17,844 \times 90\% = 16,059.60$ Owed by January 15

$$\frac{16,059.60}{12} = \underline{\$1,338.30}$$ Withholding per month

All the Math That's Fit to Learn

The Business Math Times

Volume XVIII — Taxes — One Dollar

Easy Come, Easy Go!

On or before the first Monday in February of each year, the president is required by law to submit to the Congress a budget proposal for the fiscal year that begins the following October. The budget plan sets forth the president's proposed receipts, spending, and the deficit for the federal government.

In fiscal year 1994, the Internal Revenue Service reported that federal income was $1,258 billion and outlays were $1,461 billion, leaving a deficit of $203 billion. The following pie charts show the relative sizes of the major categories of federal income and outlays for fiscal year 1994.

Income

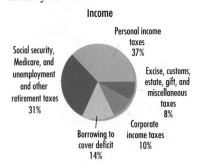

Outlays

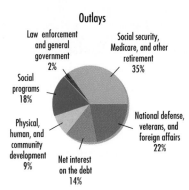

SOURCE: 1040 Forms and Instructions Booklet, Internal Revenue Service, 1995.

"Quote...Unquote"

You have to admire the Internal Revenue Service. Any organization that makes that much money without advertising deserves respect.
–Joe Griffith

The hardest thing in the world to understand is the income tax.
–Albert Einstein, 1953

Tax Facts

- **The Beginning.** To finance the Civil War, a 3 percent income tax on all incomes over $800 was enacted by the federal government in 1864. By 1872 it was discontinued. The U.S. Supreme Court declared the law unconstitutional in 1894.

- **A Great Rate.** In 1913, with the adoption of the Sixteenth Amendment, the income tax as we know it today become law. From 1913 to 1915 the rate was 1 percent.

- **An Even Greater Rate.** The countries with the lowest income tax in the world are Bahrain and Quatar, where the rate is zero, regardless of income.

- **A Not-So-Great Rate.** The highest income tax rate in United States history was levied in 1944 by the Individual Tax Act, with a 91 percent bracket.

- **A CPA's Delight.** Since 1954, Congress has changed the tax code approximately every 15 months. The rules for reporting income taxes now require over 12,000 pages.

- **1040 Time.** According to the Tax Foundation, each year nearly half the taxpayers, 56 million people, seek professional help in filing their tax returns. The average taxpayer spends 12 hours working on his or her taxes.

- **At Last, We're Free!** Tax Freedom Day is the date each year when the average taxpayer has finally earned enough money to pay all of his or her local, state, and federal tax obligations for the year. In 1996, it was May 7, 127 days into the new year.

- **11:45 Each Day.** Here's another way to look at "tax freedom." In 1996, if you worked an 8-hour day, from 9 AM to 5 PM, it took you until 11:45 AM each day to earn enough money to pay your taxes. Coffee break!!

- **Cyber Filing.** According to the IRS, 25,000 tax returns were filed electronically in 1986. By 1995, that number had jumped to 15.8 million.

- **There's No Escape.** Did you know even earnings from illegal profits are taxable? Frequently, that's how criminals are convicted—not for their original crime, but for income tax evasion. Perhaps the most famous example of this was the notorious gangster, Al Capone, who eventually wound up in prison, not for bootleg liquor trafficking and murder, but for tax evasion.

SOURCES: Internal Revenue Service; Tax Foundations.

Brainteaser

In a small town, $1/3$ of the tax revenue comes from property tax, $1/4$ comes from sales tax, and the remaining $10 million is from business income tax. What is the total amount of taxes collected by the town?

SOURCE: Adapted from Gyles Brandreth, *Classic Puzzles,* New York: Harper & Row, 1985.

Answer to Last Issue's Brainteaser
36 homes

In twelve months twelve girls can build twelve houses, and in twelve months twelve boys can build twenty-four houses.

Chapter 19

Insurance

Performance Objectives

SECTION I LIFE INSURANCE

19-1 Understanding life insurance and calculating typical premiums for various types of policies. (p. 628)

19-2 Calculating the value of various nonforfeiture options. (p. 631)

19-3 Calculating the amount of life insurance needed to cover dependents' income shortfall. (p. 633)

SECTION II PROPERTY INSURANCE

19-4 Understanding property insurance and calculating typical fire insurance premiums. (p. 636)

19-5 Calculating premiums for short-term policies, and the refunds due on canceled policies. (p. 638)

19-6 Understanding coinsurance, and computing compensation due in the event of a loss. (p. 640)

19-7 Determining each company's share of a loss when liability is divided among multiple carriers. (p. 641)

SECTION III MOTOR VEHICLE INSURANCE

19-8 Understanding motor vehicle insurance and calculating typical premiums. (p. 644)

19-9 Computing the compensation due following an accident. (p. 646)

Insurance is the promise to substitute future economic certainty for uncertainty and to replace the unknown with a sense of security. It is a mechanism for reducing financial risk and spreading financial loss due to unexpected events such as the death or disability of an individual, a home or business fire, a flood, an earthquake, an automobile accident, a negligence lawsuit, or an illness. These are only a few of the uncertainties that businesses and individuals can protect against by purchasing insurance. Companies may even purchase business interruption insurance, which covers the loss of income that may occur as a result of a multitude of perils.

Insurance is a very large and important segment of the U.S. economic system. Today there are over 6,000 insurance companies, employing more than 2 million people and collecting close to $225 billion in annual premiums. The insurance industry is second only to commercial banking as a source of investment funds, because insurance companies invest the billions of premium dollars they receive each year in a wide range of investments.

Insurance is based on the theory of **shared risk,** which means that insurance protection is purchased by many whose total payments are pooled together to pay off those few who actually incur a particular loss. Insurance companies use statisticians known as **actuaries** to calculate the **probability** or chance of a certain insurable event occurring. Based on a series of complicated calculations, insurance rates are then set. The rates are high enough to cover the cost of expected loss payments in the future, and to provide a profit for the insurance company.

This chapter will cover three major categories of insurance: life insurance, property insurance, and motor vehicle insurance. Within these three categories are several hundred different products or lines. Each year companies market new insurance products to meet the needs of a changing society. Recently, for example, insurance was made available to cover the loss of communication satellites during launch, space travel, and reentry.

Let's start with some basic terminology of the insurance industry. The company offering the insurance protection and assuring payment in the event of a loss is known as the **insurer, carrier,** or **underwriter.** The individual or business purchasing the protection is the **insured** or **policyholder.** The document stipulating the terms of the contract between the insurer and the insured is the **policy.** The amount of protection provided by the policy is the **face value,** and the amount paid at regular intervals to purchase this protection is known as the **premium.** The **beneficiary** is the person or institution to whom the proceeds of the policy are paid in the event that a loss occurs.

● insurance
A mechanism for reducing financial risk and spreading financial loss due to unexpected events.

● shared risk
The theory upon which insurance is based; protection is purchased by many whose total payments are pooled together to pay off those few who actually incur a particular loss.

● actuaries
Statisticians employed by insurance companies who calculate the probability or chance of a certain insurable event occurring.

● probability
A number expressing the likelihood or chance that a certain event will occur.

● insurer, carrier, or underwriter
The company offering the insurance protection and assuring payment in the event of a loss.

● insured, or policyholder
The individual or business purchasing the insurance protection.

● policy
The document stipulating the terms of the contract between the insurer and the insured.

● face value
The amount of protection provided by the policy.

● premium
The amount paid at regular intervals to purchase insurance protection.

● beneficiary
The person or institution to whom the proceeds of the policy are paid in the event that a loss occurs.

The average household is covered by $130,000 in life insurance.

The insurance industry is regulated by a number of authorities, including federal, state, and some inside the industry itself. This regulation is designed to promote the public welfare by maintaining the solvency of insurance companies, providing consumer protection, and ensuring fair trade practices as well as fair contracts at fair prices.

Insurance regulations, procedures, and laws vary widely from state to state. Most states have insurance commissions, departments, divisions, or boards that regulate all aspects of the insurance industry. Some of their responsibilities include premium structure and computation, insurance requirements, and salesperson education and licensing. This chapter will focus on calculating the premiums and the payouts of typical life, property, and motor vehicle insurance policies.

LIFE INSURANCE

19-1 Understanding Life Insurance and Calculating Typical Premiums for Various Types of Policies

Most people enjoy feeling that they are in control of their financial destiny. Few products are more important to that sense of security than life insurance. **Life insurance** guarantees a specified sum of money to the surviving beneficiaries upon the death of the person who is insured. Over the years, the average amount of life insurance per insured household has been steadily increasing. In 1960, for example, each insured household had an average of $13,000 in life insurance. By 1970, the average had doubled to around $26,000. By 1980, it doubled again, to over $50,000. Today the average insured household has over $130,000 in life insurance coverage.

There are two basic types of policies: those that pay only if the policyholder dies (**term insurance**) and those that pay whether the policyholder lives or dies (**permanent insurance**). Today many insurance policies combine an investment component with risk protection in order to provide the policyholder with both a death benefit if he or she dies and attractive investment returns if he or she lives. In this section we shall examine five popular types of life insurance policies: term, whole life, limited payment life, endowment, and nontraditional.

● **life insurance**

A type of insurance that guarantees a specified sum of money to the surviving beneficiaries upon the death of the person who is insured.

● **term insurance**

A type of life insurance that offers pure insurance protection, paying the face value of the policy to the beneficiaries upon the death of the insured.

● **permanent insurance**

A type of insurance that combines an investment component with risk protection in order to provide the policyholder with both a death benefit and attractive investment returns.

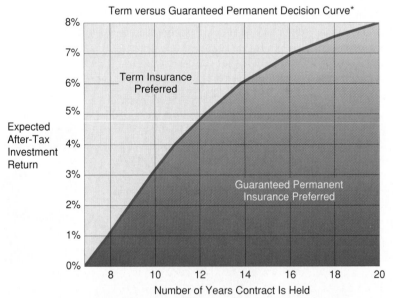

Term versus Guaranteed Permanent Decision Curve*

Expected After-Tax Investment Return

Number of Years Contract Is Held

* Graphic is based on typical quality life insurance products and related dividend scales as of April 1992. The relationship will change somewhat over time as economic conditions change.

Types of Life Insurance

Term Insurance This type of life insurance offers pure insurance protection, paying the face value of the policy to the beneficiaries upon the death of the insured. With term insurance there is no investment component. All of the premium goes toward purchasing the risk coverage. With most term policies, the premium increases periodically, because the risk of death of the insured increases with age. Term policies may be purchased with premiums increasing every year, every 5 years, every 10 years, and so on.

Renewable term insurance allows the policyholder the option of renewing the policy for another 5- or 10-year period, regardless of his or her health. The premiums on these policies are higher than nonrenewable term insurance. Because it is impossible to predict one's future health, many people opt for the renewable policy. Another common type of insurance, known as convertible term, allows the policyholder to trade in or convert the term policy for permanent insurance with an investment element and cash value, without having to prove one's health status.

Whole Life Insurance Whole life, also known as ordinary life and straight life, is the most common type of permanent insurance. With whole life insurance, policyholders agree to pay premiums for their entire lives. Whole life insurance offers a guaranteed premium and death benefit as well as a guaranteed minimum cash value, which can be borrowed against if necessary. When the insured dies, the beneficiaries receive the face value of the policy. Having cash value is like having a savings account within the policy that grows each year. If the policyholder lives long enough, the cash value can be received as an annuity to supplement retirement income in later years.

Limited Payment Life Insurance Limited payment life policies have level premiums that are limited to a certain period of time. After this period, usually 10, 20, or 30 years, the policy is paid up, and the insured is covered for the rest of his or her life. The premiums charged for limited payment policies are higher than premiums for whole life policies because they are paid for a shorter period of time. A variation of the limited payment policy is the life paid-up at 65 policy. This type is one in which the premiums are payable until the insured reaches age 65, after which no more premiums are owed.

Endowment Insurance Endowment insurance is a combination of life insurance and an accelerated savings plan. The emphasis of the endowment policy is the accumulation of money. Endowment insurance pays the face amount of the policy upon the death of the insured. It also pays the face amount if the insured is alive as of a specified date, known as the maturity date. Typical endowment periods are 10, 15, or 20 years, or to a specified age such as 65 or 70. Traditionally, this type of insurance has been purchased by families with young children in order to save money for college education, or by those who wish to set up a retirement fund with immediate life insurance protection. Because they are designed to build cash values quickly, endowment policies have comparatively high premiums.

Nontraditional Insurance In recent years, certain nontraditional policies have been introduced by insurance companies. Most of these interest-sensitive products are more flexible in design and provisions than their traditional counterparts. With these policies, the basic components of a life insurance policy, insurance (protection) and savings (investment), are separated. When premium payments are made, a portion known as the *mortality charge* is deducted to pay for the insurance coverage. This mortality charge increases with the age of the policyholder each year because the probability of death increases with age. The remaining amount, after other fees are deducted, goes to the investment *side fund.*

Universal life is the most popular interest-sensitive policy. It features a minimum guaranteed death benefit and flexible premiums and face amounts. The insurance company decides on the type of investments to make, with the earnings credited to the side fund.

Variable life is a higher-risk interest-sensitive policy that allows the policyholder to choose how the side fund will be invested. Typical choices include stocks, bonds, money market accounts, and real estate funds. Although this policy has a guaranteed death benefit, it does not have a guaranteed cash value like universal life.

Variable/universal life is a recently introduced policy that combines features of both variable life and universal life. These policies offer flexible premiums and guaranteed death benefits, both of which can be adjusted by the policyholder. The cash value is not guaranteed and depends on the investment performance of the funds selected by the policyholder.

Calculating Premiums

Insurance premiums are based on the age and sex of the insured as well as the type of policy being purchased. Premiums are less expensive for younger people because their probability of dying is lower than for older people. Females pay lower rates than males of the same age because they have a longer life expectancy than males.

Life insurance is purchased in increments of $1,000 of face value. The actuaries at insurance companies generate comprehensive rate tables, listing the premiums per $1,000 of insurance for males and females of all ages. Table 19-1 is a typical example of such a table.

| | Term Insurance | | | | Permanent Insurance | | | | | |
| | 5-Year Term | | 10-Year Term | | Whole Life | | 20-Payment Life | | 20-Year Endowment | |
Age	Male	Female	Male	Female	Male	Female	Male	Female	Male	Female
18	$2.32	$1.90	$4.33	$4.01	$13.22	$11.17	$23.14	$19.21	$33.22	$29.12
19	2.38	1.96	4.42	4.12	13.60	11.68	24.42	20.92	33.68	30.04
20	2.43	2.07	4.49	4.20	14.12	12.09	25.10	21.50	34.42	31.28
21	2.49	2.15	4.57	4.29	14.53	12.53	25.83	22.11	34.90	31.79
22	2.55	2.22	4.64	4.36	14.97	12.96	26.42	22.89	35.27	32.40
23	2.62	2.30	4.70	4.42	15.39	13.41	27.01	23.47	35.70	32.93
24	2.69	2.37	4.79	4.47	15.90	13.92	27.74	24.26	36.49	33.61
25	2.77	2.45	4.85	4.51	16.38	14.38	28.40	25.04	37.02	34.87
26	2.84	2.51	4.92	4.60	16.91	14.77	29.11	25.96	37.67	35.30
27	2.90	2.58	5.11	4.69	17.27	15.23	29.97	26.83	38.23	35.96
28	2.98	2.64	5.18	4.77	17.76	15.66	30.68	27.54	38.96	36.44
29	3.07	2.70	5.23	4.84	18.12	16.18	31.52	28.09	39.42	37.21
30	3.14	2.78	5.30	4.93	18.54	16.71	32.15	28.73	40.19	37.80
35	3.43	2.92	6.42	5.35	24.19	22.52	37.10	33.12	43.67	39.19
40	4.23	3.90	7.14	6.24	27.21	25.40	42.27	36.29	48.20	42.25
45	6.12	5.18	8.81	7.40	33.02	29.16	48.73	39.08	51.11	46.04
50	9.72	8.73	14.19	9.11	37.94	33.57	56.31	44.16	58.49	49.20
55	16.25	12.82	22.03	13.17	45.83	37.02	61.09	49.40	71.28	53.16
60	24.10	19.43	37.70	24.82	53.98	42.24	70.43	52.55	79.15	58.08

TABLE 19-1
....

ANNUAL LIFE INSURANCE PREMIUMS (PER $1,000 OF FACE VALUE)

● **premium factor**
A small surcharge added to the cost of insurance policies when the insured chooses to pay the premiums more frequently than annually; takes into account the increased cost of billing, handling, and bookkeeping.

Premium Paid	Percent of Annual Premium
Semiannually	52%
Quarterly	26%
Monthly	9%

TABLE 19-2
....

LIFE INSURANCE—PREMIUM FACTORS

Annual life insurance premiums are calculated by first determining the number of $1,000 of insurance desired and then multiplying the number of $1,000 by the rate per $1,000 found in Table 19-1. When the insured desires to pay the premiums more frequently than annually, such as semiannually, quarterly, or monthly, a small surcharge is added to account for the increased cost of billing, handling, and bookkeeping. Table 19-2 illustrates typical **premium factors** used by insurance companies for this purpose.

STEPS TO CALCULATE LIFE INSURANCE PREMIUMS:

Step 1. Calculate the number of $1,000 of insurance desired by dividing the face value of the policy by $1,000.

$$\text{Number of } \$1,000 = \frac{\text{Face value of policy}}{\$1,000}$$

Step 2. Locate the appropriate premium rate per $1,000 from Table 19-1. Choose the rate based on the type of policy desired and the age and sex of the applicant.

Step 3. Calculate annual premium by multiplying the number of $1,000 of insurance desired by the Table 19-1 rate.

$$\text{Annual premium} = \text{Number of } \$1,000 \times \text{Rate per } \$1,000$$

Step 4. For premiums other than annual, multiply the appropriate Table 19-2 premium factor by the annual premium.

$$\text{Premium other than annual} = \text{Annual premium} \times \text{Premium factor}$$

Cindy Van Patton is 24 years old. She is interested in purchasing a whole life insurance policy with a face value of $50,000. As her insurance agent, calculate the annual and monthly insurance premiums for this policy.

SOLUTION STRATEGY

Step 1.
$$\text{Number of } \$1,000 = \frac{\text{Face value of policy}}{\$1,000} = \frac{50,000}{1,000} = 50$$

Step 2. From Table 19-1 we find the premium per $1,000 for whole life insurance for a 24-year-old female to be $13.92.

Step 3. Annual premium = Number of $1,000 × Rate per $1,000 = 50 × 13.92 = $696.00

Step 4. Monthly premium = Annual premium × Monthly premium factor

Monthly premium = 696 × .09 = $62.64

TRY-IT   EXERCISE

1. Gilbert Arroyo, age 26, wants to purchase a 10-year term insurance policy with a face value of $75,000. Calculate Gilbert's annual and quarterly premiums. How much more will Gilbert pay per year if he chooses quarterly payments?

Check your answers with the solutions on page 653.

19-2 Calculating the Value of Various Nonforfeiture Options

Because all life insurance policies (except term) build up a **cash value** after the first two or three years, they should be viewed as being property with a value. Policyholders in effect own these properties, and therefore have certain **ownership rights.** For example, policyholders, or policyowners, have the right to change beneficiaries, designate how the death benefits will be paid, borrow money against the policy, assign ownership to someone else, or cancel the policy.

Let's take a closer look at what happens when a policyowner decides to cancel a policy or allows it to terminate or **lapse** by failing to make the required premium payments within 31 days of the due date. The amount of cash value that has accumulated to that point is based on the size of the policy and the amount of time it has been in force. Most policies give the policyowner three choices known as **nonforfeiture options.**

Option 1—Cash Value or Cash Surrender Option   Once a policy has accumulated cash value, the policyowner may choose to surrender (give up) the policy to the company and receive its cash value. At this point, the policy is terminated. If the insured wishes to maintain the insurance coverage, the amount of the cash value may be borrowed and later repaid with interest.

Option 2—Reduced Paid-Up Insurance   The second option is that the available cash value is used to purchase a reduced level of paid-up insurance. This policy is of the same type as the original, and continues for the life of the policyowner, with no further premiums due.

Option 3—Extended Term Insurance   With this option, the policyholder elects to use the cash value to purchase a term policy with the same face value as the original policy. The new policy will last for as long a time period as the cash value will purchase. When a policyowner simply stops paying on a policy and does not choose a nonforfeiture option, the insurance company automatically implements this extended term option.

● **cash value**
The amount of money that begins to build up in a permanent life insurance policy after the first two or three years.

● **ownership rights**
The rights of life insurance policyholders, including the right to change beneficiaries, designate how the death benefits will be paid, borrow money against the policy, assign ownership to someone else, or cancel the policy.

● **lapse**
Allowing an insurance policy to terminate by failing to make the required premium payments within 31 days of the due date.

● **nonforfeiture options**
The options available to the policyholder upon termination of a permanent life insurance policy with accumulated cash value; these include receiving the cash value, using the cash value to purchase a reduced paid-up insurance policy of the same type, or purchasing term insurance with the same face value as the original policy, for as long a time period as the cash value will purchase.

	Whole Life				20-Payment Life				20-Year Endowment			
	Option				Option				Option			
	1	2	3		1	2	3		1	2	3	
End of Year	Cash Value	Reduced Paid-up Insurance	Extended Term Years	Days	Cash Value	Reduced Paid-up Insurance	Extended Term Years	Days	Cash Value	Reduced Paid-up Insurance	Extended Term Years	Days
3	$11	$25	2	17	$29	$90	4	217	$39	$97	7	132
5	32	64	9	23	73	212	14	86	91	233	19	204
7	54	99	13	142	101	367	23	152	186	381	26	310
10	98	186	17	54	191	496	30	206	324	512	32	117
15	157	314	21	218	322	789	34	142	647	794	37	350
20	262	491	25	77	505	1,000	-Life-		1,000	1,000	-Life-	

TABLE 19-3

....

NONFORFEITURE OPTIONS (PER $1,000 OF FACE VALUE ISSUED TO FEMALE AT AGE 20)

Table 19-3 illustrates typical nonforfeiture options per $1,000 of face value, for a policy issued to a female at age 20.

STEPS TO CALCULATE THE VALUE OF VARIOUS NONFORFEITURE OPTIONS:

Step 1. Calculate the number of $1,000 of insurance by dividing the face value of the policy by $1,000.

Step 2. *Option 1—Cash Value* Locate the appropriate dollars per $1,000 in the *cash value* column of Table 19-3, and multiply this figure by the number of $1,000 of insurance.

Option 2—Reduced Paid-Up Insurance Locate the appropriate dollars per $1,000 in the *reduced paid-up insurance* column of Table 19-3, and multiply this figure by the number of $1,000 of insurance.

Option 3—Extended Term Locate the length of time of the new extended term policy in the *years* and *days* columns of Table 19-3.

EXAMPLE

Monica Mitchell purchased a $30,000 whole life insurance policy when she was 20 years old. She is now 35 years old and wishes to investigate her nonforfeiture options. As her insurance agent, use Table 19-3 to calculate the value of Monica's three options.

SOLUTION STRATEGY

Step 1.
$$\text{Number of } \$1,000 = \frac{\text{Face value of policy}}{\$1,000} = \frac{30,000}{1,000} = 30$$

Step 2. **Option 1—Cash Value** From Table 19-3 we find that after being in force for 15 years, a whole life policy issued to a female at age 20 has a cash value of $157 per $1,000 of insurance.

$$\text{Number of } \$1,000 \times \text{Table value} = 30 \times \$157 = \underline{\$4,710.00}$$

Monica's cash value option is to receive $4,710.00 in cash from the company and have no further insurance coverage.

Option 2—Reduced Paid-Up Insurance From Table 19-3 we find that after being in force for 15 years, a whole life policy issued to a female at age 20 will have enough cash value to buy $314 in paid-up whole life insurance per $1,000 of face value.

$$\text{Number of } \$1,000 \times \text{Table value} = 30 \times 314 = \underline{\$9,420.00}$$

Monica's reduced paid-up insurance option is to receive a $9,420 whole life policy, effective for her entire life, with no further payments.

Option 3—Extended Term Insurance   From Table 19-3 we find that after being in force for 15 years, a whole life policy issued to a female at age 20 will have enough cash value to buy $30,000 of term insurance for a period of <u>21 years</u> and <u>218 days</u>.

TRY-IT   EXERCISE

2. **Marcie Bader purchased a $100,000 20-payment life insurance policy when she was 20 years old. She is now 30 years old and wishes to investigate her nonforfeiture options. As her insurance agent, use Table 19-3 to determine the value of Marcie's three options.**

Check your answers with the solutions on page 653.

19-3 Calculating the Amount of Life Insurance Needed to Cover Dependents' Income Shortfall

Evaluating your life insurance needs is a fundamental part of sound financial planning. The amount of insurance, and type of policy you should purchase, are much less obvious. Life insurance is needed if you keep a household running, support a family, have a mortgage or other major debts, or expect the kids to go to college. Insurance should be used to fill the financial gap a family may incur by the death or disability of the insured.

One so-called rule of thumb is that you carry between 7 to 10 times your annual income, depending on your lifestyle, number of dependents, and other sources of income. Another estimator of the amount of insurance to purchase is based on a family's additional income requirements needed in the event of the death of the insured. These additional requirements are known as the **income shortfall.**

Let's say, for example, that a family has $30,000 in living expenses per year. If the family's total income, after the death of the insured, decreases to only $20,000, the income shortfall would be $10,000 ($30,000 − $20,000). The theory is to purchase enough life insurance so that the face value of the policy, collected by the family upon the death of the insured, can be invested at the prevailing interest rate to generate the additional income needed to overcome the $10,000 shortfall. When prevailing interest rates are low, large amounts of insurance are needed to cover the shortfall. As interest rates rise, less insurance will be needed.

● **income shortfall**
The difference between the total living expenses and the total income of a family after the death of the insured; used as an indicator of how much life insurance to purchase.

STEPS TO CALCULATE INSURANCE NEEDED TO COVER DEPENDENTS' INCOME SHORTFALL:

Step 1. Determine the dependents' total annual living expenses, including mortgages.

Step 2. Determine the dependents' total annual sources of income, including salaries, investments, and social security.

Step 3. Subtract the income from the living expenses to find the income shortfall.

$$\text{Income shortfall} = \text{Total living expenses} - \text{Total income}$$

Step 4. Calculate the insurance needed to cover the shortfall by dividing the shortfall by the prevailing interest rate (round to the nearest $1,000).

$$\text{Insurance needed} = \frac{\text{Income shortfall}}{\text{Prevailing interest rate}}$$

With a prevailing interest rate of 6%, how much life insurance is required to cover dependents' income shortfall if their living expenses amount to $48,000 per year and their total income sources amount to $33,000 per year?

SOLUTION STRATEGY

Step 1. Living expenses per year are $48,000 (given).

Step 2. Dependents' total income is $33,000 (given).

Step 3. Income shortfall = Total expenses − Total income = $48,000 − $33,000 = $15,000

Step 4.
$$\text{Insurance needed} = \frac{\text{Shortfall}}{\text{Prevailing rate}} = \frac{\$15,000}{.06} = \underline{\$250,000}$$

TRY-IT EXERCISE

3. Robert Kelly is evaluating his life insurance needs. His family's total living expenses are $54,000 per year. Mary, his wife, earns $38,000 per year in salary and receives another $5,000 per year from an endowment fund. If the prevailing interest rate is currently 5%, how much life insurance should Robert purchase to cover his dependents' income shortfall?

Check your answer with the solution on page 653.

REVIEW EXERCISES   CHAPTER 19—SECTION I

Calculate the annual, semiannual, quarterly, and monthly premiums for the following life insurance policies:

	Face Value of Policy	Sex and Age of Insured	Type of Policy	Annual Premium	Semiannual Premium	Quarterly Premium	Monthly Premium
1.	$ 5,000	Male—24	Whole Life	$79.50	$41.34	$20.67	$7.16
2.	10,000	Female—35	10-Year Term	53.50	27.82	13.91	4.82
3.	25,000	Male—19	20-Year Endowment	842.00	437.84	218.92	75.78
4.	75,000	Male—50	20-Payment Life	4,223.25	2,196.09	1,098.05	380.09
5.	100,000	Female—29	5-Year Term	270.00	140.40	70.20	24.30
6.	40,000	Male—35	Whole Life	967.60	503.15	251.58	87.08
7.	35,000	Male—30	20-Payment Life	1,125.25	585.13	292.57	101.27
8.	250,000	Female—45	20-Year Endowment	11,510.00	5,985.20	2,992.60	1,035.90

Calculate the value of the nonforfeiture options for the following life insurance policies:

	Face Value of Policy	Years in Force	Type of Policy	Cash Value	Paid-Up Insurance	Extended Term Years	Extended Term Days
9.	$50,000	10	Whole Life	$4,900.00	$9,300.00	17	54
10.	250,000	7	20-Year Endowment	46,500.00	95,250.00	26	310
11.	35,000	15	Whole Life	5,495.00	10,990.00	21	218
12.	100,000	3	20-Payment Life	2,900.00	9,000.00	4	217

13. Bob DeLucia is 35 years old and is interested in purchasing a 20-year endowment insurance policy with a face value of $120,000.

    a. Calculate the annual premium for this policy.

        Face value = $120,000, 20-year endowment, M-35

$$\text{Number of 1000s} = \frac{120,000}{1,000} = 120$$

        Annual premium = 43.67×120

                  = <u>$5,240.40</u>

    b. Calculate the semiannual premium.

        Semi-annual premium = $5,240.40 × .52

                      = <u>$2,725.01</u>

14. Carol Nolan-Fish, age 27, wants to purchase a 5-year term insurance policy with a face value of $25,000. As her insurance agent, answer the following:

    a. What is the annual premium for this policy?

        Face value = $25,000, 5-year term, F-27

        Number of 1000s = 25

        Annual premium = $2.58 × 25

                 = <u>$64.50</u>

    b. What is the monthly premium?

        Monthly premium = 64.50 × .09

                 = <u>$5.81</u>

    c. How much more will Carol pay per year if she chooses monthly payments?

        Total payments = $5.81 × 12 = 69.72$

                     69.72 − 64.50

        If paid monthly <u>$5.22</u> More will be paid

15. Maggie Talcott purchased a $75,000, 20-payment life insurance policy when she was 20 years old. She is now 30 years old and wishes to investigate her nonforfeiture options. As her insurance agent, calculate the value of Maggie's three options.

Face value = $75,000, 10 years in force, 20 payment, life

Option 1 = 191.00 × 75   Option 3 = <u>30 years 206 Days</u> extended term

        = <u>$14,325</u> Cash value

Option 2 = 496.00 × 75

        = <u>$37,200</u> Reduced paid-up insurance

16. Michael McDonald is evaluating his life insurance needs. His family's total living expenses are $37,500 per year. Vickie, his wife, earns $14,900 per year in salary and receives another $3,500 annually in disability benefits from an insurance settlement for an accident. If the prevailing interest rate is $7\frac{1}{2}\%$, how much life insurance should Michael purchase to cover his dependents' income shortfall? Round to nearest $1,000.

Total living expenses = $37,500

Total income   = $14,900 + 3,500 = $18,400

Income shortfall   = $37,500 − 18,400 = $19,100

$$\frac{\text{Income shortfall}}{\text{Prevailing interest rate}} = \frac{19,100}{.075} = \$254,666.67 = \underline{\$255,000} \text{ Insurance needed}$$

17. Stacy Spencer, a single mother, is 20 years old. She has called on you for an insurance consultation. Her objective is to purchase life insurance protection for the next ten years while her children are growing up. Stacy tells you that she can afford about $250 per year for insurance premiums. You have suggested either a 10-year term policy or a whole life policy.

    a. Rounded to the nearest thousand, how much insurance coverage can Stacy purchase under each policy? Hint: Divide her annual premium allowance by the rate per $1,000 for each policy.

10-year term policy rate = $4.20

Number of 1,000s = $\dfrac{250}{4.20} = 59.5 = 60$

She can purchase a $60,000 10-year term policy.

Whole life policy rate = $12.09

Number of 1,000s = $\dfrac{250}{12.09} = 20.6 = 21$

She can purchase a $21,000 whole life policy.

    b. If she should die in the next ten years, how much more will her children receive under the term insurance?

Term face value   = $60,000
Whole life face value = − $21,000
                     $39,000

Under term policy, $39,000 more would be paid.

    c. If she should live beyond the 10th year, what are her nonforfeiture options with the whole life policy?

Nonforfeiture options of whole life policy in force 10 years
Option 1 = $ 98.00 × 21 = $2,058 Cash value
Option 2 = $186.00 × 21 = $3,906 Reduced paid-up
Option 3 = 17 years, 54 days Extended term insurance

SECTION II

PROPERTY INSURANCE

19-4 Understanding Property Insurance and Calculating Typical Fire Insurance Premiums

Businesses and homeowners alike need insurance protection for the financial losses that may occur to their property from such perils as fire, lightning, wind, water, negligence, burglary, and vandalism. Although the probability that a particular peril will occur is quite small, no homeowner or business can afford the risk of not having **property insurance.** Most mortgage lenders, in fact, require that sufficient property insurance is purchased by the borrower as a condition for obtaining a mortgage.

    In addition to the items listed above, most property insurance policies today have provisions for liability coverage, medical expenses, and additional expenses that may be incurred while the damaged property is being repaired. For example, a business may have to move to a temporary location during reconstruction, or a family may have to stay in an apartment or motel while their house is being repaired. Insurance companies offer similar policies to meet the needs of apartment and home renters, as well as condominium owners.

    In this section, we shall focus our attention on fire insurance, and how these premiums are determined. Fire insurance rates are quoted as an amount per $100 of insurance coverage purchased. Rates are separated into two categories: (a) the structure or building itself, and (b) the contents within the building.

    A *building's* fire insurance rates are determined by a number of important factors:

1. The *dollar amount* of insurance purchased on the property.

2. The *location* of the property—city, suburbs, and rural areas.

3. The *proximity* and *quality* of fire protection available.

4. The *type of construction* materials used—masonry (brick) or wood (frame).

    The *contents* portion of the fire insurance rate is based on:

1. The *dollar amount* or value of the contents.

2. The *flammability* of the contents.

● **property insurance**
Insurance protection for the financial losses that may occur to business and homeowner's property from such perils as fire, lightning, wind, water, negligence, burglary, and vandalism.

From this rate structure we can see that a building made of concrete, bricks, and steel, located 2 or 3 miles from a fire station, would have a considerably lower rate than a building of the same value, with wood frame construction, located in a rural area, 12 miles from the nearest fire-fighting equipment. Or for that matter, a warehouse filled with explosive chemicals would cost more to insure than the same warehouse filled with Coca-Cola.

Table 19-4 illustrates typical annual fire insurance premiums. Note that the rates are per $100 of insurance coverage. The building and contents are listed separately, and divided by the structural class of the building and the location (area rating).

Most businesses and homeowners carry special insurance policies to protect against loss due to fire.

STEPS TO CALCULATE TYPICAL FIRE INSURANCE PREMIUMS:

Step 1. From Table 19-4, locate the appropriate rate, based on *structural class* and *area rating,* for both the building and the contents.

Step 2. Calculate the number of $100 of insurance coverage desired for both the building and the contents by dividing the amount of coverage for each by $100.

Step 3. Multiply the number of $100 for both the building and contents by the rates from Step 1 to find the annual premium for each.

Step 4. Add the annual premiums for the building and the contents to find the total annual premium.

Total annual fire premium = Building premium + Contents premium

---

EXAMPLE

What is the total annual fire insurance premium on a building valued at $200,000 with structural classification B and area rating 4, and contents valued at $40,000?

SOLUTION STRATEGY

Step 1. From Table 19-4 we find the following rates for structural class B and area rating 4:

Building—$.76 per $100 of coverage

Contents—$.83 per $100 of coverage

Step 2. Number of $100 of coverage:

$$\text{Building} = \frac{\text{Amount of coverage}}{\$100} = \frac{200,000}{100} = 2,000$$

$$\text{Contents} = \frac{\text{Amount of coverage}}{\$100} = \frac{40,000}{100} = 400$$

Step 3. Annual fire insurance premiums:

Building = Number of $100 × Table rate = 2,000 × .76 = $1,520.00

Contents = Number of $100 × Table rate = 400 × .83 = $332.00

Step 4.   Total annual fire premium = Building premium + Contents premium

Total annual fire premium = 1,520.00 + 332.00 = $1,852.00

| Area Rating | Structural Classification | | | | | | | |
| | A | | B | | C | | D | |
	Building	Contents	Building	Contents	Building	Contents	Building	Contents
1	$.21	$.24	$.32	$ .37	$ .38	$ .42	$ .44	$ .48
2	.38	.42	.39	.48	.43	.51	.57	.69
3	.44	.51	.55	.66	.69	.77	.76	.85
4	.59	.68	.76	.83	.87	1.04	.98	1.27
5	.64	.73	.92	1.09	1.08	1.13	1.39	1.43

TABLE 19-4

ANNUAL FIRE INSURANCE PREMIUMS (PER $100 OF FACE VALUE)

4. You are the insurance agent for McCready Enterprises, Inc. The owner, Fred Mc-Cready, would like you to give him a quote on the total annual premium for a property insurance policy on a new warehouse in the amount of $420,000, and contents valued at $685,000. The warehouse is structural classification A and area rating 2.

Check your answer with the solution on page 653.

19-5 Calculating Premiums for Short-Term Policies and the Refunds Due on Canceled Policies

● **short-term policy**
An insurance policy for less than one year.

● **short-rate**
The premium charged when a policy is canceled by the insured, or is written for less than one year.

From time to time businesses and individuals cancel insurance policies or require **short-term policies** of less than one year. For example, a family might sell their home two months after paying the annual premium, or a business may require coverage for a shipment of merchandise that will be sold within a few months. When a policy is canceled by the insured, or is written for less than one year, the premium charged is known as the **short-rate.** These premiums are more expensive than the rates charged for annual policies, because the selling and administrative expenses are being charged off over a shorter period of time.

Short-Rate Refund

Table 19-5 illustrates typical short-term policy rate factors. These rate factors should be used to calculate the premiums and refunds for short-term policies canceled by the insured. Note that these rate factors are a percentage of the annual premium.

STEPS TO CALCULATE SHORT-RATE REFUNDS—POLICIES CANCELED BY INSURED:

Step 1. Calculate the short-term premium using the short-rate from Table 19-5:

$$\text{Short-rate premium} = \text{Annual premium} \times \text{Short-rate}$$

Step 2. Calculate the short-rate refund by subtracting the short-rate premium from the annual premium:

$$\text{Short-rate refund} = \text{Annual premium} - \text{Short-rate premium}$$

TABLE 19-5
....
PROPERTY INSURANCE
SHORT-RATE SCHEDULE

Time Policy Is in Force	Percent of Annual Premium	Time Policy Is in Force	Percent of Annual Premium
5 days	8%	4 months	50%
10 days	10	5 months	60
15 days	14	6 months	70
20 days	16	7 months	75
25 days	18	8 months	80
		9 months	85
1 month	20	10 months	90
2 months	30	11 months	95
3 months	40	12 months	100

EXAMPLE

A property insurance policy has an annual premium of $500. What is the short-rate refund if the policy is canceled by the insured after 3 months?

SOLUTION STRATEGY

Step 1.
$$\text{Short-rate premium} = \text{Annual premium} \times \text{Short-rate}$$
$$\text{Short-rate premium} = 500 \times 40\% = \underline{\$200}$$

Step 2.
$$\text{Short-rate refund} = \text{Annual premium} - \text{Short-rate premium}$$
$$\text{Short-rate refund} = 500 - 200 = \underline{\$300}$$

 **TRY-IT** **EXERCISE**

5. A property insurance policy has an annual premium of $850. What is the short-rate refund if the policy is canceled by the insured after 8 months?

Check your answer with the solution on page 653.

Regular Refund

When a policy is canceled by the insurance company, rather than the insured, the company must refund the entire unused portion of the premium. This short-term refund calculation is based on the fraction of a year that the policy was in force, and is known as a regular refund.

STEPS TO CALCULATE REGULAR REFUNDS—POLICIES CANCELED BY COMPANY:

Step 1. Calculate the premium for the period of time the policy was in force, by using either:

$$\textbf{Exact time: Annual premium} \times \frac{\textbf{Days policy in force}}{\textbf{365}}$$

or

$$\textbf{Approximate time: Annual premium} \times \frac{\textbf{Months policy in force}}{\textbf{12}}$$

Step 2. Calculate refund by subtracting premium for period in force from the annual premium:

$$\textbf{Regular refund} = \textbf{Annual premium} - \textbf{Premium for period}$$

EXAMPLE

A property insurance policy has an annual premium of $500. What is the regular refund if the policy is canceled by the insurance company after 3 months?

SOLUTION STRATEGY

Step 1.
$$\text{Premium for period} = \text{Annual premium} \times \frac{\text{Months policy in force}}{12}$$
$$\text{Premium for period} = 500 \times \frac{3}{12} = \underline{\$125}$$

Step 2.   Regular refund = Annual premium − Premium for period
                           Regular refund = 500 − 125 = $\underline{\$375}$

TRY-IT   EXERCISE

6. **A property insurance policy has an annual premium of $850. What is the regular refund if the policy is canceled by the insurance company after 8 months?**

Check your answer with the solution on page 653.

19-6 Understanding Coinsurance and Computing Compensation Due in the Event of a Loss

Knowing that most fires do not totally destroy the insured property, many businesses, as a cost-saving measure, insure their buildings and contents for less than the full value. Insurance companies, in order to protect themselves from having more claims than premiums collected, write a **coinsurance clause** into most business policies. This clause stipulates a minimum amount of coverage required in order for a claim to be paid in full. The coinsurance minimum is stated as a percent of the replacement value of the property, and is usually between 70% and 90%.

Here's an example of how coinsurance works. Let's say that a building has a replacement value of $100,000. If the insurance policy has an 80% coinsurance clause, the building must be insured for $80,000 (80% of the $100,000) in order to be fully covered for any claim, up to the face value of the policy. Any coverage less than the required 80% would be paid out in proportion to the coverage ratio. The **coverage ratio** is a ratio of the amount of insurance carried by the insured to the amount of insurance required by the insurance company.

● **coinsurance clause**

A clause in a property insurance policy stipulating a minimum amount of coverage required in order for a claim to be paid in full. This requirement is stated as a percent of the replacement value of the property.

● **coverage ratio**

A ratio of the amount of insurance carried by the insured to the amount of insurance required according to the coinsurance clause of the insurance policy.

$$\text{Coverage ratio} = \frac{\text{Insurance carried}}{\text{Insurance required}}$$

If, for example, the owner had purchased only $40,000, rather than the required $80,000, the insurance company would only be obligated to pay half, or 50%, of any claim. This is because the ratio of insurance carried to insurance required was 50%.

$$\text{Coverage ratio} = \frac{\$40,000}{\$80,000} = \frac{1}{2} = 50\%$$

STEPS TO CALCULATE AMOUNT OF LOSS TO BE PAID WITH A COINSURANCE CLAUSE:

Step 1. Determine the amount of insurance required by the coinsurance clause:

Insurance required = Replacement value of property × Coinsurance percent

Step 2. Calculate the amount of the loss to be paid by the insurance company by multiplying the coverage ratio times the amount of the loss:

$$\text{Amount of loss paid by insurance} = \frac{\text{Insurance carried}}{\text{Insurance required}} \times \text{Amount of the loss}$$

The Castlerock Corporation had property valued at $500,000 and insured for $300,000. If the fire insurance policy contained an 80% coinsurance clause, how much would be paid by the insurance company in the event of a $100,000 fire?

SOLUTION STRATEGY

Step 1.   Insurance required = Value of the property × Coinsurance percent

Insurance required = 500,000 × .80 = $400,000

Step 2.   Amount of loss paid by insurance $= \dfrac{\text{Insurance carried}}{\text{Insurance required}} \times \text{Amount of loss}$

Amount of loss paid by insurance $= \dfrac{300,000}{400,000} \times 100,000 = \$75,000$

TRY-IT   **EXERCISE**

7. Consolidated Walchow Corporation had property valued at $850,000 and insured for $400,000. If the fire insurance policy contained a 70% coinsurance clause, how much would be paid by the insurance company in the event of a $325,000 fire?

Check your answer with the solution on page 653.

19-7 Determining Each Company's Share of a Loss when Liability Is Divided among Multiple Carriers

Sometimes businesses are covered by fire insurance policies from more than one company at the same time, which is known as having **multiple carriers.** This situation occurs when one insurance company is unwilling or unable to carry the entire liability of a particular property or because additional coverage was purchased from different insurance companies over a period of time as the business expanded and became more valuable.

Assuming that all coinsurance clause requirements have been met, when a claim is made against multiple carriers, each carrier is responsible for its portion of the total coverage carried. To calculate that portion, we divide the amount of each company's policy by the total insurance carried. This portion is expressed as a percent of the total coverage.

For example, if an insurance company was one of multiple carriers and had a $30,000 fire policy written on a business that had a total of $200,000 in coverage, that insurance company would be responsible for $\frac{30,000}{200,000}$, or 15%, of any loss.

● **multiple carriers**
A situation in which a business is covered by fire insurance policies from more than one company at the same time.

> **STEPS TO DETERMINE EACH COMPANY'S SHARE OF A LOSS WHEN LIABILITY IS SHARED AMONG MULTIPLE CARRIERS:**
>
> **Step 1.** Calculate each carrier's portion by dividing the amount of each policy by the total insurance carried:
>
> $$\text{Carrier's percent of total coverage} = \frac{\text{Amount of carrier's policy}}{\text{Total amount of insurance}}$$
>
> **Step 2.** Determine each carrier's share of a loss by multiplying the amount of the loss by each carrier's percent of the total coverage:
>
> $$\text{Carrier's share of loss} = \text{Amount of loss} \times \text{Carrier's percent of total coverage}$$

The Boswell Corporation had multiple carrier fire insurance coverage in the amount of **$400,000**, as follows:

Travelers—$ 80,000 policy
State Farm—$120,000 policy
Allstate—<u>$200,000</u> policy
$400,000 total coverage

Assuming that all coinsurance clause stipulations have been met, how much would each carrier be responsible for in the event of a $50,000 fire?

SOLUTION STRATEGY

Step 1. Carrier's percent of total coverage $= \dfrac{\text{Amount of carrier's policy}}{\text{Total amount of insurance}}$

$$\text{Travelers} = \frac{80,000}{400,000} = \underline{20\%}$$

$$\text{State Farm} = \frac{120,000}{400,000} = \underline{30\%}$$

$$\text{Allstate} = \frac{200,000}{400,000} = \underline{50\%}$$

Step 2. Carrier's share of loss = Amount of loss × Carrier's percent of total coverage

Travelers Share = 50,000 × .20 = <u>$10,000</u>

State Farm Share = 50,000 × .30 = <u>$15,000</u>

Allstate Share = 50,000 × .50 = <u>$25,000</u>

TRY-IT **EXERCISE**

8. **Elite Industries, Inc., had multiple carrier fire insurance coverage in the amount of $125,000, as follows:**

Aetna—$20,000 policy
USF&G—$45,000 policy
John Hancock—<u>$60,000</u> policy
$125,000 total coverage

Assuming that all coinsurance clause stipulations have been met, how much would each carrier be responsible for in the event of a $16,800 fire?

Check your answers with the solutions on page 653.

REVIEW EXERCISES CHAPTER 19—SECTION II

Calculate the building, contents, and total property insurance premiums for the following policies:

	Area Rating	Structural Class	Building Value	Building Premium	Contents Value	Contents Premium	Total Premium
1.	4	B	$88,000	<u>$668.80</u>	$21,000	<u>$174.30</u>	<u>$843.10</u>
2.	2	C	124,000	<u>533.20</u>	35,000	<u>178.50</u>	<u>711.70</u>

Complete, worked out solutions for exercises 1, 6, 7, and 11 appear in the appendix following the index.

	Area Rating	Structural Class	Building Value	Building Premium	Contents Value	Contents Premium	Total Premium
3.	1	A	215,000	451.50	29,000	69.60	521.10
4.	5	D	518,000	7,200.20	90,000	1,287.00	8,487.20
5.	3	C	309,000	2,132.10	57,000	438.90	2,571.00

Calculate the short-term premium and refund for each of the following policies:

	Annual Premium	Canceled After	Canceled By	Short-Term Premium	Short-Term Refund
6.	$ 450	3 months	insurance company	$112.50	$337.50
7.	560	20 days	insured	89.60	470.40
8.	1,280	9 months	insured	1,088.00	192.00
9.	322	5 months	insurance company	134.17	187.83
10.	630	5 days	insured	50.40	579.60

Calculate the amount to be paid by the insurance company for each of the following claims:

	Replacement Value of Building	Face Value of Policy	Coinsurance Clause	Amount of Loss	Amount of Loss Insurance Company Will Pay
11.	$200,000	$160,000	80%	$75,000	$75,000.00
12.	350,000	300,000	90%	125,000	119,047.62
13.	70,000	50,000	70%	37,000	37,000.00
14.	125,000	75,000	80%	50,000	37,500.00
15.	500,000	300,000	80%	200,000	150,000.00

16. You are the insurance agent for Southeast Furniture Manufacturing, Inc. The owner, Michael Chang, would like you to give him a quote on the total annual premium for property insurance on a new production facility in the amount of $1,640,000, and equipment and contents valued at $955,000. The building is structural classification B and area rating 4.

Building, number of 100s $= \dfrac{\$1,640,000}{100} = 16,400$

Contents, number of 100s $= \dfrac{\$955,000}{100} = 9,550$

Building premium $= 16,400 \times .76 = \$12,464$
Contents premium $= 9,550 \times .83 = \$7,926.50$
Total annual premium $= 12,464.00 + 7,926.50$
$= \$20,390.50$

17. A property insurance policy has an annual premium of $1,350. What is the short-rate refund if the policy is canceled by the insured after 9 months?

Annual premium = $1,350.00, canceled by insured
Short-rate premium = $1,350.00 \times 85\%$
$= \$1,147.50$
Short-rate refund $= 1,350.00 - 1,147.50$
$= \underline{\$202.50}$

18. Drake Enterprises has a property insurance policy with an annual premium of $1,320. In recent months, Drake has filed 4 different claims against the policy: a fire, two burglaries, and a vandalism incident. The insurance company has elected to cancel the policy, which has been in effect for 310 days. What is the regular refund due to Drake?

Annual premium = $1,320, 310 days in force, canceled by insurance company

Regular refund $= 1,320 \times \dfrac{310}{365} = 1,121.10$

$1,320.00 - 1,121.10$
$= \underline{\$198.90}$

19. Midway Electronics had multiple carrier fire insurance coverage in the amount of $500,000, as follows:

Aetna—$300,000 policy
State Farm—$125,000 policy
Liberty Mutual—$ 75,000 policy
$500,000 total coverage

Assuming that all coinsurance clause stipulations have been met, how much would each carrier be responsible for in the event of a $95,000 fire?

Aetna: $57,000   State Farm: $23,750   Liberty Mutual: $14,250

Complete, worked out solutions for exercise 19 appear in the appendix following the index.

MOTOR VEHICLE INSURANCE

19-8 Understanding Motor Vehicle Insurance and Calculating Typical Premiums

● **motor vehicle insurance**

Insurance protection for the financial losses that may be incurred due to a motor vehicle accident or damage caused by fire, vandalism, or other perils.

● **liability**

A portion of motor vehicle insurance that includes payment for bodily injury to other persons and damages to the property of others resulting from the insured's negligence.

● **collision**

A portion of motor vehicle insurance that covers damage sustained by the insured's vehicle in an accident.

● **comprehensive**

Insurance coverage that protects the insured's vehicle for damage caused by fire, wind, water, theft, vandalism, and other perils not caused by accident.

● **deductible**

A premium reduction measure in collision insurance whereby the insured pays a stipulated amount of the damage first, the *deductible,* and the insurance company pays any amount over that; common deductibles are $100, $250, $500, and $1,000.

With the steadily increasing costs of automobile and truck repairs and replacement, as well as all forms of medical services, **motor vehicle insurance** today is an absolute necessity! In fact, most states require a certain minimum amount of insurance before a vehicle may even be registered.

Motor vehicle insurance rates, regulations, and requirements vary widely from state to state, but the basic structure is the same. Vehicle insurance is divided into three main categories: **liability, collision,** and **comprehensive.**

Liability This category includes (a) payment for bodily injury to other persons resulting from the insured's negligence; and (b) damages to the property of others resulting from the insured's negligence. This property may be other vehicles damaged in the accident, or other objects such as fences, landscaping, or buildings.

Collision This category covers damage sustained by the insured's vehicle in an accident. As a premium reduction measure, collision coverage is often sold with a **deductible** amount, for example, $250 deductible. This means that the insured pays the first $250 in damages for each occurrence, and the insurance company pays the amount over $250. As the deductible amount increases, the premium for the insurance decreases.

Comprehensive This insurance coverage protects the insured's vehicle for damage caused by fire, wind, water, theft, vandalism, and other perils not caused by an accident.

Most insurance companies also offer policyholders the option of purchasing policy extras, such as uninsured motorist's protection and coverage while driving a rented or borrowed car. Some policies even offer to pay towing expenses in the event of a breakdown, or cover the cost for a rental car while the insured's vehicle is being repaired after an accident.

Liability rates are based on three primary factors: *who* is driving the vehicle, *where* the vehicle is being driven, and the *amount* of insurance coverage desired. Table 19-6 illustrates typical annual liability premiums for bodily injury and property damage. Note that the rates are listed by driver classification (age, sex, and marital status of the driver), territory (metropolitan area, suburbs, small town, rural or farm area), and amount (in thousands of dollars).

Most states require motor vehicle insurance.

Territory	Driver Class	Bodily Injury (000)					Property Damage (000)				
		10/20	15/30	25/50	50/100	100/300	5	10	25	50	100
1	1	$61	$73	$88	$92	$113	$46	$49	$53	$58	$64
	2	63	75	81	94	116	48	51	55	61	66
	3	65	78	84	98	118	52	54	58	63	69
	4	69	81	86	101	121	54	56	60	65	71
2	1	66	75	83	93	114	56	63	68	73	77
	2	69	77	88	98	117	58	64	70	75	79
	3	75	82	92	104	119	59	66	71	76	82
	4	78	86	95	109	122	62	67	73	78	84
3	1	73	77	84	95	116	64	65	72	76	81
	2	78	83	86	99	119	66	69	74	80	83
	3	84	88	92	103	124	70	73	77	82	85
	4	87	93	95	106	128	72	78	81	85	89
4	1	77	81	86	99	118	76	78	83	88	92
	2	81	86	93	103	121	79	83	87	91	95
	3	87	92	100	106	126	80	84	88	93	97
	4	90	94	103	111	132	84	86	91	94	100

Motor vehicle liability premiums are typically stated in a three-number format, such as 50/100/50, with the numbers given in thousands of dollars. The first two numbers, 50/100, refer to the bodily injury portion and means the policy will pay up to $50,000 for bodily injury caused by the insured's vehicle to any one person, with $100,000 maximum per accident, regardless of the number of people injured. The third number, 50 ($50,000), represents the maximum property damage benefits to be paid per single accident.

Table 19-7 illustrates typical collision and comprehensive premiums. Note that these rates are listed according to model class (type of vehicle—compact, luxury, truck, or van), vehicle age, territory (where driven), and the amount of the deductible.

Insurance companies often adjust premiums upward or downward by the use of **rating factors,** which are multiples of the base rates found in the tables. For example, if a vehicle is used for business purposes, the risk of an accident is increased and therefore a rating factor of say 1.5 might be applied to the base rate to adjust for this risk. A $200 base-rate premium would increase to $300, $200 times the rating factor of 1.5. On the other hand, a vehicle driven less than three miles to work each way would have less chance of having an accident, and might have a rating factor of .9 to lower the rate.

TABLE 19-6

....

MOTOR VEHICLE LIABILITY INSURANCE PREMIUMS ANNUAL—BODILY INJURY AND PROPERTY DAMAGE RATES

● **rating factors**
Multiples of the base rates for motor vehicles; used by insurance companies to adjust premiums upward (factors greater than 1) or downward (factors less than 1), depending on the amount of risk involved in the coverage.

STEPS TO CALCULATE TYPICAL MOTOR VEHICLE INSURANCE PREMIUMS:

Step 1. Use Table 19-6 to find the appropriate base premiums for bodily injury and property damage.

Step 2. Use Table 19-7 to find the appropriate base premiums for collision and comprehensive.

Step 3. Add all the individual premiums to find the total base premium.

Step 4. Multiply the total base premium by the rating factor, if any.

Total annual premium = Total base premium × Rating factor

EXAMPLE

Evie Irvin would like to purchase a motor vehicle insurance policy with bodily injury and property damage coverage in the amounts of 25/50/25. In addition, she wants collision coverage with $500 deductible, and comprehensive with no deductible. Evie is in driver classification 3, and lives in territory 1. Her vehicle, a Jeep Cherokee, is in model class P and is 3 years old. Because she has taken driver training classes, Evie qualifies for a .95 rating factor. As Evie's insurance agent, calculate her total annual premium.

Model Class	Vehicle Age	Territory 1 & 2				Territory 3 & 4			
		Collision		Comprehensive		Collision		Comprehensive	
		$250 Deductible	$500 Deductible	Full Coverage	$100 Deductible	$250 Deductible	$500 Deductible	Full Coverage	$100 Deductible
A–G	0–1	$89	$81	$63	$59	$95	$88	$67	$61
	2–3	87	79	60	57	93	84	63	58
	4–5	86	77	58	54	89	81	60	57
	6+	84	76	55	50	86	78	57	52
H–L	0–1	96	92	78	71	104	95	83	75
	2–3	93	89	76	68	101	90	80	72
	4–5	89	85	74	66	96	87	78	68
	6+	86	81	70	64	92	84	74	66
M–R	0–1	108	104	86	83	112	106	91	88
	2–3	104	101	83	79	109	104	88	82
	4–5	100	98	79	75	104	101	84	77
	6+	94	90	75	71	100	96	80	74
S–Z	0–1	120	115	111	108	124	116	119	113
	2–3	116	112	106	104	121	114	115	109
	4–5	111	107	101	99	116	110	111	106
	6+	108	103	98	96	111	107	108	101

TABLE 19-7

....

MOTOR VEHICLE INSURANCE PREMIUMS
ANNUAL—COLLISION AND COMPREHENSIVE RATES

SOLUTION STRATEGY

Step 1. From Table 19-6, we find the bodily injury premium to be $84 and the property damage premium to be $58.

Step 2. From Table 19-7, we find collision to be $101 and comprehensive to be $83.

Step 3. Total base premium = Bodily injury + Property damage + Collision + Comprehensive
Total base premium = 84 + 58 + 101 + 83 = $326

Step 4.   Total annual premium = Total base premium × Rating factor
Total annual premium = 326 × .95 = $309.70

TRY-IT   EXERCISE

9. **Don Robinson, owner of High Performance Marine, would like to purchase truck insurance with bodily injury and property damage coverage in the amounts of 100/300/100. Don also wants $250 deductible collision, and $100 deductible comprehensive. He is in driver classification 4, and lives in territory 3. His vehicle, a Chevy Blazer, is in model class F and is 4 years old. Since Don uses his truck to make dockside calls and haul boats to his shop, the insurance company has assigned a 2.3 rating factor to his policy. What is Don's total annual premium?**

Check your answer with the solution on page 653.

19-9 Computing the Compensation Due Following an Accident

When the insured is involved in a motor vehicle accident in which he or she is at fault, his or her insurance company must pay out the claims resulting from that accident. Any amounts of bodily injury or property damage that exceed the limits of the policy coverage are the responsibility of the insured.

Bill Bradley has motor vehicle insurance in the following amounts: liability, 15/30/5; $500 deductible collision; and $100 deductible comprehensive. Recently Bill was at fault in an accident in which his van hit a car stopped at a traffic light. Two people in the other vehicle, Angel and Martha Cordero, were injured. Angel's bodily injuries amounted to $6,300 while Martha's more serious injuries totaled $18,400. In addition, their car sustained $6,250 in damages. Although he was not physically injured, the damage to Bill's van amounted to $4,788.

a. How much will the insurance company have to pay, and to whom?

b. What part of the settlement will be Bill's responsibility?

SOLUTION STRATEGY

Liability Portion:

Bill's liability coverage is limited to $15,000 per person. The insurance company will pay the $6,300 for Angel's injuries; however, Bill is responsible for Martha's expenses above the limit.

$18,400	Martha's medical expenses
−$15,000	Insurance limit—bodily injury
$3,400	Bill's responsibility

Property Damage Portion

The property damage limit of $5,000 is not sufficient to cover the damage to Angel's car. Bill will have to pay the portion above the limit.

$6,250	Angel's car repairs
−$5,000	Insurance limit—property damage
$1,250	Bill's responsibility

The damage to Bill's van will be paid by the insurance company, except for the $500 deductible.

$4,788	Van repairs
− $500	Deductible
$4,288	Insurance company responsibility

TRY-IT EXERCISE

10. Joy Miller has automobile liability insurance in the amount of 25/50/10 and also carries $250 deductible collision and full-coverage comprehensive. Recently Joy was at fault in an accident in which her Oldsmobile went out of control on a rainy day and hit two cars, a fence, and the side of a house. The first car, a Lexus, had $8,240 in damages. The second car, a Ford Taurus, sustained damages of $2,540. The repairs to Joy's car amounted to $3,542. In addition, the fence repairs came to $880, while the house damages were estimated at $5,320.

a. How much will the insurance company have to pay, and to whom?

b. What part of the settlement will be Joy's responsibility?

Check your answers with the solutions on page 654.

As an insurance agent, calculate the annual premium for the following clients:

Name	Territory	Driver Class	Bodily Injury	Property Damage	Model Class	Vehicle Age	Comprehensive Deductible	Collision Deductible	Rating Factor	Annual Premium
1. Rosen	2	4	50/100	25	J	3	$100	$250	None	$343.00
2. Maples	1	2	10/20	10	R	1	Full Coverage	500	1.5	456.00
3. Lopez	3	1	25/50	5	U	5	Full Coverage	250	3.0	1,125.00
4. Zahn	2	3	100/300	25	C	4	100	250	None	330.00
5. Nadler	4	2	50/100	100	H	2	Full Coverage	500	1.7	625.60
6. Maui	1	4	15/30	50	M	3	100	250	2.5	822.50
7. Hale	2	1	10/20	10	Q	6	100	250	3.9	1,146.60
8. Coll	3	3	100/300	100	Z	1	Full Coverage	500	None	444.00

9. Shaun Taylor would like to purchase an automobile insurance policy with bodily injury and property damage coverage in the amounts of 50/100/50. In addition, he wants collision coverage with $250 deductible and comprehensive with no deductible. Shaun is in driver classification 4 and lives in territory 3. His vehicle, a Mercedes 190S, is in model class B and is 1 year old. Shaun has had two accidents and one ticket in the past 12 months and is therefore considered to be a high risk. Consequently, the insurance company has assigned a rating factor of 4.0 to his policy. As his automobile insurance agent, calculate the total annual premium for Shaun's policy.

Bodily injury	$106.00	Rating factor	4.0×353.00
Property damage	85.00	Total annual premium	= $1,412.00
Collision	95.00		
Comprehensive	67.00		
	353.00		

10. Howard Marshall's Corvette was hit by a palm tree during Hurricane Andrew. The damage was estimated at $1,544. If Howard carried $250 deductible collision and $100 deductible comprehensive, how much of the damages does the insurance company have to pay?

Total damage $1,544.00
Less comprehensive deductible   – 100.00
Insurance company responsibility = $1,444.00

Liability 50/100/50
Maximum of $50,000 per person
Maximum of 100,000 per accident
Maximum of $50,000 property

Bodily injury (liability)

Hart's injuries	$13,500	Insurance pays all
Black's injuries	11,700	Insurance pays all
Garner's injuries	4,140	Insurance pays all
Williams' injuries	57,800	Insurance pays 50,000
Morgan's injuries	3,590	Insurance pays all

Property damage (liability)

Bus damage	$12,230	Insurance pays all

Collision

Len's camper	$3,780	
Deductible	– 250	
	$3,530	Insurance portion

11. Len Hawkins has motor vehicle liability insurance in the amount of 50/100/50 and also carries $250 deductible collision coverage and full-coverage comprehensive. Recently he was at fault in an accident in which his camper hit a bus. Five people were injured on the bus and were awarded the following settlements by the courts: Hart, $13,500; Black, $11,700; Garner, $4,140; Williams, $57,800; and Morgan, $3,590. The damage to the bus was $12,230 and Len's camper sustained $3,780 in damages.

a. How much will the insurance company have to pay, and to whom?

Insurance Co.

Hart	$13,500	Morgan	3,590
Black	11,700	Bus	12,230
Garner	4,140	Camper	3,530
Williams	50,000		$98,690

b. What part of the settlement will be Len's responsibility?

Len

Williams	$7,800
Deductible	250
	$8,050

CHAPTER 19 ■ INSURANCE

FORMULAS

Life Insurance

$$\text{Number of \$1,000} = \frac{\text{Face value of policy}}{1,000}$$

Annual premium = Number of \$1,000 $\times$ Rate per \$1,000

Premium other than annual = Annual premium $\times$ Premium factor

Income shortfall = Total living expenses − Total income

$$\text{Insurance needed} = \frac{\text{Income shortfall}}{\text{Prevailing interest rate}}$$

Property Insurance

Total annual fire premium = Building premium + Contents premium

Short-rate premium = Annual premium $\times$ Short-rate

Short-rate refund = Annual premium − Short-rate premium

Regular refund = Annual premium − Premium for period in force

$$\text{Coinsurance coverage ratio} = \frac{\text{Insurance carried}}{\text{Insurance required}}$$

$$\text{Amount of loss paid by insurance} = \frac{\text{Insurance carried}}{\text{Insurance required}} \times \text{Amount of loss}$$

$$\text{Carrier's percent of total coverage} = \frac{\text{Amount of carrier's policy}}{\text{Total amount of insurance}}$$

Carrier's share of loss = Amount of loss $\times$ Carrier's percent of total coverage

---

CHAPTER 19 ■ INSURANCE	SUMMARY CHART

SECTION I   LIFE INSURANCE

Topic	P/O, Page	Important Concepts	Illustrative Examples
Calculating Various Types of Life Insurance Premiums	19–1 628	Life insurance guarantees a specified sum of money to the surviving beneficiaries, upon the death of the insured. It is purchased in increments of \$1,000. Calculating premiums: 1. Calculate the number of \$1,000 of insurance desired by dividing the face value of the policy by \$1,000. 2. Locate the appropriate premium rate per \$1,000 in Table 19-1. 3. Calculate the total annual premium by multiplying the number of \$1,000 by the Table 19-1 rate. 4. For premiums other than annual, multiply the annual premium by the appropriate Table 19-2 premium factor.	Jennifer Appleby is 20 years old. She is interested in purchasing a 20-payment life insurance policy with a face value of \$25,000. Calculate her annual and monthly premium. $\text{Number of \$1,000} = \dfrac{25,000}{1,000} = 25$ Table 20-1 rate = \$21.50. Annual premium = $25 \times 21.50 = \underline{\$537.50}$ Monthly premium = $537.50 \times 9\% = \underline{\$48.38}$

CHAPTER 19 ■ INSURANCE (continued)

I, continued

Topic	P/O, Page	Important Concepts	Illustrative Examples
Calculating Life Insurance Nonforfeiture Options	19–2 631	Life insurance policies with accumulated cash value may be converted to one of three nonforfeiture options. Use Table 19-3 and the number of $1,000 of insurance to determine the value of each option. Option 1—Take the cash value of the policy, and cancel the insurance coverage. Option 2—Reduced, paid-up amount of the same insurance. Option 3—Term policy for a certain number of years and days, with the same face value as the original policy.	Barbara Seinfeld, 30 years old, purchased a $50,000 whole life insurance policy at age 20. What is the value of her nonforfeiture options? Number of $1,000 = $\dfrac{50,000}{1,000} = 50$ Option 1: $50 \times \$98 = \underline{\$4,900 \text{ Cash}}$ Option 2: $50 \times \$186 =$ $\underline{\$9,300 \text{ Paid-up Whole Life}}$ Option 3: $\underline{17 \text{ years, } 54 \text{ days Term Policy}}$
Determining the Amount of Life Insurance Needed to Cover Dependents' Income Shortfall	19–3 633	When one of the wage-earners in a household dies, the annual living expenses of the dependents may exceed the annual income. This difference is known as the income shortfall. To calculate the amount of insurance needed to cover the shortfall, use: $\text{Insurance needed} = \dfrac{\text{Income shortfall}}{\text{Prevailing interest rate}}$	With a prevailing interest rate of 5%, how much life insurance will be needed to cover dependents' income shortfall if the annual living expenses amount to $37,600 and the total income is $21,200? Income shortfall = $37,600 - 21,200 = \underline{\$16,400}$ Insurance needed at 5% = $\dfrac{16,400}{.05} = \underline{\$328,000}$

SECTION II PROPERTY INSURANCE

Topic	P/O, Page	Important Concepts	Illustrative Examples
Calculating Typical Fire Insurance Premiums	19–4 636	Fire insurance premiums are based on type of construction, location of the property, and availability of fire protection. Fire insurance premiums are quoted per $100 of coverage, with buildings and contents listed separately. Use Table 19-4 to calculate fire insurance premiums: $\text{Premium} = \text{Number of } \$100 \times \text{Table rate}$	What is the total annual fire insurance premium on a building valued at $120,000, with structural class C and area rating 3, and contents valued at $400,000? Building: $120 \times .69 = \underline{\$82.80}$ Contents: $400 \times .77 = \underline{\$308.00}$ Total annual fire premium = $82.80 + 308.00 = \underline{\$390.80}$

650   Chapter 19 / Insurance

II, continued

Topic	P/O, Page	Important Concepts	Illustrative Examples

Computing Short-Rate Premiums, and Canceled Policy Refunds	19–5 638	Fire policies for less than one year are known as short-rate. Use Table 19-5 for these policies.
		
		a. Short-rate refund
		(Policy canceled by insured):
		
		Short-rate premium =
		   Annual premium × Table factor
		
		Short-rate refund =
		   Annual premium – Short-rate premium
		
		b. Regular refund
		(Policy canceled by insurance company):
		
		Premium for time in force =
		   Annual premium × $\dfrac{\text{Months in force}}{12}$
		
		Regular refund =
		   Annual premium – Premium for time in force
			The Atlas Company has property insurance with State Farm. The annual premium is $3,000.
			a. If Atlas cancels the policy after 2 months, what is the short-rate refund?
			b. If State Farm cancels the policy after 2 months, what is the regular refund?
			
			a. Short-rate refund
			
			Short-rate premium =
			   $3,000 × 30\% = \underline{\$900}$
			
			Short-rate refund =
			   $3,000 − 900 = \underline{\$2,100}$
			
			b. Regular refund
			Time in force premium =
			   $3,000 × \dfrac{2}{12} = \underline{\$500}$
			
			Regular refund =
			   $3,000 − 500 = \underline{\$2,500}$

Calculating Compensation Due, Using Coinsurance Clause	19–6 640	A coinsurance clause stipulates the minimum amount of coverage required for a claim to be paid in full. If less than the coinsurance requirement is carried, the pay-out is proportionately less.
		
		Amount of insurance required =
		   Replacement value × Coinsurance %
		
		Amount of loss paid =
		   $\dfrac{\text{Insurance carried}}{\text{Insurance required}}$ × Amount of loss
			The Novell Corporation has a $150,000 fire insurance policy on a property valued at $250,000. If the policy has an 80% coinsurance clause, how much would be paid in the event of a $50,000 fire?
			
			Insurance required =
			   $250,000 × .8 = \$200,000$
			
			Amount of loss paid =
			   $\dfrac{150,000}{200,000} × 50,000 = \underline{\$37,500}$

Determining a Company's Share of a Loss, When Multiple Carriers Are Used	19–7 641	When more than one insurance company covers a piece of property, the property has multiple carriers. In the event of a claim, each company is responsible for its portion of the total insurance carried.
		
		Carrier's % of total =
		   $\dfrac{\text{Amount of carrier's policy}}{\text{Total insurance}}$
		
		Carrier's share =
		   Amount of loss × Carrier's %
			West Industries had multiple carrier fire insurance on its property as follows:
			
			Southwest Mutual $300,000
			Travelers....................$100,000
			          Total.......$400,000
			
			Assuming that all coinsurance requirements have been met, how much will each carrier be responsible for in a $20,000 fire?
			
			Southwest Mutual:
			   $\dfrac{300,000}{400,000} × 20,000 = \underline{\$15,000}$
			
			Travelers:
			   $\dfrac{100,000}{400,000} × 20,000 = \underline{\$5,000}$

SECTION III   MOTOR VEHICLE INSURANCE

Topic	P/O, Page	Important Concepts	Illustrative Examples
Computing Typical Motor Vehicle Insurance Premiums	19–8 644	Motor vehicle insurance is divided into three main categories: Liability—Covers bodily injury and property damage to others. Use Table 19-6 for these rates. Collision—Covers damage to the insured's vehicle from an auto accident. Use Table 19-7. Comprehensive—Covers damage to the insured's vehicle from fire, wind, water, vandalism, theft, and so on. Use Table 19-7. Rates may be adjusted up or down by multiplying the total table rate by a rating factor.	Roni Salkind would like auto liability coverage of 25/50/25, $250 deductible collision, and $100 deductible comprehensive. She is in driver class 2, and lives in territory 3. Her vehicle, a new 300 ZX, is in model class L, and has a sports car rating factor of 1.7. What is Roni's total auto premium? $86 Bodily injury Table 19-6 $74 Property damage Table 19-6 $104 Collision Table 19-7 + $75 Comprehensive Table 19-7 $339 Total base × 1.7 Rating factor $576.30 Total premium

Computing the Compensation Due Following an Accident	19–9 646	When the policyholder is at fault in an accident, his or her insurance company is responsible for all settlements, up to the limits and deductibles of the policy. Any settlement amounts above the policy coverage are the responsibility of the insured.	Warner Johnson has auto liability coverage of 50/100/50, no deductible comprehensive, and $250 deductible collision. Recently Warner ran a red light and broadsided Sylvia Norton's car.
			   In the court settlement, Sylvia was awarded $75,000 for bodily injury and $14,500 in property damages. Warner's car sustained $7,500 in damages. How much will the insurance company be responsible to pay?
			   How much of the settlement is Warner's responsibility?
			
			Liability:
			   Warner's policy limit for bodily injury liability is $50,000.
			
			$75,000 Court settlement
			–$50,000 Paid by insurance
			$25,000 Paid by Warner
			
			   The policy limit for property damage is $50,000; therefore the insurance company will pay the full $14,500.
			
			Collision:
			
			$7,500 Collision damage
			– 250 Deductible
			$7,250 Paid by insurance

1. Number of $1,000 = $\dfrac{\text{Face value of policy}}{1,000}$

   Number of $1,000 = \dfrac{75,000}{1,000} = 75$

   Table 19-1 rate = $4.92 per $1,000

   Annual premium = Number of 1,000 × Rate per $1,000

   Annual premium = 75 × 4.92 = $369.00

   Quarterly premium = Annual premium × Quarterly factor

   Quarterly premium = 369 × .26 = $95.94

   Total payment = Quarterly payment × 4 payments

   Total payment = $95.94 × 4 = $383.76

   Gilbert will pay $14.76 ($383.76 − $369.00)
        more if paid quarterly.

2. Number of $1,000 = $\dfrac{\text{Face value of policy}}{1,000} = \dfrac{100,000}{1,000} = 100$

   Option 1

   Cash value = 100 × 191 = $19,100

   Option 2

   Paid-up insurance = 100 × 496 = $49,600

   Option 3

   Extended term = 30 years, 206 days

3. Total income = 38,000 + 5,000 = 43,000

   Income shortfall = Total expenses − Total income

   Income shortfall = 54,000 − 43,000 = $11,000

   Insurance needed = $\dfrac{\text{Shortfall}}{\text{Prevailing rate}}$

   Insurance needed = $\dfrac{11,000}{.05} = \$220,000$

4. From Table 19-4
       Building: .38
       Contents: .42

   Building = $\dfrac{\text{Amount of coverage}}{100} = \dfrac{420,000}{100} = 4,200$

   Contents = $\dfrac{\text{Amount of coverage}}{100} = \dfrac{685,000}{100} = 6,850$

   Building = Number of $100 × Rate = 4200 × .38 = $1,596

   Contents = Number of $100 × Rate = 6,850 × .42 = $2,877

   Total premium = Building + Contents

   Total premium = 1,596 + 2,877 = $4,473

5. From Table 19-5, 8 months = 80%

   Short-rate premium = Annual premium × Short-rate

   Short-rate premium = 850 × .8 = $680

   Short-rate refund = Annual premium − Short-rate premium

   Short-rate refund = 850 − 680 = $170

6. Premium for period = Annual premium × $\dfrac{\text{Months in force}}{12}$

   Premium for period = $850 \times \dfrac{8}{12} = \$566.67$

   Regular refund = Annual premium − Premium for period

   Regular refund = 850.00 − 566.67 = $283.33

7. Insurance required = Value of property × Coinsurance percent

   Insurance required = 850,000 × .7 = $595,000

   Amount of loss paid = $\dfrac{\text{Insurance carried}}{\text{Insurance required}} \times \text{Loss}$

   Amount of loss paid = $\dfrac{400,000}{595,000} \times 325,000 = \$218,487.39$

8. Carrier's percent of total = $\dfrac{\text{Amount of carrier's policy}}{\text{Total amount of insurance}}$

   Aetna = $\dfrac{20,000}{125,000} = 16\%$

   USF&G = $\dfrac{45,000}{125,000} = 36\%$

   Hancock = $\dfrac{60,000}{125,000} = 48\%$

   Carrier's share of loss = Amount of loss × Carrier's percent

   Aetna = 16,800 × .16 = $2,688

   USF&G = 16,800 × .36 = $6,048

   Hancock = 16,800 × .48 = $8,064

9. Base premium =
   Bodily injury + Property damage + Collision + Comprehensive

   Base premium = 128 + 89 + 89 + 57 = $363

   Total annual premium = Base premium × Rating factor

   Total annual premium = 363 × 2.3 = $834.90

	a. Insurance Pays			**b. Joy Pays**
10.	$10,000	Property damage	$8,240	Lexus
	+ 3,292	Joy's car *less* deductible	2,540	Taurus
	$13,292	Total insurance	880	Fence
		responsibility	+ 5,320	House
			16,980	Total property damage
			−10,000	Insurance
			$6,980	Joy's portion
			+ 250	Collision deductible
			$7,230	Joy's responsibility

Calculate the annual, semiannual, quarterly, and monthly premiums for the following life insurance policies:

Face Value of Policy	Sex and Age of Insured	Type of Policy	Annual Premium	Semiannual Premium	Quarterly Premium	Monthly Premium
1. $80,000	Male, 29	20-Payment Life	$2,521.60	$1,311.23	$655.62	$226.94
2. 55,000	Female, 21	20-Year Endowment	1,748.45	909.19	454.60	157.36
3. 38,000	Female, 40	5-Year Term	148.20	77.06	38.53	13.34
4. 175,000	Male, 30	Whole Life	3,244.50	1,687.14	843.57	292.01

Calculate the value of the nonforfeiture options for the following life insurance policies:

Face Value of Policy	Years in Force	Type of Policy	Cash Value	Paid-up Insurance	Extended Term Years	Extended Term Days
5. $130,000	15	Whole Life	$20,410	$40,820	21	218
6. 60,000	5	20-Payment Life	$4,380	$12,720	14	86

7. Brian Murphy is 19 years old and is interested in purchasing a whole life insurance policy with a face value of $80,000.

 a. Calculate the annual insurance premium for this policy.

 Annual premium = 13.60 × 80 = $1,088.00

 b. Calculate the monthly insurance premiums.

 Monthly premium = $1,088.00 × 9% = $97.92

 c. How much more will Brian pay per year if he chooses monthly payments?

 Amount more due to monthly payments =
 (97.92 × 12) = 1,175.04 − 1,088.00
 = $87.04

8. Virginia Colbourn purchased a $45,000 20-year endowment life insurance policy when she was 20 years old. She is now 35 years old and wishes to look into her nonforfeiture options. As her insurance agent, calculate the value of Virginia's three options.

 a. Option 1

 Nonforfeiture options:
 Cash value = 647 × 45 = $29,115.00

 b. Option 2

 Reduced paid-up = 794 × 45 = $35,730.00

Name_____

Class_____

ANSWERS

1. _____ Annual $2,521.60

_____ Monthly $226.94

2. _____ Annual $1,748.45

_____ Monthly $157.36

3. _____ Annual $148.20

_____ Monthly $13.34

4. _____ Annual $3,244.50

_____ Monthly $292.01

5. _____ $20,410

_____ $40,820

_____ 21 years

_____ 218 days

6. _____ $4,380

_____ $12,720

_____ 14 years

_____ 86 days

7. a. _____ $1,088.00

 b. _____ $97.92

 c. _____ $87.04

8. a. _____ $29,115.00

 b. _____ $35,730.00

Complete, worked out solutions for questions 1, 5, and 6 appear in the appendix following the index.

Complete, worked out solution to question 10 appears in the appendix following the index.

c. Option 3

Extended term = <u>37 years, 350 days</u>

9. Carl McAdams is evaluating his life insurance needs. His family's total annual living expenses are $54,500. Darlene, his wife, earns $28,900 per year in salary. If the prevailing interest rate is 5%, how much life insurance should Carl purchase to cover his dependents' income shortfall in the even of his death?

Income shortfall = $54,500
−28,900
$25,600

Insurance needed = $\frac{\$25,600}{5\%}$ = $512,000

Calculate the building, contents, and total property insurance premiums for the following property insurance policies:

	Area Rating	Structural Class	Building Value	Building Premium	Contents Value	Contents Premium	Total Premium
10.	4	B	$47,000	$357.20	$93,000	$771.90	$1,129.10
11.	2	A	125,000	475.00	160,000	672.00	1,147.00
12.	3	C	980,000	6,762.00	1,500,000	11,550.00	18,312.00

Calculate the short-term premium and refund for the following policies:

	Annual Premium	Canceled After	Canceled By	Short-Term Premium	Refund
13.	$260	8 months	insurance company	$173.33	$86.67
14.	720	15 days	insured	$100.80	$619.20

Calculate the amount to be paid by the insurance company for each of the following claims:

	Replacement Value of Building	Face Value of Policy	Coinsurance Clause	Amount of Loss	Amount of Loss Insurance Company Will Pay
15.	$260,000	$105,000	80%	$12,000	$6,057.69
16.	490,000	450,000	90%	80,000	$80,000.00

17. You are the insurance agent for Seacoast International, a company that imports men's and women's clothing from Europe and the Far East. The owner, Erin Gregg, would like you to give her a quote on the total annual premium for property insurance on a new warehouse and showroom facility in the amount of $320,000. The building is structural classification B and area rating 4. In addition, Erin will require contents insurance in the amount of $1,200,000.

Property insurance   .76 × 3,200 = $2,432
Contents insurance   .83 × 12,000 = $9,960
Total annual premium = 2,432 + 9,960 = $12,392.00

18. "Movers of the Stars" has been contracted by Premier Events, Inc., to transport the stage and sound equipment for a 4-month rock-and-roll tour by the Rolling Stones. The moving company purchased property insurance to cover this valuable equipment for an annual premium of $12,500. What is the short-rate premium due for this coverage?

Annual premium $12,500, 4 months in force, Canceled by insured
Short-term premium = $12,500 × 50%
= $6,250.00

19. The Professional Medical Center had property valued at $750,000 and insured for $600,000. The fire insurance policy contained an 80% coinsurance clause. One evening an electrical short-circuit caused a $153,000 fire. How much of the damages will be paid by the insurance company?

Amount of insurance required $= \$750,000 \times 80\%$
$= 600,000$

Amount of loss insurance company will pay $= \dfrac{600,000}{600,000} \times 153,000$
$= \underline{\$153,000}$

20. Bubbly Cola Bottling Company had multiple carrier fire insurance coverage on its plant and equipment in the amount of $2,960,000, as follows:

Kemper	$1,350,000 policy
Metropolitan	921,000 policy
The Hartford	689,000 policy
	$2,960,000 total coverage

Assuming that all coinsurance clause stipulations have been met, how much would each carrier be responsible for in the event of a $430,000 fire? (Round to the nearest whole percent.)

a. Kemper

$\dfrac{1,350,000}{2,960,000} = .456 = 46\%$

$430,000 \times .46 = \underline{\$197,800}$

b. Metropolitan

$\dfrac{921,000}{2,960,000} = .311 = 31\%$

$430,000 \times .31 = \underline{\$133,300}$

c. The Hartford

$\dfrac{689,000}{2,960,000} = .232 = 23\%$

$430,000 \times .23 = \underline{\$98,900}$

Name_____

Class_____

ANSWERS

19. _____ $153,000

20. a. _____ $197,800

b. _____ $133,300

c. _____ $98,900

21. _____ $361.80

22. _____ $629.20

23. _____ $564.40

24. _____ $300.20

As an insurance agent, calculate the annual premium for the following clients:

Name	Terri-tory	Driver Class	Bodily Injury	Property Damage	Model Class	Vehicle Age	Comprehensive Deductible	Collision Deductible	Rating Factor	Annual Premium
21. Wills	3	2	50/100	25	X	1	$100	$500	0.9	$361.80
22. Benson	1	1	10/20	5	Q	4	Full Cov.	250	2.2	$629.20
23. Mays	2	4	100/300	100	F	7	$100	500	1.7	$564.40

24. Kathleen Sharp would like to purchase an automobile insurance policy with bodily injury and property damage coverage in the amounts of 25/50/25. In addition, she wants collision coverage with $250 deductible and comprehensive with $100 deductible. Kathleen is in driver classification 2, and lives in territory 3. Her vehicle, a new Toyota Camry, is in model class B. Since the car has an airbag, an alarm, and antilock brakes, the insurance company has assigned a rating factor of .95 to the policy. As her auto insurance agent, calculate Kathleen's total annual premium.

Complete, worked out solutions to questions 21–23 appear in the appendix following the index.

Bodily injury 25/50	86.00
Property damage 25	74.00
Collision $250 deductible	95.00
Comprehensive $100 deductible	61.00
Rating factor .95	316.00 × .95
Class 2, Territory 3	
Model B, 0 years	$300.20 Annual premium

25. Winston Hill has automobile liability insurance in the amount of 50/100/50. He also carries $250 deductible collision and full comprehensive coverage. Recently he was at fault in an accident in which his car went out of control in the rain and struck four pedestrians. In an out-of-court settlement they were awarded the following: Goya, $45,000; Truman, $68,000; Copeland, $16,000; and Kelly, $11,000. Damages to Winston's car amounted to $3,900.

a. How much will the insurance company pay, and to whom?

Insurance company will pay:	
Goya	$45,000.00
Truman	50,000.00
Copeland	5,000.00
Kelly	0.00
Winston's car	3,650.00
	$103,650.00

b. What part of the settlement will be Winston's responsibility?

Winston will pay:	
Truman—Per person limit	$18,000.00
Copeland—Total limit	11,000.00
Kelly—Total limit	11,000.00
Deductible	250.00
	$40,250.00

BUSINESS DECISION
Insuring the Fleet

26. The Yellow Cab Company of Statesville is interested in purchasing $250 deductible collision insurance and full-coverage comprehensive insurance to cover its fleet of 10 taxi cabs. As a requirement for the job, all drivers already carry their own liability coverage in the amount of 100/300/100. Statesville is rated as territory 2. Five of the cabs are 4-year old Checker Towncars, model class Y. Three of them are 2-year old Chrysler station-wagons, model class R. The remaining two are new Buick sedans, in model class C. Since these vehicles are on the road almost 24 hours a day, they are considered to be very high risk, and carry a rating factor of 5.2. They are, however, subject to an 18% multi-vehicle fleet discount.

a. As the insurance agent for Yellow Cab, calculate the total annual premium for the fleet.

10 Cabs, Collision $250 deductible, Comprehensive full coverage, Territory 2

	Comprehensive	Collision
5 Cabs Model Y, 4 years old	@ $101 \times 5 = \$505$	@ $111 \times 5 = \$555$
3 Cabs Model R, 2 years old	@ $83 \times 3 = \$249$	@ $104 \times 3 = \$312$
2 Cabs Model C, 0 years old	@ $63 \times 2 = \$126$	@ $89 \times 2 = \$178$

Total annual premium = $505 + 555 + 249 + 312 + 126 + 178 = \$1,925.00$

$1,925.00 \times 5.2 = 10,010.00 \times 82\% = \underline{\$8,208.20}$

b. When the owner saw your rate quote, he exclaimed, "Too expensive! How can I save some money on this insurance?" At that point, you suggested changing the coverage to $500 deductible collision and $100 deductible comprehensive. How much can you save Yellow Cab using the new coverage?

10 Cabs, Collision $500 deductible, Comprehensive $100 deductible, Territory 2

	Comprehensive	Collision
5 Cabs Model Y, 4 years old	@ $99 \times 5 = \$495$	@ $107 \times 5 = \$535$
3 Cabs Model R, 2 years old	@ $79 \times 3 = \$237$	@ $101 \times 3 = \$303$
2 Cabs Model C, 0 years old	@ $59 \times 2 = \$118$	@ $81 \times 2 = \$162$

Total annual premium = $495 + 535 + 237 + 303 + 162 + 118 = \$1,850.00$

$1,850.00 \times 5.2 = 9,620.00 \times 82\% = \$7,888.40$

$8,208.20 - 7,888.40 = \underline{\$319.80}$ Savings

All the Math That's Fit to Learn

The Business Math Times

Volume XIX   **Insurance**   One Dollar

Career Track:
Insurance Agent

Insurance agents and brokers are professionals who sell individuals and businesses insurance policies that provide protection against loss. They help individuals, families, and businesses select the right policy that best provides insurance protection for their lives and health, as well as for their automobiles, personal valuables, household items, businesses, and other properties.

Agents and brokers prepare reports, maintain records, and, in the event of a loss, help policyholders settle insurance claims. An increasing number of insurance agents offer comprehensive financial planning services to their clients, such as retirement planning and counseling. As a result, many are also licensed to sell mutual funds, annuities, and other securities.

Training, Other Qualifications, and Advancement

For jobs selling insurance, companies prefer college graduates, particularly those who have majored in business or economics. Courses in finance, mathematics, accounting, economics, business law, government, and business administration enable insurance agents to understand changes in tax laws and government regulations which can affect the insurance needs of clients and how agents conduct business. In addition, courses in psychology, sociology, and public speaking are useful in improving sales techniques.

All insurance agents and brokers must obtain a license in the states where they plan to sell insurance. In most states, licenses are issued only to applicants who have completed specified courses and then pass written examinations covering insurance fundamentals and state insurance laws.

SOURCE: Adapted from *Occupational Outlook Handbook*, 1994-95 Edition, U.S. Department of Labor.

"Quote...Unquote"

Here's why insurance companies are mostly indestructible:
The cost of damages most times is less than the deductible.
–*G. Sterling Leiby*

Don't spend all your money today. Save some for a rainy day.
–*Umbrella Salesman*

Auto Insurance Tips

In the United States, the average automobile insurance expenditure per insured vehicle is $638 per year. The states averaging the highest rates, over $800 per year, are Connecticut, Hawaii, Washington, DC, Rhode Island, and California. The lowest, around $400, are Iowa, Idaho, North Dakota, South Dakota, and Wyoming.

Aside from moving to a cheaper state, here are some tips from the Insurance Information Institute on how to save money on your auto insurance rates.

- **Comparison Shop.** Prices for the same coverage can vary by hundreds of dollars among companies.
- **Increase Deductibles.** Higher deductibles on collision and comprehensive coverage can lower your rates substantially. For example, switching from $200 to $500 deductible could reduce your collision cost by 15 to 30 percent.
- **Drop Collision and/or Comprehensive on Older Cars.** It is not cost effective to have this coverage on cars worth less than $1,000. Any claims you make would not substantially exceed annual cost and deductible.
- **Buy a "Low Profile" Car.** Cars that are expensive to repair and those that are favorite targets for thieves have much higher insurance costs.
- **Take Advantage of Low Mileage Discounts.** Many companies offer discounts to motorists who drive fewer than a predetermined number of miles a year.
- **Inquire about Other Discounts.** Many insurers offer substantial rate savings for more than one car, no accidents in three years, drivers over 50 years of age, driver training courses, anti-theft devices and tracking systems, anti-lock brakes, and good grades for students.

SOURCES: Adapted from the *Statistical Abstract of the United States*, 1995 Edition; and the Insurance Information Institute, 110 Williams Street, New York, NY 10038.

Brainteaser

How long will it take a train one mile long to get through a tunnel one mile long, if the train is traveling at 15 miles per hour?

Answer to Last Issue's Brainteaser

The town collected **$24 million in taxes.**

$$X = \frac{1}{3}X + \frac{1}{4}X + \$10 \text{ million}$$

$$X = \frac{7}{12}X + \$10 \text{ million}$$

$$X - \frac{7}{12}X = \$10 \text{ million}$$

$$\frac{5}{12}X = \$10 \text{ million}$$

$$X = \$24 \text{ million}$$

Chapter 20

Investments

Performance Objectives

Financial risk is the chance you take of either making or losing money on an investment. In most cases, the greater the risk, the more money you stand to gain or lose. Investment opportunities range from low-risk **conservative investments,** such as government bonds or certificates of deposit, to high-risk **speculative investments,** such as stocks in new companies, junk bonds, or options and futures. Selecting the right investment depends on personal circumstances as well as general market conditions. See Exhibit 20-1.

Investments are based on *liquidity,* which indicates how easy it is to get your money out; *safety,* how much risk is involved; and *return,* how much you can expect to earn. Investment advice is available from stockbrokers, financial planners, and many other sources. It is generally agreed that over the long run, a **diversified portfolio,** with a mixture of stocks, bonds, cash equivalents, and sometimes other types of investments, is a sensible choice. Determining the correct portfolio mix is a decision that should be based on the amount of assets available, the age of the investor, and the amount of risk desired.

In this chapter, we shall investigate three major categories of investments: **stocks,** also known as **equities,** which represent an *ownership share* of a corporation; bonds, or debt, which represent *IOUs* for money borrowed from the investor; and mutual funds, which are investment *pools* of money with a wide variety of investment goals.

● **financial risk**
The chance you take of either making or losing money on an investment.

● **conservative investments**
Low-risk investments, such as government bonds or certificates of deposit.

● **speculative investments**
High-risk investments, such as stocks in new companies, junk bonds, or options and futures.

● **diversified portfolio**
An investment strategy that is a mixture of stocks, bonds, cash equivalents, and other types of investments.

● **stocks, or equities**
An investment that is an ownership share of a corporation.

SECTION I
STOCKS

20-1 Understanding Stocks and Distributing Dividends on Preferred and Common Stock

Corporations are built and expanded with money known as capital, which is raised by issuing and selling **shares** of stock. Investors' ownership in a company is measured by the number of shares they own. Each ownership portion, or share, is represented by a **stock certificate.** In

● **share**
One unit of stock or ownership in a corporation.

● **stock certificate**
The official document that represents an ownership share in a corporation.

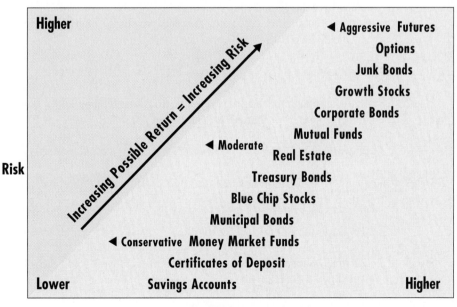

SOURCE: Adapted from Smith Barney Shearson, Inc.

EXHIBIT 20-1
....

RISK AND RETURN

shareholder

The person who owns shares of stock in a corporation.

dividends

A distribution of a company's profits to its shareholders.

publicly held corporation

A corporation whose stock is available to be bought and sold by the general investing public. The opposite of a privately held corporation.

common stock

A class of corporate stock in which the investor has voting rights and shares directly in the success or failure of the business.

preferred stock

A class of corporate stock in which the investor has preferential rights over the common shareholders to dividends and a company's assets.

par value

An arbitrary monetary figure specified in the corporate charter for each share of stock and printed on each stock certificate. The dividend for par value preferred stock is quoted as a percent of the par value.

no-par value stock

Stock that does not have a par value. The dividend for no-par value preferred stock is quoted as a dollar amount per share.

cumulative preferred stock

A type of preferred stock that receives a dividend each year. When no dividends are paid one year, the amount owed accumulates, and must be paid to cumulative preferred shareholders before any dividends can be paid to common shareholders.

dividends in arrears

The amount of dividends that accumulate and are owed to cumulative preferred shareholders for past years in which no dividends were paid.

the past, these certificates were sent to the investor, confirming the stock purchase transaction. Today, however, this confirmation comes in the form of a computerized book entry on an account statement. Investors who actually want to hold their certificates are charged extra service fees. Exhibit 20-2 is an example of a stock certificate.

Generally, if the company does well, the investor or **shareholder** will receive **dividends,** which are a distribution of the company's profits. If the share price goes up, the stockholder can sell the stock at a profit. Today over 50 million people in the United States own stock in thousands of **publicly held corporations.**

Many companies offer two classes of stock to appeal to different types of investors. These classes are known as common and preferred. With **common stock,** an investor shares directly in the success or failure of the business. When the company does well, the dividends and price of the stock may rise, and the investors make money. When the company does poorly, it does not pay dividends and the price of the stock may fall.

With **preferred stock,** the dividends are fixed, regardless of how the company is doing. When the board of directors of a company declare a dividend, the preferred stockholders are paid before the common. If the company goes out of business, the preferred stockholders have priority over the common as far as possibly getting back some of their investment.

Preferred stock is issued either with or without a **par value.** When the stock has a par value, the dividend is specified as a percent of par. For example, each share of 8%, $100 par value preferred stock pays a dividend of $8.00 per share ($100 \times .08$) per year. The dividend is usually paid on a quarterly basis; in this case, $2.00 each quarter. When preferred stock is **no-par value,** the dividend is stated as a dollar amount.

Cumulative preferred stock receives a dividend each year. When no dividends are paid one year, the amount owed, known as **dividends in arrears,** accumulates. Common stockholders cannot receive any dividends until all the dividends in arrears have been paid to cumulative preferred stockholders.

Preferred stock is further divided into categories known as nonparticipating, which means the stockholders receive only the fixed dividend and no more; and participating, which means the stockholders may receive additional dividends if the company does well. Convertible preferred means the stock may be exchanged for a specified number of common shares in the future.

STEPS TO DISTRIBUTE DIVIDENDS ON PREFERRED AND COMMON STOCK:

Step 1. If the preferred stock is *cumulative,* any dividends that are in arrears are paid first; then the preferred dividend is paid for the current period. When the dividend per share is stated in dollars (no-par stock), go to Step 2. When the dividend per share is stated as a percent (par stock), multiply the par value by the dividend rate.

$$\text{Dividend per share (preferred)} = \text{Par value} \times \text{Dividend rate}$$

Step 2. Calculate the total amount of the preferred stock dividend by multiplying the number of preferred shares by the dividend per share.

$$\text{Total preferred dividend} = \text{Number of shares} \times \text{Dividend per share}$$

Step 3. Calculate the total common stock dividend by subtracting the total preferred stock dividend from the total dividend declared.

$$\text{Total common dividend} = \text{Total dividend} - \text{Total preferred dividend}$$

Step 4. Calculate the dividends per share for common stock by dividing the total common stock dividend by the number of shares of common stock.

$$\text{Dividend per share (common)} = \frac{\text{Total common dividend}}{\text{Number of shares (common)}}$$

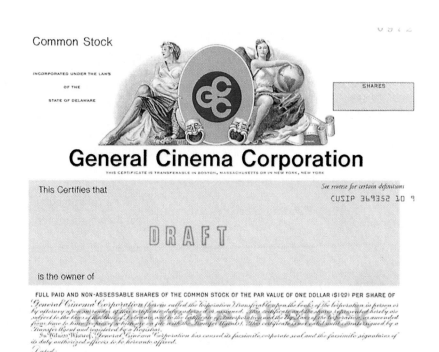

Common Stock

INCORPORATED UNDER THE LAWS
OF THE
STATE OF DELAWARE

NUMBER
FBU

SHARES

General Cinema Corporation

THIS CERTIFICATE IS TRANSFERABLE IN BOSTON, MASSACHUSETTS OR IN NEW YORK, NEW YORK

This Certifies that

See reverse for certain definitions
CUSIP 369352 10 9

DRAFT

is the owner of

FULL PAID AND NON-ASSESSABLE SHARES OF THE COMMON STOCK OF THE PAR VALUE OF ONE DOLLAR ($1.00) PER SHARE OF

COUNTERSIGNED AND REGISTERED
THE FIRST NATIONAL BANK OF BOSTON
TRANSFER AGENT AND REGISTRAR

BY

AUTHORIZED OFFICER

SPECIMEN

CHAIRMAN

SECRETARY

EXHIBIT 20-2

STOCK CERTIFICATE

EXAMPLE

The Eastman Corporation has 2,500,000 shares of common stock outstanding. If a dividend of $4,000,000 was declared by the company directors last year, what are the dividends per share of common stock?

SOLUTION STRATEGY

Since Eastman has no preferred stock, the common shareholders will receive the entire dividend. We go directly to Step 4.

$$\text{Dividend per share (common)} = \frac{\text{Total common dividend}}{\text{Number of shares (common)}} = \frac{4,000,000}{2,500,000} = \underline{\underline{\$1.60 \text{ per share}}}$$

TRY-IT   EXERCISE

1. Forsythe Computer, Inc., has 1,400,000 shares of common stock outstanding. If a dividend of $910,000 was declared by the company directors last year, what is the dividend per share of common stock?

Check your answer with the solution on page 692.

EXAMPLE

The board of directors of Waterways Developers, Inc., have declared a dividend of $300,000. The company has 60,000 shares of preferred stock that pay $.50 per share and 100,000 shares of common stock. Calculate the amount of dividends due the preferred shareholders and the dividend per share of common stock.

SOLUTION STRATEGY

Step 1. Since the preferred dividend is stated in dollars ($.50 per share), we skip to Step 2.

Step 2.   Total preferred dividend = Number of shares × Dividend per share
Total preferred dividend = 60,000 × .50 = $30,000

Step 3.   Total common dividend = Total dividend − Total preferred dividend
Total common dividend = 300,000 − 30,000 = $270,000

Step 4.

$$\text{Dividend per share (common)} = \frac{\text{Total common dividend}}{\text{Number of shares (common)}} = \frac{270,000}{100,000} = \underline{\underline{\$2.70 \text{ per share}}}$$

TRY-IT   EXERCISE

2. **The board of directors of Analog Technology, Inc., has declared a dividend of $2,800,000. The company has 600,000 shares of preferred stock that pay $1.40 per share and 1,000,000 shares of common stock. Calculate the amount of dividends due the preferred shareholders and the dividend per share of common stock.**

Check your answer with the solution on page 692.

EXAMPLE

Langley Enterprises has 100,000 shares of $100 par value, 6%, cumulative preferred stock and 2,500,000 shares of common stock. Although no dividend was declared last year, a $5,000,000 dividend has been declared this year. Calculate the amount of dividends due the preferred shareholders and the dividend per share of common stock.

SOLUTION STRATEGY

Step 1. Because the preferred stock is cumulative, and the company did not pay a dividend last year, the preferred shareholders are entitled to the dividends in *arrears* and the dividends for the *current period.*

Dividend per share (preferred) = Par value × Dividend rate
Dividend per share (preferred) = 100 × .06 = $6.00 per share

Step 2.

Total preferred dividend (per year) = Number of shares × Dividend per share
Total preferred dividend (per year) = 100,000 × 6.00 = $600,000
Total preferred dividend = 600,000 (arrears) + 600,000 (current year) = $1,200,000

Step 3.

Total common dividend = Total dividend − Total preferred dividend
Total common dividend = 5,000,000 − 1,200,000 = $3,800,000

Step 4.

$$\text{Dividend per share (common)} = \frac{\text{Total common dividend}}{\text{Number of shares (common)}} = \frac{3,800,000}{2,500,000} = \underline{\underline{\$1.52}}$$

TRY-IT EXERCISE

3. Fuller Laboratories has 300,000 shares of $100 par value, 7.5%, cumulative preferred stock and 5,200,000 shares of common stock. Although no dividend was declared for last year, a $7,000,000 dividend has been declared for this year. Calculate the amount of dividends due the preferred shareholders and the dividend per share of common stock.

Check your answers with the solutions on page 692.

20-2 Reading Stock Quotations

Stock quotation tables found in the business section of most newspapers provide investors with a daily summary of what happened in the stock market on the previous trading day. Let's take a column-by-column look at a typical day's listing for McDonald's. Exhibit 20-3 is a portion of such a table, reprinted from *The Wall Street Journal.*

Stock prices on these tables are listed in dollars and fractions (eighths, fourths, and halves) of a dollar. For calculation purposes, these fractions should be converted to decimals. The first step in reading the stock quotation table is to locate the alphabetical listing of the company whose stock you want to look up, in this case McDonald's. Each line is divided into 12 columns as follows:

Column 1 (Hi—$62\frac{1}{2}$) Highest price of the stock during the preceding 52-week period.

EXHIBIT 20-3

THE WALL STREET JOURNAL
NEW YORK STOCK EXCHANGE
COMPOSITE TRANSACTIONS

	52 Weeks Hi	52 Weeks Lo	Stock	Sym	Div	Yld %	PE	Vol 100s	Hi	Lo	Close	Net Chg
▼	48 1/2	41 1/4	JamesRiver pfL		3.50	8.6	...	84	41 1/2	40 1/2	40 1/2	- 3/4
	26 3/4	22 3/4	JamesRiver pfO		2.06	9.0	...	59	23 1/8	22 3/4	23	...
	2 7/8	7/32	vjJamesway	JMY		...	...	147	5/8	1/2	9/16	...
	18	12	JapanEquity	JEQ	1.09e	6.6	...	351	16 5/8	16 3/8	16 1/2	...
	14 1/2	8 1/4	JapanOTC	JOF		...	...	504	13	12 3/4	12 3/4	- 1/4
	26 3/4	16 5/8	JardineFlemg	JFC	1.73e	9.8	...	327	17 7/8	17 1/4	17 5/8	- 3/8
n	15 1/4	13 7/8	JardineIndia	JFI		...	...	170	14 3/8	14	14 1/8	+ 1/8
	57 7/8	43 3/8	JeffPilot	JP	1.72f	3.5	13	453	49 7/8	49 1/4	49 3/4	+ 1/2
	17 3/8	5 5/8	JennyCraig	JC	.60	9.8	6	129	6 1/4	6 1/8	6 1/8	- 1/8
▼	61 1/2	51 1/2	JerCentl pf		4.00	7.8	...	z20	51	51	51	-1
	42 1/8	18 3/8	JohnAldenFnl	JA	.40f	1.1	11	902	35 7/8	34 7/8	35 3/8	+ 3/8
	41 5/8	19 3/8	JohnNuveen	JNC	.64f	3.1	12	2131	20 3/4	20	20 3/4	+ 1/2
	45 3/4	35 5/8	JohnsJohns	JNJ	1.04	2.6	15	14264	40 3/8	38 5/8	40 3/8	+ 1 1/2
	61 3/4	45 1/2	JohnsContrl	JCI	1.44	2.8	15	831	52 3/8	50 5/8	51 3/4	+ 1 1/4
s	13 3/4	8 1/4	JohnstnInd	JII	.33	3.3	13	42	10	10	10	- 1/4
	35 3/4	18 5/8	JonesApparel	JNY		...	17	949	32 1/8	32	32	- 1/4
	27 1/8	16 1/4	Jostens	JOS	.88	5.3	dd	425	16 3/4	16 1/2	16 5/8	+ 1/8
	14	8 1/2	JoyTech	JOY		...	29	471	12 3/4	12 5/8	12 3/4	+ 1/4
	15	12 1/4	JundtGrowFd	JF	.53e	3.9	...	323	13 3/4	13 1/2	13 3/4	+ 1/4
			-K-K-K-									
s	32 3/4	17 1/8	KCS Engy	KCS	.08	.3	29	216	25 7/8	24 5/8	24 7/8	- 7/8
	27 1/4	13 1/2	KLM	KLM		...	...	628	26 1/2	26 1/8	26 3/8	+ 1/8
s▼	30	21 3/8	KN Engy	KNE	.96	4.5	14	60	21 3/4	21 1/4	21 1/4	- 1/2
	32 3/4	25 7/8	KU Engy	KU	1.64f	6.2	12	212	26 5/8	26 1/8	26 5/8	+ 1/4
	28 7/8	26 5/8	KIII pf		2.88	10.6	...	5	27 1/4	27 1/4	27 1/4	+ 1/4
	12 1/2	6 3/8	KaiserAlum	KLU		...	dd	440	8 7/8	8 3/4	8 3/4	- 1/8
n▼	8 3/4	7 1/4	KaiserAlum pfA		.65	8.8	...	128	7 3/8	7	7 3/8	...
n▼	12 1/8	9 5/8	KaiserAlum pfD		.12p	1.2	...	144	9 3/4	9 1/2	9 5/8	...
	28 3/8	22 7/8	KanebPipe	KPP	2.20	8.7	...	86	25 3/4	25 3/8	25 3/8	...
	4 1/8	2 5/8	KanebSvcs	KAB		...	7	410	3 3/8	3 1/4	3 1/4	- 1/8
	26 1/4	20 5/8	KanCityPL	KLT	1.48	6.8	14	794	21 3/4	21 1/4	21 3/4	+ 3/8
	52 5/8	**30 1/2**	**KanCitySou**	**KSU**	**.30**	**.7**	**19**	**2503**	**44 3/8**	**41 3/8**	**41 3/4**	**- 2 3/4**
	16 5/8	14	KanCitySou pf		1.00	6.9	4	z10	14 1/2	14 1/2	14 1/2	- 1/2
	10 3/4	7	KaslerHldg	KAS	.05p	.7	26	372	7 3/8	7 1/4	7 1/4	...
	28 1/8	25	KatyInd	KT	.25	1.0	dd	9	25 3/8	25 1/4	25 3/8	+ 3/8

	1	2	3	4	5	6	7	8	9	10	11	12
	52 Weeks Hi	**52 Weeks Lo**	**Stock**	**Sym**	**Div**	**Yld %**	**PE**	**Vol 100s**	**Hi**	**Lo**	**Close**	**Net Chg**
	1 3/8	1/2	MLawrencEds	MLE		...	dd	10	1	15/16	1	...
s	47 1/4	35 3/4	MartinMar	ML	.90	2.0	10	1857	44 1/2	44	44 1/4	+ 1/4
n▼	25 7/8	20 1/2	MartinMarMatl	MLM		...	...	231	20 1/2	20	20 1/8	- 3/8
s	35 3/4	12 3/8	MarvelEntn	MRV		...	29	2207	16 1/8	15 1/2	16 1/8	+ 1/4
	39 7/8	25 1/2	Masco	MAS	.68	2.4	19	7359	28 3/4	27 3/4	28	...
	28 1/8	**16 1/8**	**Mascotech**	**MSX**	**.08**	**.4**	**31**	**1821**	**20 5/8**	**19 1/2**	**19 1/2**	**- 1 1/8**
n	25 3/8	19	Mascotech pf		1.20	6.2	...	29	19 5/8	19 1/4	19 1/4	- 5/8
	33 1/4	28 1/8	MassMuInv	MCI	2.80	8.9	...	36	31 5/8	31 3/8	31 3/8	+ 1/4
	8 3/4	7 1/2	MassMuPrtInv	MPV	.68	8.9	...	131	7 7/8	7 5/8	7 5/8	- 1/4
	26 5/8	17	MaterlSci	MSC		...	22	89	22 1/8	21 3/4	22 1/8	+ 1/4
	16 1/2	9 1/4	MatlackSys	MLK		...	20	51	15 5/8	15	15 5/8	+ 1/2
	176	114	MatsuElec	MC	1.27e	.8	...	8	167	167	167	...
s	26 7/8	18 1/4	Mattel	MAT	.24	1.0	26	7958	24 3/4	23 5/8	23 7/8	- 1/4
	5 1/4	**3 7/8**	**MaunaLoa**	**NUT**	**.40**	**9.1**	**31**	**91**	**4 5/8**	**4 3/8**	**4 3/8**	**- 1/4**
	10 3/8	4 1/8	MaxusEngy	MXS		...	dd	2819	4 5/8	4 3/8	4 1/2	...
n	25 3/4	21 1/8	MaxusEngy pfA		2.50	11.4	...	17	21 7/8	21 3/4	21 7/8	+ 1/8
	49 7/8	39	MaxusEngy pf		4.00	10.2	...	5	39 3/8	39 1/4	39 1/4	- 1/8
	20 5/8	12 1/4	MaxximMed	MAM		...	16	16	16 1/4	16 1/8	16 1/4	...
s	46 1/2	33 3/8	MayDeptStrs	MA	1.04f	2.6	14	5448	41 1/4	39 1/2	39 5/8	- 3/4
	31 1/2	16 3/4	Maybelline	MAY	.24	.8	24	367	31 1/4	30 5/8	31 1/8	+ 3/8
	20	13	Maytag	MYG	.50	2.9	36	3013	17 5/8	17 1/8	17 1/8	...
n	28 1/4	22 5/8	McArthurGln	MCG	.64e	2.7	...	256	24	23 7/8	23 7/8	- 1/8
	25 5/8	18 1/8	McClatchy A	MNI	.32f	1.5	20	42	22	21 5/8	22	+ 1/8
	32 7/8	19 7/8	McDermInt	MDR	1.00	4.7	12	1786	21 1/4	20 3/4	21 1/8	+ 1/4
	35 7/8	29	McDermInt pfA		2.20	7.5	...	38	29 5/8	29 1/4	29 1/2	+ 1/8
	31 7/8	30 7/8	McDermInt pfB		2.60	8.3	...	8	31 1/4	31 1/4	31 1/4	+ 1/8
s	16 7/8	12 1/4	McDnInvst	MDD	.30	2.1	6	69	14 1/8	13 7/8	14	- 1/4
	62 1/2	45 1/2	McDonalds	MCD	.43	.8	19	5373	57 1/4	56 3/8	56 7/8	+ 3/8
	28	24 1/2	McDonalds dep pf		1.93	7.7	...	3138	24 61/64	24 5/8	24 61/64	...
	122 5/8	58	McDonDoug	MD	1.40	1.2	14	2221	115 1/8	113	113 7/8	- 1/4
	75 1/4	55 1/4	McGrawH	MHP	2.32f	3.5	cc	785	65 7/8	64 3/4	65 3/8	+ 3/8
	68 1/2	38 5/8	McKesson	MCK	1.68	2.6	18	997	64 1/4	62 7/8	63 7/8	+ 1 1/8
n	17 3/4	13 1/4	McWhortrTch wi			...	...	21	17 3/8	17 1/4	17 3/8	...
	48 1/2	39 1/8	Mead	MEA	1.00	2.5	19	974	40 3/8	39 1/2	39 5/8	- 3/4
	21	15 3/4	Measurx	MX	.44	2.4	38	45	18 3/4	18 1/8	18 1/8	- 3/4
s	10 1/4	5 5/8	MedChmPrd	MCH	1.05t	17.9	11	135	6	5 7/8	5 7/8	...

Column 2 (Lo—$45\frac{1}{2}$) Lowest price of the stock during the preceding 52-week period.

Column 3 (Stock—McDonald's) Company name and type of stock. If no symbol appears after a name, it is common stock. A "pf" after the name indicates it is preferred stock.

Column 4 (Sym—MCD) Symbol used to identify a particular stock on the stock exchange's ticker and on other references such as information systems and computer databases.

Column 5 (Div—.43) The amount of dividend paid out on the stock last year. When there were no dividends, the column is blank.

Column 6 (Yld %—.8) Yield percent. Last year's dividend as a percent of the current price of the stock. Found by dividing last year's dividend by the current price of the stock. When there were no dividends, the column shows "...".

Column 7 (PE—19) Price-earnings ratio, which indicates investor confidence in a stock. It is the ratio of the current price of the stock to the earnings per share of the company for the past 4 quarters. When a company has no earnings, the column shows "..."; dd indicates a loss.

Column 8 (Vol 100s—5373) Indicates the volume or number of shares, in hundreds, traded for the day. For example, 5373 would mean 537,300 shares (5373×100). Listings that are *underlined* indicate unusually large trading activity or volume.

Column 9 (Hi—$57\frac{1}{4}$) The highest price the stock reached during the trading day.

Column 10 (Lo—$56\frac{3}{8}$) The lowest price the stock reached during the trading day.

Column 11 (Close—$56\frac{7}{8}$) The closing or last price of the trading day.

Column 12 (Net Chg + $\frac{3}{8}$) Indicates the difference, or net change, between the closing price and the previous close.

EXAMPLE

From the following stock quotation table, explain the information listed for Exxon Corporation.

	18¾	15½	Excelsior	EIS	1.39e	8.8	...	10	15⅞	15⅞	15⅞	+ ⅛
n	12½	10⅞	ExectveRisk	ER		...	...	16	11⅜	11¼	11⅜	– ⅛
	52¼	39⅞	Exel	XL	1.20	2.7	7	371	45⅛	44⅝	45⅛	+ ⅜
n▲	42¾	20	Exide	EX	.02p	...	...	1910	45¾	43	44¾	+ 2
	28½	24¼	Extecaptl A		2.28	9.1	...	334	25⅛	24¾	25	+ ¼
	67⅜	60⅜	Exxon	XON	2.88	4.6	15	12338	63¼	62⅛	63⅛	+ ⅝

SOLUTION STRATEGY

According to the listing, the 52-week high for Exxon was $\$67\frac{3}{8}$ and the low was $\$60\frac{3}{8}$. The ticker symbol is XON. The dividend last year was $2.88 per share, the yield is 4.6%, and the PE ratio is 15. The volume for the day was 1,233,800 shares; the high for the day was $\$63\frac{1}{4}$; the low for the day was $\$62\frac{1}{8}$; and the closing price was $\$63\frac{1}{8}$, up $\frac{5}{8}$ from the previous day.

TRY-IT EXERCISE

4. From the following stock quotation table, explain the information listed for the common stock of Delta Airlines.

15⅛	13⅛	DelGpDivInco	DDF	1.10a	8.1	...	146	13½	13¼	13½	+ ⅛
25⅞	19⅞	DelmarPL	DEW	1.54	7.4	12	377	20⅞	20½	20¾	– ⅛
61⅜	39½	DeltaAir	DAL	.20	.5	dd	3304	42¼	41⅛	42¼	+ 1
58⅞	43¾	DeltaAir pf		3.50	7.7	...	1294	45⅜	44⅞	45⅜	+ ½
13⅝	9¾	DeltaWdsde	DLW	.40	3.4	dd	106	12⅛	11¾	11⅞	...

Check your answers with the solutions on page 692.

20-3 Calculating Current Yield for a Stock

One way to measure how much you are earning on a stock compared with other investments is by calculating the **current yield.** In the stock quotations, this is listed in the yield % column. The current yield is a way of evaluating the current value of a stock. It tells you how much dividend you get as a percentage of the current price of the stock. When a stock pays no dividend, there is no current yield.

- **current yield**
A percentage measure of how much an investor is earning on a stock compared with other investments. It is calculated by dividing the annual dividend per share by the current price of the stock.

STEPS TO DETERMINE THE PRICE-EARNINGS RATIO OF A STOCK:

Step 1. Divide the annual dividend per share by the current price of the stock:

$$\text{Current yield} = \frac{\textbf{Annual dividend per share}}{\textbf{Current price of the stock}}$$

Step 2. Convert the answer to a percent, rounded to the nearest tenth.

EXAMPLE

Calculate the current yield for Apex Corporation stock, which pays a dividend of **$1.70** per year and is currently selling at **$34½** per share.

SOLUTION STRATEGY

$$\text{Current yield} = \frac{\text{Annual dividend per share}}{\text{Current price of the stock}}$$

$$\text{Current yield} = \frac{1.70}{34.50} = .0492753 = \underline{\underline{4.9\%}}$$

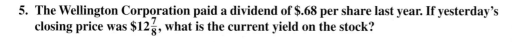

TRY-IT   EXERCISE

5. The Wellington Corporation paid a dividend of **$.68 per share last year. If yesterday's closing price was $12⅞,** what is the current yield on the stock?

Check your answer with the solution on page 692.

20-4 Determining the Price-Earnings Ratio of a Stock

One of the most widely used tools for analyzing a stock is the price-to-earnings ratio, commonly called the **price-earnings ratio** or **P/E ratio.** This number shows the relationship between the price of a stock and the company's earnings for the past 12 months. The price-earnings ratio is an important indicator because it reflects buyer confidence in a particular stock compared with the stock market as a whole. For example, a P/E ratio of 20, or 20:1, means that buyers are willing to pay 20 times the current earnings for a share of stock.

The price-earnings ratio of a stock is most useful when compared with the P/E ratios of the company in previous years and with the ratios of other companies in the same industry.

- **price-earnings ratio, or P/E ratio**
A ratio that shows the relationship between the price of a stock and a company's earnings for the past 12 months; one of the most widely used tools for analyzing stock.

STEPS TO DETERMINE THE PRICE-EARNINGS RATIO OF A STOCK:

Step 1. Divide the current price of the stock by the earnings per share for the past 12 months:

$$\text{Price-earnings ratio} = \frac{\textbf{Current price per share}}{\textbf{Earnings per share}}$$

Step 2. Round answer to the nearest whole number (may be written as a ratio, X:1).

Monarch stock is currently selling at $104\frac{3}{4}$. If the company had earnings per share of $3.60 last year, calculate the price-earnings ratio of the stock.

SOLUTION STRATEGY

$$\text{Price-earnings ratio} = \frac{\text{Current price per share}}{\text{Earnings per share}}$$

$$\text{Price-earnings ratio} = \frac{104.75}{3.60} = 29.09722 = \underline{29} \text{ or } \underline{29\!:\!1}$$

This means investors are currently willing to pay 29 times the earnings for 1 share of Monarch stock.

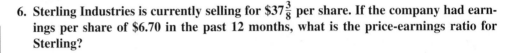

TRY-IT EXERCISE

6. Sterling Industries is currently selling for $37\frac{3}{8}$ per share. If the company had earnings per share of $6.70 in the past 12 months, what is the price-earnings ratio for Sterling?

Check your answer with the solution on page 692.

20-5 Computing the Cost, Proceeds, and Gain (or Loss) on a Stock Transaction

Investors take on the risks of purchasing stocks in the hopes of making money. Although they are more risky than many other types of investment, over the years stocks have shown they are capable of generating spectacular returns in some periods and steady returns in the long run. One investment strategy is to buy stocks and keep them for the dividends paid by the company each quarter. Another strategy is to make money from the profit (or loss) of buying and

Stock exchanges are where brokers execute investors' requests to buy and sell shares of stock.

selling the stock. Simply put, investors generally want to buy low and sell high! The gain or loss is the difference between the cost of purchasing the stock and the **proceeds** received when selling the stock.

$$\text{Gain (or loss) on stock} = \text{Proceeds} - \text{Total cost}$$

Stocks are generally purchased and sold through a **stockbroker.** Brokers have representatives at various **stock exchanges,** which are like a marketplace where stocks are bought and sold in the form of an auction. When you ask your broker to buy or sell a stock, the order is transmitted to the representative on the floor of the exchange. It is there that your request is *executed* or transacted.

The charge for this service is a **commission,** which is a percent of the cost of the transaction. Commission rates are competitive, and vary from broker to broker. **Full-service brokers,** who provide additional services such as research data and investment advice, charge higher commissions than **discount brokers,** who simply execute the transactions.

Another factor affecting the commission is whether the amount of shares purchased is a **round lot,** a multiple of 100, or an **odd lot,** less than 100. The commission rate on an odd lot is usually a bit higher than on a round lot. For example, the commission on a 400-share transaction might be 3%, while the commission on a 40-share transaction might be 4%.

STEPS TO COMPUTE THE COST, PROCEEDS, AND GAIN (OR LOSS) ON A STOCK TRANSACTION:

Cost of purchasing stock

Step 1. Calculate the cost of the shares:

Cost of shares = Price per share × Number of shares

Step 2. Compute the amount of the broker's commission:

Broker's commission = Cost of shares × Commission rate

Step 3. Determine the total cost of the stock purchase:

Total cost = Cost of shares + Broker's commission

Proceeds from selling stock

Step 1. Calculate the value of shares upon sale:

Value of shares = Price per share × Number of shares

Step 2. Compute the amount of the broker's commission.

Step 3. Determine the proceeds by subtracting the commission from the value of the shares:

Proceeds = Value of shares − Broker's commission

Gain (or loss) on the transaction

Gain (or loss) on transaction = Proceeds − Total cost

EXAMPLE

You purchase 350 shares of General Dynamo common stock at $46\frac{1}{2}$ per share. A few months later you sell the shares at $54\frac{3}{8}$. Your stockbroker charges 3% commission on round lots and 4% on odd lots. Calculate (a) the total cost, (b) the proceeds, and (c) the gain or loss on the transaction.

---

proceeds
The amount of money that an investor receives after selling a stock. It is calculated as the value of the shares less the broker's commission.

stockbroker
A professional in stock market trading and investments who acts as an agent in the buying and selling of stocks or other securities.

stock exchanges
Marketplaces where stocks, bonds, and mutual funds are bought and sold in the form of an auction.

stockbroker's commission
The fee a stockbroker charges for assisting in the purchase or sale of shares of stock; a percent of the cost of the stock transaction.

full-service broker
Stockbrokers who provide services such as research and investment advice in addition to assisting in the purchase or sale of stock. Commissions generally range from 3% to 5% of the cost of the transaction.

discount broker
Minimum service stockbrokers who simply execute stock purchase and sale transactions. Commissions generally range from 1% to 2% of the cost of the transaction.

round lot
Shares of stock purchased in multiples of 100.

odd lot
The purchase of less than 100 shares of stock.

SOLUTION STRATEGY

a. *Cost of purchasing stock*

Step 1.
$$\text{Cost of shares} = \text{Price per share} \times \text{Number of shares}$$
$$\text{Cost of shares} = 46.50 \times 350 = \underline{\$16,275.00}$$

Step 2.
$$\text{Broker's commission} = \text{Cost of shares} \times \text{Commission rate}$$
$$\text{Round lot commission} = 300 \text{ shares} \times 46.50 \times .03 = \$418.50$$
$$\text{Odd lot commission} = 50 \text{ shares} \times 46.50 \times .04 = \$93.00$$
$$\text{Broker's commission} = 418.50 + 93.00 = \underline{\$511.50}$$

Step 3.
$$\text{Total cost} = \text{Cost of shares} + \text{Broker's commission}$$
$$\text{Total cost} = 16,275 + 511.50 = \underline{\$16,786.50}$$

b. *Proceeds from selling stock*

Step 1.
$$\text{Value of shares} = \text{Price per share} \times \text{Number of shares}$$
$$\text{Value of shares} = 54.375 \times 350 = \underline{\$19,031.25}$$

Step 2.
$$\text{Broker's commission} = \text{Cost of shares} \times \text{Commission rate}$$
$$\text{Round lot commission} = 300 \text{ shares} \times 54.375 \times .03 = \$489.38$$
$$\text{Odd lot commission} = 50 \text{ shares} \times 54.375 \times .04 = \$108.75$$
$$\text{Broker's commission} = 489.38 + 108.75 = \underline{\$598.13}$$

Step 3.
$$\text{Proceeds} = \text{Value of shares} - \text{Broker's commission}$$
$$\text{Proceeds} = 19,031.25 - 598.13 = \underline{\$18,433.12}$$

c. *Gain (or loss) on the transaction*

$$\text{Gain (or loss) on transaction} = \text{Proceeds} - \text{Total cost}$$
$$\text{Gain (or loss) on transaction} = 18,433.12 - 16,786.50 = \underline{\$1,646.62}$$

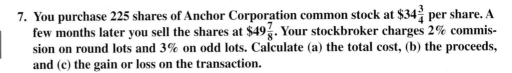

TRY-IT EXERCISE

7. You purchase 225 shares of Anchor Corporation common stock at $34\frac{3}{4}$ per share. A few months later you sell the shares at $49\frac{7}{8}$. Your stockbroker charges 2% commission on round lots and 3% on odd lots. Calculate (a) the total cost, (b) the proceeds, and (c) the gain or loss on the transaction.

Complete, worked out solutions to questions 1–2 appear in the appendix following the index.

Check your answers with the solutions on page 693.

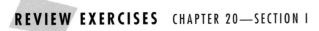

REVIEW EXERCISES CHAPTER 20—SECTION I $\boxed{S}$

Calculate the preferred and common dividend per share for the following companies:

	Company	Common Stock Shares	Preferred Stock Shares	Div. or Par	Cum.	Dividend Declared	Arrears	Preferred Div./Share	Common Div./Share
1.	Intel	5,000,000		none		$3,000,000	none	–	$.60
2.	Alcoa	10,000,000	3,000,000	$5.50	no	25,000,000	none	$5.50	$.85
3.	Pepsi	8,000,000	2,000,000	$100 6%	no	10,000,000	none	$5.00	0
4.	Wrigley	4,000,000	1,000,000	$100 4%	yes	14,000,000	1 year	$8.00	$1.50
5.	IBM	20,000,000	4,000,000	$6.25	yes	none	1 year	0	0

Answer Questions 6–10 based on the following stock quotation table:

59¾	37	Torchmark	TMK	1.12	2.9	11	1699	39⅜	38⅞	39⅛ + ¼		
30½	16¾	Toro	TTC	.48	1.9	18	776	25¾	25½	25½	...	
35	21⅜	Tosco	TOS	.60	2.0	13	1208	30¾	30	30⅜ + ½		
74	57¾	Tosco pf		4.38	6.6	...	11	65⅞	65	65⅞ + 1⅝		
▲ 29½	22½	Total	TOT	.97e	3.3	...	1127	29⅝	29⅜	29⅝ + ⅜		
s 33	17⅛	TotlSysSvc	TSS	.14	.6	37	35	23⅞	23⅜	23⅝ – ⅛		
n 23⅛	18⅝	TownCntry	TCT	1.60	8.5	...	766	19	18⅝	18⅞	...	
42⅞	32⅜	ToysRUs	TOY		...	21	9009	34⅝	33¾	34½ + ¾		
62⅜	47	TransamCp	TA	2.00	4.0	10	1450	51	49⅞	50¼ + ⅜		
28⅜	24⅝	TransamCp pf		2.13	8.4	...	289	25½	25⅛	25½	...	
26¾	22⅞	TransamInco	TAI	1.92	8.1	11	58	24¼	23¾	23¾ – ¼		

6. Town & Country—High and low for the past 52 weeks: _____ $23\frac{1}{8}$, $18\frac{5}{8}$ _____

7. Toro—Ticker symbol, PE ratio, and high for the day: _____ TTC, 18, $25\frac{3}{4}$ _____

8. Transamerica Corp. preferred—Dividend, volume, net change: $2.13, 28,900 shares, 0

9. Toys'R'Us—Percent Yield, volume, closing price: _____ 0, 900,900 shares, $34\frac{1}{2}$ _____

10. Tosco—Dividend, percent yield, low for the day: _____ .60, 2.0, 30 _____

Calculate the missing information for the following stocks:

Company	Earnings per Share	Annual Dividend	Current Price per Share	Current Yield	Price-Earnings Ratio
11. Sears	$6.59	$1.60	$46⅛	3.5%	7
12. Wendy's	$ .77	$ .24	$17⅝	1.4%	23
13. Rubbermaid	1.31	$ .45	$27½	1.6%	21
14. Ford	$4.92	$1.60	64	2.5%	13
15. Disney	1.41	.30	$42⅜	.7%	30

Complete, worked out solutions to questions 11, 13–15 appear in the appendix following the index.

Calculate the total cost, proceeds, and gain (or loss) for the following stock market transactions:

Company	Number of Shares	Purchase Price	Selling Price	Commissions Buy	Commissions Sell	Commissions Odd Lot	Total Cost	Proceeds	Gain (or Loss)
16. DuPont	100	$47½	$56½	3%	3%		$4,892.50	$5,480.50	$588.00
17. Wal-Mart	350	18¼	29⅛	2	2	add 1%	$6,524.38	$9,975.31	$3,450.93
18. Heinz	900	28⅝	36¼	3	3		$28,535.38	$31,646.25	$3,110.87
19. Goodyear	775	37½	34¾	1½	1½	add 1%	$29,526.56	$26,501.21	($3,025.35)
20. AmExpress	500	25⅞	25⅞	3	3		$13,325.63	$12,549.37	($776.26)

21. The Maxtor Corporation has 500,000 shares of common stock outstanding. If a dividend of $425,000 was declared by the company directors last year, what is the dividend per share of common stock?

$$\text{Dividend per share} = \frac{\text{Total common dividend}}{\text{Number of shares}}$$

$$= \frac{\$425,000}{500,000} = \underline{\$.85} \text{ per share}$$

22. The board of directors of Saratoga, Inc., has declared a dividend of $3,000,000. The company has 700,000 shares of preferred stock that pay $.90 per share and 1,600,000 shares of common stock.

    a. What are the dividends due the preferred shareholders?

$$\text{Total preferred dividend} = \text{number of shares} \times \text{dividend per share}$$
$$= 700,000 \times .90$$
$$= \underline{\underline{\$630,000}}$$

    b. What is the dividend per share of common stock?

$$\text{Total common dividend} = \$3,000,000 - \$630,000$$
$$= \underline{\$2,370,000}$$
$$\text{Dividend per common share} = \frac{\$2,370,000}{1,600,000}$$
$$= \underline{\underline{\$1.48}}$$

23. Keller Corporation has 1,800,000 shares of $100 par value, 5%, cumulative preferred stock and 9,750,000 shares of common stock. Although no dividend was declared for the past two years, a $44,000,000 dividend has been declared for this year.

    a. How much is due the preferred shareholders?

Dividend per share preferred $= \$100 \times 5\% = \$5.00$
Total dividend due preferred stockholders $=$
$1,800,000 \times \$5.00 \times 3 \text{ years} = \underline{\underline{\$27,000,000}}$

    b. What is the dividend per share of common stock?

Dividend per share common stock
$\$44,000,000 - \$27,000,000 = \$17,000,000$
$\dfrac{17,000,000}{9,750,000} = \underline{\underline{\$1.74}} \text{ per share}$

24. Alpha Airlines is currently selling at $47\frac{3}{8}$. The earnings per share are $3.14 and the dividend is $1.70.

    a. What is the current yield of the stock?

$$\text{Current yield} = \frac{\text{Annual dividend}}{\text{Current price}}$$
$$= \frac{\$1.70}{\$47.375} = \underline{\underline{3.6\%}}$$

    b. What is the price-earnings ratio?

$$\text{Price earnings ratio} = \frac{\text{Current price per share}}{\text{Earnings per share}}$$
$$\text{Price earnings ratio} = \frac{\$47.375}{\$3.14} = \underline{\underline{15}}$$

25. You purchase 650 shares of Prism Corporation common stock at $44\frac{1}{4}$ per share. A few months later you sell the shares at $51\frac{1}{8}$. Your stockbroker charges 3% commission on round lots and an extra $1\frac{1}{2}\%$ on odd lots.

    a. What is the total cost of the purchase?

Cost of shares $= 650 \times \$44.25$	$= \$28,762.50$	
Commission $= 600 \times \$44.25 \times 3\%$	$=+ \quad 796.50$	
$= 50 \times \$44.25 \times 4.5\%$	$=+ \quad\quad 99.56$	
Total cost	$= \underline{\underline{\$29,658.56}}$	

b. What are the proceeds on the sale?

Value of shares = $650 \times \$51.125$ = $33,231.25

Commission   = $600 \times \$51.125 \times 3\%$ = −   920.25

                    = $50 \times \$51.125 \times 4.5\%$ = −   115.03

                    Proceeds   = $32,195.97

c. What is the gain or loss on the transaction?

Gain = $32,195.97 − $29,658.56

     = $2,537.41

SECTION II

BONDS

20-6 Understanding Bonds and Reading Bond Quotations

A **bond** is a loan, or an IOU, where the bond buyer lends money to the bond issuer. With stock, the investor becomes a part-owner of the corporation; with bonds, the investor becomes a creditor. Bonds are known as fixed-income securities because the issuer promises to pay a specified amount of interest on a regular basis, usually semiannually. Although stock is issued only by corporations, bonds are issued by corporations and governments. The federal government, as well as states and local municipalities, issues bonds. The funds raised are used to finance general operations and specific projects such as schools, highways, bridges, and airports. An example of a bond certificate is shown in Exhibit 20-4.

Corporate bonds represent the number-one source of corporate borrowing for both large and small companies. Corporations use the money raised from bonds to finance modernization and expansion programs. **Secured bonds** are backed by a lien on a plant, equipment, or other corporate asset. **Unsecured bonds,** also known as **debentures,** are backed only by the general credit of the issuing corporation. Some bonds are **convertible,** which means they can be converted into, or exchanged for, a specified number of shares of common stock. **Callable** bonds give the issuer the right to call or redeem the bonds before the maturity date. Calling bonds might occur when interest rates are falling and the company can issue new bonds at a lower rate.

When bonds are issued by a corporation, they may be purchased by investors at par value, usually $1,000, and held until the maturity date; or they may be bought and sold

bond
A loan or an IOU in the form of an interest-bearing note, where the bond buyer lends money to the bond issuer. Used by corporations and governments to borrow money on a long-term basis.

secured bonds
Bonds that are backed by a lien on specific collateral such as a plant, equipment, or other corporate asset.

unsecured bonds, or debentures
Bonds that are backed only by the general credit of the issuing corporation, not on specific collateral pledged as security.

convertible bonds
Bonds that can be converted or exchanged at the owner's option for a certain number of shares of common stock.

callable bonds
Bonds that the issuer has the right to call or repurchase before the maturity date. Bonds are called when interest rates are falling and the company can issue new bonds at a lower rate.

Bonds were issued to pay part of the construction costs of the new Denver International Airport.

EXHIBIT 20-4

BOND CERTIFICATE

● **coupon rate**
A fixed percentage of the par value of a bond that is paid to the bondholder on a regular basis.

● **premium**
When a bond is selling for more than its par value it is said to be selling at a premium. This occurs during periods when prevailing interest rates are declining.

● **discount**
When a bond is selling for less than its par value it is said to be selling at a discount. This occurs during periods when prevailing interest rates are rising.

through a broker on the secondary or resale market. Bonds pay a fixed interest rate, also known as the **coupon rate.** This rate is a fixed percentage of the par value that will be paid to the bondholder on a regular basis.

For example, a company might issue a $1,000 par value, 7% bond, maturing in the year 2025. The bondholder in this case would receive a fixed interest payment of $70 per year (1,000 × .07), or $35 semiannually, until the bond matures. At maturity, the company repays the loan by paying the bondholder the par value of the bond.

During the period between the issue date and the maturity date, bond prices fluctuate in the opposite direction of prevailing interest rates. Let's say you buy a bond with a coupon rate of 8%. If interest rates in the marketplace fall to 7%, newly issued bonds will have a rate lower than yours, thus making yours more attractive and driving the price above the par value. When this occurs, the bonds are said to be selling at a **premium.** On the other hand, if interest rates rise to 9%, new bonds would have a higher rate than yours, thus making yours less attractive and pushing the price down, below par. If bonds sell below par, it is known as selling at a **discount.** Remember, at maturity the bond returns to its par value.

Just as with stocks, bond prices are listed in the financial section of most newspapers. Bonds are identified alphabetically by the abbreviated name of the issuer. Let's take a column-by-column look at a typical day's listing for Dole. Exhibit 20-5 is a portion of such a table, reprinted from *The Wall Street Journal.*

Column 1 (Bonds—Dole 7s03) Specifically identifies the issuing company, the coupon rate, and the last two numbers of the maturity date of the bond. For example, Dole 7s03 means Dole Corporation bond, with a coupon rate of 7%, maturing in the year 2003.

Column 2 (Cur Yld—7.6) The current percent yield of the bond. The yield for the Dole bond is 7.6%. As with stocks, the yield fluctuates with the current price of the bond. A cv in this column indicates the bond is convertible.

Column 3 (Vol—15) Indicates the volume or number of bonds sold. 15 Dole bonds were sold.

Column 4 (Close—$92\frac{1}{2}$) The closing or last price of the trading day. Bond prices are listed as a percent of the par value of $1,000. For example, the Dole bond, listed at $92\frac{1}{2}$, is selling for $925 (1,000 × .925). A bond selling for 126 would be $1,260 (1,000 × 1.26).

Column 5 (Net Chg.—$-\frac{3}{4}$) Indicates the difference in price from the previous close. As with closing prices, the net change is listed as a percent of the par value. The Dole bond closed down $\frac{3}{4}$, or $7.50 (1,000 × .0075).

CORPORATION BONDS
Volume, $30,630,000

Bonds	Cur Yld	Vol	Close	Net Chg.
AMR 9s16	9.1	95	99	− ⅜
AMR 8.10s98	7.9	7	102	− ⅝
ATT 4¾98	5.1	10	94	+ ¾
ATT 4⅜96	4.5	55	96¾	+ ½
ATT 4⅜99	4.8	42	90½	+ ¼
ATT 6s00	6.3	79	96	+ ⅜
ATT 5⅛01	5.6	21	91½	+ ½
ATT 8⅝31	8.2	10	105¾	+ 1¼
ATT 7⅛02	7.1	543	100⅜	...
ATT 8⅛22	8.0	289	101⅝	+ ⅛
ATT 8⅛24	8.0	65	101⅞	+ ½
ATT 4½96	4.6	103	98¼	+ ⅜
ATT 6¾04	7.0	691	96	− ⅛
Actava 9⅞97	10.1	15	97¾	− ⅛
Actava 9½98	10.3	114	92½	+ 1¼
Advst 9s08	cv	9	100¾	+ 2¾
AirbF 6¾01	cv	5	104	...
AlskAr 6⅞14	cv	8	81	+ ⅝
AlskAr zr06	...	108	38¾	...
AlbnyInt 5s02	cv	19	88½	+ ½
AlegCp 6½14	cv	10	98	− 1
Allwst 7¼14	cv	15	87⅞	− ⅛
AForP 5s30	7.9	1	63½	+ ⅛
AAir dc6¼96	6.3	15	99½	...
AmBrnd 8½03	8.3	5	102⅞	− ⅝
AmBrnd 8⅝21	8.4	15	103	− 7
Ametek 9¾04	9.8	34	100	+ 1
Anhr 8⅝16	8.5	14	101¾	− 1¼
AnnTaylr 8¾00	9.2	75	95¼	− ⅛
AshO 6¾14	cv	17	99¾	+ ¼
ARch 10⅜95	9.9	28	105	− ½
AutDt zr12	...	20	39⅜	+ ⅞
Avnet 6s12	cv	3	101¾	+ 2¼
Barnt 8½99	8.1	25	105⅛	+ ¼
BarBks 10⅞03	9.5	15	115	...
BellPa 7⅛12	7.6	4	93½	+ ¼
BellsoT 8¼32	8.1	10	102⅛	+ ¼
BellsoT 7⅞32	8.0	370	98	− ¼
BellsoT 6½00	6.6	70	99	...
BellsoT 7½33	8.0	100	94	+ ½
Bellso 5⅞09	6.7	84	88	+ 2
BstBuy 8⅝00	9.0	244	95¾	− ⅛
BethSt 9s00	9.0	19	100⅜	− ⅛
BethSt 8.45s05	8.9	29	94¾	− ¼
Bevrly 7⅝03	cv	26	100½	− ¾
BlkBst 6⅝98	6.8	7	97½	+ 1⅝
Boeing 8⅜96	7.9	10	105⅜	+ 1⅛
BoisC 7s16	cv	57	87½	− ½
Bordn 8⅜16	8.6	25	97½	+ 1½
BorgWS 9⅛03	9.5	10	96	+ ½
BwnSh 9¼05	cv	11	99¼	...

1	2	3	4	5
Bonds	Cur Yld	Vol	Close	Net Chg.
CnPw 6⅞98	7.0	5	97¾	− ¾
viCtlInf 9s06f	cv	45	9	+ ½
Coopr 10⅝05f	...	11	70	− ⅛
CrayRs 6⅛11	cv	10	83½	...
DataGn 01	cv	39	84½	− ¼
Datpnt 8⅞06	cv	27	76	+ 1
DaytP 8s03	8.0	7	100⅜	− ⅝
DeereCa 7.2s97	7.1	10	100⅞	− 2⅛
DetEd 6.4s98	6.5	8	98¾	− 1¾
DiaSTel 7s08	7.1	5	98½	− ½
Dole 7s03	7.6	15	92½	− ¾
duPnt dc6s01	6.5	352	92¾	− ¼
EMC 4¼01	cv	15	105	...
Eckerd 9¼04	9.9	749	93	+ ½
EmbSuit 11s99	10.6	9	104	...
EnqStr zr97	...	3	74⅞	− ⅛
Enron 10¾98	10.2	2	105¾	+ ¾
EthAln 8¾01	9.0	30	97½	...
Exxon 8¼94	8.1	10	102¼	+ 1 15/32
F&M 11½03	12.3	11	93⅛	− 1¾
FairCp 12s01	12.1	2	99	+ 1
FairCp 13⅛06	13.4	12	98	...
Fldcst 6s12	cv	56	89	− ¼
FreptM 10⅞01	10.1	10	107½	− 2
Frpt dc6.55s01	cv	35	89	+ 1¼
FMRP 8¾04	9.1	5	96	+ 2
GMA dc6s11	7.5	100	79¾	− ¾
GMA zr12	...	60	218⅞	− ⅛
GMA zr15	...	50	178¼	+ 1½
GMA 8¼16	8.4	135	98⅝	+ ⅝
GMA 8s94	7.9	5	101 15/16	− 3/16
GMA 8⅜97	8.0	10	104⅞	+ 1⅛
GPA Del 8¾98	10.6	173	82⅝	...
GnCorp 8s02	7.7	2	104	...
GElCap 7⅞06	7.6	10	103½	+ ⅛
GHost 11½02	11.7	210	98½	− ⅜
GHost 8s02	cv	73	86	+ 1
GnSgnl 5¾02	cv	31	100	− 1
Gene 10⅜03	12.1	85	86	+ 1
GenesisH 6s03	cv	25	114	+ 1¼
Genrad 7¼11	cv	1	78	+ 1
GaGlf 15s00	14.1	700	106¾	− ½
GaPw 10s16J	9.8	95	102½	− ½
Getty 14s00	...	13	102 25/32	...
Grancre 6½03	6.6	10	98	− ½
Hallb zr06	...	1	48½	− ¼
Hallwd na13½09	...	50	88½	...
Hallw na13½09B	...	2	90	+ ⅜
Hallwd 7s00	10.6	36	65⅞	+ 1⅞
Hlttrst 8¾05	9.6	561	91½	− ¼
HomeDp 4½97	cv	14	113¼	− 1¼
HostM 10⅝00	10.5	21	101	...
HostM 9⅛00	9.5	147	96¼	− ½
HostM 9⅞01	10.1	75	97⅝	− ⅜

EXHIBIT 20-5

THE WALL STREET JOURNAL
NEW YORK EXCHANGE BONDS

EXAMPLE

From the following bond quotation table, explain the information listed for Kmart:

IBM 7½13	8.0	144	93⅞	− ¼
IntShip 9s03	9.4	115	95⅝	+ 1⅝
IntTch 9⅜96	9.5	6	99	+ 1
InterSec 7¾11	cv	10	90	− 1
Jamswy 8s05	cv	25	20	...
JCP 6¾25	7.9	5	85	− 7
K mart 8⅜17	8.3	12	101⅜	+ 1
KaufB 10⅜99	10.2	5	101½	− 2½
KaufB 9⅜03	9.8	156	95¼	− ¼
Kenn 7⅞01	7.8	76	100½	− ⅛
Kolmrg 8¾09	cv	89	98¾	+ ¼
Kroger 9s99	8.9	36	101½	− ⅜

OwCor 9½00	9.4	6	101½	− 1¾
PhilEl 6⅛97	6.2	15	99⅜	− ⅜
PhilEl 6½03	6.9	20	94⅜	+ ⅜
PhilEl 7¾23	8.2	12	94⅜	− 2
PhilEl 7¼24	8.1	35	90	...
PacTT 7.8s07	7.8	69	100½	+ ½
PacTT 7¼08	7.6	3	95¾	− 1½
PacTT 7⅝09	7.8	91	98⅛	− ⅜
PacBell 7½33	8.1	120	92⅞	− ⅛
PacBell 6¼05	6.8	35	91½	− ⅛
PacBell 7⅛26	7.8	26	91¾	+ ¼
ParCm 7s03A	7.8	65	90	+ ½

SOLUTION STRATEGY

According to the listing, the Kmart bond has a coupon rate of $8\frac{3}{8}$% and will mature in the year 2017. The current yield is 8.3% and the volume for the day was 12 bonds traded. The bond is selling at a slight premium for $1,013.75 (1,000 × 1.01375). The net change in price from the previous trading day is up $10.00 (1,000 × .01).

TRY-IT **EXERCISE**

8. **From the following bond quotation table, explain the information listed for Home Depot:**

Hallwd 7s00	11.2	20	62¼	−	4½	NYTel 7¾06	7.8	8	100	+	½
Hlttrst 10¾02	10.1	5	106½	+	½	NYTel 7⅝23	8.1	35	94½	−	1¾
Hlttrst 8¾05	9.4	248	92¾	−	¾	NYTel 7s25	8.0	30	87¼	+	¼
HeclMn zr04	...	15	44½		...	Novacr 5½2000	cv	30	93		...
HomeDp 4½97	cv	7	117½	+	2⅜	NuevE 12½202	11.8	3	106	+	½
HostM 10⅛99	10.3	35	98½		...	OcciP 11¾11	10.5	5	112⅜		...
HostM 9⅛00	9.5	14	95⅝	−	2⅜	OcciP 11⅛19	9.6	13	116⅜	−	1

Check your answers with the solutions on page 693.

20-7 Computing the Cost of Purchasing Bonds and the Proceeds from the Sale of Bonds

Similar to stocks, when bonds are bought and sold a brokerage charge is commonly added to the price of each bond. Although there is no standard commission, the charge is generally between $5 and $10 per bond. As noted earlier, bonds pay interest semiannually, such as on January 1 and July 1. When bonds are traded between the stated interest payment dates, the interest accumulated from the last payment date must be paid to the seller by the buyer. This interest due to the seller is known as the **accrued interest.**

Accrued interest of a bond is calculated using the simple interest formula, $I = PRT$, where P is the face value of the bond, R is the coupon rate, and T is the number of days since the last payment date divided by 360. When time is stated in months, divide by 12.

● **accrued interest**

When bonds are traded between the stated interest payment dates, the interest accumulated from the last payment date that must be paid to the seller by the buyer.

STEPS TO CALCULATE THE COST OF PURCHASING A BOND:

Step 1. Calculate the accrued interest on the bond since the last payment date using $I = PRT$.

Step 2. Calculate the price to purchase the bond:

Price per bond = Current market price + Accrued interest + Commission

Step 3. Calculate total purchase price:

Total purchase price = Price per bond × Number of bonds purchased

---

EXAMPLE

What is the purchase price of ten Crystal Corporation bonds with a coupon rate of $9\frac{1}{2}$ and a current market price of 107? The commission charge is $5.00 per bond. The date of the transaction is April 1, and the bond pays interest on January 1 and July 1.

SOLUTION STRATEGY

Step 1. Because the time since the last payment is 3 months, we shall use $T = \frac{3}{12}$.

$$\text{Accrued interest} = 1,000 \times .095 \times \frac{3}{12} = \underline{\$23.75}$$

Step 2. Price per bond = Current market price + Accrued interest + Commission
Price per bond = 1,070.00 + 23.75 + 5.00 = $\underline{\$1,098.75 \text{ per bond}}$

Step 3. Total purchase price = Price per bond × Number of bonds
Total purchase price = 1,098.75 × 10 = $\underline{\$10,987.50}$

TRY-IT **EXERCISE**

9. What is the purchase price of 20 SilverLake Corporation bonds with a coupon rate of $6\frac{1}{4}$ and a current market price of $91\frac{3}{8}$? The commission charge is $10.00 per bond. The date of the transaction is October 1, and the bond pays interest on February 1 and August 1.

Check your answer with the solution on page 693.

STEPS TO CALCULATE THE PROCEEDS FROM THE SALE OF A BOND:

Step 1. Calculate the accrued interest on the bond since the last payment date using $I = PRT$.

Step 2. Calculate the proceeds per bond by:

Proceeds = Current market price + Accrued interest − Commission

Step 3. Calculate the total proceeds from the sale by:

Total proceeds = Proceeds per bond × Number of bonds sold

EXAMPLE

What are the proceeds of the sale of 15 Tornado Corporation bonds with a coupon rate of $7\frac{1}{8}$ and a current market price of 111? The commission charge is $7.50 per bond. The date of the transaction is 71 days since the last interest payment.

SOLUTION STRATEGY

Step 1.
$$\text{Accrued interest} = 1,000 \times .07125 \times \frac{71}{360} = \underline{\$14.05}$$

Step 2. Proceeds per bond = Current market price + Accrued interest − Commission
Proceeds per bond = $1,110.00 + 14.05 − 7.50 = \underline{\$1,116.55}$

Step 3. Total proceeds = Proceeds per bond × Number of bonds sold
Total proceeds = $1,116.55 × 15 = \underline{\$16,748.25}$

TRY-IT **EXERCISE**

10. What are the proceeds of the sale of five Mercantile Corporation bonds with a coupon rate of $8\frac{7}{8}$ and a current market price of 99? The commission charge is $10.00 per bond. The date of the transaction is 122 days since the last interest payment.

Check your answer with the solution on page 693.

20-8 Calculating the Current Yield for a Bond

Just as with stocks, the current yield of a bond is a simple measure of the return on investment based on the current market price. When bonds are purchased at par, the current yield is equal to the coupon rate. For example, a bond purchased at par for $1,000, with a coupon rate of 7%, pays interest of $70 per year (1,000 × .07), and has a yield of 7% ($\frac{70}{1,000}$ = .07). If the bond is purchased at a discount, say $875, it still pays $70; however, the yield is 8% ($\frac{70}{875}$ = .08). If the bond is purchased at a premium, say $1,165, it still pays $70; however, now the yield is only 6% ($\frac{70}{1165}$ = .06).

STEPS TO CALCULATE CURRENT YIELD FOR A BOND:

Step 1. Calculate the annual interest and current price of the bond.

Step 2. Divide the annual interest of the bond by the current market price:

$$\text{Current yield} = \frac{\text{Annual interest}}{\text{Current market price}}$$

Step 3. Convert the answer to a percent, rounded to the nearest tenth.

EXAMPLE

Calculate the current yield for a Revco Electronics bond with a coupon rate of $13\frac{1}{2}$% and currently selling at a premium of $107\frac{1}{4}$.

SOLUTION STRATEGY

Annual interest = Par value × Coupon rate = 1,000 × .135 = $135

Current price = Par value × Price percent = 1,000 × 1.0725 = $1,072.50

$$\text{Current yield} = \frac{\text{Annual interest}}{\text{Current market price}} = \frac{135}{1072.50} = .12587 = \underline{\underline{12.6\%}}$$

TRY-IT EXERCISE

11. Calculate the current yield for a Wakefield Industries bond with a coupon rate of $9\frac{3}{8}$% and currently selling at a discount of $84\frac{3}{4}$.

Check your answer with the solution on page 693.

REVIEW EXERCISES CHAPTER 20—SECTION II

Answer Questions 1–10 based on the following bond quotation table:

CORPORATION BONDS
Volume, $35,720,000

Bonds	Cur Yld	Vol	Close	Net Chg.
AMR 9s16	9.2	315	98⅛	− ⅜
Actava 9½98	10.5	6	90⅛	− ⅞
AirbF 6¾01	cv	45	101½	+ ½
AlskAr 6⅞14	cv	77	80½	...
AlskAr zr06	...	6	38¾	+ ¾
AlldC zr97	...	10	81	− ¼
AlldC zr03	...	5	48	+ ½
AlldC zr09	...	150	30	...
AlegCp 6½14	cv	30	99	− 1
AlgLud 02	cv	13	107	− 4
Allwst 7¼14	cv	30	88	− 1
AmBrnd 8½03	8.2	23	103½	...
AmHme 6⅞97	6.8	18	101	...
AmStor 01	cv	20	118	...
ATT 4¾98	5.1	107	93¼	− ½
ATT 4⅜96	4.5	90	96¼	− ⅛

Bonds	Cur Yld	Vol	Close	Net Chg.
IBM 7½13	8.1	806	93	+ ⅜
IntShip 9s03	9.6	50	93¾	...
IntTch 9⅜96	9.7	2	97⅛	...
Jamswy 8s05	cv	2	19	...
K mart 8⅜17	8.4	10	100	+ ¼
KaufB 10⅜99	10.1	65	102½	− 1½
KaufB 9⅜03	9.9	385	94½	− ¼
Kolmrg 8¾09	cv	180	98	...
Kroger 9s99	8.9	73	100¾	− 1⅞
Kroger 6⅜99	cv	31	128	− 5
LehmnBr 8¾02	8.3	10	105⅝	+ 1⅞
Leucadia 5¼03	...	1	96	...
Litton 12⅝05	11.5	1	109¾	...
LomasFn 9s03	9.9	1	91	...
LglsLt 7.3s99	7.3	5	100	...
LglsLt 8.9s19	9.4	147	94⅞	+ ⅝
MACOM 9¼06	cv	15	95	− ½
MGM Grd 11¾99	10.8	1	108⅞	...

1. Kmart—Coupon rate and current yield: _____ $8\frac{3}{8}\%$, 8.4%

2. AT&T $4\frac{3}{4}$98—Closing price and net change: _____ $93\frac{1}{4}$, $-\frac{1}{2}$

3. AMR—Maturity year and volume: _____ 2016, 315 Bonds

4. Leucadia—Volume and closing price: _____ 1 Bond, 96

5. Litton—Coupon rate, maturity year, and net change: _____ $12\frac{5}{8}\%$, 2005, None

6. MGM Grand—Current yield and closing price: _____ 10.8%, $108\frac{7}{8}$

7. Which bonds are selling for exactly par value? _____ Kmart and LglsLt 7.3s 99

8. Which bond has the highest current yield? _____ Litton 11.5%

9. Which bond had the greatest net change? How much? _____ Kroger $6\frac{3}{8}$99, −5

10. Which bond had the highest volume? How many were sold? _____ IBM, 806 Bonds sold

Calculate the accrued interest and the total purchase price of the following bond purchases:

Company	Coupon Rate	Market Price	Time since Last Interest	Accrued Interest	Commission per Bond	Bonds Purchased	Total Price
11. Xerox	$5\frac{1}{2}$	$86\frac{1}{4}$	2 months	$9.17	$5.00	1	$876.67
12. U.S. West	$7\frac{1}{4}$	$102\frac{1}{2}$	78 days	15.71	4.50	5	5,226.05
13. AT&T	$8\frac{3}{8}$	95	5 months	34.90	10.00	8	7,959.20
14. Hilton	$9\frac{1}{2}$	$79\frac{3}{4}$	23 days	6.07	9.75	15	12,199.80
15. Ford	$6\frac{5}{8}$	$111\frac{7}{8}$	3 months	16.56	8.00	10	11,433.10

11. Accrued interest = 1000 × Coupon rate × Time

$$I = 1000 \times .055 \times \frac{2}{12}$$
$$= \$9.17$$

Total price = (Current market price + Accrued interest + Commission) × Number of bonds
= (862.50 + 9.17 + 5.00) × 1
= $876.67

Calculate the accrued interest and the total proceeds of the following bond sales:

Company	Coupon Rate	Market Price	Time since Last Interest	Accrued Interest	Commission per Bond	Bonds Sold	Total Proceeds
16. Textron	$6\frac{1}{4}$	$91\frac{1}{2}$	21 days	$3.65	$6.00	10	$9,126.50
17. Apple	$8\frac{1}{2}$	$108\frac{3}{4}$	4 months	28.33	8.50	4	4,429.32
18. USX	$10\frac{5}{8}$	77	85 days	25.09	12.00	15	11,746.35
19. Mobil	$9\frac{3}{4}$	$89\frac{3}{8}$	1 month	8.13	7.25	7	6,262.41
20. Nabisco	$6\frac{5}{8}$	$104\frac{1}{8}$	39 days	7.18	9.00	20	20,788.60

16. $I = PRT$

Proceeds = Current market price + Accrued interest − Commission

$$I = 1000 \times .0625 \times \frac{21}{360} = \$3.65$$

Proceeds = (915.00 + 3.65 − 6.00) × 10
= $9,126.50

Calculate the annual interest and current yield for the following bonds:

Company	Coupon Rate	Annual Interest	Market Price	Current Yield
21. Kroger	$6\frac{5}{8}$	$66.25	$91\frac{1}{8}$	7.3%
22. Bordens	$9\frac{1}{4}$	92.50	108	8.6
23. Blockbuster	$7\frac{1}{2}$	75.00	$125\frac{1}{4}$	6
24. McDonald's	$11\frac{7}{8}$	118.75	$73\frac{1}{2}$	16.2
25. Pacific Telesis	$5\frac{3}{8}$	53.75	$84\frac{3}{8}$	6.4

21. Annual interest = Par value × Coupon rate
Kroger, annual interest = 1000 × .06625 = $66.25

$$\text{Current yield} = \frac{\text{Annual interest}}{\text{Current market price}}$$

$$\text{Current yield} = \frac{\$66.25}{\$911.25} = 0.0727 = 7.3\%$$

26. On March 1, Kimberly Lipscomb bought ten Slick Oil Company bonds with a coupon rate of $9\frac{1}{8}$. The purchase price was $88\frac{7}{8}$ and the commission was $6.00 per bond. Slick Oil bonds pay interest on February 1 and August 1.

a. What is the current yield of the bond?
Annual interest = Par value × Coupon rate
Annual interest = 1000 × .09125 = $91.25

$$\text{Current yield} = \frac{\text{Annual interest}}{\text{Market price}}$$

$$\text{Current yield} = \frac{\$91.25}{\$888.75} = 10.3\%$$

b. What is the total purchase price of the bonds?

Total purchase price = (Current market price + Accrued interest + Commission)
$$\times \text{Number of bonds}$$
$$\text{Accrued interest} = 1{,}000 \times .09125 \times \tfrac{1}{12} = \$7.60$$
$$\text{Total purchase price} = (888.75 + 7.60 + 6.00) \times 10$$
$$= \underline{\$9{,}023.50}$$

c. If Kimberly sold the bonds on November 1 for $93\tfrac{7}{8}$, what are the proceeds from the sale?

Proceeds of sale = Current market price + Accrued interest − Commission ×
$$\text{Number of bonds}$$
$$\text{Accrued interest} = 1{,}000 \times .09125 \times \tfrac{3}{12} = \$22.81$$
$$\text{Proceeds} = (938.75 + 22.81 - 6.00) \times 10$$
$$= \underline{\$9{,}555.60}$$

MUTUAL FUNDS

20-9 Understanding Mutual Funds and Reading Mutual Fund Quotations

● **mutual funds, or investment trusts**
Corporations that are investment pools of money with a wide variety of investment goals.

Mutual funds are a very popular way of investing. Essentially, mutual funds are professionally managed investment companies that pool the money from many people and invest it in stocks, bonds, and other securities. Most individual investors don't have the time or the ability to research the literally thousands of investment possibilities. By pooling the financial resources of thousands of shareholders, mutual funds can employ the expertise of the country's top professional money managers.

Mutual funds are corporations known as **investment trusts.** Their assets are stocks and bonds purchased with the hope that the value of these securities will increase. Investors purchase shares of stock of the fund. If the fund is successful in its investments, it pays dividends and capital gains to its shareholders.

With mutual funds, instead of choosing individual stocks and bonds, investors pick a fund with financial goals similar to their own. These range from high-risk aggressive growth goals, such as investing in new and unproven companies and industries, to more moderate-risk goals, such as steady income and balanced growth and income, which is achieved by investing in large and established companies. Most mutual fund companies offer several different funds known as a *family.* Investors are free to move their money back and forth among them as their investment goals or market conditions change.

Just as with the stock prices of other corporations, mutual fund stock prices fluctuate up and down on a daily basis and can be tracked in the financial section of most newspapers. Let's take a column-by-column look at a typical day's listing for a mutual fund in the GT Global family, known as Amer p. Exhibit 20-6 is a portion of such a table, as listed in *The Wall Street Journal.*

Column 1   Mutual fund companies are listed alphabetically by the fund's family name (GT Global), and in subcategories by the various funds available within that family (Amer p).

Column 2   (Inv. Obj.—GRO)   Investment objective is the stated goal of the fund. *The Wall Street Journal* lists 27 abbreviated objectives. The most common objectives follow:

CAP—Capital Appreciation	EQI—Equity Income
G&I—Growth and Income	S&B—Stocks and Bonds
GRO—Growth	BND—General U.S. Taxable Bonds
SML—Small Company Growth	GLM—General Municipal Bonds

● **net asset value (NAV)**
The dollar value of one share of a mutual fund's stock. It is the price investors receive when they sell their shares of the fund.

Column 3   (NAV—17.98)   **Net asset value** is the dollar value of one share of the fund's stock. This is the price you receive when you sell your shares of the fund.

● **offer price**
The price per share investors pay when purchasing a mutual fund. Offer price includes the net asset value plus the broker's commission.

Column 4   (Offer Price—18.88)   **Offer price** is the price per share investors pay when purchasing the fund. The offer price includes the net asset value plus a broker's commission charge known as a load. NL in the offer price column means no load, or no commission, when purchasing the fund. There may, however, be a sales charge when selling the shares.

Column 5   (NAV Chg.—+0.09)   This is the dollar change in the net asset value of the fund since the previous quotation.

		Inv. Obj.	NAV	Offer Price	NAV Chg.	YTD	39 wks	5 yrs	R
	1	2	3	4	5	6	7	8	9

Left table

	Inv. Obj.	NAV	Offer Price	NAV Chg.	YTD	39 wks	5 yrs	R
LtdGv	BST	9.70	NL	+0.04	-1.4	0.0	+7.9	C
LTG	BND	10.83	NL	+0.14	-10.3	-7.3	NS	..
MD Mu	SSM	9.62	NL	+0.07	-5.9	NA	NS	..
MunIn r	GLM	10.08	NL	+0.07	-6.1	-1.4	NS	..
NJHY r	MNJ	10.94	NL	+0.07	-5.9	-1.9	+8.3	C
NYHY r	DNY	10.29	NL	+0.09	-6.1	-2.4	NS	..
PAHY r	MPA	10.29	NL	+0.07	-4.9	-0.4	+8.6	B
ShtInc	BST	9.36	NL	-0.02	-4.3	-1.2	NS	..
SIntGv	BST	9.53	NL	+0.04	-2.0	-0.4	NS	..
ShtMu	STM	9.80	NL	+0.03	-1.7	+1.0	+6.5	B
FiduCap	GRO	18.46	NL	+0.13	-6.0	+2.0	+10.3	C
59 Wall St:								
EuroEq	ITL	30.02	30.02	+0.01	-5.2	+17.1	NS	..
PacBsn	ITL	39.06	39.06	-0.64	-15.3	+26.9	NS	..
Sm Co	SML	11.61	11.61	+0.20	-7.1	-0.1	NS	..
TxFSI	STM	10.14	10.14	+0.02	-1.0	+1.0	NS	..
FinHorGv t	BND	10.53	10.53	+0.09	-3.5	-2.3	+10.1	A
FinHorMu	GLM	10.34	10.34	+0.13	-8.8	NA	+7.1	E
First American Cl A:								
AstAll p	S&B	10.21	10.69	+0.13	-3.2	+1.1	NS	..
Balanced p	S&B	10.46	10.95	+0.12	-1.8	+2.4	NS	..
EqIdxA p	G&I	10.34	10.83	+0.15	-3.3	+1.5	NS	..
FxdInc p	BND	10.70	11.12	+0.05	-2.5	-0.3	+9.2	C
GovBd p	BIN	9.16	9.44	+0.04	-1.9	-0.2	+7.2	E
IntInc p	BIN	9.73	10.11	+0.03	-1.7	-0.3	NS	..
LtdInc	BST	9.92	10.12	-0.01	-0.1	+1.6	NS	..
MtgSec p	BND	9.96	10.35	+0.02	-2.0	+0.5	NS	..
MunBd p	IDM	10.43	10.75	+0.06	-3.0	+0.1	+6.4	E
RegEq p	SML	11.83	12.39	+0.08	-3.1	+6.0	NS	..
SpecEq p	CAP	15.51	16.24	+0.07	-0.8	+6.9	+11.1	C
Stock p	G&I	15.97	16.72	+0.24	-0.4	+5.8	+11.2	B
First American Cl C:								
AstAll l	S&B	10.20	NL	+0.12	NS	NS	NS	..
Balancel	S&B	10.46	NL	+0.12	NS	NS	NS	..
EqIdxl	G&I	10.34	NL	+0.15	NS	NS	NS	..
FxdIncl	BND	10.70	NL	+0.05	NS	NS	NS	..
GovBdl	BIN	9.16	NL	+0.04	NS	NS	NS	..
IntIncl	BIN	9.73	NL	+0.03	NS	NS	NS	..
LtdIncl	BST	9.92	NL	-0.01	NS	NS	NS	..
MunBd	IDM	10.43	NL	+0.06	NS	NS	NS	..
MtgSecl	BND	9.96	NL	+0.02	NS	NS	NS	..
ReqEq	SML	11.83	NL	+0.08	NS	NS	NS	..
SpecEql	CAP	15.50	NL	+0.06	NS	NS	NS	..
StockI	G&I	15.97	NL	+0.25	NS	NS	NS	..
FtBosIG	BND	9.32	9.56	+0.06	-3.1	-1.7	NS	..

Right table

	Inv. Obj.	NAV	Offer Price	NAV Chg.	YTD	39 wks	5 yrs	R
S&S PM	G&I	35.45	NL	+0.48	-4.2	+0.8	+11.1	B
GE Funds:								
IncomeA	BIN	11.57	12.08	+0.07	-2.8	NS	NS	..
Global C	WOR	18.35	NL	+0.10	-2.2	+15.7	NS	..
IntlEqD	...	14.47	NL	+0.03	NA	NA	NA	..
Strag C	S&B	15.31	NL	+0.13	-4.0	+0.6	NS	..
US Eq A	G&I	15.55	16.33	+0.21	-4.4	NS	NS	..
US Eq C	G&I	15.57	NL	+0.21	-4.2	+0.8	NS	..
US Eq D	G&I	15.58	NL	+0.21	-4.2	NS	NS	..
GIT Invst:								
EqSpc	SML	19.26	NL	+0.05	-2.5	+8.6	+7.5	E
TFNatl	HYM	10.02	NL	+0.06	-7.2	-3.5	+6.5	E
TFVA	SSM	10.86	NL	+0.08	-6.7	-2.9	+6.8	E
GT Global:								
Amer p	GRO	17.98	18.88	+0.09	+4.7	+23.2	+16.0	A
EmMktA	ITL	14.95	15.70	-0.02	-14.1	+24.7	NS	..
EmMktB	ITL	14.90	14.90	-0.02	-14.3	+24.2	NS	..
EuroA p	ITL	10.56	11.09	+0.02	-2.6	+12.5	+4.2	D
EuroB	ITL	10.49	10.49	+0.02	-2.8	+11.9	NS	..
GvIncA p	WBD	9.04	9.49	+0.03	-10.8	-1.6	+9.5	B
GovIncB	WBD	9.04	9.04	+0.03	-11.0	-2.1	NS	..
GrIncA p	WOR	6.04	6.34	...	-5.0	+7.8	NS	..
GrIncB	WOR	6.04	6.04	...	-5.3	+7.0	NS	..
HltCr p	SEC	17.51	18.38	+0.25	-7.7	+4.0	NS	..
HltCrB	SEC	17.42	17.42	+0.24	-7.9	+3.5	NS	..
HiIncA	WBD	11.32	11.88	-0.19	-24.8	-9.0	NS	..
HiIncB	WBD	11.31	11.31	-0.19	-24.9	-9.4	NS	..
IntlA p	ITL	10.33	10.85	-0.01	-6.3	+12.2	+7.3	C
IntlB	ITL	10.27	10.27	-0.01	-6.5	+11.5	NS	..
Japan p	ITL	12.92	13.56	-0.14	+11.3	+16.3	+2.1	E
LatAmG	ITL	19.23	20.19	+0.16	-16.9	+16.6	NS	..
LatAmGB	ITL	19.17	19.17	+0.16	-17.0	+16.2	NS	..
PacifA p	ITL	13.04	13.69	-0.12	-17.8	+10.8	+9.3	B
PacifB	ITL	12.96	12.96	-0.12	-17.9	+10.2	NS	..
StratA p	WBD	10.51	11.03	-0.08	-21.2	-7.2	+9.8	B
StratB	WBD	10.52	10.52	-0.07	-21.3	-7.6	NS	..
Telecom	WOR	16.04	16.84	+0.15	-6.6	+14.2	NS	..
TeleB	WOR	15.95	15.95	+0.14	-6.7	+13.6	NS	..
Wldw p	WOR	16.51	17.33	+0.02	-5.5	+7.2	+9.8	B
WldwB	WOR	16.40	16.40	+0.02	-5.7	+6.6	NS	..
Gabelli Funds:								
ABC p	GRO	10.08	10.29	+0.01	+0.5	+7.6	NS	..
Asset p	GRO	22.31	NL	+0.15	-4.2	+3.8	+10.5	C
CnvSc	S&B	11.39	NL	+0.02	-1.1	+2.6	NS	..
EqInc p	EQI	11.33	11.86	+0.07	-1.6	+4.1	NS	..

EXHIBIT 20-6

Total Return These columns indicate the performance and ranking of the fund.

Column 6 (YTD—+4.7) This is the year-to-date percent return on investment of the fund.

Columns 7 & 8 Each day *The Wall Street Journal* lists different past performance data in these columns. Exhibit 20-6, a Friday, lists the 39-week (+23.2) and annualized 5-year return (+16.0) of the fund. On Tuesdays, for example, these columns list the 4-week and 1-year percent returns of the fund.

Column 9 (R—A) This column lists the fund's ranking compared to other funds with the same investment objectives: A = top 20%; B = next 20%; C = middle 20%, D = next 20%; E = bottom 20%.

EXAMPLE

From the following mutual fund quotation table, explain the information listed for the Robertson Stephens—Em Gr fund.

	Inv. Obj.	NAV	Offer Price	NAV Chg.	YTD	26 wks	4 yrs	R
TNMuOb	SSM	9.92	10.23	...	-4.3	NA	NS	..
Robertson Stephens:								
Contra	GRO	12.27	12.27	+0.06	+7.5	+22.5	NS	..
Em Gr p	SML	18.53	NL	-0.23	+3.1	+12.4	+15.6	B
Val Pl	SML	13.55	NL	-0.13	+3.8	+8.2	NS	..
Rochester Fds:								
BdGrow p	S&B	13.10	13.54	-0.08	+0.9	+3.7	+18.0	A
RoMu p	DNY	17.50	18.23	+0.03	-6.2	-5.6	+9.3	A
LtdNY p	IDM	3.22	3.29	...	-2.0	-1.2	NS	..

According to the listing, the investment objective of this fund is investing in <u>small growth companies</u>. The net asset value is <u>$18.53</u> and the offer price is the same as the NAV since this is a <u>no-load</u> fund. The change in net asset value from the previous trading session is <u>down $.23</u>. Regarding return on investment, this fund is <u>up 3.1%</u> for the year-to-date; <u>up 12.4%</u> for the past 26 weeks; and <u>up 15.6%</u> on an annualized basis for the past 4 years. The fund has a ranking of <u>B</u> compared to similar funds.

TRY-IT EXERCISE

12. **From the following mutual fund quotation table, explain the information listed for the Oppenheimer Fd: EqIncA fund.**

	Inv. Obj.	NAV	Offer Price	NAV Chg.	YTD	26 wks	4 yrs	R
					— Total Return —			
SmCoGr	SML	16.56	NL	−0.14	−3.7	−2.4	+14.5	C
TFBdA	GLM	9.71	NL	...	−2.2	−2.1	NS	..
Oppenheimer Fd:								
AsetA p	S&B	12.55	13.32	−0.07	−3.2	−0.1	+9.3	D
CA TE A p	MCA	10.10	10.60	...	−6.4	−5.4	+7.8	D
ChHY p	BHI	12.64	13.27	−0.03	−1.2	+3.7	+16.4	B
Disc p	SML	35.69	37.87	−0.60	−9.6	−9.3	+18.2	B
EqIncA p	EQI	9.61	10.20	−0.05	−2.9	−2.7	+8.4	D
EqIncB t	...	9.58	9.58	−0.05	NA	NA	NA	..
GlBio p	SEC	20.10	21.33	−0.22	−13.9	−8.7	+13.8	B
GlGr p	S&B	14.83	15.73	−0.06	−3.5	+7.5	NS	..
GlEnv p	SEC	10.25	10.88	−0.08	−7.0	−3.0	−3.1	E
GloblA p	WOR	36.10	38.30	−0.19	−2.0	+11.2	+9.7	B
GloblB t	WOR	35.95	35.95	−0.19	−2.3	+10.8	NS	..
Gold p	SEC	13.57	14.40	−0.07	−4.8	+15.7	+4.2	D

Check your answers with the solutions on page 693.

20-10 Calculating the Sales Charge and Sales Charge Percent of a Mutual Fund

load
The sales charge or broker's commission on a mutual fund.

front-end load
The sales charge or commission on a mutual fund when it is paid at the time of purchase.

back-end load
The sales charge or commission on a mutual fund when it is paid at the time of sale.

With mutual funds, the sales charge or broker's commission is known as the **load.** These charges vary from 1% to over 8% of the amount invested. The load is paid either when purchasing the stock, in a **front-end load,** or when selling the stock, in a **back-end load.** Some mutual funds don't charge a commission and are known as no-load funds. For load funds, the difference between the offer price and the net asset value is the sales charge.

STEPS TO CALCULATE MUTUAL FUND SALES CHARGE AND SALES CHARGE PERCENT:

Step 1. Calculate mutual fund sales charge by subtracting the net asset value from the offer price:

Mutual fund sales charge = Offer price − Net asset value

Step 2. Calculate sales charge percent by dividing the sales charge by the net asset value:

$$\text{Sales charge percent} = \frac{\text{Sales charge}}{\text{Net asset value}}$$

EXAMPLE

A mutual fund has an offer price of $6.75 per share and a net asset value of $6.44. What are the sales charge and the sales charge percent?

Step 1.

Mutual fund sales charge = Offer price – Net asset value

Mutual fund sales charge = 6.75 – 6.44 = <u>$.31 per share</u>

Step 2.

$$\text{Sales charge percent} = \frac{\text{Sales charge}}{\text{Net asset value}}$$

$$\text{Sales charge percent} = \frac{.31}{6.44} = .0481 = \underline{\underline{4.8\%}}$$

TRY-IT   **EXERCISE**

13. **What are the sales charge and the sales charge percent for a mutual fund with an offer price of $9.85 per share and net asset value of $9.21?**

Check your answers with the solutions on page 693.

20-11 Calculating the Net Asset Value of a Mutual Fund

The assets of a mutual fund consist of the total current value of the stocks or bonds that the fund owns. As stated earlier, a mutual fund's net asset value is the per share price of the fund's stock.

STEPS TO CALCULATE NET ASSET VALUE OF A MUTUAL FUND:

Step 1. Calculate net asset value by subtracting the total liabilities from the total assets of the fund and dividing by the number of shares outstanding.

$$\text{Net asset value (NAV)} = \frac{\text{Total assets} - \text{Total liabilities}}{\text{Number of shares outstanding}}$$

Step 2. Round the answer to dollars and cents.

EXAMPLE

A mutual fund has total assets of $40,000,000 and liabilities of $6,000,000. If there are 12,000,000 shares outstanding, what is the net asset value of the fund?

SOLUTION STRATEGY

$$\text{Net asset value} = \frac{\text{Total assets} - \text{Total liabilities}}{\text{Number of shares outstanding}}$$

$$\text{Net asset value} = \frac{40,000,000 - 6,000,000}{12,000,000} = \underline{\$2.83 \text{ per share}}$$

14. A mutual fund has total assets of $80,000,000 and liabilities of $5,000,000. If there are 17,000,000 shares outstanding, what is the net asset value of the fund?

Check your answer with the solution on page 693.

20-12 Calculating the Number of Shares Purchased of a Mutual Fund

Investors frequently purchase shares of mutual funds using lump-sum amounts of money. To accommodate this practice, most funds sell fractional shares of their stock.

STEPS TO CALCULATE NUMBER OF SHARES PURCHASED OF A MUTUAL FUND:

Step 1. Calculate number of shares by dividing the amount of the investment by the offer price of the fund. For no-load funds, use the net asset value as the denominator.

$$\text{Number of shares purchased} = \frac{\text{Total investment}}{\text{Offer price}}$$

Step 2. Round the answer to thousandths (three decimal places).

EXAMPLE

Zoraya Cuesta invested a lump sum of $5,000 in a mutual fund with an offer price of $6.55. How many shares did Zoraya purchase?

SOLUTION STRATEGY

$$\text{Number of shares purchased} = \frac{\text{Total investment}}{\text{Offer price}}$$

$$\text{Number of shares purchased} = \frac{5,000}{6.55} = \underline{763.359 \text{ shares}}$$

15. Lois Classen invested $10,000 in a no-load mutual fund with a net asset value of $12.25. How many shares did she purchase?

● **return on investment (ROI)**
The basic measure of how well an investment is doing. Used to compare various investments on an equal basis. Calculated as a percent, by dividing the total gain on the investment by the total purchase price.

Check your answer with the solution on page 693.

20-13 Calculating Return on Investment (ROI)

Regardless of whether you are investing in stocks, bonds, or mutual funds, the basic measure of how well your investments are doing is known as the **return on investment (ROI)**. This performance yardstick allows investors to compare various investments on an equal basis. Return on investment takes into account all transaction charges, such as broker's commissions and fees, as well as income received, such as dividends and interest payments. ROI is expressed as a percent, rounded to the nearest tenth.

STEPS TO CALCULATE RETURN ON INVESTMENT:

Step 1. Calculate the dollar gain (or loss) on the sale of the investment by subtracting the total cost from the proceeds of the sale.

$$\text{Gain (or loss) on investment} = \text{Proceeds} - \text{Total cost}$$

Step 2. Compute total gain by adding any dividends received on stocks, or interest received on bonds, to the gain or loss on sale.

$$\text{Total gain (or loss)} = \text{Gain (or loss)} + \text{Dividends or interest}$$

Step 3. Calculate return on investment by dividing the total gain by the total cost of purchase. Round your answer to the nearest tenth percent.

$$\text{Return on investment (ROI)} = \frac{\text{Total gain}}{\text{Total cost of purchase}}$$

EXAMPLE

Spencer Gordon purchased 1,000 shares of Mastermind Mutual Fund for an offer price of $5.30 per share. He later sold the shares at a net asset value of $5.88 per share. During the time Spencer owned the shares, Mastermind paid a dividend of $.38 per share. What is Spencer's return on investment?

SOLUTION STRATEGY

Step 1.
$$\text{Total cost of purchase} = 1,000 \text{ shares} \times 5.30 = \$5,300$$
$$\text{Proceeds from sale} = 1,000 \text{ shares} \times 5.88 = \$5,880$$
$$\text{Gain on sale} = \text{Proceeds} - \text{Total cost}$$
$$\text{Gain on sale} = 5,880 - 5,300 = \underline{\$580}$$

Step 2. In addition to the gain on sale, Spencer also made $380 ($1,000 \times .38$) in dividends.

$$\text{Total gain} = \text{Gain on sale} + \text{Dividends}$$
$$\text{Total gain} = 580 + 380 = \underline{\$960}$$

Step 3. $\text{Return on investment} = \dfrac{\text{Total gain}}{\text{Total cost of purchase}} = \dfrac{960}{5,300} = .18113 = 18.1\%$

TRY-IT EXERCISE

16. **Bob Leshin purchased 2,000 shares of Homestead National Mutual Fund for an offer price of $8.60 per share. He later sold the shares at a net asset value of $9.18 per share. During the time Bob owned the shares, Homestead National paid dividends of $.27 and $.42 per share. What is Bob's return on investment?**

Check your answer with the solution on page 693.

Answer Questions 1–12 based on the following mutual fund quotation table:

	Inv. Obj.	NAV	Offer Price	NAV Chg.	— Total Return — YTD	39 wks	5 yrs R			Inv. Obj.	NAV	Offer Price	NAV Chg.	— Total Return — YTD	39 wks	5 yrs R
									SpEquitII	SML	10.37	10.37	+0.12	−3.9	+4.4	NS ..
Rembrandt Funds:									**Smith Barney A:**							
AsiaTI	...	9.26	NL	−0.14	NA	NA	NA ..		CapApA	CAP	13.53	14.17	+0.40	−6.7	−2.0	NS ..
Bal Tr	S&B	9.65	NL	+0.08	−3.3	+0.4	NS ..		GIGvtA	WBD	12.16	12.67	+0.02	−3.9	+2.8	NS ..
GIFxInTr	WBD	10.10	NL	+0.01	−3.2	+3.2	NS ..		IncGrA p	G&I	12.63	13.23	+0.12	−4.4	+0.9	+9.5 D
Gwth Tr	GRO	10.05	NL	+0.12	−1.2	+0.8	NS ..		IncRetA	BST	9.49	9.63	...	+0.3	+1.5	+7.7 C
IntlEqTr	ITL	12.61	NL	−0.08	+0.2	+15.4	NS ..		IntlA	ITL	17.34	18.16	−0.04	−7.3	+25.1	+16.1 A
SIGvFITr	BST	9.67	NL	+0.03	−3.0	−1.6	NS ..		MoGvtA	BND	12.29	12.80	+0.08	−2.2	−1.6	+9.9 B
SmCapTr	SML	9.84	NL	+0.06	−3.8	+5.4	NS ..		MuCalA	MCA	12.23	12.74	+0.06	−4.7	−1.2	+8.5 A
TE FITr	GLM	9.63	9.63	+0.06	−4.8	−1.8	NS ..		MuFI A	MFL	12.82	13.35	+0.10	−4.5	−0.5	NS ..
Tax FI Tr	BIN	9.76	9.76	+0.05	−3.4	−1.0	NS ..		MuLtd A	IDM	6.53	6.66	+0.02	−2.7	+0.7	+7.6 B
ValueTr	GRO	9.95	NL	+0.05	−2.6	−0.9	NS ..		MunNtA	GLM	13.30	13.85	+0.08	−4.8	−0.8	+9.1 A
Retire Invst Trust:									MuNJ A	MNJ	13.20	13.75	+0.07	−5.6	−1.8	NS ..
Balanced	S&B	16.76	16.76	+0.21	−4.6	−2.1	+8.0 E		MuNY A	DNY	12.80	13.33	+0.08	−4.9	−1.1	+8.8 A
EqGro	GRO	17.70	17.70	+0.30	−4.9	−1.4	+8.3 D		SHTSY	BST	4.04	4.04	+0.01	−1.6	−0.1	NS ..
EqIncom	EQI	17.77	17.77	+0.24	−4.0	−0.6	+8.2 D		USGvtA	BND	13.09	13.64	+0.09	−2.3	−1.6	+9.9 B
Income	BND	15.44	15.44	+0.10	−4.2	−2.5	+7.8 E		UtltyA p	SEC	12.53	13.12	+0.13	−3.7	−4.4	NS ..
Rev BC	G&I	13.88	NL	+0.39	−6.3	−2.2	+7.0 E		**Smith Barney B & C:**							
Rightime Group:									CapApB	CAP	13.39	13.39	+0.40	−6.9	−2.6	NS ..
BlueC p	G&I	32.72	34.35	−0.03	+0.2	+4.2	+10.2 C		IntlB	ITL	17.18	17.18	−0.05	−7.5	+24.6	NS ..
RT fp	G&I	35.27	NL	−0.10	−0.1	+4.9	+9.6 D		MuLtd B	IDM	6.53	6.53	+0.03	−2.9	NA	NS ..
GvSc p	BND	13.33	13.99	+0.16	−0.8	−0.7	+5.9 E		IntlC	ITL	17.33	17.33	−0.04	−7.4	+25.1	NS ..
Grth p	GRO	25.69	26.97	+0.16	−0.4	−0.2	+4.8 E									

1. Smith Barney A: MuCalA—Offer price and 39-week return: ___$12.74, −1.2%___

2. Retirement Investment Trust: Balanced—Objective and net asset value: <u>Stocks and Bonds</u> <u>$16.76</u>

3. Rightime Group: BlueC—NAV change and 5-year return: ___−0.03 +10.2%___

4. Which Rembrandt fund has the only positive return in the year-to-date? <u>IntlEqTr. +0.2%</u>

5. Which Rightime Group fund is a bond fund? What is its ranking? ___GVScp, E___

6. Which Smith Barney A funds have the best and worst 39-week returns? <u>Best: Intl A +25.1%</u> <u>Worst: Utlty A −4.4%</u>

7. What does NL mean in the offer price of some funds? ___No Load, no commission___

8. Which Rembrandt fund has the best 39-week return? ___IntlEqTr. +15.4%___

Fund	Offer Price	Net Asset Value (NAV)	Sales Charge	Sales Charge %
9. Smith Barney A: MuFl A	13.35	12.82	.53	4.1%
10. Retire Invst Trust: Income	15.44	15.44	0	0
11. Rightime Group: Grth p	26.97	25.69	1.28	5%
12. Smith Barney A: USGvtA	13.64	13.09	.55	4.2%

9. Mutual fund sales charge = Offer price − Net asset value

Sales charge = 13.35 − 12.82 = $.53

Sales charge % = Sales charge ÷ Net asset value

Sales charge % = $\frac{.53}{12.82}$ = 4.1%

Calculate the net asset value and number of shares purchased for the following funds (round shares to thousandths, three decimal places):

	Total Assets	Total Liabilities	Shares Outstanding	Net Asset Value (NAV)	Offer Price	Total Investment	Shares Purchased
13.	$80,000,000	$2,300,000	5,000,000	$15.54	$16.10	$10,000	621.118
14.	52,000,000	1,800,000	6,100,000	8.23	9.50	5,000	526.316
15.	95,400,000	4,650,000	8,500,000	10.68	11.15	50,000	4,484.305
16.	15,000,000	750,000	1,300,000	10.96	NL	25,000	2,281.022

13. Net asset value = $\dfrac{\text{Total assets} - \text{Total liabilities}}{\text{Number of shares outstanding}}$

$\dfrac{\$80,000,000 - \$2,300,000}{5,000,000}$

= $15.54

Shares purchased = $\dfrac{\text{Total investment}}{\text{Offer price}}$

= $\dfrac{\$10,000}{\$16.10}$

= 621.118 Shares

Calculate the total cost, proceeds, total gain or loss, and return on investment for the following mutual fund investments. The offer price is the purchase price of the shares and the net asset value is the price at which the shares were later sold:

	Shares	Offer Price	Total Cost	Net Asset Value (NAV)	Proceeds	Per Share Dividends	Total Gain (or Loss)	Return on Investment
17.	100	$15.30	$1,530.00	$18.80	$1,880.00	$.45	$395.00	25.8%
18.	500	10.40	5,200.00	12.90	6,450.00	.68	1,590.00	30.6%
19.	1,000	4.85	4,850.00	6.12	6,120.00	1.25	2,520.00	52%
20.	700	7.30	5,110.00	5.10	3,570.00	0	(1,540.00)	−30.1%

17. Gain (or loss) on investment = Proceeds − Total cost

Total gain (or loss) = Gain (or loss) + Dividends

Return on investment = $\dfrac{\text{Total gain}}{\text{Total cost of purchase}}$

Total cost = $100 \times \$15.30 = \$1,530.00$

Proceeds = $100 \times \$18.80 = \$1,880.00$

$1,880.00 − 1,530.00 + (.45 \times 100)$

Total gain = $395.00

Return on investment = $\dfrac{395.00}{1,530.00} = 25.8\%$

21. A mutual fund has an offer price of $13.10 and a net asset value of $12.35.

   a. What is the sales charge?

   Sales charge = $13.10 − 12.35 = \underline{\underline{\$.75}}$

   b. What is the sales charge percent?

   Sales percent = $\dfrac{.75}{12.35} = \underline{\underline{6.1\%}}$

22. A mutual fund has total assets of $25,000,000 and liabilities of $3,500,000. If there are 8,600,000 shares outstanding, what is the net asset value of the fund?

   Net asset value = $\dfrac{25,000,000 − 3,500,000}{8,600,000} = \underline{\underline{\$2.50}}$

23. William Stokes invested a lump sum of $10,000 in a mutual fund with an offer price of $14.50. How many shares did he purchase?

   Shares purchased = $\dfrac{\$10,000}{\$14.50} = \underline{\underline{689.655}}$

24. Charlie Beavin purchased 500 shares of Advantage Resource Fund for an offer price of $8.90 per share. He later sold the shares at a net asset value of $10.50 per share. During the time that he owned the shares the fund paid a dividend of $.75 per share, three times. What is Charlie's return on investment?

   Cost = $500 \times \$8.90 = \$4,450.00$

   Proceeds = $500 \times \$10.50 = \$5,250.00$

   Dividends = $(.75 \times 500) \times 3 = \$1,125.00$

   Return on investment = $\dfrac{5,250.00 − 4,450.00 + 1,125.00}{4,450.00} = \underline{\underline{43.3\%}}$

FORMULAS

Stocks

Dividend per share (preferred) = Par value $\times$ Dividend rate

$$\text{Dividend per share (common)} = \frac{\text{Total common dividend}}{\text{Number of shares (common)}}$$

$$\text{Current yield} = \frac{\text{Annual dividend per share}}{\text{Current price of the stock}}$$

$$\text{Price-earnings ratio} = \frac{\text{Current price per share}}{\text{Earnings per share}}$$

Gain (or loss) on stock = Proceeds − Total cost

Bonds

Price per bond = Current market price + Accrued interest + Commission

Proceeds = Current market price + Accrued interest − Commission

$$\text{Current yield} = \frac{\text{Annual interest}}{\text{Current market price}}$$

Mutual funds

Mutual fund sales charge = Offer price − Net asset value

$$\text{Sales charge percent} = \frac{\text{Sales charge}}{\text{Net asset value}}$$

$$\text{Net asset value (NAV)} = \frac{\text{Total assets} - \text{Total liabilities}}{\text{Number of shares outstanding}}$$

$$\text{Number of shares purchased} = \frac{\text{Total investment}}{\text{Offer price}}$$

$$\text{Return on investment (ROI)} = \frac{\text{Total gain}}{\text{Total cost of purchase}}$$

CHAPTER 20 ■ INVESTMENTS	SUMMARY CHART

SECTION I STOCKS

Topic	P/O, Page	Important Concepts	Illustrative Examples
Distributing Dividends on Preferred and Common Stock	20–1 661	Companies raise capital by selling stock. Common stock shares in the success or failure of the business. Preferred stock receives a fixed dividend and is paid before common. Cumulative preferred receives dividends in arrears, those not paid in past years. Preferred dividends are stated as a percent of par value or as a dollar amount for no-par preferred. Dividends are distributed as follows: 1. Preferred—Arrears. 2. Preferred—Current period. 3. Common—Current period.	Kensington Corp. has 100,000 shares of $100 par, 7%, cumulative preferred and 300,000 shares of common stock. No dividend was declared last year. This year a $2,000,000 dividend was declared. Distribute the dividends among the two classes of stock. Preferred stockholders receive 100 × .07 = $7.00 per share. Preferred—Arrears: 100,000 shares × 7 = $700,000

Topic	P/O, Page	Important Concepts	Illustrative Examples
			Preferred—Current: 100,000 shares × 7 = $700,000 Total due preferred = $1,400,000 Common: $2,000,000 Total dividend −1,400,000 Preferred dividend $600,000 Common dividend Div. per share = $\frac{600,000}{300,000}$ = $2.00
Calculating Current Yield for a Stock	20–3 667	Current yield is a measure of how much you are earning on a stock compared with other investments. Current Yield = $\frac{\text{Annual dividend}}{\text{Current price}}$	What is the current yield for Calder Corporation stock, which pays a dividend of $2.35 per share and is currently selling for 57\frac{1}{4}$? Current Yield = $\frac{2.35}{57.25}$ = 4.1%
Determining the Price-Earnings Ratio of a Stock	20–4 667	The price-earnings ratio of a stock shows the relationship between the price of a stock and the company's earnings for the past 12 months. P/E ratio = $\frac{\text{Current price per share}}{\text{Earnings per share}}$	Trendy Toy stock is selling at 34$\frac{1}{8}$. If the company had earnings per share of $4.27, calculate the price-earnings ratio. P/E ratio = $\frac{34.125}{4.27}$ = 7.99 = 8

Computing the Cost, Proceeds, and Gain (or Loss) on a Stock Transaction	20–5
	668
		Stocks are purchased and sold through stockbrokers, who charge a commission for these services. Round lots are purchases in multiples of 100 shares. Odd lots are purchases of less than 100 shares. Extra commission is usually charged for odd lots.
		
		Total cost of purchase =
		    Cost of shares + Broker's comm.
		
		Proceeds = Value of shares − Broker's comm.
		
		Gain (or loss) = Proceeds − Total cost
			You purchase 450 shares of G-Tech common stock at 19$\frac{3}{4}$ per share. A few months later you sell the shares at 27$\frac{1}{2}$. Your stockbroker charges 3% on round lots and 4% on odd lots. What are the total cost, the proceeds, and the gain or loss on your investment?
			
			Purchase
			Cost of shares =
			    450 × 19.75 = $8,887.50
			
			Commission =
			    400 × 19.75 × .03 = $237.00
			    50 × 19.75 × .04 = 39.50
			        Total Comm = $276.50
			
			Total cost of purchase =
			8,887.50 + 276.50 = $9,164.00
			
			Sale
			Value of shares =
			    450 × 27.50 = $12,375.00

I, continued

Topic	P/O, Page	Important Concepts	Illustrative Examples
			Commission = $400 \times 27.50 \times .03 = \$330.00$ $50 \times 27.50 \times .04 = \underline{\quad 55.00}$ Total commision = $\underline{\$385.00}$ Proceeds = $12{,}375 - 385.00 = \underline{\$11{,}990.00}$ *Gain* $11{,}990.00 - 9{,}164.00 =$ $\qquad\qquad\qquad \underline{\$2{,}826.00}$

SECTION II   BONDS

Topic	P/O, Page	Important Concepts	Illustrative Examples
Computing the Cost of Purchasing Bonds	20–7 676	Bonds are loans to companies or governments that pay fixed interest semiannually. *Buying Bonds:* 1. Calculate accrued interest since last payment by $I = PRT$. 2. Calculate the price to the bond: $\dfrac{\text{Purchase}}{\text{price per}} = \dfrac{\text{Current}}{\text{price}} + \dfrac{\text{Accrued}}{\text{interest}} + \text{Commission}$ bond 3. Calculate total purchase price: $\dfrac{\text{Total}}{\text{purchase}} = \dfrac{\text{Price}}{\text{per}} \times \dfrac{\text{Number of}}{\text{bonds}}$ price bond	What is the purchase price of 10 Tiffany bonds with a coupon rate of $5\frac{1}{2}$ and a current market price of $96\frac{1}{4}$? The commission charge is $6.00 per bond. The date of the purchase is November 1; the bond pays interest on Jan. 1 and July 1. Accrued interest = $1{,}000 \times .055 \times \dfrac{4}{12} = \$18.33$ Commission = $10 \times 6.00 = \$60$ Price per bond = $962.50 + 18.33 + 60.00 =$ $\qquad\qquad\qquad \underline{\$1{,}040.83}$ Total purchase price = $1{,}040.83 \times 10 = \underline{\$10{,}408.30}$
Computing Proceeds from the Sale of Bonds	20–7 677	*Selling Bonds:* 1. Calculate accrued interest since last payment by $I = PRT$. 2. Calculate the proceeds per bond by adding the accrued interest to the current market price and subtracting the broker's commission. 3. $\dfrac{\text{Total}}{\text{proceeds}} = \dfrac{\text{Proceeds}}{\text{per bond}} \times \dfrac{\text{Number}}{\text{of bonds}}$	What are the proceeds of the sale of five Procter & Gamble bonds with a coupon rate of $6\frac{3}{8}$ and a current market price of $107\frac{3}{4}$? The commission charge is $8 per bond. The date of sale is 100 days since the last interest payment. Accrued interest = $1{,}000 \times .06375 \times \dfrac{100}{360} = \$17.71$ Commission = $5 \times 8.00 = \$40$ Proceeds per bond = $1{,}077.50 + 17.71 - 40.00 =$ $\qquad\qquad\qquad \underline{\$1{,}055.21}$ Total proceeds = $1{,}055.21 \times 5 = \underline{\$5{,}276.05}$

II, continued

Topic	P/O, Page	Important Concepts	Illustrative Examples
Calculating the Current Yield for a Bond	20–8 677	Current yield is a simple measure of the return on investment based on the current market price of the bond. Annual interest = Par value × Coupon rate $\text{Current yield} = \dfrac{\text{Annual interest}}{\text{Market price}}$	Calculate the current yield for a Universal Foods bond with a coupon rate of $9\frac{1}{4}\%$ and currently selling at a premium of $112\frac{1}{2}$. Annual interest = $1,000 \times .0925 = \underline{\$92.50}$ $\text{Current yield} = \dfrac{92.50}{1,125} = \underline{\underline{8.2\%}}$

SECTION III MUTUAL FUNDS

Topic	P/O, Page	Important Concepts	Illustrative Examples
Calculating the Sales Charge and the Sales Charge Percent of a Mutual Fund	20–10 682	Mutual fund sales charge or load may vary from 1% to 8% of the amount invested. When it is paid at the time of purchase, it is known as a front-end load. It is the difference between the offer price and the net asset value of the fund. Sales charge = Offer price – NAV $\text{Sales charge } \% = \dfrac{\text{Sales charge}}{\text{Net asset value}}$	What are the sales charge and the sales charge percent for a mutual fund with an offer price of $12.35 per share and a net asset value of $11.60? Sales charge = $12.35 - 11.60 = \underline{\$.75 \text{ per share}}$ $\text{Sales charge } \% = \dfrac{.75}{11.60} = \underline{\underline{6.5\%}}$
Calculating Net Asset Value of a Mutual Fund	20–11 683	The assets of a mutual fund are the total current value of its investments. The net asset value is the per share figure. $\dfrac{\text{Net asset}}{\text{value (NAV)}} = \dfrac{\text{Total assets} - \text{Total liabilities}}{\text{Number of shares outstanding}}$	A mutual fund has total assets of $20,000,000 and liabilities of $5,000,000. If there are 4,000,000 shares outstanding, what is the net asset value of the fund? Net asset value = $\dfrac{20,000,000 - 5,000,000}{4,000,000} = \underline{\underline{\$3.75}}$
Computing Number of Shares Purchased of a Mutual Fund	20–12 684	Mutual fund stock is sold in fractional shares to accommodate those investing lump sums of money. Shares are rounded to thousandths (three decimal places). $\text{Number of shares} = \dfrac{\text{Total investment}}{\text{Offer price}}$ Note: For no-load funds, use net asset value as the denominator.	Mike Matthews invested a lump sum of $10,000 in a mutual fund with an offer price of $8.75. How many shares did he purchase? Number of shares = $\dfrac{10,000}{8.75} = \underline{\underline{1,142.857}}$

III, continued

Topic	P/O, Page	Important Concepts	Illustrative Examples
Calculating Return on Investment (ROI)	20–13 684	Return on investment is the basic measure of how your stocks, bonds, or mutual fund investments are doing. 1. Calculate the gain (or loss) on the investment: Gain (or loss) = Proceeds − Total cost 2. Compute total gain (or loss) by adding any dividends received on stocks, or interest received on bonds. Total gain = Gain + Dividends or interest 3. $\text{Return on investment} = \dfrac{\text{Total gain}}{\text{Total cost of purchase}}$	Gene Gomberg purchased 1,000 shares of Continental Group mutual fund for an offer price of $7.50 per share. He later sold the shares at a net asset value of $8.75. During the time he owned the shares, Continental paid a dividend of $.85 per share. What is Gene's return on investment? Total cost = $1,000 \times 7.50 = \underline{\$7,500}$ Proceeds = $1,000 \times 8.75 = \underline{\$8,750}$ Gain = $8,750 - 7,500 = \underline{\$1,250}$ Dividends = $1,000 \times .85 = \underline{\$850}$ Total gain = $1,250 + 850 = \underline{\$2,100}$ $\text{ROI} = \dfrac{2,100}{7,500} = .28 = \underline{\underline{28\%}}$

TRY-IT EXERCISE   SOLUTIONS

1. $\text{Dividend per share} = \dfrac{\text{Total dividend}}{\text{Number of shares}}$

$\text{Dividend per share} = \dfrac{910,000}{1,400,000} = \underline{\underline{\$.65}}$

2. Total preferred dividend = Number of shares × Dividend per share
Total preferred dividend = $600,000 \times 1.40 = \underline{\$840,000}$

Total common dividend = Total dividend − Total preferred dividend
Total common dividend = $2,800,000 - 840,000 = \$1,960,000$

$\text{Dividend per share} = \dfrac{\text{Total common dividend}}{\text{Number of shares}}$

$\text{Dividend per share} = \dfrac{1,960,000}{1,000,000} = \underline{\underline{\$1.96}}$

3. Dividend per share = Par value × Dividend rate
Dividend per share = $100 \times 7.5\% = \$7.50$
Total preferred div. (per year) = Number of shares × Div. per share
Total preferred div. (per year) = $300,000 \times 7.50 = \$2,250,000$
Total preferred div. = 2,250,000 (arrears) + 2,250,000 (this year) = $\underline{\$4,500,000}$
Total common div. = Total div − Preferred div.
Total common div. = $7,000,000 - 4,500,000 = \$2,500,000$

$\text{Dividend per share} = \dfrac{2,500,000}{5,200,000} = \underline{\underline{\$.48}}$

4. *Delta Airlines: Stock*

52-week high	61⅜
52-week low	39½
Ticker symbol	DAL
Dividend	$.20 per share
Yield	.5%
PE Ratio	dd indicates a loss
Volume	330,400 shares traded
High for day	42¼
Low for day	41⅛
Close for day	42¼
Change	up 1 point

5. $\text{Current yield} = \dfrac{\text{Annual dividend per share}}{\text{Current price of stock}}$

$\text{Current yield} = \dfrac{.68}{12.875} = \underline{\underline{5.3\%}}$

6. $\text{Price-earnings ratio} = \dfrac{\text{Current price per share}}{\text{Earnings per share}}$

$\text{Price-earnings ratio} = \dfrac{37.375}{6.70} = 5.57 = \underline{\underline{6}}$

7. a. *Cost of stock*

Cost of shares = Price per share × Number of shares
Cost of shares = 34.75 × 225 = $7,818.75

Broker's commission = Cost of shares × Comm. rate
Round lot = 200 × 34.75 × .02 = $139.00
Odd lot = 25 × 34.75 × .03 = $26.06
Total commission = 139.00 + 26.06 = $165.06

Total cost = Cost of shares + Commission
Total cost = 7,818.75 + 165.06 = $7,983.81

b. *Proceeds from sale*

Value of shares = Price per share × Number of shares
Value of shares = 49.875 × 225 = $11,221.88

Commission:
Round lot = 200 × 49.875 × .02 = $199.50
Odd lot = 25 × 49.875 × .03 = $37.41
Total commission = 199.50 + 37.41 = $236.91

Proceeds = Value of shares − Broker's commission
Proceeds = 11,221.88 − 236.91 = $10,984.97

c. *Gain on transaction*

Gain = Proceeds − Total cost
Gain = 10,984.97 − 7,983.81 = $3,001.16

8. *Home Depot: Bond*

Coupon rate	4½%
Maturing in	1997
cv	Convertible
Volume	7 Bonds
Closing price	$1,175.00 (1,000 × 1.175)
Net change	up $23.75 (1,000 × .02375)

9. Accrued interest = $1,000 \times .0625 \times \dfrac{2}{12} = \$10.42$

Price per bond = Market price + Accrued int + Comm.
Price per bond = 913.75 + 10.42 + 10.00 = $934.17

Total purchase price = Price per bond × Number of bonds
Total purchase price = 934.17 × 20 = $18,683.40

10. Accrued interest = $1,000 \times .08875 \times \dfrac{122}{360} = \$30.08$

Proceeds per bond = Market price + Accrued interest − Comm.
Proceeds per bond = 990 + 30.08 − 10.00 = $1,010.08

Total proceeds = Proceeds per bond × Number of bonds
Total proceeds = 1,010.08 × 5 = $5,050.40

11. Annual interest = Par value × Coupon rate
Annual interest = 1,000 × .09375 = $93.75

Current price = Par value × Price percent
Current price = 1,000 × .8475 = $847.50

Current yield = $\dfrac{\text{Annual interest}}{\text{Market price}}$

Current yield = $\dfrac{93.75}{847.50} = .1106 = 11.1\%$

12. *Oppenheimer Fund: EqInc A: Mutual Fund*

Investment objective	Equity income
Net asset value	$9.61
Offer price	$10.20
NAV change	down $.05
Year-to-date return	−2.9%
26-week return	−2.7%
4-year return	+8.4%
Rating	D

13. Mutual fund sales charge = Offer price − Net asset value
Mutual fund sales charge = 9.85 − 9.21 = $.64

Sales charge percent = $\dfrac{\text{Sales charge}}{\text{NAV}} = \dfrac{.64}{9.21} = 6.9\%$

14. Net asset value = $\dfrac{\text{Total assets} - \text{Total liabilities}}{\text{Number of shares}}$

Net asset value = $\dfrac{80,000,000 - 5,000,000}{17,000,000} = \$4.41$

15. Number of shares purchased = $\dfrac{\text{Total investment}}{\text{Offer price}}$

Number of shares purchased = $\dfrac{10,000}{12.25} = 816.327$ shares

16. Total cost of purchase = 2,000 × 8.60 = $17,200
Proceeds from sale = 2,000 × 9.18 = $18,360

Gain on sale = Proceeds − Total cost
Gain on sale = 18,360 − 17,200 = $1,160

Dividends: 2,000 × .27 = $540
              2,000 × .42 = $840
Total dividends = 540 + 840 = $1,380

Total gain = Gain on sale + Dividends
Total gain = 1,160 + 1,380 = $2,540

Return on investment = $\dfrac{\text{Total gain}}{\text{Total cost of purchase}}$

ROI = $\dfrac{2,540}{17,200} = .1476 = 14.8\%$

Name____________________

Class____________________

CHAPTER 20 ASSESSMENT TEST

Calculate the preferred and common stock dividend per share for the following companies:

Company	Common Stock Shares	Preferred Stock Shares	Preferred Stock Div. or Par.	Preferred Stock Cum.	Dividend Declared	Arrears	Preferred Div./Share	Common Div./Share
1. Goodrich	22,000,000		none		$ 7,900,000	none	0	$.36
2. Hasbro	5,000,000	1,000,000	$3.20	yes	8,500,000	1 year	$6.40	$.42
3. Chrysler	80,000,000	3,400,000	$100, 5%	yes	58,000,000	2 years	$15.00	$.09

Answer Questions 4–7 based on the following stock quotation table:

	52 Weeks Hi	52 Weeks Lo	Stock	Sym	Div	Yld %	PE	Vol 100s	Hi	Lo	Close	Net Chg
	14	**9½**	**Fiat pf**		**.32e**	**2.5**	**...**	**597**	**13¼**	**12¾**	**13**	**– ¾**
n	15⅛	15	FidAdvAsia	FAE		...	...	374	15⅛	15	15	...
s	27¼	13⅜	FideltyFnl	FNF	.28	1.6	8	626	17¼	16⅞	17¼	+ ¼
	34⅜	19½	Fieldcrst	FLD		...	14	391	32¼	31¾	31¾	– ⅜
n	**19**	**12⅛**	**FilaHldg**	**FLH**		**...**	**...**	**343**	**14⅝**	**14**	**14**	**– ¾**
	10¾	8⅜	Filtertek	FTK	.26	3.0	73	71	8⅞	8¾	8¾	...
s	33¼	19⅛	Fingerhut	FHT	.16	.5	20	1662	30⅜	29½	29¾	– ⅝

	52 Weeks Hi	52 Weeks Lo	Stock	Sym	Div	Yld %	PE	Vol 100s	Hi	Lo	Clo
	62½	32¾	GreenTree	GNT	.38	.8	13	2600	49½	48	48
	17⅜	12½	Greiner	GII	.28f	2.0	16	15	14¼	14⅛	14
	18⅞	13½	GrowGp	GRO	.28	1.8	16	234	16⅛	15¾	15
	12½	8¼	GrowFdSpn	GSP		...	...	559	10½	10¼	10
	5⅜	**2⅝**	**Grubb/Ellis**	**GBE**		**...**	**dd**	**161**	**3¼**	**3**	**3**
	66⅜	33	Grumman	GQ	1.20	1.9	36	917	61⅞	61¾	61
n	33½	19½	GrupoCasa	ATY		...	...	442	24	23⅜	23

4. GreenTree—Dividend, volume, net change: .38, 260,000, up $\frac{7}{8}$

5. Fingerhut—Dividend, percent yield, low for the day: .16, .5%, $29\frac{1}{2}$

6. Grumman—Ticker symbol, P/E ratio, and high for the day: GQ, 36, $61\frac{7}{8}$

7. Fieldcrest—Percent Yield, volume, closing price: 0, 39,100, $31\frac{3}{4}$

Calculate the missing information for the following stocks:

Company	Earnings per Share	Annual Dividend	Current Price per Share	Current Yield	Price-Earnings Ratio
8. Federal Express	$3.20	$1.50	$$69\frac{1}{4}$	2.2%	22
9. Merck	$2.09	$1.12	$$33\frac{1}{2}$	3.3%	16
10. Office Depot	$2.10	$.48	$40	1.2%	19
11. Loews Corp.	$8.98	$1.71	$$89\frac{3}{4}$	1.9%	10

Calculate the total cost, proceeds, and gain (or loss) for the following stock market transactions:

Company	Number of Shares	Purchase Price	Selling Price	Commissions Buy	Commissions Sell	Commissions Odd Lot	Total Cost	Proceeds	Gain (or Loss)
12. Olin	400	$$39\frac{1}{4}$	$$44\frac{3}{4}$	2%	2%	—	$16,014	$17,542	$1,528.00
13. Limited	630	$24\frac{1}{8}$	$19\frac{7}{8}$	3	3	add 1%	15,661.95	12,139.65	(3,522.30)
14. Exxon	200	$61\frac{1}{2}$	$71\frac{1}{4}$	2	2	—	12,546	13,965	1,419.00
15. IBM	850.	$45\frac{1}{2}$	$53\frac{3}{4}$	$1\frac{1}{2}$	$1\frac{1}{2}$	add 1%	39,277.88	44,975.31	5,697.43

16. The board of directors of Contempo Furniture has declared a dividend of $16,000,000. The company has 800,000 shares of preferred stock that pay $4.90 per share, and 8,200,000 shares of common stock.

   a. What are the dividends due the preferred shareholders?

   Preferred shareholders get $4.90 per share × 800,000 = $3,920,000

ANSWERS

1. 0 $.36
2. $6.40 $.42
3. $15.00 $.09
4. .38 260,000 $\frac{7}{8}$
5. .16 .5 $29\frac{1}{2}$
6. GQ 36 $61\frac{7}{8}$
7. 0 39,100 $31\frac{3}{4}$
8. 2.2% 22
9. 2.09 3.3%
10. 40 19
11. 8.98 1.71
12. $1,528.00
13. ($3,522.30)
14. $1,419.00
15. $5,697.43

16. a. $3,920,000

b. What is the dividend per share of common stock?

$$\text{Dividend per share common stock} = \$16,000,000 - \$3,920,000$$
$$= \frac{\$12,080,000}{8,200,000}$$
$$= \underline{\$1.47} \text{ per share}$$

17. Great Eastern Financial has 500,000 shares of $100 par value, $6\frac{1}{2}\%$, cumulative preferred stock and 8,400,000 shares of common stock. Although no dividend was declared for the past three years, a $19,000,000 dividend has been declared for this year.

a. How much is due the preferred shareholders?

$$\text{Preferred shareholders due: } \$100.00 \times 6\frac{1}{2}\% \times 4 \text{ years}$$
$$= \$26.00 \text{ per share}$$
$$\text{Total due preferred shareholders} = \$26.00 \times 500,000$$
$$= \underline{\$13,000,000}$$

b. What is the dividend per share of common stock?

$$\text{Dividend per share common stock} = 19,000,000 - 13,000,000$$
$$= \frac{\$6,000,000}{8,400,000}$$
$$= \underline{\$.71} \text{ per share}$$

18. Webster Electronics is currently selling at $27\frac{1}{8}$. The earnings per share are $2.69 and the dividend is $.70.

a. What is the current yield of the stock?

$$\text{Current yield} = \frac{\$.70}{27.125} = \underline{2.6\%}$$

b. What is the price-earnings ratio?

$$\text{Price earnings ratio} = \frac{\$27.125}{\$2.69} = \underline{10}$$

19. You purchase 350 shares of General Merchandise common stock at $12\frac{3}{8}$ per share. A few months later you sell the shares at $9\frac{7}{8}$. Your stockbroker charges 3% commission on round lots and an extra $1\frac{1}{2}\%$ on odd lots.

a. What is the total cost of the purchase?

$$\text{Total cost} = 300 \times \$12.375 = \$3,712.50 \times 103\% = \$3,823.88$$
$$50 \times \$12.375 = \quad 618.75 \times 104.5\% = \$\ \ 646.59$$
$$= \underline{\$4,470.47}$$

b. What are the proceeds on the sale?

$$\text{Proceeds} = 300 \times \$9.875 = \$2,962.50 \times 97\% = \$2,873.63$$
$$50 \times \$9.875 = \quad \$493.75 \times 95.5\% = \$\ \ 471.53$$
$$= \underline{\$3,345.16}$$

c. What is the gain or loss on the transaction?

$$\text{Loss} = \$4,470.47 - \$3,345.16 = \underline{\$1,125.31}$$

Answer Questions 20–25 based on the bond quotation table below:

CORPORATION BONDS Volume, $30,630,000					Bonds	Cur Yld	Vol	Close	Net Chg.
Bonds	Cur Yld	Vol	Close	Net Chg.	CnPw 6⅞98	7.0	5	97¾	– ¾
					vjCtlInf 9s06f	cv	45	9	+ ½
AMR 9s16	9.1	95	99	– ⅜	Coopr 10⅝05f	...	11	70	– ⅛
AMR 8.10s98	7.9	7	102	– ⅝	CrayRs 6⅛11	cv	10	83½	...
ATT 4¾98	5.1	10	94	+ ¾	DataGn 01	cv	39	84½	– ¼
ATT 4⅜96	4.5	55	96¾ +	½	Datpnt 8⅞06	cv	27	76	+ 1
ATT 4⅜99	4.8	42	90½ +	¼	DaytP 8s03	8.0	7	100⅜	– ⅝
ATT 6s00	6.3	79	96 +	⅜	DeereCa 7.2s97	7.1	10	100⅞	– 2⅛
ATT 5⅛01	5.6	21	91½ +	½	DetEd 6.4s98	6.5	8	98¾	– 1¾
ATT 8⅝31	8.2	10	105¾ +	1¼	DiaSTel 7s08	7.1	5	98½	– ½
ATT 7⅛02	7.1	543	100⅜	...	Dole 7s03	7.6	15	92½	– ¾
ATT 8⅛22	8.0	289	101⅝ +	⅛	duPnt dc6s01	6.5	352	92¾	– ¼
ATT 8⅛24	8.0	65	101⅞ +	½	EMC 4¼01	cv	15	105	...
ATT 4½96	4.6	103	98¼ +	⅜	Eckerd 9¼04	9.9	749	93	+ ½
					EmbSuit 11s99	10.6	9	104	...

20. Eckerd—Maturity year and volume: _____2004,   749_____

21. Detroit Edison—Closing price and net change: ___$98\frac{3}{4}$,   down $1\frac{3}{4}$___

22. AMR 9s16—Coupon rate, maturity year, and net change: __9%,   2016,   down $\frac{3}{8}$__

23. Data General—Volume and closing price: ___39, $84\frac{1}{2}$___

24. Dole—Coupon rate and current yield: ____7%,   7.6%____

25. Which ATT bond is selling at the greatest discount? ___ATT $4\frac{3}{8}$ 99, price $90\frac{1}{2}$___

Calculate the accrued interest and the total purchase price of the following bond purchases:

Company	Coupon Rate	Market Price	Time Since Last Interest	Accrued Interest	Commission per Bond	Bonds Purchased	Total Price
26. Conagra	$8\frac{1}{4}$	$95\frac{3}{8}$	65 days	$14.90	$5.00	10	$9,736.50
27. Gateway	$7\frac{3}{8}$	$78\frac{1}{2}$	100 days	$20.49	9.50	5	$4,074.95
28. Chevron	$5\frac{5}{8}$	$105\frac{3}{4}$	3 months	$14.06	7.00	15	$16,178.40

Calculate the accrued interest and the total proceeds of the following bond sales:

Company	Coupon Rate	Market Price	Time Since Last Interest	Accrued Interest	Commission per Bond	Bonds Sold	Total Proceeds
29. Upjohn	$7\frac{3}{8}$	$94\frac{1}{2}$	10 days	$2.05	$6.00	10	$9,410.50
30. Brunswick	$8\frac{7}{8}$	$109\frac{1}{4}$	4 months	$29.58	5.00	20	$22,341.60
31. Pet	$9\frac{1}{4}$	98	85 days	$21.84	8.00	5	$4,969.20

Calculate the annual interest and current yield for the following bonds:

Company	Coupon Rate	Annual Interest	Market Price	Current Yield
32. Duracell	$5\frac{3}{8}$	$53.75	$94\frac{1}{8}$	5.7%
33. Seaboard	$9\frac{1}{2}$	$95.00	$105\frac{3}{4}$	9%

34. On May 1, Perry Herbert bought 10 Satellite bonds with a coupon rate of $7\frac{7}{8}$. The purchase price was $101\frac{3}{8}$ and the commission was $8.00 per bond. Satellite bonds pay interest on April 1 and October 1.

a. What is the current yield of the bond?

$$\text{Current yield} = \frac{\text{Annual interest}}{\text{Current market price}}$$

Interest $= 1000 \times .07875 = \$78.75$

Yield $= \frac{\$78.75}{1013.75} = 7.8\%$

b. What is the total purchase price of the bonds?

Accrued interest $= 1,000 \times .07875 \times \frac{1}{12} = \$6.56$

Total purchase price $= (\$1,013.75 + 6.56 + 8.00) \times 10$
$= \$10,283.10$

26. Interest $= 1,000 \times .0825 \times \frac{65}{360} = \$14.90$

Total cost $= (\$953.75 + 14.90 + 5.00) \times 10$
$= \$9,736.50$

29. Interest $= 1,000 \times .07375 \times \frac{10}{360} = \$2.05$

Proceeds $= (945.00 + 2.05 - 6.00) \times 10$
$= \$9,410.50$

32. Annual interest $= 1,000 \times 5.375\% = \$53.75$

Current yield $= \frac{53.75}{941.25} = 5.7\%$

c. If Perry sold the bonds on August 1 for $109\frac{1}{2}$, what are the proceeds from the sale?

Accrued interest $= 1,000 \times .07875 \times \frac{4}{12} = \$26.25$

Proceeds $= (1,095.00 + 26.25 - 8.00) \times 10 = \underline{\$11,132.50}$

Name_____

Class_____

ANSWERS

c. _____$11,132.50_____

Answer Questions 35–40 using the following mutual fund quotation table:

	Inv. Obj.	NAV	Offer Price	NAV Chg.	– Total Return – YTD	13 wks	3 yrs R
.GlGrB †	WOR	9.22	9.22	−0.07	−2.9	−3.2	NS ..
GrInB †	G&I	12.95	12.95	+0.01	−3.6	−5.0	NS ..
HlthB †	SEC	24.56	24.56	−0.12	−7.1	−9.3	NS ..
HiYldB †	BHI	12.47	12.47	−0.01	−3.2	−4.4	NS ..
IncmB †	BND	6.74	6.74	...	−4.3	−4.9	NS ..
InvB †	GRO	7.59	7.59	−0.08	−6.6	−8.8	NS ..
MATxB †	DMA	8.99	8.99	−0.01	−5.7	−5.8	NS ..
MuniB †	GLM	8.67	8.67	−0.02	−6.0	−6.0	NS ..
NJTxB †	MNJ	8.74	8.74	−0.02	−6.0	−6.1	NS ..
NwOpB †	GRO	22.44	22.44	−0.36	−8.5	−10.0	NS ..
NYTxB †	DNY	8.63	8.63	−0.01	−7.2	−7.0	NS ..
OTC B †	SML	10.19	10.19	−0.21	−10.5	−10.5	NS ..
TxExB †	GLM	8.65	8.65	−0.02	−7.4	−7.3	NS ..
TFHYB †	HYM	14.13	14.13	−0.02	−5.3	−5.4	+8.6 B
TFInB †	ISM	14.50	14.50	−0.03	−6.3	−6.3	+6.5 E
USGvB †	BND	12.59	12.59	+0.01	−4.1	−4.4	NS ..
UtilB †	SEC	9.09	9.09	+0.04	−6.9	−5.9	NS ..
VstaB †	SML	7.02	7.02	−0.11	−6.3	−7.6	NS ..
VoyB †	CAP	10.70	10.70	−0.10	−9.4	−10.0	NS ..
Quantitative Group:							
BostFor	ITL	10.42	10.42	−0.03	+9.8	+8.0	+7.3 D
BostGrInc	G&I	13.66	13.66	−0.02	−5.6	−6.4	+6.6 D
BostNumASML		15.04	15.04	−0.27	−2.3	−4.6	NS ..
BostNumOSML		14.91	14.91	−0.26	−2.5	−4.7	NS ..
Quest For Value:							
CA TE	MCA	10.36	10.88	−0.01	−6.6	−6.9	+7.3 C

	Inv. Obj.	NAV	Offer Price	NAV Chg.	– Total Return – YTD	13 wks	3 yrs R
PATxA p	MPA	7.60	7.98	−0.01	−7.2	−7.5	+7.2 D
SCTxA	SSM	7.68	8.06	−0.02	−7.0	−7.1	+6.6 E
US Gvt A pBND		6.84	7.18	...	−3.0	−3.5	+7.0 D
H Yd B A pBHI		6.60	6.93	−0.04	−2.4	−3.5	+16.2 C
Sentinel Group:							
Balan p	S&B	14.44	15.20	...	−4.2	−4.9	+7.7 D
Bond p	BND	6.13	6.45	+0.01	−5.2	−5.9	+9.2 B
Com S p	G&I	28.34	29.83	+0.03	−4.0	−5.3	+7.4 D
EmGr p	SML	5.31	5.59	−0.03	−7.2	−6.7	NS ..
GvSecs p	BND	9.71	10.22	+0.01	−4.8	−5.3	+7.7 C
Grwth p	GRO	16.17	17.02	−0.09	−9.0	−8.9	+2.7 E
PA TF p	MPA	12.87	13.55	−0.01	−5.0	−5.0	+7.0 E
TF Inc p	GLM	12.93	13.61	−0.01	−5.9	−6.1	+7.9 B
World p	ITL	12.67	13.34	−0.05	+0.3	−0.5	NS ..
Sentry	GRO	14.67	NL	+0.04	−1.2	−1.4	+7.0 C
Sequoia	GRO	54.82	NL	+0.24	+0.3	−0.5	+12.9 A
Seven Seas Series:							
MatrixEq	GRO	11.32	NL	...	−4.7	−5.8	NS ..
SP500	G&I	10.10	NL	...	−4.4	−6.2	NS ..
S&P Mid	SML	11.18	NL	−0.14	−5.9	−6.4	NS ..
ST Gvt	BST	9.68	NL	...	−0.9	−1.2	NS ..
Yldpl	BST	9.99	NL	...	+0.9	+0.8	NS ..
1784 Funds:							
Gov Med	BIN	9.43	NL	+0.01	−4.1	−4.5	NS ..
Gr In	G&I	10.17	NL	−0.12	−4.5	−5.6	NS ..
MATEIn	DMA	9.66	NL	−0.03	−5.7	−5.7	NS ..

35. Sentinel Group: Balan—Objective, net asset value, and ranking: Stocks and Bonds, 14.44, D

36. Quantitative Group: BostGrinc—Offer price and 13-week return: 13.66, down 6.4

37. Quest for Value: CA TE—NAV, NAV change, and 3-year return: 10.36, down 0.01, 7.3%

38. Which Seven Seas Series funds have the best and worst YTD returns? Yldpl, S&P Mid

Fund	Offer Price	Net Asset Value (NAV)	Sales Charge	Sales Charge %
39. Quest for Value: CA TE	$10.88	$10.36	$.52	5%
40. Sentinel Group: EmGr	$5.59	$5.31	$.28	5.3%

35. ___Stocks and Bonds, 14.44, D___

36. ___13.66, down 6.4___

37. ___10.36, down 0.01, 7.3%___

38. ___Yldpl, S&P Mid___

39. ___$10.88 $10.36 $.52 5%___

40. ___$5.59 $5.31 $.28 5.3%___

41. ___$7.05 6,410.256___

42. ___$7.65 3,267.974___

43. ___ROI −6.3%___

44. ___ROI 25.9%___

45. ___ROI 46.6%___

Calculate the net asset value and number of shares purchased for the following funds (round shares to thousandths, three decimal places):

	Total Assets	Total Liabilities	Shares Outstanding	Net Asset Value (NAV)	Offer Price	Total Investment	Shares Purchased
41.	$30,000,000	$1,800,000	4,000,000	$7.05	$7.80	$50,000	6,410.256
42.	58,000,000	3,700,000	7,100,000	$7.65	NL	25,000	3,267.974

Calculate the total cost, proceeds, total gain or loss, and return on investment for the following mutual fund investments. The offer price is the purchase price of the shares and the net asset value is the price at which the shares were later sold.

	Shares	Offer Price	Total Cost	Net Asset Value (NAV)	Proceeds	Per Share Dividends	Total Gain (or Loss)	Return on Investment
43.	100	$13.40	$1,340	$11.80	1,180	$.75	($85.00)	−6.3%
44.	500	12.65	$6,325	15.30	7,650	.63	$1,640	25.9%
45.	1,000	9.40	$9,400	12.82	12,820	.96	$4,380	46.6%

41. N.A.V. $= \dfrac{\$30,000,000 - \$1,800,000}{4,000,000} = \$7.05$

Shares purchased $= \dfrac{\$50,000}{\$7.80} = 6,410.256$

42. N.A.V. $= \dfrac{\$58,000,000 - \$3,700,000}{\$7,100,000} = \$7.65$

Shares purchased $= \dfrac{25,000}{7.65} = 3,267.974$

ANSWERS

46. a. _____$.55_____

b. _____6.6%_____

47. _____$9.04_____

48. _____1,694.915_____

49. _____33.6%_____

46. A mutual fund has an offer price of $8.90 and a net asset value of $8.35.

a. What is the sales charge?

Sales charge = Offer price − NAV
= 8.90 − 8.35 = $.55

b. What is the sales charge percent?

$$\text{Sales charge percent} = \frac{\text{Sales charge}}{\text{NAV}} = \frac{.55}{8.35} = 6.6\%$$

47. A mutual fund has total assets of $25,000,000 and liabilities of $1,500,000. If there are 2,600,000 shares outstanding, what is the net asset value of the fund?

$$\text{NAV} = \frac{\$25,000,000 − \$1,500,000}{2,600,000} = \$9.04$$

48. Myra Gross invested a lump sum of $20,000 in a mutual fund with an offer price of $11.80. How many shares did she purchase?

$$\text{Number of shares} = \frac{20,000}{11.80} = 1,694.915$$

49. Fred Baldwin purchased 800 shares of Premium Value Fund for an offer price of $6.90 per share. He later sold the shares at a net asset value of $8.60 per share. During the time he owned the shares the fund paid dividends of $.24 and $.38 per share. What is Fred's return on investment?

Cost = 800 × $6.90 = $5,520
Proceeds = 800 × $8.60 = $6,880
Dividends = ($.24 + $.38) × 800 = $496
Gain = $6880 + $496 − $5,520 = $1,856

$$\text{Return on investment} = \frac{1,856}{5,520} = 33.6\%$$

 BUSINESS DECISION
Paper Profit

50. You have received your investment portfolio year-end statement from your broker, Rich Waldman. All investments were purchased at the January prices and held the entire year.

Portfolio Year-End Statement

Investment	Number	Dividend	Price—Jan. 1	Price—Dec. 31
Disney	400 shares	$.30	38⅜	45¾
Federal Express	500 shares	0	74½	70⅛
McDonald's	200 shares	.24	27⅞	29¼
Exxon	300 shares	3.00	68¾	64⅝
AT&T 7⅛02	20 bonds		98½	101⅜
Ryder 9⅞17	10 bonds		103⅞	100¾

a. Calculate how much profit or loss you made for the year, including stock dividends and bond interest.

Company	Value Jan.1	Value Dec.31	Dividend/ Interest	Gain/ (Loss)
Disney	$15,350.00	$18,300.00	120.00	$3,070.00
Federal Express	37,250.00	35,062.50	0	(2,187.50)
McDonald's	5,575.00	5,850.00	48.00	323.00
Exxon	20,625.00	19,387.50	900.00	(337.50)
AT&T 7⅛02	19,700.00	20,275.00	1,425.00	2,000.00
Ryder 9⅝17	10,387.50	10,075.00	987.50	675.00
	$108,887.50	$108,950.00	$3,480.50	$3,543.00

Total profit for year = $3,543.00

b. What was the total return on investment for your portfolio?

$$\text{Return on investment} = \frac{\text{Total gain}}{\text{Value Jan.1}} = \frac{\$3,543.00}{\$108,887.50} = \underline{\underline{3.3\%}}$$

c. Using a broker's commission of 3% buying and 3% selling on the stocks, and $5.00 buying and $5.00 selling per bond, how much profit or loss would you make if you liquidated your entire portfolio at the December 31 prices?

	Total cost Jan.1	Proceeds Dec.31	Dividend/ Interest	Gain/ (Loss)
Disney	$15,810.50	$17,751.00	$120.00	$2,060.50
Federal Express	38,367.50	34,010.63	0	(4,356.87)
McDonald's	5,742.25	5,674.50	48.00	(19.75)
Exxon	21,243.75	18,805.88	900.00	(1,537.87)
AT&T	19,800.00	20,175.00	1,425.00	1,800.00
Ryder	10,437.50	10,025.00	987.50	575.00
	$111,401.50	$106,442.01	$3,480.50	($1,478.99)

Total loss = $1,478.99

d. What would be the return on investment?

$$\text{Return on investment} = \frac{\$1,478.99}{\$111,401.50} = \underline{\underline{1.3\%}} \text{ Loss}$$

ANSWERS

50. a. _____ $3,543.00 _____

    b. _____ 3.3% _____

    c. _____ Total loss = $1,478.99 _____

    d. _____ 1.3% Loss _____

All the Math That's Fit to Learn

The Business Math Times

Volume XX | Investments | One Dollar

Career Track:
Stockbroker

Nature of the Work

Most investors, whether they are individuals with a few hundred dollars to invest, or large institutions with millions, use stockbrokers to handle the transactions, when buying or selling stocks, bonds, mutual funds, or other financial products. In most cases, the broker relays the buy or sell order through their firms' offices to the floor of a securities exchange, such as the New York Stock Exchange. There, floor brokers actually execute the transaction.

Stockbrokers also provide many related services for their customers, such as financial counseling, portfolio management, and supplying information about various securities their clients are interested in, as well as giving current price quotations.

Training, Other Qualifications, and Advancement

Because stockbrokers must be well informed about economic conditions and trends, a college education, with emphasis in business administration, economics, and finance, is increasingly important.

"Quote...Unquote"

If you want to make money, really big money, do what nobody else is doing. Buy when everyone else is selling and hold until everyone else is buying. This is not merely a catchy slogan, it is the very essence of successful investment.
–J. Paul Getty

Investing is not as tough as being a topnotch bridge player. All it takes is the ability to see things as they really are.
–Warren Buffet, chairman, Berkshire Hathaway

Note: In June 1996, Berkshire Hathaway was the most expensive stock on the NYSE, selling at over $30,600 per share.

Stockbrokers must meet state licensing requirements, which generally include passing examinations and in some cases, furnishing a personal bond. In addition, they must serve a 4-month apprenticeship and pass an exam administered by the National Association of Securities Dealers, Inc., before they are officially registered as representatives of their brokerage firm.

SOURCE: Adapted from *Occupational Outlook Handbook*, 1994-95 Edition, U.S. Department of Labor.

Wall Street Words

- **AMEX** American Stock Exchange.
- **Bear** An investor who expects stock prices to fall.
- **Bear market** A period of generally declining stock prices.
- **Blue chip** A widely known company that is a leader in its industry and has a proven record of profits and a long history of dividend payment.
- **Bull** An investor who expects stock prices to rise.
- **Bull market** A period of generally rising stock prices.
- **DJIA** Dow Jones Industrial Average. The average price of 30 blue chip American stocks. Often used by investors to judge the overall performance of the stock market.
- **NASDAQ** National Association of Securities Dealers Automated Quotations.

An automated information network that provides brokers with price quotations on securities traded over-the-counter.
- **NYSE** New York Stock Exchange.
- **Rally** A sharp rise following a decline in the general price level of the market, or in an individual stock.
- **Ticker** A telegraphic moving tape that continuously provides the last sale prices and volume of securities transactions on exchanges.
- **Wall Street** The street in New York City where the NYSE and many brokerage firms are located. The term is often used to describe the stock market itself. "How did Wall Street do today?"

Brainteaser

Two hungry friends were at a Pizza Hut. If they wanted the most pizza for their money, and the prices were the same, should they order a 10-inch round pizza or a 9-inch square pizza?

SOURCE: *Mathematics Teacher Magazine*, November 1986.

Answer to Last Issue's Brainteaser

8 Minutes At 15 mph, the train is traveling at 1 mile every 4 minutes. To get through a 1 mile long tunnel, the train must travel a total of 2 miles: 1 mile in, and 1 mile out. The total travel time, therefore, is 4 x 2 = 8 minutes.

Chapter 21

Business Statistics and Data Presentation

Performance Objectives

Information, the Name of the Game!

Statistical ideas and methods are used in almost every aspect of human activity, from the natural sciences to the social sciences. Statistics has special applications in such areas as medicine, psychology, education, engineering, and agriculture. In business, statistical methods are applied extensively in production, marketing, finance, and accounting.

Business statistics is the systematic process of collecting, interpreting, and presenting numerical data about business situations. In business, statistics is organized into two categories, descriptive statistics and statistical inference. **Descriptive statistics** deals with the tabular or graphical presentation of data, while **statistical inference** is the process of arriving at conclusions, predictions, forecasts, or estimates based on that data. In order to make sound managerial decisions, today's managers must understand the meaning and implications of vast amounts of numerical data generated by their companies.

Business statistics starts with the collection of raw data concerning a particular business situation or question. For example, if management wants the next annual report to present a comparison chart of company sales and profit figures with current industry trends, two types of information would be required. First are the company records of sales and profits. This data would be readily available from *internal* company sources. Most large corporations today use a vast array of computer systems to collect and store incredible amounts of information relating to all aspects of business activity. Management information systems are then used to deliver this data, upon request, in an electronic instant.

Information gathered from sources outside the firm such as current industry statistics are known as *external* data, and are readily available from a variety of private and government publications. The federal government is by far the largest researcher and publisher of business data. The Departments of Commerce and Labor periodically publish information relating to all aspects of the economy and the country. Some of these publications are the *Statistical Abstract of the United States, Survey of Current Business, Monthly Labor Review, Federal Reserve Bulletin, Census of the United States*, and the *Census of Business.*

Private statistical services such as Moody's Investors Service and Standard and Poor's offer a wealth of information for business decision making. Other private sources are periodicals such as *The Wall Street Journal, Fortune, Business Week, Forbes,* and *Money,* as well as hundreds of industry and trade publications.

Glossary terms (margin)

● **business statistics**

The systematic process of collecting, interpreting, and presenting numerical data about business situations.

● **descriptive statistics**

Statistical procedures that deal with the collection, classification, summarization, and the tabular or graphical presentation of data.

● **statistical inference**

The process of arriving at conclusions, predictions, forecasts, or estimates based on the data under study.

Government publications, financial journals, and news sources are excellent resources for business and financial data.

DATA INTERPRETATION AND PRESENTATION

Numerical data form the raw material upon which analyses, forecasts, and managerial plans are based. In business, tables and charts are used extensively to summarize and display data in a clear and concise manner. In this section you will learn to read, interpret, and construct information from tables and charts.

21-1 Reading and Interpreting Information from Tables

Tables are a collection of related data arranged for ease of reference or comparison, usually in parallel columns with meaningful titles. They are a very useful tool in summarizing statistical data and are found everywhere in business. Once the data has been obtained from the table, it can be compared to other data by arithmetic or percentage analysis.

● **tables**
A collection of related data arranged for ease of reference or comparison, usually in parallel columns with meaningful titles.

STEPS TO READING TABLES:

Step 1. Scan the titles above the columns for the category of information being sought.

Step 2. Look down the column for the specific fact required.

Table 21-1 shows the sales figures in dollars for Magnum Enterprises over a six-month period. Magnum manufactures and sells standard and deluxe computer components. Note that the table is divided into columns representing sales per month of each product type by territory.

	January		February		March		April		May		June	
	Standard	**Deluxe**	**Standard**	**Deluxe**	**Standard**	**Deluxe**	**Standard**	**Deluxe**	**Standard**	**Deluxe**	**Standard**	**Deluxe**
Northwest	$123,200	$ 86,400	$115,800	$ 73,700	$133,400	$ 91,100	$136,700	$ 92,600	$112,900	$ 65,300	$135,000	$ 78,400
Northeast	214,700	121,300	228,400	133,100	246,600	164,800	239,000	153,200	266,100	185,000	279,300	190,100
Southwest	88,300	51,000	72,100	45,700	97,700	58,300	104,000	67,800	125,000	78,300	130,400	74,500
Southeast	143,200	88,700	149,900	91,300	158,400	94,500	127,700	70,300	145,700	79,400	162,000	88,600

TABLE 21-1

MAGNUM ENTERPRISES
SIX-MONTH SALES REPORT

EXAMPLE

Answer the following questions about Magnum Enterprises from Table 21-1:

1. What were the sales of deluxe units in April in the Northeast?
2. What were the sales of standard units in May in the Southwest?
3. What were the total sales for February and March in the Southeast?
4. What months showed a decrease in sales of deluxe units in the Northwest?
5. How many more standard units were sold company-wide in June than in January?
6. What percent of the total units sold in March were deluxe?

SOLUTION STRATEGY

Questions 1, 2, and 4 can be answered by inspection. Questions 3, 5, and 6 require numerical or percentage calculations.

1. Deluxe unit sales in April in the Northeast = $153,200

2. Standard unit sales in May in the Southwest = $125,000

3. Total sales in February and March in the Southeast:

$$149,900 + 91,300 + 158,400 + 94,500 = $494,100$$

4. Decrease in sales of deluxe units in the Northwest occurred in February and May.

5. Standard unit sales in January = $569,400
Standard unit sales in June = $706,700

$$706,700 - 569,400 = \underline{\$137,300} \text{ more in June}$$

6. To solve this problem we will utilize the percentage formula Rate = Portion ÷ Base. In this case the Rate is the unknown, the total sales in March is the Base, and the deluxe sales in March is the Portion.

$$\text{Rate} = \frac{408,700}{1,044,800} = .3911 = \underline{39.1\%}$$

TRY-IT   EXERCISES

Answer the following questions about Magnum Enterprises from Table 21-1:

1. What were the sales of standard units in February in the Northeast?

2. What were the sales of deluxe units in April in the Southeast?

3. What were the total sales for May and June in the Northwest?

4. What months showed an increase in sales of standard units in the Southwest?

5. How many more deluxe units were sold company-wide in May than in April?

6. What percent of the total units sold in the Northwest were standard?

Check your answers with the solutions on page 738.

21-2 Reading and Constructing Line Charts

● **line chart**

A series of data points on a grid, continuously connected by straight lines, that display a picture of selected data changing over a period of time.

● **x-axis**

The horizontal axis of a chart, usually used to measure units of time such as days, weeks, months, or years.

● **y-axis**

The vertical axis of a chart, usually used to measure the quantity or magnitude of something, such as sales dollars or production units. The y-axis is frequently used to measure the percentage of something.

Charts are used to display a picture of the relationships among selected data. **Line charts** show data changing over a period of time. A single glance at a line chart gives the viewer a general idea of the direction or trend of the data: up, down, or up and down.

The horizontal or **x-axis** is used to measure units of time, such as days, weeks, months, or years, while the vertical or **y-axis** depicts magnitude, such as sales dollars or production units. Frequently the y-axis is used to measure the percentage of something.

Line charts are actually a series of data points on a grid, continuously connected by straight lines. They may contain a single line, representing the change of one variable such as interest rates; or they may contain multiple lines, representing the change of interrelated variables such as interest rates and stock prices or sales and profits.

STEPS FOR READING LINE CHARTS:

Step 1. Scan either the x- or y-axis for the known variable: x for time, y for amount.

Step 2. Draw a perpendicular line from that axis to the point where it intersects the chart.

Step 3. Draw a line from that point perpendicular to the opposite axis.

Step 4. The answer is read where that line intersects the opposite axis.

Exhibit 21-1 and Exhibit 21-2 are examples of single- and multiple-line charts.

EXAMPLE

Answer the following questions from the charts in Exhibits 21-1 and 21-2:

1. In what year is the U.S. population projected to be 280 million?

2. What was the U.S. population in 1995?

3. In what year did network TV viewership reach its lowest point, 800 hours per year?

4. In what year did cable TV viewership level off, and at approximately how many hours per year?

SOLUTION STRATEGY

1. Locate 280 million on the *y*-axis and then scan to the right until the line chart is intersected. Look down, perpendicular to the *x*-axis, to find the answer, <u>2002</u>.

2. Locate 1995 on the *x*-axis and then scan up until the line is intersected. Scan left to the *y*-axis to find the answer, <u>262 million</u>.

3. By inspection we see that network TV viewership reached its lowest point in <u>1990</u>.

4. Cable TV leveled off in <u>1992</u> at approximately <u>400</u> hours per year.

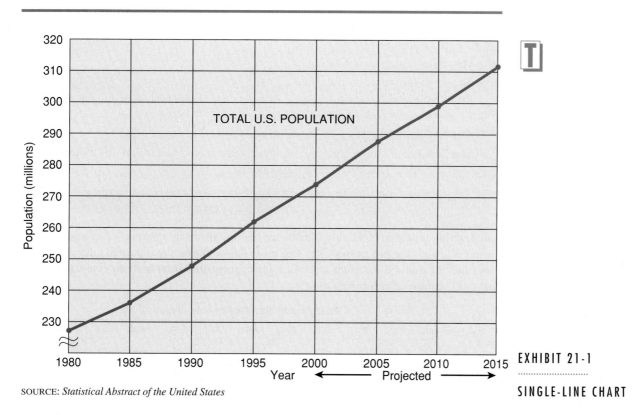

EXHIBIT 21-1

SOURCE: *Statistical Abstract of the United States*

SINGLE-LINE CHART

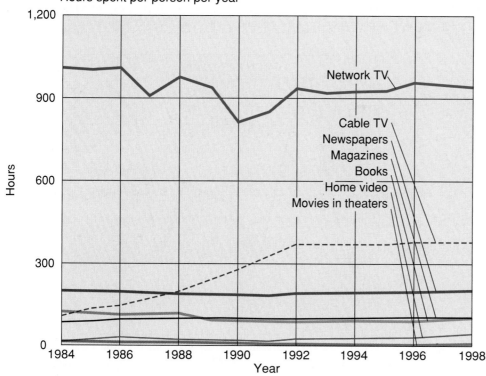

EXHIBIT 21-2

SOURCE: *Statistical Abstract of the United States*

MULTIPLE-LINE CHART

Answer the following questions from the line charts in Exhibits 21-1 and 21-2:

7. In what year is the U.S. population projected to reach 300 million?

8. Approximately how many hours per person per year was spent reading newspapers in 1994?

9. In what year were cable TV and newspaper readership the same?

Check your answers with the solutions on page 738.

STEPS TO CONSTRUCT A LINE CHART:

Step 1. Evenly space and label the time variable on the *x*-axis.

Step 2. Evenly space and label the amount variable on the *y*-axis.

Step 3. Show each data point by placing a dot above the time period and across from the corresponding amount.

Step 4. Connect the plotted points with straight lines to form the chart.

Step 5. When multiple lines are displayed, they should be labeled or differentiated by various colors or line patterns.

EXAMPLE

You are the manager of Handy Hardware Stores, Inc. The company has one store in Centerville and one in Carson City. The table below shows the monthly sales figures, in thousands of dollars, for each store last year. From this information, construct a line chart of the total sales for each month.

Handy Hardware: Monthly Sales Report (000)

	Jan.	Feb.	Mar.	Apr.	May	June	July	Aug.	Sept.	Oct.	Nov.	Dec.
Centerville	16	18	24	21	15	14	17	18	16	23	24	20
Carson City	8	11	14	12	10	15	13	13	9	13	14	17
Total	24	29	38	33	25	29	30	31	25	36	38	37

SOLUTION STRATEGY

For this chart, show the months on the *x*-axis and the sales on the *y*-axis. Use a range of 20 to 40 on the *y*-axis. Plot each month with a dot and connect all the dots with straight lines.

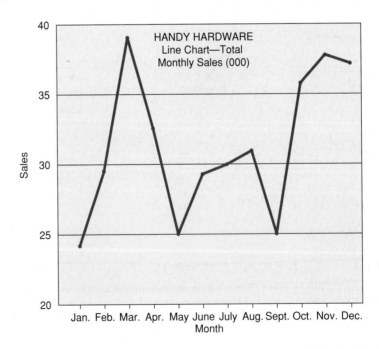

As shown in the exercises, statistical information is used in many different circumstances, including measuring attendance figures at a circus performance.

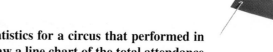

TRY-IT EXERCISE

10. The following data represent the audience statistics for a circus that performed in your town last week. Use the grid below to draw a line chart of the total attendance for each day.

	Monday	Tuesday	Wednesday	Thursday	Friday	Saturday	Sunday
Adults	2,300	2,100	1,900	2,200	2,400	2,700	2,600
Children	3,300	2,600	2,400	1,900	2,700	3,100	3,600
Total	5,600	4,700	4,300	4,100	5,100	5,800	6,200

Circus Attendance

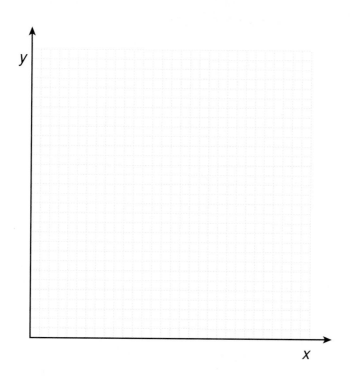

Check your chart with the solution on page 738.

From the Handy Hardware table on page 706 construct a multiple-line chart of the monthly sales for each of the stores. Show the Centerville store with a solid line and the Carson City store with a dashed line.

SOLUTION STRATEGY

As in the last example, the x-axis, time, will be months. The y-axis should range from 0 to 25 in order to include all the data.

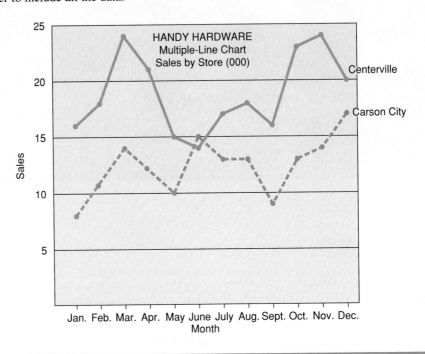

TRY-IT   EXERCISE

11. From the Circus Attendance table on page 707 draw a multiple-line chart showing the number of adults and children attending the circus last week. Use a solid line for the adults and a dashed line for the children.

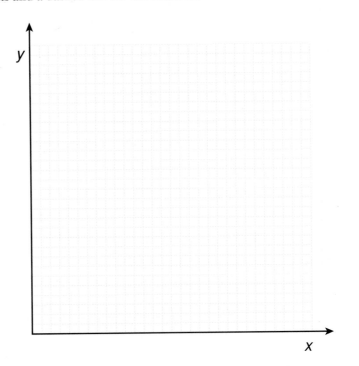

Check your chart with the solution on page 739.

One of the most common uses of statistical information and data interpretation is for business presentations.

21-3 Reading and Constructing Bar Charts

Bar charts represent quantities or percentages by the length of horizontal or vertical bars. As with line charts, bar charts often illustrate increases or decreases in magnitude of a certain variable or the relationship between similar variables. Bar charts may or may not be based on the movement of time.

Bar charts are divided into three categories: standard, component, and comparative. **Standard bar charts** are used to illustrate the change in magnitude of one variable. See Exhibit 21-3.

Component bar charts are used to illustrate parts of something that add to a total. Each bar is divided into the components, stacked on top of each other and shaded or colored differently. See Exhibit 21-4.

● **bar chart**
Graphical presentations that represent quantities or percentages by the length of horizontal or vertical bars. These charts may or may not be based on the movement of time.

● **standard bar chart**
A bar chart that illustrates increases or decreases in magnitude of one variable.

● **component bar chart**
A bar chart used to illustrate the parts of something that add to a total; each bar is divided into the components stacked on top of each other and shaded or colored differently.

U.S. College Enrollment

Enrollment (millions) — vertical axis from 12.5 to 16.0

Year (horizontal axis): 1988, 1990, 1992, 1994, 1996, 1998, 2000, 2002, 2004
Projected →

SOURCE: *Statistical Abstract of the United States*

T

EXHIBIT 21-3
....
STANDARD BAR CHART

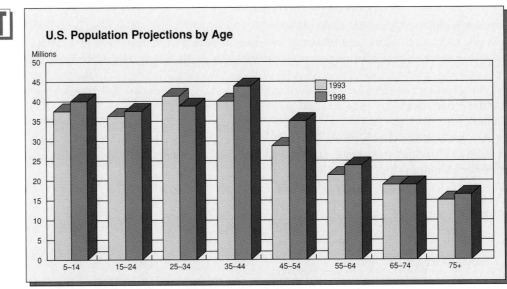

THE HOTTEST JOB PROSPECTS

Fastest-Growing Occupations	1991 Employment	Net New Jobs by 2005 (Percent change)
Health Care		
Home-Health Aides		92% (Increase)
Medical Assistants		74%
Radiologic Technicians		70%
Physical Therapists		76%
Computer Professionals and Technicians		
Computer Programmers		56%
Systems Analysts and Computer Scientists		79%
Data Processing Equipment Repairers		60%
Operations Research Analysts		73%
Management and White-Collar Professionals		
Marketing, Advertising, and Public Relations		47%
Legal Secretaries		47%
Management Analysts		52%
Paralegals		85%
Jobs in Thousands	0 200 400 600 800 1,000	

EXHIBIT 21-4
....
COMPONENT BAR CHART

U.S. Population Projections by Age

1993
1998

SOURCE: U.S. Department of Commerce, Bureau of the Census

EXHIBIT 21-5
....
COMPARATIVE BAR CHART

● **comparative bar chart**
A bar chart used to illustrate the relationship between two or more similar variables.

Comparative bar charts are used to illustrate two or more related variables. The bars representing each variable should be shaded or colored differently to make the chart easy to read and interpret. See Exhibit 21-5.

STEPS FOR READING BAR CHARTS:

Step 1. Scan the *x*- or *y*-axis for a known variable.

Step 2. Read the answer on the opposite axis directly across from the top of the appropriate bar.

EXAMPLE

From the bar charts in Exhibits 21-3, 21-4, and 21-5, answer the following questions:

1. In what year did college enrollment reach 14.5 million students?
2. What is the projected college enrollment in the year 2000?

3. What profession will show the greatest percent increase by the year 2005?

4. What profession in the Management and White-Collar Professionals category will exceed 600,000 jobs by 2005?

5. Which age category shows the greatest decrease from 1993 to 1998?

6. Which age category is the largest in 1998?

SOLUTION STRATEGY

1. Locate 14.5 million on the *y*-axis and scan across to where the chart intersects the line; now look down to the *x*-axis for the answer, <u>1992</u>.

2. Locate 2000 on the *x*-axis and scan up to the top of the bar; then scan left to the *y*-axis for the answer, <u>15.5 million</u>.

3. According to the chart, <u>home-health aides, 92%</u>.

4. <u>Marketing, advertising, and public relations</u> will exceed 600,000 jobs by 2005.

5. The <u>25–34</u> age category shows the greatest decrease from 1993 to 1998.

6. The largest age category in 1998 is <u>35–44</u>.

 TRY-IT **EXERCISES**

From the bar charts in Exhibits 21-3, 21-4, and 21-5, answer the following questions:

12. How much did college enrollment increase between 1988 and 1990?

13. What profession will total 400,000 jobs by 2005?

14. What profession will have 900,000 jobs by 2005?

15. Which age category shows the smallest amount of change from 1993 to 1998?

Check your answers with the solutions on page 739.

STEPS TO CONSTRUCT A BAR CHART:

Step 1. Evenly space and label the *x*-axis. The space between bars should be one-half the width of the bars.

Step 2. Evenly space and label the *y*-axis. Be sure to include the full range of values needed to represent the variable. The lowest values should start at the bottom of the *y*-axis and increase upward.

Step 3. Draw each bar up from the *x*-axis to the point opposite the *y*-axis that corresponds to its value.

Step 4. For comparative and component bar charts, differentiate the bars by color or shading pattern. For complex presentations, provide a key or legend that shows which pattern or color represents each variable. This will help the reader to interpret the chart.

Note: The steps above are used to construct charts with vertical bars. For charts with horizontal bars, lay out the bars on the *y*-axis and the magnitude variable on the *x*-axis.

EXAMPLE

From the Handy Hardware sales report table on page 706, construct a standard bar chart of total sales for January through June.

SOLUTION STRATEGY

For this chart the time variable, January through June, is shown on the *x*-axis. A range of 20 to 40 is used on the *y*-axis.

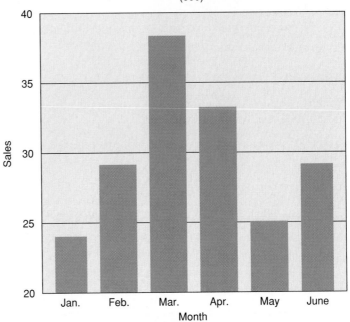

HANDY HARDWARE
Total Sales—Bar Chart
(000)

TRY-IT **EXERCISE**

16. From the table for Circus Attendance on page 707 use the following grid to construct a standard bar chart of the total attendance for each day.

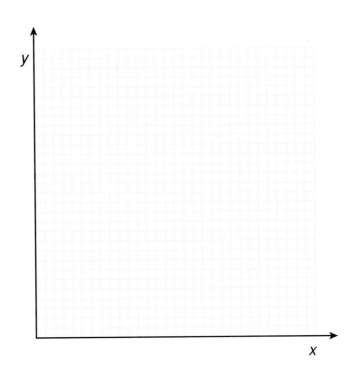

Check your chart with the solution on page 739.

EXAMPLE

From the table for Circus Attendance on page 707 construct a component bar chart that displays the adults and the children as components of each day's total audience. Plot the adults at the bottom of the bars, in dark shading, and the children stacked above the adults, in light shading.

For this chart the time variable, Monday through Sunday, is shown on the *x*-axis. A range of 0 to 7,000 is used on the *y*-axis.

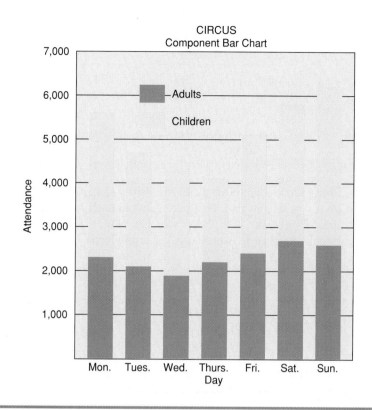

CIRCUS
Component Bar Chart

TRY-IT   EXERCISE

17. **From the Handy Hardware sales report table on page 706 construct a component bar chart that displays the Centerville and the Carson City stores as components of the total monthly sales for July through December.**

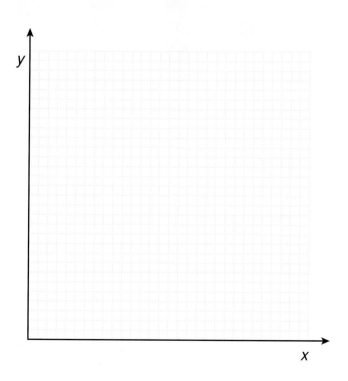

Check your chart with the solution on page 740.

From the table below, construct a comparative bar chart of the freshmen and sophomore enrollment. Let the *x*-axis represent the time variable. For each term, group the bars together and differentiate them by shading.

	Interstate Business College: Annual Enrollment			
	Fall	Winter	Spring	Summer
Freshmen	1,800	1,400	1,350	850
Sophomores	1,200	1,200	1,150	700
Juniors	1,200	1,100	750	650
Seniors	850	700	500	400

SOLUTION STRATEGY

This chart is constructed in the same way as the standard bar chart except that the variables being compared are drawn side by side. The space between the bars is one-half the width of each bar. The *y*-axis ranges from 0 to 2,000 students. Note that the bars are shaded to differentiate the variables and that an explanation key is provided.

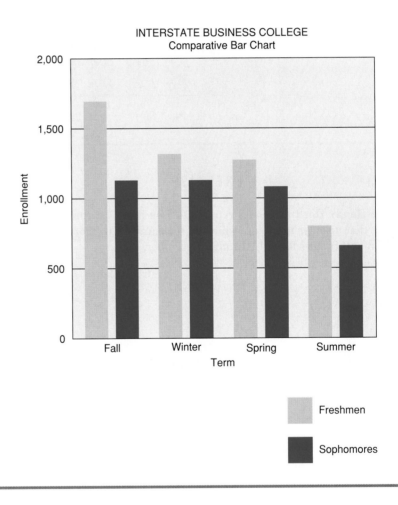

TRY-IT **EXERCISE**

18. From the Interstate Business College enrollment figures in the table on page 714, construct a comparative bar chart of the junior and senior enrollment. Let the *x*-axis represent the time variable. For each term, group the bars together and differentiate them by shading.

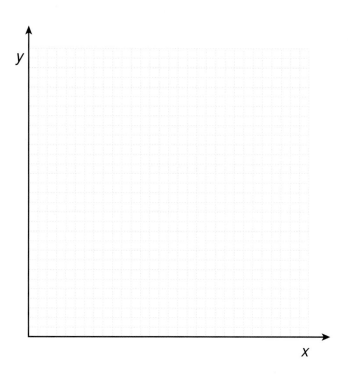

Check your chart with the solution on page 740.

21-4 Reading and Constructing Pie Charts

The **pie chart** is a circle divided into sections representing the component parts of a whole. The whole, 100%, is the circle; the parts are the wedge-shaped sections of the circle. When this type of chart is used, the data is usually converted to percentages. The size of each section of the circle is determined by the portion or percentage each component is of the whole. Pie charts are generally read by inspection since each component of the data is clearly labeled by category and percent. Exhibit 21-6 illustrates examples of pie charts.

● **pie chart**
A circle divided into sections, usually expressed in percentage form, representing the component parts of a whole.

How People Spend
(share of household consumption)

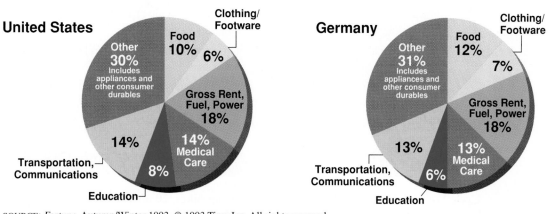

EXHIBIT 21-6
....
PIE CHARTS

From the pie charts in Exhibit 21-6, answer the following:

1. In the United States, what percent of household consumption is spent on education?

2. What category of household consumption is the same in the United States and Germany?

SOLUTION STRATEGY

By inspection,

1. <u>8%</u> of U.S. household consumption is spent on education.

2. <u>Gross rent, fuel, and power (18%)</u> is the same in the United States and Germany.

T R Y - I T   EXERCISE

19. **From the pie charts in Exhibit 21-6, answer the following:**

    a. What is the combined percent of Germany's household consumption of food and clothing?

    b. How much more, in percent, does a U.S. household spend on transportation and communications than a German household?

Check your answers with the solutions on page 740.

STEPS TO CONSTRUCT A PIE CHART:

Step 1. Convert the amount of each component to a percent using the percentage formula Rate = Portion ÷ Base. Let the portion be the amount of each component, and the base the total amount. Round each percent to hundredths.

Step 2. Since a full circle is made up of 360° representing 100%, multiply each component's percent (decimal form) by 360° to determine how many degrees each component's slice will be. Round to the nearest whole degree.

Step 3. Draw a circle with a compass and mark the center.

Step 4. Using a protractor, mark off the number of degrees on the circle that represents each component.

Step 5. Connect each point on the circle with the center by a straight line to form a segment or slice for each component.

Step 6. Label the segments clearly by name, color, or shading.

EXAMPLE

Cycle World sold 80 bicycles last week: 30 racing bikes, 20 off-road bikes, 15 standard bikes, and 15 tricycles. Construct a pie chart showing the sales breakdown for the shop.

For this chart, we must first convert the component amounts to percents and then multiply the decimal form of the percents by 360° as follows:

$$\textit{Racing bikes:} \quad \frac{30}{80} = .375 = 37.5\% \qquad .375 \times 360° = 135°$$

$$\textit{Off-road bikes:} \quad \frac{20}{80} = .25 = 25\% \qquad .25 \times 360° = 90°$$

$$\textit{Standard bikes:} \quad \frac{15}{80} = .1875 = 18.75\% \qquad .1875 \times 360° = 68°$$

$$\textit{Tricycles:} \quad \frac{15}{80} = .1875 = 18.75\% \qquad .1875 \times 360° = 68°$$

Next, draw a circle and use a protractor to mark the degree points of each component. Note that due to rounding, the degrees do not equal exactly 360°. Connect the points with the center of the circle to form the segments, and label each appropriately. The completed chart follows.

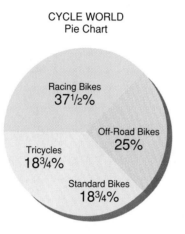

CYCLE WORLD
Pie Chart

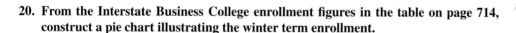

TRY-IT   EXERCISE

20. **From the Interstate Business College enrollment figures in the table on page 714, construct a pie chart illustrating the winter term enrollment.**

Check your chart with the solution on page 740.

As the sales manager for Magnum Enterprises, you have been asked by the president to prepare the following charts for the shareholders' meeting next week. Use the six-month sales report, Table 21-1, as the database for these charts. Calculate totals as required:

1. Single-line chart of the total company sales per month.

	Jan	Feb	Mar	Apr	May	Jun
Standard	$569,400	$566,200	$ 636,100	$607,400	$ 649,700	$ 706,700
Deluxe	347,400	343,800	408,700	383,900	408,000	431,600
Total	916,800	910,000	1,044,800	991,300	1,057,700	1,138,300

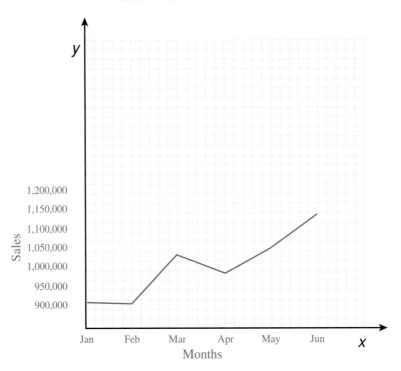

2. See sales figures in question 1 and Graph 2.

2. Multiple-line chart of the total sales per month of each model, standard and deluxe.

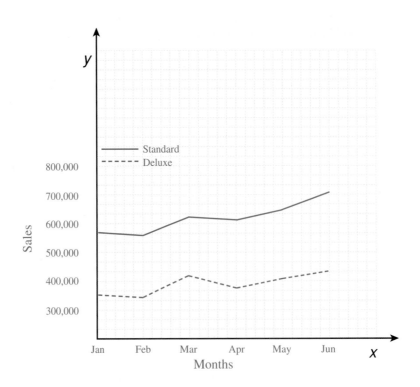

3. Standard bar chart of the deluxe sales per month in the Southeast territory.

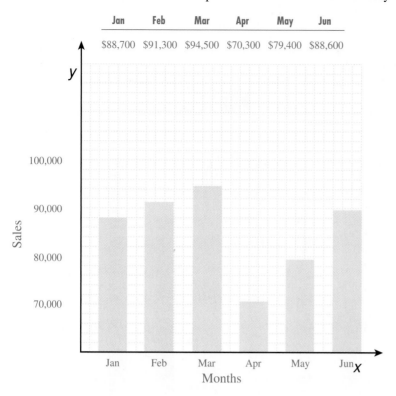

	Jan	Feb	Mar	Apr	May	Jun
	$88,700	$91,300	$94,500	$70,300	$79,400	$88,600

4. Component bar chart of the standard and deluxe model sales as components of total monthly sales in the Northeast territory.

	Jan	Feb	Mar	Apr	May	Jun
Standard	$214,700	$228,400	$246,600	$239,000	$266,100	$279,300
Deluxe	121,300	133,100	164,800	153,200	185,000	190,100
Total	336,000	361,500	411,400	392,200	451,100	469,400

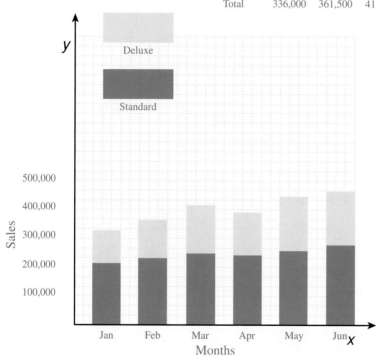

5. Comparative bar chart of the standard and deluxe model sales per month in the Northwest territory.

	Jan	Feb	Mar	Apr	May	Jun
Standard	123,200	115,800	133,400	136,700	112,900	135,000
Deluxe	86,400	73,700	91,100	92,600	65,300	78,400

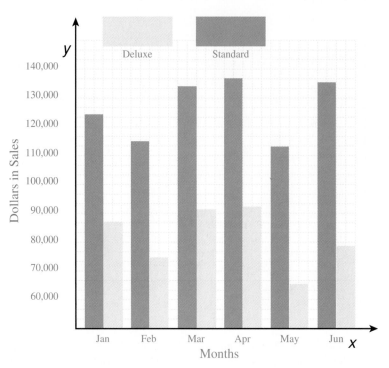

6. Pie chart of the total six-month sales of the four territories.

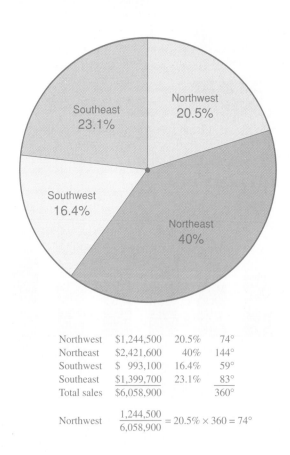

Northwest	$1,244,500	20.5%	74°
Northeast	$2,421,600	40%	144°
Southwest	$ 993,100	16.4%	59°
Southeast	$1,399,700	23.1%	83°
Total sales	$6,058,900		360°

Northwest $\dfrac{1,244,500}{6,058,900} = 20.5\% \times 360 = 74°$

7. The following table shows Magnum's stock prices on the first day of each month. Choose and prepare a chart that best illustrates this information.

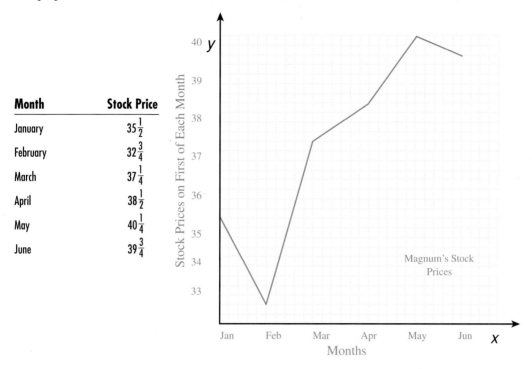

Month	Stock Price
January	$35\frac{1}{2}$
February	$32\frac{3}{4}$
March	$37\frac{1}{4}$
April	$38\frac{1}{2}$
May	$40\frac{1}{4}$
June	$39\frac{3}{4}$

MEASURES OF CENTRAL TENDENCY—UNGROUPED DATA

A numerical **average** is a value that is representative of a whole set of values. In business, managers use averages extensively to describe or represent a variety of situations. Imagine a payroll director being asked to describe the hourly wages of his 650 factory workers. On the one extreme, he might produce a list of his 650 workers along with their hourly wages. This action answers the question but it provides too much information. A more appropriate response might be to calculate the average hourly wage, and report that "$9.75 was the average hourly wage of the workers."

Because an average is numerically located within the range of values that it represents, averages are often referred to as measures of central tendency. In this section we shall study the three most commonly used averages in business statistics: the arithmetic mean, the median, and the mode. We will also study a measure of dispersion known as the range.

● **average**
A numerical value that is representative of a whole set of values.

21-5 Calculating the Arithmetic Mean of Ungrouped Data

The **arithmetic mean** corresponds to the generally accepted meaning of the word "average." It is customary to abbreviate the term *arithmetic mean* and refer to this average simply as the **mean.**

● **mean, or arithmetic mean**
The sum of the values of a set of data divided by the number of values in that set.

STEPS TO CALCULATE THE ARITHMETIC MEAN OF UNGROUPED DATA

Step 1. Find the sum of all the values in the data set.
Step 2. Divide the sum in Step 1 by the number of values in the set.

$$\text{Mean} = \frac{\text{Sum of values}}{\text{Number of values}}$$

EXAMPLE

A travel agency had daily sales of $4,635 on Monday, $3,655 on Tuesday, $3,506 on Wednesday, $2,870 on Thursday, $4,309 on Friday, and $5,475 on Saturday. What is the mean sales per day?

SOLUTION STRATEGY

To calculate the mean (average sales per day), we find the sum of the values (sales per day), and divide this sum by the number of values (6 days).

$$\text{Mean} = \frac{\text{Sum of values}}{\text{Number of values}}$$

$$\text{Mean} = \frac{4{,}635 + 3{,}655 + 3{,}506 + 2{,}870 + 4{,}309 + 5{,}475}{6} = \frac{24{,}450}{6} = \underline{\$4{,}075}$$

TRY-IT   EXERCISE

21. **The attendance figures for a series of management seminars are as follows: 432, 247, 661, 418, and 512. What was the average number of people attending per seminar?**

Check your answer with the solution on page 740.

21-6 Calculating the Median

● **median**

The *midpoint* value of a set of data when the numbers are ranked in ascending or descending order.

Another measure of central tendency, and a very useful way of describing a large quantity of data, is the median. The **median** of a set of numbers is the *midpoint* value when the numbers are ranked in ascending or descending order. The median is a more useful measure of central tendency than the mean when one or more of the values of the set is significantly higher or lower than the rest of the set. For example, if the ages of five people in a group are 22, 26, 27, 31, and 69, the mean of this set is 35. However, the median is 27, a value that better describes the set.

When there is an odd number of values in the set, the middle value is the median. For example, in a set of seven ranked values, the fourth value is the midpoint. There are three values greater than and three values less than the median.

When there is an even number of values in the set, the median is the midpoint or average between the two middle values. For example, in a set with ten values, the median is the midpoint between the fifth and the sixth value.

STEPS TO DETERMINE THE MEDIAN

Step 1. Rank the numbers in ascending or descending order.
Step 2a. For an *odd number of values*—The median is the middle value.
Step 2b. For an *even number of values*—The median is the average or midpoint of the two middle values.

$$\text{Median} = \frac{\text{Middle value} + \text{Middle value}}{2}$$

EXAMPLE

Find the median for the following set of values:

| 2 | 8 | 5 | 13 | 11 | 6 | 9 | 15 | 4 |

SOLUTION STRATEGY

Step 1. Rank the data in ascending order as follows:

| 2 | 4 | 5 | 6 | 8 | 9 | 11 | 13 | 15 |

Step 2. Because the number of values in this set is *odd* (nine), there are four values below and four values above the median. Therefore the median is the fifth value, **8**.

TRY-IT **EXERCISE**

22. Determine the median for the following set of values:

     4,589   6,558   4,237   2,430   3,619   5,840   1,220

Check your answer with the solution on page 740.

EXAMPLE

Find the median for the following set of values:

    56   34   87   12   45   49

SOLUTION STRATEGY

Step 1. Rank the data in ascending order:

    12   34   45   49   56   87

Step 2. Because the number of values in this set is *even* (six), the median is the midpoint between the third and the fourth values, 45 and 49.

$$\text{Median} = \frac{\text{Middle value} + \text{Middle value}}{2} = \frac{45 + 49}{2} = \frac{94}{2} = \underline{\underline{47}}$$

TRY-IT **EXERCISE**

23. Determine the median for the following set of values:

    12   33   42   13   79   29   101   54   76   81

Check your answer with the solution on page 741.

21-7 Determining the Mode

The **mode** is the third measure of central tendency that we shall consider. It is the value or values in a set that occur *most often*. It is possible for a set of data to have more than one mode, or no mode at all.

● **mode**
The value or values in a set of data that occur *most often*.

> **STEPS TO DETERMINE THE MODE:**
>
> **Step 1.** Count the number of times each value in a set occurs.
> **Step 2a.** If one value occurs more times than any other, it is the mode.
> **Step 2b.** If two or more values occur more times than any other, they are all modes of the set.
> **Step 2c.** If all values occur the same number of times, there is no mode.

One common business application of the mode is in merchandising, where it is used to keep track of the most frequently purchased goods, as in the following example. Note that the mean and median of this set of data would provide little useful information regarding sales.

EXAMPLE

Find the mode of the following set of values representing the wattage of light bulbs sold in a hardware store:

| 25 | 25 | 60 | 60 | 60 | 75 | 75 | 75 | 75 | 100 | 100 | 150 |

SOLUTION STRATEGY

From this data we see that the mode is <u>75 watts</u>, because the value 75 occurs most often. This would indicate to the retailer that 75-watt bulbs were the most frequently purchased.

TRY-IT   EXERCISE

24. **Calculate the mode of the following set of values representing the size, in gallons, of fish tanks sold in a pet shop:**

    10 10 20 10 55 20 10 65 85 20 10 20 55 10 125 55 10 20

Check your answer with the solution on page 741.

21-8 Determining the Range

range
The difference between the lowest and the highest values in a data set; used as a measure of *dispersion*.

Although it does not measure central tendency like the mean, median, and mode, the range is another useful measure in statistics. The **range** is a measure of *dispersion;* it is the difference between the lowest and the highest values in a data set. It is used to measure the scope or broadness of a set of data. A small range indicates that the data in a set is narrow in scope; the values are close to each other. A large range indicates that the data in a set is wide in scope; the values are spread far apart.

> **STEPS TO CALCULATE THE RANGE**
>
> **Step 1.** Locate the highest and lowest values in a set of numbers.
> **Step 2.** Subtract the lowest from the highest to get the range.
>
> Range = Highest value – Lowest value

EXAMPLE

Find the range of the following shirt prices in a department store:

$37.95 $15.75 $24.75 $18.50 $33.75 $42.50 $14.95 $27.95 $19.95

SOLUTION STRATEGY

To find the range of shirt prices, subtract the lowest price from the highest price:

Range = Highest value – Lowest value = 42.50 – 14.95 = <u>$27.55</u>

Note that the range for shirts, $27.55, is relatively large. It might be said that customers shopping in this shirt department have a wide range of prices to choose from.

TRY-IT EXERCISE

25. **Find the range of the following temperature readings from the oven of a bakery:**

367° 351° 349° 362° 366° 358° 369° 355° 354°

Check your answer with the solution on page 741.

REVIEW EXERCISES CHAPTER 21—SECTION II

Calculate the mean of the following sets of values (round to the nearest tenth where applicable):

1. 4   6   1   8   9   2   3   5   5   6   8   9   10

$= \dfrac{76}{13} = \underline{\underline{5.8}}$

2. 324 553 179 213 423 336 190 440 382 111 329 111 397

$= \dfrac{3,988}{13} = \underline{\underline{306.8}}$

3. .87   .32   1.43   2.3   5.4   3.25   .5

$= \dfrac{14.07}{7} = \underline{\underline{2}}$

Determine the median of the following sets of values (round to the nearest tenth where applicable):

4. 57   38   29   82   71   90   11   94   26   18   18
   11   18   18   26   29   (38)   57   71   82   90   94

   $\underline{\underline{38}}$ is the median.

5. $2.50 $3.25 $4.35 $1.22 $1.67 $4.59
   $1.22 $1.67 $2.50 $3.25 $4.35 $4.59

   $\dfrac{2.50 + 3.25}{2} = \dfrac{5.75}{2} = \underline{\underline{\$2.88}}$

6. 35%   51%   50%   23%   18%   67%   44%   52%
   18%   23%   35%   44%   50%   51%   52%   67%

   $\dfrac{44\% + 50\%}{2} = \underline{\underline{47\%}}$

Find the mode of the following sets of values:

7. 21   57   46   21   34   76   43   68   21   76   18   12
   12×1 (21×3) 34×1 43×1 46×1 68×1 76×2 57×1 18×1
   The mode is 21.

8. $1,200 $7,300 $4,500 $3,450 $1,675
   $1,200 \times 1$ $7,300 \times 1$ $4,500 \times 1$ $3,450 \times 1$ $1,675 \times 1$
   There is no mode in this set.

9. 4 9 3 5 4 7 1 9 9 4 7 1 8 1 4 6 7 4 6 9 9 2
   (4×5) (9×5) 3×1 5×1 7×3 1×3 8×1 6×2 2×1
   4 and 9 are both modes in this set.

Find the range of the following sets of values:

10. 12 42 54 28 112 76 95 27 36 11 96 109 210
    Highest   210
    Lowest $- 11$
    Range $\underline{\underline{199}}$

11. $2.35 $4.16 $3.42 $1.29 $.89 $4.55

Highest   4.55
Lowest   − .89
Range $3.66

12. 1,099   887   1,659   1,217   2,969   790

Highest   2,969
Lowest   − 790
Range   2,179

13. The following numbers represent the gallons of chocolate syrup used per month by a Haagen-Däzs Ice Cream Shop to make milk shakes and hot fudge sundaes:

Jan.—225   Feb.—254   March—327   April—370   May—425   June—435
July—446   Aug.—425   Sept.—359   Oct.—302   Nov.—270   Dec.—241

a. What is the mean of this set of data?

$$\frac{225 + 254 + 327 + 370 + 425 + 435 + 446 + 425 + 359 + 302 + 270 + 241}{12}$$

$$\frac{4,079}{12} = 339.9$$

b. What is the median of this set of data?

225, 241, 254, 270, 302, 327, 359, 370, 425, 425, 435, 446

$$\frac{327 + 359}{2} = 343$$

c. What is the mode of this set of data?

425 occurs twice; it is the mode.

d. What is the range of this set of data?

$446 − 225 = 221$

14. The Pleasant Dreams Mattress Company manufactured the following number of king-size mattresses last week:

2,300   2,430   2,018   2,540   2,675   4,800

a. What is the mean, median, mode, and range of this set of production data?

Mean = 2,300 + 2,430 + 2,018 + 2,540 + 2,675 + 4,800   Mode = No mode

$= \frac{16,763}{6} = 2793.8$ Mattresses   Range = 4800 − 2018 = 2,782

Median = 2,018   2,300   2,430   2,540   2,675   4,800

$\frac{2,430 + 2,540}{2} = 2,485$ Mattresses

b. Which average best describes the production at Pleasant Dreams? Why?

2485, the median best describes the production data since the last number is uncharacteristically high. The mean is therefore too high.

15. You are the owner of The Dependable Delivery Service. Your company has four vehicles:

a large and a small van and a large and a small truck. The following set of data represents the number of packages delivered last week:

	Monday	Tuesday	Wednesday	Thursday	Friday
Small Van	67	86	94	101	86
Large Van	142	137	153	165	106
Small Truck	225	202	288	311	290
Large Truck	322	290	360	348	339

a. What is the mean number of packages delivered for each van?

Small van $\dfrac{67 + 86 + 94 + 101 + 86}{5} = \underline{\underline{86.8}}$

Large van $\dfrac{142 + 137 + 153 + 165 + 106}{5} = \underline{\underline{140.6}}$

b. What is the median number of packages delivered for each truck?

Small truck   202   225   ⓐ288ⓑ   290   311
Median = $\underline{\underline{288}}$
Large truck   290   322   ⓐ339ⓑ   348   360 = $\underline{\underline{339}}$
Median = $\underline{\underline{339}}$

c. What is the mean number of packages delivered on Monday?

$\dfrac{67 + 142 + 225 + 322}{4} = \underline{\underline{189}}$ Monday

d. What is the median number of packages delivered on Thursday?

101   165   311   348
$\dfrac{165 + 311}{2} = \underline{\underline{238}}$

e. What is the mode of all the packages delivered during the week?

$\underline{\underline{86}}$ occurs twice.
$\underline{\underline{290}}$ occurs twice.
These are both modes of this set of numbers.

f. What is the range of all the packages delivered during the week?

Highest   360
Lowest $\underline{\ \ 67}$
Range $\underline{\underline{293}}$

- **ungrouped data**
  Data that has not been grouped into a distribution-type format.

- **grouped data**
  Data that has been divided into equal-size groups known as classes. Frequently used to represent data when dealing with large amounts of values in a set.

- **frequency**
  The number of values in each class of a frequency distribution.

FREQUENCY DISTRIBUTIONS—GROUPED DATA

In the previous section, the values in the sets are listed individually and are known as **ungrouped data.** Frequently business statistics deals with hundreds or even thousands of values in a set. In dealing with such a large amount of values it is often easier to represent the data by dividing the values into equal-size groups known as classes, creating **grouped data.**

The number of values in each class is called the **frequency,** with the resulting chart called a **frequency distribution** or **frequency table.** The purpose of a frequency distribution is to organize large amounts of data into a more compact form without changing the essential information contained in those values.

- **frequency distribution, or frequency table**
  The chart obtained by dividing data into equal-size classes; used to organize large amounts of data into a more compact form without changing the essential information contained in those values.

21-9 Constructing a Frequency Distribution

> **STEPS TO CONSTRUCT A FREQUENCY DISTRIBUTION:**
>
> **Step 1.** Divide the data into equal-size classes. Be sure to use a range that includes all values in the set.
>
> **Step 2.** Use tally marks to record the frequency of values within each class.
>
> **Step 3.** Rewrite the tally marks for each class numerically in a column labeled "frequency (f)." The data is now grouped.

EXAMPLE

From the following ungrouped data representing the weight of packages shipped by Monarch Manufacturing this month, construct a frequency distribution using classes with an interval of 10 pounds each.

| 13 | 16 | 65 | 45 | 44 | 35 | 22 | 46 | 36 | 49 | 56 | 26 |
| 68 | 27 | 35 | 15 | 43 | 62 | 32 | 57 | 48 | 23 | 43 | 44 |

SOLUTION STRATEGY

First, we find the range of the data by subtracting the lowest value, 13, from the highest value, 68. This gives a range of 55 pounds. Second, by using 60 pounds as the range for the classes of our frequency distribution we are sure to include all values in the set. Class intervals of 10 pounds each allow for 6 equal classes:

Frequency Distribution for Monarch Manufacturing

Class (lb)	Tally	Frequency (f)
10 to 19	III	3
20 to 29	IIII	4
30 to 39	IIII	4
40 to 49	JHT III	8
50 to 59	II	2
60 to 69	III	3

TRY-IT   EXERCISE

26. You are the manager of The Dress Code Boutique. From the following ungrouped data representing the dollar sales of each transaction at the store today, construct a frequency distribution using classes with an interval of 10 dollars each.

| 14 | 19 | 55 | 47 | 44 | 39 | 22 | 71 | 35 | 49 | 64 | 22 | 88 | 78 | 16 |
| 88 | 37 | 29 | 71 | 74 | 62 | 54 | 59 | 18 | 93 | 49 | 74 | 26 | 66 | 75 |

Check your answer with the solution on page 741.

21-10 Computing the Mean of Grouped Data

Just as with ungrouped data, we can calculate the arithmetic mean of grouped data in a frequency distribution. Keep in mind, however, that the means for grouped data are calculated using the midpoints of each class rather than the actual values of the data, and are therefore only approximations. Because the actual values of the data in each class of the distribution are lost, we must make the assumption that the midpoints of each class closely approximate the values in that class. In most cases this is true because some class values fall below the midpoint and some above, thereby canceling the inaccuracy.

STEPS TO CALCULATE THE MEAN OF A FREQUENCY DISTRIBUTION:

Step 1. Add a column to the frequency distribution listing the midpoints of each class. Label it "midpoints" (m).

Step 2. In a column labeled ($f \times m$), multiply the frequency for each class by the midpoint of that class.

Step 3. Find the sum of the frequency column.

Step 4. Find the sum of the ($f \times m$) column.

Step 5. Find the mean by dividing the sum of the ($f \times m$) column by the sum of the frequency column.

$$\text{Mean of grouped data} = \frac{\text{Sum of (frequency} \times \text{midpoint)}}{\text{Sum of frequency}}$$

EXAMPLE

Calculate the mean of the grouped data from the frequency distribution for Monarch Manufacturing in the previous example.

SOLUTION STRATEGY

Begin by attaching the midpoint (m) and frequency $\times$ midpoint ($f \times m$) columns to the frequency distribution as follows:

Frequency Distribution for Monarch Manufacturing

Class (lb)	Tally	Frequency (f)	Midpoint (m)	$f \times m$
10 to 19	III	3	14.5	43.5
20 to 29	IIII	4	24.5	98.0
30 to 39	IIII	4	34.5	138.0
40 to 49	JHT III	8	44.5	356.0
50 to 59	II	2	54.5	109.0
60 to 69	III	3	64.5	193.5
		24		938.0

After finding the sum of the frequency and $f \times m$ columns, use these sums to calculate the mean of the grouped data:

$$\text{Mean of grouped data} = \frac{\text{Sum of (frequency} \times \text{midpoint)}}{\text{Sum of frequency}} = \frac{938}{24} = \underline{\underline{39.1 \text{ lb}}}$$

TRY-IT   EXERCISE

27. **From the frequency distribution previously prepared in Try-It Exercise 26, for The Dress Code Boutique, calculate the mean of the grouped data.**

Check your answer with the solution on page 741.

21-11 Preparing a Histogram of a Frequency Distribution

● **histogram**

A special type of bar chart, without space between the bars, that is used to display the data from a frequency distribution.

A **histogram** is a special type of bar chart that is used in business to display the data from a frequency distribution. A histogram is drawn in the same way as a standard bar chart but without space between the bars. Since a frequency distribution has classes whose numbers are continuous, the histogram bars depicting that distribution are made to look continuous by drawing them adjacent to each other.

STEPS TO PREPARE A HISTOGRAM OF A FREQUENCY DISTRIBUTION:

Step 1. Locate the classes of the frequency distribution adjacent to each other along the *x*-axis, increasing from left to right.

Step 2. Evenly space the frequencies on the *y*-axis, increasing from bottom to top.

Step 3. Plot the frequency for each class in the form of a rectangular bar whose top edge is opposite the frequency of that class on the *y*-axis.

EXAMPLE

Prepare a histogram from the Monarch Manufacturing frequency distribution on page 728.

SOLUTION STRATEGY

Below is the histogram prepared from the data in the Monarch Manufacturing frequency distribution. Note that the *x*-axis displays the adjacent classes and the *y*-axis displays their frequencies.

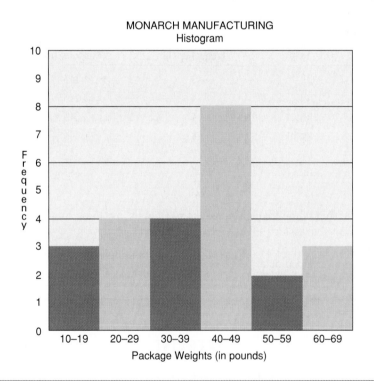

MONARCH MANUFACTURING
Histogram

TRY-IT   EXERCISE

28. Using the graph provided on the next page, construct a histogram from the data in The Dress Code Boutique frequency distribution you prepared in Try-It Exercise 26.

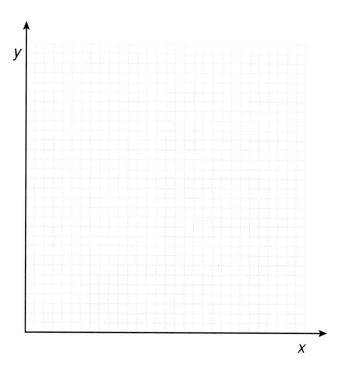

Check your answer with the solution on page 741.

1. You are the sales manager of the Esquire Sportswear Company. Last week your 30 sales-people reported the following automobile mileage while making sales calls to retail stores around the state:

385   231   328   154   283   86   415   389   575   117   75   173   247   316   357
211   432   271   93   515   376   328   183   359   136   88   438   282   375   637

a. Group the data into seven classes of equal size (1–99, 100–199, 200–299, 300–399, etc.) and construct a frequency distribution of the mileage.

Class	Tally	Frequency
1–99	IIII	4
100–199	LHT	5
200–299	LHTI	6
300–399	LHTIIII	9
400–499	III	3
500–599	II	2
600–699	I	1

b. Calculate the mean of the grouped data using 49.5, 149.5, 249.5, etc. as the midpoints.

Class	Tally	Frequency (f)	Midpoint (m)	f × m
1–99	IIII	4	49.5	198
100–199	LHT	5	149.5	747.5
200–299	LHTI	6	249.5	1,497
300–399	LHTIIII	9	349.5	3,145.5
400–499	III	3	449.5	1,348.5
500–599	II	2	549.5	1,099
600–699	I	1	649.5	649.5
		30		8,685.

Mean = $\dfrac{8,685}{30} = 289.5$

c. Using the grid provided on the next page, prepare a histogram of this data to graphically illustrate your salespeople's mileage.
See graph.

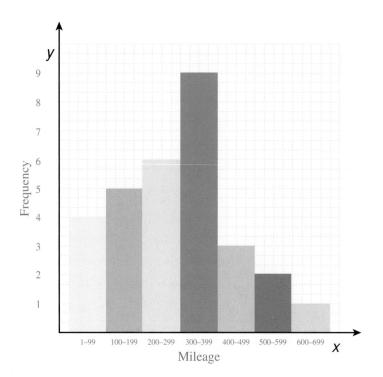

Mileage

2. You are the payroll manager for the Bilt-Rite Construction Company. Your boss has asked that you review the hourly wages of your workers and give him a report to be presented at this afternoon's board meeting. The following are the hourly wages of your construction crew:

$4.15 $5.60 $4.95 $6.70 $5.40 $7.15 $6.45 $8.25 $7.60 $6.25

$5.50 $4.90 $7.60 $6.40 $7.75 $5.25 $6.70 $8.45 $7.10 $8.80

$9.65 $8.40 $6.50 $5.25 $6.75 $8.50 $5.35 $6.80 $4.25 $9.95

a. Group the wages into six classes of equal size ($4.00–$4.99, $5.00–$5.99, etc.) and construct a frequency distribution.

Class	Tally	Frequency
$4.00–4.99	IIII	4
5.00–5.99	JHTI	6
6.00–6.99	JHTIII	8
7.00–7.99	JHT	5
8.00–8.99	JHT	5
9.00–9.99	II	2

b. Calculate the mean of the grouped data.

Class	Tally	Frequency (f)	Midpoint (m)	f × m
4.00–4.99	IIII	4	4.495	17.98
5.00–5.99	JHTI	6	5.495	32.97
6.00–6.99	JHTIII	8	6.495	51.96
7.00–7.99	JHT	5	7.495	37.475
8.00–8.99	JHT	5	8.495	42.475
9.00–9.99	II	2	9.495	18.99
		30		201.85

$$\text{Mean} = \frac{201.85}{30} = \$6.73$$

c. Using the grid provided on the next page, prepare a histogram of the hourly wages for your boss to present at his meeting.

See graph.

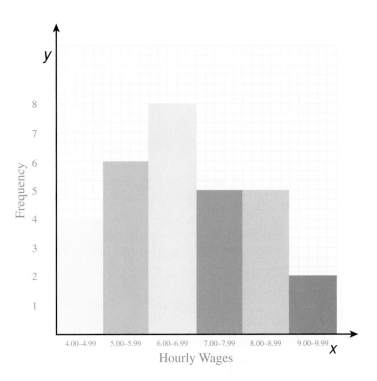

Frequency

Hourly Wages

CHAPTER 21 ■ BUSINESS STATISTICS AND DATA PRESENTATION

FORMULAS

Ungrouped Data

$$\text{Mean} = \frac{\text{Sum of values}}{\text{Number of values}}$$

Median (odd number of values) = Middle value

$$\text{Median (even number of values)} = \frac{\text{Middle value + Middle value}}{2}$$

Mode = Value or values that occur most frequently

Range = Highest value − Lowest value

Grouped Data

$$\text{Mean} = \frac{\text{Sum of (frequency} \times \text{midpoint)}}{\text{Sum of frequency}}$$

CHAPTER 21 ■ BUSINESS STATISTICS	SUMMARY CHART

SECTION I   DATA INTERPRETATION AND PRESENTATION

Topic	P/O, Page	Important Concepts	Illustrative Examples
Reading and Interpreting Information from Tables	21–1 703	Tables are a collection of related data arranged for ease of reference or comparison, usually in parallel columns with meaningful titles. They are a very useful tool in summarizing statistical data and are found everywhere in business. Reading Tables: 1. Scan the titles above the columns for the category of information being sought. 2. Look down the column for the specific fact required.	FRIENDLY AUTO SALES 90-Day Sales Report (Thousands of Dollars) |	April	May	June
Autos	56	61	64
Trucks	68	58	66
Parts	32	41	37
Total	156	160	167	

I, continued

Topic	P/O, Page	Important Concepts	Illustrative Examples
Reading and Constructing Line Charts	21–2 704	Charts are used to display a picture of the relationships among selected data. Line charts show data changing over a period of time. They are a graph of series of data points on a grid, continuously connected by straight lines. Reading Line Charts: 1. Scan either the x- or y-axis for the known variable; x for time or y for amount. 2. Draw a perpendicular line from that axis to the point where it intersects the chart. 3. Draw a line from that point perpendicular to the opposite axis. 4. The answer is read where that line intersects the opposite axis. Constructing Line Charts: 1. Evenly space and label the time variable on the x-axis. 2. Evenly space and label the amount variable on the y-axis. 3. Show each data point by placing a dot above the time period and across from the corresponding amount. 4. Connect the plotted points with straight lines to form the chart. 5. Lines should be differentiated by various line patterns or colors.	*Single-Line Chart* 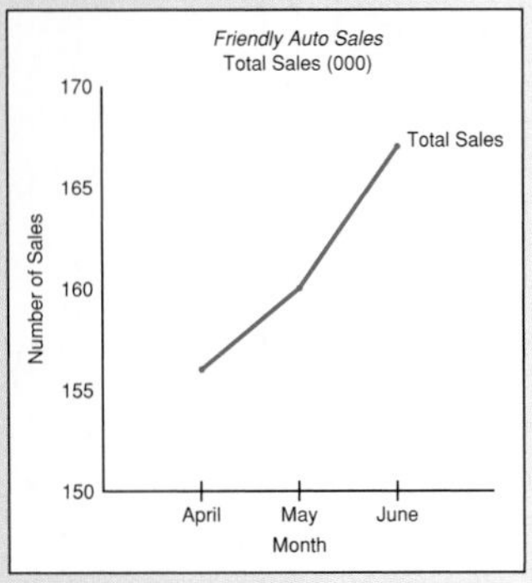 *Multiple-Line Chart* 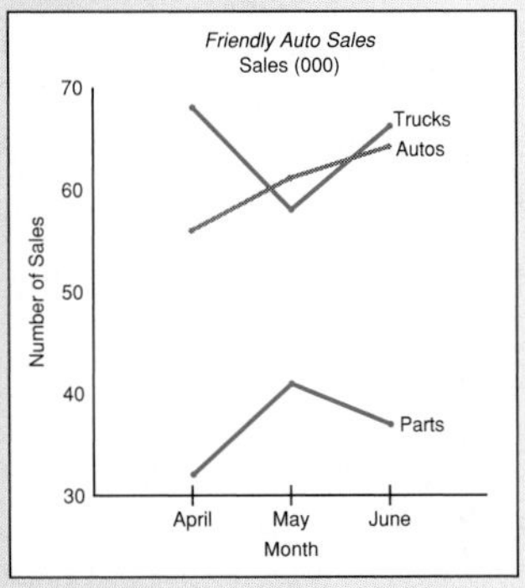
Reading and Constructing Bar Charts	21–3 709	Bar charts represent data by the length of horizontal bars or vertical columns. As with line charts, bar charts often illustrate increases or decreases in magnitude of a certain variable, or the relationship between similar variables. Component bar charts illustrate parts of something that add to a total. Each bar is divided into components stacked on top of each other and shaded or colored differently. Comparative bar charts illustrate two or more related variables. In this chart, the bars of the related variables are drawn next to each other but do not touch.	*Standard Bar Chart* 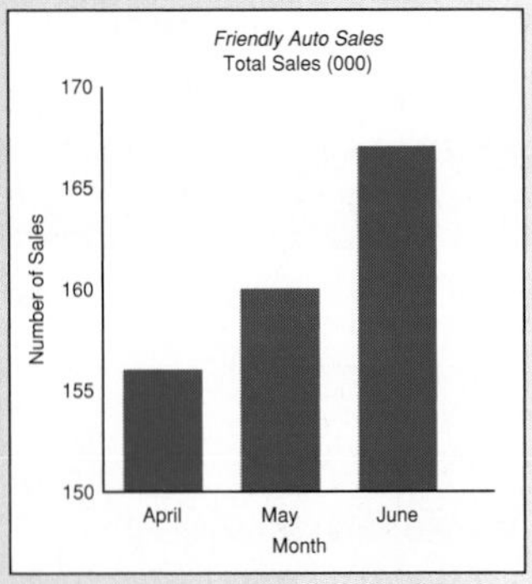

I, continued

Topic	P/O, Page	Important Concepts	Illustrative Examples
		Reading bar charts: 1. Scan the x- or y-axis for a known variable. 2. Read the answer on the opposite axis directly across from the top of the appropriate bar. Constructing Bar Charts: 1. Evenly space and label the x-axis. The space between bars should be one-half the width of the bars. 2. Evenly space and label the y-axis. 3. Draw each bar up from the x-axis to the point opposite the y-axis that corresponds to its value. 4. For comparative and component bar charts, differentiate the bars by color or shading pattern.	*Component Bar Chart* *Comparative Bar Chart*
Reading and Constructing Pie Charts	21–4 715	The pie chart is a circle divided into sections representing the component parts of a whole, usually in percentage terms. Constructing Pie Charts: 1. Convert the amount of each component to a percent using the formula Rate = Portion ÷ Base. Let the percentage be the amount of each component, and the base the total amount. Round each percent to hundredths. 2. Since a full circle is made up of 360° representing 100%, multiply each component's percent (decimal form) by 360° to determine how many degrees each component's slice will be. Round to the nearest whole degree. 3. Draw a circle with a compass and mark the center. 4. Using a protractor, mark off the number of degrees on the circle that represents each component. 5. Connect each point on the circle with the center by a straight line to form a segment or slice for each component. 6. Label the segments clearly by name, color, or shading.	$\text{April} = \dfrac{156}{483} = .322 = 32.2\%$ $\text{April} = .322 \times 360° = 116°$ $\text{May} = \dfrac{160}{483} = .331 = 33.1\%$ $\text{May} = .331 \times 360° = 119°$ $\text{June} = \dfrac{167}{483} = .346 = 34.6\%$ $\text{June} = .346 \times 360° = 125°$ *Pie Chart*

SECTION II   MEASURES OF CENTRAL TENDENCY - Ungrouped Data

Topic	P/O, Page	Important Concepts	Illustrative Examples
Calculating the Arithmetic Mean	21–5 721	A numerical average is a value that is representative of a whole set of values. The arithmetic mean corresponds to the generally accepted meaning of the word *average*. Computing the Mean: 1. Find the sum of all the values in the set. 2. Divide by the number of values in the set. $$\text{Mean} = \frac{\text{Sum of values}}{\text{Number of values}}$$	If a grocery store had sales of $4,600 on Monday, $3,650 on Tuesday, and $3,500 on Wednesday, what is the mean sales for the three days? $$\text{Mean} = \frac{4,600 + 3,650 + 3,500}{3}$$ $$= \frac{11,750}{3} = \underline{\$3,916.67}$$
Calculating the Median	21–6 722	Another measure of central tendency, and a very useful way of describing a large quantity of data, is the median. The median of a set of numbers is the *midpoint* value when the numbers are ranked in increasing or decreasing order. Determining the Median: 1. Rank the numbers in increasing or decreasing order. 2a. For an *odd number* of values in the set, the median is the middle value. 2b. For an *even number* of values in the set, the median is the average or midpoint of the two middle values. $$\text{Median} = \frac{\text{Middle value} + \text{Middle value}}{2}$$	Example 1: Find the median for the following set of values: 2 8 5 13 11 6 9 15 4 Rank the data as follows: 2 4 5 6 8 9 11 13 15 Because the number of values in the set is odd (nine), the median is the middle value, $\underline{8}$. Example 2: Find the median for the following set of values: 56 34 87 12 45 49 Rank the data as follows: 12 34 45 49 56 87 Because the number of values in this set is even (six), the median is the midpoint between the third and the fourth values, 45 and 49. $$\text{Median} = \frac{45 + 49}{2} = \frac{94}{2} = \underline{\underline{47}}$$
Determining the Mode	21–7 723	The mode is the third measure of central tendency. It is the value or values in a set that occur most often. It is possible for a set of data to have more than one mode or no mode at all. Determining the Mode: 1. Count the number of times each value in a set occurs. 2a. If one value occurs most often, it is the mode. 2b. If more than one value occur the same number of times, they are all modes of the set. 2c. If all values occur only once, there is no mode.	Find the mode of the following set representing television screen sizes sold in a Circuit City store yesterday: 25 25 27 25 17 19 12 12 17 25 17 5 25 From this data we see that the mode is $\underline{25\text{ inches}}$, since the value 25 occurs most often.

II, continued

Topic	P/O, Page	Important Concepts	Illustrative Examples
Determining the Range	21–8 724	The range is a measure of dispersion, equal to the difference between the lowest and the highest values in a set. It is used to measure the scope or broadness of a set of data. Determining the Range: 1. Locate the highest and lowest values in a set of numbers. 2. Subtract these values to determine the range. Range = Highest value − Lowest value	Find the range of the following modem prices at Computers USA: 237 215 124 185 375 145 199 Highest = \$375 Lowest = \$124 Range = 375 − 124 = <u>\$251</u>

SECTION III   FREQUENCY DISTRIBUTIONS

Topic	P/O, Page	Important Concepts	Illustrative Examples
Constructing a Frequency Distribution	21–9 728	Business statistics frequently deals with hundreds or even thousands of values in a set. In dealing with large amounts of values, it is often easier to represent the data by dividing the values into equal-size groups known as classes, forming grouped data. The number of values in each class is called the frequency, with the resulting chart called a frequency distribution. Constructing a frequency distribution: 1. Divide the data into equal-size classes. Be sure to use a range that includes all values in the set. 2. Use tally marks to record the frequency of values within each class. 3. Rewrite the tally marks for each class numerically in a column labeled "frequency." The data is now grouped.	The following ungrouped data represents the number of sales calls made by the sales force of Northwest Supply Company last month. Construct a frequency distribution of this data using six equal classes with an interval of ten. 13 26 65 45 44 35 46 36 49 56 16 68 27 35 43 62 32 57 23 43 44 <table><tr><th>Class</th><th>Tally</th><th>Freq (f)</th></tr><tr><td>10 to 19</td><td>II</td><td>2</td></tr><tr><td>20 to 29</td><td>III</td><td>3</td></tr><tr><td>30 to 39</td><td>IIII</td><td>4</td></tr><tr><td>40 to 49</td><td>JHI II</td><td>7</td></tr><tr><td>50 to 59</td><td>II</td><td>2</td></tr><tr><td>60 to 69</td><td>III</td><td>3</td></tr></table>
Computing the Mean of Grouped Data	21–10 728	Calculating the mean of a frequency distribution: 1. Add a column to the frequency distribution listing the midpoints of each class. 2. In a column labeled $(f \times m)$, multiply the frequency for each class by the midpoint of that class. 3. Find the sum of the frequency column. 4. Find the sum of the $(f \times m)$ column. 5. Find the mean by dividing the sum of the $(f \times m)$ column by the sum of the frequency column. $$\text{Mean} = \frac{\text{Sum of } (f \times m)}{\text{Sum of frequencies}}$$	Calculate the mean number of sales calls for Northwest Supply. The mean of the grouped data is computed by first attaching the midpoint (m) and frequency × midpoint $(f \times m)$ columns to the frequency distribution as follows: <table><tr><th>Class</th><th>Freq (f)</th><th>Midpt (m)</th><th>f × m</th></tr><tr><td>10–19</td><td>2</td><td>14.5</td><td>29.0</td></tr><tr><td>20–29</td><td>3</td><td>24.5</td><td>73.5</td></tr><tr><td>30–39</td><td>4</td><td>34.5</td><td>138.0</td></tr><tr><td>40–49</td><td>7</td><td>44.5</td><td>311.5</td></tr><tr><td>50–59</td><td>2</td><td>54.5</td><td>109.0</td></tr><tr><td>60–69</td><td>3</td><td>64.5</td><td>193.5</td></tr><tr><td></td><td>21</td><td></td><td>854.5</td></tr></table> $$\text{Mean} = \frac{854.5}{21} = \underline{40.7 \text{ calls}}$$

III, continued

Topic	P/O, Page	Important Concepts	Illustrative Examples
Preparing a Histogram of a Frequency Distribution	21–11 730	A histogram is a special type of bar chart that is used in business to display the data from a frequency distribution. A histogram is drawn in the same way as a standard bar chart except there are no spaces between the bars. Constructing a histogram: 1. Locate the classes of the frequency distribution adjacent to each other along the *x*-axis, increasing from left to right. 2. Evenly space the frequencies on the *y*-axis, increasing from bottom to top. 3. Plot each class's frequency in the form of a rectangular bar whose top edge is opposite the frequency of that class.	*Histogram*

TRY-IT EXERCISE   SOLUTIONS

1. Standard units—February—Northeast = <u>228,400</u>

2. Deluxe units—April—Southeast = <u>70,300</u>

3. Total sales—May and June—Northwest
May = 112,900 + 65,300 = 178,200
June = 135,000 + 78,400 = <u>213,400</u>
Total = <u>391,600</u>

4. Months with increase in standard unit sales—Southwest
<u>March, April, May, June</u>

5. April—Deluxe = 92,600 + 153,200 + 67,800 + 70,300 = 383,900
May—Deluxe = 65,300 + 185,000 + 78,300 + 79,400 = 408,000
408,000 − 383,900 = <u>24,100</u>

6. Northwest—Percent standard units = $\dfrac{\text{Standard units}}{\text{Total units}}$

Northwest—Percent standard units = $\dfrac{757,000}{1,244,500}$ = .6082 = <u>60.8%</u>

7. <u>2010</u>   **8.** <u>150 hours</u>   **9.** <u>1988</u>

10.

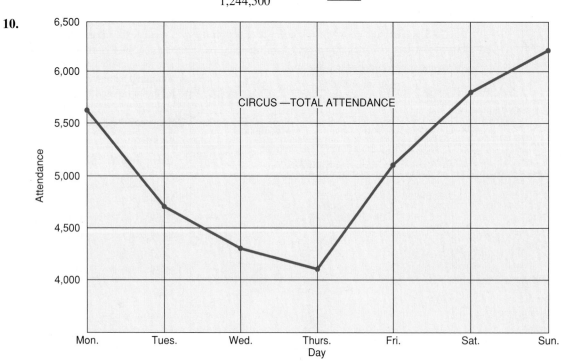

11.

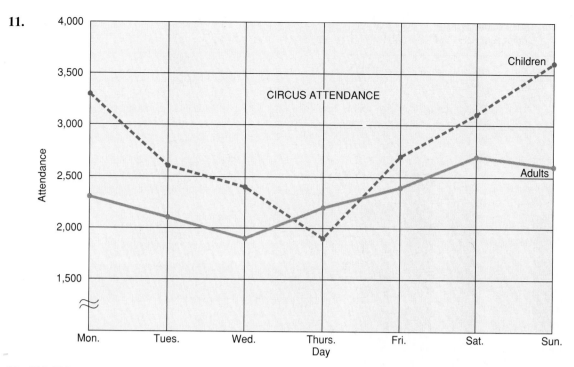

12. <u>800,000</u>

13. <u>Legal secretaries</u>

14. <u>Computer programmers</u>

15. <u>65–74</u>

16.

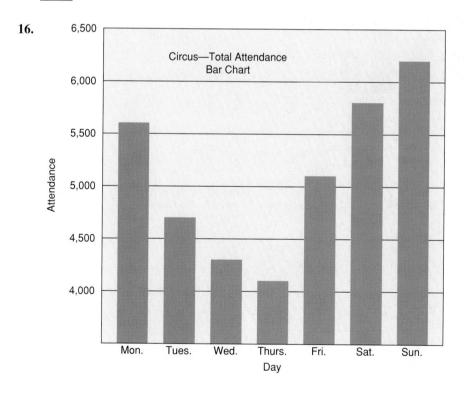

17.

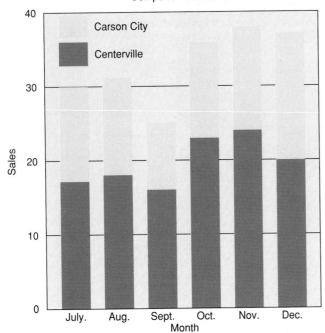

HANDY HARDWARE
Component Bar Chart

18.

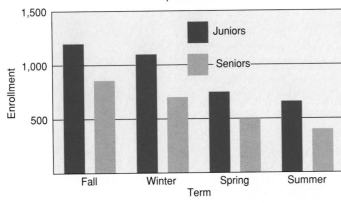

College Enrollment
Comparative Bar Chart

19. a. Food 12% + Clothing 7% = <u>19%</u>

b. U.S. 14% − Germany 13% = <u>1%</u>

20. Freshmen $= \dfrac{1,400}{4,400} = .318 = \underline{31.8\%}$ $.318 \times 360 = \underline{114°}$

Sophomores $= \dfrac{1,200}{4,400} = .273 = \underline{27.3\%}$ $.273 \times 360 = \underline{98°}$

Juniors $= \dfrac{1,100}{4,400} = .25 = \underline{25\%}$ $.25 \times 360 = \underline{90°}$

Seniors $= \dfrac{700}{4,400} = .159 = \underline{15.9\%}$ $.159 \times 360 = \underline{57°}$

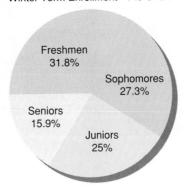

INTERSTATE BUSINESS COLLEGE
Winter Term Enrollment—Pie Chart

21. Mean $= \dfrac{\text{Sum of values}}{\text{Number of values}}$

Mean $= \dfrac{432 + 247 + 661 + 418 + 512}{5} = \dfrac{2,270}{5} = \underline{454}$

22. Ranked in increasing order:
1,220   2,430   3,619   <u>4,237</u>   4,589   5,840   6,558

Median is midpoint of odd number of values = <u>4,237</u>

23. Ranked in increasing order:
12 13 29 33 42 54 76 79 81 101
For even number of values, median is midpoint of the two middle values.

Midpoint $= \dfrac{42 + 54}{2} = \dfrac{96}{2} = \underline{\underline{48}}$

24. $\underline{10 = 7}$ $20 = 5$ $55 = 3$ $65 = 1$ $85 = 1$ $125 = 1$

The mode of these values is $\underline{\underline{10}}$ because it occurred the most number of times, 7.

25. Range = Highest value – Lowest value
Range $= 369° - 349° = \underline{\underline{20°}}$

26. *The Dress Code*
Frequency Distribution
$ Sales per transaction

Class ($)	Tally	Frequency
10–19	IIII	4
20–29	IIII	4
30–39	III	3
40–49	IIII	4
50–59	III	3
60–69	III	3
70–79	IЖI I	6
80–89	II	2
90–99	I	1

27. *The Dress Code*   *$ Sales per transaction*

Class ($)	Tally	Freq (*f*)	Midpoint (*m*)	(*f* x *m*)
10–19	IIII	4	14.5	58.0
20–29	IIII	4	24.5	98.0
30–39	III	3	34.5	103.5
40–49	IIII	4	44.5	178.0
50–59	III	3	54.5	163.5
60–69	III	3	64.5	193.5
70–79	IЖI I	6	74.5	447.0
80–89	II	2	84.5	169.0
90–99	I	1	94.5	94.5
		30		1,505.0

$\text{Mean} = \dfrac{\text{Sum of } (f \times m)}{\text{Sum of frequency}}$

$\text{Mean} = \dfrac{1,505}{30} = 50.166 = \underline{\underline{\$50.17}}$

28.

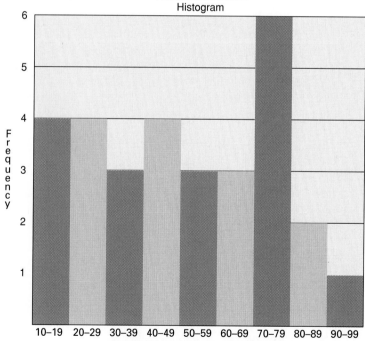

THE DRESS CODE
Histogram

1. The following data represents the monthly sales figures, in thousands, for the New York and California branches of the Discovery Corporation:

	April	May	June	July	August	September
New York	121	254	218	156	255	215
California	88	122	211	225	248	260

a. Construct a multiple-line chart depicting the monthly sales for the two branches. Show the New York branch as a solid line and the California branch as a dashed line.

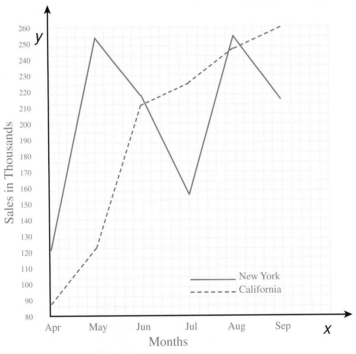

b. Construct a comparative bar chart for the same data. Highlight the bars for each branch differently.

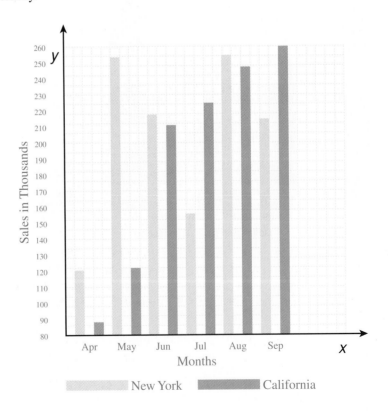

2. Construct a pie chart from the following information compiled in a recent survey of the buying habits of kids ages 8–17.

Category	Percentage
Clothing	35%
Fast food, snacks, candy	20%
Electronics products	15%
Entertainment	10%
School supplies	10%
Personal care	7%
Other	3%

Clothing $35\% \times 360° = 126°$
Fast food, etc. $20\% \times 360° = 72°$
Electronics $15\% \times 360° = 54°$
Entertainment $10\% \times 360° = 36°$
School supplies $10\% \times 360° = 36°$
Personal care $7\% \times 360° = 25°$
Other $3\% \times 360° = 11°$

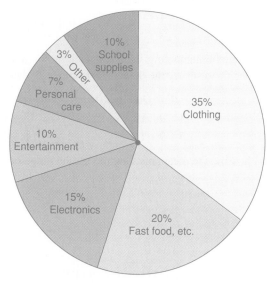

ANSWERS

3. a. _____ 50%

_____ 25%

_____ 10%

_____ 12.5%

_____ 2.5%

3. Last month Computer Village sold $150,000 in standard computers, $75,000 in portable computers, $30,000 in software, $37,500 in printers, and $7,500 in accessories.

a. What percent of the total sales does each category of merchandise represent?

Standard computers	$150,000 =	50%
Portable computers	75,000 =	25%
Software	30,000 =	10%
Printers	37,500 =	12.5%
Accessories	7,500 =	2.5%
Total sales	$300,000	

b. Construct a pie chart showing the percentage breakdown of sales by merchandise category.

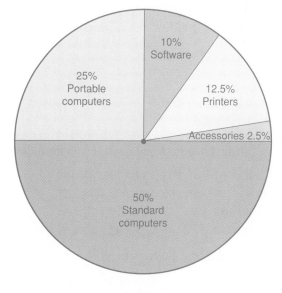

Standard $50\% \times 360° = 180°$
Portable $25\% \times 360° = 90°$
Software $10\% \times 360° = 36°$
Printers $12.5\% \times 360° = 45°$
Accessories $2.5\% \times 360° = 9°$

4. You have just been hired as the quality control manager by Blue Diamond Manufacturing, a company producing fuel injection systems for General Motors, Ford, and Chrysler. Top management has requested a status report on the number of defective units produced each day. You decide to keep track of the number of defects each day for 30 days. The following are the results of your survey:

Blue Diamond Manufacturing—Defects per day—Survey 1

11 13 17 13 15   9 14 11 13 15 11 10 14 12 15
19 15 13 17   9 20 13 14 18 16 15 14 17 18 13

a. Find the mean, median, mode, and range of this data for your report to top management.

Mean: $424 \div 30 = \underline{14.1}$

Median $= \dfrac{14 + 14}{2} = \underline{14}$ Mode: 13 occurs 6 times; it is the mode.

Range:
Highest 20
Lowest 9
Range 11

After implementing your suggestions for improved quality on the production line, you decide to survey the defects for another 30 days with the following results:

Blue Diamond Manufacturing—Defects per day—Survey 2

11	9	12	7	8	10	12	8	9	10	9	7	11	12	8
7	9	11	8	6	12	10	8	8	7	9	6	10	9	11

b. Find the mean, median, mode, and range of the new data.

Mean: $\dfrac{274}{30} = \underline{9.1}$ Mode: 8 and 9 occur 6 times each; they are the modes.

Median $= \dfrac{9 + 9}{2} = \underline{9}$

Range:
Highest 12
Lowest 6
Range 6

c. If defective units cost the company $75.00 each to fix, use the *means* of each survey to calculate the average cost per day for defects, before and after your improvements.

Before: $\$75.00 \times 14.1 = \underline{\$1,057.50}$ Per day
After: $\$75.00 \times 9.1 = \$ \underline{682.50}$ Per day

d. Theoretically, how much will your improvements save the company in a 300-day production year?

Savings over 300 days
$\$1,057.50$
$-\ \$682.50$
$\overline{\quad\$375.00} \times 300 = \underline{\$112,500.00}$

e. Congratulations! The company has awarded you a bonus amounting to 15% of the first year's savings. How much is your bonus check?

Bonus check $= \$112,500 \times 15\% = \underline{\$16,875.00}$

5. You are the personnel director for Supreme Industries. Forty applicants for employment were given an assessment test in math and English with the following results:

87	67	81	83	94	72	84	68	33	56
91	79	88	95	84	75	46	27	69	97
69	57	66	81	87	19	76	54	78	91
78	72	75	89	74	92	45	59	85	72

a. What are the range and mode of these scores?

Range: Highest 97
Lowest 19
Range 78

Mode: 72 occurs 3 times; it is the mode.

b. Group the data into nine classes of equal size (11–20, 21–30, etc.) and construct a frequency distribution.

Class	Tally	Frequency
1–10		
11–20	I	1
21–30	I	1
31–40	I	1
41–50	II	2
51–60	IIII	4
61–70	IIII	5
71–80	IIII IIII	10
81–90	IIII IIII	10
91–100	IIII I	6

c. Calculate the mean of the grouped data using 15.5, 25.5, etc., as the midpoints.

Class	Tally	Frequency (f)	Midpoint (m)	f × m
11–20	I	1	15.5	15.5
21–30	I	1	25.5	25.5
31–40	I	1	35.5	35.5
41–50	II	2	45.5	91
51–60	IIII	4	55.5	222
61–70	IIII	5	65.5	327.5
71–80	IIII IIII	10	75.5	755
81–90	IIII IIII	10	85.5	855
91–100	IIII I	6	95.5	573
		40		2,900

$$\text{Mean} = \frac{2,900}{40} = \underline{\underline{72.5}}$$

d. If company policy is to consider only those who score *10 points higher* than the mean of the data or better, how many from this group are still being considered for the job?

$\underline{\underline{14}}$ people scored higher than 72.5.

e. Construct a histogram of the assessment test scores frequency distribution.

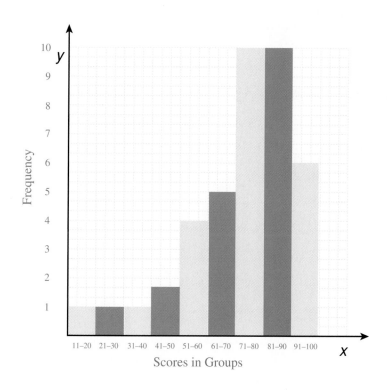

ANSWERS

Evans _____ $550

Chen _____ $550

Walker _____ $300

Black _____ $1,350

Sanchez _____ $2,450

BUSINESS DECISION
Beat the Mean Bonus!

6. You are the owner of Supreme Imports, Inc., a used car dealership specializing in expensive pre-owned automobiles, such as Mercedes Benz, BMW, and Lexus. You have a unique and quite motivating bonus plan that has worked very well over the years.

Each quarter the mean number of cars sold is calculated. The first time a salesperson sells more cars than the mean, he or she earns a $100 bonus for each car *over the mean* in that quarter. If a salesperson beats the mean a second time in a year, the bonus increases to $150 per car for that quarter. Three times over the mean in one year and the bonus is $200 per car for that quarter. If anyone beats the mean all four quarters, the fourth quarter bonus is $300 per car. Remember, the bonus is paid only for the number of cars over the mean.

Each year the program starts all over again. All bonuses are paid once per year, in January, for the previous year. The following table represents the number of cars sold by your five salespeople for each quarter last year. Calculate the bonus each person should receive for last year.

	First Quarter	Second Quarter	Third Quarter	Fourth Quarter
Evans	16	23	14	23
Chen	12	20	16	25
Walker	15	13	26	19
Black	22	20	27	19
Sanchez	25	19	32	24

Mean, 1st Quarter
$$\frac{16 + 12 + 15 + 22 + 25}{5} = 18$$

Mean, 3rd Quarter
$$\frac{14 + 16 + 26 + 27 + 32}{5} = 23$$

Mean, 2nd Quarter
$$\frac{23 + 20 + 13 + 20 + 19}{5} = 19$$

Mean, 4th Quarter
$$\frac{23 + 25 + 19 + 19 + 24}{5} = 22$$

Evans
Beat mean: 2Q + 4Q
Evans's bonus: $(4 \times \$100) + (1 \times \$150)$
               $\$400$ + $\$150$ = $\underline{\$550}$

Chen
Beat mean: 2Q + 4Q
Chen's bonus: $(1 \times \$100) + (3 \times \$150)$
               $\$100$ + $\$450$ = $\underline{\$550}$

Walker
Beat mean: 3Q
Walker's bonus: $(3 \times \$100)$ = $\underline{\$300}$

Black
Beat mean: 1Q + 2Q + 3Q
Black's bonus: $(4 \times \$100) + (1 \times \$150) + (4 \times \$200)$
               $\$400$ + $\$150$ + $\$800$ = $\underline{\$1,350}$

Sanchez
Beat mean: 1Q + 3Q + 4Q
Sanchez's bonus: $(7 \times \$100) + (9 \times \$150) + (2 \times \$200)$
               $\$700$ + $\$1,350$ + $\$400$ = $\underline{\$2,450}$

All the Math That's Fit to Learn

The Business Math Times

Volume XXI | **Business Statistics and Data Presentation** | One Dollar

Census 2000:
The $4 Billion Survey

No, it's not a misprint! That's how much it will cost for the Census Bureau to conduct the next national head count in the year 2000. The Constitution requires a census every 10 years to apportion seats in the House of Representatives. Census numbers also are used to distribute billions of dollars in federal and state money.

The 1990 census cost U.S. taxpayers $2.5 billion. Duplicating the door-to-door head counting procedure used in 1990 was estimated to cost $4.8 billion in 2000. To save money, some statistical sampling will be used.

Counting a quarter-billion people is a job that takes serious preparation. The plan is to actually count only 9 percent of the population and rely on sampling to determine the number remaining. Estimated cost for the sampling is $3.9 billion. Statistical sampling, commonly associated with public opinion polls, involves questioning a randomly selected group of people and using the information derived from them to count or describe a much larger group.

For Census 2000, forms will be sent to 120 million U.S. households. The bureau plans to simplify the forms, reducing the number of questions to about 8 on the short form, down from 17 in 1990, and 55 on the long form, down from 59. The long form is sent to about 1 in every 6 households, and contains questions that provide a wealth of data for demographers, social scientists, marketers, and government agencies.

In addition to mailing the forms, they will be available at government buildings such as libraries and police stations, as well as community centers and convenience stores. Also, for the first time, Census 2000 will allow people to phone their responses in using a toll-free telephone number. Even a web site on the Internet is being considered.

In 1990, only 65 percent of Americans mailed back the form, a significant drop from 78 percent in previous census years. The bureau is currently testing two different envelopes for mailing the forms. One, the friendly approach, is imprinted with a bright yellow circle (like a smiley-face button) that reads, "Count Me In!" The other, the authoritative approach, warns in bold black letters, "YOUR RESPONSE IS REQUIRED BY LAW."

Which do you think will be chosen? Stay close to a mailbox near you!!

SOURCES: Adapted from John Pierson, "Preparing for 2000, Census Bureau Tests Carrots vs. Sticks," *The Wall Street Journal,* May 2, 1996: B1; "No Need to Count Every Last Person," *The New York Times* editorial, March 5, 1996: A14; Steven A. Holmes, "Census, in a First, to Use Sampling in the Year 2000," *The New York Times,* February 29, 1996: A11; and "250 Million, But Who's Counting?" Associated Press, February 29, 1996: 3A.

"Lem, this town ain't big enough for two statisticians."

High Seas Origin

Did you know the word *average* is derived from maritime laws dating back to the 16th century? When a cargo vessel was in danger of sinking during a storm at sea, the heavy cargo was usually thrown overboard to save the ship.

By law, the cost of the lost or damaged goods was equally divided among all the concerned parties. In French, this practice was known as *avarié,* which later became the English word, *average!*

SOURCE: Word for Word. Syndicated cartoon.

The National Data Book

Did you know *The Statistical Abstract of the United States* is our national data book? Published since 1878, it is the standard summary of statistics on the social, political, and economic organization of the United States.

Brainteaser*

An absent-minded professor misplaced the business math test scores of his five students. However, he did remember that the mode was 90, the median was 85, and the mean was 83. If the grades ranged from 0 to 100, what is the lowest possible grade from the missing set of scores?

SOURCE: *Mathematics Teacher Magazine,* April 1987.

*Solution to this brainteaser is at the end of Appendix A, Collaborative Learning Exercises, which follows Chapter 21.

Answer to Last Issue's Brainteaser
9-Inch square

Area of a square = side^2
Area = 9 x 9 = 81 sq. in.

Area of a circle = πr^2
Area = 3.14 x 5 x 5 = 78.5 sq. in.

Appendix A

Collaborative Learning Activities

The following collaborative learning activities are designed to supplement and enhance your business math learning experience. They will introduce you to real world business applications of the material presented in each chapter as well as professionals who use these applications each day in their work.

Although the activities can be done on an individual basis, it is recommended that students break into teams of two, three, or four, and work together to accomplish each task.

For maximum effectiveness, each team's findings should be shared with the rest of the class.

Collaborative Learning Activity—Chapter 1

Using Math in Business

As a team, discuss and list the ways that math is used in the following businesses. Report your findings to the class.
a. Supermarket
b. Car dealership
c. Beauty Salon
d. Restaurant
e. Additional choice: _____

Collaborative Learning Activity—Chapter 2

Knowing Fractions Is Half the Battle

As a team, investigate and share with the class how fractions are used in the following:
a. Stock market
b. Manufacturing
c. Cooking
d. Medicine or pharmacy
e. Architecture and building construction
f. Additional choice: _____

Collaborative Learning Activity—Chapter 3

Sports Math

As a team, choose two sports.
a. Investigate how fractions and decimals are used in their record keeping and statistics.
b. Prepare a visual presentation to share with the class.

Collaborative Learning Activity—Chapter 4

Choosing a Checking Account

Have each team member call a local bank, credit union, or other financial institution offering checking accounts. Ask them to send a brochure describing the types of checking accounts they have and other banking services they offer. As a team, look over the material, and answer the following:
a. How do they compare regarding monthly service charges, interest paid, account minimums, ATM charges, and other rules and regulations?
b. Do they offer any incentives, such as a no-fee Visa or MasterCard, bounce-proof checking, or a line of credit?

c. Based on your team's research, which one seems like the best deal for a
- College student? Why?
- Small business? Why?
- Large corporation? Why?

Collaborative Learning Activity—Chapter 5

Using Formulas in Business

Have each member of the team speak with someone in one of the following professions to determine how they use equations and formulas in their business:

a. Store owner or manager
b. Real estate or insurance salesperson
c. Advertising or marketing manager
d Production manager
e. Accountant
f. Banker
g. Additional choice: _____

Collaborative Learning Activity—Chapter 6

Percents—The Language of Business!

As we learned in Chapter 6, percents are one of the most common and useful business math tools. As a team, find ten examples of their application in business from each of the following sources:

a. Business sections of your local newpaper
b. Business newspapers, such as *The Wall Street Journal* or *Barrons*
c. Business magazines, such as *Fortune* or *Business Week*
d. Company annual reports

Collaborative Learning Activity—Chapter 7

Comparing Invoices and Discounts

1. As a team, collect invoices from a number of businesses in different industries in your area.
   a. How are they similar?
   b. How are they different?

2. Have each member of the team speak with a wholesaler or a retailer in your area.
   a. What are the typical trade discounts in that industry?
   b. What are the typical cash discounts in that industry?

Collaborative Learning Activity—Chapter 8

The "Shopping" Trip

1. As a team, collect newspaper advertisements for merchandise that is "on sale" at the following types of retail stores in your area. Calculate the amount of the markdown, the markdown percent, or the original price—whichever is not given in the ad. How do the figures compare among the categories?
   a. Supermarket
   b. Drugstore
   c. Department store
   d. Specialty shop
   e. Additional choice: _____

2. Have each member of the team visit one of the stores advertising "sale" merchandise in Question 1, and answer the following:
   a. Were the items marked correctly with the advertised sale price?
   b. Did the stores make any attempt to feature the sale merchandise using in-store displays, such as signs or other eye-catching devices?
   c. Were the employees aware of the sale?
   d. Would you say the stores did a good job of coordinating their newspaper advertising with their "in-store" efforts?
   e. Overall, what can you and your team conclude about markdowns and "sales" from this "shopping" trip?

Collaborative Learning Activity—Chapter 9

The Job Hunt

1. As a team, collect help wanted ads from the classifed section of your local newpaper. (Note: Sunday editions are usually best.) Find examples of various jobs paid by salary, hourly rate, piece rate, and commission, and answer the following:
   a. How much do they pay?
   b. What pay periods are used?
   c. What fringe benefits do they offer?
   d. Did you notice any trends among similar jobs?

2. As a team, go to the library and reseach the following:
   a. Personal income of employees in various industries and in government occupations.
   b. Personal and household income by area of the country. How does your area compare?
   c. Starting salaries by amount of education, in various fields of study.
   d. Where did your team find this information?

Collaborative Learning Activity—Chapter 10

The Car Loan

As a team, choose a particular type of vehicle category that you wish to research (such as sport utility vehicle, sports car, or luxury sedan). Then have each member of the team choose a different manufacturer's competitive model within that category.

For example, if the team picked sport utility vehicles, then individual choices might be Nissan Pathfinder, Toyota 4Runner, Ford Explorer, and Chevy Blazer.
   a. From your local newspaper, collect advertisements for the purchase of the model you picked.
   b. Visit an automobile dealership for the vehicle you picked. Speak with a salesperson about the types of deals currently being offered on that model.
      • What loan rates and terms are available through the dealer?
      • Who is the actual lender?
      • How much does the dealer make on the financing?
   c. Contact various lending institutions (banks, finance companies, credit unions) and inquire about automobile loans.
      • What rates and terms are being offered?
      • Which one is offering the best deal?
      • How do these compare with those from the dealership?

Collaborative Learning Activity—Chapter 11

Putting Your Money to Work!

As a team, research the financial institutions and brokerage houses in your area to determine the various deals being offered on certificates of deposit. Assume that you want to invest $10,000, for up to 24 months.
   a. What interest rates do these CDs pay? How often is interest compounded?
   b. What is the early withdrawal penalty?
   c. Which offers a better deal: bank CDs or brokerage house CDs?
   d. Are these CDs insured? By whom? For how much?
   e. Overall, which CD would be worth the most money after 24 months?

Collaborative Learning Activity—Chapter 12

The "Personal" Sinking Fund

1. As a team, design a "personal" sinking fund for something you wish to save for in the future.
   a. What is the amount and the purpose of the fund?
   b. What interest rate is currently available in savings accounts? (Check with local lending institutions.)
   c. At that rate, calculate what monthly payment would be required to accumulate the desired amount in 1 year, 2 years, 5 years?

2. As a team, research the annual reports or speak with accountants of corporations that are using sinking funds to accumulate money for a future obligation. Answer the following questions about those funds:
   a. What is the name of the corporation?

b. What is the purpose and the amount of the sinking fund?

c. For how many years is the fund?

d. How much are the periodic payments?

e. At what interest rate are these funds growing?

Collaborative Learning Activity—Chapter 13

Plastic Choices

1. Have each member of the team contact a local bank, credit union, or retail store in your area that offers a credit card. Get a brochure and/or a copy of the credit agreement.

   a. For each card, determine the following information:
      - Annual interest rate
      - Method used for computing interest
      - Credit limit
      - Annual fee
      - "Fine-print" features

   b. Based on your research, which cards are the best and worst deals?

2. Contact Ram Research (1-800-344-7714), a company that publishes a monthly consumer newsletter called CardTrack. This newsletter lists the banks currently offering the best credit card rates and features in the country.

   a. Order a copy of CardTrack ($5.00)

   b. Compare your local banks' offers to those in the newsletter.

3. As a team, go to the library and research the rules, regulations, and recent changes in the following:

   a. The Fair Credit Reporting Act, a federal law that spells out the rules that govern credit-card issuers.

   b. Laws in your state relating to credit cards.

Collaborative Learning Activity—Chapter 14

The "Hypothetical" Mortgage

As a team, contact several lending institutions in your area that offer mortgage loans. Speak with loan officers, and ask for their help with a class project in business math.

Your assignment is to research the various types of financing deals currently being offered for a hypothetical home you plan to buy. The following assumptions apply to this project:
- The purchase price of the house you plan to buy is $100,000.
- The house was recently appraised for $105,000.
- You plan to make a 25% down payment ($25,000) and are seeking a $75,000 mortgage.
- You have a job that qualifies you for that size mortgage.

Your assignment, as a team, is to compare the current interest rates, costs, and features associated with a 15-year fixed-rate mortgage, a 30-year fixed-rate mortgage, and an adjustable-rate mortgage.

a. What are the current interest rates and discount points of the 15- and 30-year fixed-rate mortgages?

b. What are the monthly payments of the fixed-rate mortgages?

c. What is the teaser rate, discount points, adjustment period, rate caps, margin, and index for the adjustable-rate mortgage?

d. What are the fees or charges for the loan application, property appraisal, survey, credit report, inspections, title search, title insurance, and document preparation?

e. What other charges or fees can be expected at closing?

f. As a team, decide which type of mortgage is the best deal at this time? Why?

g. Which bank would you and your team choose for the mortgage? Why?

Collaborative Learning Activity—Chapter 15

Analyzing a Company

As a team, choose an industry you wish to research, such as airline, beverage, computer, entertainment, food, motor vehicle, retail, or wholesale. Next, choose three public companies that directly compete in that industry.

From the reference section of your library, research key business ratios and other available information about that industry. This may be found in the government's publication, *The Sur-*

vey of Current Business, or from private sources, such as *Moody's Index, Dunn & Bradstreet,* or *Standard & Poors.*

Next, obtain the most recent financial statements for each company. These may be found in the sources mentioned above, or, if possible, contact a stockbroker or the company directly, and obtain a copy of the most recent annual report and quarterly reports.

Based on the information your team has accumulated:

a. Calculate the current and previous years' financial ratios for each company.

b. Compare each company's ratios to the industry averages.

c. Evaluate each company's financial condition regarding liquidity, efficiency, leverage, and profitability.

d. If you and your team were going to invest in only one of these companies, which would you choose? Why?

Collaborative Learning Activity—Chapter 16

The Counting Game!

As a team, choose two or three competitive retail stores in your area, such as supermarkets, drug stores, general merchandisers, or hardware stores. Speak with an accounting and/or merchandise manager for each, and determine the following:

a. How many different items are carried in inventory?

b. What is their average inventory?

c. How often is a physical inventory count taken? Who does it?

d. Does the company have a computerized perpetual inventory system? How does it work?

e. What is the inventory turnover ratio? How does this compare with the published industry figures for a company that size? (Where did you find the published figures?)

f. What method of inventory valuation is being used? Why?

g. Which of the companies your team researched has a more efficient inventory system? Why?

Collaborative Learning Activity—Chapter 17

Going, Going, Gone!

1. Have each member of your team choose their favorite automobile and determine the price of a new one from a dealership. Then check the classified ads of your local newspaper or a publication of used car prices. Determine the price of the same car model at one, two, three, four, and five years old.

   a. Prepare a depreciation schedule based on the information you found.

   b. Calculate what percent of its original value was lost in each year.

   c. Construct a line graph of the five years of depreciation of the car.

   d. Does it seem to be straight-line or accelerated?

   e. Compare the depreciation for each team member's car. Which models depreciated the fastest? the slowest?

   f. Can any conclusions be drawn from this research?

2. Choose a local industry, and have each member of the team pick a different company within that industry and speak with an accountant who works there. Identify three major assets that are being depreciated, such as a truck, production-line equipment, a computer, office furniture and fixtures, etc. For each asset, determine the following:

   a. Original purchase price

   b. Useful life

   c. Salvage value

   d. Depreciation method used for financial statement reporting

   e. Depreciation method used for income tax purposes

   f. Can any conclusions be drawn from this research?

Collaborative Learning Activity—Chapter 18

"Your Tax Dollars at Work"

In Chapter 18, Taxes, the primary focus has been on calculating the amount of taxes that are due. Now, as a team, let's do some research into how your tax dollars are being spent, both at the local and state level.

1. **Local level.** As we have learned, local tax dollars are generally raised from property and local sales taxes. Is this true in your area? Contact your local tax assessors office and determine the following:
   a. What are the local taxing units? City, county, municipality, district, province, parish, other?
   b. How are local taxes derived for each unit?
   c. What are the tax rates for each unit?
   d. How have the rates changed over the past five years?
   e. What is the latest tax budget for each unit and how is the money being spent?
   f. List five major projects in your area that are currently, recently, or soon-to-be funded by your tax dollars.
   g. As a team, what is your overall opinion of "your local tax dollars at work"?

2. **State level.** Tax revenue in most states is derived either from sales tax, state income tax, or a combination of both. Is this true in your state? As a team, contact your state taxing authority and determine the following:
   a. How are state taxes derived?
   b. What are the tax rates?
   c. How have the rates changed over the past five years?
   d. What is the latest tax budget and how is the money being spent?
   e. List five or more major projects in your state that are currently, recently, or soon-to-be funded by tax dollars.
   f. As a team, what is your overall opinion of "your state tax dollars at work"?

Collaborative Learning Activity—Chapter 19

Insurance for Sweetie Pie

As a team, you and your partners are hypothetically going to start a company called The Sweetie Pie Corporation, a bakery that makes and distributes pies, cakes, cookies, and donuts to restaurants and food stores in your area.

The company will have property and a building valued at $200,000, baking and production-line equipment valued at $400,000, office equipment and fixtures worth $100,000, and four delivery trucks valued at $25,000 each. There will be 10 employees, and 4 partners, including yourself.

Each team member is to consult with a different insurance agent to put together a "package" of business insurance for Sweetie Pie Corporation, including property insurance, liability insurance, and business interruption insurance.

In addition, look into a health insurance program for the partners and the employees, as well as $100,000 "key man" insurance for each partner. What other types of coverage does the agent recommend?

It is only fair that you tell the agents this is a hypothetical project for your business math class and are seeking their help on this assignment. After each team member has done their research, collaborate on which insurance agent offered the best package and rates, and why. Share your findings with the class.

Collaborative Learning Activity—Chapter 20

Yesterday, Today, and Tomorrow!

In this activity, you and your team will research the meaning and direction of some of the more important investment and money indicators in our economy. Your best sources of information for this project will be the library, stockbrokers, and financial newspapers such as *The Wall Street Journal*, *Barron's*, or *The New York Times*.

Divide the indicators among the team members and do the following:
a. Research and explain what these indicators mean, and how they are derived.
b. Look up the current figure for each indicator.
c. Look up historical figures (every 3 or 6 months) and prepare a visual presentation (line-graph or bar-graph) of each indicator's performance trend since June 1996.
d. As a team, discuss and report what each trend indicates.

Indicator	June 1996
Dow Jones Industrial Average	5762.86
Standard & Poors 500	678.51
Nasdaq Composite Average	1247.80
Japanese yen (per U.S. dollar)	107.92
German mark (per U.S. dollar)	1.5437
Gold (troy oz.)	$390.60
Oil, W. Texas crude (per barrel)	$21.63
Prime rate	8.25%
Certificates of deposit (6-months)	5.25%
30-year mortgage	8.25%

Collaborative Learning Activity—Chapter 21

Conducting a Marketing Research Survey

You and your team have been hired to conduct a marketing research survey by a company that is interested in advertising its products to college students in your area. They want to know the media preferences of the students at your school, and specifically would like answers to the following questions:

• What radio station, if any, do you listen to in the morning?
• What television local news program, if any, do you watch in the evening?
• What newspaper, if any, do you read each day?

a. As a team, design a questionnaire for this research survey. For each question, list all of the local media choices, with a place for easy check-off response. Be sure to include "no preference" and "none of the above" as choices. In addition to the survey questions, design some easy check-off demographic information questions, such as male/female, age group, ethnic group, income range, and marital status.

b. Individually, have each member of the research team personally interview about 25 or 30 students. (Questionnaires can be handed out, and then collected.)

c. As a team, tabulate the results of each survey and demographic question.

d. Calculate the mean, median, and mode for each of the demographic questions.

e. Prepare a visual presentation for the class of the results of the survey questions.

f. As a team, do you think the results of your survey are valid? Why? Why not?

Answer to the Brainteaser for Chapter 21

Answer 66

The most common score (mode) was 90, so at least two scores were 90s. The middle score (median) was 85, so at least one score was 85 and the remaining two must be less than 85. The mean was 83, so the sum of all five test scores was 5×83, or 415.

$415 - 2(90) - 85 = 150$. If one score was 84, the other would be 66.

Appendix B

Answers to Odd-Numbered Exercises

CHAPTER I   A REVIEW OF BASIC OPERATIONS

REVIEW EXERCISES   CHAPTER 1—SECTION I

1. 22,938—twenty-two thousand, nine hundred thirty-eight   **3.** 184—one hundred eighty-four   **5.** 2,433,590—two million, four hundred thirty-three thousand, five hundred ninety   **7.** 183,622   **9.** 1,936   **11.** d   **13.** a   **15.** 1,760   **17.** 235,400
19. 8,000,000   **21.** 1,300,000,000   **23.** 19,000,000,000   **25.** 76,000   **27.** $45,300
29. 22,600

REVIEW EXERCISES   CHAPTER 1—SECTION II

1. 91   **3.** 19,943   **5.** 37,648   **7.** 70,928   **9.** 42,100 estimate—37,844 exact   **11a.** 7,000
11b. 6,935   **13.** 3,236 grand total   **15.** $1,627   **17.** 4,629   **19.** 278,091   **21.** $138
23. $139   **25.** 3,490,700   **27.** $20,220   **29.** 378

REVIEW EXERCISES   CHAPTER 1—SECTION III

1. 11,191   **3.** 294,300   **5.** 56,969,000   **7.** 13,110   **9.** 100,000 estimate—98,980 exact
11. 200 estimate—187 exact   **13.** 399   **15.** 70,350   **17.** 13 R67   **19.** 55
21. 2 R300 estimate—2 R339 exact   **23.** 6   **25.** $924

ASSESSMENT TEST

1. 200,049—two hundred thousand, forty-nine   **3.** 316,229   **5.** 18,300   **7.** 260,000
9. 99   **11.** 44 R28   **13.** 22,258   **15.** 714   **17.** $14,524   **19a.** 19   **19b.** 25   **21a.** $11,340
21b. $36   **23.** $1,003   **25.** $49,260   **27.** 5,040   **29.** 15

CHAPTER 2   FRACTIONS

REVIEW EXERCISES   CHAPTER 2—SECTION I

1. mixed fraction, twenty-three and four-fifths   **3.** improper fraction, fifteen-ninths
5. mixed fraction, two and one-eighth   **7.** $3\frac{1}{3}$ **9.** $4\frac{4}{15}$ **11.** $1\frac{2}{31}$ **13.** $\frac{59}{5}$ **15.** $\frac{149}{8}$

17. $\frac{1,001}{4}$ **19.** $\frac{3}{4}$ **21.** $\frac{27}{115}$ **23.** $\frac{1}{8}$ **25.** $\frac{19}{65}$ **27.** $\frac{13}{16}$ **29.** $\frac{5}{18}$ **31.** $\frac{36}{48}$ **33.** $\frac{44}{64}$ **35.** $\frac{42}{98}$

37. $\frac{40}{64}$ **39.** $\frac{126}{182}$ **41.** $\frac{16}{72}$ **43.** $\frac{3}{5}$

REVIEW EXERCISES CHAPTER 2—SECTION II

1. 15   **3.** 12   **5.** 300   **7.** $1\frac{1}{3}$ **9.** $1\frac{7}{16}$ **11.** $1\frac{13}{20}$ **13.** $2\frac{3}{20}$ **15.** $11\frac{13}{24}$ **17.** $10\frac{17}{40}$
19. $43\frac{1}{8}$ **21.** $\frac{2}{3}$ **23.** $\frac{11}{18}$ **25.** $8\frac{4}{15}$ **27.** $26\frac{29}{45}$ **29.** $35\frac{13}{15}$ **31a.** $45\frac{11}{30}$ **31b.** $90\frac{19}{30}$
33. $\frac{5}{16}$

REVIEW EXERCISES CHAPTER 2—SECTION III

1. $\frac{8}{15}$ **3.** $\frac{2}{9}$ **5.** $\frac{10}{19}$ **7.** $2\frac{2}{5}$ **9.** $21\frac{13}{15}$ **11.** $\frac{1}{125}$ **13a.** $\frac{5}{8}$ **13b.** 2,750   **15.** $43\frac{15}{16}$
17. $317\frac{9}{10}$ **19.** $2\frac{2}{9}$ **21.** $1\frac{1}{15}$ **23.** $\frac{2}{5}$ **25.** $5\frac{17}{35}$ **27.** 19   **29.** $\frac{5}{14}$ **31.** 46   **33a.** 240
33b. 90   **35.** 213   **37.** 55

ASSESSMENT TEST

1. improper fraction, eighteen elevenths   **3.** proper fraction, thirteen sixteenths   **5.** 25
7. $\frac{86}{9}$ **9.** $\frac{2}{5}$ **11.** $\frac{18}{78}$ **13.** $\frac{25}{36}$ **15.** $5\frac{1}{3}$ **17.** $4\frac{3}{10}$ **19.** $13\frac{1}{3}$ **21.** 69   **23.** $23\frac{5}{8}$ **25a.** $18\frac{3}{8}$
25b. $183,750.00   **27.** $3,325   **29.** 15 ounces, pasta; 4 tablespoons, garlic;
$3\frac{1}{8}$ cups, tomatoes; $6\frac{1}{4}$ tablespoons, cheese

CHAPTER 3   DECIMALS

REVIEW EXERCISES CHAPTER 3—SECTION I

1. twenty-one hundredths   **3.** ninety-two thousandths   **5.** ninety-eight thousand forty-five
and forty-five thousandths   **7.** nine hundred thirty-eight hundred-thousandths   **9.** fifty-seven
and one half hundred-thousandths   **11.** .8   **13.** 67,309.04   **15.** 183,000.0183   **17.** 123.007
19. .01004   **21.** $14.60   **23.** 43.01   **25.** 46

REVIEW EXERCISES CHAPTER 3—SECTION II

1. 58.033   **3.** $45.27   **5.** 152.784494   **7.** 16.349   **9.** $.87   **11.** 779.75   **13.** $138.37
15. 2.693   **17a.** 2.3091   **17b.** 1.6309   **19.** $1,636.24   **21.** 549.24   **23.** 7.3952
25. .04848   **27.** 45,007.9   **29.** 1.29   **31.** .02   **33.** 3.7   **35.** 1,555   **37.** $7,946.50
39a. $45.70   **39b.** $11.40   **41.** 316   **43a.** $45.72   **43b.** $10.06   **45a.** 15   **45b.** 27
45c. $39.96

REVIEW EXERCISES CHAPTER 3—SECTION III

1. $\frac{1}{8}$ **3.** $\frac{1}{125}$ **5.** $14\frac{41}{50}$ **7.** 5.67   **9.** 1.22   **11.** 58.43   **13.** 5   **15a.** 16   **15b.** $190.24
17a. $64,375.00   **17b.** $2,575.00   **17c.** $66,950.00   **19.** $13.10

ASSESSMENT TEST

1. sixty-one hundredths   **3.** one hundred nineteen dollars and eighty-five cents
5. four hundred ninety-five ten-thousandths   **7.** 5.014   **9.** $16.57   **11.** 99.070   **13.** 4.7
15. $37.19   **17.** 7.7056   **19.** .736   **21.** .000192   **23.** .4   **25.** $20.06   **27.** $\dfrac{441}{10,000}$
29. 3.11   **31.** $1,127.85   **33.** $1,500.36   **35.** $5,025.00   **37.** $21,773.77   **39a.** 23
39b. $41.17

CHAPTER 4   CHECKING ACCOUNTS

REVIEW EXERCISES   CHAPTER 4—SECTION I

1. $345.54   **3.** $644.30   **5.** Your Signature, 099-506-8   Blank Endorsement
7. $9,998.67 net deposit   **9.** #439—$90.68 Bal. Fwd, #440—$317.90 Bal. Fwd,
#441—$864.50 Bal. Fwd.

REVIEW EXERCISES   CHAPTER 4—SECTION II

1. $1,485.90   reconciled balance   **3.** $471.84   reconciled balance

ASSESSMENT TEST

1. $24,556.00   **3.** $935.79   net deposit   **5.** $324.57   reconciled balance

CHAPTER 5   USING EQUATIONS TO SOLVE BUSINESS PROBLEMS

REVIEW EXERCISES   CHAPTER 5—SECTION I

1. B = 13   **3.** S = 90   **5.** K = 3   **7.** Y = $7\frac{1}{2}$ **9.** G = 4   **11.** A = 3   **13.** X = 4   **15.** D = 5
17. Q = 1   **19.** 5F + 33   **21.** HP + 550   **23.** 8Y − 128   **25.** $\frac{3}{4}$B + 40   **27.** X = 5B + C
29. $5.75R = $28.75   **31.** 5X + 4 + 2X = X + 40

REVIEW EXERCISES   CHAPTER 4—SECTION II

1. 47 Karen, 39 Kathy   **3.** 114 cartons   **5.** 18 old machines   **7.** $22,400 Robbin,
$67,200 Bryant   **9.** 288 total transactions   **11.** 14 extended, 42 standard   **13a.** 220 peanut
butter, 310 oatmeal   **13b.** $352 peanut butter, $403 oatmeal   **15.** $2.60 per piece   **17.** $777
19. $114.10   **21.** 27 inches   **23.** 18,850   **25a.** 256   **25b.** $9.52

ASSESSMENT TEST

1. T = 65   **3.** K = 15   **5.** X = 8   **7.** B = 8   **9.** X = 15   **11.** 4R − 108   **13.** ZW + 24
15. X = 4C + L   **17.** 3F − 14 = 38   **19.** 14 Blue Water, 19 Atlas   **21.** $55   **23.** 95 watts
25. $1.15   **27a.** 200 banana splits, 800 sundaes   **27b.** $850 banana splits, $2,880 sundaes
29. $104,000   **31.** $1,365   **33.** 60 ft.

CHAPTER 6   PERCENTS AND THEIR APPLICATIONS IN BUSINESS

REVIEW EXERCISES   CHAPTER 6—SECTION I

1. .28   **3.** .134   **5.** .4268   **7.** .0002   **9.** 1.2517   **11.** 350%   **13.** 4,600%   **15.** .935%
17. 16,400%   **19.** 533%   **21.** $\frac{1}{20}$ **23.** $\frac{89}{100}$ **25.** $\frac{19}{50}$ **27.** $\frac{5}{8}$ **29.** $1\frac{1}{4}$ **31.** 75%
33. 240%   **35.** 125%   **37.** 18.75%   **39.** 35%

REVIEW EXERCISES   CHAPTER 6—SECTION II

1. 57   **3.** 90   **5.** 85.5   **7.** 64.77   **9.** 56.88   **11.** 32%   **13.** 250%   **15.** 13.5%   **17.** 29.9%
19. 26%   **21.** 460   **23.** 34.86   **25.** 363.64   **27.** 400   **29.** $53.65   **31.** $59,200
33. $165,000   **35.** $13,650   **37.** $142.35   **39.** 10   **41.** 1,700   **43.** $61,230.75
45. 40% chicken, 35% steak, 25% fish

REVIEW EXERCISES   CHAPTER 6—SECTION III

1. 37.5%   **3.** 25.2%   **5.** 60   **7.** 15   **9.** 10,000   **11.** 7%   **13a.** 1,105   **13b.** 442 graphite,
663 wood   **15.** 29.4%   **17a.** $110,000   **17b.** $105,600   **19a.** 11.9%   **19b.** $59.625

ASSESSMENT TEST

1. .88   **3.** .5968   **5.** .005625   **7.** 68.1%   **9.** 2,480%   **11.** $\frac{19}{100}$ **13.** $\frac{93}{1,250}$ **15.** $\frac{127}{500}$
17. 55.56%   **19.** 5,630%   **21.** 408   **23.** 103.41   **25.** 180%   **27.** 69   **29.** 2,960   **31.** 1,492
33. $122.48   **35.** 50%   **37.** 21%   **39a.** 500 lbs   **39b.** 72.2%   **41.** 18.1%
43a. $2,543.40 airport, $1,630.80 downtown, $1,225.80 suburban   **43b.** $2,464.02 airport,
$1,579.50 downtown, $1,187.78 suburban, $1,086.70 beach   **45a.** 70%   **45b.** $7,965,000
45c. 59.3% owned, 40.7% leased

CHAPTER 7   INVOICES, TRADE AND CASH DISCOUNTS

REVIEW EXERCISES   CHAPTER 7—SECTION I

1. box   **3.** drum   **5.** gross   **7.** thousand   **9.** Frasier Mfg.   **11.** June 16, 199x
13. J. M. Hardware Supply   **15.** 2051 W. Adams Blvd, Nashville, TN 96133
17. Gilbert Trucking   **19.** $61.45   **21.** $4,415.12

REVIEW EXERCISES   CHAPTER 7—SECTION II

1. $258   **3.** $7.93   **5.** $44.13   **7.** $53.92 - $80.87   **9.** $527.45 - $431.55
11. 76%, $429.65   **13.** 87.25%, $4.01   **15.** $120.50, $34.9%   **17.** $239.99
19. $1,950   **21a.** $494.80   **21b.** $192.97   **21c.** $301.83   **23.** $1,512
25a. Pro-Chef, $233.75   **25b.** $7,125.00.

REVIEW EXERCISES   CHAPTER 7—SECTION III

1. .792, $285.12   **3.** .648, $52.97   **5.** .57056, $4.14   **7.** .765, .235   **9.** .59288, .40712
11. .51106, .48894   **13.** .6324, .3676, $441.12, $758.88   **15.** .65666, .34334, $303.34,
$580.16   **17.** .5292, .4708, $1,353.53, $1,521.42   **19.** .49725   **21a.** .6   **21b.** $54,300.00
23a. .57375   **23b.** .42625   **25a.** $324.19   **25b.** .53687   **27a.** $232.96   **27b.** $291.20
29a. $1,494.90   **29b.** $687.65   **29c.** $807.25

1. $474, $15,326   **3.** $96.84, $2,324.16   **5.** $319.25, $8,802.19   **7.** $474.23, $870.37
9. $5,759.16, $1,472.92   **11.** May 8, June 22   **13.** 2%, Feb 8, 1%, Feb 18, Mar 30
15. Jan 10, Jan 30   **17.** Oct 23, Nov 12   **19.** June 25, July 15   **21a.** April 27, May 27
21b. $21.24   **21c.** $1,148.76   **23a.** Mar 22   **23b.** Apr 11   **25a.** $23,095.36
25b. June 24   **25c.** $24,134.65   **27.** July 31, Aug 15   **29.** $1,599.04, $52.852.36

ASSESSMENT TEST

1. Sunshine Patio Furniture Manufacturers   **3.** 4387   **5.** $46.55   **7.** $2,558   **9.** $11,562.45
11. $1,485   **13.** 33.76%   **15.** Ideal Shoes, $340.56, Fancy Footwear, $335.30 (lower net price)   **17a.** .6052   **17b.** .3948   **19a.** April 24   **19b.** May 9   **19c.** May 15   **19d.** June 4

CHAPTER 8   MARKUP AND MARKDOWN

REVIEW EXERCISES   CHAPTER 8—SECTION I

1. $138.45, 85.7%   **3.** $6,944.80, 77.8%   **5.** $156.22, $93.73   **7.** $2,149, 159.2%
9. $.75, $1.33   **11.** $85.90   **13.** $195   **15a.** $4.19   **15b.** 71.7%   **17.** $21.88   **19.** $583.92
21a. $65.18   **21b.** 62.9%   **23.** $322.87

REVIEW EXERCISES   CHAPTER 8—SECTION II

1. $115, 43.5%   **3.** $61.36, $136.36   **5.** 37.5%   **7.** $94.74, 133%, 57.1%
9. $9,468.74, $24,917.74, 61.3%   **11.** 60%   **13a.** $335   **13b.** 38.3%   **15.** $366.12
17. $26.46   **19.** 75.4%   **21a.** $30.49   **21b.** 141.8%   **21c.** 58.6%   **23a.** 63.3%
23b. 172.5%

REVIEW EXERCISES   CHAPTER 8—SECTION III

1. $161.45, 15%   **3.** $1.68, 23.2%   **5.** $41.10, $16.44   **7.** $80.27, 30.7%   **9.** $559.96, $1,039.92   **11a.** $45.80   **11b.** 19.4%   **13.** $44.53   **15.** $249.98   **17.** $469.68
19. $233.99   **21.** $70, $100   **23.** $152.99, $169.99

ASSESSMENT TEST

1. $152.60   **3.** $18.58   **5a.** $81.50   **5b.** 71.6%   **5c.** 41.7%   **7.** $15.95   **9a.** $32.55
9b. 26.6%   **11.** $216.06   **13.** $124.20   **15a.** 44%   **15b.** 47.3%

CHAPTER 9   PAYROLL

REVIEW EXERCISES   CHAPTER 9—SECTION I

1. $1,250, $625, $576.92, $288.46   **3.** $8,333.33, $4,166.67, $3,846.15, $1,923.08
5. $34,800, $2,900, $1,338.46, $669.23   **7.** $17,420, $1,451.67, $725.83, $670
9. $166,666.67   **11.** $491.55   **13.** 36, 0, $205.20, 0, $205.20   **15.** 48, 8, $290, $87.04, $377.04   **17.** $572   **19.** $433   **21.** $739.90   **23.** $3,664.50   **25.** $3,336   **27.** $629.97

REVIEW EXERCISES CHAPTER 9—SECTION II

1. $51.15, social security; $11.96, Medicare **3a.** $372.00, social security; $87.00, Medicare
3b. November **3c.** $167.40, social security; $87.00, Medicare **5.** $212.16, $49.62
7. $208.94, $68.15 **9.** $117 **11.** $2,088.74 **13.** $85 **15.** $511 **17.** $161.41 **19.** $181.45

REVIEW EXERCISES CHAPTER 9—SECTION III

1a. $806, social security; $188.50, Medicare **1b.** $10,478, social security;
$2,450.50, Medicare **3.** $347.20, social security; $81.20, Medicare **5a.** $378 **5b.** $56
7a. $950.13, SUTA; $140.76, FUTA **7b.** $183.87, SUTA; $27.24, FUTA
9a. $27,949.80, 1st Qtr.; $20,175, 2nd, 3rd, and 4th Qtrs. **9b.** 1040-ES

ASSESSMENT TEST

1a. $67,200 **1b.** $2,584.62 **3.** $491.76 **5.** $32,275 **7.** $3,300.10 **9.** $2,284.10
11. $44.95, social security; $10.51, Medicare **13.** $97 **15a.** $1,704.54 **15b.** $1,783.82
15c. $2,029.79 **17a.** $1,693.03, social security; $395.95, Medicare
17b. $44,018.78, social security; $10,294.70, Medicare **19a.** $378 **19b.** $56
21a. $58,589.20 **21b.** 20.8% **21c.** $3,046,638.40

CHAPTER 10   SIMPLE INTEREST AND PROMISSORY NOTES

REVIEW EXERCISES CHAPTER 10—SECTION I

1. $800 **3.** $19,050 **5.** $206.62 **7.** $1,602.74, $1,625 **9.** $1,839.79, $1,865.34
11. $15.16, $15.38 **13.** $60.82, $61.67 **15.** $882.88, $895.15 **17.** $12,852, $66,852
19. $2,362.50, $36,112.50 **21.** $1,770 **23.** $1,330,000 **25.** 98 **27.** 289 **29.** Dec. 3
31. June 24 **33.** Feb. 23 **35.** $62,005.48 **37.** $403.89

REVIEW EXERCISES CHAPTER 10—SECTION II

1. $1,250 **3.** $50,000 **5.** $12,000 **7.** 14% **9.** 12.8% **11.** 158 days **13.** 308 days
15. 180 days **17.** $13,063.16, $13,403.16 **19.** $2,390.63, $27,890.63 **21a.** 166 days
21b. Sept. 29 **23.** $10,000 **25.** 11.6% **27.** $6,147.56 **29a.** 12.5 years **29b.** 10 years

REVIEW EXERCISES CHAPTER 10—SECTION III

1. $292.50, $4,207.50 **3.** $231.25, $1,618.75 **5.** $232.38, $7,567.62 **7.** 84 days, $171.50,
$4,828.50 **9.** 100 days, $34.31, $1,265.69 **11.** $132.30, $2,567.70, 14.72% **13.** $214.28,
$3,585.72, 15.37% **15.** $4,683.85, $52,816.15, 13.88% **17.** Jan. 31, $4,057.78, 12 days,
$4,037.49 **19a.** $23,533.33 **19b.** April 10 **21a.** Dec. 16 **21b.** $41,266.67
21c. Nov. 21 **21d.** $40,836.81

ASSESSMENT TEST

1. $641.10 **3.** $672.93 **5.** $24,648 **7.** 107 **9.** Jan. 24 **11.** $11,666.67 **13.** 9.1%
15. 72 days **17.** 190 days, $13,960 **19.** 15.2%, $2,795 **21.** Jan. 20, $20,088.54,
$854,911.46 **23.** $10,544.72, $279,455.28, 12.35% **25.** Aug. 25, $5,642.31, 34 days,
$5,569.30 **27.** $99.37 **29.** 15.3% **31.** $9,393.88 **33a.** $28,970.83 **33b.** Nov. 12
33c. 13.46%

CHAPTER 11 COMPOUND INTEREST AND PRESENT VALUE

REVIEW EXERCISES CHAPTER 11—SECTION I

1. 3, 13% **3.** 24, 4% **5.** 16, 3.5% **7.** 3, 3% **9.** $11,255.09, $1,255.09
11. $11,413.29, $4,413.29 **13.** $6,721.67, $1,421.67 **15.** $119,614.75, $94,614.75
17. $29,799.88, $20,999.88 **19.** 12.17216, $231,271.04 **21.** 132.78160, $1,327,816
23. $512.50, 10.25% **25.** $4,565.88, 12.68% **27a.** 6.14% **27b.** $4,288.50 **29.** $673,925

REVIEW EXERCISES CHAPTER 11—SECTION II

1. $4,633.08, $1,366.92 **3.** $437.43, $212.57 **5.** $3,680.50, $46,319.50 **7.** $6,107.07,
$3,692.93 **9.** $209.10, $40.90 **11.** .20829, $2,499.48 **13.** .24200, $338.80 **15.** .26356,
$28,991.60 **17a.** $2,549.58 **17b.** $950.42 **19a.** $10,927 **19b.** $14,073

ASSESSMENT TEST

1. $31,530.66, $17,530.66 **3.** $3,586.86, $586.86 **5.** 5.61652, $112,330.40 **7.** $1,078.06,
12.68% **9.** $6,930, $143,070 **11.** $658.35, 241.65 **13.** .62027, $806.35 **15.** $81,392.40,
$45,392.40 **17.** $17,150.85, compound amount; $2,150.85, compound interest
19. $32,342 **21a.** 12.55% **21b.** $17,888.55 **23.** $48,545.40

CHAPTER 12 ANNUITIES

REVIEW EXERCISES CHAPTER 12—SECTION I

1. $18,639.29 **3.** $151,929.30 **5.** $74,951.37 **7.** $13,680.33 **9.** $100,226.90
11. $2,543.20 **13a.** $39,620.37 **13b.** $104,157.75 **13c.** $209,282.37 **13d.** $42,122.67
15a. $34,784.89 **15b.** $81,669.67 **15c.** $82,486.37

REVIEW EXERCISES CHAPTER 12—SECTION II

1. $2,969.59 **3.** $27,096.86 **5.** $79,773.10 **7.** $16,819.32 **9.** $110,997.88
11. $9,025.15 **13.** $380,773 **15a.** $74,387.35 **15b.** $68,388.70 **15c.** $69,756.47

REVIEW EXERCISES CHAPTER 12—SECTION III

1. $2,113.50 **3.** $55.82 **5.** $859.13 **7.** $336.36 **9.** $1,087.48 **11.** $418.24
13a. $3,769.04 **13b.** $2,385.76 **15a.** $245,770.96 **15b.** $2,135,329.28 **17a.** $12,244.45
17b. $265,333

ASSESSMENT TEST

1. $121,687.44 **3.** $86,445.14 **5.** $42,646.92 **7.** $11,593.58 **9.** $993.02 **11.** $255.66
13. $20,345.57 **15.** $6,081.72 **17a.** $195,350.02 **17b.** $7,071.39 **19a.** $19,496.56
19b. $19,351.43 **21.** $1,678.39

CHAPTER 13   CONSUMER AND BUSINESS CREDIT

REVIEW EXERCISES   CHAPTER 13—SECTION I

1. 1.5%, $2.52, $335.90   **3.** 21%, $7.96, $544.32   **5a.** $1.20   **5b.** $259.13   **7.** $636.17, $11.13, $628.75   **9.** $817.08, $14.30, $684.76   **11.** $152.29   **13a.** $6.89   **13b.** $728.23 **15a.** $157.14   **15b.** $9,957.14   **15c.** $20,042.86

REVIEW EXERCISES   CHAPTER 13—SECTION II

1. $1,050, $582, $1,982   **3.** $10,800, $2,700, $14,700   **5.** $7,437.50, $2,082.34, $10,832.34 **7.** $1,350, $270, $67.50   **9.** $15,450, $8,652, $502.13   **11.** $322, $14, 13%   **13.** $223.50, $12.02, 14.75%   **15.** $31, 11.25%   **17.** $4,940, 16.6%   **19.** 29.97, $1,498.50, $135.39 **21.** 6.20, $111.60, $159.30   **23.** 8, 36, 78, $\frac{36}{78}$ **25.** 15, 120, 300, $\frac{120}{300}$ **27.** $\frac{120}{300}$, $360, $2,077.50   **29.** $\frac{78}{1,176}$, $219.94, $2,984.06   **31a.** $411.30   **31b.** $2,310.30   **33.** $34.92 **35a.** $1,667.68   **35b.** 14.5%   **37.** $216.45, finance charge, $63.19, monthly payment **39a.** 300   **39b.** 465   **41a.** $504.00   **41b.** $152.25   **41c.** 14.75%, table; 14.64%, formula **41d.** $1,157.52

ASSESSMENT TEST

1a. 1.33%   **1b.** $4.59   **1c.** $440.38   **3.** $4.46, $724.12   **5.** $839.64, $14.02, $859.61 **7a.** $694.76   **7b.** $7.50   **7c.** $864.74   **9a.** $9,920   **9b.** $39,120   **11a.** $10,384 **11b.** 19.25%   **13a.** $66,300   **13b.** $4,646.67   **15a.** $14,144   **15b.** $1,428   **15c.** 11.75% **15d.** $32,906.45   **17a.** 14.68%   **17b.** $51,480   **17c.** $11,581.79

CHAPTER 14   MORTGAGES

REVIEW EXERCISES   CHAPTER 14—SECTION I

1. 80, 9.00, $720, $92,800   **3.** 130.9, 8.06, $1,055.05, $185,615.00   **5.** 96.8, 7.17, $694.06, $153,061.60   **7.** $639.47, $821.39   **9.** $1,189.79, $1,601.21   **11a.** 7.25% **11b.** 15.25% **13a.** Fortune Bank, $115,950; Northern Trust Bank, $120,000   **13b.** Fortune Bank, $120,450; Northern Trust Bank, $120,000 (better deal by $450.00)   **15a.** $2,512.08 **15b.** $150,400   **15c.** $51,495   **15d.** $15,275

REVIEW EXERCISES   CHAPTER 14—SECTION II

1. $89,025, $21,125   **3.** $112,960, $13,860.00   **5.** $63,700, 0   **7.** 14.32%, 24.05% **9.** 26.04%, 35%   **11a.** Johnson and Turnberry   **11b.** Johnson and Turnberry **13.** no, potential credit only $19,200

ASSESSMENT TEST

1. 134.9, 7.56, $1,019.84, $171,052   **3.** monthly payment, $1,447.85; loan balance after 3 payments, $145,955.46   **5.** $1,321.00, $1,596.67   **7.** $41,200, $13,800 **9.** 24.3%, 40.15%   **11.** Morgan, FHA; Willow, FHA and conventional   **13a.** $5,194.80 **13b.** loan balance after 2 payments, $518,704.76   **13c.** $6,147.30   **13d.** $4,052.70 **15a.** Red River Bank, $946,368; Sterling Savings & Loan, $919,584 **15b.** Sterling is a better deal by $9,346.50   **17.** 0   **19a.** 27.86%   **19b.** 39.53%   **19c.** FHA

CHAPTER 15 FINANCIAL STATEMENTS AND RATIOS

REVIEW EXERCISES CHAPTER 15—SECTION I

1. $161,600 **3.** $29,000 **5.** current asset **7.** owner's equity **9.** long-term liability
11. current liability **13.** current asset **15.** current asset **17.** fixed asset **19.** current asset
21. owner's equity **23.** owner's equity **25.** current liability

27a.

Northern Industries, Inc.
Balance Sheet
June 30, 1995

Assets

Current Assets		Percent
Cash	$ 44,300	5.5
Accounts Receivable	127,600	15.8
Merchandise Inventory	88,100	10.9
Prepaid Maintenance	4,100	.5
Office Supplies	4,000	.5
Total Current Assets	268,100	33.2
Property, Plant and Equipment		
Land	154,000	19.0
Buildings	237,000	29.3
Fixtures	21,400	2.6
Vehicles	64,000	7.9
Computers	13,000	1.6
Total Property, Plant and Equipment	489,400	60.4
Investments and Other Assets		
Investments	32,000	4.0
Goodwill	20,000	2.5
Total Assets	$809,500	100%

Liabilities and Owner's Equity

Current Liabilities		
Accounts Payable	55,700	6.9
Salaries Payable	23,200	2.9
Notes Payable	38,000	4.7
Total Current Liabilities	116,900	14.5
Long-Term Liabilities		
Mortgage Payable	91,300	11.3
Debenture Bonds	165,000	20.4
Total Long-Term Liabilities	256,300	31.7
Total Liabilities	373,200	46.2
Owner's Equity		
Common Stock	350,000	43.2
Retained Earnings	86,300	10.7
Total Owner's Equity	436,300	53.9
Total Liabilities and Owner's Equity	$809,500	100%

*Percents may vary by .1 due to rounding

27b.

Northern Industries, Inc.
Comparative Balance Sheet
June 30, 1995 and 1996

Assets	1996	1995	Increase/Decrease Amount	Increase/Decrease Percent
Current Assets				
Cash	$ 40,200	$ 44,300	($4,100)	(9.3)
Accounts Receivable	131,400	127,600	3,800	3.0
Merchandise Inventory	92,200	88,100	4,100	4.7
Prepaid Maintenance	3,700	4,100	(400)	(9.8)
Office Supplies	6,200	4,000	2,200	55.0
Total Current Assets	273,700	268,100	5,600	2.1
Property, Plant and Equipment				
Land	154,000	154,000	0	0
Buildings	231,700	237,000	(5,300)	(2.2)
Fixtures	23,900	21,400	2,500	11.7
Vehicles	55,100	64,000	(8,900)	(13.9)
Computers	16,800	13,000	3,800	29.2
Total Property, Plant and Equipment	481,500	489,400	7,900	1.6
Investments and Other Assets				
Investments	36,400	32,000	4,400	13.8
Goodwill	22,000	20,000	2,000	10.0
Total Assets	$813,600	$809,500	4,100	.5
Liabilities and Owner's Equity				
Current Liabilities				
Accounts Payable	51,800	55,700	(3,900)	(7.0)
Salaries Payable	25,100	23,200	1,900	8.2
Notes Payable	19,000	38,000	(19,000)	(50.0)
Total Current Liabilities	95,900	116,900	(21,000)	(18.0)
Long-Term Liabilities				
Mortgage Payable	88,900	91,300	(2,400)	(2.6)
Debenture Bonds	165,000	165,000	0	0
Total Long-Term Liabilities	253,900	256,300	(2,400)	(.9)
Total Liabilities				
Owner's Equity	349,800	373,200	(23,400)	(6.3)
Common Stock	350,000	350,000	0	0
Retained Earnings	113,800	86,300	27,500	31.9
Total Owner's Equity	463,800	436,300	27,500	6.3
Total Liabilities and Owner's Equity	$813,600	$809,500	4,100	.5

1. $202,200, $94,200   **3.** $675,530, $334,160   **5a.** $316,120   **5b.** $122,680   **5c.** $212,320
5d. $45,120

7a.

Tasty Treats Food Wholesalers, Inc.
Income Statement
For the year ended December 31, 1996

Revenue		
Gross Sales	$2,249,000	109.6
Less: Sales Returns and Allowances	143,500	7.0
Sales Discounts	54,290	2.6
Net Sales	$2,051,210	100.0
Cost of Goods sold		
Merchandise Inventory, Jan.1	875,330	42.7
Net Purchases	546,920	26.7
Freight In	11,320	.6
Goods Available for Sale	1,433,570	69.9
Less: Merchandise Inventory, Dec. 31	716,090	34.9
Cost of Goods Sold	717,480	35.0
Gross Margin	1,333,730	65.0
Operating Expenses		
Salaries	319,800	15.6
Rent	213,100	10.4
Depreciation	51,200	2.5
Utilities	35,660	1.7
Advertising	249,600	12.2
Insurance	39,410	1.9
Administrative Expenses	91,700	4.5
Miscellaneous Expenses	107,500	5.2
Total Operating Expenses	1,107,970	54.0
Income before Taxes	225,760	11.0
Income Tax	38,450	1.9
Net Income	$ 187,310	9.1

7b.

Tasty Treats Food Wholesalers, Inc.
Comparative Income Statement
For the years ended December 31, 1996 and 1997

	1997	1996	Increase/Decrease Amount	Increase/Decrease Percent
Revenue				
Gross Sales	$2,125,000	$2,249,000	($124,000)	(5.5)
Less: Sales Returns and Allowances	126,400	143,500	(17,100)	(11.9)
Sales Discounts	73,380	54,290	19,090	35.2
Net Sales	1,925,220	2,051,210	(125,990)	(6.1)
Cost of Goods Sold				
Merchandise Inventory, Jan. 1	716,090	875,330	(159,240)	(18.2)
Net Purchases	482,620	546,920	(64,300)	(11.8)
Freight In	9,220	11,320	(2,100)	(18.6)
Goods Available for Sale	1,207,930	1,433,570	(225,640)	(15.7)
Less: Merchandise Inventory, Dec. 31	584,550	716,090	(131,540)	(18.4)
Cost of Goods Sold	623,380	717,480	(94,100)	(13.1)
Gross Margin	1,301,840	1,333,730	(31,890)	(2.4)
Operating Expenses				
Salaries	340,900	319,800	21,100	7.0
Rent	215,000	213,100	1,900	.9
Depreciation	56,300	51,200	5,100	10.0
Utilities	29,690	35,660	(5,970)	(16.7)
Advertising	217,300	249,600	(32,300)	(13.0)
Insurance	39,410	39,410	0	0
Administrative Expenses	95,850	91,700	4,150	4.5
Miscellaneous Expenses	102,500	107,500	(5,000)	(4.7)
Total Operating Expenses	1,096,950	1,107,970	(11,020)	(1.0)
Income before Income Tax	204,890	225,760	(20,870)	(9.2)
Income Tax	44,530	38,450	6,080	15.8
Net Income	$ 160,360	$ 187,310	(26,950)	(14.4)

REVIEW EXERCISES CHAPTER 15—SECTION III

1. $51,160, 1.69:1   **3.** $2,350, 2.88:1   **5.** $95,920, 1.29:1   **7.** $2,165, 1.73:1   **9.** 44 days
11. $105,650, 6.2 times   **13.** $74,447.50, 6.6 times   **15.** .58:1   **17.** $155,390, .7:1, 2.3:1
19. $253,940, $78,530, 34.2%, 10.6%   **21.** $113,080, $27,159, 35.7%, 8.6%   **23.** 8.2%

25.

King Tire Company
Trend Analysis Chart

	1996	1995	1994	1993	1992
Net Sales	107.5	127.3	108.0	97.	100.0
Net Income	124.3	128.5	99.4	104.2	100.0
Total Assets	109.7	107.4	105.0	97.7	100.0
Stockholder's Equity	105.9	120.3	106.4	94.5	100.0

ASSESSMENT TEST

1a.

Service Master Carpet Cleaning
Balance Sheet
December 31, 1996

Assets		Percent
Current Assets	$132,500	52.2
Property, Plant and Equipment	88,760	35.0
Investments and Other Assets	32,400	12.8
Total Assets	$253,660	100%
Liabilities		
Current Liabilities	51,150	20.2
Long-Term Liabilities	87,490	34.5
Total Liabilities	138,640	54.7
Owner's Equity		
Al Mosley, Equity	115,020	45.3
Total Liabilities and Owner's Equity	$253,660	100%

1b.

Service Master Carpet Cleaning
Comparative Balance Sheet
December 31, 1996 and 1997

	1997	1996	Increase/Decrease Amount	Increase/Decrease Percent
Assets				
Current Assets	$154,300	$132,500	$21,800	16.5
Property, Plant and Equipment	124,650	88,760	35,890	40.4
Investments and Other Assets	20,000	32,400	(12,400)	(38.3)
Total Assets	$298,950	$253,660	45,290	17.9
Liabilities				
Current Liabilities	65,210	51,150	14,060	27.5
Long-Term Liabilities	83,800	87,490	(3,690)	(4.2)
Total Liabilities	149,010	138,640	10,370	7.5
Owner's Equity				
Al Mosley Equity	149,940	115,020	34,920	30.4
Total Liabilities and Owner's Equity	$298,950	$253,660	45,290	17.9

3. $185,772

5a.

Abbey Road Restaurant Supply
Income Statement
Third Quarter, 1997

Revenue		
Gross Sales	$224,400	106.8
Less: Sales Returns and Allowances	14,300	6.8
Net Sales	210,100	100.0
Cost of Goods sold		
Merchandise Inventory, July 1	165,000	78.5
Net Purchases	76,500	36.4
Goods Available for Sale	241,500	114.9
Less: Merchandise Inventory, Sept. 30	143,320	68.2
Cost of Goods Sold	98,180	46.7
Gross Margin	111,920	53.3
Operating Expenses	68,600	32.7
Income before Taxes	43,320	20.6
Income Tax	8,790	4.2
Net Income	$ 34,530	16.4

5b.

Abbey Road Restaurant Supply
Comparative Income Statement
Third and Fourth Quarter - 1997

			Increase/Decrease	
	4th Qtr.	**3rd Qtr.**	**Amount**	**Percent**
Revenue				
Gross Sales	$218,200	$224,400	($6,200)	(2.8)
Less: Sales Returns and Allowances	9,500	14,300	(4,800)	(33.6)
Net Sales	208,700	210,100	1,400	.7
Cost of Goods Sold				
Merchandise Inventory, Beginning	143,320	165,000	(21,680)	(13.1)
Net Purchases	81,200	76,500	4,700	6.1
Goods Available for Sale	224,520	241,500	(16,980)	(7.0)
Less: Merchandise Inventory, Ending	125,300	143,320	(18,020)	(12.6)
Cost of Goods Sold	99,220	98,180	1,040	1.0
Gross Margin	109,480	111,920	(2,440)	(2.2)
Operating Expenses	77,300	68,600	8,700	12.7
Income before Income Tax	32,180	43,320	(11,140)	(25.7)
Income Tax	11,340	8,790	2,550	29.0
Net Income	$ 20,840	$ 34,530	(13,690)	(39.6)

7. $653,300   **9.** 1.02:1   **11.** 1.74 times   **13.** 37.9%   **15.** 48.3%
17. 4.2%

13.

Custom Concrete, Inc.
Depreciation Schedule, MACRS
Cement Manufacturing Equipment

End of Year	Original Basis (cost)	Cost Recovery Percentage	Cost Recovery (depreciation)	Accumulated Depreciation	Book Value
				(new)	$320,000
1	$320,000	5	$16,000	$16,000	304,000
2	320,000	9.5	30,400	46,400	273,600
3	320,000	8.55	27,360	73,760	246,240
4	320,000	7.70	24,640	98,400	221,600
5	320,000	6.93	22,176	120,576	199,424

CHAPTER 18   TAXES

REVIEW EXERCISES   CHAPTER 18—SECTION I

1. $.59, $9.54   **3.** $.32, $5.20   **5.** $100.80, $15.84, $1,556.64   **7.** $9.90, $22, $251.85
9. $17,847.98, $937.02   **11a.** $70.19   **11b.** $1,045.09   **13a.** $54,871.09   **13b.** $3,017.91
15. $922,140

REVIEW EXERCISES   CHAPTER 18—SECTION II

1. $76,000, $2,614.40   **3.** $198,400, $5,138.56   **5.** $106,440, $2,267.17   **7.** $264,033,
$13,993.75   **9.** 4.92%, $4.92, $49.20, 49.2   **11.** 3.69%, $3.69, $36.90, 36.9   **13a.** $87,500
13b. $1,701   **15a.** $4,078.80   **15b.** $163.15   **15c.** $4,221.56

REVIEW EXERCISES   CHAPTER 18—SECTION III

1. $32,180, $3,900, $4,450, $2,500, $25,230   **3.** $43,910, $6,550, $5,000, $32,360
5. $6,780, $3,275, $5,000, $51,155   **7.** $4,080, $5,750, $21,230, $7,500, $55,790
9. $33,807   **11.** $16,889   **13.** $14,509   **15.** $78,513.34   **17.** $120,312.19   **19.** refund,
$651   **21.** refund, $1,438   **23.** $18,494.70, $70,460.30   **25.** $334,250,000, $620,750,000

ASSESSMENT TEST

1. $1.17, $19.05   **3.** $6.62, $141.62   **5.** $1,184.63, $755, $19,489.63   **7a.** $25.42
7b. $471.30   **9a.** $3.83, $2,221.40   **9b.** $7.50, $4,350   **9c.** $55,871.40   **11.** $52,101,
$662.72   **13.** $82,615, $2,394.18   **15.** 1.64%, $1.64, $16.40, 16.4   **17a.** .07%   **17b.** $.07
17c. $.70   **17d.** .7   **19.** $66,003, $6,550, $7,500, $49,773   **21.** $53,255.32   **23.** $3,739
25. $72,303.13   **27.** owe, $228   **29a.** $33,650   **29b.** $24,750   **29c.** $2,137
29d. $1,763 refund

CHAPTER 19   INSURANCE

REVIEW EXERCISES   CHAPTER 19—SECTION I

1. $79.50, $41.34, $20.67, $7.16   **3.** $842, $437.84, $218.92, $75.78   **5.** $270, $140.40,
$70.20, $24.30   **7.** $1,125.25, $585.13, $292.57, $101.27   **9.** $4,900, $9,300, 17 years,
54 days   **11.** $5,495.00, $10,990, 21 years, 218 days   **13a.** $5,240.40   **13b.** $2,725.01
15. $14,325.00 cash value; $37,200 reduced paid-up ins.; 30 years, 206 days extended term
17a. $60,000 10-year term, $21,000 whole life   **17b.** $39,000   **17c.** $2,058 cash value;
$3,906 reduced paid-up ins.; 17 years, 54 days extended term

REVIEW EXERCISES CHAPTER 19—SECTION II

1. $668.80, $174.30, $843.10   **3.** $451.50, $69.60, $521.10   **5.** $2,132.10, $438.90, $2,571
7. $89.60, $470.40   **9.** $134.17, $187.83   **11.** $75,000   **13.** $37,000   **15.** $150,000
17. $202.50   **19.** Aetna: $57,000, State Farm: $23,750, Liberty Mutual: $14,250

REVIEW EXERCISES CHAPTER 19—SECTION III

1. $343   **3.** $1,125   **5.** $625.60   **7.** $1,146.60   **9.** $1,412   **11a.** Hart: $13,500, Black:
$11,700, Garner: $4,140, Williams: $50,000, Morgan: $3,590, bus: $12,230, camper: $3,530
11b. Williams: $7,800, deductible: $250

ASSESSMENT TEST

1. $2,521.60, $1,311.23, $655.62, $226.94   **3.** $148.20, $77.06, $38.53, $13.34   **5.** $20,410
cash value, $40,820 reduced paid-up ins.; 21 years, 218 days extended term   **7a.** $1,088.00
7b. $97.92   **7c.** $87.04   **9.** $512.000   **11.** $475, $672, $1,147   **13.** $173.33, $86.67
15. $6,057.69   **17.** $12,392   **19.** $153,000   **21.** $361.80   **23.** $564.40
25a. Goya: $45,000, Truman: $50,000, Copeland: $5,000, Kelly: 0, Winston's car: $3,650
25b. Truman: $18,000, Copeland: $11,000, Kelly: $11,000, deductible: $250

CHAPTER 20   INVESTMENTS

REVIEW EXERCISES CHAPTER 20—SECTION I

1. none, $.60   **3.** $5.00, 0   **5.** 0, 0   **7.** TTC, 18, $25\frac{3}{4}$ **9.** 0, 900,900, $34\frac{1}{2}$ **11.** 3.5%, 7

13. $1.31, 1.6%   **15.** $1.41, $.30   **17.** $6,524.38, $9,975.31, $3,450.93   **19.** $29,526.56,
$26,501.21, ($3,025.35)   **21.** $.85   **23a.** $27,000,000   **23b.** $1.74   **25a.** $29,658.56
25b. $32,195.97   **25c.** $2,537.41

REVIEW EXERCISES CHAPTER 20—SECTION II

1. $8\frac{3}{8}$%, 8.4%   **3.** 2016, 315   **5.** $12\frac{5}{8}$%, 2005, none   **7.** Kmart, LglsLt7.3s99

9. Kroger$6\frac{3}{8}$99, down 5   **11.** $9.17, $876.67   **13.** $34.90, $7,959.20   **15.** $16.56, $11,433.10

17. $28.33, $4,429.32   **19.** $8.13, $6,262.41   **21.** $66.25, 7.3%   **23.** $75, 6%
25. $53.75, 6.4%

REVIEW EXERCISES CHAPTER 20—SECTION III

1. $12.74, 1.2%   **3.** −0.03, +10.2%   **5.** GVScp, E   **7.** no load   **9.** $13.35, $12.82,
$.53, 4.1%   **11.** $26.97, $25.69, $1.28, 5%   **13.** $15.54, 621.118   **15.** $10.68, 4,484.305
17. $1,530, $1,880, $395, 25.8%   **19.** $4,850, $6,120, $2,520, 52%   **21a.** $.75   **21b.** 6.1%
23. 689.655

ASSESSMENT TEST

1. none, \$.36 **3.** \$15, \$.09 **5.** \$.16, .5%, $29\frac{1}{2}$ **7.** 0, 39, 100, $31\frac{3}{4}$ **9.** \$2.09, 3.3%

11. \$8.98, \$1.71 **13.** \$15,661.95, \$12,139.65, (\$3,522.30) **15.** \$39,277.88, \$44,975.31, \$5,697.43 **17a.** \$13,000,000 **17b.** \$.71 **19a.** \$4,470.47 **19b.** \$3,345.16

19c. (\$1,125.31) **21.** $98\frac{3}{4}$, $-1\frac{3}{4}$ **23.** 39, $84\frac{1}{2}$ **25.** ATT $4\frac{3}{8}$99 **27.** \$20.49, \$4,074.95

29. \$2.05, \$9,410.50 **31.** \$21.84, \$4,969.20 **33.** \$95, 9% **35.** stocks & bonds, \$14.44, D
37. \$10.36, −0.01, 7.3% **39.** \$10.88, \$10.36, \$.52, 5% **41.** \$7.05, 6,410.256
43. \$1,340, \$1,180, (\$85), −6.3% **45.** \$9,400, \$12,820, \$4,380, 46.6%
47. \$9.04 **49.** 33.6%

CHAPTER 21   BUSINESS STATISTICS AND DATA PRESENTATION

REVIEW EXERCISES   CHAPTER 21—SECTION I

1.

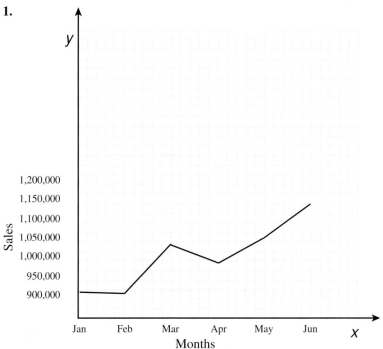

3.

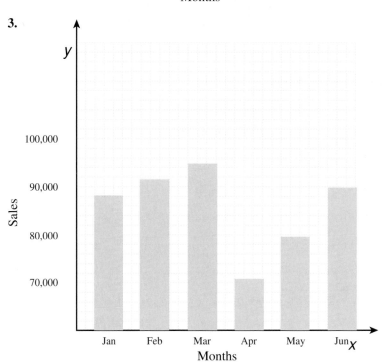

5.

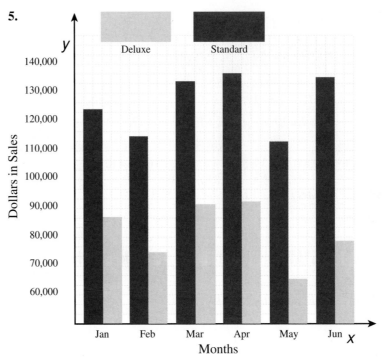

7.

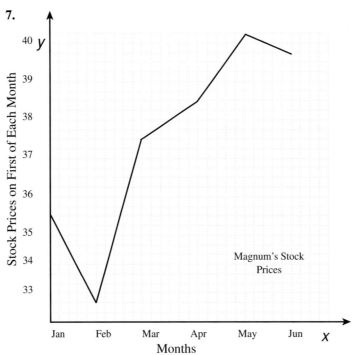

REVIEW EXERCISES CHAPTER 21—SECTION II

1. 5.8 **3.** 2 **5.** $2.88 **7.** 21 **9.** 4 and 9 **11.** $3.66 **13a.** 339.9 **13b.** 343 **13c.** 425
13d. 221 **15a.** small van: 86.8, large van: 140.6 **15b.** small truck: 288, large truck: 339
15c. 189 **15d.** 238 **15e.** 86 and 290 **15f.** 293

1a.

Class	Tally	Frequency
1–99	IIII	4
100–199	‖‖‖	5
200–299	‖‖‖ I	6
300–399	‖‖‖ IIII	9
400–499	III	3
500–599	III	2
600–699	I	1

1b.

Class	Tally	Frequency (f)	Midpoint (m)	f × m
1–99	IIII	4	49.5	198
100–199	‖‖‖	5	149.5	747.5
200–299	‖‖‖ I	6	249.5	1,497
300–399	‖‖‖ IIII	9	349.5	3,145.5
400–499	III	3	449.5	1,348.5
500–599	II	2	549.5	1,099
600–699	I	1	649.5	649.5
		30		8,685.

$$\text{Mean} = \frac{8,685}{30} = 289.5$$

1c.

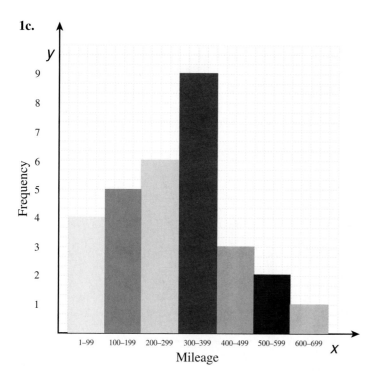

1a.

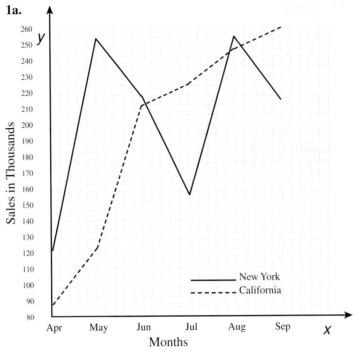

1b.

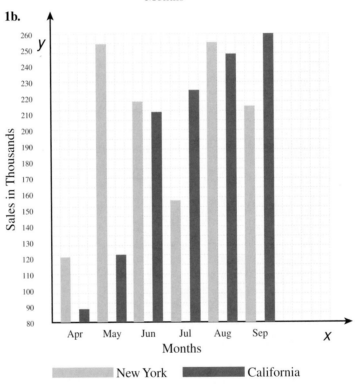

3a. standard: 50%, portable: 25%, software: 10%, printers: 12.5%, accessories: 2.5%

3b.

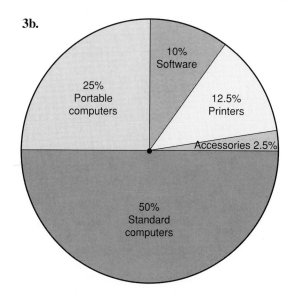

5a. range: 78, mode: 72

5b.

Class	Tally	Frequency
11–20	I	1
21–30	I	1
31–40	I	1
41–50	II	2
51–60	IIII	4
61–70	ⅢⅡ	5
71–80	ⅢⅡ ⅢⅡ	10
81–90	ⅢⅡ ⅢⅡ	10
91–100	ⅢⅡ I	6

5c. mean = 72.5   **5d.** 14

5e.

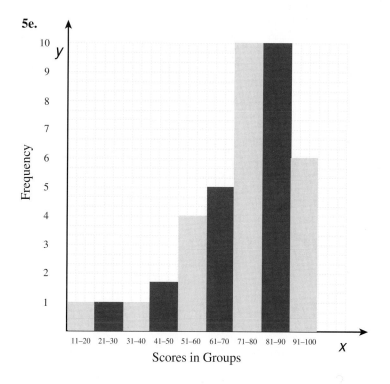

Appendix C

Worked-out Solutions

CHAPTER 5   USING EQUATIONS TO SOLVE BUSINESS PROBLEMS

REVIEW EXERCISES   CHAPTER 5—SECTION I

1.
$$B + 11 = 24$$
$$\underline{-11 \quad -11}$$
$$B \quad = 13$$
Proof:
$$13 + 11 = 24$$
$$\underline{24 = 24}$$

2.
$$C - 16 = 5$$
$$\underline{+16 \quad +16}$$
$$C \quad = 21$$
Proof:
$$21 - 16 = 5$$
$$\underline{5 = 5}$$

3.
$$S + 35 = 125$$
$$\underline{-35 \quad -35}$$
$$S \quad = 90$$
Proof:
$$90 + 35 = 125$$
$$\underline{125 = 125}$$

4.
$$M - 58 = 12$$
$$\underline{+58 \quad +58}$$
$$M \quad = 70$$
Proof:
$$70 - 58 = 12$$
$$\underline{12 = 12}$$

5.
$$21K = 63$$
$$\frac{21K}{21} = \frac{63}{21}$$
$$K = 3$$
Proof:
$$21(3) = 63$$
$$\underline{63 = 63}$$

6.
$$\frac{Z}{3} = 45$$
$$(3)\frac{Z}{3} = 45(3)$$
$$Z = 135$$
Proof:
$$\frac{135}{3} = 45$$
$$\underline{45 = 45}$$

7.
$$50Y = 375$$
$$\frac{50Y}{50} = \frac{375}{50}$$
$$Y = 7\frac{1}{2}$$
Proof: $50\left(7\frac{1}{2}\right) = 375$
$$\underline{375 = 375}$$

8.
$$\frac{L}{5} = 8$$
$$(5)\frac{L}{5} = 8(5)$$
$$L = 40$$
Proof: $\frac{40}{5} = 8$
$$\underline{8 = 8}$$

9.
$$6G + 5 = 29$$
$$\underline{-5 \quad -5}$$
$$6G \quad = 24$$
$$\frac{6G}{6} = \frac{24}{6}$$
$$G = 4$$
Proof:
$$6(4) + 5 = 29$$
$$24 + 5 = 29$$
$$\underline{29 = 29}$$

10.
$$\frac{D}{3} - 5 = 15$$
$$\underline{+5 \quad +5}$$
$$\frac{D}{3} = 20$$
$$(3)\frac{D}{3} = 20(3)$$
$$D = 60$$
Proof:
$$\frac{60}{3} - 5 = 15$$
$$20 - 5 = 15$$
$$\underline{15 = 15}$$

11.
$$25A - 11 = 64$$
$$\underline{+11 \quad +11}$$
$$25A \quad = 75$$
$$\frac{25A}{25} = \frac{75}{25}$$
$$A = 3$$
Proof:
$$25(3) - 11 = 64$$
$$75 - 11 = 64$$
$$\underline{64 = 64}$$

12.
$$\frac{R}{5} + 33 = 84$$
$$\underline{-33 \quad -33}$$
$$\frac{R}{5} = 51$$
$$(5)\frac{R}{5} = 51(5)$$
$$R = 255$$
Proof:
$$\frac{255}{5} + 33 = 84$$
$$51 + 33 = 84$$
$$\underline{84 = 84}$$

13.
$$3(4X + 5) = 63$$
$$12X + 15 = 63$$
$$\underline{-15 \quad -15}$$
$$12X \quad = 48$$
$$\frac{12X}{12} = \frac{48}{12}$$
$$X = 4$$
Proof:
$$3(4(4) + 5) = 63$$
$$3(16 + 5) = 63$$
$$3(21) = 63$$
$$\underline{63 = 63}$$

14.
$$C + 5 = 26 - 2C$$
$$\underline{+2C \qquad +2C}$$
$$3C + 5 = 26$$
$$\underline{-5 \quad -5}$$
$$3C = 21$$
$$\frac{3C}{3} = \frac{21}{3}$$
$$C = 7$$
Proof:
$$7 + 5 = 26 - 2(7)$$
$$12 = 26 - 14$$
$$\underline{12 = 12}$$

15.
$$12(2D - 4) = 72$$
$$24D - 48 = 72$$
$$\underline{+48 \quad +48}$$
$$24D \quad = 120$$
$$\frac{24D}{24} = \frac{120}{24}$$
$$D = 5$$
Proof: $12(2(5) - 4) = 72$
$$12(10 - 4) = 72$$
$$12(6) = 72$$
$$\underline{72 = 72}$$

16.
$$14V + 5 - 5V = 4(V + 5)$$
$$9V + 5 = 4V + 20$$
$$\underline{-4V \qquad -4V}$$
$$5V + 5 = 20$$
$$\underline{-5 \quad -5}$$
$$5V = 15$$
$$\frac{5V}{5} = \frac{15}{5}$$
$$V = 3$$
Proof:
$$14(3) + 5 - 5(3) = 4(3 + 5)$$
$$42 + 5 - 15 = 4(8)$$
$$\underline{32 = 32}$$

17.
$$Q + 20 = 3(9 - 2Q)$$
$$Q + 20 = 27 - 6Q$$
$$\underline{+6Q \qquad +6Q}$$
$$7Q + 20 = 27$$
$$\underline{-20 \quad -20}$$
$$7Q = 7$$
$$\frac{7Q}{7} = \frac{7}{7}$$
$$Q = 1$$
Proof:
$$1 + 20 = 3(9 - 2(1))$$
$$21 = 3(7)$$
$$\underline{21 = 21}$$

ASSESSMENT TEST

1. $T + 45 = 110$ *Proof:*

$$\frac{-45 \quad -45}{T \quad = 65} \qquad \boxed{65} + 45 = 110$$

$$110 = 110$$

2. $G - 24 = 75$ *Proof:*

$$\frac{+24 \quad +24}{G \quad = 99} \qquad \boxed{99} - 24 = 75$$

$$75 = 75$$

3. $\dfrac{\cancel{11}K}{\cancel{11}} = \dfrac{165}{11}$ *Proof:*

$$K = 15 \qquad 11(\boxed{15}) = 165$$

$$165 = 165$$

4. $3(2C - 5) = 45$ $\dfrac{\cancel{6}C}{\cancel{6}} = \dfrac{60}{6}$ *Proof:*

$$6C - 15 = 45 \qquad C = 10 \qquad 3(2(\boxed{10}) - 5) = 45$$

$$\frac{+15 \quad +15}{6C \quad = 60} \qquad\qquad\qquad 3(20 - 5) = 45$$

$$3(15) = 45$$

$$45 = 45$$

5. $8X - 15 = 49$ $\dfrac{\cancel{8}X}{\cancel{8}} = \dfrac{64}{8}$ *Proof:*

$$\frac{+15 \quad +15}{8X \quad = 64} \qquad X = 8 \qquad 8(\boxed{8}) - 15 = 49$$

$$64 - 15 = 49$$

$$49 = 49$$

6. $\dfrac{S}{7} = 12$ *Proof:* $\dfrac{84}{7} = 12$

$$(\cancel{7})\dfrac{S}{\cancel{7}} = 12(7) \qquad 12 = 12$$

$$S = 84$$

7. $B + 5 = 61 - 6B$ $7B + 5 = 61$ $\dfrac{\cancel{7}B}{\cancel{7}} = \dfrac{56}{7}$ *Proof:*

$$\frac{+6B \qquad\quad +6B}{7B + 5 = 61} \qquad \frac{-5 \quad -5}{7B = 56} \qquad B = 8 \qquad \boxed{8} + 5 = 61 - 6(8)$$

$$13 = 61 - 48$$

$$13 = 13$$

8. $\dfrac{N}{4} - 7 = 8$ $(\cancel{4})\dfrac{N}{\cancel{4}} = 15(4)$ *Proof:* $\dfrac{60}{4} - 7 = 8$

$$\frac{+7 \quad +7}{\dfrac{N}{4} \quad = 15} \qquad N = 60 \qquad 15 - 7 = 8$$

$$8 = 8$$

9. $4(3X + 8) = 212$ $\dfrac{\cancel{12}X}{\cancel{12}} = \dfrac{180}{12}$ *Proof:*

$$12X + 32 = 212 \qquad X = 15 \qquad 4(3(\boxed{15}) + 8) = 212$$

$$\frac{-32 \quad -32}{12X \quad = 180} \qquad\qquad 4(45 + 8) = 212$$

$$4(53) = 212$$

$$212 = 212$$

CHAPTER 7   INVOICES, TRADE AND CASH DISCOUNTS

REVIEW EXERCISES   CHAPTER 7—SECTION II

10. $100\% - 37\% = \underline{63\%}$ $\$3,499.00 \times .63 = \underline{\$2,204.37}$

11. $100\% - 24\% = \underline{76\%}$ $\$565.33 \times .76 = \underline{\$429.65}$

12. $100\% - 45.8\% = \underline{54.2\%}$ $\$1,244.25 \times .542 = \underline{\$674.38}$

13. $100\% - 12.75\% = \underline{87.25\%}$ $\$4.60 \times .8725 = \underline{\$4.01}$

14. $\$4,500.00 - 3,565.00 = \$935.00$ $\dfrac{935.00}{4,500.00} = .2077 = \underline{20.8\%}$

15. $\$345.50 - 225.00 = \$120.50$ $\dfrac{120.50}{345.50} = .3487 = \underline{34.9\%}$

16. $\$2.89 - 2.15 = \$.74$ $\dfrac{.74}{2.89} = .2560 = \underline{25.6\%}$

REVIEW EXERCISES   CHAPTER 7—SECTION III

12.

Net Price Factor	Single Equivalent Discount	Trade Discount	Net Price
$.85 \times .95 \times .95$ $\underline{.76713}$	$1.00 - .76713$ $.23287$	$\$7,800.00$ $\times .23287$ $\overline{\$1,816.39}$	$\$7,800.00$ $\times .76713$ $\overline{\$5,983.61}$

1. CD = $\$15,800.00 \times .03 = \underline{\underline{\$474.00}}$
  NAD = $\$15,800.00 - \$474.00 = \underline{\underline{\$15,326.00}}$

3. CD = $\$2,421.00 \times .04 = \underline{\underline{\$96.84}}$
  NAD = $\$2,421.00 - \$96.84 = \underline{\underline{\$2,324.16}}$

5. CD = $\$9,121.44 \times .035 = \underline{\underline{\$319.25}}$
  NAD = $\$9,121.44 - \$319.25 = \underline{\underline{\$8,802.19}}$

7. Credit for partial payment = $\dfrac{\$460}{.97} = \underline{\underline{\$474.23}}$
  NAD = $\$1,344.60 - \$474.23 = \underline{\underline{\$870.37}}$

9. Credit for partial payment = $\dfrac{\$5,500}{.955} = \underline{\underline{\$5,759.16}}$
  NAD = $\$7,232.08 - \$5,759.16 = \underline{\underline{\$1,472.92}}$

2. CD = $\$12,660.00 \times .02 = \underline{\underline{\$253.20}}$
  NAD = $\$12,660.00 - \$253.20 = \underline{\underline{\$12,406.80}}$

4. CD = $\$6,940.20 \times .02 = \underline{\underline{\$138.80}}$
  NAD = $\$6,940.20 - \$138.80 = \underline{\underline{\$6,801.40}}$

6. Credit for partial payment = $\dfrac{\$2,500}{.98} = \underline{\underline{\$2,551.02}}$
  NAD = $\$8,303.00 - \$2,551.02 = \underline{\underline{\$5,751.98}}$

8. Credit for partial payment = $\dfrac{\$3,200}{.96} = \underline{\underline{\$3,333.33}}$
  NAD = $\$5,998.20 - \$3,333.33 = \underline{\underline{\$2,664.87}}$

CHAPTER 8 MARKUP AND MARKDOWN

REVIEW EXERCISES CHAPTER 8—SECTION I

1. $M = SP - C = 299.95 - 161.50 = \underline{\underline{\$138.45}}$
  $\%M_C = \dfrac{M}{C} = \dfrac{138.45}{161.50} = .8572 = \underline{\underline{85.7\%}}$

2. $SP = C + M = 32.40 + 21.50 = \underline{\underline{\$53.90}}$
  $\%M_C = \dfrac{M}{C} = \dfrac{21.50}{32.40} = .6635 = \underline{\underline{66.4\%}}$

3. $C = SP - M = 12,344.80 - 5,400.00 = \underline{\underline{\$6,944.80}}$
  $\%M_C = \dfrac{M}{C} = \dfrac{5400.00}{6944.80} = .7775 = \underline{\underline{77.8\%}}$

4. $SP = C(100\% + \%M_C) = 75(100\% + 80\%) = 75(1.8) = \underline{\underline{\$135.00}}$
  $M = SP - C = 135.00 - 75.00 = \underline{\underline{\$60.00}}$

5. $C = \dfrac{SP}{100\% + \%M_C} = \dfrac{249.95}{100\% + 60\%} = \dfrac{249.95}{1.6} = \underline{\underline{\$156.22}}$
  $M = SP - C = 249.95 - 156.22 = \underline{\underline{\$93.73}}$

6. $SP = C + M = 46.25 + 50.00 = \underline{\underline{\$96.25}}$
  $\%M_C = \dfrac{M}{C} = \dfrac{50.00}{46.25} = 1.081 = \underline{\underline{108.1\%}}$

7. $M = SP - C = 3,499.00 - 1,350.00 = \underline{\underline{\$2,149.00}}$
  $\%M_C = \dfrac{M}{C} = \dfrac{2,149.00}{1,350.00} = 1.592 = \underline{\underline{159.2\%}}$

8. $C = SP - M = 2,335.00 - 880.00 = \underline{\underline{\$1,455.00}}$
  $\%M_C = \dfrac{M}{C} = \dfrac{880.00}{1,455.00} = .6048 = \underline{\underline{60.5\%}}$

9. $SP = C(100\% + \%M_C) = .58(100\% + 130\%) = .58(2.3) = \underline{\underline{\$1.33}}$
  $M = SP - C = 1.33 - .58 = \underline{\underline{\$.75}}$

10. $C = \dfrac{SP}{100\% + \%M_C} = \dfrac{44.95}{100\% + 75\%} = \dfrac{44.95}{1.75} = \underline{\underline{\$25.69}}$
  $M = SP - C = 44.95 - 25.69 = \underline{\underline{\$19.26}}$

REVIEW EXERCISES CHAPTER 8—SECTION II

1. $SP = C + M = 65.00 + 50.00 = \underline{\underline{\$115.00}}$
  $\%M_{SP} = \dfrac{M}{SP} = \dfrac{50.00}{115.00} = .4347 = \underline{\underline{43.5\%}}$

2. $M = SP - C = 51.50 - 34.44 = \underline{\underline{\$17.06}}$
  $\%M_{SP} = \dfrac{M}{SP} = \dfrac{17.06}{51.50} = .3312 = \underline{\underline{33.1\%}}$

3. $SP = \dfrac{C}{100\% - \%M_{SP}} = \dfrac{75.00}{100\% - 45\%} = \dfrac{75.00}{.55} = \underline{\underline{\$136.36}}$

$M = SP - C = 136.36 - 75.00 = \underline{\underline{\$61.36}}$

4. $C = SP(100\% - \%M_{SP}) = 133.50(100\% - 60\%) = 133.50(.4) = \underline{\underline{\$53.40}}$

$M = SP - C = 133.50 - 53.40 = \underline{\underline{\$80.10}}$

5. $\%M_{SP} = \dfrac{\%M_C}{100\% + \%M_C} = \dfrac{60\%}{100\% + 60\%} = \dfrac{.6}{1.6} = .375 = \underline{\underline{37.5\%}}$

6. $\%M_C = \dfrac{\%M_{SP}}{100\% - \%M_{SP}} = \dfrac{35\%}{100\% - 35\%} = \dfrac{.35}{.65} = .5384 = \underline{\underline{53.8\%}}$

7. $M = SP - C = 165.99 - 71.25 = \underline{\underline{\$94.74}}$ **8.** $SP = C + M = 1.18 + .79 = \underline{\underline{\$1.97}}$

$\%M_C = \dfrac{M}{C} = \dfrac{94.74}{71.25} = 1.3296 = \underline{\underline{133\%}}$ $\%M_C = \dfrac{M}{C} = \dfrac{.79}{1.18} = .6694 = \underline{\underline{66.9\%}}$

$\%M_{SP} = \dfrac{M}{SP} = \dfrac{94.74}{165.99} = .5707 = \underline{\underline{57.1\%}}$ $\%M_{SP} = \dfrac{M}{SP} = \dfrac{.79}{1.97} = .4010 = \underline{\underline{40.1\%}}$

9. $SP = \dfrac{C}{100\% - \%M_{SP}} = \dfrac{15,449.00}{100\% - 38\%} = \dfrac{15,449.00}{.62} = \underline{\underline{\$24,917.74}}$

$M = SP - C = 24,917.74 - 15,449.00 = \underline{\underline{\$9,468.74}}$

$\%M_C = \dfrac{M}{C} = \dfrac{9,468.74}{15,449.00} = .6129 = \underline{\underline{61.3\%}}$

10. $C = SP(100\% - \%M_{SP}) = 1,299.00(100\% - 55\%) = 1,299(.45) = \underline{\underline{\$584.55}}$

$M = SP - C = 1,299.00 - 584.55 = \underline{\underline{\$714.45}}$

$\%M_C = \dfrac{M}{C} = \dfrac{714.45}{584.55} = 1.2222 = \underline{\underline{122.2\%}}$

11. $\%M_{SP} = \dfrac{\%M_C}{100\% + \%M_C} = \dfrac{150\%}{100\% + 150\%} = \dfrac{1.5}{2.5} = .60 = \underline{\underline{60\%}}$

12. $\%M_C = \dfrac{\%M_{SP}}{100\% - \%M_{SP}} = \dfrac{47\%}{100\% - 47\%} = \dfrac{.47}{.53} = .8867 = \underline{\underline{88.7\%}}$

REVIEW EXERCISES   CHAPTER 8—SECTION III

1. Sale price = Original price − Markdown = $189.95 - 28.50 = \underline{\underline{\$161.45}}$

$MD\% = \dfrac{MD}{\text{Original price}} = \dfrac{28.50}{189.95} = .1500 = \underline{\underline{15\%}}$

2. MD = Original price − Sale price = $53.88 - 37.50 = \underline{\underline{\$16.38}}$

$MD\% = \dfrac{MD}{\text{Original price}} = \dfrac{16.38}{53.88} = .3040 = \underline{\underline{30.4\%}}$

3. Original sale price = Sale price + $MD = 1.29 + .39 = \underline{\underline{\$1.68}}$

$MD\% = \dfrac{MD}{\text{Original price}} = \dfrac{.39}{1.68} = .2321 = \underline{\underline{23.2\%}}$

4. Sale price = Original price$(100\% - MD\%) = 264.95(.7) = \underline{\underline{\$185.47}}$

MD = Original price − Sale price = $264.95 - 185.47 = \underline{\underline{\$79.48}}$

5. Original price = $\dfrac{\text{Sale price}}{100\% - MD\%} = \dfrac{24.66}{100\% - 40\%} = \dfrac{24.66}{.6} = \underline{\underline{\$41.10}}$

MD = Original price − Sale price = $41.10 - 24.66 = \underline{\underline{\$16.44}}$

6. MD = Original price − Sale price = $68.00 - 51.99 = \underline{\underline{\$16.01}}$

$MD\% = \dfrac{MD}{\text{Original price}} = \dfrac{16.01}{68.00} = .2354 = \underline{\underline{23.5\%}}$

7. Sale price = Original price − $MD = 115.77 - 35.50 = \underline{\underline{\$80.27}}$

$MD\% = \dfrac{MD}{\text{Original price}} = \dfrac{35.50}{115.77} = .3066 = \underline{\underline{30.7\%}}$

8. Original price = Sale price + $MD = 235.00 + 155.00 = \underline{\underline{\$390.00}}$

$MD\% = \dfrac{MD}{\text{Original price}} = \dfrac{155.00}{390.00} = .3974 = \underline{\underline{39.7\%}}$

9. Sale price = Original price$(100\% - MD\%) = 1,599.88(.65) = \underline{\underline{\$1,039.92}}$

MD = Original price − Sale price = $1,599.88 - 1,039.92 = \underline{\underline{\$559.96}}$

10. Original price = $\dfrac{\text{Sale price}}{100\% - MD\%} = \dfrac{15.90}{100\% - 25\%} = \dfrac{15.90}{.75} = \underline{\underline{\$21.20}}$

MD = Original price − Sale price = $21.20 - 15.90 = \underline{\underline{\$5.30}}$

CHAPTER 9   PAYROLL

REVIEW EXERCISES   CHAPTER 9—SECTION I

19.
$50 \times 3.60 = 180.00$
$50 \times 4.25 = 212.50$
$\underline{9 \times 4.50 = + 40.50}$
$109 \underline{\underline{\$433.00}}$

20.
$50 \times 3.60 = 180.00$
$\underline{33 \times 4.25 = + 140.25}$
$83 \underline{\underline{\$320.25}}$

21.
$50 \times 3.60 = 180.00$
$50 \times 4.25 = 212.50$
$50 \times 4.50 = 225.00$
$\underline{24 \times 5.10 = + 122.40}$
$174 \underline{\underline{\$739.90}}$

REVIEW EXERCISES   CHAPTER 9—SECTION II

16. $49.04 \times 2 = 98.08$
$594.00 - 98.08 = 495.92$
$495.92 - 124 = 371.92 \times 15\% = \underline{\underline{\$55.79}}$

18. $4,150 - 212.50 = 3,937.50$
$3,937.50 - 2,121.00 = 1,816.50$
$285.30 + 28\%(1,816.50)$
$285.30 + 508.62 = \underline{\underline{\$793.92}}$

17. $1,127 - 1,060 = 67$
$142.65 + 28\%(67)$
$142.65 + 18.76 = \underline{\underline{\$161.41}}$

19. $98.08 \times 4 = 392.32$
$1,849.00 - 392.32 = 1,456.68$
$1,456.68 - 247.00 = 1,209.68 \times 15\% = \underline{\underline{\$181.45}}$

CHAPTER 10   SIMPLE INTEREST AND PROMISSORY NOTES

REVIEW EXERCISES   CHAPTER 10—SECTION I

1. $I = PRT = 5,000 \times .08 \times 2 = \underline{\underline{\$800}}$

2. $I = PRT = 75,000 \times .1075 \times \dfrac{6}{12} = \underline{\underline{\$4,031.25}}$

3. $I = PRT = 100,000 \times .127 \times \dfrac{18}{12} = \underline{\underline{\$19,050.00}}$

4. $I = PRT = 80,000 \times .15 \times 3.5 = \underline{\underline{\$42,000.00}}$

5. $I = PRT = 6,440 \times .055 \times \dfrac{7}{12} = \underline{\underline{\$206.62}}$

6. $I = PRT = 13,200 \times .092 \times 4.75 = \underline{\underline{\$5,768.40}}$

7. $I = PRT$

Exact: $45,000 \times .13 \times \dfrac{100}{365} = \underline{\underline{\$1,602.74}}$

Ordinary: $45,000 \times .13 \times \dfrac{100}{360} = \underline{\underline{\$1,625.00}}$

8. $I = PRT$

Exact: $184,500 \times .155 \times \dfrac{58}{365} = \underline{\underline{\$4,544.26}}$

Ordinary: $184,500 \times .155 \times \dfrac{58}{360} = \underline{\underline{\$4,607.38}}$

9. $I = PRT$

Exact: $32,400 \times .086 \times \dfrac{241}{365} = \underline{\underline{\$1,839.79}}$

Ordinary: $32,400 \times .086 \times \dfrac{241}{360} = \underline{\underline{\$1,865.34}}$

10. $I = PRT \quad 7,230 \times .09 \times \dfrac{18}{365} = \underline{\underline{\$32.09}}$

Exact: $7,230 \times .09 \times \dfrac{18}{360} = \underline{\underline{\$32.54}}$

11. $I = PRT$

Exact: $900 \times .1025 \times \dfrac{60}{365} = \underline{\underline{\$15.16}}$

Ordinary: $900 \times .1025 \times \dfrac{60}{360} = \underline{\underline{\$15.38}}$

12. $I = PRT$

Exact: $100,000 \times .1 \times \dfrac{1}{365} = \underline{\underline{\$27.40}}$

Ordinary: $100,000 \times .1 \times \dfrac{1}{360} = \underline{\underline{\$27.78}}$

13. $I = PRT$

Exact: $2,500 \times .12 \times \dfrac{74}{365} = \underline{\underline{\$60.82}}$

Ordinary: $2,500 \times .12 \times \dfrac{74}{360} = \underline{\underline{\$61.67}}$

14. $I = PRT$

Exact: $350 \times .141 \times \dfrac{230}{365} = \underline{\underline{\$31.10}}$

Ordinary: $350 \times .141 \times \dfrac{230}{360} = \underline{\underline{\$31.53}}$

15. $I = PRT$

Exact: $50,490 \times .0925 \times \dfrac{69}{365} = \underline{\underline{\$882.88}}$

Ordinary: $50,490 \times .0925 \times \dfrac{69}{360} = \underline{\underline{\$895.15}}$

16. $I = PRT$

Exact: $486,000 \times .135 \times \dfrac{127}{365} = \underline{\underline{\$22,828.68}}$

Ordinary: $486,000 \times .135 \times \dfrac{127}{360} = \underline{\underline{\$23,145.75}}$

17. $I = PRT = 54,000 \times .119 \times 2 = \underline{\$12,852.00}$

$MV = P + I = 54,000 + 12,852 = \underline{\$66,852.00}$

18. $I = PRT = 125,000 \times .125 \times \dfrac{5}{12} = \underline{\$6,510.42}$

$MV = P + I = 125,000 + 6,510.42 = \underline{\$131,510.42}$

19. $I = PRT = 33,750 \times .084 \times \dfrac{10}{12} = \underline{\$2,362.50}$

$MV = P + I = 33,750.00 + 2,362.50 = \underline{\$36,112.50}$

20. $I = PRT = 91,000 \times .0925 \times 2.5 = \underline{\$21,043.75}$

$MV = P + I = 91,000.00 + 21,043.75 = \underline{\$112,043.75}$

21. $MV = P(1 + RT) = 1,500(1 + .09 \times 2) = \underline{\$1,770.00}$

22. $MV = P(1 + RT) = 18,620(1 + .105 \times \dfrac{30}{12}) = \underline{\$23,507.75}$

23. $MV = P(1 + RT) = 1,000,000(1 + .11 \times 3) = \underline{\$1,330,000.00}$

24. $MV = P(1 + RT) = 750,000(1 + .1335 \times \dfrac{11}{12}) = \underline{\$841,781.25}$

25.
```
   30
 −  5
   25 Sept
   61 Oct-Nov
 + 12 Dec
   98 Days
```

26.
```
   30
 − 27
    3 June
   92 July-Sept
 + 15 Oct
  110 Days
```

27.
```
   31
 − 23
    8 Jan
  273 Feb-Oct
 +  8 Nov
  289 Days
```

28.
```
   31
 −  9
   22 Mar
   91 Apr-June
 + 30 July
  143 Days
```

29.
```
   31
 − 19
   12 Oct
   30 Nov
 +  3 Dec ──→ December 3
   45 Days
```

30.
```
   28
 −  5
   23 Feb
   61 Mar-Apr
 + 26 May ──→ May 26
  110 Days
```

31.
```
   31
 − 26
    5 May
 + 24 June ──→ June 24
   29 Days
```

32.
```
   31
 − 21
   10 July
  184 Aug-Jan
    6 Feb ──→ February 6
  200 Days
```

33.
```
   31
 −  6
   25 Dec
   31 Jan
   23 Feb ──→ February 23
   79 Days
```

REVIEW EXERCISES CHAPTER 10—SECTION II

1. $P = \dfrac{I}{RT} = \dfrac{300}{.12 \times 2} = \underline{\$1,250.00}$

2. $P = \dfrac{I}{RT} = \dfrac{675}{.09 \times 1.5} = \underline{\$5,000.00}$

3. $P = \dfrac{I}{RT} = \dfrac{3,000}{.08 \times \dfrac{9}{12}} = \underline{\$50,000.00}$

4. $P = \dfrac{I}{RT} = \dfrac{5,350}{.107 \times \dfrac{90}{360}} = \underline{\$200,000.00}$

5. $P = \dfrac{I}{RT} = \dfrac{917}{.131 \times \dfrac{210}{360}} = \underline{\$12,000.00}$

6. $R = \dfrac{I}{PT} = \dfrac{1,200}{5,000 \times 3} = \underline{8\%}$

7. $R = \dfrac{I}{PT} = \dfrac{105}{1,800 \times \dfrac{5}{12}} = \underline{14\%}$

8. $R = \dfrac{I}{PT} = \dfrac{728}{48,000 \times \dfrac{60}{360}} = \underline{9.1\%}$

9. $R = \dfrac{I}{PT} = \dfrac{275}{4,600 \times \dfrac{168}{360}} = \underline{12.8\%}$

10. $R = \dfrac{I}{PT} = \dfrac{18,750}{125,000 \times 2} = \underline{7.5\%}$

11. $T = \dfrac{I}{PR} = \dfrac{948}{18,000 \times .12} = .4388889$
$\phantom{T = \dfrac{I}{PR} = } \times 360$
$\phantom{T = \dfrac{I}{PR} = } \underline{158 \text{ Days}}$

12. $T = \dfrac{I}{PR} = \dfrac{228}{7,900 \times .104} = .2775073$
$\phantom{T = \dfrac{I}{PR} = } \times 360$
$\phantom{T = \dfrac{I}{PR} = } \underline{100 \text{ Days}}$

13. $T = \dfrac{I}{PR} = \dfrac{375}{4,500 \times .0975} = .8547009$
$\phantom{T = \dfrac{I}{PR} = } \times 360$
$\phantom{T = \dfrac{I}{PR} = } \underline{308 \text{ Days}}$

14. $T = \dfrac{I}{PR} = \dfrac{4,450}{25,000 \times .089} = \underline{2 \text{ Years}}$

15. $T = \dfrac{I}{PR} = \dfrac{51}{680 \times .15} = .5$
$\phantom{T = \dfrac{I}{PR} = } \times 360$
$\phantom{T = \dfrac{I}{PR} = } \underline{180 \text{ Days}}$

16. $T = \dfrac{I}{PR} = \dfrac{760}{16,000 \times .13} = .3653846$
$\phantom{T = \dfrac{I}{PR} = } \times 360$
$\phantom{T = \dfrac{I}{PR} = } \underline{132 \text{ Days}}$

$MV = P + I = 16,000 + 760 = \underline{\$16,760.00}$

17. $P = \dfrac{I}{RT} = \dfrac{340}{.095 \times \dfrac{100}{365}} = \underline{\underline{\$13,063.16}}$

$MV = P + I = 13,063.16 + 340.00 = \underline{\$13,403.16}$

19. $I = PRT = 25,500 \times .1125 \times \dfrac{300}{360} = \underline{\$2,390.63}$

$MV = P + I = 25,500 + 2,390.63 = \underline{\$27,890.63}$

18. $R = \dfrac{I}{PT} = \dfrac{225}{3,600 \times \dfrac{160}{365}} = \underline{\underline{14.3\%}}$

$MV = P + I = 3,600 + 225 = \underline{\$3,825.00}$

20. $P = MV - I = 59,000 - 4,000 = \underline{\$55,000}$

$T = \dfrac{I}{PR} = \dfrac{4,000}{55,000 \times .104} = .6993007$
$$\begin{array}{r} \times\ 365 \\ \hline \underline{256\ \text{Days}} \end{array}$$

REVIEW EXERCISES CHAPTER 10—SECTION III

1. Bank Discount $= FV \times R \times T = 4,500 \times .13 \times \dfrac{6}{12} = \underline{\underline{\$292.50}}$

Proceeds $= FV - $ Discount $= 4,500 - 292.50 = \underline{\$4,207.50}$

2. Bank Discount $= FV \times R \times T = 235 \times .113 \times \dfrac{50}{360} = \underline{\underline{\$3.69}}$

Proceeds $= FV - $ Discount $= 235.00 - 3.69 = \underline{\$231.31}$

3. Bank Discount $= FV \times R \times T = 1,850 \times .125 \times 1 = \underline{\underline{\$231.25}}$

Proceeds $= FV - $ Discount $= 1,850.00 - 231.25 = \underline{\$1,618.75}$

4. Bank Discount $= FV \times R \times T = 35,000 \times .0965 \times \dfrac{11}{12} = \underline{\underline{\$3,096.04}}$

Proceeds $= FV - $ Discount $= 35,000 - 3,096.04 = \underline{\$31,903.96}$

5. Bank Discount $= FV \times R \times T = 7,800 \times .0825 \times \dfrac{130}{360} = \underline{\underline{\$232.38}}$

Proceeds $= FV - $ Discount $= 7,800 - 232.38 = \underline{\$7,567.62}$

6. Maturity date $=$
$$\begin{array}{r} 30 \\ -\ 3 \\ \hline 27\ \text{Days} \end{array}$$
$\nearrow$ 27 June
31 July
$\underline{22}$ Aug $\longrightarrow$ August 22
80 Days

Bank Discount $= FV \times R \times T = 16,800.00 \times .10 \times \dfrac{80}{360} = \underline{\underline{\$373.33}}$

Proceeds $= FV - $ Discount $= 16,800.00 - 373.33 = \underline{\$16,426.67}$

7. Term $=$
$$\begin{array}{r} 30 \\ -\ 16 \\ \hline 14\ \text{Days} \end{array}$$
$\nearrow$ 14 Apr
61 May–June
$\underline{9}$ July
84 Days

Bank Discount $= FV \times R \times T = 5,000.00 \times .147 \times \dfrac{84}{360} = \underline{\underline{\$171.50}}$

Proceeds $= FV - $ Discount $= 5,000.00 - 171.50 = \underline{\$4,828.50}$

8. Maturity date $=$
$$\begin{array}{r} 30 \\ -\ 3 \\ \hline 27\ \text{Days} \end{array}$$
$\nearrow$ 27 Sept
61 Oct–Nov
$\underline{21}$ Dec $\longrightarrow$ December 21
109 Days

Bank Discount $= FV \times R \times T = 800 \times .121 \times \dfrac{109}{360} = \underline{\underline{\$29.31}}$

Proceeds $= FV - $ Discount $= 800.00 - 29.31 = \underline{\$770.69}$

9. Term $=$
$$\begin{array}{r} 31 \\ -\ 19 \\ \hline 12\ \text{Days} \end{array}$$
$\nearrow$ 12 Aug
61 Sept–Oct
$\underline{27}$ Nov
100 Days

Bank Discount $= FV \times R \times T = 1,300 \times .095 \times \dfrac{100}{360} = \underline{\underline{\$34.31}}$

Proceeds $= FV - $ Discount $= 1,300.00 - 34.31 = \underline{\$1,265.69}$

10. Maturity date $=$
$$\begin{array}{r} 31 \\ -\ 7 \\ \hline 24\ \text{Days} \end{array}$$
$\nearrow$ 24 May
$\underline{29}$ June $\longrightarrow$ June 29
53

Bank Discount $= FV \times R \times T = 75,000 \times .15 \times \dfrac{53}{360} = \underline{\underline{\$1,656.25}}$

Proceeds $= FV - $ Discount $= 75,000.00 - 1,656.25 = \underline{\$73,343.75}$

11. Bank discount $= FV \times R \times T = 2{,}700 \times .14 \times \dfrac{126}{360} = \underline{\$132.30}$

Proceeds $= FV - \text{Discount} = 2{,}700.00 - 132.30 = \underline{\$2{,}567.70}$

Effective rate $= \dfrac{\text{Discount}}{P \times T} = \dfrac{132.30}{2{,}567.70 \times \dfrac{126}{360}} = \underline{14.72\%}$

12. Bank discount $= FV \times R \times T = 6{,}505.00 \times .1039 \times \dfrac{73}{360} = \underline{\$137.05}$

Proceeds $= FV - \text{Discount} = 6{,}505.00 - 137.05 = \underline{\$6{,}367.95}$

Effective rate $= \dfrac{\text{Discount}}{P \times T} = \dfrac{137.05}{6{,}367.95 \times \dfrac{73}{360}} = \underline{10.61\%}$

13. Bank discount $= FV \times R \times T = 3{,}800 \times .145 \times \dfrac{140}{360} = \underline{\$214.28}$

Proceeds $= FV - \text{Discount} = 3{,}800.00 - 214.28 = \underline{\$3{,}585.72}$

Effective rate $= \dfrac{\text{Discount}}{P \times T} = \dfrac{214.28}{3{,}585.72 \times \dfrac{140}{360}} = \underline{15.37\%}$

14. Bank discount $= FV \times R \times T = 95{,}000 \times .097 \times \dfrac{45}{360} = \underline{\$1{,}151.88}$

Proceeds $= FV - \text{Discount} = 95{,}000.00 - 1{,}151.88 = \underline{\$93{,}848.12}$

Effective rate $= \dfrac{\text{Discount}}{P \times T} = \dfrac{1{,}151.88}{93{,}848.12 \times \dfrac{45}{360}} = \underline{9.82\%}$

15. Bank discount $= FV \times R \times T = 57{,}500 \times .1275 \times \dfrac{230}{360} = \underline{\$4{,}683.85}$

Proceeds $= FV - \text{Discount} = 57{,}500.00 - 4{,}683.85 = \underline{\$52{,}816.15}$

Effective rate $= \dfrac{\text{Discount}}{P \times T} = \dfrac{4{,}683.85}{52{,}816.15 \times \dfrac{230}{360}} = \underline{13.88\%}$

16. Maturity date $=$
$$\begin{array}{ll} 31 & 27\ \text{Mar} \\ -\ 4 & 30\ \text{Apr} \\ \hline 27\ \text{Days} & \underline{13}\ \text{May} \longrightarrow \underline{\text{May 13}} \\ & 70\ \text{Days} \end{array}$$

$MV = FV(1 + RT) = 2{,}500\left(1 + .12 \times \dfrac{70}{360}\right) = \underline{\$2{,}558.33}$

Discount Period $=$
$$\begin{array}{ll} 30 & 15\ \text{Apr} \\ -\ 15 & \underline{13}\ \text{May} \\ \hline 15\ \text{Days} & \underline{28\ \text{Days}} \end{array}$$

Bank discount $= MV \times R \times T = 2{,}558.33 \times .13 \times \dfrac{28}{360} = \$25.87$

Proceeds $= MV - \text{Discount} = 2{,}558.33 - 25.87 = \underline{\$2{,}532.46}$

17. Maturity date $=$
$$\begin{array}{ll} 31 & 19\ \text{Dec} \\ -\ 12 & \underline{31}\ \text{Jan} \longrightarrow \underline{\text{January 31}} \\ \hline 19\ \text{Days} & 50\ \text{Days} \end{array}$$

$MV = FV(1 + RT) = 4{,}000\left(1 + .104 \times \dfrac{50}{360}\right) = \underline{\$4{,}057.78}$

Discount Period $=$
$$\begin{array}{l} 31 \\ -\ 19 \\ \hline \underline{12\ \text{Days}} \end{array}$$

Bank discount $= MV \times R \times T = 4{,}057.78 \times .15 \times \dfrac{12}{360} = \$20.29$

Proceeds $= MV - \text{Discount} = 4{,}057.78 - 20.29 = \underline{\$4{,}037.49}$

18. Maturity date =

$$\begin{array}{c} 31 \\ -\ 7 \\ \hline 23\ \text{Days} \end{array} \nearrow \begin{array}{l} 23\ \text{June} \\ 92\ \text{July–Sept} \\ \underline{10}\ \text{Oct} \longrightarrow \text{October 10} \\ 125\ \text{Days} \end{array}$$

$$MV = FV(1 + RT) = 850\left(1 + .135 \times \frac{125}{360}\right) = \underline{\$889.84}$$

Discount Period =

$$\begin{array}{c} 30 \\ -\ 3 \\ \hline 27\ \text{Days} \end{array} \nearrow \begin{array}{l} 27\ \text{Apr} \\ \underline{10}\ \text{May} \\ 37\ \text{Days} \end{array}$$

Bank discount $= MV \times R \times T = 889.84 \times .165 \times \dfrac{37}{360} = \$15.09$

Proceeds $= MV - \text{Discount} = 889.84 - 15.09 = \underline{\$874.75}$

ASSESSMENT TEST

1. $I = PRT = 15,000 \times .13 \times \dfrac{120}{365} = \underline{\$641.10}$

2. $I = PRT = 1,700 \times .125 \times \dfrac{33}{365} = \underline{\$19.21}$

3. $I = PRT = 20,600 \times .12 \times \dfrac{98}{360} = \underline{\$672.93}$

4. $I = PRT = 286,000 \times .135 \times \dfrac{224}{360} = \underline{\$24,024.00}$

5. $MV = P(1 + RT) = 15,800(1 + .14 \times 4) = \underline{\$24,648.00}$

6. $MV = P(1 + RT) = 120,740\left(1 + .1175 \times \dfrac{7}{12}\right) = \underline{\$129,015.72}$

7.
$$\begin{array}{c} 30 \\ -\ 16 \\ \hline 14\ \text{Days} \end{array} \nearrow \begin{array}{l} 14\ \text{Apr} \\ 92\ \text{May–July} \\ \underline{1}\ \text{Aug} \\ \underline{107\ \text{Days}} \end{array}$$

8.
$$\begin{array}{c} 31 \\ -\ 20 \\ \hline 11\ \text{Days} \end{array} \nearrow \begin{array}{l} 11\ \text{Oct} \\ 30\ \text{Nov} \\ \underline{18}\ \text{Dec} \\ \underline{59\ \text{Days}} \end{array}$$

9.
$$\begin{array}{c} 30 \\ -\ 30 \\ \hline 0\ \text{Days} \end{array} \nearrow \begin{array}{l} 0\ \text{Nov} \\ 31\ \text{Dec} \\ \underline{24}\ \text{Jan} \longrightarrow \text{January 24} \\ 55\ \text{Days} \end{array}$$

10.
$$\begin{array}{c} 31 \\ -\ 15 \\ \hline 16\ \text{Days} \end{array} \nearrow \begin{array}{l} 16\ \text{May} \\ 92\ \text{June–Aug} \\ \underline{3}\ \text{Sept} \longrightarrow \underline{\text{September 3}} \\ 111\ \text{Days} \end{array}$$

11. $P = \dfrac{I}{RT} = \dfrac{2,800}{.12 \times 2} = \underline{\$11,666.67}$

12. $P = \dfrac{I}{RT} = \dfrac{5,900}{.105 \times \dfrac{10}{12}} = \underline{\$67,428.57}$

13. $R = \dfrac{I}{PT} = \dfrac{800}{2,200 \times 4} = \underline{9.1\%}$

14. $R = \dfrac{I}{PT} = \dfrac{4,500}{50,000 \times \dfrac{9}{12}} = \underline{12\%}$

15. $T = \dfrac{I}{PR} = \dfrac{350}{13,500 \times .13} = .1994301$
$$\begin{array}{r} \times\ 360 \\ \hline 71.7 = \underline{72\ \text{Days}} \end{array}$$

16. $T = \dfrac{I}{PR} = \dfrac{625}{7,900 \times .104} = .7607108$
$$\begin{array}{r} \times\ 360 \\ \hline 273.8 = \underline{274\ \text{Days}} \end{array}$$

17. $T = \dfrac{I}{PR} = \dfrac{960}{13,000 \times .14} = .5274725$
$$\begin{array}{r} \times\ 360 \\ \hline 189.8 = \underline{190\ \text{Days}} \end{array}$$
$MV = P + I = 13,000 + 960 = \underline{\$13,960.00}$

18. $P = \dfrac{I}{RT} = \dfrac{1,790}{.122 \times \dfrac{133}{365}} = \underline{\$40,265.62}$
$MV = P + I = 40,265.62 + 1,790.00 = \underline{\$42,055.62}$

19. $P = \dfrac{I}{RT} = \dfrac{295}{2,500 \times \dfrac{280}{360}} = \underline{15.2\%}$
$MV = P + I = 2,500 + 295 = \underline{\$2,795.00}$

20.
$$\begin{array}{c} 30 \\ -\ 5 \\ \hline 25\ \text{Days} \end{array} \nearrow \begin{array}{l} 25\ \text{Apr} \\ 92\ \text{May–July} \\ \underline{14}\ \text{Aug} \\ \underline{131\ \text{Days}} \end{array}$$

Bank Discount $= FV \times R \times T = 50,000 \times .13 \times \dfrac{131}{360} = \underline{\$2,365.28}$

Proceeds $= FV - \text{Discount} = 50,000.00 - 2,365.28 = \underline{\$47,634.72}$

21.

$$\begin{array}{ll} 31 & \text{6 Oct} \\ -\,25 & \text{61 Nov–Dec} \\ \hline \text{6 Days} & \underline{\text{20 Jan}} \qquad \text{January 20} \\ & \text{87 Days} \end{array}$$

Bank Discount $= FV \times R \times T = 875{,}000 \times .095 \times \dfrac{87}{360} = \underline{\$20{,}088.54}$

Proceeds $= FV - \text{Discount} = 875{,}000.00 - 20{,}088.54 = \underline{\$854{,}911.46}$

22. Bank discount $= FV \times R \times T = 22{,}500 \times .105 \times \dfrac{60}{360} = \underline{\$393.75}$

Proceeds $= FV - \text{Discount} = 22{,}500.00 - 393.75 = \underline{\$22{,}106.25}$

Effective rate $= \dfrac{\text{Discount}}{P \times T} = \dfrac{393.75}{22{,}106.25 \times \dfrac{60}{360}} = \underline{10.69\%}$

23. Bank discount $= FV \times R \times T = 290{,}000 \times .119 \times \dfrac{110}{360} = \underline{\$10{,}544.72}$

Proceeds $= FV - \text{Discount} = 290{,}000.00 - 10{,}544.72 = \underline{\$279{,}455.28}$

Effective rate $= \dfrac{\text{Discount}}{P \times T} = \dfrac{10{,}544.72}{279{,}455.28 \times \dfrac{110}{360}} = \underline{12.35\%}$

24. Maturity date $=$

$$\begin{array}{ll} 30 & \text{19 Jan} \\ -\,12 & \text{59 Feb–Mar} \\ \hline \text{19 Days} & \underline{\text{5 Apr}} \qquad \text{April 5} \\ & \text{83 Days} \end{array}$$

$MV = FV(1 + RT) = 8{,}000\left(1 + .11 \times \dfrac{83}{360}\right) = \underline{\$8{,}202.89}$

Discount Period $=$

$$\begin{array}{ll} 31 & \text{30 Mar} \\ -\,1 & \text{5 Apr} \\ \hline \text{30 Days} & \underline{\text{35 Days}} \end{array}$$

Bank discount $= MV \times R \times T = 8{,}202.89 \times .15 \times \dfrac{35}{360} = \$119.63$

Proceeds $= MV - \text{Discount} = 8{,}202.89 - 119.63 = \underline{\$8{,}083.26}$

25. Maturity date $=$

$$\begin{array}{ll} 30 & \text{13 June} \\ -\,17 & \text{31 July} \\ \hline \text{13 Days} & \underline{\text{25 Aug}} \qquad \text{August 25} \\ & \text{69 Days} \end{array}$$

$MV = FV(1 + RT) = 5{,}500\left(1 + .135 \times \dfrac{69}{360}\right) = \underline{\$5{,}642.31}$

Discount Period $=$

$$\begin{array}{ll} 31 & \text{9 July} \\ -\,22 & \text{25 Aug} \\ \hline \text{9 Days} & \underline{\text{34 Days}} \end{array}$$

Bank discount $= MV \times R \times T = 5{,}642.31 \times .137 \times \dfrac{34}{360} = \$73.01$

Proceeds $= MV - \text{Discount} = 5{,}642.31 - 73.01 = \underline{\$5{,}569.30}$

CHAPTER 11 COMPOUND INTEREST AND PRESENT VALUE

REVIEW EXERCISES CHAPTER 11—SECTION I

1. Periods $=$ Years $\times$ Periods/Year $= 3 \times 1 = \underline{3}$

Rate per period $= \dfrac{\text{Nominal Rate}}{\text{Periods/Year}} = \dfrac{13}{1} = \underline{13\%}$

2. Periods $=$ Years $\times$ Periods/Year $= 5 \times 4 = \underline{20}$

Rate per period $= \dfrac{\text{Nominal Rate}}{\text{Periods/Year}} = \dfrac{16}{4} = \underline{4\%}$

3. Periods $=$ Years $\times$ Periods/Year $= 12 \times 2 = \underline{24}$

Rate per period $= \dfrac{\text{Nominal Rate}}{\text{Periods/Year}} = \dfrac{8}{2} = \underline{4\%}$

4. Periods $=$ Years $\times$ Periods/Year $= 6 \times 12 = \underline{72}$

Rate per period $= \dfrac{\text{Nominal Rate}}{\text{Periods/Year}} = \dfrac{18}{12} = \underline{1.5\%}$

5. Periods $=$ Years $\times$ Periods/Year $= 4 \times 4 = \underline{16}$

Rate per period $= \dfrac{\text{Nominal Rate}}{\text{Periods/Year}} = \dfrac{14}{4} = \underline{3.5\%}$

6. Periods $=$ Years $\times$ Periods/Year $= 9 \times 2 = \underline{18}$

Rate per period $= \dfrac{\text{Nominal Rate}}{\text{Periods/Year}} = \dfrac{10.5}{2} = \underline{5.25\%}$

7. Periods = Years × Periods/Year = .75 × 4 = <u>3</u>

Rate per period = $\dfrac{\text{Nominal Rate}}{\text{Periods/Year}} = \dfrac{12}{4} = \underline{\underline{3\%}}$

8.   4,000 Orig principal
<u>+ 400</u> Interest period 1 ($I = PRT$)(4,000 × .1 = 400)
  4,400 Principal period 2
<u>+ 440</u> Interest period 2 ($I = PRT$)(4,400 × .1 = 440)
<u>$4,840</u> Compound amount

Compound interest = Compound amount   4,840
− Principal   <u>− 4,000</u>
<u>$840</u>

9.   10,000.00 Original principal
<u>+ 300.00</u> Interest period 1 (10,000 × .12 × .25 = 300)
  10,300.00 Princiapl period 2
<u>+ 309.00</u> Interest period 2 (10,300 × .12 × .25 = 309)
  10,609.00 Princiapl period 3
<u>+ 318.27</u> Interest period 3 (10,609 × .12 × .25 = 318.27)
  10,927.27 Princiapl period 4
<u>+ 327.82</u> Interest period 4 (10,927.27 × .12 × .25 = 327.82)
<u>$11,255.09</u> Compound amount

Compound interest = Compound amount $11,255.09
− Principal   <u>− 10,000.00</u>
<u>$1,255.09</u>

10.   8,000.00 Original principal
<u>+ 320.00</u> Interest period 1 (8,000 × .08 × .5 = 320)
  8,320.00 Principal period 2
<u>+ 332.80</u> Interest period 2 (8,320 × .08 × .5 = 332.80)
  8,652.80 Principal period 3
<u>+ 346.11</u> Interest period 3 (8,652.80 × .08 × .5 = 346.11)
  8,998.91 Principal period 4
<u>+ 359.96</u> Interest period 4 (8,998.91 × .08 × .5 = 359.96)
  9,358.87 Principal period 5
<u>+ 374.35</u> Interest period 5 (9,358.87 × .08 × .5 = 374.35)
  9,733.22 Principal period 6
<u>+ 389.33</u> Interest period 6 (9,733.22 × .08 × .5 = 389.33)
<u>$10,122.55</u> Compound amount

Compound interest = Compound amount   10,122.55
− Principal   <u>− 8,000.00</u>
<u>$2,122.55</u>

11. 13%, 4 Periods
Compound amount = Table factor × Principal
1.63047 × 7,000 = <u>$11,413.29</u>

Compound interest = Compound amount − Principal
11,413.29 − 7,000.00 = <u>$4,413.29</u>

12. 7%, 12 Periods
Compound amount = Table factor × Principal
2.25219 × 11,000 = <u>$24,774.09</u>

Compound interest = Compound amount − Principal
24,774.09 − 11,000.00 = <u>$13,774.09</u>

13. 2%, 12 Periods
Compound amount = Table factor × Principal
1.26824 × 5,300 = <u>$6,721.67</u>

Compound interest = Compound amount − Principal
6,721.67 − 5,300.00 = <u>$1,421.67</u>

14. $1\frac{1}{2}\%$, 24 Periods

Compound amount = Table factor × Principal
1.42950 × 67,000 = <u>$95,776.50</u>

Compound interest = Compound amount − Principal
95,776.50 − 67,000.00 = $28,776.50

15. 11%, 15 Periods

Compound amount = Table factor × Principal
$$4.78459 \times 25{,}000 = \underline{\$119{,}614.75}$$

Compound interest = Compound amount − Principal
$$119{,}614.75 - 25{,}000.00 = \underline{\$94{,}614.75}$$

16. $\frac{1}{2}$%, 24 Periods

Compound amount = Table factor × Principal
$$1.12716 \times 400 = \underline{\$450.86}$$

Compound interest = Compound amount − Principal
$$450.86 - 400.00 = \underline{\$50.86}$$

17. 5%, 25 Periods

Compound amount = Table factor × Principal
$$3.38635 \times 8{,}800 = \underline{\$29{,}799.88}$$

Compound interest = Compound amount − Principal
$$29{,}799.88 - 8{,}800.00 = \underline{\$20{,}999.88}$$

18. Table factor required = 1%, 36 Periods

1%, 20 Periods:	1.22019
1%, 16 Periods:	× 1.17258
36 Periods	1.4307703 = 1.43077 "New" factor 1%, 36 Periods

Compound amount = Table factor × Principal
$$1.43077 \times 13{,}000 = \underline{\$18{,}600.01}$$

19. Table factor required = 9%, 29 Periods

9%, 20 Periods:	5.60441
9%, 9 Periods:	× 2.17189
29 Periods	12.172162 = 12.17216 "New" factor 9%, 29 Periods

Compound amount = Table factor × Principal
$$12.17216 \times 19{,}000 = \underline{\$231{,}271.04}$$

20. Table factor required = 4%, 44 Periods

4%, 22 Periods:	2.36992
4%, 22 Periods:	× 2.36992
44 Periods	5.6165208 = 5.61652 "New" factor 4%, 44 Periods

Compound amount = Table factor × Principal
$$5.61652 \times 34{,}700 = \underline{\$194{,}893.24}$$

21. Table factor required = 13%, 40 Periods

13%, 20 Periods:	11.52309
13%, 20 Periods:	× 11.52309
40 Periods	132.7816 = 132.78160 "New" factor 13%, 40 Periods

Compound amount = Table factor × Principal
$$132.78160 \times 10{,}000 = \underline{\$1{,}327{,}816.00}$$

22. Table factor required = 7%, 32 Periods

7%, 16 Periods:	2.95216
7%, 16 Periods:	× 2.95216
32 Periods	8.7152486 = 8.71525 "New" factor 7%, 32 Periods

Compound amount = Table factor × Principal
$$8.71525 \times 1{,}000 = \underline{\$8{,}715.25}$$

23. 5%, 2 Periods

Compound amount = Table factor × Principal
$$1.10250 \times 5{,}000 = \underline{\$5{,}512.50}$$

Compound interest = Compound amount − Principal
$$\$5{,}512.50 - 5{,}000 = \underline{\$512.50}$$

$$\text{Effective rate} = \frac{1 \text{ year interest}}{\text{Principal}} = \frac{512.50}{5{,}000.00} = \underline{10.25\%}$$

24. 13%, 1 Period

Compound amount = Table factor × Principal

$$1.13000 \times 2,000 = \$2,260.00$$

Compound interest = Compound amount − Principal

$$2,260.00 - 2,000.00 = \underline{\$260.00}$$

Effective rate = $\dfrac{1 \text{ year interest}}{\text{Principal}} = \dfrac{260.00}{2,000.00} = \underline{\underline{13\%}}$

25. 1%, 12 Periods

Compound amount = Table factor × Principal

$$1.12683 \times 36,000 = \$40,565.88$$

Compound interest = Compound amount − Principal

$$40,565.88 - 36,000.00 = \underline{\$4,565.88}$$

Effective rate = $\dfrac{1 \text{ year interest}}{\text{Principal}} = \dfrac{4,565.88}{36,000.00} = \underline{\underline{12.68\%}}$

26. 2%, 4 Periods

Compound amount = Table factor × Principal

$$1.08243 \times 1,000 = \$1,082.43$$

Compound interest = Compound amount − Principal

$$1,082.43 - 1,000.00 = \underline{\$82.43}$$

Effective rate = $\dfrac{1 \text{ year interest}}{\text{Principal}} = \dfrac{82.43}{1,000.00} = \underline{\underline{8.24\%}}$

REVIEW EXERCISES CHAPTER 11—SECTION II

1. 9%, 3 Periods

Present value = Table factor × Compound amount

$$.77218 \times 6,000 = \underline{\$4,633.08}$$

Compound interest = Compound amount − Present value

$$6,000.00 - 4,633.08 = \underline{\$1,366.92}$$

2. 7%, 12 Periods

Present value = Table factor × Compound amount

$$.44401 \times 24,000 = \underline{\$10,656.24}$$

Compound interest = Compound amount − Present value

$$24,000.00 - 10,656.24 = \underline{\$13,343.76}$$

3. 2%, 20 Periods

Present value = Table factor × Compound amount

$$.67297 \times 650 = \underline{\$437.43}$$

Compound interest = Compound amount − Present value

$$650 - 437.43 = \underline{\$212.57}$$

4. 3%, 24 Periods

Present value = Table factor × Compound amount

$$.49193 \times 2,000 = \underline{\$983.86}$$

Compound interest = Compound amount − Present value

$$2,000.00 - 983.86 = \underline{\$1,016.14}$$

5. 11%, 25 Periods

Present value = Table factor × Compound amount

$$.07361 \times 50,000 = \underline{\$3,680.50}$$

Compound interest = Compound amount − Present value

$$50,000.00 - 3,680.50 = \underline{\$46,319.50}$$

6. 5%, 3 Periods

Present value = Table factor × Compound amount

$$.86384 \times 14,500 = \underline{\$12,525.68}$$

Compound interest = Compound amount − Present value

$$14,500.00 - 12,525.68 = \underline{\$1,974.32}$$

7. 3%, 16 Periods

Present value = Table factor × Compound amount

$$.62317 \times 9,800 = \underline{\$6,107.07}$$

Compound interest = Compound amount − Present value

$$9,800.00 - 6,107.07 = \underline{\$3,692.93}$$

8. 9%, 10 Periods

Present value = Table factor × Compound amount
.42241 × 100,000 = $42,241.00

Compound interest = Compound amount − Present value
100,000.00 − 42,241.00 = $57,759.00

9. $1\frac{1}{2}$%, 12 Periods

Present value = Table factor × Compound amount
.83639 × 250 = $209.10

Compound interest = Compound amount − Present value
250.00 − 209.10 = $40.90

10. 2%, 9 Periods

Present value = Table factor × Compound amount
.83676 × 4,000 = $3,347.04

Compound interest = Compound amount − Present value
4,000.00 − 3,347.04 = $652.96

11. Table factor required = 4%, 40 Periods

4%, 20 Periods: .45639

4%, 20 Periods: × .45639

40 Periods   .2082918 = .20829   "New" factor 4%, 40 Periods

Present value = Table factor × Compound amount
.20829 × 12,000 = $2,499.48

12. Table factor required = 7%, 38 Periods

7%, 20 Periods: .25842

7%, 18 Periods: × .29586

38 Periods   .0764561 = .07646   "New" factor 7%, 38 Periods

Present value = Table factor × Compound amount
.07646 × 33,000 = $2,523.18

13. Table factor required = 3%, 48 Periods

3%, 24 Periods: .49193

3%, 24 Periods: × .49193

48 Periods   .2419951 = .24200   "New" factor 3%, 48 Periods

Present value = Table factor × Compound amount
.24200 × 1,400 = $338.80

14. Table factor required = 13%, 45 Periods

13%, 20 Periods: .08678

13%, 25 Periods: × .04710

45 Periods   .0040873 = .00409   "New" factor 13%, 45 Periods

Present value = Table factor × Compound amount
.00409 × 1,000 = $4.09

15. Table factor required = 4%, 34 Periods

20 Periods: .45639

14 Periods: × .57748

34 Periods   .2635561 = .26356   "New" factor 4%, 34 Periods

Present value = Table factor × Compound amount
.26356 × 110,000 = $28,991.60

ASSESSMENT TEST

1. 7%, 12 Periods

Compound amount = 2.25219 × 14,000 = $31,530.66

Compound interest = 31,530.66 − 14,000 = $17,530.66

2. $1\frac{1}{2}$%, 20 Periods

Compound amount = 1.34686 × 7,700 = $10,370.82

Compound interest = 10,370.82 − 7,700 = $2,670.82

3. $1\frac{1}{2}$%, 12 Periods

Compound amount = 1.19562 × 3,000 = $3,586.86

Compound interest = 3,586.86 − 3,000.00 = $586.86

4. 11%, 19 Periods

Compound amount = 7.26334 × 42,000 = $305,060.28

Compound interest = 305,060.28 − 42,000.00 = $263,060.28

5. Table factor required = 4%, 44 Periods

  4%, 22 Periods: 2.36992

  4%, <u>22</u> Periods: × <u>2.36992</u>

    44 Periods 5.6165208 = <u>5.61652</u> "New" factor 4%, 44 Periods

Compound amount = 5.61652 × 20,000 = $112,330.40

6. Table factor required = $\frac{1}{2}$%, 48 Periods

  $\frac{1}{2}$%, 24 Periods: 1.12716

  $\frac{1}{2}$%, <u>24</u> Periods: × <u>1.12716</u>

    48 Periods 1.2704897 = <u>1.27049</u> "New" factor $\frac{1}{2}$%, 48 Periods

Compound amount = 1.27049 × 10,000 = $12,704.90

7. 1%, 12 Periods

Compound amount = 1.12683 × 8,500 = $9,578.06

1 year interest = 9,578.06 − 8,500.00 = $1,078.06

Effective rate = $\dfrac{\text{1 year interest}}{\text{Principal}} = \dfrac{1,078.06}{8,500.00} = \underline{12.68\%}$

8. 2%, 4 Periods

Compound amount = 1.08243 × 1,000,000 = $1,082,430.00

1 year interest = 1,082,430.00 − 1,000,000.00 = $82,430.00

Effective rate = $\dfrac{\text{1 year interest}}{\text{Principal}} = \dfrac{82,430.00}{1,000,000.00} = \underline{8.24\%}$

9. 15%, 22 Periods

Present value = .04620 × 150,000 = $6,930.00

Compound interest = 150,000.00 − 6,930.00 = $143,070.00

10. 7%, 5 Periods

Present value = .71299 × 20,000 = $14,259.80

Compound interest = 20,000.00 − 14,259.80 = $5,740.20

11. $1\frac{1}{2}$%, 21 Periods

Present value = .73150 × 900 = $658.35

Compound interest = 900.00 − 658.35 = $241.65

12. 2%, 5 Periods

Present value = .90573 × 5,500 = $4,981.52

Compound interest = 5,500.00 − 4,981.52 = $518.48

13. Table factor required = 1%, 48 Periods

  1%, 24 Periods: .78757

  1%, <u>24</u> Periods: × <u>.78757</u>

    48 Periods .6202665 = <u>.62027</u> "New" factor 1%, 48 Periods

Present value = .62027 × 1,300 = $806.35

14. Table factor required = 5%, 50 Periods

  5%, 25 Periods: .29530

  5%, <u>25</u> Periods: × <u>.29530</u>

    50 Periods .0872021 = <u>.08720</u> "New" factor 5%, 50 Periods

Present value = .08720 × 100,000 = $8,720.00

CHAPTER 12   ANNUITIES

REVIEW EXERCISES   CHAPTER 12—SECTION II

1. $R = 5\%$ $P = 14$ $F = 9.89864$
Amount $= 300.00 \times 9.89864 = \underline{\$2,969.59}$

2. $R = 7\%$ $P = 20$ $F = 10.59401$
Amount $= 2,000.00 \times 10.59401 = \underline{\$21,188.02}$

3. $R = 3\%$ $P = 24$ $F = 16.93554$
Amount $= 1,600.00 \times 16.93554 = \underline{\$27,096.86}$

4. $R = \frac{1}{2}\%$ $P = 21$ $F = 19.88798$
Amount $= 1,000.00 \times 19.88798 = \underline{\$19,887.98}$

5. $R = 4\%$ $P = 12$ $F = 9.3850$
Amount $= 8,500.00 \times 9.38507 = \underline{\$79,773.10}$

6. $R = 11\%$ $P = 9$ $F = 5.53705 + 1.00000$
Amount $= 1,400.00 \times 6.53705 = \underline{\$9,151.87}$

7. $R = 3\%$ $P = 15$ $F = 11.93794 + 1.00000$
Amount $= 1,300.00 \times 12.93794 = \underline{\$16,819.32}$

8. $R = 1\frac{1}{2}\%$ $P = 26$ $F = 21.39863 + 1.00000$
Amount $= 500.00 \times 22.39863 = \underline{\$11,199.32}$

9. $R = 4\%$ $P = 23$ $F = 14.85684 + 1.00000$
Amount $= 7,000.00 \times 15.85684 = \underline{\$110,997.88}$

10. $R = 7\%$ $P = 17$ $F = 9.76322 + 1.00000$
Amount $= 4,000.00 \times 10.76322 = \underline{\$43,052.88}$

REVIEW EXERCISES   CHAPTER 12—SECTION III

1. $R = 5\%$ $P = 16$ $FV = 50,000.00$
Table factor $= 23.65749$
Payment $= \dfrac{50,000.00}{23.65749} = \underline{\$2,113.50}$

2. $R = 9\%$ $P = 14$ $FV = 250,000.00$
Table factor $= 26.01919$
Payment $= \dfrac{250,000}{26.01919} = \underline{\$9,608.29}$

3. $R = 3\%$ $P = 20$ $FV = 1,500.00$
Table factor $= 26.87037$
Payment $= \dfrac{1,500.00}{26.87037} = \underline{\$55.82}$

4. $R = 1\%$ $P = 18$ $FV = 4,000.00$
Table factor $= 19.61475$
Payment $= \dfrac{4,000.00}{19.61475} = \underline{\$203.93}$

5. $R = 4\%$ $P = 16$ $FV = 18,750.00$
Table factor $= 21.82453$
Payment $= \dfrac{18,750.00}{21.82453} = \underline{\$859.13}$

6. $R = 9\%$ $P = 12$ $PV = 30,000.00$
Table factor $= 7.16073$
Payment $= \dfrac{30,000.00}{7.16073} = \underline{\$4,189.52}$

7. $R = 2\%$ $P = 20$ $PV = 5,500.00$
Table factor $= 16.35143$
Payment $= \dfrac{5,500.00}{16.35143} = \underline{\$336.36}$

8. $R = 1\frac{1}{2}\%$ $P = 21$ $PV = 10,000.00$
Table factor $= 17.90014$
Payment $= \dfrac{10,000.00}{17.90014} = \underline{\$558.65}$

9. $R = 3\%$ $P = 16$ $PV = 13,660.00$
Table factor $= 12.56110$
Payment $= \dfrac{13,660.00}{12.56110} = \underline{\$1,087.48}$

10. $R = 1\%$ $P = 18$ $PV = 850.00$
Table factor $= 16.39827$
Payment $= \dfrac{850.00}{16.39827} = \underline{\$51.83}$

ASSESSMENT TEST

1. $R = 2\%$ $P = 24$ Payment $= 4,000.00$
Table factor $= 30.42186 \times 4,000.00$
FV $= \underline{\$121,687.44}$

2. $R = 5\%$ $P = 20$ Payment $= 10,000.00$
Table factor $= 33.06595 \times 10,000.00$
FV $= \underline{\$330,659.50}$

3. $R = 5\%$ $P = 25$ Payment $= 1,850.00$
Table factor $= 47.72710 - 1.00000$
          $= 46.72710 \times 1,850.00$
FV $= \underline{\$86,445.14}$

4. $R = 1\%$ $P = 22$ Payment $= 200.00$
Table factor $= 24.47159 - 1.00000$
          $= 23.47159 \times 200.00$
FV $= \underline{\$4,694.32}$

5. $R = 5\%$ $P = 9$ Payment $= 6,000.00$
Table factor $= 7.10782 \times 6,000.00$
PV $= \underline{\$42,646.92}$

6. $R = 1\frac{1}{2}\%$ $P = 12$ Payment $= 125,000.00$
Table factor $= 10.90751 \times 125,000.00$
PV $= \underline{\$1,363,438.75}$

7. $R = 1\%$ $P = 17$ Payment $= 700.00$
Table factor $= 15.56225 + 1.00000$
PV $= 16.56225 \times 700.00 = \underline{\$11,593.58}$

8. $R = 2\%$ $P = 11$ Payment $= 2,000.00$
Table factor $= 9.78685 + 1.00000$
PV $= 10.78685 \times 2,000.00 = \underline{\$21,573.70}$

9. $R = 7\%$ $P = 13$ $FV = 20,000.00$

Table factor = 20.14064

Payment = $\dfrac{20,000.00}{20.14064} = \underline{\$993.02}$

10. $R = 1\%$ $P = 27$ $FV = 7,000.00$

Table factor = 30.82089

Payment = $\dfrac{7,000.00}{30.82089} = \underline{\$227.12}$

11. $R = 2\%$ $P = 32$ Loan amount = 6,000.00

Table factor = 23.46833

Payment = $\dfrac{6,000.00}{23.46833} = \underline{\$255.66}$

12. $R = 1\frac{1}{2}\%$ $P = 30$ Loan amount = 20,000.00

Table factor = 24.01584

Payment = $\dfrac{20,000.00}{24.01584} = \underline{\$832.78}$

CHAPTER 13 CONSUMER AND BUSINESS CREDIT

ASSESSMENT TEST

6.

Date	Number of Days	Activity	Unpaid Balance	Daily Balance
Jan 1–6	6	$480.94	$480.94	2,885.64
Jan 7–11	5	+ 80.00	560.94	2,804.70
Jan 12–17	6	− 125.00	435.94	2,615.64
Jan 18–23	6	+ 97.64	533.58	3,201.48
Jan 24–28	5	− 72.00	461.58	2,307.90
Jan 29	1	+ 109.70	571.28	571.28
Jan 30–31	2	+ 55.78	627.06	1,254.12
	31			$15,640.76

Average daily balance $= \dfrac{\$15,640.76}{31} = \underline{\$504.54}$

7.

Date	Number of Days	Activity	Unpaid Balance	Daily Balance
Sept 1–3	3	$686.97	$686.97	$2,060.91
Sept 4–7	4	+ 223.49	910.46	3,641.84
Sept 8–11	4	− 350.00	560.46	2,241.84
Sept 12–20	9	+ 85.66	646.12	5,815.08
Sept 21–23	3	− 200.00	446.12	1,338.36
Sept 24–27	4	+ 347.12	793.24	3,172.96
Sept 28–30	3	+ 64.00	857.24	2,571.72
	30			$20,842.71

Average daily balance $= \dfrac{\$20,842.71}{30} = \underline{\$694.76}$

8. Periodic rate = $7.75\% + 3.25\% = \dfrac{11\%}{12} = .91\%$

Date	Number of Days	Activity Amount	Unpaid Balance	Daily Balance
Jun 1–7	7	$52,900.00	52,900.00	370,300.00
Jun 8–17	10	+ 30,600.00	83,500.00	835,000.00
Jun 18–27	10	+ 12,300.00	95,800.00	958,000.00
Jun 28–30	3	+ 35,000.00	60,800.00	182,400.00
	30			2,345,700.00

CHAPTER 14 MORTGAGES

REVIEW EXERCISES CHAPTER 14—SECTION I

6. 9%, 15 years table factor = 10.15

Number of 1,000s financed = $\dfrac{78,500}{1,000} = 78.5$

Monthly payment = $78.5 \times 10.15 = \underline{\$796.78}$

Month 1

$I = 78,500 \times .09 \times \dfrac{1}{12} = \underline{\$588.75}$

$796.78 - \$588.75 = \underline{\$208.03}$ to reduce principal

$78,500 - 208.03 = \underline{\$78,291.97}$ Loan balance

7. $\dfrac{76,400.00}{1,000} = 76.4$

8% for 20 years = 8.37×76.4

Monthly PI   = $\underline{\$639.47}$

Annual insurance   866.00

Annual tax   = $\underline{1,317.00}$

Annual TI $2,183.00 \div 12 =$ 181.92

                                                    $\underline{+639.47}$

Monthly PITI $\underline{\$821.39}$

8. $\dfrac{128,800.00}{1,000} = 128.8$

10% for 15 years = 10.75 × 128.8

Monthly PI = $\underline{\$1,384.60}$

Annual insurance 1,215.00

Annual taxes = $\underline{2,440.00}$

$\qquad\qquad\qquad\quad\$3,655.00 \div 12 = \quad 304.58$

$\qquad\qquad\qquad\qquad\qquad\qquad + 1,384.60$

Monthly PITI $\qquad\qquad\qquad \underline{\$1,689.18}$

10. $\dfrac{250,000}{1,000} = 250$

$9\frac{1}{2}\%$ for 25 years = 8.74 × 250

Monthly PI = $\underline{\$2,185.00}$

Annual insurance 2,196.00

Annual taxes = $\underline{6,553.00}$

$\qquad\qquad\qquad\quad\$8,749.00 \div 12 = \quad 729.08$

$\qquad\qquad\qquad\qquad\qquad\qquad + 2,185.00$

Monthly PITI $\qquad\qquad\qquad \underline{\$2,914.08}$

9. $\dfrac{174,200.00}{1,000} = 174.2$

$7\frac{1}{4}\%$ for 30 years = 6.83 × 174.2

Monthly PI = $\underline{\$1,189.79}$

Annual insurance 1,432.00

Annual taxes = $\underline{3,505.00}$

$\qquad\qquad\qquad\$4,937.00 \div 12 = \quad 411.42$

$\qquad\qquad\qquad\qquad\qquad\qquad + 1,189.79$

Monthly PITI $\qquad\qquad\qquad \underline{\$1,601.21}$

ASSESSMENT TEST

1. Number of 1,000s financed $= \dfrac{134,900.00}{1,000} = \underline{134.9}$

Table factor, $7\frac{3}{4}\%$ for 25 years $= \underline{7.56}$

Monthly payment = 134.9 × 7.56 = $\underline{\$1,019.84}$

Total interst = (25 × 12 × 1,019.84) − 134,900.00 = $\underline{\$171,052.00}$

2. Number of 1,000s financed $= \dfrac{79,500.00}{1,000} = \underline{79.5}$

Table factor, $8\frac{1}{4}\%$ for 20 years $= \underline{8.53}$

Monthly payment = 79.5 × 8.53 = $\underline{\$678.14}$

Total interest = (20 × 12 × 678.14) − 79,500.00 = $\underline{\$83,253.60}$

4. Monthly PI = 54.2 × 8.40 = $\underline{\$455.28}$

Monthly PITI = 455.28 + $\dfrac{719.00 + 459.00}{12} = \underline{\$553.45}$

5. Monthly PI = 132.1 × 10.00 = $\underline{\$1,321.00}$

Monthly PITI = 1,321.00 + $\dfrac{2,275.00 + 1,033.00}{12} = \underline{\$1,596.67}$

6. Percent of appraised value = 114,500.00 × .65 = $\underline{\$74,425.00}$

Potential credit = 74,425.00

$\qquad\qquad\qquad\quad \underline{-\ 77,900.00} = \underline{0}$

$\qquad\qquad\qquad\quad -\ \$3,475.00$

7. Percent of appraised value = 51,500.00 × .8 = $\underline{\$41,200.00}$

Potential credit = 41,200.00

$\qquad\qquad\qquad\quad \underline{-\ 27,400.00}$

$\qquad\qquad\qquad\quad \underline{\$13,800.00}$

8. Percent of appraised value = 81,200.00 × .7 = $\underline{\$56,840.00}$

Potential credit = 56,840.00

$\qquad\qquad\qquad\quad \underline{-\ 36,000.00}$

$\qquad\qquad\qquad\quad \underline{\$20,840.00}$

9. Housing expense ratio $= \dfrac{1,288.00}{5,300.00} = \underline{24.3\%}$

Total obligations ratio $= \dfrac{1,288.00 + 840.00}{5,300.00} = \underline{40.15\%}$

10. Housing expense ratio $= \dfrac{952.00}{3,750.00} = \underline{25.39\%}$

Total obligations ratio $= \dfrac{952.00 + 329.00}{3,750.00} = \underline{34.16\%}$

CHAPTER 15 FINANCIAL STATEMENTS AND RATIOS

26a.

Gary's Gifts
Balance Sheet
December 31, 1995

Assets

Current Assets	$157,600	67%
Property, Plant, Equipment	42,000	17.8%
Investments & Other Assets	35,700	15.2%
Total Assets	$235,300	100.0%

Liabilities & Owner's Equity

Current Liability	$ 21,200	9%
Long-Term Liability	53,400	22.7%
Total Liabilities	$ 74,600	31.7%
Owners Equity	$160,700	68.3%
Total Liabilities & Owner's Equity	$235,300	100.0%

26b.

Gary's Gifts
Comparative Balance Sheet
December 31, 1995 and 1996

Assets	1996	1995	Amount	Percent
Current Assets	$175,300	$157,600	$17,700	11.2%
Property, Plant, Equipment	43,600	42,000	1,600	3.8%
Invest. & Other Assets	39,200	35,700	3,500	9.8%
Total Assets	$258,100	$235,300	$22,800	9.7%
Liabilities & Owners Equity				
Current Liabilities	$ 27,700	$ 21,200	$ 6,500	30.7%
Long Term Liabilities	51,000	53,400	(2,400)	(4.5)
Total Liabilities	$ 78,700	$ 74,600	$ 4,100	5.5%
Owners Equity	$179,400	$160,700	$18,700	11.6%
Total Liability + Owner's Equity	$258,100	$235,300	$22,800	9.7%

27a.

Northern Industries, Inc.
Balance Sheet
June 30, 1995

Assets

Current Assets		Percent
Cash	$ 44,300	5.5
Accounts Receivable	127,600	15.8
Merchandise Inventory	88,100	10.9
Prepaid Maintenance	4,100	.5
Office Supplies	4,000	.5
Total Current Assets	268,100	33.2
Property, Plant and Equipment		
Land	154,000	19.0
Buildings	237,000	29.3
Fixtures	21,400	2.6
Vehicles	64,000	7.9
Computers	13,000	1.6
Total Property, Plant and Equipment	489,400	60.4
Investments and Other Assets		
Investments	32,000	4.0
Goodwill	20,000	2.5
Total Assets	$809,500	100%

Liabilities and Owner's Equity

Current Liabilities		
Accounts Payable	55,700	6.9
Salaries Payable	23,200	2.9
Notes Payable	38,000	4.7
Total Current Liabilities	116,900	14.5
Long-Term Liabilities		
Mortgage Payable	91,300	11.3
Debenture Bonds	165,000	20.4
Total Long-Term Liabilities	256,300	31.7
Total Liabilities	373,200	46.2
Owner's Equity		
Common Stock	350,000	43.2
Retained Earnings	86,300	10.7
Total Owner's Equity	436,300	53.9
Total Liabilities and Owner's Equity	$809,500	100%

*Percents may vary by .1 due to rounding

27b.

Northern Industries, Inc.
Comparative Balance Sheet
June 30, 1995 and 1996

Assets	1996	1995	Increase/Decrease Amount	Percent
Current Assets				
Cash	$ 40,200	$ 44,300	($4,100)	(9.3)
Accounts Receivable	131,400	127,600	3,800	3.0
Merchandise Inventory	92,200	88,100	4,100	4.7
Prepaid Maintenance	3,700	4,100	(400)	(9.8)
Office Supplies	6,200	4,000	2,200	55.0
Total Current Assets	273,700	268,100	5,600	2.1
Property, Plant and Equipment				
Land	154,000	154,000	0	0
Buildings	231,700	237,000	(5,300)	(2.2)
Fixtures	23,900	21,400	2,500	11.7
Vehicles	55,100	64,000	(8,900)	(13.9)
Computers	16,800	13,000	3,800	29.2
Total Property, Plant and Equipment	481,500	489,400	7,900	1.6
Investments and Other Assets				
Investments	36,400	32,000	4,400	13.8
Goodwill	22,000	20,000	2,000	10.0
Total Assets	$813,600	$809,500	4,100	.5
Liabilities and Owner's Equity				
Current Liabilities				
Accounts Payable	51,800	55,700	(3,900)	(7.0)
Salaries Payable	25,100	23,200	1,900	8.2
Notes Payable	19,000	38,000	(19,000)	(50.0)
Total Current Liabilities	95,900	116,900	(21,000)	(18.0)
Long-Term Liabilities				
Mortgage Payable	88,900	91,300	(2,400)	(2.6)
Debenture Bonds	165,000	165,000	0	0
Total Long-Term Liabilities	253,900	256,300	(2,400)	(.9)
Total Liabilities				
Owner's Equity	349,800	373,200	(23,400)	(6.3)
Common Stock	350,000	350,000	0	0
Retained Earnings	113,800	86,300	27,500	31.9
Total Owner's Equity	463,800	436,300	27,500	6.3
Total Liabilities and Owner's Equity	$813,600	$809,500	4,100	.5

28.

Wal-Mart
Comparative Balance Sheet
January 1993—1994

Assets	1994	1993	Amount	Percent
Current Assets				
Cash and Cash Equivalent	$ 20,115	$ 12,363	$ 7,752	62.7
Receivables	689,987	524,555	165,432	31.5
Recoverable Costs from Sale Leaseback	208,236	312,016	(103,780)	(33.3)
Inventories				
At Replacement Cost	11,483,119	9,779,981	1,703,138	17.4
Less LIFO Reserves	469,413	511,672	(42,259)	(8.3)
LIFO	11,013,706	9,268,309	1,745,397	18.8
Prepaid Expenses and Other	182,558	80,347	102,211	127
Total Current Assets	$12,114,602	$10,197,590	$1,917,012	18.8

REVIEW EXERCISES CHAPTER 15—SECTION II

6a.

Kwik-Mix Concrete, Inc.
Income Statement
January 1 to March 31, 1996

Revenue		
Gross Sales	$240,000	122.1
Less: Sales Discounts	43,500	22.1
Net Sales	$196,500	100.0
Cost of Goods Sold		
Merchandise Inventory, Jan. 1	86,400	44.0
Net Purchases	76,900	39.1
Goods Available for Sale	163,300	83.1
Less: Merchandise Inventory, Mar. 31	103,200	52.5
Cost of Goods Sold	60,100	30.6
Gross Margin	136,400	69.4
Operating Expenses	108,000	55.0
Income before Taxes	28,400	14.5
Income Tax	14,550	7.4
Net Income	$ 13,850	7.0

6b.

Kwik-Mix Concrete, Inc.
Comparative Income Statement
First and Second Quarter, 1996

	2nd Qtr.	1st Qtr	Increase/Decrease Amount	Percent
Revenue				
Gross Sales	$297,000	$240,000	$57,000	23.8
Less: Sales Discounts	41,300	43,500	(2,200)	(5.1)
Net Sales	255,700	196,500	59,200	30.1
Cost of Goods Sold				
Merchandise Inventory, Beginning	103,200	86,400	16,800	19.4
Net Purchases	84,320	76,900	7,420	9.6
Goods Available for Sale	187,520	163,300	24,220	14.8
Less: Merchandise Inventory, Ending	96,580	103,200	(6,620)	(6.4)
Cost of Goods Sold	90,940	60,100	30,840	51.3
Gross Margin	164,760	136,400	28,360	20.8
Operating Expenses	126,700	108,000	18,700	17.3
Income before Income Tax	38,060	28,400	9,660	34.0
Income Tax	16,400	14,550	1,850	12.7
Net Income	$ 21,660	$ 13,850	7,810	56.4

7a.

Tasty Treats Food Wholesalers, Inc.
Income Statement
For the year ended December 31, 1996

Revenue		
Gross Sales	$2,249,000	109.6
Less: Sales Returns and Allowances	143,500	7.0
Sales Discounts	54,290	2.6
Net Sales	$2,051,210	100.0
Cost of Goods sold		
Merchandise Inventory, Jan.1	875,330	42.7
Net Purchases	546,920	26.7
Freight In	11,320	.6
Goods Available for Sale	1,433,570	69.9
Less: Merchandise Inventory, Dec. 31	716,090	34.9
Cost of Goods Sold	717,480	35.0
Gross Margin	1,333,730	65.0
Operating Expenses		
Salaries	319,800	15.6
Rent	213,100	10.4
Depreciation	51,200	2.5
Utilities	35,660	1.7
Advertising	249,600	12.2
Insurance	39,410	1.9
Administrative Expenses	91,700	4.5
Miscellaneous Expenses	107,500	5.2
Total Operating Expenses	1,107,970	54.0
Income before Taxes	225,760	11.0
Income Tax	38,450	1.9
Net Income	$ 187,310	9.1

7b.

Tasty Treats Food Wholesalers, Inc.
Comparative Income Statement
For the years ended December 31, 1996 and 1997

	1997	1996	Increase/Decrease Amount	Increase/Decrease Percent
Revenue				
Gross Sales	$2,125,000	$2,249,000	($124,000)	(5.5)
Less: Sales Returns and Allowances	126,400	143,500	(17,100)	(11.9)
Sales Discounts	73,380	54,290	19,090	35.2
Net Sales	1,925,220	2,051,210	(125,990)	(6.1)
Cost of Goods Sold				
Merchandise Inventory, Jan. 1	716,090	875,330	(159,240)	(18.2)
Net Purchases	482,620	546,920	(64,300)	(11.8)
Freight In	9,220	11,320	(2,100)	(18.6)
Goods Available for Sale	1,207,930	1,433,570	(225,640)	(15.7)
Less: Merchandise Inventory, Dec. 31	584,550	716,090	(131,540)	(18.4)
Cost of Goods Sold	623,380	717,480	(94,100)	(13.1)
Gross Margin	1,301,840	1,333,730	(31,890)	(2.4)
Operating Expenses				
Salaries	340,900	319,800	21,100	7.0
Rent	215,000	213,100	1,900	.9
Depreciation	56,300	51,200	5,100	10.0
Utilities	29,690	35,660	(5,970)	(16.7)
Advertising	217,300	249,600	(32,300)	(13.0)
Insurance	39,410	39,410	0	0
Administrative Expenses	95,850	91,700	4,150	4.5
Miscellaneous Expenses	102,500	107,500	(5,000)	(4.7)
Total Operating Expenses	1,096,950	1,107,970	(11,020)	(1.0)
Income before Income Tax	204,890	225,760	(20,870)	(9.2)
Income Tax	44,530	38,450	6,080	15.8
Net Income	$ 160,360	$ 187,310	(26,950)	(14.4)

8.

The Walt Disney Company
Comparative Income Sheet
1992 and 1993

	1993	1992	Amount	Percent
Revenues (amounts in millions)				
Theme Parks and Resorts	$3,440.7	$3,306.9	133.8	4
Film Entertainment	3,673.4	3,115.2	558.2	17.9
Consumer Products	1,415.1	1,081.9	333.2	30.8
Total Income	8,529.2	7,504.0		

1a.

Service Master Carpet Cleaning
Balance Sheet
December 31, 1996

Assets		Percent
Current Assets	$132,500	52.2
Property, Plant and Equipment	88,760	35.0
Investments and Other Assets	32,400	12.8
Total Assets	$253,660	100%
Liabilities		
Current Liabilities	51,150	20.2
Long-Term Liabilities	87,490	34.5
Total Liabilities	138,640	54.7
Owner's Equity		
Al Mosley, Equity	115,020	45.3
Total Liabilities and Owner's Equity	$253,660	100%

1b.

Service Master Carpet Cleaning
Comparative Balance Sheet
December 31, 1996 and 1997

	1997	1996	Increase/Decrease Amount	Percent
Assets				
Current Assets	$154,300	$132,500	$21,800	16.5
Property, Plant and Equipment	124,650	88,760	35,890	40.4
Investments and Other Assets	20,000	32,400	(12,400)	(38.3)
Total Assets	$298,950	$253,660	45,290	17.9
Liabilities				
Current Liabilities	65,210	51,150	14,060	27.5
Long-Term Liabilities	83,800	87,490	(3,690)	(4.2)
Total Liabilities	149,010	138,640	10,370	7.5
Owner's Equity				
Al Mosley Equity	149,940	115,020	34,920	30.4
Total Liabilities and Owner's Equity	$298,950	$253,660	45,290	17.9

2a.

General Industries, Inc.
Balance Sheet
October 31, 1996

Assets

Current Assets		Percent*
Cash	$ 45,260	4.1
Accounts Receivable	267,580	24.5
Merchandise Inventory	213,200	19.5
Prepaid Expenses	13,400	1.2
Office Supplies	5,300	.5
Total Current Assets	544,740	49.8
Property, Plant and Equipment		
Land	87,600	8.0
Building	237,200	21.7
Equipment	85,630	7.8
Vehicles	54,700	5.0
Computers	31,100	2.8
Total Property, Plant and Equipment	496,230	45.4
Investments and Other Assets		
Investments	53,100	4.8
Total Assets	$1,094,070	100%

Liabilities and Owner's Equity

Current Liabilities		
Accounts Payable	43,200	3.9
Salaries Payable	16,500	1.5
Notes Payable (6-months)	102,400	9.4
Total Current Liabilities	162,100	14.8
Long-Term Liabilities		
Mortgage Payable	124,300	11.4
Notes Payable (3 years)	200,000	18.3
Total Long-Term Liabilities	324,300	29.6
Total Liabilities	486,400	44.5
Owner's Equity		
Common Stock	422,000	38.6
Retained Earnings	185,670	17.0
Total Owner's Equity	607,670	55.5
Total Liabilities and Owner's Equity	$1,094,070	100%

*Percents may vary by .1 due to rounding

2b.

General Industries, Inc.
Comparative Balance Sheet
October 31, 1996 and 1997

Assets	1997	1996	Increase/Decrease Amount	Percent
Current Assets				
Cash	$ 47,870	$ 45,260	2,610	5.8
Accounts Receivable	251,400	267,580	(16,180)	(6.0)
Merchandise Inventory	223,290	213,200	10,090	4.7
Prepaid Maintenance	8,500	13,400	(4,900)	(36.6)
Supplies	6,430	5,300	1,130	21.3
Total Current Assets	537,490	544,740	7,250	1.3
Property, Plant and Equipment				
Land	87,600	87,600	0	0
Building	234,500	237,200	(2,700)	(1.1)
Equipment	88,960	85,630	3,330	3.9
Vehicles	68,800	54,700	14,100	25.8
Computers	33,270	31,100	2,170	7.0
Total Property, Plant and Equipment	513,130	496,230	16,900	3.4
Investments and Other Assets				
Investments	55,640	53,100	2,540	4.8
Total Assets	$1,106,260	$1,094,070	12,190	1.1
Liabilities and Owner's Equity				
Current Liabilities				
Accounts Payable	48,700	43,200	5,500	11.3
Salaries Payable	9,780	16,500	(6,720)	(40.7)
Notes Payable (6-month)	96,700	102,400	(5,700)	(5.6)
Total Current Liabilities	155,180	162,100	(6,920)	(4.3)
Long-Term Liabilities				
Mortgage Payable	121,540	124,300	(2,760)	(2.2)
Notes Payable (3-years)	190,000	200,000	(10,000)	(5.0)
Total Long-Term Liabilities	311,540	324,300	(12,760)	(3.9)
Total Liabilities	466,720	486,400	(19,680)	(4.0)
Owner's Equity				
Common Stock	450,000	422,000	28,000	6.6
Retained Earnings	189,540	185,670	3,870	2.1
Total Owner's Equity	639,540	607,670	31,870	5.2
Total Liabilities and Owner's Equity	$1,106,260	$1,094,070	12,190	1.1

5a.

Abbey Road Restaurant Supply
Income Statement
Third Quarter, 1997

Revenue		
Gross Sales	$224,400	106.8
Less: Sales Returns and Allowances	14,300	6.8
Net Sales	210,100	100.0
Cost of Goods sold		
Merchandise Inventory, July 1	165,000	78.5
Net Purchases	76,500	36.4
Goods Available for Sale	241,500	114.9
Less: Merchandise Inventory, Sept. 30	143,320	68.2
Cost of Goods Sold	98,180	46.7
Gross Margin	111,920	53.3
Operating Expenses	68,600	32.7
Income before Taxes	43,320	20.6
Income Tax	8,790	4.2
Net Income	$ 34,530	16.4

5b.

Abbey Road Restaurant Supply
Comparative Income Statement
Third and Fourth Quarter - 1997

	4th Qtr.	3rd Qtr.	Increase/Decrease Amount	Increase/Decrease Percent
Revenue				
Gross Sales	$218,200	$224,400	($6,200)	(2.8)
Less: Sales Returns and Allowances	9,500	14,300	(4,800)	(33.6)
Net Sales	208,700	210,100	1,400	.7
Cost of Goods Sold				
Merchandise Inventory, Beginning	143,320	165,000	(21,680)	(13.1)
Net Purchases	81,200	76,500	4,700	6.1
Goods Available for Sale	224,520	241,500	(16,980)	(7.0)
Less: Merchandise Inventory, Ending	125,300	143,320	(18,020)	(12.6)
Cost of Goods Sold	99,220	98,180	1,040	1.0
Gross Margin	109,480	111,920	(2,440)	(2.2)
Operating Expenses	77,300	68,600	8,700	12.7
Income before Income Tax	32,180	43,320	(11,140)	(25.7)
Income Tax	11,340	8,790	2,550	29.0
Net Income	$ 20,840	$ 34,530	(13,690)	(39.6)

6a.

Omega Optical, Inc.
Income Statement
For the year ended December 31, 1996

Revenue		
Gross Sales	$1,243,000	108.5
Less: Sales Returns and Allowances	76,540	6.7
Sales Discounts	21,300	1.9
Net Sales	$1,145,160	100.0
Cost of Goods Sold		
Merchandise Inventory, Jan. 1	654,410	57.1
Net Purchases	318,000	27.8
Freight In	3,450	.3
Goods Available for Sale	975,860	85.2
Less: Merchandise Inventory, Dec. 31	413,200	36.1
Cost of Goods Sold	562,660	49.1
Gross Margin	582,500	50.9
Operating Expenses		
Salaries	92,350	8.1
Rent	83,100	7.3
Depreciation	87,700	7.7
Utilities	21,350	1.9
Advertising	130,440	11.4
Insurance	7,920	.7
Miscellaneous Expenses	105,900	9.2
Total Operating Expenses	528,760	46.2
Income before Taxes	53,740	4.7
Income Tax	18,580	1.6
Net Income	$ 35,160	3.1

6b.

Omega Optical, Inc.
Comparative Income Statement
For the years ended December 31, 1996 and 1997

	1997	1996	Increase/Decrease Amount	Increase/Decrease Percent
Revenue				
Gross Sales	$1,286,500	$1,243,000	43,500	3.5
Less: Sales Returns and Allowances	78,950	76,540	2,410	3.1
Sales Discounts	18,700	21,300	(2,600)	(12.2)
Net Sales	1,188,850	1,145,160	43,690	3.8
Cost of Goods Sold				
Merchandise Inventory, Jan. 1	687,300	654,410	32,890	5.0
Net Purchases	325,400	318,000	7,400	2.3
Freight In	3,980	3,450	530	15.4
Goods Available for Sale	1,016,680	975,860	40,820	4.2
Less: Merchandise Inventory, Dec. 31	401,210	413,200	(11,990)	(2.9)
Cost of Goods Sold	615,470	562,660	52,810	9.4
Gross Margin	573,380	582,500	(9,120)	1.6

(continued)

Omega Optical, Inc.
Comparative Income Statement
For the years ended December 31, 1996 and 1997

	1997	1996	Increase/Decrease Amount	Percent
Operating Expenses				
Salaries	99,340	92,350	6,990	7.6
Rent	85,600	83,100	2,500	3.0
Depreciation	81,200	87,700	(6,500)	(7.4)
Utilities	21,340	21,350	(10)	(0.05)
Advertising	124,390	130,440	(6,050)	(4.6)
Insurance	8,700	7,920	780	9.8
Miscellaneous Expenses	101,230	105,900	(4,670)	(4.4)
Total Operating Expenses	521,800	528,760	(6,960)	(1.3)
Income before Income Tax	51,580	53,740	(2,160)	(4.0)
Income Tax	12,650	18,580	(5,930)	(31.9)
Net Income	$ 38,930	$ 35,160	3,770	10.7

20.

Toys "R" Us
Vertical Analysis
For 1994

	Percent
Net Sales	100.0
Costs and Expenses	
Cost of Sales	69.2
Selling, Advertising	18.8
Depreciation and Amortization	1.7
Interest expense	.9
Interest and other increase	(.3)
Earnings before taxes on income	9.7
Taxes on income	3.6
Net earnings	6.1

CHAPTER 17 DEPRECIATION

REVIEW EXERCISES CHAPTER 17—SECTION II

4. End of Year	Orig. Cost	Cost Recov. %	Depreciation	Accum. Depreci.	Book Value
					$2,400,000
1	$2,400.000	14.29	$342.960	$ 342,960	2,057,040
2	2,400,000	24.49	587,760	930,720	1,469,280
3	2,400,000	17.49	419,760	1,350,480	1,049,520
4	2,400,000	12.49	299,760	1,650,240	749,760
5	2,400,000	8.93	214,320	1,864,560	535,440
6	2,400,000	8.92	214,080	2,078,640	321,360
7	2,400,000	8.93	214,320	2,292,960	107,040
8	2,400,000	4.46	107,040	2,400,000	0

CHAPTER 19 INSURANCE

REVIEW EXERCISES CHAPTER 19—SECTION I

1. Face value $5,000 Male-24

Number of 1,000s $= \dfrac{5,000}{1,000} = 5$

Whole life annual premium $= \$15.90 \times 5$

$\qquad\qquad\qquad\qquad = \underline{\$79.50}$

Semiannual premium $= \ 79.50 \times .52$

$\qquad\qquad\qquad\qquad = \underline{\$41.34}$

Quarterly premium $= \ 79.50 \times .26$

$\qquad\qquad\qquad\qquad = \underline{\$20.67}$

Monthly premium $= \ 79.50 \times .09$

$\qquad\qquad\qquad\qquad = \underline{\$7.16}$

9. Nonforfeiture options:

Face value $50,000   10 years in force, Whole life

Number of 1,000s = 50

Option 1, Cash value $98.00 per 1,000

$\qquad\qquad\qquad\qquad = \ 98.00 \times 50$

$\qquad\qquad\qquad\qquad = \underline{\$4,900.00}$

Option 2, Reduced, Paid up $186.00 per 1,000

$\qquad\qquad\qquad\qquad = \ 186.00 \times 50$

$\qquad\qquad\qquad\qquad = \underline{\$9,300.00}$ ins. for life

Option 3, Extended term $\underline{\text{17 years, 54 days}}$

REVIEW EXERCISES CHAPTER 19—SECTION II

1. Building value $88,000, Contents value $21,000   Area 4, Class B

Building, number of 100s $\dfrac{88,000}{100} = 880$

Contents, number of 100s $\dfrac{21,000}{100} = 210$

Building $.76 \times 880 = \underline{\$668.80}$ Annual premium

Contents $.83 \times 210 = \underline{\$174.30}$ Annual premium

Total annual premium $= 668.80 + 174.30 = \$843.10$

6. Annual premium $450 after 3 months by insurance company

Premium $= \$450.00 \times \dfrac{3}{12} = \underline{\$112.50}$

Refund due $= \ 450.00 - 112.50$

$\qquad\qquad = \underline{\$337.50}$

7. Annual premium $560 after 20 days by insured

Short-rate premium $= \$560 \times 16\%$

$\qquad\qquad\qquad\quad = \underline{\$89.60}$

Refund due $\quad = \$560.00 - 89.60$

$\qquad\qquad\quad = \underline{\$470.40}$

11. Replacement cost $= \$200,000$ Face value $= \$160,000$

Coinsurance $\quad = 80\%$ Loss $\quad = \$75,000$

Insurance required $= 200,000 \times 80\% = \$160,000$

Amount of loss paid $= \dfrac{160,000}{160,000} \times 75,000$

$\qquad\qquad\qquad\quad = \underline{\$75,000}$

19.

Aetna: $\dfrac{300,000}{500,000} = 60\%$ $.6 \times 95,000 = \underline{\$57,000}$

State Farm: $\dfrac{125,000}{500,000} = 25\%$ $.25 \times 95,000 = \underline{\$23,750}$

Liberty Mutual: $\dfrac{95,000}{500,000} = 15\%$ $.15 \times 95,000 = \underline{\$14,250}$

ASSESSMENT TEST

1. M-29, Face value $80,000, 20 payment life

Number of 1,000s $\dfrac{80,000}{1,000} = 80$

Annual premium $= 31.52 \times 80$

$\qquad\qquad\qquad = \underline{\$2,521.60}$

Semiannual $\quad = 2,521.60 \times 52\%$

$\qquad\qquad\quad = \underline{\$1,311.23}$

Quarterly $\quad = 2,521.60 \times 26\%$

$\qquad\qquad\quad = \underline{\$655.62}$

Monthly $\quad = 2,521.60 \times 9\%$

$\qquad\qquad\quad = \underline{\$226.94}$

6. Face value $60,000   5 years in force, 20 payment life

Number of 1,000s $\dfrac{60,000}{1,000} = 60$

Option 1, Cash value $\quad = \ 73 \times 60 = \underline{\$4,380}$

Option 2, Reduced, Paid up $= 212 \times 60 = \underline{\$12,720}$

Option 3, Extended term $\quad = \underline{\text{14 years, 86 days}}$

5. Nonforfeiture options:

Face value $130,000   15 years in force, Whole life

Number of 1,000s $\dfrac{130,000}{1,000} = 130$

Option 1, Cash value $\quad = 157 \times 130 = \underline{\$20,410}$

Option 2, Reduced, Paid up $= 314 \times 130 = \underline{\$40,820}$

Option 3, Extended term $\quad = \underline{\text{21 years, 218 days}}$

10. Number of 100s, Building $\dfrac{47,000}{100} = 470$

Building premium $\quad 470 \times .76 = \underline{\$357.20}$

Number of 100s, Contents $\dfrac{93,000}{100} = 930$

Contents premium $\quad 930 \times .83 = \underline{\$771.90}$

Total premium $= \$771.90 + 357.20 = \underline{\$1,129.10}$

21.	Bodily injury	50/100	99.00
	Property damage	25	74.00
	Collision	$500 deductible	116.00
	Comprehensive	$100 deductible	+ 113.00
	Rating factor	.9	$402.00 \times .9$
	Annual Premium		$361.80

22.	Bodily injury	10/20	61.00
	Property damage	5	46.00
	Collision	$250 deductible	100.00
	Comprehensive	Full coverage	+ 79.00
	Rating factor	2.2	286.00×2.2
	Annual Premium		$629.20

23.	Bodily injury	100/300	122.00
	Property damage	100	84.00
	Collision	$500 deductible	76.00
	Comprehensive	$100 deductible	+ 50.00
	Rating factor	1.7	332.00×1.7
	Annual Premium		$564.40

CHAPTER 20   INVESTMENTS

REVIEW EXERCISES   CHAPTER 20—SECTION I

1. Common dividend per share $= \dfrac{\$3,000,000}{5,000,000} = .6 = \underline{\$.60 \text{ per share}}$

2. Total preferred dividend $= 3,000,000 \times \$5.50 = \underline{\$16,500,000}$

   Total common dividend $= \$25,000,000 - \$16,500,000 = \$8,500,000$

   Common dividend per share $= \dfrac{\$8,500,000}{10,000,000} = .85 = \underline{\$.85 \text{ per share}}$

11. Current yield $= \dfrac{\text{Annual dividend}}{\text{Current price}}$

    $= \dfrac{1.60}{46.125} = .0346 = \underline{3.5\%}$

    Price earnings ratio $= \dfrac{\text{Current price per share}}{\text{Earnings per share}}$

    $= \dfrac{46.125}{6.59} = \underline{7}$

13. Earnings per share $= \dfrac{\text{Current price}}{\text{PE ratio}} = \dfrac{27.5}{21} = \underline{\$1.31}$

14. Current price $= \dfrac{\text{Dividend}}{\text{Yield}} = \dfrac{\$1.60}{2.5\%} = \underline{\$64}$

15. Dividend $= \text{Price} \times \text{Yield} = 42.375 \times .7\% = \underline{\$.30}$

ASSESSMENT TEST

27. Interest $= 1,000 \times .07375 \times \dfrac{100}{360} = \underline{\$20.49}$

    Total cost $= (\$785.00 + \$20.49 + \$9.50) \times 5 = \underline{\$4,074.95}$

28. Interest $= 1,000 \times .05625 \times \dfrac{3}{12} = \underline{\$14.06}$

    Total cost $= (\$1,057.50 + \$14.06 + \$7.00) \times 15 = \underline{\$16,178.40}$

30. Interest $= 1,000 \times .08875 \times \dfrac{4}{12} = \underline{\$29.58}$

    Proceeds $= (\$1,092.50 + \$29.58 - \$5.00) \times 20 = \underline{\$22,341.60}$

31. Interest $= 1,000 \times .0925 \times \dfrac{85}{360} = \underline{\$21.84}$

    Proceeds $= (\$980.00 + \$21.84 - \$8.00) \times 5 = \underline{\$4,969.20}$

33. Annual interest $= 1,000 \times 9.5\% = \underline{\$95.00}$

    Current yield $= \dfrac{95.00}{1,057.50} = \underline{9\%}$